P9-DND-304

Gleim Publications, Inc., offers five university-level study systems:

Auditing & Systems Exam Questions and Explanations with Exam Prep Software
Business Law/Legal Studies Exam Questions and Explanations with Exam Prep Software
Federal Tax Exam Questions and Explanations with Exam Prep Software
Financial Accounting Exam Questions and Explanations with Exam Prep Software
Cost/Managerial Accounting Exam Questions and Explanations with Exam Prep Software

The following is a list of Gleim examination review systems:

CIA Review: Part I, Internal Audit Role in Governance, Risk, and Control
CIA Review: Part II, Conducting the Internal Audit Engagement
CIA Review: Part III, Business Analysis and Information Technology
CIA Review: Part IV, Business Management Skills

CMA Review: Part 1, Business Analysis
CMA Review: Part 2, Management Accounting and Reporting
CMA Review: Part 3, Strategic Management
CMA Review: Part 4, Business Applications

CPA Review: Financial
CPA Review: Auditing
CPA Review: Business
CPA Review: Regulation

EA Review: Part 1, Individuals
EA Review: Part 2, Sole Proprietorships and Partnerships
EA Review: Part 3, Corporations, Fiduciaries, Estate and Gift Tax, and Trusts
EA Review: Part 4, IRS Administration and Other Topics

Order forms are provided at the back of this book or contact us at www.gleim.com or (800) 87-GLEIM.

REVIEWERS AND CONTRIBUTORS

Garrett Gleim, University of Pennsylvania, is our book production coordinator. Mr. Gleim coordinated the production staff, reviewed the manuscript, and provided production assistance throughout the project.

Grady M. Irwin, J.D., is a graduate of the University of Florida College of Law, and he has taught in the University of Florida College of Business. Mr. Irwin provided substantial editorial assistance throughout the project.

Lauren Jones is a graduate of the Fisher School of Accounting at the University of Florida. Ms. Jones is our book production assistant and composed the page layout and provided assistance throughout the project.

John F. Rebstock, CIA, is a graduate of the Fisher School of Accounting at the University of Florida. Mr. Rebstock reviewed portions of the manuscript.

A PERSONAL THANKS

This manual would not have been possible without the extraordinary effort and dedication of Julie Cutlip, Erin McKenna, Teresa Soard, and Heather Williams, who typed the entire manuscript and all revisions; and drafted, scanned, and laid out the diagrams and illustrations in this book.

The authors also appreciate the production and editorial assistance of Justin Ash, Clint Berg, Nicole Brake, Matthew Carty, Katharine Cicatelli, Seth Kaye, Jean Marzullo, Kevin McKinley, Shane Rapp, Sonia Santana, Christina Smart, Dilpesh Topiwala, and Polly Werner.

The authors also appreciate the critical reading assistance of Mike DeMare, Scott Grubbs, Erica Malinowski, Thomas McDuffie, and April Woodbury.

Finally, we appreciate the encouragement, support, and tolerance of our families throughout this project.

THIRTEENTH EDITION
CPA REVIEW

Auditing

by

Irvin N. Gleim, Ph.D., CPA, CIA, CMA, CFM

and

William A. Hillison, Ph.D., CPA, CMA

ABOUT THE AUTHORS

Irvin N. Gleim is Professor Emeritus in the Fisher School of Accounting at the University of Florida and is a member of the American Accounting Association, Academy of Legal Studies in Business, American Institute of Certified Public Accountants, Association of Government Accountants, Florida Institute of Certified Public Accountants, The Institute of Internal Auditors, and the Institute of Management Accountants. He has had articles published in the *Journal of Accountancy, The Accounting Review,* and *The American Business Law Journal* and is author/coauthor of numerous accounting and aviation books and CPE courses.

William A. Hillison is Professor of Accounting at Florida State University, where he holds the Andersen Chair. His primary teaching duties include graduate and undergraduate auditing and systems courses. He is a member of the Florida Institute of Certified Public Accountants, American Accounting Association, and Institute of Certified Management Accountants. He has had articles published in many journals including the *Journal of Accounting Research*, the *Journal of Accounting Literature*, the *Journal of Accounting Education*, *Cost and Management*, *The Internal Auditor*, *ABACUS*, the *Journal of Accountancy*, *The CPA Journal*, and *The Journal of Forecasting*.

Gleim Publications, Inc.
P.O. Box 12848
University Station
Gainesville, Florida 32604
(800) 87-GLEIM or (800) 874-5346
(352) 375-0772
FAX: (352) 375-6940
Internet: www.gleim.com
E-mail: admin@gleim.com

This is the first printing of the thirteenth edition of *CPA Review: Auditing*. Please e-mail update@gleim.com with **CPA AUD 13-1** included in the subject or text. You will receive our current update as a reply. Updates are available until the next edition is published.

EXAMPLE:
To: update@gleim.com
From: your e-mail address
Subject: CPA AUD 13-1

ISSN: 1547-8033

ISBN: 1-58194-404-7 *CPA Review: Auditing*
ISBN: 1-58194-398-9 *CPA Review: Regulation*
ISBN: 1-58194-401-2 *CPA Review: Financial*
ISBN: 1-58194-407-1 *CPA Review: Business*
ISBN: 1-58194-350-4 *CPA Review*, 4-Book Set

ACKNOWLEDGMENTS

Material from *Uniform Certified Public Accountant Examination Questions and Unofficial Answers*, Copyright © 1974-2003 by the American Institute of Certified Public Accountants, Inc., is reprinted and/or adapted with permission. Visit the AICPA web page at www.aicpa.org or call (212) 596-6200 for more information.

The author is indebted to the Institute of Certified Management Accountants for permission to use problem materials from past CMA examinations. Questions and unofficial answers from the Certified Management Accountant Examinations, copyright by the Institute of Certified Management Accountants, are reprinted and/or adapted with permission.

The authors are grateful for permission to reproduce Certified Internal Auditor Examination Questions, copyright © 1991-1995 by The Institute of Internal Auditors, Inc.

This publication was printed and bound by Corley Printing Company, St. Louis, MO, a registered ISO-9002 company. More information about Corley Printing Company is available at www.corleyprinting.com or by calling (314) 739-3777.

Visit our Internet site (www.gleim.com) for the latest updates and information on all of our products.

TABLE OF CONTENTS

<u>Page</u>

Preface for CPA Candidates vi
Optimizing Your Auditing Score 1

Study Unit 1. Engagement Responsibilities 17
Study Unit 2. Risk Assessment 59
Study Unit 3. Strategic Planning Issues 101
Study Unit 4. Internal Control Concepts and Information Technology 133
Study Unit 5. Internal Control -- Sales-Receivables-Cash Receipts Cycle 179
Study Unit 6. Internal Control -- Purchases-Payables-Cash Disbursements Cycle 203
Study Unit 7. Internal Control -- Payroll and Other Cycles 229
Study Unit 8. Tests Of Controls 249
Study Unit 9. Internal Control Communications 279
Study Unit 10. Evidence -- Objectives and Nature 317
Study Unit 11. Evidence -- The Sales-Receivables-Cash Cycle 351
Study Unit 12. Evidence -- The Purchases-Payables-Inventory Cycle 377
Study Unit 13. Evidence -- Other Assets, Liabilities, and Equities 395
Study Unit 14. Evidence -- Key Considerations 419
Study Unit 15. Evidence -- Sampling 451
Study Unit 16. Reports -- Standard, Qualified, Adverse, and Disclaimer 489
Study Unit 17. Reports -- Other Modifications 527
Study Unit 18. Review, Compilation, and Special Reports 557
Study Unit 19. Related Reporting Topics 593
Study Unit 20. Governmental Audits 629

Appendix A: Auditing Pronouncement Summary 657
Index 673
Order Form 679

PREFACE FOR CPA CANDIDATES

The purpose of this Gleim *CPA Review* study book is to help YOU prepare to pass the Auditing & Attestation section of the CPA examination. Our overriding consideration is to provide an inexpensive, effective, and easy-to-use study program. This book

1. Explains how to optimize your grade by focusing on the Auditing & Attestation section of the CPA exam.

2. Defines the subject matter tested on the Auditing & Attestation section of the CPA exam.

3. Outlines all of the subject matter tested on the Auditing & Attestation section in 20 easy-to-use study units.

4. Presents multiple-choice questions from recent CPA examinations to prepare you for auditing questions in future CPA exams. Our answer explanations are presented to the immediate right of each question for your convenience. Two bookmarks are provided at the back of this book. Use a bookmark to cover our answer explanations as you study the questions.

5. Presents one simulation in each study unit to acquaint you with simulation formats. Answer the simulation test questions in your book. The answers and grading instructions follow each question.

The outline format, spacing, and the question and answer formats in this book are designed to facilitate readability, learning, and understanding. Even though this review book constitutes a complete self-study program for the Auditing and Attestation section of the CPA exam, you may wish to enroll in a group study CPA review program. Check our website for live courses we recommend. This book and the Gleim *CPA Test Prep* software* are compatible with all other CPA review materials and courses that follow the AICPA Content Specification Outlines.

To maximize the efficiency and effectiveness of your CPA review program, begin by **studying** (not merely reading) *CPA Review: A System for Success*. It has been carefully organized and written to provide important information to assist you in passing the CPA examination.

Thank you for your interest in the Gleim *CPA Review* books, *CPA Test Prep* software, *CPA Review* audios, and *CPA Review Online* courses. We deeply appreciate the thousands of letters and suggestions received from CIA, CFM, CMA, EA, and CPA candidates during the last 30 years. Please send your suggestions, comments, and corrections concerning this review book. The last page has been designed to help you note corrections and suggestions during your study process. Please tear it out and mail it to us with your comments immediately after you take the CPA exam. We will respond to each letter on an individual basis.

Good Luck on the Exam,

Irvin N. Gleim
William A. Hillison

December 2004

OPTIMIZING YOUR AUDITING SCORE

Overview of Auditing 1
AICPA Content Specification Outlines (CSOs) 2
A System for Success 5
How to Study a Study Unit (books and software) 6
How to Study a Study Unit Using Gleim's Complete System 7
Gleim Audio Reviews 7
CPA Review Online 7
Multiple-Choice Question Answering Technique 8
Simulation Questions 10
Simulation Tabs 11
Simulation Question Answering Technique 12
Control: How to 13
Gleim Auditing Study Unit Listing 13
Auditing Authoritative Pronouncements Cross-References 14
Gleim's Technical Support Via E-mail 15

This introduction is a summary of Gleim's *CPA Review: A System for Success*, an 80-page book containing a detailed discussion of the steps to exam success. *A System for Success* is a necessity for all CPA candidates. It should be studied at least twice: at the start of a candidate's study program and again 1 or 2 weeks before taking the CPA exam. It is a separate book so you do not have to carry it with you when you use this book, *CPA Review: Auditing*.

Auditing is scheduled for 4 1/2 hours.

AICPA title:	Auditing & Attestation
AICPA acronym:	AUD
Gleim title:	Auditing
Question format:	90 Multiple-choice questions in 3 testlets of 30 questions each
	2 Simulations
Areas covered:	I. (25%) Engagement Planning
	II. (15%) Internal Control
	III. (35%) Forming a Conclusion
	IV. (10%) Engagement Review
	V. (15%) Required Communications

OVERVIEW OF AUDITING

The Auditing section tests candidates' knowledge of auditing procedures, auditing standards generally accepted in the United States of America (GAAS) and other standards related to attest engagements, and the skills needed to apply that knowledge in auditing and other attestation engagements. This section tests such knowledge in the context of five broad engagement tasks in the CSO outline.

The AICPA suggests that the following publications will be sources of questions for Auditing & Attestation. Our outlines and answer explanations are based on these publications.

1) AICPA Statements on Auditing Standards and Interpretations
2) AICPA Statements on Standards for Accounting and Review Services and Interpretations
3) AICPA Statements on Quality Control Standards
4) AICPA Statements on Standards for Attestation Engagements
5) U.S. General Accounting Office *Government Auditing Standards*
6) AICPA Audit and Accounting Guides:

   - *Audit Sampling*
   - *Consideration of Internal Control in a Financial Statement Audit*
   - *Analytical Procedures*
   - *Auditing Revenues in Certain Industries*

7) Current textbooks on auditing and other assurance services
8) AICPA Auditing Practice Releases
9) AICPA Audit and Accounting Manual
10) AICPA Audit Risk Alerts and Compilation and Review Alerts
11) Single Audit Act, as amended

AICPA CONTENT SPECIFICATION OUTLINES (CSOs)

The AICPA has indicated that the content specification outlines have several purposes, including:

1. *Ensure consistent coverage of subject matter from one examination to the next.*

2. *Provide guidance to those who are responsible for preparing the examination in order to ensure a balanced examination.*

3. *Assist candidates in preparing for the examination by indicating subjects that may be covered by the examination.*

4. *Alert accounting educators about the subject matter considered necessary to prepare for the examination.*

The next 2 pages contain the AICPA Auditing & Attestation CSOs and corresponding Gleim Study Units.

AICPA CONTENT SPECIFICATION OUTLINES	**GLEIM STUDY UNITS**

Auditing & Attestation

I. **Plan the engagement, evaluate the prospective client and engagement, decide whether to accept or continue the client and the engagement, and enter into an agreement with the client (25%)**

    A.   Determine nature and scope of engagement

        1)   Auditing standards generally accepted in the United States of America (GAAS)
        2)   Standards for accounting and review services
        3)   Standards for attestation engagements
        4)   Compliance auditing applicable to governmental entities and other recipients of governmental financial assistance
        5)   Other assurance services
        6)   Appropriateness of engagement to meet client's needs

    B.   Assess engagement risk and the CPA firm's ability to perform the engagement

        1)   Engagement responsibilities
        2)   Staffing and supervision requirements
        3)   Quality control considerations
        4)   Management integrity
        5)   Researching information sources for planning and performing the engagement

    C.   Communicate with the predecessor accountant or auditor
    D.   Decide whether to accept or continue the client and engagement
    E.   Enter into an agreement with the client as to the terms of the engagement
    F.   Obtain an understanding of the client's operations, business, and industry
    G.   Perform analytical procedures
    H.   Consider preliminary engagement materiality
    I.   Assess inherent risk and risk of misstatements from errors, fraud, and illegal acts by clients
    J.   Consider other planning matters

        1)   Using the work of other independent auditors
        2)   Using the work of a specialist
        3)   Internal audit function
        4)   Related parties and related party transactions
        5)   Electronic evidence
        6)   Risks of auditing around the computer

    K.   Identify financial statement assertions and formulate audit objectives

        1)   Significant financial statement balances, classes of transactions, and disclosures
        2)   Accounting estimates

    L.   Determine and prepare the work program defining the nature, timing, and extent of the procedures to be applied

II. **Consider internal control in both manual and computerized environments (15%)**

    A.   Obtain an understanding of business processes and information flows
    B.   Identify controls that might be effective in preventing or detecting misstatements
    C.   Document an understanding of internal control
    D.   Consider limitations of internal control
    E.   Consider the effects of service organizations on internal control
    F.   Perform tests of controls
    G.   Assess control risk

I. ENGAGEMENT PLANNING

1. Engagement Responsibilities
2. Risk Assessment
3. Strategic Planning Issues

II. INTERNAL CONTROL

4. Internal Control Concepts and Information Technology
5. Internal Control -- Sales-Receivables-Cash Receipts Cycle
6. Internal Control -- Purchases-Payables-Cash Disbursements Cycle
7. Internal Control -- Payroll and Other Cycles
8. Tests of Controls
9. Internal Control Communications

AICPA CONTENT SPECIFICATION OUTLINES	GLEIM STUDY UNITS

III. Obtain and document information to form a basis for conclusions (35%)

III. FORMING A CONCLUSION AND
IV. ENGAGEMENT REVIEW

  A.   Perform planned procedures

10. Evidence -- Objectives and Nature

    1.   Applications of audit sampling
    2.   Analytical procedures
    3.   Confirmation of balances and/or transactions with third parties
    4.   Physical examination of inventories and other assets
    5.   Other tests of details
    6.   Computer-assisted audit techniques, including data interrogation, extraction, and analysis
    7.   Substantive tests prior to balance sheet date
    8.   Tests of unusual year-end transactions

11. Evidence -- The Sales-Receivables-Cash Cycle

12. Evidence -- The Purchases-Payables-Inventory Cycle

13. Evidence -- Other Assets, Liabilities, and Equities

14. Evidence -- Key Considerations

15. Evidence -- Sampling

  B.   Evaluate contingencies
  C.   Obtain and evaluate lawyers' letters
  D.   Review subsequent events
  E.   Obtain representations from management
  F.   Identify reportable conditions and other control deficiencies
  G.   Identify matters for communication with audit committees
  H.   Perform procedures for accounting and review services engagements
  I.   Perform procedures for attestation engagements

IV. Review the engagement to provide reasonable assurance that objectives are achieved and evaluate information obtained to reach and to document engagement conclusions (10%)

  A.   Perform analytical procedures
  B.   Evaluate the sufficiency and competence of audit evidence and document engagement conclusions
  C.   Evaluate whether financial statements are free of material misstatements
  D.   Consider substantial doubt about an entity's ability to continue as a going concern
  E.   Consider other information in documents containing audited financial statements
  F.   Review the work performed to provide reasonable assurance that objectives are achieved

V. Prepare communications to satisfy engagement objectives (15%)

V. REQUIRED COMMUNICATIONS

  A.   Reports

16. Reports -- Standard, Qualified, Adverse, and Disclaimer

    1)   Reports on audited financial statements
    2)   Reports on reviewed and compiled financial statements
    3)   Reports required by *Government Auditing Standards*
    4)   Reports on compliance with laws and regulations
    5)   Reports on internal control
    6)   Reports on prospective financial information
    7)   Reports on agreed-upon procedures
    8)   Reports on the processing of transactions by service organizations
    9)   Reports on supplementary financial information
    10)   Special reports
    11)   Reports on other assurance services
    12)   Reissuance of reports

17. Reports -- Other Modifications

18. Review, Compilation, and Special Reports

19. Related Reporting Topics

20. Governmental Audits

  B.   Other required communications

    1)   Errors and fraud
    2)   Illegal acts
    3)   Communication with audit committees
    4)   Other reporting considerations covered by statements on auditing standards and statements on standards for attestation engagements

  C.   Other matters

    1)   Subsequent discovery of facts existing at the date of the auditor's report
    2)   Consideration after the report date of omitted procedures

A SYSTEM FOR SUCCESS

To assure your success on the Auditing section of the CPA examination, you should focus on the following steps:

1. **Understand the exam, including coverage, content, format, administration, and grading**.

    a. The better you understand the examination process from beginning to end, the better you will be able to perform.

    b. Study Gleim's *CPA Review: A System for Success*. Please be sure you have a current copy of this useful book.

2. **Learn and understand the subject matter tested**. The AICPA's CSOs for the Auditing section, along with the questions that have appeared in recent CPA examinations and the suggestions from recent CPA candidates*, are the basis for the study outlines that are presented in each of the 20 Auditing study units that make up this book. You will also learn and understand the Auditing material tested on the CPA exam by answering numerous multiple-choice questions from recent CPA exams. Multiple-choice questions with the answer explanations to the immediate right of each question are a major component of each Auditing study unit.

3. **Practice answering recent exam questions to perfect your question answering techniques**. Answering recent exam questions helps you understand the standards to which you will be held. This motivates you to learn and understand while studying (rather than reading) the outlines in each of the 20 Auditing study units.

    a. Question answering techniques are suggested for multiple-choice and simulation questions in Study Units 4 and 5 of *CPA Review: A System for Success*.

    b. Our *CPA Test Prep* software contains thousands of additional multiple-choice questions that are not offered in our books. Additionally, the software has many useful features, including documentation of your performance and the ability to simulate the CBT (computer-based testing) exam environment.

    c. Our *CPA Review Online* is a powerful Internet-based program that makes CPA candidates learn in an interactive environment and provides feedback to candidates to encourage learning. It includes simulation (constructive response) questions in Prometric's format. All *CPA Review Online* candidates have access to their very own Personal Counselor, who helps candidates organize study plans that work with their busy schedules.

4. **Plan exam execution**. Anticipate the exam environment and prepare yourself with a plan: When to arrive? How to dress? What exam supplies to bring? How many questions and what format? Order of answering questions? How much time to spend on each question? See Study Unit 6 in *CPA Review: A System for Success*.

    a. Expect the unexpected and adjust! Remember that your sole objective when taking an examination is to maximize your score. CPA exam grading is curved, and you must outperform your peers.

5. **Be in control**. Develop confidence and assure success with a controlled preparation program followed by confident execution during the examination.

---

*Please complete the form on pages 681 and 682 IMMEDIATELY after you take the CPA exam so we can adapt to changes in the exam. Our approach has been approved by the AICPA.

HOW TO STUDY A STUDY UNIT (BOOKS AND SOFTWARE)

Twenty-question tests in the *CPA Test Prep* software will help you to focus on your weaker areas. Make it a game: how much can you improve?

The software forces you to commit to your answer choice before looking at answer explanations, thus you are preparing under true exam conditions. It also keeps track of your time and performance history for each of the study units, which is available in either a table or graphical format.

Simplify the exam preparation process by following our Suggested Steps listed below. DO NOT omit the step in which you diagnose the reasons for answering questions incorrectly; i.e., learn from your mistakes while studying so you avoid making mistakes on the CPA exam.

1. In test mode of the software, answer a 20-question test from each study unit before studying any other information.

2. Study the Knowledge Transfer Outline for the corresponding study unit in your Gleim book. Place special emphasis on the weaker areas that you identified with the initial diagnostic quiz in the Test Prep software.

3. Take two or three 20-question tests in test mode after you have studied the Knowledge Transfer Outline.

4. After EACH test session, immediately switch to study mode and select "questions missed from last session." It is imperative that you analyze why you answered each question incorrectly.

5. Continue this process until you approach a predetermined proficiency level, e.g., 75%+.

6. Modify this process to suit your individual learning process.

Learning from questions you answer incorrectly is very important. Each question you answer incorrectly is an <u>opportunity</u> to avoid missing actual test questions on your CPA exam. Thus, you should carefully study the answer explanations provided until you understand why the original answer you chose is wrong, as well as why the correct answer indicated is correct. This study technique is clearly the difference between passing and failing for many CPA candidates.

Also, you **must** determine why you answered questions incorrectly and learn how to avoid the same error in the future. Reasons for missing questions include:

a. Misreading the requirement (stem)
b. Not understanding what is required
c. Making a math error
d. Applying the wrong rule or concept
e. Being distracted by one or more of the answers
f. Incorrectly eliminating answers from consideration
g. Not having any knowledge of the topic tested
h. Employing bad intuition (WHY?) when guessing

It is also important to verify that you answered correctly for the right reasons. Otherwise, if the material is tested on the CPA exam in a different manner, you may not answer it correctly.

It is imperative that you complete your predetermined number of study units per week so you can review your progress and realize how attainable a comprehensive CPA review program is when using Gleim's books and software. Remember to meet or beat your schedule to give yourself confidence.

HOW TO STUDY A STUDY UNIT USING GLEIM'S COMPLETE SYSTEM

To ensure that you are using your time effectively, we recommend following the steps listed below while using all of the materials together (books, software, audios, and *Review Online*):

1. (25-30 minutes) In the *Review Online* course, complete Multiple-Choice Quiz #1 in 20-25 minutes (excluding the review session). It is expected that your scores will be low on the first quiz.

    a. Immediately following the quiz, review both the correct and incorrect answer explanations for each question.

2. (15-30 minutes) Use the audiovisual presentation for an overview of the study unit. The Gleim *CPA Review Audios* can be substituted for audiovisual presentations and can be used while driving to work, exercising, etc.

3. (30-45 minutes) Complete the 30-question True/False quiz. It is interactive and most effective if used prior to studying the Knowledge Transfer Outline.

4. (60 minutes) Study the Knowledge Transfer Outline, specifically the troublesome areas identified from the multiple-choice questions in the *Review Online* course. The Knowledge Transfer Outlines can be studied either online or from the books.

5. (25-30 minutes) Complete Multiple-Choice Quiz #2 in the *Review Online* course.

    a. Immediately following the quiz, review both the correct and incorrect answer explanations for each question.

6. (40-50 minutes) Complete two 20-question quizzes while in Test Mode from the *CPA Test Prep* software.

7. (50 minutes plus 10 minutes for review) Complete a simulation in the *Review Online* course. (This only applies to AUD, FAR, and REG.)

When following these steps, you will complete all 20 units in about 70-80 hours. Then spend about 10-20 hours using the *CPA Test Prep* software to create customized tests for the problem areas that you identified. To review the entire section before the exam, use the *CPA Test Prep* software to create 20-question quizzes that draw questions from all twenty study units. Continue taking 20-question quizzes until you approach your desired proficiency level, e.g., 75%+.

GLEIM AUDIO REVIEWS

Gleim *CPA Review* audios provide a 15- to 40-minute introductory review for each study unit. Each review provides a comprehensive overview of the outline in the *CPA Review* book. The purpose is to get candidates "started" so they can relate to the questions they will answer before reading the study outlines in each study unit.

The audios are short and to the point, as is the entire Gleim System for Success. We are working to get you through the CPA exam with the minimum time, cost, and frustration. You can listen to an informative discussion about the CPA exam and hear a sample audio lecture (The Equity Method) on our website at www.gleim.com/accounting/demos/.

CPA REVIEW ONLINE

Our *CPA Review Online* is a powerful Internet-based program that makes CPA candidates learn in an interactive environment and provides feedback to candidates to encourage learning. All *CPA Review Online* candidates have access to their very own personal counselor who helps candidates organize study plans that work with their busy schedules. Go to www.gleim.com to learn more.

MULTIPLE-CHOICE QUESTION ANSWERING TECHNIQUE

Expect 3 testlets of 30 multiple-choice questions each on the Auditing section. See Study Unit 4 in *CPA Review: A System for Success* for additional discussion of how to maximize your score on multiple-choice questions.

1. **Budget your time**. We make this point with emphasis. Just as you would fill up your gas tank prior to reaching empty, so too would you finish your exam before time expires.

    a. Here is our suggested time allocation for Auditing

	Minutes	Start Time	
Testlet 1 (MC)	45	4 hours	0 minutes
Testlet 2 (MC)	45	3 hours	15 minutes
Testlet 3 (MC)	45	2 hours	30 minutes
Testlet 4 (Sim)	40	1 hour	45 minutes
Testlet 5 (Sim)	40	1 hour	5 minutes
*Extra time	25	0 hour	25 minutes

    b. Before beginning your first testlet of multiple-choice questions, prepare a Gleim Time Management Sheet as recommended in Study Unit 7 of *CPA Review: A System for Success*.

    c. As you work through the individual items, monitor your time. In Auditing, we suggest 45 minutes for each testlet of 30 questions. If you have answered five items in 7 minutes, you are fine, but if you spent 10 minutes on five items, you need to speed up.

    *Remember to allocate your budgeted "extra time," as needed, to each testlet. Your goal is to answer all of the items and achieve the maximum score possible.

2. **Answer the questions in consecutive order**.

    a. Do **not** agonize over any one item. Stay within your time budget.

    b. Mark any questions you are unsure of and return to them later as time allows.

        1) Once you have selected the Continue or Quit options, you will no longer be able to review/change any answers in the testlet completed.

    c. Never leave a multiple-choice question unanswered. Make your best guess in the time allowed. Remember that your score is based on the number of correct responses. An educated guess is inherently better than a blank answer.

3. **For each multiple-choice question**:

    a. **Ignore the answer choices**. Do not allow the answer choices to affect your reading of the item stem (the part of the question that precedes the answer choices).

        1) If four answer choices are presented, three of them are incorrect. They are called **distractors** for good reason. Often, distractors are written to appear correct at first glance.

    b. **Read the question** carefully to determine the precise requirement.

        1) Focusing on what is required enables you to ignore extraneous information and to proceed directly to determining the correct answer.

            a) Be especially careful to note when the requirement is an **exception**; e.g., "Which of the following is **not** a management assertion?"

        2) By adhering to these steps, you know what is required and which are the relevant facts.

c. **Determine the correct answer** before reading the answer choices.

   1) However, some multiple-choice items are structured so that the answer cannot be determined from the question alone.

d. **Read the answer choices carefully.**

   1) Even if answer (A) appears to be the correct choice, do **not** skip the remaining answer choices. Answer (B), (C), or (D) may be even better.

   2) Treat each answer choice as a true/false question as you analyze it.

e. **Click on the best answer.**

   1) If you are uncertain, guess intelligently. Improve on your 25% chance of getting the correct answer with blind guessing.

   2) For many of the multiple-choice questions, two answer choices can be eliminated with minimal effort. This can reduce the risk of random guessing and increase your chances of success.

4. After you have answered all the items in a testlet, go back to the marked questions and reconsider your answer choices.

5. **If you don't know the answer**

   Guess, but make it an educated guess, which means select the best possible answer. First, rule out answers that you think are incorrect. Second, speculate on what the AICPA is looking for and/or the rationale behind the question. Third, select the best answer, or guess between equally appealing answers. Your first guess is usually the most intuitive. If you cannot make an educated guess, read the item and each answer and pick the best or most intuitive answer. It's just a guess!

SIMULATION QUESTIONS

In Auditing, testlets 4 and 5 are simulation questions. Refer to your time budget for each simulation question. The following toolbar icons and tabs are located at the top of each screen.

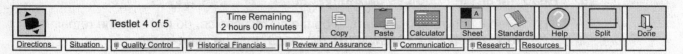

1. **Time Remaining**: This information box displays to the examinee how much time is remaining in the entire exam. Note the amount of time remaining regularly in order to keep yourself on schedule for completion.

2. **Copy**: This icon performs the same function of copying text that a standard word processing program does. It copies text from one document to insert/paste into another document.

3. **Paste**: This icon performs the same function of pasting text that a standard word processing program does. It pastes/inserts previously copied text into the selected document.

4. **Calculator**: The calculator provided is a basic tool available for simple computations. It is designed much like many common calculators used in software programs today.

5. **Spreadsheet**: The spreadsheet is much like those used in many applications, e.g., Excel, and is provided as a tool available for more complex calculations. No information is contained in the cells when the spreadsheet is opened. You may enter and execute formulas as well as text and numbers.

6. **Standards**: Simulations may include an online search of the auditing and attestation standards as a required task.

7. **Help**: This icon, when selected, provides a quick review of certain functions and tool buttons. It will also provide directions and general information, but it will not include information related specifically to the test content.

8. **Split**: This icon, when selected, will split the screen between the Situation tab and the current in-use work tab and will enable the examinee to work between screens to obtain critical information easily.

9. **Done**: There are three options when you choose this icon.

    - You may choose Review to return to the beginning of the testlet to review your answers.

    - You may choose Continue to close the current testlet and go on the next testlet. Once you have chosen continue, you may not return to that testlet. After choosing continue, you may choose Break, in order to leave the room for a break. The clock will not stop if you choose to take a break; and you may not select Break while you are currently in a testlet.

    - Finally, you may choose Quit, which means either you have completed the exam or chose not to complete it. If you choose not to complete it, security measures are in place to determine that you are intentionally not completing the exam.

SIMULATION TABS

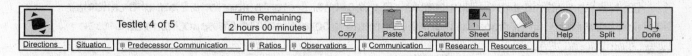

There are two types of tabs: informational tabs and work tabs. The first two tabs (Directions and Situation) are informational tabs that give directions and specific information needed to complete the simulation. In addition, the Resources tab is informational in that it contains resources and tools for use with the spreadsheet tool. Other resources and tools may be provided within the tab and will vary depending upon the situation. These tools and resources could be tax rates, present value tables, formulas, spreadsheet operators, and spreadsheet functions.

Work tabs require test-takers to respond to given information and are distinguished by a pencil icon that changes color when you enter a response. Note that the color change indicates only that a response has been made, NOT that the response is complete. Visit all tabs in each simulation to ensure your best performance.

1. Multiple Choice/Multiple Select - A work tab may contain questions and tasks that will be answered through the multiple-choice/multiple selection method. Many of these will be drop-down boxes containing the possible answers or a choice of formulas to properly complete an equation.

2. Check the Box - A work tab may have you check true or false, include or not include, etc.

3. Spreadsheet Response - A work tab may contain tasks that require completion of specific functions within a spreadsheet. This could include the completion of ratio analysis.

4. Written Communication - This tab will contain a task that requires writing or editing of existing documentation. These tasks could include the preparation of a memo to a client or editing an engagement letter.

5. Forms Completion - This tab will contain a task that requires completion of accounting or tax forms. These tasks could include the completion of certain sections of a Standard Form to Confirm Account Balance Information with Financial Institutions.

6. Research - This tab will have you answer a question or scenario through the use of the standards tool located on the toolbar. Once you search the auditing, attestation, or other standards and find the paragraph that answers the question, you will copy and paste the answer into the response area in the simulation.

Grading of Written Communication

AICPA graders are trained to look for the following 7 attributes: thesis sentence, main ideas, support ideas, punctuation, sentence structure, conciseness, and clarity.

Assign a grade of 0, 1, 2, 3, 4, or 5 to your communication response. Use zero for no response or if you did not address the issue required. Three is an average score; 4 is good; 5 is excellent; 2 is below average; 1 is poor. Divide this number by 5, then multiply the result by 30%, which is the weighting assigned to the Communication work tab by the AICPA. Example: if 5 points are possible and your grade is 3 (which is average), calculate $3/5 \times 0.30 = 0.18$.

Other work tabs will be graded similarly:

$$\frac{\text{\# Correct Responses}}{\text{\# Gradable Items}} \times \frac{\text{\% Weight Assigned to Each}}{\text{Work Tab by the AICPA}}$$

Please use Gleim's **CPA Simulation Wizard** to practice simulations under exam conditions to prepare you for your CPA exam. Go to www.gleim.com/accounting/cpa/simwizard/.

SIMULATION QUESTION ANSWERING TECHNIQUE

Do NOT be intimidated by simulations. Do your best so you outperform 2 out of 3 candidates. Practice answering simulation questions by purchasing Gleim's *CPA Review Online* at www.gleim.com/CPA.

1. Write down the time remaining (hours/minutes) on your Gleim Time Management Sheet.

2. Read the directions and situation tabs for understanding so you can use the information as you complete the work tab requirements.

3. Answer the work tabs in order from left to right. Attempt to complete each tab before moving on to the next tab. If you become frustrated, have difficulty, etc., move on to the next tab.

4. After you have completed your first pass from left to right through the tabs, return to the first work tab at the left and review and complete your answers. Move from work tab to work tab systematically, reviewing and completing each tab. Be in control.

5. Monitor your time. If you have stayed within your 45-minute allocation for each of testlets 1, 2, and 3, you will have an extra 25 minutes to allocate to testlets 4 and 5.

Be positive. You will have studied harder and practiced wiser than most candidates, and you will prevail. Do your best: no one can ask for more!

CONTROL: HOW TO

Remember, you must be in control to be successful during exam preparation and execution. Perhaps more importantly, control can also contribute greatly to your personal and other professional goals. Control is the process whereby you

1.   Develop expectations, standards, budgets, and plans.
2.   Undertake activity, production, study, and learning.
3.   Measure the activity, production, output, and knowledge.
4.   Compare actual activity with what was expected or budgeted.
5.   Modify the activity to better achieve the expected or desired outcome.
6.   Revise expectations and standards in light of actual experience.
7.   Continue the process.

Exercising control will ultimately develop the confidence you need to outperform 2 out of 3 CPA candidates and PASS the CPA exam! Obtain our *CPA Review: A System for Success* book for a more detailed discussion of control and other exam tactics.

GLEIM AUDITING STUDY UNIT LISTING

Study Unit	Title	Number of Outline Pages	Number of Questions MC	Simulation	First Page No.
1.	Engagement Responsibilities	17	63	1	17
2.	Risk Assessment	13	67	1	59
3.	Strategic Planning Issues	13	31	1	101
4.	Internal Control Concepts and Information Technology	22	58	1	133
5.	Internal Control -- Sales-Receivables-Cash Receipts Cycle	10	26	1	179
6.	Internal Control -- Purchases-Payables-Cash Disbursements Cycle	9	28	1	203
7.	Internal Control -- Payroll and Other Cycles	7	25	1	229
8.	Tests of Controls	11	40	1	249
9.	Internal Control Communications	15	45	1	279
10.	Evidence -- Objectives and Nature	13	47	1	317
11.	Evidence -- The Sales-Receivables-Cash Cycle	8	32	1	351
12.	Evidence -- The Purchases-Payables-Inventory Cycle	5	26	1	377
13.	Evidence -- Other Assets, Liabilities, and Equities	9	29	1	395
14.	Evidence -- Key Considerations	13	37	1	419
15.	Evidence -- Sampling	19	38	1	451
16.	Reports -- Standard, Qualified, Adverse, and Disclaimer	13	55	1	489
17.	Reports -- Other Modifications	12	36	1	527
18.	Review, Compilation, and Special Reports	12	49	1	557
19.	Related Reporting Topics	19	32	1	593
20.	Governmental Audits	12	25	1	629

Also see the AICPA's Content Specification Outlines on pages 3 and 4.

AUDITING AUTHORITATIVE PRONOUNCEMENTS CROSS-REFERENCES

The following listing relates AU and other auditing pronouncements to the study unit(s) where they are discussed (the subject matter may be covered without specific reference to the pronouncement). Recall that the CPA exam does not test AU numbers or SAS titles. See Appendix A, Auditing Pronouncement Summary, for a synopsis of each standard.

AU Sec. No.	Gleim Study Unit	Statements on Auditing Standards
110	A	Responsibilities and Functions of the Independent Auditor
150	1, A	Generally Accepted Auditing Standards
161	1, A	The Relationship of Generally Accepted Auditing Standards to Quality Control Standards
201	A	Nature of the General Standards
210	A	Training and Proficiency of the Independent Auditor
220	A	Independence
230	1, A	Due Professional Care in the Performance of Work
310	2, A	Appointment of the Independent Auditor
311	2, A	Planning and Supervision
312	2, A	Audit Risk and Materiality in Conducting an Audit
313	14, A	Substantive Tests Prior to the Balance-Sheet Date
315	2, A	Communications between Predecessor and Successor Auditors
316	2, A	Considerations of Fraud in a Financial Statement Audit
317	2, A	Illegal Acts by Clients
319	4, 7, 8, A	Consideration of Internal Control in a Financial Statement Audit
322	3, A	The Auditor's Consideration of the Internal Audit Function in an Audit of Financial Statements
324	9, A	Service Organizations
325	9, A	The Communication of Internal Control Related Matters Noted in an Audit
326	10, A	Evidential Matter
328	3, A	Auditing Fair Value Measurements and Disclosures
329	2, A	Analytical Procedures
330	10, 11, A	The Confirmation Process
331	12, A	Inventories
332	13, A	Auditing Derivative Instruments, Hedging Activities, and Investments in Securities
333	14, A	Management Representations
334	3, A	Related Parties
336	3, A	Using the Work of a Specialist
337	14, A	Inquiry of a Client's Lawyer Concerning Litigation, Claims, and Assessments
339	10, A	Audit Documentation
341	14, A	The Auditor's Consideration of an Entity's Ability to Continue as a Going Concern
342	3, A	Auditing Accounting Estimates
350	15, A	Audit Sampling
380	9, A	Communication with Audit Committees
390	3, A	Consideration of Omitted Procedures after the Report Date
410	A, A	Adherence to Generally Accepted Accounting Principles
411	16, A	The Meaning of *Present Fairly in Conformity with Generally Accepted Accounting Principles* in the Independent Auditor's Report
420	17, A	Consistency of Application of Generally Accepted Accounting Principles
431	16, A	Adequacy of Disclosure in Financial Statements
504	16, A	Association with Financial Statements
508	1, 16, 17, A	Reports on Audited Financial Statements
530	16, A	Dating of the Independent Auditor's Report
532	A	Restricting the Use of an Auditor's Report
534	19, A	Reporting on Financial Statements Prepared for Use in Other Countries
543	17, A	Part of Audit Performed by Other Independent Auditors
544	A	Lack of Conformity with Generally Accepted Accounting Principles
550	19, A	Other Information in Documents Containing Audited Financial Statements
551	19, A	Reporting on Information Accompanying the Basic Financial Statements in Auditor-Submitted Documents
552	19, A	Reporting on Condensed Financial Statements and Selected Financial Data
558	19, A	Required Supplementary Information
560	14, A	Subsequent Events

AU Sec. No.	Gleim Study Unit	Statements on Auditing Standards
561	14, A	Subsequent Discovery of Facts Existing at the Date of the Auditor's Report
623	18, A	Special Reports
625	19, A	Reports on the Application of Accounting Principles
634	19, A	Letters for Underwriters and Certain Other Requesting Parties
711	19, A	Filings Under Federal Securities Statutes
722	19, A	Interim Financial Information
801	20, A	Compliance Auditing Considerations in Audits of Governmental Entities and Recipients of Governmental Financial Assistance

		Statements on Standards for Attestation Engagements
AT 101	1, A	Attest Engagements
AT 201	19, A	Agreed-Upon Procedures Engagements
AT 301	1, A	Financial Forecasts and Projections
AT 401	1, A	Reporting on Pro Forma Financial Information
AT 501	9, A	Reporting on an Entity's Internal Control over Financial Reporting
AT 601	19, A	Compliance Attestation
AT 701	A	Management's Discussion and Analysis

		Statements on Standards for Accounting and Review Services
AR 50	18, A	Standards for Accounting and Review Services
AR 100	1, 18, A	Compilation and Review of Financial Standards
AR 200	18, A	Reporting on Comparative Financial Statements
AR 300	18, A	Compilation Reports on Financial Statements Included in Certain Prescribed Forms
AR 400	18, A	Communications Between Predecessor and Successor Accountants
AR 600	18, A	Reporting on Personal Financial Statements Included in Written Personal Financial Plans

		Statements on Quality Control Standards
QC 20	1	System of Quality Control for a CPA Firm's Accounting and Auditing Practice
QC 30	N/A	Monitoring a CPA Firm's Accounting and Auditing Practice
QC 40	N/A	The Personnel Management Element of a Firm's System of Quality Control -- Competencies Required by a Practitioner-in-Charge of an Attest Engagement

		Standards for Performing and Reporting on Peer Reviews
PR 100	1	Standards for Performing and Reporting on Peer Reviews

		Other Standards
	20	*Government Auditing Standards* (Yellow Book)

		Public Company Accounting Oversight Board
AS 1	1	References in Auditor's Reports to the Standards of the PCAOB
AS 2	1	An Audit of Internal Control over Financial Reporting in Conjunction with an Audit of Financial Statements
AS 3	1	Audit Documentation

GLEIM'S TECHNICAL SUPPORT VIA E-MAIL

If you e-mail us inquiries about errors, omissions, etc., we will respond by e-mail as soon as possible. Send e-mails to support@gleim.com.

STUDY UNIT ONE
ENGAGEMENT RESPONSIBILITIES

(17 pages of outline)

1.1	Attest Engagements (AT 101)	17
1.2	Audit Engagements	21
1.3	Audit Programs	23
1.4	Compilations and Reviews (AR 100)	23
1.5	Financial Forecasts and Projections (AT 301)	24
1.6	Reporting on Pro Forma Financial Information (AT 401)	27
1.7	Assurance Services	28
1.8	Quality Control	31
1.9	Practice Simulation	53

This study unit begins the consideration of engagement planning. Candidates should understand the types of services performed by CPAs. The differences among compilation, review, examination or audit, and agreed-upon procedures engagements are stressed. The list below is an overview:

> Compilation -- disclaimer of any assurance
> Review -- negative assurance
> Examination/audit -- positive assurance or opinion expressed
> Agreed-upon procedures -- results of procedures but no assurance

Assurance services are also covered in this study unit. They represent a significant enlargement of the practice of CPAs. An understanding of how these services contrast with others provided by a CPA should be obtained.

Quality control is the final subject in this study unit. The candidate must learn the five specific quality control elements and what each includes. This topic appears to be gaining importance.

1.1 ATTEST ENGAGEMENTS (AT 101)

1. **Statements on Standards for Attestation Engagements (SSAEs)** are codified in section AT of the professional standards. They are issued by the Auditing Standards Board (ASB), the Accounting and Review Services Committee, and the Management Consulting Services Executive Committee. These bodies also promulgate SASs, SSARSs, and SSCSs, respectively.

    a. SAS = Statement on Auditing Standards issued by the ASB
       SSARS = Statement on Standards for Accounting and Review Services
       SSCS = Statement on Standards for Consulting Services

    b. Synopses of the SSAEs organized by codification number are presented in Appendix A.

    c. The **Sarbanes-Oxley Act of 2002** is federal legislation that has had a dramatic effect on the engagement responsibilities of public accounting firms. This act created the **Public Company Accounting Oversight Board**. The PCAOB is responsible for registering public accounting firms within its jurisdiction; adopting standards concerning auditing reports; inspecting and investigating accounting firms; conducting disciplinary proceedings; imposing sanctions; and enforcing compliance with its rules, the act, professional standards, and securities laws relevant to audit reports and the obligations of accountants. The PCAOB has issued three auditing standards (AS 1, AS 2, and AS 3) applicable audits by public accounting firms.

2. An **attest engagement** is one in which a practitioner is engaged to issue or does issue an examination, a review, or an agreed-upon procedures report on subject matter, or an assertion about the subject matter, that is the responsibility of another party.

    a. A **practitioner** is a CPA in the practice of public accounting, which is the performance for a client while holding out as a CPA of accounting, tax, personal financial planning, litigation support, and those professional services for which standards are issued by bodies designated by the AICPA Council.

        1) Because the attestation standards apply only to attest engagements involving a practitioner as defined above, it follows that they apply only to the rendering by a CPA in public accounting of those professional services that are considered attest services (attest engagements).

            a) Attest services have traditionally been limited to expressing an opinion on historical financial statements on the basis of an audit in accordance with GAAS.

                i) But CPAs increasingly provide assurance on representations other than historical statements and in forms other than an opinion. For example, positive assurance may be provided on financial forecasts based on an **examination**, and negative assurance may be provided on historical financial statements based on a **review**.

            b) SSAEs do not cover services for which explicit standards apply, for example, SASs, SSARSs, and SSCSs.

                i) Other professional services to which the SSAEs explicitly do not apply include engagements in which the practitioner advocates a client's position, prepares tax returns or gives tax advice, has the sole function of assisting the client (e.g., to prepare information other than financial statements), or testifies as an expert witness given certain stipulated facts.

            c) Some of the assurance services being developed by the AICPA are considered attestation engagements. For example, WebTrust and SysTrust are attestation engagements.

3. The need to provide standards for the growing range of attest services resulted in the issuance of the attestation standards. These standards are a natural extension of the 10 standards that are the basis for GAAS and other standards, but do not supersede them. Thus, the candidate should master both. The following summary may be helpful in understanding the similarities and differences.

SUMMARY COMPARISON OF ATTESTATION STANDARDS WITH GAAS	
ATTESTATION (11)	**GAAS (10)**
General Standards	
1. Training in attestation	1. Training in auditing
2. Subject matter knowledge	
3. Suitable & available criteria	
4. Independence	2. Independence
5. Professional care	3. Professional care
Standards of Field Work	
1. Planning and supervision	1. Planning and supervision
	2. Consideration of internal control
2. Evidence	3. Evidence
Standards of Reporting	
1. Character of engagement	
2. Conclusions	1. Conformity with GAAP
	2. Consistency
	3. Disclosure
3. Reservations	4. Expression of opinion
4. Limitations on report use	

The following are the attestation standards:

a. **General Standards**

1) *The engagement shall be performed by a practitioner having adequate technical training and proficiency in the attest function.*

2) *The engagement shall be performed by a practitioner having adequate knowledge of the subject matter.*

3) *The practitioner shall perform an engagement only if he or she has reason to believe that the subject matter is capable of evaluation against criteria that are suitable and available to users.*

    a) Suitable criteria have the attributes of objectivity, measurability, completeness, and relevance.

        i) For example, an engagement to attest to management's representation that "workers recorded an average of 40 hours per week on a project" could be accepted by a CPA because "recorded" and "40 hours" are measurable and objectively determinable.

        ii) However, an engagement to attest that "workers worked very hard on the project" could not be accepted because "very hard" is not measurable or objectively determinable.

    b) Criteria should be available to users in one or more of the following ways:

        i) Publicly available.

        ii) Clearly included in the presentation of the subject matter or in the assertion.

        iii) Clearly included in the practitioner's report.

        iv) Well understood by most users (e.g., 40 hours per week).

        v) Available only to specified parties (in which case the report should be restricted to those parties).

4) *In all matters relating to the engagement, an independence in mental attitude shall be maintained by the practitioner.*

5) *Due professional care shall be exercised in the planning and performance of the engagement.*

b. **Standards of Field Work**

1) *The work shall be adequately planned and assistants, if any, shall be properly supervised.*

2) *Sufficient evidence shall be obtained to provide a reasonable basis for the conclusion that is expressed in the report.*

c. **Standards of Reporting**

1) *The report shall identify the subject matter or the assertion being reported on and state the character of the engagement.*

2) *The report shall state the practitioner's conclusion about the subject matter or the assertion in relation to the criteria against which the subject matter was evaluated.*

3) *The report shall state all of the practitioner's significant reservations about the engagement, the subject matter, and, if applicable, the assertion related thereto.*

4) *The report shall state that the use of the report is restricted to specified parties under the following circumstances:*

a) *When the criteria used to evaluate the subject matter are determined by the practitioner to be appropriate only for a limited number of parties who either participated in their establishment or can be presumed to have an adequate understanding of the criteria.*

b) *When the criteria used to evaluate the subject matter are available only to specified parties.*

c) *When reporting on subject matter and a written assertion has not been provided by the responsible party.*

d) *When the report is on an attest engagement to apply agreed-upon procedures to the subject matter.*

4. Two levels of attest assurance are permitted in general-distribution reports.

a. Positive (high level) assurance should be given in reports that express conclusions on the basis of an **examination**.

b. Negative (moderate level) assurance should be given in reports that express conclusions on the basis of a **review**.

5. The practitioner may report directly on the subject matter. Nevertheless, as part of the attestation procedures for examinations and reviews, the practitioner ordinarily should obtain a written assertion provided by the responsible party. A failure to obtain a written assertion is considered a scope limitation when the responsible party is the client. In addition, a representation letter is typically obtained by the practitioner from the responsible party. A failure of the responsible party or client to provide written representations is normally considered a scope limitation.

6. Attest engagements include reporting on findings based on **agreed-upon procedures** performed on subject matter. The practitioner is engaged by a client to assist specified parties to evaluate subject matter or an assertion. The report is restricted to the specified parties who have agreed to the specific procedures and taken responsibility for their sufficiency.

a. The practitioner provides neither positive nor negative assurance.

b. The practitioner must be independent.

c. A written assertion is generally not required in an agreed-upon procedures engagement unless specifically required by another attest standard.

d. The report should list the procedures performed and the related findings.

1) The procedures agreed upon should not be overly subjective or open to varying interpretations. Examples of inappropriate procedures or terminology used to describe procedures include evaluating the competency or objectivity of another party, obtaining an understanding of a subject, general review, check, or test.

2) Examples of appropriate procedures might include confirmation of information with third parties, inspection of documents for certain attributes, or mathematical computations.

7. **Attest documentation** (working papers) should be prepared and maintained. Its form and content will vary with the circumstances and the practitioner's judgment. The procedures performed, evidence gathered, and the findings reached should be documented.

8. Stop and review! You have completed the outline for this subunit. Study multiple-choice questions 1 through 6 beginning on page 34.

1.2 AUDIT ENGAGEMENTS

1. The objective of an independent, external audit in accordance with **generally accepted auditing standards (GAAS)** is to express an opinion on (attest to) whether an entity's financial statements present fairly, in all material respects, its financial position, results of operations, and cash flows in conformity with generally accepted accounting principles (GAAP).

a. As described more fully in Study Unit 10, management's assertions concerning the fairness of the financial statement components relate to

1) Completeness
2) Rights and obligations
3) Valuation or allocation
4) Existence or occurrence
5) Statement presentation and disclosure

b. An audit performed by an independent, external auditor provides assurance to external users of the financial statements of the objectivity of the auditor's opinion.

c. The auditor may make suggestions about the form or content of the financial statements or draft them based on management's information. However, the auditor's responsibility for the financial statements is confined to the expression of an opinion.

2. The standard independent auditor's report states, "An audit includes examining, on a test basis, evidence supporting the amounts and disclosures in the financial statements. An audit also includes assessing the accounting principles used and significant estimates made by management, as well as evaluating the overall financial statement presentation" (AU 508).

3. **Auditing standards** are concerned with the quality of audit performance and the objectives to be attained. Their nature requires the exercise of judgment in their application. **Auditing procedures** are performed during the audit to comply with the standards. Materiality and audit risk (Study Unit 2) underlie the application of the standards. The three general standards, three standards of field work, and four standards of reporting (**the 10 standards**) were adopted by the AICPA's members (and amended by the ASB).

a. **General Standards**

1) *The audit is to be performed by a person or persons having adequate technical training and proficiency as an auditor.*

2) *In all matters relating to the assignment, an independence in mental attitude is to be maintained by the auditor or auditors.*

3) *Due professional care is to be exercised in the planning and performance of the audit and the preparation of the report* (as amended by SAS 82 and codified in AU 230).

b. **Standards of Field Work**

1) *The work is to be adequately planned and assistants, if any, are to be properly supervised.*

2) *A sufficient understanding of internal control is to be obtained to plan the audit and to determine the nature, timing, and extent of tests to be performed.*

3) *Sufficient competent evidential matter is to be obtained through inspection, observation, inquiries, and confirmations to afford a reasonable basis for an opinion regarding the financial statements under audit.*

c. **Standards of Reporting**

1) *The report shall state whether the financial statements are presented in accordance with generally accepted accounting principles (GAAP).*

2) *The report shall identify those circumstances in which such principles have not been consistently observed in the current period in relation to the preceding period.*

3) *Informative disclosures in the financial statements are to be regarded as reasonably adequate unless otherwise stated in the report.*

4) *The report shall contain either an expression of opinion regarding the financial statements, taken as a whole, or an assertion to the effect that an opinion cannot be expressed. When an overall opinion cannot be expressed, the reasons therefor should be stated. In all cases in which an auditor's name is associated with financial statements, the report should contain a clear-cut indication of the character of the auditor's work, if any, and the degree of responsibility the auditor is taking.*

4. The 10 standards are binding on AICPA members. They are also considered standards of the profession by state boards of accountancy and the courts, so they are also binding on non-AICPA members.

a. The AICPA's *Code of Professional Conduct* includes a rule providing for enforcement of standards issued by the ASB.

b. **SASs** are standards codified within the framework of the 10 standards and are deemed to have the status of GAAS. They are summarized in Appendix A, and many are outlined in subsequent study units.

c. **Interpretive publications** do not have the status of auditing standards, but they provide recommendations on the application of the SASs. These publications include Interpretations of the SASs, appendixes to the SASs, AICPA Audit and Accounting Guides, and auditing Statements of Position. An auditor who does not follow an applicable interpretive publication should be prepared to explain how (s)he complied with the relevant SAS.

d. **Other auditing publications** have no authoritative effect, but they may provide assistance in applying the SASs. They include all other auditing literature, including articles and textbooks.

5. Stop and review! You have completed the outline for this subunit. Study multiple-choice questions 7 through 9 on page 36.

1.3 AUDIT PROGRAMS

1. The first standard of field work (GAAS) requires the auditor to plan the audit.

   a. A **written audit program** is required for all audit engagements. The program lists in reasonable detail the procedures needed to accomplish audit objectives intended to be performed to support the auditor's conclusions concerning management's assertions about the financial statements. It should be based on the auditor's judgment contingent on the assessments of inherent and control risk.

   b. The audit program will likely be adjusted as the audit progresses. The auditor may change the assessments of control risk and inherent risk as more evidence is collected. As a result, the acceptable level of detection risk may change, and the auditor may need to alter the nature, timing, and extent of substantive tests.

   c. Audit programs are part of the audit documentation.

2. Internal audit programs differ from those written by the independent external auditor.

   a. The independent external auditor's purpose is to express an opinion on the fairness of the financial statements, i.e., to evaluate the client's financial reporting.

   b. However, the internal auditor's work is more comprehensive. According to The Institute of Internal Auditors, internal auditors should evaluate and help to improve the effectiveness of risk management, control, and governance processes. Their scope of work extends to the reliability and integrity of financial and operational information; the effectiveness and efficiency of operations; the safeguarding of assets; and compliance with laws, regulations, and contracts. Consequently, the internal auditor's programs are more detailed and cover areas that normally are not considered by the independent auditor.

3. Stop and review! You have completed the outline for this subunit. Study multiple-choice questions 10 through 14 beginning on page 37.

1.4 COMPILATIONS AND REVIEWS (AR 100)

1. The AICPA bylaws designate the Accounting and Review Services Committee as the senior technical committee authorized to issue pronouncements in connection with the unaudited financial statements or other unaudited financial information of a nonpublic entity.

   a. It promulgates Statements on Standards for Accounting and Review Services (SSARSs) and is authorized to promulgate attestation standards in its area of responsibility.

2. An accountant may not permit use of his/her name in a written communication that contains the unaudited financial statements of a nonpublic entity unless

   a. (S)he has compiled or reviewed them in accordance with AR 100, *Compilation and Review of Financial Statements*, or

   b. An indication is included to the effect that the accountant has not performed such services and that (s)he assumes no responsibility.

3. AR 100 describes the accountant's procedures and reporting responsibilities relative to these services (Study Unit 18).

4.   An accountant must issue a report whenever (s)he compiles or reviews financial statements under the provisions of AR 100.

    a.   An accountant should not report on the unaudited financial statements of a nonpublic entity or submit such financial statements to the client or others unless (s)he complies with AR 100.

    b.   A **submission** of financial statements is defined as "presenting to a client or third parties financial statements that the accountant has prepared either manually or through the use of computer software."

5.   A **compilation of financial statements** is the presentation in statement form of information that is the representation of management. The accountant expresses no assurance in a compilation report.

6.   The purpose of a **review** of financial statements is to perform inquiries and analytical procedures that provide the accountant with a reasonable basis for expressing limited assurance that there are no material modifications that should be made to the statements for them to be in conformity with GAAP or, if applicable, with another comprehensive basis of accounting.

    a.   A review does not contemplate consideration of internal control, tests of transactions and account balances, and other auditing procedures.

7.   Prior to undertaking a compilation or review engagement, the accountant should establish an understanding with the entity, preferably in writing, regarding the services to be performed. The written understanding is referred to as the **engagement letter** and is discussed further in Study Unit 2. The understanding should

    a.   Describe the nature and limitations of the services to be performed

    b.   Describe the report the accountant expects to render

    c.   State that the engagement cannot be relied upon to disclose errors, fraud, or illegal acts

    d.   State that any errors, fraud, or illegal acts discovered will be reported to management or the board of directors

8.   Stop and review! You have completed the outline for this subunit. Study multiple-choice questions 15 through 22 beginning on page 38.

1.5 FINANCIAL FORECASTS AND PROJECTIONS (AT 301)

1.   An accountant must compile, examine, or apply agreed-upon procedures to **prospective financial statements (PFSs)** (financial forecasts or projections, including summaries of significant assumptions and accounting policies), if those statements are, or reasonably might be, expected to be used by another (third) party and if the practitioner

    a.   Submits to the client or others PFSs that (s)he has assembled or assisted in assembling

    b.   Reports on PFSs

2.   A **financial forecast** consists of PFSs that present, to the best of the responsible party's knowledge and belief, an entity's expected financial position, results of operations, and cash flows.

    a.   It is based on the responsible party's assumptions reflecting conditions it expects to exist and the course of action it expects to take.

        1)   The responsible party is usually management of the entity, but it may be a party outside the entity, such as a potential acquirer.

b.   It may be expressed in specific monetary amounts as a single point estimate of forecasted results or may be expressed as a range. In the latter case, the responsible party selects key assumptions to form a range within which it reasonably expects, to the best of its knowledge and belief, the item or items subject to the assumptions to actually fall.

3.   A **financial projection** differs from a forecast in that it is based on the responsible party's assumptions reflecting conditions it expects would exist and the course of action it expects would be taken given one or more hypothetical assumptions. A projection is sometimes prepared to present one or more hypothetical courses of action for evaluation, as in response to a question such as "What would happen if . . .?" A projection may be expressed as a point estimate or a range.

4.   The standard provides for **minimum presentation guidelines** for prospective financial statements.

a.   Under the guidelines, PFSs may take the form of complete basic statements or be limited to the following minimum items (when the items would be presented for the period's historical statements):

1)   Sales or gross revenues

2)   Gross profit or cost of sales

3)   Unusual or infrequently occurring items

4)   Provision for income taxes

5)   Discontinued operations or extraordinary items

6)   Income from continuing operations

7)   Net income

8)   Basic and diluted earnings per share

9)   Significant changes in financial position (neither a balance sheet nor a statement of cash flows is required)

10)   A description of what the responsible party intends the statements to present, a statement that the assumptions are based on information about circumstances and conditions existing at the time of preparation, and a caveat about achievability

11)   Summary of significant assumptions

12)   Summary of significant accounting policies

b.   A presentation is partial if it omits one or more of items 1) through 9). A **partial presentation** is ordinarily not appropriate for general use.

1)   The presentation is not deemed to be partial, and the provisions of the standard still apply, if items 10) through 12) are omitted.

5.   PFSs are for **general use** if they are for use by persons with whom the responsible party is not negotiating directly, e.g., in an offering statement of the party's securities. Only a financial forecast is appropriate for general use. All other presentations are limited use.

a.   General use prospective statements should portray expected results to the best of the responsible party's knowledge and belief.

6. **Limited use** of PFSs means use by the responsible party and those with whom that party is negotiating directly, for example, in a submission to a regulatory body or in negotiations for a bank loan. These third parties are in a position to communicate directly with the responsible party.

    a. Consequently, any type of PFSs that would be useful in the circumstances would be appropriate for limited use.

    b. A projection is appropriate only for limited use. The reason is that the presentation of a projection is based on one or more hypothetical assumptions.

        1) PFSs are appropriate for general use only if they portray, to the best of the responsible party's knowledge and belief, the expected results. A hypothetical assumption is a condition or course of action that is not necessarily expected to occur.

7. An **examination** entails evaluating the preparation of the statements, the support underlying the assumptions, and the presentation of the statements for conformity with AICPA guidelines.

    a. It also involves issuance of a report stating the practitioner's opinion on whether the PFSs conform with AICPA guidelines and whether the assumptions provide a reasonable basis for the forecast or whether the assumptions provide a reasonable basis for the projection given hypothetical assumptions.

    b. If assumptions that appear to be significant at the time are not disclosed in the presentation, including the summary of assumptions, the practitioner must express an adverse opinion. Moreover, a practitioner should not examine a presentation that omits all such disclosures.

8. A **compilation** of PFSs, such as a financial forecast, is a professional service involving assembling, to the extent necessary, the statements based on the responsible party's assumptions, performing required compilation procedures, and issuing a compilation report.

    a. The procedures include reading the statements and considering whether they meet AICPA presentation guidelines and determining that the statements are not obviously inappropriate.

        1) Other procedures consist of inquiries, testing the mathematical accuracy of the computations, and obtaining written representations.

    b. The standard report states that a compilation is limited in scope and does not enable the practitioner to express an opinion or any other form of assurance on the prospective statements or the assumptions.

        1) It adds that a compilation does not include evaluation of the support for the assumptions underlying the PFSs.

        2) A report on a projection should also include a separate paragraph that limits the use of the presentation.

9. A practitioner may accept an engagement to apply **agreed-upon procedures** to PFSs.

    a. The engagement may be accepted if the practitioner is independent and

        1) The specified parties agree to the procedures and take responsibility for their sufficiency.

        2) Report use is not intended except for specified parties.

        3) The statements include a summary of significant assumptions.

b. The report should state that the practitioner did not perform an examination and that other matters might have come to his/her attention if additional procedures had been performed.

1) It should also disclaim an opinion on conformity with AICPA presentation guidelines, etc.

2) The report lists the procedures performed and the related findings. It does not provide positive or negative assurance.

10. The standard does not provide for the **review** form of engagement with regard to prospective statements and therefore does not provide for the expression of limited assurance thereon.

11. Stop and review! You have completed the outline for this subunit. Study multiple-choice questions 23 through 36 beginning on page 40.

1.6 REPORTING ON PRO FORMA FINANCIAL INFORMATION (AT 401)

1. Pro forma information shows "what the significant effects on historical financial information would have been had a consummated or proposed transaction (or event) occurred at an earlier date." Examples of these transactions include a business combination, disposal of a segment, change in the form or status of an entity, and a change in capitalization.

2. An accountant may **examine or review** pro forma financial information if three conditions are met:

a. The document containing the pro forma financial information includes or incorporates by reference the complete historical statements for the most recent year available, and, if the pro forma financial information is for an interim period, the document should also include the interim historical information for that period.

b. The level of assurance (i.e., examine/audit or review) provided on the pro forma financial information is limited to that given on the historical statements.

c. The reporting accountant is appropriately knowledgeable about the accounting and financial reporting practices of each significant part of the combined entity.

3. A compilation of the historical statements provides no assurance; thus, it would not provide a basis for the accountant to examine or review the pro forma statements. Under the standard, only an audit or a review is contemplated.

4. The report on an examination should include an opinion (unqualified, qualified, or adverse) on whether management's assumptions provide a reasonable basis for the significant effects attributable to the transaction or event, the pro forma adjustments give appropriate effect to the assumptions, and the pro forma column reflects the proper application of those adjustments to the historical data.

a. Scope limitations, reservations about the assumptions or the presentation (including inadequate disclosure), and other matters may lead to modification of the opinion or a disclaimer.

5. A public company that discloses a material non-GAAP financial measure (a **pro forma release**) also must disclose the most directly comparable GAAP measure (SEC Regulation G).

6. Stop and review! You have completed the outline for this subunit. Study multiple-choice questions 37 through 41 beginning on page 44.

1.7 ASSURANCE SERVICES

1. Assurance services are independent professional services that improve the quality of information, or its context, for decision makers.

   a. Information might be financial or nonfinancial, historical or prospective; consist of data or relate to systems; or be internal or external to the user.

   b. Assurance services encompass audit and other attestation services but also include other, nonstandard, services.

   c. Unless the services fall under the AICPA's attestation standards, assurance services do not require written assertions.

2. Assurance services evolve naturally from attestation services, which in turn evolved from audits. The roots of all three are in independent verification.

   a. The form and content of assurance services differ.

      1) Traditional audit-related services are highly structured and considered to be relevant to a large number of users.

      2) The newer assurance services are more customized and targeted, and are intended to be highly useful in more limited circumstances.

3. Assurance services do not encompass consulting services. There are often similarities between assurance and consulting services because they are delivered using a similar body of knowledge and skills.

   a. Assurance services differ from consulting services in two ways:

      1) They focus on improving information rather than providing advice, and

      2) They usually involve situations in which one party wants to monitor another (often within the same company) rather than the two-party arrangements common in consulting engagements.

4. Assurance services can

   a. Capture information. Assurance services can capture information by using existing or improved measurement tools.

   b. Improve information reliability. Raw information is refined into reliable information. Any raw information can be refined, regardless of whether it is used for decision making at all.

   c. Improve decision making. Decision making can be improved by improving the context, such as decision models, used by the decision maker. This facet of assurance services differs from existing attestation models.

5. The following table contrasts traditional attest, assurance, and consulting services:

	Attestation	Assurance	Consulting
Result	Written conclusion about subject matter or a written assertion of another party	Better information for decision makers. Recommendations might be a byproduct	Recommendations based on the objectives of the engagement
Objective	Reliable information	Better decision making	Better outcomes
Parties to the engagement	Not specified, but generally three (the third party is usually external). CPA generally is paid by the preparer	Generally three (although the other two might be employed by the same entity). CPA is paid by the preparer or user	Generally two; CPA is paid by the user
Independence	Required by standards	Included in definition	Not required
Substance of CPA output	Conformity with established or stated criteria	Assurance about reliability or relevance of information. Criteria might be established, stated, or unstated	Recommendations; not measured against formal criteria
Form of CPA output	Written	Some form of communication	Written or oral
Critical information developed by	Asserter	Either CPA or asserter	CPA
Information content determined by	Preparer (client)	Preparer, CPA, or user	CPA
Level of assurance	Examination, review, or results of agreed-upon procedures	Flexible, for example, it might be compilation level, explicit assurance about usefulness of the information for intended purpose, or implicit from the CPA's involvement	No explicit assurance

6. **Types of assurance service.** The AICPA has identified six services to date. Some address the needs of existing customers; others are for new customers. Some are based on the types of data CPAs traditionally report on, whereas others focus on new types of data. There are likely to be many additions in the future

Assurances about Risks	Assurances about Performance	Assurances about Systems
CPA Risk Advisory ElderCare	CPA Performance Review Healthcare Effectiveness	SysTrust WebTrust

a. **CPA Risk Advisory**. Managers and investors are concerned about whether entities have identified the full scope of various business risks and taken precautions to mitigate them.

  1) This service assures that an entity's profile of business risks is comprehensive and evaluates whether the entity has appropriate systems in place to manage those risks effectively.

b. **ElderCare Services**. Older Americans prefer to live independently in their own homes. But as their capabilities decline, they require an increasingly broad range of services to do so. They and their loved ones are concerned about the comprehensiveness and quality of these services.

  1) ElderCare services assess whether specified goals regarding care for the elderly are being met by various care givers.

  2) Services provided to the elderly include accumulation of information, financial management, and assessment of nursing care.

  3) The client receiving ElderCare services may be the elderly person or another person with power of attorney.

c. **CPA Performance Review**. This service evaluates whether an entity's performance measurement system contains relevant and reliable measures for assessing the degree to which the entity's goals and objectives are achieved or how its performance compares to its competitors. It provides investors, managers, or others with a comprehensive information base and a more "balanced scorecard."

d. **Healthcare Effectiveness**. The old healthcare system (fee for service) rewarded those who delivered the most services; the new system (managed care) rewards those who deliver the fewest services.

   1) Health-care recipients and their employers are increasingly concerned about the quality and availability of health care services.

   2) This service provides assurance about the effectiveness of health care services provided by HMOs, hospitals, doctors, and other providers.

e. **SysTrust**. This service assesses whether an entity's internal information systems (financial and nonfinancial) provide reliable information for operating and financial decisions. Information systems address reporting concepts and systems, transaction processing systems, management reporting systems, and risks within a business. SysTrust is an assurance service developed under the attestation standards by the AICPA and the Canadian Institute of Chartered Accountants (CICA). SysTrust is designed to increase the comfort of management, customers, creditors, bankers, and business partners with the systems that support a business or a particular activity.

   1) The practitioner uses suitable **criteria** or benchmarks that are objective, measurable, complete, and relevant to determine whether management's assertions are fairly stated about any or all of the following principles:

      a) **Online Privacy**. Personal information obtained is collected, used, disclosed, and retained as committed or agreed.

      b) **Security**. The system is protected against unauthorized access (both physical and logical).

      c) **Processing Integrity**. System processing is complete, accurate, timely, and authorized.

      d) **Availability**. The system is available for operation and used as committed or agreed.

      e) **Confidentiality**. Information designated as confidential is protected as committed or agreed.

   2) Practitioners test the **policies, communications, procedures, and monitoring systems** using suitable criteria to assess the fairness of management's assertions about a particular principle. The report may address management's assertions or directly address the system.

f. **WebTrust**. This service, developed under the attestation standards by the AICPA and the CICA, provides Internet users, including businesses and Internet service providers, assurance about electronic commerce activities.

   1) The practitioner uses the same **criteria** as outlined for SysTrust in e.1) and 2) above.

7. Stop and review! You have completed the outline for this subunit. Study multiple-choice questions 42 through 53 beginning on page 46.

1.8 QUALITY CONTROL

1.   To be admitted to or retain membership in the AICPA, practitioners who are engaged in the practice of public accounting are required to practice in firms enrolled in an <u>AICPA approved practice-monitoring program</u> if the services performed by the firm are within the scope of the AICPA's practice-monitoring standards.

   a.   A firm (or individual) enrolled in the Center for Public Company Audit Firms Peer Review Program (Center <u>PRP</u>) or the AICPA Peer Review Program (<u>AICPA PRP</u>) is deemed to be enrolled in an approved practice-monitoring program.

   b.   Quality control over the audits of public companies will be evaluated during periodic inspections of the Public Company Accounting Oversight Board (PCAOB). The Center PRP is designed to review and evaluate those portions of a firm's accounting and auditing practice that are not inspected by the PCAOB.

   c.   Public accounting firms required to maintain a monitoring program, but without public clients, should comply with the AICPA PRP.

2.   An audit firm has a responsibility to adopt a system of quality control and establish policies and procedures to provide reasonable assurance that personnel comply with GAAS. GAAS apply to individual engagements, and quality control standards apply to the conduct of a firm's practice as a whole. Thus, quality control may affect audits. Nevertheless, deficiencies in, or instances of noncompliance with, the quality control system do not, by themselves, signify a departure from GAAS in conducting a specific audit (AU 161). NOTE: Similar rules are stated in SSAEs, SSARSs, and SQCSs.

3.   Statements on Quality Control Standards (SQCSs) require that a CPA firm have a quality control system.

   a.   Quality control for a CPA firm applies to all audit, attest, accounting and review, and other services for which standards have been established by the Auditing Standards Board or the Accounting and Review Services Committee. It does not apply explicitly to consulting or tax services.

   1)   A firm is defined broadly to include "a form of organization permitted by state law or regulation whose characteristics conform to resolutions of Council that is engaged in the practice of public accounting, including the individual owners thereof." This definition includes proprietorships, partnerships, and professional corporations.

   b.   The following are the five elements of a quality control system:

   1)   **Independence, integrity, and objectivity**. Policies and procedures should be established to provide reasonable assurance that personnel maintain independence in fact and appearance in all required circumstances, perform all professional responsibilities with integrity, and maintain objectivity in discharging professional responsibilities.

   2)   **Personnel management**. Policies and procedures should be established to provide reasonable assurance that those hired are competent, work is assigned to personnel having the necessary technical training and proficiency, employees participate in continuing education, and employees selected for advancement have the appropriate qualifications.

   3)   **Acceptance and continuance of clients and engagements**. Policies and procedures should be established to provide reasonable assurance that the likelihood of association with clients whose managers may lack integrity is minimized, that the firm undertakes only engagements it expects to complete with professional competence, and that it appropriately considers the risks of providing services.

4) **Engagement performance**. Policies and procedures should be established to provide reasonable assurance that work performed by personnel meets applicable professional standards, regulatory requirements, and the firm's standards of quality. These policies and procedures relate to planning, performing, supervising, reviewing, documenting, and communicating the results of the audit.

    a) Personnel are expected to refer to authoritative literature and consult with knowledgeable people within or outside the firm.

5) **Monitoring**. Policies and procedures should be established to provide reasonable assurance that the policies and procedures for the other quality control elements are suitably designed and are being effectively applied. Monitoring is an ongoing evaluation of relevance and adequacy of the system, appropriateness of guidance materials and practice aids, effectiveness of professional development, and compliance.

c. Administration of a quality control system requires that

    1) Responsibility for designing and maintaining policies and procedures be assigned to appropriate individuals

    2) Those policies and procedures be communicated so as to provide reasonable assurance that they are understood and complied with

    3) Consideration be given to whether and to what extent policies and procedures must be documented for effective communication

    4) The firm appropriately document compliance with quality control policies and procedures

4. A **peer review** does not substitute for monitoring, but it is a necessary part of the practice-monitoring requirement for AICPA membership. The applicable pronouncements issued by the AICPA Peer Review Board are the Standards for Performing and Reporting on Peer Reviews (PR 100). They govern peer reviews supervised by state CPA societies of firms enrolled in the AICPA Peer Review Program or the Center for Public Company Audit Firms Peer Review Program.

a. The portion of a firm's accounting and auditing practice covered by the peer review standards includes engagements under SASs, SSARSs, SSAEs, and Government Auditing Standards.

b. A **system review** is an on-site review required for a firm that performs the highest level of services. It provides the reviewer with a reasonable basis for expressing an opinion on the firm's system of quality control. An **engagement review** is for a firm not required to have a system review but not qualifying for a report review. It provides the reviewer with a reasonable basis for expressing limited assurance on whether the financial statements or information and the accountant's reports submitted materially conform with professional standards and on whether the firm's documentation conforms with the SSARSs and the SSAEs. A **report review** is for a firm that performs only compilations omitting substantially all disclosures. The report consists of comments and recommendations after review of a sample of engagements. These comments should be based on professional standards.

5. Under the federal **Sarbanes-Oxley Act of 2002**, a registered accounting firm must adopt quality control standards. Many of the provisions of Sarbanes-Oxley relate to improving the quality control of the audit and improving the quality of financial reporting. These standards relate to the audits of public companies.

    a. A **second partner review and approval** is required of audit reports.

    b. The **lead auditor** and the **reviewing partner** must be rotated off the audit every 5 years.

    c. The accounting firm must supervise any **associated person** with respect to auditing or quality control standards.

    d. **Independence rules have been expanded** by prohibiting the auditor from providing a variety of nonaudit services.

    e. The client's CEO and CFO must certify as to the appropriateness of the **financial statements and disclosures**.

    f. **Penalties** for destroying documents to impede an investigation have been expanded.

    g. Management must **assess the effectiveness of internal control** and the auditor must attest to the assessment made by management (Study Unit 9).

6. Stop and review! You have completed the outline for this subunit. Study multiple-choice questions 53 through 63 beginning on page 49.

QUESTIONS

1.1 Attest Engagements (AT 101)

1. Which of the following is a conceptual difference between the attestation standards and generally accepted auditing standards?

   A. The attestation standards provide a framework for the attest function beyond historical financial statements.

   B. The requirement that the practitioner be independent in mental attitude is omitted from the attestation standards.

   C. The attestation standards do not permit an attest engagement to be part of a business acquisition study or a feasibility study.

   D. None of the standards of field work in generally accepted auditing standards are included in the attestation standards.

Answer (A) is correct. *(CPA, adapted)*
   REQUIRED: The conceptual difference between the attestation standards and GAAS.
   DISCUSSION: Two principal conceptual differences exist between the attestation standards and GAAS. First, the attestation standards provide a framework for the attest function beyond historical financial statements. Second, the attestation standards accommodate the growing number of attest services in which the practitioner expresses assurance below the level that is expressed for the traditional audit (an opinion).
   Answer (B) is incorrect because, in any attest engagement, the practitioner must be independent in mental attitude. Answer (C) is incorrect because attestation services may be provided in conjunction with other services provided to clients. Answer (D) is incorrect because the attestation standards and GAAS require that work be adequately planned and that assistants be properly supervised. Both also require sufficient evidence.

2. Who establishes generally accepted auditing standards?

   A. Auditing Standards Board.

   B. Financial Accounting Standards Board.

   C. State Boards of Accountancy.

   D. Securities and Exchange Commission.

Answer (A) is correct. *(CPA, adapted)*
   REQUIRED: The organization that promulgates generally accepted auditing standards (GAAS).
   DISCUSSION: AICPA Conduct Rule 202, *Compliance with Standards*, requires adherence to standards promulgated by bodies designated by the AICPA Council. The Auditing Standards Board (ASB) is the body designated to issue auditing standards. They are in the form of Statements on Auditing Standards (SASs), which are codified within the framework of the 10 standards. The Public Company Accounting Oversight Board (PCAOB) was created by the Sarbanes-Oxley Act of 2002. It establishes by rule auditing, quality control, ethics, independence, and other standards relating to the preparation of audit reports for public entities. The PCAOB is required to cooperate with the AICPA and other groups in setting auditing standards and may adopt their proposals. Nevertheless, the PCAOB is authorized to amend, modify, repeal, or reject any such standards. Several auditing standards have been issued to date, the most significant requiring opinions on internal control for public companies.
   Answer (B) is incorrect because the FASB issues Statements on Financial Accounting Standards and other financial accounting pronouncements and interpretations. Answer (C) is incorrect because Boards of Accountancy in the states and territories regulate the practice of accounting. They typically grant CPA certificates and licenses. Answer (D) is incorrect because the SEC issues Financial Reporting Releases and Accounting and Auditing Enforcement Releases.

3. Which of the following is not an attestation standard?

   A. Sufficient evidence shall be obtained to provide a reasonable basis for the conclusion that is expressed in the report.

   B. The report shall identify the subject matter or the assertion being reported on and state the character of the engagement.

   C. The work shall be adequately planned and assistants, if any, shall be properly supervised.

   D. A sufficient understanding of internal control shall be obtained to plan the engagement.

Answer (D) is correct. *(CPA, adapted)*
   REQUIRED: The item not an attestation standard.
   DISCUSSION: No attestation standard mentions internal control. The second standard of field work applicable to audits in accordance with GAAS states, "A sufficient understanding of internal control is to be obtained to plan the audit and to determine the nature, timing, and extent of tests to be performed."
   Answer (A) is incorrect because the evidentiary requirement is contained in the second attestation standard of field work. Answer (B) is incorrect because the first attestation standard of reporting concerns the character of the engagement. Answer (C) is incorrect because the first attestation standard of field work concerns planning and supervision.

4. A CPA in public practice is required to comply with the provisions of the Statements on Standards for Attestation Engagements (SSAE) when

	Testifying as an expert witness in accounting and auditing matters given stipulated facts	Compiling a client's financial projection that presents a hypothetical course of action
A.	Yes	Yes
B.	Yes	No
C.	No	Yes
D.	No	No

Answer (C) is correct. *(CPA, adapted)*
REQUIRED: The services for which SSAEs establish standards or procedures.
DISCUSSION: The SSAEs cover attest engagements, including the attestation standards that relate to agreed-upon procedures engagements; financial forecasts and projections; reporting on pro forma financial information; reporting on an entity's internal control over financial reporting; compliance attestation; and management's discussion and analysis. Litigation support services are transaction services, a category of consulting services. The relevant AICPA pronouncement is the Statement on Standards for Consulting Services.
Answer (A) is incorrect because a CPA is not required to comply with the provisions of the SSAEs when testifying as an expert witness in accounting and auditing matters given stipulated facts. Such testimony is a consulting service. Answer (B) is incorrect because a CPA is not required to comply with the provisions of the SSAEs when testifying as an expert witness in accounting and auditing matters given stipulated facts. Such testimony is a consulting service. Answer (D) is incorrect because a CPA is required to comply with the provisions of the SSAEs when compiling a client's financial projection that presents a hypothetical course of action.

5. In performing an attest engagement, a CPA typically

A. Supplies litigation support services.

B. Assesses control risk at a low level.

C. Expresses a conclusion about a written assertion.

D. Provides management consulting advice.

Answer (C) is correct. *(CPA, adapted)*
REQUIRED: The usual CPA's task in an attestation engagement.
DISCUSSION: When a CPA in the practice of public accounting performs an attest engagement, the engagement is subject to the attestation standards. An attest engagement is one in which a practitioner is engaged to issue or does issue an examination, a review, or an agreed-upon procedures report on subject matter, or an assertion about the subject matter, that is the responsibility of another party. Moreover, according to the second attestation standard of reporting, "The report shall state the practitioner's conclusion about the subject matter or the assertion in relation to the criteria against which the subject matter was evaluated." However, the conclusion may refer to that assertion or to the subject matter to which the assertion relates. Furthermore, given one or more material deviations from the criteria, the practitioner should modify the report and ordinarily should express the conclusion directly on the subject matter.
Answer (A) is incorrect because litigation support services are consulting services. Answer (B) is incorrect because the CPA assesses control risk in an audit but not necessarily in all attest engagements. Furthermore, the assessment may not be at a low level. Answer (D) is incorrect because an attest engagement results in a report on subject matter or on an assertion about the subject matter.

6. Which of the following professional services is considered an attest engagement?

A. A consulting service engagement to provide computer advice to a client.

B. An engagement to report on compliance with statutory requirements.

C. An income tax engagement to prepare federal and state tax returns.

D. The compilation of financial statements from a client's accounting records.

Answer (B) is correct. *(CPA, adapted)*
REQUIRED: The attest service.
DISCUSSION: Attest services have traditionally been limited to expressing an opinion on historical financial statements on the basis of an audit in accordance with GAAS. But CPAs increasingly provide assurance on representations other than historical statements and in forms other than an opinion. Thus, attest services may extend to engagements related to management's compliance with specified requirements or the effectiveness of internal control over compliance.
Answer (A) is incorrect because the attestation standards explicitly do not apply to consulting services in which the practitioner provides advice or recommendations to a client. Answer (C) is incorrect because tax return preparation is not an attest service according to the attestation standards. Answer (D) is incorrect because a compilation of a financial statement is not an attest service according to the attestation standards.

1.2 Audit Engagements

7. Which of the following best describes what is meant by the term generally accepted auditing standards?

A. Rules acknowledged by the accounting profession because of their universal application.

B. Pronouncements issued by the Auditing Standards Board.

C. Measures of the audit quality.

D. Procedures to be used to gather evidence to support financial statements.

Answer (C) is correct.   *(CPA, adapted)*
REQUIRED: The best definition of generally accepted auditing standards.
DISCUSSION: An audit should be planned, performed, and reported on in accordance with GAAS. Auditing standards are concerned with audit quality and the objectives to be attained (AU 150).
Answer (A) is incorrect because auditing standards are not elective guidelines but standards required of all accountants during the performance of an audit. Answer (B) is incorrect because, although Statements on Auditing Standards (SASs) issued by the ASB are now deemed to be GAAS, they do not constitute all GAAS. Answer (D) is incorrect because "auditing procedures are acts that the auditor performs during the course of an audit to comply with auditing standards" (AU 150).

8. The third general standard states that due professional care is to be exercised in the planning and performance of the audit and the preparation of the report. This standard requires

A. Thorough review of the existing safeguards over access to assets and records.

B. Limited review of the indications of employee fraud and illegal acts.

C. Objective review of the adequacy of the technical training and proficiency of firm personnel.

D. Supervision of assistants by the auditor with final responsibility for the audit.

Answer (D) is correct.   *(CPA, adapted)*
REQUIRED: The requirement under the third general standard (due professional care).
DISCUSSION: According to AU 230, *Due Professional Care in the Performance of Work,* "Due professional care imposes a responsibility upon each professional within an independent auditor's organization to observe the standards of field work and reporting." The first standard of field work requires proper supervision of assistants (AU 150). Thus, AU 230 states, "The auditor with final responsibility is responsible for the assignment of tasks to, and the supervision of, assistants."
Answer (A) is incorrect because, although a review of safeguards over access to assets and records relates to the conduct of the audit, this procedure is not required specifically by the third general standard. Answer (B) is incorrect because, although a review of the likelihood of employee fraud and illegal acts relates to the conduct of the audit, this procedure is not required specifically by the third general standard. Answer (C) is incorrect because objective review of the adequacy of the technical training and proficiency of firm personnel relates to the first general standard (adequate technical training and proficiency as an auditor).

9. Which of the following statements is true concerning an auditor's responsibilities regarding financial statements?

A. Making suggestions that are adopted about the form and content of an entity's financial statements impairs an auditor's independence.

B. An auditor may draft an entity's financial statements based on information from management's accounting system.

C. The fair presentation of audited financial statements in conformity with GAAP is an implicit part of the auditor's responsibilities.

D. An auditor's responsibilities for audited financial statements are not confined to the expression of the auditor's opinion.

Answer (B) is correct.   *(CPA, adapted)*
REQUIRED: The true statement concerning the auditor's responsibilities for financial statements.
DISCUSSION: "The independent auditor may make suggestions about the form or content of the financial statements or draft them, in whole or in part, based on information from management's accounting system. However, the auditor's responsibility for the financial statements he or she has audited is confined to the expression of his or her opinion on them" (AU 110).
Answer (A) is incorrect because suggestions about the form and content of an entity's financial statements do not impair an auditor's independence as long as management takes responsibility for the financial statements. Answer (C) is incorrect because the presentation of the financial statements in conformity with GAAP is the responsibility of management. Answer (D) is incorrect because the auditor's responsibilities for audited financial statements are confined to the expression of the opinion.

1.3 Audit Programs

10. An auditor should design the written audit program so that

   A. All material transactions will be selected for substantive testing.

   B. Substantive tests prior to the balance sheet date will be minimized.

   C. The audit procedures selected will achieve specific audit objectives.

   D. Each account balance will be tested under either tests of controls or tests of transactions.

Answer (C) is correct. *(CPA, adapted)*
   REQUIRED: The purpose of a written audit program.
   DISCUSSION: In planning, the auditor should consider the nature, timing, and extent of work to be performed and should prepare a written audit program. An audit program sets forth in reasonable detail the audit procedures necessary to accomplish audit objectives.

11. Audit programs should be designed so that

   A. Most of the required procedures can be performed as interim work.

   B. Inherent risk is assessed at a sufficiently low level.

   C. The auditor can make constructive suggestions to management.

   D. The audit evidence gathered supports the auditor's conclusions.

Answer (D) is correct. *(CPA, adapted)*
   REQUIRED: The use of audit programs.
   DISCUSSION: The auditor is responsible for collecting sufficient, competent evidential matter. Audit programs describe the steps involved in that process. The evidence should support the auditor's conclusions.
   Answer (A) is incorrect because, depending on the assertion, work may be performed at interim dates or in the subsequent events period. Answer (B) is incorrect because the auditor must assess inherent risk based upon the characteristics of the client. Answer (C) is incorrect because suggestions to management are not required in an audit.

12. In designing written audit programs, an auditor should establish specific audit objectives that relate primarily to the

   A. Timing of audit procedures.

   B. Cost-benefit of gathering evidence.

   C. Selected audit techniques.

   D. Financial statement assertions.

Answer (D) is correct. *(CPA, adapted)*
   REQUIRED: The item to which specific audit objectives primarily relate.
   DISCUSSION: Most audit work consists of obtaining and evaluating evidence about financial statement assertions, which are management representations embodied in financial statement components. AU 326 states, "In obtaining evidential matter in support of financial statement assertions, the auditor develops specific audit objectives in light of those assertions."
   Answer (A) is incorrect because timing is important in meeting the objectives of the audit but does not relate to the audit objectives themselves. Answer (B) is incorrect because the cost-benefit of gathering evidence is important to the auditor but is not the primary objective. Answer (C) is incorrect because audit objectives determine the specific audit techniques.

13. The audit program usually cannot be finalized until the

   A. Consideration of the entity's internal control has been completed.

   B. Engagement letter has been signed by the auditor and the client.

   C. Reportable conditions have been communicated to the audit committee of the board of directors.

   D. Search for unrecorded liabilities has been performed and documented.

Answer (A) is correct. *(CPA, adapted)*
   REQUIRED: The time at which the audit program can be finalized.
   DISCUSSION: The nature, timing, and extent of substantive tests cannot be determined until the auditor has considered internal control, that is, obtained an understanding of internal control and assessed control risk.
   Answer (B) is incorrect because the engagement letter identifies the responsibilities of the parties and is completed before the engagement begins. Answer (C) is incorrect because reportable conditions are typically communicated upon completion of the audit. Answer (D) is incorrect because the search for unrecorded liabilities is a procedure performed during the audit.

14. In comparison with the detailed audit program of the independent auditor who is engaged to audit the financial statements of a large publicly held company, the audit client's comprehensive internal audit program is

A. More detailed and covers areas that normally are not considered by the independent auditor.

B. More detailed although it covers fewer areas than are normally covered by the independent auditor.

C. Substantially identical to the audit program used by the independent auditor because both consider substantially identical areas.

D. Less detailed and covers fewer areas than are normally considered by the independent auditor.

Answer (A) is correct. *(CPA, adapted)*
REQUIRED: The best description of the difference between the independent auditor's audit program and an internal audit program.
DISCUSSION: The independent auditor's objective is limited to expressing an opinion on the fairness of the financial statements. The internal auditor's work is more comprehensive because (s)he must evaluate and help to improve the effectiveness of the organization's risk management, control, and governance processes. Thus, an internal auditor's scope of work extends to the reliability and integrity of operational as well as financial information; the effectiveness and efficiency of operations; the safeguarding of assets; and compliance with laws, regulations, and contracts.
Answer (B) is incorrect because the internal audit program covers more areas than that of the independent auditor. Answer (C) is incorrect because the internal audit program is more detailed and covers more areas. Answer (D) is incorrect because the internal audit program is more detailed and covers more areas.

1.4 Compilations and Reviews (AR 100)

15. Which of the following accounting services most likely may an accountant perform without being required to issue a compilation or review report under the Statements on Standards for Accounting and Review Services?

I.   Preparing a working trial balance
II.   Preparing standard monthly journal entries

A. I only.

B. II only.

C. Both I and II.

D. Neither I nor II.

Answer (C) is correct. *(CPA, adapted)*
REQUIRED: The accounting services most likely to be performed without issuing a compilation or review report.
DISCUSSION: An accountant must comply with SSARSs when (s)he submits unaudited financial statements of a nonpublic entity to a client or third parties. A submission of financial statements is defined as "presenting to a client or third parties financial statements the accountant has prepared either manually or through the use of computer software." Standard monthly journal entries and a working trial balance are not financial statements, so a compilation or review report is not necessary (assuming these items are properly characterized).

16. North Co., a privately held entity, asked its tax accountant, King, a CPA in public practice, to generate North's interim financial statements on King's personal computer when King prepared North's quarterly tax return. King should not submit these financial statements to North unless, as a minimum, King complies with the provisions of

A. Statements on Standards for Accounting and Review Services.

B. Statements on Standards for Unaudited Financial Services.

C. Statements on Standards for Consulting Services.

D. Statements on Standards for Attestation Engagements.

Answer (A) is correct. *(CPA, adapted)*
REQUIRED: The standards appropriate for an accountant who generates interim financial statements.
DISCUSSION: The Statements on Standards for Accounting and Review Services apply to compilations and reviews performed by practitioners. The AICPA bylaws designate the Accounting and Review Services Committee as the senior technical committee authorized to issue pronouncements in connection with the unaudited financial statements or other unaudited financial information of a nonpublic entity.
Answer (B) is incorrect because these standards do not exist. Answer (C) is incorrect because the practitioner is providing compilation services, not consulting services. Answer (D) is incorrect because Statements on Standards for Attestation Engagements are appropriate whenever the practitioner is engaged in providing attestation services. A compilation, however, provides no assurance.

17. Blue Co., a privately held entity, asked its tax accountant, Cook, a CPA in public practice, to reproduce Blue's internally prepared interim financial statements on Cook's personal computer when Cook prepared Blue's quarterly tax return. Cook should not transmit these financial statements to Blue unless, as a minimum, Cook complies with the provisions of

A. Statements on Standards for Tax Services (SSTSs).

B. Statements on Standards for Accounting and Review Services (SSARSs).

C. Statements on Standards for Attestation Engagements (SSAEs).

D. None of the answers are correct.

Answer (D) is correct. *(CPA, adapted)*
REQUIRED: The authoritative pronouncements with which a tax accountant must comply when reproducing interim financial statements for a client.
DISCUSSION: A submission of financial statements is defined as "presenting to a client or third parties financial statements the accountant has prepared either manually or through the use of computer software." Thus, a submission includes both preparation and presentation. Accordingly, merely reproducing client-prepared financial statements, without modification, as an accommodation to a client most likely does not constitute a submission of financial statements, and the accountant need not comply with SSARSs.
Answer (A) is incorrect because SSTSs concern the preparation of tax returns. Answer (B) is incorrect because SSARSs are not applicable if the accountant is not deemed to have submitted unaudited financial statements. Answer (C) is incorrect because SSAEs apply to a report that expresses a conclusion about subject matter or an assertion that is the responsibility of another party.

18. Statements on Standards for Accounting and Review Services establish standards and procedures for which of the following engagements?

A. Assisting in adjusting the books of account for a partnership.

B. Reviewing interim financial information required to be filed by public companies with the SEC.

C. Processing financial data for clients of other accounting firms.

D. Compiling an individual's personal financial statement to be used to obtain a mortgage.

Answer (D) is correct. *(CPA, adapted)*
REQUIRED: The procedures covered under the SSARSs.
DISCUSSION: AR 100 describes the accountant's procedures and reporting responsibilities for compilations and reviews. AR 600 exempts personal financial statements from SSARS under certain conditions. The exemption applies only if the statements (1) are included in written personal financial plans, (2) will not be used to obtain credit (e.g., a mortgage), and (3) will not be used for any purposes other than developing the client's personal financial goals.
Answer (A) is incorrect because SSARSs do not apply to assisting in adjusting the books of account. Answer (B) is incorrect because SSARs apply only to nonpublic entities. Answer (C) is incorrect because SSARSs do not apply to processing financial data for clients of other accounting firms.

19. An accountant has compiled the financial statements of a nonpublic entity in accordance with Statements on Standards for Accounting and Review Services (SSARSs). Do the SSARSs require that the compilation report be printed on the accountant's letterhead and that the report be manually signed by the accountant?

	Printed on the Accountant's Letterhead	Manually Signed by the Accountant
A.	Yes	Yes
B.	Yes	No
C.	No	Yes
D.	No	No

Answer (D) is correct. *(CPA, adapted)*
REQUIRED: The requirements of a compilation report.
DISCUSSION: The compilation report need not be printed on the accountant's letterhead or manually signed by the accountant. However, the report must be signed by the accounting firm or the accountant as appropriate. Hence, the signature may be manual, stamped, electronic, or typed (AR 100).

20. May an accountant accept an engagement to compile or review the financial statements of a not-for-profit entity if the accountant is unfamiliar with the specialized industry accounting principles but plans to obtain the required level of knowledge before compiling or reviewing the financial statements?

	Compilation	Review
A.	No	No
B.	Yes	No
C.	No	Yes
D.	Yes	Yes

Answer (D) is correct. *(CPA, adapted)*
REQUIRED: The ability of an accountant to accept an engagement without the required level of knowledge.
DISCUSSION: The accountant may accept a compilation or review engagement for an entity in an industry with which the accountant has no previous experience. Acceptance, however, places upon him/her a responsibility to obtain the required level of knowledge prior to performing the engagement.

21. If requested to perform a review engagement for a nonpublic entity in which an accountant has an immaterial direct financial interest, the accountant is

A. Not independent and, therefore, may not be associated with the financial statements.

B. Not independent and, therefore, may not issue a review report.

C. Not independent and, therefore, may issue a review report, but may not express an auditor's opinion.

D. Independent because the financial interest is immaterial and, therefore, may issue a review report.

Answer (B) is correct. *(CPA, adapted)*
REQUIRED: The action of an accountant who has an immaterial direct financial interest in a potential review client.
DISCUSSION: Any attest service, including audits and reviews, requires the accountant to be independent in fact and appearance. Under an Interpretation of Conduct Rule 101, the accountant may not have a direct financial interest or a material indirect financial interest in an attest client.
Answer (A) is incorrect because an accountant may be associated with financial statements when (s)he lacks independence. Answer (C) is incorrect because an accountant lacking independence may not issue a review report. Answer (D) is incorrect because any direct interest affects independence.

22. In a review engagement, the accountant should establish an understanding with the entity, preferably in writing, regarding the services to be performed. The understanding should include all of the following except a

A. Description of the nature and limitations of the services to be performed.

B. Description of the report the accountant expects to issue.

C. Provision that the engagement cannot be relied upon to disclose errors, fraud, or illegal acts.

D. Provision that any errors, fraud, or illegal acts that come to the accountant's attention need not be reported.

Answer (D) is correct. *(Publisher)*
REQUIRED: The false statement about the accountant's understanding with the client in a review engagement.
DISCUSSION: Although the engagement cannot be relied upon to disclose errors, fraud, or illegal acts, the accountant should indicate to the client that any such acts discovered will be reported to management or the board of directors (AR 100).
Answer (A) is incorrect because the description of the nature and limitations of the services to be performed should be included in an understanding with the entity. Answer (B) is incorrect because the description of the report the accountant expects to render should be included in an understanding with the entity. Answer (C) is incorrect because a provision that the engagement cannot be relied upon to disclose errors, fraud, or illegal acts should be included in an understanding with the entity.

1.5 Financial Forecasts and Projections (AT 301)

23. The party responsible for assumptions identified in the preparation of prospective financial statements is usually

A. A third-party lending institution.

B. The client's management.

C. The reporting accountant.

D. The client's independent auditor.

Answer (B) is correct. *(CPA, adapted)*
REQUIRED: The party usually responsible for assumptions identified in the preparation of prospective financial statements.
DISCUSSION: Management is usually the responsible party, that is, the person(s) responsible for the assumptions underlying prospective financial statements. However, the responsible party may be a party outside the entity, such as a possible acquirer.

24. A financial forecast consists of prospective financial statements that present an entity's expected financial position, results of operations, and cash flows. A forecast

A. Is based on the most conservative estimates.

B. Presents estimates given one or more hypothetical assumptions.

C. Unlike a projection, may contain a range.

D. Is based on assumptions reflecting conditions expected to exist and courses of action expected to be taken.

Answer (D) is correct. *(Publisher)*

REQUIRED: The true statement about a financial forecast.

DISCUSSION: According to AT 301, a financial forecast consists of prospective financial statements "that present, to the best of the responsible party's knowledge and belief, an entity's expected financial position, results of operations, and cash flows." A forecast is based on "the responsible party's assumptions reflecting conditions it expects to exist and the course of action it expects to take."

Answer (A) is incorrect because the information presented is based on expected (most likely) conditions and courses of action rather than the most conservative estimate. Answer (B) is incorrect because a financial projection (not a forecast) is based on assumptions by the responsible party reflecting expected conditions and courses of action, given one or more hypothetical assumptions (a condition or action not necessarily expected to occur). Answer (C) is incorrect because both forecasts and projections may be stated either in point estimates or ranges.

25. An examination of a financial forecast is a professional service that involves

A. Compiling or assembling a financial forecast that is based on management's assumptions.

B. Restricting the use of the practitioner's report to management and the board of directors.

C. Assuming responsibility to update management on key events for one year after the report's date.

D. Evaluating the preparation of a financial forecast and the support underlying management's assumptions.

Answer (D) is correct. *(CPA, adapted)*

REQUIRED: The accountant's responsibility in an examination of a financial forecast.

DISCUSSION: An examination of a financial forecast entails evaluating the preparation of the statements, the support underlying the assumptions, and the presentation of the statements for conformity with AICPA guidelines (AT 301).

Answer (A) is incorrect because an examination of a financial forecast involves providing assurance on the representations of management. Answer (B) is incorrect because an examination of a financial forecast need not be limited in its distribution. Answer (C) is incorrect because the practitioner need not assume responsibility to update management on key events after the issuance of the report.

26. Prospective financial information presented in the format of historical financial statements that omit either gross profit or net income is deemed to be a

A. Partial presentation.

B. Projected balance sheet.

C. Financial forecast.

D. Financial projection.

Answer (A) is correct. *(CPA, adapted)*

REQUIRED: The nature of prospective financial information that omits gross profit or net income.

DISCUSSION: Under the minimum presentation guidelines, prospective financial statements may take the form of complete basic statements or be limited to certain minimum items (when the items would be presented for the period's historical statements). A presentation is partial if it omits one or more of the following: (1) sales or gross revenues, (2) gross profit or cost of sales, (3) unusual or infrequently occurring items, (4) provision for income taxes, (5) discontinued operations or extraordinary items, (6) income from continuing operations, (7) net income, (8) basic and diluted earnings per share, (9) significant changes in financial position.

Answer (B) is incorrect because prospective information in the form of financial statements includes more than a balance sheet even if it omits gross profit or net income. Answer (C) is incorrect because forecasts are not defined in terms of the omission of items listed in the presentation guidelines. Answer (D) is incorrect because projections are not defined in terms of the omission of items listed in the presentation guidelines.

27. Given one or more hypothetical assumptions, a responsible party may prepare, to the best of its knowledge and belief, an entity's expected financial position, results of operations, and cash flows. Such prospective financial statements are known as

- A. Pro forma financial statements.
- B. Financial projections.
- C. Partial presentations.
- D. Financial forecasts.

Answer (B) is correct. *(CPA, adapted)*
REQUIRED: The prospective statements based on one or more hypothetical assumptions.
DISCUSSION: Prospective statements include forecasts and projections. The difference between a forecast and a projection is that only the latter is based on one or more hypothetical assumptions, which are conditions or actions not necessarily expected to occur.
Answer (A) is incorrect because pro forma statements are essentially historical, not prospective, statements. Answer (C) is incorrect because partial presentations are not prospective statements. They do not meet the minimum presentation guidelines. Answer (D) is incorrect because forecasts are based on assumptions about conditions the responsible party expects to exist and the course of action it expects to take.

28. Which of the following statements concerning prospective financial statements is true?

- A. Only a financial forecast would normally be appropriate for limited use.
- B. Only a financial projection would normally be appropriate for general use.
- C. Any type of prospective financial statements would normally be appropriate for limited use.
- D. Any type of prospective financial statements would normally be appropriate for general use.

Answer (C) is correct. *(CPA, adapted)*
REQUIRED: The true statement about prospective financial statements.
DISCUSSION: Limited use of prospective financial statements means use by the responsible party and those with whom that party is negotiating directly, e.g., in a submission to a regulatory body or in negotiations for a bank loan. These third parties are in a position to communicate directly with the responsible party. Consequently, AT 100 states, "Any type of prospective financial statements that would be useful in the circumstances would be appropriate for limited use."
Answer (A) is incorrect because projections as well as forecasts are appropriate for limited use. Answer (B) is incorrect because only a forecast is appropriate for general use. Answer (D) is incorrect because only a forecast is appropriate for general use.

29. Accepting an engagement to examine an entity's financial projection most likely would be appropriate if the projection were to be distributed to

- A. All employees who work for the entity.
- B. Potential shareholders who request a prospectus or a registration statement.
- C. A bank with which the entity is negotiating for a loan.
- D. All shareholders of record as of the report date.

Answer (C) is correct. *(CPA, adapted)*
REQUIRED: The situation in which acceptance of an engagement to examine a projection is appropriate.
DISCUSSION: A projection is based on one or more hypothetical assumptions and, therefore, should be considered for limited use only. Limited use of prospective financial statements means use by the responsible party and those with whom that party is negotiating directly. Examples of appropriate use include negotiations for a bank loan and submission to a regulatory body. A projection is inappropriate for distribution to those who will not be negotiating directly with the responsible party.

30. Which of the following is a prospective financial statement for general use upon which a practitioner may appropriately report?

- A. Financial projection.
- B. Partial presentation.
- C. Pro forma financial statement.
- D. Financial forecast.

Answer (D) is correct. *(CPA, adapted)*
REQUIRED: The prospective financial statement for general use upon which a practitioner may report.
DISCUSSION: Prospective financial statements are for general use if they are for use by persons with whom the responsible party is not negotiating directly, e.g., in an offering statement of the party's securities. Only a report based on a financial forecast is appropriate for general use.
Answer (A) is incorrect because a projection is appropriate only for limited use. Answer (B) is incorrect because a presentation not in compliance with minimum guidelines is not appropriate for general use. Answer (C) is incorrect because pro forma statements are essentially historical, not prospective, statements.

31. When a practitioner examines a financial forecast that fails to disclose several significant assumptions used to prepare the forecast, the practitioner should describe the assumptions in the practitioner's report and express

    A. An "except for" qualified opinion.

    B. A "subject to" qualified opinion.

    C. An unqualified opinion with a separate explanatory paragraph.

    D. An adverse opinion.

Answer (D) is correct. *(CPA, adapted)*
    REQUIRED: The appropriate opinion if a forecast fails to disclose several significant assumptions.
    DISCUSSION: An examination results in issuance of a report stating the practitioner's opinion on whether (1) the presentation conforms with AICPA guidelines and (2) the assumptions provide a reasonable basis for the forecast. If significant assumptions are not disclosed in the presentation, including the summary of assumptions, the practitioner must express an adverse opinion. Moreover, a practitioner should not examine a presentation that omits all such disclosures.
    Answer (A) is incorrect because omission of significant assumptions requires an adverse opinion. Other departures from the presentation guidelines, however, may justify a qualified opinion. Answer (B) is incorrect because the language "subject to" is never permissible. Answer (C) is incorrect because an explanatory paragraph is insufficient when significant assumptions are omitted.

32. A practitioner's compilation report on a financial forecast should include a statement that

    A. The forecast should be read only in conjunction with the audited historical financial statements.

    B. The practitioner expresses only limited assurance on the forecasted statements and their assumptions.

    C. There will usually be differences between the forecasted and actual results.

    D. The hypothetical assumptions used in the forecast are reasonable in the circumstances.

Answer (C) is correct. *(CPA, adapted)*
    REQUIRED: The statement included in a practitioner's compilation report on a financial forecast.
    DISCUSSION: The standard report states that a compilation is limited in scope and does not enable the practitioner to express an opinion or any other form of assurance. It adds that there will usually be differences between the forecasted and actual results.
    Answer (A) is incorrect because a forecast may stand alone. Answer (B) is incorrect because a compilation provides no assurance. Answer (D) is incorrect because a financial projection, not a financial forecast, contains hypothetical assumptions.

33. When a practitioner examines projected financial statements, the report should include a separate paragraph that

    A. Describes the limitations on the usefulness of the presentation.

    B. Provides an explanation of the differences between an examination and an audit.

    C. States that the practitioner is responsible for events and circumstances up to one year after the report's date.

    D. Disclaims an opinion on whether the assumptions provide a reasonable basis for the projection.

Answer (A) is correct. *(CPA, adapted)*
    REQUIRED: The content of a separate paragraph in an examination report on projected financial statements.
    DISCUSSION: According to AT 301, when the presentation is a projection, the practitioner's "report should include a separate paragraph that describes the limitations on the usefulness of the presentation."
    Answer (B) is incorrect because the report should describe the nature of an examination. Answer (C) is incorrect because the report should not state its life expectancy. Answer (D) is incorrect because an examination report appropriately expresses an opinion on the projection.

34. A practitioner may accept an engagement to apply agreed-upon procedures to prospective financial statements provided that

    A. Use of the report is restricted to the specified parties.

    B. The prospective financial statements are also examined.

    C. Responsibility for the sufficiency of the procedures performed is taken by the practitioner.

    D. Negative assurance is expressed on the prospective financial statements taken as a whole.

Answer (A) is correct. *(CPA, adapted)*
    REQUIRED: The condition for acceptance of an engagement to apply agreed-upon procedures to prospective financial statements.
    DISCUSSION: The following conditions should be met to accept an engagement: (1) The specified parties have participated in determining its nature and scope, and they take responsibility for the adequacy of the procedures; (2) report use is restricted to those parties; and (3) the statements include a summary of significant assumptions.
    Answer (B) is incorrect because the practitioner may apply agreed-upon procedures without providing the more extensive services required by an examination. Answer (C) is incorrect because the specified parties must assume this responsibility. Answer (D) is incorrect because the practitioner should state his/her findings.

35. When third-party use of prospective financial statements is expected, a practitioner may not accept an engagement to

A. Perform a review.

B. Perform a compilation.

C. Perform an examination.

D. Apply agreed-upon procedures.

Answer (A) is correct. *(CPA, adapted)*
REQUIRED: The engagement regarding prospective statements that may not be accepted.
DISCUSSION: AT 301 does not provide for the review form of engagement with regard to prospective statements.
Answer (B) is incorrect because a compilation may be performed provided the report does not express any form of assurance. Answer (C) is incorrect because an examination report may express an opinion on presentation in conformity with AICPA guidelines and the reasonableness of assumptions. Answer (D) is incorrect because application of agreed-upon procedures is permissible.

36. A practitioner's standard report on a compilation of a projection should not include a

A. Statement that a compilation of a projection is limited in scope.

B. Disclaimer of responsibility to update the report for events occurring after the report's date.

C. Statement that the practitioner expresses only limited assurance that the results may be achieved.

D. Separate paragraph that describes the limitations on the presentation's usefulness.

Answer (C) is correct. *(CPA, adapted)*
REQUIRED: The item not in a practitioner's standard report on a compilation of a projection.
DISCUSSION: A standard report states that the compilation is limited in scope and does not enable the practitioner to express an opinion or any other form of assurance on the prospective statements. Limited assurance (e.g., based on a review) should not be provided by the practitioner based on any prospective financial statement service.
Answer (A) is incorrect because the report should state that a compilation is limited in scope and does not provide any form of assurance. Answer (B) is incorrect because the report should contain a statement that the practitioner assumes no responsibility to update the report for events and circumstances occurring after the report date. Answer (D) is incorrect because, if the practitioner has reservations about the usefulness of the statements (e.g., the statements fail to provide notes), (s)he should so indicate in a separate paragraph.

1.6 Reporting on Pro Forma Financial Information (AT 401)

37. Which of the following presents what the effects on historical financial data might have been if a consummated transaction had occurred at an earlier date?

A. Prospective financial statements.

B. Pro forma financial information.

C. Interim financial information.

D. A financial projection.

Answer (B) is correct. *(Publisher)*
REQUIRED: The kind of financial data showing what the effects of a consummated transaction would have been if it had occurred at an earlier date.
DISCUSSION: Pro forma information shows what the significant effects on historical financial information would have been had a consummated or proposed transaction (or event) occurred at an earlier date. Examples of these transactions include a business combination, disposal of a segment, a change in the form or status of an entity, and a change in capitalization.
Answer (A) is incorrect because prospective financial statements do not cover periods that have completely expired. Hence, they are not historical statements. Answer (C) is incorrect because interim financial information states actual results. Answer (D) is incorrect because a financial projection is a prospective statement and therefore is not a presentation of historical information.

38. A practitioner may report on an examination of pro forma financial information if the related historical financial statements have been

    A. Audited.

    B. Audited or reviewed.

    C. Audited, reviewed, or compiled.

    D. Reviewed or compiled.

Answer (A) is correct. *(Publisher)*
    REQUIRED: The service provided regarding the historical statements that permits an examination of pro forma financial information.
    DISCUSSION: A practitioner may examine or review pro forma financial information only if certain conditions are met. One of these conditions is that the level of assurance provided on the pro forma financial information be limited to that given on the historical statements. Accordingly, an examination of pro forma financial information, which provides a basis for giving positive assurance, is appropriate only if the historical statements have been audited.
    Answer (B) is incorrect because, if the historical statements have been reviewed, only a review of the pro forma financial information would be appropriate. Answer (C) is incorrect because a compilation of the historical statements provides no assurance; thus, it would not provide a basis for the practitioner to examine or review the pro forma statements. Answer (D) is incorrect because a compilation of the historical statements provides no assurance; thus, it would not provide a basis for the practitioner to examine or review the pro forma statements.

39. An accountant has been engaged to examine pro forma adjustments that show the effects on previously audited historical financial statements due to a proposed disposition of a significant portion of an entity's business. Other than the procedures previously applied to the historical financial statements, the accountant is required to

	Reevaluate the entity's internal control over financial reporting	Determine that the computations of the pro forma adjustments are mathematically correct
A.	Yes	Yes
B.	Yes	No
C.	No	Yes
D.	No	No

Answer (C) is correct. *(CPA, adapted)*
    REQUIRED: The procedure(s), if any, applied in an examination of pro forma financial statements.
    DISCUSSION: In an examination of pro forma financial statements, the practitioner's additional procedures include (1) understanding the underlying transaction or event, (2) discussing the assumptions about the transaction or event with management, (3) evaluating whether adjustments are included for all significant effects, (4) gathering sufficient evidence to support the adjustments, (5) evaluating whether the assumptions are sufficiently, clearly, and comprehensively presented, (6) determining that computations are correct and that the pro forma column properly reflects their application to the historical statements, (7) obtaining written management representations, and (8) evaluating the pro forma information to determine whether certain matters (the transaction or event, assumptions, adjustments, and uncertainties) have been properly described and the sources of the historical information have been properly identified. Moreover, in a business combination, the practitioner must obtain a sufficient understanding of each part of the combined entity. However, no evaluation of internal control beyond that done in the engagement performed with respect to the historical statements.

40. The practitioner's report on an examination of pro forma financial information

    A. Should have the same date as the related historical financial statements.

    B. Should be added to the report on the historical financial statements.

    C. Need not mention the report on the historical financial statements.

    D. May state an unqualified, qualified, or adverse opinion.

Answer (D) is correct. *(Publisher)*
    REQUIRED: The true statement about the practitioner's report on an examination of pro forma financial information.
    DISCUSSION: The report should include an opinion on whether (1) management's assumptions provide a reasonable basis for the significant effects attributable to the transaction or event, (2) the pro forma adjustments give appropriate effect to the assumptions, and (3) the pro forma column reflects the proper application of those adjustments to the historical data. Scope limitations, uncertainties, reservations about the assumptions or the presentation (including inadequate disclosure), and other matters may lead to modification of the opinion or a disclaimer.
    Answer (A) is incorrect because the report should be dated as of the completion of procedures. Answer (B) is incorrect because the report may appear separately. Moreover, if it is combined with the report on the historical statements, the combined report may need to be dual-dated. Answer (C) is incorrect because the report should refer to the financial statements from which the historical information is derived and state whether they were audited or reviewed.

41. A practitioner's report on a review of pro forma financial information should include a

A. Statement that the entity's internal control was not relied on in the review.

B. Disclaimer of opinion on the financial statements from which the pro forma financial information is derived.

C. Caveat that it is uncertain whether the transaction or event reflected in the pro forma financial information will ever occur.

D. Reference to the financial statements from which the historical financial information is derived.

Answer (D) is correct. *(CPA, adapted)*
REQUIRED: The statement that should be included in a review of pro forma financial information.
DISCUSSION: A practitioner's report on pro forma information should include (1) an identification of the pro forma information, (2) a reference to the financial statements from which the historical financial information is derived and a statement as to whether such financial statements were audited or reviewed, (3) a statement that the review was made in accordance with standards established by the AICPA, (4) a caveat that a review is substantially less in scope than an examination and that no opinion is expressed, (5) a separate paragraph explaining the objective of pro forma financial information and its limitations, and (6) the practitioner's conclusion providing negative assurance.
Answer (A) is incorrect because the report should not mention internal control. Answer (B) is incorrect because the practitioner should disclaim an opinion on the pro forma financial information. Answer (C) is incorrect because the transaction may already have occurred.

1.7 Assurance Services

42. Assurance services are best described as

A. Services designed for the improvement of operations, resulting in better outcomes.

B. Independent professional services that improve the quality of information, or its context, for decision makers.

C. The assembly of financial statements based on assumptions of a responsible party.

D. Services designed to express an opinion on historical financial statements based on the results of an audit.

Answer (B) is correct. *(Publisher)*
REQUIRED: The description of assurance services.
DISCUSSION: The AICPA defines assurance services as "independent professional services that improve the quality of information, or its context, for decision makers." Assurance services encompass audit and other attestation services but also include other, nonstandard, services. Assurance services do not encompass consulting services.
Answer (A) is incorrect because it is the definition of consulting services. Answer (C) is incorrect because it is the definition of compilation services. Answer (D) is incorrect because it defines the traditional audit.

43. The objective of assurance services is to

A. Provide more reliable information.

B. Enhance decision making.

C. Compare internal information and policies to those of other firms.

D. Improve the firm's outcomes.

Answer (B) is correct. *(Publisher)*
REQUIRED: The objective of assurance services.
DISCUSSION: The main objective of assurance services, as stated by the AICPA, is to provide information that assists in better decision making. Assurance services encompass audit and other attestation services but also include other, nonstandard, services. Assurance services do not encompass consulting services.
Answer (A) is incorrect because providing more reliable information is the objective of attestation services. Answer (C) is incorrect because assurance services do not involve analysis of other companies. Answer (D) is incorrect because providing information that results in better outcomes is an objective of consulting services.

44. Assurance services differ from consulting services in that they

	Focus on Providing Advice	Involve Monitoring of One Party by Another
A.	Yes	Yes
B.	Yes	No
C.	No	Yes
D.	No	No

Answer (C) is correct. *(Publisher)*
REQUIRED: The way(s) in which assurance services differ from consulting services.
DISCUSSION: Assurance services encompass attestation services but not consulting services. Assurance services differ from consulting services in two ways: (1) They focus on improving information rather than providing advice, and (2) they usually involve situations in which one party wants to monitor another rather than the two-party arrangements common in consulting engagements.

45. SysTrust is an assurance service developed by the AICPA and the Canadian Institute of Chartered Accountants. It is designed to

    A. Increase the comfort of management and other stakeholders relative to an information system.

    B. Provide an opinion on the fairness of an information system's output.

    C. Provide the SEC with information used to administer the securities laws.

    D. Allow a CPA to provide a consulting service to management relating to their information system.

Answer (A) is correct. *(Publisher)*
    REQUIRED: The purpose of SysTrust.
    DISCUSSION: The objective of SysTrust is an attestation report on management's assertion about the reliability of an information system that supports a business or a given activity. The CPA also may report directly on the reliability of the system. This assurance service is designed to increase the stakeholders' comfort relative to the system's satisfaction of the SysTrust principles: online privacy, security, processing integrity, availability, and confidentiality. The practitioner may provide assurance about any or all of these principles.
    Answer (B) is incorrect because SysTrust does not directly address the output of a system. Answer (C) is incorrect because the report is not specifically designed for any one user. Answer (D) is incorrect because assurance services are not classified as consulting services.

46. The AICPA committee on assurance services has identified a professional service called ElderCare services. One fundamental purpose of this assurance service is to assist the elderly and their families by

    A. Investing the funds of the elderly person.

    B. Reporting whether specified objectives are being met by caregivers.

    C. Choosing caregivers.

    D. Performing operational audits of health care providers.

Answer (B) is correct. *(Publisher)*
    REQUIRED: The fundamental purpose of ElderCare services.
    DISCUSSION: The AICPA committee on assurance services has developed business plans for six assurance services, one of which involves elder care. The fundamental purpose of elder care services is to gather evidence and report to concerned parties (e.g., adult children of an elderly parent) as to whether agreed-upon objectives have been met with regard to care delivery, such as medical, household, and financial services. Related services provided directly to the elderly person or to the other concerned parties may include oversight of investment of funds (but not making an investment of funds), assistance in the choice of caregivers, accounting for the elderly person's income and expenses, and arranging for care and services, such as transportation, meal delivery, or placement in a retirement facility.
    Answer (A) is incorrect because the CPA might oversee, but not make, investments. Answer (C) is incorrect because the CPA might help in the choice of caregivers but would not make the decision. Answer (D) is incorrect because an operational audit is far beyond the limits of an elder care service.

47. Which of the following qualifications is not required to provide CPA ElderCare services?

    A. Knowledge of geriatric health issues.

    B. Prior experience.

    C. Financial management skills.

    D. Mediation techniques.

Answer (B) is correct. *(Publisher)*
    REQUIRED: The item not a qualification for providing ElderCare services.
    DISCUSSION: Prior experience is not required because ElderCare services are relatively new to the CPA market. Personal skills and knowledge of issues are fundamental to providing this service to the elderly.
    Answer (A) is incorrect because knowledge of geriatric health issues are needed to provide ElderCare services. Answer (C) is incorrect because financial management skills are needed to provide ElderCare services. Answer (D) is incorrect because mediation techniques are needed to provide ElderCare services.

48. The client of the practitioner providing ElderCare services may be

	The Elderly Person	An Attorney	A Family Member
A.	Yes	No	No
B.	Yes	Yes	No
C.	No	No	Yes
D.	Yes	Yes	Yes

Answer (D) is correct. *(Publisher)*
    REQUIRED: The client(s) of the practitioner providing ElderCare.
    DISCUSSION: The client varies with the engagement. The practitioner must understand who the client is and who has final authority to resolve issues during the engagement. If the client is a family member or some third party, that person must have power of attorney over the elderly person involved.
    Answer (A) is incorrect because the elderly person may be the client of the practitioner. Answer (B) is incorrect because an attorney may be the client of the practitioner. Answer (C) is incorrect because a family member may be the client of the practitioner.

49. The AICPA assurance service called CPA Performance Review attempts to provide users with

A. A profile of the business risks and the appropriate systems in place to manage those risks.

B. An opinion on whether the financial statements are fairly stated.

C. An evaluation of whether an entity has reliable measures of performance beyond the traditional financial statements.

D. An assessment of management's assertion on internal control and whether the system is meeting the objectives of the organization.

Answer (C) is correct. *(Publisher)*
REQUIRED: The purpose of CPA Performance Review.
DISCUSSION: CPA Performance Review evaluates whether an entity's performance measurement system contains relevant and reliable measures for assessing the degree to which the entity's goals and objectives are achieved. It attempts to provide a more balanced scorecard than just the traditional financial statements.
Answer (A) is incorrect because evaluation and reporting on an entity's business risk describes the CPA Risk Advisory assurance service. Answer (B) is incorrect because an opinion on the financial statements describes the purpose of a financial audit. Answer (D) is incorrect because an assessment of management's assertion on internal control is performed in an attestation engagement to report on internal control.

50. Which of the following is a term for an attest engagement in which a CPA assesses a client's commercial Internet site for compliance with principles such as online privacy, security, and confidentiality?

A. ElectroNet.

B. EDIFACT.

C. TechSafe.

D. WebTrust.

Answer (D) is correct. *(CPA, adapted)*
REQUIRED: The attest engagement for an Internet site.
DISCUSSION: The WebTrust seal provides assurance about compliance with the principles of online privacy, security, processing integrity, availability, and confidentiality. It is a modular service that allows the practitioner to express an opinion about compliance with individual principles or combinations of principles. Online privacy is the protection of the collection, use, disclosure, and retention of personal information. Security is the protection against unauthorized access to the system (both physical and logical). Processing integrity is the assurance that system processing is complete, accurate, timely, and authorized. Availability is the assertion that the system is available for operation and used as agreed. Confidentiality is the protection of information from being viewed by non-authorized parties.
Answer (A) is incorrect because ElectroNet is a nonsense term. Answer (B) is incorrect because EDIFACT (Electronic Data Interchange For Administration Commerce and Transport) is an ISO standard for electronic data interchange (EDI). Answer (C) is incorrect because TechSafe is a nonsense term.

51. An entity engaged a CPA to determine whether the client's web sites comply with defined WebTrust principles and criteria. In performing this engagement, the CPA should apply the provisions of

A. Statements on Assurance Standards.

B. Statements on Standards for Attestation Engagements.

C. Statements on Standards for Management Consulting Services.

D. Statements on Auditing Standards.

Answer (B) is correct. *(CPA, adapted)*
REQUIRED: The pronouncements that apply to WebTrust.
DISCUSSION: An attest engagement involves reporting on subject matter, or an assurance about subject matter, that is the responsibility of another party. When providing WebTrust assurance, the accountant must address written assertions by management. Thus, Statements on Standards for Attestation Engagements are applicable.
Answer (A) is incorrect because the AICPA has not issued specific Statements on Assurance Standards. Answer (C) is incorrect because WebTrust is not considered a management consulting service. Answer (D) is incorrect because Statements on Auditing Standards are applicable to audits of financial statements.

52. A WebTrust engagement on processing integrity requires from client management a

A. Written assertion.

B. Set of financial statements.

C. Third-party verification letter.

D. Statement about the integrity of top management.

Answer (A) is correct. *(Publisher)*
REQUIRED: The requirement of management when a CPA provides the WebTrust service.
DISCUSSION: WebTrust was developed from the attestation standards and requires a written assertion by management for each principle reported on. When the assertion about a website complies with WebTrust principles, it is granted the CPA WebTrust seal to be displayed on the entity's web page. Consumers may access the examination report and CPA WebTrust principles and criteria through the entity's web page.

53. Under the assurance service WebTrust, the broad principles relating to websites are security, availability, confidentiality, processing integrity, and

    A. Information disclosure.

    B. Website performance.

    C. Online privacy.

    D. Transaction assurance.

Answer (C) is correct. *(Publisher)*
    REQUIRED: The principles relating to websites that are addressed by WebTrust.
    DISCUSSION: WebTrust provides assurance about compliance with the principles of online privacy, security, processing integrity, availability, and confidentiality. It is a modular service that allows the practitioner to express an opinion and grant the corresponding seal with respect to individual principles or combinations of principles.
    Answer (A) is incorrect because information disclosure is not included in the list of principles. Answer (B) is incorrect because website performance is not included in the list of principles. Answer (D) is incorrect because transaction assurance is not included in the list of principles.

1.8 Quality Control

54. One of a CPA firm's basic objectives is to provide professional services that conform with professional standards. Reasonable assurance of achieving this basic objective is provided through

    A. A system of quality control.

    B. A system of peer review.

    C. Continuing professional education.

    D. Compliance with generally accepted reporting standards.

Answer (A) is correct. *(CPA, adapted)*
    REQUIRED: The means of reasonably assuring that a CPA firm's services meet professional standards.
    DISCUSSION: A CPA firm must have a system of quality control that ensures that its personnel comply with professional standards applicable to its audit and accounting practice. However, a deficiency in an engagement, by itself, does not necessarily indicate that the firm's system of quality control is not sufficient (QC 20). GAAS apply to individual engagements, and quality control standards apply to the firm's practice as a whole (AU 161).
    Answer (B) is incorrect because a system of peer review is a necessary part of the practice-monitoring requirement for AICPA membership. Answer (C) is incorrect because continuing professional education is but one element of quality control. Answer (D) is incorrect because firms must comply with all pronouncements applicable to the services rendered, not just with the reporting standards.

55. Which of the following is an element of a CPA firm's quality control system that should be considered in establishing its quality control policies and procedures?

    A. Complying with laws and regulations.

    B. Using statistical sampling techniques.

    C. Managing personnel.

    D. Considering audit risk and materiality.

Answer (C) is correct. *(CPA, adapted)*
    REQUIRED: The element of quality control.
    DISCUSSION: The quality control element of personnel management requires establishment of policies and procedures to provide reasonable assurance that only qualified persons with the required technical training and proficiency perform the work (QC 20).
    Answer (A) is incorrect because the auditor considers compliance with laws and regulations. However, this consideration is not an element of quality control. Answer (B) is incorrect because an auditing firm may use statistical or nonstatistical sampling techniques in performing audits; a particular sampling technique is not an element of quality control. Answer (D) is incorrect because an auditor must consider audit risk and materiality in performing the audit, but this consideration is not an element of quality control.

56. The primary purpose of establishing quality control policies and procedures for deciding whether to accept a new client is to

    A. Enable the CPA firm to attest to the reliability of the client.

    B. Satisfy the CPA firm's duty to the public concerning the acceptance of new clients.

    C. Minimize the likelihood of association with clients whose management lacks integrity.

    D. Anticipate before performing any field work whether an unqualified opinion can be expressed.

Answer (C) is correct. *(CPA, adapted)*
    REQUIRED: The primary purpose of establishing quality control policies and procedures for deciding whether to accept a new client.
    DISCUSSION: CPA firms should have policies and procedures to determine whether to accept or continue a new client or to perform a specific engagement for a client. The objective is to minimize the likelihood of association with clients whose managers may lack integrity (QC 20).
    Answer (A) is incorrect because the CPA firm attests to the fairness of the financial statements, not to the reliability of the client. Answer (B) is incorrect because the CPA firm has a duty to the public with regard to its reporting responsibilities but not relative to client acceptance. Answer (D) is incorrect because the field work will dictate whether an unqualified opinion can be expressed.

57. A CPA firm's quality control procedures pertaining to the acceptance of a prospective audit client would most likely include

A. Inquiry of management as to whether disagreements between the predecessor auditor and the prospective client were resolved satisfactorily.

B. Consideration of whether sufficient competent evidential matter may be obtained to afford a reasonable basis for an opinion.

C. Inquiry of third parties, such as the prospective client's bankers and attorneys, about information regarding the prospective client and its management.

D. Consideration of whether internal control is sufficiently effective to permit a reduction in the extent of required substantive tests.

Answer (C) is correct. *(CPA, adapted)*
REQUIRED: The quality control procedures most likely to pertain to acceptance of a prospective audit client.
DISCUSSION: The procedures pertaining to client acceptance or continuation "should provide reasonable assurance that the likelihood of association with a client whose management lacks integrity is minimized" (QC 20). They include inquiring of the prospective client's banker, legal counsel, investment banker, underwriter, or other persons who do business with the company for information about the company and its management.
Answer (A) is incorrect because management, desirous of being accepted as a client, might not answer as objectively as a predecessor auditor. Answer (B) is incorrect because the auditor evaluates evidence during the conduct of the audit. Answer (D) is incorrect because consideration of whether internal control is sufficiently effective pertains to the assessment of control risk, which is performed after the acceptance of an audit engagement.

58. Which of the following are elements of a CPA firm's quality control that should be considered in establishing its quality control policies and procedures?

	Personnel Management	Monitoring	Engagement Performance
A.	Yes	Yes	No
B.	Yes	Yes	Yes
C.	No	Yes	Yes
D.	Yes	No	Yes

Answer (B) is correct. *(CPA, adapted)*
REQUIRED: The elements that should be considered in establishing quality control policies and procedures.
DISCUSSION: The quality control element of personnel management relates to assuring that employees have the skills needed for the responsibilities they are called upon to assume. The quality control element of monitoring is concerned with providing reasonable assurance that procedures related to the other elements are suitably designed and being effectively applied. The quality control element of engagement performance requires the firm to establish policies and procedures to ensure proper planning, performing, supervising, reviewing, documenting, and communicating the results of engagements (QC 20).
Answer (A) is incorrect because engagement performance should be considered in establishing a firm's quality control policies and procedures. Answer (C) is incorrect because personnel management should be considered in establishing a firm's quality control policies and procedures. Answer (D) is incorrect because monitoring should be considered in establishing a firm's quality control policies and procedures.

59. The nature and extent of a CPA firm's quality control policies and procedures depend on

	The CPA Firm's Size	The Nature of the CPA Firm's Practice	Cost-Benefit Considerations
A.	Yes	Yes	Yes
B.	Yes	Yes	No
C.	Yes	No	Yes
D.	No	Yes	Yes

Answer (A) is correct. *(CPA, adapted)*
REQUIRED: The factors affecting a CPA firm's quality control policies and procedures.
DISCUSSION: The nature and extent of a firm's quality control policies and procedures depend on a number of factors, such as the firm's size, the degree of operating autonomy allowed, its personnel policies, the nature of its practice and organization, and appropriate cost-benefit considerations (QC 20).

60. A CPA firm should establish procedures for conducting and supervising work at all organizational levels to provide reasonable assurance that the work performed meets the firm's standards of quality. To achieve this goal, the firm most likely would establish procedures for

A. Evaluating prospective and continuing client relationships.

B. Reviewing engagement working papers and reports.

C. Requiring personnel to adhere to the applicable independence rules.

D. Maintaining personnel files containing documentation related to the evaluation of personnel.

Answer (B) is correct. *(CPA, adapted)*
REQUIRED: The procedure necessary to provide reasonable assurance that the work performed meets the firm's standards of quality relating to supervision.
DISCUSSION: The engagement performance element of quality control includes policies and procedures that cover planning, performing, supervising, reviewing, documenting, and communicating the results of each engagement. Objectives of supervision include establishing procedures for (1) planning engagements, (2) maintaining the firm's standards of quality, and (3) reviewing engagement working papers and reports (QC 20).
Answer (A) is incorrect because evaluating client relationships relates to the quality control element of acceptance and continuance of clients and engagements. Answer (C) is incorrect because requiring adherence to independence rules relates to the quality control element of independence, integrity, and objectivity. Answer (D) is incorrect because evaluation of personnel relates to the quality control element of personnel management.

61. Quality control policies and procedures should provide the firm with reasonable assurance that the policies and procedures relating to the other elements of quality control are being effectively applied. This statement defines the quality control element of

A. Planning.

B. Supervision.

C. Independence, integrity, and objectivity.

D. Monitoring.

Answer (D) is correct. *(Publisher)*
REQUIRED: The element concerned with effective application of all elements of quality control.
DISCUSSION: The quality control element of monitoring is concerned with providing reasonable assurance that policies and procedures related to the other elements are suitably designed and being effectively applied. Monitoring involves considering and evaluating the relevance and adequacy of policies and procedures, the appropriateness of guidance materials and practice aids, the effectiveness of professional development, and the compliance with policies and procedures (QC 20).
Answer (A) is incorrect because planning is an aspect of the element of engagement performance. Answer (B) is incorrect because supervision is an aspect of the element of engagement performance. Answer (C) is incorrect because the element of independence, integrity, and objectivity provides reasonable assurance that personnel at all levels remain independent in fact and appearance, perform all professional responsibilities with integrity, and maintain objectivity in discharging those responsibilities.

62. All of the following are audit quality control requirements contained in the Sarbanes-Oxley Act of 2002 except

A. The lead audit partner must rotate off the audit every five years.

B. The audit report must be submitted to the Public Companies Accounting Oversight Board prior to issuance.

C. The audit report must be reviewed and approved by a second partner.

D. The accounting firm must supervise any associated person with respect to auditing and quality control standards.

Answer (B) is correct. *(Publisher)*
REQUIRED: The quality control issue not addressed in the Sarbanes-Oxley Act.
DISCUSSION: Audit reports must be determined appropriate for issuance by the CPA firm, but need not be approved by the PCAOB.
Answer (A) is incorrect because it represents an audit quality control issue addressed by the Sarbanes-Oxley Act. Answer (C) is incorrect because it represents an audit quality control issue addressed by the Sarbanes-Oxley Act. Answer (D) is incorrect because it represents an audit quality control issue addressed by the Sarbanes-Oxley Act.

63. When Congress passed the Sarbanes-Oxley Act of 2002, it imposed greater regulation on public companies and their auditors and required increased accountability. Which of the following is not a provision of the act?

A. Executives must certify the appropriateness of the financial statements.

B. The act provides criminal penalties for fraud.

C. Auditors may not provide specific nonaudit services for their audit clients.

D. Audit firms must be rotated on a periodic basis.

Answer (D) is correct.   *(Publisher)*
REQUIRED: The provision not included in the Sarbanes-Oxley Act.
DISCUSSION: The act requires rotation of the lead audit or coordinating partner and the reviewing partner on audits of public clients every 5 years. It also requires certain other partners to be rotated every 7 years. However, the act does not require the rotation of audit firms.
Answer (A) is incorrect because the CEO and CFO of a public company must provide a statement to accompany the audit report. This statement certifies the appropriateness of the financial statements and disclosures. However, a violation of this requirement must be knowing and intentional. Answer (B) is incorrect because Title VIII, *Corporate and Criminal Fraud Accountability Act of 2002*, creates a new crime for securities fraud with penalties of fines and up to 10 years in prison, extends the statute of limitations on securities fraud claims, and makes it a felony to create or destroy documents to impede a federal investigation. Answer (C) is incorrect because the act makes it unlawful for a registered public accounting firm to perform certain nonaudit services for audit clients, for example, bookkeeping, systems design, management functions, or any other service the Public Company Accounting Oversight Board (PCAOB) determines by regulation to be impermissible.

Use Gleim's **CPA Test Prep** for interactive testing with over 2,000 additional multiple-choice questions!

1.9 PRACTICE SIMULATION

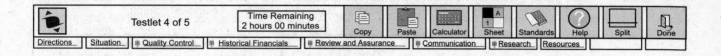

| | Testlet 4 of 5 | Time Remaining 2 hours 00 minutes | Copy | Paste | Calculator | Sheet | Standards | Help | Split | Done |

Directions | Situation | ▦ Quality Control | ▦ Historical Financials | ▦ Review and Assurance | ▦ Communication | ▦ Research | Resources

---

1. Directions

In the following simulation, you will be asked to complete various tasks related to leases and contingencies. The simulation will provide all of the information necessary to do the work. For full credit, be sure to view and complete all work tabs.

Resources are available to you under the tab marked RESOURCES. You may want to review the resources before beginning the simulation.

---

2. Situation

A CPA firm that performs a professional engagement must have a quality control system with appropriate policies and procedures. It must also adhere to other quality control standards. One of the elements of quality control is the maintenance of independence when required. Whether independence is necessary depends upon the nature of the engagement. The nature of the engagement also affects the type of report to be issued. Before undertaking the engagement, however, the firm must reach an understanding with the client about the services to be rendered.

3. Quality Control

Match the related quality control element with the associated description of a typical policy or procedure. Use each choice from the drop-down box as many times as necessary. Mark your answer in the answer column.

Policy and Procedure	Answer
1. Inquiring of third parties, such as the prospective client's bankers and attorneys	
2. Emphasizing independence of mental attitude in firm training programs and in supervision and review work	
3. Reviewing engagement working papers and reports	
4. Training and designating individuals within the firm as specialists to serve as authoritative sources	
5. Establishing qualifications and guidelines for evaluating potential entry-level employees	
6. Establishing guidelines and requirements for the firm's continuing education programs and communicating them to personnel	
7. Inspection	
8. Assuring that current employees have the skills needed for the responsibilities they are called upon to assume	
9. Requiring employees to be honest and candid within the constraints of client confidentiality	

Control Element
A) Independence, integrity, and objectivity
B) Personnel management
C) Acceptance and continuation of clients and engagements
D) Engagement performance
E) Monitoring

4. Independence

The following are various services that accountants perform. For each type of service, indicate by checking the box whether the service provided requires the accountant to be independent.

Service	Required Independence
1. Compilation	☐
2. Tax Preparation	☐
3. Review	☐
4. Examination	☐
5. Audit	☐
6. Agreed Upon Procedures	☐

5. Compilation and Review

Prior to undertaking a compilation or review engagement, the accountant should establish an understanding with the entity, preferably in writing, regarding the services to be performed. The written understanding is referred to as the **engagement letter**. It should

True	False	
☐	☐	A) Describe the nature and limitations of the services to be performed
☐	☐	B) Describe the daily duties of top management personnel
☐	☐	C) Describe the representations that management has made
☐	☐	D) Describe the report the accountant expects to issue
☐	☐	E) State that the engagement cannot be relied upon to disclose errors, fraud, or illegal acts
☐	☐	F) State that any errors, fraud, or illegal acts discovered will be reported to management or the board of directors
☐	☐	G) State that any errors, fraud, or illegal acts discovered will be reported to the proper legal authorities for prosecution

6. Communication

In a brief memo to a client, discuss the function of an audit of historical financial statements, including the assurance provided, the extent of evidence gathering, and the broad standards that govern performance of the audit work.

REMINDER: Your response will be graded for both technical content and writing skills. You should demonstrate your ability to develop, organize, and express your ideas. Do not convey information in the form of a table, bullet point list, or other abbreviated presentation.

To: Client
From: CPA
Subject: The audit function as it relates to the assurance provided, the extent of evidence
            gathering, and whether independence is required

7. Research

In the relevant Professional Standards, find the information relating to the application of the Independence Rules to Close Relatives of CPAs.

Unofficial Answers

3. Quality Control (9 Gradable Items)

1. C) Policies and procedures should be established for deciding whether to accept a client. The purpose is to minimize the likelihood of association with a client whose management lacks integrity.

2. A) Firm-sponsored training programs and supervision can help assure that personnel understand the expectation that they maintain independence both in mental attitude and in appearance.

3. D) The firm should employ policies and procedures for the conduct and supervision of work at all organizational levels to provide reasonable assurance that the work performed meets professional standards, regulatory requirements, and the firm's standards of quality.

4. D) Policies and procedures should be established to provide reasonable assurance that personnel assigned to engagements will seek assistance, to the extent required, from persons having appropriate levels of knowledge, competence, judgment, and authority.

5. B) The firm should ensure that employees possess the appropriate qualifications and characteristics to enable them to perform competently.

6. B) Policies and procedures should be established to provide reasonable assurance that personnel will have the knowledge required to enable them to fulfill assigned responsibilities. Personnel should participate in both general and industry-specific educational activities.

7. E) Inspection procedures evaluate the adequacy of quality control policies and procedures, employee understanding of them, and the extent of compliance. These procedures relate to monitoring because findings are evaluated and changes considered.

8. B) Policies and procedures should be established to provide reasonable assurance that those selected for advancement will have the qualifications necessary for the fulfillment of the responsibilities they will be called on to assume.

9. A) Policies and procedures should be established to provide reasonable assurance that personnel perform all professional responsibilities with integrity. Thus, they should be candid except as constrained by the *Code of Professional Conduct*.

4. Independence (6 Gradable Items)

1. No – Independence is not required
2. No – Independence is not required
3. Yes – Independence is required
4. Yes – Independence is required
5. Yes – Independence is required
6. Yes – Independence is required

5. Compilation and Review (7 Gradable Items)

A. <u>True</u>. The engagement letter should describe the nature and limitations of the services to be performed.

B. <u>False</u>. The engagement letter should not describe the daily duties of top management personnel.

C. <u>False</u>. The engagement letter should not describe the representations that management has made. Representations must be obtained in a review, not a compilation. In a review, representations are provided by management to the accountant in a separate letter.

D. <u>True</u>. The engagement letter should describe the report the accountant expects to issue.

E. <u>True</u>. The engagement letter should state that the engagement cannot be relied upon to disclose errors, fraud, or illegal acts.

F. <u>True</u>. The engagement letter should state that any errors, fraud, or illegal acts discovered will be reported to management or the board of directors unless they are clearly inconsequential.

G. <u>False</u>. The engagement letter should not state that any errors, fraud, or illegal acts discovered will be reported to the proper legal authorities for prosecution.

6. Communication (5 Gradable Items; For grading instructions, please refer to page 11.)

To: Client
From: CPA
Subject: The audit function as it relates to the assurance provided, the extent of evidence gathering, and whether independence is required

An audit is an examination of the financial statements. It is intended to provide positive assurance about the fairness of the financial statements. Thus, an audit provides the highest form of assurance. The audit report contains a clear-cut indication of the character of the auditor's work, if any, and the degree of responsibility the auditor is taking. The report also expresses an opinion (or states the reasons for not expressing an opinion) on whether the reporting entity's financial statements are presented fairly, in all material respects, its financial position, results of operations, and cash flows in conformity with accounting principles generally accepted in the United States of America.

An audit performed by an independent, external auditor provides assurance to external users of the financial statements. It should be performed by persons having adequate technical training and proficiency as auditors, who maintain an independence in mental attitude, in all matters related to the assignment, and who exercise due care in the planning and performance of the engagement and the preparation of the report.

Furthermore, the work must have been adequately planned and supervised, and a sufficient understanding of internal control must have been obtained. An audit is conducted in accordance with auditing standards generally accepted in the United States of America. The audit should be planned and performed to obtain sufficient competent evidence. This evidence should provide reasonable assurance about whether the financial statements are free of material misstatement. Hence, an audit includes examining, on a test basis, evidence supporting the amounts and disclosures in the financial statements. An audit also includes assessing the accounting principles used, significant management estimates, and the overall statement presentation.

7. Research (6 Gradable Items)

ET Section 101 -- *Independence*

.02 101-1 -- Interpretation of Rule 101.

Application of the Independence Rules to Close Relatives

Independence would be considered to be impaired if-

1.   An individual participating on the attest engagement team has a close relative who had

    a.   A key position with the client, or

    b.   A financial interest in the client that

        i)   Was material to the close relative and of which the individual has knowledge; or

        ii)   Enabled the close relative to exercise significant influence over the client.

2.   An individual in a position to influence the attest engagement or any partner in the office in which the lead attest engagement partner primarily practices in connection with the attest engagement has a close relative who had

    a.   A key position with the client, or

    b.   A financial interest in the client that

        i)   Was material to the close relative and of which the individual or partner has knowledge; and

        ii)   Enabled the close relative to exercise significant influence over the client.

Scoring Schedule:

	Correct Responses		Gradable Items		Weights		
Tab 3	_____	÷	9	×	20%	=	_____
Tab 4	_____	÷	6	×	20%	=	_____
Tab 5	_____	÷	7	×	20%	=	_____
Tab 6	_____	÷	5	×	30%	=	_____
Tab 7	_____	÷	6	×	10%	=	_____
							(Your Score)

Use Gleim's ***CPA Review Online*** to practice more simulations in a realistic environment.

STUDY UNIT TWO
RISK ASSESSMENT

(13 pages of outline)

2.1	Pre-Engagement Acceptance Activities	60
2.2	Planning and Supervision (AU 311)	62
2.3	Understanding the Entity's Business (AU 311)	63
2.4	Analytical Procedures (AU 329)	64
2.5	Audit Risk and Materiality (AU 312)	66
2.6	Consideration of Fraud in a Financial Statement Audit (SAS 99 Codified as AU 316)	68
2.7	Illegal Acts by Clients (AU 317)	70
2.8	Practice Simulation	93

In general, the recognition and consideration of risks related to an audit have taken on added significance on the CPA exam. The AICPA appears determined to ensure that successful candidates understand the consequences of the risks that auditors encounter. Candidates can expect to be tested on the auditor's consideration of audit risk and its components. An understanding of the interrelationship between risk and materiality is critical.

A number of risk and materiality-related topics are covered in this study unit. One example is the requirement to use analytical procedures in the planning stage of every audit to help the auditor assess risk. The auditor's expanded responsibility for the discovery of material errors, fraud, and illegal acts is an important reason for the auditor's consideration of risk and is tested regularly on the exam. (Subsequent study units cover the auditor's required control risk assessment and its effect on the audit.) Careful attention to audit planning processes and the interaction between risk assessments and materiality considerations will help the candidate establish a framework for a productive and successful study of auditing knowledge.

2.1 PRE-ENGAGEMENT ACCEPTANCE ACTIVITIES

1. The first standard of field work states, "The work is to be adequately planned and assistants, if any, are to be properly supervised" (**AU 150**).

    a. **AU 310**, *Appointment of the Independent Auditor*, indicates that an early appointment of the auditor is advantageous to both the auditor and the client. Early appointment aids the auditor in planning the work, especially work to be done before the end of the year. The client benefits from more efficient scheduling of the audit and an early completion of the work after the end of the fiscal year.

    b. Before acceptance of an engagement near or after the close of the fiscal year, an independent auditor should determine whether circumstances permit an adequate audit and expression of an unqualified opinion. If they do not, the auditor and client should discuss the possibility of a qualified opinion or a disclaimer of opinion.

2. Client acceptance includes the continued evaluation of existing clients and the evaluation of new clients. Concluding that management lacks integrity causes the auditor to reject a potential client or to end a relationship with an existing client.

    a. The successor auditor is required to communicate with the predecessor auditor before accepting the engagement (**AU 315**, *Communications between Predecessor and Successor Auditors*).

    b. The successor auditor is responsible for initiating the communication.

    c. **Conduct Rule 301**, *Confidential Client Information*, protects the confidentiality of client information. Hence, both the predecessor and successor auditors must obtain client permission to have full and frank discussions about the integrity of management as well as pertinent audit-related issues.

    d. Inquiries should include

        1) Facts that bear on the integrity of management
        2) Disagreements with management concerning accounting principles, audit procedures, or other similar matters
        3) Findings of fraud or illegal acts, or internal control problems that had been communicated by the predecessor auditor to the audit committee (or equivalent)
        4) The predecessor's **understanding** as to the reason for the change in auditors

    e. The working papers of the predecessor should normally be made available to the successor auditor.

    f. The client's refusal to grant permission or the predecessor auditor's failure to respond fully requires the successor auditor to consider the implications when deciding whether to accept the engagement.

3. The auditor is required to establish an **understanding** with the client regarding the services to be performed. If the auditor believes such an understanding has not been reached, (s)he should not accept or perform the engagement (AU 310).

    a. The audit scope, limitations, expectations, and fees for services should be set forth in a contract evidenced by an **engagement letter**. An engagement letter should be sent by the CPA to the prospective client on each engagement, audit or otherwise. Such a letter is highly recommended although not required by GAAS. If the client agrees to the contractual relationship by signing a copy of the letter and returning it to the CPA, it represents a written contract.

b. The following is an example of an engagement letter:

SWIFT, MARCH & COMPANY   *Certified Public Accountants*

[Date]
Mr. Thomas Thorp, President
Anonymous Company, Inc.
Route 32
Nowhere, New York 10000

Dear Mr. Thorp:

This will confirm our understanding of the arrangements for our audit of the financial statements of Anonymous Company, Inc., for the year ending [date].

We will audit the company's financial statements of the year ending [date], for the purpose of expressing an opinion on the fairness with which they present, in all material respects, the financial position, results of operations and cash flows in conformity with generally accepted accounting principles.

We will conduct our audit in accordance with generally accepted auditing standards. Those standards require that we obtain reasonable, rather than absolute, assurance that the financial statements are free of material misstatement, whether caused by error or fraud. Accordingly, a material misstatement may remain undetected. Also, an audit is not designed to detect error or fraud that is immaterial to the financial statements; therefore, the audit will not necessarily detect misstatements less than this materiality level that might exist due to error, fraudulent financial reporting or misappropriation of assets. If, for any reason, we are unable to complete the audit or are unable to form or have not formed an opinion, we may decline to express an opinion or decline to issue a report as a result of the engagement.

While an audit includes obtaining an understanding of internal control sufficient to plan the audit and to determine the nature, timing and extent of audit procedures to be performed, it is not designed to provide assurance on internal control or to identify reportable conditions. However, we are responsible for ensuring that the audit committee (or others with equivalent authority or responsibility) is aware of any reportable conditions that come to our attention.

The financial statements are the responsibility of the company's management. Management is also responsible for (1) establishing and maintaining effective internal control over financial reporting; (2) identifying, and ensuring the company complies with, the laws and regulations applicable to its activities; (3) making all financial records and related information available to us; and (4) providing to us at the conclusion of the engagement a representation letter that, among other things, will confirm management's responsibility for the preparation of the financial statements in conformity with generally accepted accounting principles, the availability of financial records and related data, the completeness and availability of all minutes of the board and committee meetings, and, to the best of its knowledge and belief, the absence of fraud involving management or those employees who have a significant role in the entity's internal control.

Assistance to be supplied by your personnel, including the preparation of schedules and analyses of accounts, is described on a separate attachment. Timely completion of this work will facilitate the completion of our audit.

As part of our engagement of the year ending [date], we will also prepare the federal and state income tax returns for Anonymous Company, Inc.

Our fees will be billed as work progresses and are based on the amount of time required at various levels of responsibility, plus actual out-of-pocket expenses. Invoices are payable upon presentation. We will notify you immediately of any circumstances we encounter that could significantly affect our initial estimate of total fees of $.

If this letter correctly expresses your understanding, please sign the enclosed copy and return it to us.

Very truly yours,

SWIFT, MARCH & COMPANY

_____, *Partner*

Adapted from a presentation in a January 1998 *Journal of Accounting* article by Gibson, Pany, and Smith.

APPROVED:

By: _____
Date: _____

    c.   Management is responsible for adjusting the statements to correct material misstatements. Furthermore, management's **representation letter**, which should be distinguished from the engagement letter, must assert that the effects of any uncorrected misstatements are immaterial individually or in the aggregate. An appendix to the letter should be included that summarizes all uncorrected misstatements (see Study Unit 14).

4.   Stop and review! You have completed the outline for this subunit. Study multiple-choice questions 1 through 9 beginning on page 72.

2.2 PLANNING AND SUPERVISION (AU 311)

1.   According to AU 311, *Planning and Supervision*, planning involves developing an overall strategy for the audit. The size and complexity of the entity, experience with it, and knowledge of its business affect the planning process. The auditor should also consider

    a.   Matters relating to the entity's business and its industry
    b.   Accounting policies and procedures
    c.   Methods used to process information, including the use of service organizations
    d.   Planned assessed level of control risk
    e.   Preliminary judgments about materiality
    f.   Financial statement items requiring adjustment
    g.   Conditions that may require extension or modification of audit tests
    h.   The nature of reports to be prepared

2.   Procedures considered in planning the audit include

    a.   Reviewing correspondence, prior audit documentation, permanent files, financial statements, and auditor's reports
    b.   Discussing audit matters with the CPA firm's personnel who are responsible for non-audit services to the entity
    c.   Inquiring about current business developments
    d.   Reading the current interim financial statements
    e.   Discussing the type, scope, and timing of the audit with management, the board, or the audit committee
    f.   Considering the effects of accounting and auditing pronouncements
    g.   Coordinating the assistance of entity personnel in data preparation
    h.   Determining the involvement, if any, of consultants, specialists, and internal auditors
    i.   Establishing the timing of the work
    j.   Establishing and coordinating staffing requirements

3.   In planning, the auditor should consider the nature, extent, and timing of work to be performed and is required to prepare a written audit program (or a set of programs).

    a.   An audit program sets forth in reasonable detail the audit procedures necessary to accomplish audit objectives.
    b.   The audit program's form and detail will vary.
    c.   Development of the audit program is guided by the results of planning considerations and risk assessment.
    d.   As the audit progresses, changed conditions may require modification of planned procedures.

4. Audit risk and materiality should be considered in planning the audit and designing audit procedures as well as in evaluating whether the financial statements are fairly presented, in all material respects, in conformity with GAAP.

    a. According to AU 312, "An assessment of the risk of material misstatement (whether caused by error or fraud) should be made during planning." The risk of material misstatement due to fraud should be specifically assessed.

    b. Materiality levels include an overall judgment for each statement. However, because the statements are interrelated, and for reasons of efficiency, the auditor ordinarily considers materiality for planning purposes in terms of the smallest aggregate level of misstatements that could be considered material to any one of the financial statements.

5. Supervision "involves directing the efforts of assistants who are involved in accomplishing the objectives of the audit and determining whether those objectives were accomplished" (AU 311).

6. The elements of supervision are instructing assistants, keeping informed of problems encountered, reviewing the work to determine that it is adequately performed and that it is consistent with conclusions in the report, and resolving differences of opinion.

    a. "The auditor with final responsibility for the audit and assistants should be aware of the procedures to be followed when differences of opinion concerning accounting and auditing issues exist among firm personnel involved in the audit. Such procedures should enable an assistant to document his/her disagreement with the conclusions reached if, after appropriate consultation, (s)he believes it necessary to disassociate him/herself from the resolution of the matter. In this situation, the basis for the final resolution should also be documented" (AU 311).

7. Among other things, the extent of supervision depends on the qualifications of personnel and the subject matter of the work.

8. Stop and review! You have completed the outline for this subunit. Study multiple-choice questions 10 through 19 beginning on page 75.

2.3 UNDERSTANDING THE ENTITY'S BUSINESS (AU 311)

1. "The auditor should obtain a level of knowledge of the entity's business that will enable him/her to plan and perform the audit in accordance with GAAS" (AU 311). The auditor need not acquire this understanding prior to acceptance of the engagement but must achieve it prior to completion of the engagement.

    a. This level of knowledge should enable the auditor to understand matters significantly affecting the financial statements and to

        1) Identify areas that need special consideration.

        2) Assess conditions under which accounting data are produced, processed, reviewed, and accumulated.

        3) Evaluate reasonableness of estimates and management representations.

        4) Judge the appropriateness of the principles applied and the adequacy of disclosure.

2.   The auditor should have knowledge of such matters relating to the nature of the entity's business, its organization, and its operating characteristics as the type of business; products and services; capital structure; related parties; locations; and production, distribution, and compensation methods.

   a.   Economic conditions, regulatory issues, technology change, industry accounting practices, competitive factors, and financial trends and ratios may also be relevant.

   b.   The auditor should consider the methods, including computer processing that the entity uses to process accounting information because they influence the design of internal control and the selection of audit procedures.

3.   Knowledge may be obtained from experience with the entity or its industry, prior years' audit documentation, inquiries of entity personnel, AICPA Audit and Accounting Guides, industry publications, periodicals, etc.

4.   Stop and review! You have completed the outline for this subunit. Study multiple-choice questions 20 through 23 beginning on page 77.

2.4 ANALYTICAL PROCEDURES (AU 329)

1.   Analytical procedures are evaluations of financial information made by a study of plausible relationships among both financial and nonfinancial data using models that range from simple to complex.

2.   A basic premise of analytical procedures is that plausible relationships among data may reasonably be expected to exist and continue in the absence of known conditions to the contrary. The following exhibit represents the analytical procedure decision process:

Auditor Developed Expectation	————>	Are These Materially Different?	<————	Management Reported Balance or Ratio

3.   Analytical procedures are

   a.   Required to be used in planning all financial statement audits. They assist the auditor in determining the nature, timing, and extent of other auditing procedures.

   b.   Permitted but not required to be applied as substantive tests to achieve an audit objective related to a specific financial statement assertion.

   c.   Required to be used in the final stage of the audit as a review.

4.   The auditor develops expectations or predictions of recorded balances or ratios. The candidate should learn the five sources of information used to develop analytical procedures. They are frequently tested on the CPA exam. The sources are

   a.   **Financial information from comparable prior period(s)**

      1)   For example, if a client's prior reported sales were $120,000 in year 1, $130,000 in year 2, and $140,000 in year 3, respectively, the auditor would likely predict year 4 sales to be approximately $150,000 based on the trend. If management's reported sales were materially different, the auditor would increase the assessment of the risk of misstatement and investigate the underlying causes.

   b.   **Anticipated results**, such as budgets or forecasts prepared by management (or others) prior to the end of the period

      1)   For example, if management prepared a budget at the beginning of the period reporting forecasted cost of sales to be $100,000, the auditor would expect cost of sales to approximate $100,000 at year-end.

      2)   The use of standard costs and variance analysis facilitates the application of analytical procedures in this context.

   c. **Relationships among data**, such as the interrelations among the balances on the financial statements

      1) For example, if the auditor determines that sales increased by 25% for the year, accounts receivable should increase by approximately that amount.

   d. **Comparable information from the client's industry**

      1) For example, if the usual inventory turnover ratio in the industry is 10 times per year, the auditor will expect the client's turnover ratio to be approximately 10 times.

   e. **Related nonfinancial information**

      1) For example, if the number of hours worked increased by 30%, the auditor will expect an increase in labor costs of approximately 30%.

5. **Analytical Procedures Applied in Planning the Audit**

   a. Focus on enhancing the understanding of the business and the transactions and events since the last audit.

   b. Identify areas that may represent specific audit risks.

   c. Ordinarily use data aggregated at a high level.

6. **Analytical Procedures as Substantive Tests**. Analytical procedures as well as tests of details may be used as substantive tests of management assertions.

   a. The auditor's judgment about the expected effectiveness and efficiency of the available procedures in providing the desired level of assurance determines the procedure or combination of procedures chosen. For some assertions, analytical procedures alone may provide the necessary assurance. The effectiveness and efficiency of analytical procedures depends on

      1) The nature of the assertion

         a) Analytical procedures may be effective when tests of details may not indicate potential misstatements. Thus, they may be effective for testing the completeness assertion.

      2) The plausibility and predictability of the relationship

         a) Relationships in stable environments are more predictable than those in unstable environments.

         b) Income statement accounts tend to be more predictable than balance sheet accounts.

         c) Accounts subject to management discretion may be less predictable.

      3) The availability and reliability of the data used to develop the expectation. Reliability is affected by the source of the data and the conditions under which it was gathered. For example, data are considered more reliable when

         a) Obtained from independent sources outside the entity

         b) Obtained from sources inside the entity independent of those responsible for the amount being audited

         c) Developed under reliable internal control

         d) Subjected to audit testing in current or prior years

         e) Obtained from a variety of sources

    4)   The precision of the expectation

        a)   As the expectation becomes more precise, significant differences between the expectation and management's reported number are more likely to be caused by misstatements.

        b)   Ordinarily, the more detailed the information, the more precise the expectation. For example, monthly data provide more precise expectations than annual data.

  b.   Ratios are often used in analytical analysis. Unexpected changes in a ratio should result in auditor investigation of the accounts that compromise the ratio.

  c.   Significant differences between expectations and recorded amounts should be investigated and evaluated.

    1)   Significant differences should result in inquiries to management.
    2)   Responses should be corroborated with other evidential matter.

  d.   When an analytical procedure is the principal test of a significant financial statement assertion, the auditor should document

    1)   The expectation, if not readily determinable from the documentation of the work.
    2)   The factors used to develop the expectation.
    3)   The results of the comparison of the expectation with the recorded amounts or ratios.
    4)   Any additional auditing procedures performed to resolve differences and their results.

7.   **Analytical Procedures Used in the Overall Review**

  a.   Assess conclusions and overall financial statement presentation.

  b.   Read the financial statements and notes and consider

    1)   The adequacy of evidence gathered in response to unusual or unexpected balances identified in planning or conducting the audit
    2)   Unusual or unexpected balances or relationships that were not previously identified

  c.   To be effective, analytical procedures in the overall review stage should be performed by a manager or partner having a comprehensive knowledge of the client's business and industry.

8.   Stop and review! You have completed the outline for this subunit. Study multiple-choice questions 24 through 39 beginning on page 78.

2.5 AUDIT RISK AND MATERIALITY (AU 312)

1.   Materiality and audit risk affect the application of GAAS, especially the field work and reporting standards, and are reflected in the auditor's standard report. The auditor must make judgments about materiality and audit risk in determining the nature, timing, and extent of procedures to apply and in evaluating the results.

  a.   **Audit risk** is the risk that an auditor may unknowingly fail to modify the opinion on materially misstated financial statements.

  b.   It should be distinguished from risk of malpractice litigation, adverse publicity, or erroneously concluding that financial statements are materially misstated.

    c.   Audit risk has three components that may be assessed in quantitative terms, such as percentages, or in nonquantitative terms that range, for example, from a minimum to a maximum.

        1)   **Inherent risk** is the susceptibility of an assertion to material misstatement in the absence of related controls.

        2)   **Control risk** is the risk that internal control will not prevent or detect on a timely basis a material misstatement that could occur in an assertion.

        3)   **Detection risk** is the risk that the auditor will not detect a material misstatement that exists in an assertion. It is a function of the effectiveness of an audit procedure and its application by the auditor. It can be changed at the auditor's discretion.

    d.   Inherent risk and control risk exist independently of the audit and cannot be changed by the auditor.

2.   The concept of **materiality** recognizes that some matters, but not all, are important for fair presentation of the financial statements in conformity with GAAP.

    a.   Materiality is a matter of professional judgment influenced by the needs of reasonable people who will rely on the financial statements.

    b.   Materiality judgments are made in light of surrounding circumstances and involve qualitative and quantitative considerations.

    c.   Audit risk and materiality have an inverse relationship. Thus, the risk of a large misstatement may be low, but the risk of a small misstatement may be high.

3.   Audit risk and materiality are considered in planning the audit, designing audit procedures, and evaluating whether the financial statements are presented fairly, in all material respects, in conformity with GAAP.

4.   A decrease in the acceptable level of audit risk or in the amounts considered material will result in the auditor's modifying the audit program to obtain greater assurance from substantive testing by selecting **more effective** audit procedures, applying audit procedures **nearer to year-end**, or **increasing the extent** of particular tests.

5.   Because an audit is a cumulative process, information obtained during the audit may lead to revision of auditor judgments about audit risk and materiality.

6.   When **evaluating audit findings**, the auditor considers the individual and aggregate effects of misstatements not corrected by the entity. This consideration addresses qualitative and quantitative factors. Moreover, the consideration and aggregation should include **likely misstatement**, not merely known misstatement.

7.   The auditor should document the nature and effect of **aggregated misstatements** in addition to the conclusion about whether they cause the financial statements to be materially misstated.

8.   Stop and review! You have completed the outline for this subunit. Study multiple-choice questions 40 through 49 beginning on page 83.

2.6 CONSIDERATION OF FRAUD IN A FINANCIAL STATEMENT AUDIT (SAS 99 CODIFIED AS AU 316)

1. **Responsibilities**. The auditor should plan and perform the audit to obtain **reasonable assurance** about whether the financial statements are free of material misstatement, whether caused by error or fraud. **Management** is responsible for programs and controls that prevent, deter, and detect fraud. **Management and oversight authorities** (e.g., the board and audit committee) must set the proper tone and maintain a culture of honesty.

    a. **Absolute assurance** is unattainable because of the characteristics of fraud and the limitations of audit evidence. Management may override controls in unpredictable ways or alter accounting records, and fraud may be concealed through collusion, falsifying documentation (including electronic approvals), or withholding evidence.

2. **Description and characteristics of fraud**. Fraud is intentional. The three conditions ordinarily present when fraud exists include **pressures or incentives** to commit fraud, an **opportunity**, and the capacity to **rationalize** misconduct.

3. The types of fraud relevant to the auditor include misstatements arising from

    a. **Fraudulent financial reporting**. These are intentional misstatements or omissions to deceive users such as altering accounting records or documents, misrepresenting or omitting significant information, and misapplying accounting principles.

    b. **Misappropriation of assets**. These result from theft, embezzlement, or an action that causes payment for items not received.

4. **Professional skepticism** must be maintained in considering the **risk of material misstatement due to fraud** ("fraud risk"). An auditor must critically assess evidence, continually question whether fraud has occurred, and not accept unpersuasive evidence solely because management is believed to be honest.

5. **Discussion among key engagement personnel** is required. It should emphasize professional skepticism and continual alertness to potential fraud. It may occur before or during information gathering, and communication should be ongoing.

    a. The discussion must include **brainstorming** about factors that might create the conditions for fraud, how and where the statements might be misstated, how assets might be misappropriated or financial reports fraudulently misstated, concealment, and how to respond to fraud risk.

6. Obtaining information for **identifying fraud risks** includes inquiring of management, the audit committee, the internal auditors, and others. It also involves considering the results of **planning-stage analytical procedures** and fraud risk factors.

    a. The auditor must apply analytical procedures to **revenue accounts**, e.g., by comparing recorded sales and production capacity to detect fictitious sales.

    b. **Fraud risk factors** are events or conditions indicating possible fraud. The auditor must judge whether they are present and affect the assessment of fraud risks.

    c. **Other information** may be derived from discussions among audit team members, procedures related to the acceptance and continuance of clients and engagements, reviews of interim statements, and identified inherent risks at the account-balance or class-of-transactions level.

7. The information obtained may be considered in terms of the **three conditions**, but an identifiable risk may exist when all conditions have not been observed, especially rationalization. The extent of a condition may by itself create a fraud risk, e.g., pressure to reach an earnings goal.

    a. Fraud risks vary with the entity's size, complexity, ownership, etc.

    b. Fraud risks may relate to specific assertions or to the statements as a whole.

    c.   High inherent risk of an assertion about an account balance or transaction class may exist when it is susceptible to management manipulation.

    d.   Identifying fraud risks entails considering the type of risk and its significance, likelihood, and pervasiveness.

    e.   The auditor must address the risk of **management override** of controls in all audits because of its unpredictability and ordinarily should assume the existence of a fraud risk relating to **improper revenue recognition**. In the latter case, the contrary conclusion must be documented.

8.   Identified fraud risks are assessed after the auditor's required evaluation of **relevant antifraud programs and controls**. As part of the **understanding of internal control**, the auditor must evaluate whether programs and controls have been **suitably designed and placed in operation**. The auditor then determines whether they mitigate or increase the risks.

9.   The **responses** to the assessment of fraud risks should reflect a critical evaluation of the audit evidence. Responses may have an overall effect on the audit, involve changes in audit procedures performed in response to specific fraud risks, or further address management override.

    a.   One **overall effect** is to assign more experienced personnel, or individuals with special skills, or to increase supervision. A second overall effect is to consider **accounting principles**, especially those involving subjective measurements and complex transactions, and whether they indicate a **collective bias**. Another overall effect is to make **unpredictable** choices of audit procedures.

    b.   Audit procedures vary with the risks and the balances, transactions, and assertions affected. Procedures may provide more reliable evidence or increased corroboration, be performed at year-end or throughout the reporting period, or involve larger samples or the use of computer-assisted techniques.

    c.   The auditor must further address **management override**.

        1)   Material misstatements may result from inappropriate **journal entries or adjustments**. The auditor must therefore

            a)   Understand the financial reporting process and controls.

            b)   Identify, select, and test entries and adjustments after considering the risk assessments, effectiveness of controls, nature of the reporting process, and audit evidence (electronic or manual).

            c)   Choose whether to test entries during the period.

            d)   Make inquiries about inappropriate or unusual activity.

        2)   Fraud may result from intentional misstatement of **significant accounting estimates**. The auditor must perform a retrospective review of estimates in the prior-year statements that are based on sensitive assumptions or significant management judgments.

        3)   The auditor must understand **significant unusual transactions**.

10. **Evaluating audit evidence**. The assessment of fraud risks must be ongoing because field work may reveal conditions that modify the judgment.

    a.   **Analytical procedures** performed in the overall review or as substantive tests may detect previously unrecognized fraud risks. These procedures must be applied to **revenue** through year-end. The auditor also must evaluate **responses to inquiries** about analytical relationships.

    b.   At or near the end of field work, the auditor must evaluate **earlier assessments of fraud risk**. The performance of additional procedures may result. Furthermore, the auditor responsible for the audit must determine that information about fraud risks has been properly **communicated** to team members.

   c.   The auditor must consider whether **identified misstatements** indicate fraud, with consequent effects on **materiality** judgments. If the fraud is not material, the auditor still must evaluate the implications.

      1)   If the possible fraud is material, the auditor must obtain additional evidence; consider the implications for the audit; and discuss the matter with management one level (or more) above those involved, senior management, and the audit committee.

      2)   If fraud risk is great, the auditor may consider withdrawing and communicating the reasons to the audit committee.

   d.   **Communications** about fraud are required given **evidence that fraud may exist**. Inconsequential fraud should be brought to the attention of the appropriate management. Other fraud should be reported directly to the audit committee.

   e.   **Required documentation** of the consideration of fraud:

      1)   Planning-stage discussions.
      2)   Procedures for identifying and assessing fraud risks.
      3)   Specific risks identified and the response.
      4)   Reasons for not identifying improper revenue recognition as a fraud risk.
      5)   Results of further addressing management override.
      6)   Responses to other conditions and analytical relationships.
      7)   Fraud communications.

11.   Stop and review! You have completed the outline for this subunit. Study multiple-choice questions 50 through 60 beginning on page 86.

2.7 ILLEGAL ACTS BY CLIENTS (AU 317)

1.   Illegal acts are violations of laws or governmental regulations that do not include personal misconduct by the client's personnel unrelated to their business activities. Whether an act is illegal is a determination normally beyond the auditor's competence.

2.   Illegal acts vary in their relation to the financial statements.

   a.   The further removed an illegal act is from the financial statements, the less likely the auditor is to become aware of the act or recognize its illegality.

   b.   The auditor should consider laws and regulations recognized as having a **direct and material effect** on the financial statements, such as tax laws.

      1)   Examples less likely to have a direct and material effect include laws and regulations relating to environmental protection, food and drug administration, and antitrust.

3.   The auditor's responsibility for detection of misstatements arising from illegal acts having direct and material effects is the same as that for material errors and fraud. The auditor must specifically assess the risk of material misstatements due to such illegal acts.

4.   Other illegal acts "relate more to an entity's operating aspects than to its financial and accounting aspects, and their financial statement effect is indirect."

   a.   An audit usually does not include audit procedures specifically designed to detect illegal acts that have indirect effects. Because of the nature of such illegal acts, an audit provides no assurance that they will be detected or that any contingent liabilities that may result will be disclosed.

   b.   However, an auditor must be aware of the possibility of such illegal acts.

   c.   If information comes to the auditor's attention indicating the potential for an illegal act having material but indirect effects, the auditor should apply specific audit procedures.

d. Although a financial audit does not include audit procedures specifically designed to detect illegal acts having indirect effects, the auditor should inquire of management concerning compliance with laws and regulations and obtain written representations about the absence of violations.

e. However, the auditor considers laws or regulations from the perspective of their known relationship with audit objectives rather than of legality per se.

5. The following results of normal procedures should raise questions:

a. Unauthorized or improperly recorded transactions

b. Investigation by a governmental or enforcement agency

c. Large unexplained payments to consultants, affiliates, employees, or officials

d. Large payments in cash or purchases of bank checks payable to bearer, transfers to numbered accounts, and similar transactions

e. Failure to file tax returns or pay governmental fees

f. Excessive sales commissions on agents' fees

g. Violations cited in reports by regulators

6. Audit procedures in response to a possible illegal act having indirect effects include

a. Obtaining an understanding of the act, the circumstances in which it occurred, and sufficient other information to evaluate its financial statement effects

b. Inquiring of management at a level above those involved

c. Consulting with client's legal counsel

d. Applying any other appropriate audit procedures

7. The auditor's response to detected illegal acts is to consider the effects on the financial statements and the implications for other aspects of the audit, especially the reliability of management's representations. The auditor should

a. Consider the qualitative and quantitative materiality of the act

b. Consider the adequacy of disclosure

c. Communicate material problems to the audit committee

8. If an illegal act has not been accounted for properly, the auditor should express a qualified or adverse opinion.

a. If unable to collect sufficient information, the auditor usually disclaims an opinion.

b. When the auditor concludes that an illegal act has or is likely to have occurred, (s)he should discuss the matter with the appropriate level of management and request that any necessary remedial actions be taken. If the alleged illegal act has a material effect on the financial statements or the client does not take the remedial action that the auditor considers necessary, the auditor should express a qualified or adverse opinion, depending on the level of materiality, or withdraw from the engagement.

9. Disclosure of possible illegal acts to outside parties ordinarily is not the auditor's responsibility and would violate the duty of confidentiality. However, the auditor may need

a. To comply with legal and regulatory requirements. For example, "reportable events" must be disclosed to the SEC, and reports on illegal acts may be required within one business day by the *Private Securities Litigation Reform Act of 1995*.

b. To communicate with a successor auditor

c. To respond to a subpoena

d. To report to a funding or other specified agency in accordance with governmental audit requirements, such as those established by the *Single Audit Act*. (See Study Unit 20.)

10. Stop and review! You have completed the outline for this subunit. Study multiple-choice questions 61 through 67 beginning on page 90.

QUESTIONS

2.1 Pre-Engagement Acceptance Activities

1. Before accepting an audit engagement, a successor auditor should make specific inquiries of the predecessor auditor regarding the predecessor's

    A. Opinion of any subsequent events occurring since the predecessor's audit report was issued.

    B. Understanding as to the reasons for the change of auditors.

    C. Awareness of the consistency in the application of GAAP between periods.

    D. Evaluation of all matters of continuing accounting significance.

Answer (B) is correct. *(CPA, adapted)*
REQUIRED: The specific inquiry that should be made by the successor to the predecessor auditor.
DISCUSSION: The successor auditor should inquire about reasons for the change in auditors, disagreements with management about accounting principles and auditing procedures, and facts bearing on management's integrity.
    Answer (A) is incorrect because the predecessor has no responsibility for events subsequent to the date of his/her report. Answer (C) is incorrect because the predecessor auditor would have considered consistency and reported lack of consistency in the previously issued reports. Answer (D) is incorrect because the question relates to the successor auditor's decision to accept the engagement, not the collection and evaluation of evidence.

2. Hill, CPA, has been retained to audit the financial statements of Monday Co. Monday's predecessor auditor was Post, CPA, who has been notified by Monday that Post's services have been terminated. Under these circumstances, which party should initiate the communications between Hill and Post?

    A. Hill, the successor auditor.

    B. Post, the predecessor auditor.

    C. Monday's controller or CFO.

    D. The chairman of Monday's board of directors.

Answer (A) is correct. *(CPA, adapted)*
REQUIRED: The party responsible for initiation of communications between the successor and the predecessor auditors.
DISCUSSION: AU 315 indicates that the successor auditor is required to communicate with the predecessor auditor before accepting the engagement. Initiation of the communication is the responsibility of the successor, although both must obtain client permission to communicate.
    Answer (B) is incorrect because Post, the predecessor auditor, is not required to initiate the communication. Answer (C) is incorrect because Monday's controller or CFO is not required to initiate the communication. Answer (D) is incorrect because the chairman of Monday's board of directors is not required to initiate the communication.

3. Which of the following factors most likely would cause a CPA to decide not to accept a new audit engagement?

    A. The CPA's lack of understanding of the prospective client's internal auditor's computer-assisted audit techniques.

    B. Management's disregard of its responsibility to maintain an adequate internal control environment.

    C. The CPA's inability to determine whether related party transactions were consummated on terms equivalent to arm's-length transactions.

    D. Management's refusal to permit the CPA to perform substantive tests before year-end.

Answer (B) is correct. *(CPA, adapted)*
REQUIRED: The factor that would cause a CPA to reject an audit engagement.
DISCUSSION: The control environment is the foundation for all other control components. It provides discipline and structure, sets the tone of the organization, and influences the control consciousness of employees. Management is responsible for establishing and maintaining a functioning internal control environment, which includes participation by the board of directors and the audit committee. However, management's disregard of its responsibility to maintain an adequate internal control environment may raise doubts about the auditability of the financial statements and the integrity of management. Such concerns may be sufficiently serious to cause the auditor to conclude that an audit cannot be conducted (AU 319). Thus, an auditor need not have an understanding of the client's internal control, including its internal auditing function, prior to engagement acceptance. Obtaining this understanding is part of the audit.
    Answer (A) is incorrect because the second standard of field work states, "A sufficient understanding of internal control is to be obtained to plan the audit and to determine the nature, timing, and extent of tests to be performed." Answer (C) is incorrect because the conditions surrounding a related party transaction are difficult to substantiate. However, as long as the CPA can determine that the transaction is sufficiently disclosed in the financial statements, the auditor can accept the engagement. Answer (D) is incorrect because substantive tests conducted at year-end are generally more effective than those done before year-end.

4. Which of the following factors most likely would lead a CPA to conclude that a potential audit engagement should be rejected?

A. The details of most recorded transactions are not available after a specified period of time.

B. Internal control activities requiring the segregation of duties are subject to management override.

C. It is unlikely that sufficient competent evidence is available to support an opinion on the financial statements.

D. Management has a reputation for consulting with several accounting firms about significant accounting issues.

Answer (C) is correct. *(CPA, adapted)*
REQUIRED: The factor that would cause a CPA to reject an audit engagement.
DISCUSSION: According to the third standard of field work, "Sufficient competent evidential matter is to be obtained through inspection, observation, inquiries, and confirmations to afford a reasonable basis for an opinion regarding the financial statements under audit." If the CPA is unable to obtain this evidence, the engagement most likely should be rejected.
Answer (A) is incorrect because retaining all transactional information indefinitely is not necessary to the conducting of an audit, as long as the transactions have been properly recorded. Answer (B) is incorrect because, depending on the nature of the duties, management override of internal controls will not necessitate a rejection of the engagement. However, the issue would be considered in assessing control risk. Answer (D) is incorrect because the potential for disagreements with management about the application of accounting principles is a concern, but consultation of management with other accounting firms regarding significant accounting issues would not, by itself, cause a rejection of an audit engagement.

5. Which of the following factors most likely would cause a CPA to not accept a new audit engagement?

A. The prospective client has already completed its physical inventory count.

B. The CPA lacks an understanding of the prospective client's operations and industry.

C. The CPA is unable to review the predecessor auditor's working papers.

D. The prospective client is unwilling to make all financial records available to the CPA.

Answer (D) is correct. *(CPA, adapted)*
REQUIRED: The factor that would cause a CPA to reject an audit engagement.
DISCUSSION: According to AU 310, *Appointment of the Independent Auditor*, the understanding with the client should include such matters as management's responsibility "for making all financial records and related information available to the auditor." If the prospective client is unwilling to make all financial records available to the CPA, the result may be a scope limitation that would require qualification of the opinion or a disclaimer of an opinion should the engagement be accepted.
Answer (A) is incorrect because a physical inventory can be taken after year-end, and analytical procedures can be performed to reconcile the difference between the reported year-end balance and the actual count. Answer (B) is incorrect because the auditor must gain an understanding of the client's operations and industry prior to completing the audit but need not obtain it prior to acceptance of the engagement. Answer (C) is incorrect because, with the client's authorization, the predecessor ordinarily permits the successor to review working papers having continuing accounting significance, but valid business reasons may lead the predecessor to decide not to allow such a review. Moreover, no pronouncement requires the successor to review the predecessor's working papers.

6. A financial statement audit is designed to

A. Provide assurance on internal control and to identify reportable conditions.

B. Detect error or fraud in the financial statements, regardless of whether or not the error or fraud is material.

C. Obtain reasonable assurance about whether the financial statements are free of material misstatement, whether caused by error or fraud.

D. Obtain absolute assurance on the financial statements and express an opinion on the financial statements.

Answer (C) is correct. *(Publisher)*
REQUIRED: The purpose of a financial statement audit.
DISCUSSION: The auditor is responsible for designing the audit to obtain reasonable assurance about whether the financial statements are free of material misstatement, whether caused by error or fraud.
Answer (A) is incorrect because an audit is not designed to provide assurance regarding internal control or to identify reportable conditions. However, audits of public companies (issuers subject to the reporting requirements of the Securities Exchange Act of 1934) are required to include a report expressing an opinion on internal control. Answer (B) is incorrect because an audit is only designed to detect error or fraud that is material. Answer (D) is incorrect because the auditor must obtain reasonable assurance rather than absolute assurance.

7. The scope and nature of an auditor's contractual obligation to a client is ordinarily set forth in the

A. Management representation letter.

B. Scope paragraph of the auditor's report.

C. Engagement letter.

D. Introductory paragraph of the auditor's report.

Answer (C) is correct.   *(CPA, adapted)*

REQUIRED: The form of the contractual agreement with a client.

DISCUSSION: The audit scope, audit limitations and expectations, the responsibilities of the parties, and fees for services should be set forth in a contract evidenced by an engagement letter. An engagement letter should be sent by the CPA to the prospective client on each engagement, audit or otherwise. When signed, it represents a written contract. However, GAAS do not require an engagement letter.

Answer (A) is incorrect because a management representation letter is obtained to assure that management understands its responsibility for the financial statements. Answer (B) is incorrect because the scope paragraph describes the nature of the audit. Answer (D) is incorrect because the introductory paragraph states that the financial statements were audited and the responsibilities of management and the auditor.

8. Which of the following matters generally is included in an auditor's engagement letter?

A. Management's responsibility for the entity's compliance with laws and regulations.

B. The factors to be considered in setting preliminary judgments about materiality.

C. Management's vicarious liability for illegal acts committed by its employees.

D. The auditor's responsibility to search for significant internal control deficiencies.

Answer (A) is correct.   *(CPA, adapted)*

REQUIRED: The matter generally included in an auditor's engagement letter.

DISCUSSION: The primary purpose of an engagement letter is to provide a written record of the agreement with the client as to the services to be provided by the auditor. It sets forth the rights and obligations under the contract between the client and the auditor, including the audit scope, limitations, expectations, and fees. Management's responsibility for compliance with laws and regulations applicable to its activities would be included in the agreement.

Answer (B) is incorrect because materiality judgments are made by the auditor alone and are not included in the engagement letter. Answer (C) is incorrect because the auditor is not qualified to make determinations of the legal liability of management and therefore should not include references to it in the engagement letter. Answer (D) is incorrect because the auditor performing a financial statement audit need not search for significant control deficiencies. However, the engagement letter should state that any reportable conditions coming to the auditor's attention will be reported.

9. An auditor is required to establish an understanding with a client regarding the services to be performed for each engagement. This understanding generally includes

A. Management's responsibility for errors and the illegal activities of employees that may cause material misstatement.

B. The auditor's responsibility for ensuring that the audit committee is aware of any reportable conditions that come to the auditor's attention.

C. Management's responsibility for providing the auditor with an assessment of the risk of material misstatement due to fraud.

D. The auditor's responsibility for determining preliminary judgments about materiality and audit risk factors.

Answer (B) is correct.   *(CPA, adapted)*

REQUIRED: The item required to be included in the understanding with the client.

DISCUSSION: The understanding with the client regarding services to be performed is typically documented in an engagement letter. An engagement letter should, among other things, include an understanding about reportable conditions. According to AU 310, "An audit is not designed to provide assurance on internal control or to identify reportable conditions. However, the auditor is responsible for ensuring that the audit committee or others with equivalent authority or responsibility are aware of any reportable conditions which come to his or her attention."

Answer (A) is incorrect because management is responsible for the financial statements and for maintaining effective internal control over financial reporting, not for the errors and illegal activities of employees. Answer (C) is incorrect because the auditor must assess the risk of material misstatement. Answer (D) is incorrect because the auditor must make judgments about risk and materiality in planning the audit, but responsibility for these matters is not required to be shared with the client.

2.2 Planning and Supervision (AU 311)

10. Which of the following procedures would an auditor least likely perform in planning a financial statement audit?

A. Coordinating the assistance of entity personnel in data preparation.

B. Discussing matters that may affect the audit with firm personnel responsible for non-audit services to the entity.

C. Selecting a sample of vendors' invoices for comparison with receiving reports.

D. Reading the current year's interim financial statements.

Answer (C) is correct. *(CPA, adapted)*
REQUIRED: The procedure an auditor would least likely perform in planning a financial statement audit.
DISCUSSION: Selecting a sample of vendors' invoices for comparison with receiving reports is a substantive test. Substantive testing is performed in the field work stage of a financial statement audit, not in the planning stage.
Answer (A) is incorrect because coordinating the assistance of entity personnel in data preparation is an example of a planning procedure stated in AU 311. Answer (B) is incorrect because discussing matters that may affect the audit with firm personnel responsible for non-audit services to the entity is an example of a planning procedure stated in AU 311. Answer (D) is incorrect because reading the current year's interim financial statements is an example of a planning procedure stated in AU 311.

11. During the initial planning phase of an audit, a CPA most likely would

A. Identify specific internal control activities that are likely to prevent fraud.

B. Evaluate the reasonableness of the client's accounting estimates.

C. Discuss the timing of the audit procedures with the client's management.

D. Inquire of the client's attorney as to whether any unrecorded claims are probable of assertion.

Answer (C) is correct. *(CPA, adapted)*
REQUIRED: The activity performed in the initial planning phase of an audit.
DISCUSSION: The first step in the audit process is the auditor's decision whether to accept a client. After having decided to perform an audit, the auditor enters the initial planning phase. During initial planning, AU 311, *Planning and Supervision*, states that an auditor should, among other things, meet with the client to agree on the type, scope, and timing of the engagement.
Answer (A) is incorrect because understanding internal control is subsequent to the initial planning phase. Answer (B) is incorrect because evaluation of estimates would be completed during the evidence collection phase of the audit. Answer (D) is incorrect because communication with attorneys would be completed during the evidence collection phase of the audit.

12. The senior auditor responsible for coordinating the field work usually schedules a pre-audit conference with the audit team primarily to

A. Give guidance to the staff regarding both technical and personnel aspects of the audit.

B. Discuss staff suggestions concerning the establishment and maintenance of time budgets.

C. Establish the need for using the work of specialists and internal auditors.

D. Provide an opportunity to document staff disagreements regarding technical issues.

Answer (A) is correct. *(CPA, adapted)*
REQUIRED: The purpose of a pre-audit conference.
DISCUSSION: A pre-audit conference would be useful to provide guidance to the staff regarding technical issues concerning the expected use of client personnel and the expectations of the audit team.
Answer (B) is incorrect because time budgets are prepared by supervisors based on the estimates of the time necessary to complete the tasks. Answer (C) is incorrect because the determination of the need for specialists and the use of internal auditors is made by supervisors, not the staff. Answer (D) is incorrect because disagreements regarding technical issues do not normally arise prior to the audit.

13. The element of the audit planning process most likely to be agreed upon with the client before implementation of the audit strategy is the determination of the

A. Timing of inventory observation procedures to be performed.

B. Evidence to be gathered to provide a sufficient basis for the auditor's opinion.

C. Procedures to be undertaken to discover litigation, claims, and assessments.

D. Pending legal matters to be included in the inquiry of the client's attorney.

Answer (A) is correct. *(CPA, adapted)*
REQUIRED: The element of the audit planning process most likely to be agreed upon with the client before implementation of the audit strategy.
DISCUSSION: GAAS require auditors to observe or make at least some physical counts of inventory and to become satisfied about the effectiveness of the methods of inventory-taking and the client's representations concerning quantities and condition (AU 331). Observation of inventory therefore necessitates coordination of the efforts of the auditors and the client prior to performance of the procedure.
Answer (B) is incorrect because the evidence to be gathered is not subject to the client's approval. Answer (C) is incorrect because the procedures are not subject to the client's approval. Answer (D) is incorrect because the determination of the specific legal issues to be raised in the inquiry letter is not appropriate in the planning phase.

14. In developing a preliminary audit strategy, an auditor should consider

A. Whether the allowance for sampling risk exceeds the achieved upper precision limit.

B. Findings from substantive tests performed at interim dates.

C. Whether the inquiry of the client's attorney identifies any litigation, claims, or assessments not disclosed in the financial statements.

D. The planned assessed level of control risk.

Answer (D) is correct. *(CPA, adapted)*
REQUIRED: The issue an auditor should consider when developing a preliminary audit strategy.
DISCUSSION: According to AU 311, "Audit planning involves developing an overall strategy for the expected conduct and scope of the audit. The nature, extent, and timing of planning vary with the size and complexity of the entity, experience with the entity, and knowledge of the entity's business." Among the specific matters that the audit planner should consider is the planned assessed level of control risk.
Answer (A) is incorrect because sampling risk and upper precision limits are set subsequent to developing a preliminary audit strategy. Answer (B) is incorrect because planning precedes substantive tests, including those performed at interim dates. Answer (C) is incorrect because the inquiry of the client's attorney occurs subsequent to developing a preliminary audit strategy.

15. When planning an audit, an auditor should

A. Consider whether substantive tests may be reduced based on the results of the internal control questionnaire.

B. Make preliminary judgments about materiality levels for audit purposes.

C. Conclude whether changes in compliance with prescribed controls require a change in the assessed level of control risk.

D. Prepare a preliminary draft of the management representation letter.

Answer (B) is correct. *(CPA, adapted)*
REQUIRED: The matter included in audit planning.
DISCUSSION: GAAS require the auditor to plan and perform the audit to obtain reasonable assurance about whether the financial statements are free of material misstatement. Accordingly, specific audit planning considerations include the need to make preliminary judgments about materiality levels for audit purposes (AU 311).
Answer (A) is incorrect because reducing substantive tests requires a determination of the effectiveness of internal control, a step subsequent to audit planning. Answer (C) is incorrect because procedures to determine whether changes in compliance with prescribed controls have occurred are performed subsequent to audit planning. Answer (D) is incorrect because the management representation letter is dated as of the date of the audit report.

16. The audit work performed by each assistant should be reviewed to determine whether it was adequately performed and to evaluate whether the

A. Audit procedures performed are approved in the professional standards.

B. Audit has been performed by persons having adequate technical training and proficiency as auditors.

C. Auditor's system of quality control has been maintained at a high level.

D. Results are consistent with the conclusions to be presented in the auditor's report.

Answer (D) is correct. *(CPA, adapted)*
REQUIRED: The reason for reviewing the audit work of each assistant.
DISCUSSION: The first standard of field work requires assistants to be properly supervised. Thus, the "work performed by each assistant should be reviewed to determine whether it was adequately performed and to evaluate whether the results are consistent with the conclusions to be presented in the auditor's report" (AU 311).
Answer (A) is incorrect because determination of whether the procedures are in accordance with GAAS is necessary in the planning stage. Answer (B) is incorrect because the selection of assistants having adequate technical training and proficiency concerns planning, not supervision. Answer (C) is incorrect because the review of the audit work of each assistant is only a part of quality control.

17. The in-charge auditor most likely would have a supervisory responsibility to explain to the staff assistants

A. That immaterial fraud is not to be reported to the client's audit committee.

B. How the results of various auditing procedures performed by the assistants should be evaluated.

C. What benefits may be attained by the assistants' adherence to established time budgets.

D. Why certain documents are being transferred from the current file to the permanent file.

Answer (B) is correct. *(CPA, adapted)*
REQUIRED: The responsibility of the audit supervisor.
DISCUSSION: AU 311 states "Assistants should be informed of their responsibilities and the objectives of the procedures that they are to perform." They should be informed about the matters that affect the nature, timing, and extent of procedures, including how the results of tests should be evaluated.
Answer (A) is incorrect because immaterial fraud may be reported to the client's audit committee. Answer (C) is incorrect because discussion of time budgets is not a responsibility under GAAS. Answer (D) is incorrect because, at the end of the audit, supervisors determine which documents are to be transferred to the permanent file. These decisions need not be justified to staff assistants.

18. The auditor with final responsibility for an engagement and one of the assistants have a difference of opinion about the results of an auditing procedure. If the assistant believes it is necessary to be disassociated from the matter's resolution, the CPA firm's procedures should enable the assistant to

A. Refer the disagreement to the AICPA's Peer Review Board.

B. Document the details of the disagreement with the conclusion reached.

C. Discuss the disagreement with the entity's management or its audit committee.

D. Report the disagreement to an impartial peer review monitoring team.

Answer (B) is correct. *(CPA, adapted)*
REQUIRED: The action permitted to an assistant who disagrees with the auditor in charge.
DISCUSSION: According to AU 311, audit personnel should be aware of the procedures to be followed when they have differences of opinion regarding accounting and auditing issues. An assistant should be able to document his/her disagreement with the conclusions reached if, after consultation, (s)he believes it is necessary to be disassociated from the resolution of the matter. Moreover, the basis for the final disposition of the disagreement should also be documented.
Answer (A) is incorrect because the Peer Review Board issues standards for performing and reporting on peer reviews. Answer (C) is incorrect because the client need not be informed of the disagreement about the results of an auditing procedure. Answer (D) is incorrect because there is no peer review monitoring team.

19. After field work audit procedures are completed, a partner of the CPA firm who has not been involved in the audit performs a second or wrap-up audit documentation review. This second review usually focuses on

A. The fair presentation of the financial statements in conformity with GAAP.

B. Fraud involving the client's management and its employees.

C. The materiality of the adjusting entries proposed by the audit staff.

D. The communication of internal control weaknesses to the client's audit committee.

Answer (A) is correct. *(CPA, adapted)*
REQUIRED: The purpose of a second review by an audit partner.
DISCUSSION: Analytical procedures are required in an overall review and typically performed by an audit partner. The purpose of those procedures is to assess the conclusions in the overall financial statement presentation (AU 329).
Answer (B) is incorrect because this procedure is completed by the audit team. Answer (C) is incorrect because this procedure is completed by the audit team. Answer (D) is incorrect because communication of reportable conditions is performed by the supervisor in charge of the audit.

2.3 Understanding the Entity's Business (AU 311)

20. Prior to beginning the field work on a new audit engagement in which a CPA does not possess expertise in the industry in which the client operates, the CPA should

A. Reduce audit risk by lowering the preliminary levels of materiality.

B. Design special substantive tests to compensate for the lack of industry expertise.

C. Engage financial experts familiar with the nature of the industry.

D. Obtain a knowledge of matters that relate to the nature of the entity's business.

Answer (D) is correct. *(CPA, adapted)*
REQUIRED: The action taken by an auditor who lacks experience with the client's industry.
DISCUSSION: AU 311 states, "The auditor should obtain a level of knowledge of the entity's business that will enable him/her to plan and perform the audit in accordance with GAAS."
Answer (A) is incorrect because the auditor cannot make judgments about materiality levels until (s)he has sufficient knowledge of the entity's business. Answer (B) is incorrect because the auditor cannot design substantive tests until (s)he has sufficient knowledge of the entity's business. Answer (C) is incorrect because the use of experts does not relieve the auditor of the responsibility to gain the necessary expertise to satisfy GAAS.

21. To obtain an understanding of a continuing client's business in planning an audit, an auditor most likely would

A. Perform tests of details of transactions and balances.

B. Review prior-year audit documentation and the permanent file for the client.

C. Read specialized industry journals.

D. Reevaluate the client's internal control.

Answer (B) is correct. *(CPA, adapted)*
REQUIRED: The procedure used to obtain an understanding of a continuing client's business.
DISCUSSION: Knowledge may be obtained from experience with the entity or its industry, prior years' audit documentation, inquiries of entity personnel, AICPA audit and accounting guides, and other available information.
Answer (A) is incorrect because tests of details are used to collect sufficient, competent evidential matter to support the opinion. Answer (C) is incorrect because reading specialized industry journals would provide information about the industry, but not necessarily about the specific client. Answer (D) is incorrect because a change in the assessment of control risk would occur subsequent to the planning phase.

22. An auditor obtains knowledge about a new client's business and its industry to

A. Make constructive suggestions concerning improvements to the client's internal control.

B. Develop an attitude of professional skepticism concerning management's financial statement assertions.

C. Evaluate whether the aggregation of known misstatements causes the financial statements taken as a whole to be materially misstated.

D. Understand the events and transactions that may have an effect on the client's financial statements.

Answer (D) is correct.   *(CPA, adapted)*
    REQUIRED: The reason to obtain knowledge of a new client's business and industry.
    DISCUSSION: "The auditor should obtain a level of knowledge of the entity's business that will allow him/her to plan and perform his/her audit in accordance with generally accepted auditing standards. That level of knowledge should enable him/her to obtain an understanding of the events, transactions, and practices that, in his/her judgment, may have a significant effect on the financial statements" (AU 311).
    Answer (A) is incorrect because communication of internal control-related matters occurs during and after the audit. Obtaining knowledge of the client's business occurs during audit planning. Answer (B) is incorrect because the auditor should adopt an attitude of professional skepticism in all phases of an engagement. Answer (C) is incorrect because evaluating whether the financial statements are materially misstated is done after the collection of evidence.

23. A CPA wishes to determine how various publicly-held companies have complied with the disclosure requirements of a new financial accounting standard. Which of the following information sources would the CPA most likely consult for this information?

A. AICPA Codification of Statements on Auditing Standards.

B. AICPA Accounting Trends and Techniques.

C. SEC Quality Control Review.

D. SEC Statement 10-K Guide.

Answer (B) is correct.   *(CPA, adapted)*
    REQUIRED: The publication most likely consulted for compliance information of a new financial accounting standard.
    DISCUSSION: Practical guidance for conducting accounting and audit engagements can be found in various nonauthoritative publications, such as Accounting Trends and Techniques, which describes current practice regarding corporate financial accounting and disclosure policies. It is a useful source for practitioners in industry and public practice. This annual AICPA publication is based on a survey of the annual financial reports of over 600 public companies.
    Answer (A) is incorrect because the AICPA Codification of Statements on Auditing Standards contain U.S. generally accepted auditing standards (GAAS). Answer (C) is incorrect because, although quality control extends to adherence to GAAP, the SEC Quality Control Review does not provide information about prevalent practice regarding compliance with particular disclosure requirements. Answer (D) is incorrect because consulting the actual Form 10-K filings by public companies, which contain audited financial statements, would be more useful than consulting the guidance information provided by the SEC.

2.4 Analytical Procedures (AU 329)

24. A basic premise underlying analytical procedures is that

A. These procedures cannot replace tests of balances and transactions.

B. Statistical tests of financial information may lead to the discovery of material misstatements in the financial statements.

C. The study of financial ratios is an acceptable alternative to the investigation of unusual fluctuations.

D. Plausible relationships among data may reasonably be expected to exist and continue in the absence of known conditions to the contrary.

Answer (D) is correct.   *(CPA, adapted)*
    REQUIRED: The basic premise underlying analytical procedures.
    DISCUSSION: AU 329 states, "A basic premise underlying the application of analytical procedures is that plausible relationships among data may reasonably be expected to exist and continue in the absence of known conditions to the contrary." Variability in these relationships can be explained by, for example, unusual events or transactions, business or accounting changes, misstatements, or random fluctuations.
    Answer (A) is incorrect because, for some assertions, analytical procedures alone may provide the auditor with the level of assurance (s)he desires. Answer (B) is incorrect because analytical procedures, such as simple comparisons, do not necessarily require statistical testing. Answer (C) is incorrect because the objective of analytical procedures, such as ratio analysis, is to identify significant differences for evaluation and possible investigation.

25. The objective of performing analytical procedures in planning an audit is to identify the existence of

A. Unusual transactions and events.

B. Illegal acts that went undetected because of internal control weaknesses.

C. Related party transactions.

D. Recorded transactions that were not properly authorized.

Answer (A) is correct. *(CPA, adapted)*
REQUIRED: The objective of analytical procedures.
DISCUSSION: The objective of analytical procedures "is to identify such things as the existence of unusual transactions and events, and amounts, ratios, and trends that might indicate matters that have financial statement and audit planning ramifications" (AU 329).
Answer (B) is incorrect because the objective of performing analytical procedures to plan the audit is to identify areas of specific risk, not specific illegal acts. Answer (C) is incorrect because, although the auditor should evaluate disclosures about related party transactions, analytical procedures performed to plan the audit do not necessarily detect such transactions. Answer (D) is incorrect because tests of controls are necessary to determine whether transactions were properly authorized.

26. For audits of financial statements made in accordance with generally accepted auditing standards, the use of analytical procedures is required to some extent

	In the Planning Stage	As a Substantive Test	In the Final Review Stage
A.	No	Yes	Yes
B.	Yes	Yes	No
C.	Yes	No	Yes
D.	No	No	No

Answer (C) is correct. *(CPA, adapted)*
REQUIRED: The required use of analytical procedures.
DISCUSSION: AU 329 states that analytical procedures must be applied to some extent to assist the auditor in planning other auditing procedures and as an overall review of the financial information in the final review stage of the audit. Analytical procedures may be used (but are not mandatory) as a substantive test to obtain evidential matter about particular assertions related to the account balances or classes of transactions.

27. To be effective, analytical procedures in the overall review stage of an audit engagement should be performed by

A. The staff accountant who performed the substantive auditing procedures.

B. The managing partner who has responsibility for all audit engagements at that practice office.

C. A manager or partner who has a comprehensive knowledge of the client's business and industry.

D. The CPA firm's quality control manager or partner who has responsibility for the firm's peer review program.

Answer (C) is correct. *(CPA, adapted)*
REQUIRED: The person who performs analytical procedures in the overall review stage.
DISCUSSION: To understand the complex nature of financial relationships necessary to plan, and to evaluate the results of, analytical procedures requires knowledge of the client and industry(ies) in which it operates. The purposes and limitations of those procedures also must be understood. A manager or partner with specific knowledge of the business and the industry is most likely to have such an understanding.

28. Analytical procedures used in planning an audit should focus on

A. Reducing the scope of tests of controls and substantive tests.

B. Providing assurance that potential material misstatements will be identified.

C. Enhancing the auditor's understanding of the client's business.

D. Assessing the adequacy of the available evidential matter.

Answer (C) is correct. *(CPA, adapted)*
REQUIRED: The focus of analytical procedures used in planning an audit.
DISCUSSION: Analytical procedures applied in planning an audit focus on enhancing the understanding of the business and the transactions and events since the last audit and identifying areas that may represent specific audit risks.
Answer (A) is incorrect because audit judgment is used in determining the scope of tests of controls and substantive tests. Answer (B) is incorrect because substantive tests provide reasonable assurance that material misstatements will be identified. Answer (D) is incorrect because the auditor considers the objective of the audit relative to the adequacy of the evidential matter in determining whether the objectives have been achieved.

29. Which of the following statements concerning analytical procedures is true?

A. Analytical procedures may be omitted entirely for some financial statement audits.

B. Analytical procedures used in planning the audit should not use nonfinancial information.

C. Analytical procedures usually are effective and efficient for tests of controls.

D. Analytical procedures alone may provide the appropriate level of assurance for some assertions.

Answer (D) is correct. *(CPA, adapted)*
REQUIRED: The true statement concerning analytical procedures.
DISCUSSION: AU 329 states, "For some assertions, analytical procedures are effective in providing the appropriate level of assurance." The decision is based on the auditor's judgment about the expected effectiveness and efficiency of the available procedures. The auditor must then decide which procedure(s) can provide the desired level of assurance for particular assertions.
Answer (A) is incorrect because analytical procedures are required in the planning and review stages of the audit. Answer (B) is incorrect because analytical procedures used in planning the audit often use financial data only, but relevant nonfinancial information may also be considered. Answer (C) is incorrect because analytical procedures may be used as substantive tests but not as tests of controls.

30. Which of the following procedures would an auditor most likely perform in planning a financial statement audit?

A. Inquiring of the client's legal counsel concerning pending litigation.

B. Comparing the financial statements with anticipated results.

C. Examining computer-generated exception reports to verify the effectiveness of internal control.

D. Searching for unauthorized transactions that may aid in detecting unrecorded liabilities.

Answer (B) is correct. *(CPA, adapted)*
REQUIRED: The procedure most likely performed in planning a financial statement audit.
DISCUSSION: Analytical procedures are required to be applied in the planning of all financial statement audits. Comparing the financial statements with anticipated results, that is, management budgets or forecasts prepared at the beginning of the year, is a form of analytical procedure.
Answer (A) is incorrect because inquiry of the client's legal counsel is a test of the details of transactions and balances performed during the evidence collection process. Answer (C) is incorrect because planning requires obtaining an understanding of internal control. However, the auditor is not required to obtain knowledge about operating effectiveness as part of the understanding. Answer (D) is incorrect because searching for unauthorized transactions is a test of the details of transactions and balances performed during the evidence collection process.

31. Which of the following nonfinancial information would an auditor most likely consider in performing analytical procedures during the planning phase of an audit?

A. Turnover of personnel in the accounting department.

B. Objectivity of audit committee members.

C. Square footage of selling space.

D. Management's plans to repurchase stock.

Answer (C) is correct. *(CPA, adapted)*
REQUIRED: The nonfinancial information considered in performing analytical procedures during audit planning.
DISCUSSION: AU 329 states, "Although analytical procedures used in planning the audit often use only financial data, sometimes relevant nonfinancial information is considered as well. For example, number of employees, square footage of selling space, volume of goods produced, and similar information may contribute to accomplishing the purpose of the procedures."
Answer (A) is incorrect because turnover of personnel in the accounting department is not a measure related to analytical procedures. Answer (B) is incorrect because objectivity of audit committee members is not a measure related to analytical procedures. Answer (D) is incorrect because management's plans to repurchase stock is not a measure related to analytical procedures.

32. Which of the following would not be considered an analytical procedure?

A. Estimating payroll expense by multiplying the number of employees by the average hourly wage rate and the total hours worked.

B. Projecting an error rate by comparing the results of a statistical sample with the actual population characteristics.

C. Computing accounts receivable turnover by dividing credit sales by the average net receivables.

D. Developing the expected sales based on the sales trend of the prior five years.

Answer (B) is correct. *(CPA, adapted)*
REQUIRED: The procedure not considered an analytical procedure.
DISCUSSION: Analytical procedures are evaluations of financial information made by a study of plausible relationships among both financial and nonfinancial data using models that range from simple to complex. Projecting an error rate based on a statistical sample is a sampling procedure, not an analytical procedure.
Answer (A) is incorrect because estimating payroll expense by multiplying the number of employees by the average hourly wage rate is an evaluation made by a study of a plausible relationship. Answer (C) is incorrect because computing accounts receivable turnover is an evaluation made by a study of a plausible relationship. Answer (D) is incorrect because developing expected year-end sales based upon trends is an evaluation made by a study of a plausible relationship.

33. An auditor's decision either to apply analytical procedures as substantive tests or to perform tests of transactions and account balances usually is determined by the

A. Availability of data aggregated at a high level.

B. Relative effectiveness and efficiency of the tests.

C. Timing of tests performed after the balance sheet date.

D. Auditor's familiarity with industry trends.

Answer (B) is correct. *(CPA, adapted)*
REQUIRED: The basis for choosing between analytical procedures and tests of details.
DISCUSSION: The decision is based on the auditor's judgment about the expected effectiveness and efficiency of the available procedures. The auditor considers the level of assurance required to be provided by substantive testing for a particular audit objective related to a particular assertion. (S)he must then decide which procedure or combination of procedures can provide that level of assurance. "For some assertions, analytical procedures are effective in providing the appropriate level of assurance" (AU 329).
Answer (A) is incorrect because availability of data is just one factor in evaluating effectiveness and efficiency. Answer (C) is incorrect because the timing of tests is one of many considerations in determining effectiveness and efficiency. Answer (D) is incorrect because familiarity with trends is one factor among many in determining effectiveness and efficiency.

34. An auditor's analytical procedures performed during the overall review stage indicated that the client's accounts receivable had doubled since the end of the prior year. However, the allowance for doubtful accounts as a percentage of accounts receivable remained about the same. Which of the following client explanations most likely would satisfy the auditor?

A. The client liberalized its credit standards in the current year and sold much more merchandise to customers with poor credit ratings.

B. Twice as many accounts receivable were written off in the prior year as in the current year.

C. A greater percentage of accounts receivable were currently listed in the "more than 90 days overdue" category than in the prior year.

D. The client opened a second retail outlet in the current year and its credit sales approximately equaled the older, established outlet.

Answer (D) is correct. *(CPA, adapted)*
REQUIRED: The satisfactory explanation for an increase in accounts receivable.
DISCUSSION: Analytical procedures are required to be used in the final stage of the audit as a review. A basic premise of analytical procedures is that plausible relationships among data may reasonably be expected to exist and continue in the absence of known conditions to the contrary. The only reasonable explanation proposed by the client to satisfy the auditor is the opening of a second retail outlet with sales approximating the established outlet. It is plausible that a doubling of capacity while selling to similarly creditworthy customers might have resulted in a doubling of receivables without a change in the proportion of doubtful accounts.
Answer (A) is incorrect because an increase in credit sales to less creditworthy customers would increase the proportion of doubtful accounts. Answer (B) is incorrect because this explanation suggests a lower percentage of doubtful accounts, not a constant percentage. Answer (C) is incorrect because the dating of accounts receivable would not affect the percentage relationship of the allowance to total accounts receivable.

35. Which of the following items tend to be the most predictable for purposes of analytical procedures applied as substantive tests?

A. Relationships involving balance sheet accounts.

B. Transactions subject to management discretion.

C. Relationships involving income statement accounts.

D. Data subject to audit testing in the prior year.

Answer (C) is correct. *(CPA, adapted)*
REQUIRED: The most predictable item for purposes of analytical procedures applied as substantive tests.
DISCUSSION: According to AU 329, "Relationships involving income statement accounts tend to be more predictable than relationships involving only balance sheet accounts because income statement accounts represent transactions over a period of time, whereas balance sheet accounts represent amounts at a moment in time."
Answer (A) is incorrect because relationships involving balance sheet accounts tend to be less predictable. Balance sheet accounts represent amounts at a moment in time. Answer (B) is incorrect because transactions subject to management discretion are often unpredictable. Answer (D) is incorrect because data subject to audit testing in the prior year may not reflect changed conditions.

36. Which of the following factors would least influence an auditor's consideration of the reliability of data for purposes of analytical procedures?

A. Whether the data were processed in a computer system or in a manual accounting system.

B. Whether sources within the entity were independent of those who are responsible for the amount being audited.

C. Whether the data were subjected to audit testing in the current or prior year.

D. Whether the data were obtained from independent sources outside the entity or from sources within the entity.

Answer (A) is correct. *(CPA, adapted)*
REQUIRED: The factor least likely to influence an auditor's consideration of the reliability of data for purposes of analytical procedures.
DISCUSSION: The consideration of the reliability of data should include sources of the data and the conditions under which the data were gathered. The factors influencing this consideration include the other answer choices. Other factors include whether the auditor's expectations were developed using data from a variety of sources and whether the data were developed under a reliable system with adequate controls. The mode of processing is less influential than the other factors.
Answer (B) is incorrect because whether sources within the entity were independent of those who are responsible for the amount being audited is an influential factor. Answer (C) is incorrect because whether the data were subjected to audit testing in the current or prior year is an influential factor. Answer (D) is incorrect because whether the data were obtained from independent sources outside the entity or from sources within the entity is an influential factor.

37. The primary objective of analytical procedures used in the final review stage of an audit is to

A. Obtain evidence from details testing to corroborate particular assertions.

B. Identify areas that represent specific relevant to the audit.

C. Assist the auditor in assessing the validity of the conclusions reached.

D. Satisfy doubts when questions arise about a client's ability to continue in existence.

Answer (C) is correct. *(CPA, adapted)*
REQUIRED: The primary objective of analytical procedures used in the final review stage of an audit.
DISCUSSION: Analytical procedures are required to be used as an overall review in the final review stage of the audit. They are useful in assessing the conclusions reached by the auditor and in evaluating financial statement presentation. Many procedures may be used. These ordinarily should include reading the statements and notes and considering (1) the adequacy of evidence regarding previously identified unusual or unexpected balances and (2) unusual or unexpected balances or relationships not previously noted (AU 329).
Answer (A) is incorrect because obtaining evidence to corroborate particular assertions is done before the final review stage. Answer (B) is incorrect because identifying specific areas of risk is done in the planning stage. Answer (D) is incorrect because resolving a going concern issue is a secondary objective.

38. Analytical procedures used in the overall review stage of an audit generally include

A. Considering unusual or unexpected account balances that were not previously identified.

B. Performing tests of transactions to corroborate management's financial statement assertions.

C. Gathering evidence concerning account balances that have not changed from the prior year.

D. Retesting controls that appeared to be ineffective during the assessment of control risk.

Answer (A) is correct. *(CPA, adapted)*
REQUIRED: The analytical procedure used in the final review stage.
DISCUSSION: Analytical procedures are required to be used as an overall review in the final review stage of the audit. They are useful in assessing the conclusions reached by the auditor and in evaluating financial statement presentation. Many procedures may be used. These ordinarily should include reading the statements and notes and considering (1) the adequacy of evidence regarding previously identified unusual or unexpected balances and (2) unusual or unexpected balances or relationships not previously noted (AU 329).
Answer (B) is incorrect because analytical procedures are not tests of transactions. Answer (C) is incorrect because the lack of change from the prior year may not be unusual or unexpected. Answer (D) is incorrect because analytical procedures are substantive tests, not tests of controls.

39. Analytical procedures performed in the overall review stage of an audit suggest that several accounts have unexpected relationships. The results of these procedures most likely would indicate that

A. Irregularities exist among the relevant account balances.

B. Internal control activities are not operating effectively.

C. Additional tests of details are required.

D. The communication with the audit committee should be revised.

Answer (C) is correct. *(CPA, adapted)*
REQUIRED: The implication when analytical procedures applied in the overall review stage of the audit have unexpected results.
DISCUSSION: Analytical procedures are required to be performed in the final review stage of the audit. They assist in assessing the conclusions reached and in evaluating the overall financial presentation. When analytical procedures have unexpected results, the auditor should investigate the causes. Thus, additional tests of details should be performed to gather additional evidence (AU 329).
Answer (A) is incorrect because analytical procedures can identify unexpected relationships but not their causes.
Answer (B) is incorrect because tests of controls are conducted to determine the effectiveness of their design and operation. Answer (D) is incorrect because, until the auditor determines the cause of the unexpected relationships, the auditor does not know whether the communication with the audit committee should be revised.

2.5 Audit Risk and Materiality (AU 312)

40. The existence of audit risk is recognized by the statement in the auditor's standard report that the

A. Auditor is responsible for expressing an opinion on the financial statements, which are the responsibility of management.

B. Financial statements are presented fairly, in all material respects, in conformity with GAAP.

C. Audit includes examining, on a test basis, evidence supporting the amounts and disclosures in the financial statements.

D. Auditor obtains reasonable assurance about whether the financial statements are free of material misstatement.

Answer (D) is correct. *(CPA, adapted)*
REQUIRED: The statement that recognizes the existence of audit risk.
DISCUSSION: Audit risk is the risk that an auditor may unknowingly fail to modify the opinion on materially misstated financial statements (AU 312). The exercise of due professional care allows the auditor to provide only reasonable, not absolute, assurance that the financial statements are free of material misstatement, whether caused by error or fraud. Thus, an audit performed in accordance with GAAS does not eliminate audit risk (AU 230).
Answer (A) is incorrect because the introductory paragraph of the standard audit report states the degree of the auditor's responsibility. Answer (B) is incorrect because this language indicates the auditor's belief that the statement as a whole are not materially misstated in conformity with GAAP. Answer (C) is incorrect because the scope paragraph of the audit report recognized that examining all items under audit is not feasible. This limitation is one of many inherent in the audit process.

41. The risk that an auditor's procedures will lead to the conclusion that a material misstatement does not exist in an account balance when, in fact, such misstatement does exist is

A. Audit risk.

B. Inherent risk.

C. Control risk.

D. Detection risk.

Answer (D) is correct. *(CPA, adapted)*
REQUIRED: The risk that audit procedures will fail to detect a material misstatement.
DISCUSSION: Detection risk is the risk that the auditor will not detect a material misstatement that exists in an assertion. It is affected by the auditor's procedures and can be changed at his/her discretion.
Answer (A) is incorrect because audit risk includes inherent risk and control risk, which are not affected by the auditor's procedures. Answer (B) is incorrect because inherent risk is the susceptibility of an assertion to material misstatement in the absence of related controls. Answer (C) is incorrect because control risk is the risk that a material misstatement will not be prevented or detected by internal control.

42. Inherent risk and control risk differ from detection risk in that they

    A. Arise from the misapplication of auditing procedures.

    B. May be assessed in either quantitative or nonquantitative terms.

    C. Exist independently of the financial statement audit.

    D. Can be changed at the auditor's discretion.

Answer (C) is correct.   *(CPA, adapted)*
    REQUIRED: The way in which inherent risk and control risk differ from detection risk.
    DISCUSSION: Inherent risk is the susceptibility of an assertion to a material misstatement in the absence of related controls. Control risk is the risk that internal control will not prevent or detect a material misstatement. Inherent and control risks exist independently of the audit and cannot be changed by the auditor. Detection risk is the risk that the auditor will not detect a material misstatement that exists in an assertion. It can be changed at the auditor's discretion by altering the nature, timing, or extent of the audit procedures.
    Answer (A) is incorrect because the misapplication of auditing procedures may affect detection risk but is independent of inherent and control risk. Answer (B) is incorrect because all three risks may be assessed either quantitatively or nonquantitatively. Answer (D) is incorrect because inherent risk and control risk must be assessed and cannot be changed at the auditor's discretion.

43. The acceptable level of detection risk is inversely related to the

    A. Assurance provided by substantive tests.

    B. Risk of misapplying auditing procedures.

    C. Preliminary judgment about materiality levels.

    D. Risk of failing to discover material misstatements.

Answer (A) is correct.   *(CPA, adapted)*
    REQUIRED: The relationship between detection risk and the assurance provided by substantive tests.
    DISCUSSION: An auditor considers internal control to assess control risk. (S)he also assesses inherent risk. The greater (lower) the assessed levels of control risk and inherent risk, the lower (greater) the acceptable level of detection risk. Hence, the relationship between substantive testing and detection risk is inverse.
    Answer (B) is incorrect because the risk of misapplying auditing procedures is related to the auditor's training and experience. Answer (C) is incorrect because preliminary judgments about materiality are used by the auditor to determine the acceptable level of audit risk. Detection risk is just one component of audit risk. Answer (D) is incorrect because the acceptable level of detection risk is an inverse function of the assessments of control risk and inherent risk.

44. As the acceptable level of detection risk decreases, an auditor may

    A. Reduce substantive testing by relying on the assessments of inherent risk and control risk.

    B. Postpone the planned timing of substantive tests from interim dates to the year-end.

    C. Eliminate the assessed level of inherent risk from consideration as a planning factor.

    D. Lower the assessed level of control risk from the maximum level to below the maximum.

Answer (B) is correct.   *(CPA, adapted)*
    REQUIRED: The action of the auditor as the acceptable level of detection risk decreases.
    DISCUSSION: A decrease in the acceptable level of detection risk or in the amount considered material will result in the auditor's modifying the audit program to obtain greater assurance from substantive testing by (1) selecting a more effective audit procedure, (2) applying procedures nearer to year-end, or (3) increasing the extent of particular tests.
    Answer (A) is incorrect because substantive testing would be increased. Answer (C) is incorrect because the auditor should always consider the assessed level of inherent risk in the planning phase of an audit. Answer (D) is incorrect because control risk is assessed prior to determining the acceptable level of detection risk.

45. Which of the following audit risk components may be assessed in nonquantitative terms?

	Control Risk	Detection Risk	Inherent Risk
A.	Yes	Yes	Yes
B.	No	Yes	Yes
C.	Yes	Yes	No
D.	Yes	No	Yes

Answer (A) is correct.   *(CPA, adapted)*
    REQUIRED: The audit risk components that may be assessed in nonquantitative terms.
    DISCUSSION: According to AU 312, the "components of audit risk may be assessed in quantitative terms such as percentages or in nonquantitative terms that range, for example, from a minimum to a maximum."
    Answer (B) is incorrect because control risk can be assessed in nonquantitative terms. Answer (C) is incorrect because inherent risk can be assessed in nonquantitative terms. Answer (D) is incorrect because detection risk can be assessed in nonquantitative terms.

46. Holding other planning considerations equal, a decrease in the amount of misstatements in a class of transactions that an auditor could tolerate most likely would cause the auditor to

A. Apply the planned substantive tests prior to the balance sheet date.

B. Perform the planned auditing procedures closer to the balance sheet date.

C. Increase the assessed level of control risk for relevant financial statement assertions.

D. Decrease the extent of auditing procedures to be applied to the class of transactions.

Answer (B) is correct. *(CPA, adapted)*
REQUIRED: The effect of reducing tolerable misstatement.
DISCUSSION: A decrease in the acceptable level of detection risk or in the amount considered material will result in the auditor's modifying the audit program to obtain greater assurance from substantive testing by (1) selecting a more effective audit procedure, (2) applying procedures nearer to year-end, or (3) increasing the extent of particular tests. Tolerable misstatement should not exceed the auditor's preliminary judgments about materiality, so its decrease is a reduction in materiality that requires greater assurance from substantive testing.
Answer (A) is incorrect because applying tests at interim dates reduces the assurance provided. Answer (C) is incorrect because control risk is assessed based on consideration of the client's controls. Answer (D) is incorrect because decreasing their effectiveness reduces the assurance provided.

47. Which of the following would an auditor most likely use in determining the auditor's preliminary judgment about materiality?

A. The anticipated sample size of the planned substantive tests.

B. The entity's annualized interim financial statements.

C. The results of the internal control questionnaire.

D. The contents of the management representation letter.

Answer (B) is correct. *(CPA, adapted)*
REQUIRED: The factor most likely used in determining the preliminary judgment about materiality.
DISCUSSION: AU 312 states that "the auditor's preliminary judgment about materiality might be based on the entity's annualized interim financial statements or financial statements of one or more prior periods, as long as recognition is given to the effect of major changes in the entity's circumstances (for example, a significant merger) and relevant changes in the economy as a whole or the industry in which the entity operates."
Answer (A) is incorrect because the auditor's preliminary judgment about materiality is used to determine the sample sizes for substantive tests. Sample sizes are calculated during evidence collection. Answer (C) is incorrect because results of the internal control questionnaire are considered during the assessment of control risk. Answer (D) is incorrect because the contents of the management representation letter are determined near the end of the audit.

48. When expressing an unqualified opinion, the auditor who evaluates the audit findings should be satisfied that the

A. Amount of known misstatement is documented in the management representation letter.

B. Estimate of the total likely misstatement is less than a material amount.

C. Amount of known misstatement is acknowledged and recorded by the client.

D. Estimate of the total likely misstatement includes the adjusting entries already recorded by the client.

Answer (B) is correct. *(Publisher)*
REQUIRED: The audit findings that support an unqualified opinion.
DISCUSSION: The opinion paragraph of the standard auditor's report explicitly states that the financial statements present fairly, in all material respects, the financial position, results of operations, and cash flows of the entity in conformity with GAAP. It reflects the auditor's judgment that uncorrected misstatements do not cause the financial statements to be materially misstated. The evaluation of whether the financial statements are materially misstated requires the auditor to consider the individual and aggregate effects (qualitative and quantitative) of uncorrected misstatements. This consideration and aggregation should include the best estimate of total misstatement (likely misstatement), not just the amount specifically identified (known misstatement). Moreover, the auditor must document the nature and effect of the aggregated misstatements and the conclusion about whether they cause material misstatement (AU 312).
Answer (A) is incorrect because the auditor's judgment regarding whether the financial statements are fairly presented, in all material respects, relates to his/her evaluation of likely misstatement, not known misstatement. Answer (C) is incorrect because the auditor's judgment regarding whether the financial statements are fairly presented, in all material respects, relates to his/her evaluation of likely misstatement, not known misstatement. Answer (D) is incorrect because total likely misstatement excludes material misstatements eliminated by, for example, adjusting entries.

49. Which of the following is a false statement about materiality?

A. The concept of materiality recognizes that some matters are important for fair presentation of financial statements in conformity with GAAP, while other matters are not important.

B. An auditor considers materiality for planning purposes in terms of the largest aggregate level of misstatements that could be material to any one of the financial statements.

C. Materiality judgments are made in light of surrounding circumstances and necessarily involve both quantitative and qualitative judgments.

D. An auditor's consideration of materiality is influenced by the auditor's perception of the needs of a reasonable person who will rely on the financial statements.

Answer (B) is correct.   *(CPA, adapted)*
REQUIRED: The false statement about materiality.
DISCUSSION: "Materiality levels include an overall level for each statement; however, because the statements are interrelated, and for reasons of efficiency, the auditor ordinarily considers materiality for planning purposes in terms of the smallest aggregate level of misstatements that could be considered material to any one of the financial statements" (AU 312).
Answer (A) is incorrect because the auditor's responsibility does not extend to immaterial matters. Answer (C) is incorrect because qualitative factors may cause misstatements of relatively small amounts to be material. Answer (D) is incorrect because an item is material if its misstatement or omission might affect the judgment of a reasonable person who relies on the financial statements (SFAC 2 and AU 312).

2.6 Consideration of Fraud in a Financial Statement Audit (SAS 99 Codified as AU 316)

50. Which of the following statements reflects an auditor's responsibility for detecting errors and fraud?

A. An auditor is responsible for detecting employee errors and simple fraud, but not for discovering fraudulent acts involving employee collusion or management override.

B. An auditor should plan the audit to detect errors and fraud that are caused by departures from GAAP.

C. An auditor is not responsible for detecting errors and fraud unless the application of GAAS would result in such detection.

D. An auditor should design the audit to provide reasonable assurance of detecting errors and fraud that are material to the financial statements.

Answer (D) is correct.   *(CPA, adapted)*
REQUIRED: The statement reflecting the auditor's responsibility for detecting errors and fraudulent activity.
DISCUSSION: "The auditor has a responsibility to plan and perform the audit to obtain reasonable assurance about whether the financial statements are free of material misstatements, whether caused by error or fraud" (AU 110). Thus, the consideration of fraud should be logically integrated into the overall audit process in a manner consistent with other pronouncements, e.g., those on planning and supervision, audit risk and materiality, and internal control. This consideration entails (1) understanding fraud, (2) discussing fraud risks with members of the engagement team, (3) obtaining information needed to identify fraud risks, (4) identifying those risks, (5) assessing fraud risks, (6) responding to the assessments, (7) evaluating evidence at the end of the audit, (8) making appropriate communications about fraud, and (9) documenting the consideration.

51. Because of the risk of material misstatement due to fraud, an audit of financial statements in accordance with generally accepted auditing standards should be planned and performed with an attitude of

A. Objective judgment.

B. Independent integrity.

C. Professional skepticism.

D. Impartial conservatism.

Answer (C) is correct.   *(CPA, adapted)*
REQUIRED: The attitude with which an audit in accordance with GAAS should be planned and performed.
DISCUSSION: Due professional care requires the auditor to exercise professional skepticism. Professional skepticism is an attitude that includes a questioning mind and critical assessment of audit evidence. Regardless of past experience with the entity or belief in management's honesty, the audit must be conducted with (1) an awareness that a material misstatement due to fraud may exist and (2) ongoing questioning of whether the evidence suggests that such fraud has occurred (AU 316).
Answer (A) is incorrect because, although objective judgment is a quality appropriate for practitioners, it is not required to be applied specifically in an audit. Answer (B) is incorrect because, although independent integrity is a quality appropriate for practitioners, it is not required to be applied specifically in an audit. Answer (D) is incorrect because, although impartial conservatism is a quality appropriate for practitioners, it is not required to be applied specifically in an audit.

52. Which of the following statements describes why a properly designed and executed audit may not detect a material fraud?

A. Audit procedures that are effective for detecting an unintentional misstatement may be ineffective for an intentional misstatement that is concealed through collusion.

B. An audit is designed to provide reasonable assurance of detecting material errors, but there is no similar responsibility concerning material fraud.

C. The factors considered in assessing control risk indicated an increased risk of intentional misstatements, but only a low risk of unintentional errors in the financial statements.

D. The auditor did not consider factors influencing audit risk for account balances that have effects pervasive to the financial statements taken as a whole.

Answer (A) is correct. *(CPA, adapted)*
REQUIRED: The reason a properly designed and executed audit may not detect a material fraud.
DISCUSSION: "Because of (A) the concealment of fraudulent activity, including the fact that fraud often involves collusion or falsified documents, and (B) the need to apply professional judgment in the identification and evaluation of fraud risk factors and other conditions, even a properly planned and performed audit may not detect a material misstatement resulting from fraud" (AU 316).
Answer (B) is incorrect because the auditor's responsibility is the same for fraud as for material errors. Answer (C) is incorrect because, if the risk of intentional misstatements is assessed to be high, the auditor would apply additional procedures, and thereby increase the probability of uncovering the fraud. Answer (D) is incorrect because an audit that is properly designed and executed should consider audit risk factors for accounts having pervasive effects on the statements.

53. In every audit, the members of the audit team must discuss the potential for material misstatement due to fraud. This discussion

A. Must include all members of the audit team.

B. Includes brainstorming about how assets can be misappropriated.

C. Must be deferred until the auditor begins information-gathering procedures.

D. Normally excludes consideration of how fraud might be concealed.

Answer (B) is correct. *(Publisher)*
REQUIRED: The nature of the audit team's discussion of potential fraud.
DISCUSSION: Discussion among key engagement personnel about fraud risk is required. It should emphasize professional skepticism and continual alertness to potential fraud. The discussion may occur before or during information gathering, and communication should be ongoing. The discussion must include brainstorming about factors that might create the conditions for fraud, how and where the statements might be misappropriated, how assets might be misappropriated or financial reports fraudulently misstated, how fraud could be concealed, and how the auditors might respond to fraud risk.
Answer (A) is incorrect because professional judgment should be exercised to determine the team members included. Answer (C) is incorrect because the discussion may be prior to or during gathering information to identify fraud risks. Answer (D) is incorrect because how fraud might be concealed is one topic covered when team members exchange ideas (brainstorm) about fraud.

54. During the consideration of fraud in a financial statement audit, the auditor should identify and assess risks that may result in material misstatements due to fraud. This assessment

A. Must state an overall judgment about whether an identified risk is high, medium, or low.

B. Requires an observation that the three fraud conditions are present.

C. Follows the auditor's determination that the entity's antifraud programs and controls are operating effectively.

D. Is based on evaluating whether the entity's antifraud programs and controls have been suitably designed and placed in operation.

Answer (D) is correct. *(Publisher)*
REQUIRED: The true statement about the assessment of identified fraud risks.
DISCUSSION: Identified fraud risks are assessed after the auditor's required evaluation of relevant antifraud programs and controls that relate to identified fraud risks. The entity may have broad programs or specific controls directed at specific risks. As part of the understanding of internal control, the auditor must evaluate whether controls have been suitably designed and placed in operation. The auditor should then determine whether the controls mitigate or increase the risks.
Answer (A) is incorrect because such an overall judgment is too broad to be useful. Answer (B) is incorrect because an auditor must not assume that failing to observe all three conditions signifies that no fraud risk is present. Answer (C) is incorrect because the assessment is made after evaluating whether antifraud programs and controls have been suitably designed and placed in operation.

55. Which of the following circumstances most likely would cause an auditor to consider whether material misstatements exist in an entity's financial statements?

A. Management places little emphasis on meeting earnings projections.

B. The board of directors makes all major financing decisions.

C. Reportable conditions previously communicated to management are not corrected.

D. Transactions selected for testing are not supported by proper documentation.

Answer (D) is correct. *(CPA, adapted)*
REQUIRED: The circumstance most likely to cause an auditor to consider whether material misstatements exist.
DISCUSSION: The planned scope of audit procedures should be reconsidered when conditions differ adversely from expectations. When transactions chosen for testing lack proper documentation or authorization, the likelihood of misstatement increases.
Answer (A) is incorrect because, if management places increased emphasis on meeting earnings projections, the likelihood for misstatement increases. Answer (B) is incorrect because the board's involvement in decision making reduces the likelihood of material misstatements. Answer (C) is incorrect because management should evaluate the cost and benefits of corrections in deciding whether to correct reportable conditions.

56. Which of the following characteristics most likely will heighten an auditor's concern about the risk of material misstatements due to fraud in an entity's financial statements?

A. The entity's industry is experiencing declining customer demand.

B. Employees who handle cash receipts are not bonded.

C. Bank reconciliations usually include in-transit deposits.

D. Equipment is often sold at a loss before being fully depreciated.

Answer (A) is correct. *(CPA, adapted)*
REQUIRED: The characteristic most likely to increase the auditor's concern about material misstatements due to fraud.
DISCUSSION: Certain risk factors are related to misstatements arising from fraudulent reporting. These factors may be grouped in three categories: (1) incentives/pressures, (2) opportunities, and (3) attitudes/rationalizations. One set of risk factors in the incentives/pressures category concerns threats to financial stability or profitability by economic, industry, or entity operating conditions, such as "significant declines in customer demand and increasing business failures in either industry or the overall economy" (AU 316).
Answer (B) is incorrect because failure to bond employees who handle cash receipts concerns misappropriation of assets, not fraudulent financial reporting. Answer (C) is incorrect because in-transit deposits are items requiring reconciliation. Answer (D) is incorrect because equipment is often disposed of prior to being fully depreciated.

57. Management's attitude toward aggressive financial reporting and its emphasis on meeting projected profit goals most likely would significantly influence an entity's control environment when

A. External policies established by parties outside the entity affect its accounting practices.

B. Management is dominated by one individual who is also a shareholder.

C. Internal auditors have direct access to the board of directors and the entity's management.

D. The audit committee is active in overseeing the entity's financial reporting policies.

Answer (B) is correct. *(CPA, adapted)*
REQUIRED: The factor that would most likely increase opportunities for fraudulent financial reporting.
DISCUSSION: One set of opportunity risk factors for misstatements arising from fraudulent financial reporting involves ineffective monitoring of management. One such risk factor is "domination of management by a single person or small group (in a non-owner managed business) without compensating controls" (AU 316). A compensating control in that circumstance is effective oversight by the board or audit committee of the financial reporting process and internal control.
Answer (A) is incorrect because establishment of policies by outside parties somewhat offsets the effect of an aggressive attitude toward financial reporting. Answer (C) is incorrect because the control environment is improved when internal auditors have direct access to the board of directors. Answer (D) is incorrect because the control environment is improved when the audit committee is active in overseeing policies.

58. Which of the following procedures will an auditor most likely perform when evaluating audit evidence at the completion of the audit?

    A. Obtain assurance from the entity's attorney that all material litigation has been disclosed in the financial statements.

    B. Verify the clerical accuracy of the entity's proof of cash and its bank cutoff statement.

    C. Determine whether inadequate provisions for the safeguarding of assets have been corrected.

    D. Consider whether the results of audit procedures affect the assessment of the risk of material misstatement due to fraud.

Answer (D) is correct. *(CPA, adapted)*
    REQUIRED: The procedure most likely performed when evaluating audit evidence at the completion of the audit.
    DISCUSSION: AU 316 states that the risk of material misstatement due to fraud must be specifically assessed. This assessment is ongoing. Thus, at the audit's conclusion, the results of the audit procedures and other observations should be evaluated to determine whether they alter the assessments. Furthermore, the auditor must evaluate whether analytical procedures performed as substantive tests or in the overall review indicate previously unidentified fraud risks.
    Answer (A) is incorrect because obtaining assurances from the client's attorney is a procedure performed during the audit and therefore prior to the overall review stage. Answer (B) is incorrect because conducting substantive tests of cash is a procedure performed during the audit and therefore prior to the overall review stage. Answer (C) is incorrect because determining whether inadequate controls have been improved is a procedure performed during the audit and therefore prior to the overall review stage.

59. Disclosure of fraud to parties other than a client's senior management and its audit committee ordinarily is not part of an auditor's responsibility. However, to which of the following outside parties may a duty to disclose fraud exist?

	To the SEC When the Client Reports an Auditor Change	To a Successor Auditor When the Successor Makes Appropriate Inquiries	To a Governmental Agency from Which the Client Receives Financial Assistance
A.	Yes	Yes	No
B.	Yes	No	Yes
C.	No	Yes	Yes
D.	Yes	Yes	Yes

Answer (D) is correct. *(CPA, adapted)*
    REQUIRED: The outside parties to whom a duty to disclose fraud exists.
    DISCUSSION: According to AU 316, a duty of disclosure to parties other than the client may exist when the entity reports an auditor change to the SEC on Form 8-K, and the fraud (or risk factors) is a reportable event or a source or disagreement. An auditor must also respond in accordance with the requirements for governmental audits, for example, those imposed by Government Auditing Standards. Under AU 315, a predecessor auditor must respond to inquiries by a successor if the client gives its specific permission.
    Answer (A) is incorrect because an auditor must respond to a government agency in accordance with the requirements of audits of recipients of government funds. Answer (B) is incorrect because an auditor must respond to inquiries by a successor if the client gives its specific permission. Answer (C) is incorrect because an auditor must respond to the SEC when the entity reports an auditor change on Form 8-K.

60. Which of the following must an auditor document with respect to the consideration of fraud in a financial statement audit?

    A. Reasons for not identifying management override as a fraud risk.

    B. Results of the retrospective review of accounting estimates for all years presented in the comparative statements.

    C. Instances of the auditor's exercise of professional skepticism during the consideration of fraud.

    D. Reasons for not identifying improper revenue recognition as a fraud risk.

Answer (D) is correct. *(Publisher)*
    REQUIRED: The item that must be documented.
    DISCUSSION: The auditor must document the following: (1) Planning-stage discussions among the audit team about fraud risks, including how and when they occurred, the participants, and the subject matter; (2) procedures to obtain information to identify and assess fraud risks; (3) specifically identified fraud risks; (4) the response to those risks; (5) reasons in a given situation for not identifying improper revenue recognition as a fraud risk; (6) results of procedures for further addressing the risk of management override of controls; (7) other conditions and analytical relationships leading to further audit procedures and other responses; (8) those responses deemed to be appropriate with respect to the other conditions, etc.; and (9) fraud communications to management, the audit committee, and others.
    Answer (A) is incorrect because management override is always identified as a fraud risk. Answer (B) is incorrect because the required retrospective review applies only to the prior year's significant accounting estimates. Answer (C) is incorrect because professional skepticism is a mindset with which the auditor approaches every aspect of the audit. Hence, specific, separate documentation of its exercise is not required.

2.7 Illegal Acts by Clients (AU 317)

61. Jones, CPA, is auditing the financial statements of XYZ Retailing, Inc. What assurance does Jones provide that direct-effect illegal acts that are material to XYZ's financial statements and illegal acts that have a material but indirect effect on the financial statements will be detected?

	Direct-Effect Illegal Acts	Indirect-Effect Illegal Acts
A.	Reasonable	None
B.	Reasonable	Reasonable
C.	Limited	None
D.	Limited	Reasonable

Answer (A) is correct. *(CPA, adapted)*
REQUIRED: The auditor assurance provided in connection with a client's potential illegal acts.
DISCUSSION: The auditor has the same responsibility for detecting misstatements arising from illegal acts that have a direct and material effect on the financial statements as for material errors and fraud. Thus, the auditor must plan and perform the audit to obtain reasonable assurance about whether the financial statements are free of material misstatement caused by illegal acts having direct and material effects. However, because of the nature of illegal acts that have an indirect effect, an audit in accordance with GAAS provides no assurance that such illegal acts will be detected or that any resulting contingent liabilities will be disclosed (AU 317).

62. Which of the following information discovered during an audit most likely would raise a question concerning possible illegal acts?

A. Related party transactions, although properly disclosed, were pervasive during the year.

B. The entity prepared several large checks payable to cash during the year.

C. Material internal control weaknesses previously reported to management were not corrected.

D. The entity was a campaign contributor to several local political candidates during the year.

Answer (B) is correct. *(CPA, adapted)*
REQUIRED: The information most likely to raise a question concerning possible illegal acts.
DISCUSSION: Some examples of information raising questions about possible illegal acts are unauthorized or improperly recorded transactions, a governmental investigation, violations reported by regulators, large payments for unspecified services to consultants, excessive commissions or fees, unusual cash payments or checks payable to cash, unexplained payments to government officials or employees, and failure to file tax returns or pay governmental duties or similar fees.
Answer (A) is incorrect because related party transactions are common in many entities. Answer (C) is incorrect because failure to correct material weaknesses may be based on cost and benefit considerations. Answer (D) is incorrect because donations to local candidates are permissible.

63. If specific information that implies the existence of possible illegal acts that could have a material but indirect effect on the financial statements comes to an auditor's attention, the auditor should next

A. Apply audit procedures specifically directed to ascertaining whether an illegal act has occurred.

B. Seek the advice of an informed expert qualified to practice law as to possible contingent liabilities.

C. Report the matter to an appropriate level of management at least one level above those involved.

D. Discuss the evidence with the client's audit committee, or others with equivalent authority and responsibility.

Answer (A) is correct. *(CPA, adapted)*
REQUIRED: The auditor's responsibility when (s)he becomes aware of an illegal act having a material indirect effect.
DISCUSSION: The auditor should apply audit procedures specifically directed to ascertaining whether an illegal act has occurred. When the auditor becomes aware of information concerning a possible illegal act, the auditor should obtain an understanding of the nature of the act, the circumstances in which it occurred, and sufficient other information to evaluate the effect on the financial statements.
Answer (B) is incorrect because the auditor need not consult legal counsel until after determining that an illegal act has occurred. Answer (C) is incorrect because making inquiries of management is just one possible procedure involved in determining whether an illegal act has occurred. Answer (D) is incorrect because the auditor should not discuss the evidence with the client's audit committee, or others with equivalent authority and responsibility, until after determining that an illegal act has occurred.

64. When an auditor becomes aware of a possible client illegal act, the auditor should obtain an understanding of the nature of the act to

A. Consider whether other similar acts have occurred.

B. Recommend remedial actions to the audit committee.

C. Evaluate the effect on the financial statements.

D. Determine the reliability of management's representations.

Answer (C) is correct. *(CPA, adapted)*
REQUIRED: The reason the auditor obtains an understanding of the nature of a possible illegal act.
DISCUSSION: When the auditor becomes aware of information concerning a possible illegal act, the auditor should obtain an understanding of the nature of the act, the circumstances in which it occurred, and sufficient other information to evaluate the effect on the financial statements.
Answer (A) is incorrect because the auditor may consider whether other similar acts have occurred when applying any additional procedures necessary to obtain an understanding of the nature of the act. Answer (B) is incorrect because recommending remedial actions to the audit committee is a secondary objective of the audit. Answer (D) is incorrect because if the auditor determines that an illegal act has occurred, (s)he should assess the effects on the representations of management in other areas of the audit.

65. An auditor who discovers that a client's employees paid small bribes to municipal officials most likely would withdraw from the engagement if

A. The payments violated the client's policies regarding the prevention of illegal acts.

B. The client receives financial assistance from a federal government agency.

C. Documentation that is necessary to prove that the bribes were paid does not exist.

D. Management fails to take the appropriate remedial action.

Answer (D) is correct. *(CPA, adapted)*
REQUIRED: The circumstance that would most likely cause an auditor to withdraw from an engagement.
DISCUSSION: When the auditor concludes that an illegal act has or is likely to have occurred, (s)he should discuss the matter with the appropriate level of management and request that any necessary remedial actions be taken. If the alleged illegal act has a material effect on the financial statements or the client does not take the remedial action that the auditor considers necessary, the auditor should express a qualified or adverse opinion, depending on the level of materiality, or withdraw from the engagement.
Answer (A) is incorrect because a violation of client policies regarding illegal acts by personnel does not necessitate a withdrawal from the engagement as long as management takes the proper remedial action proposed by the auditors. Answer (B) is incorrect because in some cases, auditors may need to report fraud and illegal acts to appropriate officials, oversight bodies, or funding organizations, but this duty is not in itself a basis for withdrawal when illegal acts have been detected. Answer (C) is incorrect because if the client precludes the auditor from collecting sufficient information, the auditor usually disclaims an opinion. The auditor should then withdraw if the client refuses to accept the auditor's modified report.

66. Under the Private Securities Litigation Reform Act of 1995, Baker, CPA, reported certain uncorrected illegal acts to Supermart's board of directors. Baker believed that failure to take remedial action would warrant a qualified audit opinion because the illegal acts had a material effect on Supermart's financial statements. Supermart failed to take appropriate remedial action, and the board of directors refused to inform the SEC that it had received such notification from Baker. Under these circumstances, Baker is required to

A. Resign from the audit engagement within ten business days.

B. Deliver a report concerning the illegal acts to the SEC within one business day.

C. Notify the shareholders that the financial statements are materially misstated.

D. Withhold an audit opinion until Supermart takes appropriate remedial action.

Answer (B) is correct. *(CPA, adapted)*
REQUIRED: The requirements under the Private Securities Litigation Reform Act of 1995.
DISCUSSION: Disclosure of illegal acts to outside parties is not normally the auditor's responsibility. However, under the Private Securities Litigation Reform Act of 1995, accountants must report illegal acts to the appropriate level of management and the audit committee unless they are clearly inconsequential. If senior management and the board fail to take action on reported material illegal acts, and this failure will result in a departure from a standard report or resignation from the audit, the accountants should report their conclusions to the board immediately. The board must then, within 1 business day, notify the SEC. If the accountants do not receive a copy of the notice within the 1-day period, they must furnish the SEC with a copy of their report within 1 business day.
Answer (A) is incorrect because the auditor is not required to resign from the engagement. Answer (C) is incorrect because a qualified audit opinion states that, except for the effects of the matter to which the qualification relates, the financial statements are presented fairly in all material respects. Any other notice to the shareholders is not required. Answer (D) is incorrect because the auditor should express a qualified opinion if it is justified by the lack of remedial action. GAAS do not provide for a delay in the report until remedial action is taken.

67. An auditor who discovers that a client's employees have paid small bribes to public officials most likely would withdraw from the engagement if the

A. Client receives financial assistance from a federal government agency.

B. Evidential matter that is necessary to prove that the illegal acts were committed does not exist.

C. Employees' actions affect the auditor's ability to rely on management's representations.

D. Notes to the financial statements fail to disclose the employees' actions.

Answer (C) is correct.   *(Publisher)*
REQUIRED: The event that would prompt an auditor to withdraw from an engagement.
DISCUSSION: The auditor's response to detected illegal acts is to consider the effects on the financial statements and the implications for other aspects of the audit, especially the reliability of management's representations. The auditor should consider the qualitative and quantitative materiality of the act, consider the adequacy of disclosure, and communicate material problems to the audit committee. Even when an illegal act is not material to the financial statements, the loss of management credibility may result in a need to end the relationship with the client.

Answer (A) is incorrect because in some cases, auditors may need to report fraud and illegal acts to appropriate officials, oversight bodies, or funding organizations, but this duty is not in itself a basis for withdrawal when illegal acts have been detected. Answer (B) is incorrect because if the client precludes the auditor from collecting sufficient information, the auditor usually disclaims an opinion. The auditor should then withdraw if the client refuses to accept the auditor's modified report. Answer (D) is incorrect because if an illegal act has not been disclosed properly, the auditor should express a qualified or an adverse opinion.

Use Gleim's *CPA Test Prep* for interactive testing with over 2,000 additional multiple-choice questions!

2.8 PRACTICE SIMULATION

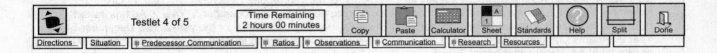

	Testlet 4 of 5	Time Remaining 2 hours 00 minutes	Copy	Paste	Calculator	Sheet	Standards	Help	Split	Done

Directions | Situation | Predecessor Communication | Ratios | Observations | Communication | Research | Resources

1. Directions

In the following simulation, you will be asked to complete various tasks related to leases and contingencies. The simulation will provide all of the information necessary to do the work. For full credit, be sure to view and complete all work tabs.

Resources are available to you under the tab marked RESOURCES. You may want to review the resources before beginning the simulation.

2. Situation

Dodd, CPA, audited Adams Company's financial statements for the year ended December 31, Year 1. On November 1, Year 2, Adams notified Dodd that it was changing auditors. On November 5, Year 2, Adams invited Hall, CPA, to make a proposal for an engagement to audit its financial statements for the year ended December 31, Year 2. Adams Company provided Hall, CPA, the following balance sheet and income statement information for engagement acceptance purposes.

Adams Company
Balance Sheet
As of October 31, Year 2

Assets

Cash	$ 240,000
Receivables	400,000
Inventory	600,000
Total current assets	$1,240,000
Plant and equipment-net	760,000
Total assets	**$2,000,000**

Liabilities and equity

Accounts payable	$ 160,000
Notes payable	100,000
Other current liabilities	140,000
Total current liabilities	$ 400,000
Long term debt	350,000
Common stock	750,000
Retained earnings	500,000
Total liabilities and equity	**$2,000,000**

Adams Company
Income Statement
For the 10 Months Ending October 31, Year 2

Sales		$3,000,000
Cost of goods sold		
Materials	$800,000	
Labor	700,000	
Overhead	300,000	1,800,000
Gross margin		$1,200,000
Selling expenses	$240,000	
General and administrative expenses	300,000	540,000
Operating income		$ 660,000
Minus interest expense		40,000
Income before taxes		$ 620,000
Minus federal income taxes		220,000
Net income		**$ 400,000**

3. Communication between the Predecessor and Successor Auditors

This question is in a true-false format. The appropriate shaded column should be checked.

Read the procedures below and determine which should be performed before accepting the engagement.

Procedures	Yes	No
1. Explain to Adams the need to make an inquiry of Dodd.		
2. Request permission from Adams to make an inquiry of Dodd.		
3. Request permission from Adams to disclose information obtained from Dodd to regulatory agencies.		
4. Ask Adams to authorize Dodd to respond fully to Hall's inquiries.		
5. Request personal financial statements from Dodd.		
6. Make inquiries of Dodd concerning the integrity of the management of Adams.		
7. Make inquiries of Dodd concerning the fee arrangements that Dodd had with Adams.		
8. Make inquiries of Dodd concerning disagreements with the management of Adams as to accounting principles and auditing procedures.		
9. Request from Dodd the reasons for the change in auditors.		
10. Demand that Dodd make available the audit documentation prepared in the prior year's audit.		

4. Ratios

This question is presented in a spreadsheet format that requires you to fill in the correct responses in the shaded cells.

Given the year-to-date financial information in the situation tab, calculate the ratios below. Calculations should be rounded if necessary to the same number of places as the prior year's ratios, which are provided for comparative purposes only.

Ratio	Adams Company's Ratios for the 10 Months Ending 10/31/Year 2	Adams Company's Ratios for the 10 Months Ending 10/31/Year 1
1. Current ratio		2.5
2. Quick ratio		1.3
3. Accounts receivable turnover		5.5
4. Inventory turnover		2.5
5. Total asset turnover		1.2
6. Gross margin percentage		35%
7. Net operating margin percentage		25%
8. Times interest earned		10.3
9. Total debt to equity percentage		50%

5. Observations

Select the most likely explanation(s) of the auditor's observations of changes in certain financial statement ratios or amounts from the prior year's ratios or amounts. For each observed change, check the number of explanations indicated. Each explanation may be used once, more than once, or not at all.

Observed Changes

1.   Inventory turnover increased substantially from the prior year. **(Choose 3 Explanations.)**

2.   Accounts receivable turnover decreased substantially from the prior year. **(Choose 3 Explanations.)**

3.   The allowance for doubtful accounts increased from the prior year, but, as a percentage of accounts receivable, it decreased from the prior year. **(Choose 3 Explanations.)**

4.   Long-term debt increased from the prior year, but interest expense increased by an amount that was proportionately greater than the increase in long-term debt. **(Choose 1 Explanation.)**

5.   Operating income increased from the prior year, although the entity was less profitable than in the prior year. **(Choose 2 Explanations.)**

6.   The gross margin percentage was unchanged from the prior year, although gross margin increased from the prior year. **(Choose 1 Explanation.)**

1	2	3	4	5	6	Explanation
						A) Items shipped on consignment during the last month of the year were recorded as sales.
						B) A significant number of credit memos for returned merchandise that were issued during the last month of the year were not recorded.
						C) Year-end purchases of inventory were overstated by incorrectly including items received in the first month of the subsequent year.
						D) Year-end purchases of inventory were understated by incorrectly excluding items received before year-end.
						E) A larger percentage of sales occurred during the last month of the year, as compared with the prior year.
						F) A smaller percentage of sales occurred during the last month of the year, as compared with the prior year.
						G) The same percentage of sales occurred during the last month of the year, as compared with the prior year.
						H) Sales increased by the same percentage as cost of goods sold, as compared with the prior year.
						I) Sales increased by a greater percentage than cost of goods sold increased, as compared with the prior year.
						J) Sales increased by a lower percentage than cost of goods sold increased, as compared with the prior year.
						K) Interest expensed decreased, as compared with the prior year.
						L) The effective income tax rate increased, as compared with the prior year.
						M) The effective income tax rate decreased, as compared with the prior year.
						N) Short-term borrowing was refinanced on a long-term basis at the same interest rate.
						O) Short-term borrowing was refinanced on a long-term basis at lower interest rates.
						P) Short-term borrowing was refinanced on a long-term basis at higher interest rates.

6. Communication

In a memorandum to a client, discuss the nature of fraud, conditions usually present when fraudulent financial reporting occurs, the types of fraud relevant to the auditor, the responsibilities of the parties for its detection, and how it may be perpetrated and concealed.

REMINDER: Your response will be graded for both technical content and writing skills. You should demonstrate your ability to develop, organize, and express your ideas. Do not convey information in the form of a table, bullet point list, or other abbreviated presentation.

To:	Client
From:	CPA
Subject:	Conditions related to fraudulent financial reporting, the types of fraud relevant to the auditor, the responsibilities of the parties for the detection, and how it may be perpetrated and concealed

7. Research

Find the answer to the following question in the AICPA Professional Standards using the materials available in the Resources tab. Print the appropriate citation in its entirety from the source you choose. This is a copy-and-paste item.

In the space provided below, find the applicable section that states whether a successor auditor must communicate with a predecessor auditor before offering a proposal for an engagement.

Unofficial Answers

3. Communications between the Predecessor and Successor Auditors (10 Gradable Items)

1.   <u>Yes</u>. Communication by the successor with the predecessor is necessary so that information can be gathered in determining whether to accept the engagement. "The successor auditor should explain to the prospective client the need to make an inquiry of the predecessor" (AU 315).

2.   <u>Yes</u>. Because the information to be communicated is considered confidential, permission should be gained by both the successor and predecessor auditors prior to the inquiry.

3.   <u>No</u>. Normally, the auditor has no obligation to report to parties external to the client. Thus, information obtained from Dodd should not be disclosed by Hall to regulatory agencies.

4.   <u>Yes</u>. Because the information obtained by the successor auditor is confidential, the client should be requested to authorize the predecessor to respond fully to the successor's inquiries.

5.   <u>No</u>. Only information about the client pertinent to the decision to accept the engagement should be requested. Personal financial information about the predecessor is not relevant.

6.   <u>Yes</u>. Inquiries by the successor should include specific questions regarding, among other things, facts that might bear on the integrity of the prospective client's management.

7.   <u>No</u>. The fee arrangement with the predecessor is unlikely to provide information that will assist the successor in determining whether to accept the engagement.

8.   <u>Yes</u>. Inquiries should include specific questions regarding facts that might bear on disagreements with the prospective client's management about accounting principles, auditing procedures, and other similarly significant matters.

9.   <u>Yes</u>. The successor auditor's inquiries should include specific questions regarding facts that might bear on the predecessor's understanding about the reason for the change in auditors.

10. <u>No</u>. The current audit may be facilitated by consideration of the prior year's audit documentation. Thus, the successor may request the client to authorize the predecessor to allow a review of the predecessor's audit documentation, and it is customary for the predecessor to cooperate. However, the successor cannot demand that Dodd make available all audit documentation prepared during the prior period's audit.

4. Ratios (9 Gradable Items)

1. Current ratio	3.1	($1,240,000 ÷ $400,000)
2. Quick ratio	1.6	[($1,240,000 − $600,000) ÷ $400,000]
3. Accounts receivable turnover	7.5	($3,000,000 ÷ $400,000)
4. Inventory turnover	3.0	($1,800,000 ÷ $600,000)
5. Total asset turnover	1.5	($3,000,000 ÷ $2,000,000)
6. Gross margin percentage	40%	($1,200,000 ÷ $3,000,000)
7. Net operating margin percentage	22%	($660,000 ÷ $3,000,000)
8. Times interest earned	16.5	[($400,000 + $40,000 + $220,000) ÷ $40,000]
9. Total debt to equity percentage	60%	[($400,000 + $350,000) ÷ ($750,000 + $500,000)]

5. Observations (13 Gradable Items)

1. <u>A), B), D)</u>. Inventory turnover is cost of sales divided by average inventory. Consignment items should still be included in inventory. However, because items shipped on consignment were recorded as sales, the items were removed from inventory. Returned merchandise should increase inventory, but, because the credit memos were not recorded, the inventory was understated. By not including year-end purchases, inventory is also understated. Hence, a lower inventory causes a higher inventory turnover ratio.

2. <u>A), B), E)</u>. Accounts receivable turnover is net credit sales divided by average accounts receivable. Goods shipped on consignment are properly included in the consignor's inventory at cost, and sales revenue from such goods should be recognized by the consignor when the merchandise is sold by recording as sales items shipped on consignment but not yet sold.

3. <u>A), B), E)</u>. If the allowance for doubtful accounts increased, and allowance for doubtful accounts as a percentage of accounts receivable decreased, accounts receivable must have increased by a greater degree than the allowance decreased. Accounts receivable would have increased if items shipped on consignment were mistakenly recorded as sales, if significant credits for returned goods were not recorded, or if a larger percentage of sales occurred during the month compared with the prior year.

4. <u>P)</u>. If short-term debt is refinanced as long-term debt at a higher interest rate, long-term debt will increase but not as significantly as interest expense will increase. This effect results from applying an increased rate to a greater amount of long-term debt.

5. <u>L), P)</u>. Operating income minus interest expense and federal income taxes yields net income for the year. If operating income increased from the prior year but net income decreased, interest expense or federal income taxes must have increased. Refinancing short-term debt as long-term debt with a higher interest rate or an increase in the effective income tax rate explain this decrease in net income.

6. <u>H)</u>. The gross margin percentage is gross margin divided by sales. If it remained constant although gross margin increased, sales also must have increased by the same proportionate amount. Because gross margin is sales minus cost of goods sold, cost of goods sold also must have increased by the same proportionate amount to maintain the relationship between sales and gross margin.

6. Communication (5 Gradable Items; For grading instructions, please refer to page 11.)

To: Client
From: CPA
Subject: Conditions related to fraudulent financial reporting, the types of fraud relevant to the auditor, the responsibilities of the parties for its detection, and how it may be perpetrated and concealed

Fraud is intentional. It results in a material misstatement of the financial statements. Under GAAS, an auditor has a responsibility to plan and perform the audit to obtain reasonable assurance about whether the financial statements are free of material misstatement, whether caused by error or fraud. Management is responsible for programs and controls that prevent, deter, and detect fraud. Management and oversight authorities (e.g., the board and audit committee) must set the proper tone and maintain a culture of honesty.

Three conditions are normally present when fraud occurs. They are incentives or pressures that provide a motive to commit fraud, opportunity, and an ability to rationalize the commission of fraud. However, not all conditions need to exist or be observed, and an auditor may not be able to observe rationalization. Circumstances, such as the balance or ineffectiveness of controls or management's ability to override controls, create opportunities. Rationalization is possible when an individual has an attitude, set of values, or character that permits intentional dishonesty.

Fraudulent misstatements may arise from fraudulent financial reporting or misappropriation of assets. The first type consists of intentional misstatements or omissions to deceive users such as altering accounting records or documents, misrepresenting or omitting significant information, and misapplying accounting principles. Misstatements of the second type result from theft, embezzlement, or an action that causes payment for items not received.

Collusion may defeat a properly performed audit because apparently persuasive evidence may be false. For example, management and employees may give false but consistent replies to inquiries or a third party may provide a false confirmation. Management may override controls over accounting records in unpredictable ways. Thus, management may direct employees to commit fraud, seek their help, or directly manipulate accounting records. Accordingly, the due professional care standard requires the auditor to obtain only reasonable assurance that the financial statements are free of material misstatements.

7. Research (6 Gradable Items)

AU Section 315 -- *Communications Between Predecessor and Successor Auditors*

Change of Auditors

.03   An auditor should not accept an engagement until the communications described in paragraphs .07 through .10 have been evaluated. However, an auditor may make a proposal for an audit engagement before communicating with the predecessor auditor. The auditor may wish to advise the prospective client (for example, in a proposal) that acceptance cannot be final until the communications have been evaluated.

Scoring Schedule:

	Correct Responses		Gradable Items		Weights		
Tab 3	_____	÷	10	×	20%	=	_____
Tab 4	_____	÷	9	×	20%	=	_____
Tab 5	_____	÷	13	×	20%	=	_____
Tab 6	_____	÷	5	×	30%	=	_____
Tab 7	_____	÷	6	×	10%	=	_____
							(Your Score)

Use Gleim's *CPA Review Online* to practice more simulations in a realistic environment.

STUDY UNIT THREE
STRATEGIC PLANNING ISSUES

(13 pages of outline)

3.1   The Auditor's Consideration of the Internal Audit Function (AU 322) 101
3.2   Using the Work of a Specialist (AU 336) 104
3.3   Related Parties (AU 334) 106
3.4   Accounting Estimates and Fair Values (AU 342 and AU 328) 109
3.5   Consideration of Omitted Procedures after the Report Date (AU 390) 113
3.6   Practice Simulation 125

This study unit considers issues that are fundamental to planning an audit. Questions about the internal audit function, related parties, and accounting estimates can be expected on the exam. Moreover, most of the issues considered in this study unit have an effect on other facets of the audit, including evidence collection and reporting. We cover the additional matters here to provide comprehensive and coherent coverage.

3.1 THE AUDITOR'S CONSIDERATION OF THE INTERNAL AUDIT FUNCTION (AU 322)

1. The independent, external auditor (hereafter referred to as "the auditor") considers the existence of an internal audit function in determining the nature, timing, and extent of audit procedures.

2. **Roles of the Auditor and the Internal Auditors**

   a. The auditor must remain independent of the entity. Internal auditors are not. However, they should be independent of audited activities.

   b. Internal auditors provide analyses, evaluations, assurances, recommendations, and other information to the management and the board. To meet this responsibility, internal auditors should be objective with respect to audited activities.

3. **Obtaining an Understanding of the Internal Audit Function**

   a. When obtaining an understanding of internal control, the auditor should obtain an understanding of the internal audit function sufficient to identify activities relevant to audit planning.

   b. Inquiries should be made about the internal auditors'

      1) Organizational status
      2) Application of professional standards
      3) Audit plan, including the nature, timing, and extent of audit work
      4) Access to records and limitations on the scope of their work

   c. Inquiring about the internal audit function's charter, mission statement, or similar directive provides information about its goals and objectives.

   d. Certain internal audit activities may not be relevant to an audit of the financial statements, e.g., evaluating the efficiency of certain management decision-making processes.

   e. Relevant internal audit activities provide

      1) Evidence about the design and effectiveness of internal control relating to the entity's ability to initiate, record, process, and report financial data consistent with the assertions in the financial statements
      2) Direct evidence about potential misstatements of such data

f.   The following are helpful in assessing the relevance of internal audit activities:

1) Considering prior-year audits
2) Reviewing how the internal auditors allocate their audit resources
3) Reading internal audit reports

g.   If the auditor concludes that the internal auditors' activities are not relevant, (s)he need not further consider their function unless the auditor requests direct assistance from the internal auditors.

1) The auditor may conclude that considering further the work of the internal auditors would be inefficient, even if some of their activities are relevant.

h.   If the auditor decides that it is efficient to consider how the internal auditors' work might affect the nature, timing, and extent of audit procedures, the auditor should assess the competence and objectivity of the internal auditors in light of the intended effect of their work on the audit.

4. **Assessing the Competence and Objectivity of the Internal Auditors**

a.   **Competence**. When assessing competence, the auditor should obtain information about

1) Educational level and professional experience
2) Professional certification and continuing education
3) Audit policies, programs, and procedures
4) Practices regarding assignment of internal auditors
5) Supervision and review
6) Quality of documentation, reports, and recommendations
7) Performance evaluation

b.   **Objectivity**. When assessing objectivity, the auditor should obtain information about

1) The organizational status of the director of internal auditing. This assessment includes whether

a) The director reports to an officer of sufficient status to ensure broad audit coverage and adequate consideration of, and action on, findings and recommendations.

b) The director has direct access and reports regularly to the board, the audit committee, or the owner-manager.

c) The board, the audit committee, or the owner-manager oversees employment decisions related to the director.

2) Policies to maintain objectivity about the areas audited. These include policies prohibiting internal auditors from auditing areas in which

a) Relatives are employed in important or audit-sensitive positions.

b) They were recently assigned or are scheduled to be assigned on completion of audit responsibilities.

c.   Assessing competence and objectivity entails considering information from previous experience with the internal audit function, from discussions with management, and from a recent external quality review.

1) The auditor also considers the need to test the effectiveness of the objectivity and competency factors listed above.

2) If the auditor determines that the internal auditors are sufficiently competent and objective, (s)he should consider how their work may affect the audit.

5. **Effect of the Internal Auditors' Work on the Audit**

    a.   The internal auditors' work may affect the nature, timing, and extent of the audit, including the procedures performed in obtaining the understanding of internal control and assessing control risk.

         1)   Because a primary objective of many internal audit functions is to review, assess, and monitor internal control, internal audit procedures may provide useful information.

    b.   Risk assessment at the financial-statement level involves an overall assessment of the risk of material misstatement and thus may affect overall audit strategy.

         1)   The internal audit function may affect the overall risk assessment and decisions about audit procedures. For example, the auditor may coordinate work with the internal auditors and reduce the number of locations at which the auditor performs procedures.

    c.   Risk assessment at the account-balance or class-of-transactions level involves obtaining and evaluating evidence about assertions. The auditor assesses control risk for each significant assertion and performs tests of controls to support assessments below the maximum.

         1)   When testing internal control, the auditor may consider the results of internal audit procedures.

    d.   Substantive procedures performed by the internal auditors may provide direct evidence about material misstatements in specific assertions.

6. **Extent of the Effect of the Internal Auditors' Work**

    a.   Reporting on the financial statements is solely the responsibility of the auditor. This responsibility cannot be shared with the internal auditors.

         1)   Judgments about assessments of risk, materiality, the sufficiency of tests, the evaluation of estimates, and other matters affecting the report should always be those of the auditor.

    b.   In judging the extent of the effect of the internal auditors' work, consideration should be given to materiality, inherent and control risk, and the degree of subjectivity involved in the evaluation of audit evidence.

         1)   For assertions related to material amounts for which the risk of material misstatement or the degree of subjectivity is high, the internal auditors' work alone cannot reduce audit risk to an acceptable level to eliminate direct tests of assertions by the auditor.

         2)   For certain assertions related to less material amounts for which the risk of material misstatement or the degree of subjectivity is low, the auditor may decide that audit risk has been reduced to an acceptable level and that direct testing by the auditor may not be necessary.

7. **Coordination of the Audit Work with Internal Auditors.** If the work of the internal auditors is expected to affect the auditor's procedures, it may be efficient for the auditor and the internal auditors to coordinate their work by

    a.   Holding periodic meetings
    b.   Scheduling audit work
    c.   Providing access to internal auditors' engagement records (documentation)
    d.   Reviewing audit reports
    e.   Discussing possible accounting and auditing issues

8.   **Evaluating and Testing the Effectiveness of the Internal Auditors' Work**

    a.   If the work of the internal auditors significantly affects the auditor's work, the auditor should evaluate the quality and effectiveness of the internal auditors' work.

    b.   When developing evaluation procedures, the auditor should consider whether the internal auditors'

        1)   Scope of work is appropriate.
        2)   Audit programs are adequate.
        3)   Documentation of the work, including supervision and review, is adequate.
        4)   Conclusions are appropriate.
        5)   Reports are consistent with results.

    c.   The auditor should test some of the internal auditors' work related to significant financial statement assertions by examining

        1)   Some of the controls, transactions, or balances that the internal auditors examined, or

        2)   Similar controls, transactions, or balances not actually examined by the internal auditors.

9.   **Using Internal Auditors to Provide Direct Assistance to the Auditor**. The auditor may request direct assistance from the internal auditors when performing an audit. When direct assistance is provided, the auditor should assess the internal auditors' competence and objectivity and supervise, review, evaluate, and test the work performed by internal auditors to the extent appropriate.

10.   Stop and review! You have completed the outline for this subunit. Study multiple-choice questions 1 through 8 beginning on page 114.

3.2 USING THE WORK OF A SPECIALIST (AU 336)

1.   **Definition of a Specialist**. A specialist is a person (or firm) possessing special skill or knowledge in a particular field other than auditing or accounting, e.g., actuaries, appraisers, attorneys, engineers, and geologists.

2.   **Decision to Use the Work of a Specialist**

    a.   The auditor is not expected to have the expertise of a person trained for or qualified to engage in the practice of another profession or occupation. The auditor may use the work of a specialist to obtain competent evidential matter.

    b.   Examples of types of matters for which the auditor may use the work of a specialist include

        1)   Valuation (works of art, special drugs, restricted securities)

        2)   Determination of physical characteristics relating to quantity or condition (mineral reserves, materials stored in piles above ground)

        3)   Determination of amounts by using special techniques or methods (certain actuarial determinations)

        4)   Interpretation of technical requirements, regulations, or agreements (the significance of contracts, legal title to property)

3.   **Selecting a Specialist**

    a.   The auditor should become satisfied about the qualifications and reputation of the specialist. Consideration should be given to

        1)   The specialist's professional certification, license, or other recognition of competence

        2)   The specialist's reputation and standing

        3)   The relationship of the client and the specialist

   b.   The auditor should attempt to obtain a specialist who is unrelated to the client. However, circumstances may permit using the work of a specialist having a relationship with the client.

   c.   The auditor, client, and specialist should have an understanding of the nature of the work to be performed by the specialist. The understanding should be documented and cover

       1)   The objectives and scope of the work

       2)   The specialist's representations as to the relationship, if any, with the client

       3)   The methods or assumptions to be used and a comparison with those used in the preceding period

       4)   The specialist's understanding of the auditor's corroborative use of the findings in relation to the financial statement assertions

       5)   The form and content of the specialist's report that would enable the auditor to make the evaluation described in the following section

4.   **Using the Findings of the Specialist**

   a.   The auditor should obtain an understanding of the methods or assumptions used to determine whether the findings are suitable for corroborative purposes. The auditor should consider whether the specialist's findings support the assertions and should test the accounting data provided by the client to the specialist.

   b.   If the specialist is related to the client, the auditor should consider performing additional procedures to determine that the findings are not unreasonable or engage an outside specialist for that purpose.

5.   **Effect of the Specialist's Work on the Auditor's Report**

   a.   If the specialist's findings support the assertions, the auditor may reasonably conclude that sufficient competent evidence has been obtained.

   b.   If there is a material difference between the specialist's findings and the assertions, or if the auditor believes that the findings are unreasonable, (s)he should apply additional procedures.

       1)   If (s)he is then unable to resolve the matter, the auditor should seek the opinion of another specialist, unless the matter cannot be resolved.

   c.   An unresolved matter is a scope limitation that will usually result in a qualified opinion or a disclaimer of an opinion.

   d.   If the auditor concludes after additional procedures that the assertions are not in conformity with GAAP, (s)he should express a qualified or adverse opinion.

6.   **Reference to the Specialist in the Auditor's Report**

   a.   When expressing an unqualified opinion, the auditor ordinarily should not refer to the work or findings of the specialist. This reference might be misunderstood to be a qualification of the opinion or a division of responsibility.

   b.   In certain circumstances, however, the auditor may express an unqualified opinion and refer to the specialist. A specialist may be referred to and identified in the report if the auditor believes the reference will facilitate an understanding of the reason for an explanatory paragraph, for example, when

       1)   Describing a substantial doubt about the entity's ability to continue as a going concern

       2)   Emphasizing a matter

   c.   The auditor may also refer to the work of a specialist if (s)he departs from an unqualified opinion.

7.   Stop and review! You have completed the outline for this subunit. Study multiple-choice questions 9 through 13 beginning on page 116.

3.3 RELATED PARTIES (AU 334)

1. **Accounting Considerations**

    a. SFAS 57, *Related Party Disclosures*, indicates that accounting principles ordinarily do not require transactions with related parties to be accounted for differently from those with unrelated parties.

        1) Primary emphasis should be on the **adequacy of disclosure**.
        2) Furthermore, the auditor should understand that the substance of a transaction could differ significantly from its form. Financial statements should recognize substance, not legal form.

    b. Transactions indicative of the existence of related parties include

        1) Borrowing or lending interest-free or at a rate significantly different from prevailing market rates at the time of the transaction
        2) Selling real estate at a price significantly different from appraised value
        3) Making nonmonetary exchanges of similar property
        4) Making loans with no scheduled terms for repayment

2. **Audit Procedures**

    a. An audit cannot provide assurance that all related party transactions will be detected, but the auditor should be aware of the possible existence of material related party transactions and of certain relationships that must be disclosed even in the absence of transactions.

        1) Many of the procedures listed in this outline are normally performed in an audit, even if the auditor has no reason to suspect that related party transactions exist.

    b. The auditor should obtain an understanding of management responsibilities and the relationship of each component to the total entity. Consideration should be given to

        1) Internal controls relevant to management activities
        2) The business purpose served by the components of the entity

    c. Business structure and operating style are occasionally designed to obscure related party transactions.

    d. In the absence of contrary evidence, transactions with related parties should not be assumed to be outside the ordinary course of business. But the auditor should be aware that such transactions may have been motivated solely or largely by

        1) Lack of sufficient working capital or credit to continue the business
        2) A desire for favorable earnings to support the company's stock price
        3) An overly optimistic earnings forecast
        4) Dependence on one or a few products, customers, or transactions for success
        5) A declining industry with many business failures
        6) Excess capacity
        7) Significant litigation, especially between shareholders and management
        8) Significant obsolescence dangers because the company is in a high-technology industry

e. Determining the existence of related parties. Emphasis should be placed on known related party transactions. Certain relationships, such as parent-subsidiary or investor-investee, may be clearly evident. Determining the existence of others requires specific audit procedures, which may include

1) Evaluating the company's procedures for identifying and properly accounting for related party transactions

2) Requesting from management the names of all related parties and inquiring whether transactions occurred with them

3) Reviewing filings with the SEC and other regulatory agencies for the names of related parties and for other businesses in which officers and directors occupy directorship or management positions

4) Determining the names of all pension and other trusts established for employees and the names of their officers and trustees

5) Reviewing shareholder listings of closely held companies to identify principal shareholders

6) Reviewing prior years' working papers for the names of known related parties

7) Inquiring of predecessor, principal, or other auditors of related entities concerning their knowledge of existing relationships and the extent of management involvement in material transactions

8) Reviewing material investment transactions during the period to determine whether they have created related parties

f. Identifying transactions with related parties. The following procedures may identify material transactions with known related parties or indicate the existence of previously unknown related parties:

1) Provide personnel performing all segments of the audit with the names of known related parties.

2) Review the minutes of meetings of the board and committees.

3) Review filings with the SEC and other regulatory agencies.

4) Review conflict-of-interest statements obtained by the company from its management.

5) Review business transacted with major customers, suppliers, borrowers, and lenders for indications of undisclosed relationships.

6) Consider whether unrecognized transactions are occurring, such as receiving or providing accounting, management, or other services at no charge or a major shareholder's absorbing corporate expenses.

7) Review accounting records for large, unusual, or nonrecurring transactions or balances, especially those near the end of the period.

8) Review confirmations of compensating balance arrangements for indications that balances are or were maintained for or by related parties.

9) Review invoices from law firms.

10) Review confirmations of loans receivable and payable for guarantees.

g. Examining identified related party transactions

1) After identifying related party transactions, the auditor should become satisfied about their purpose, nature, extent, and effect. The following should be considered:

a) Obtain an understanding of the business purpose of the transaction.

b) Examine invoices, executed copies of agreements, contracts, and other documents.

c) Determine whether the transaction has been approved by the board or other officials.

d) Test for reasonableness the compilation of amounts to be disclosed or considered for disclosure.

e) Arrange for the audits of intercompany balances to be performed as of concurrent dates, even if the fiscal years differ, and for the examination of specified, important, and representative related party transactions by the auditors for each of the parties, with appropriate exchange of relevant information.

f) Inspect or confirm and obtain satisfaction concerning the transferability and value of collateral.

2) To fully understand a particular transaction, the auditor may

a) Confirm the transaction amount and terms, including guarantees and other significant data, with the other parties.

b) Inspect evidence in possession of the other parties.

c) Confirm or discuss significant information with intermediaries, such as banks, guarantors, agents, or attorneys.

d) Refer to financial publications, trade journals, and credit agencies.

e) With respect to material uncollected balances, guarantees, and other obligations, obtain information about the financial capability of the other parties from audited financial statements, unaudited financial statements, income tax returns, and reports issued by credit agencies.

h. Disclosure

1) For transactions or relationships for which SFAS 57 requires disclosure, the auditor should consider whether (s)he has obtained sufficient competent evidence to understand the relationships and the effects of the transactions.

a) The auditor should evaluate the transactions or relationships and become satisfied on the basis of professional judgment that they are adequately disclosed in the notes to the financial statements.

2) Except for routine transactions, determining whether a transaction would have occurred if the parties had not been related, or what the terms and manner of settlement would have been, is ordinarily not possible. Accordingly, representations by management that a transaction was consummated on terms equivalent to those that prevail in arm's-length transactions are difficult to substantiate.

a) If the auditor believes that a representation is unsubstantiated, (s)he should express a qualified or adverse opinion because of a departure from GAAP, depending on materiality.

3. Stop and review! You have completed the outline for this subunit. Study multiple-choice questions 14 through 21 beginning on page 118.

3.4 ACCOUNTING ESTIMATES AND FAIR VALUES (AU 342 AND AU 328)

1. **Introduction.** Auditors must obtain and evaluate sufficient competent evidence to support significant accounting estimates.

   a. An **accounting estimate** in historical financial statements approximates an element, item, or account by measuring the effects of past transactions or events or the current status of an asset or liability.

      1) Examples include net realizable values of inventory and accounts receivable, property and casualty insurance loss reserves, revenues from contracts accounted for by the percentage-of-completion method, and pension and warranty expenses.

   b. Such estimates are often necessary because

      1) Measurement or valuation may be uncertain pending future events.

      2) Relevant data for past events cannot be accumulated on a timely, cost-effective basis.

   c. **Management is responsible** for making the judgments about accounting estimates.

      1) These judgments are normally based on subjective as well as objective factors, including knowledge about past and current events and assumptions about future conditions and courses of action.

   d. The auditor must evaluate the reasonableness of accounting estimates in the context of the financial statements taken as a whole.

      1) Even when the estimation process involves competent personnel using relevant and reliable data, potential bias exists in the subjective factors, and control may be difficult to establish.

         a) When planning and performing procedures to evaluate accounting estimates, the auditor should adopt an attitude of professional skepticism toward both the subjective and objective factors.

         b) According to AU 312, *Audit Risk and Materiality in Conducting an Audit*, the difference between the estimate best supported by the evidence and the estimate in the financial statements must be reasonable.

            i) If the amount in the financial statements is not reasonable, it should be treated as a likely error or fraud and aggregated with other likely misstatements.

            ii) If the differences are individually reasonable but collectively indicate possible bias (for example, when the effect of each difference is to increase income), the auditor must reconsider the estimates as a whole.

2. **Developing Accounting Estimates**

   a. Management's process of preparing accounting estimates, whether or not documented or formally applied, normally consists of

      1) Determining when estimates are required

      2) Identifying the relevant factors

      3) Accumulating relevant, sufficient, and reliable data

      4) Developing assumptions regarding the most likely circumstances and events with respect to the relevant factors

      5) Determining the estimated amount based on the assumptions and other relevant factors

      6) Determining that presentation and disclosure conform with applicable accounting principles

b.   The risk of material misstatement of accounting estimates varies with the

1)   Complexity and subjectivity of the process
2)   Availability and reliability of relevant data
3)   Number, significance, and degree of uncertainty of the assumptions

3.   **Internal Control Related to Accounting Estimates**

a.   Internal control may reduce the probability of material misstatements of accounting estimates. Specific aspects of internal control relevant to the process of arriving at estimates include

1)   Management communication of the need for proper estimates
2)   Accumulation of relevant, sufficient, and reliable data
3)   Preparation of estimates by qualified personnel
4)   Adequate review and approval by proper authority of

a)   Sources of relevant factors
b)   Development of assumptions
c)   Reasonableness of assumptions and resulting estimates

5)   Consideration by proper authority of the need to use the work of specialists
6)   Consideration by proper authority of changes in methods
7)   Comparison of prior estimates with results to assess the reliability of the process
8)   Consideration by management of whether the resulting estimate is consistent with operational plans

4.   **Evaluating Accounting Estimates**

a.   The auditor's objective is to obtain sufficient competent evidence to provide reasonable assurance that

1)   All material accounting estimates have been developed.
2)   Those estimates are reasonable (free from bias).
3)   Presentation and disclosure conform with applicable accounting principles.

b.   **Identifying circumstances that require accounting estimates.** In evaluating whether all material accounting estimates have been developed, the auditor considers the entity's industry, its business methods, new accounting pronouncements, and other external factors. Possible procedures include

1)   Considering financial statement assertions to determine the need for estimates
2)   Evaluating information obtained from other procedures, for example, information

a)   About changes in the entity's business and its industry indicative of the need for an accounting estimate
b)   About changes in the methods of accumulating information
c)   About litigation, claims, and assessments
d)   From reading available minutes
e)   In regulatory or examination reports, supervisory correspondence, and similar materials from regulatory agencies

3)   Inquiring of management about circumstances indicating the need for an estimate

c. **Evaluating reasonableness**

1) The evaluation concentrates on key factors and assumptions that are

    a) Significant to the estimate
    b) Sensitive to variations
    c) Deviative from historical patterns
    d) Subjective and susceptible to misstatement and bias

2) The auditor normally should also consider

    a) The entity's experience in making past estimates
    b) The auditor's experience in the industry
    c) Any changes that may cause factors different from those previously considered to become significant
    d) In some cases, the possible need to obtain written representations from management regarding the key factors and assumptions

3) The auditor should understand how management developed the estimate and then use one or more of the following approaches:

    a) Review and test the process used by management. Procedures for this purpose may include

        i) Identifying any controls over the process that might be useful in the evaluation
        ii) Identifying the sources of data and factors used in forming the assumptions and considering whether they are relevant, reliable, and sufficient in light of information from other audit tests
        iii) Considering whether other key factors or alternative assumptions exist
        iv) Evaluating whether the assumptions are consistent with each other and with relevant data
        v) Analyzing historical data used to develop assumptions to assess comparability, consistency, and reliability
        vi) Considering whether business or industry changes cause other factors to become significant to the assumptions
        vii) Reviewing documentation of the assumptions and inquiring about plans, goals, and objectives that might relate to them
        viii) Using the work of a specialist
        ix) Testing calculations used to translate assumptions and key factors into the estimate

    b) Develop an independent estimate to corroborate management's estimate by using other key factors or alternative assumptions.

    c) Review events or transactions occurring after the date of the balance sheet but prior to the completion of field work that are important in identifying and evaluating the reasonableness of accounting estimates, key factors, or assumptions.

5.   **AU 328**, *Auditing Fair Value Measurements and Disclosures*, states that FVMD arise from initial recording or from later changes in value reflected in net income or other comprehensive income.

    a.   **Fair value** is the amount at which an asset (liability) can be bought or sold (incurred or settled) in a current transaction between willing parties, not in a forced sale. An **observable market price** is the preferable measure of fair value when it is available.

    b.   **Management's responsibility** is to establish a process for (1) determining FVMD, (2) selecting proper valuation methods, (3) identifying significant assumptions, and (4) ensuring conformity with GAAP.

    c.   Absent observable market prices, **assumptions** (preferably those used in the market) must be included in **valuation methods** (e.g., discounted cash flows).

    d.   The auditor must **understand the entity's process** for making FVMD and the **relevant controls**. This understanding is used to assess the **risk of material misstatement** and determine the nature, timing, and extent of audit procedures.

    e.   To evaluate the **conformity of FVMD with GAAP** in the context of the statement as a whole, the auditor must understand the entity's business and industry, especially when items measured or valuation methods are complex (e.g., derivatives).

        1)   The auditor also must evaluate **management's intent and ability** to carry out actions relevant to FVMD. Hence, the auditor should make inquiries and corroborate responses.

        2)   When the entity uses a **valuation method**, the auditor must understand the reasons for the selection and determine whether it is appropriate and has been properly applied. The auditor evaluates whether the method has been consistently applied and, if changed, whether the change is justified.

    f.   An auditor may use the work of a **specialist** as evidence when evaluating FVMD.

    g.   The **testing** of FVMD varies with complexity and risk. Complexity depends on the nature of an item and the valuation method. For example, securities that are not actively traded may be measured using discounted cash flows.

        1)   Complexity usually means **uncertainty** about the **reliability** of the process resulting from a long forecast period, the number and subjectivity of assumptions, or the uncertainty of future events.

        2)   Evidence for understanding the reliability of the process may be obtained by **comparing prior-period FVMD with current-period results**, while allowing for changes in conditions.

    h.   The auditor evaluates internal and external evidence to determine whether **significant assumptions**, individually and in the aggregate, form a reasonable basis for FVMD.

    i.   The auditor's responsibility relative to a **valuation model** is not to act as an appraiser but to evaluate the reasonableness of the assumptions and the appropriateness of the model in the circumstances.

    j.   **Tests of the data** used to prepare the FVMD are performed to verify that they are accurate, complete, and relevant. Moreover, the auditor determines that the FVMD are consistent with the data and assumptions.

    k.   **To corroborate the FVMD**, the auditor may develop a model based on his/her assumptions or on management's. In either case, the auditor must understand management's assumptions to ensure that all significant variables are considered.

        1)   **Subsequent events and transactions** may substantiate FVMD as of the balance sheet date. An example is the sale of investments just after year-end that does not reflect a change in conditions.

    l.   The evaluation of whether **fair-value disclosures conform with GAAP** is based on the same kinds of procedures as those applied to measurements in the statements. The auditor determines the **adequacy** of disclosures and assesses whether they are sufficiently informative about measurement **uncertainty**.

    m. **Written management representations** about FVMD normally should concern the reasonableness of assumptions and whether they properly reflect the ability and intent to carry out specific relevant actions.

    n.   The auditor should **communicate with the audit committee** about the process used to develop especially sensitive fair value estimates.

6.   Stop and review! You have completed the outline for this subunit. Study multiple-choice questions 22 through 27 beginning on page 120.

3.5 CONSIDERATION OF OMITTED PROCEDURES AFTER THE REPORT DATE (AU 390)

1.   An auditor may determine, subsequent to the date of the report, that auditing procedures considered necessary at the time of the audit were omitted, but that there is no indication that the financial statements are not fairly presented.

    a.   However, an auditor has no responsibility to carry out a retrospective review of the work once (s)he has reported.

2.   When the auditor decides that a necessary procedure was omitted, (s)he should assess its importance to his/her current ability to support the previously expressed opinion.

    a.   The results of other procedures applied or audit evidence obtained in a later audit (possibly at an interim date) may compensate for an omitted procedure.

3.   If the auditor determines that the omission impairs his/her current ability to support the opinion, and (s)he believes persons are currently relying, or are likely to rely, on the report, the auditor should promptly undertake to apply the omitted procedure or alternative procedures that would provide a satisfactory basis for the opinion.

4.   If the auditor is unable to apply the previously omitted procedure or alternative procedures, (s)he should consult an attorney.

5.   Stop and review! You have completed the outline for this subunit. Study multiple-choice questions 28 through 31 beginning on page 123.

QUESTIONS

3.1 The Auditor's Consideration of the Internal Audit Function (AU 322)

1. In assessing the competence and objectivity of an entity's internal auditor, an independent auditor would least likely consider information obtained from

A. Discussions with management personnel.

B. External quality reviews of the internal auditor's activities.

C. Previous experience with the internal auditor.

D. The results of analytical procedures.

Answer (D) is correct. *(CPA, adapted)*
REQUIRED: The least likely procedure in assessing the competence and objectivity of an entity's internal auditor.
DISCUSSION: Analytical procedures are evaluations of financial information made by a study of plausible relationships among both financial and nonfinancial data, using models that range from simple to complex. They are substantive tests used by the auditor to gather evidence about the fairness of the financial statements.
Answer (A) is incorrect because AU 322 identifies discussions with management as a procedure appropriate for assessing competence and objectivity of an internal auditor. Answer (B) is incorrect because AU 322 identifies quality reviews as a procedure appropriate for assessing competence and objectivity of an internal auditor. Answer (C) is incorrect because AU 322 identifies consideration of previous experience as a procedure appropriate for assessing competence and objectivity of an internal auditor.

2. In assessing the competence of an internal auditor, an independent CPA most likely would obtain information about the

A. Quality of the internal auditor's documentation.

B. Organization's commitment to integrity and ethical values.

C. Influence of management on the scope of the internal auditor's duties.

D. Organizational levels to which the internal auditor reports.

Answer (A) is correct. *(CPA, adapted)*
REQUIRED: The information needed to assess the competence of an internal auditor.
DISCUSSION: In assessing the competence of an internal auditor, the auditor should consider such factors as educational level and professional experience; professional certification and continuing education; audit policies, programs and procedures; supervision and review of the internal auditor's activities; departmental practices regarding assignments; quality of documentation, reports, and recommendations; and evaluation of the internal auditor's performance.
Answer (B) is incorrect because the organization's commitment to integrity and ethical values relates to objectivity rather than competence. Answer (C) is incorrect because the influence of management on the scope of the internal auditor's duties relates to objectivity rather than competence. Answer (D) is incorrect because the organizational levels to which the internal auditor reports relates to objectivity rather than competence.

3. In assessing the objectivity of internal auditors, an independent auditor should

A. Evaluate the quality control program in effect for the internal auditors.

B. Examine documentary evidence of the work performed by the internal auditors.

C. Test a sample of the transactions and balances that the internal auditors examined.

D. Determine the organizational level to which the internal auditors report.

Answer (D) is correct. *(CPA, adapted)*
REQUIRED: The procedure performed to assess an internal auditor's objectivity.
DISCUSSION: If the auditor decides that it is efficient to consider how the internal auditors' work may affect the nature, timing, and extent of audit procedures, the competence and objectivity of the internal auditors should be assessed. Assessing objectivity includes obtaining information about organizational status (the level to which the internal auditors report; access to the board, audit committee, or the owner-manager; and whether these individuals oversee employment decisions related to the internal auditors) and about policies to maintain internal auditors' objectivity concerning the areas audited (AU 322).
Answer (A) is incorrect because evaluating quality control pertains to competence, not objectivity. Answer (B) is incorrect because examining internal auditors' engagement records (documentation), pertains to competence, not objectivity. Answer (C) is incorrect because testing details examined by internal auditors pertains to competence, not objectivity.

4. For which of the following judgments may an independent auditor share responsibility with an entity's internal auditor who is assessed to be both competent and objective?

	Assessment of Inherent Risk	Assessment of Control Risk
A.	Yes	Yes
B.	Yes	No
C.	No	Yes
D.	No	No

Answer (D) is correct. *(CPA, adapted)*
REQUIRED: The judgment(s) that an auditor may share with an entity's internal auditor.
DISCUSSION: The auditor may use the internal auditor to provide direct assistance in the audit as long as the auditor supervises, reviews, evaluates, and tests the work of the internal auditor. However, an internal auditor, regardless of his/her competence and objectivity, should never make any judgments concerning the audit work being conducted. All judgments must be made by the auditor.

5. For which of the following judgments may an independent auditor share responsibility with an entity's internal auditor who is assessed to be both competent and objective?

	Materiality of Misstatements	Evaluation of Accounting Estimates
A.	Yes	No
B.	No	Yes
C.	No	No
D.	Yes	Yes

Answer (C) is correct. *(CPA, adapted)*
REQUIRED: The judgment(s) for which an auditor may share responsibility with an internal auditor.
DISCUSSION: The responsibility to report on financial statements rests solely with the auditor and cannot be shared with internal auditors. Because the auditor has the ultimate responsibility to express an opinion on the financial statements, judgments about assessments of inherent and control risk, materiality of misstatements, sufficiency of tests performed, evaluation of significant accounting estimates, and other matters affecting the auditor's report should always be those of the auditor.
Answer (A) is incorrect because the auditor cannot share responsibility with the internal auditor for judgments about materiality. Answer (B) is incorrect because the auditor cannot share responsibility with the internal auditor for judgments about accounting estimates. Answer (D) is incorrect because the auditor cannot share responsibility with the internal auditor for judgments about materiality or accounting estimates.

6. During an audit, an internal auditor may provide direct assistance to an independent CPA in

	Obtaining an Understanding of Internal Control	Performing Tests of Controls	Performing Substantive Tests
A.	No	No	No
B.	Yes	No	No
C.	Yes	Yes	No
D.	Yes	Yes	Yes

Answer (D) is correct. *(CPA, adapted)*
REQUIRED: The types of direct assistance an internal auditor may provide to an independent CPA.
DISCUSSION: The auditor may request direct assistance from the internal auditor when performing the audit. Thus, the auditor may appropriately request the internal auditor's assistance in obtaining the understanding of internal control, performing tests of controls, or performing substantive tests (AU 322). The internal auditor may provide assistance in all phases of the audit as long as the internal auditor's competence and objectivity have been tested and the independent auditor supervises, reviews, evaluates, and tests the work performed by the internal auditor to the extent appropriate.

7. An internal auditor's work would most likely affect the nature, timing, and extent of an independent auditor's auditing procedures when the internal auditor's work relates to assertions about the

A. Existence of contingencies.

B. Valuation of intangible assets.

C. Existence of fixed asset additions.

D. Valuation of related party transactions.

Answer (C) is correct. *(CPA, adapted)*
REQUIRED: The assertion most likely affected by the internal auditor's work.
DISCUSSION: For assertions related to material financial statement amounts when the risk of material misstatement or the degree of subjectivity involved in the evaluation of the audit evidence is high, reliance on the internal auditor is less effective. However, for certain assertions related to less material financial statement amounts, when the risk of material misstatement or the degree of subjectivity involved is low, for example, assertions about the existence of cash, prepaid assets, and fixed asset additions, the auditor may be able to rely on the internal auditor's work.
Answer (A) is incorrect because the auditor is less likely to rely on the internal auditor's work regarding subjective issues such as existence of contingencies. Answer (B) is incorrect because the auditor is less likely to rely on the internal auditor's work regarding subjective issues such as valuation of intangible assets. Answer (D) is incorrect because the auditor is less likely to rely on the internal auditor's work regarding subjective issues such as valuation of related party transactions.

8. Miller Retailing, Inc. maintains a staff of three full-time internal auditors. If the work of the internal auditors is relevant to the audit, it is efficient to consider how that work may affect the audit, and the internal auditors are found to be competent and objective, the independent auditor most likely will

A. Nevertheless need to make direct tests of assertions about material financial statement amounts for which the risk of material misstatement is high.

B. Decrease the extent of the tests of controls needed to restrict detection risk to the acceptable level.

C. Increase the extent of the procedures needed to reduce control risk to an acceptable level.

D. Not evaluate and test the work performed by the internal auditors.

Answer (A) is correct. *(CPA, adapted)*
    REQUIRED: The true statement about the effect of the work of the internal auditors.
    DISCUSSION: The auditor has the sole reporting responsibility and must make all judgments about matters affecting the report. When amounts are material and the risk of material misstatement or the subjectivity of the evaluation of the evidence is high, "the consideration of the internal auditors' work cannot alone reduce audit risk to an acceptable level to eliminate the necessity to perform tests of those assertions directly by the auditor" (AU 322).
    Answer (B) is incorrect because the auditor performs substantive tests, not tests of controls, to restrict detection risk to the acceptable level. Answer (C) is incorrect because control risk can be assessed but not restricted by the auditor. Answer (D) is incorrect because the auditor should evaluate the quality and effectiveness of the work of the internal auditors that significantly affects the nature, timing, and extent of the audit procedures.

3.2 Using the Work of a Specialist (AU 336)

9. In using the work of a specialist, an auditor referred to the specialist's findings in the auditor's report. This would be an appropriate reporting practice if the

A. Client is not familiar with the professional certification, personal reputation, or particular competence of the specialist.

B. Auditor, as a result of the specialist's findings, adds an explanatory paragraph emphasizing a matter regarding the financial statements.

C. Client understands the auditor's corroborative use of the specialist's findings in relation to the representations in the financial statements.

D. Auditor, as a result of the specialist's findings, decides to indicate a division of responsibility with the specialist.

Answer (B) is correct. *(CPA, adapted)*
    REQUIRED: The instance in which an auditor may refer to a specialist's findings.
    DISCUSSION: An auditor ordinarily should not refer to the work or findings of a specialist. However, "The auditor may, as a result of the report or findings of the specialist, decide to add explanatory language to his/her standard report or depart from an unqualified opinion." The specialist may be identified "if the auditor believes the reference will facilitate an understanding of the reason for the explanatory paragraph or the departure from the unqualified opinion" (AU 336). Emphasizing a matter is a basis for adding an explanatory paragraph that may justify referring to a specialist.
    Answer (A) is incorrect because the auditor is required to evaluate the professional qualifications of the specialist. Answer (C) is incorrect because the specialist's awareness of the use of his/her work is independent of the decision to refer to the specialist. Answer (D) is incorrect because a division of responsibility with the specialist is inappropriate.

10. When using the work of a specialist, an auditor may refer to and identify the specialist in the auditor's report if the

A. Auditor wishes to indicate a division of responsibility.

B. Specialist's work provides the auditor greater assurance of reliability.

C. Auditor expresses a qualified opinion as a result of the specialist's findings.

D. Specialist is not independent of the client.

Answer (C) is correct. *(CPA, adapted)*
    REQUIRED: The instance when an audit report may refer to and identify a specialist.
    DISCUSSION: The auditor may refer to the specialist if (s)he departs from an unqualified opinion (AU 336). Additionally, an auditor may express an unqualified opinion and refer to a specialist if, as a result of the work of the specialist, (s)he adds an explanatory paragraph.
    Answer (A) is incorrect because an auditor may divide responsibility with other independent auditors, not with a specialist. Answer (B) is incorrect because the reference is solely to clarify the reason for the modification of the report. Answer (D) is incorrect because the specialist's lack of independence is not a basis for the reference.

11. Which of the following statements is true about the auditor's use of the work of a specialist?

    A. The specialist should not have an understanding of the auditor's corroborative use of the specialist's findings.

    B. The auditor is required to perform substantive procedures to verify the specialist's assumptions and findings.

    C. The client should not have an understanding of the nature of the work to be performed by the specialist.

    D. The auditor should obtain an understanding of the methods and assumptions used by the specialist.

Answer (D) is correct. *(CPA, adapted)*
    REQUIRED: The true statement about the auditor's use of the work of a specialist.
    DISCUSSION: AU 336 notes that the auditor should obtain an understanding of the methods and assumptions used to determine whether the findings are suitable for corroborative purposes. The auditor should consider whether the specialist's findings support the assertions and should test the accounting data provided by the client to the specialist.
    Answer (A) is incorrect because the specialist should have an understanding about the nature of the work to be performed. Answer (B) is incorrect because, if the specialist's findings support the assertions, the auditor may reasonably conclude that sufficient, competent evidential matter has been obtained. Answer (C) is incorrect because the client should have an understanding about the nature of the work to be performed.

12. Which of the following statements is true concerning an auditor's use of the work of a specialist?

    A. The auditor need not obtain an understanding of the methods and assumptions used by the specialist.

    B. The auditor may not use the work of a specialist in matters material to the fair presentation of the financial statements.

    C. The reasonableness of the specialist's assumptions and their applications are strictly the auditor's responsibility.

    D. The work of a specialist who has a contractual relationship with the client may be acceptable under certain circumstances.

Answer (D) is correct. *(CPA, adapted)*
    REQUIRED: The true statement about use of a specialist.
    DISCUSSION: A related specialist may be acceptable, but the auditor should consider additional audit procedures to assess the reliability and usefulness of a related specialist.
    Answer (A) is incorrect because the auditor should obtain an understanding of the methods or assumptions used to determine whether the findings are suitable for corroborative purposes. Answer (B) is incorrect because the auditor may use the work of a specialist in helping to collect sufficient competent evidence. Answer (C) is incorrect because, although the auditor must evaluate the assumptions and their usefulness for the auditor's purpose, the reasonableness of the specialist's assumptions and their application is the responsibility of the specialist.

13. In using the work of a specialist, an understanding should exist among the auditor, the client, and the specialist as to the nature of the specialist's work. The documentation of this understanding should cover

    A. A statement that the specialist assumes no responsibility to update the specialist's report for future events or circumstances.

    B. The conditions under which a division of responsibility may be necessary.

    C. The specialist's understanding of the auditor's corroborative use of the specialist's findings.

    D. The auditor's disclaimer as to whether the specialist's findings corroborate the representations in the financial statements.

Answer (C) is correct. *(CPA, adapted)*
    REQUIRED: The matter covered in the understanding about the work of the specialist.
    DISCUSSION: The understanding should be documented and should cover the objectives and scope of the work, the specialist's representations as to his/her relationship to the client, the methods or assumptions to be used, and a comparison with those used in the preceding period. It should also cover the specialist's understanding of the auditor's corroborative use of the findings in relation to the assertions in the financial statements, and the form and content of the specialist's report that would enable the auditor to evaluate the specialist's work (AU 336).
    Answer (A) is incorrect because the understanding need not contain a disclaimer about the specialist's responsibility to update the report. Answer (B) is incorrect because the auditor may in some cases refer to a specialist but may not divide responsibility with him/her. Answer (D) is incorrect because the understanding need not contain a disclaimer about whether the findings corroborate the representations.

3.3 Related Parties (AU 334)

14. When auditing related party transactions, an auditor places primary emphasis on

   A. Confirming the existence of the related parties.

   B. Verifying the valuation of the related party transactions.

   C. Evaluating the disclosure of the related party transactions.

   D. Ascertaining the rights and obligations of the related parties.

Answer (C) is correct. *(CPA, adapted)*
   REQUIRED: The primary concern of the auditor about related party transactions.
   DISCUSSION: The auditor's primary emphasis with regard to related party transactions should be on the presentation and disclosure assertion with respect to their nature and their effect on the financial statements. However, the FASB requires that transactions with related parties be accounted for on the same basis as would be appropriate if the parties were not related.
   Answer (A) is incorrect because, in an audit of related party transactions, the auditor places no special emphasis on existence assertions. Answer (B) is incorrect because, in an audit of related party transactions, the auditor places no special emphasis on valuation assertions. Answer (D) is incorrect because, in an audit of related party transactions, the auditor places no special emphasis on rights and obligations assertions.

15. An auditor searching for related party transactions should obtain an understanding of each subsidiary's relationship to the total entity because

   A. This may permit the audit of intercompany account balances to be performed as of concurrent dates.

   B. Intercompany transactions may have been consummated on terms equivalent to arm's-length transactions.

   C. This may reveal whether particular transactions would have taken place if the parties had not been related.

   D. The business structure may be deliberately designed to obscure related party transactions.

Answer (D) is correct. *(CPA, adapted)*
   REQUIRED: The reason for understanding parent-subsidiary relationships when searching for related party transactions.
   DISCUSSION: AU 334 states that "the auditor should obtain an understanding of management responsibilities and the relationship of each component to the total entity." The auditor should also consider internal control and the business purpose of each component of the entity. The auditor should be aware that sometimes "business structure and operating style are occasionally deliberately designed to obscure related party transactions."
   Answer (A) is incorrect because a concurrent audit is not required. Answer (B) is incorrect because the auditor's concern is that related party transactions were not at arm's-length. Answer (C) is incorrect because, except for routine transactions, determining whether a transaction would have occurred and what the terms would have been if the parties were unrelated is ordinarily not possible.

16. Which of the following auditing procedures most likely would assist an auditor in identifying related party transactions?

   A. Inspecting correspondence with lawyers for evidence of unreported contingent liabilities.

   B. Vouching accounting records for recurring transactions recorded just after the balance sheet date.

   C. Reviewing confirmations of loans receivable and payable for indications of guarantees.

   D. Performing analytical procedures for indications of possible financial difficulties.

Answer (C) is correct. *(CPA, adapted)*
   REQUIRED: The auditing procedure most likely useful in identifying related party transactions.
   DISCUSSION: AU 334 lists procedures for identifying material transactions with parties known to be related and for identifying transactions that may be indicative of previously undetermined relationships. Procedures used to determine the latter include reviewing confirmations of loans receivable and payable for indications of guarantees.
   Answer (A) is incorrect because the question indicates that the auditor is concerned about identifying related party transactions, not unreported contingent liabilities. Answer (B) is incorrect because recurring transactions recorded after the balance sheet are in the normal course of business, for example, sales transactions. Answer (D) is incorrect because analytical procedures may disclose financial difficulties but not related party transactions.

17. Which of the following most likely would indicate the existence of related parties?

A. Writing down obsolete inventory just before year-end.

B. Failing to correct previously identified internal control deficiencies.

C. Depending on a single product for the success of the entity.

D. Borrowing money at an interest rate significantly below the market rate.

Answer (D) is correct. *(CPA, adapted)*
REQUIRED: The event that most likely indicates the existence of related parties.
DISCUSSION: Exchanging property for similar property in a nonmonetary transaction, borrowing or lending at rates significantly above or below market rates, selling realty at a price materially different from its appraised value, and making loans with no scheduled repayment terms suggest possible related party transactions (AU 334).
Answer (A) is incorrect because inventory is customarily written down to lower of cost or market at year-end. Answer (B) is incorrect because the cost of correction may exceed the benefits. Answer (C) is incorrect because dependence on one product is not a transaction that by its own nature suggests the existence of related parties. However, AU 334 cites it as a possible condition motivating related party transactions.

18. Which of the following events most likely indicates the existence of related parties?

A. Borrowing a large sum of money at a variable rate of interest.

B. Selling real estate at a price that differs significantly from its book value.

C. Making a loan without scheduled terms for repayment of the funds.

D. Discussing merger terms with a company that is a major competitor.

Answer (C) is correct. *(CPA, adapted)*
REQUIRED: The item that most likely indicates the existence of related parties.
DISCUSSION: AU 334 gives examples of transactions that suggest a related party relationship. Exchanging property for similar property in a nonmonetary transaction, borrowing or lending at rates significantly above or below market rates, selling realty at a price materially different from its appraised value, and making loans with no scheduled repayment terms suggest related party transactions.
Answer (A) is incorrect because large sums of money are often borrowed at fluctuating interest rates, especially when the debt is long term. Answer (B) is incorrect because real estate's fair value is normally significantly higher than its book value. Answer (D) is incorrect because discussing merger terms indicates only that the parties may be related in the future.

19. Which of the following statements is true about related party transactions?

A. In the absence of evidence to the contrary, related party transactions should be assumed to be outside the ordinary course of business.

B. An auditor should determine whether a particular transaction would have occurred if the parties had not been related.

C. An auditor should substantiate that related party transactions were consummated on terms equivalent to those that prevail in arm's-length transactions.

D. The audit procedures directed toward identifying related party transactions should include considering whether transactions are occurring but are not being given proper accounting recognition.

Answer (D) is correct. *(CPA, adapted)*
REQUIRED: The true statement about related party transactions.
DISCUSSION: According to AU 334, the audit procedures directed toward identifying related party transactions should include considering whether transactions are occurring, but are not being given proper accounting recognition, for example, receiving or providing accounting, management, or other services at no charge or a major shareholder's payment of corporate expenses.
Answer (A) is incorrect because, in the absence of contrary evidence, related party transactions are assumed to be in the ordinary course of business. Answer (B) is incorrect because determining whether a particular transaction would have occurred if the parties had not been related is ordinarily not possible unless it is routine. Answer (C) is incorrect because related party transactions need not be consummated on terms equivalent to those that prevail in arm's-length transactions.

20. After determining that a related party transaction has, in fact, occurred, an auditor should

    A. Add a separate paragraph to the auditor's standard report to explain the transaction.

    B. Perform analytical procedures to verify whether similar transactions occurred, but were not recorded.

    C. Obtain an understanding of the business purpose of the transaction.

    D. Substantiate that the transaction was consummated on terms equivalent to an arm's-length transaction.

Answer (C) is correct.   *(CPA, adapted)*
    REQUIRED: The procedure performed after determining that a related party transaction has occurred.
    DISCUSSION: After identifying related party transactions, the auditor should become satisfied about their purpose, nature, extent, and effect. Among other things, the auditor should obtain an understanding of the business purpose of the transaction (AU 334).
    Answer (A) is incorrect because, if the related party transaction has been accounted for properly, no modification of the standard report is necessary. However, in some cases, the auditor may wish to add a separate paragraph emphasizing that the entity has had significant related party transactions (AU 508). Answer (B) is incorrect because the auditor is not responsible for undisclosed, unrecorded related party transactions. Answer (D) is incorrect because the auditor normally cannot determine whether a transaction was consummated on terms equivalent to an arm's-length transaction. The auditor's primary concern is with disclosure of related party transactions.

21. An auditor most likely would modify an unqualified opinion if the entity's financial statements include a note on related party transactions

    A. Disclosing loans to related parties at interest rates significantly below prevailing market rates.

    B. Describing an exchange of real estate for similar property in a nonmonetary related party transaction.

    C. Stating that a particular related party transaction occurred on terms equivalent to those that would have prevailed in an arm's-length transaction.

    D. Presenting the dollar volume of related party transactions and the effects of any change from prior periods in the method of establishing terms.

Answer (C) is correct.   *(CPA, adapted)*
    REQUIRED: The note most likely resulting in a modified opinion.
    DISCUSSION: Stating that a particular related party transaction occurred on terms equivalent to those that would have prevailed in an arm's-length transaction is difficult to substantiate and is contrary to SFAS 57. If such a representation is included in the statements and the auditor believes that it is unsubstantiated, (s)he should modify the opinion because of the departure from GAAP.

3.4 Accounting Estimates and Fair Values (AU 342 and AU 328)

22. In evaluating the reasonableness of an entity's accounting estimates, an auditor normally is concerned about assumptions that are

    A. Susceptible to bias.

    B. Consistent with prior periods.

    C. Insensitive to variations.

    D. Similar to industry guidelines.

Answer (A) is correct.   *(CPA, adapted)*
    REQUIRED: The auditor's normal concern about assumptions used in making accounting estimates.
    DISCUSSION: AU 342 states, "In evaluating the reasonableness of an estimate, the auditor normally concentrates on key factors and assumptions that are (1) significant to the accounting estimate, (2) sensitive to variations, (3) deviations from historical patterns, and (4) subjective and susceptible to misstatement and bias."
    Answer (B) is incorrect because assumptions consistent with those of prior periods are of less concern to the auditor. Answer (C) is incorrect because assumptions insensitive to variations are of less concern to the auditor. Answer (D) is incorrect because estimates that are similar to industry guidelines are more likely to be reasonable.

23. The auditor's evaluation of the reasonableness of accounting estimates

A. Should be in the context of individual financial statements or items.

B. Considers that management bases its judgment on both subjective and objective factors.

C. Will be unfavorable if the estimates in the financial statements are based on assumptions about future events and transactions.

D. Should be based on an attitude of conservatism.

Answer (B) is correct. *(Publisher)*
REQUIRED: The true statement about the auditor's evaluation of the reasonableness of accounting estimates.
DISCUSSION: Estimates are based on both subjective and objective factors. Hence, control over estimates may be difficult to establish. Given the potential bias in the subjective factors, the auditor should therefore adopt an attitude of professional skepticism toward both the subjective and objective factors.
Answer (A) is incorrect because the evaluation should be in the context of the financial statements taken as a whole. Answer (C) is incorrect because estimates are often based on assumptions about the future. Answer (D) is incorrect because estimates should be based on assumptions regarding the most likely circumstances and events. The auditor should evaluate those assumptions with professional skepticism.

24. Auditors must obtain and evaluate sufficient competent evidence to support significant accounting estimates. Differences between the estimates best supported by the evidence and those in the financial statements

A. Are per se unreasonable and should be treated as misstatements if collectively material.

B. May be individually reasonable but collectively indicate possible bias.

C. May be individually unreasonable, but if they collectively indicate no bias, aggregation of the differences with other likely misstatements is not required.

D. Should arouse concern only when estimates are based on hypothetical assumptions or subjective factors.

Answer (B) is correct. *(Publisher)*
REQUIRED: The true statement about differences between the estimates best supported by the evidence and those in the financial statements.
DISCUSSION: If the amount in the financial statements is not reasonable, it should be treated as a likely error or fraud and aggregated with other likely misstatements. If the differences between the best estimates and those in the financial statements are individually reasonable but collectively indicate possible bias (for example, when the effect of each difference is to increase income), the auditor must reconsider the estimates as a whole.
Answer (A) is incorrect because no estimate is considered accurate with certainty. Hence, differences may be reasonable and not considered to be likely material misstatements. Answer (C) is incorrect because an unreasonable difference should be considered a likely misstatement and aggregated with other likely misstatements. Answer (D) is incorrect because estimates are based on subjective as well as objective factors.

25. Karl, an auditor with extensive experience in the retail industry, is assigned to audit the reasonableness of accounting estimates in the year 1 financial statements of Haas Company. Haas Company, which was formed in year 1, markets fishing lures. Which of the following is the least important consideration for Karl in his audit of the reasonableness of accounting estimates?

A. An inexperienced employee at Haas prepared the financial statements and was entirely responsible for the accounting estimates.

B. Karl has never been involved in an audit of a company that sells fishing lures.

C. The accounting estimates in the financial statements of Haas Company are based on numerous significant assumptions.

D. The accounting estimates in the financial statements are susceptible to bias.

Answer (B) is correct. *(Publisher)*
REQUIRED: The least important consideration in an audit of the reasonableness of accounting estimates.
DISCUSSION: AU 311 states that an auditor should obtain a level of knowledge of the entity's business sufficient for planning and performing the audit in accordance with GAAS. This knowledge helps the auditor evaluate the reasonableness of estimates. Karl has extensive experience in the retail industry and therefore most likely has an acceptable level of competence. If necessary, Karl may seek the help of a specialist before conducting the audit.
Answer (A) is incorrect because preparation of the statements by an inexperienced employee who may not have the competence necessary to formulate accounting estimates suggests the need for additional audit effort. Answer (C) is incorrect because the significant assumptions underlying accounting estimates are crucial to the audit. The auditor is required to concentrate on the key factors and assumptions that are significant to the estimates, sensitive to variations, deviations from historical patterns, and subjective and susceptible to misstatement and bias (AU 342). Answer (D) is incorrect because estimates that are subjective or susceptible to bias require additional consideration by the auditor.

26. During the audit of fair value measurements and disclosures (FVMD), the auditor must

A. Understand the components of internal control but need not specifically obtain an understanding of the entity's process for determining FVMD.

B. Use the understanding of the audited entity's process for determining FVMD to assess the risk of material misstatement.

C. Determine that the entity has measured fair values using discounted cash flows whenever feasible.

D. Address only the initial recording of transactions.

Answer (B) is correct.   *(Publisher)*
REQUIRED: The necessary procedure in an audit of FVMD.
DISCUSSION: To meet its responsibility to make the FVMD included in the financial statements, management may need to adopt an accounting and financial reporting process that consists of (1) choosing valuation methods, (2) identifying significant assumptions, (3) preparing the valuations, and (4) ensuring conformity with GAAP. The auditor must obtain an understanding of this process and the relevant controls that is sufficient for an effective audit of FVMD. The understanding is used to assess the risk of material misstatement and to determine the nature, timing, and extent of audit procedures.
    Answer (A) is incorrect because the auditor must obtain such an understanding. Answer (C) is incorrect because GAAP do not require a specific method for measuring fair value. However, use of observable market prices is preferable. In their absence, the measurement is based on the best available information, and the entity's process will be more complex. Answer (D) is incorrect because fair value measurements also are necessary for changes in value subsequent to initial recording, e.g., adjustments at the balance sheet date for holding gains or losses on trading and available-for-sale securities.

27. As part of the audit of fair value measurements and disclosures (FVMD), an auditor may need to test the entity's significant assumptions. In these circumstances, the auditor must

A. Verify that the entity has used its own assumptions, not those of marketplace participants.

B. Obtain sufficient evidence to express an opinion on the assumptions.

C. Evaluate whether the assumptions individually and as a whole form a reasonable basis for the FVMD.

D. Identify especially sensitive assumptions.

Answer (C) is correct.   *(CPA, adapted)*
REQUIRED: The necessary step in an audit of FVMD when the auditor tests significant assumptions.
DISCUSSION: Observable market prices are not always available for fair value measurements. In this case, the entity uses valuation methods based on the assumptions that the market would employ to estimate fair values, if obtainable without excessive cost. Accordingly, GAAS require the auditor to evaluate whether the significant assumptions form a reasonable basis for the measurements. Because assumptions often are interdependent and must be consistent with each other, the auditor must evaluate them independently and as a whole. Reasonable assumptions are consistent with (1) economic conditions, (2) existing market data, (3) the entity's plans, (4) past experience, (5) prior-period assumptions, (6) cash flow risks, and (7) other matters.
    Answer (A) is incorrect because valuation methods should be based on the assumptions that participants in the market would use to estimate fair value without undue cost and effort. Answer (B) is incorrect because the procedures applied to the entity's assumptions are required merely to evaluate whether, in the context of the audit of the financial statements as a whole, the assumptions form a reasonable basis for the measurements. Answer (D) is incorrect because the auditor considers the sensitivity of valuations to changes in assumptions. Accordingly, the auditor considers using procedures to identify especially sensitive assumptions but is not always required to do so.

3.5 Consideration of Omitted Procedures after the Report Date (AU 390)

28. Six months after expressing an unqualified opinion on audited financial statements, an auditor discovered that the engagement personnel failed to confirm several of the client's material accounts receivable balances. The auditor should first

A. Request the permission of the client to undertake the confirmation of accounts receivable.

B. Perform alternative procedures to provide a satisfactory basis for the unqualified opinion.

C. Assess the importance of the omitted procedures to the auditor's ability to support the previously expressed opinion.

D. Inquire whether there are persons currently relying, or likely to rely, on the unqualified opinion.

Answer (C) is correct. *(CPA, adapted)*
REQUIRED: The responsibility of the auditor after discovery of the omission of a procedure.
DISCUSSION: When the auditor discovers that a procedure considered necessary at the time of the audit was omitted, (s)he should assess the importance of the omitted procedure to his/her ability to support the previously expressed opinion regarding the financial statements taken as a whole (AU 390).

29. An auditor is considering whether the omission of a substantive procedure considered necessary at the time of an audit may impair the auditor's present ability to support the previously expressed opinion. The auditor need not apply the omitted procedure if the

A. Financial statements and auditor's report were not distributed beyond management and the board of directors.

B. Auditor's previously expressed opinion was qualified because of a departure from GAAP.

C. Results of other procedures that were applied tend to compensate for the procedure omitted.

D. Omission is due to unreasonable delays by client personnel in providing data on a timely basis.

Answer (C) is correct. *(CPA, adapted)*
REQUIRED: The condition under which an auditor need not apply an omitted procedure.
DISCUSSION: When the auditor decides that a necessary audit procedure was omitted, (s)he should assess its importance to his/her current ability to support the previously expressed opinion. The results of other procedures applied or audit evidence obtained in a later audit, possibly at an interim date, may compensate for the omitted procedure.
Answer (A) is incorrect because the need to apply procedures to support the audit opinion is independent of the distribution of the audit report. Answer (B) is incorrect because the type of opinion originally expressed is independent of the need to support that opinion. Answer (D) is incorrect because the auditor should assess any scope limitation in determining whether to express an opinion.

30. On March 15, year 2, Kent, CPA, issued an unqualified opinion on a client's audited financial statements for the year ended December 31, year 1. On May 4, year 2, Kent's internal inspection program disclosed that engagement personnel failed to observe the client's physical inventory. Omission of this procedure impairs Kent's present ability to support the unqualified opinion. If the shareholders are currently relying on the opinion, Kent should first

A. Advise management to disclose to the shareholders that Kent's unqualified opinion should not be relied on.

B. Undertake to apply alternative procedures that would provide a satisfactory basis for the unqualified opinion.

C. Reissue the auditor's report and add an explanatory paragraph describing the departure from generally accepted auditing standards.

D. Compensate for the omitted procedure by performing tests of controls to reduce audit risk to a sufficiently low level.

Answer (B) is correct. *(CPA, adapted)*
REQUIRED: The appropriate action when an auditor discovers that a necessary audit procedure was not performed during the previous audit.
DISCUSSION: If the auditor determines that the omission impairs his/her current ability to support the opinion and (s)he believes persons are currently relying or are likely to rely on the report, the auditor should promptly undertake to apply the omitted procedure or alternative procedures that would provide a satisfactory basis for the opinion (AU 390).
Answer (A) is incorrect because notification of users would only be necessary if the auditor could not become satisfied upon applying the procedure. Answer (C) is incorrect because the auditor has followed GAAS in becoming satisfied with the application of the procedure. Answer (D) is incorrect because tests of controls do not substitute for required substantive tests.

31. An auditor concludes that a substantive auditing procedure considered necessary during the prior year's audit was omitted and there are persons currently relying on the auditor's report. The auditor most likely would promptly apply the omitted procedure if

    A. Control risk was assessed at the maximum level for the relevant financial statement assertions.

    B. The auditor's working papers will be subject to post-issuance review in connection with a peer review program.

    C. The results of other procedures that were applied tend to compensate for the one omitted.

    D. The omission of the procedure impairs the auditor's present ability to support the previously expressed opinion.

Answer (D) is correct. *(CPA, adapted)*
    REQUIRED: The appropriate action when an auditor discovers that a necessary audit procedure was not performed during the previous audit.
    DISCUSSION: If the auditor determines that the omission impairs his/her current ability to support the opinion and (s)he believes persons are currently relying or are likely to rely on the report, the auditor should promptly undertake to apply the omitted procedure or alternative procedures that would provide a satisfactory basis for the opinion (AU 390).
    Answer (A) is incorrect because assessing control risk at the maximum level does not require performance of the omitted procedure if the evidence gathered by other procedures (whether or not tests of controls were performed) permits support of the previously expressed opinion. Answer (B) is incorrect because the review of working papers in connection with a peer review program does not affect the evidence-gathering process. The auditor's attention should be on obtaining sufficient competent evidence, not on whether his/her decision is subject to review. Answer (C) is incorrect because, if the results of other procedures that were applied tend to compensate for the one omitted, the auditor is more likely not to apply the omitted procedure.

Use Gleim's *CPA Test Prep* for interactive testing with over 2,000 additional multiple-choice questions!

3.6 PRACTICE SIMULATION

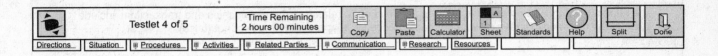

| Testlet 4 of 5 | Time Remaining 2 hours 00 minutes | Copy | Paste | Calculator | Sheet | Standards | Help | Split | Done |

Directions | Situation | Procedures | Activities | Related Parties | Communication | Research | Resources

1. Directions

In the following simulation, you will be asked to complete various tasks related to strategic planning issues. The simulation will provide all the information necessary to do the work. For full credit, be sure to view and complete all work tabs.

Resources are available to you under the tab marked RESOURCES. You may want to review the resources before beginning the simulation.

2. Situation

Temple, CPA, is auditing the financial statements of Ford Lumber Yards, Inc., a privately held corporation with 300 employees and five shareholders, three of whom are active in management. Ford has been in business for many years but has never had its financial statements audited. Temple suspects that the substance of some of Ford's business transactions differs from their form because of the pervasiveness of related party relationships and transactions in the local building supplies industry.

3. Procedures

This question is presented in a check-the-box format.

The audit procedures Temple should apply to identify Ford's related-party relationships and transactions include some of the following. Determine whether each procedure is appropriate (true) or not (false).

Procedures	True	False
1. Evaluate the company's procedures for identifying and properly reporting related party relationships and transactions.		
2. Request from management the names of all related parties and inquire whether there were any related party transactions.		
3. Review confirmations of accounts receivable, particularly for the small balances.		
4. Review tax returns and filings with other regulatory agencies for the names of related parties.		
5. Review cash receipts for a few days prior to and after year-end, particularly for significant amounts of currency.		
6. Review the stock certificate book to identify the shareholders.		
7. Review the minutes of board of directors' meetings.		
8. Review conflict-of-interest statements obtained by the company from its management.		
9. Review the extent and nature of business transacted with major customers, suppliers, borrowers, and lenders.		
10. Request from the client's competitors the names of known related parties.		
11. Review all investment transactions to determine whether the investment created related party relationships.		
12. Review accounting records for large, unusual, or nonrecurring transactions or balances, paying particular attention to transactions recognized at or near the end of the reporting period.		
13. Review invoices from law firms that have performed services for the company for indications of the existence of related party relationships or transactions.		
14. Review accounting records for consistently recurring transactions that, in the aggregate, are considered immaterial.		

4. Activities

This question has a matching format that requires you to select the correct response from a drop-down list. Write the answers in the shaded column.

The independent, external auditor decides that it is efficient to consider how the internal auditors' work might affect the nature, timing, and extent of audit procedures. Thus, the independent auditor should assess both the competence and objectivity of the internal auditors. For each of the following procedures, determine whether it is appropriate for assessing competence, objectivity, both, or neither.

Procedures	Answer
1. Update or obtain information about the supervision and review of internal auditors.	
2. Update or obtain information about the policies regarding the employment of relatives of internal auditors in audit-sensitive positions.	
3. Evaluate evidence from a recent external quality review of the internal auditors.	
4. Update or obtain information about the audit programs and procedures used by the internal auditors.	
5. Evaluate the personal financial statements of the internal auditors.	
6. Determine whether the internal auditors have direct access to the board of directors.	
7. Update or obtain information about the professional certification of the internal auditors.	
8. Update or obtain information about the continuing education programs provided to the internal auditors.	
9. Consider information obtained in previous audits about the activities of internal auditors.	
10. Consider whether the internal auditors are well paid.	

Answer Choices
A) The independent auditor should perform this procedure to test the competence and objectivity of the internal auditors.
B) The independent auditor should perform this procedure to test the competence but not the objectivity of the internal auditors.
C) The independent auditor should perform this procedure to test the objectivity but not the competence of the internal auditors.
D) The auditor would not perform this procedure.

5. Related Parties

This question has a matching format that requires you to select the correct responses from a drop-down list. Write the answers in the shaded column. A choice may be used once, more than once, or not at all.

Match each description of a possible related party transaction, motive for such a transaction, audit procedure pertinent to related party transactions, or disclosure with the appropriate answer choice.

Description	Answer
1. An overly optimistic earnings forecast.	
2. The transaction was consummated on terms equivalent to those that prevail at arm's-length.	
3. Confirm significant information with intermediaries.	
4. Review conflict-of-interest statements obtained by the company for its management.	
5. Making nonmonetary exchanges of similar property.	
6. Interest-free borrowing.	
7. Reviewing shareholder listings of closely held companies.	
8. Excess capacity.	
9. The transaction would have occurred even if the parties were not related.	
10. Determine whether the transaction was approved by the board of directors.	

Choices
A) Transactions indicative of the existence of related parties.
B) Motivation for entering into related party transactions.
C) Specific audit procedure that may uncover related parties.
D) Procedure to gain an understanding of a related party transaction.
E) Appropriate financial statement disclosure by management about related party transactions.
F) Inappropriate financial statement disclosure by management about related party transactions.

6. Communication

In a brief memorandum to your immediate supervisor, describe the procedures that you intend to use to evaluate the reasonableness of management's estimates. Type your communication in your word processor program and print out the copy in a memorandum style format.

REMINDER: Your response will be graded for both technical content and writing skills. You should demonstrate your ability to develop, organize, and express your ideas. Do not convey information in the form of a table, bullet point list, or other abbreviated presentation.

To:	Supervisor
From:	CPA
Subject:	Evaluation of reasonableness of estimates

7. Research

Use the research materials available to you to find the answers to the following question in the AICPA Professional Standards. Print the appropriate citation in its entirety from the source you choose. Use only one source. This is a copy-and-paste item.

Subsequent to the audit, the auditor discovered that certain required procedures were not performed. Cite the appropriate standard that should be applied in this situation.

Unofficial Answers

3. Procedures (14 Gradable Items)

1. <u>True</u>. It is management's responsibility to identify and report related party transactions. The auditor should evaluate the client's procedures for meeting this responsibility.

2. <u>True</u>. To begin the investigation of potential related party transactions, the auditor should inquire of management concerning the names of parties and types of transactions.

3. <u>False</u>. Accounts receivable confirmations are not likely to disclose related parties because a confirmation request does not ask for such information.

4. <u>True</u>. Filings with the SEC, IRS, and any other agency reported to by the entity should be reviewed for any named related parties.

5. <u>False</u>. Cutoff tests are effective for the completeness assertion but are not likely to disclose related parties.

6. <u>True</u>. Principal shareholders are considered related parties, and transactions with them are subject to disclosure requirements.

7. <u>True</u>. Deliberations of the board of directors should be evaluated for a number of purposes, including the possibility of discussions concerning transactions with related parties.

8. <u>True</u>. Clients often request management to submit statements about conflicts of interest. A conflict of interest by management may result from certain types of related party transactions.

9. <u>True</u>. Significant transactions should be evaluated from many perspectives related to the assertions of management. One issue is the possibility for disclosure of any related party transactions.

10. <u>False</u>. The auditor is not likely to communicate with the client's competitors.

11. <u>False</u>. Only significant (material) investment transactions are evaluated individually.

12. <u>True</u>. Significant transactions should be evaluated for disclosure implications, particularly those at or near year-end.

13. <u>True</u>. Contracts and agreements typically result in attorneys' fees represented by invoices. The auditor is interested in this type of information because of the potential for detecting related party transactions.

14. <u>False</u>. Immaterial transactions, in the aggregate, are not typically a concern to the auditor.

4. Activities (10 Gradable Items)

1. <u>B)</u>.
2. <u>C)</u>.
3. <u>A)</u>.
4. <u>B)</u>.
5. <u>D)</u>.
6. <u>C)</u>.
7. <u>B)</u>.
8. <u>B)</u>.
9. <u>A)</u>.
10. <u>D)</u>.

5. Related Parties (10 Gradable Items)

1. B).
2. F).
3. D).
4. C).
5. A).
6. A).
7. C).
8. B).
9. F).
10. D).

6. Communication (5 Gradable Items; For grading instructions, please refer to page 11.)

To: Supervisor
From: CPA
Subject: Evaluation of reasonableness of estimates

The audit of estimates requires the auditor to evaluate the reasonableness of the client's representations. The evaluation concentrates on key factors and assumptions that are significant to the estimate, sensitive to variations, inconsistent with historical patterns, and subjective and susceptible to misstatement and bias. The auditor normally should also consider the entity's experience in making past estimates; the auditor's experience in the industry; any changes that may cause factors different from those previously considered to become significant; and in some cases, the possible need to obtain written representations from management regarding the key factors and assumptions. When evaluating an estimate, the auditor should understand how management developed it and then use one or more of three approaches to test it. The auditor may review and test the process used by management. A second approach is to develop an independent estimate to corroborate management's estimate by using other key factors or alternative assumptions. A third approach is to review events or transactions occurring after the date of the balance sheet but prior to the completion of field work that are important in identifying and evaluating the reasonableness of accounting estimates, key factors, or assumptions. Indeed the subsequent event or transaction may minimize or eliminate the need for evaluating the reasonableness of the estimate, key factor, or assumption.

7. Research (6 Gradable Items)

AU Section 390 -- *Consideration of Omitted Procedures after the Report Date*

.01   This section provides guidance on the considerations and procedures to be applied by an auditor who, subsequent to the date of his report on audited financial statements, concludes that one or more auditing procedures considered necessary at the time of the audit in the circumstances then existing were omitted from his audit of the financial statements, but there is no indication that those financial statements are not fairly presented in conformity with generally accepted accounting principles or with another comprehensive basis of accounting. This circumstance should be distinguished from that described in section 561 which applies if an auditor, subsequent to the date of his report on audited financial statements, becomes aware that facts regarding those financial statements may have existed at that date that might have affected his report had he then been aware of them.

.02   Once he has reported on audited financial statements, an auditor has no responsibility to carry out any retrospective review of his work. However, reports and working papers relating to particular engagements may be subjected to post-issuance review in connection with a firm's internal inspection program, peer review, or otherwise, and the omission of a necessary auditing procedure may be disclosed.

.03   A variety of conditions might be encountered in which an auditing procedure considered necessary at the time of the audit in the circumstances then existing has been omitted; therefore, the considerations and procedures described herein necessarily are set forth only in general terms. The period of time during which the auditor considers whether this section applies to the circumstances of a particular engagement and then takes the actions, if any, that are required hereunder may be important. Because of legal implications that may be involved in taking the actions contemplated herein, the auditor would be well advised to consult with his attorney when he encounters the circumstances to which this section may apply, and, with the attorney's advice and assistance, determine an appropriate course of action.

.04   When the auditor concludes that an auditing procedure considered necessary at the time of the audit in the circumstances then existing was omitted from his audit of financial statements, he should assess the importance of the omitted procedure to his present ability to support his previously expressed opinion regarding those financial statements taken as a whole. A review of his working papers, discussion of the circumstances with engagement personnel and others, and a re-evaluation of the overall scope of his audit may be helpful in making this assessment. For example, the results of other procedures that were applied may tend to compensate for the one omitted or make its omission less important. Also, subsequent audits may provide audit evidence in support of the previously expressed opinion.

.05   If the auditor concludes that the omission of a procedure considered necessary at the time of the audit in the circumstances then existing impairs his present ability to support his previously expressed opinion regarding the financial statements taken as a whole, and he believes there are persons currently relying, or likely to rely, on his report, he should promptly undertake to apply the omitted procedure or alternative procedures that would provide a satisfactory basis for his opinion.

.06   When as a result of the subsequent application of the omitted procedure or alternative procedures, the auditor becomes aware that facts regarding the financial statements existed at the date of his report that would have affected that report had he been aware of them, he should be guided by the provisions of section 561.05-.09.

.07   If in the circumstances described in paragraph .05, the auditor is unable to apply the previously omitted procedure or alternative procedures, he should consult his attorney to determine an appropriate course of action concerning his responsibilities to his client, regulatory authorities, if any, having jurisdiction over the client, and persons relying, or likely to rely, on his report.

Scoring Schedule:

	Correct Responses		Gradable Items		Weights		
Tab 3	_____	÷	14	×	20%	=	_____
Tab 4	_____	÷	10	×	20%	=	_____
Tab 5	_____	÷	10	×	20%	=	_____
Tab 6	_____	÷	5	×	30%	=	_____
Tab 7	_____	÷	6	×	10%	=	_____

(Your Score)

Use Gleim's *CPA Review Online* to practice more simulations in a realistic environment.

STUDY UNIT FOUR
INTERNAL CONTROL CONCEPTS AND INFORMATION TECHNOLOGY

(22 pages of outline)

4.1	Definition of Internal Control (AU 319)	133
4.2	Internal Control Components and Considerations	134
4.3	Internal Control for Computer Systems	138
4.4	Understanding Internal Control (AU 319)	150
4.5	Flowcharting	153
4.6	Practice Simulation	173

AU 319, *Consideration of Internal Control in a Financial Statement Audit*, and information technology (IT) topics are extensively tested. The importance of the pervasive use of IT in control systems was emphasized by the issuance of **SAS 94**, *The Effect of Information Technology on the Auditor's Consideration of Internal Control in a Financial Statement Audit*, which amended AU 319. Accordingly, this study unit contains definitions and concepts of great significance for exam preparation. Many of these definitions and concepts were developed in the report of the Committee of Sponsoring Organizations of the Treadway Commission (**the COSO report**) and are reflected in AICPA pronouncements.

Because of the Sarbanes-Oxley Act of 2002, the concepts also are important to companies subject to the Securities Exchange Act of 1934. A public company must include in its annual report an assessment by management of whether internal control over financial reporting is effective. The auditor is required to attest to and report on management's assessment as part of the overall audit.

The general concepts described in this study unit are applied specifically in the transaction processing cycles considered in Study Units 5, 6, and 7. It is important for CPA candidates to master the material in this study unit before continuing.

4.1 DEFINITION OF INTERNAL CONTROL (AU 319)

1. In all audits, the auditor should obtain an understanding of internal control sufficient to plan the audit by performing procedures to understand the design of controls relevant to an audit of financial statements, and to determine whether they have been placed in operation. The understanding includes consideration of how the use of IT and manual procedures affects controls. The second standard of field work (GAAS) states:

   A sufficient understanding of internal control is to be obtained to plan the audit and to determine the nature, timing, and extent of tests to be performed.

2. Internal control is a process -- effected by an entity's board of directors, management, and other personnel -- designed to provide reasonable assurance regarding the achievement of **objectives** related to

   a. Reliability of financial reporting
   b. Effectiveness and efficiency of operations
   c. Compliance with applicable laws and regulations

3. Internal control consists of the following five interrelated components (a useful mnemonic is "Controls stop **CRIME**," with the E representing Environment):

   a. **Control activities** are the policies and procedures that help ensure that management directives are carried out.

   b. **Risk assessment** is the entity's identification and analysis of relevant risks as a basis for their management.

   c. **Information and communication** systems support the identification, capture, and exchange of information in a form and time frame that enable people to carry out their responsibilities.

   d. **Monitoring** is a process that assesses the quality of internal control performance over time.

   e. **Control environment** sets the tone of an organization, influencing the control consciousness of its people. It is the foundation for all other components.

4. The relationship between objectives and the components needed to achieve objectives is direct. Moreover, internal control is relevant to the whole entity (or any operating unit or business function). However, an entity generally has controls relating to objectives that are not relevant to an audit and therefore need not be considered, e.g., an airline's automated controls over flight schedules, controls over compliance with health and safety regulations, or controls over the effectiveness and efficiency of certain management decision-making processes. Furthermore, understanding internal control relevant to each operating unit or business function may not be needed to plan and perform an effective audit.

   a. Controls relevant to an audit ordinarily pertain to objectives related to the preparation of fairly presented financial statements.

   b. Controls relating to operations and compliance may be important, e.g., if they relate to nonfinancial data used by an auditor in analytical procedures or if they relate to compliance with tax laws and other regulations that may have a direct and material effect on the financial statements.

   c. In general, **relevant controls** individually or in combination are those likely to prevent or detect material misstatements in financial statement assertions. Thus, auditors are primarily concerned not with whether a control belongs in a given control component but with whether it affects assertions.

5. Controls over **safeguarding of assets** against unauthorized acquisition, use, or disposition may include those relating to financial reporting and operations objectives. However, the auditor's consideration is usually limited to controls relevant to the reliability of financial reporting, such as a lockbox system or controls that limit access to the data and programs that process cash payments.

6. Stop and review! You have completed the outline for this subunit. Study multiple-choice questions 1 through 4 beginning on page 155.

4.2 INTERNAL CONTROL COMPONENTS AND CONSIDERATIONS

1. **Control Environment**. The following factors are included in this component:

   a. **Integrity and ethical values**. Standards should be effectively communicated, e.g., by management example. Management should also remove incentives and temptations for dishonest or unethical acts.

   b. **Commitment to competence**. Management must consider the competence levels for particular jobs.

   c. **Board of directors or audit committee participation**. The independence, experience, and stature of their members are among the factors that affect the entity's control consciousness.

    d. **Management's philosophy and operating style**.

       1) Relate to management's approach to taking and monitoring business risks

       2) Include management's attitudes and actions towards financial reporting

       3) Encompass management's attitudes towards information processing and accounting functions and personnel

    e. **Organizational structure**. Key areas of authority and responsibility and appropriate lines of reporting should be considered.

    f. **Assignment of authority and responsibility**. This factor concerns how authority over and responsibility for operating activities are assigned and how reporting relationships and authorization hierarchies are established.

    g. **Human resource policies and practices** relate to hiring, orientation, training, evaluation, counseling, promoting, compensating, and remedial actions. Training policies should communicate roles and responsibilities and expected levels of performance and behavior.

2. **Risk Assessment**. Relevant risks include events and circumstances that may adversely affect an entity's ability to initiate, record, process, and report financial data consistent with financial statement assertions. The following factors affecting risk should be considered:

    a. **Changes in operating environment**. A shift in the regulatory or operating environment may require reconsideration of risks.

    b. **New personnel**. New employees may have a different focus on control issues.

    c. **New or revamped information systems**. Significant and rapid changes in information systems can affect control risk, but IT is important to the risk assessment process because it provides timely information for identifying and managing risks.

    d. **Rapid growth**. Expansion can strain controls and increase risk.

    e. **New technology**. Integrating new technology into production or information processes may change risk.

    f. **New business models, products, or activities**. New business areas may change risk.

    g. **Corporate restructurings**. Staffing changes can cause changes in risk.

    h. **Expanded foreign operations**. Expansion to foreign markets may result in changes in risk.

    i. **New accounting pronouncements**. Adoption or changes of principles may affect risk.

3. **Control Activities**. The policies and procedures helping to ensure that actions are taken to address risks to achievement of objectives are control activities. Whether automated or manual, they have various objectives and are applied at various levels.

    a. **Performance reviews** include reviews of actual performance versus budgets and prior performance.

    b. **Information processing** requires checks of accuracy, completeness, and authorization of transactions. These controls include application controls and general controls.

    c. **Physical controls** involve the security of assets and records and periodic counts and reconciliations.

    d. **Segregation of duties** involves the separation of the functions of authorization, record keeping, and asset custody so as to minimize the opportunities for a person to be able to perpetrate and conceal errors or fraud in the normal course of his/her duties.

4.   **Information and Communication**. An information system consists of physical and hardware elements (infrastructure), people, software, data, and manual and automated procedures and often uses IT extensively.

   a.   For financial reporting, the information system (including the accounting system) encompasses automated and manual procedures and records used to initiate, record, process, and report transactions, events, and conditions and to maintain accountability for assets, liabilities, and equity.

      1)   **Initiation** may be automatic through programmed methods. **Recording** includes identification and capture of relevant information. **Processing** involves edit and validation, calculation, measurement, valuation, summarization, and reconciliation by manual or automated means. **Reporting** of financial and other information for use in, for example, the monitoring function, may be in a print or electronic medium.

   b.   An **information system**

      1)   Identifies and records all valid transactions
      2)   Describes transactions sufficiently for proper classification
      3)   Measures transactions
      4)   Determines the proper reporting period for transactions
      5)   Presents transactions and related disclosures properly

   c.   **Communication** includes providing an understanding to employees about their roles and responsibilities. Communication may be through policy, manuals, financial reporting manuals, and memoranda, and by electronic and oral means or by management actions.

5.   **Monitoring**. Monitoring entails the timely assessment of internal control and the taking of corrective action so that it operates as intended and is modified for changes in conditions. Establishing and maintaining internal control is management's responsibility.

   a.   This monitoring process involves

      1)   Ongoing activities built into normal recurring actions such as supervision
      2)   The actions of internal auditors
      3)   Consideration of communications from external parties

   b.   Monitoring information may be produced by the information system. Hence, the auditor must obtain sufficient knowledge about major monitoring activities, including the source of related information, and how monitoring is used to initiate corrective action.

6.   **General Considerations**

   a.   Specific control components should be considered in view of the size of the entity; organizational and ownership characteristics; the nature of the business; diversity and complexity of operations; nature and complexity of control systems, including the use of service organizations; and legal and regulatory concerns.

7.   **Limitations of Internal Control**

   a.   **Reasonable assurance**. Because of its inherent limitations, internal control can be designed and operated to provide only reasonable assurance that control objectives are met.

   b.   **Inherent limitations**

      1)   Human judgment is faulty, and controls may fail because of simple error or mistake. For example, design changes for an automated order entry system may be faulty because the designers did not understand the system or because programmers did not correctly code the design changes. Errors may also arise when automated reports are misinterpreted by users.

2) Manual or automated controls can be circumvented by collusion.

3) Management may inappropriately override internal control.

4) Custom, culture, the corporate governance system, and an effective control environment are not absolute deterrents to fraud. For example, if the nature of management incentives increases the risk of material misstatements, the effectiveness of controls may be diminished.

c. **Costs should not exceed the benefits of control**. Although this relationship is a primary design criterion for internal control, the precise measurement of costs and benefits is not feasible.

8. **Effect of IT on Internal Control**

a. The use of IT may affect any of the components of internal control and the entity's operating units or business functions. Thus, IT may be part of discrete systems, for example, an accounts receivable system for a business unit or a system that controls factory equipment. However, the use of IT may be in integrated systems that support all financial reporting, operations, and compliance objectives.

b. IT affects the basic ways in which transactions are initiated, recorded, processed, and reported.

1) A **manual system** uses manual procedures and paper records (e.g., for recording sales orders, authorizing credit, preparing shipping documents and invoices, and maintaining receivables records), and controls are also manual (e.g., approvals and reviews, reconciliations, and follow-up of reconciling items).

2) In contrast, **automated procedures** use electronic records to replace paper purchase orders, invoices, shipping documents, and related accounting records. Controls in IT systems combine manual and automated controls (such as those embedded in programs).

a) Manual controls may be independent of IT, use IT information, or simply monitor the functioning of IT and automated controls and handle exceptions.

c. IT should result in greater effectiveness and efficiency of internal control because it

1) Permits consistent application of predefined business rules and the performance of complex calculations in high volume.

2) Improves the quality of information.

3) Permits additional analysis.

4) Improves monitoring of activities and policies and procedures.

5) Lessens the risk that controls will be circumvented.

6) Implements security controls in applications, databases, and operating systems for the purpose of segregating duties.

d. **IT risks** include

1) Reliance on faulty systems or programs.

2) Unauthorized access to data leading to destruction of data, inaccurate recording of transactions, etc.

3) Unauthorized changes in master files, systems, or programs.

4) Failure to make necessary changes in systems or programs.

5) Inappropriate manual intervention.

6) Loss of data.

4

  e. Internal control risks vary with the information system and therefore with the nature and characteristics of IT usage.

    1) For example, when many users have access to a database, ineffective control at one entry point may undermine the security of the database. Thus, if IT personnel or users have greater access than that needed to perform their duties, segregation of duties may be ineffective, and the risk of unauthorized transactions or changes in programs or data affecting the financial statements is increased.

 9. Stop and review! You have completed the outline for this subunit. Study multiple-choice questions 5 through 15 beginning on page 156.

4.3 INTERNAL CONTROL FOR COMPUTER SYSTEMS

 This subunit concerns information technology issues related to the classification of controls, the control environment, and control activities.

 1. **Characteristics of a computer system.** The basic components of a computer are its hardware and software.

  a. **Hardware** includes the following:

    1) A **central processing unit (CPU)**. All computers have at least one CPU that works in conjunction with peripheral devices. The CPU is the main element of a computer system. The major function of the CPU is to retrieve stored instructions and data, decode the instructions, and carry out the instructions in the arithmetic-logic unit (ALU). The use of multiple CPUs in a single computer can be used to reduce processing time. The principal components of the CPU are the arithmetic-logic unit and the control unit.

    2) A **server** is a computer specially configured to support a network by permitting users to share data, peripherals, and programs.

    3) **Workstations and terminals**. Workstations are desktop machines that have enhanced mathematical and graphical abilities. A terminal is online equipment that is a common input device. The terminal includes a keyboard and a monitor that allows display of user input and computer output.

    4) **Input/output (I/O) devices**. Peripheral equipment is used to transfer data in and out of the computer. Examples include pen-based or touch-screen devices, a mouse, scanners, monitors, printers, and voice-recognition devices.

    5) **Physical storage devices** maintain data for later retrieval. Examples include hard disk drives, floppy disk drives, DVDs, magnetic tape drives (an older technology now used mostly for backup), and CD-ROM drives.

    6) **Random access memory (RAM)** is the computer's internal temporary storage area that holds program data during processing.

    7) **Communication devices** allow transmission of information among computers. Examples include front-end processing, multiplexors, modems, routers, and bridges.

    b.   **Software** includes the following:

        1)   An **operating system** is essential software that acts as an interface between application software and the hardware. It manages access to the computer's resources by concurrent applications and, in a network system, concurrent users. DOS, Windows, and Unix are examples.

        2)   **Applications** consist of most other software that runs on the computer other than the operating system and peripheral device drivers. Examples include data entry, query, or report programs that process data. Application software also includes generic software (spreadsheets, word processors, database programs, etc.), as well as custom and packaged programs for payroll, billing, and other accounting purposes.

        3)   **Security software** is discussed in subunit 3.6.

2.   **Computer systems** are varied in structure. Systems may include a large mainframe computer for centralized processing or networks for decentralized (distributed) processing. For example, a **client-server system** divides processing of an application between the user or client machine and a server. This division is dictated by which tasks each is better suited to perform. User interaction is ordinarily restricted to the user interface, data entry, queries, and receipt of reports. The server manages peripheral hardware and controls access to shared databases.

    a.   **Local area networks (LANs)** and **wide area networks (WANs)** are defined by the area over which they provide communications.

    b.   **Intranets and extranets** are defined by who has access. An intranet is a network based on the same technology (connectivity standards and web software) as the Internet, but access is limited to an organization or those with specific authorization. An extranet provides web access for existing customers or specific users rather than the general public. It typically uses the public Internet as its transmission system but requires a password to gain access.

3.   The use of computers has fundamental effects on internal control but not on its objectives or basic philosophy. These effects flow from the characteristics that distinguish computer-based from manual processing.

    a.   **Transaction trails**. A complete trail useful for audit purposes might exist for only a short time or only in computer-readable form. The nature of the trail is often dependent on the transaction processing mode, for example, whether transactions are batched prior to processing or whether they are processed immediately as they happen.

    b.   **Uniform processing of transactions**. Computer processing uniformly subjects like transactions to the same processing instructions and thus virtually eliminates clerical error, but programming errors (or other similar systematic errors in either the hardware or software) will result in all like transactions being processed incorrectly when they are processed under the same conditions.

    c.   **Segregation of functions**. Many control procedures once performed by separate individuals may be concentrated in computer systems. Hence, an individual who has access to the computer may perform incompatible functions. As a result, other controls may be necessary to achieve the control objectives ordinarily accomplished by segregation of functions.

    d.   **Potential for errors and fraud**. The potential for individuals, including those performing control procedures, to gain unauthorized access to data, to alter data without visible evidence, or to gain access (direct or indirect) to assets may be greater in computer systems. Decreased human involvement in handling transactions can reduce the potential for observing errors and fraud. Errors or fraud in the design or changing of application programs can remain undetected for a long time.

e. **Potential for increased management supervision.** Computer systems offer management many analytical tools for review and supervision of operations. These additional controls may enhance internal control. For example, traditional comparisons of actual and budgeted operating ratios and reconciliations of accounts are often available for review on a more timely basis. Additionally, some programmed applications provide statistics regarding computer operations that may be used to monitor actual processing.

f. **Initiation or subsequent execution of transactions by computer.** Certain transactions may be automatically initiated or certain procedures required to execute a transaction may be automatically performed by a computer system. The authorization of these transactions or procedures may not be documented in the same way as those in a manual system, and management's authorization may be implicit in its acceptance of the design of the system.

g. **Dependence of other controls on controls over computer processing.** Computer processing may produce reports and other output that are used in performing manual control procedures. The effectiveness of these controls can be dependent on the effectiveness of controls over the completeness and accuracy of computer processing. For example, the effectiveness of a manual review of a computer-produced exception listing is dependent on the controls over the production of the listing.

4. **Classification of Controls.** "The two broad groupings of information systems control activities are general controls and application controls. **General controls** commonly include controls over data center and network operations; systems software acquisition and maintenance; access security; and application system acquisition, development, and maintenance." "**Application controls** apply to the processing of individual applications. These controls help ensure that transactions occurred, are authorized, and are completely and accurately recorded and processed" (AU 319).

a. **General controls** apply to mainframe, miniframe, and end-user environments. They support the application controls by helping to ensure the proper functioning of information systems. Thus, they should be tested prior to evaluation of application controls. If general controls are ineffective, it is unlikely that the auditor will be able to rely on the application controls and assess control risk below the maximum level. General controls may be categorized as follows:

1) Controls over operations to ensure efficient and effective operations of the computer activity. They include

a) Proper segregation of the duties and responsibilities within the computer environment. The responsibilities of systems analysts, programmers, operators, file librarians, and the control group should be performed by different individuals, and proper supervision should be provided.

b) Consideration of disaster recovery and protection for the loss of data. These controls include

i) A disaster plan, for example, one that provides for an alternative processing site, a "hot site" for immediate recovery, or a "cold site" for less immediate recovery

ii) File backup and reconstruction procedures

iii) Use of file labels, both external and internal (machine-readable header and trailer labels)

2) The procedures for acquiring, developing, testing, documenting, and approving systems or programs and changes thereto, including implementation of new releases of packaged software

      3) Controls over access to equipment, data files, and programs, including system software that restricts access to or monitors the use of system utilities

         a) Access controls provide assurance that only authorized individuals use the system and that usage is for authorized purposes. Such controls include physical safeguards of equipment, proper library security, and passwords.

      4) Other data and procedural controls affecting overall computer operations (e.g., supervision and follow-up)

  b. **Application controls** relate to specific tasks performed by the system. They should provide reasonable assurance that the initiating, recording, processing, and reporting of data are properly performed. Application controls relate to individual computerized accounting applications, for example, programmed edit controls for verifying customers' account numbers and credit limits. Application controls may be further classified as follows:

      1) **Input controls** provide reasonable assurance that data received for processing have been properly authorized, converted into machine-sensible form, and identified, and that data (including data transmitted over communication lines) have not been lost, added to, suppressed, duplicated, or otherwise improperly changed. Input controls also relate to rejection, correction, and resubmission of data initially incorrect.

      2) **Processing controls** provide reasonable assurance that processing has been performed as intended for the particular application, i.e., that all transactions are processed as authorized, that no authorized transactions are omitted, and that no unauthorized transactions are added.

      3) **Output controls** assure the accuracy of the processing result (such as account listings, reports, magnetic files, invoices, or disbursement checks) and the receipt of output by authorized personnel only.

5. **The Control Environment.** Two factors in the control environment specifically relate to computer processing.

  a. **Organizational structure.** The computer processing department should

      1) Be treated as a service department
      2) Be independent of users
      3) Report to senior-level management
      4) Not have an asset custody function
      5) Have no transactional authority

  b. **Assigning authority and responsibility** for computer processing

      1) **Segregation of duties.** This control is vital because a segregation of functions (authorization, recording, and access to assets) may not be feasible in a computer environment. For example, a computer may print checks, record disbursements, and generate information for reconciling the account balance, which are activities customarily segregated in a manual system.

         a) **Database/network/web administrators.** They are responsible for management, supervision, and oversight of computing facilities.

         b) **Data administrators.** They coordinate activities within the data administration department.

         c) **Systems analysts.** They analyze and design computer information systems. These design specifications will guide the preparation of specific programs by computer programmers. Systems analysts should not have access to computer equipment, production programs, data files, and processing controls.

10

d) **Programmers**. They design, write, test, and document the specific programs developed by the analysts. Programmers as well as analysts may be able to modify programs, data files, and controls and should therefore have no access to computer equipment, software, or files.

e) **Computer (console) operators**. They are responsible for the actual processing of data. They load data and operate the equipment. Console operators should not be assigned programming duties or responsibility for systems design and should have no opportunity to make changes in programs and systems as they operate the equipment. Ideally, computer operators should not have programming knowledge or access to documentation not strictly necessary for their work.

f) **Data conversion (key) operators**. They perform the tasks of data preparation and transmission, for example, conversion of source data to magnetic disk or tape and entry of transactions.

g) **Librarians**. They should maintain control over and accountability for documentation, programs, and data files. Librarians should have no access to equipment.

h) **Data control group**. They must be independent of systems development, programming, and operations. They receive user input, log it, transfer it to the computer center, monitor processing, review error messages, compare control totals, distribute output, and determine whether error corrections have been made by users.

6. **Risk assessment** for computer processing includes consideration of

a. **Backup and recovery policies and procedures**. A computer center should have a reconstruction and recovery plan that will allow it to regenerate important programs and database files. The center should create backup (duplicate) copies of data files, databases, programs, and documentation; store backup copies off-site; and plan for auxiliary processing on alternate systems or at another site.

1) **Batch processing**. Magnetic tape and magnetic disks are used for batch processing.

a) **Checkpoint procedures** involve capturing all the values of data and program indicators at specified points and storing these values in another file. If processing is interrupted, it can be resumed at the last checkpoint rather than at the beginning of the run.

2) **Online processing**. Magnetic disks are used for online processing.

a) **Rollback and recovery**. This procedure involves the dumping (copying) of the master file's contents and associated data structures onto a backup file. In the event of a faulty run, the dump is used together with the transaction log or file to reconstruct the master file.

3) **Database management systems** use magnetic disks for online processing.

a) **Database systems** require a more elaborate backup procedure. Normally, recovery and restart procedures must provide for continued operations during reconstruction of lost information.

b) **Dual logging** involves the use of two transaction logs written simultaneously on two separate storage media.

c) The **before-image/after-image** technique captures the data values before and after transaction processing and stores them in files. These files can be used to recreate the database in the event of data loss or corruption.

4) **Fully protected systems** have generator or battery backup to prevent data destruction and downtime from electrical power disturbances. Loss of electrical power or voltage fluctuations need not disturb the vulnerable contents of main memory if a noninterruptible system is in place.

5) **Fault-tolerant computer systems** have additional hardware and software as well as a backup power supply. A fault-tolerant computer has additional chips and disk storage. These systems are used for critical applications that involve high volume online transaction processing.

6) **Hot-site and cold-site backup facilities**. A hot site is a service bureau. It is a fully operational processing facility that is immediately available. A cold site is a shell facility where the user can quickly install computer equipment.

b. **Virus protection**. A computer virus is a software program that infects another program or a system's primary storage (main memory) by altering its logic. Infection often results in the destruction of data. Once infected, a software program can spread the virus to other software programs. Obtaining software through a shareware network or by downloading from untrustworthy sources is a typical cause of infection. Propagation of viruses through e-mail attachments is also common.

1) To protect against viruses, three types of controls should be implemented.

a) **Preventive controls** include establishing a formal security policy, using only clean and certified copies of software, not using shareware software, checking new software with antivirus software, restricting access, and educating users.

b) **Detective controls** include making file size and date/time stamp comparisons.

c) **Corrective controls** include ensuring that clean backup is maintained and having a documented plan for recovery from a virus.

c. **Worms** make copies of themselves with either benign or malignant intent. They usually exist as separate, independent programs and use operating system services as their means of replication. Threats from worms arise when an organization connects its computers to an open network. Controls are similar to those for viruses.

d. A **Trojan horse** is a computer program that appears to have a legitimate function but performs some destructive or illicit function after it begins to run.

e. **Internet security**. Connection to the Internet presents security issues.

1) The most important control is to install an organization-wide network security policy. This policy should promote the following objectives:

a) **Availability**. The intended and authorized users should be able to access data to meet organizational goals.

b) **Security, privacy, and confidentiality**. The secrecy of information that could adversely affect the organization if revealed to the public or competitors should be assured.

c) **Integrity**. Unauthorized or accidental modification of data should be prevented.

2) **User account management** involves installing a system to ensure that

a) New accounts are added correctly and assigned only to authorized users.

b) Old and unused accounts are removed promptly.

c) **Passwords** are changed periodically, and employees are educated on how to choose a password that cannot be easily guessed. For example, a password of at least six diverse characters that do not form a word should be chosen.

12

3) A **firewall** separates an internal from an external network (e.g., the Internet) and prevents passage of specific types of traffic. It identifies names, Internet Protocol (IP) addresses, applications, etc., and compares them with programmed access rules. A firewall may have any of the following features:

    a) A **packet filtering system** examines each incoming IP packet.

    b) A **proxy server** maintains copies of web pages to be accessed by specified users. Outsiders are directed there, and more important information is not available from this access point.

    c) An **application gateway** limits traffic to specific applications.

    d) A **circuit-level gateway** is a filter that connects an internal device, e.g., a network printer, with an outside TCP/IP port. It can identify a valid TCP session.

        i) TCP/IP is a suite of communications protocols used to connect computers to the Internet. It is also built into network operating systems.

    e) **Stateful inspection** stores information about the state of a transmission and uses it as background for evaluating messages from similar sources.

4) Firewall systems ordinarily produce reports on organization-wide Internet use, exception reports for unusual usage patterns, and system penetration-attempt reports. These reports are very helpful to the auditor as a method of continuous monitoring, or logging, of the system.

    a) Firewalls do not provide adequate protection against computer viruses. Thus, an organization should include one or more of the virus controls listed in its network security policy.

7. **Control activities** for computer processing include policies and procedures that management has established to provide reasonable assurance that specific entity objectives will be achieved.

    a. **Hardware controls**. Automated equipment (hardware) controls are built into the equipment by the manufacturer to detect and control errors arising from the use of the equipment itself.

        1) **Boundary (storage) protection** protects programs or data from interference (unauthorized reading or writing) caused by activity related to other programs or data stored on the same medium. Primary storage locations in the CPU may be protected by features built into the hardware, but boundary protection for disk storage is effected through programming.

        2) **Diagnostic routines** check for hardware problems. If built into the equipment, they permit the system itself to give notice of imminent failure.

        3) **Dual read**. An input device may read an input twice for comparison.

        4) **Duplicate circuitry**. Dual circuits in the arithmetic-logic unit of the CPU permit calculations to be performed twice and compared.

        5) An **echo check** provides for a peripheral device to return (echo) a signal sent by the CPU. For example, the CPU sends a signal to the printer, and the printer, just prior to printing, sends a signal back to the CPU verifying that the proper print position has been activated.

        6) **File protection**. Most data storage media have a ring, tab, or notch that can be used to prevent or allow writing on the media.

13

7) A **parity check** adds the bits in a character or message and checks the sum to determine if it is odd or even, depending on whether the computer has odd or even parity. This check verifies that all data have been transferred without loss. For example, if the computer has even parity, a bit will be added to a binary coded character or message that contains an odd number of bits. No bit is added if a character or message in binary form has an even number of bits.

8) **Preventive maintenance**. Regular servicing avoids equipment failure.

b. **Digital signatures** represent a form of encryption technology used by businesses to authenticate documents. A plaintext document is sent with an encrypted portion of the same document over the Internet. If the plaintext document is tampered with, the two will not match.

c. **Access controls**. Access controls prevent improper use or manipulation of data files and programs. They ensure that only those persons with a bona fide purpose and authorization have access to data processing.

1) Physical security controls protect against unauthorized access to information.

    a) **Keypad devices** allow entry of a password or code to gain entry to a physical location or computer system.

    b) **Card reader controls** relate to reading information from a magnetic strip on a credit, debit, or other access card. Controls can then be applied to information about the cardholder contained on the magnetic strip.

2) **Passwords and ID numbers**. The use of passwords and identification numbers (for example, a PIN used for an ATM) is an effective control in an online system to prevent unauthorized access to computer files. Lists of authorized persons are maintained in the computer. The entry of passwords or identification numbers; a prearranged set of personal questions; and the use of badges, magnetic cards, or optically scanned cards may be combined to avoid unauthorized access.

    a) A **security card** may be used with a computer so that users must sign on with an ID and a password. The card controls the machine's operating system and records access data (date, time, duration, etc.).

    b) Proper **user authentication** by means of a password requires password-generating procedures to assure that valid passwords are known only by the proper individuals. Thus, a password should not be displayed when entered at a keyboard.

    c) Password security may also be compromised in other ways. For example, because log-on procedures may be cumbersome and tedious, users often store log-on sequences on their personal computers and invoke them when they want to use mainframe or network facilities. A risk of this practice is that anyone with access to the personal computers could log on to the system.

    d) To be more effective, passwords should consist of random letters, symbols, and numbers and should not contain words or phrases.

3) **File attributes** can be assigned to control access to and the use of files. Typical attributes include read/write, read only, archive, and hidden.

14

4) **Device authorization table**. This control restricts access to those physical devices that should logically need access. For example, because it is illogical for anyone to access the accounts receivable file from a manufacturing terminal, the device authorization table will deny access even when a valid password is used.

a) Such tests are often called **compatibility tests** because they ascertain whether a code number is compatible with the use to be made of the information. Thus, a user may be authorized to enter only certain kinds of data, have access only to certain information, have access but not updating authority, or use the system only at certain times. The lists or tables of authorized users or devices are sometimes called **access control matrices**.

5) **System access log**. This log records all uses and attempted uses of the system. The date and time, codes used, mode of access, data involved, and interventions by operators are recorded.

6) **Encryption**. Encoding data before transmission over communications lines makes it more difficult for someone with access to the transmission to understand or modify its contents.

a) Encryption technology converts data into a code. Unauthorized users may still be able to access the data but, without the encryption key, they will be unable to decode the information.

b) Encryption software uses a fixed algorithm to manipulate plain text and an encryption key to introduce variation. The machine instructions necessary to encrypt and decrypt data can constitute a 20%-to-30% increase in system overhead.

c) Encryption technology may be either hardware- or software-based. Two major types of encryption software exist.

i) **Public Key Infrastructure (PKI)**. Public/private key, or asymmetric, encryption requires two keys. The public key for encrypting messages is widely known, but the private key for decrypting messages is kept secret by the recipient.

- RSA, named for its developers (Rivest, Shamir, and Adelman), is the most commonly used public/private method.

ii) **Secret-key**, or symmetric, encryption requires only a single key for each pair of entities that want to send each other encrypted messages.

- Data Encryption Standard (DES), a shared private-key method developed by the U.S. government, has been the most prevalent secret-key method.

- The Advanced Encryption Standard (AES) is a recently adopted cryptographic algorithm for use by U.S. Government organizations to protect sensitive information. The AES will be widely used on a voluntary basis by organizations, institutions, and individuals as well as by the U.S. Government.

d) A Web server (a computer that delivers Web pages to the Internet) should be secure; that is, it should support a security protocol that encrypts messages to protect transactions from third party detection or tampering.

7) **Callback**. This feature requires the remote user to call the computer, give identification, hang up, and wait for the computer to call an authorized number. This control ensures acceptance of data only from authorized modems. However, a call-forwarding device may thwart this control by transferring access from an authorized to an unauthorized number.

8) **Controlled disposal of documents**. One method of enforcing access restrictions is to destroy data when they are no longer in use. Thus, paper documents may be shredded and magnetic media may be erased.

9) **Biometric technologies**. These are automated methods of establishing an individual's identity using physiological or behavioral traits. These characteristics include fingerprints, retina patterns, hand geometry, signature dynamics, speech, and keystroke dynamics.

10) **Automatic log-off** (disconnection) of inactive data terminals may prevent the viewing of sensitive data on an unattended data terminal.

11) **Utility software restrictions**. Utility software may have privileged access and therefore be able to bypass normal security measures. Performance monitors, tape and disk management systems, job schedulers, online editors, and report management systems are examples of utility software. Management can limit the use of privileged software to security personnel and establish audit trails to document its use. The purpose is to gain assurance that its uses are necessary and authorized.

12) **Security personnel**. An organization may hire security specialists. For example, developing an information security policy for the organization, commenting on security controls in new applications, and monitoring and investigating unsuccessful access attempts are appropriate duties of the information security officer.

d. **Input controls**. Input controls are critical to auditors because they represent the most prevalent type of control. Input system activities are the most error prone and are often the targets of fraud.

1) **Edit checks** are computer-programmed controls. They include

   a) **Error listing**. Editing (validation) of data should produce a cumulative automated error listing that includes not only errors found in the current processing run but also uncorrected errors from earlier runs. Each error should be identified and described, and the date and time of detection should be given.

   b) **Field check**. These tests of the characters in a field verify that they are of an appropriate type for that field. For example, the field for a Social Security number should not contain alphabetic characters.

   c) **Financial total**. This control total summarizes dollar amounts in a group of records for subsequent comparison after processing.

   d) **Hash total**. A control total without a defined meaning, such as the total of employee numbers or invoice numbers, is used to verify the completeness of data. Thus, the hash total for the employee listing by the personnel department could be compared with the total generated during the payroll run.

   e) **Reasonableness, limit, and range checks**. These tests are based upon known limits for given information. For example, the hours worked per week is not likely to be greater than 45.

f) **Preformatting**. To avoid data entry errors in online systems, a screen prompting approach may be used that is the equivalent of the preprinted forms routinely employed as source documents. The dialogue approach, for example, presents a series of questions to the operator. The preformatted screen approach involves the display of a set of boxes for entry of specified data items. The format may even be in the form of a copy of a transaction document.

g) **Record count**. This count gives a control total of the number of records processed during the operation of a program.

h) **Check digit**. A self-checking digit system is used to detect incorrect or nonexistent identification numbers. The digit is generated by applying an algorithm to the ID number. During the input process, the check digit is recomputed by applying the same algorithm to the code actually entered.

i) **Sequence check**. This edit check is used to determine that records are in proper order. For example, a payroll input file is likely to be sorted into Social Security number order. A sequence check can then be performed to verify record order.

j) **Sign check**. These tests assure that data in a field have the appropriate arithmetic sign. For example, hours worked in a payroll record should always be a positive number.

k) **Validity check**. The validity of identification numbers or transaction codes is tested by comparison with items already known to be correct or authorized. For example, Social Security numbers on payroll input records can be compared with Social Security numbers authorized by the personnel department.

2) An **echo check** is an input control over transmission on communication lines. Data are sent back to the user's terminal for comparison with the transmitted data. Echo checks also verify that a hardware device is performance ready.

3) **Completeness checks** of transmission of data determine whether all necessary information has been sent. The software notifies the sender if something is omitted.

4) **Closed-loop verification** is the display of the amounts entered and is an input control that permits visual verification of the accuracy of the input by the operator.

e. **Processing controls**

1) Some input controls are also processing controls, e.g., limit, reasonableness, and sign tests.

2) Other tests of the logic of processing are posting, cross-footing, and zero-balance checks.

a) Comparing the contents of a record before and after updating is a **posting check**.

b) **Cross-footing** compares an amount to the sum of its components.

c) A **zero-balance check** adds the positive and negative amounts posted. The result should be zero.

3) **Internal header and trailer labels** ensure that incorrect files are not processed. A matching test should make certain an updated transaction is matched with the appropriate master file. This check is useful if the computer operator has failed to compare the external label of a file with the program specifications.

4) **Run-to-run control totals** (e.g., record counts or certain critical amounts) should be generated and checked at designated points during processing.

a) **Proof account activity listing**. In an online system, the change in a file for the day can be compared with source information.

      5)   **End-of-file procedures** should be available to avoid errors such as prematurely closing the transaction file when the end of the current master file is reached. The transaction file may contain new records to be added to the master file.

      6)   **Concurrency controls** manage situations in which two or more programs attempt to use a file or database at the same time.

      7)   An **audit trail** should be created through the use of input-output control logs, error listings, transaction logs, and transaction listings.

f.   **Output controls**

      1)   The data control group supervises output control.

           a)   Error listings and exception reports are received directly from the system by the control group, which should make any necessary inquiries and send the errors to users for correction and resubmission.

           b)   The console log should be reviewed for unusual interruptions, interventions, or other activity.

g.   **Program acquisition, development, and documentation controls**

      1)   **Documentation** supports and explains data processing applications, including systems development. It is helpful to operators and other users, control personnel, new employees, and auditors as well as to programmers and analysts who are maintaining the old or developing a new system. The auditor considers documentation to be an important internal control activity. Documentation should be secured in a library, and access should be carefully controlled. It should be subject to uniform standards regarding flowcharting techniques, coding methods, and modification procedures (including proper authorization).

           a)   **System documentation** includes narrative descriptions, flowcharts, the system definition used for development, input and output forms, file and record layouts, controls, program change authorizations, and backup procedures.

           b)   **Program documentation** contains descriptions, program flowcharts and decision tables, program listings or source code, test data, input and output forms, detailed file and record layouts (describing the data structure, e.g., field lengths and types), change requests, operator instructions, and controls.

           c)   **Operating documentation** (computer run manual) provides information about setup, necessary files and devices, input procedures, console messages and responsive operator actions, run times, recovery procedures, disposal of output, and control.

           d)   **User documentation** describes the system and procedures for data entry, error checking and correction, and formats and uses of reports.

      2)   Systems and program **acquisition and development controls**

           a)   Effective systems acquisition or development requires participation by senior management.

           b)   Standards for systems design and programming should be established. These standards represent user needs and system requirements determined during the systems analysis.

c) Changes in the computer system should be subject to strict controls **(change controls)**. For example, a written request for an application program change should be made by a user department and authorized by a designated manager or committee.

    i) The program should then be redesigned using a working copy, not the version currently in use. Also, the systems documentation must be revised.

    ii) Changes in the program should be tested by the user, the internal auditor, and a systems employee who was not involved in designing the change.

    iii) Approval of the documented change and the results of testing should be given by a systems manager. The change and test results may then be accepted by the user.

d) New and modified programs should be tested with incorrect or incomplete data as well as typical data to determine whether controls have been properly implemented in the program.

e) Unauthorized program changes can be detected by code comparison. The version in use should be periodically compared with a copy controlled by the auditors. Software can be used to perform this procedure.

8. Stop and review! You have completed the outline for this subunit. Study multiple-choice questions 16 through 46 beginning on page 159.

4.4 UNDERSTANDING INTERNAL CONTROL (AU 319)

1. "In all audits, the auditor should obtain an understanding of each of the five components of internal control sufficient to plan the audit. A sufficient understanding is obtained by performing procedures to understand the design of controls relevant to an audit of financial statements and determining whether they have been placed in operation."

    a. However, the auditor is not obligated to search for deficiencies in internal control, although (s)he must communicate any reportable conditions noted.

    b. Internal control knowledge should be used to

        1) Identify types of potential misstatements
        2) Consider factors that affect the risk of material misstatements
        3) Design tests of controls if appropriate (see Study Unit 8)
        4) Design substantive tests

    c. Placed in operation at a moment in time differs from operating effectiveness over a period of time.

        1) **Placed in operation** means the entity is using the control.

            a) Knowledge about whether the controls have been placed in operation must be gained as part of the understanding of internal control necessary to plan the audit.

        2) **Operating effectiveness** is concerned with how and by whom the control (manual or automated) was applied and the consistency of application.

            a) Knowledge about operating effectiveness need not be obtained as part of the understanding of internal control. The evaluation of the effectiveness of internal control is the process of assessing control risk. This subject is covered in Study Unit 8, Tests of Controls.

d. The understanding may raise doubts about auditability.

1) Concerns about management integrity may lead to the conclusion that the risk of misrepresentations precludes an audit.

2) The nature and extent of records may indicate that sufficient competent evidence is unlikely to be available.

e. When making a judgment about the understanding of internal control necessary to plan the audit, the auditor considers

1) Knowledge obtained from other sources, such as information from previous audits and the auditor's understanding of the industry and market

2) The risk that misstatements may occur

3) The factors influencing the design of tests of controls and substantive tests

4) Assessments of inherent risk

5) Judgments about materiality

6) The complexity and sophistication of operations and systems, including the extent of reliance on manual or automated controls

f. The judgment about the understanding needed to plan the audit also should address **IT risks** that may result in misstatements.

1) The more complex and sophisticated the operations and systems, the greater the understanding the auditor requires of the control components.

2) **Specialized skills** may be required to determine the effect of IT on the audit, to understand IT controls, and to design and perform tests of IT controls and substantive tests. These skills may be obtained from an audit staff member or an outside professional.

a) Whether an outside professional should be used depends on such factors as the complexity of systems and IT controls and their use in the business, the extent of data sharing among systems, implementation of new systems or changes in old ones, the involvement in electronic commerce, use of emerging technologies, and audit evidence available only electronically.

b) An outside professional may make inquiries of the entity's IT personnel, inspect documentation, observe operation of controls, and test IT controls.

c) The auditor must have sufficient IT expertise to communicate audit objectives, to evaluate whether the IT professional's procedures will meet those objectives, and to evaluate the results.

g. The auditor should understand the **information system relevant to financial reporting**, that is, the classes of significant transactions; the automated and manual procedures applied from the occurrence of transactions to their inclusion in the statements; the related accounting records, supporting information, and specific accounts; how the system captures other significant events and conditions; and the financial reporting process, including significant accounting estimates and disclosures.

1) Thus, the auditor must understand not only the manual procedures but also the IT systems, programs, and controls in the financial reporting process.

20.

h. **Documentation of the understanding** is required by GAAS. Its form and extent are influenced by the nature and complexity of the controls. For example, a complex information system that electronically initiates, records, processes, and reports a large volume of transactions requires extensive documentation. Accordingly, flowcharts, questionnaires, or decision tables may be appropriate for a complex information system, but a memorandum may suffice when little or no use is made of IT or few transactions are processed. In general, the more complex the controls and the more extensive the audit procedures, the more extensive the documentation.

1) **Systems (document) flowcharts** are diagrams of the client's system that track the flow of documents and processing. Advantages are that they provide a visual representation of the system and are flexible in construction. Flowcharts are introduced in subunit E and are illustrated in Study Units 5, 6, and 7.

2) **Questionnaires** consist of a series of interrelated questions about internal control policies and procedures. The questions are typically phrased so that a "Yes" indicates a control strength and a "No" indicates a potential weakness. An area is provided next to the responses for the auditor to explain the responses or cross-reference the answer with other working papers. An advantage of the questionnaire is that it helps identify control concerns and prevents the auditor from overlooking important control considerations.

3) A **narrative memorandum** is a written description of the process and flow of documents and of the control points. The advantage is flexibility. Internal control can be described; however, following the flow from the narrative may be difficult for a complex system.

4) A **decision table** identifies the contingencies considered in the description of a problem and the appropriate actions to be taken relative to those contingencies. Decision tables are logic diagrams presented in matrix form. Unlike flowcharts, they do not present the sequence of the actions described.

2. Stop and review! You have completed the outline for this subunit. Study multiple-choice questions 47 through 54 beginning on page 167.

4.5 FLOWCHARTING

1.   Flowcharting is a useful tool for systems development as well as for understanding internal control. A flowchart is a pictorial diagram of the definition, analysis, or solution of a problem in which symbols are used to represent operations, data flow, documents, records, etc.

   a.   The processing is presented sequentially from the point of origin to final output distribution.

      1)   Processing usually flows from top to bottom and from left to right in the flowchart.

   b.   Areas of responsibility (e.g., data processing or purchasing) are usually depicted in vertical columns or areas.

   c.   A **system flowchart** provides an overall view of the inputs, processes, and outputs of a system.

   d.   A **program flowchart** represents the specific steps in a program and the order in which they will be carried out.

      1)   Macro- and microflowcharts describe a program in less or greater detail, respectively.

   e.   A **document flowchart** depicts the flow of documents through an entity.

2.   An entity's organizational structure is depicted by an **organizational chart**. An example chart is presented on the next page and illustrates a typical division of duties and responsibilities to achieve internal control objectives. This division is by "functional responsibility." The chart begins with the board of directors and includes the following:

Sales Department	Controller	Industrial Relations
Sales order	Cost accounting	Personnel
Customer relations	Timekeeping	
	General ledger	Manufacturing
Treasurer	Payroll	Shipping
Mail room	Billing	Receiving
Credit manager	Inventory control	Inventory (warehouse)
Cash receipts	Accounts payable	Purchasing agent
Cash disbursements	Accounts receivable	Shops

   a.   A sales-receivables manual system flowchart, which diagrams a sales and receivables process, is on page 182. Later in Study Unit 5, we present a cash receipts manual system flowchart. A purchases-payables-cash disbursements manual system flowchart is presented in Study Unit 6 and a payroll manual system flowchart in Study Unit 7. Refer to the organizational chart on page 180 as appropriate to determine how these systems fit in the organizational structure.

3.   Why the flowcharts? They are used to understand, evaluate, and document client internal control. Many CPA questions address flowcharting itself. Other CPA questions address specific controls, audit procedures, weaknesses, etc., related to or a part of internal control.

72

4. Commonly used document flowchart symbols include

Starting or ending point or point of interruption

Input or output of a document or report

Computer operation or group of operations

Manual processing operation, e.g., prepare document

Generalized symbol for input or output used when the medium is not specified

Magnetic tape used for input or output

Magnetic disk used for storage

Decision symbol indicating a branch in the flow

Connection between points on the same page

Connection between two pages of the flowchart

Storage (file) that is not immediately accessible by computer

Flow direction of data or processing

Display on a video terminal

Manual input into a terminal or other online device

Adding machine tape (batch control)

5. Stop and review! You have completed the outline for this subunit. Study multiple-choice questions 55 through 58 beginning on page 170.

QUESTIONS

4.1 Definition of Internal Control (AU 319)

1. The primary objective of procedures performed to obtain an understanding of internal control is to provide an auditor with

   A. Knowledge necessary for audit planning.

   B. Evidential matter to use in assessing inherent risk.

   C. A basis for modifying tests of controls.

   D. An evaluation of the consistency of application of management's policies.

Answer (A) is correct. *(CPA, adapted)*
   REQUIRED: The objective of procedures performed to obtain an understanding of internal control.
   DISCUSSION: The second standard of field work states, "A sufficient understanding of internal control is to be obtained to plan the audit and to determine the nature, timing, and extent of tests to be performed."
   Answer (B) is incorrect because inherent risk is independent of internal control. Answer (C) is incorrect because the understanding is obtained to plan all aspects of the audit, not merely tests of controls. Answer (D) is incorrect because evaluating the consistency of application of management's policies is a test of controls.

2. An auditor uses the knowledge provided by the understanding of internal control and the assessed level of control risk primarily to

   A. Determine whether procedures and records concerning the safeguarding of assets are reliable.

   B. Ascertain whether the opportunities to allow any person to both perpetrate and conceal fraud are minimized.

   C. Modify the initial assessments of inherent risk and preliminary judgments about materiality levels.

   D. Determine the nature, timing, and extent of substantive tests for financial statement assertions.

Answer (D) is correct. *(CPA, adapted)*
   REQUIRED: The auditor's purpose in understanding internal control and assessing control risk.
   DISCUSSION: The second standard of field work states, "A sufficient understanding of internal control is to be obtained to plan the audit and to determine the nature, timing, and extent of tests to be performed." Substantive tests are intended to detect material misstatements in the financial statements.
   Answer (A) is incorrect because knowledge about operating effectiveness need not be obtained as part of the understanding of internal control. Answer (B) is incorrect because knowledge about operating effectiveness need not be obtained as part of the understanding of internal control. Answer (C) is incorrect because inherent risk and materiality are independent of internal control.

3. In an audit of financial statements, an auditor's primary consideration regarding an internal control is whether the control

   A. Reflects management's philosophy and operating style.

   B. Affects management's financial statement assertions.

   C. Provides adequate safeguards over access to assets.

   D. Enhances management's decision-making processes.

Answer (B) is correct. *(CPA, adapted)*
   REQUIRED: The primary consideration regarding an internal control.
   DISCUSSION: An auditor's primary concern is whether a specific control affects financial statement assertions. Much of the audit work required to form an opinion consists of gathering evidence about the assertions in the financial statements. These assertions are management representations embodied in the components of the financial statements (AU 326). Controls relevant to an audit are individually or in combination likely to prevent or detect material misstatements in financial statement assertions (AU 319).
   Answer (A) is incorrect because management's philosophy and operating style is just one factor in one component (the control environment) of internal control. Answer (C) is incorrect because restricting access to assets is only one of many physical controls, which constitute one category of one component (control activities) of internal control. Answer (D) is incorrect because many controls concerning management's decision-making process are not relevant to an audit.

4. An auditor would most likely be concerned with controls that provide reasonable assurance about the

A. Efficiency of management's decision-making process.

B. Appropriate prices the entity should charge for its products.

C. Decision to make expenditures for certain advertising activities.

D. Entity's ability to initiate, record, process, and report financial data.

Answer (D) is correct. *(CPA, adapted)*
   REQUIRED: The controls about which an auditor is most likely to be concerned.
   DISCUSSION: AU 319 states, "The information system relevant to financial reporting objectives, which includes the accounting system, consists of the procedures, whether automated or manual, and records established to initiate, record, process, and report entity transactions (as well as events and conditions) and to maintain accountability for the related assets, liabilities, and equity."
   Answer (A) is incorrect because the efficiency of certain management decision-making processes is not likely to be relevant to a financial statement audit. Answer (B) is incorrect because product pricing is not likely to be relevant to a financial statement audit. Answer (C) is incorrect because decisions about advertising are not likely to be relevant to a financial statement audit.

4.2 Internal Control Components and Considerations

5. Which of the following is a management control method that most likely could improve management's ability to supervise company activities effectively?

A. Monitoring compliance with internal control requirements imposed by regulatory bodies.

B. Limiting direct access to assets by physical segregation and protective devices.

C. Establishing budgets and forecasts to identify variances from expectations.

D. Supporting employees with the resources necessary to discharge their responsibilities.

Answer (C) is correct. *(CPA, adapted)*
   REQUIRED: The management control method most likely to improve supervision.
   DISCUSSION: The control activities component of internal control includes performance reviews. Performance reviews involve comparison of actual performance with budgets, forecasts, or prior performance. Identifying variances alerts management to the need for investigative and corrective actions. Such actions are necessary for effective supervision.
   Answer (A) is incorrect because management's supervisory responsibilities extend well beyond internal control requirements imposed by regulatory bodies. Answer (B) is incorrect because access control pertains to the physical controls component. Answer (D) is incorrect because supporting employees concerns the human resource policies and practices factor of the control environment component.

6. Which of the following are considered control environment factors?

	Detection Risk	Commitment to Competence
A.	Yes	Yes
B.	Yes	No
C.	No	Yes
D.	No	No

Answer (C) is correct. *(CPA, adapted)*
   REQUIRED: The factor(s), if any, considered part of the control environment.
   DISCUSSION: Commitment to competence is a control environment factor. It relates to the knowledge and skills needed to do the tasks included in a job and management's consideration of required competence levels.
   Answer (A) is incorrect because commitment to competence but not detection risk (a component of audit risk) is a control environment factor. Answer (B) is incorrect because commitment to competence but not detection risk (a component of audit risk) is a control environment factor. Answer (D) is incorrect because commitment to competence but not detection risk (a component of audit risk) is a control environment factor.

7. Which of the following is not a component of internal control?

A. Control risk.

B. Monitoring.

C. Information and communication.

D. The control environment.

Answer (A) is correct. *(CPA, adapted)*
   REQUIRED: The item not a component of internal control.
   DISCUSSION: Control risk is one of the elements in the audit risk model. It is the risk that a material misstatement that could occur in an assertion will not be prevented or detected on a timely basis by the entity's internal control. Hence, control risk is a function of the effectiveness of internal control, not a component thereof.

8. Which of the following factors are included in an entity's control environment?

	Audit Committee Participation	Integrity and Ethical Values	Organizational Structure
A.	Yes	Yes	No
B.	Yes	No	Yes
C.	No	Yes	Yes
D.	Yes	Yes	Yes

Answer (D) is correct. *(CPA, adapted)*
REQUIRED: The factors in a control environment.
DISCUSSION: The control environment is the foundation for all other control components. It provides discipline and structure, sets the tone of the organization, and influences the control consciousness of employees. It includes board of directors or audit committee participation, integrity and ethical values, or organizational structure, management's philosophy and operating style, assignment of authority and responsibility, human resource policies and practices, and commitment to competence.

9. Which of the following components of internal control includes development and use of training policies that communicate prospective roles and responsibilities to employees?

A. Monitoring.

B. Control environment.

C. Risk assessment.

D. Control activities.

Answer (B) is correct. *(Publisher)*
REQUIRED: The component of internal control that includes the development of training policies.
DISCUSSION: The control environment sets the tone of an organization. It includes human resource policies and practices relative to hiring, orientation, training, evaluating, counseling, promoting, compensating, and remedial actions.
Answer (A) is incorrect because monitoring assesses the quality of internal control over time. Answer (C) is incorrect because risk assessment is the identification and analysis of relevant risks. Answer (D) is incorrect because control activities are the policies and procedures that help ensure that management directives are carried out. They include performance reviews, information processing, physical controls, and segregation of duties.

10. Proper segregation of duties reduces the opportunities to allow persons to be in positions both to

A. Journalize entries and prepare financial statements.

B. Record cash receipts and cash disbursements.

C. Establish internal control and authorize transactions.

D. Perpetrate and conceal errors and fraudulent acts.

Answer (D) is correct. *(CPA, adapted)*
REQUIRED: The effects of the segregation of duties.
DISCUSSION: Segregation of duties is a category of the control activities component of internal control. Segregating responsibilities for authorization, recording, and asset custody reduces an employee's opportunity to perpetrate an error or fraud and subsequently conceal it in the normal course of his/her duties.
Answer (A) is incorrect because accountants typically journalize entries and prepare financial statements. Answer (B) is incorrect because accountants may record both cash receipts and cash disbursements as long as they do not have custody of cash. Answer (C) is incorrect because management establishes internal control and ultimately has the responsibility to authorize transactions.

11. Proper segregation of functional responsibilities to achieve effective internal control calls for separation of the functions of

A. Authorization, execution, and payment.

B. Authorization, recording, and custody.

C. Custody, execution, and reporting.

D. Authorization, payment, and recording.

Answer (B) is correct. *(CPA, adapted)*
REQUIRED: The duties separated to achieve effective internal control.
DISCUSSION: One person should not be responsible for all phases of a transaction, i.e., for authorization of transactions, recording of transactions, and custodianship of the related assets. These duties should be performed by separate individuals to reduce the opportunities to allow any person to be in a position both to perpetrate and conceal errors or fraud in the normal course of his/her duties (AU 319).
Answer (A) is incorrect because payment is a form of execution (operational responsibility). Answer (C) is incorrect because custody of assets and execution of related transactions are often not segregated. Answer (D) is incorrect because payments must be recorded when made.

12. Internal control can provide only reasonable assurance of achieving an entity's control objectives. The likelihood of achieving those objectives is affected by which limitation inherent to internal control?

- A. The auditor's primary responsibility is the detection of fraud.
- B. The board of directors is active and independent.
- C. The cost of internal control should not exceed its benefits.
- D. Management monitors internal control.

Answer (C) is correct.   *(Publisher)*
REQUIRED: The true statement about the limitation of internal control.
DISCUSSION: AU 319 states, "Internal control is influenced by the quantitative and qualitative estimates and judgments made by management in evaluating the cost-benefit relationship of an entity's internal control. The cost of an entity's internal control should not exceed the benefits that are expected to be derived. Although the cost-benefit relationship is a primary criterion that should be considered in designing internal control, the precise measurement of costs and benefits usually is not possible."
Answer (A) is incorrect because the auditor's responsibility is "to plan and perform the audit to obtain reasonable assurance about whether the financial statements are free of material misstatement, whether caused by error or fraud" (AU 110). Answer (B) is incorrect because an active and independent board strengthens the control environment. Answer (D) is incorrect because monitoring strengthens internal control.

13. Which of the following most likely would not be considered an inherent limitation of the potential effectiveness of an entity's internal control?

- A. Incompatible duties.
- B. Management override.
- C. Faulty judgment.
- D. Collusion among employees.

Answer (A) is correct.   *(CPA, adapted)*
REQUIRED: The item not considered an inherent limitation of internal control.
DISCUSSION: AU 319 discusses the inherent limitations of internal control. The performance of incompatible duties, however, is a failure to assign different people the functions of authorization, recording, and asset custody, not an inevitable limitation of internal control. Segregation of duties is a category of control activities.
Answer (B) is incorrect because management establishes internal controls. Thus, it can override those controls. Answer (C) is incorrect because human judgment in decision making may be faulty. Answer (D) is incorrect because controls, whether manual or automated, may be circumvented by collusion among two or more people.

14. An independent auditor is concerned with controls designed to safeguard assets that are relevant to the reliability of financial reporting. Adequate safeguards over access to and use of assets means protection from

- A. Any management decision that would unprofitably use company resources.
- B. Only those losses arising from fraud.
- C. Losses such as those arising from setting a product price too low and subsequently realizing operating losses from the product's sale.
- D. Losses arising from access by unauthorized persons.

Answer (D) is correct.   *(Publisher)*
REQUIRED: The meaning of adequate safeguards over access to and use of assets.
DISCUSSION: A management objective implicit in internal control is that access to assets be permitted only in accordance with management's authorization. However, elimination of access is not feasible because access to assets is necessary in normal business operations. The extent of access is determined by the nature of the assets and their susceptibility to loss through errors and fraud. Authorization of access entails limitations on both physical access and indirect access.
Answer (A) is incorrect because no audit can protect against every decision that uses resources unprofitably. Answer (B) is incorrect because the organization should be protected against losses from both errors and fraud. Answer (C) is incorrect because internal controls concerning the efficiency and effectiveness of certain management decision-making processes, such as those related to product pricing, ordinarily do not relate to a financial statement audit.

15. An entity has many employees that access a database. The database contains sensitive information concerning the customers of the entity and has numerous access points. Access controls prevent employees from entry to those areas of the database for which they have no authorization. All salespersons have certain access permission to customer information. Which of the following is a true statement regarding the nature of the controls and risks?

    A. Because there is no segregation of duties among the salespersons, risk of collusion is increased.

    B. Only one salesperson should be allowed access permission.

    C. Sales department personnel should not have access to any part of the database.

    D. A salesperson's access to customer information should extend only to what is necessary to perform his/her duties.

Answer (D) is correct. *(Publisher)*
    REQUIRED: The true statement concerning information technology controls and risks.
    DISCUSSION: Internal control risks vary with the nature and characteristics of IT usage. Employees should be allowed access to systems only to the extent necessary for them to carry out their responsibilities.
    Answer (A) is incorrect because salespersons carry out the same responsibilities. Thus, no segregation of responsibilities is expected. Answer (B) is incorrect because all salespersons may need access to fulfill their responsibilities. Answer (C) is incorrect because certain information from the database, for example, a customer's credit standing, may need to be accessed.

4.3 Internal Control for Computer Systems

16. Which of the following characteristics distinguishes computer processing from manual processing?

    A. Computer processing virtually eliminates the occurrence of computational error normally associated with manual processing.

    B. Errors or fraud in computer processing will be detected soon after their occurrence.

    C. The potential for systematic error is ordinarily greater in manual processing than in computerized processing.

    D. Most computer systems are designed so that transaction trails useful for audit purposes do not exist.

Answer (A) is correct. *(CPA, adapted)*
    REQUIRED: The feature that distinguishes computer processing from manual processing.
    DISCUSSION: Computer processing uniformly subjects like transactions to the same processing instructions. A computer program defines the processing steps to accomplish a task. Once the program is written and tested appropriately, it will perform the task repetitively and without error. However, if the program contains an error, all transactions will be processed incorrectly.
    Answer (B) is incorrect because, when an error does occur, for example, in input, it may not be discovered on a timely basis. Ordinarily, much less human intervention occurs once the transaction is processed. Answer (C) is incorrect because systematic (repetitive) errors will occur in computerized processing if an error exists in the program. Answer (D) is incorrect because adequately designed systems maintain transaction, console, and error logs that create useful audit trails.

17. Which of the following is considered a component of a local area network (LAN)?

    A. Program flowchart.

    B. Loop verification.

    C. Transmission media.

    D. Input routine.

Answer (C) is correct. *(CPA, adapted)*
    REQUIRED: The component of a LAN.
    DISCUSSION: A LAN connects a variety of computing resources for data sharing and communications purposes within a localized area such as an office complex. LANs contain computers for processing and data storage, transmission media (communications channels) to transmit information, communications electronics for message switching and routing, and various software to accomplish the network tasks.
    Answer (A) is incorrect because a program flowchart is a medium to document the understanding of internal control. Answer (B) is incorrect because a closed loop verification is an application control. Answer (D) is incorrect because an input routine captures the data as the initial phase of a transaction cycle.

18. When online, real-time processing is used, the grandfather-father-son updating backup concept is relatively difficult to implement because

A. Locating information points on files is an extremely time-consuming task.

B. Magnetic fields and other environmental factors cause off-site storage to be impracticable.

C. Information must be dumped in the form of hard copy if it is to be reviewed before used in updating.

D. The process of updating old records is destructive.

Answer (D) is correct. *(CPA, adapted)*
REQUIRED: The reason the grandfather-father-son approach is difficult to use with online, realtime processing.
DISCUSSION: When records are updated in an online real-time system, new data are customarily written over the old data. Thus, updating is destructive. Although sequential files can also be written over, the usual file processing procedures result in keeping the old master file and transaction data files intact and writing a new updated master file. The retention of several generations of files is feasible.
Answer (A) is incorrect because locating data in an online real-time system is relatively fast. Answer (B) is incorrect because storing magnetically encoded data off-site (e.g., in a safe deposit box) is feasible. Answer (C) is incorrect because data may be dumped to tape or disk and need not be transferred to hard copy.

19. Which of the following, when used in multiples in a single computer, can help a corporation reduce its processing time?

A. Input/output devices.

B. Physical storage devices.

C. Central processing units.

D. Communication devices.

Answer (C) is correct. *(Publisher)*
REQUIRED: The component that reduces a corporation's processing time.
DISCUSSION: The central processing unit (CPU) is the main component of a computer system. It retrieves stored instructions and data, decodes instructions, and carries out the instructions. The use of multiple CPUs in a single computer can be used to reduce processing time.
Answer (A) is incorrect because input/output devices are used to transfer data in and out of the computer and they do not reduce processing time. Answer (B) is incorrect because physical storage devices maintain data for later retrieval. They do not directly affect processing time. Answer (D) is incorrect because communication devices allow transmission of information among computers.

20. An auditor anticipates assessing control risk below the maximum level in an automated environment. Under these circumstances, on which of the following activities would the auditor initially focus?

A. Programmed controls.

B. Application controls.

C. Output controls.

D. General controls.

Answer (D) is correct. *(CPA, adapted)*
REQUIRED: The initial concern when the auditor anticipates assessing control risk at less than the maximum in a computer environment.
DISCUSSION: Assessing control risk below the maximum level involves identifying specific controls that are likely to prevent or detect material misstatements in specific assertions, performing tests of controls, and reaching a conclusion on the assessed level of control risk. "The two broad groupings of information systems control activities are general controls and application controls. General controls commonly include controls over data center and network operations; systems software acquisition and maintenance; access security; and application system acquisition, development, and maintenance." "Application controls apply to the processing of individual applications. These controls help ensure that transactions occurred, are authorized, and are completely and accurately recorded and processed" (AU 319). General controls apply to mainframe, miniframe, and end-user environments. They support the application controls by helping to ensure the proper functioning of information systems. Thus, they should be tested prior to evaluation of application controls.
Answer (A) is incorrect because programmed activities relate to application controls, which should be tested for effectiveness once the general controls prove to be effective. Answer (B) is incorrect because general controls are tested before application controls. Answer (C) is incorrect because output controls are application controls, which are tested after general controls.

21. Kelly Corporation needs an internal communication network that provides high speed communication among nodes. Which of the following is appropriate for Kelly?

A. Wide area network (WAN).

B. Local area network (LAN).

C. File server.

D. Value-added network (VAN).

Answer (B) is correct. *(Publisher)*
REQUIRED: The network that provides the fastest communication.
DISCUSSION: Local area networks are privately owned networks that provide high speed communication among nodes. They are usually restricted to limited areas, such as a particular floor of an office building.
Answer (A) is incorrect because wide area networks provide lower speed communication because they are spread out among larger areas than LANs. Answer (C) is incorrect because a file server is a piece of hardware which acts as an access control mechanism in a local area network. Answer (D) is incorrect because a VAN is a privately owned telecommunications carrier that provides capacity to outside users. It does not provide high-speed communication among nodes.

22. A client is concerned that a power outage or disaster could impair the computer hardware's ability to function as designed. The client desires off-site backup hardware facilities that are fully configured and ready to operate within several hours. The client most likely should consider a

A. Cold site.

B. Cool site.

C. Warm site.

D. Hot site.

Answer (D) is correct. *(CPA, adapted)*
REQUIRED: The type of off-site backup hardware facility that is an available, fully operational processing facility.
DISCUSSION: A hot site is a service bureau that is a fully operational processing facility and is promptly available in the case of a power outage or disaster.
Answer (A) is incorrect because a cold site is a shell facility suitable for quick installation of computer equipment. Installing computer equipment would take more time in a cold site than in a hot site. Answer (B) is incorrect because it is a fabricated term that does not describe actual facilities. Answer (C) is incorrect because it is a fabricated term that does not describe actual facilities.

23. The use of message encryption software

A. Guarantees the secrecy of data.

B. Requires manual distribution of keys.

C. Increases system overhead.

D. Reduces the need for periodic password changes.

Answer (C) is correct. *(CIA, adapted)*
REQUIRED: The effect of message encryption software.
DISCUSSION: Encryption software uses a fixed algorithm to manipulate plain text and an encryption key (a set of random data bits used as a starting point for the application of the algorithm) to introduce variation. The machine instructions necessary to encrypt and decrypt data constitute system overhead. As a result, processing speed may be slowed.
Answer (A) is incorrect because no encryption approach absolutely guarantees the secrecy of data. Answer (B) is incorrect because keys may also be distributed electronically via secure key transporters. Answer (D) is incorrect because periodic password changes are needed. Passwords are the typical means of validating users' access to unencrypted data.

24. Which of the following is an example of how specific internal controls in a database environment may differ from controls in a nondatabase environment?

A. Controls should exist to ensure that users have access to and can update only the data elements that they have been authorized to access.

B. Controls over data sharing by diverse users within an entity should be the same for every user.

C. The employee who manages the computer hardware should also develop and debug the computer programs.

D. Controls can provide assurance that all processed transactions are authorized, but cannot verify that all authorized transactions are processed.

Answer (A) is correct. *(CPA, adapted)*
REQUIRED: The difference between internal controls in a database environment and a nondatabase environment.
DISCUSSION: A database is a series of related files combined to eliminate unnecessary redundancy of data elements. The data dictionary states not only the meaning of a data element but also its ownership (who is responsible for its maintenance), size, format, and usage. Moreover, it states what persons, programs, reports, and functions use the data element. Thus, the issue of ownership (maintenance or updating) of, and control over access to, data elements common to many applications arises only in a database environment.
Answer (B) is incorrect because certain data should not be accessed by all individuals, and those who do have access may have different levels of authority. Thus, the controls should vary among users regardless of whether the environment includes a database. Answer (C) is incorrect because these duties should be segregated. Answer (D) is incorrect because controls can play multiple roles in a database or nondatabase environment by comparing authorized transactions with processed transactions and reporting anomalies.

25. Which of the following strategies would a CPA most likely consider in auditing an entity that processes most of its financial data only in electronic form, such as a paperless system?

    A. Continuous monitoring and analysis of transaction processing with an embedded audit module.

    B. Increased reliance on internal control activities that emphasize the segregation of duties.

    C. Verification of encrypted digital certificates used to monitor the authorization of transactions.

    D. Extensive testing of firewall boundaries that restrict the recording of outside network traffic.

Answer (A) is correct. *(CPA, adapted)*
REQUIRED: The audit strategy for an electronic environment.
DISCUSSION: An audit module embedded in the client's software routinely selects and abstracts certain transactions. They may be tagged and traced through the information system. An alternative is recording in an audit log, that is, in a file accessible only by the auditor.
Answer (B) is incorrect because the same level of segregation of duties as in a manual system is not feasible in highly sophisticated computer systems. Answer (C) is incorrect because encrypted digital signatures help ensure the authenticity of the sender of information, but verifying them is a less pervasive and significant procedure than continuous monitoring of transactions. Answer (D) is incorrect because firewalls exclude unauthorized activity from entering a system; however, such activity would be independent of the internal processing of financial information.

26. Which of the following procedures would an entity most likely include in its computer disaster recovery plan?

    A. Develop an auxiliary power supply to provide uninterrupted electricity.

    B. Store duplicate copies of critical files in a location away from the computer center.

    C. Maintain a listing of all entity passwords with the network manager.

    D. Translate data for storage purposes with a cryptographic secret code.

Answer (B) is correct. *(CPA, adapted)*
REQUIRED: The most likely procedure to follow in a computer disaster recovery plan.
DISCUSSION: Off-site storage of duplicate copies of critical files protects them from a fire or other disaster at the computing facility. The procedure is part of an overall disaster recovery plan.
Answer (A) is incorrect because the use of an uninterruptible power supply assures continued processing rather than recovery from a disaster. Answer (C) is incorrect because maintaining a safeguarded copy of passwords protects against loss of passwords by personnel. Answer (D) is incorrect because encrypting stored data files protects them from unauthorized use.

27. Robert is the data administrator (DA) for Big Time Corporation. An example of Robert's responsibilities as the DA is to monitor

    A. The database industry.

    B. The performance of the database.

    C. Database security.

    D. Backup of the system.

Answer (A) is correct. *(Publisher)*
REQUIRED: The responsibilities of a data administrator.
DISCUSSION: The DA handles administrative issues that arise regarding the database. The DA acts as an advocate by suggesting new applications and standards. One of the DA's responsibilities is to monitor the database industry for new developments. In contrast, the database administrator (DBA) deals with the technical aspects of the database.
Answer (B) is incorrect because the performance of the database is an example of the database administrator's responsibilities. Answer (C) is incorrect because database security is an example of the database administrator's responsibilities. Answer (D) is incorrect because backup of the system is an example of the database administrator's responsibilities.

28. An entity has the following invoices in a batch:

Invoice Number	Product	Quantity	Unit Price
201	F10	150	$ 5.00
202	G15	200	$10.00
203	H20	250	$25.00
204	K35	300	$30.00

Which of the following numbers represents the record count?

    A. 1

    B. 4

    C. 810

    D. 900

Answer (B) is correct. *(CPA, adapted)*
REQUIRED: The record count.
DISCUSSION: Input controls in batch computer systems are used to determine that no data are lost or added to the batch. Depending on the sophistication of a particular system, control may be accomplished by using record counts, batch totals, or hash totals. A record count establishes the number of source documents and reconciles it to the number of output records. The total number of invoices processed is an example of a record count. In this case, the record count is 4.
Answer (A) is incorrect because 1 is the number of batches. Answer (C) is incorrect because 810 is a hash total of the invoice numbers. Answer (D) is incorrect because 900 is the total quantity of items.

29. An entity has the following invoices in a batch:

Invoice Number	Product	Quantity	Unit Price
201	F10	150	$ 5.00
202	G15	200	$10.00
203	H20	250	$25.00
204	K35	300	$30.00

Which of the following most likely represents a hash total?

A. FGHK80

B. 4

C. 204

D. 810

Answer (D) is correct. *(CPA, adapted)*
REQUIRED: The example of a hash total.
DISCUSSION: Input controls in batch computer systems are used to determine that no data are lost or added to the batch. Depending on the sophistication of a particular system, control may be accomplished by using record counts, batch totals, or hash totals. The hash total is a control total without a defined meaning, such as the total of employee numbers or invoice numbers, that is used to verify the completeness of data. The hash total of the invoice numbers is 810.
Answer (A) is incorrect because a hash total is ordinarily the sum of a numeric field. Answer (B) is incorrect because 4 is a record count. Answer (C) is incorrect because 204 is an invoice number.

30. A customer intended to order 100 units of product Z96014, but incorrectly ordered nonexistent product Z96015. Which of the following controls most likely would detect this error?

A. Check digit verification.

B. Record count.

C. Hash total.

D. Redundant data check.

Answer (A) is correct. *(CPA, adapted)*
REQUIRED: The control that would detect a nonexistent product number.
DISCUSSION: Check digit verification is used to identify incorrect identification numbers. The digit is generated by applying an algorithm to the ID number. During input, the check digit is recomputed by applying the same algorithm to the entered ID number.
Answer (B) is incorrect because a record count is a control total of the number of transactions in a batch. Answer (C) is incorrect because a hash total is a control total that is the sum of a field without a defined meaning. Answer (D) is incorrect because a redundant data check searches for duplicate information in a database.

31. Which of the following is an example of a validity check?

A. The computer ensures that a numerical amount in a record does not exceed some predetermined amount.

B. As the computer corrects errors and data are successfully resubmitted to the system, the causes of the errors are printed out.

C. The computer flags any transmission for which the control field value did not match that of an existing file record.

D. After data for a transaction are entered, the computer sends certain data back to the terminal for comparison with data originally sent.

Answer (C) is correct. *(CPA, adapted)*
REQUIRED: The example of a validity check.
DISCUSSION: Validity checks test identification numbers or transaction codes for validity by comparison with items already known to be correct or authorized. For example, a validity check may identify a transmission for which the control field value did not match a preexisting record in a file.
Answer (A) is incorrect because a limit check determines whether a numerical amount exceeds a predetermined amount. Answer (B) is incorrect because an error log or error listing identifies errors that were previously detected and subsequently corrected. Answer (D) is incorrect because a closed-loop verification sends certain data back to the terminal for comparison with data originally sent by the operator.

32. Which of the following is a network node that is used to improve network traffic and to set up a boundary that prevents traffic from one segment from crossing over to another?

A. Router.

B. Gateway.

C. Firewall.

D. Heuristic.

Answer (C) is correct. *(CPA, adapted)*
REQUIRED: The network node that improves traffic and establishes boundaries.
DISCUSSION: A firewall separates an internal from an external network (e.g., the Internet) and prevents passage of specific types of traffic. It identifies names, Internet Protocol (IP) addresses, applications, etc., and compares them with programmed access rules.
Answer (A) is incorrect because a router directs and forwards network traffic. Answer (B) is incorrect because a gateway limits traffic but does not improve network traffic. Answer (D) is incorrect because a heuristic is an exploratory problem-solving technique that uses self-education methods to improve performance.

33. Which of the following controls most likely could prevent computer personnel from modifying programs to bypass programmed controls?

A. Periodic management review of computer utilization reports and systems documentation.

B. Segregation of duties for computer programming and computer operations.

C. Participation of user department personnel in designing and approving new systems.

D. Physical security of computer facilities in limiting access to computer equipment.

Answer (B) is correct. *(CPA, adapted)*
REQUIRED: The control necessary to prevent computer personnel from modifying programs to bypass controls.
DISCUSSION: Programmers and analysts can modify programs, data files, and controls, so they should have no access to programs used to process transactions. Segregation of programming and operations is necessary to prevent unauthorized modifications of programs.
Answer (A) is incorrect because, although periodic management review is appropriate, reports and systems documentation will not prevent or detect unauthorized modifications. Answer (C) is incorrect because user participation relates to new systems, not modification of existing systems. Answer (D) is incorrect because programmers may have access through data communications. Thus, physical security is not sufficient to prevent unauthorized modifications.

34. For control purposes, which of the following should be organizationally segregated from the computer operations function?

A. Data conversion.

B. Surveillance of CRT messages.

C. Systems development.

D. Minor maintenance according to a schedule.

Answer (C) is correct. *(CPA, adapted)*
REQUIRED: The activity that should be segregated from computer operations.
DISCUSSION: Systems analysts survey the existing system, analyze the organization's information requirements, and design new computer systems to meet those needs. These design specifications will guide the preparation of specific programs by computer programmers. The console operator should not be assigned programming duties, much less responsibility for systems design, and thus not have the opportunity to make changes in programs and systems as (s)he operates the equipment.
Answer (A) is incorrect because data conversion may be assigned to computer operations. Answer (B) is incorrect because surveillance of CRT messages may be assigned to computer operations. Answer (D) is incorrect because minor maintenance according to a schedule may be assigned to computer operations.

35. Able Co. uses an online sales order processing system to process its sales transactions. Able's sales data are electronically sorted and subjected to edit checks. A direct output of the edit checks most likely would be a

A. Report of all missing sales invoices.

B. File of all rejected sales transactions.

C. Printout of all user code numbers and passwords.

D. List of all voided shipping documents.

Answer (B) is correct. *(CPA, adapted)*
REQUIRED: The output of edit checks.
DISCUSSION: Edit checks test transactions prior to processing. Rejected transactions should be recorded in a file for evaluation, correction, and resubmission. Edit checks are applied to the sales transactions to test for completeness, reasonableness, validity, and other related issues prior to acceptance. A report of missing invoices, a printout of all user code numbers and passwords, and a list of all voided shipping documents are unlikely to be direct outputs of the edit routine.

36. One of the major problems in a computer system is that incompatible functions may be performed by the same individual. One compensating control is the use of

A. Echo checks.

B. A check digit system.

C. Computer-generated hash totals.

D. A computer log.

Answer (D) is correct. *(CPA, adapted)*
REQUIRED: The control compensating for inadequate segregation of duties in a computer system.
DISCUSSION: A computer (console) log is a record of computer and software usage usually produced by the operating system. Proper monitoring of the log is a compensating control for the lack of segregation of duties. For instance, the log should list operator interventions.
Answer (A) is incorrect because echo checks are hardware controls used to determine if the correct message was received by an output device. Answer (B) is incorrect because a check digit system is an input control that tests identification numbers. Answer (C) is incorrect because hash totals are control totals used to check for losses or inaccuracies arising during data movement.

37. In the accounting system of Acme Company, the amounts of cash disbursements entered at a computer terminal are transmitted to the computer, which immediately transmits the amounts back to the terminal for display on the terminal screen. This display enables the operator to

    A. Establish the validity of the account number.

    B. Verify the amount was entered accurately.

    C. Verify the authorization of the disbursement.

    D. Prevent the overpayment of the account.

Answer (B) is correct. *(CPA, adapted)*
    REQUIRED: The effect of displaying the amounts entered at a terminal.
    DISCUSSION: The display of the amounts entered is an input control that permits visual verification of the accuracy of the input by the operator. This is termed "closed-loop verification."
    Answer (A) is incorrect because displaying the amounts entered at a terminal does not establish the validity of the account number. Answer (C) is incorrect because displaying the amounts entered at a terminal does not verify the authorization of the disbursement. Answer (D) is incorrect because displaying the amounts entered at a terminal does not prevent the overpayment of the account.

38. Which of the following is the most effective user account management control in preventing the unauthorized use of a computer system?

    A. Management enforces an aggressive password policy that requires passwords to be 10 characters long, to be nonreusable, and to be changed weekly.

    B. An account manager is responsible for authorizing and issuing new accounts.

    C. The passwords and usernames of failed log-in attempts are logged and documented in order to cite attempted infiltration of the system.

    D. Employees are required to renew their accounts semiannually.

Answer (D) is correct. *(Publisher)*
    REQUIRED: The most effective user account management control.
    DISCUSSION: Management's network security policy should include measures to ensure that old and unused accounts are removed promptly. If employees' accounts expire semiannually, reasonable assurance is provided that accounts in use by unauthorized employees do not exist.
    Answer (A) is incorrect because, although passwords should be changed periodically, changing a long, non-reusable password weekly encourages employees to write each new password down in order to remember it, a practice not considered conducive to the control structure. Answer (B) is incorrect because the duties of authorization and control over assets should be separated. Answer (C) is incorrect because, although failed log-in attempts should be logged, it is considered bad practice to record the password of failed log-in attempts. Employees often mistype their passwords, and therefore access to the log by an infiltrator could facilitate breaking into a user's account.

39. An Internet firewall is designed to provide adequate protection against which of the following?

    A. A computer virus.

    B. Unauthenticated logins from outside users.

    C. Insider leaking of confidential information.

    D. A Trojan horse application.

Answer (B) is correct. *(Publisher)*
    REQUIRED: The protection provided by an Internet firewall.
    DISCUSSION: A firewall is a device that separates two networks and prevents passage of specific types of network traffic while maintaining a connection between the networks. Generally, an Internet firewall is designed to protect a system from unauthenticated logins from outside users, although it may provide several other features as well.
    Answer (A) is incorrect because a firewall cannot adequately protect a system against computer viruses. Answer (C) is incorrect because industrial spies need not leak information through the firewall. A telephone or floppy disk are much more common means of sharing confidential information. Answer (D) is incorrect because, like a virus, a firewall cannot adequately protect against a Trojan horse or any other program that can be executed in the system by an internal user.

40. Which of the following passwords would be most difficult to crack?

    A. O?Ca!FlSi

    B. language

    C. 12 HOUSE 24

    D. pass56word

Answer (A) is correct. *(CPA, adapted)*
    REQUIRED: The most effective password design.
    DISCUSSION: To be effective, passwords should consist of random letters, symbols, and numbers and should not contain words or phrases. Accordingly, computer system users should avoid employing words for or in their passwords.

41. Which of the following is a computer program that appears to be legitimate but performs some illicit activity when it is run?

    A. Hoax virus.

    B. Web crawler.

    C. Trojan horse.

    D. Killer application.

Answer (C) is correct. *(CPA, adapted)*
REQUIRED: The apparently legitimate computer program that performs an illicit activity.
DISCUSSION: A Trojan horse is a computer program that appears friendly, for example, a game, but that actually contains an application destructive to the computer system.
Answer (A) is incorrect because a hoax virus is a false notice about the existence of a computer virus. It is usually disseminated through use of distribution lists and is sent by e-mail or via an internal network. Answer (B) is incorrect because a web crawler (a spider or bot) is a computer program created to access and read information on websites. The results are included as entries in the index of a search engine.
Answer (D) is incorrect because a killer application is one that is so useful that it may justify widespread adoption of a new technology.

42. A client communicates sensitive data across the Internet. Which of the following controls would be most effective to prevent the use of the information if it were intercepted by an unauthorized party?

    A. A firewall.

    B. An access log.

    C. Passwords.

    D. Encryption.

Answer (D) is correct. *(Publisher)*
REQUIRED: The most effective control for preventing the use of intercepted information.
DISCUSSION: Encryption technology converts data into a code. Encoding data before transmission over communications lines makes it more difficult for someone with access to the transmission to understand or modify its contents.
Answer (A) is incorrect because a firewall tries to prevent access from specific types of traffic to an internal network. After someone has obtained information from the site, a firewall cannot prevent its use. Answer (B) is incorrect because an access log only records attempted usage of a system. Answer (C) is incorrect because passwords prevent unauthorized users from accessing the system. If information has already been obtained, a password cannot prevent its use.

43. Which of the following is an encryption feature that can be used to authenticate the originator of a document and ensure that the message is intact and has not been tampered with?

    A. Heuristic terminal.

    B. Perimeter switch.

    C. Default settings.

    D. Digital signatures.

Answer (D) is correct. *(CPA, adapted)*
REQUIRED: The encryption feature used to authenticate the originator of a document and ensure that the original message is intact.
DISCUSSION: Businesses and others require that documents sent over the Internet be authentic. To authenticate a document, a company or other user may transmit a complete plaintext document along with an encrypted portion of the same document or another standard text that serves as a digital signature. If the plaintext document is tampered with, the two will not match.
Answer (A) is incorrect because the term "heuristic terminal" is not meaningful in this context. Answer (B) is incorrect because the term "perimeter switch" is not meaningful in this context. Answer (C) is incorrect because, in a computer program, a default setting is a value that a parameter will automatically assume unless specifically overridden.

44. Which of the following is a password security problem?

    A. Users are assigned passwords when accounts are created, but do not change them.

    B. Users have accounts on several systems with different passwords.

    C. Users copy their passwords on note paper, which is kept in their wallets.

    D. Users select passwords that are not listed in any online dictionary.

Answer (A) is correct. *(CPA, adapted)*
REQUIRED: The password technique that poses a security problem.
DISCUSSION: Proper user authentication by means of a password requires password-generating procedures to assure that valid passwords are known only by the proper individuals. If passwords are assigned, users should change passwords frequently so that they are the only persons with access under those identifiers.
Answer (B) is incorrect because no security issue arises when different passwords are used for accounts on different systems. Answer (C) is incorrect because storing a password online would be a greater problem. Answer (D) is incorrect because storing a password online would be a greater problem.

45. A client installed the most sophisticated controls using biometric attributes of employees to gain access to their computer system. This technology most likely replaced which of the following controls?

A. Use of security specialists.

B. Reasonableness tests.

C. Passwords.

D. Virus protection software.

Answer (C) is correct. *(Publisher)*
REQUIRED: The control most likely replaced by biometric technologies.
DISCUSSION: The purpose of passwords is to prevent access by unauthorized users just as the more sophisticated control of employee biometric attributes. The use of passwords is an effective control in an online system to prevent unauthorized access to computer systems. However, biometric technologies are more sophisticated and difficult to compromise.
Answer (A) is incorrect because biometric technologies do not eliminate the need for specialists who evaluate and monitor security needs. Answer (B) is incorrect because checking to see if information is reasonable is related to input controls, not access controls. Answer (D) is incorrect because virus protection software prevents damage to data in a system, not access to a system.

46. An auditor is gaining an understanding of a client's Internet controls. Which of the following would likely be the least effective control?

A. The client requires all users to select passwords that are not easily guessed.

B. The client requires users to share potentially useful downloaded programs from public electronic bulletin boards with only authorized employees.

C. The client uses a proxy server to provide information to external web-page users.

D. The client uses a firewall system that produces reports on Internet usage patterns.

Answer (B) is correct. *(Publisher)*
REQUIRED: The least effective control for Internet security.
DISCUSSION: Sharing programs from public electronic bulletin boards with authorized employees would be a futile control. The programs are available to anyone on the public electronic bulletin board.
Answer (A) is incorrect because passwords can be an effective control against unauthorized access. Answer (C) is incorrect because a proxy server allows only certain information to be provided to external users, thereby preventing unauthorized access. Answer (D) is incorrect because firewalls separate an internal network from an external network. Reports on Internet usage patterns can help in monitoring the effectiveness of the system.

4.4 Understanding Internal Control (AU 319)

47. In obtaining an understanding of controls that are relevant to audit planning, an auditor is required to obtain knowledge about the

A. Design of the controls included in the internal control components.

B. Effectiveness of the controls that have been placed in operation.

C. Consistency with which the controls are currently being applied.

D. Controls related to each principal transaction class and account balance.

Answer (A) is correct. *(CPA, adapted)*
REQUIRED: The knowledge required in gaining an understanding of internal control.
DISCUSSION: "In all audits, the auditor should obtain an understanding of each of the five components of internal control sufficient to plan the audit. A sufficient understanding is obtained by performing procedures to understand the design of controls relevant to an audit of financial statements and determining whether they have been placed in operation" (AU 319).
Answer (B) is incorrect because the issue of the effectiveness of controls is required to be addressed when the auditor assesses control risk. Answer (C) is incorrect because the issue of the consistency of application is required to be addressed when the auditor assesses control risk. Answer (D) is incorrect because audit planning ordinarily does not require understanding every balance and transaction class or every assertion relevant thereto.

48. In obtaining an understanding of internal control in a financial statement audit, an auditor is not obligated to

A. Determine whether the controls have been placed in operation.

B. Perform procedures to understand the design of internal control.

C. Document the understanding of the entity's internal control components.

D. Search for significant deficiencies in the operation of internal control.

Answer (D) is correct.   *(CPA, adapted)*
REQUIRED: The step an auditor need not take in obtaining an understanding of internal control.
DISCUSSION: "In all audits, the auditor should obtain an understanding of each of the five components of internal control sufficient to plan the audit. A sufficient understanding is obtained by performing procedures to understand the design of controls relevant to an audit of financial statements and determining whether they have been placed in operation." In addition, the auditor should document the understanding of the entity's internal control components obtained to plan the audit (AU 319). However, in an audit of financial statements, the auditor is not obligated to search for reportable conditions (AU 325).
Answer (A) is incorrect because the auditor should determine whether the controls are in operation. Answer (B) is incorrect because the auditor should understand the design of controls. Answer (C) is incorrect because the auditor should document the understanding of the controls.

49. As part of understanding internal control, an auditor is not required to

A. Consider factors that affect the risk of material misstatement.

B. Ascertain whether internal controls have been placed in operation.

C. Identify the types of potential misstatements that can occur.

D. Obtain knowledge about the operating effectiveness of internal control.

Answer (D) is correct.   *(CPA, adapted)*
REQUIRED: The step not required in obtaining the understanding of internal control.
DISCUSSION: The understanding is used to identify types of potential misstatements; consider factors affecting the risk of material misstatements; design tests of controls, when applicable; and design substantive tests. The understanding should include not only the design of relevant controls but also whether they have been placed in operation. However, operating effectiveness is required to be addressed only when the auditor assesses control risk.
Answer (A) is incorrect because the auditor should consider factors affecting the risk of material misstatement. Answer (B) is incorrect because the auditor should determine whether controls have been placed in operation. Answer (C) is incorrect because the auditor should determine the types of possible misstatements.

50. In planning an audit of certain accounts, an auditor may conclude that specific procedures used to obtain an understanding of an entity's internal control need not be included because of the auditor's judgments about materiality and assessments of

A. Control risk.

B. Detection risk.

C. Sampling risk.

D. Inherent risk.

Answer (D) is correct.   *(CPA, adapted)*
REQUIRED: The assessed risk that may justify omission of procedures used to obtain the understanding.
DISCUSSION: The nature, timing, and extent of procedures performed to obtain the understanding vary with the size and complexity of the entity, the auditor's prior experience with the entity, the nature of specific controls used by the entity (including its use of IT), the nature and extent of changes in systems and operations, and the entity's documentation of specific controls. "The auditor's assessments of inherent risk and judgments about materiality for various account balances and transaction classes also affect the nature and extent of the procedures performed" (AU 319). Thus, if an account has a low assessed level of inherent risk and the amounts involved are not material, specific procedures for obtaining the understanding might be omitted.
Answer (A) is incorrect because obtaining the understanding precedes or is concurrent with the assessment of control risk. Answer (B) is incorrect because the assessed level of control risk is used to determine the acceptable level of detection risk. Answer (C) is incorrect because sampling risk is controllable by the auditor. The auditor assesses inherent risk and control risk, not detection risk or sampling risk.

51. When obtaining an understanding of an entity's internal controls, an auditor should concentrate on their substance rather than their form because

A. The controls may be operating effectively but may not be documented.

B. Management may establish appropriate controls but not enforce compliance with them.

C. The controls may be so inappropriate that the auditor assesses control risk at the maximum.

D. Management may implement controls whose costs exceed their benefits.

Answer (B) is correct. *(CPA, adapted)*
REQUIRED: The reason an auditor should concentrate on the substance of controls, not their form.
DISCUSSION: The auditor must concentrate on the substance rather than the form of controls because management may establish appropriate controls but not act on them. Whether controls have been placed in operation at a point in time differs from their operating effectiveness over a period of time. Thus, operating effectiveness concerns not merely whether the entity is using controls but also how the controls (manual or automated) are applied, the consistency of their application, and by whom they are applied (AU 319).
Answer (A) is incorrect because an auditor is concerned with the actual operating effectiveness of controls, not with a lack of evidence about form (documentation). Answer (C) is incorrect because, if controls are so inappropriate that the auditor assesses control risk at the maximum, their substance is irrelevant. Answer (D) is incorrect because, when considering internal control in a financial statement audit, the auditor is primarily concerned with the effectiveness of controls, not their cost-benefit relationship.

52. In obtaining an understanding of a manufacturing entity's internal control concerning inventory balances, an auditor most likely would

A. Review the entity's descriptions of inventory policies and procedures.

B. Perform test counts of inventory during the entity's physical count.

C. Analyze inventory turnover statistics to identify slow-moving and obsolete items.

D. Analyze monthly production reports to identify variances and unusual transactions.

Answer (A) is correct. *(CPA, adapted)*
REQUIRED: The step in obtaining an understanding of an entity's internal control concerning inventory balances.
DISCUSSION: The auditor should obtain a sufficient understanding of the internal control components to plan the audit, including knowledge about the design of relevant controls and whether they have been placed in operation. Reviewing the entity's descriptions of inventory policies and procedures helps the auditor understand their design.
Answer (B) is incorrect because performing test counts of inventory is a test of details (a substantive test). Answer (C) is incorrect because analysis of inventory turnover statistics is an analytical procedure performed as a substantive test.
Answer (D) is incorrect because analysis of monthly production reports to identify variances and unusual transactions is an analytical procedure performed as a substantive test.

53. An auditor should obtain sufficient knowledge of an entity's information system relevant to financial reporting to understand the

A. Safeguards used to limit access to computer facilities.

B. Process used to prepare significant accounting estimates.

C. Procedures used to assure proper authorization of transactions.

D. Policies used to detect the concealment of fraud.

Answer (B) is correct. *(CPA, adapted)*
REQUIRED: The purpose of obtaining sufficient knowledge of an entity's accounting system.
DISCUSSION: The auditor should obtain sufficient knowledge of the information system relevant to financial reporting to understand (1) the classes of significant transactions; (2) the procedures, both automated and manual, by which transactions are initiated, recorded, processed, and reported from their incurrence to their inclusion in the statements; (3) the related accounting records (whether electronic or manual) supporting information, and specific accounts involved; (4) how the information system captures other significant events and conditions; and (5) the financial reporting process used to prepare the entity's financial statements, including significant accounting estimates and disclosures (AU 319).
Answer (A) is incorrect because limiting access to computer facilities involves activities outside the accounting system relevant to financial reporting. Answer (C) is incorrect because assuring proper authorization of transactions involves activities outside the accounting system relevant to financial reporting. Answer (D) is incorrect because detecting fraud involves activities outside the accounting system relevant to financial reporting.

54. In an audit of financial statements in accordance with generally accepted auditing standards, an auditor is required to

A. Identify specific controls relevant to management's financial statement assertions.

B. Perform tests of controls to evaluate the effectiveness of the entity's accounting system.

C. Determine whether procedures are suitably designed to prevent or detect material misstatement.

D. Document the auditor's understanding of the entity's internal control.

Answer (D) is correct. *(CPA, adapted)*
REQUIRED: The requirement in an audit of financial statements in accordance with GAAS.
DISCUSSION: The auditor should document the understanding of the entity's internal control components obtained to plan the audit. The form and extent of the documentation are influenced by the nature and complexity of the entity's controls (AU 319).
Answer (A) is incorrect because an auditor need not identify specific controls unless (s)he wishes to assess control risk below the maximum level. Answer (B) is incorrect because an auditor need not perform tests of controls directed toward the effectiveness of their operation unless (s)he wishes to assess control risk below the maximum level. Answer (C) is incorrect because an auditor need not perform procedures directed toward evaluating the effectiveness of their design unless (s)he wishes to assess control risk below the maximum level.

4.5 Flowcharting

55. An auditor's flowchart of a client's accounting system is a diagrammatic representation that depicts the auditor's

A. Assessment of control risk.

B. Identification of weaknesses in the system.

C. Assessment of the control environment's effectiveness.

D. Understanding of the system.

Answer (D) is correct. *(CPA, adapted)*
REQUIRED: The purpose of an auditor's flowchart.
DISCUSSION: The auditor should document the understanding of the client's internal control components obtained to plan the audit. The form and extent of this documentation are influenced by the nature and complexity of the entity's controls. For example, documentation of the understanding of internal control of a complex information system in which many transactions are electronically initiated, recorded, processed, or reported may include questionnaires, flowcharts, or decision tables (AU 319).
Answer (A) is incorrect because the conclusions about the assessment of control risk should be documented. If it is below the maximum, the basis for the conclusions should also be documented. However, the assessment of control risk precedes or is concurrent with obtaining the understanding. Answer (B) is incorrect because the flowchart is a tool to document the auditor's understanding of internal control but does not specifically identify weaknesses in the system. Answer (C) is incorrect because the auditor's judgment is the ultimate basis for concluding that controls are effective.

56. An advantage of using systems flowcharts to document information about internal control instead of using internal control questionnaires is that systems flowcharts

A. Identify internal control weaknesses more prominently.

B. Provide a visual depiction of clients' activities.

C. Indicate whether controls are operating effectively.

D. Reduce the need to observe clients' employees performing routine tasks.

Answer (B) is correct. *(CPA, adapted)*
REQUIRED: The advantage of systems flowcharts over internal control questionnaires.
DISCUSSION: Systems flowcharts provide a visual representation of a series of sequential processes, that is, of a flow of documents, data, and operations. In many instances, a flowchart is preferable to a questionnaire because a picture is usually more easily comprehended.
Answer (A) is incorrect because a systems flowchart can present the flow of information and documents in a system, but does not specifically identify the weaknesses. Answer (C) is incorrect because the flowchart does not provide evidence of how effectively controls are actually operating. Answer (D) is incorrect because the flowchart is useful in documenting the understanding of internal control, but it does not reduce the need for observation of employees performing tasks if those tests of controls are deemed necessary.

57. The following is a section of a system flowchart for a payroll application.

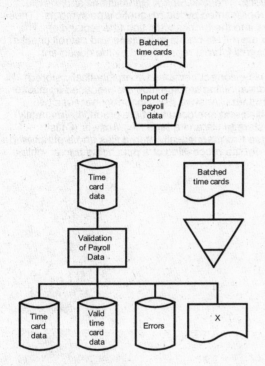

Symbol X could represent

A. Erroneous time cards.

B. An error report.

C. Batched time cards.

D. Unclaimed payroll checks.

Answer (B) is correct. *(CPA, adapted)*
   REQUIRED: The item represented by Symbol X.
   DISCUSSION: Symbol X is a document, that is, hard copy output of the validation routine shown. The time card data, the validated data, and the errors are recorded on magnetic disk after the validation process. Thus, either an error report or the valid time card information is represented by Symbol X.
   Answer (A) is incorrect because time cards were stored offline before the validation process. Answer (C) is incorrect because time cards were stored offline before the validation process. Answer (D) is incorrect because no payroll checks are shown.

58. Which of the following symbolic representations indicates that new payroll transactions and the old payroll file have been used to prepare payroll checks, prepare a printed payroll journal, and generate a new payroll file?

A.

B.

C.

D.

Answer (D) is correct. *(CPA, adapted)*

REQUIRED: The symbolic representation for updating the payroll file and generating checks and a payroll journal.

DISCUSSION: The new payroll transactions and the old payroll file are represented by the magnetic tape symbols. These files are entered into the process function (the rectangle). The output is a new payroll file on magnetic tape and payroll checks and a printed payroll journal represented by the document symbols.

Answer (A) is incorrect because two magnetically stored payroll files and two offline storage files are produced from a single document form. Answer (B) is incorrect because two offline storage files and one document are produced (manually) from an offline storage file and a tape file. Answer (C) is incorrect because two magnetically stored files and a punchcard are produced from the processing of a punchcard and an offline storage file.

4.6 PRACTICE SIMULATION

Testlet 4 of 5 | Time Remaining 2 hours 00 minutes | Copy | Paste | Calculator | Sheet | Standards | Help | Split | Done

Directions | Situation | Documentation | Audit Procedures | Control Activities | Communication | Research | Resources

1. Directions

In the following simulation, you will be asked to complete various tasks related to internal control concepts and information technology. The simulation will provide all of the information necessary to do the work. For full credit, be sure to view and complete all work tabs.

Resources may be available under the tab marked RESOURCES. You may want to review the resources before beginning the simulation.

2. Situation

As a newly hired auditor, you should obtain an understanding of internal control and information technology.

HJB, Inc., a U.S. corporation, merged with PKA International, which conducts most of its business operations in Europe and Asia. The objective of the newly-formed company is to enter new markets and eventually become the leader in its industry.

HJB, Inc. recently began using a new computer system that changed the process of recording transactions with customers and suppliers. HJB, Inc. is in the process of updating its documentation of internal control to comply with the Sarbanes-Oxley Act of 2002.

3. Internal Control Documentation Methods

HJB, Inc. may use a variety of methods for documenting internal controls. The same methods may be used by the auditor to document the understanding of the controls in a financial statement audit. Match the documentation method with the phrase or description with which it is most closely associated. Each choice may be used once, more than once, or not at all.

Phrase or Description	Documentation Method
1. A written description of a process	
2. A logic diagram in matrix form	
3. A problem and appropriate actions	
4. Diagram of a series of sequential processes	
5. Visual depiction of the flow of documents	
6. Series of interrelated queries	
7. The most flexible documentation method	
8. Control strength represented by a "Yes"	

Choices
A) Flowchart
B) Questionnaire
C) Narrative memorandum
D) Decision table

4. Audit Procedures

This question has a matching format that requires you to select the correct responses from a drop-down list. Write the answers in the shaded column. Each choice may be used once, more than once, or not at all.

Match the audit procedures for control risk assessment with the appropriate statement.

Procedures	Answer
1. The auditor performs procedures directed toward the effectiveness of the controls.	
2. The auditor prepares flowcharts, narratives, questionnaires, or other material.	
3. The auditor considers the factors affecting the risk of material misstatement.	
4. The auditor documents the reasons for assessing control risk at the maximum.	
5. The auditor designs substantive tests.	
6. The auditor collects evidence on the operating effectiveness of the procedures.	
7. The auditor records the basis for determining that the controls are working as designed.	
8. The auditor considers whether the evidence supports a further reduction in the assessed level of control risk.	
9. The auditor applies limited substantive tests to determine whether a control is operational.	
10. The auditor identifies the types of potential misstatement.	

Choices
A) Describes a reason for the auditor to obtain an understanding of internal control.
B) Describes what is required for an auditor to assess control risk below the maximum.
C) Describes the documentation requirements for the understanding of internal control and assessment of control risk.
D) Describes a procedure that would not be performed.

5. Control Activities

This question has a matching format that requires you to select the correct responses from a drop-down list. Write the answers in the shaded column. Each choice may be used once, more than once, or not at all.

For each of the following, match the control activity choice with the appropriate management action.

Management's Action	Answer
1. Investigating performance indicators	
2. Review of documents and transactions	
3. Safeguarding assets	
4. Comparing actual performance with budgeted performance	
5. Reconciliation	
6. Separating authorization of transactions and record-keeping	
7. Periodic counting of inventory.	
8. Design and use of adequate documents and records	

Choices
A) Performance reviews
B) Information processing
C) Physical controls
D) Segregation of duties

6. Communication

In a brief memorandum to the file, list the control environment factors and a brief explanation of each. Type your communication in your word processor program and print out the copy in a memorandum style format.

REMINDER: Your response will be graded for both technical content and writing skills. You should demonstrate your ability to develop, organize, and express your ideas. Do not convey information in the form of a table, bullet point list, or other abbreviated presentation.

> To: File
> From: CPA
> Subject: Control environment factors

7. Research

Use the research materials available to you to find the answers to the following question in the AICPA Professional Standards. Print the appropriate citation in its entirety from the source you choose. Use only one source. This is a copy-and-paste item.

How should an auditor obtain an understanding of internal control in an audit?

Unofficial Answers

3. Internal Control Documentation Methods (8 Gradable Items)

1. <u>C)</u>– A narrative memorandum is a written description of the processing and flow of documents and control points. The advantage of this method is its flexibility.

2. <u>D)</u>– A decision table identifies the contingencies considered in the description of a problem and the appropriate actions to be taken relative to those contingencies. Decision tables are logic diagrams presented in matrix form.

3. <u>D)</u>– A decision table identifies the contingencies considered in the description of a problem and the appropriate actions to be taken relative to those contingencies. Decision tables are logic diagrams presented in matrix form.

4. <u>A)</u>– A flowchart is a pictorial diagram of a set of sequential processes. It may be a diagram of the documents and processes of a system or of the steps in a computer program.

5. <u>A)</u>– A flowchart is a pictorial diagram of a set of sequential processes. It may be a diagram of the documents and processes of a system or of the steps in a computer program.

6. <u>B)</u>– Questionnaires consist of a series of interrelated questions about internal control polices and procedures. The questions are typically phrased so that a "Yes" response indicates a control strength and a "No" indicates a potential weakness.

7. <u>C)</u>– A narrative memorandum is a written description of the processing and flow of documents and control points. The advantage of this method is its flexibility.

8. <u>B)</u>– Questionnaires consist of a series of interrelated questions about internal control polices and procedures. The questions are typically phrased so that a "Yes" response indicates a control strength and a "No" indicates a potential weakness.

4. Audit Procedures (10 Gradable Items)

1. <u>B). Describes what is required for an auditor to assess control risk below the maximum</u>. To assess control risk below the maximum, the auditor must identify specific controls related to specific assertions, perform tests of controls, and reach a conclusion about the assessed level of control risk. A test of controls is a procedure to obtain evidence about the effectiveness of the operation of a control. Before controls are tested, the effectiveness of their design should be considered.

2. <u>C). Describes the documentation requirements for the understanding of internal control and assessment of control risk</u>. Documentation of the auditor's consideration of internal control is influenced by the nature and complexity of the entity's controls, the assessed level of control risk, and the nature of the entity's documentation of its internal control. Flowcharts, questionnaires, decision tables, and narratives are among the possible forms of documentation.

3. <u>A). Describes a reason for the auditor to obtain an understanding of internal control</u>. The auditor should obtain an understanding of the components of internal control sufficient to plan the audit. In planning the audit, this knowledge should be used to (1) determine the types of potential misstatement, (2) consider factors affecting the risk of misstatement, (3) design tests of controls (when applicable), and (4) design substantive tests.

4. D). Describes a procedure that would not be performed. Although the understanding of internal control and the conclusion that control risk is at the maximum level must be documented, the auditor need not document the basis (the reasons) for that conclusion.

5. A). Describes a reason for the auditor to obtain an understanding of internal control. The auditor should obtain an understanding of the components of internal control sufficient to plan the audit.

6. B). Describes what is required for an auditor to assess control risk below the maximum. To assess control risk below the maximum, the auditor must perform tests of controls directed toward the effectiveness of the operation of specific internal controls relevant to particular financial statement assertions.

7. C). Describes the documentation requirements for the understanding of internal control and assessment of control risk. If the auditor concludes that control risk should be assessed below the maximum, the conclusion and the basis for it must be documented.

8. B). Describes what is required for an auditor to assess control risk below the maximum. If the auditor desires to further reduce the control risk assessment, (s)he should consider whether additional evidential matter sufficient to support a further reduction is likely to be available, and whether performing tests of controls to obtain the evidential matter would be efficient.

9. D). Describes a procedure that would not be performed. The auditor performs substantive tests to detect material misstatements. The auditor assesses control risk to determine the nature, timing, and extent of the substantive tests. The auditor would not apply substantive tests in assessing control risk.

10. A). Describes a reason for the auditor to obtain an understanding of internal control. The auditor should obtain an understanding of the components of internal control sufficient to plan the audit. In planning the audit, this knowledge should be used to (1) determine the types of potential misstatement, (2) consider factors affecting the risk of misstatement, (3) design tests of controls (when applicable), and (4) design substantive tests.

5. Control Activities (8 Gradable Items)

1. A). Performance reviews
2. B). Information processing
3. C). Physical controls
4. A). Performance reviews
5. B). Information processing
6. D). Segregation of duties
7. C). Physical controls
8. B). Information processing

6. Communication (5 Gradable Items; For grading instructions, please refer to page 11.)

To: File
From: CPA
Subject: Control environment factors

The auditor considers control environment factors. One key control environmental factor is "management philosophy and operating style," which includes management's attitudes toward monitoring business risks, financial reporting, accounting, and information processing. A second factor is "organizational structure," or the entity's framework for reaching its objectives. This factor dictates that activities be planned, executed, controlled, and monitored effectively. A third factor is "integrity and ethical values" that relate to behavioral standards that should be communicated to personnel. Management should remove or reduce incentives and temptations that may prompt personnel to engage in unethical, illegal, or dishonest acts. A fourth factor is management's "commitment to competence." This factor requires management to consider the competence levels for particular jobs and activities.

A fifth and critical control environment factor is the "board of directors or audit committee participation" in the activities of the organization. The board or audit committee's independence from management, experience, and stature are factors that affect the organization's control consciousness. A sixth factor is "assignment of authority and responsibility." This factor addresses operational authority and responsibility, reporting relationships, authorization, business practices, knowledge and experience of key people, and goal congruence. Finally, the factor of "human resource policies and practices" addresses the employee-relations issues of hiring, orientation, training, evaluation, counseling, promotion, compensation, and remedial actions.

7. Research (6 Gradable Items)

AU Section 319 -- *Consideration of Internal Control in a Financial Statement Audit*

Obtaining an Understanding of Internal Control

.25   In all audits, the auditor should obtain an understanding of each of the five components of internal control sufficient to plan the audit. A sufficient understanding is obtained by performing procedures to understand the design of controls relevant to an audit of financial statements and determining whether they have been placed in operation. In planning the audit, such knowledge should be used to-

- Identify types of potential misstatement.
- . Consider factors that affect the risk of material misstatement.
- Design tests of controls, when applicable. Paragraphs .65 through .69 of this section discuss factors the auditor considers in determining whether to perform tests of controls.
- Design substantive tests.

.26   The nature, timing, and extent of procedures the auditor chooses to perform to obtain the understanding will vary depending on the size and complexity of the entity, previous experience with the entity, the nature of the specific controls used by the entity including the entity's use of IT, the nature and extent of changes in systems and operations, and the nature of the entity's documentation of specific controls. For example, the understanding of risk assessment needed to plan an audit for an entity operating in a relatively stable environment may be limited. Also, the understanding of monitoring needed to plan an audit for a small, noncomplex entity may be limited. Similarly, the auditor may need only a limited understanding of control activities to plan an audit for a noncomplex entity that has significant owner-manager approval and review of transactions and accounting records. On the other hand, the auditor may need a greater understanding of control activities to plan an audit for an entity that has a large volume of revenue transactions and that relies on IT to measure and bill for services based on a complex, frequently changing rate structure.

.27   Whether a control has been *placed in operation* at a point in time is different from its *operating effectiveness* over a period of time. In obtaining knowledge about whether controls have been placed in operation, the auditor determines that the entity is using them. Operating effectiveness, on the other hand, is concerned with how the control (whether manual or automated) was applied, the consistency with which it was applied, and by whom it was applied. The auditor determines whether controls have been placed in operation as part of the understanding of internal control necessary to plan the audit. The auditor evaluates the operating effectiveness of controls as part of assessing control risk, as discussed in paragraphs .62 through .83 of this section. Although understanding internal control and assessing control risk are discussed separately in this section, they may be performed concurrently in an audit. Furthermore, some of the procedures performed to obtain the understanding may provide evidential matter about the operating effectiveness of controls relevant to certain assertions.

.28   The auditor's understanding of internal control may sometimes raise doubts about the auditability of an entity's financial statements. Concerns about the integrity of the entity's management may be so serious as to cause the auditor to conclude that the risk of management misrepresentation in the financial statements is such that an audit cannot be conducted. Concerns about the nature and extent of an entity's records may cause the auditor to conclude that it is unlikely that sufficient competent evidential matter will be available to support an opinion on the financial statements.

Scoring Schedule:

	Correct Responses		Gradable Items		Weights		
Tab 3	_____	÷	8	×	20%	=	_____
Tab 4	_____	÷	10	×	20%	=	_____
Tab 5	_____	÷	8	×	20%	=	_____
Tab 6	_____	÷	5	×	30%	=	_____
Tab 7	_____	÷	6	×	10%	=	_____

(Your Score)

Use Gleim's *CPA Review Online* to practice more simulations in a realistic environment.

STUDY UNIT FIVE
INTERNAL CONTROL --
SALES-RECEIVABLES-CASH RECEIPTS CYCLE

(10 pages of outline)

5.1	Responsibilities/Organizational Structure	179
5.2	Sales-Receivables Flowchart	181
5.3	Cash Receipts Flowchart	184
5.4	Controls in a Cash Sale Environment	186
5.5	Other Sales-Receivables Related Transactions	186
5.6	Technology Considerations for the Sales-Receivables-Cash Receipts Cycle	187
5.7	Practice Simulation	198

A standard approach to considering internal control as well as to substantive testing is to divide the auditee's transactions, balances, and related control activities into groupings of related items. This cycle approach is consistent with how transactions are recorded in journals and ledgers. Among the relevant accounts considered are cash, trade receivables, other receivables, allowance for bad debts, sales, sales returns, and bad debt expense.

Understanding how information and documents flow through a particular cycle enables an auditor to determine what controls are in place and whether they are effective in safeguarding assets and preventing or detecting errors and fraud. Auditors are required to obtain and document an understanding of internal control. Thus, a knowledge of flowcharts is important not only in preparing for the CPA exam but also in documenting this understanding.

Some candidates may feel that information presented in flowcharts is difficult to master. It is likely that candidates will be required to consider flowcharts on future exams. CPA candidates in the past have not been required to prepare flowcharts but have been expected to evaluate them. The study materials presented here provide the foundations of understanding. They have been kept simple and straightforward. Nevertheless, they capture the information most often tested on the CPA exam. The narrative should be studied in conjunction with the flowcharts. Candidates should understand and not just memorize the various documents, flows, and control points. Although the basic concepts are derived from a manual system, they can be extended to a computer environment. The last subunit provides candidates with an understanding of the effect of technology on the sales cycle.

5.1 RESPONSIBILITIES/ORGANIZATIONAL STRUCTURE

1. Management is responsible for the establishment of the controls over the sales-receivables-cash receipts cycle to ensure

   a. Proper acceptance of the customer order
   b. Granting of credit approval in accordance with credit limits
   c. Safeguarding of assets associated with the sale
   d. Timely shipment of goods to customers
   e. Billing for shipments at authorized prices
   f. Accounting for and collection of receivables
   g. The recording, safeguarding, and depositing intact of cash (checks) received

2. The auditor is charged with obtaining an understanding of internal control, determining that controls are in place, judging whether to apply tests of controls, and ultimately assessing control risk associated with the sales-receivables-cash receipts cycle.

Organizational Chart

This is a typical organizational flowchart. It is discussed in Study Unit 4, Internal Control Concepts and Information Technology, beginning on page 133. To help you visualize the internal control of this typical organization, the following document flowcharts with explanations are presented for your study:

	Page
Study Unit 5	
Sales-Receivables Manual System Flowchart	182
Cash Receipts Manual System Flowchart	185
Sales-Receivables Computer System Flowchart	187
Study Unit 6	
Purchases-Payables-Cash Disbursements Manual System Flowchart	205
Purchases-Payables Computer System Flowchart	208
Study Unit 7	
Payroll Manual System Flowchart	231
Payroll Computer System Flowchart	233

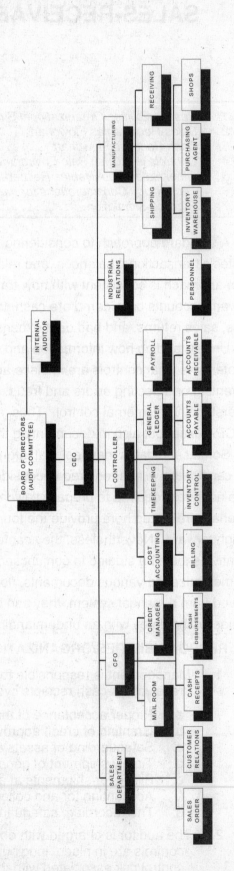

3.   The organizational structure should separate duties and responsibilities so that an individual is not in the position both to perpetrate and conceal errors or fraud. The ideal segregation of duties is

a.   Authorization of the transaction

1)   Specific authorization may be needed for some transactions, such as credit approvals, whereas a general authorization may suffice for others, such as retail cash sales.

b.   Recording of the transaction

c.   Custody over the assets (e.g., inventory, receivables, and cash) associated with the transaction

4.   However, cost-benefit considerations typically affect the organizational structure and complete separation may not be feasible. Compensating controls will likely be established when the segregation of duties is not maintained. Typical compensating controls may include

a.   More supervision

b.   Owner involvement in the process

5.   The following are the responsibilities of personnel or departments in the sales-receivables-cash receipts cycle:

a.   **Sales** prepares sales orders based on customer orders.

b.   **Credit Manager** authorizes customer credit and initiates write-off of bad debts. The credit manager should report to the treasurer.

c.   **Inventory Warehouse** maintains physical custody of products.

d.   **Shipping** prepares shipping documents and ships products based on authorized sales orders.

e.   **Billing** prepares customer invoices based on goods shipped.

f.   **Accounts Receivable** maintains the accounts receivable subsidiary ledger.

g.   **Mail Room** receives mail and prepares initial cash receipts records.

h.   **Cash Receipts** safeguards and promptly deposits cash receipts.

i.   **General Ledger** maintains the accounts receivable control account and records sales. Daily summaries of sales are recorded in a sales journal. Totals of details from the sales journal are usually posted monthly to the general ledger.

j.   **Receiving** department prepares receiving reports and handles all receipts of goods or materials, including sales returns.

6.   Stop and review! You have completed the outline for this subunit. Study multiple-choice questions 1 and 2 on page 189.

5.2 SALES-RECEIVABLES FLOWCHART

1.   Study the flowchart on the following page. Understand and visualize the sales-receivables process and controls. Read the following description as needed. Note the control activities implemented and listed on page 183.

2.   **Description of the Document Flow**. (To simplify the presentation, the flowchart does not show the disposition of all documents, for example, by filing, or other supplemental procedures.) The process begins in the upper left corner of the flowchart marked "start."

Sales-Receivables Manual System Flowchart

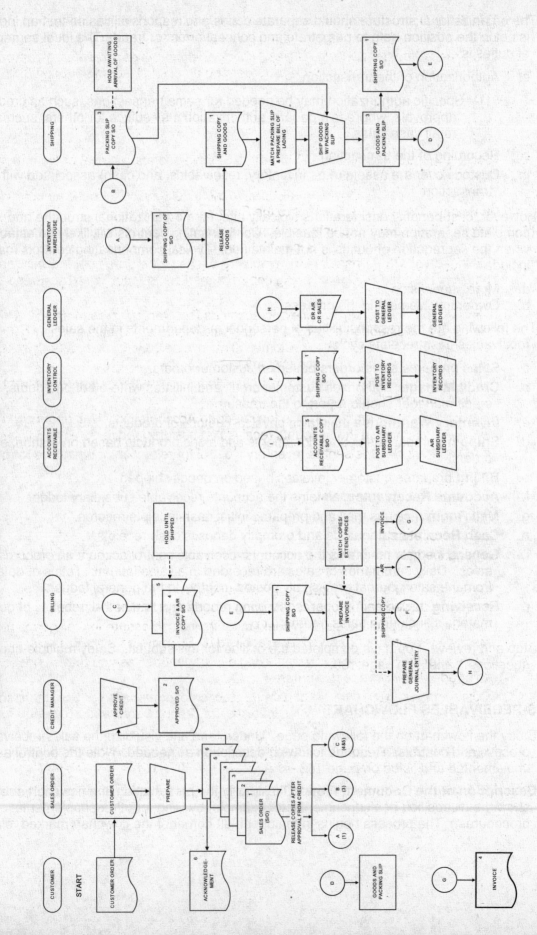

a.   The Sales Order department receives a customer order and prepares a multipart sales order. Prior to release, copy 2 of the sales order is sent to the Credit Manager.

b.   The Credit Manager performs a credit check and authorizes the order, if appropriate. The approval is conveyed to Sales Order and an acknowledgment (copy 6) is sent to the customer.

c.   Sales Order releases copies of the order. Two copies, the invoice copy and accounts receivable copy (copies 4 and 5), are sent to Billing and held awaiting notification of shipment.

d.   A copy (the packing slip copy 3) is sent to Shipping pending arrival of the goods from the Inventory Warehouse.

e.   A copy (the shipping copy 1) is released to the Inventory Warehouse as authorization to release the goods to be sent to the Shipping department.

f.   When the goods and the shipping copy 1 arrive at the Shipping department, the matching packing slip copy 3 is pulled from the file, and shipping documents (e.g., a bill of lading) are prepared. The goods are packed for shipment along with the packing slip copy 3. The shipping copy 1 is marked "shipped" and forwarded to Billing.

g.   Billing pulls the matching invoice and accounts receivable copies (4 and 5). Prices are checked and extended based on the quantities shipped. The invoice (copy 4) is completed and mailed to the customer. The invoice contains a section (a remittance advice) to be returned with the customer check.

h.   Billing prepares a journal entry to be posted by the General Ledger department (credit to sales and debit to the accounts receivable control account).

i.   The accounts receivable copy 5 is forwarded to Accounts Receivable for posting to the individual account in the accounts receivable subsidiary ledger.

j.   The shipping copy 1 is sent to Inventory Control for reduction of quantities for goods shipped.

3. **Control Activities Implemented**

a.   The division of the duties of the transaction is as follows: authorization, recording, and custody of assets.

b.   Routing the sales order copy through the Credit Manager assures that goods are shipped only to customers who are likely to pay (i.e., properly valued).

c.   Routing the shipping copy through the Inventory Warehouse helps assure that goods are safeguarded and released only upon proper approval of the order.

d.   Matching of the packing slip copy held by Shipping can assure that all goods released from the Inventory Warehouse are received by Shipping on a timely basis.

e.   Matching of the copies held by the Billing department can assure that all goods shipped are invoiced to customers.

f.   Documents are prenumbered to permit detection of unrecorded or unauthorized transactions. For example, sales invoices are prenumbered and accounted for to ensure that all orders are billed.

g.   Periodic reconciliation of the accounts receivable subsidiary ledger with the general ledger can assure that all invoices are recorded in customers' accounts.

4. Stop and review! You have completed the outline for this subunit. Study multiple-choice questions 3 through 7 beginning on page 189.

5.3 CASH RECEIPTS FLOWCHART

1. Study the flowchart on the next page. Understand and visualize the cash receipts process and controls. Read the following description as needed. Note the control activities implemented and listed below and on the next page.

2. **Description of the Document Flow**. This flowchart represents the procedures and documents for cash collections from credit customers; cash receipts from cash sales are considered in Subunit 5.4. (To simplify the presentation, the flowchart does not show the disposition of documents, for example, by filing, or other supplemental procedures.) The process begins in the upper left corner of the flowchart marked "start."

   a. The Mail Room receives all customer receipts, opens the mail, separates the checks from the remittance advices, and prepares a daily listing of the checks received (the daily remittance list). If no remittance advice is received, the mail clerks prepare one. A copy of the daily remittance list is sent to the Controller.

      1) A remittance advice is part of or a copy of the sales invoice sent to a customer and intended to be returned with the payment. It contains the customer's name, the invoice number, and its amount.

   b. Cash receipts and copy 1 of the daily remittance list are forwarded to Cash Receipts for preparation of the deposit ticket and recording in the cash receipts register.

   c. The receipts are deposited daily by Cash Receipts. The validated (by the bank) deposit ticket is returned to the Controller. The Controller reconciles the validated deposit ticket with the daily remittance list of cash received from the Mail Room.

   d. A journal voucher (entry) prepared by Cash Receipts indicating the debit to cash and credit to accounts receivable is sent to the General Ledger.

   e. The remittance advices are sent to Accounts Receivable for posting the reductions in accounts receivable to the individual customers' accounts.

3. **Control Activities Implemented**

   a. Two clerks should be present in the Mail Room during the opening and recording of the receipts.

   b. Checks are endorsed "For Deposit Only into Account Number XXXX" immediately upon opening the mail.

   c. All cash is deposited intact daily. This procedure assures that the cash received and recorded on the daily remittance list can be reconciled with the deposit ticket validated by the bank.

   d. Periodic reconciliation of the accounts receivable subsidiary ledger and the accounts receivable control account in the general ledger establishes agreement of the total amounts posted. However, the reconciliation cannot determine whether an amount was posted to the wrong account in the subsidiary ledger. Moreover, application of such a control will be ineffective if sales were not recorded in the books of original entry, e.g., the sales journal.

   e. Monthly statements are sent to customers to assure that failure to receive and/or record payments made by customers is detected (not shown on flowchart).

   f. Employees responsible for handling cash are bonded. Because the bonding company investigates employees before providing the bond, some assurance is provided concerning their integrity. Also, the bond provides insurance against losses.

Cash Receipts Manual System Flowchart

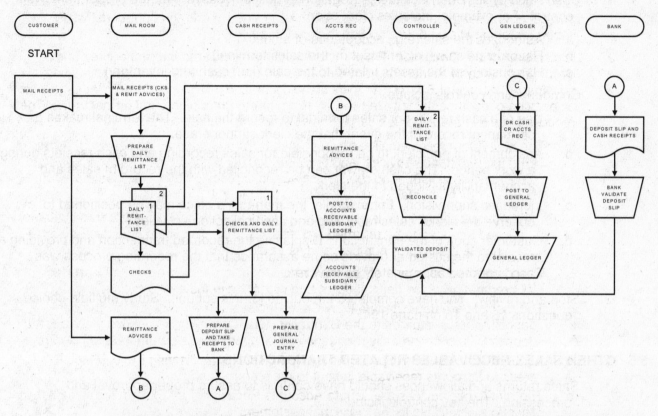

g.   A **lockbox system** (not depicted in the flowchart) can assure that cash receipts are not abstracted by mail clerks or other employees. This system provides for customer payments to be sent to a post office box and collected directly by the bank.

   1)   Hence, a lockbox system prevents lapping. **Lapping** occurs when an employee with access to both the accounts receivable subsidiary ledger and customer payments steals a portion of the receipts without recording them in the customer accounts. To conceal the theft, subsequent receipts are posted to the accounts of customers whose payments were stolen. This process of using new receipts to cover a recent theft must continue indefinitely to avoid detection.

4.   Stop and review! You have completed the outline for this subunit. Study multiple-choice questions 8 through 14 beginning on page 191.

5.4 CONTROLS IN A CASH SALE ENVIRONMENT

1. Cash sales cycles often lack the segregation of duties necessary for the proper framework of control. For example, the sales clerk often

    a. Authorizes the sale (e.g., acceptance of a check)
    b. Records the sale (i.e., enters it on the sales terminal)
    c. Has custody of the assets related to the sale (i.e., cash and inventory)

2. Compensating controls include

    a. Use of a cash register or sales terminal to record the sale. The terminal makes a permanent record of the event that the clerk cannot erase.
    b. Assignment of one clerk to be responsible for sales recording and cash receipts during a work period. The cash drawer can be reconciled with the record of sales and accountability assigned to the clerk.
    c. Increased supervision. For example, the manager's office may be positioned to observe the clerks' sales recording and cash collection activities.
    d. Customer audit of the transaction. Displaying the recorded transaction and providing a receipt to the customer provide some assurance that the recording process was accomplished appropriately by the clerk.

3. Stop and review! You have completed the outline for this subunit. Study multiple-choice questions 15 and 16 on page 194.

5.5 OTHER SALES-RECEIVABLES RELATED TRANSACTIONS

1. Sales returns and allowances should have controls to assure proper approval and processing. The key controls include

    a. Approval by the sales department to return goods
    b. Receipt of the returned goods by the receiving department and preparation of a receiving report
    c. The separate approval of the credit memo related to a sales return or allowance, that is, approval by someone not in the sales department

2. The write-off of bad debts requires strong controls. The key controls include

    a. Initiation of the write-off by the credit manager and approval by the treasurer or other officer. The credit manager will be evaluated, in part, on the amount of bad debts written off and will require significant evidence before initiating a write-off.
    b. Maintenance of a separate accounting ledger for accounts written off

3. Stop and review! You have completed the outline for this subunit. Study multiple-choice questions 17 through 20 beginning on page 194.

5.6 TECHNOLOGY CONSIDERATIONS FOR THE SALES-RECEIVABLES-CASH RECEIPTS CYCLE

1. **Overall Considerations**

   a. Computer processing typically replaces the activities of clerks performing recording functions, e.g., recording sales and accounts receivable, updating the inventory file to reflect goods sold, and recording customer receipts by posting the amounts to the accounts receivable subsidiary file.

   b. Periodic reconciliations (weekly or monthly) of the accounts receivable subsidiary file and general ledgers are usually replaced by daily reconciliations.

   c. Sophisticated systems may replace the paper flow with computer control over authorization of the release of goods for packing and shipping. ←

   1) The use of online systems expedites the response to customer orders.

   2) Batching transactions is useful for processing large volumes of data, especially when the transactions are sorted sequentially. Batch processing is appropriate when an immediate response is not necessary.

2. Study the flowchart below. Understand and visualize the sales-receivables process and controls in a normative computer environment. Read the following description as needed. Note the control activities implemented and listed on page 188.

Sales-Receivables Computer System Flowchart

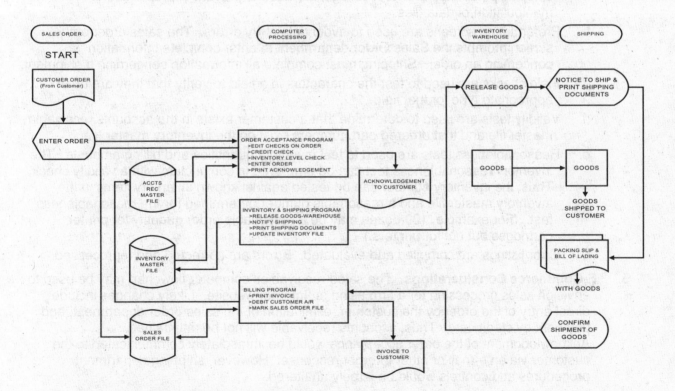

3. **Description of the Information Flow**

   a. The sales-receivables computer system flowchart above provides one view of computer processing using online systems. In this case, paper flow is replaced with electronic transmissions, and manual files and ledgers are replaced by computer disk files. The accounting departments (from the previous flowcharts) of Billing, Inventory Control, and Accounts Receivable are replaced by the Computer Processing department. Furthermore, routine credit decisions are replaced by a computer program.

b.   The Sales Order department receives a customer order and records it into the order acceptance program on a preformatted sales entry screen. Edit checks are used to assure proper entry. The accounts receivable master file is checked for current customer information and credit limits. Inventory levels are checked for availability from the inventory master file. The accepted order, along with prices determined from the inventory master file, is entered into the sales order master file, and an acknowledgment is printed and sent to the customer.

c.   Information is passed to the inventory and shipping program that sends a release authorization to the Inventory Warehouse via a computer workstation. Inventory levels are formally updated upon release of the goods from the Inventory Warehouse. An electronic shipping authorization is sent to the Shipping department. The communication also generates a packing slip and shipping documents (e.g., a bill of lading) that are printed in the Shipping department.

d.   Shipping provides the billing program with the information concerning the shipment. The billing program accesses demographic and price data from the sales order file and prepares and prints the invoice. The accounts receivable master file is also updated. (Additionally, the sale and cost of sale are recorded in the general ledger, but this step is not shown on the flowchart.)

4.   **Control Activities Implemented**. Only the major controls implemented are identified. The computer-related controls identified here are those defined in Study Unit 4.

a.   Access controls, such as passwords, device authorization tables for sales and shipping personnel, and access logs, are used to prevent improper use or manipulation of data files.

b.   Preformatted screens are used to avoid data entry errors. The sales order entry screen prompts the Sales Order department to enter complete information concerning an order. Shipping must complete all information concerning a shipment.

c.   Field checks are used to test the characters in a field to verify that they are of an appropriate type for that field.

d.   Validity tests are used to determine that a customer exists in the accounts receivable master file and that ordered part numbers exist on the inventory master file.

e.   Reasonableness tests are used to test inventory quantities and billing amounts. The inventory reasonableness test can be employed in conjunction with a validity check. Thus, the inventory number can be tested against known inventory items in the inventory master file and a reasonable number determined for the reasonableness test. (For example, 100 dozen may be a reasonable order quantity for printer cartridges but not for printers.)

f.   Error listings are compiled and evaluated. Errors are corrected and reprocessed.

5.   **E-Commerce Considerations**. The sales-receivables computer flowchart may be used to envision sales processing for a firm using an Internet website. Likely changes include direct entry of the order by the customer, elimination of the sales order department, and payment by credit card. Thus, accounts receivable will not be maintained. Acknowledgment of the order acceptance would be immediately communicated to the customer via an e-mail or other Internet response. However, shipping department procedures and controls would be largely unaltered.

a.   Additional controls include

1)   A **firewall** between the customer and internally stored client data
2)   **Passwords** for authorized or preferred customers
3)   **Encryption** procedures for transmission of sensitive information

6.   Stop and review! You have completed the outline for this subunit. Study multiple-choice questions 21 through 26 beginning on page 195.

QUESTIONS

5.1 Responsibilities/Organizational Structure

1. At which point in an ordinary sales transaction of a wholesaling business is a lack of specific authorization of least concern to the auditor in the conduct of an audit?

    A. Granting of credit.

    B. Shipment of goods.

    C. Determination of discounts.

    D. Selling of goods for cash.

Answer (D) is correct. *(CPA, adapted)*
    REQUIRED: The point in an ordinary sales transaction at which specific authorization is of least concern to an auditor.
    DISCUSSION: Selling goods for cash is the consummation of a transaction that would likely be covered by a general authorization. Thus, the risk of loss arising from lack of specific authorization of cash sales is minimal.
    Answer (A) is incorrect because granting of credit in a sales transaction may require specific authorization, i.e., special consideration before approval by the appropriate person. Answer (B) is incorrect because shipment of goods in a sales transaction may require specific authorization. Answer (C) is incorrect because determination of discounts in a sales transaction may require specific authorization.

2. During the consideration of a small business client's internal control, the auditor discovered that the accounts receivable clerk approves credit memos and has access to cash. Which of the following controls would be most effective in offsetting this weakness?

    A. The owner reviews errors in billings to customers and postings to the subsidiary ledger.

    B. The controller receives the monthly bank statement directly and reconciles the checking accounts.

    C. The owner reviews credit memos after they are recorded.

    D. The controller reconciles the total of the detail accounts receivable accounts to the amount shown in the ledger.

Answer (C) is correct. *(CPA, adapted)*
    REQUIRED: The most effective control to compensate for an employee's performance of incompatible functions.
    DISCUSSION: The clerk is in a position to both perpetrate and conceal a fraud in the normal course of his/her duties. The clerk has custody of cash, performs the record keeping function for accounts receivable, and authorizes credit memos. Thus, the clerk could conceal a theft of cash collected from customers on account by authorizing sales returns. In a small business, cost-benefit considerations ordinarily preclude establishment of formal control activities. In this situation, effective owner-management involvement may compensate for the absence of certain control activities. Accordingly, the owner should determine that credit memos are genuine.
    Answer (A) is incorrect because the clerk could commit a defalcation without errors in billing and postings to the subsidiary ledger. Answer (B) is incorrect because the bank reconciliation will not detect a theft of cash concealed by improper credit memos. Cash abstracted by the clerk would not be recorded. Answer (D) is incorrect because improper credits to accounts receivable do not cause a discrepancy between the control account and the subsidiary ledger.

5.2 Sales-Receivables Flowchart

3. Which of the following controls most likely would be effective in offsetting the tendency of sales personnel to maximize sales volume at the expense of high bad debt write-offs?

    A. Employees responsible for authorizing sales and bad debt write-offs are denied access to cash.

    B. Shipping documents and sales invoices are matched by an employee who does not have authority to write off bad debts.

    C. Employees involved in the credit-granting function are separated from the sales function.

    D. Subsidiary accounts receivable records are reconciled to the control account by an employee independent of the authorization of credit.

Answer (C) is correct. *(CPA, adapted)*
    REQUIRED: The control most effective in offsetting the tendency of sales personnel to maximize sales volume at the expense of high bad debt write-offs.
    DISCUSSION: Salespeople should be responsible for generating sales and providing service to customers. For effective control, the credit department should be responsible for monitoring the financial condition of prospective and continuing customers in the credit approval process and should report to the treasurer.
    Answer (A) is incorrect because denial of access to cash does not address the problem of the incompatibility of the sales and credit granting functions. Answer (B) is incorrect because matching of shipping and sales documents does not address the issue. Answer (D) is incorrect because reconciliation of the subsidiary and general ledgers does not address the issue.

4. An auditor tests an entity's policy of obtaining credit approval before shipping goods to customers in support of management's financial statement assertion of

A. Valuation or allocation.

B. Completeness.

C. Existence or occurrence.

D. Rights and obligations.

Answer (A) is correct. *(CPA, adapted)*
REQUIRED: The assertion related to the policy of credit approval before shipping goods to customers.
DISCUSSION: The proper approval of credit provides assurance that the account receivable is collectible; thus, it is related to the valuation assertion that accounts receivable are recorded at net realizable value.
Answer (B) is incorrect because completeness concerns whether all transactions and accounts have been represented. Answer (C) is incorrect because existence or occurrence concerns whether assets or liabilities exist and whether recorded transactions have occurred. Answer (D) is incorrect because rights and obligations assertions relate to whether assets are the rights of the entity and obligations are liabilities of the entity at a given date.

5. Which of the following internal control activities most likely would assure that all billed sales are correctly posted to the accounts receivable ledger?

A. Daily sales summaries are compared to daily postings to the accounts receivable ledger.

B. Each sales invoice is supported by a prenumbered shipping document.

C. The accounts receivable ledger is reconciled daily to the control account in the general ledger.

D. Each shipment on credit is supported by a prenumbered sales invoice.

Answer (A) is correct. *(CPA, adapted)*
REQUIRED: The control activities to assure that all billed sales are correctly posted to the accounts receivable ledger.
DISCUSSION: Daily sales summaries represent billed sales. Reconciliation with the postings to the accounts receivable ledger would provide assurance that billed sales were posted.
Answer (B) is incorrect because invoice support would assure that sales were supported by shipments. Answer (C) is incorrect because the reconciliation of the accounts receivable ledger with the general ledger would assure that the sum of the debits to the accounts receivable ledger equaled the debit to the control account. Answer (D) is incorrect because matching shipments with invoices would assure that all shipments were billed.

6. Which of the following activities most likely would not be an internal control activity designed to reduce the risk of errors in the billing process?

A. Comparing control totals for shipping documents with corresponding totals for sales invoices.

B. Using computer programmed controls on the pricing and mathematical accuracy of sales invoices.

C. Matching shipping documents with approved sales orders before invoice preparation.

D. Reconciling the control totals for sales invoices with the accounts receivable subsidiary ledger.

Answer (D) is correct. *(CPA, adapted)*
REQUIRED: The procedure not considered an internal control designed to reduce the risk of errors in the billing process.
DISCUSSION: The accounts receivable subsidiary ledger contains all receivables outstanding to date. It would not be practical to attempt to reconcile current sales invoices with the accounts receivable subsidiary ledger. The accounts receivable subsidiary ledger should be reconciled to the general ledger control account periodically, however.
Answer (A) is incorrect because the total amounts shipped should correspond to the sales invoices and can be reconciled on a daily basis. Answer (B) is incorrect because program controls would be appropriate in a computerized environment. Answer (C) is incorrect because the preparation of an invoice should be contingent on the shipment of goods.

7. Which of the following controls most likely would help ensure that all credit sales transactions of an entity are recorded?

   A. The billing department supervisor sends copies of approved sales orders to the credit department for comparison to authorized credit limits and current customer account balances.

   B. The accounting department supervisor independently reconciles the accounts receivable subsidiary ledger to the accounts receivable control account monthly.

   C. The accounting department supervisor controls the mailing of monthly statements to customers and investigates any differences reported by customers.

   D. The billing department supervisor matches prenumbered shipping documents with entries in the sales journal.

Answer (D) is correct. *(CPA, adapted)*
REQUIRED: The control to detect unrecorded sales.
DISCUSSION: The sequential numbering of documents provides a standard control over transactions. The numerical sequence should be accounted for by an independent party. A major objective is to detect unrecorded and unauthorized transactions. Moreover, comparing shipments with the sales journal also will detect unrecorded transactions.

Answer (A) is incorrect because credit approval does not ensure that sales have been recorded. Answer (B) is incorrect because the reconciliation will not detect sales that were never recorded. Answer (C) is incorrect because customers are unlikely to report understatement of their accounts.

5.3 Cash Receipts Flowchart

8. Refer to the flowchart below.

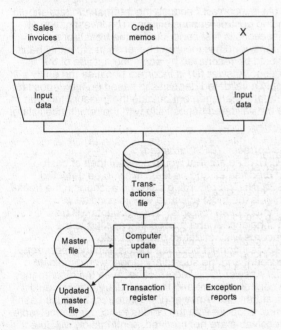

In a credit sales and cash receipts system flowchart, Symbol X could represent

   A. Auditor's test data.

   B. Remittance advices.

   C. Error reports.

   D. Credit authorization forms.

Answer (B) is correct. *(CPA, adapted)*
REQUIRED: The document in the credit sales and cash receipts flowchart represented by Symbol X.
DISCUSSION: Remittance advices (Symbol X) are sent with sales invoices to customers to be returned with cash payments. Credit memos are internal documents crediting customer accounts for returns or allowances granted. These documents are processed against the master file in the updating run.

Answer (A) is incorrect because auditor's test data are not part of the client's processing of accounts receivable payments. Answer (C) is incorrect because error reports are an output of the process. Answer (D) is incorrect because credit authorization forms are documents approving credit sales. They should be distinguished from credit memos.

9. An auditor would consider a cashier's job description to contain compatible duties if the cashier receives remittances from the mail room and also prepares the

A. Prelist of individual checks.

B. Monthly bank reconciliation.

C. Daily deposit slip.

D. Remittance advices.

Answer (C) is correct. *(CPA, adapted)*
REQUIRED: The cashier duty compatible with receiving remittances from the mail room.
DISCUSSION: Preparing the bank deposit slip is a part of the custodial function, which is the primary responsibility of a cashier. The cashier is an assistant to the treasurer and thus performs an asset custody function. The preparation of a bank deposit slip is an integral part of the custodial function, along with the depositing of remittances daily at a local bank.
Answer (A) is incorrect because the mail room prepares the prelist of checks as soon as they are received. Answer (B) is incorrect because someone independent of the custodial function (e.g., the controller) should prepare the monthly bank reconciliation. Answer (D) is incorrect because the mail room prepares remittance advices if one is not received from the customer.

10. Upon receipt of customers' checks in the mail room, a responsible employee should prepare a remittance listing that is forwarded to the cashier. A copy of the listing should be sent to the

A. Internal auditor to investigate the listing for unusual transactions.

B. Treasurer to compare the listing with the monthly bank statement.

C. Accounts receivable bookkeeper to update the subsidiary accounts receivable records.

D. Entity's bank to compare the listing with the cashier's deposit slip.

Answer (C) is correct. *(CPA, adapted)*
REQUIRED: The use of a copy of the client's remittance listing.
DISCUSSION: The individuals with record-keeping responsibility should not have custody of cash. Hence, they should use either the remittance advices or a listing of the remittances to make entries to the cash and accounts receivable control account and to the subsidiary accounts receivable records. Indeed, having different people make entries in the control account and in the subsidiary records is an effective control.
Answer (A) is incorrect because the internal auditors should have no ongoing control responsibilities. The investigation of unusual transactions is first conducted in the treasurer's department. Answer (B) is incorrect because the monthly bank statement should be reconciled by someone outside of the treasury function. Answer (D) is incorrect because the entity's bank will supply a validated deposit slip based on the deposit for the day. Company management outside the treasury function will compare the validated deposit slip with the remittance listing.

11. Cash receipts from sales on account have been misappropriated. Which of the following acts would conceal this defalcation and be least likely to be detected by an auditor?

A. Understating the sales journal.

B. Overstating the accounts receivable control account.

C. Overstating the accounts receivable subsidiary ledger.

D. Understating the cash receipts journal.

Answer (A) is correct. *(CPA, adapted)*
REQUIRED: The act that would conceal theft of cash receipts from credit sales and be least likely to be detected.
DISCUSSION: Not recording sales on account in the books of original entry is the most effective way to conceal a subsequent theft of cash receipts. The accounts will be incomplete but balanced, and procedures applied to the accounting records will not detect the defalcation.
Answer (B) is incorrect because the discrepancy between the control account and the subsidiary ledger would indicate a misstatement. Answer (C) is incorrect because the discrepancy between the control account and the subsidiary ledger would indicate a misstatement. Answer (D) is incorrect because cash receipts will not reconcile with the credits to accounts receivable. If accounts receivable are not credited, confirmation will detect the defalcation.

12. Employers bond employees who handle cash receipts because fidelity bonds reduce the possibility of employing dishonest individuals and

A. Protect employees who make unintentional errors from possible monetary damages resulting from their errors.

B. Deter dishonesty by making employees aware that insurance companies may investigate and prosecute dishonest acts.

C. Facilitate an independent monitoring of the receiving and depositing of cash receipts.

D. Force employees in positions of trust to take periodic vacations and rotate their assigned duties.

Answer (B) is correct. *(CPA, adapted)*
REQUIRED: The purpose of bonding employees.
DISCUSSION: Effective internal control, including personnel practices that stress the hiring of trustworthy people, does not guarantee against losses from embezzlement and other fraudulent acts committed by employees. Accordingly, an employer may obtain a fidelity bond to insure against losses arising from illegal acts by the covered employees. Prior to issuing this form of insurance, the underwriters investigate the individuals to be covered. Also, employees should be informed that bonding companies are diligent in prosecuting bonded individuals who commit fraud.
Answer (A) is incorrect because bonding insures employers against intentional wrongdoing. Answer (C) is incorrect because bonding is irrelevant to monitoring the receipt and deposit of cash receipts. Answer (D) is incorrect because bonding is irrelevant to periodic vacations and rotation of duties.

13. Which of the following internal controls most likely would reduce the risk of diversion of customer receipts by an entity's employees?

A. A bank lockbox system.

B. Prenumbered remittance advices.

C. Monthly bank reconciliations.

D. Daily deposit of cash receipts.

Answer (A) is correct. *(CPA, adapted)*
REQUIRED: The control that would reduce the risk of employee misappropriation of cash.
DISCUSSION: A lockbox system assures that cash receipts are not abstracted by mail clerks or other employees. Customer payments are mailed to a post office box and collected directly by the bank.
Answer (B) is incorrect because prenumbering facilitates control over remittance advices, but it would not prevent diversion of cash. Answer (C) is incorrect because a bank reconciliation reconciles the cash in the bank with the amount recorded. However, if cash is not recorded, the reconciliation does not detect its diversion. Answer (D) is incorrect because if the diversion occurs prior to the deposit, timely deposits do not necessarily reduce the risk of diversion.

14. Which of the following internal control activities most likely would deter lapping of collections from customers?

A. Independent internal verification of dates of entry in the cash receipts journal with dates of daily cash summaries.

B. Authorization of write-offs of uncollectible accounts by a supervisor independent of credit approval.

C. Segregation of duties between receiving cash and posting the accounts receivable ledger.

D. Supervisory comparison of the daily cash summary with the sum of the cash receipts journal entries.

Answer (C) is correct. *(CPA, adapted)*
REQUIRED: The best protection from lapping of collections from customers.
DISCUSSION: Lapping is the delayed recording of cash receipts to cover a cash shortage. Current receipts are posted to the accounts of customers who paid one or two days previously to avoid complaints (and discovery) when monthly statements are mailed. The best protection is for the customers to send payments directly to the company's depository bank. The next best procedure is to assure that the accounts receivable clerk has no access to cash received by the mail room. Thus, the duties of receiving cash and posting the accounts receivable ledger are segregated.
Answer (A) is incorrect because lapping delays recording cash receipts so that posting the cash receipts journal and recording in the cash summary occur on the same date and in the same amounts. Answer (B) is incorrect because lapping involves delayed posting of cash payments, not bad debt write-offs. Moreover, the credit manager should initiate write-offs to be approved by the treasurer. Answer (D) is incorrect because lapping delays recording cash receipts so that posting the cash receipts journal and recording in the cash summary occur on the same date and in the same amounts.

5.4 Controls in a Cash Sale Environment

15. In a retail cash sales environment, which of the following controls is often absent?

    A. Competent personnel.

    B. Segregation of functions.

    C. Supervision.

    D. Asset access limited to authorized personnel.

Answer (B) is correct. *(Publisher)*
REQUIRED: The control often absent in a cash sales environment.
DISCUSSION: In the usual retail cash sales situation, the sales clerk authorizes and records the transactions and takes custody of assets. However, management ordinarily employs other compensating controls to minimize the effects of the failure to segregate functions. The cash receipts function is closely supervised, cash registers provide limited access to assets, and an internal recording function maintains control over cash receipts.
Answer (A) is incorrect because competent personnel is a compensating control normally found in a cash sales environment. Answer (C) is incorrect because supervision is a compensating control normally found in a cash sales environment. Answer (D) is incorrect because limitation of access to assets is a compensating control normally found in a cash sales environment.

16. Which of the following procedures would an auditor most likely perform to test controls relating to management's assertion about the completeness of cash receipts for cash sales at a retail outlet?

    A. Observe the consistency of the employee's use of cash registers and tapes.

    B. Inquire about employee's access to recorded but undeposited cash.

    C. Trace the deposits in the cash receipts journal to the cash balance in the general ledger.

    D. Compare the cash balance in the general ledger with the bank confirmation request.

Answer (A) is correct. *(CPA, adapted)*
REQUIRED: The test of controls for the completeness assertion.
DISCUSSION: An assertion about completeness addresses whether all transactions that should be presented are included in the financial statements. To determine that controls are operating effectively to ensure that all cash receipts are being recorded for cash sales in a retail environment, the auditor may observe the activities of the employees. Controls should provide assurance that employees use cash registers that contain internal functions (e.g., tapes) to record all sales.
Answer (B) is incorrect because inquiry about employees' access to recorded cash pertains to the existence assertion. Once the sales are recorded, other controls are in place to determine that the existence of cash can be assured. Answer (C) is incorrect because tracing cash receipts to the ledger is a substantive test, not a test of controls. Answer (D) is incorrect because confirmation of cash with the bank is a substantive test, not a test of controls.

5.5 Other Sales-Receivables Related Transactions

17. An auditor noted that the accounts receivable department is separate from other accounting activities. Credit is approved by a separate credit department. Control accounts and subsidiary ledgers are balanced monthly. Similarly, accounts are aged monthly. The accounts receivable manager writes off delinquent accounts after 1 year, or sooner if a bankruptcy or other unusual circumstances are involved. Credit memoranda are prenumbered and must correlate with receiving reports. Which of the following areas could be viewed as an internal control weakness of the above organization?

    A. Handling of credit memos.

    B. Monthly aging of receivables.

    C. Credit approvals.

    D. Write-offs of delinquent accounts.

Answer (D) is correct. *(Publisher)*
REQUIRED: The area viewed as an internal control weakness of the organization.
DISCUSSION: The accounts receivable manager has the ability to perpetrate fraud because (s)he performs incompatible functions. Authorization and recording of transactions should be separate. Thus, someone outside the accounts receivable department should authorize write-offs.
Answer (A) is incorrect because the procedures regarding credit memoranda are standard controls. Answer (B) is incorrect because monthly aging is appropriate. Answer (C) is incorrect because credit approval is an authorization function that is properly segregated from the record-keeping function.

18. Which of the following most likely would be the result of ineffective internal control in the revenue cycle?

A. Final authorization of credit memos by personnel in the sales department could permit an employee defalcation scheme.

B. Fictitious transactions could be recorded, causing an understatement of revenues and an overstatement of receivables.

C. Fraud in recording transactions in the subsidiary accounts could result in a delay in goods shipped.

D. Omission of shipping documents could go undetected, causing an understatement of inventory.

Answer (A) is correct. *(CPA, adapted)*
REQUIRED: The most likely result of ineffective internal controls in the revenue cycle.
DISCUSSION: Ineffective controls in the revenue cycle, such as inappropriate division of duties and responsibilities, inadequate supervision, or deficient authorization, may result in the ability of employees to perpetrate fraud. Thus, sales personnel should approve sales returns and allowances but not the related credit memos. Moreover, no authorization for the return of goods, defective or otherwise, should be considered complete until the goods are returned as evidenced by a receiving report.
Answer (B) is incorrect because recording fictitious sales would overstate revenues. Answer (C) is incorrect because the customers' accounts are not posted until after goods are shipped. Answer (D) is incorrect because, if shipping documents are omitted, shipments of goods may not be credited to inventory, thereby overstating the account.

19. Sound internal control activities dictate that defective merchandise returned by customers be presented initially to the

A. Accounts receivable supervisor.

B. Receiving clerk.

C. Shipping department supervisor.

D. Sales clerk.

Answer (B) is correct. *(CPA, adapted)*
REQUIRED: The individual to whom customers should return defective merchandise.
DISCUSSION: For control purposes, all receipts of goods or materials should be handled by the receiving clerk. Receiving reports should be prepared for all items received.
Answer (A) is incorrect because the accounts receivable supervisor has a record keeping function incompatible with access to assets. Answer (C) is incorrect because shipping and receiving should be segregated. Answer (D) is incorrect because all returns of goods should be handled by an independent receiving function.

20. Proper authorization of write-offs of uncollectible accounts should be approved in which of the following departments?

A. Accounts receivable.

B. Credit.

C. Accounts payable.

D. Treasurer.

Answer (D) is correct. *(CPA, adapted)*
REQUIRED: The department authorizing write-offs of applicable accounts.
DISCUSSION: The write-off of uncollectible accounts requires strong controls. The initiation of the write-off is performed by the credit manager. However, authorization should be by an independent party, typically the treasurer. The credit manager will be evaluated, in part, on the amount of bad debt written off and should require significant evidence before initiating a write-off.
Answer (A) is incorrect because accounts receivable is a recording function and should not authorize transactions. Answer (B) is incorrect because the credit manager should not both initiate and approve the write-off. Answer (C) is incorrect because accounts payable is a recording function and should not authorize transactions.

5.6 Technology Considerations for the Sales-Receivables-Cash Receipts Cycle

21. An online sales order processing system most likely would have an advantage over a batch sales order processing system by

A. Detecting errors in the data entry process more easily by the use of edit programs.

B. Enabling shipment of customer orders to be initiated as soon as the orders are received.

C. Recording more secure backup copies of the database on magnetic tape files.

D. Maintaining more accurate records of customer accounts and finished goods inventories.

Answer (B) is correct. *(CPA, adapted)*
REQUIRED: The advantage of an online system over a batch system.
DISCUSSION: An online processing system can handle transactions as they are entered because of its direct connection to a computer network. Thus, shipment of customer orders may be initiated instantaneously as they are received. Batch processing is the accumulation and grouping of transactions for processing on a delayed basis.
Answer (A) is incorrect because both systems use edit programs. Answer (C) is incorrect because online systems record information on disk or other direct access memory devices. Answer (D) is incorrect because online and batch systems provide equivalent accuracy.

22. Mill Co. uses a batch processing method to process its sales transactions. Data on Mill's sales transaction file are electronically sorted by customer number and are subjected to programmed edit checks in preparing its invoices, sales journals, and updated customer account balances. One of the direct outputs of the creation of this file most likely would be a

A. Report showing exceptions and control totals.

B. Printout of the updated inventory records.

C. Report showing overdue accounts receivable.

D. Printout of the sales price master file.

Answer (A) is correct. *(CPA, adapted)*
REQUIRED: The most likely direct output of the creation of a sales transaction file.
DISCUSSION: Batch processing is useful for processing large volumes of data, especially when sorted in sequential order, for example, by customer number. Editing (validation) of data should produce a cumulative automated error listing that includes not only errors found in the current processing run but also uncorrected errors from earlier runs. Each error should be identified and described, and the date and time of detection should be given. The creation of the file will also generate various totals that will serve as controls over the accuracy of the processing.
Answer (B) is incorrect because a batch system is less appropriate for printing records that require up-to-date information. Answer (C) is incorrect because testing for overdue accounts receivable should be done prior to approving current sales orders. Answer (D) is incorrect because a complete listing of sales prices would not be found in a sales transactions file.

23. When evaluating internal control of an entity that processes sales transactions on the Internet, an auditor would be most concerned about the

A. Lack of sales invoice documents as an audit trail.

B. Potential for computer disruptions in recording sales.

C. Inability to establish an integrated test facility.

D. Frequency of archiving and data retention.

Answer (B) is correct. *(CPA, adapted)*
REQUIRED: The greatest concern about Internet controls.
DISCUSSION: Processing sales on the Internet (often called e-commerce) creates new and additional risks for clients. The client should use effective controls to ensure proper acceptance, processing, and storage of sales transactions. Threats include not only attacks from hackers but also system overload and equipment failure.
Answer (A) is incorrect because e-commerce sales transactions would not typically result in sales invoice documents. Answer (C) is incorrect because an integrated test facility is just one of many techniques for testing sales processing controls and transactions. Answer (D) is incorrect because, although archival and data retention are disaster recovery concerns, the question relates to controls over sales processing.

Questions 24 and 25 are based on the following information. A flowchart of a client's revenue cycle appears below.

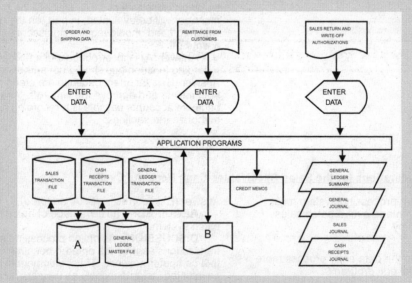

24. Symbol A most likely represents

   A. Remittance advice file.

   B. Receiving report file.

   C. Accounts receivable master file.

   D. Cash disbursements transaction file.

Answer (C) is correct. *(CPA, adapted)*
   REQUIRED: The file accessed during processing a client's revenue transactions.
   DISCUSSION: During the processing of sales orders and remittances from customers, as well as sales returns and write-off authorizations, the accounts receivable master file is accessed and updated. Thus, symbol A represents the accounts receivable master file.
   Answer (A) is incorrect because the remittance advice file is represented by the cash receipts transaction file. Answer (B) is incorrect because the receiving report file relates to the purchasing cycle. Answer (D) is incorrect because the cash disbursements transaction file relates to the purchasing cycle.

25. Symbol B most likely represents

   A. Customer orders.

   B. Receiving reports.

   C. Customer checks.

   D. Sales invoices.

Answer (D) is correct. *(CPA, adapted)*
   REQUIRED: The document represented by symbol B.
   DISCUSSION: One output of the revenue cycle is the generation of sales invoices to be sent to customers.
   Answer (A) is incorrect because customer orders are entered online and not outputted from the system. Answer (B) is incorrect because receiving reports are generated from the purchasing cycle, not the revenue cycle. Answer (C) is incorrect because customer checks are represented by remittances from customers and entered online. However, the customer checks are safeguarded and deposited daily into the bank account.

26. A CPA is gaining an understanding of the internal controls for a client that sells garden products using an Internet site. Which of the following is not likely to be found on the client's organization chart?

   A. The sales order department.

   B. The shipping department.

   C. The warehouse.

   D. Computer processing.

Answer (A) is correct. *(Publisher)*
   REQUIRED: The department or process not associated with an e-commerce client.
   DISCUSSION: The customer directly communicates the order via the Internet site. Thus, a sales order department is not needed to handle and process the order. Acceptance of the order, collection of payment, and scheduling of products for shipment are largely independent of human involvement.
   Answer (B) is incorrect because the products must be stored and subsequently shipped to the customer. Answer (C) is incorrect because the products must be stored and subsequently shipped to the customer. Answer (D) is incorrect because the order processing procedure is handled primarily by computer, and a computer processing department is likely to be found on the organization chart.

Use Gleim's ***CPA Test Prep*** for interactive testing with over 2,000 additional multiple-choice questions!

5.7 PRACTICE SIMULATION

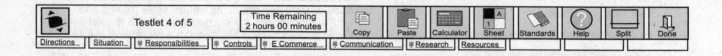

| | Testlet 4 of 5 | Time Remaining 2 hours 00 minutes | Copy | Paste | Calculator | Sheet | Standards | Help | Split | Done |

Directions | Situation | Responsibilities | Controls | E Commerce | Communication | Research | Resources

1. Directions

In the following simulation, you will be asked to complete various tasks related to the consideration of internal control for sales and receivables. The simulation will provide all of the information necessary to do the work. For full credit, be sure to view and complete all work tabs.

Resources are available to you under the tab marked RESOURCES. You may want to review the resources before beginning the simulation.

2. Situation

You are evaluating controls for a client related to the sales, receivables, and cash receipts process. To prepare documentation to support your understanding, you have collected information about the processes and departments of the organization.

3. Responsibilities

This question has a matching format that requires you to select the correct responses from a drop-down list. Write the answers in the shaded column. Each choice may be used once, more than once, or not at all.

Match each department or person involved in the sales-receivables-cash receipts cycle with the associated responsibility.

Department or Person	Answer
1. Inventory warehouse	
2. Shipping department	
3. Credit manager	
4. Sales department	
5. General ledger	
6. Cash receipts	
7. Mail room	
8. Account receivable clerk	
9. Billing department	

Responsibilities
A) Prepares sales orders
B) Authorizes customer credit
C) Prepares purchase orders to vendors
D) Maintains physical custody of products
E) Prepares shipping documents
F) Prepares customer invoices
G) Maintains accounts receivable subsidiary ledger
H) Receives initial customer receipts
I) Safeguards and deposits cash receipts
J) Maintains the accounts receivable control account

4. Controls

This question has a matching format that requires you to select the correct responses from a drop-down list. Write the answers in the shaded column. Each choice may be used once, more than once, or not at all.

Match each department or person involved in the sales-receivables-cash receipts cycle with the associated control.

Department or Person	Answer
1. Inventory warehouse	
2. Shipping department	
3. Credit manager	
4. Sales department	
5. General ledger	
6. Cash receipts	
7. Mail room	
8. Account receivable clerk	
9. Billing department	

Controls
K) Safeguards the cash and checks prior to deposit in the bank
L) Releases goods only upon receipt of a valid copy of a sales order
M) Matches copies of documents to ensure that all customers are invoiced
N) Checks are immediately endorsed "For Deposit Only" when received
O) Only remittance advices are forwarded here for posting to customer accounts
P) Approved customer orders are required before sales orders are released for processing
Q) Goods sent to customers based only on authorized sales orders
R) Goods are paid for only when proper documentation is on hand to support a payment
S) Investigates potential customers and their likelihood to pay
T) Provides the check balance for the sum of the accounts receivable

5. E-Commerce versus Manual Sales Systems

This question has a matching format that requires you to select the correct responses from a drop-down list. Write the answers in the shaded column. Each choice may be used once, more than once, or not at all.

Indicate whether the organizational arrangement or control is used in e-commerce or in manual sales systems, in both, or neither.

Organization or Control	Answer
1. Packing slips	
2. Encryption	
3. Shipping department	
4. Time cards	
5. Field checks	
6. Customer order department	
7. Firewall	
8. Credit limit	
9. Preformatted screens	
10. Purchase orders	

Responsibilities
A) Used in both manual and e-commerce sales systems
B) Used only in manual sales systems
C) Used only in e-commerce sales systems
D) Used in neither manual nor e-commerce sales systems

6. Communication

In a memo to the client, explain the benefits and costs that are associated with a lockbox system. Describe the potential problems that can be avoided by using such a system.

REMINDER: Your response will be graded for both technical content and writing skills. You should demonstrate your ability to develop, organize, and express your ideas. Do not convey information in the form of a table, bullet point list, or other abbreviated presentation.

To:	Client
From:	CPA
Subject:	A lockbox system

7. Research

Use the research materials available to you to find the answers to the following question in the AICPA Professional Standards. Print the appropriate citation in its entirety from the source you choose. Use only one source. This is a copy-and-paste item.

Research and describe the documentation alternatives relative to the understanding and evaluation of the internal controls of your client. Identify the sources of your citations from the standards.

Unofficial Answers

3. Responsibilities (9 Gradable Items)

1. D) - The inventory warehouse department maintains physical custody of products.
2. E) - The shipping department prepares shipping documents.
3. B) - The credit manager authorizes customer credit.
4. A) - The sales department prepares sales orders.
5. J) - General ledger personnel maintain accounts receivable control account.
6. I) - Cash receipts personnel safeguard and deposit cash receipts.
7. H) - Mail room personnel receive initial customer receipts.
8. G) - Accounts receivable personnel maintain the accounts receivable subsidiary ledger.
9. F) - Billing department personnel prepare customer invoices.

4. Controls (9 Gradable Items)

1. L) - The inventory warehouse releases goods only upon receipt of a valid copy of a sales order.
2. Q) - The shipping department sends goods to customers based only on authorized sales orders.
3. S) - The credit manager investigates potential customers and their likelihood to pay.
4. P) - The sales department approves customer orders before sales orders are released for processing.
5. T) - General ledger personnel provide the check balance for the sum of the accounts receivable.
6. K) - Cash receipts personnel safeguard the cash and checks prior to deposit in the bank.
7. N) - Mail room personnel ensure that checks are immediately endorsed "For Deposit Only" when received.
8. O) - The accounts receivable clerk uses only remittance advices for posting to customer accounts.
9. M) - The billing department matches a suspense copy of the sales order with the shipping copy to ensure that all customers are invoiced.

5. E-Commerce versus Manual Sales Systems (10 Gradable Items)

1. A) - Packing slips are used in manual and e-commerce sales systems.
2. C) - Encryption is used only in e-commerce sales systems.
3. A) - A shipping department is used in manual and e-commerce sales systems.
4. D) - Time cards are used neither in manual nor in e-commerce sales systems. They are part of the payroll cycle.
5. C) - Field checks are made only in e-commerce sales systems.
6. B) - A customer order department is found only in manual sales systems.
7. C) - A firewall is used only in e-commerce sales systems.
8. A) - A credit limit is used in manual and e-commerce sales systems.
9. C) - Preformatted screens are used only in e-commerce sales systems.
10. D) - Purchase orders are part of the purchases-payables-cash disbursements cycle.

6. Communication (5 Gradable Items; For grading instructions, please refer to page 11.)

To: Client
From: CPA
Subject: A lockbox system

This memorandum summarizes our presentation to you regarding your adoption of a lockbox system for the control of your cash receipts. A lockbox system may be used to expedite the receipt of funds. A company maintains mailboxes, often in numerous locations around the country, to which customers send payments. A bank retrieves customer payments from these mailboxes several times a day, and funds received are immediately deposited into the company's account without first being processed by the company's accounting system. This procedure hastens availability of the funds. Remittance advices received with the payment are forwarded to the company for internal processing of the receipt. In addition, having several lockboxes throughout the country reduces the time a payment is in the postal system (float).

Concentration banking may be useful in this context. Regional concentration banks may serve as centers for the transfer of lockbox receipts. A disbursement account at the regional center will then expedite the use of the receipts for payments in that region. Such use might be delayed if all receipts were transmitted to a national central bank.

Among the other benefits of a lockbox system is that cash receipts cannot be abstracted by mail clerks or other company employees. Thus, the system prevents lapping because receipts are recorded by an external fiduciary. Another benefit is that external audit evidence of the existence of the receipts is created. The costs of a lockbox include administrative fees based on volume and flat monthly fees.

If you have any questions about lockbox systems or other matters, please contact us at your convenience.

7. Research (6 Gradable Items)

AU Section 319 -- *Consideration of Internal Control in a Financial Statement Audit*

Documenting the Understanding

.61   The auditor should document the understanding of the entity's internal control components obtained to plan the audit. The form and extent of this documentation is influenced by the nature and complexity of the entity's controls. For example, documentation of the understanding of internal control of a complex information system in which a large volume of transactions are electronically initiated, recorded, processed, or reported may include flowcharts, questionnaires, or decision tables. For an information system making limited or no use of IT or for which few transactions are processed (for example, long-term debt), documentation in the form of a memorandum may be sufficient. Generally, the more complex the entity's internal control and the more extensive the procedures performed by the auditor, the more extensive the auditor's documentation should be.

Scoring Schedule:

	Correct Responses		Gradable Items		Weights		
Tab 3	_____	÷	9	×	20%	=	_____
Tab 4	_____	÷	9	×	20%	=	_____
Tab 5	_____	÷	10	×	20%	=	_____
Tab 6	_____	÷	5	×	30%	=	_____
Tab 7	_____	÷	6	×	10%	=	_____
							(Your Score)

STUDY UNIT SIX
INTERNAL CONTROL --
PURCHASES-PAYABLES-CASH DISBURSEMENTS CYCLE

(9 pages of outline)

6.1   *Responsibilities/Organizational Structure* *203*
6.2   *Purchases-Payables-Cash Disbursements Manual System Flowchart* *204*
6.3   *Technology Considerations for the Purchases-Payables-Cash Disbursements Cycle* *208*
6.4   *Electronic Data Interchange (EDI)* *210*
6.5   *Practice Simulation* *221*

This study unit describes control concepts in a payment system. The focus is on a traditional, manual voucher system that requires each payment to be vouched, or supported, prior to payment. This system has many variations, but the objectives and concepts of control are similar. The manual system presented here has most of the elements that are expected to be tested on future CPA exams.

The computer system described eliminates most of the paper flow from the manual system. The objectives of internal control, however, are the same. Only the methods have changed. As always, understanding the concepts rather than attempting to memorize the material is the better approach to learning.

6.1 RESPONSIBILITIES/ORGANIZATIONAL STRUCTURE

1. Management is responsible for establishing the controls over the purchases-payables-cash disbursements cycle to ensure

   a. Proper authorization of the purchase
   b. Ordering the proper quality and quantity of goods on a timely basis
   c. Acceptance only of goods that have been ordered
   d. Receipt of proper terms and prices from the vendor
   e. Payment only for those goods and services that were ordered, received, and properly invoiced
   f. Payment on a timely basis (e.g., to take advantage of cash discounts)

2. The auditor is charged with obtaining an understanding of internal control, determining that controls are in place, judging whether to test controls, and ultimately assessing control risk associated with the purchases-payables-cash disbursement cycle accounts in order to plan the audit.

3. Although much of the following information was presented in Study Unit 5, it has been repeated for the convenience of the reader.

4. Ideally, the organizational structure should separate duties and responsibilities into

   a. Authorization of the transaction
   b. Recording of the transaction
   c. Custody over the assets (e.g., inventory and cash disbursements) associated with the transaction

5. However, cost-benefit considerations may affect the organizational structure and complete separation may not be feasible. Compensating controls will likely be established when the segregation of duties is not maintained. Typical compensating controls may include

   a. More supervision
   b. Owner involvement in the process

6. Responsibilities of personnel and departments in the purchases-payables-cash disbursements cycle include

    a. **Inventory Control** provides authorization for the purchase of goods and performs an accountability function (e.g., Inventory Control is responsible for maintaining perpetual records for inventory quantities and costs).

    b. **Purchasing Agent** issues purchase orders for required goods.

    c. **Receiving** department accepts goods for approved purchases, counts and inspects the goods, and prepares the receiving report.

    d. **Inventory Warehouse** provides physical control over the goods.

    e. **Accounts Payable** (vouchers payable) assembles the proper documentation to support a payment voucher (and disbursement) and records the account payable.

    f. **Cash Disbursements** evaluates the documentation to support a payment voucher and signs and mails the check. This department cancels the documentation to prevent duplicate payment.

    g. **General Ledger** maintains the accounts payable control account and other related general ledger accounts.

7. Stop and review! You have completed the outline for this subunit. Study multiple-choice questions 1 and 2 on page 212.

6.2 PURCHASES-PAYABLES-CASH DISBURSEMENTS MANUAL SYSTEM FLOWCHART

1. **Description of the Document Flow.** The organizational chart (Study Unit 5) displays the reporting responsibilities of each function in the flowchart. To simplify the presentation, the flowchart does not show the disposition, e.g., the filing of documents, or other supplemental procedures. Some text is added to the flowchart to facilitate understanding of the flow. The flowchart begins at the point labeled "start." Copies of documents are numbered so they may be referenced through the system.

    a. Inventory Control, based on the preestablished reorder point, initiates a requisition as authorization for the purchase. The quantity authorized is the economic order quantity (EOQ). One copy of the requisition is sent to the Purchasing Agent (copy 2) and another is sent to Accounts Payable (copy 1). Inventory Control maintains a perpetual inventory by recording both reductions for sales of goods to customers and increases for receipts of goods from vendors.

    b. The Purchasing Agent provides additional authorization and determines the appropriate vendor, often through bidding, to supply the appropriate quantity and quality of goods at the optimal price. The purchasing agent then prepares a multipart (five-part) purchase order. Copies 1 and 2 are sent to the vendor with a request to return one copy as an acknowledgment. Copy 4 of the purchase order (with the quantity omitted -- a blind copy) is sent to Receiving as authorization to accept the goods when delivered. Copy 3 is sent to Accounts Payable, matched with the previously received requisition, and filed for subsequent action. Copy 5 is filed in the open purchase order file.

    c. When the goods arrive, Receiving accepts the goods based on the authorization by the Purchasing Agent (the blind copy of the purchase order). Receiving counts and inspects the goods and prepares a receiving report. A copy of the receiving report (copy 1) is sent to Inventory Control and posted to the perpetual inventory records and then sent to Accounts Payable. The copy is then matched with the requisition and purchase order being held, and the three copies are filed for subsequent action. Copy 2 of the receiving report accompanies the goods to the Inventory Warehouse.

Purchases-Payables-Cash Disbursements Manual System Flowchart

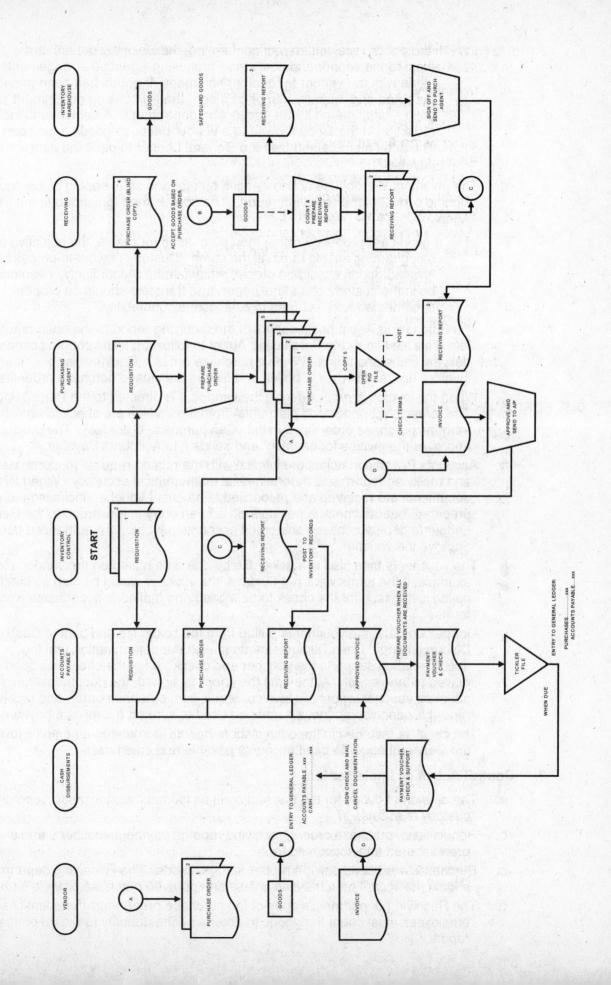

      1)   If the goods received are nonconforming, the Shipping department will return them to the vendor and notify the Purchasing Agent so arrangements can be made with the vendor for another shipment. If goods had been previously accepted and an entry had been made, the Purchasing department should send a debit memo to the Accounting department. A debit memo indicates a reduction in the amount owed to a vendor because goods have been returned. The debit memo authorizes the General Ledger to debit the appropriate payable.

d.   The Inventory Warehouse acknowledges receipt and safekeeping of the goods by signing copy 2 of the receiving report. The copy is then forwarded to the Purchasing Agent.

      1)   If goods are produced rather than purchased for resale, the objective of safeguarding assets remains the same. Custody of work-in-process and finished goods should be properly maintained. Accordingly, inventories should be in the custody of a storekeeper, and transfers should be properly documented and recorded to establish accountability.

e.   The Purchasing Agent posts copy 2 of the receiving report to the open purchase order file. This file allows the Purchasing Agent to follow up with vendors concerning delivery times and terms. When a purchase order is filled (i.e., all goods and related invoices are received), it is pulled and filed in the closed purchase order file.

f.   When the invoice is received from the vendor, it is directed to the Purchasing Agent. The terms (e.g., prices and discounts) from the invoice are checked against those from the purchase order (filed in the open purchase order file). The purchasing agent approves the invoice for payment and sends it to Accounts Payable.

g.   Accounts Payable matches the invoice with the related requisition, purchase order, and receiving report, and determines its mathematical accuracy. When all four documents are received and reconciled, a payment voucher, including a check, is prepared (but the check is not signed), and an entry is forwarded to the General Ledger to debit purchases and credit accounts payable. An authorized person should approve the voucher.

h.   The voucher is then filed in a tickler file by due date based on the vendor's terms. For example, if the terms were net 30 days, the voucher would be filed so that it would be pulled just in time for the check to be signed and mailed in accordance with the terms.

i.   On the due date, the voucher is pulled from the tickler file and sent to Cash Disbursements. Cash Disbursements makes the determination that the documentation supports the voucher and check. If so, the check is signed and mailed to the vendor. At the time the check is signed, the documentation, (i.e., payment voucher, approved invoice, requisition, purchase order, and receiving report) is canceled so that it cannot be used to support a duplicate payment.

j.   The check is recorded in the cash disbursements journal and an entry is forwarded to the General Ledger to debit accounts payable and credit cash.

2. Control Activities Implemented

a.   The division of duties for the transaction is as follows: authorization, recording, custody of assets.

b.   Requisitions, purchase orders, receiving reports, payment vouchers, and checks are prenumbered and accounted for.

c.   Purchases are based only on proper authorizations. The Receiving department should not accept merchandise unless an approved purchase order is on hand.

d.   The Receiving department's copy of the purchase order omits the quantity so that employees must count the goods to determine the quantity to record on the receiving report.

    e.   The Purchasing Agent compares prices and terms from the vendor invoice with requested and acknowledged terms from the vendor.

    f.   Vouchers and the related journal entries are prepared only when goods are received that have been authorized, ordered, and appropriately invoiced.

    g.   The tickler file permits timely payments to realize available cash discounts.

    h.   Cash Disbursements ascertains that proper support exists for the voucher and check before signing the check.

    i.   Two signatures may be required for checks larger than a preset limit.

    j.   Cash Disbursements, which reports to the treasurer, mails the checks so that no one internal to the entity can gain access to the signed checks.

    k.   Cash Disbursements cancels payment documents to prevent their use as support for duplicate vouchers and checks.

    l.   Periodic reconciliation of the vouchers in the tickler file with Accounts Payable assures proper recording in the accounts payable control account.

    m.   Periodic counts of inventory, independently reconciled with perpetual records, provide assurance that physical controls over inventory are effective.

        1)   Internal verification of inventory is independent if performed by an individual who is not responsible for custody of assets or the authorization and recording of transactions.

    n.   Accounts Payable examines the vendor invoice for mathematical errors.

    o.   Accounts Payable compares the vendor's invoice with the receiving report, the requisition, and the purchase order to assure that a valid transaction occurred.

3.   This voucher-disbursement system is applicable to virtually all required payments by the entity, not just purchases of inventory as described above. The following are additional considerations:

    a.   The authorizations may come from other departments based on a budget or policy (e.g., a utility bill might need authorization by the plant manager).

    b.   Accounts Payable would require different document(s) (e.g., a utility bill with the signature of the plant manager) to support the preparation of the payment voucher and check.

    c.   A debit other than purchases (e.g., utilities expense) would be entered on the payment voucher and recorded in the general ledger. Accounts payable would still be credited.

    d.   The use of the tickler file and the functions of Cash Disbursements would not change when other types of payments were made.

4.   Stop and review! You have completed the outline for this subunit. Study multiple-choice questions 3 through 17 beginning on page 212.

6.3 TECHNOLOGY CONSIDERATIONS FOR THE PURCHASES-PAYABLES-CASH DISBURSEMENTS CYCLE

1. Overall Considerations

   a. Computer processing ordinarily replaces the activities of clerks performing recording functions (e.g., updating the inventory file to record goods received from vendors and updating the open purchase order file). (The Computer Processing department is not shown on the Organizational Chart in Study Unit 5.)

   b. No physical voucher is prepared, the tickler file is maintained by the computer, and no check is prepared until the due date.

   c. Sophisticated systems may replace the internal paper flows with electronic transmissions.

   d. Ordinarily, the manual files and ledgers are replaced by disk files.

Purchases-Payables Computer System Flowchart

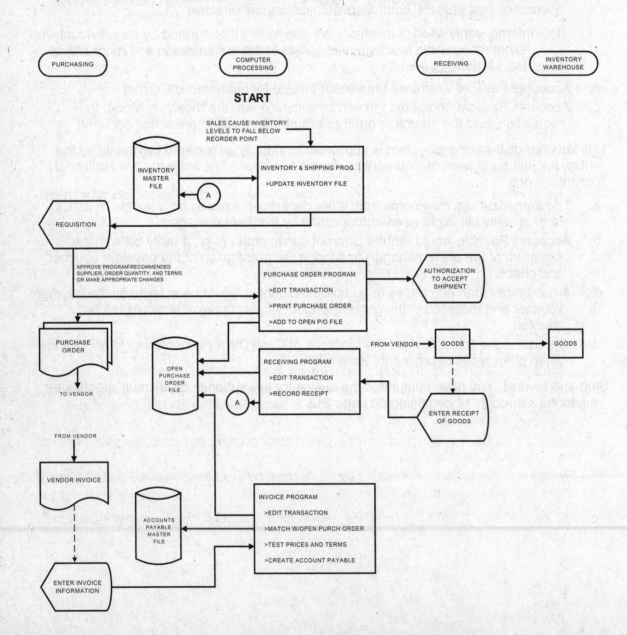

2. **Description of the Information Flow**. This purchases-payables computer system flowchart depicts one example of an online purchasing system. The accounting departments (see the previous flowchart) of Inventory Control and Accounts Payable and the Purchasing Agent's open purchase order file are replaced by the Computer Processing department. In addition, routine order decisions are replaced by computer programs.

   a. The shipping of inventory for sales orders and the related reduction of inventory on the inventory master file cause inventory levels to fall below the reorder point. As a result, a requisition request is transmitted to the Purchasing Agent. The approved vendor, economic order quantity, costs, and other relevant terms are stored in the inventory master file and provided to the Purchasing Agent. The Purchasing Agent can approve the information or make modifications based on current conditions.

   b. Once the requisition is approved, the purchase order program prints the purchase order for mailing to the vendor, records it in the open purchase order file, and authorizes Receiving to accept the shipment.

   c. When the goods arrive, Receiving accepts the shipment and enters the count and other relevant information into the receiving program. This step updates the open purchase order file and the inventory master file. The goods are taken to the Inventory Warehouse.

   d. When the invoice arrives, the Purchasing Agent enters the information into the invoice program, which tests the terms against those in the record in the open purchase order file. If the information is complete and the goods have been received, a record is created in the accounts payable master file. Furthermore, the General Ledger is updated for the debit to purchases and the credit to accounts payable. However, this step is not shown.

   e. The accounts payable program generates a check when the terms of the purchase require it to do so.

3. **Control Activities Implemented**. The major computer-related controls are identified here. The controls are defined in Study Unit 4.

   a. Access to the programs and data is restricted by password and device authorization tables. For example, the Receiving department, even with the proper password, can access only the receiving program and can change only the fields in the records affected by the receiving transactions.

   b. Access logs are maintained that automatically record each transaction, the time of the transaction, and the password of the person who entered the transaction.

   c. Preformatted computer video screens are used to ensure proper input. For example, the Receiving department's entry screen requires the quantity received to be completed (along with the other data) before the transaction is accepted.

   d. Field checks are used to test the characters in certain fields to verify that they are of an appropriate type for that field (e.g., the quantity field should contain numbers only).

   e. Validity tests are used that assure the propriety of supplier transactional data prior to accepting the input.

   f. Reasonableness tests are used to test quantities ordered and received to determine if they are within acceptable limits.

4. Stop and review! You have completed the outline for this subunit. Study multiple-choice questions 18 and 19 on page 217.

6.4 ELECTRONIC DATA INTERCHANGE (EDI)

1. EDI is the communication of electronic documents directly from a computer in one entity to a computer in another entity. EDI eliminates the paper documents, both internal and external, that are the traditional basis for many audit procedures performed in substantive testing and in tests of controls.

    a. The advantages of EDI include reduction of clerical errors, speed, and the elimination of repetitive clerical tasks. EDI also eliminates document preparation, processing, filing, and mailing costs.

    b. Moreover, an organization that has reengineered its procedures and processes to take full advantage of EDI may have eliminated even the electronic equivalents of paper documents. For example, the buyer's point-of-sale (POS) system may directly transmit information to the seller, which delivers on a JIT (just-in-time) basis. Purchase orders, invoices, and receiving reports are replaced with a long-term contract establishing quantities, prices, and delivery schedules; production schedules; advance shipment notices; evaluated receipts settlements (periodic payment authorizations transmitted to the trading partner with no need for matching purchase orders, invoices, and receiving reports); and payments by electronic funds transfer (EFT), which is a process based on EDI that transfers money from one account to another by computer.

        1) Accordingly, auditors must seek new forms of evidence to support assertions about EDI transactions, whether the evidence exists at the auditee organization, the trading partner, or a third party, such as a value-added network. Examples of such evidence are the authorized paper purchase contract, an electronic completed production schedule image, and internal and external evidence of evaluated receipts settlements sent to the trading partner.

        2) Auditors must evaluate electronic signatures and reviews when testing controls.

        3) Auditors may need to consider other subsystems when testing a particular subsystem. Thus, production cycle evidence may be needed to test the expenditure cycle.

        4) EDI often uses a **VAN (value-added network)** as a third-party service provider, and reliance on controls provided by the VAN may be critical. VANs are privately owned telecommunications carriers that sell capacity to outside users. Among other things, a VAN provides a mailbox service permitting EDI messages to be sent, sorted, and held until needed in the recipient's computer system.

            a) Encryption performed by physically secure hardware devices is more secure than encryption performed by software.

        5) Auditing an EDI application requires development of an audit trail. In addition to the elements listed above, an essential element of an EDI audit trail is an activity log. Because an audit trail allows for the tracing of a transaction from initiation to its disposition, an activity log provides a key link in the tracking process. Such a log provides information about users who have accessed the system, the files accessed, the processing accomplished, the time of access, and the amount of time the processing required.

    c. Successful implementation of EDI begins with mapping the work processes and flows that support the organization's goals. The initial phase of EDI implementation includes understanding the organization's mission and an analysis of its activities as part of an integrated solution to the organization's needs.

2. **EDI Terms and Components**

   a. The standards focus on procedures to convert written documents into a standard electronic document-messaging format to facilitate EDI.

   b. Conventions are the procedures for arranging data elements in specified formats for various accounting transactions, e.g., invoices, materials releases, and advance shipment notices. In an attempt to provide standardization and structure for EDI, organizations such as the American National Standards Institute (ANSI) have defined virtually every type of business transaction in terms of their fields and information content. These are termed transmission sets. By using such standards, communication between trading partners can be facilitated.

   c. Transmission protocols are rules on how each envelope or package of information is structured and processed by the communications devices so that messages are kept separate.

3. **Methods of Communication between Computers** (Telephone lines and modems are typically used.)

   a. **Point-to-point** is the most traditional EDI connection. Both parties have fixed computer connections, and the computers are used solely for EDI. The direct connection that is created forces all the computers to be compatible with each other. A point-to-point arrangement is very similar to networks within one company.

   b. **Value-added networks** (VAN) are mailbox-type services in which the sender's and receiver's computers are never directly connected to each other. Instead, both parties to the EDI arrangement subscribe to a third-party VAN provider. Because of the third-party buffer, the VAN users are not required to conform to the same standards, conventions, and protocols. Also, value-added networks can store messages (in a mailbox), so the parties can batch outgoing and incoming messages.

   c. The **Internet** is a means of conducting business directly with a trading partner. It can be used in a more open environment in which one firm transmits documents to another. This approach is based on less formal agreements between the trading partners than in EDI and requires the sending firm to format the documents into the format of the receiving firm.

4. **XML and XBRL**. XML (extensible markup language) was developed by an international consortium as an open standard usable with many programs and platforms. XML codes all information in such a way that a user can determine not only how it should be presented but also what it is. Thus, all computerized data may be tagged with identifiers. Unlike HTML, XML uses codes that are extensible, not fixed. Accordingly, if an industry can agree on a set of codes, software for that industry can be written that incorporates those codes.

   a. XBRL (extensible business reporting language) for Financial Statements is the specification developed by an AICPA-led consortium for U.S. commercial and industrial companies that report in accordance with U.S. GAAP. It is a variation of XML that is expected to decrease the costs of generating financial reports, reformulating information for different uses, and sharing business information using electronic media.

5. Stop and review! You have completed the outline for the subunit. Study multiple-choice questions 20 through 28 beginning on page 217.

QUESTIONS

6.1 Responsibilities/Organizational Structure

1. The objectives of internal control for a production cycle are to provide assurance that transactions are properly executed and recorded, and that

A. Independent internal verification of activity reports is established.

B. Transfers to finished goods are documented by a completed production report and a quality control report.

C. Production orders are prenumbered and signed by a supervisor.

D. Custody of work-in-process and of finished goods is properly maintained.

Answer (D) is correct. *(CPA, adapted)*
REQUIRED: The objectives of the internal control for a production cycle.
DISCUSSION: A principal objective of internal control is to safeguard assets. In the production cycle, control activities must be in place to ensure that inventory is protected from misuse and theft. Accordingly, inventories should be in the custody of a storekeeper, and transfers should be properly documented and recorded to establish accountability.
Answer (A) is incorrect because independent internal verification of activity reports is a control activity, not an objective. Answer (B) is incorrect because documenting transfers to finished goods is a control activity, not an objective. Answer (C) is incorrect because the use of prenumbered production orders signed by a supervisor is a control activity, not an objective.

2. Which of the following control activities is not usually performed with regard to vouchers payable in the accounting department?

A. Determining the mathematical accuracy of the vendor's invoice.

B. Having an authorized person approve the voucher.

C. Controlling the mailing of the check and remittance advice.

D. Matching the receiving report with the purchase order.

Answer (C) is correct. *(CPA, adapted)*
REQUIRED: The procedure not usually performed with respect to vouchers by the accounting department.
DISCUSSION: The cash disbursements department, which is responsible to the treasurer, has an asset custody function that should be segregated from the recording function of the accounting department. Consequently, checks for disbursements should be signed by a responsible person in that department after necessary supporting evidence has been examined. This individual should also be responsible for canceling the supporting documentation and mailing the signed checks and remittance advices. The documentation typically consists of a payment voucher, requisition, purchase order, receiving report, and vendor invoice.
Answer (A) is incorrect because the accounting department determines the mathematical accuracy of the vendor's invoice. Answer (B) is incorrect because the accounting department has an authorized person approve the voucher. Answer (D) is incorrect because the accounting department matches the receiving report with the purchase order.

6.2 Purchases-Payables-Cash Disbursements Manual System Flowchart

3. When the shipping department returns nonconforming goods to a vendor, the purchasing department should send to the accounting department the

A. Unpaid voucher.

B. Debit memo.

C. Vendor invoice.

D. Credit memo.

Answer (B) is correct. *(CPA, adapted)*
REQUIRED: The document that purchasing sends to accounting when shipping returns nonconforming goods.
DISCUSSION: A debit memo indicates a reduction in the amount owed to a vendor because goods have been returned. The debit memo authorizes the accounting department to debit the appropriate payable.
Answer (A) is incorrect because the purchasing department does not have custody of the unpaid voucher. Answer (C) is incorrect because the purchasing department does not have custody of the vendor invoice. Answer (D) is incorrect because a credit memo is a document indicating a reduction in the amount due from a customer.

4. Which of the following controls would be most effective in assuring that recorded purchases are free of material errors?

A. The receiving department compares the quantity ordered on purchase orders with the quantity received on receiving reports.

B. Vendors' invoices are compared with purchase orders by an employee who is independent of the receiving department.

C. Receiving reports require the signature of the individual who authorized the purchase.

D. Purchase orders, receiving reports, and vendors' invoices are independently matched in preparing vouchers.

Answer (D) is correct. *(CPA, adapted)*
REQUIRED: The control most effective in assuring that recorded purchases are free of material errors.
DISCUSSION: A voucher should not be prepared for payment until the vendor's invoice has been matched against the corresponding purchase order and receiving report (and often the requisition). This procedure provides assurance that a valid transaction has occurred and that the parties have agreed on the terms, such as price and quantity.
Answer (A) is incorrect because the receiving department should receive a blind copy of the purchase order. Answer (B) is incorrect because it is not as comprehensive as the correct answer. Answer (C) is incorrect because the receiving report is prepared by the receiving department.

5. In a properly designed internal control system, the same employee most likely would match vendors' invoices with receiving reports and also

A. Post the detailed accounts payable records.

B. Recompute the calculations on vendors' invoices.

C. Reconcile the accounts payable ledger.

D. Cancel vendors' invoices after payment.

Answer (B) is correct. *(CPA, adapted)*
REQUIRED: The control procedures that could be performed by the same employee.
DISCUSSION: The vouchers payable clerk would typically match purchase orders, vendors' invoices, and receiving reports; test the calculations and terms on the vendors' invoices; and prepare a disbursement voucher.
Answer (A) is incorrect because a different employee should post the accounts payable records. Answer (C) is incorrect because a different employee should reconcile the accounts payable ledger with the general ledger. Answer (D) is incorrect because an employee in the treasurer's department should cancel vendors' invoices and other documentation after signing the check for payment.

6. For effective internal control, the accounts payable department ordinarily should

A. Obliterate the quantity ordered on the receiving department copy of the purchase order.

B. Establish the agreement of the vendor's invoice with the receiving report and purchase order.

C. Stamp, perforate, or otherwise cancel supporting documentation after payment is mailed.

D. Ascertain that each requisition is approved as to price, quantity, and quality by an authorized employee.

Answer (B) is correct. *(CPA, adapted)*
REQUIRED: The procedure performed by the accounts payable department.
DISCUSSION: The accounts payable department is responsible for matching the vendor's invoice against the corresponding purchase order and receiving report. This procedure provides assurance that a valid transaction has occurred and that the parties have agreed on the terms, such as price and quantity.
Answer (A) is incorrect because the purchasing department is responsible for sending copies of the purchase order to the different departments. Answer (C) is incorrect because the cash disbursements department is responsible for canceling supporting documentation when checks are signed. Answer (D) is incorrect because the purchasing department is responsible for approving each requisition.

7. Which of the following internal control activities is not usually performed in the vouchers payable department?

A. Matching the vendor's invoice with the related receiving report.

B. Approving vouchers for payment by having an authorized employee sign the vouchers.

C. Indicating the asset and expense accounts to be debited.

D. Accounting for unused prenumbered purchase orders and receiving reports.

Answer (D) is correct. *(CPA, adapted)*
REQUIRED: The control not usually performed in the vouchers payable department.
DISCUSSION: Employees in the vouchers payable department should have no responsibilities related to purchasing or receiving goods. The purchasing department accounts for unused prenumbered purchase orders. The receiving department accounts for unused prenumbered receiving reports.
Answer (A) is incorrect because matching the vendor's invoice with the related receiving report, purchase requisition, and purchase order is a function of the vouchers payable department. Answer (B) is incorrect because signing of vouchers by an authorized employee to signify that information has been verified is a function of the vouchers payable department. Answer (C) is incorrect because indicating the affected accounts on the voucher is a function of the vouchers payable department.

8. In a well-designed internal control system, the same employee may be permitted to

A. Mail signed checks and also cancel supporting documents.

B. Prepare receiving reports and also approve purchase orders.

C. Approve vouchers for payment and also have access to unused purchase orders.

D. Mail signed checks and also prepare bank reconciliations.

Answer (A) is correct. *(CPA, adapted)*
REQUIRED: The functions the same employee may be permitted to perform in a well-designed control system.
DISCUSSION: The cash disbursements department has an asset custody function. Consequently, this department is responsible for signing checks after verification of their accuracy by reference to the supporting documents. The supporting documents should then be canceled and the checks mailed. Cancellation prevents the documentation from being used to support duplicate payments. Moreover, having the party who signs the checks place them in the mail reduces the risk that they will be altered or diverted.
Answer (B) is incorrect because the receiving department should not know how many units have been ordered. Answer (C) is incorrect because accounts is responsible for approving vouchers, and purchasing is the only department with access to the purchase orders. The same employee should not approve the purchase and approve payment. Answer (D) is incorrect because the bank reconciliation is performed by someone with no asset custody function.

9. Which of the following internal control activities most likely addresses the completeness assertion for inventory?

A. Work-in-process is periodically reconciled with subsidiary records.

B. Employees responsible for custody of finished goods do not perform the receiving function.

C. Receiving reports are prenumbered and periodically reconciled.

D. There is a separation of duties between payroll department and inventory accounting personnel.

Answer (C) is correct. *(CPA, adapted)*
REQUIRED: The internal control procedure that most likely addresses the completeness assertion for inventory.
DISCUSSION: The completeness assertion concerns whether all transactions and accounts that should be presented are included. For inventory, the assertion is that inventory quantities include all products, materials, and supplies on hand or that are owned by the company but are in transit or stored elsewhere. The use of prenumbered receiving reports makes it possible to detect unrecorded (incomplete) inventory.
Answer (A) is incorrect because reconciling work-in-process with the subsidiary records relates most closely to the existence assertion. Answer (B) is incorrect because separation of custody of finished goods from the receiving function relates to the existence assertion. Answer (D) is incorrect because a separation of duties between payroll department and inventory accounting personnel addresses the issue of proper recording of inventoriable labor cost, a matter related to the valuation assertion.

10. Which of the following questions would most likely be included in an internal control questionnaire concerning the completeness assertion for purchases?

A. Is an authorized purchase order required before the receiving department can accept a shipment or the vouchers payable department can record a voucher?

B. Are purchase requisitions prenumbered and independently matched with vendor invoices?

C. Is the unpaid voucher file periodically reconciled with inventory records by an employee who does not have access to purchase requisitions?

D. Are purchase orders, receiving reports, and vouchers prenumbered and periodically accounted for?

Answer (D) is correct. *(CPA, adapted)*
REQUIRED: The most likely control over the completeness of purchases.
DISCUSSION: The completeness assertion concerns whether all transactions and accounts that should be presented are so included. Thus, management asserts that all purchases are recorded and included in the accounts. A standard control procedure related to the completeness assertion for purchases is the use of prenumbered documents. Items missing from the numerical sequence may represent unrecorded transactions and accounts.
Answer (A) is incorrect because the authorization of purchases concerns the rights and obligations assertion. Answer (B) is incorrect because purchase orders should be matched with vendor invoices and receiving reports. Answer (C) is incorrect because reconciliation of the voucher file with the inventory records verifies that recorded liabilities are obligations of the entity.

11. The authority to accept incoming goods in receiving should be based on a(n)

A. Vendor's invoice.

B. Materials requisition.

C. Bill of lading.

D. Approved purchase order.

Answer (D) is correct. *(CPA, adapted)*

REQUIRED: The document on which the authority to accept incoming goods in receiving should be based.

DISCUSSION: A company's receiving department should accept merchandise only if a purchase order or approval granted by the purchasing department is on hand.

Answer (A) is incorrect because the vendor's invoice does not indicate whether purchase of the goods was properly authorized by someone outside the receiving department. Answer (B) is incorrect because materials requisition does not indicate whether purchase of the goods was properly authorized by someone outside the receiving department. Answer (C) is incorrect because the carrier's bill of lading does not indicate whether purchase of the goods was properly authorized by someone outside the receiving department.

12. In a well-designed internal control system, employees in the same department most likely would approve purchase orders, and also

A. Reconcile the open invoice file.

B. Inspect goods upon receipt.

C. Authorize requisitions of goods.

D. Negotiate terms with vendors.

Answer (D) is correct. *(CPA, adapted)*

REQUIRED: The task appropriately performed by employees who approve purchase orders.

DISCUSSION: To prevent or detect errors or fraud in the performance of assigned responsibilities, duties are often segregated. Approving purchase orders and negotiating terms with vendors are part of the authorization process performed by the purchasing department.

Answer (A) is incorrect because reconciling the open invoice file is the accounting department's function. Answer (B) is incorrect because inspection of goods upon receipt is the receiving department's function. Answer (C) is incorrect because authorization of the requisition is inventory control's function.

13. Internal control is strengthened when the quantity of merchandise ordered is omitted from the copy of the purchase order sent to the

A. Department that initiated the requisition.

B. Receiving department.

C. Purchasing agent.

D. Accounts payable department.

Answer (B) is correct. *(CPA, adapted)*

REQUIRED: The department that should receive a copy of the purchase order from which the quantity of merchandise ordered has been omitted.

DISCUSSION: A company's receiving department should accept merchandise only if a purchase order or approval granted by the purchasing department is on hand. A standard control is to delete the quantity from the receiving department's copy of the purchase order. If the receiving clerk does not know the quantity ordered, an independent count is more likely.

Answer (A) is incorrect because the department that initiated the requisition presumably knows what amount was ordered. Answer (C) is incorrect because the purchasing agent is responsible for authorizing the purchase order. Answer (D) is incorrect because the accounts payable department must compare a duplicate of the original purchase order with the receiving report and other documents before it can prepare a payment voucher.

14. In testing controls over cash disbursements, an auditor most likely would determine that the person who signs checks also

A. Reviews the monthly bank reconciliation.

B. Returns the checks to accounts payable.

C. Is denied access to the supporting documents.

D. Is responsible for mailing the checks.

Answer (D) is correct. *(CPA, adapted)*

REQUIRED: The test of controls over cash payments.

DISCUSSION: The person responsible for signing the checks should also be responsible for assuring that the checks are mailed. This precaution assures limited access to the checks once they are signed.

Answer (A) is incorrect because the bank reconciliation should not be reviewed by someone with responsibility for custody of assets. Answer (B) is incorrect because checks should be returned to the treasury department. Answer (C) is incorrect because supporting documentation should be presented to the check signer as authorization to sign the check. That documentation should be canceled after the check is signed.

15. To provide assurance that each voucher is submitted and paid only once, an auditor most likely would examine a sample of paid vouchers and determine whether each voucher is

    A. Supported by a vendor's invoice.

    B. Stamped "paid" by the check signer.

    C. Prenumbered and accounted for.

    D. Approved for authorized purchases.

Answer (B) is correct. *(CPA, adapted)*
    REQUIRED: The observation necessary to determine whether a voucher was paid only once.
    DISCUSSION: To assure that voucher documentation is not used to support a duplicate payment, the individual responsible for cash disbursements should examine the voucher and determine the appropriateness of the supporting documents, sign the check, cancel the payment documents, and mail the check to the vendor.
    Answer (A) is incorrect because each voucher should be supported by a vendor's invoice, but if the invoice is not canceled, it may be recycled to support a second voucher. Answer (C) is incorrect because, if additional vouchers are prepared and supported with recycled documentation, accounting for the prenumbered vouchers would not assure that duplicates do not exist. Answer (D) is incorrect because, although vouchers should be approved, unless the documentation is canceled, duplicate payments may be possible.

16. Which of the following internal control activities is not usually performed in the treasurer's department?

    A. Verifying the accuracy of checks and vouchers.

    B. Controlling the mailing of checks to vendors.

    C. Approving vendors' invoices for payment.

    D. Canceling payment vouchers when paid.

Answer (C) is correct. *(CPA, adapted)*
    REQUIRED: The control procedure not usually performed in the treasurer's department.
    DISCUSSION: The accounts payable department is responsible for compiling documentation to support an account payable. This approval process is performed in the accounting department.
    Answer (A) is incorrect because verifying the accuracy of checks and vouchers is a procedure typically performed in the treasurer's department. Answer (B) is incorrect because controlling the mailing of checks to vendors is a procedure typically performed in the treasurer's department. Answer (D) is incorrect because canceling payment vouchers when paid is a procedure typically performed in the treasurer's department.

17. Which of the following control procedures most likely would assist in reducing control risk related to the existence or occurrence of manufacturing transactions?

    A. Perpetual inventory records are independently compared with goods on hand.

    B. Forms used for direct materials requisitions are prenumbered and accounted for.

    C. Finished goods are stored in locked limited-access warehouses.

    D. Subsidiary ledgers are periodically reconciled with inventory control accounts.

Answer (A) is correct. *(CPA, adapted)*
    REQUIRED: The control most likely to reduce control risk related to the existence or occurrence assertion.
    DISCUSSION: The recorded accountability for assets should be compared with existing assets at reasonable intervals. If assets are susceptible to loss through errors and fraud, the comparison should be made independently. An independent comparison is one made by persons not having responsibility for asset custody or the authorization or recording of transactions.
    Answer (B) is incorrect because accounting for prenumbered forms relates more to the completeness assertion than the existence or occurrence assertion. This control procedure provides assurance that all transactions were recorded. Answer (C) is incorrect because, although limitation of access is appropriate for safeguarding certain assets, it does not establish accountability, and locking raw materials and work-in-process inventories in limited-access warehouses may not be feasible. Answer (D) is incorrect because periodic reconciliation of subsidiary ledgers with control accounts is related to the completeness assertion.

6.3 Technology Considerations for the Purchases-Payables-Cash Disbursements Cycle

18. In the accounting system of Apogee Company, the quantities counted by the receiving department and entered at a terminal are transmitted to the computer, which immediately transmits the amounts back to the terminal for display on the terminal screen. This display enables the operator to

A. Establish the validity of the account number.

B. Verify that the amount was entered accurately.

C. Verify the authorization of the disbursement.

D. Prevent the overpayment of the account.

Answer (B) is correct. *(CPA, adapted)*
REQUIRED: The effect of displaying the amounts entered at a terminal.
DISCUSSION: The display of the amounts entered is an input control that permits visual verification of the accuracy of the input by the operator. This is termed closed-loop verification.
Answer (A) is incorrect because displaying the amounts entered at a terminal does not establish the validity of the account number. Answer (C) is incorrect because displaying the amounts entered at a terminal does not verify the authorization of the disbursement. Answer (D) is incorrect because displaying the amounts entered at a terminal does not prevent the overpayment of the account.

19. A client's program that recorded receiving report information entered directly by the receiving department on vendor shipment receipt included a reasonableness or limit test. Which of the following errors would this test likely detect?

A. The receipt was for a shipment from an unauthorized vendor.

B. The vendor shipped the wrong item.

C. The receiving department clerk entered the quantity of the product received as 0.

D. The shipment received from the vendor was past due by 2 weeks.

Answer (C) is correct. *(Publisher)*
REQUIRED: The error likely to be detected by a reasonableness or limit test.
DISCUSSION: Reasonableness or limit tests are used to test quantities received to determine if they are within acceptable limits. Entry of a product number with 0 received would be identified as probable error.
Answer (A) is incorrect because a validity test should be performed before order acceptance to determine if the vendor is an authorized vendor. Answer (B) is incorrect because the received products should be compared with the product numbers ordered to determine if they were ordered. Answer (D) is incorrect because the purchasing department should follow up on past due orders.

6.4 Electronic Data Interchange (EDI)

20. An audit of the electronic data interchange (EDI) area of a purchasing department revealed the facts listed below. Which one indicates the need for improved internal control?

A. Employees may access the computer system only via an ID and an encrypted password.

B. The system employs message sequencing as a way to monitor data transmissions.

C. Certain types of transactions may be made only at specific terminals.

D. Branch office employees may access the server with a single call via modem.

Answer (D) is correct. *(Publisher)*
REQUIRED: The condition that indicates the need for improved internal control.
DISCUSSION: The system should employ automatic dial-back to prevent intrusion by unauthorized parties. This procedure accepts an incoming modem call, disconnects, and automatically dials back a prearranged number to establish a permanent connection for data transfer or inquiry.
Answer (A) is incorrect because employee access to the computer system via an ID and an encrypted password is considered acceptable. Encrypted passwords further decrease the likelihood of unauthorized access. Answer (B) is incorrect because message sequencing detects unauthorized access by numbering each message and incrementing each message by one more than the last one sent. This procedure will detect a gap or duplicate. Answer (C) is incorrect because allowing certain types of transactions to be made only at specific terminals minimizes the likelihood of unauthorized access.

21. Which of the following statements is correct concerning internal control in an electronic data interchange (EDI) system?

A. Preventive controls generally are more important than detective controls in EDI systems.

B. Control objectives for EDI systems generally are different from the objectives for other information systems.

C. Internal controls in EDI systems rarely permit control risk to be assessed below the maximum.

D. Internal controls related to the segregation of duties generally are the most important controls in EDI systems.

Answer (A) is correct. *(CPA, adapted)*
REQUIRED: The true statement about EDI controls.
DISCUSSION: In general, preventive controls are more important than detective controls because the benefits typically outweigh the costs. In electronic processing, once a transaction is accepted, there is often little opportunity to apply detective controls. Thus, preventing errors or fraud before they happen is important.
Answer (B) is incorrect because the basic control objectives are the same regardless of the nature of the processing: to ensure the integrity of the information and to safeguard the assets. Answer (C) is incorrect because, to gather sufficient evidence in a sophisticated computer system, reliance on the controls is often necessary. Control risk may be assessed below the maximum if relevant controls are identified and tested and if the resulting evidential matter provides the degree of assurance necessary to support the assessed level of control risk.
Answer (D) is incorrect because the level of segregation of duties achieved in a manual system is usually not feasible in a computer system.

22. Which of the following is usually a benefit of transmitting transactions in an electronic data interchange (EDI) environment?

A. A compressed business cycle with lower year-end receivables balances.

B. A reduced need to test computer controls related to sales and collections transactions.

C. An increased opportunity to apply statistical sampling techniques to account balances.

D. No need to rely on third-party service providers to ensure security.

Answer (A) is correct. *(CPA, adapted)*
REQUIRED: The benefit of EDI.
DISCUSSION: EDI transactions are typically transmitted and processed in real time. Thus, EDI compresses the business cycle by eliminating delays. The time required to receive and process an order, ship goods, and receive payment is greatly reduced compared with that of a typical manual system. Accordingly, more rapid receipt of payment minimizes receivables and improves cash flow.
Answer (B) is incorrect because use of a sophisticated processing system increases the need to test computer controls. Answer (C) is incorrect because computer technology allows all transactions to be tested rather than just a sample. Answer (D) is incorrect because EDI often uses a VAN (value-added network) as a third-party service provider, and reliance on controls provided by the VAN may be critical.

23. Many entities use the Internet as a network to transmit electronic data interchange (EDI) transactions. An advantage of using the Internet for electronic commerce rather than a traditional value-added network (VAN) is that the Internet

A. Permits EDI transactions to be sent to trading partners as transactions occur.

B. Automatically batches EDI transactions to multiple trading partners.

C. Possesses superior characteristics regarding disaster recovery.

D. Converts EDI transactions to a standard format without translation software.

Answer (A) is correct. *(CPA, adapted)*
REQUIRED: The advantage of using the Internet to transmit EDI transactions.
DISCUSSION: VAN services have typically used a proprietary network or a network gatewayed with a specific set of other proprietary networks. A direct Internet connection permits real-time computer-to-computer communication for client-server applications, so transactions can be sent to trading partners as they occur.
Answer (B) is incorrect because the Internet does not automatically batch EDI transactions, although multiple trading partners are possible. Answer (C) is incorrect because the use of the Internet affects the entity's disaster recovery plan. Answer (D) is incorrect because, regardless of the network used to transmit transactions, they first must be translated into a standard format for transmission.

24. Which of the following statements is true concerning the security of messages in an electronic data interchange (EDI) system?

A. When confidentiality of data is the primary risk, message authentication is the preferred control rather than encryption.

B. Encryption performed by physically secure hardware devices is more secure than encryption performed by software.

C. Message authentication in EDI systems performs the same function as segregation of duties in other information systems.

D. Security in the transaction phase in EDI systems is not necessary because problems at that level will usually be identified by the service provider.

Answer (B) is correct. *(CPA, adapted)*
REQUIRED: The true statement about the security of messages in an EDI system.
DISCUSSION: Physically secure hardware devices for performing encryption are under the direct control of the client. Software is not easily controlled because it is portable. More control is achieved with the hardware approach. However, in the business environment, most encryption applications rely on software.
Answer (A) is incorrect because, when confidentiality is a concern, encryption and access controls should be used. Answer (C) is incorrect because authentication relates to authorization, not security issues. Answer (D) is incorrect because security in the EDI transaction phase is also an issue. The transmission of information to the service provider, such as a VAN, is subject to a variety of problems, for example, interception or alteration, that may not be detected by the service provider.

25. In building an electronic data interchange (EDI) system, what process is used to determine which elements in the entity's computer system correspond to the standard data elements?

A. Mapping.

B. Translation.

C. Encryption.

D. Decoding.

Answer (A) is correct. *(CPA, adapted)*
REQUIRED: The process used in the implementation phase of an EDI system to determine the elements in the entity's computer system corresponding to the standard data elements.
DISCUSSION: Conventions are the procedures for arranging data elements in specified formats for various accounting transactions, e.g., invoices, materials releases, and advance shipment notices. In an attempt to provide standardization and structure for EDI, organizations such as the American National Standards Institute (ANSI) have defined virtually every type of business transaction in terms of their fields and information content. These are termed transmission sets. By using such standards, communication between trading partners can be facilitated. Mapping entails determining which data elements used by the entity correspond to the standard data elements.
Answer (B) is incorrect because translation occurs during processing of transactions. Answer (C) is incorrect because encryption occurs during processing of transactions. Answer (D) is incorrect because decoding occurs during processing of transactions.

26. Which of the following is usually a benefit of using electronic funds transfer for international cash transactions?

A. Improvement of the audit trail for cash receipts and disbursements.

B. Creation of self-monitoring access controls.

C. Reduction of the frequency of data entry errors.

D. Off-site storage of source documents for cash transactions.

Answer (C) is correct. *(CPA, adapted)*
REQUIRED: The benefit of using EFT for international cash transactions.
DISCUSSION: The processing and transmission of electronic transactions, such as EFTs, virtually eliminates human interaction. This process not only helps eliminate errors but also allows for the rapid detection and recovery from errors when they do occur.
Answer (A) is incorrect because the audit trail is typically less apparent in an electronic environment than in a manual environment. Answer (B) is incorrect because a key control is management's establishment and monitoring of access controls. Answer (D) is incorrect because source documents are often eliminated in EFT transactions.

27. Which of the following is an essential element of the audit trail in an electronic data interchange (EDI) system?

A. Disaster recovery plans that ensure proper backup of files.

B. Encrypted hash totals that authenticate messages.

C. Activity logs that indicate failed transactions.

D. Hardware security modules that store sensitive data.

Answer (C) is correct. *(CPA, adapted)*
REQUIRED: The essential element in an EDI audit trail.
DISCUSSION: Because an audit trail allows for the tracing of a transaction from initiation to its disposition, an activity log provides a key link in the tracking process. Such a log provides information about users who have accessed the system, the files accessed, the processing accomplished, the time of access, and the amount of time the processing required.
Answer (A) is incorrect because disaster recovery plans are an important control for any system but do not relate to the audit trail. Answer (B) is incorrect because encrypted hash totals ensure the integrity of the transmission but do provide for an audit trail. Answer (D) is incorrect because security of storage is an important control, but it does not relate to the audit trail.

28. Which of the following characteristics distinguishes electronic data interchange (EDI) from other forms of electronic commerce?

A. EDI transactions are formatted using standards that are uniform worldwide.

B. EDI transactions need not comply with generally accepted accounting principles.

C. EDI transactions ordinarily are processed without the Internet.

D. EDI transactions are usually recorded without security and privacy concerns.

Answer (A) is correct. *(CPA, adapted)*
REQUIRED: The distinguishing characteristic of an EDI system.
DISCUSSION: Organizations such as the American National Standards Institute (ANSI) have defined virtually every type of business transaction in terms of their fields and information content. These definitions are termed transmission sets. When a trading partner sends a transmission set, the receiving computer can expect to receive the specified information in a specified format.
Answer (B) is incorrect because EDI transactions must comply with GAAP. Answer (C) is incorrect because the Internet is frequently used in EDI transactions. Answer (D) is incorrect because the use of EDI does not eliminate security and privacy concerns.

Use Gleim's **CPA Test Prep** for interactive testing with over 2,000 additional multiple-choice questions!

6.5 PRACTICE SIMULATION

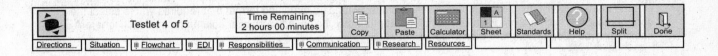

	Testlet 4 of 5	Time Remaining 2 hours 00 minutes	Copy	Paste	Calculator	Sheet	Standards	Help	Split	Done

| Directions | Situation | Flowchart | EDI | Responsibilities | Communication | Research | Resources | | | |

1. Directions

In the following simulation, you will be asked to complete various tasks related to the purchases-payables-cash distribution cycles. The simulation will provide all of the information necessary to do the work. For full credit, be sure to view and complete all work tabs.

Resources are available to you under the tab marked RESOURCES. You may want to review the resources before beginning the simulation.

2. Situation

Your client is contemplating establishing a fully integrated Electronic Data Interchange (EDI) system for its purchases, payables, and cash disbursements. It will be designed to take advantage of technology to facilitate purchases from supplier trading partners.

Currently, the client uses a manual system that has been documented by a flowchart. You have been discussing the issues related to the change from a manual system to an EDI system. The client is particularly interested in whether various management responsibilities in a purchases-payables-cash distribution cycle can be delegated to employees. The client's decision about the extent of automation of the new system will be influenced by these considerations.

The client is planning to make the change in the coming year, and you are concerned about the effect the change will have on your audit. You realize that it will require a reconsideration of internal control and a new assessment of control risk.

3. Flowchart

Below is a flowchart for the client's current purchasing and cash disbursement transactions. Within the flowchart are lettered blanks signifying missing information. This question has a matching format that requires you to select the correct response from a drop-down list. Write the appropriate choice in the answer column next to each letter. A choice may be used once, more than once, or not at all.

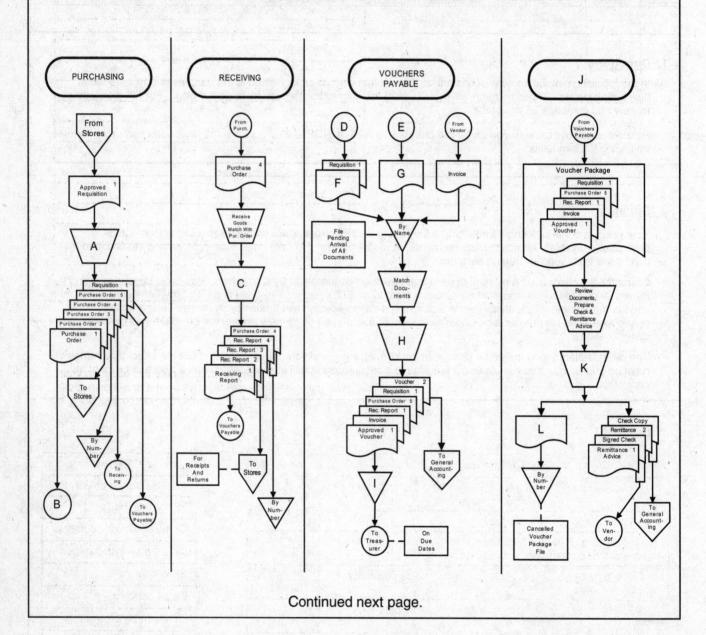

Continued next page.

3. Flowchart -- Continued

Letter	Answer
A	
B	
C	
D	
E	
F	
G	
H	
I	
J	
K	
L	

Choices
1. Purchase order No. 5
2. Unpaid voucher file, filed by due date
3. Sign checks and cancel voucher package documents
4. File by number
5. Prepare purchase order
6. From Purchasing
7. Treasurer
8. Stores
9. Receiving report No. 1
10. Canceled voucher purchase
11. To purchasing agent
12. From Receiving
13. Prepare receiving report
14. Prepare and approve voucher
15. To vendor

4. EDI System

Use the following phrases to complete the sentences relating to the new EDI system and its potential effect on your audit. This question has a matching format that requires you to select the correct response from a drop-down list. Write the appropriate choice in the answer column next to each sentence. Each choice may be used once, more than once, or not at all.

Phrases	Answer
1. An EDI system is often used to support the production system of _____.	
2. An advantage of EDI includes _____.	
3. One piece of evidence that the auditor should inspect to assure proper agreements with trading partners is _____.	
4. EDI often uses _____ as a third-party service provider.	
5. Auditing an EDI application requires the development of _____.	
6. _____ provides information about users who have accessed the EDI system.	
7. EDI eliminates _____ both internal and external.	
8. EDI messages should be _____ to insure privacy.	
9. Rules on how each "package of information" is structured are referred to as _____.	
10. An open environment would be created when EDI is conducted on _____.	

Choices
A) reduction of errors
B) the Internet
C) transmission protocols
D) a value-added network
E) encrypted
F) an audit trail
G) a written contract
H) paper documents
I) just-in-time
J) an activity log

5. Responsibilities

For each of the following, determine whether the responsibility belongs to management (M) or employees (E) in the purchases-payables-cash disbursements cycle. This question is presented in a check-the-box format that requires you to select the correct response from a given list.

Item	M	E
1. Preparation of purchase orders for required goods.		
2. Matching the documentation to support a payment voucher.		
3. Proper authorization of the purchase.		
4. Approval of the payment for those goods and services that were ordered, received, and properly invoiced.		
5. Monitor ordering the proper quality and quantity of goods on a timely basis.		
6. Provide physical control over the goods.		
7. Count and inspect the goods and prepare the receiving report.		
8. Approve payment to receive discount.		
9. Record the purchase transaction.		
10. Contract for proper terms and prices from the vendor.		

6. Communication

In a brief memorandum to your client's management team, discuss the control and audit implications of EDI. Type your communication in your word processor program and print out the copy in a memorandum style format.

REMINDER: Your response will be graded for both technical content and writing skills. You should demonstrate your ability to develop, organize, and express your ideas. Do not convey information in the form of a table, bullet point list, or other abbreviated presentation.

To: Client Management
From: CPA
Subject: Objectives of a properly operating purchases-payables-cash disbursements cycle

7. Research

Use the research materials available to you to find the answers to the following question in the AICPA Professional Standards. Print the appropriate citation in its entirety from the source you choose. Use only one source. This is a copy-and-paste item.

Information that supports a financial statement assertion may be electronically generated, for example, in an EDI system. What guidelines must an auditor follow with regard to obtaining an understanding of the component of internal control that is most directly relevant to automated information systems?

Unofficial Answers

3. Flowchart (12 Gradable Items)

A) 5. Prepare purchase order: The trapezoid symbol represents a manual (offline) activity. The input is the approved purchase requisition, and the output of this process in Purchasing is the purchase order. Accordingly, the activity is "Prepare purchase order."

B) 15. To vendor: Purchase order 1 is sent to the vendor of the goods ordered. All other copies of the purchase order are accounted for. The circle is a connection symbol. Thus, copy 1 of the purchase order goes "To vendor."

C) 13. Prepare receiving report: The goods are received in Receiving, and the output of the manual activity in trapezoid C is the receiving report. Consequently, the activity is "Prepare receiving report."

D) 6. From Purchasing: Circle D in the vouchers payable section of the flowchart represents documents transferred from some other location. Copy 1 of the requisition and copy 5 of the purchase order came from Purchasing where the documents were previously identified. Hence, circle D is "From Purchasing."

E) 12. From Receiving: Circle E in the vouchers payable section represents a document transferred from some other location. Copy 1 of the receiving report came from Receiving. Because circle D reflects the transfer of requisition 1 and purchase order 5, the only unidentified document is the receiving report. Thus, circle E is "From Receiving."

F) 1. Purchase order No. 5: The documents sent from Purchasing to Vouchers Payable are requisition 1 and purchase order 5. Requisition 1 is shown with document F. Document F must therefore be "Purchase order No. 5."

G) 9. Receiving report No. 1 As noted in the answer to question 5, circle E represents "From Receiving." The document sent from Receiving is "Receiving report No. 1."

H) 14. Prepare and approve voucher: The responsibility of Vouchers Payable is to assemble documentation appropriate to support a payment voucher. Once the requisition, purchase order, receiving report, and invoice have been matched, a voucher is created.

I) 2. Unpaid voucher file, filed by due date: The inverted triangle represents a file. The voucher and related supporting documents are filed. The vouchers will be filed by due date, retrieved when due, and sent to the treasurer for payment.

J) 7. Treasurer: Vouchers Payable sends the voucher and related supporting documentation to the treasurer (item J. on the flowchart) on the due date.

K) 3. Sign checks and cancel voucher package documents: The treasurer reviews the documentation in support for the payment. A check is then prepared and signed, and the support for the voucher is canceled so that it cannot be used to support a duplicate payment.

L) 10. Canceled voucher package: Once the check has been mailed, the supporting canceled voucher documentation is filed.

4. EDI System (10 Gradable Items)

1. I) just-in-time
2. A) reduction of errors
3. G) a written contract
4. D) a value-added network
5. F) an audit trail
6. J) an activity log
7. H) paper documents
8. E) encrypted
9. C) transmission protocols
10. B) the Internet

5. Responsibilities (10 Gradable Items)

1. E - Employees
2. E - Employees
3. M - Management
4. M - Management
5. M - Management
6. E - Employees
7. E - Employees
8. M - Management
9. E - Employees
10. M - Management

6. Communication (5 Gradable Items; For grading instructions, please refer to page 11.)

To: Client management
From: CPA
Subject: Control and audit implications of EDI

An organization that has reengineered its procedures and processes to take full advantage of EDI may have eliminated even the electronic equivalents of paper documents. For example, the buyer's point-of-sale (POS) system may directly transmit information to the seller, which delivers on a JIT (just-in-time) basis. Purchase orders, invoices, and receiving reports are replaced with (1) a long-term contract establishing quantities, prices, and delivery schedules; (2) production schedules; (3) advance shipment notices; (4) evaluated receipts settlements (periodic payment authorizations transmitted to the trading partner with no need for matching purchase orders, invoices, and receiving reports); and (5) payments by electronic funds transfer (EFT) that transfer money from one account to another by computer.

Accordingly, auditors must seek new forms of evidence to support assertions about EDI transactions, whether the evidence exists at the auditee organization, the trading partner, or a third party, such as a value-added network. Examples of such evidence are (1) the authorized paper purchase contract; (2) an electronic completed production schedule image; and (3) internal and external evidence of evaluated receipts settlements sent to the trading partner. Furthermore, auditors must evaluate electronic signatures and reviews when testing controls. Auditors also may need to consider other subsystems when testing a particular subsystem. Thus, production cycle evidence may be needed to test the expenditure cycle.

EDI often uses a VAN (value-added network) as a third-party service provider, and reliance on controls provided by the VAN may be critical. VANs are privately owned telecommunications carriers that sell capacity to outside users. Among other things, a VAN provides a mailbox service permitting EDI messages to be sent, sorted, and held until needed in the recipient's computer system.

Auditing an EDI application requires consideration of the audit trail. In addition to the elements listed above, an essential element of an EDI audit trail is an activity log. Because an audit trail allows for the tracing of a transaction from initiation to its disposition, an activity log provides a key link in the tracking process. Such a log provides information about users who have accessed the system, the files accessed, the processing accomplished, the time of access, and the amount of time the processing required.

7. Research (6 Gradable Items)

AU Section 319 – *Consideration of Internal Control in a Financial Statement Audit*

Information and Communication

.47 The information system relevant to financial reporting objectives, which includes the accounting system, consists of the procedures, whether automated or manual, and records established to initiate, record, process, and report entity transactions (as well as events and conditions) and to maintain accountability for the related assets, liabilities, and equity. The quality of system-generated information affects management's ability to make appropriate decisions in controlling the entity's activities and to prepare reliable financial reports.

.48 Communication involves providing an understanding of individual roles and responsibilities pertaining to internal control over financial reporting.

.49 The auditor should obtain sufficient knowledge of the information system relevant to financial reporting to understand-
• The classes of transactions in the entity's operations that are significant to the financial statements.
• The procedures, both automated and manual, by which transactions are initiated, recorded, processed, and reported from their occurrence to their inclusion in the financial statements.
• The related accounting records, whether electronic or manual, supporting information, and specific accounts in the financial statements involved in initiating, recording, processing, and reporting transactions.
• How the information system captures other events and conditions that are significant to the financial statements.
• The financial reporting process used to prepare the entity's financial statements, including significant accounting estimates and disclosures.

.50 When IT is used to initiate, record, process, or report transactions or other financial data for inclusion in financial statements, the systems and programs may include controls related to the corresponding assertions for significant accounts or may be critical to the effective functioning of manual controls that depend on IT.

.51 In obtaining an understanding of the financial reporting process, the auditor should understand the automated and manual procedures an entity uses to prepare financial statements and related disclosures, and how misstatements may occur. Such procedures include-
• *The procedures used to enter transaction totals into the general ledger.* In some information systems, IT may be used to automatically transfer such information from transaction processing systems to general ledger or financial reporting systems. The automated processes and controls in such systems may reduce the risk of inadvertent error but do not overcome the risk that individuals may inappropriately override such automated processes, for example, by changing the amounts being automatically passed to the general ledger or financial reporting system. Furthermore, in planning the audit, the auditor should be aware that when IT is used to automatically transfer information there may be little or no visible evidence of such intervention in the information systems.
• *The procedures used to initiate, record, and process journal entries in the general ledger.* An entity's financial reporting process used to prepare the financial statements typically includes the use of standard journal entries that are required on a recurring basis to record transactions such as monthly sales, purchases, and cash disbursements, or to record accounting estimates that are periodically made by management such as changes in the estimate of uncollectible accounts receivable. An entity's financial reporting process also includes the use of nonstandard journal entries to record nonrecurring or unusual transactions or adjustments such as a business combination or disposal, or a nonrecurring estimate such as an asset impairment. In manual, paper-based general ledger systems, such journal entries may be identified through inspection of ledgers, journals, and supporting documentation. However, when IT is used to maintain the general ledger and prepare financial statements, such entries may exist only in electronic form and may be more difficult to identify through physical inspection of printed documents.
• *Other procedures used to record recurring and nonrecurring adjustments to the financial statements.* These are procedures that are not reflected in formal journal entries, such as consolidating adjustments, report combinations, and reclassifications.

.52 The auditor also should obtain sufficient knowledge of the means the entity uses to communicate financial reporting roles and responsibilities and significant matters relating to financial reporting.

Scoring Schedule:

	Correct Responses		Gradable Items		Weights		
Tab 3	_____	÷	12	×	20%	=	_____
Tab 4	_____	÷	10	×	20%	=	_____
Tab 5	_____	÷	10	×	20%	=	_____
Tab 6	_____	÷	5	×	30%	=	_____
Tab 7	_____	÷	6	×	10%	=	_____
							(Your Score)

Use Gleim's *CPA Review Online* to practice more simulations in a realistic environment.

STUDY UNIT SEVEN
INTERNAL CONTROL -- PAYROLL AND OTHER CYCLES

(7 pages of outline)

7.1	Responsibilities and Organizational Structure	229
7.2	Payroll Manual System Flowchart	230
7.3	Technology Considerations for the Payroll Cycle	232
7.4	Other Cycles	234
7.5	Practice Simulation	243

The focus of this study unit is on payroll. Flowcharts are used to gain a perspective on the document and information flow. However, the flowcharts are limited to essential points, particularly the payroll computer system flowchart. The narrative should be studied in conjunction with the flowcharts. Candidates should stress gaining an understanding of the objectives of the controls.

Controls related to other accounts, not previously included in the study units, are also covered at the end of this study unit. Only the major controls are addressed, giving consideration to the questions traditionally asked on the CPA exam.

7.1 RESPONSIBILITIES AND ORGANIZATIONAL STRUCTURE

1. Management is responsible for the establishment of the controls to ensure

   a. Proper authorization of the payroll
   b. Appropriate calculation of the payroll
   c. Safeguarding of assets associated with the payment of payroll
   d. Proper distribution of the payroll
   e. Proper accounting for the payroll transactions

2. For audit planning purposes, the auditor is responsible for obtaining an understanding of internal control for payroll, determining that controls are in place, judging whether to test controls, and assessing control risk related to the payroll cycle.

3. Although the following information is similar to that in the previous two study units, it has been repeated for the reader's convenience.

4. The organizational structure should separate duties and responsibilities into

   a. Authorization of payroll transactions
   b. Recording of payroll transactions
   c. Custody of the assets (e.g., payroll checks) associated with payroll transactions

5. Duties and responsibilities for payroll have traditionally been appropriately separated. However, cost-benefit considerations may affect the organizational structure and complete separation may not be feasible. Compensating controls will likely be established when segregation of duties is not maintained. Typical compensating controls may include

   a. More supervision
   b. Owner involvement in the payroll process

6. Responsibilities of the organizational subunits involved in the payroll cycle include

   a. **Personnel** provides an authorized list of employees and associated pay rates, deductions, and exemptions.
   b. **Payroll** is an accounting function responsible for calculating the payroll (i.e., preparing the payroll register) based on authorizations from Personnel and the authorized time records from Timekeeping.

c.   **Timekeeping** is an accounting function overseeing the employees' recording of hours on time cards (using the time clock) and receiving and reconciling the job time tickets from Manufacturing.

d.   **Cost Accounting** is an accounting function that accumulates direct materials, direct labor, and overhead costs on job order cost sheets to determine the costs of production.

e.   **Accounts Payable** prepares the payment voucher based on the payroll register prepared by Payroll.

f.   **Cash Disbursements** signs and deposits a check based on the payment voucher into a separate payroll account, prepares individual employee paychecks, and distributes paychecks.

7.   Stop and review! You have completed the outline for this subunit. Study multiple-choice questions 1 and 2 on page 235.

7.2 PAYROLL MANUAL SYSTEM FLOWCHART

1.   Study the flowchart on the next page. Understand and visualize the payroll process and controls. The Organizational Chart in Study Unit 5 displays the reporting responsibilities of each function in the flowchart. Read the following description as needed. Note the control activities implemented.

2.   **Description of Document Flow.** To simplify the presentation, the flowchart does not show the disposition, e.g., the filing of documents, or other supplemental procedures. The process begins at the point labeled "start."

a.   Personnel provides authorizations of employees, pay rates, and deductions to Payroll just prior to calculation of the payroll.

b.   Employees punch their time cards in Timekeeping before and after each shift.

c.   The shop supervisor assigns employees production order tasks to be performed, and each employee completes a job time ticket for each task performed. Indirect labor (e.g., down time, cleaning machines, and setup) is also reported on job time tickets. At the end of the shift, the shop supervisor determines that employees have submitted job time tickets to account for all time. The job time tickets are then forwarded to Timekeeping.

d.   Timekeeping reconciles the clock cards with the job time tickets to assure that employees were present and working. Clock cards are approved (e.g., initialed) by Timekeeping.

e.   Clock cards are forwarded to Payroll as authorization of the hours worked. The authorized employees, rates, and deductions from Personnel, together with the authorized hours from Timekeeping, are used to calculate the payroll for the period. A payroll register is prepared listing each employee, gross pay, all deductions, and net pay. The payroll register is then sent to Accounts Payable.

f.   Accounts Payable uses the payroll register as authorization to prepare a payment voucher and check for the payroll equal to the total of the net pay to employees. (Actually, a number of separate vouchers and checks will be prepared for each required payment generated from the payroll; e.g., a check will be prepared with the IRS as payee for withholding taxes, and a check may be prepared with the union as payee for withheld union dues, etc.).

g.   The check, voucher, and supporting documentation will be sent to Cash Disbursements for signing. The check for the net payroll drawn on the general cash account is deposited in a separate payroll account. Checks drawn on this special account are prepared for each employee; that is, an imprest payroll checking account is used. The checks are distributed to the employees.

Payroll Manual System Flowchart

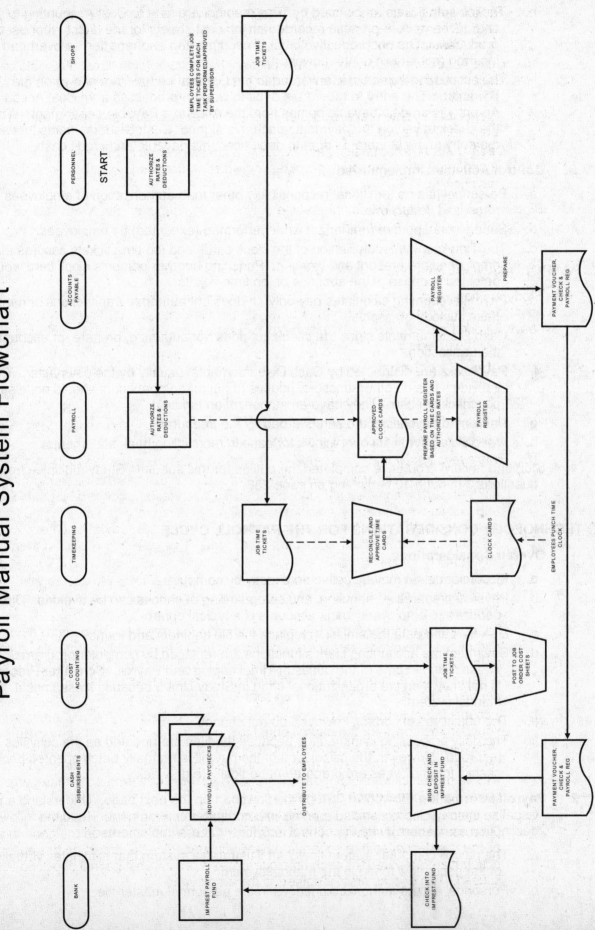

h.   The job time tickets, once used by Timekeeping, are sent to Cost Accounting to charge the work-in-process recorded on job cost sheets for the direct labor used in production. The nonproductive labor is accumulated and reported as overhead incurred (not shown on the flowchart).

i.   The accounting entries are forwarded to the General Ledger (not shown on the flowchart). The entry to record the debit to work-in-process is from Cost Accounting. An entry to credit a payable comes from the Accounts Payable department. When the check based on the payment voucher is signed, Cash Disbursements forwards the entry to the General Ledger to debit accounts payable and credit cash.

3.   **Control Activities Implemented**

a.   Personnel has no functional responsibility other than authorization of employees, pay rates, and deductions.

b.   Supervisors approve (authorize) work performed (executed) by employees.

c.   The Timekeeping reconciliation of the clock cards and job time tickets assures that employees are present and working. Punching another person's clock card would be detected because of the absence of job time tickets.

d.   Payroll accounting calculates pay only. It does not authorize transactions or handle (take custody of) assets.

e.   Cash Disbursements signs the check but does not authorize, prepare, or account for the transaction.

f.   Paychecks are distributed by Cash Disbursements, usually by the paymaster. This individual has no other functions relative to payroll. Supervisors should not distribute paychecks because they have an authorization function.

g.   Unclaimed paychecks are safeguarded by the treasurer.

h.   A separate payroll account allows for ease in reconciling bank statements.

4.   Stop and review! You have completed the outline for this subunit. Study multiple-choice questions 3 through 10 beginning on page 236.

7.3 TECHNOLOGY CONSIDERATIONS FOR THE PAYROLL CYCLE

1.   **Overall Considerations**

a.   Most information may be collected directly by computer.

b.   Physical preparation, handling, and safeguarding of checks can be avoided. Direct deposit into employees' bank accounts is a typical control.

c.   Disk files and data transmission replace the file cabinets and forms.

d.   Several of the accounting clerk's functions are replaced by computer programs. These include some of the duties of Timekeeping and Payroll. Computer Processing is not shown on the organizational chart in Study Unit 5 because it assumes a manual system.

e.   The objectives of control, however, do not change.

f.   The daily processing is immediate because the files are updated as the activities are recorded. However, the calculation of the payroll is normally batch oriented because checks to employees are prepared periodically (e.g., weekly).

2.   **Payroll Information Flowchart**. Study the flowchart on the next page. Understand and visualize the payroll process and controls in a computer environment. Read the following description as needed. Note the control activities that are implemented.

a.   The payroll computer system flowchart illustrates a system that eliminates virtually all of the paper flow found in the manual system.

b.   Personnel makes authorized changes in the personnel master file.

c. As the employee enters the plant, a clock card record is initiated by passing an ID card through a terminal that contains the timekeeping program.

d. Production orders, based on the production schedule, are released to the shops via terminal. Shop supervisors assign production employees to the tasks. Prior to beginning, the production employee logs in to the system using his/her ID card. When the production job is complete, the employee logs out, thereby updating the production record. Information is passed to the timekeeping program to be reconciled with the time records and to update the payroll master file.

e. Periodically (e.g., weekly), information from the payroll master file is matched with wage rate, deduction, and exemption information to calculate the payroll. The checks are printed and the general ledger updated (not shown on flowchart).

Payroll Computer System Flowchart

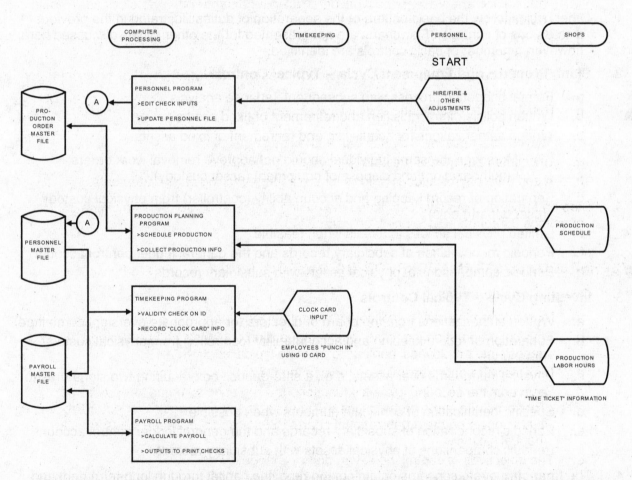

3. **Control Activities Implemented.** The major computer-related controls are identified here. The controls are defined in Study Unit 4.

a. Access controls are used requiring passwords and identification numbers. Only the Personnel department has access to the personnel master file and can make changes. Other departments are limited to the changes that can be made to files. Each shop employee is issued an identification card used as input to initiate timekeeping transactions.

b. Preformatted computer video screens are used for inputs.

    c.   Validity checks are made to assure that an employee record exists on the personnel file before any transactions are accepted.

    d.   Time records from Timekeeping are automatically reconciled with the production time logged in the shops.

    e.   Reasonableness tests are made when appropriate, e.g., testing at the end of the week to assure that total hours recorded for an employee are not in excess of 40 hours or the acceptable limit.

    f.   Exception reports are printed, identifying all questionable and potentially incorrect transactions. These transactions are investigated and any corrections are made for reprocessing.

4.   Stop and review! You have completed the outline for this subunit. Study multiple-choice questions 11 through 13 on page 238.

7.4 OTHER CYCLES

1.   Other cycles follow the basic pattern of the separation of duties illustrated in the previous discussions of controls. Flowcharts are not presented for the other cycles discussed here; however, a number of basic controls are identified.

2.   **Plant, Property, and Equipment Cycle -- Typical Controls**

    a.   Formal budgeting process with subsequent variance analysis

    b.   Written policies for acquisition and retirement of fixed assets

    c.   Written authorizations for acquisition and retirement of fixed assets

        1)   Moreover, the same individual should not approve removal work orders (authorization) and dispose of equipment (asset custody).

    d.   Separation of record keeping and accountability (controller) from physical custody (user departments)

    e.   Limited physical access to assets when feasible

    f.   Periodic reconciliation of subsidiary records and the general ledger control account

    g.   Periodic comparisons of physical assets with subsidiary records

3.   **Investing Cycle -- Typical Controls**

    a.   Written authorizations from the board of directors (or appropriate oversight committee)

    b.   Separation of record keeping and accountability (controller) from physical custody (treasury)

    c.   Physical safeguards over assets, e.g., a safe-deposit box requiring two signatures to gain admittance

    d.   Specific identification of certificate numbers when possible

    e.   Periodic reconciliation of subsidiary records and the general ledger control account

    f.   Periodic comparisons of physical assets with subsidiary records

4.   The **financing cycle** concerns obtaining and repaying capital through long-term debt and shareholders' equity transactions. These major transactions are authorized by the board of directors or other ultimate authority.

5. **Inventory and Warehousing Cycle**

a. Transfers of raw materials, finished goods, and costs are subject to cost accounting internal control activities.

b. The objectives of internal control include safeguarding assets and promoting the reliability of financial reporting. Thus, internal control includes physical controls over storage, assignment of custody to specific individuals, use of prenumbered documents for authorization of transfers, and perpetual inventory records.

    1) For example, requisitions and other documents should evidence proper authorizations, quantities, descriptions, and dates, and subsidiary ledgers should be independently reconciled with control accounts.

6. Stop and review! You have completed the outline for this subunit. Study multiple-choice questions 14 through 25 beginning on page 239.

QUESTIONS

7.1 Responsibilities and Organizational Structure

1. The purpose of segregating the duties of hiring personnel and distributing payroll checks is to separate the

A. Authorization of transactions from the custody of related assets.

B. Operational responsibility from the record-keeping responsibility.

C. Human resources function from the controllership function.

D. Administrative controls from the internal accounting controls.

Answer (A) is correct. *(CPA, adapted)*
    REQUIRED: The purpose of segregating the duties of hiring personnel and distributing payroll checks.
    DISCUSSION: In principle, the payroll function should be divided into its authorization, recording, and custody functions. Authorization of hiring, wage rates, and deductions is provided by personnel. Authorization of hours worked (executed by employees) is provided by production. Based upon these authorizations, accounting calculates and records the payroll. Based on the calculated amounts, the treasurer prepares and distributes payroll checks.
    Answer (B) is incorrect because neither hiring personnel (authorization) nor distributing checks (asset custody) is a record-keeping activity. Answer (C) is incorrect because controllership is a record-keeping activity. Neither the controller nor the personnel department (human resources function) should distribute checks. Answer (D) is incorrect because the professional standards no longer recognize the distinction between administrative controls and internal accounting controls.

2. In determining the effectiveness of an entity's policies and procedures relating to the existence or occurrence assertion for payroll transactions, an auditor most likely would inquire about and

A. Observe the segregation of duties concerning personnel responsibilities and payroll disbursement.

B. Inspect evidence of accounting for prenumbered payroll checks.

C. Recompute the payroll deductions for employee fringe benefits.

D. Verify the preparation of the monthly payroll account bank reconciliation.

Answer (A) is correct. *(CPA, adapted)*
    REQUIRED: The audit procedure to test controls relating to the existence or occurrence assertion for payroll transactions.
    DISCUSSION: In considering whether transactions actually occurred, the auditor is most concerned about the proper separation of duties between the personnel department (authorization) and the payroll department (processing the transactions).
    Answer (B) is incorrect because accounting for prenumbered payroll checks is related to the completeness assertion. Answer (C) is incorrect because recomputation of the payroll deductions is related to the valuation assertion. Answer (D) is incorrect because the bank reconciliation is related to the completeness and valuation assertions.

7.2 Payroll Manual System Flowchart

3. The sampling unit in a test of controls pertaining to the existence of payroll transactions ordinarily is a(n)

A. Clock card or time ticket.

B. Employee Form W-2.

C. Employee personnel record.

D. Payroll register entry.

Answer (D) is correct. *(CPA, adapted)*
REQUIRED: The evidence required to verify the existence of payroll transactions.
DISCUSSION: Determining the existence of payroll transactions is an internal control objective of the personnel and payroll cycle. The payroll register records each payroll transaction for each employee. Thus, an entry in the payroll register verifies an existing payroll transaction.
Answer (A) is incorrect because clock cards and job time tickets are records of hours worked. Answer (B) is incorrect because W-2 forms provide withholding and exemption information. Answer (C) is incorrect because personnel records contain employment data.

4. Effective internal control activities over the payroll function may include

A. Reconciliation of totals on job time tickets with job reports by employees responsible for those specific jobs.

B. Verification of agreement of job time tickets with employee clock card hours by a timekeeping department employee.

C. Preparation of payroll transaction journal entries by an employee who reports to the supervisor of the personnel department.

D. Custody of rate authorization records by the supervisor of the payroll department.

Answer (B) is correct. *(CPA, adapted)*
REQUIRED: The effective internal control over the payroll function.
DISCUSSION: The total time spent on jobs should closely approximate the total time indicated on time cards. Timekeeping's comparison of these records should provide an independent check of the accuracy of time reported on the time cards.
Answer (A) is incorrect because an independent party should perform the review function; employees should not check themselves. Answer (C) is incorrect because the payroll department should prepare the payroll transaction journal entries. If the personnel department performed this task, authorization and record keeping would be combined. Answer (D) is incorrect because personnel authorizes the pay rates used in the payroll calculation.

5. Which of the following internal control activities most likely would prevent direct labor hours from being charged to manufacturing overhead?

A. Periodic independent counts of work in process for comparison to recorded amounts.

B. Comparison of daily journal entries with approved production orders.

C. Use of time tickets to record actual labor worked on production orders.

D. Reconciliation of work-in-process inventory with periodic cost budgets.

Answer (C) is correct. *(CPA, adapted)*
REQUIRED: The control activity to prevent direct labor hours from being charged to manufacturing overhead.
DISCUSSION: Time tickets should specifically identify labor hours as direct or indirect.
Answer (A) is incorrect because independent counts of work in process for comparison with recorded amounts provide assurance that all inventories are accounted for but do not assure proper classification of the costs within the account. Answer (B) is incorrect because comparison of daily journal entries with approved production orders only provides assurance that costs are being assigned to production orders. Answer (D) is incorrect because reconciliation of work-in-process inventory with periodic cost budgets is an analytical procedure that might detect but would not prevent the problem.

6. Which of the following activities most likely would be considered a weakness in an entity's internal control over payroll?

A. A voucher for the amount of the payroll is prepared in the general accounting department based on the payroll department's payroll summary.

B. Payroll checks are prepared by the accounts payable department and signed by the treasurer.

C. The employee who distributes payroll checks returns unclaimed payroll checks to the payroll department.

D. The personnel department sends employees' termination notices to the payroll department.

Answer (C) is correct. *(CPA, adapted)*
REQUIRED: The ineffective internal control over payroll.
DISCUSSION: The payroll department assembles payroll information, which is a recording function. Custody of assets, such as unclaimed payroll checks, is incompatible with record keeping.
Answer (A) is incorrect because preparation of a voucher is appropriately performed by the accounting department, which has a record-keeping function. Answer (B) is incorrect because the treasurer's signing of checks is consistent with the asset custody function. Answer (D) is incorrect because the personnel department properly performs the authorization function regarding employment transactions.

7. Which of the following departments most likely would approve changes in pay rates and deductions from employee salaries?

    A. Personnel.

    B. Treasurer.

    C. Controller.

    D. Payroll.

Answer (A) is correct. *(CPA, adapted)*
    REQUIRED: The department that most likely would approve changes in pay rates and deductions.
    DISCUSSION: The personnel department provides the authorization for payroll-related transactions, e.g., hiring, termination, and changes in pay rates and deductions.
    Answer (B) is incorrect because the treasurer performs a custody function for payroll-related transactions. Answer (C) is incorrect because the payroll department, which is overseen by the controller, has a record keeping function for payroll-related transactions. Answer (D) is incorrect because the payroll department, which is overseen by the controller, has a record keeping function for payroll-related transactions.

8. In meeting the control objective of safeguarding of assets, which department should be responsible for

	Distribution of Paychecks	Custody of Unclaimed Paychecks
A.	Treasurer	Treasurer
B.	Payroll	Treasurer
C.	Treasurer	Payroll
D.	Payroll	Payroll

Answer (A) is correct. *(CPA, adapted)*
    REQUIRED: The department(s) responsible for the distribution of paychecks and the custody of unclaimed paychecks.
    DISCUSSION: Separating paycheck preparation from distribution makes it more difficult for fictitious employees to receive checks. In principle, the payroll function should be divided into its authorization, recording, and custody functions. Authorization of hiring, wage rates, and deductions is provided by personnel. Authorization of hours worked is provided by production. Based upon these authorizations, accounting calculates and records the payroll. Based on the calculated amounts, the treasurer prepares and distributes payroll checks. Consistent with its asset custody function, the treasurer should distribute paychecks so as to prevent payments to fictitious employees. Furthermore, the treasurer rather than the payroll department should receive unclaimed paychecks for safeguarding.

9. An auditor most likely would assess control risk at the maximum if the payroll department supervisor is responsible for

    A. Examining authorization forms for new employees.

    B. Comparing payroll registers with original batch transmittal data.

    C. Authorizing payroll rate changes for all employees.

    D. Hiring all subordinate payroll department employees.

Answer (C) is correct. *(CPA, adapted)*
    REQUIRED: The payroll department supervisor's responsibility that would cause assessment of control risk at the maximum.
    DISCUSSION: The payroll department should be independent of the personnel department, which would be responsible for authorizing all payroll rate changes for the employees of the entity. A supervisor would be authorized, however, to initiate requests for rate increases for supervised employees.
    Answer (A) is incorrect because the mere examination of authorization forms would not cause control risk concerns. Answer (B) is incorrect because it would be appropriate for the payroll department to compare payroll registers with original batch transmittal data and to reconcile any differences. Answer (D) is incorrect because a supervisor's function typically includes the hiring and firing of subordinate employees.

10. Which of the following is a control activity that most likely could help prevent employee payroll fraud?

    A. The personnel department promptly sends employee termination notices to the payroll supervisor.

    B. Employees who distribute payroll checks forward unclaimed payroll checks to the absent employees' supervisors.

    C. Salary rates resulting from new hires are approved by the payroll supervisor.

    D. Total hours used for determination of gross pay are calculated by the payroll supervisor.

Answer (A) is correct. *(CPA, adapted)*
    REQUIRED: The control to prevent payroll fraud.
    DISCUSSION: The personnel department should forward personnel changes to payroll promptly to ensure that proper authorizations are used to calculate the payroll.
    Answer (B) is incorrect because unclaimed payroll checks should be returned to the treasury department for safeguarding, not to supervisors. Answer (C) is incorrect because the personnel department, not the payroll supervisor, approves salary rates. Answer (D) is incorrect because the calculation of batch totals in the payroll department is too late in the payroll process to effectively prevent fraud.

7.3 Technology Considerations for the Payroll Cycle

11. Matthews Corp. has changed from a system of recording time worked on clock cards to a computerized payroll system in which employees record time in and out with magnetic cards. The computer system automatically updates all payroll records. Because of this change

    A. A generalized computer audit program must be used.

    B. Part of the audit trail is altered.

    C. The potential for payroll-related fraud is diminished.

    D. Transactions must be processed in batches.

Answer (B) is correct. *(CPA, adapted)*
    REQUIRED: The effect of computerization of a payroll system.
    DISCUSSION: In a manual payroll system, a paper trail of documents would be created to provide audit evidence that controls over each step in processing were in place and functioning. One element of a computer system that differentiates it from a manual system is that a transaction trail useful for auditing purposes might exist only for a brief time or only in computer-readable form.
    Answer (A) is incorrect because use of generalized audit software is only one of many ways of auditing through a computer. Answer (C) is incorrect because conversion to a computer system may actually increase the chance of fraud by eliminating segregation of incompatible functions and other controls. Answer (D) is incorrect because automatic updating indicates that processing is not in batch mode.

12. An auditor most likely would introduce test data into a computerized payroll system to test internal controls related to the

    A. Existence of unclaimed payroll checks held by supervisors.

    B. Early cashing of payroll checks by employees.

    C. Discovery of invalid employee I.D. numbers.

    D. Proper approval of overtime by supervisors.

Answer (C) is correct. *(CPA, adapted)*
    REQUIRED: The most likely reason an auditor would introduce test data into a computerized payroll system.
    DISCUSSION: Test data would be used to test programmed controls. Both valid and invalid transactions would be contrived and processed against the master file and the authorizations maintained by the personnel department to determine whether invalid I.D. numbers exist within the system.
    Answer (A) is incorrect because unclaimed payroll checks are held by supervisors external to the computerized payroll system. Answer (B) is incorrect because the inspection of bank statements would allow the auditor to determine whether payroll checks had been cashed prior to the dates of the checks. Answer (D) is incorrect because authorization of overtime would be performed by supervisors external to the computerized payroll system.

13. Which of the following activities most likely would detect whether payroll data were altered during processing?

    A. Monitor authorized distribution of data control sheets.

    B. Use test data to verify the performance of edit routines.

    C. Examine source documents for approval by supervisors.

    D. Segregate duties between approval of hardware and software specifications.

Answer (B) is correct. *(CPA, adapted)*
    REQUIRED: The activity most likely to detect alteration of payroll data during processing.
    DISCUSSION: The test data approach uses the computer to test the processing logic and controls within the system and the records produced. The auditor prepares a set of dummy transactions specifically designed to test the control activities that management claims to have incorporated into the processing programs. The auditor can expect the controls to be applied to the transactions in the prescribed manner. Thus, the auditor is testing the effectiveness of the controls over the payroll data.
    Answer (A) is incorrect because these control measures detect alteration of data outside the computer, not during processing. Answer (C) is incorrect because these control measures detect alteration of data outside the computer, not during processing. Answer (D) is incorrect because segregation of duties between hardware and software approval will not affect data during processing.

7.4 Other Cycles

14. Equipment acquisitions that are misclassified as maintenance expense most likely would be detected by an internal control activity that provides for

A. Segregation of duties for employees in the accounts payable department.

B. Independent verification of invoices for disbursements recorded as equipment acquisitions.

C. Investigation of variances within a formal budgeting system.

D. Authorization by the board of directors of significant equipment acquisitions.

Answer (C) is correct. *(CPA, adapted)*
REQUIRED: The control activity to detect misclassification of equipment acquisitions as maintenance expense.
DISCUSSION: A formal planning and budgeting system that estimates maintenance expense at a certain level will report a significant variance if capital expenditures are charged to the account. Investigation of the variance is likely to disclose the misclassification.
Answer (A) is incorrect because accounts payable assembles the required payment documentation, but is unlikely to question the classification of the expenditure. Answer (B) is incorrect because testing the population of recorded equipment acquisitions will not detect items misclassified as maintenance expense. Answer (D) is incorrect because the misclassification would occur subsequent to authorization.

15. Which of the following activities is most likely to prevent the improper disposition of equipment?

A. A separation of duties between those authorized to dispose of equipment and those authorized to approve removal work orders.

B. The use of serial numbers to identify equipment that could be sold.

C. Periodic comparison of removal work orders with authorizing documentation.

D. A periodic analysis of the scrap sales and the repairs and maintenance accounts.

Answer (A) is correct. *(CPA, adapted)*
REQUIRED: The activity most likely to prevent the improper disposition of equipment.
DISCUSSION: Segregation of duties reduces the opportunity for an individual both to perpetrate and to conceal errors or fraud. Accordingly, the authorization, recording, and asset custody functions should be separated (AU 319). Thus, the same individual should not approve removal work orders (authorization) and dispose of equipment (asset custody).
Answer (B) is incorrect because the use of serial numbers to identify equipment that could be sold may detect but will not prevent improper dispositions. Answer (C) is incorrect because periodic comparison of removal work orders with authorizing documentation may detect but will not prevent improper dispositions. Answer (D) is incorrect because a periodic analysis of the scrap sales and the repairs and maintenance accounts may detect but will not prevent improper dispositions.

16. Which of the following internal control activities most likely would justify a reduced assessed level of control risk concerning plant and equipment acquisitions?

A. Periodic physical inspection of plant and equipment by the internal audit staff.

B. Comparison of current-year plant and equipment account balances with prior-year actual balances.

C. The review of prenumbered purchase orders to detect unrecorded trade-ins.

D. Approval of periodic depreciation entries by a supervisor independent of the accounting department.

Answer (A) is correct. *(CPA, adapted)*
REQUIRED: The internal control activity that would justify reducing an assessed level of control risk.
DISCUSSION: A periodic physical inspection by the internal audit staff is the best activity for verifying the existence of plant and equipment. Direct observation by an independent, competent, and objective internal audit staff helps to reduce the potential for fictitious acquisitions or other fraudulent activities. The result is a lower assessed level of control risk.
Answer (B) is incorrect because comparing records of assets may not detect nonexistent assets. Answer (C) is incorrect because reviewing purchase orders is less effective than direct verification. Answer (D) is incorrect because depreciation is based on recorded amounts. If they are misstated, depreciation will also be misstated.

17. Which of the following questions would an auditor least likely include on an internal control questionnaire concerning the <u>initiation</u> and <u>execution</u> of equipment transactions?

   A. Are requests for major repairs approved at a higher level than the department initiating the request?

   B. Are prenumbered purchase orders used for equipment and periodically accounted for?

   C. Are competitive bids solicited for purchases of equipment?

   D. Are procedures in place to monitor and properly restrict access to equipment?

Answer (D) is correct. *(CPA, adapted)*
   REQUIRED: The question least likely to be included on an internal control questionnaire concerning initiation and execution of equipment transactions.
   DISCUSSION: Although access to equipment should be restricted to authorized personnel only, the issue is the initiation and execution of equipment transactions, not custody of the assets.
   Answer (A) is incorrect because approval of major repairs is related to transaction initiation and execution. Answer (B) is incorrect because use of prenumbered purchase orders is related to transaction initiation and execution. Answer (C) is incorrect because competitive bidding is related to transaction initiation and execution.

18. Which of the following questions would an auditor most likely include on an internal control questionnaire for notes payable?

   A. Are assets that collateralize notes payable critically needed for the entity's continued existence?

   B. Are two or more authorized signatures required on checks that repay notes payable?

   C. Are the proceeds from notes payable used for the purchase of noncurrent assets?

   D. Are direct borrowings on notes payable authorized by the board of directors?

Answer (D) is correct. *(CPA, adapted)*
   REQUIRED: The question most likely included on an internal control questionnaire for notes payable.
   DISCUSSION: Control is enhanced when different persons or departments authorize, record, and maintain custody of assets for a class of transactions. Authorization of notes payable transactions is best done by the board of directors.
   Answer (A) is incorrect because the importance of specific assets to the entity is an operational matter and not a primary concern of an auditor when (s)he is considering internal control. Answer (B) is incorrect because questions about the payment function are likely to be on the questionnaire relating to cash disbursements. Answer (C) is incorrect because the use of funds is an operating decision made by management and is not a primary concern of the auditor when considering internal control.

19. Which of the following controls would an entity most likely use in safeguarding against the loss of trading securities?

   A. An independent trust company that has no direct contact with the employees who have record-keeping responsibilities has possession of the securities.

   B. The internal auditor verifies the trading securities in the entity's safe each year on the balance sheet date.

   C. The independent auditor traces all purchases and sales of trading securities through the subsidiary ledgers to the general ledger.

   D. A designated member of the board of directors controls the securities in a bank safe-deposit box.

Answer (A) is correct. *(CPA, adapted)*
   REQUIRED: The most likely control over trading securities.
   DISCUSSION: Assigning custody of trading securities to a bank or trust company provides the greatest security because such an institution normally has strict controls over assets entrusted to it and access to its vaults.
   Answer (B) is incorrect because verification of the existence of securities does not prevent their removal between the verification dates, for example, to be used as collateral for unauthorized loans. Answer (C) is incorrect because the independent auditor's procedures are not part of the client's internal control. Answer (D) is incorrect because access to a safe-deposit box should require the presence of two authorized persons.

20. Which of the following controls would a company most likely use to safeguard marketable securities when an independent trust agent is not employed?

    A. The investment committee of the board of directors periodically reviews the investment decisions delegated to the treasurer.

    B. Two company officials have joint control of marketable securities, which are kept in a bank safe-deposit box.

    C. The internal auditor and the controller independently trace all purchases and sales of marketable securities from the subsidiary ledgers to the general ledger.

    D. The chairman of the board verifies the marketable securities, which are kept in a bank safe-deposit box, each year on the balance sheet date.

Answer (B) is correct. *(CPA, adapted)*
    REQUIRED: The control to safeguard marketable securities.
    DISCUSSION: The safeguarding of assets requires physical controls, for example, the use of a safe-deposit box requiring two signatures to gain admittance.
    Answer (A) is incorrect because proper authorization does not physically safeguard an asset. Answer (C) is incorrect because independent tracing of purchases and sales to the accounting records assures proper recording but does not safeguard the asset. Answer (D) is incorrect because reconciliation once per year is likely to be insufficient to provide adequate control.

21. Which of the following internal control activities would an entity most likely use to assist in satisfying the completeness assertion related to long-term investments?

    A. Senior management verifies that securities in the bank safe-deposit box are registered in the entity's name.

    B. The internal auditor compares the securities in the bank safe-deposit box with recorded investments.

    C. The treasurer vouches the acquisition of securities by comparing brokers' advices with canceled checks.

    D. The controller compares the current market prices of recorded investments with the brokers' advices on file.

Answer (B) is correct. *(CPA, adapted)*
    REQUIRED: The control activity to assist in satisfying the completeness assertion for long-term investments.
    DISCUSSION: An interpretation of AU 326 states, "Substantive tests designed primarily to obtain evidence about the completeness assertion include analytical procedures and tests of details of related populations." The related population consists of the assets in the safe-deposit box. This population should be compared with the records of the investments to provide assurance that the balance is complete, that is, contains all long-term investments.
    Answer (A) is incorrect because verification that securities are registered in the entity's name relates to the rights assertion. Answer (C) is incorrect because comparing canceled checks with brokers' advices pertains to the rights assertion. Answer (D) is incorrect because comparing market prices with brokers' advices relates most directly to the valuation assertion.

22. An auditor's tests of controls over the issuance of raw materials to production would most likely include

    A. Reconciling raw materials and work-in-process perpetual inventory records to general ledger balances.

    B. Inquiring of the custodian about the procedures followed when defective materials are received from vendors.

    C. Observing that raw materials are stored in secure areas and that storeroom security is supervised by a responsible individual.

    D. Examining materials requisitions and reperforming client controls designed to process and record issuances.

Answer (D) is correct. *(CPA, adapted)*
    REQUIRED: The tests of controls performed with regard to issuance of raw materials.
    DISCUSSION: The internal transfer of raw materials is part of the inventory and warehousing cycle, which encompasses the physical flow of goods and the flow of costs. The transfer of raw materials (and costs) is subject to cost accounting internal controls. These include physical controls over storage, assignment of custody to specific individuals, use of prenumbered documents for authorization of transfers, and perpetual inventory records. Thus, prenumbered materials requisitions should be examined for proper authorizations, quantities, descriptions, and dates. Reperformance of relevant control activities is another possible test. For example, subsidiary ledgers and control accounts should be reconciled by an independent party. The auditor should reperform this control.
    Answer (A) is incorrect because reconciling account balances is a substantive test. Answer (B) is incorrect because tests of controls over issuance of raw materials do not provide evidence about activities followed when defective materials are received. Answer (C) is incorrect because the question concerns issuance, not storage, of raw materials.

23. In obtaining an understanding of a manufacturing entity's internal control concerning inventory balances, an auditor most likely would

    A. Analyze the liquidity and turnover ratios of the inventory.

    B. Perform analytical procedures designed to identify cost variances.

    C. Review the entity's descriptions of inventory policies and procedures.

    D. Perform test counts of inventory during the entity's physical count.

Answer (C) is correct. *(CPA, adapted)*
    REQUIRED: The activity for understanding a manufacturer's controls relevant to inventory.
    DISCUSSION: The auditor makes inquiries of personnel, observes activities and operations, and reviews an entity's documentation of controls relevant to the management of inventories to obtain an understanding of internal control.
    Answer (A) is incorrect because analytical procedures relate to substantive testing, not the evaluation of controls. Answer (B) is incorrect because analytical procedures relate to substantive testing, not the evaluation of controls. Answer (D) is incorrect because test counts relate to substantive testing, not internal controls.

24. Which of the following internal control activities most likely would be used to maintain accurate inventory records?

    A. Perpetual inventory records are periodically compared with the current cost of individual inventory items.

    B. A just-in-time inventory ordering system keeps inventory levels to a desired minimum.

    C. Requisitions, receiving reports, and purchase orders are independently matched before payment is approved.

    D. Periodic inventory counts are used to adjust the perpetual inventory records.

Answer (D) is correct. *(CPA, adapted)*
    REQUIRED: The internal control activity most useful in maintaining accurate inventory records.
    DISCUSSION: The recorded accountability for assets should be compared with existing assets at reasonable intervals. If assets are susceptible to loss through errors or fraud, the comparison should be made independently. Thus, periodic inventory accounts reconciled to the perpetual inventory records provides assurance that the inventory records properly reflect the inventory on hand.
    Answer (A) is incorrect because periodic comparison of inventory records with current cost information may provide assurance that inventories are maintained at lower of cost or market but does not assure the accuracy of the records. Answer (B) is incorrect because a JIT system may provide assurance that inventory levels are maintained at the desired minimum but does not assure the accuracy of the records. Answer (C) is incorrect because this control provides assurance that only goods that are authorized and received are paid for but does not assure the accuracy of the inventory records.

25. Independent internal verification of inventory occurs when employees who

    A. Issue raw materials, obtain materials requisitions for each issue, and prepare daily totals of materials issued.

    B. Compare records of goods on hand with physical quantities do not maintain the records or have custody of the inventory.

    C. Obtain receipts for the transfer of completed work to finished goods prepare a completed production report.

    D. Are independent of issuing production orders update records from completed job cost sheets and production cost reports on a timely basis.

Answer (B) is correct. *(CPA, adapted)*
    REQUIRED: The employee functions that permit independent internal verification of inventory.
    DISCUSSION: The recorded accountability for assets should be compared with existing assets at reasonable intervals. If assets are susceptible to loss through errors or fraud, the comparison should be made independently. An independent comparison is one made by persons not having responsibility for asset custody or the authorization or recording of transactions. If these functions are segregated and an independent reconciliation is made, the opportunity for any person to be in a position to both perpetrate and conceal errors or fraud in the normal course of his/her duties will be reduced.
    Answer (A) is incorrect because employees who have custody of raw materials cannot perform an independent verification of inventory. Answer (C) is incorrect because employees who have custody of finished goods cannot perform an independent verification of inventory. Answer (D) is incorrect because employees who maintain inventory records, job cost sheets, and production cost reports are not independent with respect to inventory.

7.5 PRACTICE SIMULATION

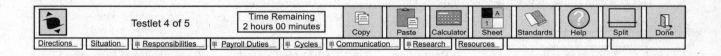

| Testlet 4 of 5 | Time Remaining 2 hours 00 minutes | Copy | Paste | Calculator | Sheet | Standards | Help | Split | Done |

Directions | Situation | Responsibilities | Payroll Duties | Cycles | Communication | Research | Resources

1. Directions

In the following simulation, you will be asked to complete various tasks related to payroll and other cycles. The simulation will provide you with all of the information necessary to do your work. For full credit, be sure to view and complete all work tabs.

Resources may be available under the tab marked RESOURCES. You may want to review the resources before beginning the simulation.

2. Situation

Butler, CPA, has been engaged to audit the financial statements of Young Computer Outlets, Inc., a new client. Young is a privately owned chain of retail stores that sells a variety of computer software and video products. Young uses an in-house payroll department at its corporate headquarters to compute payroll data and to prepare and distribute payroll checks to its 300 salaried employees. Butler is preparing an internal control questionnaire to assist in obtaining an understanding of Young's internal control and in assessing control risk.

3. Responsibilities

This question is presented in a check-the-box format.

Indicate whether management (column M) or the auditor (column A) is responsible for the following payroll activities.

Payroll Activities	M	A
1. Gain an understanding of the control procedures related to payroll transactions.		
2. Authorize the payroll.		
3. Calculate the proper amount for the payroll.		
4. Safeguard assets associated with the payment of payroll.		
5. Determine that the control activities described in the payroll procedures manual are in place.		
6. Assess control risk related to payroll.		
7. Distribute the payroll.		
8. Account for the payroll transactions.		

4. Payroll Duties

This question is presented in a check-the-box format.

Determine the responsibility (authorization, recording, or asset custody) of each organizational subunit.

A) Authorization	B) Recording	C) Asset Custody	Organizational Subunits
			1. Personnel
			2. Payroll
			3. Timekeeping
			4. Cost accounting
			5. Accounts payable
			6. Cash disbursements

5. Cycles

This question has a matching format that requires you to select the correct response from a drop-down list. Write the answers in the shaded column. Each choice may be used once, more than once, or not at all.

Determine which of the following control activities pertain to which cycle.

Control Activities	Answer
1. Formal budgeting process with subsequent variance analysis.	
2. Cash disbursements signs the check but does not authorize, prepare, or account for the transaction.	
3. Limited physical access to fixed assets when feasible.	
4. Authorization of repayment of capital by board of directors.	
5. Prenumbered document use for authorization transfers.	
6. Specific identification of certificate numbers when possible.	
7. Supervisors' approval of work performed by employees.	
8. Treasurer safeguards unclaimed checks.	
9. Written authorization for acquisition and retirement of fixed assets.	
10. Use of perpetual methods of recording.	

Cycle Choices
A) Payroll cycle
B) Plant, property, and equipment cycle
C) Investing cycle
D) Financing cycle
D) Inventory and warehousing cycle

6. Communication

Prepare an internal control questionnaire for Young's payroll department that will help Butler in understanding Young's internal control and in assessing risk. Use a yes/no format. Type your communication in your word processor program and print out the copy in a memorandum style format. *REMINDER: Your response will be graded for both technical content and writing skills. You should demonstrate your ability to develop, organize, and express your ideas. Do not convey information in the form of a table, bullet point list, or other abbreviated presentation.*

7. Research

Use the research materials available to you to find the answers to the following question in the AICPA Professional Standards. Print the appropriate citation in its entirety from the source you choose. Use only one source. This is a copy-and-paste item.

According to AU 319, how might an auditor obtain an understanding of internal control necessary to plan an audit engagement?

Unofficial Answers

3. Responsibilities (8 Gradable Items)

1.   A) - Auditor. The auditor is responsible for gaining an understanding of the control procedures related to payroll transactions.
2.   M) - Management. Management is responsible for authorizing transactions.
3.   M) - Management. Management is responsible for calculating the proper amount for the payroll.
4.   M) - Management. Management is responsible for safeguarding the assets associated with the payment of payroll.
5.   A) - Auditor. The auditor is responsible for determining that the control activities described in the payroll procedures manual are in place.
6.   A) - Auditor. The auditor is responsible for assessing control risk related to payroll.
7.   M) - Management. Management is responsible for distributing the payroll.
8.   M) - Management. Management is responsible for accounting for the payroll transactions.

4. Payroll Duties (9 Gradable Items)

1.   A) - Authorization. The personnel subunit is responsible for authorization.
2.   B) - Recording. The payroll subunit is responsible for recording.
3.   B) - Recording. The timekeeping subunit is responsible for recording.
4.   B) - Recording. The cost accounting subunit is responsible for recording.
5.   B) - Recording. The accounts payable subunit is responsible for recording.
6.   C) - Asset Custody. The cash disbursements subunit is responsible for asset custody. It signs the check but does not authorize, prepare, or account for the transaction.

5. Cycles (10 Gradable Items)

1.   B) - The plant, property, and equipment cycle pertains to the control activity of a formal budgeting process with subsequent variance analysis.
2.   A) - The payroll cycle pertains to the control activity of allowing cash disbursements to sign the check but not authorizing, preparing, or accounting for the transaction.
3.   B) - The plant, property, and equipment cycle pertains to the control activity of limiting physical access to assets when feasible.
4.   D) - The financing cycle pertains to the control activity requiring authorization of repayment of capital by board of directors.
5.   E) - The inventory and warehousing cycle pertains to the control activity involving prenumbered document use for authorization transfers.
6.   C) - The investing cycle pertains to the control activity of using specific identification of certificate numbers when possible.
7.   A) - The payroll cycle pertains to the control activity of requiring supervisor's approval of work performed by employees.
8.   A) - The payroll cycle pertains to the control activity in which the treasurer safeguards unclaimed checks.
9.   B) - The plant, property, and equipment cycle pertains to the control activity involving written authorization for acquisition and retirement of fixed assets.
10. E) - The inventory and warehousing cycle pertains to the control activity involving the use of perpetual methods of recording.

6. Communication (5 Gradable Items; For grading instructions, please refer to page 11.)

Young Computer Outlets, Inc.
Payroll Internet Control Questionnaire

1. Are payroll changes resulting from hires, separations, salary changes, overtime, bonuses, promotions, etc., properly authorized and approved?

2. Are discretionary payroll deductions and withholdings authorized in writing by employees?

3. Are the employees who perform each of the following payroll functions independent of the other five functions?

   - Approval of payroll changes
   - Preparation of payroll data
   - Approval of payroll
   - Signing of paychecks
   - Distribution of paychecks
   - Reconciliation of the payroll account

4. Are changes in the standard data on which payroll is based (hires, separations, salary changes, promotions, deductions, withholdings, etc.) promptly entered into the system to process the payroll?

5. Is gross pay determined by using authorized salary rates and time and attendance records?

6. Is a suitable chart of accounts or set of established guidelines used for determining salary account distribution and for recording payroll withholding liabilities?

7. Are clerical operations in payroll preparation verified?

8. Is payroll preparation and recording reviewed by supervisors or internal audit personnel?

9. Are payrolls approved by a responsible official before payroll checks are issued?

10. Are payrolls disbursed through an imprest account?

11. Is the payroll bank account reconciled monthly to the general ledger?

12. Are the payroll bank reconciliations properly approved and differences promptly followed up?

13. Are the custody and follow-up of unclaimed salary checks assigned to a responsible official?

14. Are differences reported by employees followed up on a timely basis by persons not involved in payroll preparation?

15. Does the entity use tickler files or another means to assure proper and timely payment of withholdings to appropriate bodies and to file required information returns?

16. Are employee compensation records reconciled to control accounts?

17. Is access to personnel and payroll records, checks, forms, signature plates, etc., limited?

7. Research (6 Gradable Items)

AU Section 319 – *Consideration of Internal Control in a Financial Statement Audit*

Understanding of Internal Control Necessary to Plan the Audit

.29   In making a judgment about the understanding of internal control necessary to plan the audit, the auditor considers the knowledge obtained from other sources about the types of misstatement that could occur, the risk that such misstatements may occur, and the factors that influence the design of tests of controls, when applicable, and substantive tests. Other sources of such knowledge include information from previous audits and the auditor's understanding of the industry and market in which the entity operates. The auditor also considers his or her assessment of inherent risk, judgments about materiality, and the complexity and sophistication of the entity's operations and systems, including the extent to which the entity relies on manual controls or on automated controls.

.30   In making a judgment about the understanding of internal control necessary to plan the audit, the auditor also considers IT risks that could result in misstatements. For example, if an entity uses IT to perform complex calculations, the entity receives the benefit of having the calculations consistently performed. However, the use of IT also presents risks, such as the risk that improperly authorized, incorrectly defined, or improperly implemented changes to the system or programs performing the calculations, or to related program tables or master files, could result in consistently performing those calculations inaccurately. As an entity's operations and systems become more complex and sophisticated, it becomes more likely that the auditor would need to increase his or her understanding of the internal control components to obtain the understanding necessary to design tests of controls, when applicable, and substantive tests.

.31   The auditor should consider whether specialized skills are needed for the auditor to determine the effect of IT on the audit, to understand the IT controls, or to design and perform tests of IT controls or substantive tests. A professional possessing IT skills may be either on the auditor's staff or an outside professional. In determining whether such a professional is needed on the audit team, the auditor considers factors such as the following:

- The complexity of the entity's systems and IT controls and the manner in which they are used in conducting the entity's business
- The significance of changes made to existing systems, or the implementation of new systems
- The extent to which data is shared among systems
- The extent of the entity's participation in electronic commerce
- The entity's use of emerging technologies
- The significance of audit evidence that is available only in electronic form

.32   Procedures that the auditor may assign to a professional possessing IT skills include inquiring of an entity's IT personnel how data and transactions are initiated, recorded, processed, and reported and how IT controls are designed; inspecting systems documentation; observing the operation of IT controls; and planning and performing tests of IT controls. If the use of a professional possessing IT skills is planned, the auditor should have sufficient IT-related knowledge to communicate the audit objectives to the professional, to evaluate whether the specified procedures will meet the auditor's objectives, and to evaluate the results of the procedures as they relate to the nature, timing, and extent of other planned audit procedures.

.33   Paragraphs .34 through .57 of this section provide an overview of the five internal control components and the auditor's understanding of the components relating to a financial statement audit. A more detailed discussion of these components is provided in the appendix [paragraph .110].

Scoring Schedule:

	Correct Responses		Gradable Items		Weights		
Tab 3	_____	÷	8	×	20%	=	_____
Tab 4	_____	÷	9	×	20%	=	_____
Tab 5	_____	÷	10	×	20%	=	_____
Tab 6	_____	÷	5	×	30%	=	_____
Tab 7	_____	÷	6	×	10%	=	_____
							_____
							(Your Score)

Use Gleim's *CPA Review Online* to practice more simulations in a realistic environment.

STUDY UNIT EIGHT
TESTS OF CONTROLS

(11 pages of outline)

8.1	Assessing Control Risk (AU 319)	249
8.2	Evidence to Support the Assessed Level of Control Risk (AU 319)	252
8.3	Correlation of Control Risk and Detection Risk	254
8.4	Assessing Control Risk in a Computer Environment	255
8.5	Practice Simulation	273

This study unit describes the auditor's assessment of control risk. A key theme is that the auditor must have assurance that controls are being effectively applied before control risk can be assessed below the maximum. This assurance must be obtained regardless of whether the client's controls are manual or automated.

This study unit also describes the relationship of control risk with the other component risks in the audit risk model. If difficulty is encountered in understanding the issues in this study unit, the candidate should review the material in Study Units 4 through 7 before continuing.

8.1 ASSESSING CONTROL RISK (AU 319)

1. An independent financial statement audit entails obtaining and evaluating evidence about management's **assertions**. Assertions are incorporated in the account balance, transaction class, and disclosure components of financial statements. The following classification of assertions is given in AU 326:

   a. Existence or occurrence
   b. Completeness
   c. Rights and obligations
   d. Valuation or allocation
   e. Presentation and disclosure

   NOTE: These classifications are explained in Study Unit 10, Evidence -- Objectives and Nature.

2. **Audit risk** is the risk that the auditor may unknowingly fail to modify the opinion on financial statements that are materially misstated. The components of audit risk are inherent risk, control risk, and detection risk.

   a. **Inherent risk** is the susceptibility of an assertion to a material misstatement assuming no related controls exist.

   b. **Control risk** is the risk that a material misstatement that could occur in an assertion will not be prevented or detected on a timely basis by the entity's internal control.

   c. **Detection risk** is the risk that the auditor will not detect a material misstatement that exists in an assertion.

3. The **assessed level of control risk** is an evaluation of the effectiveness of internal control in preventing or detecting material misstatements.

   a. It is stated in terms of financial statement assertions.

   b. It is stated quantitatively [such as from 0% to 100% (0 to 1.0)] or nonquantitatively (such as a range from minimum to maximum).

      1) For example, the auditor may decide that the probability is 10% (.1) that the controls relevant to an assertion will not prevent or detect a possible material misstatement of that assertion. However, in the absence of any relevant controls, control risk would be 100% (1.0); that is, failure to prevent or detect would be certain.

   c. After obtaining the understanding of internal control, the auditor may **assess control risk at the maximum** (1.0 or 100%) for some or all assertions for any of the following reasons:

      1) Controls are unlikely to pertain to an assertion.
      2) Controls are unlikely to be effective.
      3) Evaluating effectiveness would be inefficient.

   d. When the auditor assesses control risk at the maximum level, (s)he must become satisfied that performing only substantive tests will be effective in restricting detection risk to an acceptable level. The auditee's use of information technology (IT) such that evidence of initiating, recording, processing, or reporting of data supporting financial statement assertions exists only in electronic form may prevent the auditor from giving the necessary assurance solely on the basis of substantive testing.

      1) In these circumstances, the competence and sufficiency of the evidence ordinarily depend on the effectiveness of controls over its accuracy and completeness. For example, substantive tests alone may not suffice when the entity's automated system initiates orders for goods and settles payables automatically without any other documentation.

   e. In an audit of the financial statements of a public company (an issuer as defined in the securities acts), the auditor's procedures must be sufficient to express an opinion on the client's required assessment of its internal control structure and procedures for financial reporting (Section 404 of the Sarbanes-Oxley Act of 2002).

4. **Assessing control risk below the maximum** for certain assertions requires the auditor to obtain evidence about the effectiveness of the design and operation of controls. Accordingly, the auditor must

   a. Identify specific controls relevant to specific assertions

      1) The identified controls should be those that are likely to prevent or detect material misstatement in specific assertions.

      2) Some controls have pervasive effects, whereas others affect only a specific assertion.

         a) For example, the establishment of an effective internal audit function is pervasive, but the periodic reconciliation of the accounts receivable subsidiary ledger with the general ledger control account is specific to the completeness assertion for accounts receivable.

      3) An auditor must consider the direct or indirect relationships a control (manual or automated) has with an assertion. The more indirect the relationship, the less effective that control.

      4) Assessing control risk at a low level ordinarily permits the auditor to reduce the audit effort devoted to substantive testing.

      5) The auditor should consider the need to identify relevant general controls as well as application controls.

3

    b.   Test controls

        1)   **Tests of controls** are procedures to obtain evidence about the effectiveness of the operation of controls. However, the auditor also must consider their design.

        2)   Procedures to evaluate the effectiveness of a control's **design** are concerned with whether the control is suitably designed to prevent or detect material misstatements. When directed toward the effectiveness of the design of a control, the performance of any of the following procedures is not considered to be a test of controls:

            a)   Inquiry of entity personnel

            b)   Inspection of documents, reports, or electronic files

            c)   Observation of the application of the control

            d)   In the case of complex internal control, use of flowcharts, questionnaires, or decision tables

        3)   Tests of controls are concerned with the manner in which controls (manual or automated) were applied, the consistency of application, and by whom they were applied.

            a)   When directed toward the operating effectiveness of a control, the performance of any of the following procedures is a test of controls:

               i)   Inquiry of entity personnel

               ii)   Inspection of documents, reports, or electronic files indicating performance

               iii)   Observation of the application of the control

               iv)   Reperformance by the auditor

            b)   The auditor must consider not only the effective operation of direct controls (e.g., user review of an exception report) but the indirect controls on which they depend (e.g., general controls).

            c)   The auditor may be able to reduce the extent of tests of an automated control given the inherent consistency of IT processing. However, the auditor must determine that the control continues to be effective, for example, by verifying that program change controls are in place and that the authorized version of the program is in use.

            d)   Tests of automated controls may require methods and specialized skills different from those used to test manual controls, for example, computer-assisted audit techniques or IT-generated reports.

    c.   Reach a conclusion on the assessed level of control risk

        1)   The assessed level of control risk is the conclusion resulting from assessing control risk.

5.   The auditor should document the conclusions about the assessed level of control risk.

    a.   The nature and extent of the auditor's documentation are influenced by the assessed level of control risk, the nature of controls, and the nature of the entity's documentation.

    b.   If control risk is assessed **at the maximum level**, the auditor should document the conclusion but need not document the basis (i.e., the reason) for that conclusion.

    c.   If control risk is assessed **below the maximum level**, the auditor should document the conclusion **and** the basis for the conclusion.

6.   Stop and review! You have completed the outline for this subunit. Study multiple-choice questions 1 through 12 beginning on page 260.

8.2 EVIDENCE TO SUPPORT THE ASSESSED LEVEL OF CONTROL RISK (AU 319)

1. The auditor should obtain sufficient evidence to support an assessed level of control risk that is below the maximum.

2. The lower the assessed level of control risk (the closer to zero), the more assurance audit evidence must provide that controls relevant to an assertion are designed and operating effectively.

3. **Relationship of the Understanding to Assessing Control Risk**

   a. Understanding internal control and assessing control risk may be done concurrently. Thus, some procedures performed to obtain the understanding and not specifically planned as tests of controls may nevertheless provide evidence about the effectiveness of the design and operation of controls relevant to certain assertions. For example, determining whether an automated control has been placed in operation also may test its operating effectiveness, depending on whether the program has been changed or whether the risk of improper intervention is significant.

      1) Such procedures will be sufficient to support an assessed level of control risk below the maximum level only if they provide sufficient evidence to evaluate the effectiveness of both the design and operation of a control relevant to an assertion.

   b. **Further reduction of the assessment.** The auditor may seek a further reduction of the assessed level of control risk for certain assertions after obtaining the understanding and assessing control risk. Accordingly, the auditor should consider whether evidence is available to support the further reduction and whether it would be efficient to gather such evidence by testing controls.

      1) The purpose of seeking a lower assessment of control risk is to reduce the audit effort devoted to substantive tests. Thus, the auditor should weigh the costs of performing additional tests of controls against the expected savings from devoting less audit effort to substantive testing.

4. The **sufficiency** of evidence is a matter of judgment.

   a. The degree of assurance provided is a function of the type of evidence, its source, its timeliness, and the availability of other evidence related to the conclusion.

   b. These characteristics influence the nature, timing, and extent of tests of controls.

   c. The auditor selects such tests from techniques such as inquiry, observation, inspection, and reperformance of a control that pertains to an assertion. No single test of controls is always necessary, applicable, or equally effective in all cases.

5. The **nature of particular controls** influences the type of evidence available to evaluate the effectiveness of the design or operation of those controls.

   a. For example, documentation about assignment of authority and responsibility, monitoring controls, or controls performed by a computer may not be available, so observation, inquiry, or computer-assisted audit techniques may be used to obtain information about effectiveness.

6. **Sources.** Evidence about the effectiveness of the design and operation of controls obtained directly by the auditor (e.g., through observation) usually provides more assurance than evidence obtained indirectly or by inference, such as through inquiry.

   a. For example, evidence may be obtained through the auditor's direct observation of an individual who applies a control. This evidence is usually more reliable than that gathered through inquiries about the application of the control.

   b. However, the observed application of a control might differ from that when the auditor is not present.

c. When the auditor determines that a specific control may have a significant effect in reducing assessed control risk, (s)he usually needs to perform additional tests instead of relying on inquiries alone.

7. **Timeliness** of evidence concerns when it was obtained and the portion of the audit period to which it applies.

   a. The evidence obtained by some tests of controls, such as observation, pertains only to the moment in time at which the auditing procedure was applied. Thus, such evidence may be insufficient for periods not subjected to such tests.

      1) In such circumstances, the auditor may supplement those tests with other tests that provide evidence about the entire period. For example, the auditor may test general controls related to the modification and use of computer programs to determine whether an application control performed by a program operated consistently during the period.

   b. Evidence obtained in prior audits may be considered.

      1) The auditor should consider the significance of the assertion, the controls evaluated, the degree to which effective design and operation were evaluated, the results of the tests of controls, and the evidence that may be obtained from current period substantive tests.

      2) The auditor should consider that the longer the time elapsed since the tests of controls, the less assurance they may provide.

      3) The auditor should also obtain evidence in the current period about changes in internal control subsequent to the prior audits.

   c. When obtaining evidence about the design or operation of internal control during an **interim period**, the auditor should determine what additional evidence should be obtained for the remaining period. The auditor should consider the

      1) Length of the remaining period
      2) Significance of the assertion involved
      3) Specific controls evaluated during the interim period
      4) Extent of the evaluation
      5) Results of the tests of controls used in making the evaluation
      6) Evidence from substantive tests to be performed during the remaining period

8. The auditor should consider the **interrelationship** of various types of evidence relating to an assertion in evaluating the degree of assurance provided.

   a. If a single type of evidence is not sufficient, the auditor may perform other tests of controls.

   b. The interrelationship of an entity's five control components -- control environment, risk assessment, control activities, information and communication, and monitoring -- should be considered in the evaluation of the degree of assurance provided by evidence.

   c. When various types of evidence support the same conclusion, the degree of assurance provided usually increases.

   d. Evidence indicating that the control environment is ineffective may adversely affect otherwise effective control components for a particular assertion. In this circumstance, the auditor may decide to obtain additional evidence about the design and operation of that system or procedure during the audit period.

   e. An audit of financial statements is a cumulative process. Thus, as the auditor assesses control risk or performs substantive tests, the information obtained may cause him/her to modify the nature, timing, or extent of the planned tests of controls or substantive tests.

9. Stop and review! You have completed the outline for this subunit. Study multiple-choice questions 13 through 18 beginning on page 264.

8.3 CORRELATION OF CONTROL RISK AND DETECTION RISK

1. The ultimate purpose of assessing control risk (and inherent risk) is to contribute to the evaluation of the overall risk that the financial statements contain material misstatements. The assessed levels of control risk and inherent risk determine the acceptable level of detection risk for financial statement assertions.

    a. Based on the level to which the auditor seeks to restrict the risk of a material misstatement (audit risk) and the assessed levels of inherent risk and control risk, substantive tests are performed to restrict detection risk to an acceptable level. **Substantive tests** are performed to detect material misstatements in financial statement assertions. They consist of tests of details of classes of transactions and account balances (tests of details) and analytical procedures.

        1) The risk of material misstatement of an assertion, or **audit risk (AR)**, can be expressed algebraically as the product of inherent risk (IR), control risk (CR), and the acceptable detection risk (DR). Accordingly, if the auditor decides to restrict the risk of misstatement (that is, the risk of incorrect acceptance) to 5% and assesses inherent risk and control risk at 50% and 30%, respectively, the following calculation determines the acceptable level of detection risk:

        $$AR = IR \times CR \times DR$$

        $$DR = \frac{AR}{IR \times CR}$$

        $$DR = \frac{5\%}{50\% \times 30\%}$$

        $$DR = 33\ 1/3\%$$

        2) The **acceptable level of detection risk**, which is inversely related to control risk and inherent risk, determines the nature, timing, and extent of substantive tests. Thus, a lower acceptable level of detection risk increases the assurance to be provided by substantive tests. To obtain greater assurance, the auditor may change the tests'

            a) **Nature** to a more effective procedure, such as directing tests toward independent parties rather than parties within the entity

            b) **Timing**, such as from interim dates to year-end

            c) **Extent**, such as using a larger sample

    b. **Risk of substantive test of details.** AU 350, *Audit Sampling*, expanded the risk formula for a given substantive test of details to divide detection risk (DR) into the risk for the test of details (TD) and the risk for analytical procedures and other substantive tests (AP).

        1) The TD and AP terms replace the DR term as follows:
        $$AR = IR \times CR \times AP \times TD$$

        2) This risk formula is typically solved for the auditor's acceptable risk for the test of details (TD).

            a) The expectation is that the auditor will change the nature, timing, or extent of tests of details to achieve the acceptable level of audit risk (AR).

        3) AP is the risk that analytical procedures and other relevant substantive tests do not detect misstatements equal to tolerable misstatements that could occur in an assertion, given that they are not detected by internal control.

4) Following the previous example, assume that the auditor assessed AP at 60%. The following acceptable level of risk for the test of details is

$$TD = \frac{AR}{IR \times CR \times AP}$$

$$TD = \frac{5\%}{50\% \times 30\% \times 60\%}$$

$$TD = 55.5\%$$

2. The assessed level of control risk usually cannot be sufficiently low to eliminate the need for all substantive tests. Consequently, critical assertions for significant account balances and transaction classes must be tested regardless of the assessed level of control risk.

    a. In assessing control risk, the auditor also may use tests of details of transactions concurrently as tests of controls (i.e., as **dual-purpose tests**).

        1) As substantive tests, tests of details of transactions detect material misstatements in the financial statements.

        2) As tests of controls, they evaluate whether a control operated effectively.

3. Stop and review! You have completed the outline for this subunit. Study multiple-choice questions 19 through 27 beginning on page 266.

8.4 ASSESSING CONTROL RISK IN A COMPUTER ENVIRONMENT

1. There are many similarities between assessing control risk in a computer environment and in a manual system. The candidate should build on these similarities. Most of the terms used here are defined in Study Unit 4, Internal Control Concepts and Information Technology.

    a. The objectives are the same. Control risk is assessed by the auditor to help determine the nature, timing, and extent of the substantive tests appropriate to support the opinion regardless of the nature of the system.

    b. The concept is the same. After obtaining an understanding of internal control and determining that the controls are in place, the auditor considers whether testing the effectiveness of the controls and potentially assessing control risk below the maximum is more efficient than forgoing tests of controls and assessing control risk at the maximum. However, the auditee's use of IT requires the auditor to consider whether omitting tests of controls will enable him/her to provide the necessary assurance.

        1) The conventional procedure is first to assess control risk relative to the control environment (often referred to as the general controls). If the control environment is ineffective, the auditor should not assess control risk for individual controls (application controls) below the maximum.

c.   Many procedures are the same. Numerous controls in a computer environment are outside the computer system and can be tested using procedures applicable to a manual system.

1)   These procedures include

a)   Inquiries of entity personnel
b)   Inspection of documents, reports, and electronic files
c)   Observation of the application of specific controls
d)   Reperformance by the auditor

2)   Computer controls to which traditional tests of controls are applicable include those found in the control environment and control activities components of internal control.

a)   The control environment

i)   Organizational structure. The auditor inspects documentation and observes operations demonstrating that the computer processing department has no custody of assets or transaction authority and is actually

- Operating as a service department independently of users
- Reporting to senior-level management

ii)   Assignment of authority and responsibility. The auditor inquires and observes whether the following employees are performing functions consistent with their assigned responsibilities (and have no incompatible responsibilities):

- Systems analyst
- Programmer
- Computer (console) operator
- Data conversion (key) operator
- Librarian
- Data control group

b)   Control activities

i)   Information processing

- The auditor observes the backup copies of files and programs to determine that they are safeguarded.
- The auditor inspects the written security policy concerning virus protection and observes the existence of available anti-virus software.
- The auditor inspects program acquisition and development requests for the proper authorization, assignment of responsibility for design and coding, testing, and acceptance.
- The auditor inspects program documentation to determine whether it is complete and up-to-date.

ii)   The auditor tests access controls by

- Attempting to sign on to the computer system using various passwords and ID numbers
- Inspecting the system access log for completeness and appropriate use and follow-up (passwords required to be consistent with employees' responsibilities)
- Observing that disposal of sensitive documents and printouts is controlled so that unauthorized persons cannot gain information concerning passwords or ID numbers

2.   Certain controls relating to the input, processing, and output of data are internal to the computer system. They should be tested by procedures that are not traditionally performed in a manual environment. Such techniques have been characterized as auditing around the computer or auditing through the computer.

    a.   **Auditing around the computer** is not appropriate when systems are sophisticated or the major controls are included in the computer programs. It may be appropriate for very simple systems that produce appropriate printed outputs for the auditor.

        1)   The auditor manually processes transactions and compares the results with the client's computer processed results.

        2)   Because only a small number of transactions can ordinarily be processed, the effectiveness of the tests of controls must be questioned.

        3)   The computer is treated as a black box, and only inputs and outputs are evaluated.

    b.   **Auditing through the computer** uses the computer to test the processing logic and controls within the system and the records produced. This approach may be accomplished in several ways, including

        1)   Running test data
        2)   Parallel simulation
        3)   Creation of an integrated test facility
        4)   Programming embedded audit modules

3.   The **Test Data Approach**. The auditor prepares a set of dummy transactions specifically designed to test the control activities that management claims to have incorporated into the processing programs. The auditor can expect the controls to be applied to the transactions in the prescribed manner. Thus, the auditor is testing the effectiveness of the controls.

    a.   EXAMPLE:

        1)   Management may have represented that the following edit checks were included in the payroll processing program:

            a)   Field checks for all numeric and alphabetic fields

            b)   Reasonableness test on hours worked over 40 hours

            c)   Validity check on employee numbers compared with known employees in the personnel master file

            d)   Error listings of all transactions that fail a test

        2)   The auditor will create and process a set of transactions, including ones that should pass the edit checks and be processed and some that should fail the edit checks and be printed on the error listing.

    b.   The primary advantage of this method is that it directly tests the controls.

    c.   The primary disadvantage is that it tests processing at only one moment in time. That is, the auditor does not have assurance that the program tested is the one used throughout the year to process client transactions.

10

d.   The following illustrates a test data approach in flowchart form.

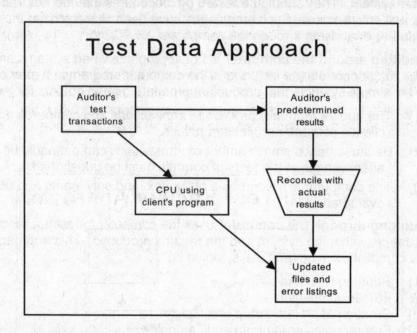

4.   **Parallel simulation** uses a controlled program to reprocess sets of client transactions and compares the auditor-achieved results with those of the client. The key is for the auditor's program to include the client's edit checks. Thus, the client's results of processing, rejected transactions, and error listing should be the same as the auditor's.

a.   The auditor's controlled program may be a copy of the client's program that has been tested. An expensive alternative is for the auditor to write a program that includes management's controls. Also, a program may be created from generalized audit software.

b.   The primary advantage of parallel simulation is that transactions from throughout the period may be reprocessed. The results can then be compared with the client's results to provide assurance that the edit checks (controls) have been applied during the period.

c.   The primary disadvantages of this method are the cost of obtaining the program and the coordination effort required to obtain transactions to reprocess.

d.   The following illustrates the parallel simulation method in flowchart form.

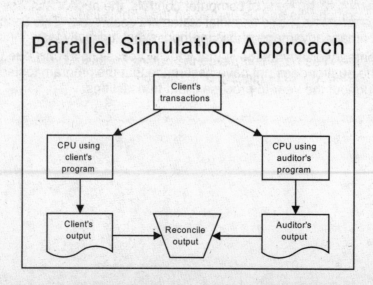

5.   Using the **integrated test facility (ITF)** method, the auditor creates a dummy record within the client's actual system (e.g., a fictitious employee in the personnel and payroll file). Dummy and actual transactions are processed (e.g., time records for the dummy employee and for actual employees). The auditor can test the edit checks by altering the dummy transactions and evaluating error listings.

a.   The primary advantage of this method is that it tests the actual program in operation.

b.   The primary disadvantages are that the method requires considerable coordination, and the dummy transactions must be purged prior to internal and external reporting. Thus, the method is not used extensively by external auditors.

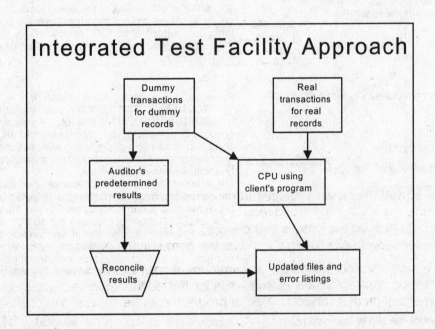

6.   An **embedded audit module** is an integral part of an application system that is designed to identify and report actual transactions and other information that meet criteria having audit significance.

a.   An advantage is that it permits continuous monitoring of online, real-time systems.

b.   A disadvantage is that **audit hooks** must be programmed into the operating system and applications programs to permit insertion of audit modules.

7.   Upon completion of the tests of computer controls, the auditor assesses computer control risk and relates it to specific financial statement assertions. This control risk assessment is a primary factor in determining the appropriate substantive tests.

8.   Stop and review! You have completed the outline for this subunit. Study multiple-choice questions 28 through 40 beginning on page 269.

QUESTIONS

8.1 Assessing Control Risk (AU 319)

1. The ultimate purpose of assessing control risk is to contribute to the auditor's evaluation of the risk that

A. Tests of controls may fail to identify procedures relevant to assertions.

B. Material misstatements may exist in the financial statements.

C. Specified controls requiring segregation of duties may be circumvented by collusion.

D. Entity policies may be inappropriately overridden by senior management.

Answer (B) is correct. *(CPA, adapted)*
REQUIRED: The purpose of assessing control risk.
DISCUSSION: "The ultimate purpose of assessing control risk is to contribute to the auditor's evaluation of the risk that material misstatements exist in the financial statements." The assessment of control risk and inherent risk provides evidence about this risk. The auditor uses the evidence as part of the reasonable basis for an opinion (AU 319).
Answer (A) is incorrect because tests of controls are performed when the auditor wishes to assess control risk below the maximum level. An auditor must identify specific controls relevant to specific assertions before (s)he can obtain evidence about the effectiveness of the design and operation of the controls. Answer (C) is incorrect because collusion is an inherent limitation of internal control. Answer (D) is incorrect because inappropriate management override is an inherent limitation of internal control.

2. Control risk should be assessed in terms of

A. Specific controls.

B. Types of potential fraud.

C. Financial statement assertions.

D. Control environment factors.

Answer (C) is correct. *(CPA, adapted)*
REQUIRED: The approach used in assessing control risk.
DISCUSSION: AU 319 states, "Assessing control risk is the process of evaluating the effectiveness of an entity's internal control in preventing or detecting material misstatements in the financial statements. Control risk is assessed in terms of financial statement assertions."
Answer (A) is incorrect because specific controls relevant to the assertions must be identified and tested before control risk for those assertions can be assessed below the maximum. Answer (B) is incorrect because the auditor should use knowledge obtained from the understanding of internal control to identify types of potential misstatements. Answer (D) is incorrect because the auditor considers the control environment in assessing risk but does not assess risk in terms of control environment factors.

3. After assessing control risk below the maximum level, an auditor desires to further reduce the assessed level of control risk. At this time, the auditor considers whether

A. It would be efficient to obtain an understanding of the entity's accounting system.

B. The entity's internal controls have been placed in operation.

C. The entity's internal controls pertain to any financial statement assertions.

D. Additional evidential matter sufficient to support a further reduction is likely to be available.

Answer (D) is correct. *(CPA, adapted)*
REQUIRED: The consideration when a further reduction in assessed control risk is desired.
DISCUSSION: According to AU 319, an auditor may wish to reduce the assessed level of control risk for some assertions. Accordingly, the auditor considers whether additional evidence is likely to be available to support the further reduction and whether it is efficient to gather such evidence by performing tests of controls.
Answer (A) is incorrect because the auditor should have already obtained an understanding of the entity's accounting system as part of obtaining an understanding of the information and communication component of internal control. Answer (B) is incorrect because the auditor determines whether controls have been placed in operation while obtaining the understanding. Answer (C) is incorrect because the auditor identifies specific controls relevant to specific assertions when assessing control risk below the maximum.

4. An auditor may decide to assess control risk at the maximum level for certain assertions because the auditor believes

    A. Controls are unlikely to pertain to the assertions.

    B. The entity's control components are interrelated.

    C. Sufficient evidential matter to support the assertions is likely to be available.

    D. More emphasis on tests of controls than substantive tests is warranted.

Answer (A) is correct. *(CPA, adapted)*
    REQUIRED: The reason an auditor may decide to assess control risk at the maximum.
    DISCUSSION: "After obtaining the understanding of internal control, the auditor may assess control risk at the maximum level for some or all assertions because (s)he believes controls are unlikely to pertain to an assertion or are unlikely to be effective, or because evaluating the effectiveness of controls would be inefficient" (AU 319).
    Answer (B) is incorrect because the integration of control procedures may be a valuable consideration in assessing control risk below the maximum. Answer (C) is incorrect because, if sufficient evidential matter is likely to be available, the auditor is more likely to be able to assess control risk below the maximum. Answer (D) is incorrect because assessing control risk at the maximum level reflects the auditor's decision not to perform procedures to obtain evidence about the effectiveness of controls. However, the auditor must be satisfied that performing only substantive tests will be effective in reducing detection risk to an acceptable level.

5. Which of the following is a step in an auditor's decision to assess control risk below the maximum?

    A. Apply analytical procedures to both financial data and nonfinancial information to detect conditions that may indicate weak controls.

    B. Perform tests of details of transactions and account balances to identify potential errors and fraud.

    C. Identify the controls that are likely to detect or prevent material misstatements.

    D. Document that the additional audit effort to perform tests of controls exceeds the potential reduction in substantive testing.

Answer (C) is correct. *(CPA, adapted)*
    REQUIRED: The step necessary to assess control risk below the maximum.
    DISCUSSION: Assessing control risk below the maximum requires that the auditor (1) identify specific controls relevant to specific assertions, (2) perform procedures to evaluate the effectiveness of the design of the controls, (3) perform tests of controls, and (4) reach a conclusion about the assessed level of control risk. In assessing control risk, the auditor should identify the controls that are likely to detect or prevent material misstatements in specific assertions (AU 319).
    Answer (A) is incorrect because analytical procedures are substantive tests. Answer (B) is incorrect because tests of details are substantive tests. The auditor must perform tests of controls to assess control risk below the maximum. Answer (D) is incorrect because, if the cost of tests of controls exceeds the potential benefit from a reduction in substantive testing, assessing control risk at the maximum is justified.

6. Which of the following is not a step in an auditor's decision to assess control risk below the maximum?

    A. Evaluate the effectiveness of the control activity with tests of controls.

    B. Obtain an understanding of the entity's control environment.

    C. Perform tests of details of transactions to detect material misstatements in the financial statements.

    D. Consider whether controls can have a pervasive effect on financial statement assertions.

Answer (C) is correct. *(CPA, adapted)*
    REQUIRED: The item not a step in assessing control risk below the maximum.
    DISCUSSION: Every financial statement audit requires that the auditor obtain an understanding of the components of the entity's internal control. If the auditor wishes to assess control risk below the maximum level, (s)he must also (1) identify specific controls relevant to specific assertions, (2) perform procedures to evaluate the effectiveness of the design of the controls, (3) perform tests of controls, and (4) reach a conclusion about the assessed level of control risk (AU 319). Tests of details are substantive tests and are not required to assess control risk below the maximum.
    Answer (A) is incorrect because tests of controls is a step in the decision to assess control risk below the maximum level. Answer (B) is incorrect because understanding the entity's control environment is a step in the decision to assess control risk below the maximum level. Answer (D) is incorrect because identifying relevant controls is a step in the decision to assess control risk below the maximum level.

7. Samples to test controls are intended to provide a basis for an auditor to conclude whether

A. The controls are operating effectively.

B. The financial statements are materially misstated.

C. The risk of incorrect acceptance is too high.

D. Materiality for planning purposes is at a sufficiently low level.

Answer (A) is correct. *(CPA, adapted)*
REQUIRED: The reason for sampling to test controls.
DISCUSSION: Tests of controls are procedures to obtain evidence about the effectiveness of the operation of controls in preventing or detecting material misstatements in the financial statements. Tests of controls (whether manual or automated) are concerned with how they were applied, by whom they were applied, and the consistency of their application during the audit period. Prior to performing tests of controls, the auditor employs procedures directed toward the effectiveness of the design of controls to evaluate whether they are suitably designed to prevent or detect material misstatements in specific assertions (AU 319).
Answer (B) is incorrect because substantive tests determine whether material misstatements exist. Answer (C) is incorrect because the risk of incorrect acceptance is an aspect of sampling risk with which the auditor is concerned when performing substantive tests of details. Answer (D) is incorrect because materiality is established during planning, not as a result of tests of controls.

8. Which of the following tests of controls most likely will help assure an auditor that goods shipped are properly billed?

A. Scan the sales journal for sequential and unusual entries.

B. Examine shipping documents for matching sales invoices.

C. Compare the accounts receivable ledger to daily sales summaries.

D. Inspect unused sales invoices for consecutive prenumbering.

Answer (B) is correct. *(CPA, adapted)*
REQUIRED: The test of controls most likely to assure that goods shipped are properly billed.
DISCUSSION: The proper starting point to determine whether all goods shipped were properly billed is the shipping documents. Tracing the shipping documents to the matching sales invoices provides assurance that controls worked effectively to ensure that all goods shipped were billed.
Answer (A) is incorrect because scanning the sales journal provides evidence concerning shipments that were billed but no evidence about unbilled shipments. Answer (C) is incorrect because the accounts receivable ledger represents shipments that were billed. Answer (D) is incorrect because unbilled shipments do not create gaps in the prenumbered sales invoices.

9. An auditor is least likely to test controls that provide for

A. Approval of the purchase and sale of trading securities.

B. Classification of revenue and expense transactions by product line.

C. Segregation of the functions of recording disbursements and reconciling the bank account.

D. Comparison of receiving reports and vendors' invoices with purchase orders.

Answer (B) is correct. *(CPA, adapted)*
REQUIRED: The controls that are least likely to be tested.
DISCUSSION: The independent auditor is primarily concerned with the fairness of external financial reporting. (S)he is less likely to test controls over records used solely for internal management purposes than those used to prepare financial statements for external distribution. Assertions about the presentation of transactions by product line are not typically made. Thus, the independent auditor is unlikely to expend significant audit effort in testing such classifications.
Answer (A) is incorrect because a basic management objective is proper authorization of transactions. Answer (C) is incorrect because a basic management objective is to compare recorded accountability with existing assets at reasonable intervals, such as by reconciling the bank account and the accounting records. Reconciliations should be performed by an independent employee. Answer (D) is incorrect because comparison of receiving reports, vendors' invoices, and purchase orders is a control over purchasing.

10. After obtaining an understanding of a client's internal control, an auditor may decide not to test the effectiveness of the computer control procedures. Which of the following is not a valid reason for choosing to omit tests of controls?

A. The controls duplicate operative controls existing elsewhere in the system.

B. There appear to be major weaknesses that would preclude assessing control risk below the maximum level.

C. The time and dollar costs of testing exceed the time and dollar savings in substantive testing if the tests of controls show the controls to be operative.

D. The operating effectiveness of controls appears to support a reduced assessment of control risk.

Answer (D) is correct. *(CPA, adapted)*
REQUIRED: The invalid reason for omitting tests of controls.
DISCUSSION: Although controls appear to be operating effectively based on the understanding of internal control, the auditor must perform tests of controls for those assertions for which control risk is to be assessed below the maximum level. The assessment of control risk affects the acceptable level of detection risk used in determining the nature, timing, and extent of substantive tests.
Answer (A) is incorrect because compensating controls may appropriately limit control risk. Answer (B) is incorrect because, if the auditor intends to assess control risk at the maximum level, tests of controls are unnecessary, but the auditor must be satisfied that performing only substantive tests will be effective and more efficient in restricting detection risk to an acceptable level. Furthermore, when a significant amount of information supporting assertions is electronically initiated, recorded, processed, or reported, the auditor may determine that it is not possible to design substantive tests that by themselves provide sufficient evidence that the assertions are not materially misstated. Answer (C) is incorrect because, if tests of controls are not cost effective, the auditor should expand substantive testing.

11. When assessing control risk below the maximum level, an auditor is required to document the auditor's

	Understanding of the Entity's Control Environment	Basis for Concluding That Control Risk is Below the Maximum Level
A.	Yes	No
B.	No	Yes
C.	Yes	Yes
D.	No	No

Answer (C) is correct. *(CPA, adapted)*
REQUIRED: The item(s) that should be documented when assessing control risk below the maximum.
DISCUSSION: The understanding of the components of internal control, including the control environment, should be documented regardless of the assessed level of control risk. If control risk is assessed at the maximum level, the auditor should document the conclusion but need not document the basis for that conclusion. If control risk is assessed below the maximum level, the auditor should document the conclusion and the basis for the conclusion.

12. When control risk is assessed at the maximum level for all financial statement assertions, an auditor should document the auditor's

	Understanding of the Entity's Internal Control Components	Conclusion That Control Risk is at the Maximum Level	Basis for Concluding That Control Risk is at the Maximum Level
A.	Yes	No	No
B.	Yes	Yes	No
C.	No	Yes	Yes
D.	Yes	Yes	Yes

Answer (B) is correct. *(CPA, adapted)*
REQUIRED: The items that should be documented when control risk is assessed at the maximum level.
DISCUSSION: The auditor should document the understanding of internal control and the conclusions about the assessed level of control risk for specific assertions. If the assessed level is below the maximum, the basis for the conclusion must also be documented.

8.2   Evidence to Support the Assessed Level of Control Risk (AU 319)

13. Which of the following procedures is an auditor most likely to include in the planning phase of a financial statement audit?

A. Obtain an understanding of the entity's risk assessment process.

B. Identify specific controls designed to prevent fraud.

C. Evaluate the reasonableness of the entity's accounting estimates.

D. Perform cutoff tests of the entity's sales and purchases.

Answer (A) is correct. *(CPA, adapted)*
REQUIRED: The procedure most likely to be performed during the planning phase of a financial statement audit.
DISCUSSION: According to the second standard of field work, "A sufficient understanding of internal control is to be obtained to plan the audit and to determine the nature, timing, and extent of tests to be performed." Risk assessment is a component of internal control. For financial reporting purposes, it is an entity's identification, analysis, and management of risks relevant to preparing financial statements that are fairly presented in conformity with GAAP. An auditor must obtain an understanding of the entity's risk assessment process as well as the other components of internal control when planning a financial statement audit (AU 319).
Answer (B) is incorrect because an auditor should specifically assess the risk of material misstatement due to fraud and should consider that assessment in designing audit procedures. When considering fraud risk factors, the auditor may assess whether specific controls exist to mitigate that risk (AU 316). Identifying specific controls is necessary only when the auditor plans to assess control risk below the maximum level. Answer (C) is incorrect because an auditor must perform procedures in a phase of the audit subsequent to planning before evaluating estimates. Answer (D) is incorrect because cutoff tests are substantive tests normally performed subsequent to planning.

14. After obtaining an understanding of an entity's internal control and assessing control risk, an auditor may next

A. Perform tests of controls to verify management's assertions that are embodied in the financial statements.

B. Consider whether evidential matter is available to support a further reduction in the assessed level of control risk.

C. Apply analytical procedures as substantive tests to validate the assessed level of control risk.

D. Evaluate whether the internal controls detected material misstatements in the financial statements.

Answer (B) is correct. *(CPA, adapted)*
REQUIRED: The audit step that may follow obtaining the understanding and assessing control risk.
DISCUSSION: According to AU 319, an auditor may wish to further reduce the assessed level of control risk for some assertions. Accordingly, the auditor should consider whether evidence is available to support the further reduction and whether it is efficient to gather such evidence by tests of controls. The purpose of seeking a lower assessment of control risk is to diminish the audit effort expended in substantive testing. Thus, the increased effort (costs) associated with additional tests of controls should be less than the benefits (reduced costs) from devoting less audit effort to substantive tests.
Answer (A) is incorrect because substantive tests are performed to test assertions about account balances. Answer (C) is incorrect because substantive tests are used to restrict detection risk. Answer (D) is incorrect because evaluating whether controls detected material misstatements would most likely occur earlier in the audit.

15. Which of the following procedures most likely will provide an auditor with evidence about whether an entity's controls are suitably designed to prevent or detect material misstatements?

A. Reperforming the controls for a sample of transactions.

B. Performing analytical procedures using data aggregated at a high level.

C. Vouching a sample of transactions directly related to the controls.

D. Observing the entity's personnel applying the controls.

Answer (D) is correct. *(CPA, adapted)*
REQUIRED: The procedure evaluating the effectiveness of the design of controls.
DISCUSSION: AU 319 states, "Generally, evidential matter about the effectiveness of the design and operation of controls obtained directly by the auditor, such as through observation, provides more assurance than evidential matter obtained indirectly or by inference, such as through inquiry."
Answer (A) is incorrect because reperformance is a test of controls that relates to the effectiveness of their application rather than their design. Answer (B) is incorrect because analytical procedures are substantive tests rather than procedures directed at the effectiveness of the design of controls. Answer (C) is incorrect because vouching is a substantive test rather than procedures directed at the effectiveness of the design of controls.

16. In assessing control risk, an auditor ordinarily selects from a variety of techniques, including

A. Inquiry and analytical procedures.

B. Reperformance and observation.

C. Comparison and confirmation.

D. Inspection and verification.

Answer (B) is correct. *(CPA, adapted)*
REQUIRED: The procedures associated with the assessment of control risk.
DISCUSSION: According to AU 319, the auditor selects tests of controls "from a variety of techniques such as inquiry, observation, inspection, and reperformance of a control that pertains to an assertion. No one specific test of controls is always necessary, applicable, or equally effective in every circumstance."
Answer (A) is incorrect because analytical procedures are more closely associated with substantive testing. Answer (C) is incorrect because comparison and confirmation are more closely associated with substantive testing. Answer (D) is incorrect because inspection and verification are more closely associated with substantive testing.

17. An auditor generally tests the segregation of duties related to inventory by

A. Personal inquiry and observation.

B. Test counts and cutoff procedures.

C. Analytical procedures and invoice recomputation.

D. Document inspection and reconciliation.

Answer (A) is correct. *(CPA, adapted)*
REQUIRED: The audit test of the segregation of duties for inventory.
DISCUSSION: The segregation of duties reduces the opportunity for an individual to perpetrate and conceal errors or fraud in the normal course of his/her duties. Authorization of transactions, recording of transactions, and custody of assets should be segregated. The best evidence that controls based on segregation of duties are operating as planned is provided by the auditor's own observation and inquiries.
Answer (B) is incorrect because test counts and cutoff procedures are substantive tests, not tests of controls. Answer (C) is incorrect because analytical procedures and recomputations are substantive tests, not tests of controls. Answer (D) is incorrect because, although document inspection may be useful as a test of controls, it is not effective to test the segregation of duties.

18. Which of the following procedures concerning accounts receivable is an auditor most likely to perform to obtain evidential matter in support of an assessed level of control risk below the maximum level?

A. Observing an entity's employee prepare the schedule of past due accounts receivable.

B. Sending confirmation requests to an entity's principal customers to verify the existence of accounts receivable.

C. Inspecting an entity's analysis of accounts receivable for unusual balances.

D. Comparing an entity's uncollectible accounts expense with actual uncollectible accounts receivable.

Answer (A) is correct. *(CPA, adapted)*
REQUIRED: The procedure used to obtain evidential matter in support of an assessed level of control risk below the maximum level.
DISCUSSION: To assess control risk below the maximum, an auditor must perform tests of controls. Tests of controls include inquiry, observation, inspection, and reperformance of a control by the auditor. Thus, observing an entity's employee prepare the schedule of past due accounts receivable provides evidence of the effectiveness of certain controls over accounts receivable.
Answer (B) is incorrect because sending confirmation requests to verify the existence of accounts receivable is a test of the details of balances, which is a substantive test. Answer (C) is incorrect because inspecting an entity's analysis of accounts receivable for unusual balances is a test of the details of balances, which is a substantive test. Answer (D) is incorrect because comparing uncollectible accounts expense with actual uncollectible accounts receivable is a form of analytical procedure, which is used to determine whether the auditor's expectation is supported by client data.

8.3 Correlation of Control Risk and Detection Risk

19. An auditor assesses control risk because it

A. Is relevant to the auditor's understanding of the control environment.

B. Provides assurance that the auditor's materiality levels are appropriate.

C. Indicates to the auditor where inherent risk may be the greatest.

D. Affects the level of detection risk that the auditor may accept.

Answer (D) is correct. *(CPA, adapted)*
REQUIRED: The reason for assessing control risk.
DISCUSSION: The assessed levels of control risk and inherent risk determine the acceptable level of detection risk. In the audit risk model, allowable audit risk (specified by the auditor) equals the product of control risk, inherent risk, and detection risk. This equation can be solved for detection risk when the other values are specified.
   Answer (A) is incorrect because the understanding of the control environment provides evidence for assessing control risk. Answer (B) is incorrect because materiality levels are based upon auditor judgment. Answer (C) is incorrect because inherent risk is independent of internal control.

20. On the basis of audit evidence gathered and evaluated, an auditor decides to increase the assessed level of control risk from that originally planned. To achieve an overall audit risk level that is substantially the same as the planned audit risk level, the auditor would

A. Increase inherent risk.

B. Increase materiality levels.

C. Decrease inherent risk.

D. Decrease detection risk.

Answer (D) is correct. *(CPA, adapted)*
REQUIRED: The step to achieve an overall audit risk that is substantially the same as the planned audit risk given an increase in the assessed control risk.
DISCUSSION: Audit risk is a function of inherent risk, control risk, and detection risk. The only risk the auditor directly controls is detection risk. (S)he can only assess what control risk and inherent risk are believed to be, but (s)he can change detection risk directly. Hence, the auditor can achieve the desired audit risk based on the assessed levels of inherent risk and control risk and the acceptable level of detection risk. Because detection risk has an inverse relationship with control risk, increasing the assessed control risk requires a decrease in the acceptable detection risk if overall audit risk is held constant.
   Answer (A) is incorrect because inherent risk is not under the control of the auditor and can only be assessed. Answer (B) is incorrect because materiality and risk are interrelated. However, as risk increases, the auditor will likely reduce the level of materiality. Answer (C) is incorrect because inherent risk is not under the control of the auditor and can only be assessed.

21. An auditor uses the knowledge provided by the understanding of internal control and the final assessed level of control risk primarily to determine the nature, timing, and extent of the

A. Attribute tests.

B. Compliance tests.

C. Tests of controls.

D. Substantive tests.

Answer (D) is correct. *(CPA, adapted)*
REQUIRED: The auditor's use of the understanding of internal control and the final assessed level of control risk.
DISCUSSION: The auditor uses the understanding obtained and the assessment of control risk to plan the nature, timing, and extent of substantive tests. Substantive tests are "tests of details of transactions and balances and analytical procedures" (AU 319).
   Answer (A) is incorrect because testing of controls is an application of attribute sampling. Answer (B) is incorrect because compliance tests determine whether an entity is complying with laws and regulations (AU 801). Answer (C) is incorrect because tests of controls must be performed before control risk is assessed below the maximum.

22. The objective of tests of details of transactions performed as tests of controls is to

A. Monitor the design and use of entity documents such as prenumbered shipping forms.

B. Determine whether internal controls have been placed in operation.

C. Detect material misstatements in the account balances of the financial statements.

D. Evaluate whether internal controls operated effectively.

Answer (D) is correct. *(CPA, adapted)*
REQUIRED: The objective of tests of details of transactions performed as tests of controls.
DISCUSSION: When the auditor wishes to assess control risk for specific financial statement assertions below the maximum level, or when performing only substantive tests would not be effective in restricting detection risk to an acceptable level, the auditor gathers information about the effectiveness of the design and operation of controls. Tests of controls are defined as procedures to obtain evidence about operational effectiveness (AU 319). A test of details of the transactions reflected in relevant financial statement assertions clearly addresses the operational effectiveness of controls.
Answer (A) is incorrect because the client's controls should monitor the use of entity documents. Answer (B) is incorrect because determination of whether controls have been placed in operation is made in conjunction with the auditor's understanding of internal control. Answer (C) is incorrect because the purpose of substantive tests is to detect material misstatements in the account balances.

23. When an auditor increases the planned assessed level of control risk because certain controls were determined to be ineffective, the auditor will most likely increase the

A. Extent of tests of details.

B. Level of inherent risk.

C. Extent of tests of controls.

D. Level of detection risk.

Answer (A) is correct. *(CPA, adapted)*
REQUIRED: The effect of an increase in the planned assessed level of control risk.
DISCUSSION: An auditor considers internal control to assess control risk. The greater (lower) the assessed level of control risk, the lower (greater) the acceptable level of detection risk. In turn, the acceptable level of detection risk affects substantive testing. For example, as the acceptable level of detection risk decreases, the auditor changes the nature, timing, or extent of substantive tests to increase the assurance they provide.
Answer (B) is incorrect because inherent risk is not affected by control risk. Answer (C) is incorrect because, once controls are determined to be ineffective, further tests of controls are unnecessary. Answer (D) is incorrect because the acceptable detection risk decreases when the assessed level of control risk increases.

24. When numerous property and equipment transactions occur during the year, an auditor who plans to assess control risk at a low level usually performs

A. Tests of controls and extensive tests of property and equipment balances at the end of the year.

B. Analytical procedures for current year property and equipment transactions.

C. Tests of controls and limited tests of current-year property and equipment transactions.

D. Analytical procedures for property and equipment balances at the end of the year.

Answer (C) is correct. *(CPA, adapted)*
REQUIRED: The type of testing performed when an auditor plans to assess control risk at a low level.
DISCUSSION: When transactions are numerous and the auditor plans to assess control risk below the maximum level, tests of controls are performed to determine their operating effectiveness. If control risk is assessed below the maximum, the assurance to be provided by substantive testing is reduced. Thus, the auditor must have determined that assessing control risk below the maximum for certain assertions is effective and more efficient than performing only substantive tests (AU 319).
Answer (A) is incorrect because the substantive tests are reduced, not expanded. Answer (B) is incorrect because analytical procedures are applied regardless of the level at which control risk is assessed. Answer (D) is incorrect because analytical procedures are applied regardless of the level at which control risk is assessed.

25. A client maintains perpetual inventory records in both quantities and dollars. If the assessed level of control risk is high, an auditor will probably

  A. Apply gross profit tests to ascertain the reasonableness of the physical counts.

  B. Increase the extent of tests of controls relevant to the inventory cycle.

  C. Request the client to schedule the physical inventory count at the end of the year.

  D. Insist that the client perform physical counts of inventory items several times during the year.

Answer (C) is correct. *(CPA, adapted)*
  REQUIRED: The auditor's action if control risk for inventory is high.
  DISCUSSION: If control risk is high, the acceptable level of detection risk decreases for a given level of audit risk. The auditor should change the nature, timing, or extent of substantive tests to increase the assurance they provide. Thus, extending work done at an interim date to year-end might be inappropriate. Observation of inventory at year-end would provide greater assurance.
  Answer (A) is incorrect because comparing the gross profit test results with the prior year's results provides evidence about sales and cost of goods sold but not inventory. Answer (B) is incorrect because, if the auditor believes controls are unlikely to be effective, tests of controls may not be performed. However, the auditor needs to be satisfied that performing only substantive tests will be effective in restricting detection risk to an acceptable level. Answer (D) is incorrect because the risk is that year-end inventory is misstated.

26. An auditor may compensate for a high assessed level of control risk by increasing the

  A. Level of detection risk.

  B. Extent of tests of controls.

  C. Preliminary judgment about audit risk.

  D. Extent of analytical procedures.

Answer (D) is correct. *(CPA, adapted)*
  REQUIRED: The method an auditor may use to compensate for a high assessed level of control risk.
  DISCUSSION: The higher the assessed level of control risk, the lower the acceptable level of detection risk. As the acceptable level of detection risk decreases, the auditor should obtain greater assurance from substantive tests, which may include analytical procedures, by changing their nature, timing, or extent.
  Answer (A) is incorrect because the acceptable level of detection risk decreases when the assessed level of control risk increases. Answer (B) is incorrect because the auditor should change the nature, timing, or extent of substantive tests. Answer (C) is incorrect because the auditor plans the audit so as to reduce the risk of material misstatement of financial statement assertions to an appropriate level. This risk is not necessarily changed because of a high assessed level of control risk.

27. Regardless of the assessed level of control risk, an auditor should perform some

  A. Tests of controls to determine the effectiveness of controls.

  B. Analytical procedures to verify the design of controls.

  C. Substantive tests to restrict detection risk for significant transaction classes.

  D. Dual-purpose tests to evaluate both the risk of monetary misstatement and preliminary control risk.

Answer (C) is correct. *(CPA, adapted)*
  REQUIRED: The procedures performed regardless of the assessed level of control risk.
  DISCUSSION: AU 319 states, "Although the inverse relationship between control risk and detection risk may permit the auditor to change the nature or the timing of substantive tests or limit their extent, ordinarily the assessed level of control risk cannot be sufficiently low to eliminate the need to perform any substantive tests to restrict detection risk for all of the assertions relevant to significant account balances or transaction classes."

8.4 Assessing Control Risk in a Computer Environment

28. In a computerized payroll system environment, an auditor is least likely to use test data to test controls related to

A. Missing employee numbers.

B. Proper approval of overtime by supervisors.

C. Time tickets with invalid job numbers.

D. Agreement of hours per clock cards with hours on time tickets.

Answer (B) is correct. *(CPA, adapted)*
REQUIRED: The least likely use of test data to test controls in a computerized payroll system environment.
DISCUSSION: Approval of overtime by supervisors most likely entails initialing of time cards. Inspection by the auditor is the appropriate test of this control.
Answer (A) is incorrect because the auditor uses test data to determine whether programmed controls were effective in checking for missing numbers. Answer (C) is incorrect because the auditor would use test data to determine whether programmed controls were effective in checking for invalid numbers. Answer (D) is incorrect because the auditor uses test data to determine whether programmed controls were effective in checking for agreement of sets of numbers.

29. Which of the following types of evidence should an auditor most likely examine to determine whether internal controls are operating as designed?

A. Gross margin information regarding the client's industry.

B. Confirmations of receivables verifying account balances.

C. Client records documenting the use of computer programs.

D. Anticipated results documented in budgets or forecasts.

Answer (C) is correct. *(CPA, adapted)*
REQUIRED: The items tested to determine the operating effectiveness of internal controls.
DISCUSSION: In testing controls over the computer processing function, the auditor should obtain evidence of proper authorization of access to computer programs and files.
Answer (A) is incorrect because analytical procedures are applied as substantive tests to gross margin information and anticipated results. Answer (B) is incorrect because confirmations customarily request information regarding account balances and are substantive tests, not tests of controls. Answer (D) is incorrect because analytical procedures are applied as substantive tests to gross margin information and anticipated results.

30. To obtain evidence that online access controls are properly functioning, an auditor most likely will

A. Create checkpoints at periodic intervals after live data processing to test for unauthorized use of the system.

B. Examine the transaction log to discover whether any transactions were lost or entered twice because of a system malfunction.

C. Enter invalid identification numbers or passwords to ascertain whether the system rejects them.

D. Vouch a random sample of processed transactions to assure proper authorization.

Answer (C) is correct. *(CPA, adapted)*
REQUIRED: The procedure an auditor will most likely use to obtain evidence that user online access controls are functioning as designed.
DISCUSSION: Employees with access authority to process transactions that change records should not also have asset custody or program modification responsibilities. The auditor should determine that password authority is consistent with other assigned responsibilities. The auditor can directly test whether password controls are working by attempting entry into the system by using invalid identifications and passwords.
Answer (A) is incorrect because checkpoints are used as a recovery procedure in batch processing applications. Answer (B) is incorrect because testing for missing or duplicate transactions will not determine whether online access controls were functioning effectively. Answer (D) is incorrect because unauthorized transactions may be entered by someone having knowledge of valid passwords, etc.

31. When an accounting application is processed by computer, an auditor cannot verify the reliable operation of automated controls by

A. Manually comparing detail transaction files used by an edit program with the program's generated error listings to determine that errors were properly identified by the edit program.

B. Constructing a processing system for accounting applications and processing actual data from throughout the period through both the client's program and the auditor's program.

C. Manually reperforming, as of a moment in time, the processing of input data and comparing the simulated results with the actual results.

D. Periodically submitting auditor-prepared test data to the same computer process and evaluating the results.

Answer (C) is correct.   *(CPA, adapted)*
REQUIRED: The procedure that would not verify the reliable operation of automated controls.
DISCUSSION: This procedure describes what is termed auditing around the computer. The computer is treated as a black box, and only the inputs and outputs are evaluated. Because the actual controls may not be understood or tested, the technique is ordinarily inappropriate if the effectiveness of automated controls is important to the understanding of internal control and the assessment of control risk. Moreover, the auditor is concerned with the reliable operation of the controls throughout the audit period, not at a single moment in time.
Answer (A) is incorrect because a manual comparison of the computer generated output of an auditor-controlled edit program with the error listings generated by the client's program provides evidence that the client's automated controls were operating as planned. Answer (B) is incorrect because parallel simulation can be an effective method of testing the reliability of controls. Answer (D) is incorrect because submitting auditor-prepared test data to the client's computer process is an effective method of assessing the reliability of controls.

32. To obtain evidence that user identification and password controls are functioning as designed, an auditor should

A. Review the online transaction log to ascertain whether employees using passwords have access to data files and computer programs.

B. Examine a sample of password holders and access authority to determine whether they have access authority incompatible with their other responsibilities.

C. Extract a random sample of processed transactions and ensure that transactions are appropriately authorized.

D. Observe the file librarian's activities to discover whether other systems personnel are permitted to operate computer equipment without restriction.

Answer (B) is correct.   *(CPA, adapted)*
REQUIRED: The procedure an auditor should use to obtain evidence that user identification and password controls are functioning as designed.
DISCUSSION: Employees with access authority to process transactions that change records should not also have asset custody or program modification responsibilities. The auditor should determine that password authority is consistent with other assigned responsibilities. In addition, the auditor can directly test whether password controls are working by attempting entry into the system by using invalid identifications and passwords.
Answer (A) is incorrect because password assignment properly provides employees with access to files and programs. Answer (C) is incorrect because testing transactions for proper authorization does not ensure that user identification controls were functioning effectively. Answer (D) is incorrect because the file librarian oversees the physical protection of files, programs, and documentation, not the operation of computer equipment.

33. An auditor most likely should test for the presence of unauthorized computer program changes by running a

A. Program with test data.

B. Check digit verification program.

C. Source code comparison program.

D. Program that computes control totals.

Answer (C) is correct.   *(CPA, adapted)*
REQUIRED: The method used to test for the presence of unauthorized computer program changes.
DISCUSSION: The best way to test for unauthorized computer program changes is to examine the program itself. By comparing a program under his/her control with the program used for operations, the auditor can determine whether unauthorized changes have been made. This procedure is simple and inexpensive, and it does not require advanced computer expertise.
Answer (A) is incorrect because the test data may not trigger the unauthorized changes. Answer (B) is incorrect because check digit verification tests the accuracy of data transcription, not programs. Answer (D) is incorrect because control totals test the reasonableness and accuracy of processing but will not necessarily detect program changes.

34. Which of the following statements is not true of the test data approach to testing an accounting system?

A. Test data are processed by the client's computer programs under the auditor's control.

B. The test data need consist of only those valid and invalid conditions that interest the auditor.

C. Only one transaction of each type need be tested.

D. The test data must consist of all possible valid and invalid conditions.

Answer (D) is correct. *(CPA, adapted)*
REQUIRED: The false statement about the test data approach.
DISCUSSION: The test data approach includes preparation of dummy transactions by the auditor. These transactions are processed by the client's computer programs under the auditor's control. The test data consist of one transaction for each valid and invalid condition that interests the auditor. Consequently, the test data need not consist of all possible valid and invalid conditions.
Answer (A) is incorrect because the test data are processed by the client's computer programs under the control of the auditor. Answer (B) is incorrect because only those controls deemed important to the auditor need be tested. Answer (C) is incorrect because the computer processes all similar transactions in the same way. Accordingly, only one transaction needs to be tested to determine whether a control is working effectively.

35. When an auditor tests a computerized accounting system, which of the following is true of the test data approach?

A. Several transactions of each type must be tested.

B. Test data are processed by the client's computer programs under the auditor's control.

C. Test data must consist of all possible valid and invalid conditions.

D. The program tested is different from the program used throughout the year by the client.

Answer (B) is correct. *(CPA, adapted)*
REQUIRED: The true statement about the test data approach.
DISCUSSION: In using the test data approach, the auditor prepares a set of dummy transactions specifically tailored to test the control procedures that management claims to have incorporated into the processing program. The auditor then processes these transactions using management's program and compares the expected results with the actual output of the program.
Answer (A) is incorrect because the computer processes each transaction in a consistent manner. Thus, only one type of transaction for each condition to be tested need be included. Answer (C) is incorrect because the test data should consist of those control procedures that the auditor desires to test. Answer (D) is incorrect because the auditor expects to test the program that the client has used throughout the year to gain assurance that the controls are in place and working.

36. Processing data through the use of simulated files provides an auditor with information about the operating effectiveness of controls. One of the techniques involved in this approach makes use of

A. Controlled reprocessing.

B. An integrated test facility.

C. Input validation.

D. Program code checking.

Answer (B) is correct. *(CPA, adapted)*
REQUIRED: The process that uses simulated files to determine the operating effectiveness of controls.
DISCUSSION: The ITF or minicompany technique is a development of the test data method. It permits dummy transactions to be processed at the same time as live transactions but requires additional programming to ensure that programs will recognize the specially coded test data. Also, dummy files must be established (the test facility or dummy entity). Nevertheless, output (for example, control totals) is affected by the existence of the ITF transactions.
Answer (A) is incorrect because controlled reprocessing involves the use of a copy of the client's program to reprocess actual data. Answer (C) is incorrect because the client's input controls should accomplish input validation. Answer (D) is incorrect because program code checking compares the code of the current client program with the original; it does not use simulated files.

37. An auditor who is testing computer controls in a payroll system will most likely use test data that contain conditions such as

A. Deductions not authorized by employees.

B. Overtime not approved by supervisors.

C. Time tickets with invalid job numbers.

D. Payroll checks with unauthorized signatures.

Answer (C) is correct. *(CPA, adapted)*
REQUIRED: The most likely conditions in test data used in a test of computer controls over payroll.
DISCUSSION: The auditor will most likely test computer controls for detection of time tickets with invalid job numbers. The validity of codes can be determined by the computer system. Testing of approvals, authorizations, and signatures usually require manual procedures.
Answer (A) is incorrect because testing of authorizations usually requires manual procedures. Answer (B) is incorrect because testing of approvals usually requires manual procedures. Answer (D) is incorrect because testing of signatures usually requires manual procedures.

38. Which of the following computer-assisted auditing techniques allows fictitious and real transactions to be processed together without the knowledge of client operating personnel?

    A. Integrated test facility (ITF).

    B. Input controls matrix.

    C. Parallel simulation.

    D. Data entry monitor.

Answer (A) is correct. *(CPA, adapted)*
    REQUIRED: The technique that processes fictitious and real transactions without the knowledge of client personnel.
    DISCUSSION: The ITF or minicompany technique is a development of the test data method. It permits dummy transactions to be processed at the same time as live transactions but requires additional programming to ensure that programs will recognize the specially coded test data. The test transactions may be submitted without the computer operators' knowledge.
    Answer (B) is incorrect because input controls matrix is not a method typically used by auditors to test a client's computer systems. Answer (C) is incorrect because parallel simulation reprocesses only real, not fictitious, transactions. Answer (D) is incorrect because data entry monitor is not a method typically used by auditors to test a client's computer systems.

39. An auditor who wishes to capture an entity's data as transactions are processed and continuously test the entity's computerized information system most likely would use which of the following techniques?

    A. Snapshot application.

    B. Embedded audit module.

    C. Integrated data check.

    D. Test data generator.

Answer (B) is correct. *(CPA, adapted)*
    REQUIRED: The technique that captures an entity's data as transactions are processed and continuously tests the information system.
    DISCUSSION: Continuous monitoring and analysis of transaction processing can be achieved with an embedded audit module. An audit module embedded in the client's software routinely selects and abstracts certain actual transactions and other information with audit significance. They may be tagged and traced through the information system. A disadvantage is that audit hooks must be programmed into the operating system and applications. An alternative is recording in an audit log, that is, in a file accessible only by the auditor.

40. The following flowchart depicts

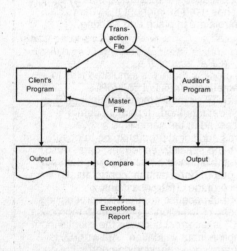

    A. Program code checking.

    B. Parallel simulation.

    C. Integrated test facility.

    D. Controlled reprocessing.

Answer (B) is correct. *(CPA, adapted)*
    REQUIRED: The audit technique depicted by the flowchart.
    DISCUSSION: Parallel simulation is a test of the controls in a client's application program. An auditor-developed program is used to process actual client data and compare the output and the exceptions report with those of the client's application program. If the client's programmed controls are operating effectively, the two sets of results should be reconcilable.
    Answer (A) is incorrect because program code checking refers to checking the client's application program code to determine if it contains the appropriate controls. Answer (C) is incorrect because an ITF introduces dummy records into the client's files and then processes dummy transactions to update the records. The auditor can test the controls by including various types of transactions to be processed. Answer (D) is incorrect because controlled reprocessing is a variant of parallel simulation that uses an authenticated copy of the auditee's program. The flowchart indicates that the auditor's program is being used.

8.5 PRACTICE SIMULATION

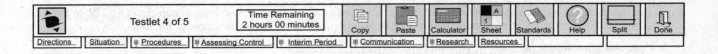

| | Testlet 4 of 5 | Time Remaining 2 hours 00 minutes | Copy | Paste | Calculator | Sheet | Standards | Help | Split | Done |

Directions | Situation | Procedures | Assessing Control | Interim Period | Communication | Research | Resources

1. Directions

In the following simulation, you will be asked to complete various tasks related to tests of controls and control risk. The simulation will provide all of the information necessary to do the work. For full credit, be sure to view and complete all work tabs.

Resources are available to you under the tab marked RESOURCES. You may want to review the resources before beginning the simulation.

2. Situation

Lauren Jones, CPA, has been engaged to perform the first audit of the financial statements of Chips R' Us, Inc., a privately held manufacturer of custom computer processors. Founded only five years ago, Chips is already one of the largest privately held corporations in its industry. With over 40 locations nationwide, Chips relies heavily on its computer networks to assist in the consolidation of financial data among offices. Jones and her team are preparing an audit program to assist in gaining an understanding of controls and assessing control risk for the engagement.

3. Procedures

This question has a matching format that requires you to select the correct response from a drop-down list. Write the letter of the answer in the shaded column. An answer may be used once, more than once, or not at all.

Some procedures listed below are used to gain an understanding of internal controls. Other procedures are used solely as tests of controls. Still others are not typically considered in testing controls. Match each procedure with an objective.

Procedures	Answer
1. Inspection of purchase orders for the authorization of the purchasing agent	
2. Confirmation of accounts receivable with debtors	
3. Observation of the taking of inventory	
4. Reading policy and procedure manuals	
5. Observation of an employee's preparation of a daily deposit ticket	
6. Inspection of a report listing customers that were denied credit	
7. Reperformance of the extension of approved pay rates times approved hours worked	
8. Inquire about how new employees are trained	

Objectives
U) Gain an understanding of controls
T) Test of controls
N) Used neither to gain an understanding nor to test controls

4. Assessing Control Risk in a Computer Environment

This question has a matching format that requires you to select the correct response from a drop-down list. Write the letter of the answer in the shaded column. An answer may be used once, more than once, or not at all.

Complete each statement below by choosing the proper word or phrase.

Computer Testing	Answer
1. To test _____, the auditor should enter invalid passwords.	
2. To test whether unauthorized computer program changes have been made, the auditor should run _____.	
3. _____ should include dummy transactions of both valid and invalid transactions.	
4. The _____ processes both fictitious and real transactions without the knowledge of client personnel.	
5. An auditor-developed program used to process actual client data to compare with the client's output and exceptions reports is _____.	
6. _____ is a procedure that does not effectively verify the reliable operation of automated controls.	
7. The use of _____ oversees the physical protection of files.	
8. An example of an edit check is _____.	

Word/Phrase
A) The test data approach
B) Auditing through the computer
C) Online access controls
D) Auditing around the computer
E) A reasonable test
F) The ITF or minicompany technique
G) Parallel simulation
H) A media librarian
I) A source code comparison program

5. Interim Period Considerations

This question is presented in a check-the-box format. Select the correct response from the given list.

When obtaining evidence about the effectiveness of the design or operation of internal control during an interim period, the auditor should determine what additional evidence should be obtained for the remaining period. The auditor should consider which of the following?

Considerations for Interim Period	Yes	No
1. Length of the remaining period		
2. Significance of the assertion involved		
3. Financial well-being of the corporation at the interim		
4. Specific controls evaluated during the interim period		
5. Extent of the evaluation		
6. Results of the tests of controls used in making the evaluation		
7. Cost of the specific controls implemented during period		
8. Evidence from substantive tests to be performed during remaining period		

6. Communication

A staff member has asked whether the effectiveness of controls for the payroll cycle of a client should be tested. Explain in a memorandum when not testing controls is appropriate, the effect of the client's use of information technology on this assessment, and whether the status of the client as an issuer is relevant. Type your communication in your word processor program and print out a copy in a memorandum style format.

REMINDER: Your response will be graded for both technical content and writing skills. You should demonstrate your ability to develop, organize, and express your ideas. Do not convey information in the form of a table, bullet point list, or other abbreviated presentation.

To: Staff
From: CPA
Subject: When not testing a nonpublic client's controls is appropriate

7. Research

Use the research materials available to you to find the answer to the following question in the AICPA Professional Standards. Print the appropriate citation in its entirety from the source you choose. Use only one source. This is a copy-and-paste type item in a simulation.

The audit risk model defines the level of detection risk as a function of other risks. Research, document, and define the relation of detection risk to other risks is an audit.

Unofficial Answers

3. Procedures (8 Gradable Items)

1. T)– Inspection of purchase orders for the authorization of the purchasing agent is used as a test of controls.

2. N)– Confirmation of accounts receivable with debtors is used neither to gain an understanding nor to test controls. Confirmations are typically for the purpose of collecting substantive evidence rather than testing the effectiveness of the controls.

3. N)– Observation of the taking of inventory is used neither to gain an understanding nor to test controls. Observation of the taking of the inventory is a substantive test to provide assurance that the inventory exists.

4. U)– Reading policy and procedure manuals is used to gain an understanding of controls.

5. T)– Observation of an employee's preparation of a daily deposit ticket is used as a test of controls.

6. T)– Inspection of a report listing customers that were denied credit is used as a test of controls.

7. T)– Reperformance of the extension of approved pay rates times approved hours worked is used as a test of controls.

8. U)– Inquiring about how new employees are trained is used to gain an understanding of controls.

4. Assessing Control Risk in a Computer Environment (8 Gradable Items)

1. C), "online access controls" best completes this statement

2. I), "a source code comparison program" best completes this statement

3. A), "a test data approach" best completes this statement

4. F), "ITF or minicompany technique" best completes this statement

5. G), "parallel simulation" best completes this statement

6. D), "auditing around the computer" best completes this statement

7. H), "a media librarian" best completes this statement

8. E), "reasonableness test" best completes this statement

5. Interim Period Considerations (8 Gradable Items)

1) <u>Yes</u>. The considerations for the interim period are length of the remaining period, significance of the assertion involved, specific controls evaluated during the interim period, extent of the evaluation, results of the tests of controls used in making the evaluation, and evidence from substantive tests to be performed during the remaining period.

2) <u>Yes</u>. The considerations for the interim period are length of the remaining period, significance of the assertion involved, specific controls evaluated during the interim period, extent of the evaluation, results of the tests of controls used in making the evaluation, and evidence from substantive tests to be performed during the remaining period.

3) <u>No</u>. The considerations for the interim period are length of the remaining period, significance of the assertion involved, specific controls evaluated during the interim period, extent of the evaluation, results of the tests of controls used in making the evaluation, and evidence from substantive tests to be performed during the remaining period.

4) <u>Yes</u>. The considerations for the interim period are length of the remaining period, significance of the assertion involved, specific controls evaluated during the interim period, extent of the evaluation, results of the tests of controls used in making the evaluation, and evidence from substantive tests to be performed during the remaining period.

5) <u>Yes</u>. The considerations for the interim period are length of the remaining period, significance of the assertion involved, specific controls evaluated during the interim period, extent of the evaluation, results of the tests of controls used in making the evaluation, and evidence from substantive tests to be performed during the remaining period.

6) <u>Yes</u>. The considerations for the interim period are length of the remaining period, significance of the assertion involved, specific controls evaluated during the interim period, extent of the evaluation, results of the tests of controls used in making the evaluation, and evidence from substantive tests to be performed during the remaining period.

7) <u>No</u>. The considerations for the interim period are length of the remaining period, significance of the assertion involved, specific controls evaluated during the interim period, extent of the evaluation, results of the tests of controls used in making the evaluation, and evidence from substantive tests to be performed during the remaining period.

8) <u>Yes</u>. The considerations for the interim period are length of the remaining period, significance of the assertion involved, specific controls evaluated during the interim period, extent of the evaluation, results of the tests of controls used in making the evaluation, and evidence from substantive tests to be performed during the remaining period.

6. Communication (5 Gradable Items; For grading instructions, please refer to page 11.)

To: Staff
From: CPA
Subject: When not testing a nonpublic client's controls is appropriate

After obtaining the understanding of internal control, the auditor may assess control risk at the maximum level for some or all financial statement assertions. Under current AICPA auditing standards, this assessment of control risk of a nonpublic client (one not subject to the reporting requirements of the securities acts) is an appropriate reason not to perform tests of controls. Control risk may be assessed at the maximum because controls are unlikely to pertain to an assertion, controls are unlikely to be effective, or evaluating effectiveness would be inefficient. When the auditor assesses control risk for a nonpublic client at the maximum level, (s)he must become satisfied that performing only substantive tests will be effective in restricting detection risk to an acceptable level.

The client's use of information technology (IT) may be such that evidence of initiating, recording, processing, or reporting of data supporting financial statement assertions exists only in electronic form. Thus, the use of IT may prevent the auditor from giving the necessary assurance solely on the basis of substantive testing. In these circumstances, the competence and sufficiency of the evidence ordinarily depend on the effectiveness of controls over its accuracy and completeness. For example, substantive tests alone may not suffice when the entity's automated system initiates orders for goods and settles payables automatically without any other documentation.

In an audit of the financial statements of a public company (an issuer as defined in the securities acts), the auditor's procedures must be sufficient to express an opinion on the client's required assessment of its internal control structure and procedures for financial reporting (Section 404 of the Sarbanes-Oxley Act of 2002).

7. Research (6 Gradable Items)

AU Section 319 -- *Consideration of Internal Control in a Financial Statement Audit*

Correlation of Control Risk with Detection Risk

.105   The ultimate purpose of assessing control risk is to contribute to the auditor's evaluation of the risk that material misstatements exist in the financial statements. The process of assessing control risk (together with assessing inherent risk) provides evidential matter about the risk that such misstatements may exist in the financial statements. The auditor uses this evidential matter as part of the reasonable basis for an opinion referred to in the third standard of field work, which follows: Sufficient competent evidential matter is to be obtained through inspection, observation, inquiries, and confirmations to afford a reasonable basis for an opinion regarding the financial statements under audit.

.106   After considering the level to which he or she seeks to restrict the risk of a material misstatement in the financial statements and the assessed levels of inherent risk and control risk, the auditor performs substantive tests to restrict detection risk to an acceptable level. As the assessed level of control risk decreases, the acceptable level of detection risk increases. Accordingly, the auditor may alter the nature, timing, and extent of the substantive tests performed.

.107   Although the inverse relationship between control risk and detection risk may permit the auditor to change the nature or the timing of substantive tests or limit their extent, ordinarily the assessed level of control risk cannot be sufficiently low to eliminate the need to perform any substantive tests to restrict detection risk for all of the assertions relevant to significant account balances or transaction classes. Consequently, regardless of the assessed level of control risk, the auditor should perform substantive tests for significant account balances and transaction classes.

.108   The substantive tests that the auditor performs consist of tests of details of transactions and balances, and analytical procedures. In assessing control risk, the auditor also may use tests of details of transactions as tests of controls. The objective of tests of details of transactions performed as substantive tests is to detect material misstatements in the financial statements. The objective of tests of details of transactions performed as tests of controls is to evaluate whether a control operated effectively. Although these objectives are different, both may be accomplished concurrently through performance of a test of details on the same transaction. The auditor should recognize, however, that careful consideration should be given to the design and evaluation of such tests to ensure that both objectives will be accomplished.

Scoring Schedule:

	Correct Responses		Gradable Items		Weights		
Tab 3	_____	÷	8	×	20%	=	_____
Tab 4	_____	÷	8	×	20%	=	_____
Tab 5	_____	÷	8	×	20%	=	_____
Tab 6	_____	÷	5	×	30%	=	_____
Tab 7	_____	÷	6	×	10%	=	_____
							(Your Score)

Use Gleim's **CPA Review Online** to practice more simulations in a realistic environment.

STUDY UNIT NINE
INTERNAL CONTROL COMMUNICATIONS

(15 pages of outline)

9.1	Communication of Internal Control Related Matters Noted in an Audit (AU 325)	279
9.2	Communication with Audit Committees (AU 380)	282
9.3	Reporting on an Entity's Internal Control over Financial Reporting (AT 501)	285
9.4	Service Organizations (AU 324)	290
9.5	Practice Simulation	309

This study unit concerns various auditor communications, most involving internal control. During the conduct of an audit, the auditor may observe control deficiencies. If so, the auditor has a responsibility, ancillary to the audit itself, to communicate these reportable conditions to the client as defined by **AU 325**, *Communication of Internal Control Related Matters Noted in an Audit*. Other issues relating to the conduct of the audit also should be communicated to the audit committee. Some of these are closely related to internal control, but others relate to the audit in general as described in **AU 380**, *Communication with Audit Committees*. The CPA may be engaged to provide a report on the effectiveness of an entity's internal control over financial reporting (or an assertion thereon) that is appropriate for general distribution. This service and the reports issued are described in **AT 501**, *Reporting on an Entity's Internal Control over Financial Reporting*. Furthermore, public companies are required by Sarbanes-Oxley to provide an assessment of the effectiveness of internal control over financial reporting in annual reports. They also must include an auditor's opinion on the assessment and an opinion on the effectiveness of internal control. The auditor's reporting responsibility is similar to that described in AT 501, but the PCAOB's **Auditing Standard No. 2**, *An Audit of Internal Control Over Financial Reporting Performed in Conjunction with an Audit of Financial Statements*, provides additional guidance on the required process and reporting. The CPA may be either a user or a preparer of a report prepared in accordance with AU 324, *Service Organizations*. Such a report may affect the user CPA's assessment of a client's control risk.

9.1 COMMUNICATION OF INTERNAL CONTROL RELATED MATTERS NOTED IN AN AUDIT (AU 325)

1. AU 325 concerns identifying and reporting reportable conditions in internal control observed during an audit.

   a. The communication is expected to be to the audit committee or its equivalent.

   b. The client and auditor may agree to communicate on other issues not discussed in this standard or based on the application of agreed-upon procedures.

2. **Reportable conditions** are matters coming to the auditor's attention that relate to significant deficiencies in the design or operation of internal controls that, in the auditor's judgment, could adversely affect the organization's ability to initiate, record, process, and report financial data consistent with the assertions of management in the financial statements.

   a. Such deficiencies may involve all five internal control components (recall "controls stop CRIME"):

      1) **C**ontrol activities
      2) **R**isk assessment
      3) **I**nformation and communication
      4) **M**onitoring
      5) Control **E**nvironment

   b. The auditor should also consider matters coming to his/her attention that relate to interim reporting outside the entity.

   c. Matters that are not reportable conditions may also be communicated for the benefit of management and others.

   d. Auditors are not required to communicate suggested corrective action for reportable conditions.

3. **Identifying Reportable Conditions**. Although an auditor need not search for reportable conditions, (s)he may become aware of them during the audit.

   a. The awareness will depend on many factors, such as the nature and extent of audit procedures, size and complexity of the entity, and nature and diversity of the business.

   b. In judging which matters are reportable, the auditor should consider various factors, for example, the size, complexity, and diversity of the entity; organizational structure; and ownership characteristics.

   c. The existence of reportable conditions may reflect a conscious management decision, of which the audit committee is aware, to accept a degree of risk because of cost or other considerations.

      1) If the audit committee has acknowledged the deficiencies and the related risks, the matter may not need to be reported, but changes in management or the audit committee or the passage of time may make it appropriate to report such matters.

   d. If an auditor becomes aware of a potential future internal control deficiency while performing an audit, the auditor is not required to report the problem as a reportable condition unless it affects the applicable period under audit. However, the auditor should document all communication about the matter that (s)he has with the client.

   e. The following are some examples of reportable conditions:

      1) Inadequate overall internal control design
      2) Absence of appropriate segregation of duties
      3) Absence of appropriate reviews and approvals of transactions, accounting entries, or systems output
      4) Inadequate procedures for assessing and applying accounting principles or intentional misapplication thereof
      5) Inadequate provisions for the safeguarding of assets
      6) Failure of the system to provide complete and accurate output because of design flaws or misapplication of control procedures
      7) Failure of identified controls
      8) Intentional override of controls by those in authority
      9) Failure to perform tasks that are part of internal control

3

10) Willful wrongdoing by employees or management, such as manipulation, falsification, or alteration of accounting records or supporting documents
11) Misrepresentation by client personnel to the auditor
12) Unqualified personnel
13) Insufficient control consciousness within the organization
14) Failure to follow up and correct deficiencies
15) Significant undisclosed related party transactions
16) Lack of objectivity by accounting decision makers

Report on Reportable Conditions

In planning and performing our audit of the financial statements of the ABC Corporation for the year ended December 31, year 1, we considered its internal control in order to determine our auditing procedures for the purpose of expressing our opinion on the financial statements and not to provide assurance on internal control. However, we noted certain matters involving internal control and its operation that we consider to be reportable conditions under standards established by the AICPA. Reportable conditions involve matters coming to our attention relating to significant deficiencies in the design or operation of internal control that, in our judgment, could adversely affect the organization's ability to initiate, record, process, and report financial data consistent with the assertions of management in the financial statements.

[Insert paragraphs here describing the reportable conditions.]

This report is intended solely for the information and use of the audit committee (board of directors, board of trustees, or owners in owner-managed enterprises), management, and others within the organization (or specified regulatory agency) and is not intended to be and should not be used by anyone other than these specified parties.

4. **Agreed-Upon Criteria**. Clients may request the auditor to be alert for and report matters that are not reportable conditions. The auditor may also report matters of value to management absent a specific request. The auditor may be requested to

    a. Visit specific locations
    b. Assess specific control procedures
    c. Perform procedures not otherwise planned
    d. Report matters of less significance than provided for in AU 325
    e. Report on conditions specified by the client
    f. Report on further investigation of matters noted to identify causes

5. **Reporting -- Form and Content**. Reporting should preferably be in writing, and oral communications should be reflected in memoranda or notations in the audit documentation.

    a. A report on reportable conditions should

       1) State that the purpose of the audit is to report on the financial statements, not to provide assurance on internal control
       2) Define reportable conditions
       3) Describe the reportable conditions
       4) State that use is intended solely for persons within the organization, such as management and the audit committee

          a) When requirements are established by governmental authorities to furnish such reports, the report may refer to these authorities.

    b. EXAMPLE

       1) An auditor may also wish to include statements about other matters, such as the inherent limitations of internal control and the specific extent and nature of the consideration of internal control.

c.   If a reportable condition is of such magnitude as to be a material weakness, it may be, but is not required to be, separately identified and communicated if the auditor chooses or the client so requests.

        1)   A **material weakness** in internal control is a reportable condition in which the design or operation of one or more of the internal control components does not reduce to a relatively low level the risk that errors or fraud in amounts that would be material in relation to the financial statements being audited may occur and not be detected within a timely period by employees in the normal course of performing their assigned functions.

        2)   When the auditor wishes, or has been requested, to advise that reportable conditions have been identified but none is a material weakness, the report should include

            a)   The first paragraph in the sample report on the previous page
            b)   Paragraphs describing the reportable conditions noted
            c)   The definition of a material weakness
            d)   The following comments, if appropriate:

> Our consideration of internal control would not necessarily disclose all matters in internal control that might be reportable conditions and, accordingly, would not necessarily disclose all reportable conditions that are also considered to be material weaknesses as defined above. However, none of the reportable conditions described above is believed to be a material weakness.

            e)   The final paragraph in the example on the previous page

    d.   **Important**: Because of possible misinterpretation of the limited assurance given by stating in a written report that no reportable conditions were noted, the auditor should not make such a representation, and no report should be issued (but the report would be issued in a governmental audit).

    e.   When timely communication is important, the auditor may communicate significant matters during the audit. The decision is influenced by the significance of the matters noted and the urgency of corrective action.

    f.   AU 325 does not preclude an auditor from communicating observations and suggestions unrelated to internal control matters, such as those dealing with operational or administrative efficiencies, business strategies, and other items beneficial to the client.

6.   Stop and review! You have completed the outline for this subunit. Study multiple-choice questions 1 through 13 beginning on page 294.

9.2 COMMUNICATION WITH AUDIT COMMITTEES (AU 380)

1.   **Introduction**. Certain matters related to the audit must be communicated to those responsible for oversight of the financial reporting and disclosure process for which management is responsible (the audit committee).

    a.   The required communications apply to entities with an audit committee or the equivalent and to all SEC engagements.

    b.   The auditor must ensure that the audit committee receives additional information about the audit that may assist in its oversight process.

        1)   AU 380 does not preclude communications with others who may benefit therefrom.

c.   If the communication is oral, it should be reflected in memoranda or notations in the audit documentation. The auditor may want to review any minutes prepared by the audit committee to determine that they are consistent with the auditor's understanding of the communication. If the report is written, it should state that it is intended solely for the audit committee, the board, and, if appropriate, management.

d.   Because the specified communications are incidental to the audit, they may be made after the issuance of the audit report if they are timely, but earlier discussion of some matters may be desirable.

e.   It may be appropriate for management to communicate certain matters to the audit committee, and the auditor should be satisfied that such communications have occurred.

   1)   Although communication of recurring matters need not be repeated yearly, the auditor should periodically consider whether changes in the audit committee or the passage of time may justify timely reporting of such matters.

f.   AU 380 is not intended to restrict the communication of other matters.

2.   **Matters to Be Communicated to the Audit Committee**

   a.   **Auditor's responsibility under GAAS.** An audit addresses many matters of interest to an audit committee, e.g., internal control and whether the financial statements contain material misstatements.

      1)   For the audit committee to understand the nature of the assurance provided, the level of responsibility assumed must be communicated.

         a)   The audit is designed to provide reasonable, not absolute, assurance.

   b.   **Significant accounting policies.** The auditor should determine that the audit committee is informed about the

      1)   Selection of, changes in, and application of significant accounting policies
      2)   Methods used to account for significant unusual transactions
      3)   Effects of significant accounting policies in controversial or emerging areas that lack authoritative guidance or consensus, such as revenue recognition, off-balance-sheet financing, and accounting for equity investments

   c.   **Management judgments and accounting estimates.** Certain management estimates are particularly sensitive because they are significant to the financial statements, and future events affecting them may differ from current judgments. The audit committee should be informed about

      1)   The process used in formulating sensitive estimates
      2)   The basis for the auditor's conclusions concerning their reasonableness

   d.   **Audit adjustments.** The audit committee should be informed about audit adjustments that could, individually or in the aggregate, significantly affect the entity's financial reporting process. It should also be informed about uncorrected misstatements pertaining to the latest period that management regarded as immaterial, both individually and in the aggregate.

      1)   An audit adjustment, whether or not recorded, is a proposed correction of the financial statements that the auditor judges may not have been detected except during the audit.

         a)   Matters underlying adjustments proposed but not recorded could cause future statements to be materially misstated, although the adjustments are not material to the current statements.

6

e. **Other information in documents containing audited financial statements**. Other information prepared by management may accompany the financial statements.

1) For example, annual reports that certain entities file with the SEC must contain a section labeled Management's Discussion and Analysis of Financial Condition and Results of Operations.

a) The auditor should discuss with the audit committee his/her responsibility for the other information, the procedures performed, and the results.

f. **Auditor's judgments about the quality of the entity's accounting principles**. For SEC clients, the auditor should discuss these matters with the audit committee. Management is normally a participant in the discussion. Matters covered may include the consistency of principles and their application; the clarity and completeness of the statements; and items significantly affecting representational faithfulness, verifiability, and neutrality. Because objective criteria have not been developed to permit consistent evaluation, the discussion should address the unique circumstances of the auditee.

g. **Disagreements with management**. Management and the auditor may disagree about the application of accounting principles, the basis for accounting estimates, the scope of the audit, disclosures in the financial statements, and the wording of the audit report. The auditor and the audit committee should discuss any disagreements about matters significant to the statements or the audit report.

h. **Management consultation with other accountants**. When the auditor is aware of such a consultation, (s)he should discuss with the audit committee his/her views about the significant matters involved.

i. **Major issues discussed with management prior to retention**. The auditor and the audit committee should discuss any major issues discussed with management in connection with the initial or recurring retention of the auditors.

j. **Difficulties encountered in performing the audit**

1) The audit committee should be informed of serious difficulties encountered in dealing with management, such as unreasonable delays in permitting commencement of the audit or providing needed information, and an unreasonable timetable set by management.

2) Other significant problems may include unavailability of client personnel, and failure of client personnel to complete client-prepared schedules on a timely basis.

3. The **Sarbanes-Oxley Act of 2002** requires the accountant of a firm subject to the act to report the following to the audit committee:

a. All critical accounting policies and practices to be used.

b. All material alternative treatments of financial information within GAAP discussed with management.

c. Ramification of the use of alternative disclosures and treatments.

d. The treatment preferred by the accountant.

4. Stop and review! You have completed the outline for this subunit. Study multiple-choice questions 14 through 21 beginning on page 298.

9.3 REPORTING ON AN ENTITY'S INTERNAL CONTROL OVER FINANCIAL REPORTING (AT 501)

1. **Applicability.** A practitioner may be engaged to issue an examination report on the effectiveness of an entity's internal control over financial reporting (or on an assertion thereon).

   a. An entity's internal control over financial reporting includes those policies and procedures that pertain to an entity's ability to initiate, record, process, and report financial data consistent with the assertions in the financial statements.

   b. As part of the **engagement performance**, the practitioner should obtain from the responsible party a **written assertion** about the effectiveness of internal control. The written assertion may be in a report that accompanies the practitioner's report or in a representation letter to the practitioner. The assertion is usually made as of year-end, but may be made about effectiveness during a period of time, e.g., for a year.

   c. The assertion may be phrased in a variety of ways, for example, "Management's assertion that X Company maintained effective internal control over financial reporting as of a specific date," or "Management's assertion that X Company's internal control over financial reporting is sufficient to meet the stated objectives."

      1) The practitioner should not, however, provide assurance about "an assertion that is so subjective that people having competence in and using the same or similar criteria would not ordinarily be able to arrive at similar conclusions" (for example, "very effective control" would not be appropriate).

2. **Other Attest Services.** A practitioner may examine or apply agreed-upon procedures relating to the effectiveness of internal control but should not perform a review. The scope and level of assurance could vary, and the review report would be susceptible to misinterpretation.

   a. The guidance in Study Unit 18 applies to an agreed-upon procedures engagement relating to internal control.

3. **Conditions for Engagement Acceptance.** A practitioner may accept an examination engagement when the following conditions are met:

   a. Management accepts responsibility for the effectiveness of the entity's internal control.

   b. The responsible party (the management personnel accepting responsibility) evaluates the effectiveness of internal control using suitable criteria (**control criteria**) established by a recognized body of experts. One recognized body is the Committee of Sponsoring Organizations (COSO), which included the American Institute of Certified Public Accountants, the American Accounting Association, Financial Executives Institute, the Institute of Management Accountants, and The Institute of Internal Auditors. The organization sponsored the National Commission on Fraudulent Financial Reporting. In 1992, the commission, also known as the Treadway Commission, issued the document, "Internal Control Integrated Framework." The final report is usually referred to as the COSO Report and represents the basic definitions found in the generally accepted auditing standards.

   c. Sufficient evidential matter exists or could be developed to support the responsible party's evaluation.

4. **Components of an Entity's Internal Control.** The components of an entity's internal control are a function of the definition of internal control selected by management. One possibility is the definition established by COSO.

5. **Limitations of an Entity's Internal Control.** Inherent limitations of internal control are described in Study Unit 4 beginning on page 133.

6. In an **examination** engagement, the practitioner's objective is to express an opinion on whether internal control is effective, in all material respects, based on the control criteria or whether the responsible party's assertion about the effectiveness of internal control is fairly stated, in all material respects, based on the control criteria. However, the assertion may also relate to a segment of internal control.

    a. To express an opinion, the practitioner accumulates sufficient evidence about the design and operating effectiveness of internal control to limit attestation risk to an appropriately low level.

        1) Design effectiveness concerns whether the control is suitably designed to prevent or detect material misstatements on a timely basis.

        2) Operating effectiveness concerns how the control was applied, the consistency with which it was applied, and by whom it was applied.

    b. Performing an examination involves

        1) Planning

            a) An overall strategy should be developed.

            b) If operations are in multiple locations, the practitioner should consider factors similar to those (s)he would consider in performing an audit of the financial statements of an entity with multiple locations. It is not always necessary to understand and test controls at each site.

            c) The practitioner should consider whether the entity has an internal audit function when planning the engagement.

            d) Controls should be appropriately documented by management and serve as the basis for management's and the practitioner's reports.

        2) Obtaining an understanding of internal control
        3) Evaluating design effectiveness
        4) Testing and evaluating operating effectiveness
        5) Forming an opinion

7. **Deficiencies in an entity's internal control** should be communicated.

    a. The presence of a material weakness will preclude the practitioner from concluding that the entity has effective internal control. Depending on the significance and effects of the material weakness, the practitioner may qualify the opinion ("except for") or express an adverse opinion.

    b. The practitioner should communicate reportable conditions to the audit committee and identify the reportable conditions that are also considered to be material weaknesses, preferably in writing.

8. **Responsible Party's Representations**

    a. The practitioner should obtain written representations from the responsible party

        1) Acknowledging responsibility for establishing and maintaining internal control
        2) Stating that the responsible party has performed an evaluation of internal control and specifying the control criteria
        3) Stating the assertion based on the control criteria as of a specified date
        4) Stating that the responsible party has disclosed all reportable conditions and identified those believed to be material weaknesses
        5) Describing any fraudulent activities that are material or that involve management or other employees with a significant role in internal control
        6) Stating whether, subsequent to the date being reported on, changes occurred in internal control or other factors that might significantly affect internal control, including any corrective actions taken by the responsible party

b. Refusal to furnish all appropriate written representations is a scope limitation that precludes an unqualified opinion. It usually suffices to cause issuance of a disclaimer of opinion or withdrawal from the engagement. The practitioner should also consider the effects of the refusal on his/her ability to rely on other representations.

9. **Reporting Standards**. The report may express an opinion directly on the effectiveness of internal control or on the responsible party's assertion as to effectiveness.

a. The standard form given by AT 501 includes introductory, scope, inherent limitations, and opinion paragraphs.

Report Expressing an Opinion Directly on the Effectiveness of Internal Control

> <u>Independent Accountant's Report</u>
>
> We have examined the effectiveness of W Company's internal control over financial reporting as of December 31, 20XX, based on [identify criteria, for example, COSO]. W Company's management is responsible for maintaining effective internal control over financial reporting. Our responsibility is to express an opinion on the effectiveness of internal control based on our examination.
>
> Our examination was conducted in accordance with attestation standards established by the American Institute of Certified Public Accountants and, accordingly, included obtaining an understanding of the internal control over financial reporting, testing, and evaluating the design and operating effectiveness of internal control, and performing such other procedures as we considered necessary in the circumstances. We believe that our examination provides a reasonable basis for our opinion.
>
> Because of inherent limitations in any internal control, misstatements due to errors or fraud may occur and not be detected. Also, projections of any evaluation of internal control over financial reporting to future periods are subject to the risk that the internal control may become inadequate because of changes in conditions, or that the degree of compliance with the policies or procedures may deteriorate.
>
> In our opinion, W Company maintained, in all material respects, effective internal control over financial reporting as of December 31, 20XX, based on [identify criteria, for example, COSO].

b. If the practitioner expresses an opinion on a written assertion, the above report should be modified appropriately (for example, identify the assertion in the first paragraph and change the last paragraph to "In our opinion, management's assertion that...").

10. **Report Modifications**

a. Material weaknesses

1) If the examination discloses material weaknesses, the practitioner should modify the report and express his/her opinion directly on the effectiveness of internal control, not on the assertion. The modification depends on the weakness and its effect on the achievement of the objectives of the control criteria.

2) A modified report should include an explanatory paragraph describing the material weakness(es) and the effect on the achievement of the objectives of the control criteria. The paragraph should also state, "We believe such condition represents a material weakness. A material weakness is a condition that precludes the entity's internal control from providing reasonable assurance that material misstatements in the financial statements will be prevented or detected on a timely basis."

3) Depending on the significance of the weakness(es) the practitioner would express either a qualified or an adverse opinion.

4)   If the assertion contains a statement that management believes the cost of correcting the weakness would exceed the benefits, the practitioner should disclaim an opinion on management's cost-benefit statement.

5)   If the practitioner's report on his/her examination of the effectiveness of internal control is included within the same document that includes his/her audit report, the following should be included in the paragraph of the examination report that describes the material weakness:

> These conditions were considered in determining the nature, timing, and extent of audit tests applied in our audit of the 20XX financial statements, and the report does not affect our report dated [**date of report**] on these financial statements.

b.   Scope limitations

1)   The practitioner should qualify or disclaim an opinion or withdraw from the engagement depending on the importance of the omitted procedures.

c.   Opinion based in part on the report of another practitioner

1)   When the practitioner decides to refer to the report of the other practitioner as a basis, in part, for his/her opinion, (s)he should disclose this fact when describing the scope of the examination and should refer to the report of the other practitioner when expressing the opinion.

d.   Subsequent events

1)   The practitioner should obtain the responsible party's representations relating to any changes in internal control or other factors that might affect internal control if they occurred subsequent to the date as of which internal control is being examined but prior to the date of the report.

2)   If the practitioner obtains knowledge about subsequent events that (s)he believes significantly affect the effectiveness of internal control as of the date of the assertion, the practitioner should report directly on the effectiveness of internal control and express a qualified or adverse opinion. If the effects of the subsequent event cannot be determined, an opinion should be disclaimed.

3)   If the practitioner becomes aware of conditions that existed at the date of the report that might have affected the opinion had (s)he known about them, (s)he must determine whether the information is reliable and whether there are persons relying on the practitioner's report on the effectiveness of the entity's internal control. Guidance about these matters is contained in AU 561, which is covered in Study Unit 14.

e.   Reporting on the effectiveness of a segment of the entity's internal control

1)   If the practitioner is engaged to examine the effectiveness of only a segment of an entity's internal control (e.g., internal control over financial reporting of an entity's operating division), the practitioner's report should refer to the segment of the entity's internal control examined.

f.   Reporting on the suitability of design of the entity's internal control

1)   When evaluating the suitability of design of the entity's internal control, the practitioner should obtain an understanding of the components of internal control that the responsible party should implement to meet the control objectives and identify the controls relevant to those control objectives.

2)   When reporting on the suitability of design of the entity's internal control that has already been placed in operation, the practitioner should modify the report by adding the following to the scope paragraph of the report:

> We were not engaged to examine and report on the operating effectiveness of W Company's internal control over financial reporting as of December 31, 20XX, and, accordingly, we express no opinion on operating effectiveness.

g. Reporting on internal control based on criteria specified by a regulatory agency

1) If criteria specified by a regulatory agency have been subjected to due process procedures, a practitioner should use the report form illustrated in 9.1. If such criteria have not been subjected to due process procedures, the practitioner should modify the report by adding a separate paragraph that restricts the use to the regulatory agency and to those within the entity.

2) A practitioner who identifies material weaknesses in internal control that are not covered by the criteria set by the agency should include these material weaknesses in the report. (S)he does not, however, assume responsibility for the comprehensiveness of the agency's criteria.

3) If a regulatory agency requires the reporting of all conditions that are not in conformity with the agency's criteria, the practitioner should describe all conditions of which (s)he is aware in the report.

11. **Other Information in a Client-Prepared Document Containing the Practitioner's Report**

a. The practitioner's responsibility with respect to other information in such a document does not extend beyond the information identified in the report, and (s)he has no obligation to perform any procedures to corroborate any other information contained in the document.

b. The practitioner should read the other information not covered by the practitioner's report or by the report of the other practitioner and consider whether it, or the manner of its presentation, is materially inconsistent with the information appearing in the practitioner's report, or whether such information contains a material misstatement of fact.

12. **Relationship of the Examination of Internal Control to the Opinion Obtained in an Audit**

a. The two engagements differ in purpose.

1) The purpose of an examination of the effectiveness of internal control is to express an opinion about whether the entity maintained, in all material respects, effective control based on the control criteria.

2) The purpose of the consideration of internal control in a financial statement audit is to enable the auditor to plan the audit and determine the nature, timing, and extent of tests to be performed.

b. The two engagements also differ in scope.

1) In an examination of management's assertion about internal control, the practitioner must both gain an understanding of internal control and test the effectiveness of the controls.

2) The auditor in a financial statement audit is required to obtain an understanding of the controls relevant to audit planning and then to assess control risk. If control risk is assessed below the maximum level, the auditor tests the controls. If control risk is assessed at the maximum, the auditor performs only substantive tests.

3) Accordingly, the consideration in an audit is usually more limited than that undertaken to express an opinion.

4) However, the procedures performed in the two engagements are similar.

13. **Relationship to the Foreign Corrupt Practices Act of 1977 (FCPA)**

    a.   Whether an entity is in compliance with the provisions of the FCPA is a legal determination made by management, the board, and legal counsel.

14. **Reporting on internal control under the Sarbanes-Oxley Act of 2002.** The PCAOB's **AS No. 2**, *An Audit of Internal Control Over Financial Reporting Performed in Conjunction with an Audit of Financial Statements*, provides guidance on the required process and reporting. Conceptually, AS No. 2 is similar to AT 501. However, it provides more direction and some significant differences. Key issues are outlined here.

    a.   Management must assess the design and effectiveness of internal control over financial reporting. The assessment must be performed using a suitable framework, such as the Committee of Sponsoring Organizations (COSO) of the Treadway Commission's *Internal Control – Integrated Framework*. Management then issues a report on effectiveness as of a date (e.g., 12/31/x1).

    b.   The CPA evaluates the assessment and expresses an opinion on management's assertion. In the same report, the CPA expresses a second opinion directly on the effectiveness of internal control over financial reporting.

    c.   Management cannot use the auditor's procedures as part of the basis for its assessment of internal control effectiveness.

    d.   Levels of deficiencies in the effectiveness of internal control are defined.

        1)   A **control deficiency** exists when the design or operation of a control does not allow management or employees to prevent or detect misstatements on a timely basis.

        2)   A **significant deficiency** is a control deficiency, or combination of control deficiencies, that adversely affects the company's ability to initiate, authorize, record, process, or report external financial data reliably.

        3)   A **material weakness** is a significant deficiency, or combination of significant deficiencies, that results in more than a remote likelihood that a material misstatement of the annual or interim statements will not be prevented.

    e.   A material weakness requires the auditor to express an adverse opinion on internal control and precludes management from assessing that internal control is effective.

    f.   The opinion on internal control must be issued in conjunction with the audit of the financial statements. A single report or two separate reports may be issued.

    g.   Ineffective oversight of financial reporting by the audit committee should be at least a significant deficiency and is a strong indicator of a material weakness.

    h.   The auditor must communicate all significant deficiencies and material weaknesses to management and the audit committee in writing.

15. Stop and review! You have completed the outline for this subunit. Study multiple-choice questions 22 through 38 beginning on page 301.

9.4 SERVICE ORGANIZATIONS (AU 324)

1.   This pronouncement applies to a financial statement audit of an entity that uses another organization's services as part of its own information system ("outsourcing").

    a.   A service organization's services are part of the client's information system if they have an effect on

        1)   Initiation of transactions.
        2)   Accounting records, supporting information, and specific accounts.
        3)   Processing from initiation to inclusion of transactions in the statements.
        4)   The process used to prepare statements, including estimates and disclosures.

13

    b.   The standard concerns

        1)   Factors to be considered by an auditor whose client uses a service organization to process certain transactions

        2)   Guidance to auditors who issue reports on the processing of transactions by a service organization for use by other auditors (Practitioners commonly call this a "SAS 70 engagement.")

2.   **Definitions**

    a.   **User organization** is an entity that is a user of a service organization and whose financial statements are being audited.

    b.   **User auditor** is the auditor of the user organization.

    c.   **Service organization** is an entity that provides services to user organizations.

    d.   **Service auditor** is an auditor who reports on the processing of transactions by a service organization.

    e.   **Report on controls placed in operation** is the service auditor's report on a service organization's description of its internal controls, on whether they were suitably designed to achieve specified control objectives, and on whether they had been placed in operation as of a specific date.

    f.   **Report on controls placed in operation and tests of operating effectiveness** is the service auditor's report on a service organization's description of its internal controls, on whether they were suitably designed, on whether they had been placed in operation, and on whether the controls tested were operating with sufficient effectiveness to provide reasonable, but not absolute, assurance that the related objectives were achieved.

3.   **Effect on a User Organization's Internal Control**

    a.   The significance of the service organization's controls depends primarily on the transactions it processes for the user and the degree of interaction between its activities and those of the user.

        1)   When the user initiates transactions, and the service organization executes and processes such transactions, the degree of interaction is high. In this case, the user may be able to implement effective controls for those transactions.

        2)   If the service organization initiates, executes, and processes the user's transactions, the degree of interaction is lower, and the user may not be able to implement effective controls.

4.   **Control Risk Assessment in Planning the Audit When the Client Uses a Service Organization**

    a.   The auditor must obtain an understanding of internal control to assess control risk and plan the audit. This understanding may extend not only to controls placed in operation by the client but also by service organizations.

    b.   Sufficient information about the nature of the services that are part of the user organization's information system and the service organization's controls may be available from many sources, such as the contract between the parties or the reports of service auditors, internal auditors, or regulators.

    c.   If not, the auditor may

        1)   Request information, through the client, from the service organization

        2)   Visit the service organization and perform necessary procedures

        3)   Request that a service auditor be engaged to perform procedures and provide a report

d. To assess control risk below the maximum, the auditor must apply tests of controls. If those controls exist at the service organization, the auditor must acquire evidence of effectiveness by

1) Applying the tests.
2) Obtaining a service auditor's report on the effectiveness of the controls.

a) A report on the controls placed in operation is not sufficient to allow assessment of control risk at below the maximum because it does not consider the effectiveness of the controls.

e. If the user auditor is unable to obtain sufficient evidence to achieve audit objectives, for example, if the service auditor's report does not address relevant assertions, (s)he should qualify or disclaim the opinion because of the scope limitation.

f. The ultimate responsibility for assessment of risk rests with the user auditor.

5. The results of the performance of substantive tests by service auditors may be used by the user auditor as part of the evidence to support the opinion on the financial statements.

6. **Considerations in Using a Service Auditor's Report**

a. The user auditor should make inquiries concerning the service auditor's professional reputation.

b. The user auditor may request agreed-upon procedures.

c. Reportable conditions may be identified as a result of the user auditor's consideration of the service auditor's report.

d. The user auditor should not refer to the service auditor's report as a basis, in part, for his/her own opinion because the service auditor was not responsible for examining any portion of the user organization's statements.

7. **Responsibilities of Service Auditors**

a. The engagement differs from an audit of financial statements, but the service auditor should follow applicable GAAS. Moreover, the service auditor must make inquiries of management about **subsequent events** (changes in controls affecting users' information systems after the period covered by the service auditor's report but prior to its date).

b. If the service auditor becomes aware of errors, fraud, or illegal acts that may affect the user organization, the auditor should determine from management of the service organization whether the information has been communicated to the users. If not, the service auditor should inform the service organization's audit committee and, if not satisfied with the response, consider resigning.

c. Reports that may be issued

1) **Reports on controls placed in operation**. These reports may be relevant to the user auditor's understanding of internal control, but they do not permit the user auditor to assess control risk at below the maximum. The report expressing an opinion on a description of the controls placed in operation includes

a) A reference to the aspects of the service organization covered.
b) A description of the service auditor's procedures.
c) Identification of the party stating the control objectives.
d) A statement of purposes of the engagement.
e) A disclaimer of opinion on operating effectiveness.

15

      f)   An opinion on whether the service organization's description fairly presents, in all material respects, the relevant aspects of the controls placed in operation at a specific date and whether they were suitably designed to provide reasonable assurance that the control objectives would be achieved if complied with satisfactorily.

      g)   A statement of inherent limitations.

      h)   Identification of the parties for whom the report is intended.

2)   **Reports on controls placed in operation and tests of operating effectiveness**. These reports may be relevant to a user auditor in obtaining understanding and determining the effectiveness of internal control. They may allow the user auditor to assess control risk below the maximum level. The report expressing an opinion on a description of the controls and tests of operating effectiveness includes all the components in 7.c.1), except for the disclaimer of opinion, on the previous page, as well as those that follow.

      a)   A reference to a description of tests of specified service organization controls designed to obtain evidence about their operating effectiveness. The description should include the controls that were tested, the control objectives, the tests applied, and the results of the tests. The description should include an indication of the nature, timing, and extent of the tests, as well as sufficient detail to enable a user auditor to determine the effect of such tests on his/her assessment of control risk.

      b)   A statement of the period covered by the service auditor's report on the operating effectiveness of the specified controls

      c)   The service auditor's opinion on whether the controls that were tested were operating with sufficient effectiveness to provide reasonable, but not absolute, assurance that the related control objectives were achieved during the period specified

      d)   A limitation on the opinion for controls not tested

      e)   A statement that the effectiveness and significance of the service organization's controls are dependent on their interaction with factors present at individual user organizations

      f)   A statement that the service auditor has performed no procedures to evaluate the effectiveness of controls at individual user organizations

3)   Regardless of the type of report issued, the service auditor should obtain **written representations** from the service organization's management about its responsibility for the controls; the appropriateness of specified control objectives; the fairness of the description of relevant controls; placement of controls in operation at a given date; changes in controls since the last examination; subsequent events; disclosures of fraud, illegal acts, or uncorrected errors; and design deficiencies.

8.   Stop and review! You have completed the outline for this subunit. Study multiple-choice questions 39 through 45 beginning on page 306.

QUESTIONS

9.1 Communication of Internal Control Related Matters Noted in an Audit (AU 325)

1. An auditor's communication of internal control related matters noted in an audit usually should be addressed to the

A. Audit committee.

B. Director of internal auditing.

C. Chief financial officer.

D. Chief accounting officer.

Answer (A) is correct. *(CPA, adapted)*
REQUIRED: The recipient of the auditor's communication of internal control related matters noted in an audit.
DISCUSSION: The communication is ordinarily made to the audit committee. However, it may be made to individuals at a level of authority and responsibility equivalent to an audit committee if the organization does not have one.

2. Reportable conditions are matters that come to an auditor's attention that should be communicated to an entity's audit committee because they represent

A. Disclosures of information that significantly contradict the auditor's going concern assumption.

B. Material fraud or illegal acts perpetrated by high-level management.

C. Significant deficiencies in the design or operation of internal control.

D. Manipulation or falsification of accounting records or documents from which financial statements are prepared.

Answer (C) is correct. *(CPA, adapted)*
REQUIRED: The definition of a reportable condition.
DISCUSSION: Reportable conditions are matters coming to the auditor's attention that relate to significant deficiencies in the design or operation of internal control that, in the auditor's judgment, could adversely affect the organization's ability to initiate, record, process, and report financial data consistent with the assertions of management in the financial statements (AU 325).
Answer (A) is incorrect because reportable conditions should not include disclosures that contradict auditor assumptions or findings. Answer (B) is incorrect because, although material fraud or illegal acts are considered reportable conditions, reportable conditions include more than just errors or fraud. Answer (D) is incorrect because, although material fraud or illegal acts are considered reportable conditions, reportable conditions include more than just errors or fraud.

3. Which of the following matters would an auditor most likely consider to be a reportable condition to be communicated to the audit committee?

A. Management's failure to renegotiate unfavorable long-term purchase commitments.

B. Recurring operating losses that may indicate going concern problems.

C. Evidence of a lack of objectivity by those responsible for accounting decisions.

D. Management's current plans to reduce its ownership equity in the entity.

Answer (C) is correct. *(CPA, adapted)*
REQUIRED: The reportable condition.
DISCUSSION: Reportable conditions are matters coming to the auditor's attention that relate to significant deficiencies in the design or operation of internal control that, in the auditor's judgment, could adversely affect the organization's ability to record, process, summarize, and report financial data consistent with the assertions of management in the financial statements. Categories of reportable conditions include deficiencies in internal control design, failures in the operation of internal control, and others. An example of the latter is "evidence of undue bias or lack of objectivity by those responsible for accounting decisions" (AU 325).
Answer (A) is incorrect because management's failure to renegotiate unfavorable long-term purchase commitments is not a reportable condition. Answer (B) is incorrect because recurring operating losses that may indicate going concern problems is not a reportable condition. Answer (D) is incorrect because management's current plans to reduce its ownership equity in the entity is not a reportable condition.

4. During consideration of internal control in a financial statement audit, an auditor is not obligated to

    A. Search for significant deficiencies in the operation of internal control.

    B. Understand the internal control environment.

    C. Determine whether the control activities relevant to audit planning have been placed in operation.

    D. Perform procedures to understand the design of the internal control policies.

Answer (A) is correct. *(CPA, adapted)*
    REQUIRED: The task not required during the auditor's consideration of the internal control.
    DISCUSSION: The auditor must obtain an understanding of internal control and assess control risk to plan the audit. The limited purpose of this consideration does not include the search for significant deficiencies or reportable conditions.
    Answer (B) is incorrect because the auditor must gain an understanding of the five components of internal control. Answer (C) is incorrect because obtaining the understanding of controls relevant to audit planning includes performing procedures to provide sufficient knowledge of the design of the relevant controls pertaining to the internal control components. It also includes determining whether they have been placed in operation. Answer (D) is incorrect because the understanding also includes knowledge about whether relevant controls have been placed in operation.

5. A previously communicated reportable condition that has not been corrected ordinarily should be communicated again if

    A. The deficiency has a material effect on the auditor's assessment of control risk.

    B. The entity accepts that degree of risk because of cost-benefit considerations.

    C. The weakness could adversely affect the entity's ability to report financial data.

    D. There has been major turnover in upper-level management and the board of directors.

Answer (D) is correct. *(CPA, adapted)*
    REQUIRED: The reason a previously communicated reportable condition that has not been corrected should be communicated again.
    DISCUSSION: AU 325 requires communication about reportable conditions and makes no exception solely for previous reporting of a condition. But, "provided the audit committee has acknowledged its understanding and consideration of such deficiencies and the associated risks, the auditor may decide the matter does not need to be reported." However, the auditor should periodically consider whether the passage of time or changes in management or the audit committee make reporting such matters appropriate.
    Answer (A) is incorrect because, if the audit committee has acknowledged its understanding and consideration of the risks, the auditor may decide not to report the matter despite its adverse effects. Answer (B) is incorrect because, if the audit committee has acknowledged its understanding and consideration of the risks, the auditor may decide not to report the matter despite its adverse effects. Answer (C) is incorrect because, if the audit committee has acknowledged its understanding and consideration of the risks, the auditor may decide not to report the matter despite its adverse effects.

6. Which of the following statements is true concerning an auditor's required communication of reportable conditions?

    A. A reportable condition previously communicated during the prior year's audit that remains uncorrected causes a scope limitation.

    B. An auditor should perform tests of controls on reportable conditions before communicating them to the client.

    C. An auditor's report on reportable conditions should include a restriction on the use of the report.

    D. An auditor should communicate reportable conditions after tests of controls, but before commencing substantive tests.

Answer (C) is correct. *(CPA, adapted)*
    REQUIRED: The true statement concerning the auditor's required communication of reportable conditions.
    DISCUSSION: A report on reportable conditions should (1) state that the purpose of the audit was to report on the financial statements, not to provide assurance on internal control; (2) give the definition of reportable conditions; and (3) state that the report is intended solely for the information and use of the audit committee, management, and others within the organization (or a specified regulatory agency) and is not intended to be and should not be used by anyone other than these specified parties (AU 325).
    Answer (A) is incorrect because, although a reportable condition previously communicated may require continued communication in the following year, it does not necessarily cause a scope limitation in the audit. Answer (B) is incorrect because tests of controls are performed on internal controls, not on reportable conditions. Answer (D) is incorrect because reportable conditions are typically reported at the conclusion of the audit. However, they may be communicated during the conduct of the audit if such information is considered useful to the client.

7. An auditor's letter issued on reportable conditions relating to an entity's internal control observed during a financial statement audit should

   A. Include a brief description of the tests of controls performed in searching for reportable conditions and material weaknesses.

   B. Indicate that the reportable conditions should be disclosed in the annual report to the entity's shareholders.

   C. Include a paragraph describing management's assertion concerning the effectiveness of internal control.

   D. Indicate that the audit's purpose was to report on the financial statements and not to provide assurance on internal control.

Answer (D) is correct.   *(CPA, adapted)*
   REQUIRED: The content of an auditor's letter concerning reportable conditions.
   DISCUSSION: AU 325 states, "Any report issued on reportable conditions should indicate that the purpose of the audit was to report on the financial statements and not to provide assurance on internal control."
   Answer (A) is incorrect because the report on reportable conditions should not describe the tests performed by the auditor. Answer (B) is incorrect because the reportable conditions need not be reported to shareholders in the annual report. Answer (C) is incorrect because management need not make assertions relative to the reportable conditions or the effectiveness of internal control in the audited financial statements.

8. Which of the following statements concerning material weaknesses and reportable conditions is true?

   A. An auditor should identify and communicate material weaknesses separately from reportable conditions.

   B. All material weaknesses are reportable conditions.

   C. An auditor should immediately report material weaknesses and reportable conditions discovered during an audit.

   D. All reportable conditions are material weaknesses.

Answer (B) is correct.   *(CPA, adapted)*
   REQUIRED: The true statement concerning reportable conditions.
   DISCUSSION: According to AU 325, all material weaknesses are reportable conditions, but not all reportable conditions are material weaknesses.
   Answer (A) is incorrect because an auditor may, but is not required to, identify material weaknesses separately from other reportable conditions. Answer (C) is incorrect because whether an interim communication is made depends on the relative significance of the matters noted and the urgency of corrective action. Thus, immediate reporting may not be necessary. Answer (D) is incorrect because not all reportable conditions are material weaknesses.

9. Which of the following statements is true concerning reportable conditions noted in an audit?

   A. Reportable conditions are material weaknesses in the design or operation of specific internal control components.

   B. The auditor is obligated to search for reportable conditions that could adversely affect the entity's ability to record and report financial data.

   C. Reportable conditions should be recommunicated each year, even if management has acknowledged its understanding of such deficiencies.

   D. The auditor may separately communicate those reportable conditions considered to be material weaknesses.

Answer (D) is correct.   *(CPA, adapted)*
   REQUIRED: The true statement concerning reportable conditions.
   DISCUSSION: An auditor may, but is not required to, separately identify material weaknesses, which are reportable conditions in which the design or operation of the specific internal control components do not reduce to a relatively low level the risk that errors or fraud in amounts that could be material in relation to the financial statements being audited may occur and not be detected.
   Answer (A) is incorrect because all material weaknesses are reportable conditions, but not all reportable conditions are material weaknesses. Answer (B) is incorrect because the auditor is not obligated to search for reportable conditions. Answer (C) is incorrect because, if management has acknowledged the deficiencies and their risks, the auditor may choose not to continue to report such matters.

10. Which of the following statements is true concerning the auditor's required communication of a material weakness in internal control?

A. A weakness that management refuses to correct should be included in a separate paragraph of the auditor's report.

B. A weakness previously communicated during the prior year's audit that has not been corrected should be communicated again in writing.

C. Suggested corrective action for management's consideration concerning a material weakness need not be communicated to the client.

D. The auditor should test the controls that constitute a material weakness before communicating it to the client.

Answer (C) is correct. *(CPA, adapted)*
REQUIRED: The true statement concerning the required communication of a material internal control weakness.
DISCUSSION: Although the auditor is required to communicate reportable conditions to the audit committee, there is no requirement to communicate suggested corrective action.
Answer (A) is incorrect because a weakness that management refuses to correct is not, by itself, sufficient to require a separate explanatory paragraph. Answer (B) is incorrect because, if the audit committee has acknowledged its understanding and consideration of the weakness, the auditor may decide not to communicate it again. Answer (D) is incorrect because the auditor should communicate reportable conditions of which (s)he becomes aware. Testing controls is not a prerequisite of the communication.

11. Which of the following representations should not be included in a report on internal control related matters noted in an audit?

A. Reportable conditions related to internal control design exist, but none is deemed to be a material weakness.

B. There are no significant deficiencies in the design or operation of internal control.

C. Corrective follow-up action is recommended due to the relative significance of material weaknesses discovered during the audit.

D. The auditor's consideration of internal control would not necessarily disclose all reportable conditions that exist.

Answer (B) is correct. *(CPA, adapted)*
REQUIRED: The item not included in a report on internal control related matters.
DISCUSSION: The report should describe the reportable conditions noted but should not offer any assurance about internal control, whether limited or otherwise. If no reportable conditions are noted during the audit, no report should be issued.
Answer (A) is incorrect because the report may state that the reportable conditions noted are not material weaknesses. Answer (C) is incorrect because an interim communication may be the appropriate means for recommending corrective follow-up action on significant matters noted. Answer (D) is incorrect because the language in the standard report states that the consideration of internal control might not disclose all reportable conditions.

12. Which of the following statements is true concerning an auditor's communication of internal control related matters (reportable conditions) noted in an audit?

A. The auditor may issue a written report to the audit committee representing that no reportable conditions were noted during the audit.

B. Reportable conditions should be recommunicated each year even if the audit committee has acknowledged its understanding of such deficiencies.

C. Reportable conditions may not be communicated in a document that contains suggestions regarding activities that concern other topics such as business strategies or administrative efficiencies.

D. The auditor may choose to communicate significant internal control related matters either during the course of the audit or after the audit is concluded.

Answer (D) is correct. *(CPA, adapted)*
REQUIRED: The true statement concerning an auditor's communication of reportable conditions noted in an audit.
DISCUSSION: Timely communication of reportable conditions may be desirable. Hence, the auditor has the option of making an interim communication before conclusion of the engagement. The timing of the communication is determined by the significance of the matters noted and the urgency of corrective action.
Answer (A) is incorrect because AU 325 prohibits issuance of a report declaring that no reportable conditions were noted (except in an audit in accordance with Government Auditing Standards). The limited assurance that would be provided could be misinterpreted. Answer (B) is incorrect because reportable conditions may be known to management, and their existence may reflect a decision to accept the risk because of cost or other considerations. If the audit committee has acknowledged the deficiencies and their risks, the auditor may choose not to continue to report such matters. Answer (C) is incorrect because items beneficial to the client may be communicated even though they are not related to internal control.

13. The development of constructive suggestions to a client for improvements in its internal control is

- A. A task addressed by the auditor only during a special engagement.

- B. A requirement as important as assessing control risk.

- C. A requirement of the auditor's consideration of internal control.

- D. A desirable by-product of an audit engagement.

Answer (D) is correct. *(CPA, adapted)*
REQUIRED: The true statement about constructive suggestions to a client for improvements in its internal control.
DISCUSSION: During an audit, the auditor may become aware of matters related to internal control that may be of interest to the audit committee. AU 325 requires that those matters meeting the definition of reportable conditions be communicated. However, the auditor may identify other matters not constituting reportable conditions and report them for the benefit of management or others.
Answer (A) is incorrect because, at a minimum, the auditor must communicate reportable conditions noted in an audit. Answer (B) is incorrect because constructive suggestions are not required, but the auditor must assess control risk. Answer (C) is incorrect because constructive suggestions are not required.

9.2 Communication with Audit Committees (AU 380)

14. An auditor would least likely initiate a discussion with a client's audit committee concerning

- A. The methods used to account for significant unusual transactions.

- B. The maximum dollar amount of misstatements that could exist without causing the financial statements to be materially misstated.

- C. Indications of fraud and illegal acts committed by a corporate officer that were discovered by the auditor.

- D. Disagreements with management as to accounting principles that were resolved during the current year's audit.

Answer (B) is correct. *(CPA, adapted)*
REQUIRED: The item least likely to be discussed with the audit committee.
DISCUSSION: The auditor is responsible for determining the levels of materiality appropriate in the audit of a client's financial statements. This decision is made in relation to the acceptable level of audit risk but need not be communicated to the audit committee.
Answer (A) is incorrect because methods used to account for significant unusual transactions is an item communicated to the client's audit committee. Answer (C) is incorrect because indications of fraud and illegal acts is an item communicated to the client's audit committee. Answer (D) is incorrect because disagreements with management is an item communicated to the client's audit committee.

15. Which of the following statements is true about an auditor's required communication with an entity's audit committee?

- A. Any matters communicated to the entity's audit committee are also required to be communicated to the entity's management.

- B. The auditor is required to inform the entity's audit committee about misstatements discovered by the auditor and not subsequently corrected by management.

- C. Disagreements with management about the application of accounting principles are required to be communicated in writing to the entity's audit committee.

- D. Weaknesses in internal control previously reported to the entity's audit committee are required to be communicated to the audit committee after each subsequent audit until the weaknesses are corrected.

Answer (B) is correct. *(CPA, adapted)*
REQUIRED: The true statement about an auditor's required communication with an entity's audit committee.
DISCUSSION: The matters to be discussed with the audit committee include the auditors' responsibility under GAAS; significant accounting policies; sensitive accounting estimates; audit adjustments, including not only adjustments having a significant effect on financial reports but also uncorrected misstatements pertaining to the latest period presented that were determined by management to be immaterial; the quality of the accounting principles used by management (in SEC engagements); other information in documents containing audited statements; auditor disagreements with management, whether or not satisfactorily resolved; management's consultations with other accountants; issues discussed with management prior to the auditors' retention; and any serious difficulties the auditors may have had with management during the audit (AU 380).
Answer (A) is incorrect because the requirement is that certain information be communicated to the entity's audit committee, not management. Answer (C) is incorrect because communication with the entity's audit committee may be oral or written. Answer (D) is incorrect because communication of recurring matters ordinarily need not be repeated.

16. Which of the following statements is true concerning an auditor's required communication with an entity's audit committee?

A. This communication is required to occur before the auditor's report on the financial statements is issued.

B. This communication should include management changes in the application of significant accounting policies.

C. Any significant matter communicated to the audit committee also should be communicated to management.

D. Audit adjustments proposed by the auditor, whether or not recorded by management, need not be communicated to the audit committee.

Answer (B) is correct. *(CPA, adapted)*
REQUIRED: The true statement concerning an auditor's required communication with the audit committee.
DISCUSSION: The auditor should communicate to the audit committee, among other things, management's selection of and changes in significant accounting policies or their application. The auditor should also determine that the committee is informed about the methods used to account for significant unusual transactions and the effects of significant accounting policies in controversial or emerging areas. Moreover, in an SEC engagement, the auditor should discuss the quality of the auditee's accounting principles as applied in its financial reports (AU 380).
Answer (A) is incorrect because the communication typically comes near the end of the audit, after the auditor has identified the items that should be communicated. Answer (C) is incorrect because the communication is required to be made only to the audit committee or others with similar oversight authority. Answer (D) is incorrect because audit adjustments, whether or not recorded, should be communicated to the audit committee.

17. Which of the following statements is true concerning an auditor's required communication with an entity's audit committee?

A. This communication should include disagreements with management about audit adjustments, whether or not satisfactorily resolved.

B. If matters are communicated orally, it is necessary to repeat the communication of recurring matters each year.

C. If matters are communicated in writing, the report is required to be distributed to both the audit committee and management.

D. This communication is required to occur before the auditor's report on the financial statements is issued.

Answer (A) is correct. *(CPA, adapted)*
REQUIRED: The true statement about an auditor's required communication with an entity's audit committee.
DISCUSSION: The matters to be discussed with the audit committee include the auditors' responsibility under GAAS; significant accounting policies; sensitive accounting estimates; audit adjustments; the quality of the accounting principles used by management (in SEC engagements); other information in documents containing audited statements; auditor disagreements with management, whether or not satisfactorily resolved; management's consultations with other accountants; issues discussed with management prior to the auditors' retention; and any serious difficulties the auditors may have had with management during the audit.
Answer (B) is incorrect because the oral or written communication of recurring matters ordinarily need not be repeated. Answer (C) is incorrect because communications with management are neither required nor precluded. Answer (D) is incorrect because, as long as the communication is timely, it need not be made prior to issuance.

18. An auditor is obligated to communicate a proposed audit adjustment to an entity's audit committee only if the adjustment

A. Has not been recorded before the end of the auditor's field work.

B. Has a significant effect on the entity's financial reporting process.

C. Is a recurring matter that was proposed to management the prior year.

D. Related to an uncorrected misstatement, was determined to be immaterial by management, and pertained to the earliest period presented.

Answer (B) is correct. *(CPA, adapted)*
REQUIRED: The circumstances in which a proposed audit adjustment must be communicated.
DISCUSSION: The auditor should inform the audit committee about adjustments arising from the audit that could in his/her judgment have a significant effect on the entity's financial reporting process, either individually or in the aggregate. Furthermore, the auditor should communicate to the audit committee any uncorrected misstatements aggregated during the current engagement and pertaining to the latest period presented that management determined to be immaterial, either individually or in the aggregate (AU 380).
Answer (A) is incorrect because the entries affecting the year-end financial statement balances may be made subsequent to year-end. Answer (C) is incorrect because the oral or written communication of recurring matters ordinarily need not be repeated. Answer (D) is incorrect because the auditor should communicate such an adjustment if it pertained to the latest period presented.

19. Which of the following matters is an auditor required to communicate to an entity's audit committee?

    A.   The basis for assessing control risk below the maximum.

    B.   The process used by management in formulating sensitive accounting estimates.

    C.   The auditor's preliminary judgments about materiality levels.

    D.   The justification for performing substantive procedures at interim dates.

Answer (B) is correct.   *(CPA, adapted)*
    REQUIRED: The required communication.
    DISCUSSION: Certain management estimates are particularly sensitive because they are significant to the financial statements, and future events affecting them may differ from current judgments. The audit committee should be informed about the process used in formulating sensitive estimates and the basis for the auditor's conclusions concerning their reasonableness (AU 380).
    Answer (A) is incorrect because the basis for assessing control risk need not be communicated to the audit committee. Answer (C) is incorrect because the preliminary judgments about materiality need not be communicated to the audit committee. Answer (D) is incorrect because the reasons for interim procedures need not be communicated to the audit committee.

20. During the planning phase of an audit, an auditor is identifying matters for communication to the entity's audit committee. The auditor most likely would ask management whether

    A.   There was significant turnover in the accounting department.

    B.   It consulted with another CPA firm about installing a new computer system.

    C.   There were changes in the application of significant accounting policies.

    D.   It agreed with the auditor's selection of fraud detection procedures.

Answer (C) is correct.   *(CPA, adapted)*
    REQUIRED: The issue relative to communication with the audit committee.
    DISCUSSION: The auditor should determine that the audit committee is informed about the initial selection of and changes in significant accounting policies or their application. Moreover, in an SEC engagement, the auditor should discuss the quality of the auditee's accounting principles as applied in its financial reports (AU 380).
    Answer (A) is incorrect because the auditor would be concerned about significant turnover in the accounting department in the assessment of risk, but the matter is not likely of sufficient concern to justify disclosure to the audit committee. Answer (B) is incorrect because the auditor would communicate the consultation with other CPAs about accounting and auditing matters, not about choice of a new computer system. Answer (D) is incorrect because the auditor need not seek approval from management of audit procedures.

21. In an SEC engagement, should an auditor communicate the following matters to an audit committee of a public entity?

	Auditors' Judgments About the Quality of the Client's Accounting Principles	Issues Discussed with Management Prior to the Auditor's Retention
A.	Yes	Yes
B.	Yes	No
C.	No	Yes
D.	No	No

Answer (A) is correct.   *(CPA, adapted)*
    REQUIRED: The matter(s), if any, to be communicated to the audit committee.
    DISCUSSION: The matters to be discussed with the audit committee include the quality of the accounting principles used by management in SEC engagements. Management is normally a participant in the discussion. Matters covered may include the consistency of principles and their application; the clarity and completeness of the statements; and items significantly affecting representational faithfulness, verifiability, and neutrality. However, objective criteria have not been developed to permit consistent evaluation of the application of principles to a given entity's statements. Thus, the discussion should address the unique circumstances of the auditee. Furthermore, in any audit engagement, the auditor and the audit committee should discuss any major issues discussed with management in connection with the initial or recurring retention of the auditors, for example, issues concerning the application of accounting principles and auditing standards.

9.3 Reporting on an Entity's Internal Control over Financial Reporting (AT 501)

22. A practitioner, without auditing an entity's financial statements, may accept an engagement to examine the effectiveness of an entity's internal control over financial reporting in effect

	As of a Specified Date	During a Specified Period of Time
A.	Yes	Yes
B.	Yes	No
C.	No	Yes
D.	No	No

Answer (A) is correct. *(CPA, adapted)*
REQUIRED: The applicability of a report on an examination of the effectiveness of internal control.
DISCUSSION: The engagement is usually to examine the effectiveness of internal control as of the end of the entity's fiscal year, but the client may choose a different date. Furthermore, a practitioner may be engaged to examine the effectiveness of internal control during a period of time.

23. Which of the following best describes a CPA's engagement to report on an entity's internal control over financial reporting?

A. An attestation engagement to examine the effectiveness of its internal control.

B. An audit of the financial statement that results in communicating reportable conditions.

C. A prospective engagement to project, for a period of time not to exceed one year, and report on the expected benefits of the entity's internal control.

D. A consulting engagement to provide constructive advice to the entity on its internal control.

Answer (A) is correct. *(CPA, adapted)*
REQUIRED: The best description of an engagement to report on an entity's internal control over financial reporting.
DISCUSSION: In an attestation engagement to examine the effectiveness of an entity's internal control over financial reporting, the practitioner's objective is to express an opinion on (1) whether internal control is effective, in all material respects, based on the control criteria or (2) whether the responsible party's assertion regarding internal control is fairly stated, in all material respects, based on the control criteria.
Answer (B) is incorrect because an engagement to report on internal control is a service separate and distinct from a traditional financial statement audit. Answer (C) is incorrect because the opinion expressed by the CPA should not extend into the future. Answer (D) is incorrect because consulting engagements do not result in the expression of an opinion.

24. A practitioner's report on internal control is least likely to be issued as a result of

A. An engagement to examine the effectiveness of an entity's internal control based on criteria established by a regulatory body.

B. A review of the annual financial statements of a large corporation.

C. A request to apply agreed-upon procedures relating to the effectiveness of an entity's internal control.

D. A request by management to report on the fairness of its assertion about internal control effectiveness.

Answer (B) is correct. *(CPA, adapted)*
REQUIRED: The engagement that would least likely result in a report related to internal control.
DISCUSSION: Practitioners are engaged to audit and express an opinion on, rather than review, the annual statements of large corporations. A review is appropriate for nonpublic entities that seek a report expressing only limited assurance. Moreover, a review does not contemplate consideration of internal control (AR 100). According to AT 501, a practitioner may examine or apply agreed-upon procedures relating to, but not review, the effectiveness of an entity's internal control.
Answer (A) is incorrect because a regulatory body may establish its own criteria, which may or may not have been subjected to due process procedures. Answer (C) is incorrect because a practitioner may apply agreed-upon procedures relating to the effectiveness of internal control. However, the report should be in the form of procedures and findings and not provide positive or negative assurances. Answer (D) is incorrect because a practitioner may examine and express a positive opinion on an assertion about the effectiveness of internal control.

25. Which of the following conditions is necessary for a practitioner to accept an attest engagement to examine an entity's internal control over financial reporting?

A. The practitioner anticipates relying on the entity's internal control in a financial statement audit.

B. The responsible party evaluates the effectiveness of internal control.

C. The practitioner is a continuing auditor who previously has audited the entity's financial statements.

D. Management agrees not to include the practitioner's report in a general-use document.

Answer (B) is correct.   *(CPA, adapted)*
REQUIRED: The condition necessary for a practitioner to accept an attest engagement to examine and report on an entity's internal control.
DISCUSSION: A practitioner may accept an examination engagement when the following conditions are met: (1) management accepts responsibility for the effectiveness of internal control, (2) the responsible party evaluates the effectiveness of internal control using suitable criteria, and (3) sufficient evidence exists or could be developed. Subsequently, as part of engagement performance, the practitioner must obtain from the responsible party a written assertion about internal control effectiveness.
Answer (A) is incorrect because this engagement is separate from the audit of the financial statements and may be conducted and reported on separately and independently. Answer (C) is incorrect because this engagement is separate from the audit of the financial statements and may be conducted and reported on separately and independently. Answer (D) is incorrect because the report is for general distribution if the conditions are met.

26. The Committee of Sponsoring Organizations (COSO) of the Treadway Commission issued a document in 1992 that has been embraced by numerous organizations, including the AICPA and the GAO. That document is titled

A. The Yellow Book.

B. Internal control--Integrated Framework.

C. Statements on Auditing Standards.

D. *Code of Professional Conduct.*

Answer (B) is correct.   *(Publisher)*
REQUIRED: The document issued by the COSO.
DISCUSSION: Many professional and regulatory bodies have recognized the COSO's internal control framework by incorporating its terms, definitions, and concepts into their policies, procedures, pronouncements, and other literature.
Answer (A) is incorrect because the Yellow Book, or **Government Auditing Standards**, is issued by the GAO. Answer (C) is incorrect because Statements on Auditing Standards are issued by the Auditing Standards Board of the AICPA. Answer (D) is incorrect because the *Code of Professional Conduct* has been adopted by the members of the AICPA.

27. When engaged to express an opinion about the effectiveness of an entity's internal control, the practitioner should

A. Obtain the responsible party's written representation acknowledging responsibility for establishing and maintaining internal control.

B. Not directly express an opinion on the effectiveness of internal control.

C. Keep informed of events subsequent to the date of the report that might have affected the opinion.

D. Accept responsibility for the establishment of the control procedures tested.

Answer (A) is correct.   *(CPA, adapted)*
REQUIRED: The true statement about an engagement to examine the effectiveness of internal control.
DISCUSSION: The practitioner should obtain the responsible party's written representation acknowledging its responsibility for establishing and maintaining internal control. The representation letter also should include the assertion about the evaluation of control effectiveness and the specification of the control criteria used. Failure to provide these representations constitutes a scope limitation.
Answer (B) is incorrect because an opinion may be expressed either on the responsible party's assertion or directly on the effectiveness of internal control. Answer (C) is incorrect because the practitioner is not responsible for keeping informed of events subsequent to the date of the report. Answer (D) is incorrect because the responsible party, not the practitioner, is responsible for the establishment of internal control.

28. Brown, CPA, has accepted an engagement to examine the effectiveness of Crow Company's internal control and to issue a report on such examination. In what form may Crow present its written assertion about effectiveness?

I. In a separate report that will accompany Brown's report

II. In a representation letter to Brown

A. I only.

B. II only.

C. Either I or II.

D. Neither I nor II.

Answer (C) is correct.   *(CPA, adapted)*
REQUIRED: The form of a written assertion by management on the effectiveness of internal control.
DISCUSSION: The responsible party may present its written assertion about the effectiveness of an entity's internal control over financial reporting in a separate report accompanying the practitioner's report or in a representation letter.

29. A practitioner has been engaged to report on an examination of the effectiveness of an entity's internal control over financial reporting without performing an audit of the financial statements. The responsible party presents its written assertion in a separate report that will accompany the practitioner's report. The assertion is based on control criteria that have been subjected to due process procedures. What restrictions, if any, should the practitioner place on the use of this report?

   A. This report should be restricted for use by management.

   B. This report should be restricted for use by the audit committee.

   C. This report should be restricted for use by a specified regulatory agency.

   D. The practitioner does not need to place any restrictions on the use of this report.

Answer (D) is correct. *(CPA, adapted)*
   REQUIRED: The restrictions, if any, on the use of a report on an examination of the effectiveness of internal control.
   DISCUSSION: Practitioners are allowed to provide assurances about (1) whether internal control is effective based on the control criteria or (2) whether the responsible party's assertion about internal control is fairly stated in all material respects based on the control criteria. Such a report will have no restrictions on its use if the responsible party evaluated the effectiveness of control using suitable criteria. Ordinarily, criteria that have been subjected to due process procedures are suitable. However, a limitation may be necessary when the control criteria have been established by a regulatory agency that did not follow due process.

30. Snow, CPA, was engaged by Master Co. to examine the effectiveness of Master's internal control over financial reporting. Snow's report should state that

   A. Because of inherent limitations of internal control, errors or fraud may occur and not be detected.

   B. Management's evaluation of the effectiveness of internal control is based on criteria established by the American Institute of Certified Public Accountants.

   C. The results of Snow's tests will form the basis for Snow's opinion on the fairness of Master's financial statements in conformity with GAAP.

   D. The purpose of the engagement is to enable Snow to plan an audit and determine the nature, timing, and extent of tests to be performed.

Answer (A) is correct. *(CPA, adapted)*
   REQUIRED: The statement in a CPA's report on an examination of the effectiveness of internal control over financial reporting.
   DISCUSSION: The independent accountant's report should contain an introductory paragraph describing the subject matter and the responsible party, a scope paragraph describing the standards applied and the nature of the procedures performed, a paragraph describing the inherent limitations of internal control, and an opinion paragraph indicating whether the entity maintained effective internal control, in all material respects over financial reporting based on the control criteria.
   Answer (B) is incorrect because the CPA's examination is based on attestation standards established by the AICPA. Answer (C) is incorrect because the results of the CPA's tests will form a basis for the opinion either on the fairness of management's assertion about internal control or directly on the effectiveness of internal control. Answer (D) is incorrect because the purpose of the engagement is to enable the CPA to collect sufficient, competent evidential matter to support his/her opinion on whether the entity maintained effective internal control.

31. When a practitioner expresses an unqualified opinion on management's assertion that internal control over financial reporting is sufficient to meet the entity's stated objectives, it is implied that the

   A. Entity has not violated provisions of the Foreign Corrupt Practices Act.

   B. Likelihood of management fraud is minimal.

   C. Practitioner has engaged in an improper form of reporting because the assertion is too subjective.

   D. Practitioner believes that management's assertion about the effectiveness of internal control is fairly stated.

Answer (D) is correct. *(CPA, adapted)*
   REQUIRED: The implication of an unqualified opinion on management's assertion on internal control.
   DISCUSSION: An entity's internal control should provide reasonable assurance that specific entity objectives are achieved. The unqualified opinion on management's assertion (as opposed to an opinion expressed directly on the effectiveness of internal control) states that management's assertion as to effectiveness is fairly stated in all material respects, based on the identified control criteria. According to AT 501, the language given in the question stem is an alternative to the effectiveness wording in management's assertion.
   Answer (A) is incorrect because whether a company is in compliance with the provisions of the FCPA is a legal determination that a practitioner is not normally competent to make. Answer (B) is incorrect because the inherent limitations of internal control, such as possible collusion, prevent absolute assurance about management fraud. Answer (C) is incorrect because the language given in the question stem is an alternative form of management's assertion. An assertion that internal control is "very effective" is one that is too subjective.

32. Cain Company's management engaged Bell, CPA, to examine the effectiveness of Cain's internal control over financial reporting. Bell's report, which was accompanied by the responsible party's separate report presenting its written assertion about the effectiveness of internal control, described several material weaknesses and potential errors and fraudulent activities that could occur. Subsequently, management included Bell's report in its annual report to the board of directors with a statement that the cost of correcting the weaknesses would exceed the benefits. Bell should

A. Disclaim an opinion as to management's cost-benefit statement.

B. Advise the board that Bell either agrees or disagrees with management's statement.

C. Express an adverse opinion as to management's cost-benefit statement.

D. Advise both management and the board that Bell was withdrawing the opinion.

Answer (A) is correct. *(CPA, adapted)*
REQUIRED: The practitioner's action when the report is included in the client's annual report with a statement that the cost of corrective action exceeds the benefits.
DISCUSSION: If the assertion accompanying the practitioner's report includes a statement that the cost of corrective action exceeds the benefits of implementing new controls, the practitioner should include as the last paragraph of the report language that disclaims an opinion on the cost-benefit statement.
Answer (B) is incorrect because the practitioner would discuss the matter with management if (s)he believes that the statement is a material misstatement of fact. Answer (C) is incorrect because an adverse opinion should be expressed when the practitioner believes that the internal controls are not effective. Answer (D) is incorrect because, even assuming that the practitioner believes that the statement is a material misstatement, withdrawal of the opinion is not a necessary immediate action.

33. When an independent auditor reports on an examination of the effectiveness of an entity's internal control over financial reporting based on criteria established by a regulatory agency, the report should

A. State that the practitioner assumes responsibility for the comprehensiveness of the criteria if they have not been subjected to due process procedures.

B. Modify the inherent limitations paragraph.

C. Contain a statement of restriction on use if the criteria have not been subjected to due process procedures and are appropriate only for a limited number of users.

D. Identify the control criteria in the scope paragraph.

Answer (C) is correct. *(Publisher)*
REQUIRED: The true statement about a report on internal control based on criteria established by a governmental agency.
DISCUSSION: If the criteria were established by a regulatory agency after following due process procedures, including distribution of proposed criteria for public comment, and the criteria are available to users, a standard form of reporting may be used. If the control criteria have not been subjected to due process procedures, and the practitioner determines that the criteria are appropriate only for a limited group of users (e.g., those who participated in their establishment), the appropriate form of the standard report must be modified to include a restriction on use stated in a paragraph following the opinion paragraph.
Answer (A) is incorrect because the practitioner assumes no responsibility for the control criteria in these circumstances. Answer (B) is incorrect because AT 501 lists seven conditions for modification of the standard reports, but none requires omission or amendment of the inherent limitations paragraph. Answer (D) is incorrect because the control criteria are identified in the introductory and opinion paragraphs but not the scope paragraph.

34. A CPA's consideration of internal control in a financial statement audit of a nonpublic client

A. Is usually more limited than that made in connection with an engagement to examine the effectiveness of internal control.

B. Is usually more extensive than that made in connection with an engagement to examine the effectiveness of internal control.

C. Will usually be identical to that made in connection with an engagement to examine the effectiveness of internal control.

D. Will usually result in a report on whether management's written assertion about the effectiveness of internal control is fairly stated.

Answer (A) is correct. *(CPA, adapted)*
REQUIRED: The scope of the consideration of internal control in an audit.
DISCUSSION: The scope of the consideration of internal control in an audit of a nonpublic client is usually less than that in an engagement to examine the effectiveness of internal control. The auditor must test controls in such an engagement. In the consideration of internal control during an audit, the auditor may not test controls if (s)he assesses control risk for the related assertions at the maximum level.
Answer (B) is incorrect because procedures are more extensive in an engagement to report on the effectiveness of internal control. Answer (C) is incorrect because procedures are more extensive in an engagement to report on the effectiveness of internal control. Answer (D) is incorrect because an audit does not result in a report on management's written assertion about the effectiveness of internal control unless the requirements of an engagement for that purpose are also met.

35. King Corp. has received a local government grant and asked you, as a CPA, to examine the effectiveness of internal control that is required by the terms of the grant. The governmental agency responsible for the grant has prepared written criteria for such a report that have not been subjected to due process procedures. During your consideration of internal control to prepare the report, you find what you consider to be a material weakness in accounting for the grant. This weakness was not covered by the criteria established by the governmental agency. What action should you take in your report to the governmental agency?

- A. Include the weakness in the report even though it is not covered by the agency's criteria.

- B. Do not include the weakness in the report because it is outside the criteria established by the agency.

- C. Advise King Corp.'s audit committee but do not include the weakness in the report.

- D. Include a comment in the report that you do not believe the criteria established by the agency are comprehensive but do not include the weakness in the report.

Answer (A) is correct. *(CPA, adapted)*
REQUIRED: The proper action when a material weakness is discovered that was not covered by the applicable criteria established by a governmental agency.
DISCUSSION: According to AT 501, a material weakness in this context is "a condition in which the design or operation of one or more of the specific internal control components does not reduce to a relatively low level the risk that misstatements due to error or fraud in amounts that would be material in relation to the applicable grant or program might occur and not be detected on a timely basis by employees in the normal course of performing their assigned functions." A material weakness is also "a condition in which the lack of conformity with the regulatory agency's criteria is material in accordance with any guidelines for determining materiality that are included in such criteria." A practitioner who identifies material weaknesses in internal control that are not covered by the criteria set by the agency should include these material weaknesses in the report. (S)he does not, however, assume responsibility for the comprehensiveness of the agency's criteria.
Answer (B) is incorrect because professional standards require that this weakness be included. Answer (C) is incorrect because, although the CPA should advise King's audit committee about the problem, (s)he should also include it in the report. Answer (D) is incorrect because it is inappropriate to comment about the criteria established by the agency.

36. How do the scope, procedures, and purpose of an engagement to report on the effectiveness of an entity's internal control compare with those for the consideration of internal control in a financial statement audit of a nonpublic client?

	Scope	Procedures	Purpose
A.	Similar	Different	Similar
B.	Different	Similar	Similar
C.	Different	Different	Different
D.	Different	Similar	Different

Answer (D) is correct. *(CPA, adapted)*
REQUIRED: The comparison of an engagement to report on internal control and the consideration of internal control in an audit of a nonpublic client.
DISCUSSION: The purpose of an examination of internal control is to express an opinion either directly on the examination of internal control or on the responsible party's assertion about the effectiveness of internal control. The purpose of the consideration of internal control in a financial statement audit is to enable the auditor to plan the audit. The two engagements also differ in scope. In the latter, the auditor is only required to obtain an understanding of internal control and assess control risk. Accordingly, the consideration in an audit is usually more limited than that undertaken to express an opinion. However, the procedures typically performed are similar.

37. The Sarbanes-Oxley Act of 2002 requires management to include a report on internal control in the firm's annual report. It also requires auditors to evaluate management's internal control report. Which of the following statements concerning these requirements is false?

- A. The auditor should provide recommendations for improving internal control in their assessment.

- B. Management should identify significant deficiencies and material weaknesses in their report.

- C. Management's report should state their responsibility for establishing and maintaining an adequate internal control system.

- D. The auditor should evaluate whether internal controls are effective in accurately and fairly reflecting the firm's transactions.

Answer (A) is correct. *(Publisher)*
REQUIRED: The false statement about the Sarbanes-Oxley Act.
DISCUSSION: The auditor may provide management with recommendations for improving controls, but the Sarbanes-Oxley Act does not require such a communication in their report.
Answer (B) is incorrect because management's report should include any significant deficiencies and material weaknesses as well as any corrective action taken. Answer (C) is incorrect because management's report should state that they are responsible for establishing and maintaining internal controls. Answer (D) is incorrect because the auditor should evaluate and express an opinion on the effectiveness of internal control over financial reporting.

38. Firms subject to the reporting requirements of the Securities Exchange Act of 1934 are required by the Foreign Corrupt Practices Act of 1977 to maintain satisfactory internal control. Moreover, the Sarbanes-Oxley Act of 2002 requires that annual reports include (1) a statement of management's responsibility for establishing and maintaining adequate internal control and procedures for financial reporting, and (2) management's assessment of their effectiveness. The role of the registered auditor relative to the assessment made by management is to

A. Disclaim an opinion on the assessment and controls.

B. Report clients with unsatisfactory internal control to the SEC.

C. Express an opinion on whether the client is subject to the Securities Exchange Act of 1934.

D. Attest to, and report on, the assessment made by management.

Answer (D) is correct. *(Publisher)*
REQUIRED: The role of the auditor relative to reporting on the assessment by the management of a public client of internal control and procedures for financial reporting.
DISCUSSION: The registered auditor that issues the audit report for a public client must attest to, and report on, the assessment made by management in the internal control report. The attestation must be made in accordance with standards for attestation engagements issued or adopted by the Public Company Accounting Oversight Board (PCAOB). However, the auditor's evaluation must not be the subject of a separate engagement. The auditor must determine whether the entity's transactional records are (1) accurate and fair and (2) provide reasonable assurance that financial statements may be prepared in conformity with GAAP. The auditor also must describe material weaknesses in internal control.
Answer (A) is incorrect because the auditor is required to attest to internal control of public client. Answer (B) is incorrect because the auditor's report on internal control is issued in conjunction with the audit report on the financial statements. Answer (C) is incorrect because public clients must report to the SEC, but the auditor need not express an opinion on whether the client is subject to the Securities Exchange Act of 1934.

9.4 Service Organizations (AU 324)

39. AU 324, *Service Organizations*, applies to a financial statement audit of an entity that uses services of another organization as part of its information system. For this purpose, the user auditor may need to obtain the service auditor's report. Which of the following is a true statement about a service auditor's report?

A. It provides the user auditor with assurance regarding whether control procedures have been placed in operation at the client organization.

B. It should include an opinion.

C. If it proves to be inappropriate for the user auditor's purposes, (s)he must personally perform procedures at the service organization.

D. A user auditor need not inquire about the service auditor's professional reputation.

Answer (B) is correct. *(Publisher)*
REQUIRED: The true statement about a service auditor's report regarding internal control.
DISCUSSION: A service auditor's report on policies and procedures at the service organization should be helpful in providing a sufficient understanding to plan the audit of the user organization. The service auditor's report may express an opinion on the fairness of the description of the controls placed in operation at the service organization and whether they were suitably designed. If the service auditor has also tested controls, the report may also express an opinion on the operating effectiveness of the controls.
Answer (A) is incorrect because a service auditor's report is helpful to the user auditor in obtaining an understanding of internal control at the service organization, but it does not provide assurance regarding conditions at the client organization. Answer (C) is incorrect because audit procedures at the service organization may be applied by the service auditor on the request of (and under the direction of) the user auditor. Answer (D) is incorrect because the user auditor should inquire about the service auditor's professional reputation.

40. Computer Services Company (CSC) processes payroll transactions for schools. Drake, CPA, is engaged to report on CSC's controls placed in operation as of a specific date. These controls are relevant to the schools' internal control, so Drake's report will be useful in providing the schools' independent auditors with information necessary to plan their audits. Drake's report expressing an opinion on CSC's controls placed in operation as of a specific date should contain a(n)

A. Description of the scope and nature of Drake's procedures.

B. Statement that CSC's management has disclosed to Drake all design deficiencies of which it is aware.

C. Opinion on the operating effectiveness of CSC's controls.

D. Paragraph indicating the basis for Drake's assessment of control risk.

Answer (A) is correct. *(CPA, adapted)*
REQUIRED: The item in a service auditor's report on controls placed in operation.
DISCUSSION: The report expressing an opinion on the description of controls placed in operation includes (1) a reference to the aspects of the service organization covered, (2) a description of the service auditor's procedures, (3) identification of the party stating the control objectives, (4) a statement of purposes of the engagement, (5) a disclaimer of opinion on operating effectiveness, (6) an opinion on whether the service organization's description fairly presents the controls placed in operation, (7) a statement of inherent limitations, and (8) the parties for whom the report is intended.
Answer (B) is incorrect because the service auditor need not conclude whether management has disclosed all design deficiencies. Answer (C) is incorrect because the report on controls placed in operation does not contain an opinion on operating effectiveness. Answer (D) is incorrect because the report contains no assessment of control risk, only an opinion on the controls placed in operation.

41. Lake, CPA, is auditing the financial statements of Gill Co. Gill uses the EDP Service Center, Inc. to process its payroll transactions. EDP's financial statements are audited by Cope, CPA, who recently issued a report on EDP's internal control. Lake is considering Cope's report on EDP's internal control in assessing control risk on the Gill engagement. What is Lake's responsibility concerning making reference to Cope as a basis, in part, for Lake's own opinion?

   A. Lake may refer to Cope only if Lake is satisfied as to Cope's professional reputation and independence.

   B. Lake may refer to Cope only if Lake relies on Cope's report in restricting the extent of substantive tests.

   C. Lake may refer to Cope only if Lake's report indicates the division of responsibility.

   D. Lake may not refer to Cope under the circumstances above.

Answer (D) is correct. *(CPA, adapted)*
   REQUIRED: The reference, if any, in an auditor's report to a service auditor's report on internal control.
   DISCUSSION: The service auditor was not responsible for examining any portion of the user organization's financial statements. Hence, the user auditor should not refer to the service auditor's report as a basis in part for his/her own opinion on those financial statements (AU 324).
   Answer (A) is incorrect because, although the user auditor should make inquiries concerning the service auditor's professional reputation and consider the service auditor's independence, no reference to the service auditor should be made in the user auditor's report. Answer (B) is incorrect because the user auditor should not refer to the service auditor's report even if (s)he uses that report in assessing control risk and in determining the nature, timing, and extent of the substantive tests. Answer (C) is incorrect because the user auditor should not divide responsibility with the service auditor.

42. A service organization may maintain internal control that interacts with that of the client. The user auditor

   A. Is not required to evaluate the service organization's controls.

   B. Should obtain absolute assurance that the service organization's controls will prevent or detect errors or fraud.

   C. Should not consider weaknesses in the service organization's internal control to be weaknesses in the client's structure.

   D. Need not be concerned with the service organization's internal control if the client has effective controls related to service organization processing.

Answer (D) is correct. *(Publisher)*
   REQUIRED: The true statement about the interaction of the internal controls at the service and the client organization.
   DISCUSSION: When the client has effective controls related to service organization processing, the user auditor may be able to assess control risk at an acceptably low level and forgo the use of a service auditor's report.
   Answer (A) is incorrect because, when controls of the client and the service organization interact, the service organization's controls must be evaluated in conjunction with the client's. Answer (B) is incorrect because reasonable, not absolute, assurance should be obtained that the service organization's controls will prevent or detect errors and fraud. Answer (C) is incorrect because the user auditor should consider the combination of controls at the client and service organizations.

43. Payroll Data Co. (PDC) processes payroll transactions for a retailer. Cook, CPA, is engaged to express an opinion on a description of PDC's internal controls placed in operation as of a specific date. These controls are relevant to the retailer's internal control, so Cook's report may be useful in providing the retailer's independent auditor with information necessary to plan a financial statement audit. Cook's report should

   A. Contain a disclaimer of opinion on the operating effectiveness of PDC's controls.

   B. State whether PDC's controls were suitably designed to achieve the retailer's objectives.

   C. Identify PDC's controls relevant to specific financial statement assertions.

   D. Disclose Cook's assessed level of control risk for PDC.

Answer (A) is correct. *(CPA, adapted)*
   REQUIRED: The components of a service report.
   DISCUSSION: Service auditors may (1) report on controls placed in operation or (2) report on controls placed in operation and tests of operating effectiveness. The report limited to controls placed in operation should include a disclaimer of an opinion related to operating effectiveness of the controls.
   Answer (B) is incorrect because the report should state whether PDC's controls were suitably designed to provide reasonable assurance of achieving the specified control objectives of the service organization. Answer (C) is incorrect because specific controls relevant to specific financial statement assertions need not be identified in the service auditor's report. Answer (D) is incorrect because the assessed level of control risk is not disclosed.

44. A service auditor's report on internal control may be issued on controls placed in operation or on controls placed in operation and tests of operating effectiveness. Which of the following is true of a report on controls placed in operation?

    A. It should disclaim an opinion on whether internal control, taken as a whole, meets the control objectives.

    B. It should include an opinion concerning the design of internal control as well as conclusions from tests of controls.

    C. It will include a list of all errors and frauds discovered.

    D. It need not be restricted in its use and may be made available to any third party.

Answer (A) is correct. *(Publisher)*
REQUIRED: The true statement about a service auditor's report on internal control.
DISCUSSION: A service auditor's report on controls placed in operation should contain (1) a reference to the aspects of the service organization covered; (2) a description of the service auditor's procedures; (3) identification of the party stating the control objectives; (4) a statement of purposes of the engagement; (5) a disclaimer of opinion on operating effectiveness; (6) an opinion on the description of internal control at the service organization; (7) a statement of inherent limitations; and (8) identification of the parties for whom the report is intended.
    Answer (B) is incorrect because the service auditor should determine whether controls are suitably designed to achieve specified control objectives and whether they have been placed in operation. However, no tests of controls have been performed, and no conclusions as to effectiveness can be expressed. Answer (C) is incorrect because a clearly inconsequential rate of deviations or errors or frauds that have been detected and corrected in the normal functioning of the system need not be identified. Answer (D) is incorrect because a service auditor's report is intended solely for the use of service organization management, client organizations, and the independent auditors of client organizations.

45. Dunn, CPA, is auditing the financial statements of Taft Co. Taft uses Quick Service Center (QSC) to process its payroll. Price, CPA, is expressing an opinion on a description of the controls placed in operation at QSC regarding the processing of its customers' payroll transactions. Dunn expects to consider the effects of Price's report on the Taft engagement. Price's report should contain a (an)

    A. Description of the scope and nature of Price's procedures.

    B. Statement that Dunn may assess control risk based on Price's report.

    C. Assertion that Price assumes no responsibility to determine whether QSC's controls are suitably designed.

    D. Opinion on the operating effectiveness of QSC's internal controls.

Answer (A) is correct. *(CPA, adapted)*
REQUIRED: The content of a service auditor's report on controls placed in operation.
DISCUSSION: Service auditors may (1) report on controls placed in operation or (2) report on controls placed in operation and tests of operating effectiveness. A service auditor's report on controls placed in operation should contain (1) a reference to the aspects of the service organization covered; (2) a description of the scope and nature of the service auditor's procedures; (3) identification of the party stating the control objectives; (4) a statement of purposes of the engagement; (5) a disclaimer of opinion on operating effectiveness; (6) an opinion on the description of internal control at the service organization; (7) a statement of inherent limitations; and (8) identification of the parties for whom the report is intended.
    Answer (B) is incorrect because Price did not examine the operating effectiveness of the internal controls. Answer (C) is incorrect because the purpose of Price's examination is to determine whether QSC's controls were suitably designed. Answer (D) is incorrect because Price did not examine the operating effectiveness of the internal controls.

Use Gleim's *CPA Test Prep* for interactive testing with over 2,000 additional multiple-choice questions!

9.5 PRACTICE SIMULATION

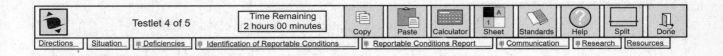

| Testlet 4 of 5 | Time Remaining 2 hours 00 minutes | Copy | Paste | Calculator | Sheet | Standards | Help | Split | Done |

Directions | Situation | Deficiencies | Identification of Reportable Conditions | Reportable Conditions Report | Communication | Research | Resources

1. Directions

In the following simulation, you will be asked to complete various tasks related to audit communication. The simulation will provide all the information necessary to do your work. For full credit, be sure to view and complete all work tabs.

Resources are available under the tab marked RESOURCES. You may want to review the resources before beginning the simulation.

2. Situation

Land & Hale, CPAs, are auditing the financial statements of Stone Co., a nonpublic entity, for the year ended December 31, year 1. Edwin Land, the engagement supervisor, anticipates expressing an unqualified opinion on May 20, year 2. Ed Wood, an assistant on the engagement, drafted the auditor's communication of internal control related matters that Land plans to send to Stone's board of directors with the May 20th auditor's report. Land reviewed Wood's draft and indicated in the *Supervisor's Review Notes* that Wood's draft contained deficiencies.

Independent Auditor's Report

To the Board of Directors of Stone Company:

   In planning and performing our audit of the financial statements of Stone, Co. for the year ended December 31, year 1, we considered its internal control in order to determine our auditing procedures for the purpose of expressing our opinion on the financial statements and to provide assurance on internal control. However, we noted certain matters involving internal control and its operations that we consider to be reportable conditions under standards established by the American Institute of Certified Public Accountants. Reportable conditions involve matters coming to our attention relating to significant deficiencies in the design or operation of internal control that, in our judgment, could adversely affect the organization's ability to initiate, record, process, and report financial data consistent with our assessment of control risk.

   We noted that deficiencies in internal control design included inadequate provisions for the safeguarding of assets, especially concerning cash receipts and inventory stored at remote locations. Additionally, we noted failures in the operation of internal control. Reconciliations of subsidiary ledgers to control accounts were not timely prepared, and senior employees in authority intentionally overrode internal control concerning cash payments to the detriment of the overall objectives of internal control.

   A material weakness is not necessarily a reportable condition but a design defect in which the internal control components do not reduce to a relatively low level the risk that errors or fraud in amounts that would be material in relation to the financial statements being audited may occur and not be detected by the auditor during the audit.

   Our consideration of internal control would not necessarily disclose all matters in internal control that might be reportable conditions and, accordingly, would not necessarily disclose all reportable conditions that are also considered to be material weaknesses as defined above. However, none of the reportable conditions described above is believed to be a material weakness.

   This report is intended solely for the information and use of the Board of Directors of Stone Co. Accordingly, it is not intended to be used by shareholders, management, or those who are not responsible for these matters.

Land & Hale, CPAs
May 4, Year 2

3. Deficiencies

This question has a true-false format.

Indicate in the shaded column whether Land is correct or incorrect in his criticisms of Wood's draft.

Potential Deficiencies	*Answer*
In the first paragraph:	
1. The report should not refer to "our audit of the financial statements."	
2. The report should indicate that providing assurance is not the purpose of the consideration of internal control.	
3. The reference to "our assessment of control risk" at the end of the paragraph should have been a reference to "the assertions of management in the financial statements."	
4. The report should refer to "conformity with generally accepted accounting principles."	
In the second paragraph:	
5. The report should not refer to deficiencies because such a reference is inconsistent with the expression of an unqualified opinion on the financial statements.	
6. When deficiencies (reportable conditions) are noted, the report should include a description of the assessed level of control risk.	
In the third paragraph:	
7. The definition of "material weakness" is incorrect. A material weakness is a reportable condition.	
8. The report should indicate that the auditor assumes no responsibility for errors or fraud resulting from the deficiencies (reportable conditions) identified in the report.	
9. The report should refer to detection by the entity's employees at the end of the paragraph, not detection by the auditor.	
In the fourth paragraph:	
10. The report should indicate that the consideration of internal control is expected to disclose all reportable conditions.	
11. It is inappropriate to state that "none of the reportable conditions...is believed to be a material weakness."	
In the final paragraph:	
12. The restriction on the report's use is inappropriate because management ordinarily would receive the report.	
13. The report should indicate that the financial statement audit resulted in an unqualified opinion.	
14. The report should indicate that the auditor is not responsible for updating the report for events or circumstances occurring after the date of the report.	
Dating the report:	
15. The report may not be dated before the auditor's report on the financial statements.	

Choices
Correct
Incorrect

4. Identification of Reportable Conditions

This question is presented in a check-the-box format.

State whether each of the following issues is considered a reportable condition under AU 325, *Communication of Internal Control Related Matters Noted in an Audit.*

Issues	Yes	No
1. Inadequate provisions for the safeguarding of assets		
2. Failure of management to provide the auditor with personal financial statements		
3. Intentional override of controls		
4. Unqualified personnel		
5. Write off of customer accounts determined to be bad debts		
6. Separation of the accounting function from the finance function		
7. Undisclosed related party transactions		
8. Failure of management to provide confidential information to competitors		
9. Lack of objectivity by accounting decision makers		
10. Failure of management to maximize profits		

5. Reportable Conditions Report

This question has a true-false (yes-no) format.

The report on reportable conditions required by AU 325 should preferably be in writing. The written report should contain certain language. Indicate in the table below which language is appropriate for this report.

Report Language	Answer
1. We considered internal control in order to determine our auditing procedures.	
2. An additional purpose was to provide assurance on internal controls.	
3. Reportable conditions could adversely affect the entity's ability to initiate, record, process and report financial information.	
4. The auditor is responsible for instituting proper controls.	
5. These reportable conditions could affect the reporting of the auditor's financial statements.	
6. Our consideration was made in accordance with standards established by the American Institute of Certified Public Accountants.	
7. This report is intended solely for the use of the audit committee.	
8. We will update this report if conditions change subsequent to the audit year.	

Choices
A) Yes
B) No

6. Communication

In a brief memorandum to a client, identify and describe the various components of internal control. Type your communication in your word processor program and print out the copy in a memorandum style format.

REMINDER: Your response will be graded for both technical content and writing skills. You should demonstrate your ability to develop, organize, and express your ideas. Do not convey information in the form of a table, bullet point list, or other abbreviated presentation.

To: Client
From: CPA
Subject: Internal control components

7. Research

Use the research materials available to find the answers to the following question in the AICPA Professional Standards. Print the appropriate citation in its entirety from the source you choose. Use only one source. This is a copy-and-paste item.

Research and report the difference relationship between reportable conditions and material weaknesses. Cite the appropriate literature to support your findings.

Unofficial Answers

3. Deficiencies (15 Gradable Items)

1. <u>Incorrect</u>. The report should indicate that the purpose of the audit was to report on the financial statements and not to provide assurance on internal control.

2. <u>Correct</u>. The report on reportable conditions should indicate that internal control was considered for the purpose of planning the audit.

3. <u>Correct</u>. The last sentence in the paragraph should read, "Reportable conditions involve matters coming to our attention relating to significant deficiencies in the design or operation of internal control that in our judgment could adversely affect the organization's ability to initiate, record, process, and report financial data consistent with the assertions of management in the financial statements."

4. <u>Incorrect</u>. The report communicates reportable conditions, not whether the financial statements are in conformity with GAAP.

5. <u>Incorrect</u>. The purpose of the report is to communicate reportable conditions. Thus, it is appropriate to reference control deficiencies in the report.

6. <u>Incorrect</u>. The auditor assesses the level of control risk to determine the nature, extent, and timing of the substantive procedures performed in an audit. However, this need not be described in the report on reportable conditions.

7. <u>Correct</u>. A reportable condition may be of such magnitude as to be considered a material weakness. A material weakness in internal control is a reportable condition in which the design or operation of one or more of the internal control components does not reduce to a relatively low level the risk that errors or fraud in amounts that would be material in relation to the financial statements being audited may occur and not be detected within a timely period by employees in the normal course of performing their assigned functions.

8. <u>Incorrect</u>. Although the auditor assumes no responsibility for errors or fraud resulting from deficiencies identified in the report, the report does not explicitly state this.

9. <u>Correct</u>. The statement should end with "and not be detected within a timely period by employees in the normal course of performing their assigned functions."

10. <u>Incorrect</u>. It would be appropriate for the report to indicate that all reportable conditions would not necessarily be identified during the audit of the financial statements.

11. <u>Incorrect</u>. The auditor may state, "However, none of the reportable conditions described above is believed to be a material weakness," if the auditor has so concluded.

12. <u>Correct</u>. The report may be intended for the information and use by the audit committee, board of directors, board of trustees, or owners in owner-managed enterprises, management, and others within the organization (or specified regulatory agency) and is not intended to be used and should not be used by anyone other than these specified parties (AU 325).

13. <u>Incorrect</u>. The report need not identify the type of opinion that was expressed on the financial statements.

14. <u>Incorrect</u>. The report should not contain a statement concerning the auditor's responsibility for updating the report. The auditor has no such obligation.

15. <u>Incorrect</u>. Because timely communication may be important, the auditor may choose to communicate significant matters during the course of the audit rather than after the audit is concluded. The decision on whether an interim communication should be issued would be influenced by the relative significance of the matters noted and the urgency for corrective follow-up action.

4. Identification of Reportable Conditions (10 Gradable Items)

1. Yes.
2. No.
3. Yes.
4. Yes.
5. No.
6. No.
7. Yes.
8. No.
9. Yes.
10. No.

5. Reportable Conditions Report (8 Gradable Items)

1. A) Yes.
2. B) No.
3. A) Yes.
4. B) No.
5. B) No.
6. A) Yes.
7. A) Yes.
8. B) No.

6. Communication (5 Gradable Items; For grading instructions, please refer to page 11.)

> To: Client
> From: CPA
> Subject: Internal control components

This brief memorandum describes the authoritative control model adopted by the AICPA. It provides common analytical components and terminology for a discussion of control by auditors, clients, regulators, and others.

According to AICPA pronouncements, the five internal control components are control activities, risk assessment, information and communication, monitoring, and the control environment. Control activities are the policies and procedures that help ensure that management directives are carried out. Risk assessment is the entity's identification and analysis of relevant risks as a basis for their management. Information and communication systems support the identification, capture, and exchange of information in a form and time frame that enable people to carry out their responsibilities. Monitoring is a process that assesses the quality of internal control performance over time. The control environment sets the tone of an organization, influencing the control consciousness of its people. It is the foundation for all other components.

If you have any questions or comments about the matters described in this memorandum, please contact us at your convenience.

7. Research (6 Gradable Items)

AU Section 325 – *Communication of Internal Control Related Matters Noted in an Audit*

Reportable Conditions

.02   During the course of an audit, the auditor may become aware of matters relating to internal control that may be of interest to the audit committee. The matters that this section requires for reporting to the audit committee are referred to as *reportable conditions*. Specifically, these are matters coming to the auditor's attention that, in his judgment, should be communicated to the audit committee because they represent significant deficiencies in the design or operation of internal control, which could adversely affect the organization's ability to initiate, record, process, and report financial data consistent with the assertions of management in the financial statements. Such deficiencies may involve aspects of the five internal control components of (*a*) the control environment, (*b*) risk assessment, (*c*) control activities, (*d*) information and communication, and (*e*) monitoring. [As amended, effective for audits of financial statements for periods beginning on or after January 1, 1997, by Statement on Auditing Standards No. 78. Revised, April 2002, to reflect conforming changes necessary due to the issuance of Statement on Auditing Standards No. 94.]

Reporting-Form and Content

.15   A reportable condition may be of such magnitude as to be considered a material weakness. A *material weakness in internal control* is a reportable condition in which the design or operation of one or more of the internal control components does not reduce to a relatively low level the risk that misstatements caused by error or fraud in amounts that would be material in relation to the financial statements being audited may occur and not be detected within a timely period by employees in the normal course of performing their assigned functions. Although this section does not require that the auditor separately identify and communicate material weaknesses, the auditor may choose or the client may request the auditor to separately identify and communicate as material weaknesses those reportable conditions that, in the auditor's judgment, are considered to be material weaknesses. [As modified, June 1990, by the Audit Issues Task Force.]

Scoring Schedule:

	Correct Responses		Gradable Items		Weights		
Tab 3	_____	÷	15	×	20%	=	_____
Tab 4	_____	÷	10	×	20%	=	_____
Tab 5	_____	÷	8	×	20%	=	_____
Tab 6	_____	÷	5	×	30%	=	_____
Tab 7	_____	÷	6	×	10%	=	_____
							(Your Score)

Use Gleim's ***CPA Review Online*** to practice more simulations in a realistic environment.

STUDY UNIT TEN
EVIDENCE -- OBJECTIVES AND NATURE

(13 pages of outline)

10.1   Nature, Competence, and Sufficiency (AU 326) 317
10.2   The Confirmation Process (AU 330) 320
10.3   Audit Documentation (AU 339) 324
10.4   The Computer as an Audit Tool 327
10.5   Practice Simulation 345

The primary purpose of the collection of evidence is to test management's assertions related to the balances reported on the financial statements. The sufficiency and competence of required evidence are judged by the auditor based on the acceptable level of detection risk, which is based on (1) the level to which the auditor wishes to restrict the risk of a material misstatement and (2) the assessments of inherent risk and control risk.

10.1 NATURE, COMPETENCE, AND SUFFICIENCY (AU 326)

1. The third standard of field work declares "sufficient competent evidential matter is to be obtained through inspection, observation, inquiries, and confirmations to afford a reasonable basis for an opinion regarding the financial statements under audit."

2. **Nature of Assertions**

   a. Most audit work consists of obtaining and evaluating evidence about financial statement assertions. The measure of the validity of this evidence lies in the auditor's judgment. The assertions are representations by management that are embodied in financial statement components and can be either explicit or implicit.

   b. The five assertions (use the mnemonic COVES to help you remember) are classified as follows:

      1) **C**ompleteness -- whether all transactions and accounts that should be presented in the financial statements are included

      2) Rights and **O**bligations -- whether, at a given date, all assets are the rights of the entity and all liabilities are the obligations of the entity

      3) **V**aluation or Allocation -- whether the assets, liabilities, revenues, and expenses of an entity have been included in the financial statements at the appropriate amounts in conformity with GAAP

      4) **E**xistence or Occurrence -- whether assets/liabilities exist at a given date and whether recorded transactions have occurred during a given period

      5) **S**tatement Presentation and Disclosure -- whether financial statement components have been properly classified, described, and disclosed

3. **Use of Assertions in Developing Audit Objectives and Designing Substantive Tests**

   a. Development of audit objectives. The auditor develops specific audit objectives considering the specific circumstances of the entity, including the nature of its economic activity and the accounting practices unique to its industry.

      1) There is not necessarily a one-to-one relationship between audit objectives and procedures. Some auditing procedures may relate to more than one objective.

         a) On the other hand, a combination of auditing procedures may be needed to achieve a single objective.

b. Selecting substantive tests. Substantive tests consist of tests of the details of transactions and balances (tests of details) and analytical procedures. After developing the audit objectives, the auditor should select appropriate substantive tests after considering the risk of material misstatement of the financial statements, including the assessed levels of inherent and control risk, and the expected effectiveness and efficiency of such tests.

1) The auditor should consider

   a) The nature and materiality of the items being tested
   b) The kinds and competence of available evidence
   c) The nature of the audit objective to be achieved

2) For example, a substantive test related to existence would entail selecting items included in a financial statement amount and then searching for relevant evidence (proof of the financial event). The direction of testing, from the records to the evidence, is critical in meeting the objective.

   a) A substantive test related to completeness would involve selecting evidence indicating that an item should be included in an amount (proof of the financial event) and then investigating whether it is so included in the account balance.

   b) The direction of testing for existence and completeness assertions is illustrated below.

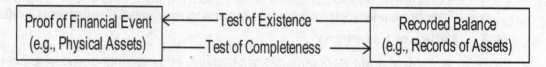

c. Influence of data processing methods. The auditor's audit objectives do not change based on the method of processing information (i.e., manually or electronically).

1) Methods of applying audit procedures to gather evidence, however, may be influenced by the data processing method. The more computerized an accounting system, the more the auditor must use information technology-assisted audit techniques to obtain evidence.

d. The nature, timing, and extent of audit procedures in the given circumstances are determined by the auditor's professional judgment.

e. Procedures should be adequate to achieve the audit objectives developed by the auditor.

f. Evidence should be sufficient to form conclusions concerning the validity of the individual assertions.

g. The evidence collected and documented should provide a reasonable basis for the opinion.

h. In entities that use significant information technology, the potential for improper and undetected initiation or alteration of information may be increased. In such circumstances, substantive tests alone may be insufficient to reduce detection risk to an acceptable level for one or more assertions. The auditor should perform tests of controls to gather evidential matter to use in assessing control risk, or consider the effect on the report. Thus, in these circumstances, the auditor may not forgo tests of controls, assess control risk at the maximum, and rely totally on substantive tests.

4.   **Nature of Evidential Matter**. Evidence supporting the financial statements (F/S) consists of underlying accounting data and all corroborating information available to the auditor.

   a.   **Underlying accounting data** consist of the books of original entry (e.g., journals and registers), the general and subsidiary ledgers, related accounting manuals, and records such as work sheets and spreadsheets supporting cost allocations, computations, and reconciliations, often in electronic form.

   1)   Accounting data alone cannot be considered sufficient support for financial statements.

   2)   The auditor tests underlying accounting data by

   a)   Analysis and review

   b)   Retracing the procedural steps followed in the accounting process and in developing the work sheets and allocations involved

   c)   Recalculation

   d)   Reconciling related types and applications of the same information

   b.   **Corroborating evidential matter** includes both written and electronic information (e.g., checks, invoices, EFTs, contracts, and minutes of meetings); confirmations and other written representations by knowledgeable people; information obtained by the auditor from inquiry, observation, inspection, and physical examination; and other information developed by, or available to, the auditor that permits conclusions through valid reasoning.

   c.   Accounting data and corroborating evidence may be available only in electronic form (e.g., EDI systems or image processing systems) and may exist only at a certain moment in time. When choosing audit procedures, the auditor should consider that evidence may not be retrievable after a specified period of time.

   d.   The diagram below illustrates the relationship of data in the accounting process on the left and the related direction of the completeness and existence tests on the right.

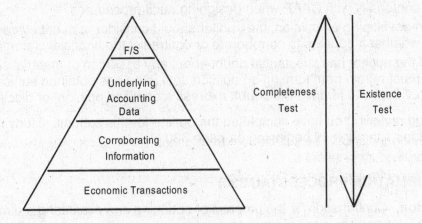

5. **Competence of Evidential Matter**. Competent evidence, regardless of its form, must be both valid (objective and reliable) and relevant (i.e., timely and related to the issue). Its validity is dependent on the circumstances under which it is obtained. Subject to exceptions, the following presumptions can be made about the validity of evidence:

   a. Evidence obtained from independent sources outside an entity provides greater assurance of reliability for the purposes of an independent audit than evidence secured solely within the entity.

   b. The more effective the internal control, the more assurance it provides about the reliability of the accounting data and financial statements.

   c. The independent auditor's direct personal knowledge, obtained through physical examination, observation, computation, and inspection, is more persuasive than information obtained indirectly.

6. **Sufficiency of Evidential Matter**

   a. The amounts and kinds of evidence needed are matters to be determined in the exercise of the professional judgment of the auditor.

   b. The auditor typically has to rely on persuasive, rather than convincing, evidence.

   c. The auditor must decide whether the evidence available within time and cost limits is sufficient to justify the opinion.

   d. A rational relationship should exist between the cost of obtaining evidence and the usefulness of the information obtained. However, the difficulty and the expense involved in testing a particular item are not in themselves a valid basis for omitting the test.

7. **Evaluation of Evidential Matter**. Through this evaluation, the auditor considers whether the specific audit objectives have been achieved.

   a. The independent auditor should be thorough in the search for evidence and unbiased in its evaluation.

   b. The auditor should recognize the possibility that the financial statements may not be in conformity with GAAP when designing audit procedures.

   c. In developing an opinion, the auditor should consider relevant evidence regardless of whether it appears to corroborate or contradict the financial statement assertions.

   d. If the auditor has substantial doubt about any assertion of material significance, (s)he must refrain from forming an opinion until (s)he has obtained sufficient competent evidence to remove the doubt, express a qualified opinion, or disclaim an opinion.

8. Stop and review! You have completed the outline for this subunit. Study multiple-choice questions 1 through 19 beginning on page 330.

10.2 THE CONFIRMATION PROCESS (AU 330)

1. **Definition**. Confirmation "is the process of obtaining and evaluating a direct communication from a third party in response to a request for information about a particular item affecting financial statement assertions." This process includes

   a. Selecting items for confirmations

   b. Designing the request

   c. Communicating the request to the appropriate third party

   d. Obtaining the response

   e. Evaluating the information, or lack thereof, provided by the third party about the audit objectives, including its reliability

2. **Confirmation and the Assessment of Audit Risk**

    a.   The auditor uses the audit risk assessment to determine the appropriate audit procedures, including confirmation.

    b.   The greater the combined assessed level of inherent and control risk, the greater the assurance to be provided by substantive tests. Thus, confirmation might be used when a more effective procedure is needed instead of or in conjunction with tests directed toward documents or parties within the entity.

    c.   If the entity has entered into an unusual or complex transaction and the combined assessed level of inherent and control risk is high, the auditor should consider confirming the terms of the transaction with the other parties in addition to examining documents.

    d.   The auditor should assess whether the evidence provided by confirmations reduces audit risk to an acceptably low level. The materiality of the account balance and the inherent and control risk assessments should be considered. If the evidence provided by confirmations alone is not sufficient, additional procedures should be performed.

    e.   As the combined assessed level of inherent and control risk decreases, the auditor may modify substantive tests by changing their nature from more effective to less effective (and less costly) tests.

    f.   Assertions addressed by confirmations

        1)   Even properly designed confirmation requests do not address all assertions with equal effectiveness.

            a)   For example, confirming goods on consignment is likely to be more effective for testing existence and rights than for valuation, and confirming receivables is likely to be more effective for testing existence than for completeness and valuation.

        2)   When obtaining evidence for assertions not adequately addressed by confirmations, the auditor should consider other audit procedures to complement or replace confirmation procedures.

        3)   Confirmation requests can be designed to provide evidence for the completeness assertion. Their effectiveness in this regard depends on whether the auditor selects items from an appropriate population, for example, from a list of vendors when accounts payable are confirmed.

            a)   However, some confirmations are not designed to elicit evidence on completeness; e.g., the Standard Form to Confirm Account Balance Information with Financial Institutions does not provide assurance about information not listed on the form.

3. **Designing Requests and Applying Confirmation Procedures**

    a.   The auditor should exercise an appropriate level of professional skepticism throughout the confirmation process.

    b.   Designing the confirmation request

        1)   Requests should be specific to particular audit objectives.

        2)   The assertions addressed and the factors likely to affect the reliability of the confirmations should be considered.

        3)   The following factors affect the design of the request because they directly affect the reliability of the evidence obtained.

            a)   The form of the request
            b)   Prior experience on the audit or similar engagements
            c)   The nature of information being confirmed
            d)   The intended respondent

4) The **positive confirmation** requests a reply regardless of whether the respondent agrees with the information stated. It may ask the respondent to state whether (s)he agrees with the information given or request that the recipient fill in an account balance (termed a **blank form**) or provide other information.

a) Positive forms provide evidence only when responses are received from the recipients.

b) Blank forms mitigate the risk that the recipients of a positive confirmation request will sign and return the request without verifying the information.

5) The **negative confirmation** requests the recipient to respond only if (s)he disagrees with the information stated.

a) Negative forms are used to reduce audit risk to an acceptable level when the combined assessed level of inherent and control risk is low, a large number of small balances is involved, and the auditor has no reason to believe that the recipients are unlikely to give them consideration.

i) The auditor should consider performing other substantive procedures to supplement the use of negative confirmation.

b) The auditor should investigate relevant information provided on negative confirmations that have been returned to determine its effect on the audit. For example, given a pattern of misstatements, the auditor should reconsider the combined assessed level of inherent and control risk and consider the effect on planned audit procedures.

c) Unreturned negative confirmation requests rarely provide significant evidence about assertions other than existence.

i) An unreturned negative confirmation request provides some evidence of existence because it has not been returned with an indication that the addressee is unknown; however, it provides no explicit evidence that the intended recipient verified the information.

6) The auditor may consider information from prior years' audits or audits of similar entities when determining the effectiveness and efficiency of employing confirmation procedures.

7) When designing requests, the auditor should consider the types of information respondents will be readily able to confirm. The nature of the information may directly affect the competence of the evidence obtained and the response rate.

a) Understanding the substance of the client's arrangements and transactions with third parties is fundamental to determining the information to be confirmed. The auditor should also consider

i) Requesting confirmation of the terms of unusual agreements or transactions as well as the amounts

ii) Ascertaining whether there may be oral modifications to agreements

8) The auditor should direct the confirmation request to a knowledgeable third party.

a) Information about the respondent's competence, knowledge, motivation, ability, willingness to respond, objectivity, or freedom from bias may affect the design of the confirmation request and the evaluation of the results, including the determination as to whether other procedures are necessary.

    c.   Performing confirmation procedures

        1)   The auditor should control confirmation requests and responses during the performance of procedures.

            a)   Control means direct communication between the intended recipient and the auditor to minimize possible bias because of interception and alteration of the requests or responses.

        2)   When responses other than written communications mailed to the auditor (e.g., FAX responses) are received, additional evidence may be required to support their validity. For example, the auditor may wish to verify the sources by calling the purported senders, or by having the sender mail the original confirmation directly to the auditor.

            a)   Oral confirmations should be documented in the working papers, and if the information in the oral confirmations is significant, the auditor should request written confirmation directly to the auditor.

        3)   When using positive confirmations, the auditor should usually follow up with a second and, if applicable, a third request to parties who did not respond.

4. **Alternative Procedures**

    a.   When the auditor has not received replies to positive confirmation requests, (s)he should apply alternative procedures to the nonresponses to reduce audit risk to an acceptably low level.

    b.   The omission of alternative procedures may be warranted when

        1)   The auditor has not identified unusual qualitative factors or systematic characteristics related to the nonresponses.

        2)   Given testing for overstatement, treating the aggregate nonresponses as 100% misstatements would not affect the auditor's decision about whether the financial statements are materially misstated.

    c.   The nature of alternative procedures varies with the account and the assertion.

5. **Evaluating the Results of Confirmation Procedures**

    a.   The auditor should evaluate the evidence provided by confirmations and alternative procedures to determine whether sufficient evidence has been obtained about all the applicable financial statement assertions.

    b.   Consideration should be given to

        1)   The reliability of the confirmations and alternative procedures

        2)   The nature of any exceptions, including the quantitative and qualitative implications

        3)   The evidence provided by other procedures

        4)   The possibility of a need for additional evidence

    c.   If the evidence gathered is not sufficient, the auditor should request additional confirmations or extend other tests.

6. **Confirmation of Accounts Receivable**

   a. **Accounts receivable** are the entity's claims against customers arising from the sale of goods or services in the normal course of business.

      1) They include the loans of a financial institution.

   b. Confirmation of accounts receivable is a generally accepted auditing procedure. The presumption is that the auditor will confirm accounts receivable unless one of the following is true:

      1) They are immaterial.
      2) Confirmation would be ineffective.
      3) The combined assessed level of inherent and control risk is low, and that level, together with the evidence expected to be obtained from analytical procedures or other substantive tests of details, is sufficient to reduce audit risk to an acceptably low level.

   c. An auditor who has not requested confirmations in the examination of accounts receivable should document how (s)he overcame this presumption.

   d. Confirmation of accounts receivable is also considered in Study Unit 11.

7. Stop and review! You have completed the outline for this subunit. Study multiple-choice questions 20 through 28 beginning on page 335.

10.3 AUDIT DOCUMENTATION (AU 339)

1. Audit documentation (working papers) should be prepared and maintained. It is the

   a. Principal record of the auditing procedures applied,
   b. Evidence obtained, and
   c. Conclusions reached.

2. Audit documentation serves mainly to

   a. Provide the principal support for the auditor's report, and
   b. Aid in the conduct and supervision of the audit.

3. Documentation should be sufficient to

   a. Enable engagement team supervisors and reviewers to understand the nature, timing, extent, and results of the procedures performed and the evidence obtained.
   b. Indicate who performed and reviewed the work.
   c. Show that the accounting records agree or reconcile with the financial statements or other information reported on.

4. Examples include audit programs, analyses, memoranda, confirmations, letters of representation, abstracts or copies of documents (e.g., copies of contracts), schedules, and commentaries. Documentation may be on paper or electronic or other media (e.g., tapes, disks, or film).

   a. A **working trial balance** is ordinarily used to record the year-end ledger balances prior to audit. Reclassifications and adjustments are accumulated on the trial balance to reflect the final audited balances.

   b. **Lead schedules** are summaries of detailed schedules. For example, a cash lead schedule may summarize findings recorded on the cash in bank, petty cash, and count of cash on hand detail schedules.

5. Audit documentation should be sufficient to show that the standards of field work (the acronym is PIE) have been met.

    a. **P** -- The engagement was adequately **planned and supervised**.

    b. **I** -- A sufficient understanding of **internal control** was obtained to plan the audit and determine the nature, timing, and extent of tests.

    c. **E** -- The **evidence** obtained through the procedures performed is sufficient and competent and provides a reasonable basis for an opinion.

6. Audit findings or significant issues to be documented include

    a. Identification of items tested to determine the operating effectiveness of controls or to perform substantive tests of details that consist of inspection of documents or confirmations.

        1) The source of the items and the specific selection criteria should be stated, for example, those for a particular type of sample.

    b. Management's selection, application, and consistency of application of GAAP, for example,

        1) Accounting for complex or unusual transactions.
        2) Treatment of estimates and uncertainties (and any related assumptions).

    c. Evidence that the financial statements or disclosures may be materially misstated.

    d. Evidence that the auditing procedures required modification.

    e. Difficulty in applying necessary auditing procedures.

    f. Other findings that could result in modification of the report.

7. The nature and extent of documentation are determined by the

    a. Risk of material misstatement of an assertion or an account or class of transactions.

    b. Extent of judgment involved in performing the work and evaluating the results.

    c. Nature of the auditing procedures.

    d. Significance of the evidence obtained.

    e. Nature and extent of exceptions identified.

    f. Need to document a conclusion or the basis for a conclusion not readily determinable from other documentation of the work.

8. Audit documentation is typically classified into permanent and current files.

    a. **Permanent files** are schedules, documents, and records with continuing audit significance for a specific client. These may include the articles of incorporation, bylaws, contracts (including debt agreements), schedules of ongoing importance (e.g., plant, property, and equipment), the organization chart, and internal control analyses.

    b. **Current files** include schedules and analyses that relate to the current year under audit. For example, results of substantive tests such as confirmations and inventory observation and test counts are kept in the current files.

9. The following techniques are essential for preparing and maintaining proper audit documentation.

   a. Heading. The heading should include the name of the client, a title identifying a description of the working paper, and the period covered by the audit.

   b. Index numbers. The working papers should be given an index or reference number for identification, cross-referencing, and filing purposes.

   c. Tick marks. A tick mark is used to show that the auditor has performed a procedure. All of the tick marks should be disclosed in a legend on the working papers to explain the work identified by each tick mark.

   d. Signature and dates. Each working paper, upon completion, should be signed and dated by both the preparer and reviewer.

10. Audit documentation is the property of the auditor.

11. The financial statements are primarily supported by the client's accounting records, and audit documentation is not a part of, or a substitute for, the client's accounting records.

12. The auditor should retain audit documentation "for a period of time sufficient to meet the needs of his or her practice and to satisfy any applicable legal or regulatory requirements for records retention."

13. An auditor should take reasonable steps to preserve the confidentiality of documented client information, including prevention of unauthorized access thereto.

14. The **Sarbanes-Oxley Act of 2002** states additional documentation requirements for registered public accountants. The PCAOB's Auditing Standard No. 3, *Audit Documentation*, which applies to audit engagements and reviews of interim financial information, reflects these considerations.

   a. Audit documentation must contain sufficient information to enable an **experienced auditor**, having no previous connection with the engagement, to understand the work performed and conclusions reached and to determine who performed and reviewed the work and the relevant dates.

      1) Audit documentation must not only support final conclusions but also include auditor-identified information about significant findings and issues that is inconsistent with or contradicts the auditor's final conclusions.

   b. The auditor must identify all **significant findings or issues** in an **engagement completion document**.

   c. Audit documentation must be retained for at least 7 years from the **report release date**.

   d. A complete and final set of audit documentation should be assembled for retention as of a date **(the documentation completion date)** not more than 45 days after the report release date.

   e. Audit documentation must **not** be deleted or discarded after the documentation completion date. However, information may be added.

   f. AS 3 does not address the issue of whether audit documentation is the property of the auditor. AS 3 also is silent on the confidentiality of audit documentation. (Note: The PCAOB adopted as interim ethics standards only the AICPA's provisions in its Code of Professional Conduct on integrity and objectivity. Thus, Conduct Rule 301, *Confidential Client Information*, is not a PCAOB standard.

15. Still other documentation standards may apply, for example, those of the SEC regarding retention of memoranda, communications (sent or received), other documents, and records related to the engagements.

16. Stop and review! You have completed the outline for this subunit. Study multiple-choice questions 29 through 40 beginning on page 338.

10.4 THE COMPUTER AS AN AUDIT TOOL

1. Many auditors use personal computers (PCs) to perform audit functions more efficiently and effectively. For this purpose, auditors must select tasks appropriate for personal computer capabilities and the software for those tasks. The use of software by the auditor is often termed a **computer-assisted audit technique (CAAT)**.

    a. Advantages

        1) The auditor can work independently of the auditee.
        2) The confidentiality of auditor procedures can be maintained.
        3) Audit work does not depend on the availability of auditee personnel.
        4) The auditor has access to records at remote sites.

    b. Disadvantages

        1) The auditor must have a working understanding of the computer system, e.g., a complicated database system (may also be an advantage).
        2) Supervisory review may be more difficult.

2. Audit procedures include

    a. Directly accessing the company's database (interrogation)
    b. Scanning files for certain types of records, items, etc.
    c. Building and using predictive models to identify high-risk areas
    d. Applying statistical sampling item selection and analysis routines
    e. Using input/output routines to provide hard copy and to reformat data (extraction)
    f. Preparing financial statements and other reports with spreadsheet routines
    g. Illustrating analyses with graphs and other pictorial displays
    h. Writing customized audit programs
    i. Storing audit programs, routines, and results electronically
    j. Implementing other types of audit procedures and analyses electronically
    k. Preparing and storing working papers
    l. Communicating data through networks
    m. Using specialized audit software to, among other things, compare source code with object code to detect unauthorized program changes, to analyze unexecuted code, or to generate test data
    n. Embedding code in the auditee's programs to routinely extract/select certain transactions or details to be recorded in a file accessible only by the auditor
    o. Employment of expert systems software to automate the knowledge and logic of experts in a certain field to help an auditor with decision making and risk analysis

3. **Generalized Audit Software** (GAS)

    a. Generalized audit software is useful for both tests of controls and substantive tests. It is software that is written to interface with many different client systems.
    b. Generalized audit software can be used to perform audit tasks such as

        1) Sampling and selecting items (e.g., confirmations)
        2) Testing extensions, footings, and calculations
        3) Examining records, for example, accounts receivable for amounts in excess of credit limits
        4) Summarizing and sorting data
        5) Performing analytical procedures, such as comparing inventory records with transaction details
        6) File access and file reorganization

     c.   Advantages of generalized audit software are that

        1)   It is independent of the client's programs and personnel. Thus, information can be accessed without detailed knowledge of the client's hardware and software.

        2)   Less computer expertise is needed in comparison with writing programs from scratch.

        3)   It can run on different systems.

     d.   Significant disadvantages are that

        1)   Some software packages may process only sequential files.
        2)   Modifications may be necessary for a specific audit.
        3)   Audit software cannot examine items not in machine-readable form.
        4)   It has limited application in an online, real-time system.

4.   A discussion of the test data approach, parallel simulation, and integrated test facilities, was presented in Study Unit 8.

5.   The leading CAAT software packages are currently Audit Command Language (ACL)® and Interactive Data Extraction and Analysis (IDEA)™ software.

     a.   These software packages, designed specifically for use in auditing, perform 11 major functions.

        1)   Aging. An auditor can test the aging of accounts receivable.

        2)   Duplicate identification. Duplicate data can be organized by data field and subsequently identified.

        3)   Exportation. Data can be transferred to other software.

        4)   Extraction. Data can be extracted for exception analysis.

        5)   Gap identification. Gaps in information can be automatically noted.

        6)   Joining and merging. Two separate data files may be joined or merged to combine and match information.

        7)   Sampling. Samples of the data can be prepared and analyzed.

        8)   Sorting. Information can be sorted by any data field.

        9)   Stratification. Large amounts of data can be organized by specific factors, thereby facilitating analysis.

        10) Summarization. Data can be organized to identify patterns.

        11) Total fields. Totals for numeric fields can be quickly and accurately calculated.

6.   **Artificial intelligence (AI)** is computer software designed to perceive, reason, and understand. In the business area, emphasis has been on the particular form of AI termed **expert systems**. The development of artificial intelligence and its subfield, expert systems, has been identified by the AICPA Future Issues Committee as one of the major concerns facing the accounting profession. Expert systems in taxation, financial accounting, managerial accounting, and auditing have long been in use in major CPA firms.

     a.   An expert system is an interactive system that asks a series of questions and uses knowledge gained from a human expert to analyze answers and make a decision. Its components are the knowledge database, domain database, database management system, inference engine, user interface, and knowledge acquisition facility.

        1)   The **knowledge database** contains the rules used when making decisions on certain topics. The facts about certain topics are contained in the **domain database**. These facts are used as a basis for comparison when the system matches a pattern of events or facts with a decision situation.

        2)   The **inference engine** is the heart of the expert system's processing. It performs the deductive thinking and logic portion of the processing.

3) Rules from the knowledge database, facts from the domain database, and input from the system user are all used by the inference engine.

4) Expert systems use symbolic processing based on **heuristics**. A heuristic procedure is an exploratory problem-solving technique that uses self-education methods, e.g., the evaluation of feedback, to improve performance.

b. Expert systems allow auditors and accountants to perform their duties in less time and with more uniformity. An expert system makes it more likely that different decision makers will reach the same conclusions given the same set of facts.

1) An expert system can be used to choose an audit program, select a test sample type and size, determine the level of misstatement, perform analytical procedures, and make a judgment based on the findings.

7. **Neural networks** are another form of artificial intelligence. A neural network learns from its mistakes in that it changes its knowledge database when informed of the accuracy of its decisions.

a. Whereas an expert system imitates a human expert and relies on many programmed rules, a neural network has a generalized learning capacity. It learns by experience.

8. **Specialized audit software** is written in a procedure- or problem-oriented language to fulfill a specific set of audit tasks. The purposes and users of the software are well defined before the software is written. Auditors develop specialized audit software for the following reasons:

a. Unavailability of alternative software
b. Functional limitations of alternative software
c. Efficiency considerations
d. Increased understanding of systems
e. Opportunity for easy implementation
f. Increased auditor independence and prestige

9. Stop and review! You have completed the outline for this subunit. Study multiple-choice questions 41 through 47 beginning on page 342.

QUESTIONS

10.1 Nature, Competence, and Sufficiency (AU 326)

1. The third standard of field work requires the auditor to collect sufficient competent evidential matter in support of the opinion. Which procedure is not identified in this standard?

    A. Inspection.

    B. Inquiries.

    C. Observation.

    D. Reconciliation.

Answer (D) is correct. *(Publisher)*
REQUIRED: The procedure not identified in the third standard of field work.
DISCUSSION: The third standard of field work identifies inspection, observation, inquiries, and confirmations. Although reconciliations are often made by the auditor in collecting evidence, the procedure is not explicitly mentioned in the third standard of field work.
Answer (A) is incorrect because inspection is identified in the third standard of field work as appropriate procedures for the collection of sufficient competent evidence. Answer (B) is incorrect because inquiries are identified in the third standard of field work as appropriate procedures for the collection of sufficient competent evidence. Answer (C) is incorrect because observation is identified in the third standard of field work as appropriate procedures for the collection of sufficient competent evidence.

2. Which of the following statements concerning audit evidence is true?

    A. To be competent, audit evidence should be either persuasive or relevant, but it need not be both.

    B. The measure of the validity of audit evidence lies in the auditor's judgment.

    C. The difficulty and expense of obtaining audit evidence concerning an account balance is a valid basis for omitting the test.

    D. A client's accounting data can be sufficient audit evidence to support the financial statements.

Answer (B) is correct. *(CPA, adapted)*
REQUIRED: The true statement concerning audit evidence.
DISCUSSION: Concerning audit evidence, AU 326 states, "The measure of the validity of such evidence for audit purposes lies in the judgment of the auditor." Unlike legal evidence, audit evidence is not circumscribed by rigid rules. In determining whether evidence is competent and sufficient, the auditor must make many judgments about relevance, objectivity, timeliness, the existence of corroboration, etc.
Answer (A) is incorrect because, to be competent, audit evidence must be both valid and relevant. Moreover, an auditor is often compelled to rely on evidence that is persuasive rather than convincing. Answer (C) is incorrect because, although there should be a rational relationship between the cost of obtaining evidence and its usefulness, difficulty and expense are not in themselves a valid basis for omitting a test. Answer (D) is incorrect because accounting data must be supported by corroborating information. Accounting data alone cannot support the financial statements.

3. Which of the following is a false statement about audit objectives?

    A. There should be a one-to-one relationship between audit objectives and procedures.

    B. Audit objectives should be developed in light of management assertions about the financial statement components.

    C. Selection of tests to meet audit objectives should depend upon the understanding of internal control.

    D. The auditor should resolve any substantial doubt about any of management's material financial statement assertions.

Answer (A) is correct. *(Publisher)*
REQUIRED: The false statement about audit objectives.
DISCUSSION: There is not necessarily a one-to-one relationship between audit objectives and procedures (AU 326). Some procedures may relate to more than one objective, and multiple procedures may be needed to achieve a single objective.
Answer (B) is incorrect because assertions made by management should be considered when the auditor develops objectives. Answer (C) is incorrect because the understanding of internal control and the assessed control risk affect the nature, timing, and extent of substantive tests. Answer (D) is incorrect because the auditor must refrain from forming an opinion until (s)he has gathered sufficient competent evidence to remove any substantial doubt about a material assertion by management. Otherwise, (s)he must qualify the opinion or disclaim an opinion.

4. AU 326, *Evidential Matter*, states that management makes certain assertions that are embodied in financial statement components; for example, two such categories of assertions are completeness and valuation or allocation. Which of the following is not a broad category of management assertions according to AU 326?

    A. Rights and obligations.

    B. Presentation and disclosure.

    C. Existence or occurrence.

    D. Errors or fraud.

Answer (D) is correct. *(Publisher)*
    REQUIRED: The category of assertions not explicitly listed in AU 326.
    DISCUSSION: Management implicitly represents that the financial statements are free from material misstatements. But this representation is not explicitly noted in AU 326 as a category of management assertions. AU 326 states that management assertions in the financial statements can be classified according as follows: (1) existence or occurrence, (2) completeness, (3) rights and obligations, (4) valuation or allocation, and (5) presentation and disclosure.
    Answer (A) is incorrect because rights and obligations is a category listed in AU 326. Answer (B) is incorrect because presentation and disclosure is a category listed in AU 326. Answer (C) is incorrect because existence or occurrence is a category listed in AU 326.

5. The objective of tests of details of transactions performed as substantive tests is to

    A. Comply with generally accepted auditing standards.

    B. Attain assurance about the reliability of the accounting system.

    C. Detect material misstatements in the financial statements.

    D. Evaluate whether management's policies and procedures operated effectively.

Answer (C) is correct. *(CPA, adapted)*
    REQUIRED: The objective of tests of details.
    DISCUSSION: Substantive tests are (1) tests of the details of transactions and balances and (2) analytical procedures. They are performed to detect material misstatements in the financial statement assertions (AU 319).
    Answer (A) is incorrect because the auditor may use a variety of techniques and is not required to use tests of the details of transactions to comply with GAAS. Answer (B) is incorrect because tests of controls are applied to test the reliability of the accounting system and other elements of internal control. Answer (D) is incorrect because tests of controls are used to determine whether policies or procedures operated effectively.

6. In testing the existence assertion for an asset, an auditor ordinarily works from the

    A. Financial statements to the potentially unrecorded items.

    B. Potentially unrecorded items to the financial statements.

    C. Accounting records to the supporting evidence.

    D. Supporting evidence to the accounting records.

Answer (C) is correct. *(CPA, adapted)*
    REQUIRED: The usual procedure testing the existence assertion for an asset.
    DISCUSSION: The existence assertion concerns whether assets or liabilities of the entity exist at a given time. The direction of testing is ordinarily from the accounting records to the supporting evidence, including direct observation of the inventory. Thus, "the auditor selects from items contained in a financial statement amount and searches for relevant evidential matter" (AU 326).
    Answer (A) is incorrect because unrecorded items relate to the completeness assertion. The auditor should select evidence indicating that an item should be included in an amount and then investigate. Answer (B) is incorrect because unrecorded items relate to the completeness assertion. The auditor should select evidence indicating that an item should be included in an amount and then investigate. Answer (D) is incorrect because proceeding from the supporting evidence to the accounting records might detect unrecorded assets.

7. An auditor observes the mailing of monthly statements to a client's customers and reviews evidence of follow-up on errors reported by the customers. This test of controls most likely is performed to support management's financial statement assertion(s) of

	Presentation and Disclosure	Existence or Occurrence
A.	Yes	Yes
B.	Yes	No
C.	No	Yes
D.	No	No

Answer (C) is correct. *(CPA, adapted)*
    REQUIRED: The financial statement assertion(s) related to observing the client's follow-up on errors reported on monthly statements.
    DISCUSSION: The existence assertion relates to whether the related balance exists at the balance sheet date. Observation of the mailing of monthly statements as well as observing the correction of reported errors provides evidence that controls may be effective in ensuring that there are actual client customers.
    Answer (A) is incorrect because the observation of client activities related to customer statements provides little evidence concerning presentation or disclosure in the financial statements. Answer (B) is incorrect because the observation of client activities related to customer statements provides little evidence concerning presentation or disclosure in the financial statements. Answer (D) is incorrect because the mailing and follow-up procedures provide evidence that controls may be effective in ensuring that there are actual client customers.

8. In determining whether transactions have been recorded, the direction of the audit testing should be from the

A. General ledger balances.

B. Adjusted trial balance.

C. Original source documents.

D. General journal entries.

Answer (C) is correct. *(CPA, adapted)*
REQUIRED: The direction of testing to determine whether transactions have been recorded.
DISCUSSION: Determining whether transactions have been recorded is a test of the completeness assertion. Thus, beginning with the original source documents and tracing the transactions to the appropriate records would determine whether they were recorded.

9. Which of the following elements ultimately determines the specific auditing procedures that are necessary in the circumstances to afford a reasonable basis for an opinion?

A. Auditor judgment.

B. Materiality.

C. Audit risk.

D. Reasonable assurance.

Answer (A) is correct. *(CPA, adapted)*
REQUIRED: The ultimate determinant of specific auditing procedures.
DISCUSSION: The third standard of field work states, "Sufficient competent evidential matter is to be obtained through inspection, observation, inquiries, and confirmations to afford a reasonable basis for an opinion regarding the financial statements." The nature, timing, and extent of the specific procedures to be applied to obtain sufficient competent evidential matter are matters of professional judgment (AU 326).
Answer (B) is incorrect because materiality is among the considerations in exercising professional judgment. Answer (C) is incorrect because audit risk is among the considerations in exercising professional judgment. Answer (D) is incorrect because, although the audit should be planned and performed to obtain reasonable assurance about whether the financial statements are free of material misstatement, whether such assurance has been obtained is itself ultimately a matter of auditor judgment.

10. A client uses a suspense account for unresolved questions whose final accounting has not been determined. If a balance remains in the suspense account at year-end, the auditor would be most concerned about

A. Suspense debits that management believes will benefit future operations.

B. Suspense debits that the auditor verifies will have realizable value to the client.

C. Suspense credits that management believes should be classified as "current liability."

D. Suspense credits that the auditor determines to be customer deposits.

Answer (A) is correct. *(CPA, adapted)*
REQUIRED: The accounting disposition of year-end suspense items most troublesome for an auditor.
DISCUSSION: Although the auditor must evaluate management's assertions about all accounts, the greatest risks are overstated assets and understated liabilities. The unverified suspense debits represent assets that may not exist.
Answer (B) is incorrect because the auditor has verified that the debits (assets) have future value. Thus, they are properly classified as assets. Answer (C) is incorrect because, for each suspense credit, a liability is reflected. Consequently, liabilities are not understated. Answer (D) is incorrect because, for each suspense credit, a liability is reflected. Consequently, liabilities are not understated.

11. Which of the following statements about evidential matter is true?

A. Competent evidence supporting management's assertions should be convincing rather than merely persuasive.

B. Effective internal control contributes little to the reliability of the evidence created within the entity.

C. The cost of obtaining evidence is not an important consideration to an auditor in deciding what evidence should be obtained.

D. A client's accounting data cannot be considered sufficient audit evidence to support the financial statements.

Answer (D) is correct. *(CPA, adapted)*
REQUIRED: The true statement about evidence.
DISCUSSION: Evidence supporting the financial statements consists of underlying accounting data (books of original entry, ledgers, spreadsheets, accounting manuals, etc.) and corroborating information (documents, confirmations, records of EFTs, etc.). Accounting data alone are not sufficient support. However, without adequate attention to its propriety and accuracy, an opinion would not be warranted.
Answer (A) is incorrect because the auditor must usually rely on evidence that is merely persuasive. It is seldom possible to become convinced beyond all doubt regarding all aspects of the audited statements. Answer (B) is incorrect because the more effective the controls, the more assurance they provide about the reliability of the accounting data and financial statements. Answer (C) is incorrect because the auditor will consider the cost of evidence relative to its usefulness.

12. Which of the following is an example of corroborating information that could be used by an auditor as evidential matter supporting the financial statements?

    A. Worksheets supporting cost allocations.

    B. Confirmation of accounts receivable.

    C. General and subsidiary ledgers.

    D. Accounting manuals.

Answer (B) is correct. *(Publisher)*
    REQUIRED: The example of corroborating information.
    DISCUSSION: Corroborating information includes both written and electronic information, such as checks, invoices, contracts, minutes of meetings, confirmations, and data obtained from inquiry, observation, inspection, and physical examination. It may also include any other information developed by or available to the auditor that permits valid reasoning (AU 326).
    Answer (A) is incorrect because worksheets supporting cost allocations are examples of underlying accounting data, not corroborating information. Answer (C) is incorrect because general and subsidiary ledgers are examples of underlying accounting data, not corroborating information. Answer (D) is incorrect because accounting manuals are examples of underlying accounting data, not corroborating information.

13. A retail entity uses electronic data interchange (EDI) in executing and recording most of its purchase transactions. The entity's auditor recognizes that the documentation of the transactions will be retained for only a short period of time. To compensate for this limitation, the auditor most likely would

    A. Increase the sample of EDI transactions to be selected for cutoff tests.

    B. Perform tests several times during the year, rather than only at year-end.

    C. Plan to make a 100% count of the entity's inventory at or near the year-end.

    D. Decrease the assessed level of control risk for the existence or occurrence assertion.

Answer (B) is correct. *(CPA, adapted)*
    REQUIRED: The auditor's response to limited retention time of documentation supporting EDI transactions.
    DISCUSSION: According to AU 326, accounting data and corroborating evidence may be available only in electronic form. For example, if EDI is used, purchase, shipping, billing, cash receipt, and cash payment transactions often occur by exchange of electronic messages instead of source documents. In an image processing system, documents are scanned and converted into electronic form for storage purposes, and the source documents may not be retained. Thus, electronic evidence may exist at a given moment in time, but it may not be retrievable after a specified period if files are changed and no backups exist. Consequently, the auditor should consider the time during which information is available to determine the nature, timing, and extent of substantive tests and tests of controls. For example, the auditor may change the timing of audit tests by performing them several times during the year instead of only at year-end.
    Answer (A) is incorrect because increasing the sample of transactions does not compensate for the lack of documentation. Answer (C) is incorrect because inventory is not the only affected balance. Answer (D) is incorrect because the auditor would likely increase the assessed level of control risk for the existence or occurrence assertion in light of this information.

14. Audit evidence can come in different forms with different degrees of persuasiveness. Which of the following is the least persuasive type of evidence?

    A. Bank statement obtained from the client.

    B. Test counts of inventory made by the auditor.

    C. Prenumbered purchase order forms.

    D. Correspondence from the client's attorney about litigation.

Answer (C) is correct. *(CPA, adapted)*
    REQUIRED: The least persuasive type of evidence.
    DISCUSSION: When documentation, such as purchase order forms, is prepared solely by client personnel, its persuasiveness will be less than that prepared by the auditor or an independent party. Ordinarily, the most reliable documentation is created outside the entity and has never been within the client's control.
    Answer (A) is incorrect because, although a bank statement obtained from the client has been within the client's control, it is an externally generated document and is preferable to an internally prepared document. Answer (B) is incorrect because, in principle, evidence is more likely to be valid when it consists of the auditor's direct personal knowledge. Answer (D) is incorrect because correspondence from the client's attorney about litigation is externally generated and therefore preferable to an internally generated document.

15. Which of the following types of audit evidence is the most persuasive?

A. Prenumbered client purchase order forms.

B. Client work sheets supporting cost allocations.

C. Bank statements obtained from the client.

D. Client representation letter.

Answer (C) is correct. *(CPA, adapted)*
REQUIRED: The most persuasive evidence.
DISCUSSION: Evidence from independent sources outside the entity provides greater assurance of reliability for purposes of an audit than evidence secured or prepared solely within the entity. Although the bank statements are in the possession of the client, they originated outside of the client and, relative to the other responses, they are the most persuasive.

Answer (A) is incorrect because prenumbered client purchase order forms is evidence prepared solely within the entity. Answer (B) is incorrect because client work sheets is evidence prepared solely within the entity. Answer (D) is incorrect because the client representation letter supports inquiries during the audit but is viewed as less persuasive than documentary evidence.

16. Which of the following presumptions does not relate to the competence of audit evidence?

A. The more effective internal control, the more assurance it provides about the accounting data and financial statements.

B. An auditor's opinion, to be economically useful, is formed within reasonable time and based on evidence obtained at a reasonable cost.

C. Evidence obtained from independent sources outside the entity is more reliable than evidence secured solely within the entity.

D. The independent auditor's direct personal knowledge, obtained through observation and inspection, is more persuasive than information obtained indirectly.

Answer (B) is correct. *(CPA, adapted)*
REQUIRED: The presumption not relating to the competence of audit evidence.
DISCUSSION: Competent evidence is both valid and relevant. Ordinarily, evidence obtained from independent sources, developed under effective internal control, or generated through the auditor's personal experience is presumed to be the most competent (AU 326). However, cost-benefit considerations relate to the sufficiency, not the competence, of evidence.

Answer (A) is incorrect because the more effective the controls, the more assurance they provide about the reliability of the accounting data and financial statements. Answer (C) is incorrect because evidence obtained from independent sources outside an entity provides greater assurance of reliability than evidence secured solely within the entity. Answer (D) is incorrect because the independent auditor's direct personal knowledge, obtained through physical examination, observation, computation, and inspection, is more persuasive than information obtained indirectly.

17. Which of the following presumptions is correct about the reliability of evidential matter?

A. Information obtained indirectly from outside sources is the most reliable evidential matter.

B. To be reliable, evidential matter should be convincing rather than persuasive.

C. Reliability of evidential matter refers to the amount of corroborative evidence obtained.

D. Effective internal control provides more assurance about the reliability of evidential matter.

Answer (D) is correct. *(CPA, adapted)*
REQUIRED: The correct presumption about the reliability of evidential matter.
DISCUSSION: AU 326 indicates that the more effective the internal control, the more assurance it provides about the reliability of the accounting data and financial statements.

Answer (A) is incorrect because an independent auditor's direct personal knowledge, obtained through physical examination, observation, computation, and inspection, is more persuasive than information obtained indirectly. However, it is not necessarily the most reliable evidential matter. Answer (B) is incorrect because evidence at best is only persuasive rather than convincing. Answer (C) is incorrect because reliability relates to the faith that the auditor can place in the evidence and is not necessarily based on the amount of corroborative evidence obtained.

18. Which statement about evidential matter is invalid?

A. The auditor is seldom convinced beyond all doubt with respect to all aspects of the statements being audited.

B. The auditor would not undertake a procedure that would provide persuasive evidence only.

C. The auditor evaluates the degree of risk involved in deciding the kind of evidence to gather.

D. The auditor evaluates the usefulness of the evidence against the cost to obtain it.

Answer (B) is correct. *(Publisher)*
REQUIRED: The invalid statement about evidential matter.
DISCUSSION: In most cases, evidential matter that is obtained to afford a reasonable basis for an opinion is necessarily persuasive rather than convincing. The cost of obtaining convincing evidence may outweigh the benefits. There must be a rational relationship between the cost and usefulness. Nevertheless, the difficulty and expense of testing an item are not in themselves a valid basis for omitting an audit test (AU 326).
Answer (A) is incorrect because the auditor is seldom persuaded beyond all doubt given the high cost of absolute certainty. Answer (C) is incorrect because the auditor should assess the risk of misstatement before determining the kind and amount of evidence necessary to form an opinion. Answer (D) is incorrect because a rational relationship should exist between the cost and usefulness of evidence.

19. Each of the following might, by itself, form a valid basis for an auditor to decide to omit a test except for the

A. Difficulty and expense involved in testing a particular item.

B. Assessment of control risk at a low level.

C. Inherent risk involved.

D. Relationship between the cost of obtaining evidence and its usefulness.

Answer (A) is correct. *(CPA, adapted)*
REQUIRED: The consideration that is not a valid reason for omission of an audit test.
DISCUSSION: A rational relationship should exist between the costs of obtaining evidence and the usefulness of the information obtained. However, the difficulty and expense of performing a test are not in themselves considered valid reasons for omitting it if the test is necessary to obtain sufficient competent evidential matter to afford a reasonable basis for an opinion (AU 326).
Answer (B) is incorrect because the lower the control risk, the higher the acceptable detection risk, and the greater the justification for omitting a substantive test. Answer (C) is incorrect because a test might be omitted if the susceptibility to errors and fraud is slight. Answer (D) is incorrect because "There should be a rational relationship between the cost of obtaining evidence and the usefulness of the information obtained" (AU 326).

10.2 The Confirmation Process (AU 330)

20. In which of the following circumstances would the use of the negative form of accounts receivable confirmation most likely be justified?

A. A substantial number of accounts may be in dispute and the accounts receivable balance arises from sales to a few major customers.

B. A substantial number of accounts may be in dispute and the accounts receivable balance arises from sales to many customers with small balances.

C. A small number of accounts may be in dispute and the accounts receivable balance arises from sales to a few major customers.

D. A small number of accounts may be in dispute and the accounts receivable balance arises from sales to many customers with small balances.

Answer (D) is correct. *(CPA, adapted)*
REQUIRED: The circumstances in which negative accounts receivable confirmations are most likely justified.
DISCUSSION: AU 330 states, "Negative confirmation requests may be used to reduce audit risk to an acceptable level when (1) the combined assessed level of inherent and control risk is low, (2) a large number of small balances is involved, and (3) the auditor has no reason to believe that the recipients of the requests are unlikely to give them consideration."

21. In auditing accounts receivable, the negative form of confirmation request most likely would be used when

A. Recipients are likely to return positive confirmation requests without verifying the accuracy of the information.

B. The combined assessed level of inherent and control risk relative to accounts receivable is low.

C. A small number of accounts receivable are involved but a relatively large number of errors are expected.

D. The auditor performs a dual-purpose test that assesses control risk and obtains substantive evidence.

Answer (B) is correct. *(CPA, adapted)*
REQUIRED: The most likely use of the negative form of confirmation.
DISCUSSION: The negative form of confirmation is used to reduce audit risk to an acceptable level when the combined assessed level of inherent and control risk is low, a large number of small balances is involved, and the auditor has no reason to believe the recipients are unlikely to give the confirmations consideration.
Answer (A) is incorrect because, when the recipients are likely to return confirmations without verifying information, the auditor may consider other procedures to test existence. Answer (C) is incorrect because, when the risk of error is high, the positive form of confirmation should be used. Answer (D) is incorrect because confirmations are a substantive test used to collect evidence, not to assess control risk.

22. Auditors may use positive or negative forms of confirmation requests. An auditor most likely will use

A. The positive form to confirm all balances regardless of size.

B. The negative form for small balances.

C. A combination of the two forms, with the positive form used for trade balances and the negative form for other balances.

D. The positive form when the combined assessed level of inherent and control risk for related assertions is acceptably low, and the negative form when it is unacceptably high.

Answer (B) is correct. *(CPA, adapted)*
REQUIRED: The true statement about the use of positive and negative confirmations.
DISCUSSION: The negative confirmation asks for a response only when the debtor disagrees. The negative form may be used when the combined assessed level of inherent and control risk is low, many small balances are involved, and the auditor has no reason to believe that recipients are unlikely to give confirmations their consideration (AU 330). A combination of the two forms is often used.
Answer (A) is incorrect because the negative form is often used, e.g., when many small balances are involved. Answer (C) is incorrect because the nature of the balances does not dictate the form used. Answer (D) is incorrect because the positive form is used when control risk is high.

23. Which of the following strategies most likely could improve the response rate of the confirmation of accounts receivable?

A. Including a list of items or invoices that constitute the account balance.

B. Restricting the selection of accounts to be confirmed to those customers with relatively large balances.

C. Requesting customers to respond to the confirmation requests directly to the auditor by fax or e-mail.

D. Notifying the recipients that second requests will be mailed if they fail to respond in a timely manner.

Answer (A) is correct. *(CPA, adapted)*
REQUIRED: The strategy most likely to improve confirmation response rates.
DISCUSSION: According to AU 330, the auditor should consider what respondents are most readily able to confirm so as to improve the response rate and the competence of the evidence obtained. Thus, some customers may use a voucher system that makes it more convenient to respond to individual invoices rather than the total balance.
Answer (B) is incorrect because, although the auditor will likely focus on the larger balances, this emphasis is not likely to improve the response rate. Answer (C) is incorrect because, when responses other than written communications mailed to the auditor (e.g., e-mail or faxes) are received, additional evidence may be required to support their validity, for example, verifying the response by a telephone call to the purported sender. Answer (D) is incorrect because notifying the recipients that second requests will be mailed if they fail to respond in a timely manner is threatening. It may reduce the response rate.

24. Which of the following statements is correct concerning the use of negative confirmation requests?

A. Unreturned negative confirmation requests rarely provide significant explicit evidence.

B. Negative confirmation requests are effective when detection risk is low.

C. Unreturned negative confirmation requests indicate that alternative procedures are necessary.

D. Negative confirmation requests are effective when understatements of account balances are suspected.

Answer (A) is correct. *(CPA, adapted)*
REQUIRED: The true statement about negative confirmation requests.
DISCUSSION: Unreturned negative confirmation requests rarely provide significant evidence about assertions other than certain aspects of existence. However, unreturned negative confirmations do not provide explicit evidence that the intended parties received the requests and verified the information provided.
Answer (B) is incorrect because, when desired detection risk is low, positive confirmations are more effective. Answer (C) is incorrect because the auditor assumes the account is fairly stated when negative confirmations are not returned, thus indicating alternative procedures are not necessary. Answer (D) is incorrect because positive confirmations are more effective when understatements of account balances are suspected.

25. An auditor decides to use the blank form of accounts receivable confirmation rather than the positive form. The auditor should be aware that the blank form may be less efficient because

A. Subsequent cash receipts need to be verified.

B. Statistical sampling may not be used.

C. A higher assessed level of detection risk is required.

D. More nonresponses are likely to occur.

Answer (D) is correct. *(CPA, adapted)*
REQUIRED: The disadvantage of a blank form confirmation request.
DISCUSSION: The blank form of accounts receivable confirmation requests the recipient to complete the confirmation by providing the balance due the client. This procedure may require more effort by the recipient and thus limit response rates. Accordingly, the auditor may have to perform alternative procedures (AU 330).
Answer (A) is incorrect because verification of subsequent cash receipts is an alternative procedure performed when the response rate is too low. Answer (B) is incorrect because statistical sampling may be used with any form of confirmation. Answer (C) is incorrect because detection risk is the risk that a material misstatement may not be detected. It is a function of the effectiveness, not the efficiency, of an auditing procedure and its application by the auditor. The blank form of positive confirmation tends to reduce detection risk.

26. The confirmation of customers' accounts receivable rarely provides reliable evidence about the completeness assertion because

A. Many customers merely sign and return the confirmation without verifying its details.

B. Recipients usually respond only if they disagree with the information on the request.

C. Customers may not be inclined to report understatement errors in their accounts.

D. Auditors typically select many accounts with low recorded balances to be confirmed.

Answer (C) is correct. *(CPA, adapted)*
REQUIRED: The reason confirmations rarely provide evidence about completeness.
DISCUSSION: Confirmations do not address all assertions with equal effectiveness. For example, confirmations of accounts receivable do not necessarily provide reliable evidence about the completeness assertion because customers may not report understatement errors. Also, confirmations may not be designed to provide assurance about information not given in the request forms.
Answer (A) is incorrect because failure to confirm the accounts is related to the valuation assertion. Answer (B) is incorrect because positive confirmations ask the customer to return the confirmation whether it is correct or not. Answer (D) is incorrect because auditors typically select accounts with material balances. The existence assertion is normally tested by confirmation.

27. To reduce the risks associated with accepting e-mail responses to requests for confirmation of accounts receivable, an auditor most likely would

A. Request the senders to mail the original forms to the auditor.

B. Examine subsequent cash receipts for the accounts in question.

C. Consider the e-mail responses to the confirmations to be exceptions.

D. Mail second requests to the e-mail respondents.

Answer (A) is correct. *(CPA, adapted)*
REQUIRED: The most likely method of reducing the risks associated with e-mail responses to confirmation requests.
DISCUSSION: According to AU 330, *The Confirmation Process*, when responses other than written communications mailed to the auditor (e.g., e-mail or faxes) are received, additional evidence may be required to support their validity. For example, the auditor may wish to verify the sources by calling the purported senders or by having the senders mail the original confirmations directly to the auditor.
Answer (B) is incorrect because subsequent collections provide evidence as to valuation once the existence assertion has been tested using confirmations. Answer (C) is incorrect because the responses, if from bona fide debtors, are not exceptions. Answer (D) is incorrect because the respondents should still have the original requests.

28. In confirming accounts receivable, an auditor decided to confirm customers' account balances rather than individual invoices. Which of the following most likely would be included with the client's confirmation letter?

    A. An auditor-prepared letter explaining that a nonresponse may cause an inference that the account balance is correct.

    B. A client-prepared letter reminding the customer that a nonresponse will cause a second request to be sent.

    C. An auditor-prepared letter requesting the customer to supply missing and incorrect information directly to the auditor.

    D. A client-prepared statement of account showing the details of the customer's account balance.

Answer (D) is correct. *(CPA, adapted)*
    REQUIRED: The nature of a confirmation of an accounts receivable balance.
    DISCUSSION: A confirmation must be requested by the client because the receiving party has no relationship with the client's auditor. In confirming the customer's receivables account balance, display of the details of the balance would likely help the customer in reconciling the amount and may increase response rates.
    Answer (A) is incorrect because the request should come from the client. Answer (B) is incorrect because no threats should be included in a confirmation. Answer (C) is incorrect because the request should come from the client.

10.3 Audit Documentation (AU 339)

29. Audit documentation serves mainly to

    A. Provide the principal support for the auditor's report.

    B. Satisfy the auditor's responsibilities concerning the *Code of Professional Conduct*.

    C. Monitor the effectiveness of the CPA firm's quality control procedures.

    D. Document the level of independence maintained by the auditor.

Answer (A) is correct. *(CPA, adapted)*
    REQUIRED: The purpose of audit documentation.
    DISCUSSION: Audit documentation provides the principal record of the auditing procedures applied, evidence obtained, and the conclusions reached. It should be designed to meet the circumstances of a particular engagement. AU 339 states audit documentation "serves mainly to provide the principal support for the auditor's report, including the representation regarding observance of the standards of field work."
    Answer (B) is incorrect because, although audit documentation is required to be prepared for each engagement by GAAS, it is not specifically required by the *Code of Professional Conduct*. Answer (C) is incorrect because the creation of audit documentation to satisfy quality control standards is a secondary purpose. Answer (D) is incorrect because the auditor must be independent to perform an audit. An auditor either is or is not independent.

30. Which of the following factors would least likely affect the nature and extent of audit documentation?

    A. The risk of material misstatement.

    B. The extent of exceptions identified.

    C. The nature of the auditing procedures.

    D. The medium in which it is recorded and maintained.

Answer (D) is correct. *(CPA, adapted)*
    REQUIRED: The least likely factor affecting the nature and extent of audit documentation.
    DISCUSSION: The medium used to prepare and maintain the audit documentation, e.g., paper or magnetic disk, does not affect its nature and extent. The nature and extent of documentation are determined by (1) the risk of material misstatement, (2) the extent of judgment involved in performing the work and evaluating the results, (3) the nature of the auditing procedures, (4) the significance of the evidence obtained, (5) the nature and extent of exceptions identified, and (6) the need to document a conclusion or the basis for a conclusion.

31. An auditor ordinarily uses a working trial balance resembling the financial statements without notes, but containing columns for

A. Cash flow increases and decreases.

B. Audit objectives and assertions.

C. Reclassifications and adjustments.

D. Reconciliations and tickmarks.

Answer (C) is correct. *(CPA, adapted)*
REQUIRED: The columns contained on a working trial balance in the audit documentation.
DISCUSSION: A working trial balance is ordinarily used to record the year-end ledger balances prior to audit in the audit documentation. Reclassifications and adjustments are accumulated on the trial balance to reflect the final audited balances.
Answer (A) is incorrect because cash flow increases or decreases are reflected on the client's statement of cash flows. Answer (B) is incorrect because the audit objectives and tests of management's assertions are determined in the planning stage of the audit and reflected in the audit documentation. Answer (D) is incorrect because the working trial balance has no column for either reconciliations or tickmarks.

32. The audit working paper that reflects the major components of an amount reported in the financial statements is the

A. Interbank transfer schedule.

B. Carryforward schedule.

C. Supporting schedule.

D. Lead schedule.

Answer (D) is correct. *(CPA, adapted)*
REQUIRED: The working paper that reflects the major components of a reported amount.
DISCUSSION: Lead schedules help to eliminate detail from the auditor's working trial balance by classifying and summarizing similar or related items that are contained on the supporting schedules. A lead schedule contains the detailed accounts from the general ledger making up the line item total in the financial statements; e.g., the cash account in the financial statements might consist of petty cash, cash-general, cash-payroll, etc.
Answer (A) is incorrect because an interbank transfer schedule is a working paper prepared for several days before and after the end of the period to determine that both parts of these transactions are recorded in the same period. Answer (B) is incorrect because a carryforward schedule is a continuing schedule of an account with a balance carried forward for several years. Answer (C) is incorrect because supporting schedules provide details aggregated in the lead schedule.

33. In creating lead schedules for an audit engagement, a CPA often uses automated audit documentation software. What client information is needed to begin this process?

A. Interim financial information such as third quarter sales, net income, and inventory and receivables balances.

B. Specialized journal information, such as the invoice and purchase order numbers of the last few sales and purchases of the year.

C. General ledger information, such as account numbers, prior-year account balances, and current-year unadjusted information.

D. Adjusting entry information, such as deferrals and accruals, and reclassification journal entries.

Answer (C) is correct. *(CPA, adapted)*
REQUIRED: The client information needed to begin the creation of lead schedules.
DISCUSSION: Lead schedules are summaries of detailed schedules. To create these summaries, general ledger information is needed. A lead schedule contains the detailed accounts from the general ledger making up the line item total. For example, a cash lead schedule may summarize findings recorded on the cash in bank, petty cash, and count of cash on hand detail schedules.
Answer (A) is incorrect because interim information is used in review engagements of interim financial information. Answer (B) is incorrect because specific transactions are reflected in detailed audit documentation and results are summarized on lead schedules. Answer (D) is incorrect because specific transactions are reflected in detailed audit documentation and results are summarized on lead schedules.

34. Which of the following documentation is required for an audit in accordance with generally accepted auditing standards?

A. A flowchart or an internal control questionnaire that evaluates the effectiveness of the entity's internal controls.

B. A client engagement letter that summarizes the timing and details of the auditor's planned field work.

C. An indication that the accounting records agree or reconcile with the financial statements.

D. The basis for the auditor's conclusions when the assessed level of control risk is at the maximum level for all financial statement assertions.

Answer (C) is correct. *(CPA, adapted)*
REQUIRED: The audit documentation required by GAAS.
DISCUSSION: Audit documentation should be sufficient to "show that the accounting records agree or reconcile with the financial statements or other information being reported on" (AU 339). It also should be sufficient to permit supervisors and reviewers to understand the nature, timing, extent, and results of the procedures performed and to identify the individuals who performed or reviewed the work. Furthermore, audit documentation should be sufficient to indicate adherence to the standards of field work.
Answer (A) is incorrect because, although an auditor must document that a sufficient understanding of internal control has been obtained, GAAS do not require a flowchart or questionnaire. Answer (B) is incorrect because under GAAS, an engagement letter is highly recommended, but not required, for all types of engagements. Answer (D) is incorrect because GAAS require the documentation of the conclusions, but not the basis for the auditor's conclusions, when the assessed level of control risk is at the maximum level for all financial statement assertions.

35. Which of the following statements concerning audit documentation is false?

A. An auditor may support an opinion by other means in addition to audit documentation.

B. The form of audit documentation should be designed to meet the circumstances of a particular engagement.

C. Audit documentation may not serve as a reference source for the client.

D. Audit documentation should show that the auditor has obtained an understanding of internal control.

Answer (C) is correct. *(CPA, adapted)*
REQUIRED: The false statement concerning audit documentation.
DISCUSSION: "Certain audit documentation may sometimes serve as a useful reference source for the client, but it should not be regarded as a part of, or a substitute for, the client's accounting records."
Answer (A) is incorrect because audit documentation provides the principal support for the auditor's report, but additional means may be used to support an opinion. Answer (B) is incorrect because the form and content of audit documentation vary with the circumstances. Answer (D) is incorrect because audit documentation should be sufficient to show that the auditor has followed the field work standards, for example, that a sufficient understanding of internal control has been obtained to plan the audit and determine the nature, timing, and extent of substantive tests.

36. Although the quantity and content of audit documentation vary with each engagement, an auditor's permanent files most likely include

A. Schedules that support the current year's adjusting entries.

B. Prior years' accounts receivable confirmations that were classified as exceptions.

C. Documentation indicating that the audit work was adequately planned and supervised.

D. Analyses of capital stock and other owners' equity accounts.

Answer (D) is correct. *(CPA, adapted)*
REQUIRED: The component of the permanent section of audit documentation.
DISCUSSION: The permanent section of audit documentation usually contains copies of important company documents. They may include the articles of incorporation, stock options, contracts, and bylaws; the engagement letter, which is the contract between the auditor and the client; analyses from previous audits of accounts of special importance to the auditor, such as long-term debt, PP&E, and equity; and information concerning internal control, e.g., flowcharts, organization charts, and questionnaires.
Answer (A) is incorrect because schedules that support the current year's adjusting entries are not carried forward in the permanent file. They are unlikely to have continuing significance. Answer (B) is incorrect because prior years' accounts receivable confirmations that were classified as exceptions are not carried forward in the permanent file. They are unlikely to have continuing significance. Answer (C) is incorrect because documentation indicating that the audit work was adequately planned and supervised is always included in the current files.

37. The permanent (continuing) file of an auditor's audit documentation most likely would include copies of the

- A. Lead schedules.
- B. Attorney's letters.
- C. Bank statements.
- D. Debt agreements.

Answer (D) is correct. *(CPA, adapted)*

REQUIRED: The component of the permanent section of the auditor's audit documentation.

DISCUSSION: The permanent section of the audit documentation usually contains copies of important company documents. The section may include the articles of incorporation, stock options, contracts, and bylaws; the engagement letter; analyses from previous audits of accounts of special importance to the auditor; and information concerning internal control, e.g., flowcharts.

Answer (A) is incorrect because the current file of an auditor's audit documentation includes all audit documentation applicable to the current year under audit, including lead schedules. Answer (B) is incorrect because the current file of an auditor's audit documentation includes all audit documentation applicable to the current year under audit, including attorneys' letters. Answer (C) is incorrect because the current file of an auditor's audit documentation includes all audit documentation applicable to the current year under audit, including bank statements.

38. The current file of the auditor's audit documentation ordinarily should include

- A. A flowchart of the internal control procedures.
- B. Organization charts.
- C. A copy of the financial statements.
- D. Copies of bond and note indentures.

Answer (C) is correct. *(CPA, adapted)*

REQUIRED: The item included in the current file of the auditor's audit documentation.

DISCUSSION: The current file of the auditor's audit documentation includes all working papers applicable to the current year under audit. A copy of the financial statements must be included in the current file because the amounts included in these statements are the focus of the audit.

Answer (A) is incorrect because a flowchart of the internal control procedures would be included in the permanent file. Answer (B) is incorrect because organization charts would be included in the permanent file. Answer (D) is incorrect because copies of bond and note indentures would be included in the permanent file.

39. The auditor is required to retain audit documentation

- A. For a period to satisfy applicable legal or regulatory requirements.
- B. For as long as the client remains a client and continues to pay audit fees on a timely basis.
- C. In perpetuity.
- D. For a period to be agreed upon in the engagement letter.

Answer (A) is correct. *(Publisher)*

REQUIRED: The retention period for audit documentation.

DISCUSSION: GAAS require the auditor to retain audit documentation for a period sufficient to meet the needs of his/her practice and to satisfy any applicable legal or regulatory requirements. For example, the PCAOB's AS 3, *Audit Documentation*, implements the requirement of the Sarbanes-Oxley Act of 2002 that registered public accounting firms when performing engagements under PCAOB standards retain audit documentation for 7 years from the audit report release date.

Answer (B) is incorrect because the auditor must retain the audit documentation beyond the date the auditor is succeeded by a new auditor. Answer (C) is incorrect because audit documentation need not be maintained in perpetuity. Answer (D) is incorrect because the auditor determines the retention period necessary to meet his/her needs subject to legal and regulatory requirements.

40. Which of the following statements ordinarily is true concerning the content of audit documentation?

    A. Whenever possible, the auditor's staff should prepare schedules and analyses rather than the entity's employees.

    B. It is preferable to have negative figures indicated in red figures instead of parentheses to emphasize amounts being subtracted.

    C. It is appropriate to use calculator tapes with names or explanations on the tapes rather than writing separate lists onto working papers.

    D. The analysis of asset accounts and their related expense or income accounts should not appear on the same working paper.

Answer (C) is correct. *(CPA, adapted)*
    REQUIRED: The true statement concerning the content of audit documentation.
    DISCUSSION: The quantity, type, and content of audit documentation vary with the circumstances, but it should be sufficient to show that the accounting records agree or reconcile with the financial statements or other information reported on. It also should be sufficient to permit supervisors and reviewers to understand the nature, timing, extent, and results of the procedures performed and to identify the individuals who performed or reviewed the work. Furthermore, audit documentation should be sufficient to indicate adherence to the standards of field work. As long as calculator tapes containing names or explanations achieve this purpose, separate lists need not be written onto working papers.
    Answer (A) is incorrect because the client's staff may be used to prepare schedules whenever appropriate to control costs. Answer (B) is incorrect because negative figures may be in parentheses. Answer (D) is incorrect because the analysis of asset accounts and their related expense or income accounts should appear on the same working paper.

10.4 The Computer as an Audit Tool

41. The two requirements crucial to achieving audit efficiency and effectiveness with a personal computer are selecting

    A. The appropriate audit tasks for personal computer applications and the appropriate software to perform the selected audit tasks.

    B. The appropriate software to perform the selected audit tasks and audit procedures that are generally applicable to several clients in a specific industry.

    C. Client data that can be accessed by the auditor's personal computer and audit procedures that are generally applicable to several clients in a specific industry.

    D. Audit procedures that are generally applicable to several clients in a specific industry and the appropriate audit tasks for personal computer applications.

Answer (A) is correct. *(CPA, adapted)*
    REQUIRED: The two requirements necessary to achieve audit efficiency and effectiveness using a personal computer.
    DISCUSSION: The question relates to using the computer as an audit tool. To use a personal computer for this purpose effectively and efficiently, the auditor must have the appropriate hardware and software.
    Answer (B) is incorrect because selection of standardized procedures for the industry does not relate directly to the efficient and effective use of a personal computer. Answer (C) is incorrect because access to the client's records and selection of standardized audit procedures pertain more to the use of generalized audit software to perform substantive tests than to using the personal computer as an audit tool. Answer (D) is incorrect because selection of standardized procedures for the industry does not relate directly to the efficient and effective use of a personal computer.

42. An auditor would least likely use computer software to

    A. Construct parallel simulations.

    B. Access data files.

    C. Prepare spreadsheets.

    D. Assess computer control risk.

Answer (D) is correct. *(CPA, adapted)*
    REQUIRED: The task least likely to be done with computer software.
    DISCUSSION: The auditor is required to obtain an understanding of internal control and assess control risk to plan the audit. This assessment is a matter of professional judgment that cannot be accomplished with a computer.
    Answer (A) is incorrect because parallel simulation involves using an auditor's program to reproduce the logic of the client's program. Answer (B) is incorrect because computer software makes accessing client files much faster and easier. Answer (C) is incorrect because many audit spreadsheet programs are available.

43. A primary advantage of using generalized audit software packages to audit the financial statements of a client that uses an computer system is that the auditor may

   A. Consider increasing the use of substantive tests of transactions in place of analytical procedures.

   B. Substantiate the accuracy of data through self-checking digits and hash totals.

   C. Reduce the level of required tests of controls to a relatively small amount.

   D. Access information stored on computer files while having a limited understanding of the client's hardware and software features.

Answer (D) is correct. *(CPA, adapted)*
   REQUIRED: The advantage of using generalized audit software (GAS).
   DISCUSSION: These packages permit the auditor to audit through the computer, e.g., to extract, compare, analyze, and summarize data and generate output for use in the audit. Although generalized audit software requires the auditor to provide certain specifications about the client's records, computer equipment, and file formats, a detailed knowledge of the client's system may be unnecessary because the audit package is designed to be used in many environments.
   Answer (A) is incorrect because the auditor is required to apply analytical procedures in the planning and overall review phases of the audit. Answer (B) is incorrect because self-checking digits and hash totals are application controls used by clients. Answer (C) is incorrect because audit software may permit far more comprehensive tests of controls than in a manual audit.

44. Which of the following is an engagement attribute for an audit of an entity that processes most of its financial data in electronic form without any paper documentation?

   A. Discrete phases of planning, interim, and year-end fieldwork.

   B. Increased effort to search for evidence of management fraud.

   C. Performance of audit tests on a continuous basis.

   D. Increased emphasis on the completeness assertion.

Answer (C) is correct. *(CPA, adapted)*
   REQUIRED: The engagement attribute for auditing in an electronic environment.
   DISCUSSION: The audit trail for transactions processed in electronic form may be available for only a short period of time. The auditor may conclude that it is necessary to time audit procedures so that they correspond to the availability of the evidence. Thus, audit modules may be embedded in the client's software for this purpose.
   Answer (A) is incorrect because this engagement attribute would be appropriate for any type of client. Answer (B) is incorrect because processing transactions in electronic form does not inherently increase the risk of management fraud. Answer (D) is incorrect because no inherent additional concern arises about the completeness assertion as a result of processing transactions in electronic form.

45. Using personal computers in auditing may affect the methods used to review the work of staff assistants because

   A. Supervisory personnel may not have an understanding of the capabilities and limitations of personal computers.

   B. Audit documentation may not contain readily observable details of calculations.

   C. The audit field work standards for supervision may differ.

   D. Documenting the supervisory review may require assistance of consulting services personnel.

Answer (B) is correct. *(CPA, adapted)*
   REQUIRED: The reason using personal computers may affect the review of the work of staff assistants.
   DISCUSSION: The first standard of field work requires assistants to be properly supervised. Thus, the "work performed by each assistant should be reviewed to determine whether it was adequately performed and to evaluate whether the results are consistent with the conclusions to be presented in the auditor's report" (AU 311). With the introduction of computers, accountants have been able to perform fewer manual calculations. Usually, the necessary numbers are entered into computer spreadsheets, and the answer is produced. Thus, the use of computers makes the review of a staff assistant's work different from that needed when the calculations are done manually.
   Answer (A) is incorrect because supervisors of the audit staff typically have the skills to evaluate the appropriate use of personal computers. Answer (C) is incorrect because the audit field work standards for supervision are the same whether or not a computer is used. Answer (D) is incorrect because audit staff typically have skills appropriate for the use of personal computers in documenting the work product of the audit.

46. A bank implemented an expert system to help account representatives consolidate the bank's relationships with each customer. The expert system has

- A. A sequential control structure.
- B. Distinct input-output variables.
- C. A knowledge base.
- D. Passive data elements.

Answer (C) is correct. *(CIA, adapted)*
REQUIRED: The component of an expert system.
DISCUSSION: An expert system relies on a computer's ability to make decisions in a human way. An expert system has the following components: knowledge base, domain database, database management system, inference engine, user interface, and knowledge acquisition facility. The knowledge base contains the rules used when making decisions.

Answer (A) is incorrect because traditional programs, e.g., in COBOL, have sequential control structures; expert systems do not. Answer (B) is incorrect because traditional programs, not expert systems, have distinct input-output variables. Answer (D) is incorrect because traditional programs, not expert systems, have passive data elements.

47. Specialized audit software

- A. Is written to interface with many different client systems.
- B. May be written while its purposes and users are being defined.
- C. Requires the auditor to have less computer expertise than generalized audit software.
- D. May be written in a procedure-oriented language.

Answer (D) is correct. *(Publisher)*
REQUIRED: The true statement regarding specialized audit software.
DISCUSSION: Specialized audit software is written in a procedure- or problem-oriented language to fulfill a specific set of audit tasks. The purposes and users of the software are well defined before the software is written. Auditors develop specialized audit software for the following reasons:

1. Unavailability of alternative software
2. Functional limitations of alternative software
3. Efficiency considerations
4. Increased understanding of systems
5. Opportunity for easy implementation
6. Increased auditor independence and prestige

Answer (A) is incorrect because generalized audit software is written to interface with many different client systems. Answer (B) is incorrect because the purposes and users of this software must be defined before it is written. Answer (C) is incorrect because generalized audit software purchased "off the shelf" requires less computer expertise than specialized software created by the auditor.

Use Gleim's *CPA Test Prep* for interactive testing with over 2,000 additional multiple-choice questions!

10.5 PRACTICE SIMULATION

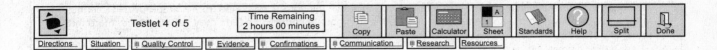

		Time Remaining						
	Testlet 4 of 5	2 hours 00 minutes	Copy	Paste	Calculator	Sheet	Standards	Help	Split	Done

Directions | Situation | Quality Control | Evidence | Confirmations | Communication | Research | Resources

1. Directions

In the following simulation, you will be asked to complete various tasks related to leases and contingencies. The simulation will provide all of the information necessary to do the work. For full credit, be sure to view and complete all work tabs.

Resources are available to you under the tab marked RESOURCES. You may want to review the resources before beginning the simulation.

2. Situation

Rex King, CPA, is auditing the financial statements of Cycle Co. Most of King's work in forming his opinion on Cycle's financial statements consists of obtaining and evaluating evidential matter concerning Cycle's management assertions in the financial statements

3. Quality Control

This question has a matching format that requires you to select the correct response from a drop-down list. Write the letter for each answer in the shaded column next to the appropriate assertion. Each choice may be used once, more than once, or not at all.

For each of the following, determine which assertion that management is making relative to the financial statements.

Assertions	Answer
1. Cycle Co. asserts that all transactions and accounts that should be present in the financial statements are included.	
2. Cycle Co. asserts that its assets and liabilities exist and the recorded transactions occurred during the current year.	
3. Cycle Co. asserts that the components of the financial statements are properly classified, described, and disclosed.	
4. Cycle Co. asserts that assets reported are owned by the entity and the liabilities are the obligations of the entity as of year-end.	
5. Cycle Co. asserts that all assets, liabilities, revenues, and expenses have been included in the financial statements at the appropriate amounts.	

Choices
A) Rights and obligations
B) Presentation and disclosure
C) Completeness
D) Existence or occurrence
E) Valuation or allocation

4. Evidence

This question has a matching format that requires you to select the correct response from a drop-down list. Write the letter for each answer in the shaded column next to the appropriate item. Each term may be used once, more than once, or not at all.

Each of the following items relating to audit evidence should be matched with the term with which it is most likely associated.

Evidence-Related Item	Answer
1. Test count of inventory	
2. Ownership rights	
3. Payroll register	
4. Employee payroll check	
5. Completeness	
6. Measure of importance	
7. Tracing a purchase into the ledger	
8. Confirmation of an accounts receivable	
9. Occurrence	
10. Invoice	

Terms
A) Assertion
B) Underlying accounting data
C) Information technology
D) Materiality
E) Test of the details of a balance
F) Corroborating evidential matter
G) Test of the details of a transaction

5. Confirmation Process

This question is presented in a check-the-box format.

Determine which statements about the confirmation process are correct. Check the shaded box to the right if the statement is correct.

Statement	Correct
1. A confirmation is the process of obtaining and evaluating a direct communication from the client.	
2. Confirmations provide primary evidence concerning the existence assertion.	
3. Positive confirmation requests a reply regardless of whether the respondent agrees with the information stated.	
4. The client should control the confirmations during the process to ensure that they are mailed properly.	
5. When using negative confirmations, the auditor should send a second request if the first is not returned.	
6. A FAX could be considered a confirmation if received from an appropriate party.	
7. Confirmation of accounts receivable need not be performed if the balance is immaterial.	
8. An auditor never sends a third confirmation request if previous requests have not been answered.	
9. The auditor uses the audit risk assessment to determine the appropriate form and extent of confirmations.	
10. The auditor can use information from the audits of similar entities in determining the expected effectiveness of the use of confirmations.	

6. Communication

In a brief memorandum to a staff member, describe the appropriate alternative procedures to be performed when some customers of the client do not respond to positive accounts receivable confirmations. Type your communication in your word processor program and print out the copy in a memorandum style format.

REMINDER: Your response will be graded for both technical content and writing skills. You should demonstrate your ability to develop, organize, and express your ideas. Do not convey information in the form of a table, bullet point list, or other abbreviated presentation.

To: Staff
From: CPA
Subject: Nature of positive receivables confirmation requests and alternative procedures when customers do not respond to them.

7. Research

Find the answer to the following question in the AICPA Professional Standards using the materials available in the Resources tab. What are the illustrative audit objectives and examples of substantive tests for the completeness assertion?

Print the appropriate citation in its entirety. This is a copy-and-paste item. Write the corresponding AU section numbers in the boxes provided below. Cite the three appropriate auditing standards (out of the ten) that should be demonstrated in the auditor's documentation (working papers)

AU Section

AU Section

AU Section

Unofficial Answers

3. Assertions (5 Gradable Items)

1. <u>C) - Completeness</u>. The completeness assertion relates to whether the account balance contains all the transactions for the reporting period.

2. <u>D) - Existence or occurrence</u>. The existence or occurrence assertion relates to whether the assets and liabilities reported on the financial statements exist and whether the transactions in the statements occurred.

3. <u>B) - Presentation and disclosure</u>. The statement presentation and disclosure assertion relates to proper descriptions and classifications in the financial statements, including appropriate footnotes.

4. <u>A) - Rights and obligations</u>. The rights and obligations assertion relates to whether the client has ownership rights to the assets and has obligations for the reported liabilities.

5. <u>E) - Valuation or allocation</u>. The valuation or allocation assertion relates to whether the assets, liabilities, and capital accounts are reported in accordance with GAAP and whether proper allocations have been made (e.g., depreciation).

4. Evidence (10 Gradable Items)

1. <u>E) - Test of the details of a balance</u> is the term most associated with a test count of inventory.

2. <u>A) - Assertion</u> is the term most associated with ownership rights.

3. <u>B) - Underlying accounting data</u> is the term most associated with payroll register.

4. <u>F) - Corroborating evidential matter</u> is the term most associated with employee payroll check.

5. <u>A) - Assertion</u> is the term most associated with completeness.

6. <u>D) - Materiality</u> is the term most associated with measure of importance.

7. <u>G) - Test of the details of a transaction</u> is the term most associated with tracing a purchase into the ledger.

8. <u>E) - Test of the details of a balance</u> is the term most associated with confirmation of an accounts receivable.

9. <u>A) - Assertion</u> is the term most associated with occurrence.

10. <u>F) - Corroborating evidential matter</u> is the term most associated with invoice.

5. Confirmation Process (10 Gradable Items)

A. This statement is <u>not correct</u> because a confirmation is the process of obtaining and evaluating a direct communication from a third party in response to a request for information about a particular item.

B. This statement is <u>correct</u>.

C. This statement is <u>correct</u>.

D. This statement is <u>not correct</u> because, the auditor should control the confirmations during the process to ensure that they are mailed properly.

E. This statement is <u>not correct</u> because, when negative confirmations are sent, the recipient is only to respond if (s)he disagrees with the information stated.

F. This statement is <u>correct</u>.

G. This statement is <u>correct</u>.

H. This statement is <u>not correct</u> because when positive confirmations are sent, the auditor should usually follow up with a second and, if applicable, a third request to parties who did not respond.

I. This statement is <u>correct</u>.

J. This statement is <u>correct</u>.

6. Communication (5 Gradable Items; For grading instructions, please refer to page 11.)

To: Staff
From: CPA
Subject: Nature of positive receivables confirmation requests and alternative procedures when customers do not respond to them.

The positive confirmation requests a reply regardless of whether the respondent agrees with the information stated. It may ask the respondent to state whether (s)he agrees with the information given or request that the recipient fill in an account balance (termed a blank form) or provide other information. Positive forms provide evidence only when responses are received from the recipients. Blank forms mitigate the risk that the recipients of a positive confirmation request will sign and return the request without verifying the information. However, blank forms tend to have lower response rates because recipients must take additional effort. Thus, more alternative procedures may be needed.

When the auditor has not received replies to positive confirmation requests, (s)he should apply alternative procedures to the nonresponses to reduce audit risk to an acceptably low level. The omission of alternative procedures may be warranted when the auditor has not identified unusual qualitative factors or systematic characteristics related to the nonresponses. Omission also may be appropriate when, given testing for overstatement, treating the aggregate nonresponses as 100% misstatements would not affect the auditor's decision about whether the financial statements are materially misstated. The nature of alternative procedures varies with the account and the assertion. Comparison of subsequent receipts of accounts receivable with actual items being paid is an acceptable alternative to positive confirmations. Another alternative is the review of shipping and other client source documents to verify that the goods/services were ordered (purchase orders) and shipped (bills of lading).

7. Research (6 Gradable Items)

AU 326 – *Evidential Matter*

Completeness

Inventory quantities include all products, materials and supplies on hand.

- Observing physical inventory counts.
- Analytically comparing the relationship of inventory balances to recent purchasing, production, and sales activities.
- Testing shipping and receiving cutoff procedures.

Inventory quantities include all products, materials, and supplies owned by the company that are in transit or stored at outside locations.

- Obtaining confirmation of inventories at locations outside the entity.
- Analytically comparing the relationship of inventory balances to recent purchasing, production, and sales activities.
- Testing shipping and receiving cutoff procedures.

Illustrative Audit Objectives

Inventory listings are accurately compiled and the totals are properly included in the inventory accounts.

Examples of Substantive Tests

- Tracing test counts recorded during the physical inventory observation to the inventory listing.
- Accounting for all inventory tags and count sheets used in recording the physical inventory counts.
- Testing the clerical accuracy of inventory listings.
- Reconciling physical counts to perpetual records and general ledger balances and investigating significant fluctuations.

Scoring Schedule:

	Correct Responses		Gradable Items		Weights		
Tab 3	_____	÷	5	×	20%	=	_____
Tab 4	_____	÷	10	×	20%	=	_____
Tab 5	_____	÷	10	×	20%	=	_____
Tab 6	_____	÷	5	×	30%	=	_____
Tab 7	_____	÷	6	×	10%	=	_____

(Your Score)

Use Gleim's *CPA Review Online* to practice more simulations in a realistic environment.

STUDY UNIT ELEVEN
EVIDENCE -- THE SALES-RECEIVABLES-CASH CYCLE

(8 pages of outline)

11.1	Substantive Testing of Sales and Receivables	.351
11.2	Substantive Testing of Cash	.354
11.3	Practice Simulation	.369

The primary purpose of the collection of evidence is to test management's assertions about the balances in the financial statements. Development of the audit program requires the determination of specific objectives related to the assertions. Many audit tests are directed toward the detection of the overstatement of sales, receivables, and cash in recognition of the related audit risks. The purpose of this study unit is to develop a comprehensive audit program for the sales-receivables-cash cycle. The program includes the customary procedures assuming no unusual risks. Some of the CPA questions that follow the study outlines in this study unit concern special risks that require modification of the audit program. The candidate should consider those questions and problems and practice modification of programs to address special risks.

The technique described below is a plan for audit program development that may be used in answering CPA exam questions. Application of the assertions model (COVES is the mnemonic for the five categories of assertions) assures that all assertions are tested. However, other formats for presentation of the steps are acceptable.

11.1 SUBSTANTIVE TESTING OF SALES AND RECEIVABLES

1. **Accounts receivable** are the entity's claims against customers that have arisen from the sale of goods or services in the normal course of business and from a financial institution's loans.

2. Revenues result from an entity's ongoing major or central operations, for example, sales of goods or services. Testing assertions about accounts receivable results in evidence relevant to the assertions about sales revenues and vice versa. Thus, testing for the completeness of sales also tests the completeness of receivables because a credit to sales ordinarily is accompanied by a debit to receivables, an entry that is recorded in the sales journal. Special journals are designed to record a large volume of similar items. Entries not suitable for one of the special journals are recorded in the general journal.

   a. **SEC Staff Accounting Bulletin (SAB) 101** provides guidance for the reporting of revenue in financial statements filed with the SEC, including the criteria for revenue recognition. SAB 101 follows current GAAP but applies them to transactions not addressed in the authoritative literature.

   b. Special consideration of sales-related accounts follows this audit program.

3. The following is a standard program for sales and receivables that tests management's assertions about COVES:

   a. **C**ompleteness. Do the balances of sales and receivables contain all transactions for the period?

      1) Compare (reconcile) the total recorded amounts in the subsidiary ledger with the accounts receivable amount recorded in the general ledger.

      2) Sales cutoff test. Test to determine that a sale and receivable were recorded when title passed to the customer, which often occurs when goods are shipped (i.e., when terms are **FOB shipping point**). Shipping documents are traced to the accounting records for several days prior to and after year-end to determine proper recognition in the appropriate period of the sale and receivable. This test detects inflated sales.

      3) Analytical procedures. Use the appropriate sources of data (e.g., prior experience, budgets prepared by management at the beginning of the period, nonfinancial data, industry information, and interrelationships) to develop expectations to compare with management's presentations. Calculate and compare ratios for the current period, for example, the accounts receivable turnover ratio (net credit sales ÷ average accounts receivable), with those of prior periods and industry norms.

      4) Cash receipts cutoff test. Test the recording of the receipts of cash and the associated reduction in accounts receivable. Inspection and tracing of the daily remittance list for several days prior to and after year-end will provide evidence of proper recording.

      5) Account for the numerical sequence of sales-related documents such as sales orders, shipping documents, and invoices.

      6) Vouch shipping documents back to sales invoices and journal entries to test whether the related sales were recorded at the time of sale.

   b. Rights and **O**bligations. Does the entity have the right to collect receivables?

      1) Inquiries of management. Consider the motivation and opportunity for factoring or selling the receivables and inquire of management as to whether such transactions have occurred.

      2) Track cash receipts to determine that the entity is collecting and depositing the proceeds into bank accounts controlled by the entity.

      3) Determine whether sales have been made with a right of return and what the expected and actual returns are after year-end.

   c. **V**aluation or allocation. Are accounts receivable valued in accordance with GAAP, e.g., net realizable value (gross accounts receivable – allowance for uncollectible accounts)?

      1) Age the accounts receivable. Classify the receivables by age and compare percentages within classifications with those of the prior year.

      2) Trace subsequent cash receipts. Cash receipts after the balance sheet date provide the best evidence of collectibility. By the end of the field work, the auditor should be able to judge the likely collections of the outstanding balances and determine whether the allowance for uncollectibles is sufficient to properly value the year-end balance of receivables.

      3) Review delinquent customers' credit ratings. This step provides evidence for assessing uncollectibility.

d. **E**xistence or Occurrence. Are the accounts receivable valid assets? Did sales occur?

1) Confirm accounts receivable (also tests the rights and valuation assertions).

   a) Confirmation of accounts receivable is a generally accepted auditing procedure. Moreover, confirmation at year-end provides greater assurance than at an interim date. The auditor will confirm accounts receivable unless they are immaterial, confirmation would be ineffective, or risk of misstatement based on other procedures is judged to be sufficiently low.

   b) An auditor who has not confirmed accounts receivable should document how (s)he overcame this presumption.

   c) Confirming receivables may detect lapping because the company's and customer's records of lapped accounts will differ. **Lapping** is the theft of a cash payment from one customer concealed by crediting that customer's account when a second customer makes a payment.

   d) Confirmation may also detect an improper cutoff. If the client held open the sales journal after year-end and improperly recorded sales and receivables for the period under audit rather than for the subsequent period, responses to confirmations would indicate that the amounts owed as of year-end are smaller than the recorded amounts.

   e) When customers fail to answer a second request for a positive confirmation, the accounts may be in dispute, uncollectible, or fictitious. The auditor should then apply alternative procedures (examination of subsequent cash receipts, shipping documents, and other client documentation of existence to obtain evidence about the validity of nonresponding accounts.

2) Vouch recorded accounts receivable to shipping documents. Because shipment of goods is typically the event creating the sale and receivable, vouching recorded receivables to shipping documents, such as bills of lading, tests for existence.

3) Vouch a sample of recorded sales transactions to customer orders and shipping documents. Large and unusual sales should be included in the sample selected for testing. This test is directed toward the occurrence assertion concerning sales and is useful for detecting overstatements.

e. **S**tatement Presentation and Disclosure. Are sales and receivables presented properly on the financial statements?

1) Inspect the income statement and balance sheet to determine that sales are shown on the income statement as a revenue, minus returns and allowances. Accounts receivable should be presented as a current asset, minus the allowance for uncollectible accounts.

2) Read note disclosures to determine that accounting policies are disclosed (e.g., accounts receivable should be presented at net realizable value). Pledges of accounts receivable should be disclosed. Any significant sales or receivables transactions with related parties should also be disclosed.

3) Obtain a management representations letter that includes assertions relating to sales and receivables.

4) Determine whether an entity has appropriately identified its reportable operating segments in accordance with SFAS 131 and evaluate management's disclosures about reportable operating segments and related information, including products and services, geographic areas, and major customers.

4. **Tests of Assertions and Specific Objectives for Accounts Related to the Sales and Receivables Cycle**

    a. Sales returns and allowances. Although the auditor should test all assertions, if control risk is low, the primary tests will concern the existence or occurrence assertion. Was there a proper authorization for the return of goods, and were those goods actually returned?

        1) The auditor ordinarily tests the documentation that supports the return to determine whether proper authorization exists and the credit to the customer's account was supported by a receiving report representing the return of goods.

    b. Write-off of bad debts. If control risk is relatively low, the audit program for accounts receivable described above should provide sufficient competent evidence about bad debts. However, if controls are weak, for example, if the accounting function (the accounts receivable bookkeeper) is allowed to approve write-offs, the auditor will perform specific tests to control for the risks.

        1) Thus, the auditor might decide to attempt to confirm the receivables previously written off. If the write-offs were legitimate, most requests will be marked *Return to Sender* because the debtors will probably not be in business.

5. Stop and review! You have completed the outline for this subunit. Study multiple-choice questions 1 through 21 beginning on page 359.

11.2 SUBSTANTIVE TESTING OF CASH

1. **C**ompleteness. Does the balance at the end of the accounting period reflect all cash transactions?

    a. Cash cutoff tests. For cash receipts, trace the daily remittance list to the last validated deposit ticket for the period. For cash disbursements, determine the last check written for the period and trace the effect to the accounting records. Determine that all outstanding checks have been listed on the bank reconciliation.

    b. Analytical procedures. Use of analytical procedures is not typically as effective for cash as for most other accounts because it is a managed account. However, the auditor may be able to use management's budget, prepared at the beginning of the period, as an expectation with which to compare the year-end balance.

2. Rights and **O**bligations. Does the entity have ownership rights to the cash? In most cases, risks related to ownership are low and few specific tests are applied. However, confirmation procedures discussed with respect to the existence assertion provide evidence for this assertion. Inquiries of management are also appropriate.

3. **V**aluation or allocation. Is the asset valued in accordance with GAAP? U.S. currency has low inherent risk relative to this assertion. However, special circumstances, such as holdings of foreign currency, may require additional testing.

4. **E**xistence or occurrence. Does cash exist? Because inherent risk is high for cash, most audit procedures are directed toward existence.

    a. Count cash on hand.

        1) Control all cash and negotiable securities to protect against substitution.

        2) Determine that all received checks are payable to the client.

        3) Determine that all received checks are endorsed "For Deposit Only into Account Number XXXX."

b.   Bank confirmation. The AICPA Standard Form to Confirm Account Balance Information with Financial Institutions is used for specific deposits and loans.

   1)   A confirmation is requested by (i.e., signed by) the client, but it should be sent by the CPA to any bank with which the client has had business during the period.

   2)   The form confirms the account name, account number, interest rate, and balance for deposits.

   3)   For direct liabilities on loans, the form confirms account number/description, balance, due date, interest rate, date through which interest is paid, and description of collateral.

   4)   To confirm other transactions and written or oral arrangements, such as contingent liabilities, lines of credit, compensating balances, and security agreements, auditors send a separate letter, signed by the client, to an official responsible for the financial institution's relationship with the client.

   5)   According to AU 330, the standard form (and separate letter) is designed to substantiate only the information that is stated on the confirmation request. Thus, the auditor should be aware that the standard form is not intended to elicit evidence about the completeness assertion.

       a)   Nevertheless, the standard confirmation form contains this language: "Although we do not request or expect you to conduct a comprehensive, detailed search of your records, if during the process of completing this confirmation, additional information about other deposit and loan accounts we may have with you comes to your attention, please include such information below."

c.   Bank reconciliation. Inspect or prepare bank reconciliations for each account.

   1)   A bank reconciliation verifies the agreement of the bank statements obtained directly from the institution and the amount of cash reported in the financial statements. These amounts should be equal after adjustment for deposits in transit, outstanding checks, bank charges, etc.

d.   Cutoff bank statement. It should be requested directly from the bank for the period 7 to 10 days after year-end. Use this statement to test reconciling items on the year-end bank reconciliation, e.g., deposits in transit and outstanding checks.

   1)   Search for checks written before year-end but not listed as outstanding on the bank reconciliation. These checks are often evidence of a fraud termed **kiting**, which results from an improper recording of a bank transfer.

       a)   To cover a shortage of cash (cash is recorded in the accounting records but not in the bank's), an employee would write a check just prior to year-end on the disbursing bank but not record the disbursement in the accounting records in the current year. Furthermore, the check would not appear as a disbursement on the disbursing bank's year-end bank statement because it would not have cleared. However, the receipt would be recorded by the receiving bank (at least as a deposit in transit), thereby covering the shortage. In the short term, the cash balance will appear to reconcile.

       b)   To uncover the fraud, the auditor should match the returned checks written prior to year-end from the cutoff bank statement with the outstanding checks on the bank reconciliation of the disbursing bank. Since the kited check was not recorded, it will not be listed as outstanding.

   2)   Consider the number of checks returned in the cutoff bank statement. This procedure may provide evidence of window dressing, that is, trying to improve the current ratio. The client may write checks to pay current liabilities but not mail them until the next accounting period.

STANDARD FINANCIAL INSTITUTION CONFIRMATION FORM

STANDARD FORM TO CONFIRM ACCOUNT
BALANCE INFORMATION WITH FINANCIAL INSTITUTIONS

ORIGINAL
To be mailed to accountant

CUSTOMER NAME

We have provided to our accountants the following information as of

the close of business on _____, 20 _____,
regarding our deposit and loan balances. Please confirm the
accuracy of the information, noting any exceptions to the information
provided. If the balances have been left blank, please complete this
form by furnishing the balance in the appropriate space below.*
Although we do not request nor expect you to conduct a
comprehensive, detailed search of your records, if during the process
of completing this confirmation additional information about other
deposit and loan accounts we may have with you comes to your
attention, please include such information below. Please use the
enclosed envelope to return the form directly to our accountants.

Financial
Institution's   [   ]
Name and
Address

                   [   ]

1. At the close of business on the date listed above, our records indicated the following deposit balance(s):

ACCOUNT NAME	ACCOUNT NO.	INTEREST RATE	BALANCE*

2. We were directly liable to the financial institution for loans at the close of business on the date listed above as follows:

ACCOUNT NO./ DESCRIPTION	BALANCE*	DATE DUE	INTEREST RATE	DATE THROUGH WHICH INTEREST IS PAID	DESCRIPTION OF COLLATERAL

_____   _____
(Customer's Authorized Signature)   (Date)

The information presented above by the customer is in agreement with our records. Although we have not conducted a comprehensive, detailed search of our records, no other deposit or loan accounts have come to our attention except as noted below.

_____   _____
(Financial Institution Authorized Signature)   Date)

_____
(Title)

EXCEPTIONS AND/OR COMMENTS

Please return this form directly to our accountants: [   ]

*Ordinarily, balances are intentionally left blank if they are not   [   ]
available at the time the form is prepared.

Approved 1990 by American Bankers Association, American Institute of Certified Public Accountants, and Bank Administration   D451 5951
Institute. Additional forms available from: AICPA - Order Department, P.O. Box 1003, NY, NY 10108-1003

EXAMPLE OF LETTER TO CONFIRM OTHER FINANCIAL INSTITUTION INFORMATION

(Date)
Financial Institution Official
First United Bank
Anytown, USA 00000

Dear Financial Institution Official:

In connection with an audit of the financial statements of *(name of customer)* as of *(balance sheet date)* and for the *(period)* then ended, we have advised our independent auditors of the information listed below, which we believe is a complete and accurate description of our contingent liabilities, including oral and written guarantees, with your financial institution. Although we do not request nor expect you to conduct a comprehensive, detailed search of your records, if during the process of completing this confirmation additional information about other contingent liabilities, including oral and written guarantees, between *(name of customer)* and your financial institution comes to your attention, please include such information below.

Name of Maker	Date of Note	Due Date	Current Balance

Interest Rate	Date Through Which Interest Is Paid	Description of Collateral	Description of Purpose of Note

Information related to oral and written guarantees is as follows:

_____

_____

_____

Please confirm whether the information about contingent liabilities presented above is correct by signing below and returning this directly to our independent auditors *(name and address of CPA firm)*.

Sincerely,

(Name of Customer)

_____

By: _____
        (Authorized Signature)

Dear CPA Firm:

The above information listing contingent liabilities, including oral and written guarantees, agrees with the records of this financial institution. Although we have not conducted a comprehensive, detailed search of our records, no information about other contingent liabilities, including oral and written guarantees, came to our attention. [Note exceptions below or in an attached letter.]

_____

_____

_____

_____
(Name of Financial Institution)

By: _____ _____
        (Officer and Title)   *(Date)*

e. Prepare a schedule of interbank transfers. This procedure can help detect errors in transfers but may not be effective in the detection of kiting because the disbursement has not been recorded. For this procedure to be effective, the auditor should be assured that all transfers have been identified.

f.   Proof of cash. When control risk is high (when control activities for the transaction process are not effective), a proof of cash may be prepared. It provides direct evidence that both the beginning and ending balances as well as deposit and disbursement transactions recorded by the bank reconcile with transactions recorded in the accounting records for a period of time, typically a month.

5.   **S**tatement Presentation and Disclosure. Is cash properly classified, described, and disclosed in the financial statements?

a.   Inquire of management about disclosure. Include references to cash in the management representations letter.

b.   Determine that restricted cash (e.g., sinking funds and compensating balances) is reported in the noncurrent asset section of the balance sheet.

c.   Assess statement of cash flows.

1)   Determine proper presentation: direct or indirect method.

2)   Reconcile information with income statement and balance sheet presentations.

3)   Examine elements of statement of cash flows classifications: operating activities, investing activities, and financing activities.

d.   Read financial statement note disclosures.

6.   Stop and review! You have completed the outline for this subunit. Study multiple-choice questions 22 through 32 beginning on page 365.

QUESTIONS

11.1 Substantive Testing of Sales and Receivables

1. Which of the following comparisons would be most useful to an auditor in evaluating the results of an entity's operations?

A. Prior-year accounts payable to current-year accounts payable.

B. Prior-year payroll expense to budgeted current-year payroll expense.

C. Current-year revenue to budgeted current-year revenue.

D. Current-year warranty expense to current-year contingent liabilities.

Answer (C) is correct. *(CPA, adapted)*
REQUIRED: The best comparison for evaluating the results of operations.
DISCUSSION: Revenues result from an entity's ongoing major or central operations. These operations reflect numerous activities and affect many accounts. Consequently, comparing current-year revenue with the budgeted current-year revenue provides evidence as to the completeness of revenue. Revenue is a broad measure of the effects of the entity's main activities and is a primary component of the results of operations.
Answer (A) is incorrect because the change in accounts payable is too narrow a measure to be useful in this evaluation. Answer (B) is incorrect because payroll expense is too narrow a measure to be useful in this evaluation. Answer (D) is incorrect because the relationship of warranty expense and contingent liabilities is too narrow a measure to be useful in this evaluation.

2. An auditor most likely would limit substantive audit tests of sales transactions when control risk is assessed as low for the existence or occurrence assertion concerning sales transactions and the auditor has already gathered evidence supporting

A. Opening and closing inventory balances.

B. Cash receipts and accounts receivable.

C. Shipping and receiving activities.

D. Cutoffs of sales and purchases.

Answer (B) is correct. *(CPA, adapted)*
REQUIRED: The evidence related to the existence or occurrence assertion for sales transactions.
DISCUSSION: Cash receipts and accounts receivable have a direct relationship with sales. A cash sale results in a debit to cash and a credit to sales. A sale on account results in a debit to accounts receivable and a credit to sales. Thus, evidence related to cash receipts and accounts receivable provides assurances about sales.
Answer (A) is incorrect because the opening and closing inventory balances do not directly affect the sales transactions. Answer (C) is incorrect because, although shipping activities are related to sales, receiving activities are not. Answer (D) is incorrect because, although cutoffs of sales provide evidence as to sales transactions, cutoffs of purchases do not.

3. If the objective of a test of details is to detect overstatements of sales, the auditor should compare transactions in the

A. Cash receipts journal with the sales journal.

B. Sales journal with the cash receipts journal.

C. Source documents with the accounting records.

D. Accounting records with the source documents.

Answer (D) is correct. *(CPA, adapted)*
REQUIRED: The appropriate test to detect overstatement of sales.
DISCUSSION: Overstatements of sales likely result from entries with no supporting documentation. The proper direction of testing is to sample entries in the sales account and vouch them to the shipping documents. The source documents represent the valid sales.
Answer (A) is incorrect because the cash receipts journal and the sales journal are books of original entry, not source documents. Answer (B) is incorrect because the cash receipts journal and the sales journal are books of original entry, not source documents. Answer (C) is incorrect because the proper direction of testing is from the accounting records to the source documents.

4. Tracing shipping documents to prenumbered sales invoices provides evidence that

A. No duplicate shipments or billings occurred.

B. Shipments to customers were properly invoiced.

C. All goods ordered by customers were shipped.

D. All prenumbered sales invoices were accounted for.

Answer (B) is correct. *(CPA, adapted)*
REQUIRED: The evidence provided by tracing shipping documents to prenumbered sales invoices.
DISCUSSION: The direction of testing to determine that shipments to customers were properly invoiced is from the shipping documents to the sales invoices.
Answer (A) is incorrect because tracing a sample of customer orders to the shipping documents provides evidence about duplicate shipments. Answer (C) is incorrect because tracing sales orders to shipping documents provides evidence that all goods ordered by customers were shipped. Answer (D) is incorrect because accounting for all the numbered invoices provides assurance that no invoices were lost or misplaced.

5. An auditor most likely would review an entity's periodic accounting for the numerical sequence of shipping documents and invoices to support management's financial statement assertion of

A. Existence or occurrence.

B. Rights and obligations.

C. Valuation or allocation.

D. Completeness.

Answer (D) is correct. *(CPA, adapted)*

REQUIRED: The assertion supported by reviewing the numerical sequence of shipping documents and invoices.

DISCUSSION: The completeness assertion concerns whether all transactions that should be presented are included. Testing the numerical sequence of shipping documents and invoices is a means of detecting omitted items.

Answer (A) is incorrect because the existence or occurrence assertion deals with whether assets or liabilities exist at a given date and whether recorded transactions have occurred. Answer (B) is incorrect because the rights and obligations assertion concerns whether assets are the rights of the entity and liabilities are obligations at a given date. Answer (C) is incorrect because the valuation or allocation assertion concerns whether assets, liabilities, revenues, and expenses have been included at appropriate amounts.

6. An entity's financial statements were misstated over a period of years because large amounts of revenue were recorded in journal entries that involved debits and credits to an illogical combination of accounts. The auditor could most likely have been alerted to this fraud by

A. Scanning the general journal for unusual entries.

B. Performing a revenue cutoff test at year-end.

C. Tracing a sample of journal entries to the general ledger.

D. Examining documentary evidence of sales returns and allowances recorded after year-end.

Answer (A) is correct. *(CPA, adapted)*

REQUIRED: The procedure to detect misstatement of revenue as a result of illogical entries.

DISCUSSION: The general journal is a book of original entry used for transactions not suitable for recording in the special journals (sales, purchases, cash receipts, cash disbursements). Entries involving unusual combinations of accounts are more likely to appear in the general journal than in one of the special journals, which are designed to record large numbers of similar items. For example, credit sales (debit accounts receivable, credit sales) are entered in the sales journal.

Answer (B) is incorrect because a revenue cutoff is a test of the timing of recognition. Moreover, it applies to transactions at year-end only. Answer (C) is incorrect because tracing journal entries will only test whether recorded transactions were posted to the ledger. Answer (D) is incorrect because this procedure applies to year-end transactions only.

7. Which of the following might be detected by an auditor's review of the client's sales cutoff?

A. Excessive goods returned for credit.

B. Unrecorded sales discounts.

C. Lapping of year-end accounts receivable.

D. Inflated sales for the year.

Answer (D) is correct. *(CPA, adapted)*

REQUIRED: The condition that might be detected by review of the client's sales cutoff.

DISCUSSION: Sales cutoff tests are designed to detect the client's manipulation of sales. By examining recorded sales for several days before and after the balance sheet date and comparing them with sales invoices and shipping documents, the auditor may detect the recording of a sale in a period other than that in which title passed. The completeness assertion is the primary focus of the cutoff tests.

Answer (A) is incorrect because sales returns are not examined in the sales cutoff test. Answer (B) is incorrect because examination of cash receipts would reveal unrecorded discounts. Answer (C) is incorrect because lapping may be detected by the confirmation of customer balances and tracing amounts received according to duplicate deposit slips to the accounts receivable subsidiary ledger.

8. Cutoff tests designed to detect credit sales made before the end of the year that have been recorded in the subsequent year provide assurance about management's assertion of

A. Presentation.

B. Completeness.

C. Rights.

D. Existence.

Answer (B) is correct. *(CPA, adapted)*

REQUIRED: The management assertion about which assurance is provided by cutoff tests.

DISCUSSION: The completeness assertion is tested by examining recorded sales for several days before and after the balance sheet date and comparing them with sales invoices and shipping documents. The auditor may detect the recording of a sale in a period other than that in which title passed.

Answer (A) is incorrect because the assertion about presentation and disclosure concerns whether financial statement components are properly classified, described, and disclosed. Answer (C) is incorrect because the rights and obligations assertion concerns whether assets are the rights of the entity and liabilities are obligations at a given date. Answer (D) is incorrect because the existence or occurrence assertion concerns whether assets or liabilities exist at a given date and whether recorded transactions have occurred.

9. Which of the following most likely would give the most assurance concerning the valuation assertion of accounts receivable?

A. Vouching amounts in the subsidiary ledger to details on shipping documents.

B. Comparing receivable turnover ratios with industry statistics for reasonableness.

C. Inquiring about receivables pledged under loan agreements.

D. Assessing the allowance for uncollectible accounts for reasonableness.

Answer (D) is correct. *(CPA, adapted)*
REQUIRED: The procedure providing the most assurance about the valuation of accounts receivable.
DISCUSSION: Assertions about valuation or allocation concern whether financial statement components have been included at appropriate amounts. For example, management asserts that trade accounts receivable are stated at net realizable value (gross accounts receivable minus allowance for uncollectible accounts). Hence, assessing the allowance provides assurance about the valuation of the account.
Answer (A) is incorrect because vouching amounts in the subsidiary ledger to details on shipping documents provides evidence about the occurrence assertion for transactions. Answer (B) is incorrect because comparing receivable turnover ratios with industry statistics for reasonableness provides evidence as to completeness. Answer (C) is incorrect because inquiring about receivables pledged under loan agreements pertains to presentation and disclosure assertions.

10. In evaluating the adequacy of the allowance for doubtful accounts, an auditor most likely reviews the entity's aging of receivables to support management's financial statement assertion of

A. Existence or occurrence.

B. Valuation or allocation.

C. Completeness.

D. Rights and obligations.

Answer (B) is correct. *(CPA, adapted)*
REQUIRED: The assertion tested by reviewing the entity's aging of receivables.
DISCUSSION: Assertions about valuation or allocation concern whether financial statement components have been included at appropriate amounts in accordance with GAAP. For example, management asserts that trade accounts receivable are stated at net realizable value (gross accounts receivable minus allowance for uncollectible accounts). Aging the receivables is a procedure for assessing the reasonableness of the allowance.
Answer (A) is incorrect because the existence or occurrence assertion deals with whether assets or liabilities exist at a given date and whether recorded transactions have occurred. Answer (C) is incorrect because the completeness assertion concerns whether all transactions that should be presented are included. Answer (D) is incorrect because the rights and obligations assertion concerns whether assets are the rights of the entity and liabilities are obligations at a given date.

11. An auditor's purpose in reviewing credit ratings of customers with delinquent accounts receivable most likely is to obtain evidence concerning management's assertions about

A. Presentation and disclosure.

B. Existence or occurrence.

C. Rights and obligations.

D. Valuation or allocation.

Answer (D) is correct. *(CPA, adapted)*
REQUIRED: The assertion about which evidence is provided by reviewing credit ratings of delinquent customers.
DISCUSSION: Assertions about valuation or allocation concern whether financial statement components have been included at appropriate amounts. Determining the realizable value of accounts receivable includes assessing whether the client's allowance for uncollectibility is reasonable. Reviewing the credit ratings of delinquent customers provides evidence for that purpose.
Answer (A) is incorrect because the assertion about presentation and disclosure concerns whether financial statement components are properly classified, described, and disclosed. Answer (B) is incorrect because the existence or occurrence assertion concerns whether assets or liabilities exist at a given date and whether recorded transactions have occurred. Answer (C) is incorrect because the rights and obligations assertion concerns whether assets are the rights of the entity and liabilities are obligations at a given date.

12. AU 330, *The Confirmation Process*, defines confirmation as "the process of obtaining and evaluating a direct communication from a third party in response to a request for information about a particular item affecting financial statement assertions." Two assertions for which confirmation of accounts receivable balances provides primary evidence are

A. Completeness and valuation.

B. Valuation and rights and obligations.

C. Rights and obligations and existence.

D. Existence and completeness.

Answer (C) is correct.   *(CPA, adapted)*
REQUIRED: The assertions tested by confirming receivables.
DISCUSSION: Confirmation by means of direct (independent) communication with debtors is the generally accepted auditing procedure for accounts receivable. Properly designed requests may address any assertion in the financial statements, but they are most likely to be effective for the existence and rights and obligations assertions. Thus, confirmation provides evidence that receivables are valid, that the client has ownership of the accounts and the right of collection, and that the debtor has the obligation to pay.
Answer (A) is incorrect because confirmation is not effective for the completeness assertion. It is unlikely to detect unrecorded accounts. Answer (B) is incorrect because confirmation is less effective for the valuation assertion than the existence and rights and obligations assertions. Answer (D) is incorrect because confirmation is less effective for the completeness assertion than the existence and rights and obligations assertions.

13. An auditor confirms a representative number of open accounts receivable as of December 31 and investigates respondents' exceptions and comments. By this procedure the auditor would be most likely to learn of which of the following?

A. One of the cashiers has been covering a personal embezzlement by lapping.

B. One of the sales clerks has not been preparing charge slips for credit sales to family and friends.

C. One of the computer control clerks has been removing all sales invoices applicable to his account from the data file.

D. The credit manager has misappropriated remittances from customers whose accounts have been written off.

Answer (A) is correct.   *(CPA, adapted)*
REQUIRED: The fraud most likely to be detected by confirming receivables.
DISCUSSION: Lapping is the theft of a cash payment from one customer concealed by crediting that customer's account when a second customer makes a payment. When lapping exists at the balance sheet date, the confirmation of customer balances will probably detect the fraud because the customers' and companies' records of lapped accounts will differ.
Answer (B) is incorrect because, if a charge slip has not been prepared, no accounts receivable balance will exist to be confirmed. Answer (C) is incorrect because, if a sales invoice is not processed, no account balance will appear in the records. Answer (D) is incorrect because, once the account has been written off, the account is no longer open.

14. An auditor suspects that a client's cashier is misappropriating cash receipts for personal use by lapping customer checks received in the mail. In attempting to uncover this embezzlement scheme, the auditor most likely would compare the

A. Dates checks are deposited per bank statements with the dates remittance credits are recorded.

B. Daily cash summaries with the sums of the cash receipts journal entries.

C. Individual bank deposit slips with the details of the monthly bank statements.

D. Dates uncollectible accounts are authorized to be written off with the dates the write-offs are actually recorded.

Answer (A) is correct.   *(CPA, adapted)*
REQUIRED: The procedure to detect lapping.
DISCUSSION: Lapping involves recording current cash payments on accounts receivable as credits to prior customers' accounts to conceal an abstraction of cash. Comparing the date that a customer's check was deposited with the date a record was made to reduce the balance would determine whether the deposit was made prior to the recording date.
Answer (B) is incorrect because the total cash received and deposited for any one day will reconcile when lapping occurs. Answer (C) is incorrect because the total cash received and deposited for any one day will reconcile when lapping occurs. Answer (D) is incorrect because lapping does not involve unauthorized write-offs.

15. An auditor who has confirmed accounts receivable may discover that the sales journal was held open past year-end if

A. Positive confirmations sent to debtors are not returned.

B. Negative confirmations sent to debtors are not returned.

C. Most of the returned negative confirmations indicate that the debtor owes a larger balance than the amount being confirmed.

D. Most of the returned positive confirmations indicate that the debtor owes a smaller balance than the amount being confirmed.

Answer (D) is correct. *(Publisher)*
REQUIRED: The result of confirmation indicating that the sales journal was held open past year-end.
DISCUSSION: When the majority of the returned positive confirmations indicate smaller balances at year-end than those in the client's records, the client may have held open the sales journal after year-end and debited customers' accounts for the period under audit rather than for the subsequent period. The effect is to overstate sales and receivables.
Answer (A) is incorrect because the failure to receive replies to positive confirmations may cause the auditor concern about the existence assertion. Answer (B) is incorrect because the failure to return negative confirmations provides some evidence about the existence assertion. Answer (C) is incorrect because replies indicating balances larger than those confirmed suggest that the sales journal was closed prior to year-end.

16. During the process of confirming receivables as of December 31, year 1, a positive confirmation was returned indicating the "balance owed as of December 31 was paid on January 9, year 2." The auditor would most likely

A. Determine whether there were any changes in the account between January 1 and January 9, year 2.

B. Determine whether a customary trade discount was taken by the customer.

C. Reconfirm the zero balance as of January 10, year 2.

D. Verify that the amount was received.

Answer (D) is correct. *(CPA, adapted)*
REQUIRED: The auditor action when a confirmation response states that the year-end balance was paid.
DISCUSSION: Responses to confirmations that involve significant differences are investigated by the auditor. Others are delegated to client employees with a request that explanations be given to the auditor. Such differences often arise because of recent cash payments. In that event, the auditor should trace remittances to verify that stated amounts were received.
Answer (A) is incorrect because the auditor wishes to confirm a year-end balance, not transactions in the subsequent period. Also, the reply does not suggest a discrepancy in the account. Answer (B) is incorrect because the auditor is more concerned with confirming the balance due at year-end than with whether a customer took a discount. Answer (C) is incorrect because reconfirmation is not required.

17. The auditor may consider confirming accounts receivable balances at an interim date if

A. Collections subsequent to year-end are to be reviewed.

B. The combined assessed level of inherent and control risk relative to financial statement assertions about receivables is acceptably low.

C. Negative confirmations are to be used for a sample of the accounts.

D. Cash and accounts receivable are audited at the same time.

Answer (B) is correct. *(Publisher)*
REQUIRED: The basis for confirming accounts receivable at an interim date.
DISCUSSION: If the combined assessed level of inherent and control risk for assertions about receivables is acceptably low, the auditor may decide to change the timing of the procedure, for example, by confirming these balances at interim dates rather than at year-end. The auditor is then expected to gain assurance that conclusions formed at the interim date are still valid at the balance sheet date.
Answer (A) is incorrect because a review of subsequent collections is typically performed to test the valuation assertion whether confirmations are performed at an interim date or year-end. Answer (C) is incorrect because negative confirmation is a less effective procedure than positive confirmation. Hence, it provides no basis for interim-date confirmation. Answer (D) is incorrect because cash should be audited with other highly liquid assets such as trading securities, not with accounts receivable.

18. To reduce the risks associated with accepting fax responses to requests for confirmations of accounts receivable, an auditor most likely would

A. Examine the shipping documents that provide evidence for the existence assertion.

B. Verify the sources and contents of the faxes in telephone calls to the senders.

C. Consider the faxes to be nonresponses and evaluate them as unadjusted differences.

D. Inspect the faxes for forgeries or alterations and consider them to be acceptable if none are noted.

Answer (B) is correct. *(CPA, adapted)*
REQUIRED: The procedure to reduce the risk of accepting false confirmations by fax.
DISCUSSION: Because establishing the source of a fax is often difficult, the auditor should ensure that the confirmations returned by fax are genuine. One way is to verify the sources by following up with telephone calls to the senders.
Answer (A) is incorrect because the purpose of the confirmation is to test the existence of the receivable by direct communication with the debtor. Answer (C) is incorrect because a fax is considered a valid response if the source can be verified. Answer (D) is incorrect because faxes may not be signed. Furthermore, the auditor is unlikely to be qualified to recognize forgeries.

19. Cooper, CPA, is auditing the financial statements of a small rural municipality. The receivable balances represent residents' delinquent real estate taxes. Internal control at the municipality is ineffective. To determine the existence of the accounts receivable balances at the balance sheet date, Cooper would most likely

A. Send positive confirmation requests.

B. Send negative confirmation requests.

C. Examine evidence of subsequent cash receipts.

D. Inspect the internal records such as copies of the tax invoices that were mailed to the residents.

Answer (A) is correct. *(CPA, adapted)*
REQUIRED: The best procedure to determine the existence of accounts receivable given an ineffective internal control.
DISCUSSION: The presumption that the auditor will request confirmation of receivables cannot be overcome unless the receivables are not material, confirmation is unlikely to be effective, or the combined assessed level of inherent risk and control risk is low. None of these conditions apply. Thus, the auditor should confirm the receivables. However, negative confirmations are not used unless the combined assessed level of inherent risk and control risk is low. Because control risk for the municipality is high, the auditor should send positive confirmation requests.
Answer (B) is incorrect because a negative confirmation does not require a reply if the balance is in agreement and therefore decreases the level of confidence of evidence. Answer (C) is incorrect because this procedure relates more to the valuation of accounts. Answer (D) is incorrect because replies to positive confirmation requests constitute independent external evidence that is more persuasive than that derived from inspection of internally generated documents.

20. When an auditor does not receive replies to positive requests for year-end accounts receivable confirmations, the auditor most likely would

A. Inspect the allowance account to verify whether the accounts were subsequently written off.

B. Increase the assessed level of detection risk for the valuation and completeness assertions.

C. Send the customer a second confirmation.

D. Increase the assessed level of inherent risk for the revenue cycle.

Answer (C) is correct. *(CPA, adapted)*
REQUIRED: The auditor action when positive confirmation requests are not returned.
DISCUSSION: When first requests for positive confirmation are not returned, the auditor should consider a second request. The request will be signed by the client, requesting the debtor to respond directly to the auditor.
Answer (A) is incorrect because it is premature to conclude that the account is uncollectible. Answer (B) is incorrect because the auditor must collect sufficient evidence to achieve the desired level of detection risk. It would be inappropriate to increase the level of risk. Answer (D) is incorrect because inherent risk is independent of control risk or the audit process.

21. Which of the following procedures would an auditor most likely perform for year-end accounts receivable confirmations when the auditor did not receive replies to second requests?

A. Review the cash receipts journal for the month prior to year-end.

B. Intensify the study of internal control concerning the revenue cycle.

C. Increase the assessed level of detection risk for the existence assertion.

D. Inspect the shipping records documenting the merchandise sold to the debtors.

Answer (D) is correct. *(CPA, adapted)*
REQUIRED: The most appropriate audit procedure when customers fail to reply to second request forms.
DISCUSSION: When customers fail to answer a second request for a positive confirmation, the accounts may be in dispute, uncollectible, or fictitious. The auditor should then apply alternative procedures (examination of subsequent cash receipts, shipping documents, and other client documentation of existence) to obtain evidence about the validity of nonresponding accounts (AU 330).
Answer (A) is incorrect because previous collections cannot substantiate year-end balances. Answer (B) is incorrect because nonresponse to a confirmation request is not proof of ineffective controls. Nonresponses do occur and are expected. Answer (C) is incorrect because control risk and inherent risk are assessed but detection risk is not. However, the acceptable level of detection risk may be decreased if the assessment of inherent risk or control risk is increased as a result of nonresponses to confirmation requests.

11.2 Substantive Testing of Cash

22. The best evidence regarding year-end bank balances is documented in the

A. Cutoff bank statement.

B. Bank reconciliations.

C. Interbank transfer schedule.

D. Bank deposit lead schedule.

Answer (B) is correct. *(CPA, adapted)*
REQUIRED: The best source of evidence regarding year-end bank balances.
DISCUSSION: A bank reconciliation verifies the agreement of the bank statements obtained directly from the institution and the amount of cash reported in the financial statements. These amounts should be equal after adjustment for deposits in transit, outstanding checks, bank charges, etc. Thus, a bank reconciliation documents direct (primary) evidence of the year-end bank balance.
Answer (A) is incorrect because the cutoff bank statement covers a brief period after the end of the period. Answer (C) is incorrect because only the record of transfer activity between banks is recorded on this schedule. Answer (D) is incorrect because the bank deposit lead schedule contains details supporting the cash amount in the working trial balance, but it is the bank reconciliation that supports the amounts in the lead schedule.

23. Which of the following sets of information does an auditor usually confirm on one form?

A. Accounts payable and purchase commitments.

B. Cash in bank and collateral for loans.

C. Inventory on consignment and contingent liabilities.

D. Accounts receivable and accrued interest receivable.

Answer (B) is correct. *(CPA, adapted)*
REQUIRED: The information confirmed on one form.
DISCUSSION: The AICPA Standard Form to Confirm Account Balance Information with Financial Institutions is used by auditors to confirm the deposit balance held by the bank for a client. In addition, this confirmation requests loan information, such as a description of the collateral securing the loan.
Answer (A) is incorrect because a confirmation of accounts payable balances requests information about purchase commitments. Answer (C) is incorrect because inventory on consignment is confirmed by a form sent to the consignee holding the inventory, and contingent liabilities are confirmed by a form sent to an official responsible for a financial institution's relationship with the client. Answer (D) is incorrect because a confirmation of accounts receivable does not provide information about interest that is owed to the client.

24. The primary purpose of sending a standard confirmation request to financial institutions with which the client has done business during the year is to

A. Detect kiting activities that may otherwise not be discovered.

B. Corroborate information regarding deposit and loan balances.

C. Provide the data necessary to prepare a proof of cash.

D. Request information about contingent liabilities and secured transactions.

Answer (B) is correct. *(CPA, adapted)*
REQUIRED: The primary purpose of sending a standard confirmation request to financial institutions.
DISCUSSION: The AICPA Standard Form to Confirm Account Balance Information with Financial Institutions is used to confirm specifically listed deposit and loan balances. The form confirms the account name, account number, interest rate, and balance for deposits.
Answer (A) is incorrect because kiting activities are best detected by inspecting checks returned in the cutoff bank statement. Answer (C) is incorrect because a proof of cash is based on information from the client's books and the bank statements. Answer (D) is incorrect because the auditor sends a separate letter, signed by the client, to request information about contingent liabilities and secured transactions.

25. An auditor ordinarily sends a standard confirmation request to all banks with which the client has done business during the year under audit, regardless of the year-end balance. A purpose of this procedure is to

A. Provide the data necessary to prepare a proof of cash.

B. Request that a cutoff bank statement and related checks be sent to the auditor.

C. Detect kiting activities that may otherwise not be discovered.

D. Seek information about other deposit and loan amounts that come to the attention of the institution in the process of completing the confirmation.

Answer (D) is correct. *(CPA, adapted)*
REQUIRED: The reason confirmations are sent to all banks used by the client.
DISCUSSION: The AICPA Standard Form to Confirm Account Balance Information with Financial Institutions is used to confirm specifically listed deposit and loan balances. Nevertheless, the standard confirmation form contains this language: "Although we do not request or expect you to conduct a comprehensive, detailed search of your records, if during the process of completing this confirmation, additional information about other deposit and loan accounts we may have with you comes to your attention, please include such information below."
Answer (A) is incorrect because the information for a proof of cash is in the month-end bank statement. Answer (B) is incorrect because a cutoff bank statement is for some period subsequent to the balance sheet date. Answer (C) is incorrect because the auditor should compare the returned checks in the cutoff bank statement with those listed as outstanding on the bank reconciliation, as well as prepare a bank transfer schedule for a few days before and after the balance sheet date.

26. The usefulness of the standard bank confirmation request may be limited because the bank employee who completes the form may

A. Not believe that the bank is obligated to verify confidential information to a third party.

B. Sign and return the form without inspecting the accuracy of the client's bank reconciliation.

C. Not have access to the client's cutoff bank statement.

D. Be unaware of all the financial relationships that the bank has with the client.

Answer (D) is correct. *(CPA, adapted)*
REQUIRED: The reason for the limited usefulness of the standard bank confirmation request.
DISCUSSION: According to AU 330, the standard form is designed to substantiate only the information that is stated on the confirmation request. Thus, the auditor should be aware that the standard form is not intended to elicit evidence about the completeness assertion because the individual completing the form may not be aware of all the financial relationships that the bank has with the client.
Answer (A) is incorrect because the client requests the information from the bank, and the bank must provide that information. Answer (B) is incorrect because the bank is not responsible for the accuracy of the client's bank reconciliation. Answer (C) is incorrect because the cutoff bank statement is not necessary to complete the form.

27. The standard AICPA form directed to financial institutions requests all of the following except

A. Due date of a direct liability.

B. The principal amount paid on a direct liability.

C. Description of collateral for a direct liability.

D. The interest rate of a direct liability.

Answer (B) is correct. *(Publisher)*
REQUIRED: The item not requested on a standard financial institution confirmation form.
DISCUSSION: The principal amount paid on a direct liability is not listed on the Standard Form to Confirm Account Balance Information with Financial Institutions. The auditor is not concerned with the amount of a liability already paid. The form confirms account number/description, balance, due date, interest rate, date through which interest is paid, and description of collateral.
Answer (A) is incorrect because the due date of a direct liability is requested on a standard confirmation form to obtain third-party evidence. Answer (C) is incorrect because a description of the collateral is requested on a standard confirmation form to obtain third-party evidence. Answer (D) is incorrect because the interest rate is requested on a standard confirmation form to obtain third-party evidence.

Questions 28 and 29 are based on the following information. The following was taken from the bank transfer schedule prepared during the audit of Fox Co.'s financial statements for the year ended December 31, year 1. Assume all checks are dated and issued on December 30, year 1.

| Check No. | Bank Accounts | | Disbursement Date | | Receipt Date | |
	From	To	Per Books	Per Bank	Per Books	Per Bank
101	National	Federal	Dec. 30	Jan. 4	Dec. 30	Jan. 3
202	County	State	Jan. 3	Jan. 2	Dec. 30	Dec. 31
303	Federal	American	Dec. 31	Jan. 3	Jan. 2	Jan. 2
404	State	Republic	Jan. 2	Jan. 2	Jan. 2	Dec. 31

28. Which of the following checks might indicate kiting?

A. #101 and #303.

B. #202 and #404.

C. #101 and #404.

D. #202 and #303.

Answer (B) is correct. *(CPA, adapted)*
REQUIRED: The checks that might indicate kiting.
DISCUSSION: Kiting is the recording of a deposit from an interbank transfer in the current period, while failing to record the related disbursement until the next period. It is a fraud that exploits the lag (float period) between the deposit of a check in one account and the time it clears the bank on which it is drawn. Checks #202 and #404 may indicate kiting because they were recorded by the receiving banks before year-end, although the disbursing banks did not record the payments until the next year.
Answer (A) is incorrect because checks #101 and #303 were recorded as received after year-end. Answer (C) is incorrect because check #101 was recorded as received after year-end. Answer (D) is incorrect because check #303 was recorded as received after year-end.

29. Which of the following checks illustrate deposits/transfers in transit at December 31, year 1?

A. #101 and #202.

B. #101 and #303.

C. #202 and #404.

D. #303 and #404.

Answer (B) is correct. *(CPA, adapted)*
REQUIRED: The checks indicating deposits/transfers in transit.
DISCUSSION: A deposit/transfer in transit is one recorded in the entity's books as a receipt by the balance sheet date but not recorded as a deposit by the bank until the next period. Check #101 is a deposit/transfer in transit because the check was recorded in the books before the end of the year but not recorded by either bank until January. Check #303 is also a deposit/transfer in transit, because the check was deducted from Federal's balance in December, but it was not added to American's balance until January.
Answer (A) is incorrect because check #202 was recorded in the books after the balance sheet date. Answer (C) is incorrect because checks #202 and #404 were recorded in the books after the balance sheet date. Answer (D) is incorrect because check #404 was recorded in the books after the balance sheet date.

30. An auditor should test bank transfers for the last part of the audit period and first part of the subsequent period to detect whether

A. The cash receipts journal was held open for a few days after year-end.

B. The last checks recorded before year-end were actually mailed by year-end.

C. Cash balances were overstated because of kiting.

D. Any unusual payments to or receipts from related parties occurred.

Answer (C) is correct. *(CPA, adapted)*
REQUIRED: The reason for testing bank transfers at year-end.
DISCUSSION: Kiting is the recording of a deposit from an interbank transfer in the current period, while failing to record the related disbursement until the next period. It is a fraud that exploits the lag (float period) between the deposit of a check in one account and the time it clears the bank on which it is drawn. To detect kiting, the auditor should examine a schedule of bank transfers for a period covering a few days before and after the balance sheet date. For the procedure to be effective, however, the auditor should be assured that all transfers have been identified.
Answer (A) is incorrect because a cutoff bank statement should be examined to determine whether the cash receipts journal was held open for a few days after year-end. Answer (B) is incorrect because a cutoff bank statement should be examined to determine whether the last checks recorded before year-end were actually mailed by year-end. Answer (D) is incorrect because unusual payments to or receipts from related parties can occur at any time of the year.

31. Which of the following cash transfers results in a misstatement of cash at December 31, year 1?

Bank Transfer Schedule

	Disbursement		Receipt	
	Recorded in Books	Paid by Bank	Recorded in Books	Received by Bank
A.	12/31/Y1	1/4/Y2	12/31/Y1	12/31/Y1
B.	1/4/Y2	1/5/Y2	12/31/Y1	1/4/Y2
C.	12/31/Y1	1/5/Y2	12/31/Y1	1/4/Y2
D.	1/4/Y2	1/11/Y2	1/4/Y2	1/4/Y2

Answer (B) is correct. *(CPA, adapted)*
REQUIRED: The interbank cash transfer that indicates an error in cash cutoff.
DISCUSSION: An error in cash cutoff occurs if one half of the transaction is recorded in the current period and one half in the subsequent period. Inspection of the Recorded in Books columns indicates that transfer (B) was recorded as a receipt on 12/31/Y1 but not as a disbursement until 1/4/Y2. This discrepancy is an error in cutoff called a kite, and it overstates the cash balance.

32. Which of the following procedures would an auditor most likely perform in auditing the statement of cash flows?

A. Compare the amounts included in the statement of cash flows to similar amounts in the prior year's statement of cash flows.

B. Reconcile the cutoff bank statements to verify the accuracy of the year-end bank balances.

C. Vouch all bank transfers for the last week of the year and first week of the subsequent year.

D. Reconcile the amounts included in the statement of cash flows to the other financial statements' balances and amounts.

Answer (D) is correct. *(CPA, adapted)*
REQUIRED: The procedure useful in auditing the statement of cash flows.
DISCUSSION: The information presented on a statement of cash flows is taken from the income statement and balance sheet. Indeed, a reconciliation of net income and net operating cash flow is required to be presented. Thus, reconciliation of amounts in the statement of cash flows with other financial statements' balances and amounts is an important procedure in the audit of the statement of cash flows.
Answer (A) is incorrect because analytical procedures for cash are not effective. Cash is a managed account. Answer (B) is incorrect because reconciling the cutoff bank statements to verify the accuracy of year-end bank balances is an appropriate procedure to audit the cash account but not necessarily the statement of cash flows. Answer (C) is incorrect because vouching all bank transfers for the last week of the year and the first week of the subsequent year is effective for detecting cutoff misstatements, such as those arising from kiting, but not for auditing the statement of cash flows.

Use Gleim's **CPA Test Prep** for interactive testing with over 2,000 additional multiple-choice questions!

11.3 PRACTICE SIMULATION

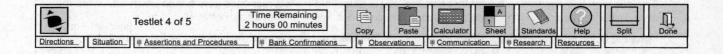

| | Testlet 4 of 5 | Time Remaining 2 hours 00 minutes | Copy | Paste | Calculator | Sheet | Standards | Help | Split | Done |

Directions | Situation | ▦ Assertions and Procedures | ▦ Bank Confirmations | ▦ Observations | ▦ Communication | ▦ Research | Resources |

---

1. Directions

In the following simulation, you will be asked to complete various tasks related to the collection of evidence in the sales-receivables-cash cycle. The simulation will provide you with all of the information necessary to do your work. For full credit, be sure to view and complete all work tabs.

Resources are available to you under the tab marked RESOURCES. You may want to review what is included in the resources before beginning the simulation.

---

2. Situation

You are collecting evidence in your audit of a client's sales, receivables, and cash receipts. To properly test management's assertions about the balances in the financial statements, you are preparing to perform substantive testing of the sales, receivables, and cash cycle.

The following is a bank reconciliation prepared by your client, who has a September 30 year-end:

General Company
Bank Reconciliation
1st National Bank of U.S. Bank Account
September 30, 20X1

Balance per bank				$28,375
Deposits in transit				
9/29/20X1			$4,500	
9/30/20X1			1,525	6,025
				34,400
Outstanding checks				
# 988	8/31/20X1		2,200	
#1281	9/26/20X1		675	
#1285	9/27/20X1		850	
#1289	9/29/20X1		2,500	
#1292	9/30/20X1		7,225	(13,450)
				20,950
Customer note collected by bank				(3,000)
Error: Check #1282, written on 9/26/20X1 for $270, was erroneously charged by bank as $720; bank was notified on 10/2/20X1				450
Balance per books				$18,400

Assume the following:

- The client prepared the bank reconciliation on 10/2/20X1.
- The bank reconciliation is mathematically accurate.
- The auditor received a cutoff bank statement dated 10/7/20X1 directly from the bank on 10/11/20X1.
- The 9/30/20X1 deposit in transit, outstanding checks #1281, #1285, #1289, and #1292, and the correction of the error regarding check #1282 appeared on the cutoff bank statement.
- The auditor assessed control risk concerning the financial statement assertions related to cash at the maximum.

3. Audit Procedures and Management Assertions

This question has a matching format that requires you to select the correct response from a drop-down list. Write the answer in the shaded column. Each choice may be used once, more than once, or not at all.

For each of the audit procedures listed below, choose the assertion that is most likely tested by the procedure.

Audit Procedures	Answer
1. The auditor reviewed delinquent customers' credit ratings.	
2. The auditor confirmed accounts receivable.	
3. The auditor performed a sales cutoff test to assure that all sales transactions for the year were included in the balance.	
4. The auditor accounted for the numerical sequence of sales orders.	
5. The auditor vouched the recorded accounts receivables to shipping documents.	
6. The auditor determined that accounts receivable was presented on the balance sheet as a current asset.	
7. The auditor aged the accounts receivable.	
8. The auditor inquired of management about the possibility that the receivables had been sold or factored.	
9. The auditor reconciled the total receivables from the subsidiary ledger to the balance in the general ledger.	
10. The auditor determined that a note was included describing any sales with related parties.	

Assertion Choices
A) Completeness
B) Rights and obligations
C) Valuation or allocation
D) Existence or occurrence
E) Statement presentation and disclosure

4. Bank Confirmation

This question is presented in a check-the-box format that requires you to select the correct response from a given list.

For each of the following items, determine whether the information is typically included on the Standard Form to Confirm Account Balance Information with Financial Institutions (Bank Confirmation) sent by the auditor to all the banks that a client has done business with during the year.

Items of Information	*Included*	*Not Included*
1. A place for the signature of the auditor.		
2. The following statement: "Please use the enclosed envelope to return the form directly to the auditor."		
3. An area on the form for the bank to list any outstanding checks.		
4. An area on the form for a deposit balance to be placed.		
5. A place for the signature of the bank official.		
6. An area on the form to describe any collateral for loans.		
7. A statement on the form that requests the bank to be alert for any fraudulent transactions.		
8. The following statement: "Although we do not request nor expect you to conduct a comprehensive, detailed search..."		
9. An area on the form for the bank to note exceptions or comments.		
10. A statement on the form that requests the bank to keep the information confidential.		

5. Bank Reconciliation

This question has a matching format that requires you to select the correct response from a drop-down list. Write the answer in the shaded column. Each choice may be used once, more than once, or not at all.

Based on the bank confirmation information given in the situation tab, select one or more procedures (as indicated), for each of the following items that the auditor most likely should perform to gather sufficient, competent, and relevant evidence.

Item	Answer(s)				
1. Balance per bank – **select 2 procedures**					
2. Deposits in transit – **select 5 procedures**					
3. Outstanding checks – **select 5 procedures**					
4. Customer note collected by bank – **select 1 procedure**					
5. Error – **select 2 procedures**					
6. Balance per books – **select 1 procedure**					

Choices
A) Trace to cash receipts journal.
B) Trace to cash disbursements journal.
C) Compare with 9/30/20X1 general ledger.
D) Confirm directly with bank.
E) Inspect bank credit memo.
F) Inspect bank debit memo.
G) Ascertain reason for unusual delay.
H) Inspect supporting documents for reconciling item not appearing on cutoff statement.
I) Trace items on the bank reconciliation to cutoff statement.
J) Trace items on the cutoff statement to bank reconciliation.

6. Communication

In the audit of your client, you requested and obtained an aged accounts receivable schedule listing the total amount owed by each customer as of September 30, 20X1. You also sent positive confirmation requests to a sample of the customers. In a memorandum to an audit associate, describe the additional substantive audit procedures that should be applied in auditing the accounts receivable. Type your communication in your word processor program and print out the copy in a memorandum-style format.

REMINDER: Your response will be graded for both technical content and writing skills. You should demonstrate your ability to develop, organize, and express your ideas. Do not convey information in the form of a table, bullet point list, or other abbreviated presentation.

To: Audit Associate
From: CPA
Subject: Additional substantive audit procedures

7. Research

Find the answer to the following question in the AICPA Professional Standards using the materials available in the Resources tab. Print the appropriate citation in its entirety from the source you choose. This is a cut-and-paste item.

Cite the appropriate auditing standard that outlines the auditor's responsibility for confirming accounts receivable during an audit.

Unofficial Answers

3. Audit Procedures and Management Assertions (10 Gradable Items)

1. <u>C) – Valuation or allocation</u>
2. <u>D) – Existence or occurrence</u>
3. <u>A) – Completeness</u>
4. <u>A) – Completeness</u>
5. <u>D) – Existence or occurrence</u>
6. <u>E) – Statement presentation and disclosure</u>
7. <u>C) – Valuation or allocation</u>
8. <u>B) – Rights and obligations</u>
9. <u>A) – Completeness</u>
10. <u>E) – Statement presentation and disclosure</u>

4. Bank Confirmation (10 Gradable Items)

1. <u>Not included</u> on confirmation
2. <u>Included</u> on confirmation
3. <u>Not included</u> on confirmation
4. <u>Included</u> on confirmation
5. <u>Included</u> on confirmation
6. <u>Included</u> on confirmation
7. <u>Not included</u> on confirmation
8. <u>Included</u> on confirmation
9. <u>Included</u> on confirmation
10. <u>Not included</u> on confirmation

5. Bank Reconciliation (16 Gradable Items)

1) <u>D) and I) - Confirm directly with bank and trace items on the bank reconciliation to cutoff statement</u>. The balance per bank should be confirmed directly with the bank using a "Standard Form to Confirm Account Balance Information with Financial Institutions." Moreover, the cutoff bank statement gives the balance per bank at September 30, 20X1.

2) <u>A), G), H), I), and J) - Trace to cash receipts journal; ascertain reason for unusual delay; inspect supporting documents for reconciling item not appearing on cutoff statement; trace items on the bank reconciliation to cutoff statement; and trace items on the cutoff statement to bank reconciliation</u>. Each deposit should be supported by an entry in the cash receipts journal. The 9/29/20X1 deposit in transit should be investigated to determine the reason for the delay. It should have been reported on the cutoff bank statement. The 9/29/20X1 deposit in transit should also be investigated to determine why it did not appear on the cutoff bank statement. The deposits in transit on the bank reconciliation should be compared with items in the cutoff bank statement to test for their existence. In addition, a test should be performed in the opposite direction. The deposits in transit on the cutoff bank statement should be compared with items in the bank reconciliation to test the completeness of the deposits in transit.

3) <u>B), G), H), I), and J) - Trace to cash disbursements journal; ascertain reason for unusual delay; inspect supporting documents for reconciling item not appearing on cutoff statement; trace items on the bank reconciliation to cutoff statement; and trace items on the cutoff statement to bank reconciliation</u>. Each check should be supported by an entry in the cash disbursements journal. Check #988 should be investigated to determine the reason for its delay in clearing and to determine why it did not appear on the cutoff bank statement. Outstanding checks on the bank reconciliation should be compared with the cutoff bank statement to test the existence of the outstanding checks. In addition, a test should be performed in the opposite direction. Outstanding checks on the cutoff bank statement should be compared with the bank reconciliation to test for the completeness of the listed outstanding checks.

4) <u>E) - Inspect bank credit memo</u>. The problem involves reconciling the balance per bank to the balance per books. The proceeds of the customer note collected by the bank increased the balance per bank, so the amount of the note must be subtracted to arrive at the balance per books. The amount collected on the note can be verified by inspecting the bank's credit memo. The bank credited the customer's account (a liability to the bank) when it collected the proceeds of the note.

5) <u>E) and I) - Inspect bank credit memo and trace items on the bank reconciliation to cutoff statement.</u> The credit memo issued in October should be inspected and the credit given to the customer for $450 should be compared with the cutoff bank statement.

6) <u>C) - Compare to 9/30/20X1 general ledger</u>. The balance per books should be compared with the 9/30/20X1 cash balance in the general ledger.

6. Communication (5 Gradable Items; For grading instructions, please refer to page 11.)

To: Audit Associate
From: CPA
Subject: Additional substantive audit procedures

The auditor should consider applying additional substantive procedures in an audit of accounts receivable. The auditor should test the accuracy of aged accounts receivable and send second requests to customers who did not answer positive confirmation requests. After receiving the responses to the majority of the second confirmation requests, the auditor should perform alternative auditing procedures for any unanswered second confirmation requests and reconcile and investigate exceptions reported on the confirmations. The auditor should follow up by projecting the results of the sample confirmation procedures to the population and evaluating the results. Also, the auditor should determine whether any account debtors are employees or related parties.

To determine whether the balances of sales and receivables contain all the transactions for the period, the auditor should test the cutoff of sales, cash receipts, and sales returns and allowances. The auditor also should apply analytical procedures to accounts receivable. In addition, the auditor should evaluate the reasonableness of the allowance for doubtful accounts, identify any differences between the carrying amounts and tax bases of the allowance for doubtful accounts and related expenses, review activity after the balance sheet date for unusual transactions, and determine that the presentation and disclosure of accounts receivable are in conformity with GAAP.

7. Research (6 Gradable Items)

AU Section 330 -- *The Confirmation Process*

Confirmation of Accounts Receivable

.34 For the purpose of this section, *accounts receivable* means:

a.   The entity's claims against customers that have arisen from the sale of goods or services in the normal course of business, and

b.   A financial institution's loans.

Confirmation of accounts receivable is a generally accepted auditing procedure. As discussed in paragraph .06, it is generally presumed that evidence obtained from third parties will provide the auditor with higher-quality audit evidence than is typically available from within the entity. Thus, there is a presumption that the auditor will request the confirmation of accounts receivable during an audit unless one of the following is true:

● Accounts receivable are immaterial to the financial statements.

● The use of confirmations would be ineffective.

● The auditor's combined assessed level of inherent and control risk is low, and the assessed level, in conjunction with the evidence expected to be provided by analytical procedures or other substantive tests of details, is sufficient to reduce audit risk to an acceptably low level for the applicable financial statement assertions. In many situations, both confirmation of accounts receivable and other substantive tests of details are necessary to reduce audit risk to an acceptably low level for the applicable financial statement assertions.

.35 An auditor who has not requested confirmations in the examination of accounts receivable should document how (s)he overcame this presumption.

Scoring Schedule:

	Correct Responses		Gradable Items		Weights		
Tab 3	_____	÷	10	×	20%	=	_____
Tab 4	_____	÷	10	×	20%	=	_____
Tab 5	_____	÷	16	×	20%	=	_____
Tab 6	_____	÷	5	×	30%	=	_____
Tab 7	_____	÷	6	×	10%	=	_____
							_____
							(Your Score)

Use Gleim's ***CPA Review Online*** to practice more simulations in a realistic environment.

STUDY UNIT TWELVE
EVIDENCE --
THE PURCHASES-PAYABLES-INVENTORY CYCLE

(5 pages of outline)

12.1	Substantive Testing of Accounts Payable and Purchases	377
12.2	Substantive Testing of Inventory	379
12.3	Practice Simulation	389

The primary purpose of the collection of evidence is to test management's assertions about the balances in the financial statements. Development of the audit program requires not only consideration of the assertions but also the development of specific objectives related to the assertions. In general, most testing in the inventory-acquisition process is applied to accounts payable and inventory, with a focus on the likelihood of understatement of accounts payable and overstatement of inventory. Evidence about the debit in the payables transaction (i.e., inventory in a perpetual system and purchases in a periodic system) is gathered when the credit (accounts payable) is tested. The interrelationship is apparent in the opposite direction as well. As the debit is tested, evidence about the credit is also produced. The objective of this study unit is to develop a comprehensive audit program for the accounts payable and inventory accounts. The program includes the customary procedures assuming no unusual risks. Some of the questions at the end of this study unit concern special risks that require modification of the audit program. The candidate should consider those questions and problems and practice the modification of programs to address special risks.

The technique described below is a plan for audit program development that may be used in answering CPA exam questions. Application of the assertions model (COVES is the mnemonic for the five categories of assertions) assures that all assertions are tested. However, other formats for presentation of the steps are acceptable.

12.1 SUBSTANTIVE TESTING OF ACCOUNTS PAYABLE AND PURCHASES

1. Testing assertions about accounts payable provides evidence concerning the assertions about purchases and ultimately cost of goods sold. Purchases obviously result in ending inventory, but because inventory is a significant item on the balance sheet, a separate audit program is typically developed for the account. An audit program for inventory follows this section. Candidates should understand the interrelationship of these accounts and the overlap of the audit procedures.

2. Accounts payable, sometimes termed trade payables, represent the most significant current liability of most firms.

3. The following is a standard program for accounts payable and purchases that tests management's assertions about COVES.

   a. **C**ompleteness. Do the balances contain all transactions for the period? (This is typically the major detection risk for the auditor in testing payables.)

      1) Reconcile accounts payable ledger with general ledger control account. ✓ Compare the total recorded amounts in the subsidiary ledger with the amount recorded in the general ledger.

      2) Purchases cutoff test. Test to determine that all goods for which title has passed to the client at year-end are recorded in inventory and accounts payable.

      a)   Goods shipped **FOB shipping point** should be recorded in the period of shipment to the client. Thus, receipts for several days after year-end should be evaluated to determine whether the goods should be recorded in the current year.

      b)   Goods shipped **FOB destination** should be recorded in the period received. Receiving documents are traced to the accounting records by the auditor for several days prior to and after year-end to determine proper recognition of inventory and accounts payable.

3)   Analytical procedures. The auditor should use appropriate sources of data (e.g., prior experience, budgets prepared by management at the beginning of the period, nonfinancial information, industry data, and interrelationships) to form expectations with which to compare management's presentations. Ratios may be used (e.g., the accounts payable turnover ratio). Unexpected findings should be investigated.

4)   Cash disbursements cutoff test. Test the recording of cash disbursements and the associated reduction in accounts payable. Inspecting the last check written and tracing it to the accounts payable subsidiary ledger will provide evidence of proper recording.

5)   Trace subsequent payments to recorded payables. A primary test is to match the payments (checks) issued after year-end with the related payables. Checks should be issued only for recorded payables. Any checks that cannot be matched are likely indications of unrecorded liabilities.

      a)   Management may be motivated to delay recording of liabilities to improve the current ratio. However, unrecorded accounts payable must still be paid, and financial statements that fail to report all liabilities at year-end are misstated.

      b)   This procedure is often tested.

6)   Search for unvouchered payables. The accounts payable department prepares and records a voucher (with a debit to purchases and a credit to accounts payable) when all the supporting documentation is assembled. The auditor should search the suspense files for unmatched documents to determine whether relevant documents have been lost, misplaced, or misfiled. A suspense file contains transactions the classification and treatment of which are in doubt, for example, because of missing documents.

      a)   For example, a requisition, receiving report, and invoice may be held by accounts payable, but no voucher should be prepared or entry made if the purchase order has not been matched with the other documents. This situation results in an unrecorded liability.

b.   Rights and **O**bligations. Does the balance of accounts payable reflect the liability of this entity? Because the risk is relatively low that management would present liabilities of others, the procedures testing this assertion are not as consequential as those for other assertions.

1)   Inquiries. Obtain management representations about the nature of the recorded payables.

c.   **V**aluation or Allocation. Are accounts payable valued in accordance with generally accepted accounting principles? GAAP require that debts be stated at the amount necessary to satisfy the obligation.

1)   Detection risk for this assertion is reduced if the other assertions are tested in accordance with GAAS. The valuation or allocation assertion is interrelated with those for existence and completeness.

    d.   **E**xistence or Occurrence. Do the recorded accounts payable represent valid liabilities at the balance sheet date?

        1)   Confirmation is not a generally accepted auditing procedure because it is not likely to disclose unrecorded payables. Normally, the auditor can become satisfied as to the existence of recorded payables using evidence available directly from the client.

            a)   If confirmation is undertaken, small and zero balances should be sampled as well as larger balances. The auditor should use the activity in the account as a gauge for selection. That is, if orders are placed with a vendor on a consistent basis, a confirmation should be sent to that vendor regardless of the recorded balance due at year-end.

            b)   The blank form of positive confirmations should be used. It requests that the balance due be provided by the creditor (e.g., the vendor).

        2)   Vouch recorded payables to documentation. A sample of recorded payables should be reconciled with documentary support (e.g., requisitions, purchase orders, receiving reports, and approved invoices).

    e.   **S**tatement Presentation and Disclosure. Is the accounts payable balance presented properly on the financial statements?

        1)   Inspect the financial statements. Accounts payable should be presented as a current liability on the balance sheet. Purchases should be used in the determination of cost of sales for the income statement.

        2)   Read note disclosures. Any unusual significant transactions or events should be described by management in the notes (e.g., significant accounts payable to related parties).

        3)   Obtain a management representations letter with assertions related to purchases and payables.

  4.   Stop and review! You have completed the outline for this subunit. Study multiple-choice questions 1 through 13 beginning on page 382.

12.2 SUBSTANTIVE TESTING OF INVENTORY

  1.   The primary purpose of the collection of evidence for inventory is to test management's assertions about the presentation of the balance in the financial statements.

  2.   Inventory consists of the goods held for resale by the client and is presented as a current asset on the balance sheet.

  3.   The following is a standard audit program for inventory that tests management assertions about COVES.

    a.   **C**ompleteness. Does the inventory balance contain all inventory owned by the entity at year-end?

        1)   Analytical procedures. The calculation of amounts and ratios and their comparison with expectations can identify unusual findings indicative of misstatements.

            a)   The inventory turnover ratio (cost of sales ÷ average or ending inventory) should be compared with that of the prior period.

                i)   Industry averages for the client's industry can be compared with the client's ratio.

            b)   Vertical analysis (e.g., the percentage of inventory to total assets), using industry information, can identify unusual conditions.

            c)   Information from the client's previously prepared budgets can provide the basis for expectations.

       d)   Nonfinancial information (e.g., the volume, in boxes or pounds) may provide expectations about the flow of inventory as well as sales and receivables.

   2)   Purchases and sales cutoff tests. Cutoff tests should provide evidence that the inventory owned by the entity was actually reflected in the balance. Goods should be excluded if the title has not yet passed from vendors or if it has already passed to customers.

       a)   The appropriate procedure is to trace receiving and shipping documents for several days prior to and after year-end.

  b.   Rights and **O**bligations. Does the entity own the inventory reported on the balance sheet?

   1)   Vouch recorded purchases to documentation. Vouch a sample of recorded inventory items to payment records. Payment vouchers for inventory should have supporting documentation (e.g., requisition, purchase order, receiving report, and vendor invoice) and canceled checks (if payment has been made).

   2)   Consider the industry or client practices for consigned goods. When the nature of the client or industry suggests the possibility of consignment transactions (e.g., the client has held or shipped consigned goods in the past), the auditor should review the client's correspondence, evaluate sales and receivables records, and consider the results of vouching purchases to detect unrecognized consignment activity.

       a)   For example, if the client has recorded consignment shipments as sales, the auditor would likely find a pattern of large sales on account and many small, periodic cash receipts for the receivables.

  c.   **V**aluation or Allocation. Is inventory recorded at lower of cost or market?

   1)   Compare recorded costs with current cost to replace the goods. Current vendor price lists should be compared with recorded inventory costs to determine that current prices are not less than recorded costs.

   2)   Calculate the turnover ratio. An applicable analytical procedure is to calculate the inventory turnover ratio for the individual inventory items. Excessive inventory results in small turnover ratios and provides evidence of potentially obsolete items.

   3)   Test costs of manufactured items. Manufactured goods should be costed to include direct materials, direct labor, and an allocation of overhead. The overhead allocation rate should be tested for reasonableness.

  d.   **E**xistence or Occurrence. Does the inventory exist at a given date?

   1)   Observation of inventories is a generally accepted auditing procedure (AU 331, *Inventories*). The auditor should observe and make test counts but is not responsible for taking inventory.

       a)   If the entity uses the periodic inventory method, test counts should be made at or very close to year-end because the counted inventory value is used to calculate cost of sales. If control risk is high, inventory counts should be done at year-end.

       b)   If the entity uses the perpetual inventory method, counts may be made at interim dates if records are well kept.

           i)   The client may use methods, including statistical sampling, that are sufficiently reliable to make an annual count of all items unnecessary. The auditor must be assured these methods are reasonable and statistically valid and have been properly applied. Observations and test counts must still be performed.

    c) Observations should encompass all significant inventory locations.

        i) The auditor must observe and make test counts even if inventory is taken by independent specialists (i.e., businesses that perform inventory counts as their service).

2) The client's plan for taking inventory should make effective use of, and exercise control over, prenumbered inventory tags and summary sheets.

    a) The plan should include provisions for handling receipts and shipments during the count.

    b) Goods not owned by the client, such as goods held on consignment, should be separated.

    c) Appropriate instructions and supervision should be given to employees conducting the count.

3) Performing tests of the count should include

    a) Observing employees following the plan

    b) Assuring that all items are tagged

    c) Observing employees making counts and recording amounts on tags

    d) Determining that tags and inventory summary sheets are controlled

    e) Making test counts, comparing test counts with amounts recorded on the tags and summary sheets, and reconciling amounts with records

    f) Being alert for empty boxes, empty squares (i.e., boxes stacked to suggest the block of boxes is solid when the middle does not contain boxes), and inventory defects (e.g., damaged or dirty items)

    g) Establishing a cutoff by documenting the last receiving report and shipping document

4) The performance of procedures should be documented in the working papers.

5) The auditor should confirm or investigate inventories held in public warehouses.

    a) The auditor ordinarily obtains confirmation by direct communication with the custodian. When a significant portion of current or total assets is held in a public warehouse, the auditor should consider testing the client's procedures by evaluating the warehouseman, obtaining an independent accountant's report on the warehouseman's internal control, visiting the warehouse and observing physical counts, and investigating the use of warehouse receipts (e.g., whether they are being used for collateral). The auditor should confirm with lenders the details of any pledged receipts.

e. **S**tatement Presentation and Disclosure. Are inventories properly displayed as current assets, and has cost of sales been properly reflected in the income statement? Have adequate disclosures been made concerning inventory valuation, cost flow assumptions, and significant transactions, such as pledging of inventory?

1) Read financial statements. The auditor should read the financial statements to determine that accounts are properly reflected and notes adequately informative.

2) Inquire of management. The auditor should inquire of management about consigned goods, major purchase commitments, pledging of inventory, and other significant transactions or events.

3) Obtain a management representations letter that includes assertions relating to inventory and cost of sales.

4. Stop and review! You have completed the outline for this subunit. Study multiple-choice questions 14 through 26 beginning on page 385.

QUESTIONS

12.1 Substantive Testing of Accounts Payable and Purchases

1. Which of the following is a substantive test that an auditor most likely would perform to verify the existence and valuation of recorded accounts payable?

A. Investigating the open purchase order file to ascertain that prenumbered purchase orders are used and accounted for.

B. Receiving the client's mail, unopened, for a reasonable period of time after year-end to search for unrecorded vendor's invoices.

C. Vouching selected entries in the accounts payable subsidiary ledger to purchase orders and receiving reports.

D. Confirming accounts payable balances with known suppliers who have zero balances.

Answer (C) is correct. *(CPA, adapted)*
REQUIRED: The substantive test for the existence and valuation of recorded accounts payable.
DISCUSSION: Vouching a sample of recorded accounts payable to purchase orders and receiving reports provides evidence that the obligations exist at a given date. The purchase orders evidence the initiation of the transactions, and the receiving reports indicate that goods were received and that liabilities were thereby incurred. Thus, these documents provide evidence that amounts are owed to others, that the transactions occurred, and that the liabilities have been included at appropriate amounts.
Answer (A) is incorrect because ascertaining that prenumbered documents are used and accounted for relates most directly to the completeness assertion. Answer (B) is incorrect because searching for unrecorded liabilities relates most directly to completeness. Answer (D) is incorrect because confirming payables with known suppliers having zero balances is a procedure for detecting unrecorded liabilities. Thus, it relates most directly to completeness.

2. To determine whether accounts payable are complete, an auditor performs a test to verify that all merchandise received is recorded. The population of documents for this test consists of all

A. Payment vouchers.

B. Receiving reports.

C. Purchase requisitions.

D. Vendors' invoices.

Answer (B) is correct. *(CPA, adapted)*
REQUIRED: The population of documents for a test to verify that all merchandise received is recorded.
DISCUSSION: The population to be tested consists of receiving reports. An accounts payable record should be available for each receiving report.
Answer (A) is incorrect because a payment voucher is prepared for each account payable. A payment voucher would not exist for an unrecorded payable. Answer (C) is incorrect because the goods requisitioned may not have been ordered. If ordered, they may not have been received. Hence, a payable may not exist for each requisition. Answer (D) is incorrect because a vendor's invoice does not provide evidence that the goods have been received and a liability incurred. Thus, a payable need not exist for every vendor's invoice.

3. An auditor traced a sample of purchase orders and the related receiving reports to the purchases journal and the cash disbursements journal. The purpose of this substantive audit procedure most likely was to

A. Identify unusually large purchases that should be investigated further.

B. Verify that cash disbursements were for goods actually received.

C. Determine that purchases were properly recorded.

D. Test whether payments were for goods actually ordered.

Answer (C) is correct. *(CPA, adapted)*
REQUIRED: The purpose of tracing purchase orders and receiving reports to the related journals.
DISCUSSION: The auditor tests the completeness assertion for accounting records by tracing supporting documents to the entries in the records.
Answer (A) is incorrect because sampling purchase orders and receiving reports would not necessarily identify large purchases. Answer (B) is incorrect because the direction of tests would be from the records (in this case, journals) to the receiving reports to determine whether the goods recorded were properly supported. Answer (D) is incorrect because, to test whether payments were for goods actually ordered, a sample of cash disbursements would be vouched to purchase orders.

4. An auditor performs a test to determine whether all merchandise for which the client was billed was received. The population for this test consists of all

A. Merchandise received.

B. Vendors' invoices.

C. Canceled checks.

D. Receiving reports.

Answer (B) is correct. *(CPA, adapted)*
REQUIRED: The population for a test to determine whether all merchandise for which the client was billed was received.
DISCUSSION: Vendors' invoices are the billing documents received by the client. They describe the items purchased, the amounts due, and the payment terms. The auditor should trace these invoices to the related receiving reports.
Answer (A) is incorrect because testing merchandise received will not detect merchandise billed but not received. Answer (C) is incorrect because tracing canceled checks to the related receiving reports tests whether goods paid for, not goods billed, were received. Answer (D) is incorrect because tracing receiving reports to vendors' invoices tests whether all goods received were billed.

5. In auditing accounts payable, an auditor's procedures most likely would focus primarily on management's assertion of

A. Existence or occurrence.

B. Presentation and disclosure.

C. Completeness.

D. Valuation or allocation.

Answer (C) is correct. *(CPA, adapted)*
REQUIRED: The assertion that is the focus of an audit of accounts payable.
DISCUSSION: The primary audit risk for accounts payable is the potential for understatement of the liability. Thus, the auditor will most likely focus on the completeness assertion.
Answer (A) is incorrect because the existence or occurrence assertion concerns whether liabilities exist at a given date and whether transactions occurred during the period. The audit risk for accounts payable is not great for that assertion because management is unlikely to record payables for which no liability exists. Answer (B) is incorrect because the risk of inappropriate presentation and disclosure on the financial statements is not as great as the risk that some items are not included. Answer (D) is incorrect because the risk that accounts payable are not valued in accordance with GAAP is less than the risk that the balance may not be complete.

6. Which of the following procedures would an auditor most likely perform in searching for unrecorded liabilities?

A. Trace a sample of accounts payable entries recorded just before year-end to the unmatched receiving report file.

B. Compare a sample of purchase orders issued just after year-end with the year-end accounts payable trial balance.

C. Vouch a sample of cash disbursements recorded just after year-end to receiving reports and vendor invoices.

D. Scan the cash disbursements entries recorded just before year-end for indications of unusual transactions.

Answer (C) is correct. *(CPA, adapted)*
REQUIRED: The procedure most likely to detect unrecorded liabilities.
DISCUSSION: The greatest risk in the audit of payables is that unrecorded liabilities exist. Omission of an entry to record a payable is an error or fraud that is more difficult to detect than an inaccurate or false entry. The search for unrecorded payables should include (1) examining cash disbursements made after the balance sheet date and comparing them with the accounts payable trial balance, (2) sending confirmations to vendors with small and zero balances, and (3) reconciling payable balances with vendors' documentation.
Answer (A) is incorrect because sampling from known accounts payable provides little evidence as to unrecorded liabilities. Answer (B) is incorrect because a sample of purchase orders issued after year-end is expected to be recorded in the subsequent year, not in the current year. Answer (D) is incorrect because payments in the current year represent satisfied liabilities, not unrecorded liabilities.

7. An auditor's purpose in reviewing the renewal of a note payable shortly after the balance sheet date most likely is to obtain evidence concerning management's assertions about

A. Existence or occurrence.

B. Presentation and disclosure.

C. Completeness.

D. Valuation or allocation.

Answer (B) is correct. *(CPA, adapted)*
REQUIRED: The auditor's purpose in reviewing the renewal of a note payable shortly after year-end.
DISCUSSION: Events such as the renewal of the note payable do not require adjustment of the financial statements but may require disclosure (AU 560). Accordingly, the auditor should determine that the renewal had essentially the same terms and conditions as the recorded debt at year-end. A significant change may affect the presentation of notes payable (e.g., as current or noncurrent), the interpretation of the statements, and the required disclosures.
Answer (A) is incorrect because the renewal does not raise an issue as to whether the note existed. Answer (C) is incorrect because the renewal does not raise an issue as to whether all notes were reported. Answer (D) is incorrect because the renewal does not affect the valuation of notes payable.

8. Which of the following procedures would an auditor least likely perform before the balance sheet date?

A. Confirmation of accounts payable.

B. Observation of merchandise inventory.

C. Assessment of control risk.

D. Identification of related parties.

Answer (A) is correct. *(CPA, adapted)*
REQUIRED: The audit procedure least likely to be performed prior to the balance sheet date.
DISCUSSION: AU 313 states, "The auditor should consider whether the year-end balances of the particular assets or liability accounts that might be selected for interim examination are reasonably predictable with respect to amount, relative significance, and composition." Accounts payable are relatively less predictable than many other accounts. Moreover, the most important assertion regarding accounts payable is completeness, which is best tested at year-end.
Answer (B) is incorrect because the balances of inventory are reasonably predictable based on expectations of recorded purchases and sales. Answer (C) is incorrect because the auditor may assess risks prior to year-end. Answer (D) is incorrect because the auditor may identify related parties prior to year-end.

9. When using confirmations to provide evidence about the completeness assertion for accounts payable, the appropriate population most likely is

A. Vendors with whom the entity has previously done business.

B. Amounts recorded in the accounts payable subsidiary ledger.

C. Payees of checks drawn in the month after the year-end.

D. Invoices filed in the entity's open invoice file.

Answer (A) is correct. *(CPA, adapted)*
REQUIRED: The appropriate population when confirmations of accounts payable are used to test the completeness assertion.
DISCUSSION: When sending confirmations for accounts payable, the population of accounts should include small and zero balances as well as large balances. The auditor should use the activity in the account as a gauge for sample selection. That is, if orders are placed with a vendor on a consistent basis, a confirmation should be sent to that vendor regardless of the recorded balance due.
Answer (B) is incorrect because the auditor, in testing the completeness assertion, is concerned with balances that have not been recorded or invoices that have not been filed. Answer (C) is incorrect because the payees of checks are not an appropriate population for the confirmation process. Payments in the month after year-end do not necessarily reflect year-end liabilities. Answer (D) is incorrect because the auditor, in testing the completeness assertion, is concerned with balances that have not been recorded or invoices that have not been filed.

10. An auditor suspects that certain client employees are ordering merchandise for themselves over the Internet without recording the purchase or receipt of the merchandise. When vendors' invoices arrive, one of the employees approves the invoices for payment. After the invoices are paid, the employee destroys the invoices and the related vouchers. In gathering evidence regarding the fraud, the auditor most likely would select items for testing from the file of all

A. Cash disbursements.

B. Approved vouchers.

C. Receiving reports.

D. Vendors' invoices.

Answer (A) is correct. *(CPA, adapted)*
REQUIRED: The file tested to determine whether checks are being issued for unauthorized expenditures.
DISCUSSION: The best procedure to test whether any checks have been issued without supporting vouchers, purchase orders, and receiving reports is to select an appropriate sample of canceled checks (cash disbursements) and trace them to the related supporting documentation.
Answer (B) is incorrect because the approved vouchers relating to the fraudulent transactions have been destroyed and therefore could not be chosen for audit. Answer (C) is incorrect because the receipt of the merchandise is not recorded. Answer (D) is incorrect because the vendors' invoices relating to the fraudulent transactions have been destroyed and therefore could not be chosen for audit.

11. Cutoff tests designed to detect purchases made before the end of the year that have been recorded in the subsequent year most likely would provide assurance about management's assertion of

A. Valuation or allocation.

B. Existence or occurrence.

C. Completeness.

D. Presentation and disclosure.

Answer (C) is correct. *(CPA, adapted)*
REQUIRED: The purpose of cutoff tests.
DISCUSSION: The completeness assertion is concerned with whether balances reflect all transactions for the period. To determine that all goods for which title has passed to the client at year-end are recorded in inventory and accounts payable, a purchases cutoff test is appropriate.
Answer (A) is incorrect because cutoff tests do not directly test the assertion of valuation or allocation. Answer (B) is incorrect because cutoff tests do not directly test the assertion of existence or occurrence. Answer (D) is incorrect because cutoff tests do not directly test the assertion of statement presentation and disclosure.

12. An internal control narrative indicates that an approved voucher is required to support every check request for payment of merchandise. Which of the following procedures provides the greatest assurance that this control is operating effectively?

    A. Select and examine vouchers and ascertain that the related canceled checks are dated no later than the vouchers.

    B. Select and examine vouchers and ascertain that the related canceled checks are dated no earlier than the vouchers.

    C. Select and examine canceled checks and ascertain that the related vouchers are dated no earlier than the checks.

    D. Select and examine canceled checks and ascertain that the related vouchers are dated no later than the checks.

Answer (D) is correct. *(CPA, adapted)*
    REQUIRED: The procedure giving the greatest assurance that approved vouchers support check requests.
    DISCUSSION: Payment vouchers bearing the required approvals should be supported by a properly authorized purchase requisition, a purchase order executing the transaction, a receiving report indicating all goods ordered have been received in good condition, and a vendor invoice confirming the amount owed. To determine that check requests are valid, the appropriate audit procedure is therefore to compare checks and the related vouchers. The direction of testing should be from a sample of checks to the approved vouchers. If the date of a voucher is later than the date of the related check, the inference is that a check was issued without proper support.
    Answer (A) is incorrect because tracing from vouchers to canceled checks does not give assurance that all checks are supported by approved vouchers. This test will not detect canceled checks unsupported by approved vouchers, although it will permit comparison of the dates of the respective documents. Answer (B) is incorrect because tracing from vouchers to canceled checks does not give assurance that all checks are supported by approved vouchers. This test will not detect canceled checks unsupported by approved vouchers, although it will permit comparison of the dates of the respective documents. Answer (C) is incorrect because the checks should be dated no earlier than the vouchers. Each voucher should be dated earlier than (or have the same date as) the related check.

13. When performing procedures to test assertions about purchases, an auditor vouches a sample of entries in the voucher register to the supporting documents. Which assertion would this procedure most likely support?

    A. Completeness.

    B. Existence or occurrence.

    C. Valuation or allocation.

    D. Rights and obligations.

Answer (B) is correct. *(CPA, adapted)*
    REQUIRED: The assertion tested by vouching.
    DISCUSSION: A voucher signifies a liability. Its issuance is recorded in the voucher register after comparison of the vendor's invoice with the purchase requisition, purchase order, and receiving report. The direction of testing is an important consideration in meeting specific audit objectives regarding assessment of the controls over the process. Selecting a sample of recorded entries in the voucher register to vouch to the supporting documentation provides evidence that the transactions occurred.
    Answer (A) is incorrect because sampling recorded transactions to vouch to supporting documents does not test for unrecorded transactions. Answer (C) is incorrect because sampling recorded transactions provides evidence regarding the amount owed and whether the entry reflects an obligation of the company, but it most directly supports the existence assertion. Answer (D) is incorrect because sampling recorded transactions provides evidence regarding the amount owed and whether the entry reflects an obligation of the company, but it most directly supports the existence assertion.

12.2 Substantive Testing of Inventory

14. The element of the audit-planning process most likely to be agreed upon with the client before implementation of the audit strategy is the determination of the

    A. Evidence to be gathered to provide a sufficient basis for the auditor's opinion.

    B. Procedures to be undertaken to discover litigation, claims, and assessments.

    C. Pending legal matters to be included in the inquiry of the client's attorney.

    D. Timing of inventory observation procedures to be performed.

Answer (D) is correct. *(CPA, adapted)*
    REQUIRED: The element of audit planning most likely agreed upon with the client before implementation.
    DISCUSSION: The client is responsible for taking the physical inventory. The auditor is responsible for observing this process and performing test counts. The audit procedures are contingent upon management's plans; thus, the auditor must coordinate the collection of this evidence with management.
    Answer (A) is incorrect because the evidence to be gathered is a matter of audit judgment to be determined solely by the auditor. Answer (B) is incorrect because the procedures to be undertaken to discover litigation, claims, and assessments are matters of audit judgment to be determined solely by the auditor. Answer (C) is incorrect because pending legal matters to be included in the inquiry of the client's attorney are matters of audit judgment to be determined solely by the auditor.

15. When auditing inventories, an auditor would least likely verify that

A. All inventory owned by the client is on hand at the time of the count.

B. The client has used proper inventory pricing.

C. The financial statement presentation of inventories is appropriate.

D. Damaged goods and obsolete items have been properly accounted for.

Answer (A) is correct.   *(CPA, adapted)*
REQUIRED: The item not an objective of an audit of inventories.
DISCUSSION: An auditor does not expect all inventory to which the auditee has title to be on hand at the date of the count. Some purchased goods may still be in transit at that time. Also, some inventory may be on consignment or in public warehouses although properly included in the count.
Answer (B) is incorrect because the auditor should test management's assertions about valuation of inventory. Answer (C) is incorrect because the auditor should test management's assertions about presentation in the financial statements. Answer (D) is incorrect because the auditor should test management's assertions about valuation of inventory.

16. A client maintains perpetual inventory records in quantities and in dollars. If the assessed level of control risk is high, an auditor would probably

A. Apply gross profit tests to ascertain the reasonableness of the physical counts.

B. Increase the extent of tests of controls relevant to the inventory cycle.

C. Request the client to schedule the physical inventory count at the end of the year.

D. Insist that the client perform physical counts of inventory items several times during the year.

Answer (C) is correct.   *(CPA, adapted)*
REQUIRED: The auditor's action if control risk for inventory is high.
DISCUSSION: If control risk is high, a more timely audit procedure may be necessary, and extending the results of work done on an interim basis to year-end might be inappropriate. Thus, observation of inventory at year-end would provide the best evidence as to existence.
Answer (A) is incorrect because comparing the gross profit test results with the prior year's results provides evidence about sales and cost of goods sold but not inventory. Answer (B) is incorrect because, if the auditor believes control policies and procedures are unlikely to be effective, tests of controls would not be performed. Answer (D) is incorrect because the risk is that year-end inventory would be misstated.

17. To gain assurance that all inventory items in a client's inventory listing schedule are valid, an auditor most likely would vouch

A. Inventory tags noted during the auditor's observation to items listed in the inventory listing schedule.

B. Inventory tags noted during the auditor's observation to items listed in receiving reports and vendors' invoices.

C. Items listed in the inventory listing schedule to inventory tags and the auditor's recorded count sheets.

D. Items listed in receiving reports and vendors' invoices to the inventory listing schedule.

Answer (C) is correct.   *(CPA, adapted)*
REQUIRED: The step to provide assurance that all inventory items in a client's inventory listing are valid.
DISCUSSION: Validity relates to the existence assertion. To determine that the items exist, the direction of testing should be from the schedule to the inventory tags, and ultimately to the auditor's count sheet.
Answer (A) is incorrect because tracing tags to the inventory listing schedule would provide evidence of completeness; that is, all items counted are included on the listing sheet. Answer (B) is incorrect because tracing inventory tags to receiving reports and vendors' invoices would provide information useful in determining whether inventory was recorded at cost. Answer (D) is incorrect because tracing inventory items on receiving reports and vendors' invoices to the inventory listing schedule would not be an effective test. Many items received would be sold by the inventory date.

18. An auditor selected items for test counts while observing a client's physical inventory. The auditor then traced the test counts to the client's inventory listing. This procedure most likely obtained evidence concerning management's assertion of

A. Rights and obligations.

B. Completeness.

C. Existence or occurrence.

D. Valuation.

Answer (B) is correct.   *(CPA, adapted)*
REQUIRED: The assertion relevant to tracing test counts to the client's inventory listing.
DISCUSSION: Tracing the details of test counts to the final inventory schedule assures the auditor that items in the observed physical inventory are included in the inventory records. The auditor should compare the inventory tag sequence numbers in the final inventory schedule to those in the records of his/her test counts made during the client's physical inventory.
Answer (A) is incorrect because the reconciliation of the test counts with the inventory listing does not provide assurance that the inventory is owned by the client. Answer (C) is incorrect because, although the observation of inventory provides evidence as to existence, specifically tracing test counts to the inventory listing provides evidence of completeness. Answer (D) is incorrect because the valuation assertion is tested by determining whether inventory items are included in inventory at LCM.

19. While observing a client's annual physical inventory, an auditor recorded test counts for several items and noticed that certain test counts were higher than the recorded quantities in the client's perpetual records. This situation could be the result of the client's failure to record

A. Purchase discounts.

B. Purchase returns.

C. Sales.

D. Sales returns.

Answer (D) is correct. *(CPA, adapted)*
REQUIRED: The transaction type not recorded when test counts are greater than recorded quantities.
DISCUSSION: Failure to record sales returns for goods returned to the physical inventory will result in test counts greater than the quantities reported by the perpetual inventory system.
Answer (A) is incorrect because purchase discounts relate to the value of inventory, not to the quantity. Answer (B) is incorrect because failure to record purchase returns would result in lower quantities in the physical inventory than in the perpetual records. Answer (C) is incorrect because failure to record sales would result in lower quantities in the physical inventory than in the perpetual records.

20. Which of the following audit procedures probably would provide the most reliable evidence concerning the entity's assertion of rights and obligations related to inventories?

A. Trace test counts noted during the entity's physical count to the entity's summarization of quantities.

B. Inspect agreements to determine whether any inventory is pledged as collateral or subject to any liens.

C. Select the last few shipping advices used before the physical count and determine whether the shipments were recorded as sales.

D. Inspect the open purchase order file for significant commitments that should be considered for disclosure.

Answer (B) is correct. *(CPA, adapted)*
REQUIRED: The procedure providing the most reliable evidence concerning rights and obligations related to inventories.
DISCUSSION: The major audit objective of testing the assertion of rights and obligations for inventories is to determine that the entity has legal title or similar rights of ownership to the inventories. Typically, the auditor will examine paid vendors' invoices, consignment agreements, and contracts.
Answer (A) is incorrect because tracing test counts to the summarization of quantities tests the assertion of completeness. Answer (C) is incorrect because examining cutoff procedures tests the assertion of completeness. Answer (D) is incorrect because determining whether commitments should be disclosed in the footnotes is concerned with the assertion of statement presentation and disclosure.

21. To measure how effectively an entity employs its resources, an auditor calculates inventory turnover by dividing average inventory into

A. Net sales.

B. Cost of goods sold.

C. Operating income.

D. Gross sales.

Answer (B) is correct. *(CPA, adapted)*
REQUIRED: The calculation of the inventory turnover ratio.
DISCUSSION: Inventory turnover is calculated by dividing cost of goods sold by average inventory. It provides a measure of how many times inventory turns over and requires replacement.
Answer (A) is incorrect because the numerator in the inventory turnover ratio is cost of goods sold, not net sales. Answer (C) is incorrect because the numerator in the inventory turnover ratio is cost of goods sold, not operating income. Answer (D) is incorrect because the numerator in the inventory turnover ratio is cost of goods sold, not gross sales.

22. An auditor most likely would analyze inventory turnover rates to obtain evidence concerning management's assertions about

A. Existence or occurrence.

B. Rights and obligations.

C. Presentation and disclosure.

D. Valuation or allocation.

Answer (D) is correct. *(CPA, adapted)*
REQUIRED: The assertion about which analysis of inventory turnover rates provides evidence.
DISCUSSION: Assertions about valuation or allocation concern whether asset, liability, revenue, and expense components have been included in the financial statements at appropriate amounts. An examination of inventory turnover pertains to the audit objective of identifying slow-moving, excess, defective, and obsolete items included in inventories. This audit objective relates to the valuation or allocation assertion (AU 326).
Answer (A) is incorrect because analysis of inventory turnover does not test existence. Answer (B) is incorrect because analysis of inventory turnover does not test whether the entity has rights to the inventory. Answer (C) is incorrect because the presentation and disclosure assertion concerns whether the items in the financial statements are properly classified, described, and disclosed.

23. An auditor most likely would make inquiries of production and sales personnel concerning possible obsolete or slow-moving inventory to support management's financial statement assertion of

    A. Valuation or allocation.

    B. Rights and obligations.

    C. Existence or occurrence.

    D. Presentation and disclosure.

Answer (A) is correct. *(CPA, adapted)*
    REQUIRED: The assertion tested when considering obsolete or slow-moving inventory.
    DISCUSSION: The valuation or allocation assertion is directed towards whether inventory is recorded at lower of cost or market. The discovery of obsolete or slow-moving inventory suggests that the cost of inventory be written down to its market value.

24. An auditor most likely would inspect loan agreements under which an entity's inventories are pledged to support management's financial statement assertion of

    A. Existence or occurrence.

    B. Completeness.

    C. Presentation and disclosure.

    D. Valuation or allocation.

Answer (C) is correct. *(CPA, adapted)*
    REQUIRED: The assertion tested by inspection of loan agreements under which inventories are pledged.
    DISCUSSION: According to AU 326, "Assertions about presentation and disclosure address whether particular components of the financial statements are properly classified, described, and disclosed." Determining that the pledge or assignment of inventories is appropriately disclosed is an audit objective related to the presentation and disclosure assertion.
    Answer (A) is incorrect because inspection of loan agreements does not determine whether inventories physically exist. Answer (B) is incorrect because inspection of loan agreements does not determine whether the inventory includes all items owned by the company. Answer (D) is incorrect because inspection of loan agreements does not determine whether inventory is included at proper amounts.

25. An auditor concluded that no excessive costs for an idle plant were charged to inventory. This conclusion most likely related to the auditor's objective to obtain evidence about the financial statement assertions regarding inventory, including presentation and disclosure and

    A. Valuation and allocation.

    B. Completeness.

    C. Existence or occurrence.

    D. Rights and obligations.

Answer (A) is correct. *(CPA, adapted)*
    REQUIRED: The assertion related to the conclusion that no excessive costs for an idle plant were inventoried.
    DISCUSSION: Inventory should properly include the costs of direct labor, direct materials, and manufacturing overhead. Thus, to be properly valued, an appropriate amount of manufacturing overhead should be charged to inventory. Costs of an idle plant should not be included in manufacturing overhead.
    Answer (B) is incorrect because excessive costs for an idle plant do not affect the completeness assertion. Answer (C) is incorrect because excessive costs for an idle plant do not affect the existence or occurrence assertion. Answer (D) is incorrect because excessive costs for an idle plant do not affect the rights and obligations assertion.

26. Which of the following auditing procedures most likely would provide assurance about a manufacturing entity's inventory valuation?

    A. Testing the entity's computation of standard overhead rates.

    B. Obtaining confirmation of inventories pledged under loan agreements.

    C. Reviewing shipping and receiving cutoff procedures for inventories.

    D. Tracing test counts to the entity's inventory listing.

Answer (A) is correct. *(CPA, adapted)*
    REQUIRED: The procedure that provides assurance about a manufacturing entity's inventory valuation.
    DISCUSSION: Manufactured goods should be recorded at cost, including direct materials, direct labor, and an allocation of overhead. The overhead allocation rate should be tested for reasonableness.
    Answer (B) is incorrect because obtaining confirmation of inventories pledged under loan agreements tests the assertion of rights and obligations. Answer (C) is incorrect because reviewing shipping and receiving cutoff procedures tests the assertion of completeness. Answer (D) is incorrect because tracing test counts to the inventory listing tests the assertion of completeness.

Use Gleim's ***CPA Test Prep*** for interactive testing with over 2,000 additional multiple-choice questions!

12.3 PRACTICE SIMULATION

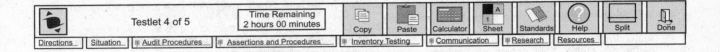

Testlet 4 of 5 | Time Remaining 2 hours 00 minutes | Copy | Paste | Calculator | Sheet | Standards | Help | Split | Done

Directions | Situation | Audit Procedures | Assertions and Procedures | Inventory Testing | Communication | Research | Resources

1. Directions

In the following simulation, you will be asked to complete various tasks related to the purchases-payables-inventory cycle. The simulation will provide all of the information necessary to do the work. For full credit, be sure to view and complete all work tabs.

Resources are available to you under the tab marked RESOURCES. You may want to review what is included in the resources before beginning the simulation.

2. Situation

Kay Bee, CPA, is auditing McGraw Wholesaling Company's financial statements and is about to perform substantive audit procedures on McGraw's trade accounts payable balances. After obtaining an understanding of McGraw's internal control for accounts payable, Kay Bee assessed control risk near the maximum. Kay Bee requested and received from McGraw a schedule of the trade accounts payable prepared using the trade accounts payable subsidiary ledger (voucher register).

3. Audit Procedures

Match each of the following descriptions with the appropriate audit procedure. This question is presented in a spreadsheet format that requires you to fill in the correct responses in the shaded cells provided.

Description	Answer
1. An auditor combines amounts in meaningful ways to allow the application of audit judgment, such as the determination of whether a proper inventory cutoff was performed.	
2. An auditor examines documents relating to transactions and balances, such as shipping and receiving records to establish ownership of inventory.	
3. An auditor obtains acknowledgments in writing from third parties of transactions or balances, such as inventory in public warehouses or on consignment.	
4. An auditor recomputes certain amounts, such as the multiplication of quantity times price to determine inventory amounts.	
5. An auditor questions client personnel about events and conditions, such as obsolete inventory.	
6. An auditor relates two or more amounts, such as inventory cost in perpetual inventory records to costs as shown on vendor invoices as part of the evaluation of whether inventory is priced at the lower of cost or market.	
7. An auditor watches the performance of some function, such as a client's annual inventory count.	

Procedure Choices

A) Observation
B) Analysis
C) Comparison
D) Inquiry
E) Confirmation
F) Inspection
G) Calculation

4. Audit Procedures and Management Assertions

This question is presented in a matching format that requires you to select the correct response from a drop-down list. Write each answer in the shaded answer column.

Match the following management assertions with the audit procedures. Choose the assertion most likely being tested by the procedure. Each choice may be used once, more than once, or not at all.

Audit Procedure	Answer
1. The auditor determined that pledged inventory was identified in a note.	
2. The auditor confirmed goods held by the client in a public warehouse.	
3. The auditor performed a purchases cutoff test to assure all purchase transactions for the year were included in the balance.	
4. The auditor accounted for the numerical sequence of purchase orders.	
5. The auditor vouched the recorded payables to receiving documents.	
6. The auditor determined that accounts payable was presented on the balance sheet as a current liability.	
7. The auditor observed the taking of the physical inventory.	
8. The auditor preformed an analytical procedure comparing this year's balance of payable with the previous year's.	
9. The auditor reconciled the total payables from the subsidiary ledger to the balance in the general ledger.	
10. The auditor compared the recorded inventory costs to the replacement costs of inventory.	

Assertion Choices

A) Completeness

B) Rights and obligations

C) Valuation or allocation

D) Existence or occurrence

E) Statement presentation and disclosure

5. Testing Inventory Cutoff

This question is presented in a check-the-box format that requires you to select the correct response from a given list.

The auditor tests the cutoff of inventory and determines whether it should be included in the final balance of the client. The client may ship and receive inventory based on a variety of shipping terms. Determine whether the inventory should be included in the 12/31/X0 balance of inventory for your client based on the following descriptions. Use "Yes" to include the inventory and "No" to exclude the inventory.

Descriptions	Yes	No
1. A shipment was made on 12/30/X0 to a customer FOB receiving point. The shipment was received by the customer on 1/3/X1.		
2. A shipment was made on 12/29/X0 to a customer FOB shipping point. The shipment was received by the customer on 12/31/X0.		
3. A shipment was received from a vendor on 1/4/X1. It was shipped from the vendor FOB shipping point on 1/2/X1.		
4. A shipment was received from a vendor on 1/4/X1. It was shipped from the vendor FOB shipping point on 12/29/X0.		
5. A shipment was received from a vendor on 1/6/X1. It was shipped from the vendor FOB receiving point on 12/29/X0.		
6. A shipment was made on 12/28/X0 to a customer FOB receiving point. The shipment was received by the customer on 12/31/X0.		
7. A shipment was made on 1/2/X1 to a customer FOB shipping point. The shipment was received by the customer on 1/3/X1.		
8. A shipment was received from a vendor on 12/31/X0. It was shipped from the vendor FOB receiving point on 12/30/X0.		

6. Communication

Describe in a memo to Kay Bee, CPA, the substantive audit procedures she should apply to McGraw's trade accounts payable balances. Type your communication in your word processor program and print out the copy in a memorandum style format.

REMINDER: Your response will be graded for both technical content and writing skills. You should demonstrate your ability to develop, organize, and express your ideas. Do not convey information in the form of a table, bullet point list, or other abbreviated presentation.

> To: Kay Bee, CPA
> From: CPA Supervisor
> Subject: Substantive procedures for McGraw's financial statements

7. Research

Use the research materials available to you to find the answers to the following question in the AICPA Professional Standards. Print the appropriate citation in its entirety from the source you choose. Use only one source. This is a copy-and-paste item.

According to the auditing standards, what should an auditor consider when evaluating the results of confirmations? Cite the appropriate literature to support your findings.

Unofficial Answers

3. Audit Procedures (7 Gradable Items)

1. B) Analysis. Analysis is combining information in ways that have meaning.

2. F) Inspection. Inspection includes the examination of documents.

3. E) Confirmation. Confirmations are communications, typically in writing, with third parties requesting information.

4. G) Calculation. Calculations are computations of values and amounts.

5. D) Inquiry. Inquiries are questions, typically posed to management and others with information of interest to the auditor.

6. C) Comparison. Comparison relates two or more amounts and interprets the difference.

7. A) Observation. Observation means watching activities or procedures. It provides the auditor with direct personal knowledge.

4. Audit Procedures and Management Assertions (10 Gradable Items)

1. E) - Statement presentation and disclosure is the assertion being tested when the auditor determines that pledged inventory was identified in a note.

2. D) - Existence or occurrence is the assertion being tested when the auditor confirmed goods held by the client in a public warehouse.

3. A) - Completeness is the assertion being tested when the auditor performed a purchases cutoff test to assure all purchase transactions for the year were included in the balance.

4. A) - Completeness is the assertion being tested when the auditor accounted for the numerical sequence of purchase orders.

5. D) - Existence or occurrence is the assertion being tested when the auditor vouched the recorded payables to receiving documents.

6. E) - Statement presentation and disclosure is the assertion being tested when the auditor determined that accounts payable was presented on the balance sheet as a current liability.

7. D) - Existence or occurrence is the assertion being tested when the auditor observed the taking of the physical inventory.

8. A) - Completeness is the assertion being tested when the auditor performed an analytical procedure comparing this year's balance of payable with the previous year's.

9. A) - Completeness is the assertion being tested when the auditor reconciled the total payables from the subsidiary ledger to the balance in the general ledger.

10. C) - Valuation or allocation is the assertion being tested when the auditor compared the recorded inventory costs to the replacement costs of inventory.

5. Testing Inventory Cutoff (8 Gradable Items)

A. Yes. The shipment should be included in the year-end inventory balance.

B. No. The shipment should not be included in the year-end inventory balance.

C. No. The shipment should not be included in the year-end inventory balance.

D. Yes. The shipment should be included in the year-end inventory balance.

E. No. The shipment should not be included in the year-end inventory balance.

F. No. The shipment should not be included in the year-end inventory balance.

G. Yes. The shipment should be included in the year-end inventory balance.

H. Yes. The shipment should be included in the year-end inventory balance.

6. Communication (5 Gradable Items; For grading instructions, please refer to page 11.)

To: Kay Bee, CPA
From: CPA Supervisor
Subject: Substantive procedures for McGraw's financial statements

The substantive audit procedures Kay Bee should apply to McGraw's trade accounts payable balances include the following:

The auditor should foot the schedule of trade accounts payable and reconcile the total of the schedule with the general ledger trial balance. The next step is to compare a sample of individual balances from the schedule with the accounts payable subsidiary ledger. The auditor also should compare a sample of individual balances from the subsidiary ledger with the schedule. Any old or disputed payables should be investigated and discussed with management. The auditor also should investigate debit balances and, if significant, consider requesting positive confirmations and propose reclassification of the amounts. Additional procedures include reviewing the minutes of directors' meetings and any written agreements, inquiring of key employees as to whether any assets are security for payables, cutoff tests, and analytical procedures.

The auditor should confirm or verify recorded accounts payable balances. Procedures for this purpose include reviewing the voucher register or subsidiary accounts payable ledger and confirming payables of a sample of vendors. The auditor should request that a sample of vendors provide statements of account balances as of the date selected. The auditor then investigates and reconciles differences discovered during the confirmation process. The auditor also tests a sample of unconfirmed balances by examining the related vouchers, invoices, purchase orders, and receiving reports.

The auditor should perform a search for unrecorded liabilities. One procedure involves examining files of receiving reports unmatched with vendors' invoices and searching for items received before the balance sheet date but not yet billed or on the schedule. Another procedure applied for this purpose is to inspect files of unprocessed invoices, purchase orders, and vendors' statements. The auditor also reviews support for the cash disbursements journal, the voucher register, or canceled checks for disbursements after the balance sheet date. The reason for the review is to identify transactions that should have been recorded at the balance sheet date but were not. A final procedure is to inquire of key employees about additional sources of unprocessed invoices or other trade payables.

7. Research (6 Gradable Items)

AU Section 330 -- *The Confirmation Process*

Evaluating the Results of Confirmation Procedures

.33   After performing any alternative procedures, the auditor should evaluate the combined evidence provided by the confirmations and the alternative procedures to determine whether sufficient evidence has been obtained about all the applicable financial statement assertions. In performing that evaluation, the auditor should consider (a) the reliability of the confirmations and alternative procedures; (b) the nature of any exceptions, including the implications, both quantitative and qualitative, of those exceptions; (c) the evidence provided by other procedures; and (d) whether additional evidence is needed. If the combined evidence provided by the confirmations, alternative procedures, and other procedures is not sufficient, the auditor should request additional confirmations or extend other tests, such as tests of details or analytical procedures.

Scoring Schedule:

	Correct Responses		Gradable Items		Weights		
Tab 3	_____	÷	7	×	20%	=	_____
Tab 4	_____	÷	10	×	20%	=	_____
Tab 5	_____	÷	8	×	20%	=	_____
Tab 6	_____	÷	5	×	30%	=	_____
Tab 7	_____	÷	6	×	10%	=	_____
							(Your Score)

Use Gleim's **CPA Review Online** to practice more simulations in a realistic environment.

STUDY UNIT THIRTEEN
EVIDENCE --
OTHER ASSETS, LIABILITIES, AND EQUITIES

(9 pages of outline)

13.1	Substantive Testing of Property, Plant, and Equipment	395
13.2	Substantive Testing of Investments (AU 332)	397
13.3	Substantive Testing of Long-Term Debt	400
13.4	Substantive Testing of Equity	401
13.5	Substantive Testing of Payroll	402
13.6	Practice Simulation	412

The objective of this study unit is to develop a comprehensive audit program for a number of accounts not previously considered. The programs include the customary procedures assuming no unusual risks. Some of the questions at the end of this study unit concern special risks that require modification of the audit programs. The candidate should consider these questions and practice the modification of audit procedures and programs to address special risks.

The technique described below is a plan for audit program development that may be used in answering CPA exam questions. Application of the assertions model (COVES is the mnemonic for the five categories of assertions) assures that all assertions are tested. However, other formats for presentation of the steps are acceptable.

13.1 SUBSTANTIVE TESTING OF PROPERTY, PLANT, AND EQUIPMENT

1. The balances included in this audit program are

    a. Buildings, equipment, improvements, and vehicles, including associated depreciation expense, repairs and maintenance, and accumulated depreciation

    b. Land

    c. Capital leases and associated amortization expense

2. The following is a standard audit program for property, plant, and equipment that tests management assertions about COVES.

    a. **C**ompleteness. Are all transactions affecting property, plant, and equipment for the period reflected in the balance?

        1) Perform analytical procedures. The five sources of data for analytical procedures (prior experience, anticipated results, nonfinancial information, industry data, and account interrelationships) can be used to develop expectations. Some typical ratios are rate of return on plant assets and plant assets to total assets.

        2) Reconcile subsidiary and general ledgers. The client will usually maintain records for individual assets or classes of assets. The subsidiary records, including cost, current depreciation expense, and accumulated depreciation, should reconcile with the general ledger and the amounts to be included on the financial statements.

            a) A schedule of fixed assets is typically prepared from the subsidiary records to be used in testing and is included in the working papers.

        3)   Analyze repairs and maintenance. The auditor should vouch significant debits from the repairs and maintenance expense account to determine whether any should have been capitalized.

            a)   Vouching additions to property, plant, and equipment also tests the completeness assertion because debits may have been for non-capital items.

  b.   Rights and **O**bligations. Does the entity have ownership rights in the reported property, plant, and equipment?

        1)   Examine titles and leases. Certain property should have titles (e.g., autos and trucks) indicating owners. The lease documents should allow the auditor to determine whether leases have been properly recorded as capital or operating leases.

        2)   Inspect records of purchase. The purchase of fixed assets should result in payments. Vouching the entries to the payment records supports the assertion that the entity owns the assets.

        3)   Inspect insurance policies. The entity should insure assets in which it has an interest. Vouching the recorded assets to insurance policies supports the rights assertion.

            a)   When liens are placed on equipment or property, the lienholder often requires that the assets be insured and that the lienholder be named as the beneficiary. Hence, the policy would likely be held by the lienholder even though the client is required to pay the premiums.

        4)   Inspect property tax records. Many states assess property tax on certain fixed assets. Paying taxes helps assure the auditor that the client has rights in the assets.

  c.   **V**aluation or Allocation. Are balances of property, plant, and equipment reported in accordance with GAAP (historical cost minus accumulated depreciation)?

        1)   Vouch additions and disposals. These are tests of the details of transactions. In a continuing audit, the prior year's balance of property, plant, and equipment is an audited balance. If the auditor tests the details of the transactions that changed the balance, (s)he has progressed towards meeting the valuation assertion (as well as other assertions such as completeness and existence).

            a)   The auditor tests the authorization, execution, recording, and custody aspects of the transaction.

        2)   Test depreciation. Fixed assets (except certain nondepreciable assets such as land) are usually measured at cost minus accumulated depreciation. The depreciation methods and their application should be tested to determine that they are generally accepted and applied consistently.

  d.   **E**xistence or Occurrence. Do the assets reflected in property, plant, and equipment exist at the balance sheet date?

        1)   Inspect plant additions. As discussed in testing the valuation and allocation assertion, tests of the details of transactions are appropriate. Thus, the focus is on additions to property, plant, and equipment.

            a)   The auditor vouches a sample from the recorded asset additions by examining the supporting documents and inspecting the physical assets. Testing in the opposite direction, i.e., by tracing from the supporting documentation to the general ledger, would not provide evidence that recorded assets exist.

            b)   Initial audits require inspection of significant assets reflected in the beginning balance as well as additions.

        2)   Test the cutoff. Additions and disposals should be recorded in the proper periods.

    e.   **S**tatement Presentation and Disclosure. Is the balance of property, plant, and equipment reflected on the balance sheet in the noncurrent section, and are adequate disclosures presented for methods of depreciation, commitments of assets, and capital lease terms?

        1)   Read financial statements. Determine that property, plant, and equipment is presented as a long-term asset. Depreciable assets should be reported at cost minus accumulated depreciation. Land should be shown at cost. Notes to the financial statements should describe classes of assets, lease agreements, depreciation methods, and any property mortgaged or used as collateral for loans.

        2)   Make inquiries of management regarding appropriate footnote disclosures and other reporting issues. Significant items should be included in the management representation letter.

3.   Stop and review! You have completed the outline for this subunit. Study multiple-choice questions 1 through 9 beginning on page 404.

13.2 SUBSTANTIVE TESTING OF INVESTMENTS (AU 332)

1.   The balances included in this audit program are

    a.   **Noncurrent items**. These include capital stock or other equity interests represented by the fair value or equity methods, bonds and similar debt instruments, and loans and advances that are in the nature of investments.

    b.   **Current items**. These include trading, held-to-maturity, and available-for-sale securities classified as current.

    c.   **Derivatives and hedges**. Derivatives are financial instruments that derive their value from other securities or financial activities. Hedges are defensive strategies to protect an entity against the risk of adverse price or interest rate movements on certain assets, liabilities, or anticipated transactions.

    d.   **Revenues** generated from investments

2.   "The appropriate classification of investments depends on management's intent in purchasing and holding the investment, on the entity's actual investment activities, and, for certain debt securities, on the entity's ability to hold the investment to maturity" (**SFAS 115**, *Accounting for Certain Investments in Debt and Equity Securities*). The auditor should obtain an understanding of the process used by management to classify investments before determining the substantive procedures.

3.   **AU 332**, *Auditing Derivative Instruments, Hedging Activities, and Investments in Securities*, provides guidance for planning and performing audit procedures to test assertions about derivatives and hedging activities accounted for under SFAS 133. The guidance also applies to all debt and equity securities, as defined by SFAS 115, but it extends to assertions about securities not accounted for under SFAS 115, e.g., equity-based investments.

    a.   An auditor may require **special skill or knowledge** regarding some assertions, for example, an understanding of GAAP for derivatives or of the measurement and disclosure issues for derivatives with complex features.

b. The **assessment of inherent risk** for derivatives and securities depends on such factors as

   1) Their complexity,
   2) Management's objectives,
   3) Whether the pertinent transactions involved a cash exchange,
   4) The extent of the entity's experience with derivatives and securities,
   5) Whether a derivative is embedded in a host contract,
   6) External matters (credit risk, market risk, hedging ineffectiveness, legal risk, etc.),
   7) The further evolution of derivatives and relevant GAAP,
   8) The entity's reliance on the expertise of outsiders, and
   9) Assumptions required by GAAP.

c. The **assessment of control risk** requires considering whether controls, including those of service organizations, have been implemented that provide for

   1) Independent monitoring of derivatives activities,
   2) Independent approval when derivatives personnel wish to exceed limits,
   3) Senior management's attention to situations in which limits are exceeded and divergences occur from approved derivatives strategies,
   4) Reconciliations over the full range of derivatives, and
   5) High-level review of the identified controls and the results of derivatives activities.

d. The **design of substantive procedures based on the risk assessments** addresses types of assertions about derivatives and securities. Examples are confirmations with issuers, holders, or counterparties; confirmation of settled and unsettled transactions; physical inspection of contracts and other documentation; analytical procedures; inquiries of frequently used counterparties or holders; confirmation of significant terms with a counterparty or holder; tests of valuation based on the method required by GAAP for the measurement or disclosure, such as cost, the investee's financial results, or fair value; and evaluation of whether presentation and disclosure requirements have been met, such as classification of securities and reporting of changes in fair value in either earnings or other comprehensive income.

   1) The auditor should perform procedures to determine whether **hedging activities**, including the designation and documentation requirements, have been carried out in accordance with GAAP and therefore qualify for hedge accounting.
   2) The auditor must also gather evidence about **management's intent and ability**, for example, to hold debt securities to maturity, to exercise significant influence over an equity-based investee, to enter into a forecasted transaction, or to dispose of securities classified as trading in the near term.
   3) Furthermore, the auditor must obtain written **management representations** confirming various aspects of derivatives and securities transactions.

4. The following is a standard audit program for investments that tests management's assertions about COVES.

   a. **C**ompleteness. Are all transactions affecting investments for the period reflected in the balance?

      1) Perform analytical procedures. Prior-period amounts held should be compared with current amounts. The expected return on investments held can be compared with actual recorded amounts.

        2)   Reconcile subsidiary and control accounts. Prepare a schedule from the subsidiary records and reconcile the amounts with the balance in the general ledger and financial statements.

        3)   Evaluate contracts and agreements. Determine whether all derivatives and hedges have been identified and reported.

b.   Rights and **O**bligations. Does the entity own the reported investments?

        1)   Recalculate interest revenue. Determine that interest revenue, based on stated rates for recorded investments, has been properly recorded.

        2)   Trace dividend revenue. Determine that dividends declared and paid by investees have been properly recorded.

c.   **V**aluation or Allocation. Are balances reported in accordance with generally accepted accounting principles, e.g., with SFAS 115?

        1)   Vouch recorded costs to documentation. The cost of recorded securities can be established by comparing recorded amounts with broker invoices, canceled checks, and other evidence of purchase.

        2)   Vouch recorded amounts for trading securities and available-for-sale securities to market quotations if available. When market quotations are unavailable, the auditor can obtain fair-value estimates from broker-dealers and other third-party sources who derive the fair value of a security by using modeling or a similar technique. The auditor must evaluate the appropriateness of the valuation models and the variables and assumptions used in the model (AU 332). Determine that unrealized holding gains and losses (changes in fair value) for trading securities are included in earnings. Determine that unrealized holding gains and losses for available-for-sale securities are reported in other comprehensive income until realized. (An exception is provided for all or part of the unrealized holding gain or loss on an available-for-sale security designated as hedged in a fair value hedge in accordance with SFAS 133.)

        3)   Vouch recorded costs for held-to-maturity securities to market quotations. Determine that the entity measures these securities at amortized cost only if it has the positive intent and ability to hold them to maturity. Recalculate the premium or discount.

        4)   Determine that transfers between categories of investments are at fair value.

        5)   Determine that, if individual available-for-sale or held-to-maturity securities suffer a nontemporary decline in fair value below their cost basis, the securities are written down to fair value, the fair value is treated as the new cost basis, and the amount of the write-down is reflected in earnings.

        6)   Obtain audited financial statements from the investees if investments are accounted for by the equity method. Determine the proper increases or decreases in the investment accounts based on percentage ownership in the investee and reported income or loss of the investee.

d.   **E**xistence or Occurrence. Do investments reported at the balance sheet date exist?

        1)   Physically inspect and count securities in the client's possession. Serial numbers should be recorded and compared with the entity's records. Inspection and counting also should be performed when counting other liquid assets (e.g., cash). The client's representative should be available to acknowledge that the securities have been returned intact.

        2)   Confirm securities. Confirmation may be made to the issuer, custodian, counterparty, or broker-dealer for unsettled transactions.

        3)   Read executed partnership or similar agreements.

e.   **S**tatement Presentation and Disclosure. Are balances related to investments reflected on the balance sheet in the current or noncurrent section depending on management expectations?

1)   Read financial statements. Determine that individual trading, available-for-sale, and held-to-maturity securities are reported as current or noncurrent as appropriate. Determine whether derivatives, hedges, and other financial instruments are adequately described in the notes to the financial statements.

2)   Direct inquiries of management toward intentions for the disposition of investments because classification often is based on the actions of management. The responses should be documented in the management representation letter. Also, the auditor should consider whether investment activities corroborate or conflict with management's stated intent.

5.   Stop and review! You have completed the outline for this subunit. Study multiple-choice questions 10 through 18 beginning on page 406.

13.3 SUBSTANTIVE TESTING OF LONG-TERM DEBT

1.   The balances included in this audit program are

a.   Long-term notes payable, mortgages payable, and bonds payable
b.   Related interest expense

2.   The following is a standard audit program for long-term debt.

a.   **C**ompleteness. Are all transactions affecting long-term debt reflected in the balances at the end of the period?

1)   Perform analytical procedures. Prior-period amounts recorded should be compared with current amounts. A key procedure to detect unrecorded debt is to recalculate interest expense based on recorded debt and compare it with recorded interest expense. Significant unexpected interest expense recorded in the general ledger suggests the existence of unrecorded debt.

2)   Reconcile subsidiary and control accounts. Prepare a schedule from the subsidiary records and reconcile the amounts with the balance in the general ledger and financial statements.

b.   Rights and **O**bligations. Are the debts recorded on the balance sheet actually obligations of the entity being audited? (Inherent risk is ordinarily low for this assertion.)

1)   Evaluate existing contracts and agreements for indications that the debt is the obligation of the auditee.

2)   Examine any bond trust indenture to determine that the client is meeting the conditions of the contract and is in compliance with the law. Thus, the client should have obtained an attorney's opinion on compliance with the law. The bond trust indenture contains information concerning contractual arrangements made with bondholders, such as the face amount of the bonds, interest rates, payment dates, descriptions of collateral, provisions for conversion or retirement, trustee duties, and sinking-fund requirements.

3)   Make inquiries of management. Questions directed at the sources and uses of the recorded debt may be addressed to management.

    c. **V**aluation or Allocation. Are balances reported in accordance with GAAP?

        1) Vouch recorded debt to debt instruments. Bonds should be recorded at face value, with separate recognition of premium or discount. Additionally, long-term debt due in the next year should be reclassified as short-term debt (also a statement presentation issue).

        2) Test amortization. Recalculate recorded debt premium or discount to determine that it is being amortized using appropriate GAAP (the interest method).

    d. **E**xistence or Occurrence. Do the outstanding debt-balance-related accounts exist at the balance sheet date?

        1) Confirm debt. Debt is confirmed with investment bankers, lenders, and bond trustees. Long-term notes payable may be confirmed directly with the holders of the notes.

        2) Review contracts and agreements. Debt should be supported by appropriate documentation identifying interest rates, payment dates, collateral, and other terms.

    e. **S**tatement Presentation and Disclosure. Are balances properly reflected on the balance sheet, is interest expense properly reflected on the income statement, and are adequate disclosures provided?

        1) Read financial statements. Determine that long-term and short-term debt are properly classified.

        2) Inspect footnote disclosures. Determine that appropriate footnote disclosures are made concerning the terms of the debt and collateral pledged to support the debt.

3. Stop and review! You have completed the outline for this subunit. Study multiple-choice questions 19 and 20 on page 409.

13.4 SUBSTANTIVE TESTING OF EQUITY

1. The typical balances included in this audit program when the auditee is a corporation are

    a. Common and preferred stock
    b. Additional paid-in capital
    c. Retained earnings
    d. Treasury stock
    e. Accumulated other comprehensive income

2. The following is a standard audit program for equity:

    a. **C**ompleteness. Are all transactions affecting equity reflected in the balances at the end of the period?

        1) Perform analytical procedures. Prior-period amounts recorded should be compared with current amounts.

        2) Reconcile subsidiary and control accounts. Prepare a schedule from the subsidiary records of equity accounts and reconcile the amounts with the balances in the general ledger and financial statements.

    b. Rights and **O**bligations. Are the equity balances properly reflective of the owners' interests in the entity?

        1) Inspect the articles of incorporation and bylaws of a corporation. These documents provide evidence concerning the legal status of the shareholders and their relationship(s) to the entity that the auditor should document in the working papers.

    c.   **V**aluation or Allocation. Are balances reported in accordance with GAAP?

        1)   Trace entries to equity accounts. The closing entries should be tested to determine that the net income has been closed to retained earnings. Any designations (appropriations) of retained earnings should be traced to the related account.

        2)   Test sales of treasury stock. Determine that gains or losses on the sale of treasury stock are recognized directly in the capital section of the balance sheet and not in earnings.

    d.   **E**xistence or Occurrence. Do the outstanding equity-balance-related accounts exist at the balance sheet date?

        1)   Confirm shares issued and outstanding with the registrar and transfer agent. The auditor should have direct communication with external parties responsible for contact with the shareholders to request information about the number of shares issued and outstanding and payment of dividends.

        2)   Inspect stock certificates held in treasury. Treasury stock should be counted.

        3)   Inspect stock certificate book. If the client keeps its own stock records, the shares outstanding and stubs should be reconciled.

    e.   **S**tatement Presentation and Disclosure. Are balances reflected on the balance sheet and adequate disclosures provided?

        1)   Read minutes of meetings of the board of directors. Authorizations of actions concerning equity (e.g., issuances of additional shares, purchases or sales of treasury shares, and declarations of dividends) should be documented in the minutes. Many of these issues have implications concerning disclosure.

        2)   Make inquiries of management concerning the actions and activities related to equity.

        3)   Inspect disclosure of treasury stock. Determine the proper use of the method (cost or par value) to report treasury stock.

        4)   Search for restrictions. Restrictions on retained earnings may arise from loans, agreements, or state law. The auditor should determine that appropriate disclosure is made.

3.   Stop and review! You have completed the outline for this subunit. Study multiple-choice questions 21 through 23 beginning on page 409.

13.5 SUBSTANTIVE TESTING OF PAYROLL

1.   Payroll processing has traditionally included control procedures that have allowed the auditor to assess control risk at a low level and thereby reduce the audit effort devoted to substantive testing. Most firms recognize that the benefits of controls exceed the costs related to the payroll processing system. One key control is a division of duties that includes the establishment of a separate personnel department. This control procedure separates record keeping from authorization. The balances directly related to the audit of payroll are

    a.   Payroll expense
    b.   Inventories (for manufacturing firms)
    c.   Accrued payroll and vacation
    d.   Payroll tax liability
    e.   Pension costs and other post-employment benefit (OPEB) costs

2.   The following is a standard audit program for payroll and related accounts.

   a.   **C**ompleteness. Are all transactions affecting payroll included in the appropriate balances?

      1)   Perform analytical procedures. Compare current expense with expectations from prior periods. Compare management-prepared budgets from the beginning of the period with actual results. Use total hours worked to develop an expectation for total payroll expense. Compare this expectation with recorded expense. Compare industry percentages for labor-related ratios with the client's results.

      2)   Test payroll cutoff. Recalculate amounts to be accrued for the period from the last payroll date to year-end. Determine that amounts have been recorded as payroll expense and accrued payroll.

      3)   Reconcile payroll tax expense with payroll tax returns (income tax, FICA, and unemployment taxes).

   b.   Rights and **O**bligations. Are the assets (inventories), expenses, and payables those of the client?

      1)   Inspect canceled checks indicating payment to employees, government, and others relating to payroll.

   c.   **V**aluation or Allocation. Are balances reported in accordance with GAAP?

      1)   Trace costs to inventories (for manufacturing firms) to determine that they contain direct labor costs.

      2)   Recalculate pension and OPEB costs. Determine that appropriate amounts have been recorded and funded based on the appropriate agreements.

   d.   **E**xistence or Occurrence. Did transactions occur to support the balances?

      1)   Vouch a sample of employee transactions recorded in the payroll-related balances to the supporting documentation, including approved time cards, time tickets, and notations in the personnel records. The purpose is to verify that employees worked the number of hours for which they were paid.

      2)   Observe the distribution of paychecks. A surprise observation of the distribution will provide assurance that bona fide employees only are being paid.

   e.   **S**tatement Presentation and Disclosure. Are payroll costs properly reflected as an expense in the income statement (or properly allocated to inventory and cost of sales for manufacturing firms)? Are liabilities properly displayed as current or noncurrent on the balance sheet, and are notes presented adequately?

      1)   Read the financial statements. Determine the appropriate presentation of balances. Notes should include a description of accounting policies and pension-related transactions.

      2)   Make inquiries of management. Questions include those relating to the reporting and disclosure of contractual arrangements with officers, union contracts, pension, and OPEB agreements.

3.   Stop and review! You have completed the outline for this subunit. Study multiple-choice questions 24 through 29 beginning on page 410.

QUESTIONS

13.1 Substantive Testing of Property, Plant, and Equipment

1. Which of the following combinations of procedures would an auditor most likely perform to obtain evidence about fixed asset additions?

 A. Inspecting documents and physically examining assets.

 B. Recomputing calculations and obtaining written management representations.

 C. Observing operating activities and comparing balances with prior period balances.

 D. Confirming ownership and corroborating transactions through inquiries of client personnel.

Answer (A) is correct. *(CPA, adapted)*
REQUIRED: The combination of procedures most likely to obtain evidence about fixed asset additions.
DISCUSSION: The auditor's direct observation of fixed assets is one means of determining whether additions have been made. Tracing to the detailed records determines whether additions have been recorded. Inspection of deeds, lease agreements, insurance policies, invoices, canceled checks, and tax notices may also reveal additions.
Answer (B) is incorrect because recomputations are based on book amounts and will not reveal unrecorded additions. Answer (C) is incorrect because analytical procedures may not detect additions offset by disposals. Answer (D) is incorrect because the auditor must become aware of additions before confirming ownership or corroborating transactions.

2. In testing plant and equipment balances, an auditor may inspect new additions listed on the analysis of plant and equipment. This procedure is designed to obtain evidence concerning management's assertions about

	Existence or Occurrence	Presentation and Disclosure
A.	Yes	Yes
B.	Yes	No
C.	No	Yes
D.	No	No

Answer (B) is correct. *(CPA, adapted)*
REQUIRED: The management assertion(s), if any, tested by inspection of new additions of plant and equipment.
DISCUSSION: Assertions about existence address whether assets or liabilities of the entity exist at a particular date. Assertions about presentation and disclosure concern whether financial statement components are appropriately classified, described, and disclosed (AU 326). Thus, inspection by the auditor provides direct evidence that new plant and equipment assets exist but is irrelevant to the presentation and disclosure assertions. Reading the financial statements and related footnotes provides evidence about the latter assertions.

3. A weakness in internal control over recording retirements of equipment may cause an auditor to

 A. Inspect certain items of equipment in the plant and trace those items to the accounting records.

 B. Review the subsidiary ledger to ascertain whether depreciation was taken on each item of equipment during the year.

 C. Trace additions to the "other assets" account to search for equipment that is still on hand but no longer being used.

 D. Select certain items of equipment from the accounting records and locate them in the plant.

Answer (D) is correct. *(CPA, adapted)*
REQUIRED: The procedure performed as a result of ineffective control over equipment retirements.
DISCUSSION: Failure to record retirements results in overstating equipment in the subsidiary records because the physical assets are not in the entity's possession. Thus, vouching items from the accounting records by locating the physical assets they represent provides evidence of whether retirements are unrecorded.
Answer (A) is incorrect because the test is in the wrong direction to discover the failure to record retirements. Answer (B) is incorrect because depreciation should not be taken on equipment that is no longer in possession of the entity. Answer (C) is incorrect because equipment should be in the equipment account, not other assets. Thus, a search of additions to other assets would provide no evidence of retirements to equipment.

4. Determining that proper amounts of depreciation are expensed provides assurance about management's assertions of valuation or allocation and

 A. Presentation and disclosure.

 B. Completeness.

 C. Rights and obligations.

 D. Existence or occurrence.

Answer (A) is correct. *(CPA, adapted)*
REQUIRED: The assertion tested by consideration of the amounts of depreciation that are expensed.
DISCUSSION: The presentation and disclosure assertion concerns whether particular components of the financial statements are properly classified, described, and disclosed. For example, if expenses reflected on the income statement include depreciation, the auditor should determine that the presentation is appropriate and that depreciation methods are properly disclosed.

5. In performing a search for unrecorded retirements of fixed assets, an auditor most likely would

A. Inspect the property ledger and the insurance and tax records, and then tour the client's facilities.

B. Tour the client's facilities, and then inspect the property ledger and the insurance and tax records.

C. Analyze the repair and maintenance account, and then tour the client's facilities.

D. Tour the client's facilities, and then analyze the repair and maintenance account.

Answer (A) is correct. *(CPA, adapted)*
REQUIRED: The step performed in a search for unrecorded retirements of fixed assets.
DISCUSSION: In a search for unrecorded retirements, that is, a test of the existence assertion, the auditor should first determine from the property ledger what assets are recorded and then tour the facilities to determine whether those assets are physically present.
Answer (B) is incorrect because touring the facilities and then inspecting the property ledger and insurance and tax records tests to determine whether existing assets are recorded. Answer (C) is incorrect because analyzing the repair and maintenance account provides evidence as to whether capital assets have been inappropriately expensed. Answer (D) is incorrect because analyzing the repair and maintenance account provides evidence as to whether capital assets have been inappropriately expensed.

6. Which of the following explanations most likely would satisfy an auditor who questions management about significant debits to the accumulated depreciation accounts?

A. The estimated remaining useful lives of plant assets were revised upward.

B. Plant assets were retired during the year.

C. The prior year's depreciation expense was erroneously understated.

D. Overhead allocations were revised at year-end.

Answer (B) is correct. *(CPA, adapted)*
REQUIRED: The explanation for significant debits to the accumulated depreciation accounts.
DISCUSSION: Plant assets retired during the year should be removed from the records. The removal will result in a credit to plant assets and a debit to the related accumulated depreciation.
Answer (A) is incorrect because revision of useful lives upward does not affect accumulated depreciation at the time of the change. Answer (C) is incorrect because if depreciation expense is erroneously understated, credits to accumulated depreciation are expected. Answer (D) is incorrect because revision of overhead allocations is a change in estimate affecting subsequent transactions only.

7. When auditing prepaid insurance, an auditor discovers that the original insurance policy on plant equipment is not available for inspection. The policy's absence most likely indicates the possibility of a(n)

A. Insurance premium due but not recorded.

B. Deficiency in the coinsurance provision.

C. Lien on the plant equipment.

D. Understatement of insurance expense.

Answer (C) is correct. *(CPA, adapted)*
REQUIRED: The likely reason an insurance policy is not available for inspection.
DISCUSSION: When liens are placed on equipment or property, the lienholder often requires that the assets be insured and that the lienholder be named as the beneficiary. Hence, the policy would likely be held by the lienholder even though the client is required to pay the premiums.
Answer (A) is incorrect because the premium has been paid and recorded as prepaid insurance. Answer (B) is incorrect because coinsurance provisions require that the policy holder maintain coverage of a certain percentage of the value of the property (often 80-90%). Answer (D) is incorrect because the issue is not the recording of insurance, but the physical existence of the policy.

8. An auditor analyzes repairs and maintenance accounts primarily to obtain evidence in support of the audit assertion that all

A. Noncapitalizable expenditures for repairs and maintenance have been recorded in the proper period.

B. Expenditures for property and equipment have been recorded in the proper period.

C. Noncapitalizable expenditures for repairs and maintenance have been properly charged to expense.

D. Expenditures for property and equipment have not been charged to expense.

Answer (D) is correct. *(CPA, adapted)*
REQUIRED: The reason an auditor analyzes repairs and maintenance expense.
DISCUSSION: The auditor should vouch significant debits from the repairs and maintenance expense account to determine whether any should have been capitalized.
Answer (A) is incorrect because an improper cutoff of repairs and maintenance expenses is not typically a major risk. Answer (B) is incorrect because the repairs and maintenance expense accounts are not the appropriate sources of evidence regarding the cutoff of expenditures for property and equipment. Answer (C) is incorrect because vouching additions to plant, property, and equipment provides evidence of whether any expense has been inappropriately charged as a capital item.

9. In auditing intangible assets, an auditor most likely would review or recompute amortization and determine whether the amortization period is reasonable in support of management's financial statement assertion of

    A. Valuation or allocation.

    B. Existence or occurrence.

    C. Completeness.

    D. Rights and obligations.

Answer (A) is correct. *(CPA, adapted)*
    REQUIRED: The assertion tested in examining intangible assets and recomputing amortization.
    DISCUSSION: Amortization is an allocation process which the auditor tests by recomputing the amortization based upon the recorded assets and the useful lives.
    Answer (B) is incorrect because amortization is not directly related to the existence or occurrence assertion. Answer (C) is incorrect because amortization is not directly related to the completeness assertion. Answer (D) is incorrect because amortization is not directly related to the rights and obligations assertion.

13.2 Substantive Testing of Investments (AU 332)

10. Which of the following pairs of accounts would an auditor most likely analyze on the same working paper?

    A. Notes receivable and interest income.

    B. Accrued interest receivable and accrued interest payable.

    C. Notes payable and notes receivable.

    D. Interest income and interest expense.

Answer (A) is correct. *(CPA, adapted)*
    REQUIRED: The pairs of accounts that an auditor most likely analyzes on the same working paper.
    DISCUSSION: The auditor analyzes information and presents the analysis for related accounts on the same working paper. Notes receivable and interest thereon are such related accounts.
    Answer (B) is incorrect because interest receivable and interest payable are independent of one another and are not likely to be analyzed on the same working paper. Answer (C) is incorrect because notes payable and notes receivable are independent of one another and are not likely to be analyzed on the same working paper. Answer (D) is incorrect because interest income and interest expense are independent of one another and are not likely to be analyzed on the same working paper.

11. An auditor would most likely verify the interest earned on bond investments by

    A. Vouching the receipt and deposit of interest checks.

    B. Confirming the bond interest rate with the issuer of the bonds.

    C. Recomputing the interest earned on the basis of face amount, interest rate, and period held.

    D. Testing internal controls relevant to cash receipts.

Answer (C) is correct. *(CPA, adapted)*
    REQUIRED: The method most likely used to verify bond interest earned.
    DISCUSSION: The audit program for long-term investments includes making an independent computation of revenue (such as dividends and interest). For example, bond certificates contain information about interest rates, payment dates, issue date, and face amount that the auditor can use to recalculate bond interest earned, including amounts accrued but not collected during the period the auditee has held the investment.
    Answer (A) is incorrect because vouching the receipt and deposit of interest checks does not consider accrued interest. Answer (B) is incorrect because confirming the rate would not, by itself, verify interest earned, which must be recomputed. Answer (D) is incorrect because verification of interest earned requires substantive testing, not tests of controls.

12. An auditor usually tests the reasonableness of dividend income from investments in publicly held companies by computing the amounts that should have been received by referring to

    A. Dividend record books produced by investment advisory services.

    B. Stock indentures published by corporate transfer agents.

    C. Stock ledgers maintained by independent registrars.

    D. Annual audited financial statements issued by the investee companies.

Answer (A) is correct. *(CPA, adapted)*
    REQUIRED: The source of information for a test of dividend income.
    DISCUSSION: Investment advisory services, such as Dun & Bradstreet, publish dividend amounts and payment dates for publicly traded entities. The auditor can obtain this information to test whether the client has properly recorded investment income.
    Answer (B) is incorrect because a registrar and transfer agent handles the recording of routine stock trades among shareholders. Answer (C) is incorrect because stock ledgers maintained by registrars are records of original purchasers of stock from a corporation. Answer (D) is incorrect because audited financial statements from investee companies would be necessary to determine income for investments accounted for under the equity method.

13. A client has a large and active investment portfolio that is kept in a bank safe-deposit box. If the auditor is unable to count the securities at the balance sheet date, the auditor most likely will

A. Request the bank to confirm to the auditor the contents of the safe-deposit box at the balance sheet date.

B. Examine supporting evidence for transactions occurring during the year.

C. Count the securities at a subsequent date and confirm with the bank whether securities were added or removed since the balance sheet date.

D. Request the client to have the bank seal the safe-deposit box until the auditor can count the securities at a subsequent date.

Answer (D) is correct. *(CPA, adapted)*
REQUIRED: The procedure most likely performed when the auditor cannot count securities at the balance sheet date.
DISCUSSION: Securities should be inspected simultaneously with the verification of cash and the count of other liquid assets to prevent transfers among asset categories for the purpose of concealing a shortage. If this procedure is not possible but the securities are kept by a custodian in a bank safe-deposit box, the client may instruct the custodian that no one is to have access to the securities unless in the presence of the auditor. Thus, when the auditor finally inspects the securities, (s)he may conclude that they represent what was on hand at the balance sheet date.
Answer (A) is incorrect because the bank does not have access to the contents of the client's safe-deposit box. Answer (B) is incorrect because supporting evidence for transactions occurring during the year is not a substitute for inspection of the securities. Answer (C) is incorrect because the bank does not have access to the contents of the client's safe-deposit box.

14. In performing a count of negotiable securities, an auditor records the details of the count on a security count worksheet. What other information is usually included on this worksheet?

A. An acknowledgment by a client representative that the securities were returned intact.

B. An analysis of realized gains and losses from the sale of securities during the year.

C. An evaluation of the client's internal control concerning physical access to the securities.

D. A description of the client's procedures that prevent the negotiation of securities by just one person.

Answer (A) is correct. *(CPA, adapted)*
REQUIRED: The information usually included on a security count worksheet.
DISCUSSION: A securities count worksheet should include a record of all the significant information from the securities, such as names, amounts, and interest rates. Also, to ensure a clear chain of custody, it should contain an acknowledgment by a client representative that the securities were returned intact when the count was complete.
Answer (B) is incorrect because the gains and losses are typically analyzed on a separate working paper. Answer (C) is incorrect because documentation of internal control is in separate working papers. Answer (D) is incorrect because documentation of internal control is in separate working papers.

15. An auditor testing long-term investments would ordinarily use analytical procedures to ascertain the reasonableness of the

A. Existence of unrealized gains or losses.

B. Completeness of recorded investment income.

C. Classification as available-for-sale or trading securities.

D. Valuation of trading securities.

Answer (B) is correct. *(CPA, adapted)*
REQUIRED: The use of analytical procedures when an auditor tests long-term investments.
DISCUSSION: The auditor may develop expectations regarding the completeness assertion for recorded investment income from stocks by using dividend records published by standard investment advisory services to recompute dividends received. Interest income from bond investments can be calculated from interest rates and payment dates noted on the certificates. Income from equity-based investments can be estimated from audited financial statements of the investees. Thus, applying an expected rate of return to the net investment amount may be an effective means of estimating total investment income.
Answer (A) is incorrect because unrealized gains or losses are dependent on the fair values of specific securities and cannot be calculated based on plausible relationships among the data. Answer (C) is incorrect because available-for-sale securities may meet the definition of current assets. Answer (D) is incorrect because individual trading securities may meet the definition of current assets.

16. In confirming with an outside agent, such as a financial institution, that the agent is holding investment securities in the client's name, an auditor most likely gathers evidence in support of management's financial statement assertions of existence or occurrence and

    A. Valuation or allocation.

    B. Rights and obligations.

    C. Completeness.

    D. Presentation and disclosure.

Answer (B) is correct. *(CPA, adapted)*
    REQUIRED: The assertion tested by confirming investments to determine if they are in the client's name.
    DISCUSSION: Confirmations may be designed to test any financial statement assertion (AU 330). However, a given confirmation request does not test all assertions equally well. For example, if the issue is whether securities are being held in the client's name by an outside agent, the completeness assertion with regard to the investment account is not adequately addressed by a confirmation request. Other agents may be holding securities for the client. Moreover, the agent may be holding other securities not specified in the request. Thus, the request tends to be most effective for testing the existence (whether the assets exist at a given date) assertion and the rights (whether the client has a specified ownership interest in the assets) assertion.
    Answer (A) is incorrect because confirmations concerning securities in the client's name are not directly related to the valuation or allocation assertions. Answer (C) is incorrect because confirmations concerning securities in the client's name are not directly related to the completeness assertion. Answer (D) is incorrect because confirmations concerning securities in the client's name are not directly related to the presentation and disclosure assertions.

17. To satisfy the valuation assertion when auditing an investment accounted for by the equity method, an auditor most likely would

    A. Inspect the stock certificates evidencing the investment.

    B. Examine the audited financial statements of the investee company.

    C. Review the broker's advice or canceled check for the investment's acquisition.

    D. Obtain market quotations from financial newspapers or periodicals.

Answer (B) is correct. *(CPA, adapted)*
    REQUIRED: The procedure to test the valuation assertion for an equity-based investment.
    DISCUSSION: The equity method recognizes undistributed income arising from an investment in an investee. Under the equity method, investor income is recorded as the investee reports income. Consequently, the audited financial statements of the investee company provide the auditor with the undistributed income from the investee.
    Answer (A) is incorrect because inspection of stock certificates provides evidence about existence, not valuation. Answer (C) is incorrect because reviewing the broker's advice or canceled check provides evidence about rights. Answer (D) is incorrect because equity-based investments are not accounted for at fair value.

18. Auditors may need to plan and perform auditing procedures for financial statement assertions about derivatives and hedging activities. Which of the following substantive procedures most clearly tests the completeness assertion about derivatives?

    A. Assessing the reasonableness of the use of an option-pricing model.

    B. Determining whether changes in the fair value of derivatives designated and qualifying as hedging instruments have been reported in earnings or in other comprehensive income.

    C. Requesting counterparties to provide information about them, such as whether side agreements have been made.

    D. Physically inspecting the derivative contract.

Answer (C) is correct. *(Publisher)*
    REQUIRED: The substantive procedure that most clearly tests the completeness assertion about derivatives.
    DISCUSSION: An audit of the completeness assertion addresses whether derivatives are recognized or disclosed in the financial statements, that is, in earnings, other comprehensive income, or cash flows or through disclosure. An example of a substantive procedure for the completeness assertion about derivatives and securities is a request to the counterparty to a derivative or the holder of a security for information about it, for example, whether an agreement exists to repurchase securities sold or whether side agreements have been made. A request might also be made to counterparties or holders who are frequently used, but who the accounting records indicate do not currently stand in that relationship to the reporting entity.
    Answer (A) is incorrect because assessing the reasonableness of the use of an option-pricing model tests the valuation assertion. Answer (B) is incorrect because determining whether changes in the fair value of derivatives designated and qualifying as hedging instruments have been reported in earnings or in other comprehensive income tests the presentation assertion. Answer (D) is incorrect because physically inspecting the derivative contract tests the existence assertion.

13.3 Substantive Testing of Long-Term Debt

19. An auditor's program to audit long-term debt should include steps that require

    A. Examining bond trust indentures.

    B. Inspecting the accounts payable subsidiary ledger.

    C. Investigating credits to the bond interest income account.

    D. Verifying the existence of the bondholders.

Answer (A) is correct. *(CPA, adapted)*
    REQUIRED: The procedure to be included in the audit program for long-term debt.
    DISCUSSION: The bond trust indenture contains information concerning contractual arrangements made with bondholders, such as the face amount of the bonds, interest rates, payment dates, descriptions of collateral, provisions for conversion or retirement, trustee duties, and sinking fund requirements. The auditor should examine any bond trust indenture to determine that the client is meeting the conditions of the contract and is in compliance with the law.
    Answer (B) is incorrect because accounts payable are current liabilities, not long-term debt. Answer (C) is incorrect because credits to bond interest income do not pertain to long-term debt (income relates to investments, not debt). Answer (D) is incorrect because the existence of bondholders is implied by the reporting of bonded debt.

20. In auditing for unrecorded long-term bonds payable, an auditor most likely will

    A. Perform analytical procedures on the bond premium and discount accounts.

    B. Examine documentation of assets purchased with bond proceeds for liens.

    C. Compare interest expense with the bond payable amount for reasonableness.

    D. Confirm the existence of individual bondholders at year-end.

Answer (C) is correct. *(CPA, adapted)*
    REQUIRED: The appropriate procedure for testing long-term bonds payable.
    DISCUSSION: The recorded interest expense should reconcile with the outstanding bonds payable. If interest expense appears excessive relative to the recorded bonds payable, unrecorded long-term liabilities may exist.
    Answer (A) is incorrect because analytical procedures on bond premium and discount accounts are not likely to uncover unrecorded payables. Answer (B) is incorrect because the examination of documentation related to asset additions is considered in the audit of assets, not bonds payable. Answer (D) is incorrect because confirmation tests existence, but the greatest risk is that the bonds payable balance is not complete.

13.4 Substantive Testing of Equity

21. During an audit of a company's equity accounts, the auditor determines whether restrictions have been imposed on retained earnings resulting from loans, agreements, or state law. This audit procedure most likely is intended to verify management's assertion of

    A. Existence or occurrence.

    B. Completeness.

    C. Valuation or allocation.

    D. Presentation and disclosure.

Answer (D) is correct. *(CPA, adapted)*
    REQUIRED: The assertion that the auditor tests relative to restrictions on retained earnings.
    DISCUSSION: The presentation and disclosure assertion concerns the classification, description, and disclosure of financial statement components (AU 326). Hence, when restrictions have been placed on retained earnings, the auditor should determine that they are properly disclosed in the notes to the financial statements.
    Answer (A) is incorrect because restrictions on retained earnings have little relevance to the existence assertion. Answer (B) is incorrect because restrictions on retained earnings have little relevance to the completeness assertion. Answer (C) is incorrect because restrictions on retained earnings have little relevance to the valuation assertion.

22. When a client's company does not maintain its own stock records, the auditor should obtain written confirmation from the transfer agent and registrar concerning

A. Restrictions on the payment of dividends.

B. The number of shares issued and outstanding.

C. Guarantees of preferred stock liquidation value.

D. The number of shares subject to agreements to repurchase.

Answer (B) is correct. *(CPA, adapted)*
REQUIRED: The information confirmed by the transfer agent and registrar.
DISCUSSION: The independent stock registrar is a financial institution employed to prevent improper issuances of stock, especially over-issuances. The transfer agent maintains detailed shareholder records and facilitates transfer of shares. Both are independent and reliable sources of evidence concerning total shares issued and outstanding.
Answer (A) is incorrect because evidence about the payment of dividends would be confirmed, but dividend restrictions would be found in the articles of incorporation, bylaws, and minutes of directors' and shareholders' meetings. Answer (C) is incorrect because guarantees of preferred stock liquidation value are beyond the purview of the transfer agent and registrar. Answer (D) is incorrect because the number of shares subject to agreements to repurchase is not the concern of the transfer agent and registrar.

23. An auditor usually obtains evidence of a company's equity transactions by reviewing its

A. Minutes of board of directors meetings.

B. Transfer agent's records.

C. Canceled stock certificates.

D. Treasury stock certificate book.

Answer (A) is correct. *(CPA, adapted)*
REQUIRED: The source of evidence about equity transactions.
DISCUSSION: Equity transactions are typically few in number and large in amount. They require authorization by the board of directors. Thus, an auditor would review the minutes of the board meetings to identify transactions.
Answer (B) is incorrect because, although the auditor might confirm certain transactions with the client's transfer agent, the agent's records are not typically made available to the auditor. Answer (C) is incorrect because canceled stock certificates only represent those shares that were retired. Answer (D) is incorrect because treasury stock records include only those transactions involving reacquisition and resale of the company's own stock.

13.5 Substantive Testing of Payroll

24. An auditor vouched data for a sample of employees in a payroll register to approved clock card data to provide assurance that

A. Payments to employees are computed at authorized rates.

B. Employees work the number of hours for which they are paid.

C. Segregation of duties exist between the preparation and distribution of the payroll.

D. Internal controls relating to unclaimed payroll checks are operating effectively.

Answer (B) is correct. *(CPA, adapted)*
REQUIRED: The purpose of vouching payroll register information to approved clock card data.
DISCUSSION: To test the existence assertion, an auditor would vouch a sample of employee transactions recorded in the payroll-related balances to supporting documentation, including approved time cards, time tickets, and notations in personnel records. The purpose is to verify that employees worked the number of hours for which they were paid.
Answer (A) is incorrect because the auditor would compare the pay rates used in calculating payments to employees with the authorized rates in the personnel files to determine if they were authorized. Answer (C) is incorrect because the auditor tests segregation of duties by inquiry and observation. Answer (D) is incorrect because the auditor would observe the activities of the treasurer to determine if unclaimed payroll checks were being properly controlled.

25. When control risk is assessed as low for assertions related to payroll, substantive tests of payroll balances most likely would be limited to applying analytical procedures and

A. Observing the distribution of paychecks.

B. Footing and crossfooting the payroll register.

C. Inspecting payroll tax returns.

D. Recalculating payroll accruals.

Answer (D) is correct. *(CPA, adapted)*
REQUIRED: The audit procedure for payroll when control risk is assessed as low.
DISCUSSION: When controls are judged to be effective, the auditor's procedures are typically limited to analytical procedures and testing for completeness of the year-end accruals.
Answer (A) is incorrect because the auditor would consider the observation of the distribution of the paychecks if control risk were assessed as high. Answer (B) is incorrect because effective controls should provide assurance of proper reporting. Additionally, analytical procedures should indicate likely misstatements. Answer (C) is incorrect because effective controls should provide assurance of proper reporting. Additionally, analytical procedures should indicate likely misstatements.

26. An auditor most likely would perform substantive tests of details on payroll transactions and balances when

A. Cutoff tests indicate a substantial amount of accrued payroll expense.

B. The assessed level of control risk relative to payroll transactions is low.

C. Analytical procedures indicate unusual fluctuations in recurring payroll entries.

D. Accrued payroll expense consists primarily of unpaid commissions.

Answer (C) is correct. *(CPA, adapted)*
REQUIRED: The situation in which the auditor would most likely perform substantive tests of details on payroll transactions and balances.
DISCUSSION: The auditor should evaluate significant unexpected differences revealed by analytical procedures. The first step is to reconsider the methods and factors used in developing the expectations and to make inquiries of management. If a suitable explanation is not received, additional procedures to investigate the differences are necessary.
Answer (A) is incorrect because a substantial amount of accrued payroll expense is not an abnormal condition. Answer (B) is incorrect because a low assessed level of control risk may permit the auditor to devote less effort to substantive tests. Answer (D) is incorrect because the existence of unpaid earned commissions provides no indication of a misstatement.

27. In auditing payroll when control risk is assessed as low, an auditor most likely will

A. Verify that checks representing unclaimed wages are mailed.

B. Trace individual employee deductions to entity journal entries.

C. Observe entity employees during a payroll distribution.

D. Compare payroll costs with entity standards or budgets.

Answer (D) is correct. *(CPA, adapted)*
REQUIRED: The procedure most likely performed during the audit of payroll.
DISCUSSION: Comparing payroll costs with budgeted amounts is a standard analytical procedure that is performed in most audits of payroll.
Answer (A) is incorrect because checks representing unclaimed wages should be maintained by the treasurer until claimed by the appropriate employees. Answer (B) is incorrect because the individual employee deductions do not result in entity journal entries, but cumulative journal entries record the sum of the payroll. Answer (C) is incorrect because observation of payroll distribution is a standard procedure but is not necessary when assessed control risk is low.

28. An auditor most likely increases substantive tests of payroll when

A. Payroll is extensively audited by the state government.

B. Payroll expense is substantially higher than in the prior year.

C. Overpayments are discovered in performing tests of details.

D. Employees complain to management about too much overtime.

Answer (C) is correct. *(CPA, adapted)*
REQUIRED: The point at which the auditor would likely extend substantive tests of payroll.
DISCUSSION: During the application of substantive tests, the auditor may decide to extend the tests when unexpected findings (e.g., overpayments) are made. The purpose is to determine the extent of any fraud.
Answer (A) is incorrect because, when payroll is audited by external parties, the auditor may decide to do less testing in the area. Answer (B) is incorrect because, although an analytical procedure in the planning stage might suggest more testing, the question indicates that substantive tests have already begun. Answer (D) is incorrect because employees' concern about too much overtime is not likely to affect the auditor's testing of the payroll.

29. Which of the following circumstances most likely will cause an auditor to suspect an employee payroll fraud scheme?

A. There are significant unexplained variances between standard and actual labor cost.

B. Payroll checks are disbursed by the same employee each payday.

C. Employee time cards are approved by individual departmental supervisors.

D. A separate payroll bank account is maintained on an imprest basis.

Answer (A) is correct. *(CPA, adapted)*
REQUIRED: The circumstance most likely to cause the auditor to suspect an employee payroll fraud scheme.
DISCUSSION: Analytical procedures, such as variance analysis, alert the auditor when actual results were not anticipated. Thus, the auditor should consider the possibility that payroll is fraudulently overstated.
Answer (B) is incorrect because the payroll checks should be disbursed by the paymaster each pay period. Answer (C) is incorrect because supervisors should approve individual time cards. Answer (D) is incorrect because a separate payroll account using an imprest basis provides additional control over payroll.

13.6 PRACTICE SIMULATION

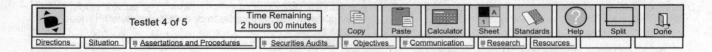

| | Testlet 4 of 5 | Time Remaining 2 hours 00 minutes | Copy | Paste | Calculator | Sheet | Standards | Help | Split | Done |

Directions | Situation | ⊞ Assertations and Procedures | ⊞ Securities Audits | ⊞ Objectives | ⊞ Communication | ⊞ Research | Resources

1. Directions

In the following simulation, you will be asked to complete various tasks related to evidence – other assets, liabilities, and equities. The simulation will provide all the information necessary to do the work. For full credit, be sure to view and complete all work tabs.

Resources are available under the tab marked RESOURCES. You may want to review the resources before beginning the simulation.

2. Situation

Kyba Inc. is a global designer and manufacturer of fine jewelry. Kyba is a continuing engagement of the Shubert CPA firm, which has identified several new audit-relevant issues that have arisen in the current year: (1) Kyba entered into several loan agreements to finance the construction of a smelting plant in Arizona. (2) In a strategy to improve efficiency, Kyba has begun buying up interests in several of its suppliers and entering into derivative contracts with retail customers to smooth effects of volatile raw materials prices. Shubert is amending the prior year's audit program to fulfill its responsibility for collecting sufficient competent evidential matter relating to this year's other assets, liabilities, and equity.

3. Matching Management Assertions to Audit Procedures

This question has a matching format that requires you to select the correct response from a drop-down list. Write each answer in the shaded column. Each choice may be used once, more than once, or not at all. Match the most likely assertion being tested with the audit procedure in the table below.

Audit Procedure	Answer
1. The auditor tested equipment by vouching significant debits to repairs and maintenance to determine whether any should have been capitalized.	
2. The auditor tested depreciation related to equipment to determine that it is generally accepted and applied consistently.	
3. The auditor examined titles related to vehicles reported in the equipment account.	
4. The auditor determined that equipment was displayed in the long-term asset category on the balance sheet.	
5. The auditor applied an analytical procedure to long-term debt by comparing the current year's balance with that of the previous year.	
6. The auditor tested the amortization of the recorded premium on long-term debt by recalculating the amount.	
7. The auditor reconciled the amounts of debt in the subsidiary ledger with the total in the general ledger account.	
8. The auditor confirmed shares of common stock issued and outstanding with the registrar and transfer agent of the client.	
9. The auditor determined that restrictions on the issuance of dividends were properly described in the financial statement notes.	
10. The auditor determined that the loss associated with the sale of treasury stock was properly calculated.	

Assertion
A) Completeness
B) Rights and obligations
C) Valuation or allocation
D) Existence or occurrence
E) Statement presentation and disclosure

4. Audit of Securities

This question is presented in a check-the-box format that requires you to select the correct response from a given list.

Indicate whether each statement about the audit of securities is correct or incorrect. None of the statements relates to securities being held as a hedge.

Statement	Correct	Incorrect
1. The auditor should determine that trading securities are recorded at cost at the balance sheet date.		
2. The auditor should determine that the client has both the positive intent and ability to hold held-to-maturity securities.		
3. The auditor should determine that available-for-sale securities are measured at fair value.		
4. The auditor expects to find a client holding common stock in the held-to-maturity category.		
5. The auditor should determine that a transfer from the held-to-maturity to trading category is made at fair value.		
6. The auditor should consider obtaining audited financial statements from an investee if investments are accounted for by the equity method.		
7. The auditor typically concludes that market quotations are the best evidence of fair value estimates.		
8. The auditor expects premium or discount for available-for-sale securities to be amortized.		
9. The auditor expects to find a nontemporary decline in the value of held-to-maturity securities reflected in current earnings.		
10. The auditor should determine that holding gains on an available-for-sale security are included in other comprehensive income.		

5. Audit Objectives

This question has a multiple-choice format that requires you to select the correct response from a drop-down list. Write the answer in the shaded column next to the audit objective.

Items 1 through 10 represent audit objectives for the investments, accounts receivable, and property and equipment accounts. Select the audit procedure that primarily achieves each objective. Select only one procedure for each audit objective. A procedure may be selected only once or not at all.

Audit Objectives for Investments	*Answer*
1. Investments are properly described and classified in the financial statements.	
2. Recorded investments represent investments actually owned at the balance sheet date.	
3. Available-for-sale securities are properly measured at fair value at the balance sheet date.	

Audit Objectives for Accounts Receivable	*Answer*
4. Accounts receivable represent all amounts owed to the entity at the balance sheet date.	
5. The entity has a legal right to all accounts receivable at the balance sheet date.	
6. Accounts receivable are stated at net realizable value.	
7. Accounts receivable are properly described and presented in the financial statements.	

Audit Objectives for Property and Equipment	*Answer*
8. The entity has a legal right to property and equipment acquired during the year.	
9. Recorded property and equipment represent assets that actually exist at the balance sheet date.	
10. Net property and equipment are properly valued at the balance sheet date.	

Choices – Investments

A) Trace investment transactions to minutes of the board of directors' meetings to determine that transactions were properly authorized.

B) Obtain positive confirmations as of the balance sheet date of investments held by independent custodians.

C) Determine that any other-than-temporary impairments of the price of investments have been properly recorded.

D) Verify that available-for-sale securities are properly classified as current or noncurrent.

Choices – Accounts Receivable

A) Review the aged trial balance for significant past due accounts.

B) Review the accounts receivable trial balance for amounts due from officers and employees.

C) Perform sales cutoff tests to obtain assurance that sales transactions and corresponding entries for inventories and cost of goods sold are recorded in the same and proper period.

D) Review loan agreements for indications of whether accounts receivable have been factored or pledged.

Choices – Property and Equipment

A) Review the provision for depreciation expense and determine that depreciable lives and methods used in the current year are consistent with those used in the prior year.

B) Physically examine all major property and equipment additions.

C) Examine deeds and title insurance certificates.

6. Communication

In a brief memorandum to a client regarding the audit of derivatives, list at least four factors considered by an auditor when assessing inherent risk in an audit of derivatives. Also list at least three factors considered by an auditor when assessing control risk in such an engagement. Type your communication in your word processor program and print out the copy in a memorandum style format.

REMINDER: Your response will be graded for both technical content and writing skills. You should demonstrate your ability to develop, organize, and express your ideas. Do not convey information in the form of a table, bullet point list, or other abbreviated presentation.

To: Client
From: CPA
Subject: Inherent risk and control risk in an audit of derivatives

7. Research

Find the answer to the following question using the AICPA Professional Standards available in the Research tab. Print the appropriate citation in its entirety from the source you choose. This is a copy-and-paste item.

Research the information concerning derivatives and securities that should be included in the management representation letter. Cite the appropriate auditing standard.

Unofficial Answers

3. Matching Management Assertions to Audit Procedures (10 Gradable Items)

1.   A) Completeness - The auditor tested equipment by vouching significant debits to repairs and maintenance to determine whether any should have been capitalized.

2.   C) Valuation or allocation - The auditor tested depreciation related to equipment to determine that it is generally accepted and applied consistently.

3.   B) Rights and obligations - The auditor examined titles related to vehicles in equipment.

4.   E) Statement presentation and disclosure - The auditor determined that equipment was displayed in the long-term asset category on the balance sheet.

5.   A) Completeness - The auditor applied an analytical procedure to long-term debt by comparing the current year's balance with that of the previous year.

6.   C) Valuation or allocation - The auditor tested the amortization of the recorded premium on long-term debt by recalculating the amount.

7.   A) Completeness - The auditor reconciled the amounts of debt in the subsidiary ledger with the total in the general ledger account.

8. <u>D) Existence or occurrence</u> - The auditor confirmed shares of common stock issued and outstanding of the client with the registrar and transfer agent.

9. <u>E) Statement presentation and disclosure</u> - The auditor determined that restrictions on the issuance of dividends were properly described in the financial statement notes.

10. <u>C) Valuation or allocation</u> - The auditor determined that the loss associated with the sale of treasury stock was properly calculated.

4. Audit of Securities (10 Gradable Items)

1. <u>Incorrect</u> - The auditor should not determine that trading securities are recorded at cost at the balance sheet date.

2. <u>Correct</u> - The auditor should determine that the client has both the positive intent and ability to hold held-to-maturity securities.

3. <u>Correct</u> - The auditor should determine that available-for-sale securities are held at fair value.

4. <u>Incorrect</u> - The auditor would not expect to find a client holding common stock securities in the category of held-to-maturity.

5. <u>Correct</u> - The auditor should determine that a transfer from the held-to-maturity to trading category is made at fair value.

6. <u>Correct</u> - The auditor should consider obtaining audited financial statements from an investee if investments are accounted for by the equity method.

7. <u>Correct</u> - The auditor would typically conclude that market quotations are the best evidence of fair value estimates.

8. <u>Incorrect</u> - The auditor would not expect to find amortization of premium or discount for available-for-sale securities.

9. <u>Correct</u> - The auditor would expect to find a nontemporary decline in the value of held-to-maturity securities reflected in current earnings.

10. <u>Correct</u> - The auditor should determine that holding gains on an available-for-sale security is included in other comprehensive income.

5. Audit Objectives (10 Gradable Items)

1. <u>D)</u> Proper description and classification of investments relates to the statement presentation and disclosure assertion. Proper disclosure relates to the appropriate classification of assets as current or noncurrent.

2. <u>B)</u> Confirmations are most effective for the existence and rights and obligation assertions.

3. <u>C)</u> Impairment of the price of investments means that fair value is less than the recorded cost. If available-for-sale securities are subject to an other-than-temporary impairment, their cost basis is written down and the change is included in earnings, not in a separate component of equity.

4. <u>C)</u> Cutoff tests typically relate to the completeness assertion. The objective is to determine that all transactions occurring during a period are recorded in that period.

5. <u>D)</u> Legal titles relates to the assertion of rights and obligations. Pledging or factoring may convey the right of the creditor to collect the receivables. Hence, the client may not have ownership rights in the assets.

6. <u>A)</u> Aging of receivables analyzes the probability of collection of receivables and is therefore related to the valuation assertion. Accounts receivable should be reported at net realizable value.

7. <u>B)</u> Accounts receivable should be presented as a current asset with any significant issues reported in the financial statement notes. One required disclosure is the existence of related party transactions. Significant amounts due from officers and employees should be disclosed in the notes.

8. <u>C)</u> Deeds and title insurance provide evidence that the client has rights related to property.

9. <u>B)</u> Physical examination of property provides strong evidence supporting the existence assertion. The auditor usually inspects all major additions of property recorded during the period.

10. <u>A)</u> Property and equipment (except land) should be recorded at cost and depreciated over their useful lives. The auditor reviews depreciation procedures during the testing of the valuation and allocation assertion.

6. Communication (5 Gradable Items; For grading instructions, please refer to page 11.)

> To: Client
> From: CPA
> Subject: Inherent risk and control risk in an audit of derivatives

This memorandum summarizes our discussion of the guidance followed by an external independent auditor when assessing inherent risk and control risk in a financial statement audit.

AU 332, *Auditing Derivative Instruments, Hedging Activities, and Investments in Securities*, provides guidance for planning and performing audit procedures to test assertions about derivatives and hedging activities accounted for under SFAS 133. The guidance also applies to all debt and equity securities.

The assessment of inherent risk for derivatives depends on such factors as their complexity, management's objectives, whether the pertinent transactions involved a cash exchange, and the extent of the entity's experience with derivatives and securities. Other factors to be considered are whether a derivative is embedded in a host contract, external matters (credit risk, market risk, etc.), the further evolution of derivatives and relevant GAAP, the entity's reliance on the expertise of outsiders, and assumptions required by GAAP.

The assessment of control risk for derivatives requires consideration of whether controls provide for independent monitoring of derivatives activities, independent approval of transactions in excess of limits, and high-level review of the identified controls and the results of derivatives activities. Other factors to be considered are senior management's attention to situations in which limits are exceeded and divergences occur from approved derivatives strategies, and reconciliations over the full range of derivatives.

If you have any questions or comments about the approach described above, please contact us at your convenience.

7. Research (7 Gradable Items)

AU Section 332 -- *Auditing Derivative Instruments, Hedging Activities, and Investments in Securities*

Management Representations

.58   Section 333, *Management Representations*, provides guidance to auditors in obtaining written representations from management. The auditor ordinarily should obtain written representations from management confirming aspects of management's intent and ability that affect assertions about derivatives and securities, such as its intent and ability to hold a debt security until its maturity or to enter into a forecasted transaction for which hedge accounting is applied. In addition, the auditor should consider obtaining written representations from management confirming other aspects of derivatives and securities transactions that affect assertions about them.

Scoring Schedule:

	Correct Responses		Gradable Items		Weights		
Tab 3	_____	÷	10	×	20%	=	_____
Tab 4	_____	÷	10	×	20%	=	_____
Tab 5	_____	÷	10	×	20%	=	_____
Tab 6	_____	÷	5	×	30%	=	_____
Tab 7	_____	÷	7	×	10%	=	_____
							_____
							(Your Score)

Use Gleim's ***CPA Review Online*** to practice more simulations in a realistic environment.

STUDY UNIT FOURTEEN
EVIDENCE -- KEY CONSIDERATIONS

(13 pages of outline)

14.1 Substantive Tests Prior to the Balance Sheet Date (AU 313) 419
14.2 Inquiry of a Client's Lawyer Concerning Litigation, Claims, and Assessments (AU 337) 421
14.3 Subsequent Events (AU 560) 423
14.4 Subsequent Discovery of Facts Existing at the Date of the Auditor's Report (AU 561) 425
14.5 Management Representations (AU 333) 426
14.6 Auditor's Consideration of an Entity's Ability to Continue as a Going Concern (AU 341) 428
14.7 Practice Simulation 444

Study Unit 14 presents a number of topics related to the collection of evidence. Of these issues, inquiry of the client's lawyer, going concern evidence, and client representations have been tested most consistently on recent exams and are the most likely candidates for future exams. All topics presented here are likely subjects of future multiple-choice questions.

14.1 SUBSTANTIVE TESTS PRIOR TO THE BALANCE SHEET DATE (AU 313)

1. **General Considerations**

   a. Interim testing may permit early consideration of significant matters affecting the year-end statements (e.g., related party transactions, changed conditions, recent accounting pronouncements, and financial statement items likely to require adjustment). Much of the audit planning, including obtaining an understanding of internal control, assessing control risk, and applying substantive tests, can be done before the balance sheet date.

   b. Applying substantive tests at an interim date potentially increases the risk that misstatements may not be detected at year-end.

      1) The longer the period of time from interim to year-end, the greater the potential audit risk.

      2) This incremental risk can be controlled if the substantive tests for the remaining period are designed to provide a reasonable basis for extending conclusions drawn from tests of details (both transactions and balances) at the interim date.

2. **Factors Considered before Substantive Testing of Details at Interim Dates**

   a. The auditor should assess the difficulty, cost, and benefits of controlling the incremental audit risk.

   b. Assessing control risk at below the maximum is not required to have a reasonable basis for extending audit conclusions from an interim date to the balance sheet date. But, if the auditor assesses control risk at the maximum for the remaining period, (s)he should consider whether the effectiveness of certain substantive tests to cover that period will be impaired.

   c. Consideration should be given to whether

      1) Rapidly changing business conditions or circumstances might predispose management to misstate financial statements in the remaining period

      2) The year-end balances of accounts selected for interim examination are reasonably predictable as to amount, relative significance, and composition

      3) The procedures for analyzing and adjusting such accounts at interim dates and for establishing cutoffs are appropriate

      4)   The accounting system provides information about year-end balances and the transactions in the remaining period that is sufficient for the investigation of

          a)   Significant unusual transactions or entries (including those at or near year-end)

          b)   Other causes of significant fluctuations

          c)   Changes in the composition of balances

3.   **Extending Audit Conclusions**

    a.   The audit work should achieve the year-end audit objectives. Tests ordinarily should include

        1)   Comparison of information about year-end and interim balances to identify unusual amounts

        2)   Investigation of any such unusual amounts

        3)   Other analytical procedures or substantive tests of details, or a combination, to provide a reasonable basis for extending audit conclusions about the assertions tested at the interim date to year-end

    b.   Factors to be considered in selecting procedures include

        1)   The nature of the transactions and balances relative to the assertions

        2)   The availability of historical data or other criteria used in analytical procedures

        3)   The availability of records required for tests of details and the nature of the applicable tests

    c.   Detection of misstatements at interim dates may require modification of the planned nature, timing, or extent of substantive tests for the remaining period or reperformance of certain auditing procedures at the year-end.

    d.   The assessment of possible misstatement at year-end should be based on the

        1)   Implications of the nature and cause of the interim misstatements
        2)   Possible relationship to other aspects of the audit
        3)   Corrections made by the auditee
        4)   Results of auditing procedures for the remaining period

4.   **Coordinating the Timing of Procedures**

    a.   Audit procedures should be properly timed and coordinated given the assessed level of control risk and the possible procedures that could be applied.

    b.   For example, the tests of interrelated accounts and cutoffs should be coordinated. Another example is the simultaneous control over negotiable assets and the testing of those items and cash on hand and in banks, bank loans, and related items.

5.   Stop and review! You have completed the outline for this subunit. Study multiple-choice questions 1 through 5 beginning on page 432.

14.2 INQUIRY OF A CLIENT'S LAWYER CONCERNING LITIGATION, CLAIMS, AND ASSESSMENTS (AU 337)

1. **Accounting Considerations**

   a. Management is responsible for adopting policies and procedures to identify, evaluate, and account for litigation, claims, and assessments.

      1) Relevant accounting principles are set forth in SFAS 5, *Accounting for Contingencies.*

2. **Auditing Considerations**

   a. The independent auditor should obtain evidence relevant to

      1) Circumstances indicating an uncertainty as to possible loss from litigation, claims, and assessments

      2) The period in which the underlying cause for legal action occurred

      3) The probability of an unfavorable outcome

      4) The amount or range of potential loss

   b. The independent auditor's procedures include

      1) Inquiring about, and discussing with management, the policies and procedures adopted for identifying, evaluating, and accounting for litigation, claims, and assessments

      2) Obtaining from management a description and evaluation of litigation, claims, and assessments that existed at period-end, and from then to the date the information is furnished, including an identification of matters referred to legal counsel

         a) The auditor should also obtain assurances from management, ordinarily in writing, that all such matters required to be disclosed by SFAS 5 have been disclosed.

      3) Examining documents in the client's possession (e.g., correspondence and invoices from lawyers)

      4) Obtaining assurance from management, usually in writing, that it has disclosed all unasserted claims that the lawyer has advised them are probable of assertion and that must be disclosed in accordance with SFAS 5

      5) Applying related procedures. An audit normally includes procedures undertaken for other purposes that might also produce evidence about litigation, claims, and assessments. Some examples are

         a) Reading minutes of meetings of shareholders, directors, and appropriate committees held during and subsequent to the period being audited

         b) Reading contracts, loan agreements, leases, and correspondence from governmental agencies, and similar documents

         c) Obtaining information about guarantees from bank confirmations

         d) Inspecting other documents for possible guarantees by the client

      6) Requesting the client's management to send a letter of inquiry to lawyers with whom management consulted. An auditor usually cannot make legal judgments.

c. Inquiry of a client's lawyer

1) A letter of audit inquiry to the client's lawyer is the auditor's primary means of obtaining corroboration of the information furnished by management.

2) The **letter of audit inquiry** includes

    a) Identification of the company and its subsidiaries and the date of the audit

    b) A management list (or a request by management that the lawyer prepare a list) that describes and evaluates **pending** or **threatened** litigation, claims, and assessments with respect to which the lawyer has been engaged and to which (s)he has devoted substantive attention on behalf of the company in the form of legal consultation or representation. For each matter, the lawyer should be requested either to provide the following information or comment on disagreements with management.

        i) The nature of the matter, the progress of the case, and the company's intended action

        ii) The probability of an unfavorable outcome and an estimate, if possible, of the amount or range of loss

        iii) Omission of any pending or threatened litigation, claims, and assessments from management's list

    c) A management list that describes and evaluates **unasserted** claims and assessments that management considers to be probable of assertion, and that would have at least a reasonable possibility of an unfavorable outcome, with respect to which the lawyer has been engaged and to which (s)he has devoted substantive attention on behalf of the company in the form of legal consultation or representation. Also included is a request that the lawyer comment on those matters that are the basis for disagreements with management.

    d) A client statement to the effect that the client understands that the lawyer will advise the client when an unasserted claim or assertion with respect to which (s)he has provided legal services requires the client to disclose or consider disclosure in accordance with SFAS 5. The letter of audit inquiry should request the lawyer to confirm this understanding.

    e) A request that the lawyer explain any limitation on his/her response

3) An example of the text of a letter of audit inquiry to the client's lawyer is presented on the next page.

4) Inquiry need not be made about immaterial matters if the client and the auditor have an understanding about the limits of materiality.

d. **Limitations on the scope of a lawyer's response.** A lawyer's refusal to furnish the information requested in an inquiry letter either in writing or orally would be a limitation on the scope of the audit sufficient to preclude an unqualified opinion.

ILLUSTRATIVE TEXT FOR AUDIT INQUIRY LETTER TO CLIENT'S LAWYER

In connection with an audit of our financial statements at (balance sheet date) and for the (period) then ended, management of the Company has prepared, and furnished to our auditors (name and address of auditors), a description and evaluation of certain contingencies, including those set forth below involving matters with respect to which you have been engaged and to which you have devoted substantive attention on behalf of the Company in the form of legal consultation or representation. These contingencies are regarded by management of the Company as material for this purpose (management may indicate a materiality limit if an understanding has been reached with the auditor). Your response should include matters that existed at (balance sheet date) and during the period from that date to the date of your response.

Pending or Threatened Litigation (excluding unasserted claims)

[Ordinarily the information would include the following: (1) the nature of the litigation, (2) the progress of the case to date, (3) how management is responding or intends to respond to the litigation (for example, to contest the case vigorously or to seek an out-of-court settlement), and (4) an evaluation of the likelihood of an unfavorable outcome and an estimate, if one can be made, of the amount or range of potential loss.] Please furnish to our auditors such explanation, if any, that you consider necessary to supplement the foregoing information, including an explanation of those matters as to which your views may differ from those stated and an identification of the omission of any pending or threatened litigation, claims, and assessments or a statement that the list of such matters is complete.

Unasserted Claims and Assessments (considered by management to be probable of assertion, and that, if asserted, would have at least a reasonable possibility of an unfavorable outcome)

[Ordinarily management's information would include the following: (1) the nature of the matter, (2) how management intends to respond if the claim is asserted, and (3) an evaluation of the likelihood of an unfavorable outcome and an estimate, if one can be made, of the amount or range of potential loss.] Please furnish to our auditors such explanation, if any, that you consider necessary to supplement the foregoing information, including an explanation of those matters as to which your views may differ from those stated.

We understand that whenever, in the course of performing legal services for us with respect to a matter recognized to involve an unasserted possible claim or assessment that may call for financial statement disclosure, if you have formed a professional conclusion that we should disclose or consider disclosure concerning such possible claim or assessment, as a matter of professional responsibility to us, you will so advise us and will consult with us concerning the question of such disclosure and the applicable requirements of Statement of Financial Accounting Standards No. 5. Please specifically confirm to our auditors that our understanding is correct.

Please specifically identify the nature of and reasons for any limitation on your response.

[The auditor may request the client to inquire about additional matters, for example, unpaid or unbilled charges or specified information on certain contractually assumed obligations of the company, such as guarantees of indebtedness of others.]

3.   Stop and review! You have completed the outline for this subunit. Study multiple-choice questions 6 through 13 beginning on page 433.

14.3 SUBSEQUENT EVENTS (AU 560)

1.   Subsequent events are material events or transactions that occur after the balance sheet date, but prior to the issuance of the financial statements, that require adjustment of, or disclosure in, the statements.

2.   **Types of Subsequent Events**

    a.   One type consists of events providing additional evidence about conditions at the date of the balance sheet and affecting the estimates inherent in statement preparation. An example is a loss on an uncollectible receivable as a result of a customer's deteriorating financial condition leading to bankruptcy subsequent to the balance sheet date.

        1)   The financial statements should be adjusted for any changes in estimates resulting from such events.

b.   A second type consists of events providing evidence about conditions that did not exist at the date of the balance sheet but that arose subsequent to that date. Some of these events require disclosure but not adjustment.

1)   Examples include

a)   Sale of a bond or capital stock issue

b)   Purchase of a business

c)   Settlement of litigation when the precipitating event occurred after the balance sheet date

d)   Loss of plant or inventories as a result of fire or flood

e)   Losses on receivables resulting from conditions (e.g., a customer's major casualty) arising after the balance sheet date

2)   Some events of the second type may be so significant that the most appropriate form of disclosure is to supplement the historical statements with pro forma financial data.

3.   Subsequent events affecting the realization of assets such as receivables and inventories or the settlement of estimated liabilities ordinarily require adjustment. They usually are the culmination of conditions that existed over a relatively long time.

4.   **Auditing Procedures in the Subsequent Period**

a.   The **subsequent period** is the period after the balance sheet date and extending to the report date with which the auditor must be concerned in completing the audit.

b.   Specific procedures applied to transactions occurring after the balance sheet date include the examination of data

1)   To assure proper cutoffs

2)   To gather information to aid the auditor in the evaluation of the assets and liabilities as of the balance sheet date

c.   Procedures that should be performed at or near the completion of the field work include

1)   Reading the latest interim financial statements and comparing them with the financial statements being reported upon

2)   Inquiring of and discussing with responsible executives as to

a)   Whether the interim statements were prepared on the same basis as the statements being reported on

b)   Whether any substantial contingent liabilities or commitments existed at the dates of the balance sheet or the inquiry

c)   Whether any significant change occurred in capital stock, long-term debt, or working capital prior to the date of inquiry

d)   Whether any unusual adjustments were made during the subsequent period

e)   The current status of items that were accounted for on the basis of tentative, preliminary, or inconclusive data

3)   Reading the available minutes of meetings of shareholders, directors, and appropriate committees

4)   Inquiring of client's legal counsel about litigation, claims, and assessments

5)   Obtaining a letter of representations, dated as of the date of the auditor's report, from appropriate officials as to whether any subsequent events occurred. This is one of several written representations obtained from the client. Representations are discussed in subunit 14.5.

       6)   Making any inquiries or performing any procedures the auditor deems necessary to dispose of questions resulting from the foregoing procedures, inquiries, and discussions

    5.   Stop and review! You have completed the outline for this subunit. Study multiple-choice questions 14 through 18 beginning on page 436.

14.4 SUBSEQUENT DISCOVERY OF FACTS EXISTING AT THE DATE OF THE AUDITOR'S REPORT (AU 561)

1.   After the date of the report, the auditor is not obligated to make further inquiries or perform other procedures with respect to the audited financial statements unless new information that may affect the report comes to the auditor's attention. However, if these facts are discovered after the report date but before the issuance of the statements, AU 560 applies.

2.   An auditor may become aware of information relating to the financial statements that was not known to the auditor at the date of the report.

      a.   If it is of such a nature and from such a source that the auditor would have investigated it had it come to his/her attention during the audit, (s)he should determine whether the information is reliable and whether the facts existed at the report date.

3.   If the auditor decides that action should be taken to prevent future reliance on the report, (s)he should advise the client to make appropriate disclosures to persons who are known to be currently relying or who are likely to rely on the financial statements and the related report. When the client makes the appropriate disclosures, one of the following should be done:

      a.   If the effect of the subsequently discovered information can promptly be determined, revised financial statements and an auditor's report should be issued as soon as possible.

          1)   Reasons for the revision should be stated in a note and referred to in the report.

      b.   When issuance of financial statements for a subsequent period is imminent, appropriate disclosure can be made in those statements.

      c.   When the effect on the financial statements of the subsequently discovered information cannot be determined without a prolonged investigation, persons who are known to be relying or who are likely to rely on the financial statements and the related report should be notified by the client.

4.   If the client refuses to make the disclosures, the auditor should notify each member of the board of the refusal and of the auditor's intent to prevent future reliance upon the report. The steps the auditor should take include

      a.   Notifying the client that the report must no longer be associated with the financial statements

      b.   Notifying applicable regulatory agencies that the report should no longer be relied upon

      c.   Notifying each person known to be relying on the financial statements that the report should no longer be relied upon

          1)   In many instances, the auditor will be unable to notify stockholders or investors at large, whose identities ordinarily are unknown. Notification to a regulatory agency will usually be the only practicable method of disclosure.

    5.   Stop and review! You have completed the outline for this subunit. Study multiple-choice questions 19 through 23 beginning on page 437.

14.5 MANAGEMENT REPRESENTATIONS (AU 333)

1. The independent auditor is required to obtain **written representations** from management as a part of an audit in accordance with GAAS.

2. **Reliance on Management Representations**

    a. Management representations are part of the audit evidence but do not substitute for necessary auditing procedures.

    b. The representation letter is management's acknowledgment of responsibility for the assertions made in the financial statements.

    c. Written representations from management ordinarily.

        1) Confirm oral representations given to the auditor
        2) Document the continuing appropriateness of the representations
        3) Reduce the possibility of misunderstandings

    d. The auditor often applies auditing procedures specifically designed to obtain corroboration concerning matters that are the subject of written representations.

3. **Obtaining Written Representations**

    a. The specific representations obtained will depend on the circumstances. However, the sample representation letter on the next page, which is taken from AU 333, contains many items typically covered.

        1) Although addressed to the auditor, the letter is drafted by the auditor. It should be signed by client personnel.
        2) The letter assumes that no matters require specific disclosure to the auditor. If such matters exist, they should be indicated by listing them following the representation, referring to accounting records or financial statements, etc.

    b. Representations may be limited to matters that are considered either individually or collectively material to the financial statements, provided management and the auditor have reached an understanding on the limits of materiality for this purpose.

        1) These limits do not apply to fraud, communications from regulatory agencies, or to representations not directly related to financial statement amounts.

    c. The auditor may determine, based on the circumstances, that other matters should be specifically included among the written representations.

    d. If the auditor reports on consolidated statements, the representations obtained from the parent should specify that they pertain to the consolidated statements and, if applicable, to the parent's separate statements.

EXAMPLE OF A MANAGEMENT REPRESENTATION LETTER

Date of Auditor's Report
To Independent Author (Named)

We are providing this letter in connection with your audit(s) of the [identification of financial statements] of [name of entity] as of [dates] and for the [periods] for the purpose of expressing an opinion as to whether the [consolidated] financial statements present fairly, in all material respects, the financial position, results of operations, and cash flows of [name of entity] in conformity with accounting principles generally accepted in the United States of America. We confirm that we are responsible for the fair presentation in the [consolidated] financial statements of financial position, results of operations, and cash flows in conformity with generally accepted accounting principles.

Certain representations in this letter are described as being limited to matters that are material. Items are considered material, regardless of size, if they involve an omission or misstatement of accounting information that, in the light of surrounding circumstances, makes it probable that the judgment of a reasonable person relying on the information would be changed or influenced by the omission or misstatement.

We confirm, to the best of our knowledge and belief, [as of (date of auditor's report),] the following representations made to you during your audit(s).

1. The financial statements referred to above are fairly presented in conformity with accounting principles generally accepted in the United States of America.

2. We have made available to you all –

   a. Financial records and related data.

   b. Minutes of the meetings of stockholders, directors, and committees of directors, or summaries of actions of recent meetings for which minutes have not yet been prepared.

3. There have been no communications from regulatory agencies concerning noncompliance with or deficiencies in financial reporting practices.

4. There are no material transactions that have not been properly recorded in the accounting records underlying the financial statements.

5. We believe that the effects of the uncorrected financial statement misstatements summarized in the accompanying schedule are immaterial, both individually and in the aggregate, to the financial statements taken as a whole.

6. We acknowledge our responsibility for the design and implementation of programs and controls to prevent and detect fraud.

7. We have no knowledge of any fraud or suspected fraud affecting the entity involving –

   a. Management,
   b. Employees who have significant roles in internal control, or
   c. Others if the fraud could have a material effect on the financial statements.

8. We have no knowledge of any allegations of fraud or suspected fraud affecting the entity received in communications from employees, former employees, analysts, regulators, short sellers, or others.

9. The company has no plans or intentions that may materially affect the carrying value or classification of assets and liabilities.

10. The following have been properly recorded or disclosed in the financial statements:

    a. Related-party transactions, including sales, purchases, loans, transfers, leasing arrangements, and guarantees, and amounts receivable from or payable to related parties.

    b. Guarantees, whether written or oral, under which the company is contingently liable.

    c. Significant estimates and material concentrations known to management that are required to be disclosed in accordance with the AICPA's Statement of Position 94-6, Disclosure of Certain Significant Risks and Uncertainties. [Significant estimates are estimates at the balance sheet date that could change materially within the next year. Concentrations refer to volumes of business, revenues, available sources of supply, or markets or geographic areas for which events could occur that would significantly disrupt normal finances within the next year. This SOP is outlined in *CPA Review: Financial*.]

11. There are no –

    a. Violations or possible violations of laws or regulations whose effects should be considered for disclosure in the financial statements or as a basis for recording a loss contingency.

    b. Unasserted claims or assessments that our lawyer has advised us are probable of assertion and must be disclosed in accordance with Financial Accounting Standards Board (FASB) Statement No. 5, *Accounting for Contingencies*.

    c. Other liabilities or gain or loss contingencies that are required to be accrued or disclosed by FASB Statement No. 5.

12. The company has satisfactory title to all owned assets, and there are no liens or encumbrances on such assets nor has any asset been pledged as collateral.

13. The company has complied with all aspects of contractual agreements that would have a material effect on the financial statements in the event of noncompliance.

[Add additional representations that are unique to the entity's business or industry.]

To the best of our knowledge and belief, no events have occurred subsequent to the balance-sheet date and through the date of this letter that would require adjustment to or disclosure in the aforementioned financial statements.

_____   _____
(Name of Chief Executive Officer and Title)   (Name of Chief Financial Officer and Title)

    e.   The written representations should be

        1)   Addressed to the auditor

        2)   Dated as of the date of the audit report

        3)   Signed by responsible and knowledgeable members of management. The chief executive officer and the chief financial officer usually should sign the representations.

    f.   The auditor may want to obtain written representations from other individuals, for example, about the completeness of the minutes of meetings from the person responsible for the minutes.

4. **Scope Limitations**

    a.   Management's refusal to provide written representations is a scope limitation that precludes an unqualified opinion. The auditor should also consider the effects of the refusal on his/her ability to rely on other representations.

    b.   If the auditor is precluded from performing necessary procedures regarding a material matter, even though management has made representations about the matter, the scope limitation requires the auditor to qualify the opinion or disclaim an opinion.

5. CEOs and CFOs must certify to the SEC that annual and quarterly reports filed in accordance with the Securities Exchange Act of 1934 contain no material misstatements.

6. Stop and review! You have completed the outline for this subunit. Study multiple-choice questions 24 through 31 beginning on page 439.

14.6 AUDITOR'S CONSIDERATION OF AN ENTITY'S ABILITY TO CONTINUE AS A GOING CONCERN (AU 341)

1. The auditor must evaluate whether a substantial doubt exists about an entity's ability to continue as a **going concern**.

    a.   Continuation as a going concern is assumed in financial reporting absent significant contrary information. Such information relates to the inability to continue to meet obligations as they fall due without, for example, one of the following:

        1)   Substantial disposal of assets outside the ordinary course of business
        2)   Debt restructuring
        3)   Externally forced revisions of operations

    b.   The standard does not apply to an audit of financial statements prepared on the liquidation basis.

        1)   It applies to audits of financial statements prepared in accordance with GAAP or a comprehensive basis other than GAAP (excluding the liquidation basis).

2. **The Auditor's Responsibility**. The auditor must "evaluate whether there is substantial doubt about the entity's ability to continue as a going concern for a reasonable period of time, not to exceed **one year beyond the date of the financial statements** being audited" (hereafter, the term "substantial doubt" will be used when referring to this quoted language).

    a.   The evaluation is based on relevant conditions and events as of the completion of field work.

        1)   Necessary information is obtained by applying the auditing procedures planned and performed to achieve the audit objectives related to management's assertions in the financial statements.

b. The process of evaluation is as follows:

1) The auditor considers whether the results of normal auditing procedures identify conditions and events that, in the aggregate, indicate that substantial doubt could exist (hereafter, simply "conditions and events").

a) Additional information about the conditions and events, as well as evidence supporting information that mitigates the substantial doubt, may need to be gathered.

2) If the auditor believes a substantial doubt exists, (s)he should obtain information about management's plans to mitigate the effect of such conditions or events and assess the likelihood that the plans will be effective.

3) After evaluating management's plans, the auditor concludes whether (s)he has a substantial doubt.

a) If so, (s)he should

i) Consider the adequacy of disclosure about the going concern issue.

ii) Include an explanatory paragraph (after the opinion paragraph) in the audit report. Also, a disclaimer of an opinion is possible.

b) If not, (s)he should still consider the need for disclosure, but need not include an explanatory paragraph in the audit report.

c. Because an auditor is not responsible for predicting the future, the entity's failure to continue as a going concern, even within the year after the date of the statements, does not, in itself, indicate inadequate auditor performance.

1) Thus, omission of the reference to substantial doubt provides no assurance of continuation as a going concern.

3. **Audit Procedures**. Procedures need not be designed solely to identify conditions and events because other procedures should be sufficient. Such procedures may include

a. Analytical procedures
b. Review of subsequent events
c. Review of compliance with debt and loan agreements
d. Reading minutes of meetings of shareholders, the board, and committees
e. Inquiry of legal counsel about litigation, claims, and assessments
f. Confirmation with related and third parties of arrangements for financial support

4. **Consideration of Conditions and Events**. The significance of conditions and events depends on the circumstances, and some may be significant only in conjunction with others. Such conditions and events include

a. **Negative trends**, e.g., recurring operating losses, working capital deficiencies, negative cash flows from operations, and poor key financial ratios

b. **Financial difficulties**, e.g., default on loans, unpaid dividends, denial of normal trade credit by suppliers, debt restructuring, noncompliance with statutory capital requirements, and the need to seek new financing or to dispose of substantial assets

c. **Internal matters**, e.g., labor difficulties, substantial dependence on the success of one project, uneconomic long-term commitments, and the need to significantly revise operations

d. **External matters**, e.g., litigation, legislation, or similar matters jeopardizing operating ability; loss of a key franchise, license, or patent; loss of a principal customer or supplier; and an uninsured or underinsured catastrophe, such as a drought, earthquake, or flood

5. **Consideration of Management's Plans.** If the auditor believes there is substantial doubt, (s)he should consider management's plans for dealing with the adverse effects of the conditions and events, obtain information about the plans, and consider the likelihood that the adverse effects will be mitigated and the plans can be effectively implemented.

    a. The auditor's considerations may include

        1) Plans to dispose of assets

            a) Restrictions thereon, such as covenants in loan agreements or encumbrances
            b) Marketability of the assets to be sold
            c) Direct or indirect effects of disposal

        2) Plans to borrow money or restructure debt

            a) Availability of debt financing, including existing or committed credit arrangements, such as lines of credit, factoring receivables, or sale-leasebacks
            b) Existing or committed arrangements to restructure or subordinate debt or to guarantee loans to the entity
            c) Existing restrictions on borrowing or the sufficiency of available collateral

        3) Plans to reduce or delay expenditures

            a) Feasibility of plans to reduce overhead or administrative expenses, postpone maintenance or research and development, or lease rather than purchase
            b) Direct or indirect effects thereof

        4) Plans to increase ownership equity

            a) Feasibility of such plans, including existing or committed arrangements to obtain capital
            b) Existing or committed arrangements to reduce dividends or accelerate cash receipts from affiliates or other investors

    b. The elements of plans that are particularly significant to overcoming the adverse effects should be identified and procedures performed to obtain evidence about them, for example, about the ability to obtain additional financing.

    c. Prospective financial information may be particularly significant to management's plans, and the auditor should request such information and consider the adequacy of support for significant underlying assumptions.

        1) Particular attention must be given to assumptions that are

            a) Material
            b) Especially sensitive or susceptible to change
            c) Inconsistent with historical trends

        2) The consideration should be based on knowledge of the entity, its business, and its management. The auditor should

            a) Read the prospective information and assumptions.
            b) Compare prospective information for prior periods with results and for the current period with results to date.

        3) If the effects of certain factors are not reflected in the prospective information, the auditor should discuss them with management, and, if necessary, request revision.

6. **Consideration of Financial Statement Effects**. After considering management's plans, the auditor may conclude there is substantial doubt and should consider the possible effects on the statements and the adequacy of disclosure.

   a. Information disclosed might include

      1) The conditions and events on which the substantial doubt is based, their possible effects, and management's evaluation of their significance and of any mitigating factors

      2) Possible discontinuance of operations

      3) Management's plans, including prospective information

         a) The information need not meet guidelines for prospective financial statements, and the consideration need not go beyond that required by GAAS.

      4) Information about recoverability or classification of recorded assets or the amounts or classification of liabilities

   b. If, primarily because of the consideration of management's plans, the substantial doubt is mitigated, the auditor should consider disclosure of the principal conditions and events that led to the belief that a substantial doubt existed, their possible effects, and any mitigating factors, including management's plans.

7. **Consideration of the Effects on the Auditor's Report**. If the auditor concludes that substantial doubt exists, the audit report should include an explanatory paragraph following the opinion paragraph (described more fully in Study Unit 17).

   a. Also, the auditor is not precluded from disclaiming an opinion in cases involving uncertainties.

8. **Documentation**. If the auditor believes that a substantial doubt exists about the ability of the entity to continue as a going concern for a reasonable time (even if that doubt is mitigated by management actions), the following should be documented:

   a. The conditions or events causing the belief.

   b. The particularly significant elements of management's plans to overcome the problem considered by the auditor.

   c. The auditing procedures performed and evidence obtained.

   d. The auditor's conclusions, including any effects on the financial statements or disclosures and any effect on the audit report.

9. Stop and review! You have completed the outline for this subunit. Study multiple-choice questions 32 through 37 beginning on page 442.

QUESTIONS

14.1 Substantive Tests Prior to the Balance Sheet Date (AU 313)

1. Periodic or cycle counts of selected inventory items are made at various times during the year rather than a single inventory count at year-end. Which of the following is necessary if the auditor plans to observe inventories at interim dates?

    A. Complete recounts by independent teams are performed.

    B. Perpetual inventory records are maintained.

    C. Unit cost records are integrated with production accounting records.

    D. Inventory balances are rarely at low levels.

Answer (B) is correct. *(CPA, adapted)*
REQUIRED: The situation in which inventory counts prior to year-end are acceptable.
DISCUSSION: "When the well-kept perpetual inventory records are checked by the client periodically by comparisons with physical counts, the auditor's observation procedures usually can be performed either during or after the end of the period under audit" (AU 331). If substantive tests are applied at an interim date, the detection risk at the balance sheet date is increased. The incremental risk may be reduced if substantive tests can be designed to cover the remaining period.
Answer (A) is incorrect because complete recounts of inventory by independent teams would rarely be necessary. Answer (C) is incorrect because, although integrating cost records into the production records may provide for increased coordination, the process is not necessary to rely on cycle counts of inventory. Answer (D) is incorrect because cycle inventory counts can be accomplished regardless of inventory levels.

2. Before applying principal substantive tests to the details of accounts at an interim date prior to the balance sheet date, an auditor should

    A. Assess control risk as below the maximum for the assertions embodied in the accounts selected for interim testing.

    B. Determine that the accounts selected for interim testing are not material to the financial statements taken as a whole.

    C. Consider whether the amounts of the year-end balances selected for interim testing are reasonably predictable.

    D. Obtain written representations from management that all financial records and related data will be made available.

Answer (C) is correct. *(CPA, adapted)*
REQUIRED: The auditor action prior to applying principal substantive tests at an interim date.
DISCUSSION: Among the auditor's considerations is whether the year-end balances of accounts selected for interim examination are reasonably predictable as to amount, relative significance, and composition.
Answer (A) is incorrect because assessing control risk below the maximum is not required. However, if the auditor assesses control risk at the maximum for the remaining period, (s)he should consider whether the effectiveness of certain substantive tests to cover that period will be impaired. Answer (B) is incorrect because the accounts selected for interim testing are likely to be material. Answer (D) is incorrect because written representations will be obtained from the client regardless of when testing is done.

3. Before applying substantive tests to the details of asset accounts at an interim date, an auditor should assess

    A. Control risk below the maximum level.

    B. Inherent risk at the maximum level.

    C. The difficulty in controlling the incremental audit risk.

    D. Materiality for the accounts tested as insignificant.

Answer (C) is correct. *(CPA, adapted)*
REQUIRED: The procedure performed prior to applying substantive tests at an interim date.
DISCUSSION: AU 313 notes certain factors that should be considered before substantive tests of details are performed at interim dates. For example, the auditor should assess the difficulty, cost, and benefits of controlling the incremental audit risk from the time of the application of the procedures to year-end.
Answer (A) is incorrect because assessing control risk below the maximum is not required to have a reasonable basis for extending audit conclusions from an interim date to the balance sheet date. Answer (B) is incorrect because the auditor need not assess inherent risk at the maximum in order to apply tests at interim. Answer (D) is incorrect because, if materiality of the accounts was insignificant, the accounts need not be tested.

4. Which of the following procedures is least likely to be performed before the balance sheet date?

    A. Observation of inventory.

    B. Testing internal control over cash.

    C. Search for unrecorded liabilities.

    D. Confirmation of receivables.

Answer (C) is correct. *(CPA, adapted)*
    REQUIRED: The procedure least likely to be performed before the balance sheet date.
    DISCUSSION: A significant risk is that all payables may not be reflected in the year-end balance. The auditor will review cash disbursements made subsequent to year-end to determine if payments are for previously unrecorded liabilities.
    Answer (A) is incorrect because, if controls are effective and the client maintains well-kept perpetual records, the auditor's observation procedures usually can be performed during the period under audit (AU 331). Answer (B) is incorrect because the understanding of internal control is customarily obtained prior to the balance sheet date to permit the auditor to plan the audit and determine the nature, extent, and timing of tests. Answer (D) is incorrect because receivables confirmation may be made either during (if controls are effective), at the end of, or after the period under audit.

5. As the acceptable level of detection risk increases, an auditor may change the

    A. Assessed level of control risk from below the maximum to the maximum level.

    B. Assurance provided by tests of controls by using a larger sample size than planned.

    C. Timing of substantive tests from year-end to an interim date.

    D. Nature of substantive tests from a less effective to a more effective procedure.

Answer (C) is correct. *(CPA, adapted)*
    REQUIRED: The effect of an increase in the acceptable level of detection risk.
    DISCUSSION: The acceptable level of detection risk affects substantive testing. For example, as the acceptable level of detection risk increases, the audit effort devoted to substantive tests may be reduced. Hence, the auditor may change the nature, timing, or extent of substantive tests, for example, by changing the timing to an interim date.
    Answer (A) is incorrect because control risk is assessed in the determination of the acceptable level of detection risk, not vice versa. Answer (B) is incorrect because an increase in the acceptable level of detection risk permits the use of a smaller sample size. Answer (D) is incorrect because an increase in the acceptable level of detection risk may permit the auditor to change to a less effective procedure.

14.2 Inquiry of a Client's Lawyer Concerning Litigation, Claims, and Assessments (AU 337)

6. The primary source of information to be reported about litigation, claims, and assessments is the

    A. Client's lawyer.

    B. Court records.

    C. Client's management.

    D. Independent auditor.

Answer (C) is correct. *(CPA, adapted)*
    REQUIRED: The primary source of information to be reported about litigation, claims, and assessments.
    DISCUSSION: According to AU 337, "Management is responsible for adopting policies and procedures to identify, evaluate, and account for litigation, claims, and assessments as a basis for the preparation of financial statements in conformity with generally accepted accounting principles."
    Answer (A) is incorrect because the client's lawyer is the auditor's primary source of evidence to corroborate the information furnished by management. Answer (B) is incorrect because the auditor does not ordinarily examine court records. Answer (D) is incorrect because the auditor collects evidence to support management's assertions concerning litigation, claims, and assessments.

7. A lawyer's response to an auditor's inquiry concerning litigation, claims, and assessments may be limited to matters that are considered individually or collectively material to the client's financial statements. Which parties should reach an understanding on the limits of materiality for this purpose?

    A. The auditor and the client's management.

    B. The client's audit committee and the lawyer.

    C. The client's management and the lawyer.

    D. The lawyer and the auditor.

Answer (D) is correct. *(CPA, adapted)*
    REQUIRED: The parties responsible for setting materiality limits for litigation inquiries.
    DISCUSSION: A lawyer's response to an auditor's inquiry concerning litigation, claims, and assessments may be limited to those that are considered individually or collectively material to the financial statements, provided the lawyer and auditor have reached an understanding on the limits of materiality for this purpose (AU 337).
    Answer (A) is incorrect because an inquiry (versus the response) need not be made about items considered immaterial, provided the auditor and client have an understanding about the limits of materiality for this purpose. Answer (B) is incorrect because the auditor must judge whether items are material relative to the financial statements. Answer (C) is incorrect because the auditor must judge whether items are material relative to the financial statements.

8. Which of the following is an audit procedure that an auditor most likely would perform concerning litigation, claims, and assessments?

   A. Request the client's lawyer to evaluate whether the client's pending litigation, claims, and assessments indicate a going concern problem.

   B. Examine the legal documents in the client's lawyer's possession concerning litigation, claims, and assessments to which the lawyer has devoted substantive attention.

   C. Discuss with management its policies and procedures adopted for evaluating and accounting for litigation, claims, and assessments.

   D. Confirm directly with the client's lawyer that all litigation, claims, and assessments have been recorded or disclosed in the financial statements.

Answer (C) is correct. *(CPA, adapted)*
   REQUIRED: The procedure to be performed concerning litigation, claims, and assessments.
   DISCUSSION: The independent auditor's procedures relative to litigation, claims, and assessments include inquiring about and discussing with management the policies and procedures adopted for identifying, evaluating, and accounting for various contingencies. The auditor will corroborate that information with communications to the client's lawyer.
   Answer (A) is incorrect because the lawyer has little information concerning the client's ability to continue as a going concern. Answer (B) is incorrect because the auditor is not responsible for examining legal documents that are in the possession of the client's lawyer. Answer (D) is incorrect because the client's lawyer would not have the ability to corroborate the proper recording of transactions in the financial statements.

9. The primary reason an auditor requests letters of inquiry be sent to a client's attorneys is to provide the auditor with

   A. The probable outcome of asserted claims and pending or threatened litigation.

   B. Corroboration of the information furnished by management about litigation, claims, and assessments.

   C. The attorneys' opinions of the client's historical experiences in recent similar litigation.

   D. A description and evaluation of litigation, claims, and assessments that existed at the balance sheet date.

Answer (B) is correct. *(CPA, adapted)*
   REQUIRED: The primary reason an auditor requests letters of audit inquiry to be sent to a client's attorneys.
   DISCUSSION: AU 337 notes that a letter of audit inquiry to a client's lawyer is the auditor's primary means of obtaining corroboration of information furnished by management concerning litigation, claims, and assessments.
   Answer (A) is incorrect because management provides information about the probable outcome of asserted claims and impending or threatened litigation. Answer (C) is incorrect because the auditor is concerned with current litigation, not recent similar litigation. Answer (D) is incorrect because management provides a description and evaluation of litigation, claims, and assessments that existed at the balance sheet date. The letter of audit inquiry provides corroboration of that information.

10. Which of the following is not an audit procedure that the independent auditor would perform with respect to litigation, claims, and assessments?

   A. Inquire of and discuss with management the policies and procedures adopted for litigation, claims, and assessments.

   B. Obtain from management a description and evaluation of litigation, claims, and assessments that existed at the balance sheet date.

   C. Obtain assurance from management that it has disclosed all unasserted claims that the lawyer has advised are probable of assertion and must be disclosed.

   D. Confirm directly with the client's lawyer that all claims have been recorded in the financial statements.

Answer (D) is correct. *(CPA, adapted)*
   REQUIRED: The procedure not performed regarding legal matters.
   DISCUSSION: Under SFAS 5, a loss contingency is recorded in the financial statements only if it is probable and its amount can be reasonably estimated. Hence, many contingent claims will not be recorded, although some may require disclosure in notes.
   Answer (A) is incorrect because inquiring of and discussing with management the policies and procedures adopted for litigation, claims, and assessments is a required procedure (AU 337). Answer (B) is incorrect because obtaining from management a description and evaluation of litigation, claims, and assessments that existed at the balance sheet date is a procedure required by AU 337. Answer (C) is incorrect because obtaining assurance from management that it has disclosed all unasserted claims that the lawyer has advised are probable of assertion is a procedure required by AU 337.

11. Which of the following statements extracted from a client's lawyer's letter concerning litigation, claims, and assessments most likely would cause the auditor to request clarification?

A. "I believe that the possible liability to the company is nominal in amount."

B. "I believe that the action can be settled for less than the damages claimed."

C. "I believe that the plaintiff's case against the company is without merit."

D. "I believe that the company will be able to defend this action successfully."

Answer (B) is correct. *(CPA, adapted)*
REQUIRED: The lawyer's statement most likely causing an auditor's request for clarification.
DISCUSSION: The letter of audit inquiry requests, among other things, that the lawyer evaluate the likelihood of unfavorable outcomes of pending or threatened litigation, claims, and assessments. It also requests that the lawyer estimate, if possible, the amount or range of potential loss (AU 337). Thus, the auditor is concerned about the amount of the expected settlement as well as the likelihood of the outcome.
Answer (A) is incorrect because the lawyer's statement that the amount of possible liability will not be material states an amount or range of loss. Answer (C) is incorrect because the lawyer has stated that no liability is expected. Answer (D) is incorrect because the lawyer has stated that no liability is expected.

12. The scope of an audit is not restricted when an attorney's response to an auditor as a result of a client's letter of audit inquiry limits the response to

A. Matters to which the attorney has given substantive attention in the form of legal representation.

B. An evaluation of the likelihood of an unfavorable outcome of the matters disclosed by the entity.

C. The attorney's opinion of the entity's historical experience in recent similar litigation.

D. The probable outcome of asserted claims and pending or threatened litigation.

Answer (A) is correct. *(CPA, adapted)*
REQUIRED: The appropriate limitations on the lawyer's response to the auditor's inquiry.
DISCUSSION: AU 337 states that two limitations on the lawyer's response will not be considered scope limitations. The response may be limited to matters to which the lawyer has given substantive attention on behalf of the client in the form of legal consultation or representation. Also, if the lawyer and auditor have reached an understanding as to the limits of materiality, the response may be limited to matters that are individually or collectively material.
Answer (B) is incorrect because an evaluation of the likelihood of an unfavorable outcome of the matters disclosed by the entity is just one matter covered in a letter of audit inquiry. Answer (C) is incorrect because a response should be made regarding all material litigation, claims, and assessments to which the lawyer has given substantive attention. Answer (D) is incorrect because the probable outcome of asserted claims and pending or threatened litigation is just one matter covered in a letter of audit inquiry.

13. The refusal of a client's attorney to provide information requested in an inquiry letter generally is considered

A. Grounds for an adverse opinion.

B. A limitation on the scope of the audit.

C. Reason to withdraw from the engagement.

D. Equivalent to a reportable condition.

Answer (B) is correct. *(CPA, adapted)*
REQUIRED: The nature of the refusal of a client's attorney to provide information requested.
DISCUSSION: A lawyer's refusal to furnish the information requested in an inquiry letter either in writing or orally is a limitation on the scope of the audit sufficient to preclude an unqualified opinion.
Answer (A) is incorrect because a scope limitation never leads to an adverse opinion. Answer (C) is incorrect because the refusal is not immediate grounds for withdrawal from an engagement. The auditor should attempt to become satisfied by alternative means. Answer (D) is incorrect because reportable conditions are deficiencies in internal control.

14.3 Subsequent Events (AU 560)

14. Which of the following procedures should an auditor ordinarily perform regarding subsequent events?

A. Compare the latest available interim financial statements with the financial statements being audited.

B. Send second requests to the client's customers who failed to respond to initial accounts receivable confirmation requests.

C. Communicate material weaknesses in internal control to the client's audit committee.

D. Review the cutoff bank statements for several months after the year-end.

Answer (A) is correct. *(CPA, adapted)*
REQUIRED: The subsequent events procedure.
DISCUSSION: Subsequent events procedures include reading the latest interim statements and comparing them with the statements being reported on; inquiring about and discussing with management various financial and accounting matters; reading the minutes of directors', shareholders', and committee meetings; obtaining a letter of representations from management; inquiring of client's legal counsel; and performing any further procedures deemed necessary.
Answer (B) is incorrect because second confirmation requests would not disclose subsequent events. Answer (C) is incorrect because communication of material weaknesses is not a subsequent events procedure. Answer (D) is incorrect because cutoff bank statements are requested from banks 7 to 10 days after year-end. They are used to verify the client's bank reconciliations.

15. Which of the following procedures would an auditor most likely perform to obtain evidence about the occurrence of subsequent events?

A. Confirming a sample of material accounts receivable established after year-end.

B. Comparing the financial statements being reported on with those of the prior period.

C. Investigating personnel changes in the accounting department occurring after year-end.

D. Inquiring as to whether any unusual adjustments were made after year-end.

Answer (D) is correct. *(CPA, adapted)*
REQUIRED: The subsequent events procedure.
DISCUSSION: Procedures performed at or near the completion of field work normally include inquiring of management as to (1) whether the interim statements were prepared on the same basis as the statements being reported on, (2) whether any substantial contingent liabilities or commitments existed at the date of the balance sheet, (3) whether any significant change had occurred in equity, (4) whether any unusual adjustments had been made during the subsequent period, and (5) the current status of items that were accounted for on a basis of tentative, preliminary, or inconclusive data.
Answer (A) is incorrect because the auditor confirms receivables before year-end. Answer (B) is incorrect because this analytical procedure is performed at the beginning of the audit. Answer (C) is incorrect because personnel changes after year-end do not typically relate to the recording of subsequent events.

16. Which of the following procedures would an auditor most likely perform to obtain evidence about the occurrence of subsequent events?

A. Recomputing a sample of large-dollar transactions occurring after year-end for arithmetic accuracy.

B. Investigating changes in equity occurring after year-end.

C. Inquiring of the entity's legal counsel concerning litigation, claims, and assessments arising after year-end.

D. Confirming bank accounts established after year-end.

Answer (C) is correct. *(CPA, adapted)*
REQUIRED: The auditing procedure for the subsequent events period.
DISCUSSION: Procedures applied after the balance sheet date should include the examination of data to determine that proper cutoffs have been made and to evaluate assets and liabilities as of the balance sheet date. The auditor should also perform procedures with respect to the subsequent events period to ascertain whether events have occurred that may require adjustment or disclosure essential to fair presentation of the financial statements. Such procedures include inquiring of the client's legal counsel (AU 560).
Answer (A) is incorrect because testing the arithmetic accuracy of known events does not generate evidence about the occurrence of other subsequent events. Answer (B) is incorrect because the auditor should inquire of officers and other executives as to significant changes in equity, but an investigation of such changes is less likely than the inquiry of legal counsel. Answer (D) is incorrect because a bank account established after year-end is not an asset that existed at the balance sheet date.

17. Which of the following procedures would an auditor most likely perform in obtaining evidence about subsequent events?

    A. Determine that changes in employee pay rates after year-end were properly authorized.

    B. Recompute depreciation charges for plant assets sold after year-end.

    C. Inquire about payroll checks that were recorded before year-end but cashed after year-end.

    D. Investigate changes in long-term debt occurring after year-end.

Answer (D) is correct. *(CPA, adapted)*
    REQUIRED: The procedure likely to be performed in obtaining evidence about subsequent events.
    DISCUSSION: Procedures that should be performed upon or near the completion of the field work include investigating any significant change in capital stock, long-term debt, or working capital. Events related to these accounts may require revision in the year-end financial statements or disclosures in the notes.
    Answer (A) is incorrect because issues concerning employee pay rates are not typically considered important subsequent events. Answer (B) is incorrect because depreciation charges for a given period do not change as a result of sale of plant assets in the subsequent period. Answer (C) is incorrect because issues concerning employee paychecks are not typically considered important subsequent events.

18. Zero Corp. suffered a loss that would have a material effect on its financial statements on an uncollectible trade account receivable due to a customer's bankruptcy. This occurred suddenly due to a natural disaster ten days after Zero's balance sheet date but one month before the issuance of the financial statements. Under these circumstances,

	The Financial Statements Should Be Adjusted	The Event Requires Financial Statement Disclosure, but No Adjustment	The Auditor's Report Should Be Modified for a Lack of Consistency
A.	Yes	No	No
B.	Yes	No	Yes
C.	No	Yes	Yes
D.	No	Yes	No

Answer (D) is correct. *(CPA, adapted)*
    REQUIRED: The effect on the financial statements and the auditor's report.
    DISCUSSION: Certain subsequent events may provide additional evidence about conditions at the date of the balance sheet and affect estimates inherent in the preparation of statements. These events require adjustment by the client in the financial statements at year-end. Other subsequent events provide evidence about conditions not existing at the date of the balance sheet but arising subsequent to that date and affecting the interpretation of the year-end financial statements. These events may require disclosure in notes to the financial statements but do not require adjustment of the financial statement balances. Thus, in this case, the financial statements should not be adjusted, but disclosure should be made in the notes. The auditor's report is unaffected.
    Answer (A) is incorrect because the financial statements are not adjusted and the matter is disclosed. Answer (B) is incorrect because the financial statements are not adjusted, the matter is disclosed, and the auditor's report is not affected. Answer (C) is incorrect because the auditor's report is not affected.

14.4 Subsequent Discovery of Facts Existing at the Date of the Auditor's Report (AU 561)

19. After the issuance of a nonpublic client's financial statements, the client decided to sell the shares of a subsidiary that accounts for 30% of its revenue and 25% of its net income. The auditor should

    A. Determine whether the information is reliable and, if determined to be reliable, request that revised financial statements be issued.

    B. Notify the entity that the auditor's report may no longer be associated with the financial statements.

    C. Describe the effects of this subsequently discovered information in a communication with persons known to be relying on the financial statements.

    D. Take no action because the auditor has no obligation to make any further inquiries.

Answer (D) is correct. *(CPA, adapted)*
    REQUIRED: The auditor's responsibility for an event occurring after the issuance of a nonpublic client's financial statements.
    DISCUSSION: AU 561 states, "After the date of the report, the auditor has no obligation to make any further or continuing inquiry or perform any other auditing procedures with respect to the audited financial statements covered by that report, unless new information that may affect the report comes to his/her attention."
    Answer (A) is incorrect because determining whether the information is reliable and requesting that revised statements be issued would be appropriate if the auditor had subsequently discovered facts existing at the date of the report. Answer (B) is incorrect because notifying the entity that the report may no longer be associated with the financial statements would be appropriate if the auditor had subsequently discovered facts existing at the date of the report. Answer (C) is incorrect because communicating the effects of subsequently discovered information to persons known to be relying on the statements would be appropriate if the auditor had subsequently discovered facts existing at the date of the report.

20. After the date of the audit report, an auditor has no obligation to make continuing inquiries or perform other procedures concerning the audited financial statements, unless

A. Information that existed at the report date and may affect the report comes to the auditor's attention.

B. Management of the entity requests the auditor to reissue the auditor's report in a document submitted to a third party that contains information in addition to the basic financial statements.

C. Information about an event that occurred after the end of field work comes to the auditor's attention.

D. Final determinations or resolutions are made of contingencies that had been disclosed in the financial statements.

Answer (A) is correct. *(CPA, adapted)*
REQUIRED: The basis for the obligation to perform procedures after the date of the report.
DISCUSSION: Although the auditor may need to extend subsequent events procedures when public companies make filings under the Securities Act of 1933 (AU 711), (s)he ordinarily need not apply any procedures after the date of the report. But if the auditor becomes aware of information that relates to the financial statements previously reported on, that (s)he did not know at the date of the report, and that is of such a nature and from such a source that (s)he would have investigated if it had come to light during the audit, (s)he should, as soon as practicable, determine whether the information is reliable and whether the facts existed at the date of the report (AU 561).
Answer (B) is incorrect because additional audit procedures are ordinarily not necessary prior to reissuing a report. Answer (C) is incorrect because the subsequent event must have occurred prior to the date of the auditor's report (ordinarily, the date of the completion of field work) for the auditor to have additional responsibilities. Answer (D) is incorrect because the auditor has no continuing responsibility to monitor disclosed contingencies.

21. Which of the following events occurring after the issuance of the financial statement most likely would cause the auditor to make further inquiries about previously issued financial statements?

A. An uninsured natural disaster occurs that may affect the entity's ability to continue as a growing concern.

B. A contingency is resolved that had been disclosed in the audited financial statements.

C. New information is discovered concerning undisclosed lease transactions of the audited period.

D. A subsidiary is sold that accounts for 25% of the entity's consolidated net income.

Answer (C) is correct. *(CPA, adapted)*
REQUIRED: The event occurring after the issuance of the financial statement most likely resulting in further inquiries.
DISCUSSION: When the auditor becomes aware of information that relates to prior financial statements, but that was not known to him/her at the date of the report, and that (s)he would have investigated if it had been discovered during the audit, the auditor should undertake to determine whether the information is reliable and whether the facts existed at the report date (AU 561).
Answer (A) is incorrect because an event occurring after the date of the report need not be considered by the auditor if it would not affect the report. Answer (B) is incorrect because the auditor need not consider final determinations or resolutions of contingencies that were disclosed in the financial statements or that resulted in a departure from the auditor's standard report. Answer (D) is incorrect because an event occurring after the date of the report need not be considered by the auditor if it would not affect the report.

22. Soon after Boyd's audit report was issued, Boyd learned of certain related party transactions that occurred during the year under audit. These transactions were not disclosed in the notes to the financial statements. Boyd should

A. Plan to audit the transactions during the next engagement.

B. Recall all copies of the audited financial statements.

C. Determine whether the lack of disclosure would affect the auditor's report.

D. Ask the client to disclose the transactions in subsequent interim statements.

Answer (C) is correct. *(CPA, adapted)*
REQUIRED: The step taken when the auditor discovers previously unknown facts existing at the report date.
DISCUSSION: The auditor should, as soon as practicable, undertake to determine whether the information is reliable and whether the facts existed at the date of the report. If these criteria are met, the auditor must take appropriate action if the report would have been affected and if (s)he believes persons who are currently relying or likely to rely on the statements would consider the information important (AU 561).
Answer (A) is incorrect because the auditor must take more immediate action. Answer (B) is incorrect because recall of the audited financial statements is not feasible. However, client revision of the statements and notice to appropriate parties may be necessary. Answer (D) is incorrect because issuance of revised statements is preferable, but only if the auditor has determined that the original statements are affected.

23. On February 25, a CPA issued an auditor's report expressing an unqualified opinion on financial statements for the year ended January 31. On March 2, the CPA learned that on February 11 the entity incurred a material loss on an uncollectible trade receivable as a result of the deteriorating financial condition of the entity's principal customer that led to the customer's bankruptcy. Management then refused to adjust the financial statements for this subsequent event. The CPA determined that the information is reliable and that there are creditors currently relying on the financial statements. The CPA's next course of action most likely would be to

A. Notify the entity's creditors that the financial statements and the related auditor's report should no longer be relied on.

B. Notify each member of the entity's board of directors about management's refusal to adjust the financial statements.

C. Issue revised financial statements and distribute them to each creditor known to be relying on the financial statements.

D. Issue a revised auditor's report and distribute it to each creditor known to be relying on the financial statements.

Answer (B) is correct. *(CPA, adapted)*
REQUIRED: The actions of an auditor related to an event discovered subsequent to the issue of the financial statements.
DISCUSSION: If the auditor decides that action should be taken to prevent future reliance on the report, (s)he should advise the client to make appropriate disclosures to persons who are known to be currently relying or who are likely to rely on the financial statements and the related report. However, if the client fails to take appropriate action, the auditor, who has determined the information's reliability and creditors' reliance on the statements, should notify each member of the board of directors of the refusal. Failing a satisfactory settlement, the auditor should notify the client that the report must no longer be associated with the statements. The auditor also should notify appropriate regulatory agencies and each person known to be relying on the financial statements that the auditor's report should no longer be relied on.
Answer (A) is incorrect because the board of directors should be notified first. Answer (C) is incorrect because the auditor has no authority to revise management's financial statements. Answer (D) is incorrect because the auditor should not revise the report, but subsequently notify those relying on the report that it is no longer valid.

14.5 Management Representations (AU 333)

24. Which of the following documentation is required for an audit in accordance with generally accepted auditing standards?

A. An internal control questionnaire.

B. A client engagement letter.

C. A planning memorandum or checklist.

D. A management representation letter.

Answer (D) is correct. *(CPA, adapted)*
REQUIRED: The requirement of an audit made in accordance with GAAS.
DISCUSSION: AU 333 requires that the auditor obtain certain written representations from management. The written representations corroborate information received orally from management but do not substitute for the procedures necessary to afford a reasonable basis for the opinion.
Answer (A) is incorrect because GAAS do not require an internal control questionnaire. Answer (B) is incorrect because GAAS do not require an engagement letter. Answer (C) is incorrect because GAAS do not require a planning memorandum or checklist.

25. A purpose of a management representation letter is to reduce

A. Audit risk to an aggregate level of misstatement that could be considered material.

B. An auditor's responsibility to detect material misstatements only to the extent that the letter is relied on.

C. The possibility of a misunderstanding concerning management's responsibility for the financial statements.

D. The scope of an auditor's procedures concerning related party transactions and subsequent events.

Answer (C) is correct. *(CPA, adapted)*
REQUIRED: The purpose of a management representation letter.
DISCUSSION: Management's written representations confirm representations given to the auditor, indicate and document their continuing appropriateness, and reduce the possibility of misunderstanding about the subject matter of the representations. That subject matter includes management's acknowledgment of responsibility for the financial statements.
Answer (A) is incorrect because a management representation letter is not a substitute for the procedures necessary to afford a reasonable basis for an opinion. Answer (B) is incorrect because a management representation letter is not a substitute for the procedures necessary to afford a reasonable basis for an opinion. Answer (D) is incorrect because a management representation letter is not a substitute for the procedures necessary to afford a reasonable basis for an opinion.

26. Which of the following statements ordinarily is included among the written management representations obtained by the auditor?

    A. Management acknowledges that there are no material weaknesses in internal control.

    B. Sufficient evidential matter has been made available to permit the expression of an unqualified opinion.

    C. Guarantees for which the company is potentially liable have been properly recorded or disclosed.

    D. Management acknowledges responsibility for illegal actions committed by employees.

Answer (C) is correct. *(Publisher)*
REQUIRED: The statement included among written management representations.
DISCUSSION: AU 333 lists the concerns ordinarily addressed in management representation letters, if applicable. The list includes disclosure of "guarantees, whether written or oral, under which the entity is contingently liable."
Answer (A) is incorrect because representations about internal control are not among those listed in AU 333. Answer (B) is incorrect because the auditor judges the sufficiency of evidence. Answer (D) is incorrect because, assuming illegal acts have occurred, management will rarely acknowledge responsibility for employees' behavior. However, the letter should make representations to the auditor about actual or possible violations of laws or regulations whose effects should be considered for disclosure or as a basis for a contingent loss.

27. Which of the following matters would an auditor most likely include in a management representation letter?

    A. Communications with the audit committee concerning weaknesses in internal control.

    B. The completeness and availability of minutes of shareholders' and directors' meetings.

    C. Plans to acquire or merge with other entities in the subsequent year.

    D. Management's acknowledgment of its responsibility to report but not detect employee fraud.

Answer (B) is correct. *(CPA, adapted)*
REQUIRED: The item included in a management representation letter.
DISCUSSION: The management representation letter is a part of audit evidence but not a substitute for necessary audit procedures. The letter includes a number of representations, including that management has made available all financial records and related data and minutes of the meetings.
Answer (A) is incorrect because communication with the audit committee is the responsibility of the auditor, not a required representation by management. Answer (C) is incorrect because plans to acquire or merge with other entities in the subsequent year affects the following but not the current year. Answer (D) is incorrect because management should make specific representations about (1) acknowledgment of its responsibility for designing and implementing programs and controls to prevent and detect fraud; (2) knowledge of fraud or suspected fraud involving management, employees with significant roles in internal control, or others if the fraud could materially affect the financial statements; and (3) knowledge of allegations about fraud or suspected fraud.

28. To which of the following matters would an auditor not apply materiality limits when obtaining specific written management representations?

    A. Disclosure of compensating balance arrangements involving restrictions on cash balances.

    B. Information concerning related party transactions and related amounts receivable or payable.

    C. The absence of errors and unrecorded transactions in the financial statements.

    D. Fraud involving employees with significant roles in internal control.

Answer (D) is correct. *(CPA, adapted)*
REQUIRED: The matter to which an auditor would not apply materiality limits.
DISCUSSION: Management's representations may be limited to matters that are considered individually or collectively material on the condition that management and the auditor have reached an understanding concerning the limits of materiality. Such limitations do not apply to certain representations not directly related to amounts in the financial statements, e.g., acknowledgment of responsibility for fair presentation, availability of records, and knowledge of fraud or suspected fraud affecting the entity involving (1) management, (2) employees with significant roles in internal control, or (3) others if the fraud could materially affect the statements (AU 333).
Answer (A) is incorrect because materiality limits apply to disclosure of compensating balance arrangements involving restrictions on cash balances. Answer (B) is incorrect because materiality limits apply to information concerning related party transactions and related amounts receivable or payable. Answer (C) is incorrect because materiality limits apply to the absence of errors and unrecorded transactions in the financial statements.

29. For which of the following matters should an auditor obtain written management representations?

A. Management's cost-benefit justifications for not correcting internal control weaknesses.

B. Management's knowledge of future plans that may affect the price of the entity's stock.

C. Management's compliance with contractual agreements that may affect the financial statements.

D. Management's acknowledgment of its responsibility for employees' violations of laws.

Answer (C) is correct. *(CPA, adapted)*
REQUIRED: The item included in written management representations.
DISCUSSION: The auditor should obtain written representations in the form of a management representation letter to complement other auditing procedures. In an audit of GAAP-based financial statements, the client's management should make, among many others, a specific representation about compliance with contractual agreements that may affect the financial statements (AU 333).
Answer (A) is incorrect because the auditor need not obtain written representations of the cost and benefit justifications of internal controls. Answer (B) is incorrect because the issue does not directly affect the fairness of the financial statements. It might, however, be addressed in management's discussion and analysis. Thus, a practitioner who examines or reviews an MD&A presentation might obtain written representations about such forward-looking information. Answer (D) is incorrect because the client is not necessarily responsible for the violations of laws by the employees, but the client should provide representations about violations or possible violations of laws or regulations that should be considered for disclosure or as bases for recognition of a loss contingency.

30. To which of the following matters would materiality limits not apply in obtaining written management representations?

A. The availability of minutes of shareholders' and directors' meetings.

B. Losses from purchase commitments at prices in excess of market value.

C. The disclosure of compensating balance arrangements involving related parties.

D. Reductions of obsolete inventory to net realizable value.

Answer (A) is correct. *(CPA, adapted)*
REQUIRED: The matter to which materiality limits do not apply when obtaining written management representations.
DISCUSSION: The availability of minutes to shareholders' meetings and directors' meetings is independent of amounts in the financial statements. Thus, materiality limits do not apply.
Answer (B) is incorrect because losses from purchase commitments relate to dollar amounts to which the materiality judgment applies. Answer (C) is incorrect because disclosure of compensating balances relates to dollar amounts to which the materiality judgment applies. Answer (D) is incorrect because reduction of obsolete inventory to net realizable values relates to dollar amounts to which the materiality judgment applies.

31. Key Co. plans to present comparative financial statements for the years ended December 31, year 1, and year 2, respectively. Smith, CPA, audited Key's financial statements for both years and plans to report on the comparative financial statements on May 1, year 3. Key's current management team was not present until January 1, year 2. What period of time should be covered by Key's management representation letter?

A. January 1, year 1 through December 31, year 2.

B. January 1, year 1 through May 1, year 3.

C. January 1, year 2 through December 31, year 2.

D. January 1, year 2 through May 1, year 3.

Answer (B) is correct. *(CPA, adapted)*
REQUIRED: The dates to be covered by a management representation letter.
DISCUSSION: "Because the auditor is concerned with events occurring through the date of his or her report that may require adjustment to or disclosure in the financial statements, the representations should be made as of a date no earlier than the date of the auditor's report." Moreover, "If current management was not present during all periods covered by the auditor's report, the auditor should nevertheless obtain written representations from current management on all such periods" (AU 333).
Answer (A) is incorrect because the representation letter should cover all periods covered by the audit through the date of the audit report. Answer (C) is incorrect because the representation letter should cover all periods covered by the audit through the date of the audit report. Answer (D) is incorrect because the representation letter should cover all periods covered by the audit through the date of the audit report.

14.6 Auditor's Consideration of an Entity's Ability to Continue as a Going Concern (AU 341)

32. Which of the following auditing procedures most likely would assist an auditor in identifying conditions and events that may indicate substantial doubt about an entity's ability to continue as a going concern?

A. Inspecting title documents to verify whether any assets are pledged as collateral.

B. Confirming with third parties the details of arrangements to maintain financial support.

C. Reconciling the cash balance per books with the cutoff bank statement and the bank confirmation.

D. Comparing the entity's depreciation and asset capitalization policies to other entities in the industry.

Answer (B) is correct.   *(CPA, adapted)*
REQUIRED: The audit procedure that may identify conditions indicating substantial doubt about an entity's continuation as a going concern.
DISCUSSION: The procedures typically employed to identify going concern issues include (1) analytical procedures, (2) review of subsequent events, (3) review of compliance with debt and loan agreements, (4) reading minutes of meetings, (5) inquiry of legal counsel, and (6) confirmation with related and third parties of arrangements for financial support.
Answer (A) is incorrect because searching for pledged assets is related to disclosure issues. Answer (C) is incorrect because reconciling the cash balance with cutoff bank statements and the bank confirmation tests the existence of cash. Answer (D) is incorrect because this comparison might identify conditions needing additional consideration but would not provide evidence about going concern issues.

33. Which of the following conditions or events most likely would cause an auditor to have substantial doubt about an entity's ability to continue as a going concern?

A. Significant related party transactions are pervasive.

B. Usual trade credit from suppliers is denied.

C. Arrearages in preferred stock dividends are paid.

D. Restrictions on the disposal of principal assets are present.

Answer (B) is correct.   *(CPA, adapted)*
REQUIRED: The event or condition causing substantial doubt about an entity's ability to continue as a going concern.
DISCUSSION: AU 341 requires auditors to evaluate whether substantial doubt exists about an entity's ability to continue as a going concern, based on procedures planned and performed to obtain evidence about the management assertions embodied in the financial statements. An auditor should examine negative trends, indications of possible financial difficulties, internal problems, and external problems. Denial of normal trade credit by suppliers is an indication of possible financial difficulty.
Answer (A) is incorrect because related party transactions do not indicate an internal problem or financial difficulty. Answer (C) is incorrect because the payment of arrearages in preferred stock dividends is a sign of financial strength. Answer (D) is incorrect because restrictions on the disposal of assets concern the liquidity of the assets. They do not raise a question as to the ability of the entity to continue operations.

34. Cooper, CPA, believes there is substantial doubt about the ability of Zero Corp. to continue as a going concern for a reasonable period of time. In evaluating Zero's plans for dealing with the adverse effects of future conditions and events, Cooper most likely will consider, as a mitigating factor, Zero's plans to

A. Discuss with lenders the terms of all debt and loan agreements.

B. Strengthen internal controls over cash disbursements.

C. Purchase production facilities currently being leased from a related party.

D. Postpone expenditures for research and development projects.

Answer (D) is correct.   *(CPA, adapted)*
REQUIRED: The managerial action that will mitigate adverse effects of future conditions and events.
DISCUSSION: Once an auditor has identified conditions and events indicating that substantial doubt exists about an entity's ability to continue as a going concern, the auditor should consider management's plans to mitigate their adverse effects. The auditor should consider plans to dispose of assets, borrow money or restructure debt, reduce or delay expenditures, and increase equity.
Answer (A) is incorrect because discussion with lenders is not a sufficient action to mitigate the circumstances. Answer (B) is incorrect because internal control improvements do not increase cash flows or postpone expenditures. Answer (C) is incorrect because the purchase of facilities may exacerbate the company's problems.

35. When an auditor concludes there is substantial doubt about a continuing audit client's ability to continue as a going concern for a reasonable period of time, the auditor's responsibility is to

A. Express a qualified or adverse opinion, depending upon materiality, due to the possible effects on the financial statements.

B. Consider the adequacy of disclosure about the client's possible inability to continue as a going concern.

C. Report to the client's audit committee that management's accounting estimates may need to be adjusted.

D. Reissue the prior year's auditor's report and add an explanatory paragraph that specifically refers to "substantial doubt" and "going concern."

Answer (B) is correct. *(CPA, adapted)*
REQUIRED: The auditor's action given substantial doubt about a client's ability to continue as a going concern.
DISCUSSION: If, after considering (1) identified conditions and events in the aggregate that raise going-concern issues and (2) management's plans for coping with their adverse effects, the auditor may conclude there is substantial doubt about the entity's ability to continue as a going concern for a reasonable period of time. In that case, the auditor should consider the possible effects on the financial statements and the adequacy of disclosure. The auditor should also include an explanatory paragraph in the report.
Answer (A) is incorrect because an auditor may still express an unqualified opinion and refer to the going concern issue in an explanatory paragraph. Answer (C) is incorrect because going concern considerations are independent of the accounting estimates that may need adjustment. Answer (D) is incorrect because the prior year's audit report should not be changed. The auditor's opinion on the prior year has not been altered.

36. Davis, CPA, believes there is substantial doubt about the ability of Hill Co. to continue as a going concern for a reasonable period of time. In evaluating Hill's plans for dealing with the adverse effects of future conditions and events, Davis most likely will consider, as a mitigating factor, Hill's plans to

A. Accelerate research and development projects related to future products.

B. Accumulate treasury stock at prices favorable to Hill's historic price range.

C. Purchase equipment and production facilities currently being leased.

D. Negotiate reductions in required dividends being paid on preferred stock.

Answer (D) is correct. *(CPA, adapted)*
REQUIRED: The managerial action that best mitigates adverse effects of future conditions and events.
DISCUSSION: Once an auditor has identified conditions and events indicating that a substantial doubt exists about an entity's ability to continue as a going concern, the auditor should consider management's plans to mitigate their adverse effects. The auditor should consider managerial actions relating to plans to dispose of assets, borrow money or restructure debt, reduce or delay expenditures, and increase equity. Plans to negotiate reductions in required dividends being paid on preferred stock are intended to increase ownership equity.
Answer (A) is incorrect because postponement of R&D projects would be a mitigating factor. Answer (B) is incorrect because increasing owners' equity would be a mitigating factor. Answer (C) is incorrect because leasing would be a mitigating factor.

37. After considering an entity's negative trends and financial difficulties, an auditor has substantial doubt about the entity's ability to continue as a going concern. The auditor's considerations relating to management's plans for dealing with the adverse effects of these conditions most likely would include management's plans to

A. Increase current dividend distributions.

B. Reduce existing lines of credit.

C. Increase ownership equity.

D. Purchase assets formerly leased.

Answer (C) is correct. *(CPA, adapted)*
REQUIRED: The managerial action that mitigates adverse effects of future conditions and events.
DISCUSSION: Once an auditor identifies conditions and events indicating that a substantial doubt exists about an entity's ability to continue as a going concern, (s)he should consider management's plans to mitigate their adverse effects. Increasing equity is likely to be a mitigating factor (AU 341). Thus, the auditor should consider the feasibility of such a plan, including arrangements to raise capital, and any arrangements to reduce dividends or to accelerate cash receipts from investors or affiliates.
Answer (A) is incorrect because increasing the current dividend distributions would reduce the company's available cash. Answer (B) is incorrect because increasing, not reducing, existing lines of credit would be a mitigating factor. Answer (D) is incorrect because plans to reduce or delay expenditures are more likely to include leasing, not purchasing. The purchase of assets may exacerbate the company's problems.

Use Gleim's *CPA Test Prep* for interactive testing with over 2,000 additional multiple-choice questions!

14.7 PRACTICE SIMULATION

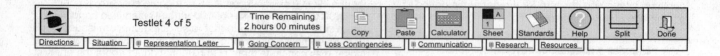

| | | Testlet 4 of 5 | Time Remaining 2 hours 00 minutes | Copy | Paste | Calculator | Sheet | Standards | Help | Split | Done |

Directions | Situation | ▓ Representation Letter | ▓ Going Concern | ▓ Loss Contingencies | ▓ Communication | ▓ Research | Resources

1. Directions

In the following simulation, you will be asked to complete various tasks related to key considerations related to substantive tests prior to the balance sheet date. The simulation will provide all the information necessary to do the work. For full credit, be sure to view and complete all work tabs.

Resources are available to you under the tab marked RESOURCES. You may want to review the resources before beginning the simulation.

2. Situation

On November 19, year 1, Wall, CPA, was engaged to audit the financial statements of Trendy Auto Imports, Inc., for the year ended December 31, year 1. Trendy is one of many regional dealers who specialize in foreign auto sales, an industry that has been closely followed in business periodicals because of the difficulties it is experiencing as the "buy American SUVs" trend has swept the nation. In considering Trendy's ability to continue as a going concern, Wall is gathering evidence that may relate to any loss contingencies, subsequent events, or other relevant conditions.

3. Management Representation Letter

This question is presented in a check-the-box format that requires you to select the correct responses from a given list.

Determine which of the following statements is typically included in the management representation letter obtained by the auditor. Check the box to the right of the statement if the item is included.

Statement	Included
1. The company is not independent with regard to the financial statements.	
2. The company approved all estimates made by the auditor in the financial statements.	
3. The company has made available to the auditor all minutes of the meetings of the board of directors.	
4. All information in the notes to the financial statements is the representation of the auditor.	
5. The company has no plans that may materially affect the carrying amount of assets or liabilities.	
6. We have no knowledge of alleged fraud or suspected fraud.	
7. All items included in this letter are assumed to be immaterial.	
8. Related party transactions have been properly disclosed in the financial statements.	
9. No events have occurred subsequent to the balance-sheet date that would require disclosure in the financial statements.	
10. We have recorded no transactions with a negative effect on earnings.	

4. Evaluation of Going Concern Issue

This question has a matching format that requires you to select the correct response from a drop-down list. Write the answer in the shaded column. Each answer choice may be used once, more than once, or not at all.

The following statements deal with the auditor's evaluation of whether the client is a going concern. For each one, determine which descriptions from the choices listed below best describe the statement.

Statement	Answer
1. Restructuring existing debt to attain more favorable conditions.	
2. Negative trends in earnings.	
3. Inquiry of legal counsel.	
4. Review of subsequent events.	
5. Resolve any substantial doubt.	
6. Delay expenditures.	
7. Loss of a key patent.	
8. Accelerate cash receipts from affiliates.	
9. Document findings.	
10. Testing management's assertions relative to going concern issues.	

Choices
A) A procedure performed by the auditor.
B) An objective of the auditor's procedures.
C) An expectation of the client.
D) A condition or event that will cause the auditor concern relative to going concern issues.
E) A management plan to address adverse effects of conditions or events.

5. Loss Contingencies

This question is presented in a check-the-box format that requires you to select the correct responses from a given list.

For each of the audit procedures listed below, determine whether it should be applied when testing for loss contingencies relating to litigation, claims, and assessments. Check the box to the right of the description if the item should be applied.

Audit Procedure	Apply
1. Read minutes of meetings of shareholders, directors, and committees.	
2. Inquire of officials at the courthouse in the county of the client.	
3. Read contracts, loan agreements, leases, and other documents.	
4. Read client correspondence with taxing and other governmental agencies.	
5. Read client correspondence with insurance and bonding companies.	
6. Read legal briefs of all suits filed against competitors of the client.	
7. Read confirmation replies for information concerning guarantees.	
8. Obtain from management or inside general counsel a description and evaluation of litigation, claims, and assessments.	
9. Obtain representation letters from all staff and professional employees of the client.	
10. Obtain an analysis of professional fee expenses and review supporting invoices for indications of contingencies.	
11. Inquire of SEC officials concerning reported violations creating claims or assessments.	
12. Request the client's management to prepare for transmittal a letter of inquiry to those lawyers consulted by the client concerning litigation, claims, and assessments.	
13. Determine that the financial statements include proper accruals and disclosures of contingencies.	
14. Obtain written or oral assurance from the audit committee that the financial statements include all accruals and disclosures required by SFAS 5.	

6. Communication

In a brief memorandum to an audit associate, describe the types of subsequent events and state examples and related considerations. Type your communication in your word processor program and print out the copy in a memorandum style format.

REMINDER: Your response will be graded for both technical content and writing skills. You should demonstrate your ability to develop, organize, and express your ideas. Do not convey information in the form of a table, bullet point list, or other abbreviated presentation.

> To: Audit associate
> From: CPA
> Subject: Subsequent events

7. Research

Find the answer to the following question in the AICPA Professional Standards using the materials available in the Resources tab. Print the appropriate citation in its entirety from the source you choose. This is a copy-and-paste item.

Cite the appropriate auditing standard that describes the audit procedures that may identify conditions and events indicative of a substantial doubt about the entity's ability to continue as a going concern.

Unofficial Answers

3. Management Representation Letter (10 Gradable Items)

1. Not included.
2. Not included.
3. Included.
4. Not included.
5. Included.
6. Included.
7. Not included.
8. Included.
9. Included.
10. Not included.

4. Evaluation of Going Concern Issue (10 Gradable Items)

1. E) - a management plan to deal with adverse effects of conditions or events.
2. D) - a condition or event that would cause the auditor concern relative to going concern.
3. A) - a procedure performed by the auditor.
4. A) - a procedure performed by the auditor.
5. B) - an objective of the auditor's procedures.
6. E) - a management plan to deal with adverse effects of conditions or events.
7. D) - a condition or event that would cause the auditor concern relative to going concern.
8. E) - a management plan to deal with adverse effects of conditions or events.
9. A) - a procedure performed by the auditor.
10. B) - an objective of the auditor's procedures.

5. Loss Contingencies (14 Gradable Items)

1. Does apply. Minutes of the meetings of the board of directors, shareholders, and various committees often provide evidence about unusual events giving rise to potential contingencies.

2. Does not apply. Inquiring of local officials is not a normal procedure. However, in certain instances the auditor may find it necessary to gather evidence from public records.

3. Does apply. Contracts, agreements, and leases often contain provisions that commit the client to contingencies.

4. Does apply. Correspondence with governmental agencies should be read and evaluated for numerous reasons (e.g., potential violations of laws or regulations, taxes or fees due, and claims or assessments on property).

5. Does apply. Insurance companies and bonding agencies often insure clients against potential losses. These losses should be identified and evaluated relative to potential financial reporting requirements.

6. Does not apply. Reading all legal briefs for suits filed against the client's competitors is not feasible or necessary.

7. Does apply. Confirmations may disclose certain guarantees offered to customers that would create contingent liabilities.

8. Does apply. AU 337 states that the auditor should "obtain from management a description and evaluation of litigation, claims, and assessments that existed at the date of the balance sheet being reported on."

9. Does not apply. AU 337 requires the auditor to obtain written representations from management, usually the chief executive officer and chief financial officer. The auditor would not normally obtain written representations from all client staff.

10. <u>Does apply</u>. Professional fees (for example, fees paid to lawyers) should be evaluated to determine their purpose. Often, the services are in relation to contingencies.

11. <u>Does not apply</u>. Normally, the auditor will not inquire of SEC officials. However, written correspondence, available from the client, should be evaluated by the auditor.

12. <u>Does apply</u>. AU 337 states, "A letter of audit inquiry to the client's lawyer is the auditor's primary means of obtaining corroboration of the information furnished by management concerning litigation, claims, and assessments."

13. <u>Does apply</u>. The auditor should consider the accounting treatment for each contingency, relative to SFAS 5, and determine that the financial statements are consistent with that treatment.

14. <u>Does not apply</u>. It is management's responsibility, not the audit committee's, to assure that appropriate accounting treatment is accorded contingencies.

6. Communication (5 Gradable Items; For grading instructions, please refer to page 11.)

To: Audit associate
From: CPA
Subject: Subsequent events

Two kinds of subsequent events require consideration by management and the auditor. The first consists of events that provide additional evidence about conditions existing at the balance-sheet date and affecting the estimates inherent in preparing financial statements. All information available prior to the issuance of the statements should be used by management to make those estimates. The financial statements should be adjusted for any changes in estimates resulting from the use of such evidence.

Recognizing events leading to adjustment of the financial statements requires judgment and knowledge of the facts. For example, a loss on an uncollectible receivable as a result of a customer's poor financial condition leading to subsequent bankruptcy is suggestive of conditions existing at the balance-sheet date and requiring adjustment. However, a similar loss from a customer's major casualty, such as a fire or flood, is not indicative of conditions existing at the balance-sheet date. The settlement of litigation for an amount different from the recorded liability requires adjustment if the events, such as personal injury or patent infringement litigation, had occurred before the balance-sheet date.

The second kind of subsequent events provides evidence about conditions not existing at the balance-sheet date. These events do not result in adjustment. Some, however, may be significant enough to require disclosure to prevent the financial statements from being misleading. Moreover, the event may be so significant that disclosure is best achieved by reporting pro forma financial data giving effect to the event as if it had occurred on the balance-sheet date. Presenting pro forma statements, usually only a balance-sheet, in column form on the face of the historical statements is another potential form of disclosure.

7. Research (6 Gradable Items)

AU Section 341 – *The Auditor's Consideration of an Entity's Ability to Continue as a Going Concern*

.05   It is not necessary to design audit procedures solely to identify conditions and events that, when considered in the aggregate, indicate there could be substantial doubt about the entity's ability to continue as a going concern for a reasonable period of time. The results of auditing procedures designed and performed to achieve other audit objectives should be sufficient for that purpose. The following are examples of procedures that may identify such conditions and events:

- Analytical procedures
- Review of subsequent events
- Review of compliance with the terms of debt and loan agreements
- Reading of minutes of meetings of stockholders, board of directors, and important committees of the board
- Inquiry of an entity's legal counsel about litigation, claims, and assessments
- Confirmation with related and third parties of the details of arrangements to provide or maintain financial support

Scoring Schedule:

	Correct Responses		Gradable Items		Weights		
Tab 3	_____	÷	10	×	20%	=	_____
Tab 4	_____	÷	10	×	20%	=	_____
Tab 5	_____	÷	14	×	20%	=	_____
Tab 6	_____	÷	5	×	30%	=	_____
Tab 7	_____	÷	6	×	10%	=	_____
							_____
							(Your Score)

Use Gleim's **CPA Review Online** to practice more simulations in a realistic environment.

STUDY UNIT FIFTEEN
EVIDENCE -- SAMPLING

(19 pages of outline)

15.1 Sampling Fundamentals (AU 350) 451
15.2 Statistical Sampling in Tests of Controls (Attribute Sampling) 454
15.3 Classical Variables Sampling (Mean-per-Unit) 459
15.4 Probability-Proportional-to-Size (PPS) or Dollar-Unit Sampling (DUS) 462
15.5 Practice Simulation 483

Subunit 15.1 defines terms, describes the purpose of and approach to sampling, and presents the basic concepts traditionally tested on the CPA exam. A study of these fundamentals is an effective way to prepare for most sampling-related questions. Periodically, however, more comprehensive questions are asked, including those requiring basic calculations or the consideration of tables.

The remaining three subunits contain study materials related to more extensive questions and simulations. They describe, in more detail, specific sampling techniques and provide several examples. Although more comprehensive than the first subunit, they are not intended to be an exhaustive treatment of sampling. These sections are based on concepts that have been tested in the past or are likely to be tested on future CPA exams and are discussed in the AICPA Auditing Practice Release, *Audit Sampling* (1999).

15.1 SAMPLING FUNDAMENTALS (AU 350)

1. **Audit sampling** applies an audit procedure to fewer than 100% of the items under audit for the purpose of drawing an inference about a characteristic of the population. Sampling may be statistical or nonstatistical.

   a. **Judgment (nonstatistical) sampling** uses the auditor's subjective judgment to determine the sample size (number of items examined) and sample selection (which items to examine). This subjectivity is not always a weakness. The auditor, based on other audit work, may be able to test the most material and risky transactions and to emphasize the types of transactions subject to high control risk.

   b. **Statistical (probability or random) sampling** provides an objective method of determining sample size and selecting the items to be examined. Unlike judgment sampling, it also provides a means of quantitatively assessing precision (how closely the sample represents the population) and reliability (confidence level, the percentage of times the sample will adequately reflect the population).

      1) Random-based selection is the primary characteristic of statistical sampling. It includes random sampling, stratified random sampling, sampling with probability proportional to size, and systematic sampling.

      2) Statistical sampling helps the auditor to design an efficient sample, to measure the sufficiency of the evidence obtained, and to evaluate the sample results. The third standard of field work requires auditors to obtain sufficient competent evidence. Sufficiency relates to the design and size of the sample. Statistical sampling permits the auditor to measure sampling risk and therefore to design more efficient samples (i.e., the minimum samples necessary to provide sufficient evidence).

2. Statistical sampling is applicable to both **tests of controls** (attribute sampling) and **substantive testing** (variables sampling).

3. The auditor expects the sample to be representative of the population. Thus, the sample should have the same characteristics (e.g., deviation rate or average value) as the population, and a conclusion or inference can be drawn from the sample about the population.

4. **Sampling risk** is the probability that a properly drawn sample may not be representative of the population. The inferences from the sample may differ from those made if all the items in the population are examined. Sampling risk is to be measured and controlled. The auditor controls sampling risk by specifying the acceptable level when developing the sampling plan.

    a. For tests of controls, sampling risk has the following aspects:

        1) "The **risk of assessing control risk too low** is the risk that the assessed level of control risk based on the sample is less than the true operating effectiveness of internal control." In other words, it is the risk that the actual control risk is greater than that indicated by the sample. This risk relates to audit effectiveness and **could cause audit failure**.

            a) Control risk is the risk that controls do not prevent or detect material misstatements on a timely basis.

            b) This risk is also termed a Type II error or Beta risk.

        2) "The **risk of assessing control risk too high** is the risk that the assessed level of control risk based on the sample is greater than the true operating effectiveness of internal control." In other words, it is the risk that actual control risk is less than that indicated by the sample. This risk concerns audit efficiency and is likely to result in greater audit effort.

            a) The auditor's overassessment of control risk may lead to an unnecessary extension of the substantive tests.

            b) This risk is also termed a Type I error or Alpha risk.

    b. For substantive tests of account balances, sampling risk has the following aspects:

        1) The **risk of incorrect acceptance** is the risk that the sample supports the conclusion that the recorded account balance is not materially misstated when it is materially misstated.

            a) This risk relates to audit effectiveness and could cause an **audit failure**.
            b) This risk is also termed a Type II error or Beta risk.

        2) The **risk of incorrect rejection** is the risk that the sample supports the conclusion that the recorded account balance is materially misstated when it is not materially misstated. After an incorrect rejection, the client would likely maintain that the balance is properly stated. The auditor would then expend more audit effort, ultimately to conclude that the balance is fairly stated.

            a) This risk relates to the efficiency, not the effectiveness, of the audit. If the cost and effort of selecting additional sample items are low, a higher risk of incorrect rejection may be acceptable.

            b) This risk is also termed a Type I error or Alpha risk.

    c. The **confidence level**, also termed the reliability level, is the complement of the applicable sampling risk factor. Thus, for a test of controls, if the risk of assessing control risk too low is 5%, the auditor's confidence level is 95% (100% − 5%). For a substantive test, if the risk of incorrect rejection is 5%, the auditor's confidence level is 95% (100% − 5%).

5. **Nonsampling risk** concerns all aspects of audit risk not caused by sampling, such as the auditor's inability to recognize noncompliance or the application of inappropriate procedures.

6. **Basic Steps in a Statistical Plan**

   a. **Determine the objectives of the plan**.

      1) For example, for a test of controls, to conclude that control is reasonably effective.

      2) For example, for a substantive test, to conclude that a balance is not misstated by more than a material amount.

   b. **Define the population**. This step includes defining the sampling unit and considering the completeness of the population.

      1) For tests of controls, it includes defining the period covered.

      2) For substantive tests, it includes identifying individually significant items.

   c. **Determine acceptable levels of sampling risk** (e.g., 5% or 10%).

   d. **Calculate the sample size** using tables or sample-size formulas.

      1) In some cases, it is efficient to divide the population into subpopulations or strata. The primary objective of **stratification** is to minimize variability. Because the variance within each subpopulation or stratum is lower than in the population as a whole, the auditor may sample a smaller number of items while holding precision and the confidence level constant.

   e. **Select the sampling approach**, e.g., random number, systematic, or block.

      1) In **random sampling**, each item in the population has an equal and nonzero probability of selection. Random selection is usually accomplished by generating random numbers from a random number table or computer program and tracing them to associated documents or items in the population.

      2) **Systematic sampling** begins with selecting a random start and then taking every n^{th} item in the population. The value of n is computed by dividing the population by the number of sampling units. The random start should be in the first interval. Because the sampling technique only requires counting in the population, no correspondence between random numbers and the items in the population is necessary as in random number sampling. A systematic sampling plan assumes the items are arranged randomly in the population. If the auditor discovers that this is not true, a random selection method should be used.

      3) **Block sampling** (cluster sampling) randomly selects groups of items as the sampling units rather than individual items. An example is the inclusion in the sample of all cash payments for May and September. One possible drawback is that the variability of items within the blocks may not be representative of the variability within the population. The advantage of block sampling is that it avoids the need to assign random numbers to individual items in the population. Instead, blocks (clusters) are randomly selected.

   f. **Take the sample**, i.e., select the items to be evaluated.

   g. **Evaluate the sample results**. Draw conclusions about the population.

   h. **Document the sampling procedures**. Prepare appropriate working papers.

7. In general, all sample sizes are dependent on

   a. The population size. As the population size increases, the required sample increases but at a decreasing rate.

   b. The acceptable risk (1 – the required confidence level). The smaller the acceptable risk, the larger the sample size.

   c. The variability in the population. The more variability in the population, measured by the standard deviation for variables sampling (or the expected deviation rate for attribute sampling), the larger the required sample size.

d.   The tolerable misstatement in variables sampling (or tolerable deviation rate in attribute sampling). The smaller the acceptable misstatement amount or deviation rate, the larger the required sample size.

8.   **The Primary Methods of Variables Sampling**. Variables sampling applies to dollar values or other quantities in contrast with the binary propositions tested by attribute sampling (see next subunit).

a.   **Mean-per-unit** averages the audit values of the sample items and multiplies the average by the number of items in the population to estimate the population value. An allowance for sampling risk is then determined.

b.   **Difference estimation and ratio estimation**

1)   Difference estimation (of population misstatement) determines differences between the audit and book values for items in the sample, adding the differences, calculating the mean difference, and multiplying the mean by the number of items in the population. An allowance for sampling risk (achieved precision at the desired level of confidence based on the normal distribution) is also calculated.

2)   Ratio estimation is similar to difference estimation except that it estimates the population misstatement by multiplying the book value of the population by the ratio of the total audit value of the sample items to their total book value.

c.   **Probability-proportional-to-size (PPS) or dollar-unit sampling (DUS)** uses the dollar as the sampling unit. PPS sampling is appropriate for testing account balances (typically assets) for overstatement when some items may be far larger than others in the population. In effect, it stratifies the population because the larger account balances have a greater chance of being selected. PPS is most useful if few misstatements are expected.

1)   Also, the method does not require the use of a measure of dispersion (e.g., standard deviation) to determine sample size or interpret the results.

9.   Stop and review! You have completed the outline for this subunit. Study multiple-choice questions 1 through 11 beginning on page 470.

15.2 STATISTICAL SAMPLING IN TESTS OF CONTROLS (ATTRIBUTE SAMPLING)

1.   **Attribute sampling** tests binary, yes/no, or error/nonerror questions. It is used to test the effectiveness of controls because it can estimate a rate of occurrence of control deviations in a population. Attribute sampling requires the existence of evidence indicating performance of the control procedure being tested (e.g., a control indicating that the purchasing agent has signed all purchase orders before sending them to the vendor). It is most helpful for a large population of documentary evidence. In general, the performance of any task that leaves evidence of its execution is suitable for attribute sampling. In such cases, the auditor can form conclusions about the population by examining a sample.

a.   Examples of tests in which attribute sampling is used include tests of controls for

1)   Billing
2)   Voucher processing
3)   Payroll
4)   Inventory pricing

2. **Steps for Testing Controls**

    a.   **Define the objectives of the plan**. The auditor should clearly state what is to be accomplished, for example, to determine that the deviation rate from an approval process for a transaction is at an acceptable level.

    b.   **Define the population**. The population is the focus of interest. The accountant wants to reach conclusions about all the items (typically documents) in the population.

        1)   The sampling unit is the individual item that will be included in the sample. Thus, the population may consist of all the transactions for the fiscal year. The sampling unit would be each document representing a transaction and containing the required evidence that a control procedure was performed (e.g., an approval signature).

    c.   **Define the deviation conditions**. The characteristic indicative of performance of a control is the attribute of interest, for example, the supervisor's signature of approval on a document. Careful definition of the attribute is important so that deviations (departures) from the control procedure may be determined and the sample items properly evaluated. For example, is it acceptable for another person to sign for the supervisor during vacation periods, and must the signature be in a certain place on the form for it to be considered approved?

    d.   **Determine the sample size**. Four factors determine the necessary sample size: the allowable risk of assessing control risk too low, the tolerable deviation rate, the expected population deviation rate, and population size. Tables are ordinarily used to calculate the appropriate sample size based on these factors. Tables 1 and 2 on the next page are derived from Appendix A of AICPA, Auditing Practice Release, *Audit Sampling* (1999).

        1)   Allowable risk of assessing control risk too low. This risk has an inverse effect on sample size. The higher the acceptable risk, the smaller the sample size. The usual risk level accepted and specified by auditors is 5% or 10%. The auditor can specify other levels of risk, but the tables most often presented use only these two.

        2)   Tolerable deviation rate. This is the maximum rate of deviations from the prescribed control that the auditor would be willing to accept without altering the planned assessed level of control risk. Deviations increase the likelihood of misstatements in the accounting records but do not always cause misstatements.

            a)   If the auditor cannot tolerate any deviations, the concept of sampling is inappropriate and the whole population must be investigated.

        3)   Expected population deviation rate. An estimate of the deviation rate in the current population is necessary to determine the appropriate sample size. This estimate can be based on the prior year's findings or a pilot sample of approximately 30 to 50 items.

            a)   The expected rate should be less than the tolerable rate. Otherwise, tests of the control should be omitted, and control risk should be assessed at the maximum.

Table 1 -- Sample Sizes for Tests of Controls -- 5% Risk of Assessing Control Risk Too Low

Expected Population Deviation Rate	Tolerable Deviation Rate								
	2%	3%	4%	5%	6%	7%	8%	9%	10%
0.00	149	99	74	59	49	42	36	32	29
.25	236	157	117	93	78	66	58	51	46
.50	*	157	117	93	78	66	58	51	46
.75	*	208	117	93	78	66	58	51	46
1.00	*	*	156	93	78	66	58	51	46
1.25	*	*	156	124	78	66	58	51	46
1.50	*	*	192	124	103	66	58	51	46
1.75	*	*	227	153	103	88	77	51	46
2.00	*	*	*	181	127	88	77	68	46
2.25	*	*	*	208	127	88	77	68	61
2.50	*	*	*	*	150	109	77	68	61
2.75	*	*	*	*	173	109	95	68	61
3.00	*	*	*	*	195	129	95	84	61
3.25	*	*	*	*	*	148	112	84	61
3.50	*	*	*	*	*	167	112	84	76
3.75	*	*	*	*	*	185	129	100	76
4.00	*	*	*	*	*	*	146	100	89
5.00	*	*	*	*	*	*	*	158	116
6.00	*	*	*	*	*	*	*	*	179

Table 2 -- Results Evaluation for Tests of Controls -- Upper Limits at 5% Risk of Assessing Control Risk Too Low

Sample Size	Actual Number of Deviations Found										
	0	1	2	3	4	5	6	7	8	9	10
25	11.3	17.6	*	*	*	*	*	*	*	*	*
30	9.5	14.9	19.6	*	*	*	*	*	*	*	*
35	8.3	12.9	17.0	*	*	*	*	*	*	*	*
40	7.3	11.4	15.0	18.3	*	*	*	*	*	*	*
45	6.5	10.2	13.4	16.4	19.2	*	*	*	*	*	*
50	5.9	9.2	12.1	14.8	17.4	19.9	*	*	*	*	*
55	5.4	8.4	11.1	13.5	15.9	18.2	*	*	*	*	*
60	4.9	7.7	10.2	12.5	14.7	16.8	18.8	*	*	*	*
65	4.6	7.1	9.4	11.5	13.6	15.5	17.4	19.3	*	*	*
70	4.2	6.6	8.8	10.8	12.6	14.5	16.3	18.0	19.7	*	*
75	4.0	6.2	8.2	10.1	11.8	13.6	15.2	16.9	18.5	20.0	*
80	3.7	5.8	7.7	9.5	11.1	12.7	14.3	15.9	17.4	18.9	*
90	3.3	5.2	6.9	8.4	9.9	11.4	12.8	14.2	15.5	16.8	18.2
100	3.0	4.7	6.2	7.6	9.0	10.3	11.5	12.8	14.0	15.2	16.4
125	2.4	3.8	5.0	6.1	7.2	8.3	9.3	10.3	11.3	12.3	13.2
150	2.0	3.2	4.2	5.1	6.0	6.9	7.8	8.6	9.5	10.3	11.1
200	1.5	2.4	3.2	3.9	4.6	5.2	5.9	6.5	7.2	7.8	8.4

4) Population size. The total number of sampling units in the population should be known. However, the sample size is relatively insensitive to size changes in large populations. For populations over 5,000, a standard table (e.g., Table 1, which assumes a large population) can be used. Use of the standard tables (based on the assumption of large populations) for sampling plans based on a smaller population size is a conservative approach because the sample size will be overstated. Hence, the risk of assessing control risk too low is not affected.

    a) A change in the size of the population has a very small effect on the required sample size when the population is large.

5) EXAMPLE: Assume the risk of assessing control risk too low is 5%, the tolerable rate is 6%, the expected population deviation rate is 2.5%, and the population size is over 5,000. Given these data, the sample size determined from Table 1 is 150. This is the intersection of the 6% Tolerable Deviation Rate column and the 2 1/2% Expected Population Deviation Rate row.

e. **Perform the sampling plan**. A random sample should be taken. Each item in the population should have an equal and nonzero chance of being selected. A random number table can be used to identify the items to be selected if a correspondence can be established between the random number and the item in the population.

1) A statistical consideration is whether to use sampling **with** or **without** replacement. The tables are designed for sampling without replacement, which results in a conservative sample size because a slightly larger sample size than necessary will be indicated.

2) Sampling without replacement means that a population item cannot be selected again after it is selected in the sampling process.

f. **Evaluate and document sample results**. The steps include calculating the sample deviation rate and determining the achieved upper deviation limit.

1) **Sample deviation rate**. The number of deviations observed is divided by the sample size to determine the sample deviation rate. This rate is the best estimate of the population deviation rate. For example, if three deviations were discovered, the auditor's best estimate of the population deviation rate would be 2% (3 ÷ 150). The auditor cannot state with certainty that the sample rate is the population rate because the sample may not be representative of the population. However, (s)he can state that the rate is not likely to be greater than a specified upper limit.

2) **Achieved upper deviation limit**. The achieved upper deviation limit is based on the sample size and the number of deviations discovered. See Table 2. The intersection of the sample size and the number of deviations indicates the upper achieved deviation limit. Accordingly, if the auditor discovers three deviations in a sample of 150, (s)he can state at a 95% confidence level (the complement of a 5% risk of assessing control risk too low) that the true occurrence rate is not greater than 5.1%.

    a) The difference between the achieved upper deviation limit determined from a standard table and the sample rate is the allowance for sampling risk (achieved precision).

    b) When the sample deviation rate exceeds the expected population deviation rate, the achieved upper deviation limit will exceed the tolerable rate at the given risk level. In that case, the sample does not support the planned assessed level of control risk.

    c) When the sample deviation rate does not exceed the expected population deviation rate, the achieved upper deviation limit will not exceed the tolerable rate at the given risk level. Thus, the sample supports the planned assessed level of control risk.

3) Each deviation should be analyzed to determine its nature, importance, and probable cause. Obviously, some are much more significant than others. Sampling provides a vehicle for forming a conclusion concerning the overall population but should not be used as a substitute for good judgment.

3. The following presentation has become a popular method for testing sampling concepts related to tests of controls. It is used to explain how to analyze the information. A variety of questions can be answered based on the analysis.

a. The table below depicts the possible combinations of the sample results and the true state of the population.

Auditor's Estimate Based on Sample Results	True State of Population	
	Deviation rate is less than tolerable rate.	Deviation rate exceeds tolerable rate.
Maximum deviation rate is less than tolerable rate.	I. Correct	III. Incorrect
Maximum deviation rate exceeds tolerable rate.	II. Incorrect	IV. Correct

b. The following definitions and explanations should be understood:

1) The true state of the population is the actual rate of deviations in the population.

2) If the true deviation rate is less than the tolerable rate, the auditor should assess control risk at less than the maximum.

3) If the true deviation rate exceeds the tolerable rate, the auditor should not assess control risk at less than the maximum.

4) The auditor's estimate based on the sample is the auditor's conclusion about the deviation rate in the population based on taking and evaluating a sample.

5) Cell I represents a correct decision to assess control risk at less than the maximum. The population actually has a deviation rate less than the tolerable rate.

6) Cell II represents an incorrect decision to assess control risk at the maximum when it could be assessed at less than the maximum. The population has an acceptable deviation rate; but, because of sampling risk, the sample indicates that the population deviation rate is greater than acceptable. This error will compel the auditor to expand substantive testing even though the controls are effective. Thus, it relates to the efficiency rather than the effectiveness of the audit.

   a) This is known as Type I error or Alpha risk.

7) Cell III represents an incorrect decision (and a critical one) to assess control risk at less than the maximum. The population has a greater than acceptable deviation rate, but the sample indicates that the deviation rate is less than the tolerable rate. Because control risk would be inappropriately assessed at less than maximum, substantive testing would be reduced and an audit failure could result.

   a) This is known as Type II error or Beta risk.

8) Cell IV represents a correct decision to assess control risk at the maximum. The population has an unacceptable deviation rate, and the sample properly indicates this condition.

    c.   A CPA exam question may take a variety of forms, but the following is representative:

        1)   As a result of tests of controls, the auditor assesses control risk higher than necessary and thereby increases substantive testing. This is illustrated by which situation? Answer: Cell II

4.   Stop and review! You have completed the outline for this subunit. Study multiple-choice questions 12 through 27 beginning on page 473.

15.3 CLASSICAL VARIABLES SAMPLING (MEAN-PER-UNIT)

1.   Sampling for substantive testing attempts to provide evidence about whether an account balance is materially misstated. Management presents an assertion about an account balance, for example, the amount of accounts receivable. The amount is expected to represent the value of the receivables, but the true value of the receivables is not known (and will never be known without a 100% audit). The auditor collects evidence as to whether management's assertion is a fair representation of the true but unknown value of the population. By taking a sample and drawing an inference about the population, the auditor either supports or rejects the conclusion that management's reported number is a fair representation.

    a.   Examples are as follows:

        1)   Is management's recorded balance of accounts receivable valued at net realizable value?

        2)   Is management's recorded balance of inventory valued at lower of cost or market?

2.   **Steps and an Example** (These are similar to the basic steps identified previously.)

    a.   **Define the objectives of the plan**. The auditor intends to estimate the book value of the population, for example, a client's accounts receivable balance.

    b.   **Define the population and the sampling unit**. For example, the population might consist of 4,000 accounts receivable with a reported book value of $3,500,000. Each customer account is a sampling unit.

    c.   **Determine the sample size**. The sample size formula for mean-per-unit variables sampling is as follows:

$$n = \left[\frac{C \times S \times N}{A} \right]^2$$

    If: n = Sample size
           C = Confidence coefficient or number of standard deviations related to the required confidence level (1 – the risk of incorrect rejection)
           S = Standard deviation of the population (an estimate based on a pilot sample or from the prior year's sample)
           N = Number of items in the population
           A = Allowance for sampling risk. This allowance is a total. In some representations, the allowance (precision) is stated in the denominator on a per-item basis (A ÷ N), and N would not be included in the formula.

        1)   The allowance for sampling risk, also termed the precision or confidence interval, is an interval around the sample statistic that is expected to include the true value of the population at the specified confidence level. When using classical variables sampling, the allowance for sampling risk is calculated based on the normal distribution.

a)   This allowance is a function of the tolerable misstatement or the maxi-mum misstatement that may exist without causing the financial statements to be materially misstated. Tolerable misstatement should not exceed the auditor's preliminary judgments about materiality.

b)   The allowance for sampling risk is established as a function of materiality to control the risk of incorrect acceptance. C in the formula is based on the risk of incorrect rejection, but the more important risk to the auditor is that of incorrect acceptance.

   i)   The allowance for sampling risk equals the product of tolerable misstatement and a ratio determined in accordance with Table 3 below (Appendix E of the AICPA Auditing Practice Release). This ratio is based on the allowable risk of incorrect acceptance and the risk of incorrect rejection, both of which are values specified by the auditor.

Table 3 -- Ratio of Desired Allowance for Sampling Risk to Tolerable Misstatement				
Risk of Incorrect Acceptance	Risk of Incorrect Rejection			
	.20	.10	.05	.01
.01	.355	.413	.457	.525
.025	.395	.456	.500	.568
.05	.437	.500	.543	.609
.075	.471	.532	.576	.641
.10	.500	.561	.605	.668
.15	.533	.612	.653	.712
.20	.603	.661	.700	.753
.25	.653	.708	.742	.791
.30	.707	.756	.787	.829
.35	.766	.808	.834	.868
.40	.831	.863	.883	.908
.45	.907	.926	.937	.953
.50	1.000	1.000	1.000	1.000

   ii)   For example, at a confidence level of 90% (10% risk of incorrect rejection), setting A at 50% (.500 in Table 3) of materiality (tolerable misstatement) controls the risk of incorrect acceptance at 5%.

2)   The confidence coefficient, C, is derived from probability theory and is based on the risk of incorrect rejection as follows:

Risk of Incorrect Rejection	Confidence Level	Confidence Coefficient
20%	80%	1.28
10%	90%	1.64 X
5%	95%	1.96
1%	99%	2.58

3) EXAMPLE: The number of sampling units is 4,000; the estimated population standard deviation is $125 based on a pilot sample; and the number of standard deviations related to the desired 90% confidence level (10% risk of incorrect rejection) is 1.64. Assuming tolerable misstatement of $100,000 and a planned risk of incorrect acceptance of 5%, the planned allowance for sampling risk (desired precision) can be determined using Table 3 on the previous page. The intersection of 10% risk of incorrect rejection and 5% allowable risk of incorrect acceptance is .500. Multiplying .500 by the $100,000 tolerable misstatement results in a $50,000 allowance for sampling risk.

Thus, the sample size is

$$n = \left[\frac{C \times S \times N}{A}\right]^2$$

$$= \left[\frac{1.64 \times \$125 \times 4,000}{\$50,000}\right]^2$$

$$= 268.96 \text{ or } 269$$

d. **Select the sample, execute the plan, and evaluate and document the results**.

1) Randomly select and audit the accounts, e.g., send confirmations.
2) Calculate the average confirmed accounts receivable amount (assume $880).
3) Calculate the sample standard deviation (assume $125).
4) Evaluate the sample results.

   a) The best estimate of the population value is the average accounts receivable value from the sample times the number of items in the population. Thus, the amount estimated is

   $$Est. \text{ of } pop. \text{ } value = Average \text{ } sample \text{ } value \times No. \text{ of items in } pop.$$

   $$= \$880 \times 4,000$$

   $$= \$3,520,000$$

   b) The calculated allowance for sampling risk (achieved precision) is determined by solving the sample size formula for A.

   $$A = \frac{C \times S \times N}{\sqrt{n}}$$

   $$= \frac{1.64 \times \$125 \times 4,000}{\sqrt{269}}$$

   $$= \$820,000 \div 16.4 = \$50,000$$

   N, C, and S are the same values used to calculate the original sample size, n. Hence, the allowance for sampling risk, A, will be the same as planned, or $50,000. A will be different only when the standard deviation, c, of the sample differs from the estimate used to calculate n. Differences in the standard deviation derived from the sample can result in changes in the levels of risk faced by the auditor, but these issues are beyond the scope of the materials presented here (and are usually not covered on the CPA exam).

          c)   The audit conclusion is that the auditor is 90% confident that the true value of the population is $3,520,000 plus or minus $50,000, for an interval of $3,470,000 to $3,570,000. Management's recorded value was $3,500,000. Consequently, the auditor cannot reject the hypothesis that the recorded value is not materially misstated, and management's recorded value would be accepted as fairly stated.

3.   Stop and review! You have completed the outline for this subunit. Study multiple-choice questions 28 through 33 beginning on page 479.

15.4 PROBABILITY-PROPORTIONAL-TO-SIZE (PPS) OR DOLLAR-UNIT SAMPLING (DUS)

1.   The PPS approach to variables sampling is distinct from the classical approach because it is a hybrid method that uses attribute sampling methods to estimate dollar amounts. PPS is based on the Poisson distribution, which is used in attribute sampling to approximate the binomial distribution.

    a.   PPS uses a dollar as the sampling unit, but the item (invoice, check, etc.) containing the sampled dollar is selected for audit. The classical approach uses items themselves (e.g., invoices, checks, etc.) as the sampling units.

        1)   PPS sampling gives each individual dollar in the population an equal chance of selection. As a practical matter, however, the auditor does not examine an individual dollar. The individual dollar identifies an entire transaction or balance to audit. Because a systematic selection method is used (i.e., every nth dollar is selected), the larger the transactions or amounts in the population, the more likely a transaction or amount will be selected for audit.

        2)   PPS is appropriate for account balances that may include only a few overstated items, such as may be expected in inventory and receivables.

            a)   PPS is only useful for tests of overstatements (e.g., of assets) because the sample selection method dictates that the larger the transaction or balance, the more likely that it will be selected. The method is inappropriate for testing liabilities because understatement is the primary audit consideration.

        3)   In contrast, the classical approach to variables sampling is not always appropriate.

            a)   When only a few differences between recorded and audit amounts are found, difference and ratio estimation sampling may not be efficient.

            b)   Mean-per-unit estimation sampling may also be difficult in an unstratified sampling situation.

        4)   PPS is also termed dollar-unit sampling (DUS), cumulative monetary amount (CMA), and combined attribute variables (CAV) sampling.

        5)   PPS is used to reach a conclusion regarding the probability of overstating an account balance by a specified dollar amount.

b.   Advantages of PPS include

1)   Automatically selects the largest items for testing (i.e., stratifies the population)
2)   Is ideal for the audit objective of testing for overstatement
3)   Allows consideration of small sample sizes, especially when no misstatements are expected
4)   Is relatively easy to apply, especially if no misstatements are discovered
5)   Permits calculation of the sample size and sample evaluation without dependence on the estimated variation (standard deviation) of the population
6)   Allows the sample selection process to begin even before the complete population is available for testing

c.   Disadvantages of PPS sampling include

1)   Items with zero or negative balances have no chance of selection.
2)   It is useful only for detecting overstatement errors.
3)   Sample sizes become relatively large if a significant amount of misstatement is expected.
4)   The calculated allowance for sampling risk tends to be overstated when a significant amount of misstatement is found in the sample.

   a)   This is an inherent limitation of PPS sampling.

d.   Overview. The steps in PPS sampling are similar to other sampling methods:

1)   Determine the objective of the plan.
2)   Define the population and sampling unit.
3)   Determine the sampling interval and sample size.
4)   Select the sample.
5)   Execute the sampling plan.
6)   Evaluate the results.

2.   The following is a simple example of the application of PPS sampling. This example is then extended to the case in which overstatement errors are detected. The CPA candidate should strive to understand the concepts rather than the details.

a.   The following assumptions apply in an audit of Seminole, Inc.:

1)   The auditor's specific objective is to conclude that Seminole's accounts receivable balance is not overstated by more than $35,000 (tolerable misstatement).
2)   The population contains $900,000 (sampling units) and over 1,000 individual accounts receivable (logical sampling units), all with debit balances.
3)   The risk of incorrect acceptance specified by the auditor is 5%. Thus, the auditor desires to be 95% confident that the recorded balance is not overstated by more than $35,000.

b.   The sample size is determined by the formula:

Sample size = Recorded amount of population ÷ Sampling interval

Sampling interval (SI) is a function of the risk of incorrect acceptance and tolerable misstatement (TM). SI is determined by dividing tolerable misstatement by a reliability factor (RF) associated with the risk level.

Sampling interval = Tolerable misstatement ÷ Reliability factor

The reliability factors (Appendix D of the AICPA Auditing Practice Release) for several risk levels, assuming no overstatements are expected, are

Risk of Incorrect Acceptance	Reliability Factor
1%	4.61
5%	3.00
10%	2.31

Because the risk of incorrect acceptance for Seminole is established at 5%, the reliability factor is 3.00. Thus, the sampling interval for Seminole is

$$SI = TM \div RF$$

$$= \$35,000 \div 3.00$$

$$= \$11,667$$

The sample size (n) for Seminole is

$$n = Recorded\ amount\ of\ population \div SI$$

$$= \$900,000 \div \$11,667$$

$$= 77$$

c.   The auditor uses systematic sampling (discussed in the extension of the example that follows) to select 77 dollars (actually 77 account balances) to audit.

d.   If no misstatements are discovered, the auditor can form the following conclusion: "I am 95% confident that the recorded accounts receivable balance of $900,000 is not overstated by more than $35,000." There is still a 5% risk that the account balance is overstated by more than $35,000.

1)   The $35,000 is termed the allowance for sampling risk (also known as precision or confidence interval). Because the sample contains no misstatements, the conclusion is that the population has no misstatements. But, because the sample may not be perfectly representative of the population, an allowance for sampling risk must be considered. Thus, the more accurate conclusion is that the auditor is 95% confident that the misstatements are not greater than the allowance for sampling risk.

2)   Given that the allowance for sampling risk is less than or equal to the tolerable misstatement, the objective of the audit test has been met.

3.   The Seminole, Inc. example is extended on the next page to consider anticipated misstatements by the auditor and to demonstrate the extrapolation of the sample results to the population when misstatements are discovered in the sampling units.

4.   **Objectives, Definition of the Population, and Sampling Unit**. In the extended example, Seminole's basic information remains the same. However, the auditor anticipates misstatements in the population to be $10,000 based on the prior audit.

5. **Determining Sampling Interval and Sample Size**

    a.   When no misstatements are expected, the sampling interval equals tolerable misstatement divided by the reliability factor. However, any anticipated misstatements must be considered in the determination of the sampling interval. Moreover, the anticipated misstatements (AM) must be multiplied by an expansion factor (EF) appropriate for the risk of incorrect acceptance. The revised sampling interval (SI) calculation is given below. The reliability factor is the same as when no overstatements are expected.

         SI = [Tolerable misstatement – (Anticipated misstatement × Expansion factor)] ÷ Reliability factor

    b.   The expansion factors (Appendix D of the AICPA Auditing Practice Release) for several risk levels are

Risk of Incorrect Acceptance	Reliability Factor	Expansion Factor
1%	4.61	1.9
5%	3.00	1.6
10%	2.31	1.5

    c.   Accordingly, for Seminole the revised sampling interval is

         SI = [TM – (AM × EF)] ÷ RF

           = [$35,000 – ($10,000 × 1.6)] ÷ 3.00

           = $6,333

    d.   As before, the sample size is calculated as

         Sample size = Recorded amount of population ÷ Sampling interval

           = $900,000 ÷ $6,333

           = 142

    e.   The effects of changes in the factors in the sample size formula should be understood. For example, the greater the auditor's allowable risk of incorrect acceptance, the smaller the sample size, and the larger the anticipated misstatement, the larger the sample size.

6. **Selecting the Sample**

    a.   Use SI to determine logical sampling units to select from the population.

    b.   The rationale is that, if every 6,333rd cumulative dollar is selected from the population of $900,000, a total of 142 items (the sample size) will be selected. The auditor should therefore start randomly between 1 and 6,333. Given a random start at the 2,733rd cumulative dollar, the sample will be the following:

        The first dollar selected will be $2,733.
        The next dollar should be $2,733 + $6,333 = $9,066.
        The next dollar should be $9,066 + $6,333 = $15,399.
        The next dollar should be $15,399 + $6,333 = $21,732.
        All subsequent dollars, add $6,333 to prior dollar selected.

c.   Although the sampling unit (a dollar) is identified, the logical sampling unit (an account receivable) is actually selected for audit from the population. The account containing the selected dollar is chosen. Table 4 below demonstrates this selection process. When the **cumulative balance** is equal to or greater than the dollar selected, the account is selected because it contains the sampling unit. If an account contains two or more sampling units, for example, an account receivable of $15,000, it would be selected, but it would be given no special consideration. The ultimate sample of logical sampling units may contain fewer items than the calculated n.

| Table 4 -- Systematic Selection for Seminole, Inc. | | | | |
Customer Number	A/R Recorded Amount	Cumulative Balance	Dollar Selected	Recorded Amount of Sample Item
001	$ 2,000	$ 2,000		
002	1,225	3,225	2,733	1,225
003	3,500	6,725		
004	2,500	9,225	9,066	2,500
005	10,000	19,225	15,399	10,000
006	915	20,140		
etc.	etc.	etc.	etc.	etc.
Total	$900,000			

7.   Executing the Audit Plan

a.   Audit the items (e.g., send confirmations to the selected accounts).

b.   Identify the overstatement errors (any understatement errors require special consideration, but the issue is beyond the scope of this outline).

8.   Evaluating and Documenting Results

a.   The evaluation process depends on whether any misstatements are found in the sample. The following summarizes that process:

1)   Project the misstatement from sample to population.
2)   Determine the allowance for sampling risk.

   a)   *Allowance for sampling risk = Basic precision (BP) + Incremental allowance (IA)*

3)   Calculate the upper misstatement limit (UML).

   a)   *Upper misstatement limit = Projected misstatement + Allowance for sampling risk*

b.   If no overstatement errors are discovered, the upper misstatement limit equals only the basic precision because

1)   The projected misstatement to the population is $0.
2)   The allowance for sampling risk equals basic precision (i.e., the incremental allowance is $0).
3)   The calculation for basic precision (BP) is

$$BP = RF \times SI$$

BP = Basic precision
RF = Reliability factor
SI   = Sampling interval

4) If no misstatements were found for Seminole, Inc., the basic precision (and upper misstatement limit) would be

$$BP = 3.0 \times \$6,333$$
$$= \$18,999$$

5) The conclusion is that the auditor is 95% confident that the balance of accounts receivable is not overstated by more than $18,999, which meets the overall objective of the audit because the amount is within the tolerable misstatement of $35,000. Again, the $18,999 is the allowance for sampling risk.

c. If some misstatements are discovered, the evaluation procedure is more involved but follows the summary presented above.

1) Project the sample results to the population if misstatements are discovered.

a) Tainting. Because each selected dollar represents a group of dollars (the sampling interval), the percentage of misstatement in the logical unit (the account selected) represents the percentage of misstatement in the sampling interval that it represents. This is termed "tainting."

i) However, if a logical unit (the account selected) equals or exceeds the sampling interval, the projected misstatement is the actual misstatement for the sampling interval and no tainting is calculated.

b) For each logical unit with a recorded amount (RA) less than the sampling interval (SI), calculate the tainting percentage (i.e., the percentage of misstatement of the sampling unit that the sample item represents):

$$Tainting \% = \frac{(RA - AA)}{RA} \text{ if } AA = Audit \ amount$$

i) Projected misstatement = SI × Tainting %

c) For each logical unit equal to or greater than the SI, use actual misstatements in the projected misstatement calculation.

d) Add the individual projected misstatements to determine the projected population misstatement.

e) EXAMPLE:

Table 5 -- Seminole, Inc., Calculation of Projected Misstatement				
Recorded Amount	Audit Amount	Tainting % = (RA − AA) ÷ RA	Sampling Interval	Projected Misstatement
$ 1,000	$ 800	20%	$6,333	$ 1,267
10,000	6,000	N/A	N/A	4,000
300	0	100%	6,333	6,333
$11,300	$6,800			$11,600

i) The first and third projected misstatements equal the tainting percentage times SI because the recorded amount of the sample item is less than SI. The second projected misstatement included is the actual misstatement. The recorded amount of the sample item is greater than SI.

ii) The total projected misstatement to the population is $11,600, but the allowance for sampling risk must be added to derive the upper misstatement limit.

2) Calculate the allowance for sampling risk and determine the upper misstatement limit.

    a) Allowance for sampling risk has two components: **basic precision** (BP) and the **incremental allowance for misstatements** (IA).

    b) BP is the same as when no misstatements are found (i.e., SI × RF).

    c) IA is based on projected misstatements related to logical sampling units less than SI. (The misstatements related to logical sampling units greater than SI are not considered in the calculation of IA.)

       i) Projected misstatements are ranked by size (but only for misstatements related to logical sampling units less than SI).

       ii) Each projected misstatement is multiplied by a factor that gives greater weights to the larger amounts. The first few factors for the 5% risk of incorrect acceptance, sufficient to calculate the allowance for sampling risk for Seminole, are presented in Table 6 below. Each factor equals the incremental change in the reliability factor minus one. For misstatements equaling 0, 1, 2, and 3 given a 5% risk of incorrect acceptance, the reliability factors are 3.00, 4.75, 6.30, and 7.76, respectively.

       • For Seminole, two misstatements are related to logical sampling units less than the SI of $6,333.

       • The ranked projected misstatements are multiplied by the factors from Table 6 and added to determine IA in Table 7.

Table 6 -- Misstatement Factors 5% Risk of Incorrect Acceptance		
Misstatement Number	Change in Reliability Factor	Change in RF – 1.0
1	1.75 (4.75 – 3.00)	.75
2	1.55 (6.30 – 4.75)	.55
3	1.46 (7.76 – 6.30)	.46
etc.	etc.	etc.

d)   The allowance for sampling risk is the sum of BP and IA.

Allowance for sampling risk = *BP + IA*

= *$18,999 + $5,447*

= *$24,446*

Table 7 -- Calculation of the Incremental Allowance for Misstatements (AI)		
Ranked Projected Misstatements	Factor	Incremental Allowance
$6,333	.75	$4,750
1,267	.55	697
Total IA (rounded)		$5,447

e)   The total projected misstatement (PM) plus the allowance for sampling risk equals the upper misstatement limit (UML).

ULM = BP + Allowance for sampling risk

= *$11,600 + $24,446*

= *$23,046*

i)   Conclusion. The auditor's conclusion is that (s)he is 95% confident that the balance of accounts receivable is not overstated by more than $36,046. However, the auditor has a tolerable misstatement of only $35,000. Thus, the auditor cannot conclude, within the acceptable level of risk, that the balance is fairly presented. (The auditor would likely require the client to make adjustments to the account before presentation on the balance sheet.)

9.   Stop and review! You have completed the outline for the subunit. Study multiple-choice questions 34 through 38 beginning on page 481.

QUESTIONS

15.1 Sampling Fundamentals (AU 350)

1. An advantage of statistical over nonstatistical sampling methods in tests of controls is that the statistical methods

- A. Afford greater assurance than a nonstatistical sample of equal size.
- B. Provide an objective basis for quantitatively evaluating sample risks.
- C. Can more easily convert the sample into a dual-purpose test useful for substantive testing.
- D. Eliminate the need to use judgment in determining appropriate sample sizes.

Answer (B) is correct. *(CPA, adapted)*
REQUIRED: The advantage of statistical over nonstatistical sampling methods.
DISCUSSION: The results of statistical (probability) sampling are objective and subject to the laws of probability. Hence, sampling risk can be quantified and controlled, and the degree of reliability desired (the confidence level) can be specified. Sampling risk is the risk that the sample selected does not represent the population.
Answer (A) is incorrect because a nonstatistical method may permit the auditor to test the most material and risky transactions and therefore may provide equal or greater assurance. However, that assurance cannot be quantified. Answer (C) is incorrect because statistical sampling provides no advantage for converting to dual-purpose testing. Answer (D) is incorrect because sample size is subject to judgments about the desired confidence level.

2. An advantage of statistical sampling over nonstatistical sampling is that statistical sampling helps an auditor to

- A. Minimize the failure to detect errors and fraud.
- B. Eliminate the risk of nonsampling errors.
- C. Reduce the level of audit risk and materiality to a relatively low amount.
- D. Measure the sufficiency of the evidential matter obtained.

Answer (D) is correct. *(CPA, adapted)*
REQUIRED: The advantage of statistical sampling over nonstatistical sampling.
DISCUSSION: Statistical sampling helps the auditor to design an efficient sample, to measure the sufficiency of the evidence obtained, and to evaluate the sample results. The third standard of field work requires auditors to obtain sufficient competent evidence. Sufficiency relates to the design and size of the sample. Statistical sampling permits the auditors to measure sampling risk and therefore to design more efficient samples, that is, samples of a size necessary to provide sufficient evidence.
Answer (A) is incorrect because, in some circumstances, professional judgment may indicate that nonstatistical methods are preferable to minimize the failure to detect errors and fraud. Answer (B) is incorrect because statistical sampling is irrelevant to nonsampling errors. Answer (C) is incorrect because statistical sampling is irrelevant to materiality. Moreover, nonstatistical methods may be used to reduce audit risk.

3. A principal advantage of statistical methods of attribute sampling over nonstatistical methods is that they provide a scientific basis for planning the

- A. Risk of assessing control risk too low.
- B. Tolerable rate.
- C. Expected population deviation rate.
- D. Sample size.

Answer (D) is correct. *(CPA, adapted)*
REQUIRED: The item for which statistical methods provide a scientific basis for planning.
DISCUSSION: Statistical theory permits the auditor to measure sampling risk and to restrict it to an acceptable level. Statistical methods determine the sample size that will accomplish the auditor's objectives.
Answer (A) is incorrect because the risk of assessing control risk too low is the risk of believing a control is effective when it is not. Answer (B) is incorrect because the tolerable rate is a function of the auditor's judgment about the planned assessed level of control risk and the desired degree of assurance to be provided by the evidence, not of the statistical methods used. Answer (C) is incorrect because the expected population deviation rate prior to sampling is a function of auditor judgment.

4. The risk of incorrect acceptance and the likelihood of assessing control risk too low relate to the

    A. Effectiveness of the audit.

    B. Efficiency of the audit.

    C. Preliminary estimates of materiality levels.

    D. Tolerable misstatement.

Answer (A) is correct. *(CPA, adapted)*
    REQUIRED: The true statement about the risks of incorrect acceptance and assessing control risk too low.
    DISCUSSION: If an account balance is erroneously accepted as fairly stated based upon a sample, additional audit work and the chances of exposing the mistake will probably be minimal. However, rejection of a fairly stated balance typically results in further audit investigation and ultimately the acceptance of the balance. Similarly, assessing control risk too low leads to an unjustified reduction in substantive testing, thereby decreasing the effectiveness of the audit. Assessing control risk too high results in an unneeded increase in substantive testing but most likely will not decrease the ultimate audit effectiveness.
    Answer (B) is incorrect because these risks relate to effectiveness. Answer (C) is incorrect because preliminary judgments about materiality are considered when planning a sample for a substantive test. The risk of assessing control risk too low relates directly to tests of controls. Answer (D) is incorrect because the tolerable misstatement is considered when planning a sample for a substantive test. The risk of assessing control risk too low relates directly to tests of controls.

5. The likelihood of assessing control risk too high is the risk that the sample selected to test controls

    A. Does not support the auditor's planned assessed level of control risk when the true operating effectiveness of internal control justifies such an assessment.

    B. Contains misstatements that could be material to the financial statements when aggregated with misstatements in other account balances or transactions classes.

    C. Contains proportionately fewer deviations from prescribed internal controls than exist in the balance or class as a whole.

    D. Does not support the tolerable misstatement for some or all of management's assertions.

Answer (A) is correct. *(CPA, adapted)*
    REQUIRED: The condition under which the auditor would assess control risk too high.
    DISCUSSION: According to AU 350, one aspect of sampling risk in performing tests of controls is the risk of assessing control risk too high. It is the risk that the assessed level of control risk based on the sample is greater than the true operating effectiveness of the control.
    Answer (B) is incorrect because substantive tests are directed towards misstatements in management's assertions. Answer (C) is incorrect because, if the sample deviation rate is lower than the population rate, the auditor may assess control risk too low. Answer (D) is incorrect because substantive tests are directed towards misstatements in management's assertions.

6. While performing a test of details during an audit, the auditor determined that the sample results supported the conclusion that the recorded account balance was materially misstated. It was, in fact, not materially misstated. This situation illustrates the risk of

    A. Incorrect rejection.

    B. Incorrect acceptance.

    C. Assessing control risk too low.

    D. Assessing control risk too high.

Answer (A) is correct. *(CPA, adapted)*
    REQUIRED: The risk of erroneously concluding that a balance is materially misstated.
    DISCUSSION: An auditor is concerned with two aspects of sampling risk in performing substantive tests of details: the risk of incorrect acceptance and the risk of incorrect rejection. The latter is the risk that the sample supports the conclusion that the recorded account balance is materially misstated when it is not materially misstated.
    Answer (B) is incorrect because the risk of incorrect acceptance is the risk that an auditor will erroneously conclude that a balance is not materially misstated. Answer (C) is incorrect because the risk of assessing control risk too low is an aspect of sampling risk in performing tests of controls.
Answer (D) is incorrect because the risk of assessing control risk too high is an aspect of sampling risk in performing tests of controls.

7. An auditor established a $60,000 tolerable misstatement for an asset with an account balance of $1,000,000. The auditor selected a sample of every twentieth item from the population that represented the asset account balance and discovered overstatements of $3,700 and understatements of $200. Under these circumstances, the auditor most likely would conclude that

A. There is an unacceptably high risk that the actual misstatements in the population exceed the tolerable misstatement because the total projected misstatement is more than the tolerable misstatement.

B. There is an unacceptably high risk that the tolerable misstatement exceeds the sum of actual overstatements and understatements.

C. The asset account is fairly stated because the total projected misstatement is less than the tolerable misstatement.

D. The asset account is fairly stated because the tolerable misstatement exceeds the net of projected actual overstatements and understatements.

Answer (A) is correct. *(CPA, adapted)*
REQUIRED: The conclusion based on a sample.
DISCUSSION: By taking every twentieth item, the auditor chose a sample containing 5% (1 ÷ 20) of the items in the population. If the sample contains $3,700 of overstatements and $200 of understatements, the projected overstatements and understatements are $74,000 and $4,000, respectively, a projected misstatement of $78,000. Furthermore, sampling risk should be considered. The allowance for sampling risk calculated for a specified level of confidence is an interval around the sample result that is expected to contain the true amount of misstatement. The upper limit of this interval equals $78,000 plus the calculated allowance. Accordingly, given that projected misstatement exceeds tolerable misstatement, the auditor most likely will conclude that the risk that actual misstatement exceeds tolerable misstatement is unacceptably high.

8. An auditor may decide to increase the risk of incorrect rejection when

A. Increased reliability from the sample is desired.

B. Many differences (audit value minus recorded value) are expected.

C. Initial sample results do not support the planned level of control risk.

D. The cost and effort of selecting additional sample items are low.

Answer (D) is correct. *(CPA, adapted)*
REQUIRED: The reason to increase the risk of incorrect rejection.
DISCUSSION: The risk of incorrect rejection is the risk that the sample supports the conclusion that the recorded account balance is materially misstated when it is not. This risk relates to the efficiency, not the effectiveness, of the audit. Incorrect rejection ordinarily results in the application of additional procedures that finally lead the auditor to the proper conclusion. If the cost and effort of selecting additional sample items are low, a higher risk of incorrect rejection may be acceptable.
Answer (A) is incorrect because an increase in the desired reliability (confidence level) for a substantive test of details requires a decrease in the risk of incorrect rejection. This risk is the complement of the confidence level for a substantive test of details. Answer (B) is incorrect because, if many differences are expected, the account balance is more likely to be materially misstated and incorrect rejection is less likely. Answer (C) is incorrect because the risk of incorrect rejection is associated with substantive testing. Control risk is associated with tests of controls.

9. In statistical sampling methods used in substantive testing, an auditor most likely would stratify a population into meaningful groups if

A. Probability-proportional-to-size (PPS) sampling is used.

B. The population has highly variable recorded amounts.

C. The auditor's estimated tolerable misstatement is extremely small.

D. The standard deviation of recorded amounts is relatively small.

Answer (B) is correct. *(CPA, adapted)*
REQUIRED: The condition under which the auditor would stratify a population.
DISCUSSION: The primary objective of stratification is to reduce the effect of high variability by dividing the population into subpopulations. Reducing the effect of the variance within each subpopulation allows the auditor to sample a smaller number of items while holding precision and the confidence level constant.
Answer (A) is incorrect because PPS sampling automatically stratifies the population. Answer (C) is incorrect because, when the tolerable misstatement is extremely small, the auditor will take relatively large sample sizes. Answer (D) is incorrect because, when the standard deviation of recorded amounts is relatively small, the auditor would consider the population in total when selecting samples.

10. An auditor is performing substantive tests of pricing and extensions of perpetual inventory balances consisting of a large number of items. Past experience indicates numerous pricing and extension errors. Which of the following statistical sampling approaches is most appropriate?

    A. Unstratified mean-per-unit.

    B. Probability-proportional-to-size.

    C. Stop or go.

    D. Ratio or difference estimation.

Answer (D) is correct. *(CPA, adapted)*
    REQUIRED: The appropriate sampling method for substantive tests of pricing and extensions of perpetual inventory balances.
    DISCUSSION: Difference estimation of population misstatement entails determining the differences between the audit and book values for items in the sample, adding the differences, calculating the mean difference, and multiplying the mean by the number of items in the population. An allowance for sampling risk is also calculated. Ratio estimation is similar except that it estimates the population misstatement by multiplying the book value of the population by the ratio of the total audit value of the sample items to their total book value. It has been demonstrated that ratio or difference estimation is both reliable and efficient when small misstatements predominate and they are not skewed.
    Answer (A) is incorrect because unstratified mean-per-unit requires sample sizes that may be too large to be cost effective. Answer (B) is incorrect because PPS sampling may result in a larger sample size than a classical variables sampling approach when the estimated misstatement is relatively large. Answer (C) is incorrect because stop-or-go sampling is an attribute sampling mode. It is appropriate when few deviations are expected. The method is not applicable in these circumstances.

11. The use of the ratio estimation sampling technique is most effective when

    A. The calculated audit amounts are approximately proportional to the client's book amounts.

    B. A relatively small number of differences exist in the population.

    C. Estimating populations whose records consist of quantities but not book values.

    D. Large overstatement differences and large understatement differences exist in the population.

Answer (A) is correct. *(CPA, adapted)*
    REQUIRED: The most effective use of ratio estimation sampling.
    DISCUSSION: Ratio estimation calculates the population misstatement by multiplying the book value of the population by the ratio of the total audit value of the sample items to their total book value. The precision is determined by considering the variances of the ratios of book value to audited value. Thus, the more homogeneous the ratios, the smaller the precision.
    Answer (B) is incorrect because the population of differences must be fairly large in order for ratio estimation to be useful. Answer (C) is incorrect because each audited value must have a book value so that a ratio may be calculated. Answer (D) is incorrect because the ratios are important to the process, not the specific values of the population.

15.2 Statistical Sampling in Tests of Controls (Attribute Sampling)

12. Which of the following combinations results in a decrease in sample size in an attribute sample?

	Allowable Risk of Assessing Control Risk Too Low	Tolerable Rate	Expected Population Deviation Rate
A.	Increase	Decrease	Increase
B.	Decrease	Increase	Decrease
C.	Increase	Increase	Decrease
D.	Increase	Increase	Increase

Answer (C) is correct. *(CPA, adapted)*
    REQUIRED: The combination that results in a decrease in size in an attribute sample.
    DISCUSSION: To determine the sample size for a test of controls, the auditor considers (1) the tolerable rate of deviations from the control being tested, (2) the expected actual rate of deviations, and (3) the allowable risk of assessing control risk too low. An increase in the allowable risk of assessing control risk too low, an increase in the tolerable rate, and a decrease in the expected rate each has the effect of reducing the required sample size.

13. In determining the number of documents to select for a test to obtain assurance that all sales returns have been properly authorized, an auditor should consider the tolerable rate of deviation from the control activity. The auditor should also consider the

I.   Likely rate of deviations
II. Allowable risk of assessing control risk too high

   A. I only.

   B. II only.

   C. Both I and II.

   D. Either I or II.

14. In planning a statistical sample for a test of controls, an auditor increased the expected population deviation rate from the prior year's rate because of the results of the prior year's tests of controls and the overall control environment. The auditor most likely would then increase the planned

   A. Tolerable deviation rate.

   B. Allowance for sampling risk.

   C. Risk of assessing control risk too low.

   D. Sample size.

15. Which of the following statements is true concerning statistical sampling in tests of controls?

   A. As the population size increases, the sample size should increase proportionately.

   B. Deviations from specific control activities at a given rate ordinarily result in misstatements at a lower rate.

   C. There is an inverse relationship between the expected population deviation rate and the sample size.

   D. In determining the tolerable rate, an auditor considers detection risk and the sample size.

Answer (A) is correct. *(CPA, adapted)*
REQUIRED: The factor(s) in determining sample size.
DISCUSSION: The factors necessary to determine sample size in an attribute sampling plan for a large population include the tolerable deviation rate, the acceptable risk of assessing control too low, and the expected deviation rate.
   Answer (B) is incorrect because the allowable risk of assessing control risk too high relates to the risk of underreliance on the controls and is not specified in the sampling plan. Answer (C) is incorrect because the allowable risk of assessing control risk too high relates to the risk of underreliance on the controls and is not specified in the sampling plan. Answer (D) is incorrect because the allowable risk of assessing control risk too high relates to the risk of underreliance on the controls and is not specified in the sampling plan.

Answer (D) is correct. *(CPA, adapted)*
REQUIRED: The effect of an increase in the expected population deviation rate.
DISCUSSION: To determine the sample size for a test of controls, the auditor considers (1) the tolerable rate of deviations, (2) the expected actual rate of deviations, and (3) the allowable risk of assessing control risk too low. An increase in the expected rate has the effect of increasing the degree of assurance to be provided by the sample and therefore increasing the planned sample size.
   Answer (A) is incorrect because the tolerable rate is a function of the planned assessed level of control risk and the degree of assurance sought from the evidence. It does not necessarily increase with the expected population deviation rate. Answer (B) is incorrect because the allowance for sampling risk is the difference between the calculated upper deviation rate and the sample rate. According to standard tables, it increases as the actual number of deviations found increases. Answer (C) is incorrect because the risk of assessing control risk too low is specified by the auditor. It does not necessarily increase with the expected rate.

Answer (B) is correct. *(CPA, adapted)*
REQUIRED: The true statement concerning statistical sampling in tests of controls.
DISCUSSION: Deviations from a specific control increase the risk of misstatements in the accounting records but do not always result in misstatements. Thus, deviations from a specific control at a given rate ordinarily result in misstatements at the financial statement level at a lower rate (AU 350).
   Answer (A) is incorrect because, as population size increases, the required sample size increases at a decreasing rate. Answer (C) is incorrect because the relationship between the expected population deviation rate and the required sample size is direct. Answer (D) is incorrect because the tolerable rate depends on the planned assessed level of control risk and the assurance to be provided by the evidence in the sample.

16. The sample size of a test of controls varies inversely with

	Expected Population Deviation Rate	Tolerable Rate
A.	Yes	Yes
B.	No	No
C.	Yes	No
D.	No	Yes

Answer (D) is correct. *(CPA, adapted)*
REQUIRED: The factor or factors that vary inversely with sample size.
DISCUSSION: The expected population deviation rate directly affects the sample size. As the expected deviation rate increases, the sample size increases. Conversely, the tolerable deviation rate varies inversely to sample size; that is, as the tolerable deviation rate decreases, the sample size increases.
Answer (A) is incorrect because the expected population deviation rate varies directly with sample size, while the tolerable rate varies inversely with sample size. Answer (B) is incorrect because the expected population deviation rate varies directly with sample size, while the tolerable rate varies inversely with sample size. Answer (C) is incorrect because the expected population deviation rate varies directly with sample size, while the tolerable rate varies inversely with sample size.

17. For which of the following audit tests would an auditor most likely use attribute sampling?

A. Making an independent estimate of the amount of a LIFO inventory.

B. Examining invoices in support of the valuation of fixed asset additions.

C. Selecting accounts receivable for confirmation of account balances.

D. Inspecting employee time cards for proper approval by supervisors.

Answer (D) is correct. *(CPA, adapted)*
REQUIRED: The appropriate use of attribute sampling.
DISCUSSION: The auditor uses attribute sampling to test the effectiveness of controls. Attribute sampling enables the auditor to estimate the occurrence rate of deviations and to determine its relation to the tolerable rate. Thus, a control such as proper approval of time cards by supervisors can be tested for effectiveness using attribute sampling.
Answer (A) is incorrect because variables sampling is useful in estimating the amount of inventory. Answer (B) is incorrect because examining invoices in support of the valuation of fixed asset additions is a substantive test for which variables sampling is appropriate. Answer (C) is incorrect because the selection of accounts receivable for confirmation is a substantive test.

18. Which of the following factors is usually not considered in determining the sample size for a test of controls?

A. Population size, when the population is large.

B. Tolerable deviation rate.

C. Risk of assessing control risk too low.

D. Expected population deviation rate.

Answer (A) is correct. *(CPA, adapted)*
REQUIRED: The factor not considered in determining the sample size for a test of controls.
DISCUSSION: A test of controls is an application of attribute sampling. The initial size for an attribute sample is based on sampling risk in the form of the risk of assessing control risk too low (the complement of the confidence level for attribute sampling), the tolerable deviation rate, the expected population deviation rate, and the population size. However, a change in the size of the population has a very small effect on the required sample size when the population is large. Consequently, population size is often not considered unless it is small.
Answer (B) is incorrect because the tolerable rate must always be considered. Answer (C) is incorrect because the risk of assessing control risk too low must always be considered. Answer (D) is incorrect because the expected population deviation rate must always be considered.

19. An auditor should consider the tolerable rate of deviation when determining the number of check requests to select for a test to obtain assurance that all check requests have been properly authorized. The auditor should also consider

	The Average Dollar Value of the Check Requests	The Allowable Risk of Assessing Control Risk Too Low
A.	Yes	Yes
B.	Yes	No
C.	No	Yes
D.	No	No

Answer (C) is correct. *(CPA, adapted)*

REQUIRED: The issue(s), if any, to consider in determining the size of a sample in a test of controls.

DISCUSSION: Tests of controls, such as tests whether check requests have been properly authorized, are binary in nature; that is, the auditor determines whether the control has been applied. Dollar values are irrelevant in this form of testing. However, in sampling, the auditor must consider the acceptable risk of assessing control risk too low to determine sample size. The auditor also must estimate a population deviation rate.

Answer (A) is incorrect because the auditor need not consider the average dollar value of the check requests but must consider the allowable risk of assessing control risk too low. Answer (B) is incorrect because the auditor need not consider the average dollar value of the check requests but must consider the allowable risk of assessing control risk too low. Answer (D) is incorrect because the auditor need not consider the average dollar value of the check requests but must consider the allowable risk of assessing control risk too low.

20. What is an auditor's evaluation of a statistical sample for attributes when a test of 50 documents results in three deviations if the tolerable rate is 7%, the expected population deviation rate is 5%, and the allowance for sampling risk is 2%?

A. Modify the planned assessed level of control risk because the tolerable rate plus the allowance for sampling risk exceeds the expected population deviation rate.

B. Accept the sample results as support for the planned assessed level of control risk because the sample deviation rate plus the allowance for sampling risk exceeds the tolerable rate.

C. Accept the sample results as support for the planned assessed level of control risk because the tolerable rate minus the allowance for sampling risk equals the expected population deviation rate.

D. Modify the planned assessed level of control risk because the sample deviation rate plus the allowance for sampling risk exceeds the tolerable rate.

Answer (D) is correct. *(CPA, adapted)*

REQUIRED: The evaluation of an attribute sample given the deviations in the sample, sampling risk, the tolerable rate, and the expected rate.

DISCUSSION: The sample has a 6% (3 ÷ 50) deviation rate. The auditor's upper precision limit is 8% (6% + the 2% allowance for sampling risk). The allowance for sampling risk (achieved precision limit) may be calculated from a standard table as the difference between the upper deviation limit and the sample rate. However, the allowance is given. Thus, the true deviation rate could be as large as 8% and exceed the tolerable rate. Accordingly, the auditor should revise the planned assessed level of control risk for the relevant assertions and possibly alter the nature, timing, and extent of substantive tests (AU 350).

Answer (A) is incorrect because the precision interval is constructed around the sample rate, not the tolerable rate. Answer (B) is incorrect because a deviation rate that may be as large as 8% is a reason for revising the planned assessed level of control risk. Answer (C) is incorrect because the sample deviation rate, which is the best estimate of the true rate, must not be ignored.

21. Which of the following statements is true concerning statistical sampling in tests of controls?

A. The population size has little or no effect on determining sample size except for very small populations.

B. The expected population deviation rate has little or no effect on determining sample size except for very small populations.

C. As the population size doubles, the sample size also should double.

D. For a given tolerable rate, a larger sample size should be selected as the expected population deviation rate decreases.

Answer (A) is correct. *(CPA, adapted)*

REQUIRED: The true statement concerning statistical sampling.

DISCUSSION: A change in the size of the population has a very small effect on the required sample size when the population is large. Tables are available for smaller population sizes providing appropriate smaller sample sizes.

Answer (B) is incorrect because the expected population deviation rate is a variable in the sample size formula. Answer (C) is incorrect because the population size and the sample size are not proportionate. Answer (D) is incorrect because a lower expected population deviation rate results in a smaller sample size.

Questions 22 and 23 are based on the following information. An auditor desired to test credit approval on 10,000 sales invoices processed during the year. The auditor designed a statistical sample that would provide 1% risk of assessing control risk too low (99% confidence) that not more than 7% of the sales invoices lacked approval. The auditor estimated from previous experience that about 2.5% of the sales invoices lacked approval. A sample of 200 invoices was examined and seven of them were lacking approval. The auditor then determined the achieved upper precision limit to be 8%.

22. In the evaluation of this sample, the auditor decided to increase the level of the preliminary assessment of control risk because the

A. Tolerable rate (7%) was less than the achieved upper precision limit (8%).

B. Expected deviation rate (7%) was more than the percentage of errors in the sample (3.5%).

C. Achieved upper precision limit (8%) was more than the percentage of errors in the sample (3.5%).

D. Expected deviation rate (2.5%) was less than the tolerable rate (7%).

Answer (A) is correct. *(CPA, adapted)*
REQUIRED: The reason for increasing the preliminary assessment of control risk.
DISCUSSION: The sample results support the planned assessed level of control risk only if the achieved upper precision limit is equal to or less than the tolerable rate. The achieved upper precision limit is a value that may be derived from a standard table based on the actual deviations, the specified risk, and the sample size. In this case, it signifies that the auditor is 99% confident that not more than 8% of the invoices lacked approval. Hence, the sample does not support the planned assessed level of control risk.
Answer (B) is incorrect because the expected rate is 2.5%. Answer (C) is incorrect because, by definition, the achieved upper precision limit equals the sample deviation rate plus an allowance for sampling risk. Answer (D) is incorrect because the expected rate is not used in the evaluation of the sample.

23. The allowance for sampling risk was

A. 5.5%

B. 4.5%

C. 3.5%

D. 1%

Answer (B) is correct. *(CPA, adapted)*
REQUIRED: The allowance for sampling risk.
DISCUSSION: The allowance for sampling risk equals the achieved upper precision limit (8%) minus the sample deviation rate (7 ÷ 200 = 3.5%), or 4.5%.
Answer (A) is incorrect because 5.5% assumes a sample deviation rate of 2.5%. Answer (C) is incorrect because 3.5% is the sample deviation rate. Answer (D) is incorrect because 1% is the excess of the achieved upper precision limit over the tolerable rate.

24. An auditor who uses statistical sampling for attributes in testing internal controls should reduce the planned reliance on a prescribed control when the

A. Sample rate of deviation plus the allowance for sampling risk equals the tolerable rate.

B. Sample rate of deviation is less than the expected rate of deviation used in planning the sample.

C. Tolerable rate less the allowance for sampling risk exceeds the sample rate of deviation.

D. Sample rate of deviation plus the allowance for sampling risk exceeds the tolerable rate.

Answer (D) is correct. *(CPA, adapted)*
REQUIRED: The reason for the auditor to increase the planned assessed level of control risk.
DISCUSSION: If the sample deviation rate plus the allowance for sampling risk exceeds the tolerable deviation rate, the sample results do not support the planned assessed level of control risk. Thus, control risk should be assessed at a higher level. The result is a lower acceptable level of detection risk and an increase in the assurance to be provided by substantive testing.
Answer (A) is incorrect because, if the sample rate is equal to or less than the tolerable rate or the expected rate, the planned assessed level of control risk need not be increased. Answer (B) is incorrect because, if the sample rate is equal to or less than the tolerable rate or the expected rate, the planned assessed level of control risk need not be increased. Answer (C) is incorrect because, if the sample rate is equal to or less than the tolerable rate or the expected rate, the planned assessed level of control risk need not be increased.

25. The diagram below depicts the auditor's estimated maximum deviation rate compared with the tolerable rate and also depicts the true population deviation rate compared with the tolerable rate.

True State of Population

Auditor's Estimate Based on Sample Results	Deviation Rate Is Less than Tolerable Rate	Deviation Rate Exceeds Tolerable Rate
Maximum Deviation Rate Is Less than Tolerable Rate	I.	III.
Maximum Deviation Rate Exceeds Tolerable Rate	II.	IV.

As a result of tests of controls, the auditor assesses control risk higher than necessary and thereby increases substantive testing. This is illustrated by situation

A. I

B. II

C. III

D. IV

Answer (B) is correct. *(CPA, adapted)*
REQUIRED: The situation that involves assessing control risk too high.
DISCUSSION: The risk of assessing control risk too high is one aspect of sampling risk in testing controls. According to AU 350, it is the risk that the assessed level of control risk based on the sample is greater than the true operating effectiveness of the control. Like the risk of incorrect rejection in substantive testing, the risk of assessing control risk too high is a form of alpha (Type I) error. Alpha error concerns the efficiency, not the effectiveness, of the audit because it ordinarily leads to application of further audit procedures and ultimate arrival at the correct conclusion.
Answer (A) is incorrect because, in situation I, the auditor would properly assess control risk at less than the maximum level. Answer (C) is incorrect because, in situation III, the sample would lead to assessing control risk too low. Answer (D) is incorrect because, in situation IV, the auditor would properly assess control risk at a high level.

26. As a result of sampling procedures applied as tests of controls, an auditor incorrectly assesses control risk lower than appropriate. The most likely explanation for this situation is that

A. The deviation rates of both the auditor's sample and the population exceed the tolerable rate.

B. The deviation rates of both the auditor's sample and the population are less than the tolerable rate.

C. The deviation rate in the auditor's sample is less than the tolerable rate, but the deviation rate in the population exceeds the tolerable rate.

D. The deviation rate in the auditor's sample exceeds the tolerable rate, but the deviation rate in the population is less than the tolerable rate.

Answer (C) is correct. *(CPA, adapted)*
REQUIRED: The most likely explanation for assessing control risk lower than appropriate.
DISCUSSION: When the deviation rate in the sample is less than the tolerable rate, the auditor concludes that the control activities tested are effective. If, in fact, the true deviation rate is greater than the tolerable rate, the auditor would assess control risk lower than appropriate.
Answer (A) is incorrect because, if the sample rate and the population rate are both greater than the tolerable rate, the auditor's conclusion should be accurate. Answer (B) is incorrect because, if the sample rate and the population rate are both less than the tolerable rate, the auditor's conclusion should be accurate. Answer (D) is incorrect because, if the sample rate exceeds the population rate, the auditor is likely to assess control risk too high.

27. In addition to evaluating the frequency of deviations in tests of controls, an auditor should also consider certain qualitative aspects of the deviations. The auditor most likely would give broader consideration to the implications of a deviation if it was

A. The only deviation discovered in the sample.

B. Identical to a deviation discovered during the prior year's audit.

C. Caused by an employee's misunderstanding of instructions.

D. Initially concealed by a forged document.

Answer (D) is correct. *(CPA, adapted)*
REQUIRED: The aspect of a deviation requiring broader consideration.
DISCUSSION: The discovery of a fraud ordinarily requires broader consideration than the discovery of an error. The discovery of an initially concealed forged document raises concerns because it indicates that the integrity of employees may be in doubt.
Answer (A) is incorrect because a single error discovered in a sample may not cause major concern. Answer (B) is incorrect because errors are often repetitive. Discovery of an identical deviation in a subsequent year is not unusual. Answer (C) is incorrect because a misunderstanding is an error rather than a fraud and does not necessarily arouse concern.

15.3 Classical Variables Sampling (Mean-per-Unit)

28. Which of the following sampling methods is used to estimate a numerical measurement of a population, such as a dollar value?

    A. Attribute sampling.

    B. Stop-or-go sampling.

    C. Variables sampling.

    D. Random-number sampling.

Answer (C) is correct. *(CPA, adapted)*
    REQUIRED: The sampling method used to estimate a numerical measurement of a population.
    DISCUSSION: Variables sampling samples dollar amounts or other quantities. The purpose of variables sampling is to estimate a measure of a population.
    Answer (A) is incorrect because attribute sampling is a method to test the internal control. Answer (B) is incorrect because stop-or-go sampling is a method to test the internal control. Answer (D) is incorrect because random number sampling is a generic term relating to the selection of the sampling units.

29. Stratified mean-per-unit (MPU) sampling is a statistical technique that may be more efficient than unstratified MPU because it usually

    A. May be applied to populations in which many monetary errors are expected to occur.

    B. Produces an estimate having a desired level of precision with a smaller sample size.

    C. Increases the variability among items in a stratum by grouping sampling units with similar characteristics.

    D. Yields a weighted sum of the strata standard deviations that is greater than the standard deviation of the population.

Answer (B) is correct. *(CPA, adapted)*
    REQUIRED: The reason for using stratification in sampling.
    DISCUSSION: The primary objective of stratification is to reduce the effect of high variability by dividing the population into subpopulations. Reducing the variance within each subpopulation allows the auditor to sample a smaller number of items while holding precision and confidence level constant.
    Answer (A) is incorrect because the number of errors in the population is independent of the advantages of stratification. Answer (C) is incorrect because stratification is used to decrease the effects of variation within the strata. Answer (D) is incorrect because the standard deviation, which measures variation, should be less within the strata than for the population as a whole.

30. Which of the following statements is true concerning the auditor's use of statistical sampling?

    A. An auditor needs to estimate the dollar amount of the standard deviation of the population to use classical variables sampling.

    B. An assumption of PPS sampling is that the underlying accounting population is normally distributed.

    C. A classical variables sample needs to be designed with special considerations to include negative balances in the sample.

    D. The selection of zero balances usually does not require special sample design considerations when using PPS sampling.

Answer (A) is correct. *(CPA, adapted)*
    REQUIRED: The true statement concerning statistical sampling.
    DISCUSSION: Variables sampling is used to estimate the amount of misstatement in, or the value of, a population. In auditing, this process entails estimating the monetary value of an account balance or other accounting total. The estimated population standard deviation is used in the sample size formula for variables estimation. Hence, it should be stated in dollar terms.
    Answer (B) is incorrect because PPS sampling is based on the Poisson distribution, which approximates the binomial distribution, not the normal distribution. Answer (C) is incorrect because classical variables samples do not require special design considerations for negative balances. Answer (D) is incorrect because PPS sampling is not designed to deal with understatements or negative values without special modifications.

31. When planning a sample for a substantive test of details, an auditor should consider tolerable misstatement for the sample. This consideration should

    A. Be related to the auditor's business risk.

    B. Not be adjusted for qualitative factors.

    C. Be related to preliminary judgments about materiality levels.

    D. Not be changed during the audit process.

Answer (C) is correct. *(CPA, adapted)*
REQUIRED: The true statement about the consideration of tolerable misstatement.
DISCUSSION: When planning a sample for substantive tests, the auditor should consider how much monetary misstatement in the related account balance or class of transactions may exist without causing the financial statements to be materially misstated. This maximum misstatement is the tolerable misstatement for the sample. It is used in audit planning to determine the necessary precision and sample size. Tolerable misstatement, combined for the entire audit plan, should not exceed the auditor's preliminary judgments about materiality (AU 350).
Answer (A) is incorrect because the auditor's business risk is irrelevant. Answer (B) is incorrect because qualitative factors should be considered, for example, the nature and cause of misstatements and their relationship to other phases of the audit. Answer (D) is incorrect because, if sample results suggest that planning assumptions were incorrect, the auditor should take appropriate action.

32. An auditor is determining the sample size for an inventory observation using mean-per-unit estimation, which is a variables sampling plan. To calculate the required sample size, the auditor usually determines the

	Variability in the Dollar Amounts of Inventory Items	Risk of Incorrect Rejection
A.	Yes	Yes
B.	Yes	No
C.	No	Yes
D.	No	No

Answer (A) is correct. *(CPA, adapted)*
REQUIRED: The factor(s), if any, used to determine a mean-per-unit sample size.
DISCUSSION: Four factors are considered in determining the sample size for mean-per-unit estimation. Those factors include the population size, an estimate of population variation (the standard deviation), the risk of incorrect rejection (its complement is the confidence level), and the tolerable misstatement (the desired allowance for sampling risk is a percentage thereof, and this percentage is a function of the risk of incorrect rejection and the allowable risk of incorrect acceptance).
Answer (B) is incorrect because both the variability in the dollar amounts of inventory items and the risk of incorrect rejection are factors in determining sample size for mean-per-unit estimation. Answer (C) is incorrect because both the variability in the dollar amounts of inventory items and the risk of incorrect rejection are factors in determining sample size for mean-per-unit estimation. Answer (D) is incorrect because both the variability in the dollar amounts of inventory items and the risk of incorrect rejection are factors in determining sample size for mean-per-unit estimation.

33. How would an increase in tolerable misstatement and an increase in assessed level of control risk affect the sample size in a substantive test of details?

	Increase in Tolerable Misstatement	Increase in Assessed Level of Control Risk
A.	Increase sample size	Increase sample size
B.	Increase sample size	Decrease sample size
C.	Decrease sample size	Increase sample size
D.	Decrease sample size	Decrease sample size

Answer (C) is correct. *(CPA, adapted)*
REQUIRED: The effects of increases in tolerable misstatement and the assessed level of control risk.
DISCUSSION: An increase in tolerable misstatement or the level of materiality decreases the sample size necessary to collect sufficient competent evidential matter. An increase in the assessed level of control risk increases the assurance to be provided by substantive tests and therefore the necessary sample size.

15.4 Probability-Proportional-to-Size (PPS) or Dollar-Unit Sampling (DUS)

34. Which of the following statements is true concerning probability-proportional-to-size (PPS) sampling, also known as dollar-unit sampling?

A. The sampling distribution should approximate the normal distribution.

B. Overstated units have a lower probability of sample selection than units that are understated.

C. The auditor controls the risk of incorrect acceptance by specifying that risk level for the sampling plan.

D. The sampling interval is calculated by dividing the number of physical units in the population by the sample size.

Answer (C) is correct. *(CPA, adapted)*
REQUIRED: The true statement about dollar-unit sampling.
DISCUSSION: AU 350 considers PPS sampling (or dollar-unit sampling) to be an appropriate random-based method. Dollar-unit sampling is one technique whereby the auditor can measure and control the risks associated with observing less than 100% of the population. The auditor can quantify and measure the risk of accepting a client's recorded amount as fair when it is materially misstated.
Answer (A) is incorrect because PPS requires no assumptions about the population or sampling distribution. Answer (B) is incorrect because, as the size of the units in the population increases, so does the probability of selection. Answer (D) is incorrect because the sampling interval is calculated by dividing the total dollars, not units, in the population by the sample size. Every nth dollar is then selected after a random start.

35. In a probability-proportional-to-size sample with a sampling interval of $10,000, an auditor discovered that a selected account receivable with a recorded amount of $5,000 had an audited amount of $4,000. If this were the only misstatement discovered by the auditor, the projected misstatement of this sample is

A. $1,000

B. $2,000

C. $5,000

D. $10,000

Answer (B) is correct. *(CPA, adapted)*
REQUIRED: The projected misstatement of the PPS sample.
DISCUSSION: PPS (or dollar-unit) sampling is a commonly used method of statistical sampling for tests of details of balances because it provides a simple statistical result expressed in dollars. Given that only one misstatement was detected, the projected misstatement for this sample is the product of the tainting percentage and the sampling interval. The tainting percentage is calculated as the difference between the recorded and the audited amount, divided by the recorded amount. In this sample, the tainting percentage is 20% [($5,000 − $4,000) ÷ $5,000]. Multiplying this number by the sampling interval results in a projected misstatement based on the sample of $2,000 (20% × $10,000).
Answer (A) is incorrect because $1,000 is the difference between the recorded amount and the audited amount. Answer (C) is incorrect because $5,000 is the difference between the sampling interval and the audited amount. Answer (D) is incorrect because $10,000 is the sampling interval.

36. Which of the following most likely would be an advantage in using classical variables sampling rather than probability-proportional-to-size (PPS) sampling?

A. An estimate of the standard deviation of the population's recorded amounts is not required.

B. The auditor rarely needs the assistance of a computer program to design an efficient sample.

C. Inclusion of zero and negative balances usually does not require special design considerations.

D. Any amount that is individually significant is automatically identified and selected.

Answer (C) is correct. *(CPA, adapted)*
REQUIRED: The advantage of using classical variables sampling rather than PPS sampling.
DISCUSSION: PPS is most useful if few misstatements are expected and overstatement is the most likely kind of misstatement. One disadvantage of PPS sampling is that it is designed to detect overstatements. It is not effective for estimating understatements. The smaller the item, the less likely it will be selected in the sample, but the more likely the item is understated.
Answer (A) is incorrect because the sample size formula for estimation of variables includes the standard deviation of the population. Answer (B) is incorrect because a computer program is helpful in many sampling applications. Answer (D) is incorrect because, in classical variables sampling, every item has an equal and nonzero probability of selection.

Questions 37 and 38 are based on the following information.

An auditor has been assigned to take a dollar-unit sample of a population of vouchers in the purchasing department. The population has a total recorded amount of $300,000. The auditor believes that a maximum misstatement of $900 is acceptable and would like to have 95% confidence in the results. (The reliability factor at 95% and zero misstatements = 3.00.) Additional information is provided in the opposite column.

Table of First 10 Vouchers in Population		
Voucher #	Balance	Cumulative Balance
1	$100	$ 100
2	150	250
3	40	290
4	200	490
5	10	500
6	290	790
7	50	840
8	190	1,030
9	20	1,050
10	180	1,230

37. Given a random start of $50 as the first dollar amount, what is the number of the fourth voucher to be selected, assuming that the sample size will be 1,000?

A. 4

B. 6

C. 7

D. 8

Answer (D) is correct. *(CIA, adapted)*
REQUIRED: The number of the fourth voucher selected using dollar-unit sampling.
DISCUSSION: The vouchers have a recorded amount of $300,000, and 1,000 items are to be sampled, so every 300th dollar will be chosen. Given a random start of $50, the vouchers containing the 50th, 350th, 650th, and 950th dollars will be selected. The cumulative amount of the first eight vouchers is $1,030. Accordingly, voucher 8 should be the fourth voucher audited because it contains the 950th dollar.
Answer (A) is incorrect because voucher 4 contains the 350th dollar and should be the second voucher selected. Answer (B) is incorrect because voucher 6 contains the 650th dollar and should be the third voucher selected. Answer (C) is incorrect because voucher 7 should not be selected.

38. In examining the sample, one overstatement was detected causing an extension of $270 to the tolerable misstatement. Assuming a sample size of 1,000 and assuming that the maximum dollar amount of overstatement, if no misstatements were found, was established to be $900 before the sampling analysis, what conclusion can the auditor now make from the sampling evidence?

A. (S)he is 95% confident that the dollar amount of overstatement in the population of vouchers is between $900 and $1,170.

B. (S)he is 95% confident that the dollar amount of overstatement in the population of vouchers exceeds $1,170.

C. (S)he is 95% confident that the dollar amount of overstatement in the population of vouchers is less than $1,170.

D. An insufficient number of misstatements were detected to warrant a conclusion.

Answer (C) is correct. *(CIA, adapted)*
REQUIRED: The conclusion from the audit evidence given an extension of tolerable misstatement.
DISCUSSION: Had the auditor detected no misstatements in the sample, (s)he could have been 95% confident that the dollar amount of overstatement in the balance was less than $900. Given discovery of an overstatement causing an extension to the tolerable misstatement of $270, the auditor can conclude with 95% confidence that the overstatement is less than $1,170 ($900 + $270).
Answer (A) is incorrect because the auditor is 95% confident that the overstatement is less than $1,170. Answer (B) is incorrect because the auditor is 95% confident that the overstatement is less than $1,170. Answer (D) is incorrect because a conclusion is warranted even if no misstatements were found.

Use Gleim's *CPA Test Prep* for interactive testing with over 2,000 additional multiple-choice questions!

15.5 PRACTICE SIMULATION

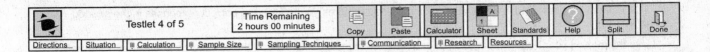

Directions | Situation | Calculation | Sample Size | Sampling Techniques | Communication | Research | Resources

1. Directions

In the following simulation, you will be asked to complete various tasks related to sampling. The simulation will provide you with all the information necessary to do your work. For full credit, be sure to view and complete all work tabs.

Resources may be available under the tab marked RESOURCES. You may want to review the resources before beginning the simulation.

2. Situation

Edward Prince, CPA has been engaged to perform an audit of a client. In performance of his auditing techniques, Edward has decided to use probability-proportional-to-size (PPS) sampling, sometimes called dollar-unit sampling, in the audit of a client's accounts receivable balance. Few, if any, misstatements of account balance overstatements are expected.

Edward plans to use the following PPS sampling table:

Reliability Factors for Misstatements
Risk of Incorrect Acceptance

# of Misstatements	1.00%	5.00%	10.00%	15.00%	20.00%
0	4.61	3.00	2.31	1.90	1.61
1	6.64	4.75	3.89	3.38	3.00
2	8.41	6.30	5.33	4.72	4.28
3	10.05	7.76	6.69	6.02	5.52
4	11.61	9.16	8.00	7.27	6.73

Other information for the current year's audit is outlined below:

Tolerable misstatement	$15,000
Risk of incorrect acceptance	5%
Number of misstatements allowed	0
Recorded amount of accounts receivable	$300,000

3. Calculation

This question is presented in a spreadsheet format that requires you to fill in the correct responses in the shaded cells.

In the prior year, Edward found the three misstatements listed below. Given this information, calculate the total projected misstatement.

	Recorded Amount	Audit Amount	Tainting	Sampling Interval	Projected Misstatement
1st Error	$400.00	$320.00		$1,000.00	
2nd Error	$500.00	$0.00		$1,000.00	
3rd Error	$3,000.00	$2,500.00		$1,000.00	
				Total Projected	

4. Sample Size

This question is presented in a spreadsheet format that requires you to fill in the correct responses in the shaded cells.

Use the current year's audit information to calculate the sampling interval and the sample size. On lines 1 through 5, fill in the proper amounts as given or calculated.

1. Reliability factor	
2. Tolerable misstatement	
3. Sampling interval	
4. Recorded amount	
5. Sample size	

5. Define and Differentiate Types of Sampling Techniques

This question has a matching format that requires you to select the correct response from a drop-down list. Write the answer in the shaded column. Each response may be used once, more than once, or not at all.

From the sampling explanations, accounts receivable, choose from the sampling choices column the sampling technique that best fits the explanation.

Sampling Explanations	Answer
1. The larger the item in the population, the more likely it will be included in the sample.	
2. Replace(s) the need for the use of judgment by the auditor.	
3. Use(s) the average value of sampled items to estimate the value of the population.	
4. Use(s) results from a portion of the population to draw an inference about the total population.	
5. Allow(s) the auditor to measure and control the risk of accepting a materially misstated balance.	
6. Require(s) the auditor to estimate the population standard deviation to determine the appropriate sample size.	
7. Is (are) equally useful for selecting samples and drawing inferences about asset and liability balances.	
8. Eliminate(s) the need for the auditor to consider materiality.	
9. Automatically stratify(ies) the population during sample selection.	
10. Require(s) documentation of results in the working papers.	

Sampling Choices
A) Classical variables or mean-per-unit (MPU)
B) Probability-proportional-to-size (PPS) sampling only
C) Both MPU and PPS sampling
D) Neither MPU nor PPS sampling

6. Communication

In a brief memorandum to a new auditing staff member who has limited knowledge of statistics, describe the advantages and disadvantages of using PPS sampling. Type your communication in your word processor program and print out the copy in a memorandum style format.

REMINDER: Your response will be graded for both technical content and writing skills. You should demonstrate your ability to develop, organize, and express your ideas. Do not convey information in the form of a table, bullet point list, or other abbreviated presentation.

> To: New Staff Member
> From: CPA
> Subject: Advantages and disadvantages of PPS sampling

7. Research

Use the research materials available to you to find the answers to the following question in the AICPA Professional Standards. Print the appropriate citation in its entirety from the source you choose. This is a copy-and-paste item.

Locate the applicable AU section describing the approaches to sampling and how it relates to the third standard of field work.

Unofficial Answers

3. Calculation (7 Gradable Items)

	Recorded Amount	Audit Amount	Tainting	Sampling Interval	Projected Misstatement
1st Error	$400.00	$320.00	20% [1]	$1,000.00	$200 [4]
2nd Error	$500.00	$0.00	100% [2]	$1,000.00	$1,000 [5]
3rd Error	$3,000.00	$2,500.00	-0- [3]	$1,000.00	$500 [6]
				Total Projected	$1,700 [7]

[1] $320 ÷ 400 = 80%, 100% − 80% = 20% tainted
[2] $0 ÷ 500 = 0%, 100% − 0% = 100% tainted
[3] The recorded amount is greater than the sampling interval; therefore, the projected misstatement equals the actual misstatement.
[4] $1,000 × 20% = $200
[5] $1,000 × 100% = $1,000
[6] $3,000 − $2,500 = $500
[7] $200 + $1,000 + $500 = $1,700

4. Sample Size (5 Gradable Items)

1. Reliability factor	3.00
2. Tolerable misstatement	$15,000.00
3. Sampling interval	$5,000.00
4. Recorded amount	$300,000.00
5. Sample size	60

1.   The risk of incorrect acceptance is 5% and 0 misstatements are allowed; therefore, the reliability factor is 3.00.
2.   Tolerable misstatement is $15,000.
3.

$$\text{Sampling Interval} = \frac{\text{Tolerable Misstatement}}{\text{Reliability Factor or Misstatements}}$$

$$= \frac{\$15,000}{3.00}$$

$$= \underline{\$5,000}$$

4.   Recorded amount is $300,000.
5.

$$\text{Sampling Size} = \frac{\text{Recorded Amount}}{\text{Sampling Interval}}$$

$$= \frac{\$300,000}{\$5,000}$$

$$= \underline{60}$$

5. Define and Differentiate Types of Sampling Techniques (10 Gradable Items)

1. <u>B) Probability-proportional-to-size sampling only</u>. Probability-proportional-to-size means that the probability of selection is related to size of the item.

2. <u>D) Neither MPU nor PPS sampling</u>. As noted in AU 350, "Evaluating the competence of evidential matter is solely a matter of auditing judgment and is not determined by the design and evaluation of an audit sample."

3. <u>A) Classical variables or mean-per-unit (MPU) sampling only</u>. MPU sampling determines the average value of sampled items (total audited value of the sample ÷ number of items in the sample) and then multiplies this average impairment, their cost basis is written down, and the change is included in earnings, not in a separate component of equity.

4. <u>C) Both MPU and PPS sampling</u>. AU 350 states, "Audit sampling is the application of an audit procedure to less than 100% of the items within an account balance or class of transactions for the purpose of evaluating some characteristic of the balance or class."

5. <u>C) Both MPU and PPS sampling</u>. As noted in AU 350, "By using statistical theory, the auditor can quantify sampling risk to assist him/herself in limiting it to a level (s)he considers acceptable."

6. <u>A) Classical variables or mean-per-unit (MPU) sampling only</u>. MPU sampling requires the auditor to estimate the population's standard deviation to determine the sample size and evaluate the results. PPS, however, does not require the use of the population standard deviation.

7. <u>A) Classical variables or mean-per-unit (MPU) sampling only</u>. PPS is appropriate only for accounts subject to the risk of overstatement (e.g., assets). Because the focus of liability accounts is ordinarily on the risk of understatement, PPS does not meet the objectives for liabilities.

8. <u>D) Neither MPU nor PPS sampling</u>. The auditor must quantify the amount considered material for either sampling method. The amount considered material is one of the factors used in calculating the appropriate sample size.

9. <u>B) Probability-proportional-to-size sampling only</u>. Because PPS increases the probability of selecting large items, it effectively stratifies the population.

10. <u>C) Both MPU and PPS sampling</u>. All important evidence and conclusions must be documented in the working papers, regardless of what tools or techniques are used by the auditor.

6. Communication (5 Gradable Items; For grading instructions, please refer to page 11.)

To:	New Staff Member
From:	CPA
Subject:	Advantages and disadvantages of PPS sampling

One advantage is that PPS sampling is generally easier to use than classical variables sampling, especially when misstatements are not found. Moreover, the size of a PPS sample and the evaluation of the sample are not based on the estimated variation (the standard deviation) of the audited amount. Because it selects the largest items for testing, PPS sampling automatically results in a stratified sample. Thus, in PPS sampling, individually significant items are automatically identified. However, PPS sampling is not as effective for understatements as for overstatements. Another advantage is that, if no misstatements are expected, PPS sampling will usually result in a smaller sample size than classical variables sampling. In addition, sample selection can begin before the complete population is available.

A disadvantage of PPS sampling is that items with zero or negative balances have no chance of selection. Moreover, it is useful only for detecting overstatement errors because the sample selection method dictates that the larger the transaction or balance, the more likely that it will be selected. Thus, PPS sampling is inappropriate for testing liabilities because understatement is the primary audit consideration for that financial statement element. Another disadvantage of PPS sampling is that sample sizes become relatively large if a significant amount of misstatement is expected. Furthermore, the calculated allowance for sampling risk tends to be overstated when a significant amount of misstatement is found in the sample. This overstatement is an inherent limitation of PPS sampling.

7. Research (6 Gradable Items)

AU Section 350 -- *Audit Sampling*

.03   There are two general approaches to audit sampling: nonstatistical and statistical. Both approaches require that the auditor use professional judgment in planning, performing, and evaluating a sample and in relating the evidential matter produced by the sample to other evidential matter when forming a conclusion about the related account balance or class of transactions. The guidance in this section applies equally to nonstatistical and statistical sampling.

.04   The third standard of field work states, "Sufficient competent evidential matter is to be obtained through inspection, observation, inquiries, and confirmations to afford a reasonable basis for an opinion regarding the financial statements under audit." Either approach to audit sampling, when properly applied, can provide sufficient evidential matter.

Scoring Schedule:

	Correct Responses		Gradable Items		Weights		
Tab 3	_____	÷	7	×	20%	=	_____
Tab 4	_____	÷	5	×	20%	=	_____
Tab 5	_____	÷	10	×	20%	=	_____
Tab 6	_____	÷	5	×	30%	=	_____
Tab 7	_____	÷	6	×	10%	=	_____
							(Your Score)

Use Gleim's **CPA Review Online** to practice more simulations in a realistic environment.

STUDY UNIT SIXTEEN
REPORTS --
STANDARD, QUALIFIED, ADVERSE, AND DISCLAIMER

(13 pages of outline)

16.1	GAAS -- The Reporting Standards	490
16.2	The Auditor's Standard Report (AU 508)	492
16.3	Addressing and Dating the Report (AU 530)	493
16.4	Qualified Opinions (AU 508)	494
16.5	Adverse Opinions (AU 508)	499
16.6	Disclaimers of Opinion (AU 508)	500
16.7	Practice Simulation	519

This study unit presents interrelated reporting issues. Subunit 16.2 should be studied carefully. Virtually all subsequent reporting topics are based on the standard audit report. For example, the other subunits of this study unit and all of Study Unit 17 build on the understanding of the standard report to present typical modifications of the report. Study Unit 18 concerns the reporting requirements for review and compilation engagements as well as special reports. Many of the matters considered in Study Unit 19 relate to standard reporting issues. Governmental audit reports, which are the topic of Study Unit 20, are variations of the standard audit report.

Summary of Departures from the Standard Audit Report

Study Unit 16: Reports -- Standard, Qualified, Adverse, and Disclaimer

Unqualified opinions with separate paragraph -- justified departure from GAAP
Qualified opinions

1) Scope limitation
2) Departure from GAAP (including inadequate disclosure)

Adverse opinions -- departure from GAAP
Disclaimers of opinion

1) Scope limitation
2) Association with unaudited financial statements
3) Lack of independence
4) Going concern

Study Unit 17: Reports -- Other Modifications

Unqualified opinions with explanatory language but no separate paragraph

1) Part of audit performed by other auditors
2) Predecessor's report on comparative statements not presented

Unqualified opinions with separate paragraph

1) Consistency
2) Going concern
3) Change in opinion
4) Emphasis of a matter (optional)

16.1 GAAS -- THE REPORTING STANDARDS

1.   The **first standard of reporting**: *The report shall state whether the financial statements are presented in accordance with GAAP.*

   a.   GAAP encompass the conventions, rules, and procedures necessary to define accepted accounting practice at a particular time. It includes not only broad guidelines of general application, but also detailed practices and procedures. Those conventions, rules, and procedures provide a standard by which to measure financial presentations (AU 411).

   b.   Financial statements should

      1)   Use principles that have general acceptance
      2)   Use principles that are appropriate in the circumstances
      3)   Include adequate disclosure
      4)   Classify and summarize information in a reasonable manner
      5)   Reflect underlying events and transactions within an acceptable range

   c.   **U.S. GAAP hierarchy for nongovernmental entities**. The report should identify the country of origin of GAAP, for example, accounting principles generally accepted in the United States of America or U.S. generally accepted accounting principles. The order of items in the GAAP hierarchy is important and has been tested on recent CPA exams.

      1)   **Established accounting principles**

         a)   Officially established accounting principles consisting of FASB Statements and Interpretations, APB Opinions, and AICPA Accounting Research Bulletins

         b)   FASB Technical Bulletins and, if cleared by the FASB, AICPA Audit and Accounting Guides and AICPA Statements of Position

NOTE: The AICPA has agreed to focus on industry-specific audit and accounting guidance and not to issue general-purpose accounting SOPs.

         c)   Consensus positions of the FASB Emerging Issues Task Force and, if cleared by the FASB, Practice Bulletins of the AICPA's Accounting Standards Executive Committee (AcSEC)

         d)   AICPA accounting interpretations, "Qs and As" (Questions and Answers) published by the FASB staff, as well as industry practices widely recognized and prevalent

      2)   **Other accounting literature**

         a)   FASB Concepts Statements; AICPA Issue Papers; International Accounting Standards issued by the International Accounting Standards Committee; GASB Statements, Interpretations, and Technical Bulletins; Federal Accounting Standards Advisory Board (FASAB) Statements, Interpretations, and Technical Bulletins; accounting textbooks, handbooks, and articles; etc.

    d.   Conduct Rule 203 prohibits expression of an opinion that financial statements are in conformity with GAAP if they contain a material departure from a principle promulgated by the body designated by the AICPA Council to establish such principles (e.g., the FASB).

        1)   However, an exception is permitted when the auditor can demonstrate that, because of unusual circumstances, the statements would otherwise have been misleading.

            a)   Given these circumstances, and if no other basis for modifying the opinion exists, the CPA may express an unqualified opinion, provided that (s)he describes in a separate paragraph of the report the departure, its effects, and the reasons compliance with GAAP would have been misleading.

            b)   The client should disclose the departure and the effects in a footnote to the financial statements.

2.   The **second standard of reporting**: *The report shall identify those circumstances in which such principles have not been consistently observed in the current period in relation to the preceding period.*

    a.   The user has the right to expect that changes in the account balances have resulted from transactions, not changes in principle.

    b.   Management has the responsibility to disclose the effects of changes.

    c.   The auditor's report should include an additional paragraph whenever a material change in principle has occurred.

3.   The **third standard of reporting**: *Informative disclosures in the financial statements are to be regarded as reasonably adequate unless otherwise stated in the report.*

    a.   Presenting statements in conformity with GAAP includes adequate disclosure of material matters related to the form, arrangement, and content of the statements and notes.

        1)   If management omits information required by GAAP, the auditor should provide the necessary disclosures in the report, if practicable, and express a qualified or adverse opinion (AU 431).

4.   The **fourth standard of reporting**: *The report shall either contain an expression of opinion regarding the financial statements, taken as a whole, or an assertion to the effect that an opinion cannot be expressed. When an overall opinion cannot be expressed, the reasons therefor should be stated. In all cases in which an auditor's name is associated with financial statements, the report should contain a clear-cut indication of the character of the auditor's work, if any, and the degree of responsibility the auditor is taking.*

    a.   The objective of the fourth standard is to prevent misinterpretation of the degree of responsibility the auditor is assuming when his/her name is associated with financial statements.

        1)   An accountant may be associated with financial statements of a public entity that (s)he has not audited or reviewed. If the accountant is aware that his/her name is to be included in a client-prepared written communication of a public company containing financial statements that have not been audited or reviewed, (s)he should request that either

            a)   His/her name not be included in the communication, or

            b)   The financial statements be marked as unaudited and that a notation be included to the effect that (s)he does not express an opinion on them (AU 504).

    2)   The statement in the introductory paragraph of the standard report about management's responsibility should not be elaborated upon in the standard report or referenced to management's report. Such a modification might lead users to the erroneous belief that the auditor is giving assurances about management's representations concerning matters discussed in the management report.

  b.   "Taken as a whole," as referred to in the fourth standard of reporting, applies equally to a complete set of financial statements, to an individual financial statement, and to financial statements for different periods presented comparatively.

  c.   The auditor may express an unqualified opinion on one of the financial statements and express a qualified or adverse opinion or disclaim an opinion on another if the circumstances warrant.

  d.   The auditor's report is customarily issued in connection with an entity's basic financial statements. Each financial statement audited should be specifically identified in the introductory paragraph of the auditor's report.

    1)   If the basic financial statements include a separate statement of changes in equity accounts, it should be identified in the introductory paragraph of the report but need not be reported on separately in the opinion paragraph because such changes are part of the presentation of financial position, results of operations, and cash flows.

5.   Stop and review! You have completed the outline for this subunit. Study multiple-choice questions 1 through 7 beginning on page 502.

16.2 THE AUDITOR'S STANDARD REPORT (AU 508)

1.   The standard report on comparative financial statements should be memorized:

Standard Audit Report

Independent Auditor's Report

To: <----------- Addressed to the Board of Directors and/or Stockholders

We have audited the accompanying balance sheets of X Company as of December 31, year 2 and year 1, and the related statements of income, retained earnings, and cash flows for the years then ended. These financial statements are the responsibility of the Company's management. Our responsibility is to express an opinion on these financial statements based on our audits.

We conducted our audits* in accordance with auditing standards generally accepted in the United States of America. Those standards require that we plan and perform the audit to obtain reasonable assurance about whether the financial statements are free of material misstatement. An audit includes examining, on a test basis, evidence supporting the amounts and disclosures in the financial statements. An audit also includes assessing the accounting principles used and significant estimates made by management, as well as evaluating the overall financial statement presentation. We believe that our audits provide a reasonable basis for our opinion.

In our opinion, the financial statements referred to above present fairly, in all material respects, the financial position of X Company as of [at] December 31, year 2 and year 1, and the results of its operations and its cash flows for the years then ended in conformity with accounting principles generally accepted in the United States of America.

Signature   <----------- May be signed, typed, or printed

Date   <----------- Date of completion of field work

---

*The PCAOB's Auditing Standard No. 1, *References in Auditors' Reports to the Standards of the Public Company Accounting Oversight Board*, requires the report of a client subject to the Sarbanes-Oxley Act to refer to "the standards of the Public Company Accounting Oversight Board (United States)" rather than to GAAS. Auditors of clients not subject to the Sarbanes-Oxley Act also may include the statement along with the reference to GAAS if they voluntarily follow the PCAOB standards. Furthermore, the report on an audit of a nonissuer may contain language to clarify that internal control is not required. Such an engagement does not require performance of procedures sufficient to express an opinion on the effectiveness of internal control over financial reporting.

2. **Paragraphs in the Standard Report**

   a. **Introductory or opening.** The introductory paragraph identifies the financial statements and period(s) under audit and describes the responsibilities of management and the auditor. It contains three sentences.

      1) We have audited . . . .
      2) Statements . . . responsibility . . . management.
      3) Our responsibility . . . opinion.

   b. **Scope.** The scope paragraph describes the nature of the audit. It contains five sentences.

      1) Conducted . . . GAAS.
      2) Standards . . . reasonable assurance.
      3) Audit . . . examining on a test basis.
      4) Audit . . . assessing principles and significant estimates by management.
      5) We believe . . . reasonable basis.

   c. **Opinion.** The opinion paragraph presents the auditor's conclusion. It contains one sentence.

      1) In our opinion, the financial statements . . . present fairly . . . .GAAP.

3. **Types of Reports**

   a. **Unqualified opinion.** An unqualified opinion states that the financial statements present fairly, in all material respects, the financial position, results of operations, and cash flows of the entity in conformity with GAAP.

   b. **Explanatory language added to the auditor's standard report.** Certain circumstances, although not affecting the auditor's unqualified opinion, may require that the auditor add an explanatory paragraph (or other explanatory language) to the report.

   c. **Qualified opinion.** A qualified opinion states that, **except for** the effects of the matter(s) to which the qualification relates, the financial statements present fairly, in all material respects, the financial position, results of operations, and cash flows of the entity in conformity with GAAP.

   d. **Adverse opinion.** An adverse opinion states that the financial statements do not present fairly the financial position, results of operations, or cash flows of the entity in conformity with GAAP.

   e. **Disclaimer of opinion.** A disclaimer of opinion states that the auditor does not express an opinion on the financial statements.

4. If only single-year financial statements are presented, the report is adjusted to reference only those statements.

5. Unless otherwise required, an explanatory paragraph may precede or follow the opinion paragraph in the auditor's report.

6. Stop and review! You have completed the outline for this subunit. Study multiple-choice questions 8 through 15 beginning on page 504.

16.3 ADDRESSING AND DATING THE REPORT (AU 530)

1. The auditor's report should be addressed to the company whose statements are being audited or to its board of directors or stockholders. If the client is an unincorporated entity, the report should be addressed as circumstances dictate, e.g., to the partners or the proprietor.

   a. If an auditor is retained to audit the financial statements of a company that is not his/her client, the report customarily is addressed to the client and not to the board of directors or stockholders of the company whose financial statements are being audited.

2.   The date of the audit report is generally the date of completion of field work. This date is important because the user has a right to expect that the auditor has performed certain procedures to detect subsequent events that would materially affect the financial statements through the date of the report.

    a.   The auditor is ordinarily not responsible for making inquiries or carrying out any audit procedures after the date of the report.

3.   When a **subsequent event** disclosed in the financial statements occurs after the completion of field work but before the issuance of the related financial statements, the auditor may use dual dating. (S)he may date the report as of the completion of field work except for the matters affected by the subsequent event, which would be assigned the appropriate later date.

    a.   In that case, the auditor's responsibility for events after the completion of field work would be limited to the specific event.

    b.   If the auditor is willing to accept responsibility to the later date and accordingly extends subsequent events procedures to that date, the auditor may choose the later date as the date for the entire report.

4.   Under AU 530, use of the original date in a **reissued report** removes any implication that records, transactions, or events after such date have been audited or reviewed. The auditor will thus have no responsibility to carry out procedures relating to the period between original issuance and reissuance.

    a.   An exception exists for filings under the Securities Act of 1933. This is covered in AU 711.

5.   Stop and review! You have completed the outline for this subunit. Study multiple-choice questions 16 through 20 beginning on page 506.

16.4 QUALIFIED OPINIONS (AU 508)

1.   **General Concepts**. Financial statements may be fairly presented **except for** the effects of a certain matter. If the opinion is qualified because of such effects, all substantive reasons should be disclosed in one or more separate explanatory paragraph(s) preceding the opinion paragraph.

    a.   The opinion paragraph should contain qualifying language and refer to the explanatory paragraph.

        1)   It should include the word "except" or "exception" in a phrase such as "except for" or "with the exception of."

        2)   "Subject to," "with the foregoing explanation," and similar phrases lack clarity and forcefulness and shall **not** be used.

        3)   Notes are part of the statements, and language such as "fairly presented when read in conjunction with Note 1" should **not** be used because of the likelihood of misunderstanding.

2.   **Scope Limitations**. A qualified opinion may be based on a lack of sufficient competent evidence or restrictions on the audit's scope.

    a.   An unqualified opinion requires the application of all procedures the auditor considers necessary in the circumstances.

        1)   Scope restrictions leading to a qualified opinion or a disclaimer may be imposed by the client or by circumstances, for example, by the

            a)   Timing of the work
            b)   Inability to obtain sufficient competent evidence
            c)   Inadequacy of the accounting records

b. Whether to qualify the opinion or disclaim an opinion depends on the assessment of the importance of the omitted procedure(s).

    1) This assessment will be affected by the nature and magnitude of the potential effects of the matters in question and their significance to the statements.

c. Some common scope restrictions relate to the inability to observe inventory, confirm accounts receivable, or obtain audited statements of an investee.

    1) When significant restrictions are imposed by the client, the auditor usually should disclaim an opinion.

d. When a qualified opinion results from a scope limitation or insufficient evidence, the situation is described in an explanatory paragraph preceding the opinion paragraph and referred to in the scope and opinion paragraphs.

    1) The scope limitation or insufficiency of evidence is not explained in a note to the statements because the description is the responsibility of the auditor.

e. The wording in the opinion paragraph should indicate that the qualification pertains to the possible effects on the financial statements and not to the scope limitation itself.

f. Example of a report in which the opinion is qualified for a scope limitation concerning an investment in a foreign affiliate

    1) The introductory paragraph is unchanged.

    2) The scope paragraph is unchanged except that it begins with the clause:

        Except as discussed in the following paragraph, . . .

    3) The explanatory paragraph and the qualifying language and reference in the opinion paragraph are as follows:

Language to Qualify an Audit Report for a Scope Limitation

We were unable to obtain audited financial statements supporting the Company's investment in a foreign affiliate stated at $___ and $___ at December 31, year 2 and year 1, respectively, or its equity in earnings of that affiliate of $___ and $___, which is included in net income for the years then ended as described in Note X to the financial statements; nor were we able to satisfy ourselves as to the carrying value of the investment in the foreign affiliates or the equity in its earnings by other auditing procedures.

In our opinion, except for the effects of such adjustments, if any, as might have been determined to be necessary had we been able to examine evidence regarding the foreign affiliate investment and earnings, the financial statements referred to in the first paragraph above present fairly...

g. Other scope limitations. If the notes to the statements contain unaudited information that should be audited, such as a material share of an investee's earnings recognized on the equity method, the auditor should apply the procedures (s)he deems necessary.

    1) If the procedures cannot be applied, (s)he should qualify the opinion or disclaim an opinion because of a scope limitation.

    2) If the disclosures, for example, the pro forma effects of a business combination or of a subsequent event, are not necessary to fair presentation, they may be identified as "unaudited" or "not covered by the auditor's report." Thus, the event or transaction would be audited but not the related pro forma disclosures.

        a) With regard to a material subsequent event, however, the only options are to dual date the report or date the report as of the date of the subsequent event and extend subsequent events procedures to that date.

h.   Limited reporting engagements. The auditor may report on one basic financial statement and not on the others.

    1)   These engagements do not involve scope limitations *per se* but rather limited reporting objectives.

    2)   If an auditor reports on the balance sheet only, (s)he may express an opinion on the balance sheet only.

    3)   References in the introductory and opinion paragraphs of the report are made only to those statements being audited.

3.   **Departures from GAAP**. A material departure from GAAP results in a qualified (or an adverse) opinion with the basis therefor stated in the report.

    a.   The materiality of the effects of a departure involves qualitative as well as quantitative judgments, for example, the

        1)   Significance of an item to an entity (e.g., inventories to a manufacturer)
        2)   Pervasiveness (e.g., whether it affects numerous items)
        3)   Effect on the statements as a whole

    b.   In addition to the substantive reasons for qualifying the opinion, the explanatory paragraph(s) should disclose the principal effects of the subject matter of the qualification, if practicable.

        1)   If the effects are not reasonably determinable, the report should so state.

        2)   The paragraph should precede the opinion paragraph.

        3)   The explanatory paragraph(s) may be shortened by referring to relevant disclosures made in a note to the statements.

        4)   Example of a report in which the opinion is qualified because of a departure from GAAP

            a)   The introductory and scope paragraphs are unchanged.

            b)   The explanatory paragraph and the qualifying language and reference in the opinion paragraph are as follows:

Language to Qualify an Audit Report for a Departure from U.S. GAAP

> The Company has excluded, from property and debt in the accompanying balance sheets, certain lease obligations that, in our opinion, should be capitalized in order to conform with U.S. generally accepted accounting principles. If these obligations were capitalized, property would be increased by \$____ and \$____, long term debt by \$____ and \$____, and retained earnings by \$____ and \$____. Additionally, net income would be increased (decreased) by \$____ and \$____, and earnings per share would be increased (decreased) by \$____ and \$____, respectively, for the years then ended.
>
> In our opinion, except for the effects of not capitalizing certain lease obligations as discussed in the preceding paragraph, the financial statements referred to above present fairly, in all material respects, the financial position of X Company as of December 31, year 2 and year 1, and the results of its operations and its cash flows for the three years then ended in conformity with accounting principles generally accepted in the United States of America.

            c)   If disclosures are made in a note to the financial statements, the separate paragraph might read as follows:

Separate Paragraph Referencing a Note Describing a Departure from U.S. GAAP

> As more fully described in Note X to the financial statements, the Company has excluded certain lease obligations from property and debt in the accompanying balance sheets. In our opinion, U.S. generally accepted accounting principles require that such obligations be included in the balance sheets.

c. Inadequate disclosure. If the financial statements, including accompanying notes, omit disclosures required by GAAP, a qualified (or adverse) opinion should be expressed and the omitted information should be provided by the auditor in the report, if practicable, unless the omission is permitted by a specific SAS.

1) Example of a report qualified for inadequate disclosure

a) The introductory and scope paragraphs are unchanged.

b) The explanatory paragraph and the qualifying language and reference in the opinion paragraph are as follows:

Language to Qualify an Audit Report for Inadequate Disclosure

> The Company's financial statements do not disclose (describe the nature of the omitted disclosures). In our opinion, disclosure of this information is required by U.S. generally accepted accounting principles.
>
> In our opinion, except for the omission of the information discussed in the preceding paragraph, the financial statements referred to above present fairly...

2) If the statements of financial position and results of operations are issued without a statement of cash flows, the omission normally requires a qualified opinion.

3) The auditor need not prepare and include in the report a basic financial statement omitted by management, such as a statement of cash flows. The following is an example of a report in these circumstances:

a) The introductory and scope paragraphs are unchanged except that the former does not mention the statement of cash flows.

b) The explanatory and opinion paragraphs are as follows:

Language to Qualify an Audit Report for Failure to Present a Statement of Cash Flows

> The Company declined to present a statement of cash flows for the years ended December 31, year 2 and year 1. Presentation of such statement summarizing the company's operating, investing, and financing activities is required by U.S. generally accepted accounting principles.
>
> In our opinion, except that the omission of a statement of cash flows results in an incomplete presentation as explained in the preceding paragraph, the financial statements referred to above present fairly, in all material respects, the financial position of X Company as of December 31, year 2 and year 1, and the results of its operation for the years then ended in conformity with accounting principles generally accepted in the United States of America.

4) According to an Interpretation of AU 326 that addresses **segment disclosures**, the auditor's standard report on financial statements prepared in conformity with GAAP implicitly applies to segment information included in those statements. The FASB requires the operating segment approach to disclosure of segment information. The auditor should not refer to segment information unless the audit reveals a related material misstatement or omission, or unless the audit was subject to a scope limitation.

d. Inappropriate accounting changes

1) A qualified opinion (or, if the effect of the change is sufficiently material, an adverse opinion) should be expressed if one of the following applies:

a) A newly adopted accounting principle is not generally accepted.

b) The method of accounting for the effect of the change is not in conformity with GAAP.

c) Management's justification for the change is not reasonable.

2) Example of a report qualified for lack of a reasonable justification for an accounting change

    a) The introductory and scope paragraphs are unchanged.

    b) The explanatory paragraph and the qualifying language and reference in the opinion paragraph are as follows:

Language to Qualify an Audit Report for Inappropriate Change in Accounting Principle

> As disclosed in Note X to the financial statements, the Company adopted, in year 2, the first-in, first-out method of accounting for its inventories, whereas it previously used the last-in, first-out method. Although use of the first-in, first-out method is in conformity with generally accepted accounting principles, in our opinion, the Company has not provided reasonable justification, as required by generally accepted accounting principles, for making this change.
>
> In our opinion, except for the change in accounting principles discussed in the preceding paragraph...

    c) In effect, both a change in accounting principle and a departure from GAAP results. The explanatory paragraph in the previous example meets the requirements for a consistency paragraph when simply a change in GAAP is encountered. Hence, a separate paragraph on consistency following the opinion paragraph (as would normally be required for acceptable changes) is not necessary.

3) Whenever an accounting change results in a qualified or adverse opinion for the year of change, the possible effects should be considered in reporting on financial statements for subsequent years.

    a) If the statements for the year of change are presented and reported on with a subsequent year's statements, the report should disclose the auditor's reservations about the earlier statements.

    b) The continued use of an unacceptable accounting principle might have a material effect in a subsequent year, and the independent auditor should express a qualified (or an adverse) opinion, depending on the materiality of the departure.

    c) If an entity departs from GAAP by accounting for a change prospectively rather than by restatement or inclusion of the cumulative effect in the year of change, the subsequent year's statements could improperly include a material charge or credit that requires a qualified (or an adverse) opinion.

    d) If reasonable justification for a change to an otherwise acceptable principle has not been provided, the auditor should continue to express the exception regarding the year of change as long as the statements are presented and reported on.

        i) The opinion on the subsequent years' statements need not express an exception to adoption of the principle. Hence, if such a change was made in year 1, and comparative statements for year 1, year 2, and year 3 are presented and reported on, the change will be a basis for a qualified opinion on the year 1 but not the year 2 and year 3 statements.

4. Stop and review! You have completed the outline for this subunit. Study multiple-choice questions 21 through 44 beginning on page 508.

16.5 ADVERSE OPINIONS (AU 508)

1.   An adverse opinion is expressed when, in the judgment of the auditor, the financial statements taken as a whole are not presented fairly in conformity with GAAP.

   a.   The auditor should include in a separate explanatory paragraph(s) preceding the opinion paragraph all substantive reasons for the adverse opinion and the principal effects of its subject matter, if practicable. If the effects are not reasonably determinable, a statement to that effect should be included.

   b.   **Example of an adverse opinion**

   1)   The introductory and scope paragraphs are unchanged.

   2)   The opinion paragraph should directly refer to a separate paragraph disclosing the basis for the adverse opinion.

   3)   The explanatory and opinion paragraphs are as follows (in this example, the departures from GAAP are described in two explanatory paragraphs):

Language to Express an Adverse Opinion for Departures from GAAP

As discussed in Note X to the financial statements, the Company carries its property, plant, and equipment accounts at appraisal values and provides depreciation on the basis of such values. Further, the company does not provide for income taxes with respect to differences between financial income and taxable income arising because of the use, for income tax purposes, of the installment method of reporting gross profit from certain types of sales. U.S. generally accepted accounting principles require that property, plant, and equipment be stated at an amount not in excess of cost, reduced by depreciation based on such amount, and that deferred income taxes be provided.

Because of the departures from U.S. generally accepted accounting principles identified above, as of December 31, year 2 and year 1, inventories have been increased $___ and $___ by inclusion in manufacturing overhead depreciation in excess of that based on cost; property, plant, and equipment, less accumulated depreciation, is carried at $___ and $___ in excess of an amount based on cost to the company; and deferred income taxes of $___ and $___ have not been recorded; resulting in an increase of $___ and $___, in retained earnings and in appraisal surplus of $___ and $___, respectively. For the years ended December 31, year 2 and year 1, cost of goods sold has been increased $___ and $___, respectively, because of the effects of depreciation accounting referred to above and deferred income taxes of $___ and $___ have not been provided, resulting in an increase in net income of $___ and $___, respectively.

In our opinion, because of the effects of the matters disclosed in the preceding paragraphs, the financial statements referred to above do not present fairly, in conformity with accounting principles generally accepted in the United States of America, the financial position of X Company as of December 31, year 2 and year 1, or the results of its operations and its cash flows for the years then ended.

2.   Stop and review! You have completed the outline for this subunit. Study multiple-choice questions 45 through 48 beginning on page 516.

16.6 DISCLAIMERS OF OPINION (AU 508)

1. **Disclaimer of Opinion Because of a Scope Limitation**

   a. States that the auditor does not express an opinion on the financial statements

   b. Is appropriate when the auditor has not performed an audit sufficient in scope to enable him/her to form an opinion

   c. Is not appropriate when the auditor believes there are material departures from GAAP

   d. Should not include a scope paragraph describing the nature of the audit

   e. Includes a separate paragraph that

      1) Provides reasons that the audit did not comply with GAAS

      2) States that the scope was not sufficient to warrant the expression of an opinion

      3) Does not identify the procedures performed

      4) Discloses any other reservations the auditor has regarding fair presentation in accordance with GAAP (e.g., that the auditor concludes that land is at appraised value rather than cost)

   f. Still carries the title "Independent Auditor's Report"

   g. Is presented as follows:

Disclaimer of Opinion Due to a Scope Limitation

<u>Independent Auditor's Report</u>

To: <----------- Addressed to owner or party who engaged accountant

We were engaged to audit the accompanying balance sheets of X Company as of December 31, year 2 and year 1, and the related statements of income, retained earnings, and cash flows for the years then ended. These financial statements are the responsibility of the Company's management. [OMIT "**Our responsibility...**"]

[Scope paragraph of standard report should be omitted.]

The Company did not make a count of its physical inventory in year 2 or year 1, stated in the accompanying financial statements at $___ as of December 31, year 2, and at $___ as of December 31, year 1. Further, evidence supporting the cost of property and equipment acquired prior to December 31, year 1, is no longer available. The Company's records do not permit the application of other auditing procedures to inventories or property and equipment.

Since the Company did not take physical inventories and we were not able to apply other auditing procedures to satisfy ourselves as to inventory quantities and the cost of property and equipment, the scope of our work was not sufficient to enable us to express, and we do not express, an opinion on these financial statements.

Signature   <----------- May be signed, typed, or printed

Date   <----------- Date of completion of engagement

2. **Piecemeal opinions** (expressions of opinion as to certain identified items) should not be expressed when the auditor has disclaimed an opinion (or has expressed an adverse opinion) because they would overshadow or contradict the report issued.

3. **Disclaimer When the Accountant Is Associated with the Unaudited Financial Statements of a Public Entity**. If the entity is nonpublic, the accountant should not consent to the use of his/her name in these circumstances unless (s)he has compiled or reviewed the statements, or the statements are accompanied by an indication that (s)he has not compiled or reviewed them and that (s)he assumes no responsibility for them.

    a.   A disclaimer should be attached to the financial statements of a public company when an accountant is associated with those statements and has not audited or reviewed them. Association means that the accountant has consented to the use of his/her name in a report, document, or written communication containing the statements.

        1)   An accountant might become associated by performing consulting services for a nonaudit client, for example, structuring a purchase transaction for a new subsidiary firm.

    b.   Each page of the financial statements should be marked as unaudited.

    c.   The accountant has no responsibility to apply any procedures beyond reading the statements for obvious material misstatements. Any procedures that may have been performed should not be described.

    d.   Any reservations known to the accountant regarding fair presentation in accordance with GAAP (e.g., that management has elected to omit substantially all of the disclosures) should be disclosed.

    e.   The report has no title or salutation.

    f.   The following is an example of a disclaimer on unaudited financial statements of a public entity.

Disclaimer of Opinion When Associated with a Public, Nonaudit Client's Financial Statements

> The accompanying balance sheet of X Company as of December 31, year 1, and the related statements of income, retained earnings, and cash flows for the year then ended were not audited by us and, accordingly, we do not express an opinion on them.
>
> Signature
>
> Date

4. **Disclaimer of Opinion on Financial Statements of a Public Company When the Accountant Is Not Independent**. An accountant must not express an opinion when (s)he is not independent.

    a.   The reasons for the lack of an opinion should not be described.

    b.   Each page of the financial statements should be marked as unaudited.

    c.   Any procedures that may have been performed should not be described.

    d.   Any reservations known to the accountant regarding fair presentation in accordance with GAAP (e.g., that management has elected to omit substantially all of the disclosures) should be disclosed.

    e.   The report has no title or salutation.

    f.   The following is an example of a disclaimer on financial statements of a public company when the accountant is not independent.

Disclaimer of Opinion When Not Independent with Public, Nonaudit Client's Financial Statements

> We are not independent with respect to XYZ Company, and the accompanying balance sheet as of December 31, year 1, and the related statements of income, retained earnings, and cash flows for the year then ended were not audited by us and, accordingly, we do not express an opinion on them.
>
> Signature
>
> Date

5. Stop and review! You have completed the outline for this subunit. Study multiple-choice questions 49 through 55 beginning on page 517.

QUESTIONS

16.1 GAAS -- The Reporting Standards

1. For a particular entity's financial statements to be presented fairly in conformity with GAAP, it is not required that the principles selected

    A. Be appropriate in the circumstances for the particular entity.

    B. Reflect transactions in a manner that presents the financial statements within a range of acceptable limits.

    C. Present information in the financial statements that is classified and summarized in a reasonable manner.

    D. Be applied on a basis consistent with those followed in the prior year.

Answer (D) is correct. *(CPA, adapted)*
REQUIRED: The item not required for statements to be in conformity with GAAP.
DISCUSSION: A lack of consistency does not preclude fair presentation in accordance with GAAP. For example, if the entity changes from one generally accepted accounting principle to another and the auditor concurs with the change, a reference in the auditor's report is required, but the financial statements will conform with GAAP.
Answer (A) is incorrect because the accounting principles should be appropriate in the circumstances. Answer (B) is incorrect because the financial statements should "reflect the underlying transactions and events in a manner that presents the financial position, results of operations, and cash flows stated within a range of acceptable limits" (AU 411). Answer (C) is incorrect because the information presented in the financial statements should be classified and summarized in a reasonable manner; that is, it should be neither too detailed nor too condensed.

2. For an entity's financial statements to be presented fairly in conformity with generally accepted accounting principles, the principles selected should

    A. Be applied on a basis consistent with those followed in the prior year.

    B. Be approved by the Auditing Standards Board or the appropriate industry subcommittee.

    C. Reflect transactions in a manner that presents the financial statements within a range of acceptable limits.

    D. Match the principles used by most other entities within the entity's particular industry.

Answer (C) is correct. *(CPA, adapted)*
REQUIRED: The requirement for an entity's financial statements to be presented fairly in conformity with GAAP.
DISCUSSION: The auditor's judgments about GAAP include "whether the financial statements reflect the underlying transactions and events in a manner that presents the financial position, results of operations, and cash flows stated within a range of acceptable limits, that is, limits that are reasonable and practicable to attain in financial statements" (AU 411).
Answer (A) is incorrect because lack of consistency does not preclude fair presentation. Answer (B) is incorrect because the Auditing Standards Board promulgates auditing standards, not GAAP. Answer (D) is incorrect because GAAP should meet the test of general acceptance and need not be the most prevalent used in the industry.

3. Several sources of GAAP consulted by an auditor are in conflict as to the application of an accounting principle. Which of the following should the auditor consider the most authoritative?

    A. FASB Technical Bulletins.

    B. AICPA Accounting Interpretations.

    C. FASB Statements of Financial Accounting Concepts.

    D. International Accounting Standards.

Answer (A) is correct. *(CPA, adapted)*
REQUIRED: The most authoritative source of GAAP.
DISCUSSION: AU 411 establishes the GAAP hierarchy. FASB Technical Bulletins are in the second tier. FASB Statements and Interpretations, APB Opinions, and AICPA Accounting Research Bulletins are in the first tier of GAAP for nongovernmental entities.
Answer (B) is incorrect because AICPA Accounting Interpretations are in the fourth tier of GAAP. Answer (C) is incorrect because FASB Statements of Financial Accounting Concepts are in the fifth tier of GAAP. Answer (D) is incorrect because International Accounting Standards are in the fifth tier of GAAP.

4. A scope limitation sufficient to preclude an unqualified opinion always will result when management

- A. Prevents the auditor from reviewing the working papers of the predecessor auditor.

- B. Engages the auditor after the year-end physical inventory is completed.

- C. Requests that certain material accounts receivable not be confirmed.

- D. Refuses to acknowledge its responsibility for the fair presentation of the financial statements in conformity with GAAP.

Answer (D) is correct. *(CPA, adapted)*
REQUIRED: The scope limitation that would preclude an unqualified opinion.
DISCUSSION: A scope limitation arises when an auditor has not been able to perform all of the procedures necessary in the circumstances. One such necessary procedure is the obtaining of certain written representations from management. Among those specific representations are management's acknowledgment of its responsibility for the fair presentation of the financial statements in conformity with GAAP. Management's refusal to provide a written representation that acknowledges its responsibility for compliance with GAAP is a scope limitation "sufficient to preclude an unqualified opinion and is ordinarily sufficient to cause an auditor to disclaim an opinion or withdraw from the engagement" (AU 333).
Answer (A) is incorrect because, if a prospective client refuses to allow a predecessor auditor to respond (or limits the response) to a successor auditor's inquiries, the successor "should inquire as to the reasons and consider the implications of that refusal in deciding whether to accept the engagement" (AU 315). Thus, the issue is engagement acceptance, not a scope limitation. Answer (B) is incorrect because engaging the auditor after the year-end physical inventory is completed does not necessarily result in a scope limitation. For example, the limitation may be remedied by taking another physical inventory that the auditor can observe (AU 310). Answer (C) is incorrect because confirmation of accounts receivable is presumed to be part of an audit in accordance with GAAS, but that presumption may be overcome. For example, confirmation is not required when the accounts are not material or when it would be ineffective. Confirmation also is not required when the combined assessed risk is low and, together with other evidence, is sufficient to reduce audit risk to an acceptable level for the pertinent assertions (AU 330).

5. The fourth standard of reporting requires the auditor's report to contain either an expression of opinion regarding the financial statements taken as a whole or an assertion to the effect that an opinion cannot be expressed. The objective of the fourth standard is to prevent

- A. Misinterpretations regarding the degree of responsibility the auditor is assuming.

- B. An auditor from reporting on one basic financial statement and not the others.

- C. An auditor from expressing different opinions on each of the basic financial statements.

- D. Restrictions on the scope of the audit, whether imposed by the client or by the inability to obtain evidence.

Answer (A) is correct. *(CPA, adapted)*
REQUIRED: The overall purpose of the fourth standard of reporting.
DISCUSSION: The fourth standard of reporting states, "In all cases in which an auditor's name is associated with financial statements, the report should contain a clear-cut indication of the character of the auditor's work, if any, and the degree of responsibility the auditor is taking." The objective of this standard is to prevent misinterpretations of the degree of responsibility the auditor is assuming when his/her name is associated with financial statements.
Answer (B) is incorrect because limited reporting engagements are permissible. Answer (C) is incorrect because the requirement to report on the financial statements "taken as a whole" applies equally to a complete set and to a single statement. Thus, an unqualified opinion may be expressed on one statement, and a qualified or adverse opinion or a disclaimer may be expressed on another if warranted. Answer (D) is incorrect because standards cannot prevent scope limitations imposed by the client or by the inability to obtain evidence.

6. Green, CPA, is aware that Green's name is to be included in the interim report of National Company, a publicly held entity. National's quarterly financial statements are contained in the interim report. Green has not audited or reviewed these interim financial statements. Green should request that

I.   Green's name not be included in the communication

II.   The financial statements be marked as unaudited, with a notation that no opinion is expressed on them

    A.   I only.

    B.   II only.

    C.   Both I and II.

    D.   Either I or II.

Answer (D) is correct. *(CPA, adapted)*
    REQUIRED: The request(s) that an accountant should make when (s)he is associated with financial statements of a public entity that (s)he has not audited or reviewed.
    DISCUSSION: If the accountant is aware that his/her name is to be included in a client-prepared written communication of a public company containing financial statements that have not been audited or reviewed, (s)he should request either (1) that his/her name not be included in the communication or (2) that the financial statements be marked as unaudited, with a notation included to the effect that (s)he does not express an opinion of them (AU 504).

---

7. An annual shareholders' report includes audited financial statements and contains a management report asserting that the financial statements are the responsibility of management. Is it permissible for the auditor's report to refer to the management report?

    A.   No, because the reference may lead to the belief that the auditor is providing assurances about management's representations.

    B.   No, because the auditor has no responsibility to read the other information in a document containing audited financial statements.

    C.   Yes, provided the reference is included in a separate explanatory paragraph of the auditor's report.

    D.   Yes, provided the auditor reads the management report and discovers no material misrepresentation of fact.

Answer (A) is correct. *(CPA, adapted)*
    REQUIRED: The true statement about a reference in the auditor's report to the management report.
    DISCUSSION: According to an Interpretation of AU 508, such a modification of the standard report may lead users to the erroneous belief that the auditor is giving assurances about management's representations concerning matters discussed in the management report. The statement in the introductory paragraph about management's responsibility should not be elaborated upon in the standard report or referenced to management's report.
    Answer (B) is incorrect because the auditor should read the other information (AU 550). Answer (C) is incorrect because no reference should be made in the auditor's report. Answer (D) is incorrect because no reference should be made in the auditor's report.

16.2 The Auditor's Standard Report (AU 508)

8. How are management's responsibility and the auditor's responsibility represented in the standard auditor's report?

	Management's Responsibility	Auditor's Responsibility
A.	Explicitly	Explicitly
B.	Implicitly	Implicitly
C.	Implicitly	Explicitly
D.	Explicitly	Implicitly

Answer (A) is correct. *(CPA, adapted)*
    REQUIRED: The representation of the responsibilities of management and the auditor in the standard audit report.
    DISCUSSION: The introductory paragraph of the independent auditor's report explicitly states, "These financial statements are the responsibility of the Company's management. Our responsibility is to express an opinion on these financial statements based on our audit" (AU 508).

9. An auditor's responsibility to express an opinion on the financial statements is

A. Implicitly represented in the auditor's standard report.

B. Explicitly represented in the opening paragraph of the auditor's standard report.

C. Explicitly represented in the scope paragraph of the auditor's standard report.

D. Explicitly represented in the opinion paragraph of the auditor's standard report.

Answer (B) is correct. *(CPA, adapted)*

REQUIRED: The representation in the standard report of the auditor's responsibility to express an opinion.

DISCUSSION: The introductory (opening) paragraph of the independent auditor's report explicitly states, "These financial statements are the responsibility of the Company's management. Our responsibility is to express an opinion on these financial statements based on our audit."

10. Under the AICPA standards, which paragraphs of an auditor's standard report on financial statements should refer to generally accepted auditing standards (GAAS) and generally accepted accounting principles (GAAP)?

	GAAS	GAAP
A.	Opening	Scope
B.	Scope	Scope
C.	Scope	Opinion
D.	Opening	Opinion

Answer (C) is correct. *(CPA, adapted)*

REQUIRED: The paragraphs in the auditor's standard report that refer to GAAS and GAAP.

DISCUSSION: The auditor's report should contain a clear-cut indication of the character of the auditor's work, if any, and state the degree of responsibility assumed. Under the AICPA standards, GAAS are referred to only in the scope paragraph because they relate to the nature of the audit. The opinion paragraph contains an opinion as to whether the statements as a whole are fairly presented, in all material respects, in conformity with GAAP. Neither GAAS nor GAAP are mentioned in the introductory paragraph, which identifies the financial statements audited and describes the responsibilities of management and of the auditor (AU 508).

11. Which of the following statements is a basic element of the auditor's standard report?

A. The disclosures provide reasonable assurance that the financial statements are free of material misstatement.

B. The auditor evaluated the overall internal control.

C. An audit includes assessing significant estimates made by management.

D. The financial statements are consistent with those of the prior period.

Answer (C) is correct. *(CPA, adapted)*

REQUIRED: The statement that is an element of the auditor's standard report.

DISCUSSION: The auditor's standard report includes the statement, "An audit also includes assessing the accounting principles used and significant estimates made by management, as well as evaluating the overall financial statement presentation."

12. The existence of audit risk is recognized by the statement in the auditor's standard report that the auditor

A. Obtains reasonable assurance about whether the financial statements are free of material misstatement.

B. Assesses the accounting principles used and also evaluates the overall financial statement presentation.

C. Realizes some matters, either individually or in the aggregate, are important while other matters are not important.

D. Is responsible for expressing an opinion on the financial statements, which are the responsibility of management.

Answer (A) is correct. *(CPA, adapted)*

REQUIRED: The statement that relates to the element of audit risk.

DISCUSSION: AU 312 states, "The existence of audit risk is recognized by the statement in the auditor's standard report that the auditor obtained reasonable assurance about whether the financial statements are free of material misstatement." Audit risk is "the risk that the auditor may unknowingly fail to appropriately modify the opinion on financial statements that are materially misstated." Audit risk exists because the assurance is not absolute.

Answer (B) is incorrect because the statement about assessing accounting principles relates to the first standard of reporting. Answer (C) is incorrect because materiality is mentioned in the standard audit report, but a statement defining materiality is not. Answer (D) is incorrect because the statement about the responsibilities of the auditor and management does not pertain to audit risk.

13. For a private company that does not receive governmental financial assistance, an auditor's standard report on financial statements generally would not refer to

A. Significant estimates made by management.

B. An assessment of the entity's accounting principles.

C. Management's responsibility for the financial statements.

D. The entity's internal control.

Answer (D) is correct. *(CPA, adapted)*
REQUIRED: The reference not made in the auditor's standard report.
DISCUSSION: Although the auditor has gained an understanding of internal control and assessed control risk, the standard auditor's report on a private company does not refer to internal control.
Answer (A) is incorrect because the report states that "an audit also includes assessing the accounting principles used and the significant estimates made by management, as well as evaluating the overall financial statement presentation" (AU 508). Answer (B) is incorrect because the report states that "an audit also includes assessing the accounting principles used and the significant estimates made by management, as well as evaluating the overall financial statement presentation" (AU 508). Answer (C) is incorrect because the introductory paragraph states, "These financial statements are the responsibility of the company's management" (AU 508).

14. Which of the following representations does an auditor make explicitly and which implicitly when expressing an unqualified opinion?

	Conformity with GAAP	Adequacy of Disclosure
A.	Explicitly	Explicitly
B.	Implicitly	Implicitly
C.	Implicitly	Explicitly
D.	Explicitly	Implicitly

Answer (D) is correct. *(CPA, adapted)*
REQUIRED: The explicit and implicit representations an auditor makes when expressing an unqualified opinion.
DISCUSSION: The opinion paragraph of the standard auditor's report explicitly states whether the financial statements are in conformity with GAAP. The third standard of reporting states, "Informative disclosures in the financial statements are to be regarded as reasonably adequate unless otherwise stated in the report." Thus, adequacy of disclosure is implicit in the standard report.

15. When single-year financial statements are presented, an auditor ordinarily would express an unqualified opinion in an unmodified report if the

A. Auditor is unable to obtain audited financial statements supporting the entity's investment in a foreign affiliate.

B. Entity declines to present a statement of cash flows with its balance sheet and related statements of income and retained earnings.

C. Auditor wishes to emphasize an accounting matter affecting the comparability of the financial statements with those of the prior year.

D. Prior year's financial statements were audited by another CPA whose report, which expressed an unqualified opinion, is not presented.

Answer (D) is correct. *(CPA, adapted)*
REQUIRED: The conditions under which an unqualified opinion would be expressed in an unmodified report.
DISCUSSION: When single-year financial statements are presented, the auditor's reporting responsibility is limited to those statements. If the prior year's financial statements are not presented for comparative purposes, the current-year auditor should not refer to the prior year's statements and the report thereon. Furthermore, the failure to present comparative statements is not a basis for modifying the opinion or the report.
Answer (A) is incorrect because an inability to obtain audited financial statements supporting an entity's investment in a foreign affiliate is a scope limitation requiring either a qualified opinion or a disclaimer of opinion. Answer (B) is incorrect because, if the entity declines to present a statement of cash flows, the auditor should express a qualified opinion. Answer (C) is incorrect because adding an additional paragraph to emphasize a matter results in a modified report.

16.3 Addressing and Dating the Report (AU 530)

16. March, CPA, is engaged by Monday Corp., a client, to audit the financial statements of Wall Corp., a company that is not March's client. Monday expects to present Wall's audited financial statements with March's auditor's report to 1st Federal Bank to obtain financing in Monday's attempt to purchase Wall. In these circumstances, March's auditor's report would usually be addressed to

A. Monday Corp., the client that engaged March.

B. Wall Corp., the entity audited by March.

C. 1st Federal Bank.

D. Both Monday Corp. and 1st Federal Bank.

Answer (A) is correct. *(CPA, adapted)*
REQUIRED: The addressee of an auditor's report when the auditee is not the client.
DISCUSSION: If an auditor is retained to audit the financial statements of a company that is not his/her client, the report customarily is addressed to the client and not to the board of directors or shareholders of the company whose financial statements are being audited.
Answer (B) is incorrect because the report would be addressed to the client, not to the entity being audited. Answer (C) is incorrect because the report would not be addressed to the intended user of the financial statements but to the client who engaged the CPA. Answer (D) is incorrect because the report would not be addressed to the intended user of the financial statements but to the client who engaged the CPA.

17. Wilson, CPA, completed the field work of the audit of Abco's December 31, year 1 financial statements on March 6, year 2. A subsequent event requiring adjustment of the year 1 financial statements occurred on April 10, year 2, and came to Wilson's attention on April 24, year 2. The subsequent event occurred prior to the issuance of the related financial statements. If the adjustment is made without disclosure of the event, Wilson's report ordinarily should be dated

A. March 6, year 2.

B. April 10, year 2.

C. April 24, year 2.

D. Using dual dating.

Answer (A) is correct. *(CPA, adapted)*
REQUIRED: The date of the report if the statements are adjusted for a subsequent event without disclosure.
DISCUSSION: If a subsequent event requiring adjustment occurs after the date of the report and prior to the issuance of the related financial statements, and the event comes to the auditor's attention, the statements should be adjusted or the opinion should be modified or a disclaimer issued. When the adjustment is made without disclosure, the report should usually be dated as of the completion of field work (AU 530).
Answer (B) is incorrect because, when a subsequent event of the type requiring adjustment is not disclosed, the related financial statements should usually be dated as of the completion of field work. Answer (C) is incorrect because, when a subsequent event of the type requiring adjustment is not disclosed, the related financial statements should usually be dated as of the completion of field work. Answer (D) is incorrect because dual dating is not permitted when the subsequent event is not disclosed.

18. On August 13, a CPA completed field work on an engagement to audit financial statements for the year ended June 30. On August 27, an event came to the CPA's attention that should be disclosed in the notes to the financial statements. The event was properly disclosed by the entity, but the CPA decided not to dual-date the auditor's report and dated the report August 27. Under these circumstances, the CPA was taking responsibility for

A. All subsequent events that occurred through August 27.

B. Only the specific subsequent event disclosed by the entity.

C. All subsequent events that occurred through August 13 and the specific subsequent event disclosed by the entity.

D. Only the subsequent events that occurred through August 13.

Answer (A) is correct. *(CPA, adapted)*
REQUIRED: The responsibility assumed by dating the audit report as of the date of a subsequent event requiring disclosure.
DISCUSSION: Subsequent events are material events or transactions that occur after the balance sheet date but prior to the issuance of the financial statements; they require adjustment or disclosure in the financial statements. If the auditor dates the report August 27, the auditor is assuming responsibility for all subsequent events that occurred through August 27.
Answer (B) is incorrect because, when the report is dual-dated, the auditor's subsequent-events responsibility is for only the specific subsequent event disclosed by the entity. Answer (C) is incorrect because dating the report August 27 makes the auditor responsible for all subsequent events occurring from June 30th through August 27th. Answer (D) is incorrect because dating the report August 27 makes the auditor responsible for all subsequent events occurring from June 30th through August 27th.

19. An auditor issued an audit report that was dual-dated for a subsequent event occurring after the completion of field work but before issuance of the related financial statements. The auditor's responsibility for events occurring subsequent to the completion of field work was

A. Limited to the specific event referenced.

B. Limited to include only events occurring before the date of the last subsequent event referenced.

C. Extended to subsequent events occurring through the date of issuance of the related financial statements.

D. Extended to include all events occurring since the completion of field work.

Answer (A) is correct. *(CPA, adapted)*
REQUIRED: The auditor's responsibility for events occurring subsequent to the completion of field work when the report is dual-dated.
DISCUSSION: Subsequent to the completion of field work, the auditor is responsible only for the specific subsequent event for which the report was dual-dated. (S)he is responsible for other subsequent events only up to the date of the completion of field work (AU 530).
Answer (B) is incorrect because the auditor's post-field-work responsibility extends only to the specified subsequent event. Answer (C) is incorrect because the date(s) of the report determines the auditor's responsibility. Answer (D) is incorrect because the auditor's post-field-work responsibility extends only to the specified subsequent event.

20. In May year 3, an auditor reissues the auditor's report on the year 1 financial statements at a continuing client's request. The year 1 financial statements are not restated, and the auditor does not revise the wording of the report. The auditor should

A. Dual-date the reissued report.

B. Use the release date of the reissued report.

C. Use the original report date on the reissued report.

D. Use the current-period auditor's report date on the reissued report.

Answer (C) is correct. *(CPA, adapted)*
REQUIRED: The date of a reissued report.
DISCUSSION: Under AU 530, use of the original date in a reissued report removes any implication that records, transactions, or events after such date have been audited or reviewed. The auditor will thus have no responsibility to carry out procedures relating to the period between original issuance and reissuance (but see AU 711 regarding filings under the Securities Act of 1933).
Answer (A) is incorrect because the report is dual-dated only if it has been revised since the original reissue date. Answer (B) is incorrect because using the release date of the reissued report implies that additional audit procedures have been applied. Answer (D) is incorrect because use of the current report date implies that the report has been updated for additional audit procedures applied between the original issue date and the current auditor's report date.

16.4 Qualified Opinions (AU 508)

21. Which of the following phrases should be included in the opinion paragraph when an auditor expresses a qualified opinion?

	When Read in Conjunction with Note X	With the Foregoing Explanation
A.	Yes	No
B.	No	Yes
C.	Yes	Yes
D.	No	No

Answer (D) is correct. *(CPA, adapted)*
REQUIRED: The phrase(s) used in a qualified opinion.
DISCUSSION: According to AU 508, the auditor should use a phrase such as "with the exception of" or "except for" to qualify an opinion. Wording such as "with the foregoing explanation" is neither clear nor forceful enough and is unacceptable. Moreover, the notes are part of the financial statements, and a reference such as "when read in conjunction with the footnotes" in the opinion paragraph is likely to be misunderstood.

22. An auditor may reasonably express a "subject to" qualified opinion for

	Lack of Consistency	Departure from Generally Accepted Accounting Principles
A.	Yes	Yes
B.	Yes	No
C.	No	Yes
D.	No	No

Answer (D) is correct. *(CPA, adapted)*
REQUIRED: The type of opinion that uses the phrase "subject to."
DISCUSSION: The phrase "subject to" should not be used in any report. It is not clear or forceful enough (AU 508).

23. An auditor may express a qualified opinion under which of the following circumstances?

	Lack of Sufficient Competent Evidential Matter	Restrictions on the Scope of the Audit
A.	Yes	Yes
B.	Yes	No
C.	No	Yes
D.	No	No

Answer (A) is correct. *(CPA, adapted)*
REQUIRED: The circumstances in which the auditor may express a qualified opinion.
DISCUSSION: A qualified opinion is expressed because of a departure from GAAP, a lack of sufficient competent evidence, or a restriction on the scope of the audit. AU 508 states that the auditor may be required to qualify the opinion or disclaim an opinion because of scope restrictions, "whether imposed by the client or by circumstances, such as the timing of the work, the inability to obtain sufficient competent evidential matter, or an inadequacy in the records."

24. In which of the following circumstances would an auditor usually choose between expressing a qualified opinion or disclaiming an opinion?

A. Departure from generally accepted accounting principles.

B. Inadequate disclosure of accounting policies.

C. Inability to obtain sufficient competent evidential matter.

D. Unreasonable justification for a change in accounting principle.

Answer (C) is correct. *(CPA, adapted)*
REQUIRED: The circumstance in which the auditor chooses between a disclaimer and a qualified opinion.
DISCUSSION: Scope restrictions, whether client-imposed or the result of circumstances such as the timing of the work, the inability to obtain sufficient competent evidence, or inadequate accounting records, may require a qualification of the opinion or a disclaimer. The choice depends on the assessment of the importance of the omitted procedure(s) to the auditor's ability to form an opinion.
Answer (A) is incorrect because a departure from GAAP usually requires a choice between a qualified or an adverse opinion. Answer (B) is incorrect because inadequate disclosure usually requires a choice between a qualified or an adverse opinion. Answer (D) is incorrect because an unjustified change in accounting principle usually requires a choice between a qualified or an adverse opinion.

25. Morris, CPA, suspects that a pervasive scheme of illegal bribes exists throughout the operations of Worldwide Import-Export, Inc., a new audit client. Morris notified the audit committee and Worldwide's legal counsel, but neither could assist Morris in determining whether the amounts involved were material to the financial statements or whether senior management was involved in the scheme. Under these circumstances, Morris should

A. Express an unqualified opinion with a separate explanatory paragraph.

B. Disclaim an opinion on the financial statements.

C. Express an adverse opinion on the financial statements.

D. Issue a special report regarding the illegal bribes.

Answer (B) is correct. *(CPA, adapted)*
REQUIRED: The auditor action when (s)he cannot determine the amounts involved in illegal acts or the extent of management's involvement.
DISCUSSION: If an auditor is precluded from applying necessary procedures or, after applying extended procedures, (s)he is unable to determine whether fraud or illegal acts may materially affect the statements, (s)he should disclaim or qualify an opinion. When the auditor cannot determine the role of management in the events, the auditor should ordinarily disclaim an opinion.
Answer (A) is incorrect because an unqualified opinion is not justified. Answer (C) is incorrect because an adverse opinion would be expressed only when the financial statements are not presented fairly. Answer (D) is incorrect because special reports as defined in AU 623 are not issued on such topics.

26. In which of the following circumstances would an auditor not express an unqualified opinion?

A. There has been a material change between periods in accounting principles.

B. Quarterly financial data required by the SEC have been omitted.

C. The auditor wishes to emphasize an unusually important subsequent event.

D. The auditor is unable to obtain audited financial statements of a consolidated investee.

Answer (D) is correct. *(CPA, adapted)*
REQUIRED: The circumstances in which an auditor would not express an unqualified opinion.
DISCUSSION: A qualified opinion may be based on a lack of sufficient competent evidence or restrictions on the audit's scope. Some common scope restrictions relate to the inability to observe inventory, confirm accounts receivable, or obtain audited statements of an investee.
Answer (A) is incorrect because a change in accounting principle results in an unqualified opinion with an additional paragraph added to explain the change. Answer (B) is incorrect because omission of quarterly data required by the SEC necessitates inclusion of an additional paragraph but does not preclude an unqualified opinion (AU 722). Answer (C) is incorrect because the auditor may add an additional paragraph to an otherwise unqualified opinion to emphasize an unusually important subsequent event.

27. When qualifying an opinion because of an insufficiency of audit evidence, an auditor should refer to the situation in the

	Opening (Introductory) Paragraph	Scope Paragraph
A.	No	No
B.	Yes	No
C.	Yes	Yes
D.	No	Yes

Answer (D) is correct. *(CPA, adapted)*
REQUIRED: The effect on the auditor's report when qualified because of an insufficiency of evidence.
DISCUSSION: When an opinion is qualified for a scope limitation, the introductory paragraph is unchanged. The scope paragraph is unchanged except that it begins with the clause, "Except as discussed in the following paragraph." An explanatory paragraph is added, followed by the opinion paragraph with appropriate qualifying language (AU 508).

28. A limitation on the scope of an audit sufficient to preclude an unqualified opinion will usually result when management

A. Presents financial statements that are prepared in accordance with the cash receipts and disbursements basis of accounting.

B. States that the financial statements are not intended to be presented in conformity with generally accepted accounting principles.

C. Does not make the minutes of the board of directors' meetings available to the auditor.

D. Asks the auditor to report on the balance sheet and not on the other basic financial statements.

Answer (C) is correct. *(CPA, adapted)*
REQUIRED: The basis for a scope limitation sufficient to preclude an unqualified opinion.
DISCUSSION: An auditor should ordinarily disclaim an opinion because of a client-imposed scope limitation (AU 508).
Answer (A) is incorrect because a special report on financial statements prepared on a comprehensive basis of accounting other than GAAP, for example, the cash basis, may express an unqualified opinion unless the statements contain a departure from that basis of accounting (AU 623). Answer (B) is incorrect because stating that the financial statements are not intended to be presented in conformity with GAAP does not constitute a scope limitation. Answer (D) is incorrect because a limitation on the reporting engagement is not a scope limitation if the auditor is able to apply necessary procedures and his/her access to information is not limited.

29. An auditor decides to express a qualified opinion on an entity's financial statements because a major inadequacy in its computerized accounting records prevents the auditor from applying necessary procedures. The opinion paragraph of the auditor's report should state that the qualification pertains to

A. A client-imposed scope limitation.

B. A departure from generally accepted auditing standards.

C. The possible effects on the financial statements.

D. Inadequate disclosure of necessary information.

Answer (C) is correct. *(CPA, adapted)*
REQUIRED: The wording in the opinion paragraph when the opinion is qualified because of a scope limitation.
DISCUSSION: AU 508 states that, when an auditor qualifies his/her opinion because of a scope limitation, the wording in the opinion paragraph should indicate that the qualification pertains to the possible effects on the financial statements and not to the scope limitation itself.
Answer (A) is incorrect because the qualification should not pertain to the scope limitation. Answer (B) is incorrect because the auditor apparently has followed GAAS in the conduct of the audit. Answer (D) is incorrect because the lack of sufficient competent evidence does not constitute inadequate disclosure.

30. In which of the following situations would an auditor ordinarily choose between expressing a qualified opinion or an adverse opinion?

A. The auditor did not observe the entity's physical inventory and is unable to become satisfied about its balance by other auditing procedures.

B. Conditions that cause the auditor to have substantial doubt about the entity's ability to continue as a going concern are inadequately disclosed.

C. There has been a change in accounting principles that has a material effect on the comparability of the entity's financial statements.

D. The auditor is unable to apply necessary procedures concerning an investor's share of an investee's earnings recognized in accordance with the equity method.

Answer (B) is correct. *(CPA, adapted)*
REQUIRED: The situation ordinarily involving a choice between a qualified opinion and an adverse opinion.
DISCUSSION: When the auditor concludes that there is substantial doubt about an entity's ability to continue as a going concern for a reasonable period of time, (s)he should include an explanatory paragraph (following the opinion paragraph) in the auditor's report to describe the uncertainty. By itself, this doubt does not require a departure from an unqualified opinion. However, if the entity's disclosures about the issue are inadequate, the departure from GAAP may result in a qualified or an adverse opinion.
Answer (A) is incorrect because a scope limitation requires the auditor to choose between a qualified opinion or a disclaimer of opinion. Answer (C) is incorrect because a justified change in accounting principle requires the auditor to add an explanatory paragraph to the standard report but not to depart from an unqualified opinion. Answer (D) is incorrect because a scope limitation requires the auditor to choose between a qualified opinion or a disclaimer of opinion.

31. An auditor did not observe a client's taking of beginning physical inventory and was unable to become satisfied about the inventory by means of other auditing procedures. Assuming no other scope limitations or reporting problems, the auditor could express an unqualified opinion on the current year's financial statements for

A. The balance sheet only.

B. The income statement only.

C. The income and retained earnings statements only.

D. All of the financial statements.

Answer (A) is correct. *(CPA, adapted)*
REQUIRED: The financial statement(s) for which the auditor can express an unqualified opinion.
DISCUSSION: A scope restriction, e.g., on the observation of inventories, may prevent the auditor from obtaining the evidence required to support an unqualified opinion. If (s)he cannot become satisfied regarding inventory, a qualified opinion or a disclaimer of opinion must be expressed, depending on the importance of the omitted procedure. Because the balance sheet reports only the ending inventory balance, the auditor can express an unqualified opinion on it alone, assuming (s)he is satisfied with the ending balance.

32. Under which of the following circumstances would a disclaimer of opinion not be appropriate?

A. The auditor is engaged after fiscal year-end and is unable to observe physical inventories or apply alternative procedures to verify their balances.

B. The auditor is unable to determine the amounts associated with fraud committed by the client's management.

C. The financial statements fail to contain adequate disclosure concerning related party transactions.

D. The client refuses to permit its attorney to furnish information requested in a letter of audit inquiry.

Answer (C) is correct. *(CPA, adapted)*
REQUIRED: The circumstances in which a disclaimer is inappropriate.
DISCUSSION: A disclaimer is inappropriate when the financial statements contain material departures from GAAP (AU 508). Inadequacy of the disclosures required by GAAP is such a departure (AU 431). Because SFAS 57 requires certain disclosures about related party transactions, the inadequacy of such disclosures is a basis for expressing a qualified or an adverse opinion.
Answer (A) is incorrect because a significant scope limitation, such as a failure to perform a generally accepted auditing procedure (observing inventory) and not becoming satisfied by alternative procedures, may result in a qualified opinion or in a disclaimer. Answer (B) is incorrect because a disclaimer or qualified opinion (and communication with the audit committee or the board) should be expressed in these circumstances if the auditor (1) is precluded from applying necessary procedures or (2) has applied extended procedures and is still unable to conclude whether fraud materially affects the statements (AU 316). Answer (D) is incorrect because a client-imposed scope limitation ordinarily results in a disclaimer.

33. When a publicly held company refuses to include in its audited financial statements any of the segment information that the auditor believes is required, the auditor should express a(n)

A. Unqualified opinion with a separate explanatory paragraph emphasizing the matter.

B. Qualified opinion because of inadequate disclosure.

C. Adverse opinion because of a significant uncertainty.

D. Disclaimer of opinion because of the significant scope limitation.

Answer (B) is correct. *(CPA, adapted)*
REQUIRED: The effect on the report of the client's failure to include required segment information.
DISCUSSION: According to an Interpretation of AU 326 that addresses segment disclosures, the auditor's standard report on financial statements prepared in conformity with GAAP implicitly applies to segment information included in those statements. The auditor should not refer to segment information unless the audit reveals a related material misstatement or omission or was subject to a scope limitation. Under AU 508, if material information is not included that the auditor believes should be disclosed, the auditor should modify the opinion for inadequate disclosure and include the omitted information in the audit report, if practicable.
Answer (A) is incorrect because inadequate disclosure requires an opinion modification if it is material in relation to the financial statements taken as a whole. Answer (C) is incorrect because a material uncertainty would typically result in an additional paragraph in the auditor's report but not an opinion modification. Answer (D) is incorrect because inadequate disclosure does not constitute a scope limitation.

34. When a client will not permit inquiry of outside legal counsel, the audit report will ordinarily contain a(n)

A. Disclaimer of opinion.

B. "Except for" qualified opinion.

C. "Subject to" qualified opinion.

D. Unqualified opinion with a separate explanatory paragraph.

Answer (A) is correct. *(CPA, adapted)*
REQUIRED: The report issued when a client will not permit inquiry of outside legal counsel.
DISCUSSION: The auditor may be unable to determine the legality of certain acts or the amounts associated with them because of an inability to gather sufficient competent evidential matter; e.g., the client may not permit inquiry of outside legal counsel. In these circumstances, the scope limitation requires a qualified opinion or a disclaimer, although a client-imposed scope limitation ordinarily results in a disclaimer.
Answer (B) is incorrect because a client-imposed scope limitation usually results in a disclaimer. Answer (C) is incorrect because the wording "subject to" is not acceptable in any report. Answer (D) is incorrect because a scope limitation results in a qualified opinion or disclaimer.

35. Green, CPA, was engaged to audit the financial statements of Essex Co. after its fiscal year had ended. The timing of Green's appointment as auditor and the start of field work made confirmation of accounts receivable by direct communication with the debtors ineffective. However, Green applied other procedures and was satisfied as to the reasonableness of the account balances. Green's auditor's report most likely contained a(n)

A. Unqualified opinion.

B. Unqualified opinion with an explanatory paragraph.

C. Qualified opinion because of a scope limitation.

D. Qualified opinion because of a departure from GAAS.

Answer (A) is correct. *(CPA, adapted)*
REQUIRED: The opinion expressed when an auditor becomes satisfied as to receivables by using alternate procedures.
DISCUSSION: Because the CPA is satisfied as to the amounts of receivables, no scope limitation exists. Accordingly, the report need not refer to the omission of the procedures or the use of alternative procedures, and the CPA may express an unqualified opinion (AU 508).
Answer (B) is incorrect because no basis is given for including an explanatory paragraph. Answer (C) is incorrect because no scope limitation exists. Answer (D) is incorrect because the auditor has not departed from GAAS. The presumption that confirmation requests will be made is overcome if the use of confirmations would be ineffective (AU 330).

36. In which of the following situations would an auditor ordinarily choose between expressing a qualified opinion or an adverse opinion?

A. The auditor did not observe the entity's physical inventory and is unable to become satisfied as to its balance by other auditing procedures.

B. The financial statements fail to disclose information that is required by generally accepted accounting principles.

C. The auditor is asked to report only on the entity's balance sheet and not on the other basic financial statements.

D. Events disclosed in the financial statements cause the auditor to have substantial doubt about the entity's ability to continue as a going concern.

Answer (B) is correct. *(CPA, adapted)*
REQUIRED: The situation in which an auditor would choose between expressing a qualified opinion or an adverse opinion.
DISCUSSION: Departures from GAAP, including inadequate disclosures, may result in either a qualified or an adverse opinion. The auditor must exercise judgment as to the materiality of the departure, weighing factors such as dollar magnitude, significance to the entity, pervasiveness of misstatements, and impact on the statements taken as a whole (AU 508). If the departure from GAAP is not sufficiently material to require an adverse opinion, the auditor should express a qualified opinion.
Answer (A) is incorrect because a scope limitation is not a basis for an adverse opinion. Answer (C) is incorrect because a limited reporting engagement may result in the expression of an unqualified opinion. Answer (D) is incorrect because substantial doubt about the entity's ability to continue as a going concern would normally result in the addition of a paragraph to the end of the report.

37. Which of the following phrases would an auditor most likely include in the auditor's report when expressing a qualified opinion because of inadequate disclosure?

A. Subject to the departure from generally accepted accounting principles, as described above.

B. With the foregoing explanation of these omitted disclosures.

C. Except for the omission of the information discussed in the preceding paragraph.

D. Does not present fairly in all material respects.

Answer (C) is correct. *(CPA, adapted)*
REQUIRED: The phrase included when the opinion is qualified because of inadequate disclosure.
DISCUSSION: A report qualified for inadequate disclosure includes a separate paragraph preceding the opinion paragraph. The opinion paragraph states, "In our opinion, except for the omission of information discussed in the preceding paragraph, the financial statements referred to above present fairly...."
Answer (A) is incorrect because a "subject to" opinion should not be expressed in any circumstance. Answer (B) is incorrect because the phrase "with the foregoing explanation" is not forceful enough, lacks clarity, and should not be used. Answer (D) is incorrect because the phrase "does not present fairly" indicates an adverse opinion.

38. If a publicly held company issues financial statements that purport to present its financial position and results of operations but omits the statement of cash flows, the auditor ordinarily will express a(n)

A. Disclaimer of opinion.

B. Qualified opinion.

C. Review report.

D. Unqualified opinion with a separate explanatory paragraph.

Answer (B) is correct. *(CPA, adapted)*
REQUIRED: The reporting responsibility when the statement of cash flows is omitted.
DISCUSSION: SFAS 95 requires presentation of a statement of cash flows if statements of financial position and income are issued. Thus, the omission of the cash flow statement is normally a basis for qualifying the opinion. If the statements fail to disclose information required by GAAP, the auditor should provide the information in the report, if practicable. However, the auditor is not required to prepare a basic financial statement. Accordingly, (s)he should qualify the opinion and explain the reason in a separate paragraph (AU 508).
Answer (A) is incorrect because a departure from GAAP is not a basis for a disclaimer. Answer (C) is incorrect because the auditor has been engaged to conduct an audit. Answer (D) is incorrect because inadequate disclosure is the basis for an opinion modification.

39. Harris, CPA, has been asked to audit and report on the balance sheet of Fox Co. but not on the statements of income, retained earnings, or cash flows. Harris will have access to all information underlying the basic financial statements. Under these circumstances, Harris may

A. Not accept the engagement because it would constitute a violation of the profession's ethical standards.

B. Not accept the engagement because it would be tantamount to rendering a piecemeal opinion.

C. Accept the engagement because such engagements merely involve limited reporting objectives.

D. Accept the engagement but should disclaim an opinion because of an inability to apply the procedures considered necessary.

Answer (C) is correct. *(CPA, adapted)*
REQUIRED: The action taken when a CPA has been asked to audit and report on the balance sheet only.
DISCUSSION: An auditor may report on one basic financial statement and not on the others. These engagements do not involve scope limitations per se, but rather limited reporting objectives.
Answer (A) is incorrect because the auditor may conduct an audit in accordance with GAAS. Answer (B) is incorrect because an auditor will express an opinion on the balance sheet; thus, it is not a piecemeal opinion. Answer (D) is incorrect because the audit is not subject to a scope limitation.

40. An auditor would express an unqualified opinion with an explanatory paragraph added to the auditor's report for

	An Unjustified Accounting Change	A Material Weakness in Internal Control
A.	Yes	Yes
B.	Yes	No
C.	No	Yes
D.	No	No

Answer (D) is correct. *(CPA, adapted)*
REQUIRED: The reason(s), if any, for adding an explanatory paragraph to the auditor's report.
DISCUSSION: An unjustified accounting change requires a modified opinion because of the departure from GAAP. Thus, an unqualified opinion with an explanatory paragraph would not be appropriate. A material weakness in internal control does not require an additional paragraph but should be considered in planning the audit.

41. Tread Corp. accounts for the effect of a material accounting change prospectively when the inclusion of the cumulative effect of the change is required in the current year. The auditor would choose between expressing a(n)

A. Qualified opinion and a disclaimer of opinion.

B. Disclaimer of opinion and an unqualified opinion with an explanatory paragraph.

C. Unqualified opinion with an explanatory paragraph and an adverse opinion.

D. Adverse opinion and a qualified opinion.

Answer (D) is correct. *(CPA, adapted)*
REQUIRED: The auditor's reporting options when a client fails to comply with GAAP.
DISCUSSION: APB 20 defines accounting changes and the GAAP for reporting an accounting change. When an audit client's financial statements contain a material departure from GAAP, the auditor should express a qualified or adverse opinion.
Answer (A) is incorrect because a disclaimer is expressed only when the audit scope is insufficient to form an opinion. Answer (B) is incorrect because a disclaimer or unqualified opinion would be inappropriate for a departure from GAAP. Answer (C) is incorrect because an unqualified opinion can be expressed only if the financial statements contain no material departure from GAAP.

42. When management does not provide reasonable justification for a change in accounting principle, and it presents comparative financial statements, the auditor should express a qualified opinion

A. Only in the year of the accounting principle change.

B. Each year that the financial statements initially reflecting the change are presented.

C. Each year until management changes back to the accounting principle formerly used.

D. Only if the change is to an accounting principle that is not generally accepted.

Answer (B) is correct. *(CPA, adapted)*
REQUIRED: The year(s) or circumstance in which an unjustified accounting change requires a qualified opinion.
DISCUSSION: If management has not provided reasonable justification for a change, the new principle is not generally accepted, or the method of accounting for the effect of the change does not conform with GAAP, the auditor should express a qualified or an adverse opinion in the report for the year of change and add (an) explanatory paragraph(s) preceding the opinion paragraph. Also, "the auditor should continue to express the exception with respect to the financial statements for the year of change as long as they are presented and reported on" (AU 508).

43. An auditor concludes that a client's illegal act, which has a material effect on the financial statements, has not been properly accounted for or disclosed. Depending on the materiality of the effect on the financial statements, the auditor should express either a(n)

A. Adverse opinion or a disclaimer of opinion.

B. Qualified opinion or an adverse opinion.

C. Disclaimer of opinion or an unqualified opinion with a separate explanatory paragraph.

D. Unqualified opinion with a separate explanatory paragraph or a qualified opinion.

Answer (B) is correct. *(CPA, adapted)*
REQUIRED: The opinion(s) expressed when an illegal act has not been properly accounted for or disclosed.
DISCUSSION: When an illegal act having a material effect on the financial statements has been detected but not properly reported, the auditor should insist upon revision of the financial statements. Failure to revise the statements precludes an unqualified opinion. Depending on the pervasiveness of the misstatement, the auditor should express either a qualified opinion or an adverse opinion.
Answer (A) is incorrect because a disclaimer of opinion is inappropriate. The auditor has concluded that the statements are materially misstated. Answer (C) is incorrect because a disclaimer of opinion is inappropriate. The auditor has concluded that the statements are materially misstated. Answer (D) is incorrect because an unqualified opinion is inappropriate for materially misstated financial statements.

44. An auditor may not express a qualified opinion when

A. A scope limitation prevents the auditor from completing an important audit procedure.

B. The auditor's report refers to the work of a specialist.

C. An accounting principle at variance with generally accepted accounting principles is used.

D. The auditor lacks independence with respect to the audited entity.

Answer (D) is correct. *(CPA, adapted)*
REQUIRED: The situation in which an auditor may not express a qualified opinion.
DISCUSSION: Conduct Rule 101 and the second general auditing standard require the auditor to be independent. If (s)he is not, any procedures (s)he might perform would not be in accordance with GAAS. Accordingly, (s)he is precluded from expressing an opinion when not independent and must disclaim an opinion and state that (s)he is not independent (AU 504).
Answer (A) is incorrect because a scope limitation is the basis for a qualified opinion or a disclaimer depending upon the auditor's assessment of the importance of the omitted procedure(s) (AU 508). Answer (B) is incorrect because the audit report may refer to and identify a specialist if the auditor departs from an unqualified opinion. Answer (C) is incorrect because a material departure from GAAP requires a qualified or an adverse opinion.

16.5 Adverse Opinions (AU 508)

45. In which of the following circumstances would an auditor be most likely to express an adverse opinion?

A. Information comes to the auditor's attention that raises substantial doubt about the entity's ability to continue as a going concern.

B. The chief executive officer refuses the auditor access to minutes of board of directors' meetings.

C. Tests of controls show that the entity's internal control is so poor that it cannot be relied upon.

D. The financial statements are not in conformity with the FASB Statements regarding the capitalization of leases.

Answer (D) is correct. *(CPA, adapted)*
REQUIRED: The basis for an adverse opinion.
DISCUSSION: An adverse opinion is expressed "when, in the auditor's judgment, the financial statements taken as a whole are not presented fairly in conformity with GAAP." SFASs are in the highest GAAP category.
Answer (A) is incorrect because substantial doubt about the entity's ability to continue as a going concern requires an explanatory paragraph following the opinion paragraph, not an adverse opinion. Answer (B) is incorrect because a client-imposed scope limitation ordinarily results in a disclaimer of opinion. Answer (C) is incorrect because assessing control risk at the maximum may affect the nature, timing, and extent of substantive tests but is not a basis for an adverse opinion. Ineffective internal control does not, by itself, indicate that the financial statements are not fairly presented.

46. An auditor's report includes the following statement: "The financial statements do not present fairly the financial position, results of operations, or cash flows in conformity with U.S. generally accepted accounting principles." This auditor's report was most likely issued in connection with financial statements that are

A. Inconsistent.

B. Based on prospective financial information.

C. Misleading.

D. Affected by a material uncertainty.

Answer (C) is correct. *(CPA, adapted)*
REQUIRED: The nature of the financial statements on which the quoted report was issued.
DISCUSSION: The language quoted states an adverse opinion. The essence of an adverse opinion is that the statements reported on, taken as a whole, are not fairly presented in accordance with GAAP (AU 508). The financial statements should be based on principles having general acceptance that are appropriate in the circumstances. If financial statements fail to meet the standards, they are misleading.
Answer (A) is incorrect because an inconsistency, by itself, results in no modification of the standard opinion paragraph. Answer (B) is incorrect because the accountant's standard examination report on a financial forecast or projection refers to guidelines for the presentation of a forecast (or projection) established by the AICPA, not to GAAP (AT 301). Answer (D) is incorrect because a material uncertainty, if properly disclosed, does not require modification of the report.

47. An auditor should disclose the substantive reasons for expressing an adverse opinion in an explanatory paragraph

A. Preceding the scope paragraph.

B. Preceding the opinion paragraph.

C. Following the opinion paragraph.

D. Within the notes to the financial statements.

Answer (B) is correct. *(CPA, adapted)*
REQUIRED: The proper reporting of the substantive reasons for expressing an adverse opinion in an explanatory paragraph.
DISCUSSION: When an adverse opinion is expressed, the opinion paragraph should include a direct reference to a separate paragraph(s) that discloses the basis for the adverse opinion. This paragraph should precede the opinion paragraph and state (1) all the substantive reasons for the adverse opinion and (2) the principal effects of the subject matter of the adverse opinion, if practicable (AU 508).

48. When an auditor expresses an adverse opinion, the opinion paragraph should include

A. The principal effects of the departure from generally accepted accounting principles.

B. A direct reference to a separate paragraph disclosing the basis for the opinion.

C. The substantive reasons for the financial statements being misleading.

D. A description of the uncertainty or scope limitation that prevents an unqualified opinion.

Answer (B) is correct. *(CPA, adapted)*
REQUIRED: The matter included in the opinion paragraph when an adverse opinion is expressed.
DISCUSSION: When an adverse opinion is expressed, the opinion paragraph should include a direct reference to a separate paragraph that discloses the basis for the adverse opinion. This paragraph should precede the opinion paragraph and state (1) all the substantive reasons for the adverse opinion and (2) the principal effects of the subject matter of the adverse opinion, if practicable (AU 508).
Answer (A) is incorrect because the principal effects of the subject matter of the adverse opinion, if practicable, should be stated in the explanatory paragraph. Answer (C) is incorrect because all the substantive reasons for the adverse opinion should be stated in the explanatory paragraph. Answer (D) is incorrect because an adverse opinion is not expressed as a result of an uncertainty or scope limitation.

16.6 Disclaimers of Opinion (AU 508)

49. Under which of the following circumstances would a disclaimer of opinion not be appropriate?

A. The auditor is unable to determine the amounts associated with an employee fraud scheme.

B. Management does not provide reasonable justification for a change in accounting principles.

C. The client refuses to permit the auditor to confirm certain accounts receivable or apply alternative procedures to verify their balances.

D. The chief executive officer is unwilling to sign the management representation letter.

Answer (B) is correct. *(CPA, adapted)*
REQUIRED: The circumstances under which a disclaimer of opinion would be inappropriate.
DISCUSSION: When management does not provide reasonable justification for a change in accounting principles, a qualified or adverse opinion should be expressed. This failure is a departure from generally accepted accounting principles.
Answer (A) is incorrect because, when the auditor is unable to determine amounts associated with an employee fraud scheme, the standards suggest that a disclaimer is appropriate. Answer (C) is incorrect because refusal to permit access to evidence results in scope limitations that necessitate a disclaimer. Answer (D) is incorrect because unwillingness to sign a management representation letter results in scope limitations that necessitate a disclaimer.

50. When disclaiming an opinion because of a client-imposed scope limitation, an auditor should indicate in a separate paragraph why the audit did not comply with generally accepted auditing standards. The auditor should also omit the

	Scope Paragraph	Opinion Paragraph
A.	No	Yes
B.	Yes	Yes
C.	No	No
D.	Yes	No

Answer (D) is correct. *(CPA, adapted)*
REQUIRED: The paragraph(s), if any, omitted from a disclaimer.
DISCUSSION: When a scope limitation exists, the auditor may express a qualified opinion or disclaim an opinion, depending on the materiality of the scope limitation. If an opinion is disclaimed, the introductory and opinion paragraphs are modified and the scope paragraph is omitted.

51. When an independent CPA is associated with the financial statements of a publicly held entity but has not audited or reviewed such statements, the appropriate form of report to be issued must include a(n)

A. Regulation S-X exemption.

B. Report on pro forma financial statements.

C. Unaudited association report.

D. Disclaimer of opinion.

Answer (D) is correct. *(CPA, adapted)*
REQUIRED: The form of report when a CPA is associated with the financial statements that have not been audited or reviewed.
DISCUSSION: A disclaimer should be attached to the financial statements of a public company when an accountant is associated with those statements and has not audited or reviewed them. Association means that the accountant has consented to the use of his/her name in a report, document, or written communication containing the statements (AU 504).
Answer (A) is incorrect because Regulation S-X describes the content of SEC registration statements. Answer (B) is incorrect because a report on pro forma financial statements may be issued in the context of an examination or review of those statements. Answer (C) is incorrect because accountants do not issue unaudited association reports.

52. When an independent CPA assists in preparing the financial statements of a publicly held entity, but has not audited or reviewed them, the CPA should issue a disclaimer of opinion. In such situations, the CPA has no responsibility to apply any procedures beyond

A. Ascertaining whether the financial statements are in conformity with GAAP.

B. Determining whether management has elected to omit substantially all required disclosures.

C. Documenting that internal control is not being relied on.

D. Reading the financial statements for obvious material misstatements.

Answer (D) is correct. *(CPA, adapted)*
REQUIRED: The procedure applied by a CPA to public-company financial statements that (s)he has assisted in preparing.
DISCUSSION: AU 504 states that the accountant has no responsibility to apply any procedures beyond reading the financial statements for obvious material misstatements. Any procedures applied should not be described.
Answer (A) is incorrect because an audit is conducted to ascertain whether the financial statements are in conformity with GAAP. Answer (B) is incorrect because the disclaimer is modified if the accountant concludes on the basis of facts known to him/her that the unaudited financial statements do not conform with GAAP. Lack of adequate disclosure is a departure from GAAP. Answer (C) is incorrect because the CPA need not consider internal control or assess control risk and has no responsibility for documentation related to these activities.

53. Due to the scope limitation, an auditor disclaimed an opinion on the financial statements taken as a whole, but the auditor's report included a statement that the current asset portion of the entity's balance sheet was fairly stated. The inclusion of this statement is

A. Not appropriate because it may tend to overshadow the auditor's disclaimer of opinion.

B. Not appropriate because the auditor is prohibited from reporting on only one basic financial statement.

C. Appropriate provided the auditor's scope paragraph adequately describes the scope limitation.

D. Appropriate provided the statement is in a separate paragraph preceding the disclaimer of opinion paragraph.

Answer (A) is correct. *(CPA, adapted)*
REQUIRED: The suitability of a statement in an auditor's disclaimer concerning whether an element was stated fairly.
DISCUSSION: "Piecemeal opinions (expressions of an opinion as to certain identified items in a financial statement) should not be expressed when the auditor has disclaimed an opinion or has expressed an adverse opinion on the financial statements taken as a whole because piecemeal opinions tend to overshadow or contradict a disclaimer of opinion or an adverse opinion" (AU 508).
Answer (B) is incorrect because the auditor can report on one basic financial statement and not on the others. Such a limited reporting engagement is acceptable. Answer (C) is incorrect because a piecemeal opinion is inappropriate in this circumstance. Answer (D) is incorrect because a piecemeal opinion is inappropriate in this circumstance.

54. Park, CPA, was engaged to audit the financial statements of Tech Co., a new client, for the year ended December 31, year 1. Park obtained sufficient audit evidence for all of Tech's financial statement items except Tech's opening inventory. Due to inadequate financial records, Park could not verify Tech's January 1, year 1 inventory balances. Park's opinion on Tech's year 1 financial statements most likely will be

	Balance Sheet	Income Statement
A.	Disclaimer	Disclaimer
B.	Unqualified	Disclaimer
C.	Disclaimer	Adverse
D.	Unqualified	Adverse

Answer (B) is correct. *(CPA, adapted)*
REQUIRED: The appropriate opinion on each financial statement when the auditor cannot verify opening inventory.
DISCUSSION: Because the balance sheet presents information as of a specific moment in time, the auditor should be able to become satisfied regarding the balances presented at year-end. However, beginning inventory enters materially into the determination of the statements of income, retained earnings, and cash flows. Thus, the auditor will probably not be able to form an opinion as to the fairness of these statements and should issue a disclaimer on them.

55. Restrictions imposed by a retail entity that is a new client prevent an auditor from observing any physical inventories. These inventories account for 40% of the entity's assets. Alternative auditing procedures cannot be applied due to the nature of the entity's records. Under these circumstances, the auditor should express a(n)

A. Disclaimer of opinion.

B. Qualified opinion.

C. Adverse opinion.

D. Unqualified opinion with an explanatory paragraph.

Answer (A) is correct.
REQUIRED: The appropriate report when inventory cannot be observed as a result of client restrictions.
DISCUSSION: A scope limitation, such as an inability to observe inventories, a mandatory procedure under GAAS, requires the auditor to determine whether (s)he has examined sufficient competent evidence to permit expression of an unqualified opinion or a qualified opinion. However, "when restrictions that significantly limit the scope of the audit are imposed by the client, ordinarily the auditor should disclaim an opinion on the financial statements" (AU 508). This client-imposed restriction is significant because it applies to 40% of the assets, an important element of the financial statements.
Answer (B) is incorrect because, ordinarily, the auditor disclaims an opinion when a client-imposed scope restriction is significant. Answer (C) is incorrect because an adverse opinion is expressed when the financial statements taken as a whole are not presented fairly in conformity with GAAP. Answer (D) is incorrect because an unqualified opinion cannot be expressed when a client-imposed scope limitation is significant.

16.7 PRACTICE SIMULATION

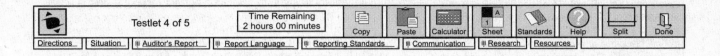

1. Directions

In the following simulation, you will be asked to complete various tasks related to standard, qualified, adverse, and disclaimer reports. The simulation will provide you with all of the information necessary to do your work. For full credit, be sure to view and complete all work tabs.

Resources may be available to you under the tab marked RESOURCES. You may want to review the resources before beginning the simulation.

2. Situation

Your firm has many clients and many audit reporting obligations. The audits of most clients result in a standard report. However, the audits of certain clients result in report modifications. The following draft represents the standard report that you contemplate for your non-public clients.

Independent Auditor's Report

To: The Board of Directors

We have (1) the accompanying balance sheet of X Company as of December 31, year 1, and the (2) statements of income, retained earnings, and cash flows for the year then ended. These financial statements are the responsibility of (3). Our responsibility is to express an opinion on these financial statements based on our audit.

We conducted our audit in accordance with U.S. (4). Those standards require that we plan and perform the audit to obtain (5) assurance about whether the financial statements are (6) misstatement. An audit includes examining, on a (7) basis, evidence supporting the amounts and disclosures in the financial statements. An audit also includes (8) the accounting principles used and significant estimates made by (9), as well as evaluating the overall financial statement presentation. We believe that our audit provides (10) basis for our opinion.

In our opinion, the financial statements referred to above present fairly, (11) the financial position of X Company as of its operations and its cash flows for the year then ended in conformity with U.S. (12).

Signature
Date

3. Auditor's Report

This question will be presented in a check-the-box format that requires you to select the correct response from a given list.

Check the appropriate box for each item. Each of the following corresponds to a number in the Independent Auditor's Report given in the situation tab. Check which is the appropriate letter indicating the word or phrase that should be included in the standard report.

Correct Word or Phrase	A	B
1. A) Examined		
B) Audited		
2. A) Related		
B) Accompanying		
3. A) The auditor		
B) The company's management		
4. A) Generally accepted auditing standards		
B) Generally accepted accounting principles		
5. A) Reasonable		
B) Absolute		
6. A) Free of		
B) Free of material		
7. A) Sample		
B) Test		
8. A) Examining		
B) Assessing		
9. A) Management		
B) The auditor		
10. A) An absolute		
B) A reasonable		
11. A) In all respects		
B) In all material respects		
12. A) Generally accepted auditing standards		
B) Generally accepted accounting principles		

4. Report Language

This question has a matching format that requires you to select the correct response from a drop-down list. Write the answer in the column next to the item or question. Each choice may be used once, more than once, or not at all.

Each of the following is a phrase from a paragraph taken from an auditor's report. Assume that, except for the information indicated in the phrase, the report would have been a standard audit report. Match the statement with the most likely report type.

Phrase	Answer
1. In our opinion, except for the omission of the statement of cash flows ...	
2. ... the scope of our work was not sufficient to enable us ...	
3. As discussed in Note 12, the Company changed its method of computing depreciation.	
4. We are not independent with respect to XYZ company ...	
5. ... except for the effects of not capitalizing certain lease obligations as discussed in the preceding paragraph ...	
6. ... based on our audit and the report of other auditors ...	
7. ... for the year then ended were not audited by us ...	
8. ... raises substantial doubt about its ability to continue as a going concern.	
9. ... presents fairly, in all material respects ...	
10. ... In our opinion, except for the effects of such adjustments, if any, ...	

Choices
A) Unqualified
B) Qualified
C) Adverse
D) Disclaimer

5. Reporting Standards

This question has a fill-in response format. Select the correct response from the phrases given. A phrase may be used only once.

Three of the reporting standards relate to the issues of application of GAAP, consistency of GAAP, and disclosure. Below is a list of phrases from the three standards.

Phrases
A) in the financial statements
B) in relation to the preceding period
C) those circumstances
D) whether the financial statements are presented
E) are to be regarded as reasonably adequate
F) Identify those circumstances in which such principles
G) observed in the current period
H) in accordance with GAAP
I) unless otherwise stated in the report
J) have not been consistently

First standard of reporting - application of GAAP
The report shall state [1] _____ [2] _____

Second standard of reporting - consistency of GAAP
The report shall [3] _____ [4] _____ [5] _____ [6] _____

Third standard of reporting - disclosing
Informative disclosures [7] _____ [8] _____ [9] _____

6. Communication

Your client suggested that you date your audit report as of the date of the financial statements and address it to the client. Explain in a memo to your client the proper dating and addressing of the report and their significance. Also, briefly discuss the implications of the date of a reissued report. Type your communication in your word processor program and print out the copy in a memorandum style format.

REMINDER: Your response will be graded for both technical content and writing skills. You should demonstrate your ability to develop, organize, and express your ideas. Do not convey information in the form of a table, bullet point list, or other abbreviated presentation.

> To: Client
> From: CPA
> Subject: Addressing and dating the report

7. Research

Use the research materials available to you to find the answers to the following question in the AICPA Professional Standards. Print the appropriate citation in its entirety from the source you choose. Use only one source. This is a copy-and-paste item.

Cite the appropriate language in the professional standards that explains when piecemeal opinions should not be expressed.

Unofficial Answers

3. Quality Control (12 Gradable Items)

1. <u>B)</u> The standard report uses the term audited.
2. <u>A)</u> The statements of income, retained earnings, and cash flows are related to the balance sheet of the entity.
3. <u>B)</u> The financial statements are the responsibility of management.
4. <u>A)</u> The audit is conducted in accordance with U.S. GAAS.
5. <u>A)</u> Reasonable, not absolute, assurance should be obtained by the auditor.
6. <u>B)</u> The financial statements are expected to be free of material misstatement. The auditor need not be concerned with immaterial matters.
7. <u>B)</u> Audit evidence is examined on a test basis.
8. <u>B)</u> The accounting principles used are assessed to determine that they are appropriate in the circumstances.
9. <u>A)</u> Management is responsible for the estimates and other assertions in the financial statements.
10. <u>B)</u> The audit provides a reasonable basis for the opinion rendered. An auditor is seldom convinced beyond all doubt with respect to all aspects of the statements audited.
11. <u>B)</u> The opinion that the financial statements are presented fairly is subject to the limitation of materiality.
12. <u>B)</u> The financial statements should be in conformity with U.S. GAAP.

4. Report Language (10 Gradable Items)

1. <u>B) Qualified</u>
2. <u>D) Disclaimer</u>
3. <u>A) Unqualified</u>
4. <u>D) Disclaimer</u>
5. <u>B) Qualified</u>
6. <u>A) Unqualified</u>
7. <u>D) Disclaimer</u>
8. <u>A) Unqualified</u>
9. <u>A) Unqualified</u>
10. <u>B) Qualified</u>

5. Reporting Standards (9 Gradable Items)

First standard of reporting - application of GAAP
The report shall state [1] <u>D) whether the financial statements are presented</u> [2] <u>H) in accordance with GAAP</u>.

Second standard of reporting - consistency of GAAP
The report shall [3] <u>F) identify those circumstances in which such principles</u> [4] <u>J) have not been consistently</u> [5] <u>G) observed in the current period</u> [6] <u>B) in relation to the preceding period</u>.

Third standard of reporting - disclosing
Informative disclosures [7] <u>A) in the financial statements</u> [8] <u>E) are to be regarded as reasonably adequate</u> [9] <u>I) unless otherwise stated in the report</u>.

6. Communication (5 Gradable Items; For grading instructions, please refer to page 11.)

To: Client
From: CPA
Subject: Addressing and dating the report

The auditor's report should be addressed to the company whose statements are being audited or to its board of directors or stockholders. If the client is an unincorporated entity, the report should be addressed as circumstances dictate, e.g., to the partners or the proprietor.

If an auditor is retained to audit the financial statements of a company that is not his/her client, the report customarily is addressed to the client and not to the board of directors or stockholders of the company whose financial statements are being audited.

The date of the audit report is generally the date of completion of field work. This date is important because the user has a right to expect that the auditor has performed certain procedures to detect subsequent events that would materially affect the financial statements through the date of the report. The auditor is ordinarily not responsible for making inquiries or carrying out any audit procedures after the date of the report.

When a subsequent event disclosed in the financial statements occurs after the completion of field work but before the issuance of the related financial statements, the auditor may use dual-dating. (S)he may date the report as of the completion of field work except for the matters affected by the subsequent event, which would be assigned the appropriate later date. In that case, the auditor's responsibility for events after the completion of field work would be limited to the specific event. If the auditor is willing to accept responsibility to the later date and accordingly extends subsequent events procedures to that date, the auditor may choose the later date as the date for the entire report.

Under AU 530, use of the original date in a reissued report removes any implication that records, transactions, or events after such date have been audited or reviewed. The auditor will thus have no responsibility to carry out procedures relating to the period between original issuance and reissuance. An exception exists for filings under the Securities Act of 1933.

The independent accountant whose report is included in a registration statement has a statutory responsibility that is determined in light of the circumstances on the effective date of the registration statement. To sustain the burden of proof that (s)he has made a "reasonable investigation," an auditor should extend his/her subsequent events procedures from the date of the report up to the effective date of the registration statement.

7. Research (6 Gradable Items)

AU Section 508 -- *Reports on Auditing Financial Statements*

Piecemeal Opinions

.64   Piecemeal opinions (expressions of opinion as to certain identified items in financial statements) should not be expressed when the auditor has disclaimed an opinion or has expressed an adverse opinion on the financial statements *taken as a whole* because piecemeal opinions tend to overshadow or contradict a disclaimer of opinion or an adverse opinion.

Scoring Schedule:

	Correct Responses		Gradable Items		Weights		
Tab 3	_____	÷	12	×	20%	=	_____
Tab 4	_____	÷	10	×	20%	=	_____
Tab 5	_____	÷	9	×	20%	=	_____
Tab 6	_____	÷	5	×	30%	=	_____
Tab 7	_____	÷	6	×	10%	=	_____
							(Your Score)

Use Gleim's **CPA Review Online** to practice more simulations in a realistic environment.

STUDY UNIT SEVENTEEN
REPORTS -- OTHER MODIFICATIONS

(12 pages of outline)

17.1   Part of Audit Performed by Other Independent Auditors (AU 543) 527
17.2   Consistency of Application of GAAP (AU 420) 530
17.3   Uncertainties and Going Concern (AU 508 and AU 341) 533
17.4   Comparative Financial Statements (AU 508) 534
17.5   Emphasis of a Matter (AU 508) 538
17.6   Practice Simulation 551

This study unit covers explanatory language added to the auditor's report. These modifications normally do not affect the auditor's opinion on the financial statements. They permit the users of the financial statements and readers of the auditor's report to better understand the responsibility assumed by the auditor. They also provide information about the client's financial statements that the auditor considers important. The following summarizes these modifications:

1.   Auditor's opinion is based in part on the report of another auditor -- Modify all three paragraphs, but do not add an additional paragraph.

2.   A material accounting change affects consistency -- Add an additional paragraph.

3.   Substantial doubt exists about the entity's ability to continue as a going concern -- Add an additional paragraph.

4.   The auditor changes the opinion for a prior period when reporting on current statements in comparative form -- Add an additional paragraph.

5.   Predecessor auditor's report for a prior period is not presented when reporting on current financial statements in comparative form -- Add sentence to introductory paragraph.

6.   A matter needs to be emphasized -- Add an additional paragraph.

17.1 PART OF AUDIT PERFORMED BY OTHER INDEPENDENT AUDITORS (AU 543)

1.   The independent auditor must make professional judgments about whether (s)he may serve as principal auditor and use the work and reports of other independent auditors who have audited the financial statements of one or more subsidiaries, divisions, branches, components, or investments included in the financial statements presented.

2.   **Principal Auditor's Course of Action**

   a.   When other auditors have performed a significant part of the audit, the auditor must decide whether his/her own participation is sufficient to justify serving as the principal auditor. The auditor should consider

      1)   The materiality of the portion of the financial statements (s)he has audited
      2)   His/her knowledge of the overall financial statements
      3)   The importance of the components (s)he audited

b.   If the auditor decides to serve as the principal auditor, (s)he must then decide whether to refer to the audit of the other auditor.

1)   If the principal auditor assumes responsibility for the other's work, no reference should be made.

2)   If responsibility is not assumed, the report should refer to the audit of the other auditor and should indicate clearly the **division of responsibility**.

3)   The other auditor remains responsible for his/her own work and report.

3.   **Decision Not to Make Reference**. If the principal auditor becomes satisfied as to the independence and professional reputation of the other auditor and the audit performed, (s)he may be able to express an opinion without referring to the other auditor. In that case, stating that part of the audit was made by another auditor might cause misinterpretation of the responsibility assumed.

a.   The principal auditor may take this position when the other auditor is an associated or correspondent firm whose work is acceptable, the other auditor was retained by the principal auditor who guided and controlled the work, the principal auditor becomes satisfied as to the audit and work of the other auditor, and the portion of the statements audited by the other auditor is not material.

b.   In an **audit of a public company under AS 3**, the principal auditor must, before the report release date, obtain, review, and retain an engagement completion document and other documents from the other auditor. For example, these other documents should include sufficient information about findings that contradict audit conclusions, a list of significant fraud risk factors and the auditor's response, a schedule of audit adjustments, significant deficiencies and weaknesses in internal control, and reconciling information about amounts audited by the other auditor.

4.   **Decision to Make Reference**

a.   The principal auditor may decide to refer to the audit of the other auditor because

1)   It may be impracticable for the principal auditor to review the other's work or perform the other procedures necessary to become satisfied about the other's audit.

2)   The financial statements of a component audited by another auditor may be material in relation to the total.

b.   When the audit of the other auditor is referred to, the report should indicate clearly, in the introductory, scope, and opinion paragraphs, the division of responsibility. The report also should disclose the magnitude of the audit of the other auditor, e.g., in dollar amounts or percentages of total assets, total revenues, or other appropriate criteria, whichever provides the clearest disclosure.

c.   The other auditor may be named if (s)he gives express permission and provided his/her report is presented.

d.   Reference to the other auditor is not a qualification of the opinion.

e. The following is an example of a report that refers to another auditor:

Audit Report with Reference to Other Auditors

Independent Auditor's Report

To: <-------------- Board of Directors or Shareholders

We have audited the consolidated balance sheet of X Company and subsidiaries as of December 31, year 2, and the related consolidated statements of income, retained earnings and cash flows for the year then ended. These financial statements are the responsibility of the Company's management. Our responsibility is to express an opinion on these financial statements based on our audits. **We did not audit the financial statements of B Company, a wholly owned subsidiary, which statements reflect total assets and revenues constituting 20% and 22%, respectively, of the related consolidated totals. Those statements were audited by other auditors whose report has been furnished to us, and our opinion, insofar as it relates to the amounts included for B Company, is based solely on the report of the other auditors.**

We conducted our audit . . . We believe the audit **and the report of the other auditors** provides a reasonable basis for our opinion.

In our opinion, based on our audit **and the report of the other auditors**, the consolidated financial statements referred to above present fairly, in all material respects, the financial position of X Company as of [at] December 31, year 2, and the results of its operations and its cash flows for the year then ended in conformity with accounting principles generally accepted in the United States of America.

Signed <------------ May be signed, typed, or printed

Date <------------ Date of completion of field work

---

5. **Procedures Applicable to Both Methods of Reporting**

a. Whether or not the principal auditor refers to the audit of the other auditor, (s)he should inquire about the professional reputation and independence of the other auditor and coordinate their activities.

b. Procedures included are

1) Making inquiries as to the professional reputation and standing of the other auditor to the AICPA, state societies, other practitioners, bankers, etc., unless known to the principal auditor

2) Obtaining a representation from the other auditor that (s)he is independent

3) Communicating with the other auditor to determine that (s)he is aware

a) Of reliance upon, and possible reference to, his/her report

b) Of applicable GAAP, GAAS, and regulatory requirements

c) Of the need for a review of uniformity of accounting practices and the elimination of intercompany transactions and balances

c. If the principal auditor concludes that (s)he can neither assume responsibility for the work of the other auditor nor refer to the audit of the other auditor, (s)he should qualify the opinion or disclaim an opinion.

1) The reasons should be stated, and the magnitude of the portion of the financial statements to which the qualification relates should be disclosed (i.e., a scope limitation exists).

6. **Additional Procedures under Decision Not to Make Reference**. When the principal auditor decides not to refer to the audit of the other auditor, (s)he should consider the following procedures:

a. Visit the other auditor and discuss the audit procedures followed and the results.

b. Review the audit programs and working papers of the other auditor.

c. Make supplemental tests of accounts.

7. **Investments.** An auditor who uses another auditor's report to report on an investor's equity in underlying net assets and its share of earnings or losses and other transactions of the investee is in the position of a principal auditor using the work and reports of other auditors.

8. **Departure of Other Auditor's Report from Standard Report.** If the report of the other auditor is other than a standard report, the principal auditor should decide whether the reason for the departure requires recognition in his/her own report.

    a. If the reason for the departure is not material and the other auditor's report is not presented, the principal auditor need not refer in the report to such departure.

9. Stop and review! You have completed the outline for this subunit. Study multiple-choice questions 1 through 7 beginning on page 539.

17.2 CONSISTENCY OF APPLICATION OF GAAP (AU 420)

1. **Consistency versus Comparability**

    a. Comparability is a broad term relating to whether one set of financial statements is comparable with another, e.g., from one period to the next or within each period. Many matters affect comparability, such as accounting changes, errors, changes in classification, and events or transactions substantially different from those previously accounted for.

    b. Consistency is a technical term that relates to the expectation of consistent application of accounting principles from one period to the next. The second standard of reporting is applicable: *The report shall identify those circumstances in which such principles have not been consistently observed in the current period in relation to the preceding period.*

    c. A change in an accounting principle or in the method of its application having a material effect on comparability of the financial statements is a departure from the consistency standard. It is described in an explanatory paragraph (following the opinion paragraph) stating the nature of the change and referring to a financial statement note that discusses the change in detail.

        1) The auditor is deemed to concur with the change unless (s)he takes exception to it in expressing a qualified opinion.

        2) A lack of consistency, by itself, is not a basis for expressing a qualified or an adverse opinion or disclaiming an opinion.

    d. The following is an explanatory paragraph (following the opinion paragraph) for a change in principle:

    Paragraph Added to Audit Report for a Change in Principle

    As discussed in Note X to the financial statements, the Company changed its method of computing depreciation in year 3.

    e. An explanatory paragraph of this kind is required to be included as long as the year of the change is presented and reported on.

        1) An exception is a change in principle not requiring a cumulative effect adjustment, such as from FIFO to LIFO, that is made at the beginning of the earliest year presented and reported on. In such a case, the principle has been applied consistently in the comparative statements, and the paragraph may be subsequently omitted.

            a) If the change is accounted for by retroactive restatement, the explanatory paragraph is required only in the year of the change. All periods presented will be comparable in subsequent years.

    f.   In first year audits, the auditor should extend procedures to gather evidence about consistency between the current and the preceding year. Given consistency, no report modification is necessary.

2.   **Accounting Issues Related to Comparability and Consistency**

    a.   In general, accounting standards require preparers of financial statements to make them as useful as possible, thereby sometimes necessitating changes in prior-period statements presented comparatively.

    b.   **APB 20**, *Accounting Changes*, provides guidance on accounting for changes in accounting principles. Other SFASs are also pertinent. Most changes require a cumulative-effect adjustment that flows through the income statement.

       1) How to account for normal APB 20 changes

          a) Report effect on net income of the year of change.

          b) Report cumulative effect on all prior years (catch-up adjustment).

          c) Report per-share cumulative effect of the change on the face of the income statement or in the notes.

          d) Report pro forma effects of retroactive application on face of income statement.

          e) Adequately disclose the change in the notes.

    c.   However, some changes are pervasive and require the prior period's financial statements to be restated to reflect a change made in the current year when the statements are presented in comparative form.

       1) Sample changes requiring restatement of prior period's financial statements

          a) Change from LIFO to any other cost flow method

          b) Change in accounting for long-term construction contracts

          c) Change to or from the full cost method in the extractive industries

       2) How to account for these exceptions

          a) In comparative statements, adjust net income, its components, retained earnings, and other affected balances to reflect the change.

          b) In single-period statements, report net effect as an adjustment directly to the beginning balance of retained earnings.

          c) Adequately disclose the change in the notes.

d.   The table below describes various changes and how they are reflected in the current and prior years' statements. All shaded items are changes in principle requiring an additional consistency paragraph at the end of the report. The bottom portion includes matters that affect comparability and have accounting implications but do not require modification of the report **unless the accounting departs from GAAP**. Disclosure is usually by notes to the financial statements.

	Factor	Current Year's Financial Statements	Prior Years' Financial Statements
A D D P A R A G R A P H	1. Change in Principle • Typical APB 20 GAAP to GAAP • Exceptions to APB 20 • Non GAAP to GAAP (Correction of Error in Principle)	Report Catch-up Effects and Disclosure Prior-Period Adjustment and Disclosure Prior-Period Adjustment and Disclosure	Do Not Restate Restate Restate
	2. Change in Entity Not from a Transaction or Event (e.g., presenting consolidated statements instead of individual company statements)	Prior-Period Adjustment and Disclosure	Restate
	3. Change in Principle Inseparable from Change in Estimate	Disclosure (Accounted for as a Change in Estimate)	Do Not Restate
	4. Changes in Presentation of Cash Flows (Items Treated as Cash Equivalents)	Disclosure	Restate
D O N O T A D D P A R A G R A P H	1. Change in Accounting Estimate	Disclosure	Do Not Restate
	2. Correction of Error Not Involving Principle	Prior-Period Adjustment and Disclosure	Restate
	3. Change in Classification	Disclosure	Restatement Permitted
	4. Different (New) Transactions	None	Not Applicable
	5. Changes Not Material to Current but May Affect Future Financial Statements	None	Not Applicable
	6. Change in Entity from a Transaction or Event (e.g., a purchase)	Prior-Period Adjustment and Disclosure	Restate

3.   Stop and review! You have completed the outline for this subunit. Study multiple-choice questions 8 through 16 beginning on page 541.

17.3 UNCERTAINTIES AND GOING CONCERN (AU 508 AND AU 341)

1. A matter involving an uncertainty is expected to be resolved at a future date. At that time, conclusive evidence about its outcome is expected to become available. If the auditor concludes that sufficient evidence supports management's assertions about the nature of a matter involving an uncertainty, an unmodified report is ordinarily appropriate. (However, the auditor always has the option of adding a paragraph to emphasize a matter.)

   a. The auditor must distinguish between situations involving uncertainties that require no report modification and those that require a departure from an unqualified opinion because of a scope limitation or departure from GAAP. An uncertainty, by itself, does not require such a departure.

      1) **Uncertainties and scope limitations.** A scope limitation occurs when sufficient evidence about management's assertions regarding the uncertainty does or did exist but was unavailable, for example, because of record retention policies or a client-imposed restriction.

         a) Although sufficient evidence about the outcome of an uncertainty cannot be expected to exist at the time of the audit, management must analyze relevant existing conditions and their effects, and the auditor must assess whether the evidence is sufficient to support the analysis. A scope limitation arises when the auditor is prevented from making that assessment and results in a qualification or disclaimer.

      2) **Uncertainties and departures from GAAP.** Departures from GAAP result in a qualified or an adverse opinion when

         a) Disclosure is inadequate.

         b) Inappropriate accounting principles or unreasonable estimates cause the statements to be materially misstated.

2. The auditor's consideration of an entity's ability to continue as a going concern was described in Study Unit 14. If the auditor concludes that substantial doubt exists, an additional paragraph should be added to the end of the auditor's standard report.

   a. But the auditor is not precluded from disclaiming an opinion.

   b. The auditor's explanatory paragraph should include the terms "substantial doubt" and "going concern."

   c. In the explanatory paragraph, the auditor should not use conditional language such as, "If the company is unable to obtain refinancing, there may be substantial doubt about the company's ability to continue as a going concern."

   d. The following is an example of an explanatory paragraph:

   Paragraph Added to Audit Report Expressing Substantial Doubt about Going Concern

The accompanying financial statements have been prepared assuming that the Company will continue as a going concern. As discussed in Note X to the financial statements, the Company has suffered recurring losses from operations and has a net capital deficiency that raises substantial doubt about its ability to continue as a going concern. Management's plans in regard to these matters are also described in Note X. The financial statements do not include any adjustments that might result from the outcome of this uncertainty.

e. If disclosures are inadequate, the departure from GAAP may result in a qualified or an adverse opinion.

f. Substantial doubt arising in the current period does not imply that such doubt existed in the prior period and should not affect the report on the prior-period statements.

g. If substantial doubt existed at the date of prior-period statements and that doubt has been removed in the current period, the explanatory paragraph in the report for the prior period should not be repeated.

3. Stop and review! You have completed the outline for this subunit. Study multiple-choice questions 17 through 26 beginning on page 544.

17.4 COMPARATIVE FINANCIAL STATEMENTS (AU 508)

1. The phrase "financial statements taken as a whole" in the fourth reporting standard applies not only to the current-period statements but also to those of prior periods presented comparatively.

   a. Thus, a continuing auditor should update the report for the one or more prior periods presented.

      1) If audit firms merge and the new firm becomes the auditor of a former client of one of the merged firms, the new firm may accept responsibility as a continuing auditor. The new firm may indicate that a merger took place and name the firm that was merged with it.

         a) Otherwise, the guidance on reports of predecessor auditors should be followed.

      2) An updated report is not a reissuance of a previous report. The updated report considers information from the audit of the current-period statements and is issued with the report on those statements.

      3) A continuing auditor need not report if only summarized comparative information of the prior period(s) is presented. For example, state and local governmental units and not-for-profit entities often present total-all-funds information rather than information by individual funds.

         a) If the client requests an opinion on the prior period(s), the auditor should consider whether the information contains sufficient detail for a fair presentation. To avoid modification of the report, additional columns or separate detail by fund will usually be needed.

   b. Ordinarily, the report on comparative statements should be dated as of the date of completion of field work for the most recent audit.

   c. During the audit, the auditor should be alert for circumstances or events affecting the prior-period financial statements presented and should consider their effects when updating the report.

2. **Different Reports on Comparative Financial Statements Presented.** The report applies to individual financial statements, so an auditor may express a qualified or an adverse opinion, disclaim an opinion, or include an explanatory paragraph for one or more statements for one or more periods while issuing a different report on the other statements. The following are examples of such reports:

   a. Standard report on the prior-year financial statements and a qualified opinion on the current-year financial statements

      1) The introductory and scope paragraphs are unchanged.

2) The explanatory paragraph and the modification of the opinion paragraph are as follows:

Language to Qualify 1 Year of a Comparative Set of Financial Statements

> The Company has excluded, from property and debt in the accompanying year 3 balance sheet, certain lease obligations that were entered into in year 3 which, in our opinion, should be capitalized in order to conform with U.S. generally accepted accounting principles. If these lease obligations were capitalized, property would be increased by $_____, long-term debt by $_____, and retained earnings by $_____ as of December 31, year 3, net income, basic earnings per share, and diluted earnings per share would be increased (decreased) by $_____ , $_____, and $_____, respectively, for the year then ended.
>
> In our opinion, except for the effects on the year 3 financial statements of not capitalizing certain lease obligations as described in the preceding paragraph . . . .

b. Standard report on the current-year financial statements with a disclaimer of opinion on the prior-year statements of income, retained earnings, and cash flows

1) The introductory paragraph is unchanged.
2) The scope paragraph is modified by adding the following clause:

> Except as explained in the following paragraph . . . .

3) The explanatory and opinion paragraphs are as follows:

Language to Disclaim an Opinion on Selected Statements of a
Comparative Set of Financial Statements

> We did not observe the taking of the physical inventory as of December 31, year 1, since that date was prior to our appointment as auditors for the Company, and we were unable to satisfy ourselves regarding inventory quantities by means of other auditing procedures. Inventory amounts as of December 31, year 1, enter into the determination of net income and cash flows for the year ended December 31, year 2.
>
> Because of the matter discussed in the preceding paragraph, the scope of our work was not sufficient to enable us to express, and we do not express, an opinion on the results of operations and cash flows for the year ended December 31, year 2.
>
> In our opinion, the balance sheets of ABC Company as of December 31, year 3 and year 2, and the related statements of income, retained earnings, and cash flows for the year ended December 31, year 3, present fairly, in all material respects, the financial position of ABC Company as of December 31, year 3 and year 2, and the results of its operations and its cash flows for the year ended December 31, year 3, in conformity with accounting principles generally accepted in the United States of America.

3. **Opinion on Prior-Period Financial Statements Different from the Opinion Previously Issued.** An auditor may become aware of circumstances or events affecting the statements of a prior period and should consider them when updating the report.

a. For example, if the opinion was modified because of a departure from GAAP, and the statements are restated in the current period to conform with GAAP, the updated report should indicate the restatement and express an unqualified opinion. An explanatory paragraph(s) preceding the opinion paragraph should disclose

1) All substantive reasons for the different opinion
2) The date of the previous report
3) The type of opinion previously expressed
4) The circumstances or events that resulted in a different opinion
5) Notification that the updated opinion differs from the previous opinion

b.   The following is a possible explanatory paragraph:

Language to Change a Previously Expressed Opinion

> In our report dated March 1, year 3, we expressed an opinion that the year 2 financial statements did not fairly present financial position, results of operations, and cash flows in conformity with U.S. generally accepted accounting principles: (1) the Company carried its property, plant, and equipment at appraisal values, and provided for depreciation on the basis of such values, and (2) the Company did not provide for deferred income taxes with respect to differences between income for financial reporting purposes and taxable income. As described in Note X, the Company has changed its method of accounting for these items and has restated its year 2 financial statements to conform with U.S. generally accepted accounting principles. Accordingly, our present opinion on the year 2 financial statements, as presented herein, is different from that expressed in our previous report.

c.   The introductory, scope, and opinion paragraphs are the same as in the standard report.

4.   **Report of Predecessor Auditor**

a.   A predecessor auditor can ordinarily reissue the report for a prior period at the request of the former client if satisfactory arrangements are made to perform this service and if the procedures described below are performed.

1)   A predecessor auditor's report may not be reissued in certain circumstances, e.g., because the CPA is no longer in public practice.

b.   Predecessor auditor's report reissued. Before reissuing (or consenting to the reuse of) the report, the predecessor auditor should consider whether the report is still appropriate in light of the current form or presentation of the prior-period statements and any subsequent events.

1)   The predecessor auditor should

a)   Read the current-period statements.

b)   Compare the prior-period statements reported on with those to be presented comparatively.

c)   Obtain a representation letter from the successor auditor.

i)   The letter should state whether the audit revealed matters that might materially affect, or require disclosure in, the statements reported on by the predecessor auditor.

d)   Obtain a representation letter from management.

i)   The letter should state whether any new information has caused management to believe that previous representations should be modified and whether any events have occurred subsequent to the balance sheet date of the latest prior-period financial statements reported on by the predecessor that would require adjustment to, or disclosure in, those financial statements.

2)   The predecessor auditor may wish to consider the matters described in AU 543, *Part of Audit Made by Other Independent Auditors* (subunit 17.1), but should not refer in the reissued report to the report or work of the successor auditor.

3)   Events or transactions subsequent to the date of the previous report that may affect the report require the predecessor auditor to make inquiries and perform other necessary procedures, such as reviewing the relevant portions of the successor's working papers.

a)   If the predecessor auditor decides to revise the report, (s)he should follow the guidance described in this subunit about changing a previously expressed opinion.

4) Because a predecessor auditor's knowledge of the former client is limited, (s)he should use the date of the previous report to avoid implications that (s)he has examined any records, transactions, or events after that date. Thus, a reissued report carries the date of the original report.

    a) If the report is revised or the statements are restated, the report should be dual dated.

c. Predecessor auditor's report not presented

    1) The introductory paragraph of the successor's report should

        a) Indicate that the prior-period statements were audited by another auditor

            i) But the successor auditor should not name the predecessor auditor unless the predecessor's practice was acquired by, or merged with, that of the successor.

        b) Give the date of the predecessor's report
        c) Disclose the type of report issued by the predecessor
        d) Describe the substantive reasons therefor, if it was not the standard report

    2) Example of a successor auditor's unqualified report when the predecessor's report is not presented

        a) The following language is added to the standard introductory paragraph (as the last sentence) for a report on the year 3 statements:

Language Added to Introductory Paragraph of Successor's Report to Reference Predecessor's Report

> The financial statements of ABC Company as of December 31, year 2, were audited by other auditors whose report dated March 31, year 3, expressed an unqualified opinion of those statements.

        b) The scope paragraph is unchanged.

        c) The opinion paragraph is unchanged except that the first line is as follows:

> In our opinion, the year 3 financial statements referred to above . . . .

    3) If the predecessor did not issue a standard report, the successor should describe the nature of, and reasons for, the explanatory paragraph added to that report or the opinion qualification. The following illustrates the possible wording added to the introductory paragraph:

Language Added to Introductory Paragraph of Successor's Report to Reference Predecessor's Modified Report

> The financial statements of ABC Company as of December 31, year 2 were audited by other auditors whose report dated March 1, year 3, on those statements included an explanatory paragraph that described the change in the Company's method of computing depreciation discussed in Note X to the financial statements.

    4) If the statements have been restated, the introductory paragraph should indicate that a predecessor reported on them before restatement. Also, if the successor becomes satisfied as to the propriety of the restatement, (s)he may also include the following paragraph in the report:

Language Added to Introductory Paragraph of Successor's Report to Express Opinion on Restatement of Prior Year's Financial Statements

> We also audited the adjustments described in Note X that were applied to restate the year 2 financial statements. In our opinion, such adjustments are appropriate and have been properly applied.

    d.   Misstatement on prior financial statements by a predecessor auditor

        1)   If the successor auditor becomes aware of information that leads him/her to believe that the financial statements of the prior periods reported on by the predecessor auditor need revision, the successor auditor should request that the client inform the predecessor auditor and arrange for the three parties to discuss and resolve the matter. At the meeting, the successor auditor should disclose any information that the predecessor may need to consider.

        2)   AU 561 discusses the procedures to be followed when there is a subsequent discovery of facts.

5.   **Comparative Presentation of Unaudited Prior-Year Financial Statements with Audited Current-Year Statements.** In these circumstances, the audit report on comparative statements presented in documents filed with the SEC would not refer to the unaudited statements, and these statements should be clearly marked as unaudited.

    a.   In all other cases, the unaudited statements (that may have been reviewed or compiled) should also be clearly marked to indicate their status, and either the report on the prior period should be reissued (AU 530) or the report on the current period should include as a separate paragraph a description of the responsibility assumed for the prior-period statements (AU 504).

6.   Stop and review! You have completed the outline for this subunit. Study multiple-choice questions 27 through 35 beginning on page 547.

17.5 EMPHASIS OF A MATTER (AU 508)

1.   A matter regarding the financial statements may be emphasized in a separate paragraph without modifying the opinion. But phrases such as "with the foregoing explanation" should not be included in the opinion paragraph. Matters emphasized may include

    a.   The information that the entity is a component of a larger enterprise
    b.   Significant related party transactions
    c.   An important subsequent event
    d.   An accounting matter affecting comparability

2.   The following is an example of a separate paragraph that emphasizes a matter:

Separate Paragraph Emphasizing a Matter

Company A is a subsidiary of Company ABC, and the financial statements reported on here are a component part of the consolidated financial statements of Company ABC reported on by other auditors.

3.   Stop and review! You have completed the outline for this subunit. Study multiple-choice question 36 on page 550.

QUESTIONS

17.1 Part of Audit Performed by Other Independent Auditors (AU 543)

1. An auditor may issue the standard audit report when the

   A. Auditor refers to the findings of a specialist.

   B. Financial statements are derived and condensed from complete audited financial statements that are filed with a regulatory agency.

   C. Financial statements are prepared on the cash receipts and disbursements basis of accounting.

   D. Principal auditor assumes responsibility for the work of another auditor.

Answer (D) is correct. *(CPA, adapted)*
   REQUIRED: The situation in which an auditor may issue the standard audit report.
   DISCUSSION: If the principal auditor can become satisfied regarding the independence, professional reputation, and the audit performed by the other auditor, (s)he may be able to express an opinion on the financial statements taken as a whole without referring to the audit of the other auditor. If (s)he assumes responsibility for the work of the other auditor, a standard report is appropriate (AU 543).
   Answer (A) is incorrect because the auditor does not refer to a specialist in the standard audit report. Answer (B) is incorrect because an auditor is not permitted to report on condensed statements in the same manner as (s)he reported on the complete statements. Answer (C) is incorrect because a special report may be appropriate.

2. Pell, CPA, decides to serve as principal auditor in the audit of the financial statements of Tech Consolidated, Inc. Smith, CPA, audits one of Tech's subsidiaries. In which situation(s) should Pell refer to Smith's audit?

   I. Pell reviews Smith's working papers and assumes responsibility for Smith's work but expresses a qualified opinion on Tech's financial statements.

   II. Pell is unable to review Smith's working papers; however, Pell's inquiries indicate that Smith has an excellent reputation for professional competence and integrity.

   A. I only.

   B. II only.

   C. Both I and II.

   D. Neither I nor II.

Answer (B) is correct. *(CPA, adapted)*
   REQUIRED: The situations, if any, in which a principal auditor refers to another auditor's audit.
   DISCUSSION: Once the principal auditor is able to become satisfied as to the independence and professional reputation of the other auditor, (s)he may decide to refer to the other auditor's audit because it may be impracticable for the principal auditor to review the other auditor's work or to use other procedures that (s)he deems necessary to obtain satisfaction as to the other auditor's audit. Such a reference indicates a division of responsibility between the auditors. The reference to the other auditor does not prohibit an unqualified opinion (AU 543).
   Answer (A) is incorrect because, if the principal auditor accepts responsibility for the other auditor's audit, (s)he should not state in the report that another auditor performed part of the audit. Such a reference might lead to misinterpretation of the degree of responsibility assumed. The type of opinion expressed is not relevant to the decision to make reference. Answer (C) is incorrect because, if the principal auditor accepts responsibility for the other auditor's audit, (s)he should not state in the report that another auditor performed part of the audit. Such a reference might lead to misinterpretation of the degree of responsibility assumed. The type of opinion expressed is not relevant to the decision to make reference. Answer (D) is incorrect because the principal auditor may refer to the other auditor's audit when (s)he wishes to divide responsibility.

3. Which of the following procedures would the principal auditor most likely perform after deciding to make reference to another CPA who audited a subsidiary of the entity?

   A. Review the working papers and the audit programs of the other CPA.

   B. Visit the other CPA and discuss the results of the other CPA's audit procedures.

   C. Make inquiries about the professional reputation and independence of the other CPA.

   D. Determine that the other CPA has a sufficient understanding of the subsidiary's internal control.

Answer (C) is correct. *(CPA, adapted)*
   REQUIRED: The procedure most likely to be performed after deciding to make reference to another auditor.
   DISCUSSION: When the principal auditor decides to divide reporting responsibility and to make reference to another auditor, (s)he should inquire about the professional reputation and independence of the other auditor to one or more of the following: the AICPA, a state society, a local chapter, or a foreign auditor's corresponding professional organization; other practitioners; credit grantors; or other appropriate sources (AU 543).
   Answer (A) is incorrect because, if the principal auditor decides not to divide responsibility and not make reference to the other auditor's audit in the report, (s)he should consider visiting the other auditor and reviewing the working papers and audit programs. Answer (B) is incorrect because, if the principal auditor decides not to divide responsibility and not make reference to the other auditor's audit in the report, (s)he should consider visiting the other auditor and reviewing the working papers and audit programs. Answer (D) is incorrect because, if the principal auditor decides to make reference to the audit of the other auditor, (s)he does not accept responsibility for the other auditor's work and need not test it.

4. In which of the following situations would a principal auditor least likely make reference to another auditor who audited a subsidiary of the entity?

A. The other auditor was retained by the principal auditor and the work was performed under the principal auditor's guidance and control.

B. The principal auditor finds it impracticable to review the other auditor's work or otherwise be satisfied as to the other auditor's work.

C. The financial statements audited by the other auditor are material to the consolidated financial statements covered by the principal auditor's opinion.

D. The principal auditor is unable to be satisfied as to the independence and professional reputation of the other auditor.

Answer (A) is correct.   *(CPA, adapted)*
REQUIRED: The situation in which a principal auditor is least likely to refer to another auditor.
DISCUSSION: According to AU 543, the principal auditor normally does not refer to another auditor when the other auditor is an associate or correspondent firm whose work is acceptable to the principal auditor or when the other auditor was retained by the principal auditor and the work was performed under the principal auditor's guidance and control.
Answer (B) is incorrect because, if the principal finds it impracticable to review the work of the other auditor, the other auditor will likely be referred to in the principal auditor's report. Answer (C) is incorrect because the more material the items audited by the other auditor, the more likely reference will be made in the principal auditor's report. Answer (D) is incorrect because, when the auditor cannot become satisfied about the independence and professional reputation of the other auditor, the opinion should be qualified or an opinion should be disclaimed.

5. When a principal auditor decides to refer to another auditor's audit, the principal auditor's report should always indicate clearly, in the introductory, scope, and opinion paragraphs, the

A. Magnitude of the portion of the financial statements examined by the other auditor.

B. Disclaimer of responsibility concerning the portion of the financial statements examined by the other auditor.

C. Name of the other auditor.

D. Division of responsibility.

Answer (D) is correct.   *(CPA, adapted)*
REQUIRED: The disclosure requirement when reference to another auditor is made.
DISCUSSION: The division of responsibility between the portion of the financial statements covered by the principal auditor's own audit and that covered by the other auditor should be clearly defined in the introductory, scope, and opinion paragraphs (AU 543).
Answer (A) is incorrect because the portion audited by the other auditor should be disclosed by stating the dollar amounts of total assets, total revenues, or other appropriate criteria in the introductory paragraph. Answer (B) is incorrect because a division of responsibility, not a disclaimer, is indicated. Answer (C) is incorrect because naming the other auditor is not required; (s)he may be named only if (s)he gives express permission and if his/her report is presented together with that of the principal auditor.

6. In which of the following situations would an auditor ordinarily express an unqualified audit opinion without an explanatory paragraph?

A. The auditor wishes to emphasize that the entity had significant related party transactions.

B. The auditor decides to make reference to the report of another auditor as a basis, in part, for the auditor's opinion.

C. The entity issues financial statements that present financial position and results of operations but omits the statement of cash flows.

D. The auditor has substantial doubt about the entity's ability to continue as a going concern, but the circumstances are fully disclosed in the financial statements.

Answer (B) is correct.   *(CPA, adapted)*
REQUIRED: The situation in which an auditor ordinarily expresses an unqualified opinion without an explanatory paragraph.
DISCUSSION: A reference to the report of another auditor as a basis, in part, for the auditor's opinion is not a qualification of the opinion. Moreover, the addition of an explanatory paragraph is not required in these circumstances.
Answer (A) is incorrect because emphasis of a matter is made in an explanatory paragraph. Answer (C) is incorrect because the omission is the basis for a qualification of the opinion, which requires an explanatory paragraph. Answer (D) is incorrect because a substantial doubt about the entity's ability to continue as a going concern requires an explanatory paragraph.

7. The introductory paragraph of an auditor's report contains the following: "We did not audit the financial statements of EZ Inc., a wholly owned subsidiary, which statements reflect total assets and revenues constituting 27% and 29%, respectively, of the related consolidated totals. Those statements were audited by other auditors whose report has been furnished to us, and our opinion, insofar as it relates to the amounts included for EZ Inc., is based solely on the report of the other auditors." These sentences

   A. Indicate a division of responsibility.

   B. Assume responsibility for the other auditor.

   C. Require a departure from an unqualified opinion.

   D. Are an improper form of reporting.

Answer (A) is correct. *(CPA, adapted)*
   REQUIRED: The effect of the quoted language.
   DISCUSSION: The quoted language is from an introductory paragraph provided as an example in AU 543 of appropriate reporting of the decision to refer to the work of another auditor. It meets the requirement that the reference indicate clearly the division of responsibility.
   Answer (B) is incorrect because the statement attempts to divide responsibility, so the principal auditor does not assume responsibility for the other auditor. Answer (C) is incorrect because a division of responsibility does not preclude an unqualified opinion. Answer (D) is incorrect because the wording is standard.

17.2 Consistency of Application of GAAP (AU 420)

8. In the first audit of a client, an auditor was not able to gather sufficient evidence about the consistent application of accounting principles between the current and the prior year, as well as the amounts of assets or liabilities at the beginning of the current year. This was due to the client's record retention policies. If the amounts in question could materially affect current operating results, the auditor would

   A. Be unable to express an opinion on the current year's results of operations and cash flows.

   B. Express a qualified opinion on the financial statements because of a client-imposed scope limitation.

   C. Withdraw from the engagement and refuse to be associated with the financial statements.

   D. Specifically state that the financial statements are not comparable to the prior year due to an uncertainty.

Answer (A) is correct. *(CPA, adapted)*
   REQUIRED: The effect on the report of insufficient evidence about beginning balances and consistency of GAAP.
   DISCUSSION: The second standard of reporting states that the report shall "identify circumstances in which principles have not been consistently observed in the current accounting period in relation to the preceding period." An auditor must be able to identify accounting changes that affect consistency. When an auditor is unable to gather evidence about the consistent application of accounting principles due to the client's failure to retain the information, the auditor will be unable to express an opinion on the results of operations and cash flows. The auditor may, however, be able to become satisfied as to the ending balances reported on the balance sheet.
   Answer (B) is incorrect because a disclaimer of opinion on the income statement and statement of cash flows is appropriate when the audit is not sufficient to permit the formation of an opinion. Answer (C) is incorrect because no ethical or other reason is given to justify withdrawal. Answer (D) is incorrect because any potential lack of comparability is not due to an uncertainty.

9. The following explanatory paragraph was included in an auditor's report to indicate a lack of consistency:

   As discussed in note T to the financial statements, the company changed its method of computing depreciation in year 1.

How should the auditor report on this matter if the auditor concurred with the change?

	Type of Opinion	Location of Explanatory Paragraph
A.	Unqualified	Before opinion paragraph
B.	Unqualified	After opinion paragraph
C.	Qualified	Before opinion paragraph
D.	Qualified	After opinion paragraph

Answer (B) is correct. *(CPA, adapted)*
   REQUIRED: The proper reporting of a lack of consistency.
   DISCUSSION: AU 508 states that a change in accounting principles or in the method of their application having a material effect on comparability requires the auditor to refer to the change in an explanatory paragraph of the report. However, no opinion modification is necessary if the auditor concurs with the change. The paragraph should follow the opinion paragraph and identify the nature of the change and refer to a footnote that discusses the change.
   Answer (A) is incorrect because the explanatory paragraph should follow the opinion paragraph. Answer (C) is incorrect because the opinion should be unqualified and the paragraph should follow the opinion paragraph. Answer (D) is incorrect because the opinion paragraph should be unqualified.

10. For which of the following events would an auditor issue a report that omits any reference to consistency?

   A. A change in the method of accounting for inventories.

   B. A change from an accounting principle that is not generally accepted to one that is generally accepted.

   C. A change in the useful life used to calculate the provision for depreciation expense.

   D. Management's lack of reasonable justification for a change in accounting principle.

Answer (C) is correct. *(CPA, adapted)*
REQUIRED: The event not requiring a reference to consistency in the auditor's report.
DISCUSSION: A change in an accounting estimate that is not inseparable from a change in an accounting principle, for example, in the useful life of an asset, is not a change that affects consistency. This change is accounted for prospectively and may require disclosure in a note to the financial statements but is not referred to in the auditor's report (AU 420).
Answer (A) is incorrect because a change in the method of accounting for inventory, for example, from FIFO to LIFO, is a change in accounting principle. Such a change affects consistency and requires an explanatory paragraph in the auditor's report. Answer (B) is incorrect because a correction of an error in principle is a change affecting consistency. It is accounted for as a correction of an error, and it requires an explanatory paragraph in the auditor's report. Answer (D) is incorrect because lack of justification for a change in accounting principle requires the auditor to express a qualified or adverse opinion. The middle paragraph explaining the reasons for the opinion modification contains all the information needed in a paragraph on consistency, so a separate paragraph following the opinion paragraph is not necessary (AU 508).

11. When there has been a change in accounting principles, but the effect of the change on the comparability of the financial statements is not material, the auditor should

   A. Refer to the change in an explanatory paragraph.

   B. Explicitly concur that the change is preferred.

   C. Not refer to consistency in the auditor's report.

   D. Refer to the change in the opinion paragraph.

Answer (C) is correct. *(CPA, adapted)*
REQUIRED: The reference, if any, in the auditor's report to a change in accounting principle not considered material.
DISCUSSION: The standard report implies that comparability between or among periods has not been materially affected by changes in accounting principles because either no change has occurred or there has been a change in principles or in the method of their application, but its effect on comparability is not material (AU 508). Moreover, changes not material to the current financial statements that may be material to future statements require no reference in the auditor's report (AU 420).
Answer (A) is incorrect because an additional paragraph is added following the opinion paragraph only if the change is material. Answer (B) is incorrect because the auditor should not refer to consistency when the effect on comparability is immaterial. Answer (D) is incorrect because the auditor should refer to the change in the opinion paragraph only if (s)he takes exception to it in expressing the opinion.

12. When an entity changes its method of accounting for income taxes, which has a material effect on comparability, the auditor should refer to the change in an explanatory paragraph added to the auditor's report. This paragraph should identify the nature of the change and

   A. Explain why the change is justified under generally accepted accounting principles.

   B. Describe the cumulative effect of the change on the audited financial statements.

   C. State the auditor's explicit concurrence with or opposition to the change.

   D. Refer to the financial statement note that discusses the change in detail.

Answer (D) is correct. *(CPA, adapted)*
REQUIRED: The content of an explanatory paragraph added because of a change in an accounting principle.
DISCUSSION: When a change in accounting principle has a material effect on comparability, the auditor should add an explanatory paragraph after the opinion paragraph that identifies the nature of the change and refers the reader to the note in the financial statements that discusses the change in detail.
Answer (A) is incorrect because the auditor's concurrence with the change is implicit unless (s)he takes exception to the change in expressing the opinion. Answer (B) is incorrect because the cumulative effect of a change is described in the financial statements, not the audit report. Answer (C) is incorrect because the auditor's concurrence with the change is implicit unless (s)he takes exception to the change in expressing the opinion.

13. When the auditor concurs with a change in accounting principle that materially affects the comparability of the comparative financial statements, the auditor should

	Concur Explicitly with the Change	Express a Qualified Opinion	Refer to the Change in an Explanatory Paragraph
A.	No	No	Yes
B.	Yes	No	Yes
C.	Yes	Yes	No
D.	No	Yes	No

Answer (A) is correct. *(CPA, adapted)*

REQUIRED: The appropriate report when the auditor concurs with a change in accounting principle.

DISCUSSION: A material change in accounting principle raises a consistency issue. Thus, a report with a separate explanatory paragraph is required. Unless the change is unjustified, however, it does not require a modification of the opinion. Thus, a qualified opinion would not be appropriate. Furthermore, an auditor does not concur explicitly with the change in the report. An explanatory paragraph will suffice.

14. Digit Co. uses the FIFO method of costing for its international subsidiary's inventory and LIFO for its domestic inventory. Under these circumstances, the auditor's report on Digit's financial statements should express an

A. Unqualified opinion.

B. Opinion qualified because of a lack of consistency.

C. Opinion qualified because of a departure from GAAP.

D. Adverse opinion.

Answer (A) is correct. *(CPA, adapted)*

REQUIRED: The effect on the report of using different inventory methods for two business segments.

DISCUSSION: A difference between the accounting principles used by two segments of an entity does not raise a consistency issue. The second standard of reporting concerns the consistent observation of principles in the current period in relation to the preceding period. Thus, the use of LIFO for one segment and FIFO for another does not, by itself, affect comparability. Assuming that the use of different methods is appropriate, an unqualified opinion is not precluded, and no explanatory paragraph relevant to consistency need be added to the report.

15. An entity changed from the straight-line method to the declining balance method of depreciation for all newly acquired assets. This change has no material effect on the current year's financial statements but is reasonably certain to have a substantial effect in later years. If the change is disclosed in the notes to the financial statements, the auditor should issue a report with a(n)

A. Qualified opinion.

B. Explanatory paragraph.

C. Unqualified opinion.

D. Consistency modification.

Answer (C) is correct. *(CPA, adapted)*

REQUIRED: The report issued when a change in accounting principle has no material effect on the current year's statements.

DISCUSSION: If a change in accounting principle has no material effect on the current financial statements but is reasonably certain to have a substantial effect in future years, the change should be disclosed but need not be recognized in the report (AU 420).

Answer (A) is incorrect because a change in accounting principle does not result in a qualified opinion. Answer (B) is incorrect because, if an accounting change has no material effect on the current financial statements but is likely to affect future financial statements, the auditor need not modify the report. Answer (D) is incorrect because, if an accounting change has no material effect on the current financial statements but is likely to affect future financial statements, the auditor need not modify the report.

16. An auditor includes an explanatory paragraph in an otherwise unmodified report to emphasize that the financial statements are not comparable with those of prior years because of a court-ordered divestiture that is already fully explained in the notes to the financial statements. The inclusion of this paragraph

A. Should be followed by a consistency modification in the opinion paragraph.

B. Requires a revision of the opinion paragraph to include the phrase "with the foregoing explanation."

C. Is not appropriate and may confuse the readers or lead them to believe the report was qualified.

D. Is appropriate and would not negate the unqualified opinion.

Answer (D) is correct. *(CPA, adapted)*
REQUIRED: The effect on the report of including an explanatory paragraph to emphasize a matter.
DISCUSSION: An auditor may emphasize a matter in an explanatory paragraph and express an unqualified opinion. Matters to be emphasized might include that the entity is a component of a larger enterprise, or that it has had significant related party transactions. Accounting matters affecting comparability, other than a change in principle, and subsequent events are other matters suitable for this treatment (AU 508). Thus, a divestiture is appropriate for emphasis because it affects comparability. However, "A change in the reporting entity resulting from a transaction or event, such as a pooling of interests, or the creation, cessation, or complete or partial purchase or disposition of a subsidiary or other business unit, does not require that an explanatory paragraph about consistency be included in the auditor's report" (AU 420).
Answer (A) is incorrect because a change in the reporting entity as a result of a divestiture does not require a consistency modification of any part of the report. Moreover, lack of consistency, by itself, does not justify an opinion modification. Answer (B) is incorrect because the phrase "with the foregoing explanation" is an inappropriate form of reporting. Answer (C) is incorrect because confusion is avoided by not modifying the opinion paragraph.

17.3 Uncertainties and Going Concern (AU 508 and AU 341)

17. Management believes and the auditor is satisfied that a material loss probably will occur when pending litigation is resolved. Management is unable to make a reasonable estimate of the amount or range of the potential loss but fully discloses the situation in the notes to the financial statements. If management does not make an accrual in the financial statements, the auditor should express a(n)

A. Qualified opinion due to a scope limitation.

B. Qualified opinion due to a departure from GAAP.

C. Unqualified opinion with an explanatory paragraph.

D. Unqualified opinion in a standard auditor's report.

Answer (D) is correct. *(CPA, adapted)*
REQUIRED: The auditor's reporting consideration of a material loss that is probable but not subject to estimation.
DISCUSSION: If the auditor concludes that sufficient evidential matter supports management's assertions about the nature of a matter involving an uncertainty, an unmodified report is ordinarily appropriate.
Answer (A) is incorrect because inability to make a reasonable estimate of the potential loss is not a scope limitation. Answer (B) is incorrect because no departure from GAAP has occurred. An accrual of the loss contingency is not required in these circumstances, and full disclosure has been made. Answer (C) is incorrect because no basis for including an additional paragraph to the report is given.

18. An auditor most likely would express an unqualified opinion and would not add explanatory language to the report if the auditor

A. Wishes to emphasize that the entity had significant transactions with related parties.

B. Concurs with the entity's change in its method of computing depreciation.

C. Discovers that supplementary information required by FASB has been omitted.

D. Believes that there is a remote likelihood of a material loss resulting from an uncertainty.

Answer (D) is correct. *(CPA, adapted)*
REQUIRED: The condition under which an explanatory paragraph is not added to the report.
DISCUSSION: Normally, an uncertainty does not require the auditor to add a paragraph to the report.
Answer (A) is incorrect because emphasis of a matter is accomplished with an additional paragraph added to the auditor's report. Answer (B) is incorrect because a change in accounting principle requires an additional paragraph describing the lack of consistency. Answer (C) is incorrect because AU 558 requires the auditor to add an additional paragraph when supplementary information that is required by FASB or GASB has been omitted.

19. If an auditor is satisfied that there is only a remote likelihood of a loss resulting from the resolution of a matter involving an uncertainty, the auditor should express a(n)

- A. Unqualified opinion.

- B. Unqualified opinion with a separate explanatory paragraph.

- C. Qualified opinion or disclaimer of opinion, depending upon the materiality of the loss.

- D. Qualified opinion or disclaimer of opinion, depending on whether the uncertainty is adequately disclosed.

Answer (A) is correct. *(CPA, adapted)*
REQUIRED: The opinion expressed when the likelihood of a loss from resolution of an uncertainty is remote.
DISCUSSION: In the absence of a scope limitation or a departure from GAAP, an uncertainty does not require modification of the opinion or a disclaimer.
Answer (B) is incorrect because a separate paragraph is not required. Answer (C) is incorrect because a disclaimer is appropriate only when the scope of the audit was too limited to warrant expression of an opinion. Moreover, even an uncertainty that entails a probable chance of material loss does not, by itself, require a qualified opinion. Answer (D) is incorrect because a disclaimer is appropriate only when the scope of the audit was too limited to warrant expression of an opinion. Moreover, even an uncertainty that entails a probable chance of material loss does not, by itself, require a qualified opinion.

20. Tech Company has disclosed an uncertainty arising from pending litigation. The auditor's decision to express a qualified opinion rather than an unqualified opinion most likely would be determined by the

- A. Lack of sufficient evidence.

- B. Inability to estimate the amount of loss.

- C. Entity's lack of experience with such litigation.

- D. Lack of insurance coverage for possible losses from such litigation.

Answer (A) is correct. *(CPA, adapted)*
REQUIRED: The basis for expressing a qualified opinion.
DISCUSSION: By definition, sufficient evidence regarding the outcome of an uncertainty cannot be expected to exist at the time of an audit. However, management must analyze existing conditions, including uncertainties, and their financial statement effects. The auditor must therefore determine whether the evidence is sufficient to support these analyses. If, as a result of a scope limitation, sufficient evidence is not available to the auditor to make this determination, a qualification or disclaimer of opinion is appropriate.
Answer (B) is incorrect because an inability to estimate the amount of loss is neither a scope limitation nor a departure from GAAP and does not justify an opinion qualification. Answer (C) is incorrect because the entity's lack of experience with such litigation is neither a scope limitation nor a departure from GAAP and does not justify an opinion qualification. Answer (D) is incorrect because the lack of insurance is neither a scope limitation nor a departure from GAAP and does not justify an opinion qualification.

21. When an auditor concludes that substantial doubt exists about an entity's ability to continue as a going concern for a reasonable period of time, the auditor's responsibility is to

- A. Prepare prospective financial information to verify whether management's plans can be effectively implemented.

- B. Project future conditions and events for a period of time not to exceed 1 year following the date of the financial statements.

- C. Express a qualified or adverse opinion, depending on materiality, because of the possible effects on the financial statements.

- D. Consider the adequacy of disclosure about the entity's possible inability to continue as a going concern.

Answer (D) is correct. *(CPA, adapted)*
REQUIRED: The auditor's responsibility given a substantial doubt about an entity's ability to continue as a going concern.
DISCUSSION: If the auditor reaches this conclusion after identifying conditions and events that create such doubt and after evaluating management's plans to mitigate their effects, (s)he should consider the adequacy of disclosure and include an explanatory paragraph (after the opinion paragraph) in the report that includes the words "substantial doubt" and "going concern." If disclosure is inadequate, the departure from GAAP requires modification of the opinion. By itself, however, the substantial doubt does not require a modified opinion paragraph or a disclaimer of opinion.
Answer (A) is incorrect because the auditor should consider management's plans but need not prepare prospective financial information. Answer (B) is incorrect because the auditor is not responsible for predicting future conditions or events. Answer (C) is incorrect because the opinion is not modified solely for a going concern issue.

22. In which of the following circumstances would an auditor most likely add an explanatory paragraph to the standard report while expressing an unqualified opinion?

A. The auditor is asked to report on the balance sheet but not on the other basic financial statements.

B. There is substantial doubt about the entity's ability to continue as a going concern.

C. Management's estimates of the effects of future events are unreasonable.

D. Certain transactions cannot be tested because of management's records retention policy.

Answer (B) is correct. *(CPA, adapted)*
REQUIRED: The situation most likely resulting in an explanatory paragraph and an unqualified opinion.
DISCUSSION: If the auditor reaches this conclusion after identifying conditions and events that create such doubt and after evaluating management's plans to mitigate their effects, (s)he should consider the adequacy of disclosure and include an explanatory paragraph (after the opinion paragraph) in the report. The auditor must use language in the explanatory paragraph that includes the words "substantial doubt" and "going concern." By itself, however, the substantial doubt is not a basis for modifying the opinion.
Answer (A) is incorrect because an auditor may be asked to report on one financial statement. In that event, (s)he may appropriately express an unqualified opinion without adding an explanatory paragraph. Answer (C) is incorrect because the statements are not fairly presented if the estimates included in them are unreasonable. An unqualified opinion could not then be expressed. Answer (D) is incorrect because a qualification or disclaimer of opinion is appropriate when the scope of the audit is limited.

23. An auditor's report included the following paragraph relative to a client's going concern:

The accompanying financial statements have been prepared assuming that the Company will continue as a going concern. If the Company is not able to renew the contract described in Note X, there may be substantial doubt about the company's ability to continue as a going concern.

Which of the following statements is true?

A. The paragraph should not refer to a footnote to the financial statements.

B. The report should not contain conditional language.

C. The report should refer to a qualification of the opinion.

D. The report should not use the phrase "substantial doubt."

Answer (B) is correct. *(Publisher)*
REQUIRED: The true statement about a going concern paragraph.
DISCUSSION: The report should not contain conditional language. "If the Company is not able to renew the contract..." is not permissible language.
Answer (A) is incorrect because the report may refer to a footnote that describes the issues. Answer (C) is incorrect because the opinion should not be qualified for a going concern doubt. Rather, an additional paragraph should be included in the report. Answer (D) is incorrect because the report should include the phrases "substantial doubt" and "going concern."

24. Green, CPA, concludes that there is substantial doubt about JKL Co.'s ability to continue as a going concern. If JKL's financial statements adequately disclose its financial difficulties, Green's auditor's report should

	Include an Explanatory Paragraph Following the Opinion Paragraph	Specifically Use the Words "Going Concern"	Specifically Use the Words "Substantial Doubt"
A.	Yes	Yes	Yes
B.	Yes	Yes	No
C.	Yes	No	Yes
D.	No	Yes	Yes

Answer (A) is correct. *(CPA, adapted)*
REQUIRED: The effects of a substantial doubt about an entity's ability to continue as a going concern.
DISCUSSION: When there is substantial doubt about an entity's ability to continue as a going concern, the auditor should consider the adequacy of disclosure and include an explanatory paragraph (after the opinion paragraph) in the report. The auditor must use language in the explanatory paragraph that includes the words "substantial doubt" and "going concern."

25. Kane, CPA, concludes that there is substantial doubt about Lima Co.'s ability to continue as a going concern for a reasonable period of time. If Lima's financial statements adequately disclose its financial difficulties, Kane's auditor's report is required to include an explanatory paragraph that specifically uses the phrase(s)

	"Possible Discontinuance of Operations"	"Reasonable Period of Time, Not to Exceed One Year"
A.	Yes	Yes
B.	Yes	No
C.	No	Yes
D.	No	No

Answer (D) is correct. *(CPA, adapted)*
REQUIRED: The phrase(s), if any, required to be included in a paragraph describing a substantial doubt about a firm's ability to continue as a going concern.
DISCUSSION: If the auditor has a substantial doubt about the firm's ability to continue as a going concern for a reasonable period of time and therefore includes an additional paragraph at the end of the report, this explanatory paragraph should include the terms "substantial doubt" and "going concern." The specific phrases included in the question are not required.

26. An auditor concludes that there is substantial doubt about an entity's ability to continue as a going concern for a reasonable period of time. If the entity's disclosures concerning this matter are adequate, the audit report may include a(n)

	Disclaimer of Opinion	Qualified Opinion
A.	Yes	Yes
B.	No	No
C.	No	Yes
D.	Yes	No

Answer (D) is correct. *(CPA, adapted)*
REQUIRED: The nature of the report given a substantial going concern doubt.
DISCUSSION: By itself, a substantial doubt about an entity's ability to continue as a going concern does not require a modification of the opinion paragraph. Hence, a qualified opinion would be inappropriate. However, nothing precludes the auditor from disclaiming an opinion in these circumstances.

17.4 Comparative Financial Statements (AU 508)

27. How does an auditor make the following representations when issuing the standard auditor's report on comparative financial statements?

	Examination of Evidence on a Test Basis	Consistent Application of Accounting Principles
A.	Explicitly	Explicitly
B.	Implicitly	Implicitly
C.	Implicitly	Explicitly
D.	Explicitly	Implicitly

Answer (D) is correct. *(CPA, adapted)*
REQUIRED: The required representations when issuing the standard auditor's report on comparative financial statements.
DISCUSSION: The scope paragraph of the standard auditor's report on comparative statements explicitly states, "An audit includes examining, on a test basis, evidence supporting the amounts and disclosures in the financial statements." Changes in the application of accounting principles are recognized in the audit report by a separate explanatory paragraph. However, when GAAP have been consistently observed, the standard report makes no mention of consistency (AU 508). Thus, consistency is implicit when no explanatory paragraph is included.

28. Mead, CPA, had substantial doubt about Tech Co.'s ability to continue as a going concern when reporting on Tech's audited financial statements for the year ended June 30, year 1. That doubt has been removed in year 2. What is Mead's reporting responsibility if Tech is presenting its financial statements for the year ended June 30, year 2, on a comparative basis with those of year 1?

A. The explanatory paragraph included in the year 1 auditor's report should not be repeated.

B. The explanatory paragraph included in the year 1 auditor's report should be repeated in its entirety.

C. A different explanatory paragraph describing Mead's reasons for the removal of doubt should be included.

D. A different explanatory paragraph describing Tech's plans for financial recovery should be included.

Answer (A) is correct. *(CPA, adapted)*
REQUIRED: The effect on an updated report when substantial doubt about the auditee's ability to continue as a going concern has been removed.
DISCUSSION: AU 341 indicates that the explanatory paragraph included in the previous report should not be repeated in subsequent reports if the doubt has been resolved.
Answer (B) is incorrect because the doubt has been resolved, and the current report should not repeat the explanatory paragraph. Answer (C) is incorrect because the reasons for the removal of doubt need not be included. Answer (D) is incorrect because the paragraph should be removed, and a different explanatory paragraph describing the plans for financial recovery is not necessary.

29. When a predecessor auditor reissues the report on the prior period's financial statements at the request of the former client, the predecessor should

A. Indicate in the introductory paragraph of the reissued report that the financial statements of the subsequent period were audited by another CPA.

B. Obtain a representation letter from the successor auditor but not from management.

C. Compare the prior period's financial statements that the predecessor reported on with the financial statements to be presented for comparative purposes.

D. Add an explanatory paragraph to the reissued report stating that the predecessor has not performed additional auditing procedures on the prior period's financial statements.

Answer (C) is correct. *(CPA, adapted)*
REQUIRED: The procedure performed by the predecessor auditor before reissuing a report.
DISCUSSION: AU 508 requires the predecessor auditor to perform certain procedures before reissuing a report on prior-period financial statements. (S)he must read the current period's financial statements and compare the prior and current financial statements. Moreover, (s)he must obtain a representation letter from the successor auditor stating whether the successor has discovered matters having a material effect on, or requiring disclosure in, the statements reported on by the predecessor. Finally, the predecessor auditor must obtain a representation letter from management confirming past representations and stating whether post-balance-sheet events require adjustment to or disclosure in the financial statements.
Answer (A) is incorrect because the reissued report should not refer to the successor auditor. Answer (B) is incorrect because the predecessor auditor should obtain a representation letter from the successor auditor and from management. Answer (D) is incorrect because the report should not be modified unless the auditor's previous conclusions have changed.

30. When reporting on comparative financial statements, an auditor ordinarily should change the previously expressed opinion on the prior year's financial statements if the

A. Prior year's financial statements are restated to conform with generally accepted accounting principles.

B. Auditor is a predecessor auditor who has been requested by a former client to reissue the previously issued report.

C. Prior year's opinion was unqualified and the opinion on the current year's financial statements is modified due to a lack of consistency.

D. Reporting entity has changed as a result of the sale of a subsidiary.

Answer (A) is correct. *(CPA, adapted)*
REQUIRED: The event that causes an auditor to change a previously expressed opinion.
DISCUSSION: If the previous opinion was modified because of a departure from GAAP, but the prior year's statements were restated to remove the basis for the modification, the updated report should express an unqualified opinion.
Answer (B) is incorrect because the predecessor's report should normally be reissued with the original report date without revision, if the report is still appropriate. Answer (C) is incorrect because a change in accounting principle in the current period has no effect on the opinion expressed in the prior year. Answer (D) is incorrect because a change in the reporting entity resulting from a transaction or event, for example, a purchase or disposition of a business unit, does not require inclusion in the audit report of an explanatory paragraph about consistency (AU 420). Furthermore, such a transaction or event in the current year is not a circumstance that affects the prior period's statements. Thus, it presents no basis for modifying the opinion expressed on those statements.

31. The predecessor auditor, who is satisfied after properly communicating with the successor auditor, has reissued a report because the audit client desires comparative financial statements. The predecessor auditor's report should

A. Refer to the report of the successor auditor only in the scope paragraph.

B. Refer to the work of the successor auditor in the scope and opinion paragraphs.

C. Refer to both the work and the report of the successor auditor only in the opinion paragraph.

D. Not refer to the report or the work of the successor auditor.

Answer (D) is correct. *(CPA, adapted)*
REQUIRED: The true statement about reference to the successor auditor in a reissued report.
DISCUSSION: A predecessor auditor who has been asked to reissue his/her report should (1) read the current-period statements, (2) compare the statements (s)he reported on with other statements to be presented comparatively, (3) obtain a letter of representations from the successor auditor, and (4) obtain a representation letter from management. The predecessor auditor may also wish to consider the professional reputation and standing of the successor auditor and other matters discussed in AU 543, but the reissued report should not refer to the report or work of the successor auditor.

32. Jewel, CPA, audited Infinite Co.'s prior-year financial statements. These statements are presented with those of the current year for comparative purposes without Jewel's auditor's report, which expressed a qualified opinion. In drafting the current year's auditor's report, Crain, CPA, the successor auditor, should

I. Not name Jewel as the predecessor auditor

II. Indicate the type of report issued by Jewel

III. Indicate the substantive reasons for Jewel's qualification

A. I only.

B. I and II only.

C. II and III only.

D. I, II, and III.

Answer (D) is correct. *(CPA, adapted)*
REQUIRED: The matter(s) included in a successor auditor's report.
DISCUSSION: The successor auditor should state in the introductory paragraph that the prior year's financial statements were audited by another auditor but should not give the name of the predecessor auditor. (S)he should give the date and the type of report and, if the report was modified, the reasons for modification. If the predecessor auditor expressed a qualified opinion, the nature of and the reasons for the opinion qualification should be described.

33. In auditing the financial statements of Star Corp., Land discovered information leading Land to believe that Star's prior year's financial statements, which were audited by Tell, require substantial revisions. Under these circumstances, Land should

A. Notify Star's audit committee and shareholders that the prior year's financial statements cannot be relied on.

B. Request Star to reissue the prior year's financial statements with the appropriate revisions.

C. Notify Tell about the information and make inquiries about the integrity of Star's management.

D. Request Star to arrange a meeting among the three parties to resolve the matter.

Answer (D) is correct. *(CPA, adapted)*
REQUIRED: The successor auditor's action when financial statements from a prior period require revision.
DISCUSSION: Because the prior year's financial statements appear to require restatement, the successor auditor should discuss the matter with the predecessor auditor. (S)he should communicate any information that the predecessor auditor may need to meet the responsibilities imposed by AU 561, *Subsequent Discovery of Facts Existing at the Date of the Auditor's Report*. AU 315 states that a meeting of the three parties should be requested.
Answer (A) is incorrect because the current auditor need not notify shareholders. Answer (B) is incorrect because the financial statements should not be revised until the parties have discussed the matter. Answer (C) is incorrect because the current auditor should request that the client communicate with the prior auditor.

34. When unaudited financial statements are presented in comparative form with audited financial statements in a document filed with the Securities and Exchange Commission, such statements should be

	Marked as "Unaudited"	Withheld Until Audited	Referred to in the Auditor's Report
A.	Yes	No	No
B.	Yes	No	Yes
C.	No	Yes	Yes
D.	No	Yes	No

Answer (A) is correct. *(CPA, adapted)*
REQUIRED: The treatment of unaudited statements presented comparatively with audited statements in a document filed with the SEC.
DISCUSSION: AU 504 states, "When unaudited financial statements are presented in comparative form with audited statements in documents filed with the Securities and Exchange Commission, such statements should be clearly marked as 'unaudited' but should not be referred to in the auditor's report."

35. When unaudited financial statements of a nonpublic entity are presented in comparative form with audited financial statements in the subsequent year, the unaudited financial statements should be clearly marked to indicate their status and

I. The report on the unaudited financial statements should be reissued.

II. The report on the audited financial statements should include a separate paragraph describing the responsibility assumed for the unaudited financial statements.

A. I only.

B. II only.

C. Neither I nor II.

D. Either I or II.

Answer (D) is correct. *(CPA, adapted)*
REQUIRED: The appropriate reporting when unaudited financial statements are presented in comparative form with audited financial statements.
DISCUSSION: The financial statements that have not been audited should be clearly marked to indicate their status and either (1) the report on the prior period should be reissued, or (2) the report on the current period should include as a separate paragraph an appropriate description of the responsibility assumed for the financial statements of the prior period (AU 504).

17.5 Emphasis of a Matter (AU 508)

36. An auditor includes a separate paragraph in an otherwise unmodified report to emphasize that the entity being reported on had significant transactions with related parties. The inclusion of this separate paragraph

A. Is considered an "except for" qualification of the opinion.

B. Violates generally accepted auditing standards if this information is already disclosed in footnotes to the financial statements.

C. Necessitates a revision of the opinion paragraph to include the phrase "with the foregoing explanation."

D. Is appropriate and would not negate the unqualified opinion.

Answer (D) is correct. *(CPA, adapted)*
REQUIRED: The effect of a separate paragraph in an otherwise unmodified report.
DISCUSSION: A matter regarding the financial statements may be emphasized in a separate paragraph without modifying the auditor's opinion on the financial statements. Matters to be emphasized might include that the entity is a component of a larger enterprise or that it has had significant related party transactions. Subsequent events and accounting matters affecting comparability (e.g., a divestiture) are other matters suitable for this treatment.
Answer (A) is incorrect because, if the opinion were modified with an "except for" qualification, the opinion would not be "otherwise unmodified." Answer (B) is incorrect because the auditor can emphasize a matter without violating GAAS. Answer (C) is incorrect because the phrase "with the foregoing explanation" would lend doubt in the reader's mind as to whether the report was intended to be qualified.

Use Gleim's ***CPA Test Prep*** for interactive testing with over 2,000 additional multiple-choice questions!

17.6 PRACTICE SIMULATION

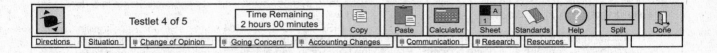

Directions | Situation | Change of Opinion | Going Concern | Accounting Changes | Communication | Research | Resources

1. Directions

In the following simulation, you will be asked to complete various tasks related to reports and other modifications. The simulation will provide all the information necessary to do the work. For full credit, be sure to view and complete all work tabs.

Resources may be available under the tab marked RESOURCES. You may want to review the resources before beginning the simulation.

2. Situation

Each of the following problems or issues relates to the auditor's responsibility to express an opinion on the client's financial statements.

3. Change of Opinion from Previous Year

This question is presented in a check-the-box format that requires you to select the correct responses from a given list.

An auditor has become aware of events affecting the financial statements of a prior year and has changed the opinion from unqualified to qualified. Indicate whether the current year's report on the comparative financial statements should address each of the issues below.

Issue	Yes	No
1. The audit procedure used to discover the event causing the change in opinion in the auditor's report.		
2. The date of the previous auditor's report.		
3. The substantive reason for the different opinion in the auditor's report.		
4. The type of opinion previously expressed.		
5. Indication that the updated opinion differs from that previously expressed.		
6. The reason the auditor did not discover the event in the previous year.		
7. Management's response to the change in opinion.		
8. Identification of the event that caused the change in opinion.		
9. The effect that the change in opinion will likely have on future periods.		
10. The date that the event that caused the change in opinion was discovered.		

4. Going Concern

The following additional paragraph was included in the auditor's report because of a substantial doubt about the entity's ability to continue as a going concern. Rewrite the paragraph and remove or change incorrect phrases.

The accompanying financial statements have been prepared by us assuming that the Company will continue as a profitable entity. As discussed in Note 12 to the Annual Report, the Company has suffered recurring losses from operations that raise some doubt about its ability to continue as a going concern. The financial statements include adjustments that will likely result from this uncertainty.

5. Accounting Changes

This question has a matching and true-false format that requires you to select the correct responses from a drop-down list. Write the answers in the columns provided. Each answer choice may be used once, more than once, or not at all.

The second standard of reporting applies to various types of accounting changes. It states, "The report shall identify those circumstances in which such principles have not been consistently observed in the current period in relation to the preceding period." Assume that the following changes have a material effect on the financial statements for the current year.

Three answers are required for each of the eight accounting changes. In column 1, fill in the letter of the type of change [A) through H)] that best matches each accounting change. In column 2, write M) if any modification is required in the auditor's report as it relates to the second standard of reporting. Write N) if no modification is required. In column 3, write R) if the prior year's financial statements should be restated when presented in comparative form with the current year's statements. Write S) if no restatement is necessary.

1)	2)	3)	Accounting Changes
			1. A change from the completed-contract method to the percentage-of-completion method of accounting for long-term construction contracts
			2. A change in the estimated useful life of previously recorded fixed assets based on newly acquired information
			3. Correction of a mathematical error in inventory pricing made in the prior period
			4. A change from prime costing to full absorption costing for inventory valuation
			5. A change from presentation of statements of individual companies to presentation of consolidated statements
			6. A change from deferring and amortizing pre-production costs to recording such costs as an expense when incurred because future benefits of the costs have become doubtful. The new accounting method was adopted in recognition of the change in estimated future benefits.
			7. A change to including the employer share of FICA taxes as *Retirement Benefits* on the income statement from including it with *Other Taxes*
			8. A change from the FIFO method of inventory pricing to the LIFO method of inventory pricing

1) Types of Changes
A) Change in accounting estimate
B) Change from GAAP to GAAP
C) Correction of an error in principle
D) Change in entity
E) Change in accounting estimate inseparable from change in principle
F) Change in classification
G) Correction of an error not involving a principle
H) New and different transactions

2) Modification Choices
M) Modification Required
N) No Modification Required

3) Restatement Choices
R) Restatement Required
S) No Restatement Required

6. Communication

Describe in a memo to your client's audit committee the auditor's responsibility when management is contemplating a change in accounting principle.

REMINDER: Your response will be graded for both technical content and writing skills. You should demonstrate your ability to develop, organize, and express your ideas. Do not convey information in the form of a table, bullet point list, or other abbreviated presentation.

To: Audit Committee
From: CPA
Subject: Change in accounting principle

7. Research

Find the answer to the following question in the Professional Standards using the materials available in the research tab. Print the appropriate citation in its entirety from the source you choose. This is a cut-and-paste item.

Certain changes made by the client may affect comparability of the financial statements, but not consistency. For those situations, the auditor does not add an additional paragraph to the standard report. Copy the paragraph that describes the auditor's consideration of changes in accounting estimates.

Unofficial Answers

3. Opinion is Changed from that of the Previous Year (10 Gradable Items)

1. <u>No</u>.
2. <u>Yes</u>.
3. <u>Yes</u>.
4. <u>Yes</u>.
5. <u>Yes</u>.
6. <u>No</u>.
7. <u>No</u>.
8. <u>Yes</u>.
9. <u>No</u>.
10. <u>No</u>.

4. Going Concern (5 Gradable Items)

The accompanying financial statements have been (1) <u>prepared assuming</u> that the Company will continue as a (2) <u>going concern</u>. As discussed in Note 12 to the (3) <u>financial statements</u>, the Company has suffered recurring losses from operations that raise (4) <u>substantial doubt</u> about its ability to continue as a going concern. The financial statements (5) <u>do not</u> include adjustments that will likely result from this uncertainty.

(Any substantive item changed that should stay the same should result in point reduction. For each one of these errors up to four, deduct 1 point from the 4 points you are given for communication.)

5. Accounting Changes (18 Gradable Items)

1. <u>1) B) Change from GAAP to GAAP</u>
    <u>2) M) Modification of the auditor's report is required.</u>
    <u>3) R) Prior statements need to be restated.</u>

2. <u>1) A) Change in accounting estimate</u>
    <u>2) N) Modification of the auditor's report is not required.</u>
    <u>3) S) No prior restatement is necessary.</u>

3. <u>1) G) Correction of an error not involving a principle</u>
    <u>2) N) Modification of the auditor's report is not required.</u>
    <u>3) R) Prior statements need to be restated.</u>

4. <u>1) C) Correction of an error in principle</u>
    <u>2) M) Modification of the auditor's report is required.</u>
    <u>3) R) Prior statements need to be restated.</u>

5. <u>1) D) Change in entity</u>
    <u>2) M) Modification of the auditor's report is required.</u>
    <u>3) R) Prior statements need to be restated.</u>

6. <u>1) E) Change in accounting estimate inseparable from change in principle</u>
    <u>2) M) Modification of the auditor's report is required.</u>
    <u>3) S) No prior restatement is necessary.</u>

7. <u>1) F) Change in classification</u>
    <u>2) N) Modification of the auditor's report is not required.</u>
    <u>3) S) No prior restatement is necessary.</u>

8. <u>1) B) Change from GAAP to GAAP</u>
    <u>2) M) Modification of the auditor's report is required.</u>
    <u>3) S) No prior restatement is necessary.</u>

6. Communication (5 Gradable Items; For grading instructions, please refer to page 11.)

To: Audit committee
From: CPA
Subject: Change of accounting principle

Independent external auditors must communicate with the audit committee about certain matters. These matters include changes in significant accounting policies. This memorandum clarifies the auditor's responsibilities in these circumstances.

When evaluating a change of accounting principle, the auditor must determine that the new principle is generally accepted. The auditor must then determine that management can justify the change to the new principle. The change is justified only if the alternative principle is preferable. Accordingly, the second standard of reporting requires that the audit report identify circumstances in which accounting principles have not been consistently observed in the current period in relation to the preceding period. The purpose of this standard is to ensure that a lack of comparability of financial statements between periods caused by changes in accounting principles will be properly reported by the auditor. A failure of the report to mention consistency implies that no change in accounting principles has occurred or that such a change in principles (or in the method of their application) had no material effect. Thus, the report must include an explanatory paragraph when a change in principle has a material effect on comparability. This paragraph is included even if the auditor concurs with the change. The paragraph follows the opinion paragraph, states the nature of the change, and refers to a financial statement note that discusses the change in detail. Furthermore, the lack of consistency, by itself, is not a basis for expressing a qualified or adverse opinion or disclaiming an opinion. However, if the auditor does not concur with the change in principle, (s)he may modify the opinion.

If you have questions or comments, please contact us at your convenience.

7. Research (6 Gradable Items)

AU Section 420 -- *Consistency of Application of Generally Accepted Accounting Principles*

Change in Accounting Estimate

.15 Accounting estimates (such as service lives and salvage values of depreciable assets and provisions for warranty costs, uncollectible receivables, and inventory obsolescence) are necessary in the preparation of financial statements. Accounting estimates change as new events occur and as additional experience and information are acquired. This type of accounting change is required by altered conditions that affect comparability but do not involve the consistency standard. The independent auditor, in addition to becoming satisfied with respect to the conditions giving rise to the change in accounting estimate, should determine that the change does not include the effect of a change in accounting principle. Provided the auditor is so satisfied, she or he need not comment on the change in the report. However, an accounting change of this type having a material effect on the financial statements may require disclosure in a note to the financial statements.

Scoring Schedule:

	Correct Responses		Gradable Items		Weights		
Tab 3	_____	÷	10	×	20%	=	_____
Tab 4	_____	÷	5	×	20%	=	_____
Tab 5	_____	÷	18	×	20%	=	_____
Tab 6	_____	÷	5	×	30%	=	_____
Tab 7	_____	÷	6	×	10%	=	_____
							(Your Score)

Use Gleim's *CPA Review Online* to practice more simulations in a realistic environment.

STUDY UNIT EIGHTEEN
REVIEW, COMPILATION, AND SPECIAL REPORTS

(12 pages of outline)

18.1	Compilation	557
18.2	Review	559
18.3	Other Considerations	562
18.4	Uses of Special Reports (AU 623)	564
18.5	Financial Statements Prepared in Conformity with an Other Comprehensive Basis of Accounting (OCBOA) (AU 623)	565
18.6	Specified Elements, Accounts, or Items of a Financial Statement (AU 623)	566
18.7	Other Presentations (AU 623)	567
18.8	Financial Information Presented in Prescribed Forms or Schedules that Require a Prescribed Form of Auditor's Report (AU 623)	568
18.9	Practice Simulation	585

Review and compilation services are provided in conjunction with the dissemination of financial statements. These services are not as comprehensive as an audit (which provides positive assurance that financial statements are in accordance with GAAP). These accounting services with respect to unaudited financial statements are governed by Statements on Standards for Accounting and Review Services (SSARSs), which are codified as AR 50, 100, 200, etc. SSARS 1 (AR 100) is the basic pronouncement on reviews and compilations and is outlined in the next few pages.

Regardless of the service provided, the CPA should establish an understanding with the client, preferably in writing, describing the nature and limitations of the services to be performed and the report to be issued. The understanding should also provide that the engagement is not intended to disclose errors, fraud, or illegal acts. The CPA must be independent to perform a review but need not be to perform a compilation.

The effective study of special reports requires little additional effort. The basis of virtually all special reports is the standard, three-paragraph audit report (one more reason to memorize the standard audit report). Several of these reports have been tested on the exam. Most often, other comprehensive basis of accounting (OCBOA) statements prepared on a cash basis have been the subject of questions.

In general, if an auditor can form an opinion on the fairness of financial information prepared on an OCBOA; specified elements, accounts, or items; or information presented in other formats, the auditor can express an opinion on the fairness of the presentation.

18.1 COMPILATION

1. The accountant should not submit unaudited financial statements to the client or others unless, as a minimum, (s)he has complied with the provisions of AR 100 concerning compilations.

   a. A submission is defined as "presenting to a client or third parties financial statements that the accountant has prepared, either manually or through the use of computer software."

   b. Compilations are "accounting services" described by AR 100 and are often referred to by practitioners as "write-up services."

2. **Accountant's Understanding of the Client and Industry.** The accountant

    a. Should possess or obtain, prior to completing the compilation, an appropriate level of knowledge of the accounting principles and practices of the client's industry and an understanding of the client's business

    b. Should possess a general understanding of the nature of the entity's business transactions, the form of its accounting records, the stated qualifications of its accounting personnel, the accounting basis on which the financial statements are to be presented, and the form and content of the financial statements

3. **Compilation Procedures.** The accountant

    a. Is not required to make inquiries or perform other procedures to verify, corroborate, or review information provided by the entity

    b. May learn from performing procedures for other purposes or become aware that the information supplied by the entity is incorrect, incomplete, or otherwise unsatisfactory for the purpose of compiling the financial statements

        1) If so, the accountant should obtain additional or revised information.

        2) If the entity refuses to provide the information, the accountant should withdraw from the engagement.

    c. Should read the compiled financial statements and consider whether the statements appear to be in appropriate form and free of obvious material errors, such as arithmetical or clerical mistakes or mistakes in the application of GAAP, including inadequate disclosure

4. **Standard Compilation Report**

    a. The standard report contains two paragraphs.

To: <---------- Addressed to owner or person who engaged accountant
We (or I) have completed the accompanying balance sheet of XYZ Company as of December 31, year 1, and the related statements of income, retained earnings, and cash flows for the year then ended, in accordance with Statements on Standards for Accounting and Review Services issued by the American Institute of Certified Public Accountants.
A compilation is limited to presenting in the form of financial statements information that is the representation of management (owners). We (I) have not audited or reviewed the accompanying financial statements and, accordingly, do not express an opinion or any other form of assurance on them.
Signature <---------- May be manual, stamped, electronic, or typed
Date   <---------- Date of completion of the compilation

    b. A **statement of retained earnings** may be omitted. If the required disclosure of changes in capital is accomplished other than in a retained earnings statement, no reference to that statement should be made in a compilation report.

    c. A compilation report should refer to a **statement of comprehensive income** if one is presented.

    d. Any other procedures that the accountant might have performed should not be described in the report.

    e. The report does not have a title. (Recall that the audit report has the title, Independent Auditor's Report.)

    f. The date of the report is the date of the completion of the compilation.

    g. Each page of financial statements should contain language such as "See Accountant's Compilation Report."

    h. The accountant may accept an engagement to issue a compilation report on one financial statement, e.g., balance sheet.

    i.   If compiled financial statements are not expected to be used by a third party, the accountant may submit them to a client without a compilation report, provided that the limitation on their use is documented in an engagement letter, preferably signed by management.

        1)   The term **third party** excludes members of management who are knowledgeable about the nature of the procedures applied and the basis of accounting and assumptions used in the preparation of the financial statements. Thus, even certain client managers may be defined as third parties because they lack knowledge about the procedures applied, etc.

    j.   The report must be signed by the accounting firm or the accountant.

5. **Modified Report**

    a.   An accountant may accept an engagement to compile financial statements that omit substantially all of the disclosures (e.g., notes) required by GAAP or another comprehensive basis of accounting if the omission is clearly indicated in the report and was not intended to mislead users.

    b.   The paragraph at the top of the next page is added as a third paragraph to the standard report:

Language to Modify Compilation Report for Lack of Disclosures

> Management has elected to omit substantially all of the disclosures required by generally accepted accounting principles. If the omitted disclosures were included in the financial statements, they might influence the user's conclusions about the company's financial position, results of operations, and cash flows. Accordingly, these financial statements are not designed for those who are not informed about such matters.

6.   When the accountant is not independent, (s)he

    a.   May perform a compilation because no assurance is provided
    b.   Should disclose the lack of independence

        1)   For example, the last paragraph should read as follows:

> We are not independent with respect to XYZ Company.

        2)   Hence, a report that does not mention independence implies that the accountant is independent.

    c.   Should not disclose the reason for lack of independence

7.   Stop and review! You have completed the outline for this subunit. Study multiple-choice questions 1 through 14 beginning on page 569.

18.2 REVIEW

1. **Accountant's Understanding of the Client and Industry**. The accountant should

    a.   Possess or obtain, prior to completing the review, an appropriate level of knowledge of the accounting principles and practices of the client's industry and an understanding of the client's business

    b.   Have a general understanding of the entity's organization, its operating characteristics, and the nature of its assets, liabilities, revenues, and expenses. This would ordinarily involve a general knowledge of the entity's production, distribution, and compensation methods, types of products and services, operating locations, and material transactions with related parties.

2.   Review procedures consist of **inquiries** and **analytical procedures**.

    a.   The following inquiries should be made to members of management who have responsibility for financial and accounting matters:

        1)   Whether the financial statements have been prepared in conformity with GAAP consistently applied.

        2)   The accounting principles and practices used and procedures for recording, classifying, and summarizing transactions and for accumulating information for disclosure.

        3)   Unusual or complex situations that may affect the statements.

        4)   Significant transactions occurring or recognized near the end of the period.

        5)   The status of uncorrected misstatements identified in the previous engagement.

        6)   Questions that have arisen during the review.

        7)   Events subsequent to the date of the financial statements that could have a material effect on the financial statements.

        8)   Their knowledge of any material fraud or suspected fraud.

        9)   Significant journal entries or other adjustments.

       10) Communications from regulators.

    b.   Analytical procedures should include developing expectations based on plausible relationships that are reasonably expected to exist and comparing recorded amounts (or ratios developed from them) with the expectations. For the purposes of AR 100, analytical procedures may consist of

        1)   Comparison of the financial statements with those from prior periods.

        2)   Comparison of the statements with anticipated results, such as previously prepared budgets or forecasts.

        3)   Comparing relationships among elements in the current financial statements with corresponding prior-period information.

        4)   Comparison of current financial information with relevant nonfinancial information.

        5)   Comparison of ratios and indicators for the current period with expectations based on prior periods or with those of entities in the same industry.

    c.   The accountant must obtain **written representations** from management. They should be addressed to the accountant, dated no earlier than the report's date, and signed by the CEO or CFO. Specific representations should address

        1)   Management's responsibility for fair presentation.

        2)   Management's belief that the statements are fairly presented.

        3)   Management's acknowledgment of its responsibility to prevent and detect fraud.

        4)   Knowledge of any material fraud or suspected fraud.

        5)   Management's full and truthful responses to inquiries.

        6)   The completeness of information.

        7)   Information about subsequent events.

    NOTE: An example of a management representation letter is in Study Unit 14. It should be modified to meet the circumstances.

    d.   Other procedures include obtaining reports from other accountants, if any; reading the financial statements to consider whether they appear to conform with GAAP; and inquiring about actions taken at shareholders' and directors' meetings.

    e.   Neither a review nor a compilation contemplates obtaining an understanding of internal control or assessing control risk, testing accounting records, responding to inquiries by obtaining corroborating evidence, or performing other audit procedures.

f. If, however, the accountant becomes aware that information appears incorrect, incomplete, or unsatisfactory, (s)he should perform the additional procedures deemed necessary to achieve the limited assurance that no material modifications should be made to the financial statements for them to be in conformity with GAAP.

g. **Documentation** should be prepared that addresses the engagement's circumstances, including any findings or issues judged to be significant.

3. **Standard Review Report**

a. The standard report contains three paragraphs.

To: <---------- Addressed to owner or person who engaged accountant

We (or I) have reviewed the accompanying balance sheet of XYZ Company as of December 31, year 1, and the related statements of income, retained earnings, and cash flows for the year then ended, in accordance with Statements on Standards for Accounting and Review Services issued by the American Institute of Certified Public Accountants. All information included in these financial statements is the representation of the management (owners) of XYZ Company.

A review consists principally of inquiries of company personnel and analytical procedures applied to financial data. It is substantially less in scope than an examination in accordance with generally accepted auditing standards, the objective of which is the expression of an opinion regarding the financial statements taken as a whole. Accordingly, we (I) do not express such an opinion.

Based on our (my) review, we are (I am) not aware of any material modifications that should be made to the accompanying financial statements in order for them to be in conformity with generally accepted accounting principles.

Signature <---------- May be manual, stamped, electronic, or typed

Date <---------- Date of completion of the review procedures

---

b. The **statement of retained earnings** may be omitted. If the required disclosure of changes in capital is accomplished other than in a retained earnings statement, no reference to that statement should be made in the review report.

c. A review report should refer to a **statement of comprehensive income** if one is presented.

d. The report does not have a title.

e. Each page of financial statements should contain language such as "See Accountant's Review Report."

f. The date of the report is the date of the completion of the review procedures.

g. The accountant may accept an engagement to issue a review report on one financial statement, e.g., the balance sheet, if the scope of his/her procedures has not been limited.

h. If the accountant is unable to perform necessary procedures or the client does not provide a representation letter, the review will be incomplete, a review report cannot be issued, and the accountant may consider whether a compilation report may be issued.

i. The report must be signed in some manner by the accounting firm or the accountant.

4. **Modified Report**

    a. The accountant may become aware of a material departure from GAAP.

        1) The departure, including its effects, should be disclosed in a separate paragraph.

        2) The conclusion paragraph should use the phrase "with the exception of" or "except for."

        3) The accountant is not required to determine the effects of the departure. If management has not done so, the accountant should state that a determination has not been made.

        4) The following is an example of an additional paragraph and a conclusion paragraph (the introduction and scope paragraphs are unchanged):

            Language to Modify Review Report for a Departure from GAAP

            > Based on our review, with the exception of the matter(s) described in the following paragraph(s), we are not aware of any material modifications that should be made to the accompanying financial statements in order for them to be in conformity with generally accepted accounting principles.
            >
            > As disclosed in note X to the financial statements, generally accepted accounting principles require that inventory cost consist of material, labor, and overhead. Management has informed us that the inventory of finished goods and work-in-process is stated in the accompanying financial statements as material and labor cost only, and that the effects of this departure from GAAP on financial position, results of operations, and cash flows have not been determined.

        5) Given proper disclosure, uncertainties about the going concern assumption and inconsistencies in the application of accounting principles do not normally require modification of the standard report.

        6) If the accountant believes that the modification is not adequate to indicate the deficiencies in the financial statements, (s)he should withdraw from the engagement (there is no provision for an adverse review report).

5. Stop and review! You have completed the outline for this subunit. Study multiple-choice questions 15 through 30 beginning on page 573.

18.3 OTHER CONSIDERATIONS

1. An accountant may be asked to change the engagement from a higher level of service (audit or review) to a lower level of service (review or compilation).

    a. The request may result from a change in circumstances affecting the entity's requirements, a misunderstanding as to the nature of one of the services, or a scope restriction, whether imposed by the client or circumstances.

    b. Before an accountant engaged to perform a higher level of service agrees to change to a lower level, the following should be considered:

        1) The reason for the client's request, particularly the implications of a scope restriction, whether imposed by the client or by circumstances

        2) The additional effort required to complete the original engagement

        3) The estimated additional cost to complete the original engagement

    c. A change in circumstances that affects the entity's requirement for the service or a misunderstanding about the nature of a service is ordinarily a reasonable basis for requesting a change in the engagement.

    d.   In considering the implications of a scope restriction, the accountant should evaluate the possibility that the information affected may be incorrect, incomplete, or otherwise unsatisfactory.

        1)   But, if an auditor has been prohibited by the client from contacting the client's legal counsel, (s)he ordinarily would be precluded from issuing a review or compilation report.

        2)   If the client in an audit or review engagement that has been changed to a review or compilation does not provide a signed representation letter, the accountant is not permitted to issue a review report and is ordinarily precluded from issuing a compilation report.

    e.   If the cost to complete the higher level of service is insignificant, the accountant should consider the propriety of accepting a change.

    f.   The report on the changed engagement should not mention

        1)   The original engagement
        2)   Any auditing or review procedures performed
        3)   Scope limitations that led to the changed engagement

2.   **AR 50, *Standards for Accounting and Review Services***

    a.   See Appendix A for a summary of the hierarchy of pronouncements applicable to these engagements.

3.   **AR 200, *Reporting on Comparative Financial Statements***

    a.   Much of the guidance on reporting on comparative statements given in **AU 508**, *Reports on Audited Financial Statements*, also applies here.

    b.   A continuing accountant who performs the same or higher level of service for the current period should update his/her report for the prior period.

        1)   A continuing accountant who performs a lower level of service should either include a separate paragraph describing the responsibility assumed for the financial statements of the prior period or reissue the previous report.

    c.   Compiled financial statements that omit substantially all of the disclosures required by GAAP are not comparable with financial statements that include such disclosures. Accordingly, the accountant ordinarily should not issue a report on comparative financial statements when statements for one or more, but not all, of the periods presented omit substantially all of the disclosures required by GAAP.

4.   **AR 300, *Compilation Reports on Financial Statements Included in Certain Prescribed Forms***

    a.   An alternative form of the standard compilation report is used when a prescribed form or related instructions call for departure from GAAP by specifying a measurement principle not in conformity with GAAP or failing to require disclosures in accordance with GAAP.

    b.   The presumption is that the information required in a prescribed form is sufficient to meet the needs of the body that designed or adopted the form.

    c.   In the standard report on statements included in such a form, the accountant should indicate that the statements are in a prescribed form and that they may differ from those presented in accordance with GAAP, but (s)he need not describe the differences in the report.

5. **AR 400,** *Communications between Predecessor and Successor Accountants*

   a. The successor accountant may decide to communicate with the predecessor accountant before accepting a review or compilation engagement.

      1) In an audit, the communication is required.

   b. The predecessor is required to respond promptly and fully on the basis of known facts.

   c. Both accountants, however, must have the client's specific consent to disclose confidential information.

   d. Most other provisions of AU 315, *Communications between Predecessor and Successor Auditors* (which is discussed in Study Unit 2), are applicable to these communications.

   e. A successor who believes the statements reported on by the predecessor may require revision must request that the client communicate this information to the predecessor.

6. **AR 600,** *Reporting on Personal Financial Statements Included in Written Personal Financial Plans*

   a. An accountant may submit a written personal financial plan containing unaudited personal financial statements to a client without complying with the requirements of SSARS 1 (AR 100) if the accountant

      1) Has an understanding with the client about its use

      2) Has no reason to believe that the financial statements will be used to obtain credit or for any other purpose except the financial plan

      3) Attaches a report describing the engagement

7. Stop and review! You have completed the outline for this subunit. Study multiple-choice questions 31 through 36 beginning on page 578.

18.4 USES OF SPECIAL REPORTS (AU 623)

1. Special reports may be issued on

   a. Financial statements that are prepared in conformity with a comprehensive basis of accounting other than generally accepted accounting principles (OCBOA)

   b. Specified elements, accounts, or items of a financial statement

   c. Compliance with aspects of contractual agreements or regulatory requirements related to audited financial statements

   d. Financial presentations to comply with contractual agreements or regulatory provisions

   e. Financial information presented in prescribed forms or schedules that require a prescribed form of auditor's report

2. **Financial Statements Prepared in Conformity with an OCBOA**

   a. GAAS are applicable when an auditor audits and reports on any financial statement.

      1) A **financial statement** is "a presentation of financial data, including notes, derived from accounting records and intended to communicate an entity's economic resources or obligations at a moment in time or the changes therein for a period of time in conformity with a comprehensive basis of accounting."

2) In addition to the basic financial statements, the following financial presentations are considered to be financial statements for reporting purposes:

    a) Statement of assets and liabilities that does not include owners' equity
    b) Statement of revenue and expenses
    c) Summary of operations
    d) Statement of operations by product lines
    e) Statement of cash receipts and disbursements

b. An auditor's judgment about the overall presentation of financial statements is ordinarily applied within the framework of GAAP, but an OCBOA is sometimes used. An OCBOA is one of the following:

1) A basis of accounting that the reporting entity uses to comply with the requirements or financial reporting provisions of a regulatory agency, for example, a basis of accounting insurance companies use under the rules of a state insurance commission

2) A basis of accounting used for tax purposes

3) The cash basis and modifications of the cash basis having substantial support, such as recording depreciation on fixed assets or accruing income taxes

4) A definite set of criteria having substantial support that is applied to all material items, for example, the price-level basis

3. Stop and review! You have completed the outline for this subunit. Study multiple-choice question 37 on page 580.

18.5 FINANCIAL STATEMENTS PREPARED IN CONFORMITY WITH AN OTHER COMPREHENSIVE BASIS OF ACCOUNTING (OCBOA) (AU 623)

1. The only differences from the standard audit report are described below.

a. The specific financial statements being audited (identified in the introductory paragraph) may differ from the traditional statements.

b. A paragraph is added before the opinion paragraph that

1) States the basis of presentation and refers to the note to the financial statements that describes the basis

2) Discloses that the basis of presentation is a comprehensive basis of accounting other than GAAP

c. In the opinion paragraph, the auditor should express an opinion (or disclaim an opinion) on whether the financial statements are presented fairly, in all material respects, **in conformity with the basis of accounting described**.

d. If the financial statements are in accordance with the requirements or reporting provisions of a regulatory agency, a paragraph that restricts the distribution of the report should be added. In this case, the report is a "restricted-use report" because it must state that it is intended solely for the information and use of the specified parties who are identified in the report (AU 532).

2. Unless the statements meet the conditions for presentation in conformity with an OCBOA, the auditor should use the standard form of the audit report modified appropriately for the departures from GAAP (i.e., express a qualified or adverse opinion).

3. Terms such as **balance sheet**, **statement of financial position**, **statement of income**, **statement of operations**, and **statement of cash flows** or other similar unmodified titles are understood to apply only to statements in conformity with GAAP (i.e., accrual basis). Consequently, the auditor should consider whether the financial statements that (s)he is reporting on are suitably titled.

a. If the statements are not suitably titled, the auditor should qualify the opinion.

4.   The following is an example of reporting on a statement prepared on the cash basis. (The modifications made to the standard report are in bold.)

Independent Auditor's Report

To: <---------- Addressed to the Board of Directors, Stockholders, or Owner

We have audited the **accompanying statements of assets and liabilities arising from cash transactions of XYZ Company as of December 31, year 2 and year 1, and the related statements of revenue collected and expenses paid for the years then ended.** These financial statements are the responsibility of the Company's management. Our responsibility is to express an opinion on these financial statements based on our audits.

A review consists principally of inquiries of company personnel and analytical procedures applied to financial data. It is substantially less in scope than an examination in accordance with generally accepted auditing standards, the objective of which is the expression of an opinion regarding the financial statements taken as a whole. Accordingly, we (I) do not express such an opinion.

As described in Note X, these financial statements were prepared on the basis of cash receipts and disbursements, which is a comprehensive basis of accounting other than generally accepted accounting principles.

In our opinion, the financial statements referred to above present fairly, in all material respects, **the assets and liabilities arising from cash transactions of XYZ Company as of December 31, year 2 and year 1, and its revenue collected and expenses paid during the years then ended, on the basis of accounting described in Note X.**

Signature   <---------- May be signed, typed or printed

Date   <---------- Date of completion of field work

---

5.   **Evaluating the Adequacy of Disclosure in Financial Statements Prepared in Conformity with an OCBOA**

a.   The auditor should apply essentially the same criteria as applied to financial statements prepared in conformity with GAAP.

b.   The financial statements should include, in the accompanying notes, a summary of significant accounting policies that discusses the basis of presentation and describes how it differs from GAAP. However, the effects of the differences need not be quantified.

6.   Stop and review! You have completed the outline for this subunit. Study multiple-choice questions 38 through 42 beginning on page 581.

18.6 SPECIFIED ELEMENTS, ACCOUNTS, OR ITEMS OF A FINANCIAL STATEMENT (AU 623)

1.   An independent auditor may express an opinion on one or more specified elements, accounts, or items of a financial statement, which may be presented in the report or in an accompanying document.

a.   Examples of the elements, accounts, or items that may be reported on based on an audit include rentals, royalties, receivables, a profit participation, or a provision for income taxes.

2.   The auditor should plan and perform the audit and prepare the report with a view to the purpose of the engagement. With the exception of the first standard of reporting (conformity with GAAP), the 10 GAAS are applicable.

3.   The engagement may be undertaken separately or in conjunction with an audit of the financial statements.

4. The measurement of materiality must relate to each element, account, or item because the auditor expresses an opinion on each element, etc., covered by the report.

    a. For example, if the auditor expresses an opinion of the fairness of a client's current assets, the materiality of each account (i.e., cash, accounts receivable, etc.) that constitutes current assets would be judged relative to current assets.

    b. Thus, an audit of a specified element, etc., is ordinarily more extensive than the consideration of the same information in an audit of the financial statements.

    c. The auditor must become satisfied that elements, etc., interrelated with those on which (s)he expresses an opinion have been considered.

5. If expressing an opinion on specified elements, etc., is equivalent to expressing a piecemeal opinion on the financial statements, an auditor who has expressed an adverse opinion or disclaimed an opinion on those statements should avoid such reporting.

    a. However, an auditor may nevertheless be able to express an opinion in these circumstances if a major portion of the financial statements is not involved. For example, an auditor who has disclaimed an opinion on the financial statements may be able to express an opinion on the accounts receivable balance. However, the report would be presented separately.

    b. If the preparation of the element, account, or item complies with the requirements or provisions of a contract or agreement that results in a presentation not in conformity with GAAP or an OCBOA, a restricted-use report is necessary (AU 532).

6. Stop and review! You have completed the outline for this subunit. Study multiple-choice questions 43 through 46 beginning on page 582.

18.7 OTHER PRESENTATIONS (AU 623)

1. **Compliance with Aspects of Contractual Agreements or Regulatory Requirements Related to Audited Financial Statements**

    a. Entities may be required by contractual agreements, such as bond indentures and certain types of loan agreements, or by regulatory agencies to furnish compliance reports by independent auditors.

        1) For example, loan agreements usually impose on borrowers a variety of covenants involving matters such as payments into sinking funds, payments of interest, maintenance of current ratios, restrictions of dividend payments, and the use of proceeds from sales of property. They also usually require audited financial statements.

        2) Reports based upon compliance with aspects of contractual agreements or regulatory provisions should be provided in conjunction with an ordinary audit of financial statements.

        3) The report envisioned provides negative assurance that may be given in a separate paragraph(s) in the audit report on the financial statements or in a separate report.

            a) But this assurance should not be given unless an audit of the statements has been made and should not extend to any covenants relating to matters that have not been subjected to audit procedures in the audit (AU 623).

        4) A restricted-use report is required (AU 532).

2. **Financial Presentations to Comply with Contractual Agreements or Regulatory Provisions**

    a. These statements may not constitute a complete presentation but may otherwise be prepared in conformity with GAAP or an OCBOA. An audit on these statements results in an opinion being expressed by the auditor.

        1) An example is a schedule of gross income and certain expenses of a real estate operation that excludes interest, depreciation, and income tax expense but is otherwise in conformity with GAAP.

        2) The special-purpose presentation may be prepared on a basis that results in a presentation not in conformity with GAAP or an OCBOA.

            a) For example, an acquisition agreement may require the acquired entity to prepare statements in which certain assets are reported at a valuation basis stated in the agreement.

        3) The report should include a paragraph that restricts the use of the report to those knowledgeable of the agreements or provisions (see AU 532).

3. Stop and review! You have completed the outline for this subunit. Study multiple-choice questions 47 and 48 on page 584.

18.8 FINANCIAL INFORMATION PRESENTED IN PRESCRIBED FORMS OR SCHEDULES THAT REQUIRE A PRESCRIBED FORM OF AUDITOR'S REPORT (AU 623)

1. Printed forms designed by the bodies with which they will be filed often prescribe the wording of the auditor's report. Many are unacceptable to auditors because they conflict with reporting standards.

    a. When a report form calls upon an auditor to make an unjustified assertion, (s)he should reword the form or attach a separate report (AU 623).

2. Stop and review! You have completed the outline for this subunit. Study multiple-choice question 49 on page 584.

QUESTIONS

18.1 Compilation

1. Statements on Standards for Accounting and Review Services (SSARSs) require an accountant to report when the accountant has

A. Typed client-prepared financial statements, without modification, as an accommodation to the client.

B. Provided a client with a financial statement format that does not include dollar amounts, to be used by the client in preparing financial statements.

C. Proposed correcting journal entries to be recorded by the client that change client-prepared financial statements.

D. Prepared, through the use of computer software, financial statements to be used by third parties.

Answer (D) is correct. *(CPA, adapted)*
REQUIRED: The situation in which an accountant must issue a report.
DISCUSSION: An accountant may (1) be engaged to report on compiled financial statements or (2) submit statements reasonably expected to be used by a third party. In both cases, the accountant must issue a report. A submission is defined as "presenting to a client or third parties financial statements that the accountant has prepared, either manually or through the use of computer software."
Answer (A) is incorrect because typing or reproducing client-prepared financial statements, without modification, as an accommodation to a client does not constitute a submission of financial statements. Answer (B) is incorrect because, without dollar amounts, the presentation is not a financial statement. Answer (C) is incorrect because journal entries are not a financial statement.

2. An accountant is required to comply with the provisions of Statements on Standards for Accounting and Review Services when

I. Reproducing client-prepared financial statements, without modification, as an accommodation to a client

II. Preparing standard monthly journal entries for depreciation and expiration of prepaid expenses

A. I only.

B. II only.

C. Both I and II.

D. Neither I nor II.

Answer (D) is correct. *(CPA, adapted)*
REQUIRED: The services that require compliance with SSARSs.
DISCUSSION: An accountant should not submit unaudited financial statements to his/her client or others without compliance with SSARSs. A submission is defined as "presenting to a client or third parties financial statements that the accountant has prepared, either manually or through the use of computer software." Thus, typing or reproducing client-prepared financial statements, without modification, as an accommodation to a client and preparing standard monthly journal entries (e.g., standard entries for depreciation and expiration of prepaid expenses) do not constitute a submission of financial statements.

3. When an accountant performs more than one level of service (for example, a compilation and a review, or a compilation and an audit) concerning the financial statements of a nonpublic entity, the accountant ordinarily should issue the report that is appropriate for

A. The lowest level of service rendered.

B. The highest level of service rendered.

C. A compilation engagement.

D. A review engagement.

Answer (B) is correct. *(CPA, adapted)*
REQUIRED: The report issued when an accountant performs more than one level of service.
DISCUSSION: The report communicates the degree of responsibility, if any, that the accountant accepts regarding the financial statements. If more than one service is performed, (s)he "should issue the report that is appropriate for the highest level of service rendered" (AR 100). An exception is permitted, however, if an accountant has both compiled and reviewed the financial statements of a nonpublic entity and if the compilation report for the same period concerns financial statements included in a prescribed form that requires a departure from GAAP (AR 300).

4. An accountant should not submit unaudited financial statements to the management of a nonpublic company unless, at a minimum, the accountant

- A. Assists in adjusting the books of account and preparing the trial balance.
- B. Types or reproduces the financial statements.
- C. Complies with the standards applicable to compilation engagements.
- D. Applies analytical procedures to the financial statements.

Answer (C) is correct. *(CPA, adapted)*
REQUIRED: The action required of an accountant who submits unaudited financial statements to the management of a nonpublic company.
DISCUSSION: The accountant should not submit unaudited financial statements of a nonpublic entity to the client or others unless, as a minimum, (s)he complies with the standards set forth in AR 100 applicable to compilation engagements. If the statements are intended for third-party use, a compilation report must be attached. If not intended for third-party use and the limitation on use is documented in the engagement letter, the statements may be submitted to the client without the report.
Answer (A) is incorrect because assisting in adjusting the books of account and preparing the trial balance is not a prerequisite for submission of unaudited statements. Answer (B) is incorrect because typing or reproducing client-prepared financial statements, without modification, does not constitute a submission of financial statements. Answer (D) is incorrect because application of analytical procedures is not required by the standards for compilations.

5. When engaged to compile the financial statements of a nonpublic entity, an accountant is required to possess a level of knowledge of the entity's accounting principles and practices. This requirement most likely will include obtaining a general understanding of the

- A. Stated qualifications of the entity's accounting personnel.
- B. Design of the entity's internal controls placed in operation.
- C. Risk factors relating to misstatements arising from illegal acts.
- D. Internal control awareness of the entity's senior management.

Answer (A) is correct. *(CPA, adapted)*
REQUIRED: The knowledge required to perform a compilation.
DISCUSSION: To perform a compilation, the accountant should possess an understanding of the nature of the entity's business, its accounting records, the qualifications of its accounting personnel, and the content and accounting basis of the financial statements.
Answer (B) is incorrect because the consideration of internal control is not necessary to perform compilation services. Answer (C) is incorrect because no assessment of risk or application of auditing procedures is required in a compilation. Answer (D) is incorrect because the consideration of internal control is not necessary to perform compilation services.

6. When compiling a nonpublic entity's financial statements, an accountant is least likely to

- A. Perform analytical procedures designed to identify relationships that appear to be unusual.
- B. Read the compiled financial statements and consider whether they appear to include adequate disclosure.
- C. Omit substantially all of the disclosures required by generally accepted accounting principles.
- D. Issue a compilation report on one or more, but not all, of the basic financial statements.

Answer (A) is correct. *(CPA, adapted)*
REQUIRED: The procedure least likely to be performed in a compilation.
DISCUSSION: In a compilation engagement, the accountant is not required to make inquiries or perform analytical or other procedures to verify, corroborate, or review information supplied by the entity. However, analytical procedures are necessary in review and audit engagements.
Answer (B) is incorrect because the accountant should read the compiled statements and consider whether they are free from obvious material errors, including inadequate disclosure. Answer (C) is incorrect because a compilation may omit substantially all disclosures required by GAAP provided the omission is clearly indicated in the report and, to the accountant's knowledge, is not undertaken with an intent to mislead. Answer (D) is incorrect because an accountant may be asked and is permitted to issue a compilation report on one or more, but not all, of the basic financial statements.

7. Which of the following should not be included in an accountant's standard report based upon the compilation of an entity's financial statements?

A. A statement that a compilation is limited to presenting in the form of financial statements information that is the representation of management.

B. A statement that the compilation was performed in accordance with Statements on Standards for Accounting and Review Services issued by the AICPA.

C. A statement that the accountant has not audited or reviewed the statements.

D. A statement that the accountant does not express an opinion but provides only negative assurance on the statements.

Answer (D) is correct. *(CPA, adapted)*
REQUIRED: The statement not made in the standard compilation report.
DISCUSSION: A compilation report does not express an opinion or any other form of assurance (AR 100). A review report may provide negative assurance.
Answer (A) is incorrect because the report should include a statement that a compilation is limited to presenting in the form of financial statements information that is the representation of management. Answer (B) is incorrect because the report should include a statement that the compilation was performed in accordance with the SSARSs. Answer (C) is incorrect because the report should include a statement that the accountant has not audited or reviewed the statements.

8. How does an accountant make the following representations when issuing the standard report for the compilation of a nonpublic entity's financial statements?

	The Financial Statements Have Not Been Audited	The Accountant Has Compiled the Financial Statements
A.	Implicitly	Implicitly
B.	Explicitly	Explicitly
C.	Implicitly	Explicitly
D.	Explicitly	Implicitly

Answer (B) is correct. *(CPA, adapted)*
REQUIRED: The correct form of the representations.
DISCUSSION: A standard report for the compilation of a nonpublic entity's financial statements should state that the financial statements have not been audited or reviewed. The report should also state that a compilation has been performed in accordance with the SSARSs issued by the AICPA.

9. A report on compiled financial statements should state that

A. A compilation is limited to presenting in the form of financial statements information that is the representation of management.

B. The accountant has compiled the financial statements in accordance with standards established by the Auditing Standards Board.

C. A compilation is substantially less in scope than a review or an audit in accordance with generally accepted auditing standards.

D. The accountant does not express an opinion but expresses only limited assurance on the compiled financial statements.

Answer (A) is correct. *(CPA, adapted)*
REQUIRED: The statement made in the compilation report.
DISCUSSION: According to AR 100, the report should state that a compilation is limited to presenting in the form of financial statements information that is the representation of management (owners).
Answer (B) is incorrect because the report should state that the compilation has been performed in accordance with the SSARSs issued by the AICPA. Answer (C) is incorrect because the report must state that the financial statements have not been audited or reviewed. Answer (D) is incorrect because the accountant does not express an opinion or any other form of assurance on the financial statements.

10. Compiled financial statements of a nonpublic entity intended for third-party use should be accompanied by a report stating that

A. The scope of the accountant's procedures has not been restricted in testing the financial information that is the representation of management.

B. The accountant assessed the accounting principles used and significant estimates made by management.

C. The accountant does not express an opinion or any other form of assurance on the financial statements.

D. A compilation consists principally of inquiries of entity personnel and analytical procedures applied to financial data.

Answer (C) is correct. *(CPA, adapted)*
REQUIRED: The language included in a compilation report.
DISCUSSION: A compilation report contains a disclaimer stating that the accountant has not audited or reviewed the financial statements and does not express an opinion or any other form of assurance on them.
Answer (A) is incorrect because a compilation does not entail testing the financial information. Answer (B) is incorrect because a financial statement audit, not a compilation, involves assessing the accounting principles used and the estimates made by management. Answer (D) is incorrect because a review, not a compilation, consists principally of inquiries and analytical procedures.

11. When an accountant attaches a compilation report to a nonpublic entity's financial statements that omit substantially all disclosures required by GAAP, the accountant should indicate in the compilation report that the financial statements are

A. Not designed for those who are uninformed about the omitted disclosures.

B. Prepared in conformity with a comprehensive basis of accounting other than GAAP.

C. Not compiled in accordance with Statements on Standards for Accounting and Review Services.

D. Special-purpose financial statements that are not comparable to those of prior periods.

Answer (A) is correct. *(CPA, adapted)*
REQUIRED: The statement in a report on a compilation omitting substantially all GAAP disclosures.
DISCUSSION: When disclosures are omitted, a third paragraph is added to the standard compilation report stating that management has elected to omit substantially all disclosures required by GAAP and that, if the omissions were included, they might influence the users' conclusions.
Answer (B) is incorrect because the basis of accounting is not at issue. Answer (C) is incorrect because a compilation in accordance with SSARSs is not inconsistent with omission of GAAP disclosures. Answer (D) is incorrect because financial statements that omit disclosures are not special-purpose.

12. An accountant may compile a nonpublic entity's financial statements intended for third-party use that omit all of the disclosures required by GAAP only if the omission is

I. Clearly indicated in the accountant's report

II. Not undertaken with the intention of misleading the financial statement users

A. I only.

B. II only.

C. Both I and II.

D. Either I or II.

Answer (C) is correct. *(CPA, adapted)*
REQUIRED: The situation in which an accountant may compile a nonpublic entity's financial statements that omit all of the disclosures required by GAAP.
DISCUSSION: An accountant may accept an engagement to compile financial statements that omit substantially all disclosures required by GAAP, "provided the omission is clearly indicated in the report and is not, to his/her knowledge, undertaken with the intention of misleading those who might reasonably be expected to use such financial statements" (AR 100).

13. Which of the following representations does an accountant make implicitly when issuing the standard report for the compilation of a nonpublic entity's financial statements?

A. The accountant is independent with respect to the entity.

B. The financial statements have not been audited.

C. A compilation consists principally of inquiries and analytical procedures.

D. The accountant does not express any assurance on the financial statements.

Answer (A) is correct. *(CPA, adapted)*
REQUIRED: The implicit representation in a standard compilation report.
DISCUSSION: Although an accountant who lacks independence is not precluded from issuing a compilation report, (s)he should specifically disclose the lack of independence. Thus, the standard report is silent with respect to independence.
Answer (B) is incorrect because a compilation explicitly states that the financial statements have not been audited. Answer (C) is incorrect because a compilation does not include application of inquiry and analytical procedures. Answer (D) is incorrect because a compilation explicitly states that no assurance is expressed.

14. Miller, CPA, is engaged to compile the financial statements of Web Co., a nonpublic entity, in conformity with the income tax basis of accounting. If Web's financial statements do not disclose the basis of accounting used, Miller should

A. Disclose the basis of accounting in the accountant's compilation report.

B. Clearly label each page "Distribution Restricted--Material Modifications Required."

C. Issue a special report describing the effect of the incomplete presentation.

D. Withdraw from the engagement and provide no further services to Web.

Answer (A) is correct. *(CPA, adapted)*
REQUIRED: The effect on a compilation report of failure to disclose the basis of accounting used.
DISCUSSION: Although the accountant is expected to perform no procedures, if (s)he is aware of misapplications of GAAP or the absence of required disclosures, (s)he should disclose that information in the compilation report.
Answer (B) is incorrect because each page of the financial statements should contain the statement, "See Accountant's Compilation Report." Answer (C) is incorrect because a special report is issued in conjunction with an audit. Answer (D) is incorrect because the accountant need not withdraw from the engagement.

18.2 Review

15. When providing limited assurance that the financial statements of a nonpublic entity require no material modifications to be in accordance with generally accepted accounting principles, the accountant should

A. Understand the accounting principles of the industry in which the entity operates.

B. Develop audit programs to determine whether the entity's financial statements are fairly presented.

C. Assess the risk that a material misstatement could occur in a financial statement assertion.

D. Confirm with the entity's lawyer that material loss contingencies are disclosed.

Answer (A) is correct. *(CPA, adapted)*
REQUIRED: The accountant's responsibility in a review engagement.
DISCUSSION: According to AR 100, "The accountant should possess a level of knowledge of the accounting principles and practices of the industry in which the entity operates and an understanding of the entity's business that will provide, through the performance of inquiry and analytical procedures, a reasonable basis for expressing limited assurance that there are no material modifications that should be made to the financial statements in order for the statements to be in conformity with GAAP."
Answer (B) is incorrect because audit programs are not developed in a review engagement. Answer (C) is incorrect because a review engagement does not involve an assessment of audit risk. Answer (D) is incorrect because the inquiry of an entity's lawyer is not required in a review engagement.

16. In reviewing the financial statements of a nonpublic entity, an accountant is required to modify the standard review report for which of the following matters?

	Inability to Assess the Risks of Material Misstatement Due to Fraud	Discovery of Significant Deficiencies in the Design of the Internal Control
A.	Yes	Yes
B.	Yes	No
C.	No	Yes
D.	No	No

Answer (D) is correct. *(CPA, adapted)*
REQUIRED: The accountant's responsibility in a review engagement.
DISCUSSION: A review does not involve obtaining an understanding of internal control or assessing control risk. It also does not involve testing accounting records and responses to inquiries by obtaining corroborating evidence or other tests ordinarily performed in an audit (AR 100). Thus, an auditor must specifically identify and assess the risks of material misstatement due to fraud (AU 316) and must perform procedures to evaluate the effectiveness of the design of controls (AU 319). Because a review consists primarily of inquiries of management and analytical procedures, the review report need not be modified for the matters specified in the question.
Answer (A) is incorrect because a review does not include assessing control risk or the risk of material misstatement due to fraud. Answer (B) is incorrect because a review does not include assessing control risk or the risk of material misstatement due to fraud. Answer (C) is incorrect because a review does not include assessing control risk or the risk of material misstatement due to fraud.

17. Which of the following procedures should an accountant perform during an engagement to review the financial statements of a nonpublic entity?

A. Communicating reportable conditions discovered during the assessment of control risk.

B. Obtaining a client representation letter from members of management.

C. Sending bank confirmation letters to the entity's financial institutions.

D. Examining cash disbursements in the subsequent period for unrecorded liabilities.

Answer (B) is correct. *(CPA, adapted)*
REQUIRED: The procedure performed in a review.
DISCUSSION: A review primarily consists of inquiries and analytical procedures. In addition, the accountant must obtain a sufficient knowledge of the accounting principles and practices of the client's industry and an understanding of the client's business. The accountant also must obtain written representations from management for all statements and periods to be covered by the report. The letter should be signed by the current managers (usually the CEO and CFO or the equivalent) responsible for, and knowledgeable about, the matters covered (AR 100).
Answer (A) is incorrect because reportable conditions must be communicated in an audit, not a review. Answer (C) is incorrect because confirmations to financial institutions are normally sent in an audit, not a review. Answer (D) is incorrect because tests of details, e.g., tests of subsequent payments, are performed in an audit, not a review.

18. Which of the following procedures is usually performed by the accountant in a review engagement of a nonpublic entity?

A. Sending a letter of inquiry to the entity's lawyer.

B. Comparing the financial statements with statements for comparable prior periods.

C. Confirming a significant percentage of receivables by direct communication with debtors.

D. Communicating reportable conditions discovered during the consideration of internal control.

Answer (B) is correct. *(CPA, adapted)*
REQUIRED: The procedure performed by the accountant in a review engagement.
DISCUSSION: An accountant should perform inquiries of company personnel and analytical procedures in a review engagement. Among the analytical procedures mentioned in AR 100 is the comparison of the financial statements with statements for comparable prior periods and with anticipated results.
Answer (A) is incorrect because AR 100 does not require that inquiries be made of an entity's lawyer. Answer (C) is incorrect because AR 100 does not require the confirmation of receivables. Answer (D) is incorrect because a review engagement does not contemplate obtaining an understanding of internal control.

19. Performing inquiry and analytical procedures is the primary basis for an accountant to issue a

A. Report on compliance with requirements governing major federal assistance programs in accordance with the Single Audit Act.

B. Review report on prospective financial statements that present an entity's expected financial position, given one or more hypothetical assumptions.

C. Management advisory report prepared at the request of a client's audit committee.

D. Review report on comparative financial statements for a nonpublic entity in its second year of operations.

Answer (D) is correct. *(CPA, adapted)*
REQUIRED: The report issued on the basis of inquiry and analytical procedures.
DISCUSSION: A review engagement consists primarily of inquiries of management limited and analytical procedures applied to financial data. Among other things, inquiries should be made about changes in the entity's business activities or accounting principles and practices. Analytical procedures are performed to identify relationships and items that appear to be unusual. One common analytical procedure is the comparison of the financial statements with statements for prior periods.
Answer (A) is incorrect because this report must be based on an audit. Answer (B) is incorrect because a practitioner may not issue a review report on a financial projection or a financial forecast (AT 301). Answer (C) is incorrect because inquiry and analytical procedures of the kind ordinarily performed by accountants are typically not the basis for a report on the results of a consulting service.

20. Which of the following inquiry or analytical procedures ordinarily are performed in an engagement to review a nonpublic entity's financial statements?

A. Analytical procedures designed to test the accounting records by obtaining corroborating evidential matter.

B. Inquiries concerning unusual or complex situations that may have an effect on the financial statements.

C. Analytical procedures designed to test management's assertions regarding continued existence.

D. Inquiries of the entity's attorney concerning contingent liabilities.

Answer (B) is correct. *(CPA, adapted)*
REQUIRED: The inquiries or analytical procedures ordinarily performed during a review.
DISCUSSION: These procedures include inquiries to members of management with responsibility for financial and accounting matters that concern, among other things, unusual or complex situations that may affect the financial statements.
Answer (A) is incorrect because a review does not contemplate gathering corroborating evidential matter. Answer (C) is incorrect because a review does not contemplate the application of procedures concerning management's assertions regarding continued existence. Answer (D) is incorrect because AR 100 does not require that inquiries be made of the entity's attorney.

21. Which of the following statements is true concerning both an engagement to compile and an engagement to review a nonpublic entity's financial statements?

A. The accountant does not contemplate obtaining an understanding of internal control.

B. The accountant must be independent in fact and appearance.

C. The accountant expresses no assurance on the financial statements.

D. The accountant should obtain written management representations.

Answer (A) is correct. *(CPA, adapted)*
REQUIRED: The true statement about both compilations and reviews.
DISCUSSION: A compilation requires the accountant to have a general understanding of the business, the form of its accounting records, the qualifications of its personnel, the accounting basis of the statements, and their form and content. A review is a higher level of service that also requires the accountant to perform inquiry and analytical procedures as a basis for providing limited assurance. However, neither a compilation nor a review contemplates obtaining an understanding of internal control and assessing control risk.
Answer (B) is incorrect because an accountant must be independent with respect to a review but not a compilation engagement. Answer (C) is incorrect because no expression of assurance is contemplated in a compilation, but limited assurance is expressed as a result of a review. Answer (D) is incorrect because written management representations are required in a review but not necessarily in a compilation engagement.

22. Financial statements of a nonpublic entity that have been reviewed by an accountant should be accompanied by a report stating that a review

A. Provides only limited assurance that the financial statements are fairly presented.

B. Includes examining, on a test basis, information that is the representation of management.

C. Consists principally of inquiries of company personnel and analytical procedures applied to financial data.

D. Does not contemplate obtaining corroborating evidential matter or applying certain other procedures ordinarily performed during an audit.

Answer (C) is correct. *(CPA, adapted)*
REQUIRED: The statement included in the review report.
DISCUSSION: The review report contains a second paragraph describing the review process. It states, "A review consists principally of inquiries of company personnel and analytical procedures applied to financial data."
Answer (A) is incorrect because the report states that the accountant is not aware of material modifications that should be made to the financial statements for them to be in conformity with GAAP. Answer (B) is incorrect because a review engagement does not include examining information that is the representation of management. Answer (D) is incorrect because the report does not contain an explicit description of the difference between an audit and a review.

23. An accountant who reviews the financial statements of a nonpublic entity should issue a report stating that a review

A. Is substantially less in scope than an audit.

B. Provides negative assurance that internal control is functioning as designed.

C. Provides only limited assurance that the financial statements are fairly presented.

D. Is substantially more in scope than a compilation.

Answer (A) is correct. *(CPA, adapted)*
REQUIRED: The statement included in an accountant's review report.
DISCUSSION: According to AR 100, "Financial statements reviewed by an accountant should be accompanied by a report stating that a review is substantially less in scope than an audit, the objective of which is the expression of an opinion regarding the financial statements taken as a whole, and, accordingly, no such opinion is expressed."
Answer (B) is incorrect because a review does not contemplate obtaining an understanding of internal control. Answer (C) is incorrect because the report should state that the accountant is not aware of any material modifications that should be made to the financial statements in order for them to be in conformity with GAAP. Answer (D) is incorrect because the report does not mention a compilation.

24. Financial statements of a nonpublic entity that have been reviewed by an accountant should be accompanied by a report stating that

A. The scope of the inquiry and analytical procedures performed by the accountant has not been restricted.

B. All information included in the financial statements is the representation of the management of the entity.

C. A review includes examining, on a test basis, evidence supporting the amounts and disclosures in the financial statements.

D. A review is greater in scope than a compilation, the objective of which is to present financial statements that are free of material misstatements.

Answer (B) is correct. *(CPA, adapted)*
REQUIRED: The true statement included in an accountant's report based upon a review.
DISCUSSION: According to AR 100, the first paragraph of the standard review report should include a statement that all information included in the financial statements is the representation of the management (owners) of the entity.
Answer (A) is incorrect because the report does not need to state that the scope of the inquiry and analytical procedures performed by the accountant has not been restricted.
Answer (C) is incorrect because an audit, not a review, includes examining, on a test basis, evidence supporting the amounts and disclosures in the financial statements. Answer (D) is incorrect because the standard review report does not mention a compilation.

25. An accountant's standard report on a review of the financial statements of a nonpublic entity should state that the accountant

A. Does not express an opinion or any form of limited assurance on the financial statements.

B. Is not aware of any material modifications that should be made to the financial statements for them to conform with GAAP.

C. Obtained reasonable assurance about whether the financial statements are free of material misstatement.

D. Examined evidence, on a test basis, supporting the amounts and disclosures in the financial statements.

Answer (B) is correct. *(CPA, adapted)*
REQUIRED: The statement in a standard review report.
DISCUSSION: The standard review report states, "Based on my review, I am not aware of any material modifications that should be made to the accompanying financial statements in order for them to be in conformity with generally accepted accounting principles" (AR 100).
Answer (A) is incorrect because a review provides negative assurance. Answer (C) is incorrect because an audit provides reasonable assurance about whether the financial statements are free of material misstatement. Answer (D) is incorrect because an audit entails gathering sufficient competent evidence to support the amounts and disclosures in the financial statements.

26. During an engagement to review the financial statements of a nonpublic entity, an accountant becomes aware that several leases that should be capitalized are not capitalized. The accountant considers these leases to be material to the financial statements. The accountant decides to modify the standard review report because management will not capitalize the leases. Under these circumstances, the accountant should

A. Express an adverse opinion because of the departure from GAAP.

B. Express no assurance of any kind on the entity's financial statements.

C. Emphasize that the financial statements are for limited use only.

D. Disclose the departure from GAAP in a separate paragraph of the accountant's report.

Answer (D) is correct. *(CPA, adapted)*
REQUIRED: The modification to a review report for a departure from GAAP.
DISCUSSION: When a departure from GAAP precludes an unmodified review report, and modification of the standard report is sufficient to disclose the departure, the accountant should add an additional paragraph to the report disclosing the departure, including its effects on the financial statements if they have been determined by management or are known as the result of the accountant's procedures.
Answer (A) is incorrect because unless an audit has been conducted, an opinion may not be expressed. If modification of the report is not adequate to indicate the deficiencies, the auditor should withdraw from the engagement. Answer (B) is incorrect because the accountant provides negative assurance in a review report. Answer (C) is incorrect because a review report need not be limited in distribution.

27. Baker, CPA, was engaged to review the financial statements of Hall Company, a nonpublic entity. Evidence came to Baker's attention that indicated substantial doubt as to Hall's ability to continue as a going concern. The principal conditions and events that caused the substantial doubt have been fully disclosed in the notes to Hall's financial statements. Which of the following statements best describes Baker's reporting responsibility concerning this matter?

A. Baker is not required to modify the accountant's review report.

B. Baker is not permitted to modify the accountant's review report.

C. Baker should issue an accountant's compilation report instead of a review report.

D. Baker should express a qualified opinion in the accountant's review report.

Answer (A) is correct. *(CPA, adapted)*
REQUIRED: The accountant's reporting responsibility in a review engagement if (s)he concludes that a substantial doubt exists as to whether the entity is a going concern.
DISCUSSION: AR 100 states that, normally, neither an uncertainty about an entity's ability to continue as a going concern nor an inconsistency in the application of accounting principles should cause the accountant to modify the standard report, provided the financial statements appropriately disclose such matters. Nothing in this statement, however, is intended to preclude an accountant from emphasizing in a separate paragraph of the report a matter regarding the financial statements.
Answer (B) is incorrect because the accountant may emphasize a matter. Answer (C) is incorrect because if appropriate procedures have been applied and the accountant has formed a conclusion, a review report may be issued. Answer (D) is incorrect because unless an audit has been conducted, an opinion may not be expressed.

28. Baker, CPA, was engaged to review the financial statements of Hall Company, a nonpublic entity. During the engagement, Baker uncovered a complex scheme involving client illegal acts and fraud that materially affect Hall's financial statements. If Baker believes that modification of the standard review report is not adequate to indicate the deficiencies in the financial statements, Baker should

A. Disclaim an opinion.

B. Express an adverse opinion.

C. Withdraw from the engagement.

D. Express a qualified opinion.

Answer (C) is correct. *(CPA, adapted)*
REQUIRED: The auditor action when modification of the standard review report is not adequate to indicate deficiencies in the financial statements.
DISCUSSION: AR 100 states that, if the accountant believes that modification is not adequate to indicate the deficiencies in the financial statements, (s)he should withdraw from the engagement. The SSARSs do not provide for an adverse review report.

29. Each page of a nonpublic entity's financial statements reviewed by an accountant should include the following reference:

A. See Accountant's Review Report.

B. Reviewed, No Accountant's Assurance Expressed.

C. See Accompanying Accountant's Notes.

D. Reviewed, No Material Modifications Required.

Answer (A) is correct. *(CPA, adapted)*
REQUIRED: The reference on each page of a nonpublic entity's financial statements reviewed by an accountant.
DISCUSSION: Each page should include a reference such as "See Accountant's Review Report" (AR 100).
Answer (B) is incorrect because a review report ordinarily expresses limited assurance. Answer (C) is incorrect because notes are part of the financial statements, not the accountant's report. Answer (D) is incorrect because the review report states that the accountant is not aware of any modifications that should be made other than those indicated in the report.

30. Moore, CPA, has been asked to issue a review report on the balance sheet of Dover Co., a nonpublic entity. Moore will not be reporting on Dover's statements of income, retained earnings, and cash flows. Moore may issue the review report provided the

A. Balance sheet is presented in a prescribed form of an industry trade association.

B. Scope of the inquiry and analytical procedures has not been restricted.

C. Balance sheet is not to be used to obtain credit or distributed to creditors.

D. Specialized accounting principles and practices of Dover's industry are disclosed.

Answer (B) is correct. *(CPA, adapted)*
REQUIRED: The condition under which an accountant may issue a review report on a single financial statement.
DISCUSSION: An accountant may issue a report on one or more of the financial statements and not on the others. This form of reporting is not considered a limitation on scope but a limited reporting engagement. However, the accountant must not be restricted in the procedures to be applied, which, in a review, consist primarily of inquiries and analytical procedures.
Answer (A) is incorrect because the decision is independent of whether the balance sheet is to be presented in a prescribed form. Answer (C) is incorrect because a reviewed financial statement may be used for any appropriate purpose. Answer (D) is incorrect because a review report may be issued on a comprehensive basis of accounting other than GAAP. The specialized principles, however, need not be disclosed.

18.3 Other Considerations

31. An accountant began an audit of the financial statements of a nonpublic entity and was asked to change the engagement to a review because of a restriction on the scope of the audit. If there is reasonable justification for the change, the review report should include reference to the

	Original Engagement That Was Agreed To	Scope Limitation That Caused the Changed Engagement
A.	Yes	Yes
B.	Yes	No
C.	No	Yes
D.	No	No

Answer (D) is correct. *(CPA, adapted)*
REQUIRED: The item(s), if any, that should be referred to in the accountant's review report.
DISCUSSION: AR 100 states, "If the accountant concludes, based upon his/her professional judgment, that there is reasonable justification to change the engagement and if (s)he complies with the standards applicable to the changed engagement, (s)he should issue an appropriate review report. The report should not include reference to the original engagement, any auditing procedures that may have been performed, or scope limitations that resulted in the changed engagement."

32. Davis, CPA, accepted an engagement to audit the financial statements of Tech Resources, a nonpublic entity. Before the completion of the audit, Tech requested Davis to change the engagement to a compilation of financial statements. Before Davis agrees to change the engagement, Davis is required to consider the

	Additional Audit Effort Necessary to Complete the Audit	Reason Given for Tech's Request
A.	No	No
B.	Yes	Yes
C.	Yes	No
D.	No	Yes

Answer (B) is correct. *(CPA, adapted)*

REQUIRED: The matter(s) considered before changing an engagement from an audit to a compilation.

DISCUSSION: Before an accountant who was engaged to perform an audit in accordance with GAAS agrees to change the engagement to a compilation or a review, at least the following should be considered: (1) the reason given for the client's request, particularly the implications of a restriction on the scope of the audit, whether imposed by the client or by circumstances; (2) the additional audit effort required to complete the audit; and (3) the estimated additional cost to complete the audit (AR 100).

33. Clark, CPA, compiled and properly reported on the financial statements of Green Co., a nonpublic entity, for the year ended March 31, year 1. These financial statements omitted substantially all disclosures required by GAAP. Green asked Clark to compile the statements for the year ended March 31, year 2, and to include all GAAP disclosures for the year 2 statements only, but otherwise present both years' financial statements in comparative form. What is Clark's responsibility concerning the proposed engagement? Clark may

A. Not report on the comparative financial statements because the year 1 statements are not comparable with the year 2 statements that include the GAAP disclosures.

B. Report on the comparative financial statements provided the year 1 statements do not contain any obvious material misstatements.

C. Report on the comparative financial statements provided an explanatory paragraph is added to Clark's report on the comparative financial statements.

D. Report on the comparative financial statements provided Clark updates the report on the year 1 statements that do not include the GAAP disclosures.

Answer (A) is correct. *(CPA, adapted)*

REQUIRED: The accountant's responsibility when compiled financial statements are presented comparatively but the earlier year's statements omit most disclosures required by GAAP.

DISCUSSION: Compiled financial statements that omit substantially all of the disclosures required by GAAP are not comparable with financial statements that include such disclosures. Accordingly, the accountant ordinarily should not issue a report on comparative financial statements when statements for one or more, but not all, of the periods presented omit substantially all of the disclosures required by GAAP (AR 200).

34. An accountant has been asked to compile the financial statements of a nonpublic company on a prescribed form that omits substantially all the disclosures required by GAAP. If the prescribed form is a standard preprinted form adopted by the company's industry trade association, and is to be transmitted only to such association, the accountant

A. Need not advise the industry trade association of the omission of all disclosures.

B. Should disclose the details of the omissions in separate paragraphs of the compilation report.

C. Is precluded from issuing a compilation report when all disclosures are omitted.

D. Should express limited assurance that the financial statements are free of material misstatements.

Answer (A) is correct. *(CPA, adapted)*

REQUIRED: The accountant's responsibility when (s)he compiles statements on a prescribed form to be transmitted only to the prescribing authority.

DISCUSSION: An alternative form of the standard compilation report is used when a prescribed form or related instructions call for departure from GAAP by specifying a measurement principle not in conformity with GAAP or failing to require disclosures in accordance with GAAP. The presumption is that the information required in a prescribed form is sufficient to meet the needs of the body that designed or adopted the form. In the standard report on statements included in such a form, the accountant should indicate that the statements are in a prescribed form and that they may differ from those presented in accordance with GAAP, but (s)he need not describe the differences in the report (AR 300).

Answer (B) is incorrect because this disclosure is unnecessary. Answer (C) is incorrect because the report may be issued in these circumstances. Answer (D) is incorrect because a compilation report expresses no assurance.

35. Gole, CPA, is engaged to review the year 2 financial statements of North Co., a nonpublic entity. Previously, Gole audited North's year 1 financial statements and expressed an unqualified opinion. Gole decides to include a separate paragraph in the year 2 review report because North plans to present comparative financial statements for year 2 and year 1. This separate paragraph should indicate that

    A. The year 2 review report is intended solely for the information of management and the board of directors.

    B. The year 1 auditor's report may no longer be relied on.

    C. No auditing procedures were performed after the date of the year 1 auditor's report.

    D. There are justifiable reasons for changing the level of service from an audit to a review.

Answer (C) is correct. *(CPA, adapted)*
    REQUIRED: The reference in a separate paragraph in a review report when comparative statements are presented and an audit was performed in the previous year.
    DISCUSSION: A continuing accountant who performs a lower level of service should include a separate paragraph describing the responsibility assumed for the financial statements of the prior period or reissue the previous report. The paragraph included in the review report should indicate that no auditing procedures were performed after the date of the original auditor's report.
    Answer (A) is incorrect because a review report may be distributed to any user. Answer (B) is incorrect because the previous auditor's report may still be relied upon. Answer (D) is incorrect because no mention of the reasons for the change of service should be made in the review report.

36. Kell engaged March, CPA, to submit to Kell a written personal financial plan containing unaudited personal financial statements. March anticipates omitting certain disclosures required by GAAP because the engagement's sole purpose is to assist Kell in developing a personal financial plan. For March to be exempt from complying with the requirements of SSARS 1, *Compilation and Review of Financial Statements*, Kell is required to agree that the

    A. Financial statements will not be presented in comparative form with those of the prior period.

    B. Omitted disclosures required by GAAP are not material.

    C. Financial statements will not be disclosed to a non-CPA financial planner.

    D. Financial statements will not be used to obtain credit.

Answer (D) is correct. *(CPA, adapted)*
    REQUIRED: The circumstances under which an accountant may depart from the requirements of SSARS 1.
    DISCUSSION: AR 600, *Reporting on Personal Financial Statements Included in Written Personal Financial Plans*, states that an accountant may submit a written personal financial plan containing unaudited personal financial statements to a client without complying with the requirements of SSARS 1 if the accountant (1) has an understanding with the client about its use and (2) has no reason to believe that the financial statements will be used to obtain credit or for any other purpose except developing the financial plan.
    Answer (A) is incorrect because the financial statements may be presented in comparative form. Answer (B) is incorrect because the exemption is appropriate regardless of the disclosures and their materiality level. Answer (C) is incorrect because the financial plan is likely to be used by the client and potentially a financial planner.

18.4 Uses of Special Reports (AU 623)

37. An auditor who conducts an audit in accordance with generally accepted auditing standards and concludes that the financial statements are fairly presented in accordance with a comprehensive basis of accounting other than generally accepted accounting principles (OCBOA), such as the cash basis of accounting, should issue a

    A. Special report.

    B. Report disclaiming an opinion.

    C. Review report.

    D. Report expressing a qualified opinion.

Answer (A) is correct. *(CPA, adapted)*
    REQUIRED: The report issued on financial statements presented in accordance with an OCBOA.
    DISCUSSION: An auditor's judgment (opinion) about the fair presentation of financial statements is applied within an identifiable framework, which is usually provided by GAAP. However, an OCBOA (e.g., cash basis) may sometimes be used. A special report is appropriate for reporting on statements prepared on an OCBOA.
    Answer (B) is incorrect because the auditor should not disclaim an opinion if (s)he is able to conclude that the statements are fairly presented. Answer (C) is incorrect because an audit results in a positive opinion. A review results in the expression of negative assurance. Answer (D) is incorrect because the auditor should not qualify the opinion if (s)he is able to conclude that the statements are fairly presented.

18.5 Financial Statements Prepared in Conformity with an Other Comprehensive Basis of Accounting (OCBOA) (AU 623)

38. When an auditor reports on financial statements prepared on an entity's income tax basis, the auditor's report should

A. Disclaim an opinion on whether the statements were examined in accordance with generally accepted auditing standards.

B. Not express an opinion on whether the statements are presented in conformity with the comprehensive basis of accounting used.

C. Include an explanation of how the results of operations differ from the cash receipts and disbursements basis of accounting.

D. State that the basis of presentation is a comprehensive basis of accounting other than GAAP.

Answer (D) is correct. *(CPA, adapted)*
REQUIRED: The statement in an auditor's report on financial statements prepared on an income tax basis.
DISCUSSION: An auditor may report on financial statements prepared in conformity with an other comprehensive basis of accounting (OCBOA). In addition to an introductory paragraph and a standard scope paragraph, the report should include a separate paragraph (after the scope paragraph) that states the basis of the presentation, refers to a note in the statements explaining the basis chosen, and states that the basis of the presentation is a comprehensive basis other than GAAP. Finally, the auditor should include a paragraph expressing an opinion that the statements are presented fairly in conformity with the OCBOA.
Answer (A) is incorrect because the auditor follows GAAS in the engagement. Answer (B) is incorrect because an opinion is expressed on whether the statements are presented in conformity with the OCBOA. Answer (C) is incorrect because, although a note in the financial statements should explain how the basis of accounting differs from GAAP, the auditor's report need only refer to that note.

39. An auditor's special report on financial statements prepared in conformity with the cash basis of accounting should include a separate explanatory paragraph before the opinion paragraph that

A. Justifies the reasons for departing from generally accepted accounting principles.

B. States whether the financial statements are fairly presented in conformity with another comprehensive basis of accounting.

C. Refers to the note to the financial statements that describes the basis of accounting.

D. Explains how the results of operations differ from financial statements prepared in conformity with generally accepted accounting principles.

Answer (C) is correct. *(CPA, adapted)*
REQUIRED: The content of an explanatory paragraph in a special report on statements prepared on an OCBOA.
DISCUSSION: A special report on statements prepared on an OCBOA should contain a paragraph stating the basis of presentation, referring to the note to the financial statements that describes the basis, and stating that the basis is a comprehensive one other than GAAP.
Answer (A) is incorrect because the auditor should not express an opinion on the propriety of the basis of accounting used but may express an opinion on whether the statements are presented fairly in conformity with the basis of accounting described. Answer (B) is incorrect because the opinion paragraph states whether the financial statements are fairly presented in conformity with another comprehensive basis of accounting. Answer (D) is incorrect because AU 623 contains no requirement to explain how the results of operations differ.

40. If compiled financial statements presented in conformity with the cash receipts and disbursements basis of accounting do not disclose the basis of accounting used, the accountant should

A. Recompile the financial statements using generally accepted accounting principles.

B. Disclose the basis in the notes to the financial statements.

C. Clearly label each page "unaudited."

D. Disclose the basis of accounting in the accountant's report.

Answer (D) is correct. *(CPA, adapted)*
REQUIRED: The accountant's action if compiled statements do not disclose that the cash basis was used.
DISCUSSION: An accountant may compile financial statements that omit disclosures required by GAAP or an OCBOA. AR 100 states two requirements: (1) The omission must be clearly indicated in the report, and (2) it is not, to the accountant's knowledge, made with deceptive intent. In addition, if the statements are compiled in conformity with an OCBOA but do not disclose the basis used, the accountant must disclose the basis in the report.
Answer (A) is incorrect because a compilation in conformity with another comprehensive basis of accounting is acceptable. Answer (B) is incorrect because the notes are the responsibility of management, not the accountant. Answer (C) is incorrect because each page "should include a reference such as 'See Accountant's Compilation Report'" (AR 100).

41. An auditor's report on financial statements prepared on the cash receipts and disbursements basis of accounting should include all of the following except

    A. A reference to the note to the financial statements that describes the cash receipts and disbursements basis of accounting.

    B. A statement that the cash receipts and disbursements basis of accounting is not a comprehensive basis of accounting.

    C. An opinion as to whether the financial statements are fairly presented in conformity with the cash receipts and disbursements basis of accounting.

    D. A statement that the audit was conducted in accordance with auditing standards generally accepted in the U.S.

Answer (B) is correct.   *(CPA, adapted)*
    REQUIRED: The statement not included on an auditor's special report on cash-basis (OCBOA) financial statements.
    DISCUSSION: A statement indicating that the cash receipts and cash disbursements basis of accounting is a comprehensive basis of accounting other than GAAP should be included in the auditor's report.
    Answer (A) is incorrect because a reference to the note of the financial statements that describes the basis should be included in the auditor's report. Answer (C) is incorrect because an opinion as to whether the financial statements are fairly presented should be included in the auditor's report. Answer (D) is incorrect because a statement that the audit was conducted in accordance with GAAS should be included in the auditor's report.

42. Delta Life Insurance Co. prepares its financial statements on an accounting basis insurance companies use pursuant to the rules of a state insurance commission. If Wall, CPA, Delta's auditor, discovers that the statements are not suitably titled, Wall should

    A. Disclose any reservations in an explanatory paragraph and qualify the opinion.

    B. Apply to the state insurance commission for an advisory opinion.

    C. Issue a special statutory basis report that clearly disclaims any opinion.

    D. Explain in the notes to the financial statements the terminology used.

Answer (A) is correct.   *(CPA, adapted)*
    REQUIRED: The proper action when statements prepared on an OCBOA are not suitably titled.
    DISCUSSION: Terms such as balance sheet, statement of income, or other unmodified titles are ordinarily understood to apply to statements presented in conformity with GAAP. Consequently, the auditor of statements prepared under another comprehensive basis should consider whether the statements are suitably titled. If (s)he believes they are not, the auditor should disclose his/her reservations in an explanatory paragraph and qualify the opinion (AU 623).
    Answer (B) is incorrect because AU 623 does not require the auditor to apply to the state insurance commission for an advisory opinion. Answer (C) is incorrect because the opinion should be qualified. Answer (D) is incorrect because the notes are the responsibility of management, not the auditor.

18.6 Specified Elements, Accounts, or Items of a Financial Statement (AU 623)

43. A CPA is permitted to accept a separate engagement (not in conjunction with an audit of financial statements) to audit an entity's

	Schedule of Accounts Receivable	Schedule of Royalties
A.	Yes	Yes
B.	Yes	No
C.	No	Yes
D.	No	No

Answer (A) is correct.   *(CPA, adapted)*
    REQUIRED: The separate engagement(s), if any, a CPA is permitted to accept.
    DISCUSSION: An auditor may be requested to express an opinion on one or more specified elements, accounts, or items of a financial statement. The report should be a special report (AU 623).

44. When an auditor is requested to express an opinion on the rental and royalty income of an entity, the auditor may

   A. Not accept the engagement because to do so would be tantamount to agreeing to express a piecemeal opinion.

   B. Not accept the engagement unless also engaged to audit the full financial statements of the entity.

   C. Accept the engagement provided the auditor's opinion is expressed in a special report.

   D. Accept the engagement provided use of the auditor's report is restricted to the entity's management.

Answer (C) is correct. *(CPA, adapted)*
   REQUIRED: The true statement about accepting an engagement to express an opinion on rental and royalty income.
   DISCUSSION: A special report may be issued in connection with an engagement to express an opinion on specified elements, accounts, or items of a financial statement. Examples of specified elements, accounts, or items on which an auditor may report based on an audit in accordance with GAAS include rentals, royalties, a profit participation, or a provision for income taxes.
   Answer (A) is incorrect because an opinion may be expressed if the auditor has not expressed an adverse opinion or disclaimed an opinion on the financial statements or if the matters to be reported on do not constitute a major portion of the statements. Answer (B) is incorrect because this engagement may be undertaken separately or in conjunction with an audit. Answer (D) is incorrect because the restriction is necessary only if the presentation is not in conformity with GAAP or an OCBOA or if it is prepared on a basis prescribed by a regulatory agency.

45. Field is an employee of Gold Enterprises. Hardy, CPA, is asked to express an opinion on Field's profit participation in Gold's net income. Hardy may accept this engagement only if

   A. Hardy also audits Gold's complete financial statements.

   B. Gold's financial statements are prepared in conformity with GAAP.

   C. Hardy's report is available for use by Gold's other employees.

   D. Field owns a controlling interest in Gold.

Answer (A) is correct. *(CPA, adapted)*
   REQUIRED: The requirement to accept an engagement.
   DISCUSSION: AU 623 states, "If a specified element, account, or item is, or is based upon, an entity's net income or stockholders' equity or the equivalent thereof, the auditor should have audited the complete financial statements to express an opinion on the specified element, account, or item."
   Answer (B) is incorrect because the financial statements could be based on an other comprehensive basis of accounting. Answer (C) is incorrect because the use of the report may be restricted. An auditor may perform many services that result in restricted-use reports, that is, those intended only for specified parties (see AU 532). Answer (D) is incorrect because whether Field owns a controlling interest in Gold is irrelevant.

46. An auditor may express an opinion on an entity's accounts receivable balance even if the auditor has disclaimed an opinion on the financial statements taken as a whole provided the

   A. Report on the accounts receivable discloses the reason for the disclaimer of opinion on the financial statements.

   B. Use of the report on the accounts receivable is restricted.

   C. Auditor also reports on the current asset portion of the entity's balance sheet.

   D. Report on the accounts receivable is presented separately from the disclaimer of opinion on the financial statements.

Answer (D) is correct. *(CPA, adapted)*
   REQUIRED: The condition for expressing an opinion on an account balance despite disclaiming an opinion on the financial statements as a whole.
   DISCUSSION: An auditor may be able to express an opinion in these circumstances if a major portion of the financial statements is not involved. For example, an auditor who has disclaimed an opinion on the financial statements may be able to express an opinion on the accounts receivable balance. However, the report would be presented separately.
   Answer (A) is incorrect because the report on accounts receivable should have introductory, scope, and opinion paragraphs. It may also require paragraphs describing the basis of presentation and limiting distribution, but it need not describe any reasons for the disclaimer on the financial statements as a whole. Answer (B) is incorrect because use of the report need not be restricted to specified parties unless the presentation does not conform with GAAP or another comprehensive basis of accounting. Answer (C) is incorrect because a report may be presented on one or more specified elements, accounts, or items of a financial statement.

18.7   Other Presentations (AU 623)

47. An auditor's report is designated a special report when it is issued in connection with

A. Interim financial information of a publicly held company that is subject to a limited review.

B. Compliance with aspects of regulatory requirements related to audited financial statements.

C. Application of accounting principles to specified transactions.

D. Limited use prospective financial statements such as financial projection.

Answer (B) is correct. *(CPA, adapted)*
REQUIRED: The auditor's service that results in a special report.
DISCUSSION: Entities may be required by contractual agreements, such as bond indentures and certain types of loan agreements, or by regulatory agencies to furnish compliance reports by independent auditors. These reports should be issued in conjunction with an ordinary audit. The report envisioned provides negative assurance that may be given in the report on the financial statements or in a separate report. But this assurance should not be given unless an audit has been performed and should not extend to any covenants relating to matters that have not been subjected to audit procedures in the audit (AU 623).
Answer (A) is incorrect because special reports are not issued in connection with reviews of interim financial information. AU 722 discusses the report appropriate for such a review. Answer (C) is incorrect because a report on the application of accounting principles is governed by AU 625. Answer (D) is incorrect because AT 300 applies to projections.

48. An auditor's report issued in connection with which of the following is generally not considered to be a special report?

A. Compliance with aspects of contractual agreements unrelated to audited financial statements.

B. Specified elements, accounts, or items of a financial statement presented in a document.

C. Financial statements prepared in accordance with an entity's income tax basis.

D. Financial information presented in a prescribed schedule that requires a prescribed form of auditor's report.

Answer (A) is correct. *(CPA, adapted)*
REQUIRED: The report not considered to be a special report.
DISCUSSION: Special reports are issued in connection with, among other things, compliance with aspects of contractual agreements or regulatory requirements related to audited statements. Such a report provides negative assurance that may be given in the report on the financial statements or in a separate report. But this assurance should not be given unless an audit of the statements has been performed.
Answer (B) is incorrect because a special report may be issued on specified elements, accounts, or items of a financial statement presented in a document. Answer (C) is incorrect because a special report may be issued on financial statements prepared in accordance with an entity's income tax basis. Answer (D) is incorrect because a special report may be issued on financial information presented in a prescribed schedule that requires a prescribed form of auditor's report.

18.8   Financial Information Presented in Prescribed Forms or Schedules that Require a Prescribed Form of Auditor's Report (AU 623)

49. Financial information is presented in a printed form that prescribes the wording of the independent auditor's report. The form is not acceptable to the auditor because the form calls for statements that are inconsistent with the auditor's responsibility. Under these circumstances, the auditor most likely would

A. Withdraw from the engagement.

B. Reword the form or attach a separate report.

C. Express a qualified opinion with an explanation.

D. Limit use of the report to the party who designed the form.

Answer (B) is correct. *(CPA, adapted)*
REQUIRED: The auditor action regarding a prescribed report form that is inconsistent with his/her responsibility.
DISCUSSION: Printed forms or schedules to be filed with a regulatory body may prescribe the wording of the auditor's report. However, this language may not conform with professional reporting standards. Consequently, AU 623 states, "Some report forms can be made acceptable by inserting additional wording; others can be made acceptable only by complete revision. When a printed report form calls upon an independent auditor to make a statement that she or he is not justified in making, the auditor should reword the form or attach a separate report."
Answer (A) is incorrect because the auditor need not withdraw if the report can be modified to be consistent with the auditor's responsibility. Answer (C) is incorrect because the auditor need not express a qualified opinion unless the financial statements were materially misstated. Answer (D) is incorrect because if the audit was in accordance with generally accepted auditing standards, a general-use report may be issued.

Use Gleim's ***CPA Test Prep*** for interactive testing with over 2,000 additional multiple-choice questions!

18.9 PRACTICE SIMULATION

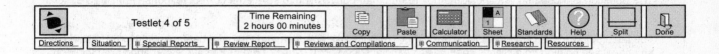

Directions | Situation | ⊞ Special Reports | ⊞ Review Report | ⊞ Reviews and Compilations | ⊞ Communication | ⊞ Research | Resources

1. Directions

In the following simulation, you will be asked to complete various tasks related to engagement acceptance. The simulation will provide all of the information necessary to do the work. For full credit, be sure to view and complete all work tabs.

Resources are available to you under the tab marked RESOURCES. You may want to review the resources before beginning the simulation.

2. Situation

Jane Doe, CPA, is discussing the advantages of either a review or compilation with Little Britches, Inc., a privately held chain of retail clothing shops specializing in consigned children's apparel. Little Britches has suggested that, instead of traditional financial statements, it may present only a cash-basis statement of assets and liabilities. This statement would not include equity accounts. If this presentation is made, Little Britches may want Doe to perform an audit of the statement. At this time, Doe is not sure whether she will be engaged to perform a review or compilation of traditional financial statements or to provide a special report on the cash-basis statement of assets and liabilities. Doe has decided to gather information and report drafts from prior engagements to assist in the decision process.

3. Issues about Special Reports

This question is presented in a check-the-box format that requires you to select the correct response from a given list.

The table below makes statements that are either True or False about an audit engagement resulting in expression of an unqualified opinion on a client's cash-basis financial statements. Check True or False in the shaded area for each statement.

Statement	True	False
1. The auditor provides less assurance in the report than for a traditional audit report on GAAP-based statements.		
2. The introductory paragraph identifies management's responsibility relative to the financial statements.		
3. The scope paragraph is unchanged from that of a traditional audit report on GAAP-based statements.		
4. The report should include a separate paragraph stating that the financial statements were prepared on the cash basis.		
5. The auditor should avoid the phrase "present fairly" in the opinion.		
6. The auditor should avoid the phrase "in all material respects" in the opinion.		
7. The report should have the heading "Independent Auditor's Report."		
8. The report should be dated as of the date of the financial statements.		
9. Management should sign the report.		
10. The report should contain a statement limiting its use.		

4. Review Report

The following draft of a review engagement report has been submitted by a staff member to the manager for review. The table below contains the comments by the manager about the draft. Indicate whether the original draft is correct, the audit manager's comment is correct, or if neither is correct.

We have reviewed the accompanying balance sheet of ABC Company as of December 31, 200X, and the related statements of income, retained earnings, and cash flows for the year then ended, in accordance with Statements on Standards for Accounting and Review Services. All information included in these financial statements is the representation of management of ABC Company.

A review consists principally of inquiries of company personnel. It is substantially less in scope than an examination in accordance with generally accepted accounting standards, the objective of which is the expression of an opinion regarding the financial statements. Accordingly, we do not express such an opinion.

Based on our examination, we are not aware of any material modifications that should be made to the accompanying financial statements in order for them to be in conformity with generally accepted accounting principles.

Manager's Comments	Answer
1. The report should not refer to the statement of cash flows because a private company does not prepare this statement.	
2. The first sentence in the first paragraph should state that the accounting and review standards are established by the federal government.	
3. The last sentence in the first paragraph should indicate that the financial statements are the representation of the CPA firm.	
4. The first sentence in the middle paragraph also should refer to analytical procedures.	
5. The second sentence in the second paragraph should state that the review is "substantially greater in scope..."	
6. The second sentence in the second paragraph should refer to "generally accepted auditing standards," not "generally accepted accounting standards."	
7. The third paragraph should state "Based on our study..." rather than "Based on our examination..."	
8. The third paragraph should state, "conformity with standards established by the Auditing Standards Board" rather than "conformity with generally accepted accounting principles."	

Choices
A. The original draft is correct.
B. The manager's comment is correct.
C. Neither the original draft nor the manager's comment is correct.

5. Reviews and Compilations

This question has a true-false format that requires you to select the correct responses from a drop-down list. Write the answer in the shaded columns next to the item or question.

Items 1 through 15 represent a series of unrelated procedures that an accountant may consider performing in separate engagements to review the financial statements of a nonpublic entity (a review) and to compile the financial statements of a nonpublic entity (a compilation). Select, as the best answer for each item, whether the procedure is required or not required for both review and compilation engagements. Make two selections for each item.

Review Choices
A) Procedure is required.
B) Procedure is not required.

Compilation Choices
C) Procedure is required.
D) Procedure is not required.

Procedure	Review A) or B)	Compilation C) or D)
1. The accountant should establish an understanding with the entity regarding the nature and limitations of the services to be performed.		
2. The accountant should make inquiries concerning actions taken at the board of directors' meetings.		
3. The accountant, as the entity's successor accountant, should communicate with the predecessor accountant to obtain access to the predecessor's working papers.		
4. The accountant should obtain a level of knowledge of the accounting principles and practices of the entity's industry.		
5. The accountant should obtain an understanding of the entity's internal control.		
6. The accountant should perform analytical procedures designed to identify relationships that appear to be unusual.		
7. The accountant should make an assessment of control risk.		
8. The accountant should send a letter of inquiry to the entity's attorney to corroborate the information furnished by management concerning litigation.		
9. The accountant should obtain written representations from management of the entity.		
10. The accountant may compare relationships among elements in the current financial statements with corresponding prior-period information.		
11. The accountant should communicate to the entity's senior management illegal employee acts discovered by the accountant that are clearly inconsequential.		
12. The accountant should make inquiries about events subsequent to the date of the financial statements that would have a material effect on the financial statements.		
13. The accountant should modify the accountant's report if there is a change in accounting principles that is adequately disclosed.		
14. The accountant should submit a hard copy of the financial statements and accountant's report when the financial statements and accountant's report are submitted on a computer disk.		
15. The accountant should perform specific procedures to evaluate whether there is substantial doubt about the entity's ability to continue as a going concern.		

6. Communication

In a memo to the audit file, describe the circumstances in which a special report is required. Also, describe the differences between the standard auditor's report and a special report on financial statements presented in accordance with the cash basis of accounting.

REMINDER: Your response will be graded for both technical content and writing skills. You should demonstrate your ability to develop, organize, and express your ideas. Do not convey information in the form of a table, bullet point list, or other abbreviated presentation.

To: Audit file
From: CPA
Subject: Special reports and differences between the standard report and the report on
          cash-basis statements

7. Research

Find the answer to the following question in the Professional Standards using the materials available in the standards button. Print the appropriate citation in its entirety from the source you choose. This is a copy-and-paste item.

Research the meaning of a "financial statement" as used by the auditor. Copy the paragraph that describes those presentations that are considered to be a financial statement other than the traditional balance sheet, statement of income, statement of retained earnings, and statement of cash flows.

Unofficial Answers

3. Issues about Special Reports (10 Gradable Items)

1.   <u>False.</u>
2.   <u>True.</u>
3.   <u>True.</u>
4.   <u>True.</u>
5.   <u>False.</u>
6.   <u>False.</u>
7.   <u>True.</u>
8.   <u>False.</u>
9.   <u>False.</u>
10. <u>False.</u>

4. Review Report (8 Gradable Items)

1.   <u>A</u> – A private company also is required to present a statement of cash flows, and the review report should refer to the statement.

2.   <u>C</u> – The report should state that the SSARSs are issued by the American Institute of Certified Public Accountants.

3.   <u>C</u> – The information in the financial statements is the representation of management.

4.   <u>B</u> – The sentence should read, "A review consists principally of inquiries of company personnel and analytical procedures applied to financial data."

5.   <u>A</u> – The draft is correct as stated.

6.   <u>B</u> – The manager is correct that the audit is conducted in accordance with generally accepted auditing standards.

7.   <u>C</u> – The paragraph should begin, "Based on our review..."

8.   <u>A</u> – The draft is correct as stated.

5. Reviews and Compilations (7 Gradable Items)

1.   <u>A), C)</u>; According to AR 100, *Compilation and Review of Financial Statements*, an accountant is required to establish with the entity an understanding regarding the nature and limitation of the services to be performed.

2.   <u>A), D)</u>; When performing review services for a client, an accountant should make "inquiries concerning actions taken at meetings of shareholders, board of directors, or comparable meetings that may affect the financial statements." When performing a compilation, "The accountant is not required to make inquiries" (AR 100).

3.   <u>B), D)</u>; "A successor accountant is not required to communicate with a predecessor accountant in connection with acceptance of a compilation or review engagement, but (s)he may decide to do so" (AR 400).

4.   <u>A), C)</u>; A level of knowledge of the accounting principles and practices of the entity's industry is required (1) to enable the accountant to compile statements that are appropriate in form for an entity in that industry or (2) to provide the accountant, through inquiries and analytical procedures, with the reasonable basis for limited assurance sought in a review.

5.   <u>B), D)</u>; Auditors, not accountants performing review engagements or compilation services, require an understanding of the entity's internal control.

6.   <u>A), D)</u>; In performing review services, an accountant is required to perform inquiries and analytical procedures in support of the limited assurance provided on the financial statements. In a compilation engagement, an accountant prepares the financial statements of an entity. No assurance is provided; therefore, no analytical procedures are required.

7.   <u>B), D)</u>; An audit, not a compilation or review, requires an assessment of control risk.

8. B). D); During a review engagement, an accountant is required to obtain written representations from management but not to obtain corroborating evidence. In providing compilation services, an accountant is not required to make any inquiries about information provided by the entity.

9. A). D); When performing a review of an entity's financial statements, the accountant must obtain written representations from responsible and knowledgeable members of management (e.g., the CEO or the CFO or the equivalent). However, in compiling financial statements, the accountant is not required to obtain written representations from management.

10. A). D); When reviewing an entity's financial statements, the accountant must perform analytical procedures, which may include comparing the relationships among elements in the current financial statements with prior-period financial information. A compilation engagement requires that an accountant prepare the financial statements based only on the information provided by management.

11. B). D); The accountant should establish an understanding with the entity, preferably in writing, regarding the services to be performed. The understanding should provide that the accountant will inform the appropriate level of management of any illegal acts that come to his/her attention, unless they are clearly inconsequential (AR 100).

12. A). D); The accountant's inquiry and analytical procedures for review engagements should consist of inquiries of persons having responsibility for financial and accounting matters concerning events subsequent to the date of the financial statements that would have a material effect on the financial statements. Compilations do not require the accountant to make inquiries or perform other procedures to verify, corroborate, or review information about events prior or subsequent to the date of the financial statements.

13. B). D); Given proper disclosure, inconsistencies in the application of accounting principles do not normally require modification of the standard report.

14. B). D); The form of the financial statement is not important. For example, the copy may be on a computer disk, fax, or other medium.

15. B). D); In providing compilation and review services, the accountant provides no positive assurance about the financial statements taken as a whole. Hence, (s)he is not required to assess the entity's ability to continue as a going concern.

6. Communication (5 Gradable Items; For grading instructions, please refer to page 11.)

To:	Audit file
From:	CPA
Subject:	Special reports and differences between the standard report and the report on cash-basis statements

Special reports may be issued on financial statements that are prepared in conformity with a comprehensive basis of accounting other than GAAP. Examples of such bases are the cash basis and the income tax basis. Special reports also are issued on specified elements, accounts, or items of a financial statement. A third type of special report concerns compliance with aspects of contractual agreements or regulatory requirements related to audited financial statements. Other special reports may be issued on financial presentations to comply with contractual agreements or regulatory provisions and on financial information presented in prescribed forms or schedules that require a prescribed form of auditor's report.

A special report on cash-basis statements differs from the standard report in various ways. For example, the statements identified in the introductory paragraph and in the opinion paragraph are the statement of assets and liabilities arising from cash transactions and the related statement of revenue collected and expenses paid. Titles such as income statement, balance sheet, and statement of cash flows are not suitable because they imply that statements are accrual-based. Accordingly, an additional paragraph is added preceding the opinion paragraph stating the basis of accounting used and referring to a note that explains that basis. A third difference is that the opinion paragraph refers to the basis of accounting described in the appropriate note, not to GAAP.

7. Research (6 Gradable Items)

AU Section 623 -- *Special Reports*

Financial Statements Prepared in Conformity with a Comprehensive Basis of Accounting Other than Generally Accepted Accounting Principles

.02   Generally accepted auditing standards are applicable when an auditor conducts an audit of and reports on any financial statement. A financial statement may be, for example, that of a corporation, a consolidated group of corporations, a combined group of affiliated entities, a not-for-profit organization, a governmental unit, an estate or trust, a partnership, a proprietorship, a segment of any of these, or an individual. The term *financial statement* refers to a presentation of financial data, including accompanying notes, derived from accounting records and intended to communicate an entity's economic resources or obligations at a point in time or the changes therein for a period of time in conformity with a comprehensive basis of accounting. For reporting purposes, the independent auditor should consider each of the following types of financial presentations to be a financial statement:

a.   Balance sheet
b.   Statement of income or statement of operations
c.   Statement of retained earnings
d.   Statement of cash flows
e.   Statement of changes in owners' equity
f. .   Statement of assets and liabilities that does not include owners' equity accounts
g.   Statement of revenue and expenses
h.   Summary of operations
i.   Statement of operations by product lines
j.   Statement of cash receipts and disbursements

Scoring Schedule:

	Correct Responses		Gradable Items		Weights		
Tab 3	_____	÷	10	×	20%	=	_____
Tab 4	_____	÷	8	×	20%	=	_____
Tab 5	_____	÷	7	×	20%	=	_____
Tab 6	_____	÷	5	×	30%	=	_____
Tab 7	_____	÷	6	×	10%	=	_____
							_____
							(Your Score)

Use Gleim's ***CPA Review Online*** to practice more simulations in a realistic environment.

STUDY UNIT NINETEEN
RELATED REPORTING TOPICS

(19 pages of outline)

19.1	Interim Financial Information (AU 722)	593
19.2	Letters for Underwriters and Certain Other Requesting Parties (AU 634)	596
19.3	Filings Under Federal Securities Statutes (AU 711)	598
19.4	Other Information in Documents Containing Audited Financial Statements (AU 550)	599
19.5	Required Supplementary Information (RSI) (AU 558)	600
19.6	Reporting on Information Accompanying the Basic Financial Statements in Auditor-Submitted Documents (AU 551)	601
19.7	Reporting on Condensed Financial Statements and Selected Financial Data (AU 552)	602
19.8	Reporting on Financial Statements Prepared for Use in Other Countries (AU 534)	603
19.9	Reports on the Application of Accounting Principles (AU 625)	605
19.10	Compliance Attestation (AT 601)	606
19.11	Engagements to Apply Agreed-Upon Procedures (AT 201)	609
19.12	Practice Simulation	622

This study unit addresses miscellaneous reporting issues. Subunit 19.1 applies the field work and reporting standards to a review of interim (e.g., quarterly) financial information of a public entity. The procedures and the report are similar to those of a review of annual statements of private entities. See Study Unit 20. Subunits 19.2 and 19.3 relate to SEC engagements. The next four subunits (19.4 through 19.7) apply to information outside the basic financial statements. Subunit 19.8 outlines the auditor's responsibilities for financial statements prepared for use in other countries. Subunit 19.9 discusses the accountant's responsibility when requested to provide an evaluation of, or a conclusion on, how accounting principles will be applied to specific transactions of a particular entity. Subunit 19.10 concerns the applicability and scope of compliance engagements. It covers both agreed-upon procedures and examination engagements. Subunit 19.11 addresses the nature of agreed-upon procedures engagements in general.

19.1 INTERIM FINANCIAL INFORMATION (AU 722)

1. **Interim financial information** (IFI) is financial information for less than a full year or for the 12 months ending on a date other than fiscal year-end. The IFI may be in statement form. It may also be in a summarized form purportedly in conformity with GAAP and applicable regulations.

   a. Before accepting an engagement to review interim financial information, the accountant must make inquiries of his/her **predecessor** (Study Unit 2).

   b. An accountant may review the IFI of an entity that files under the Securities Exchange Act of 1934 if the latest annual statements are audited.

2. **The objective of a review of IFI** is to enable the accountant to provide **negative assurance**, i.e., to state whether (s)he is aware of any material modifications that should be made for the IFI to conform with GAAP.

   a. A review primarily involves performing analytical and inquiry procedures. It does not entail testing accounting records and the effectiveness of controls, obtaining corroborating evidence, or applying certain other auditing procedures.

3. **An understanding with the client** must be established regarding the services to be performed. Absent such an understanding, the engagement must not be undertaken.

   a. The understanding includes the **objectives and limitations** of the engagement and the **responsibilities** of management and the accountant.

   b. The preferable form of the **required documentation** of the understanding is a written communication with the client (e.g., an engagement letter).

   c. **Management's responsibilities** include the IFI and the effectiveness of internal control, compliance with laws and regulations, making information available, providing a **representation letter**, and adjusting the IFI for material misstatements.

   d. The **accountant's responsibility** is to comply with AICPA standards.

4. **The accountant's knowledge of the entity's business and internal controls** must be sufficient to identify types of misstatements, consider the likelihood of their occurrence, and select inquiries and analytical procedures. This knowledge must relate to preparation of annual information as well as IFI. However, the review is not intended to provide assurance about internal control or identify reportable conditions. Procedures must include

   a. Reading documentation of the prior audit and of prior reviews with specific consideration of corrected and uncorrected misstatements, identified fraud risks (e.g., management override), and significant matters of continuing interest (e.g., control weaknesses).

   b. Reading the recent annual information and prior IFI.

   c. Considering current audit results.

   d. Inquiries of management about changes in the business or in internal control.

   e. In an initial review, inquiries of the predecessor accountant and review of his/her documentation if permitted.

   f. Obtaining knowledge of the relevant aspects of the five components of internal control relating to annual information and IFI.

5. **Analytical procedures** must be applied to identify unusual relationships and items. However, the accountant's expectations developed in a review are less precise than in an audit, and management responses generally are not corroborated. The reasonableness and consistency of the responses are considered.

   a. The following **inquiries and other procedures** are required:

      1) Reading the minutes of meetings of shareholders, the board, and committees, and inquiring about the results of meetings for which minutes are unavailable.

      2) Obtaining reports of accountants who have reviewed IFI of components of the entity or its investees. If their reports are unissued, inquiries should be made of such accountants.

      3) Inquiring of management about **financial and accounting matters**, such as (a) unusual or complex situations, (b) significant recent transactions, (c) status of uncorrected misstatements, (d) knowledge of fraud, (e) deficiencies in control, (f) significant entries and other adjustments, (g) questions arising from application of review procedures, (h) events subsequent to the date of the IFI, (i) communications from regulators, and (j) preparation of the IFI in conformity with GAAP.

      4) Reconciling the IFI and the accounting records.

      5) Reading the IFI to consider, based on information coming to the accountant's attention, whether it conforms with GAAP.

      6) Reading **other information** accompanying the IFI.

   b. Inquiries about **litigation, claims, and assessments** and **going-concern issues** ordinarily are not made unless the accountant becomes aware of reasons for such inquiries.

    c.   The accountant **extends procedures** if (s)he believes that the IFI does not conform with GAAP.

    d.   The same accountant usually performs the **audit** of the annual statements and the review of the IFI, and may be able to coordinate them.

    e.   The accountant must obtain **written representations from management** about specific matters. See Study Unit 14 for an example representation letter that addresses most of the same matters.

6.   **Evaluating results**. If the accountant becomes aware of **likely misstatements**, (s)he should accumulate them for further evaluation. Misstatements, including inadequate disclosure, are evaluated individually and in the aggregate to determine whether the IFI must be materially modified.

    a.   A **scope restriction** may arise from significant control weaknesses, inability to perform necessary procedures, or the client's failure to provide written representations. The result is an incomplete review, and no report is issued.

7.   Possible **communications to management, the audit committee, and others** include (a) the inability to complete the review, (b) the need for material modification of IFI, (c) the accountant's awareness of fraud or illegal acts, (d) internal-control-related matters, and (e) certain other matters required to be communicated to audit committees.

8.   Any discussion of the **quality of the entity's accounting principles** as applied to its interim reports is ordinarily limited to the effects of significant events, transactions, and changes in estimates considered in performing the review.

9.   If the accountant has reviewed the IFI to be filed with a regulator, for example, in an SEC Form 10-Q, (s)he should attempt to communicate to the audit committee (or its chair) and a representative of management the matters identified in 7.(a)-(e) above. This communication (written or oral and documented) should occur prior to the filing or as soon as practicable.

10.   **The Accountant's Report on a Review of IFI**

    a.   An accountant need not report in writing on a review of IFI. However, the SEC requires a registrant to hire an independent accountant to review its IFI to be included in quarterly reports to the SEC. A review report must be filed if the registrant states in a filing that the IFI was reviewed.

    b.   The following is an independent accountant's review report:

We have reviewed the accompanying [describe the interim financial information or statements reviewed] of ABC Company and consolidated subsidiaries as of September 30, 20X1, and for the 3-month and 9-month periods then ended. These financial statements are the responsibility of the company's management. We conducted our review in accordance with standards established by the American Institute of Certified Public Accountants. A review of interim financial information consists principally of applying analytical procedures and making inquiries of persons responsible for financial and accounting matters. It is substantially less in scope than an audit conducted in accordance with generally accepted auditing standards, the objective of which is the expression of an opinion regarding the financial statements taken as a whole. Accordingly, we do not express such an opinion.

Based on our review, we are not aware of any material modifications that should be made to the accompanying interim financial information (statements) for it (them) to be in conformity with accounting principles generally accepted in the United States of America.

---

    c.   Each page of the IFI must be clearly **marked as unaudited**.

    d.   The accountant **modifies the review report** for material **departures from GAAP**, including inadequate disclosure. The modification describes the departure and, if practicable, states its effects or provides the necessary information.

11.   Stop and review! You have completed the outline for this subunit. Study multiple-choice questions 1 through 3 on page 612.

19.2 LETTERS FOR UNDERWRITERS AND CERTAIN OTHER REQUESTING PARTIES (AU 634)

1. Independent accountants audit financial statements and schedules contained in registration statements filed with the SEC under the **Securities Act of 1933**. Thus, accountants often confer with clients, underwriters, and counsel concerning the accounting and auditing requirements of the act and of the SEC.

    a. In conjunction with the audit, they may issue **comfort letters** for underwriters and certain other requesting parties. Comfort letters are not required by law and are not filed with the SEC, but underwriting agreements often request them.

    b. Accountants are limited in the comments they can make in comfort letters on unaudited financial information. However, underwriters may wish to perform a reasonable investigation of financial and accounting data not **expertized** (covered by an audit report of independent accountants, who consent to be named) as a defense under the act.

        1) Accountants may issue comfort letters for other parties, e.g., a party with a **due diligence** defense under the 1933 act who submits either a written attorney's opinion stating that the party has such a defense or a suitable representation letter.

        2) When a party with a due diligence defense requests a comfort letter but does not furnish a representation letter, the accountant may not provide negative assurance but may describe procedures performed.

        3) Because the nature of a reasonable investigation has not been established, only the underwriter can determine what is sufficient.

        4) The assistance provided in a comfort letter is limited. Accountants can comment only on matters to which their expertise is relevant, and the procedures permit the expression of, at most, negative assurance.

2. **Format and Content of Comfort Letters**

    a. Dating. The letter ordinarily is dated on or shortly before the effective date of the registration statement.

        1) The procedures described in the letter relate to a cutoff date prior to the date of the letter.

    b. Addressee. The letter should not be addressed or given to anyone other than the client and the named underwriters, broker-dealer, intermediary, or buyer or seller.

        1) The appropriate addressee is the intermediary who has negotiated the agreement with the client and with whom the accountants will deal in discussions regarding the letter.

    c. Independence. Accountants customarily make a statement concerning their independence in the letter.

    d. Compliance with SEC requirements. A typical comfort letter expresses an opinion on whether audited financial statements and schedules included in the registration statement comply as to form in all material respects with the applicable accounting requirements of the act and the related rules and regulations adopted by the SEC. However, the comfort letter does not state or repeat an opinion about the fairness of presentation of the statements.

    e. Accountants' reports. Underwriters may request the accountants to repeat in the comfort letter their opinion on the audited financial statements included in the registration statement. Because of the significance of the date of the auditor's report, the accountants should not repeat their opinion or give negative assurance about the report.

f. Comments on information other than audited financial statements

    1) Unaudited condensed interim financial statements. Comments in the comfort letter about unaudited condensed interim financial statements appearing in the registration statement should always be in the form of negative assurance.

    2) Knowledge of the internal control system. The accountants should have knowledge of the client's internal controls if they comment on unaudited condensed information, capsule information, financial forecasts, or changes in capital stock, increases in long-term debt, and decreases in selected items (but would not comment on internal control).

    3) Capsule financial information. Capsule information is unaudited summarized interim information for subsequent periods used to supplement the audited financial statements or unaudited condensed interim financial information in a registration statement. The accountant may give negative assurance regarding conformity with GAAP and consistency with regards to the audited financial statements if the capsule information is in accordance with the disclosure requirements of APB 28, *Interim Financial Reporting*, and if the accountants have performed a review of the underlying financial statements in accordance with AU 722, *Interim Financial Information*.

    4) Pro forma financial information. The accountants should not comment on this information unless they have acquired the appropriate level of knowledge of the accounting and financial reporting practices of the entity, e.g., by auditing or reviewing the historical statements. This topic is covered by AT 401, which is discussed in Study Unit 1.

    5) Forecasts. To apply agreed-upon procedures to a forecast and comment thereon in a comfort letter, the accountants must perform compilation procedures for a forecast and should attach the report to the comfort letter. Negative assurance on the results of the procedures may not be provided.

    6) Management's discussion and analysis (MD&A). Comments that attestations are in accordance with AT 701, *Management's Discussion and Analysis*, may be made. No comments on the compliance of the MD&A with the forms required by SEC rules should be made. Furthermore, no comments should be made on nonfinancial data in the MD&A.

    7) Subsequent changes. Comments on these matters ordinarily concern whether a change has occurred in capital stock, long-term debt has increased, or other specified financial statement items have increased/decreased during the change period (the period subsequent to the latest financial statements included in the registration statement). Accountants are usually requested to read minutes and make inquiries.

g. Tables, statistics, and other financial information. The underwriting agreement may call for a comfort letter commenting on tables, statistics, and other financial information in the registration statement.

    1) The accountants should comment only with respect to information

        a) Expressed in dollars (or percentages derived therefrom) and obtained from records subject to the internal controls of the entity's accounting system

        b) Derived directly from the accounting records by analysis or computation

h. Concluding paragraph. The comfort letter should conclude with a paragraph that the "letter is solely for the information of the addressees and to assist the underwriters" to avoid misunderstanding of the purpose and intended use of the comfort letter.

3. Stop and review! You have completed the outline for this subunit. Study multiple-choice questions 4 through 8 beginning on page 612.

19.3 FILINGS UNDER FEDERAL SECURITIES STATUTES (AU 711)

1. **Division of Responsibilities**

   a. The responsibility for the financial representations contained in documents filed under the federal securities statutes lies with management.

   b. The accountant's responsibility is ordinarily similar to that for other types of reporting, but the statutes specify that responsibility in detail.

      1) For example, the Securities Act of 1933 imposes responsibility for false or misleading statements in an effective registration statement.

   c. The independent accountant has a responsibility as an expert when his/her report is included in a registration statement. The 1933 act states that no person shall be liable

      1) If (s)he, after reasonable investigation, had reasonable grounds to believe that the statements in the registration statement were true and that there was no omission to state a material fact required to be stated therein or necessary to make the statements therein not misleading

      2) If the part of the registration statement for which (s)he had responsibility did not fairly represent his/her statement as an expert or was not a fair copy of or extract from his/her report or valuation as an expert

   d. The standard of reasonableness is that required of a prudent individual in the management of his/her own property.

   e. The independent accountant whose report is included in a registration statement has a statutory responsibility that is determined in light of the circumstances on the effective date of the registration statement.

      1) A report based on a review of interim financial information is not deemed to be a report or part of the registration statement for this purpose. The SEC requires that the prospectus contain language to this effect.

         a) Accounting principles applied must have substantial authoritative support.

         b) The SEC now requires that registrants obtain reviews of interim financial information by their independent auditors prior to filing quarterly reports in Form 10-Q or Form 10-QSB.

   f. The independent accountant should be certain that his/her name is not being used in a way that indicates that his/her responsibility is greater than intended.

2. **Subsequent Events Procedures in 1933 Act Filings**

   a. To sustain the burden of proof that (s)he has made a "reasonable investigation," an auditor should extend his/her subsequent events procedures from the date of the report up to the effective date of the registration statement.

   b. Following the completion of field work, the independent auditor may rely mostly on inquiries. The auditor should

      1) Apply the normal subsequent events procedures.

      2) Read the prospectus and other pertinent portions of the registration statement.

      3) Obtain written representations from responsible individuals about whether any events have occurred having a material effect on the audited financial statements or that should be disclosed.

   c. An auditor who has audited the financial statements for prior periods but not for the most recent period included in the registration statement has a responsibility for material subsequent events affecting the prior period statements.

3. Stop and review! You have completed the outline for this subunit. Study multiple-choice questions 9 through 11 on page 614.

NOTE: **The following is a brief overview of the next four subunits: 19.4, 19.5, 19.6, and 19.7**. The candidate should use the table to assure that the differences among the types of information and the auditor's responsibility are fully understood.

Subunit	AU Section	Type of Information/Example	Accountant's Procedures	Reporting Responsibility
19.4	AU 550	**Other**/President's letter	Read for consistency with financial statements.	Add paragraph to audit report only if other information is not consistent with financial statements.
19.5	AU 558	**Required Supplementary**/Oil and gas reserve information	Apply limited procedures.	Add paragraph to audit report only if information is omitted or departs from requirements.
19.6	AU 551	**Accompanying in Auditor-Submitted Document**/Schedule of fixed assets	Audit.	Refer to and report on fair presentation in audit report.
19.7	AU 552	**Condensed or Selected**/Summary of financial results	Determine if stated fairly relative to complete financial statements.	In a separate report, refer to audit report and state conclusion about fairness to complete financial statements.

19.4 OTHER INFORMATION IN DOCUMENTS CONTAINING AUDITED FINANCIAL STATEMENTS (AU 550)

1. **General Considerations**

   a. This section is applicable to other information in addition to audited financial statements and the auditor's report ("other" is a technical term as used in AU 550) contained in either annual reports or other documents published by the reporting entity to which the auditor is requested to devote attention by the client.

   b. AU 550 is not applicable when the financial statements and report appear in a registration statement filed under the Securities Act of 1933 or when the auditor is engaged to express an opinion on the other information (but see 19.4.4.).

2. An entity may publish many such documents, for example, the president's letter in the annual report.

3. The auditor's responsibility with respect to other information does not extend beyond the financial information identified in the report, and the auditor has no obligation to perform any procedures to corroborate the other information. However, (s)he should read the other information and consider whether it and its manner of presentation are materially inconsistent with the financial statements.

   a. If the auditor determines that a material inconsistency exists, (s)he should determine whether the statements, the auditor's report, or both require revision.

   b. If they do not, (s)he should request the client to revise the other information. If it is not corrected, (s)he should consider such actions as revising the report to include an explanatory paragraph, withholding the report, and withdrawing from the engagement.

4. An auditor may express an opinion on the other information **in relation to the basic financial statements taken as a whole** if it has been subjected to procedures applied in the audit of those statements. The auditor may follow the guidance in 19.6 in such circumstances.

5. Stop and review! You have completed the outline for this subunit. Study multiple-choice questions 12 and 13 on page 615.

19.5 REQUIRED SUPPLEMENTARY INFORMATION (RSI) (AU 558)

1.   Authoritative bodies have developed GAAP for certain information supplementary to financial statements. This pronouncement describes procedures to be applied in an audit of financial statements appearing in a document with RSI.

   a.   It does not govern an engagement that includes the audit of the RSI.

   b.   However, this pronouncement describes the circumstances in which the auditor should report on RSI.

   c.   The provisions of AU 558 also apply to a voluntary presentation in a document including audited financial statements of information required of other entities. It does not apply in this case if the auditor has not performed the relevant procedures described in the pronouncement or the auditor presents a disclaimer in the report.

2.   **Involvement with Information outside Financial Statements.** The auditor need not audit information outside the basic statements, but (s)he does have certain responsibilities depending on the nature of the information and the document containing the statements (as per AU 550 and 551).

3.   **Involvement with RSI.** This information is essential to reporting, and guidelines have been established for its measurement and presentation. The auditor should apply **limited procedures** and report deficiencies in, or the omission of, such information. Examples of procedures include

   a.   Inquiring of management about the methods of preparing the information, including whether it is measured and presented within prescribed guidelines.

   b.   Comparing the information for consistency with audited financial statements.

4.   The auditor need not add an explanatory paragraph to the report to refer to the RSI or to the limited procedures, unless the

   a.   Information is omitted.
   b.   Measurement or presentation departs materially from prescribed guidelines.
   c.   Auditor is unable to complete the prescribed procedures.
   d.   Auditor has substantial doubt about conformity with prescribed guidelines.

5.   Deficiencies in the RSI do not affect the opinion on the basic statements, and the auditor need not present the information if it is omitted.

   a.   An example of an additional explanatory paragraph added to the standard audit report for the omission of RSI follows:

   > The (Company or Governmental Unit) has not presented [describe the supplementary information required by GAAP] that accounting principles generally accepted in the United States has determined is necessary to supplement, although not required to be part of, the basic financial statements.

   b.   The additional explanatory paragraph is modified appropriately for incorrect or misleading presentations.

6.   An auditor may perform auditing procedures on the RSI in connection with the audit of the basic statements. If they are sufficient for expression of an opinion, the auditor may expand the audit report accordingly.

7.   Stop and review! You have completed the outline for this subunit. Study multiple-choice questions 14 and 15 beginning on page 615.

19.6 REPORTING ON INFORMATION ACCOMPANYING THE BASIC FINANCIAL STATEMENTS IN AUDITOR-SUBMITTED DOCUMENTS (AU 551)

1. **General Considerations**. An auditor may submit to the client or to others a document containing information in addition to the basic financial statements and the auditor's report.

   a. The information covered is presented outside the basic statements and is not considered necessary for a fair presentation in conformity with GAAP. It includes additional details or explanations related to the basic statements, consolidating information, historical summaries, and statistical data. It may also include other material that may be from outside the accounting system or the entity.

   b. This information includes required supplementary information (RSI) described in subunit 19.5 when included in an auditor-submitted document.

2. **Reporting Responsibility**. When an auditor submits a document containing audited financial statements, (s)he must report on **all** the information included. (When the client includes information along with the financial statements, it is "other" information and the auditor's responsibility is defined by AU 550.)

   a. The report has the same objective as a report on the basic statements. It should describe the character of the work and the degree of responsibility taken. Although the auditor may prepare the accompanying information and the basic statements, both are representations of management.

   b. The report, which may be added to the report on the basic statements or appear separately in an auditor-submitted document, includes the following:

      1) A statement that the audit purpose is to form an opinion on the basic statements taken as a whole

      2) An identification of the accompanying information

      3) A statement that the accompanying information is presented for additional analysis and is not required

      4) An opinion on whether the accompanying information is fairly stated in all material respects in relation to the basic financial statements taken as a whole or a disclaimer

         a) The choice depends on whether the information has been audited. The auditor may express an opinion on part and disclaim an opinion on the rest.

         b) The following is an example of an opinion paragraph:

         > Our audit was conducted for the purpose of forming an opinion on the basic financial statements taken as a whole. The **[identify accompanying information]** is presented for purposes of additional analysis and is not a required part of the basic financial statements. Such information has been subjected to the auditing procedures applied in the audit of the basic financial statements and, in our opinion, is fairly stated in all material respects in relation to the basic financial statements taken as a whole.

         c) The following is an example of disclaiming an opinion on all of the information:

         > Our audit was conducted for the purpose of forming an opinion on the basic financial statements taken as a whole. The **[identify the accompanying information]** is presented for purposes of additional analysis and is not a required part of the basic financial statements. Such information has not been subjected to the auditing procedures applied in the audit of the basic financial statements, and, accordingly, we express no opinion on it.

   c. The same measure of materiality is used as in forming an opinion on the basic statements.

d.   If the accompanying information is materially misstated, the auditor should discuss the matter with the client and propose revisions. If the client will not revise the information, the auditor should either modify the report and describe the misstatement or refuse to include the information.

e.   The report may be affected by modifications of the report on the basic statements.

1)   A qualified opinion on the basic statements requires the auditor to clarify the effects on the accompanying information.

2)   An adverse opinion or a disclaimer precludes an opinion on the accompanying information. Like a piecemeal opinion, such an opinion might overshadow or contradict the disclaimer or adverse opinion on the basic statements.

3.   Stop and review! You have completed the outline for this subunit. Study multiple-choice questions 16 through 19 beginning on page 616.

19.7 REPORTING ON CONDENSED FINANCIAL STATEMENTS AND SELECTED FINANCIAL DATA (AU 552)

1.   This pronouncement applies to

a.   Condensed annual or interim financial statements derived from audited financial statements of a public entity

b.   Selected financial data derived from audited financial statements of a public or a nonpublic entity and presented in a document that includes audited financial statements

2.   **Condensed Financial Statements**

a.   These financial statements are considerably less detailed than complete financial statements. They should be read with the entity's most recent complete statements that include all GAAP disclosures.

b.   An auditor may report on condensed financial statements but, because they do not constitute a fair presentation, not in the same manner as on the complete statements.

c.   The auditor's report should

1)   State that the auditor has audited and expressed an opinion on the complete statements

2)   Provide the date of the report on the complete statements

3)   Indicate the type of opinion expressed on the complete statements

4)   Express an opinion as to whether the information in the condensed statements is fairly stated in all material respects in relation to the complete statements

d.   If a client names the auditor in a client-prepared document and also states that condensed statements have been derived from audited statements, the auditor need not report on the condensed statements if they are included in a document that contains audited statements.

e.   Condensed statements of a public entity may be presented comparatively with interim information as of a subsequent date that is accompanied by the auditor's review report.

1)   The auditor should report on the condensed statements in each period in a manner appropriate to the service provided.

3. **Selected Financial Data**

     a.   An auditor may report on selected data included in a client-prepared document containing audited statements.

         1)   Selected financial data are not a required part of the basic statements, and management is responsible for determining the specific data to be presented.

         2)   The report should be limited to data derived from audited statements.

         3)   If the selected financial data include other information (such as number of employees or square footage of facilities), the report should specifically identify the data on which the auditor is reporting.

         4)   The report should

             a)   State that the auditor has audited and expressed an opinion on the complete statements

             b)   Indicate the type of opinion expressed on the complete statements

             c)   Express an opinion as to whether the information in the selected financial data is fairly stated in all material respects in relation to the complete statements

     b.   In introductory material included in a client-prepared document, an entity might name the auditor and state that the data are derived from financial statements that (s)he audited. This statement does not require the auditor to report on the selected data if they are in a document that contains audited statements.

4.   Stop and review! You have completed the outline for this subunit. Study multiple-choice questions 20 through 22 beginning on page 617.

19.8 REPORTING ON FINANCIAL STATEMENTS PREPARED FOR USE IN OTHER COUNTRIES (AU 534)

1.   An independent auditor practicing in the U.S. may report on the financial statements of a U.S. entity prepared in conformity with accounting principles generally accepted in another country for use outside the U.S.

     a.   The auditor must clearly understand the purpose and uses of the statements and obtain written representations from management.

     b.   If the statements are for general distribution and the standard report of the foreign country will be used, the auditor must consider any additional legal responsibilities.

2.   **General and Field Work Standards**

     a.   The auditor's procedures should comply with the general and field work standards of U.S. GAAS.

     b.   The procedures performed under U.S. GAAS may require modification; for example, accounting principles generally accepted in another country may require that certain assets be revalued to adjust for inflation. The auditor would then need to test the adjustments.

     c.   The auditor should understand the other accounting principles.

3.   **Compliance with Auditing Standards of Another Country**. The auditor may be requested to apply the auditing standards of the other country. In that case, the auditor should comply with the general and field work standards of that country as well as with U.S. GAAS.

4. **Reporting Standards**

    a. The auditor may use either a modified U.S.-style report or the report form of the other country.

    b. The auditor may report on financial statements prepared in accordance with U.S. GAAP and financial statements prepared in conformity with accounting principles generally accepted in the other country.

    c. **Use limited to outside the United States.** A modified U.S.-style report should include

        1) A title including the word "independent"

        2) A statement that the identified statements were audited

        3) A reference to the note describing the basis of presentation, including identification of the nationality of the principles

        4) A statement that the financial statements are the responsibility of management and that the auditor's responsibility is to express an opinion based on the audit

        5) A statement that the audit was in accordance with GAAS (and, if appropriate, with the auditing standards of the other country)

        6) A statement that U.S. standards require the auditor to plan and perform the audit to obtain reasonable assurance about whether the financial statements are free of material misstatement

        7) A statement that an audit includes

            a) Examining, on a test basis, evidence supporting the amounts and disclosures in the financial statements

            b) Assessing the accounting principles used and significant estimates made by management

            c) Evaluating the overall financial statement presentation

        8) A statement that the auditor believes that the audit provides a reasonable basis for the opinion

        9) A paragraph expressing an opinion on whether the financial statements are presented fairly, in all material respects, in conformity with the basis of accounting described (including an identification of the country of origin of the accounting principles)

            a) If the statements are not fairly presented, the substantive reasons should be disclosed in an additional explanatory paragraph (preceding the opinion paragraph), and the opinion paragraph should include modifying language and refer to the explanatory paragraph.

        10) If comparative financial statements are presented, the described basis of accounting has not been applied consistently, and the change materially affects comparability, an explanatory paragraph (following the opinion paragraph) that describes the change in accounting principle and refers to the note that discusses the change and its effects

        11) The signature of the auditor's firm

        12) The date (usually the date of the completion of field work)

    d. **Use in the United States.** If the auditor reports on fair presentation in conformity with the accounting principles generally accepted in another country, the auditor should use a U.S.-style report, modified because of departures from accounting principles generally accepted in the United States. The auditor may express an opinion on whether the financial statements are presented in conformity with accounting principles generally accepted in the other country.

5. Stop and review! You have completed the outline for this subunit. Study multiple-choice questions 23 and 24 beginning on page 618.

19.9 REPORTS ON THE APPLICATION OF ACCOUNTING PRINCIPLES (AU 625)

1. Management and others may consult with accountants to learn how to apply accounting principles to new transactions and financial products or to increase their knowledge about specific financial reporting issues.

2. **Applicability**

   a. This pronouncement should be applied by an accountant in public practice (**reporting accountant**) when preparing a **written report** on the

      1) Application of accounting principles to **specific transactions**, whether completed or proposed, "involving facts and circumstances of a particular entity."

      2) Type of opinion that may be expressed on a **specific entity's financial statements**.

   b. This pronouncement also applies to **oral advice** believed to be an important factor in the decisions described in 2.a. above made by a principal to the transaction.

   c. It does not apply to a **continuing accountant** engaged to report on a specific entity's financial statements, assistance in litigation involving accounting matters or to related expert testimony, or professional advice provided to another public accountant.

   d. It also does not apply to position papers (e.g., newsletters, articles, speeches and texts), lectures and other forms of public presentations, and letters for the public record to professional and governmental standard-setting bodies.

   e. An accountant must not provide a written report on the application of accounting principles to a **hypothetical transaction**.

3. **Performance Standards**

   a. In performing the engagement, the reporting accountant should consider the circumstances in which the report or advice is requested, the purpose, and the intended use. Also, the reporting accountant should

      1) Exercise due professional care.
      2) Have adequate technical training and proficiency.
      3) Plan the engagement adequately.
      4) Supervise assistants.
      5) Accumulate sufficient information to provide a reasonable basis for the professional judgment rendered.
      6) Consider the circumstances and purpose of the request for a written report or oral advice and its intended use.
      7) Obtain an understanding of the form and substance of the transaction(s).
      8) Review applicable GAAP.
      9) Consult with other professionals or experts, if appropriate.
      10) Ascertain and consider the existence of creditable precedents or analogies.
      11) Consult with the continuing accountant of the entity to determine all the available relevant facts, including disputes with management.

         a) The reporting accountant should explain to the management of the entity the need for consultation with the continuing accountant, request permission, and request authorization for the continuing accountant to respond fully.

4. **Reporting Standards**. The addressee of the accountant's written report is the requesting entity. The report should accomplish the following:

   a. Briefly describe the engagement and state that it was in accordance with applicable AICPA standards.

   b. Identify the specific entity; describe the transaction(s); state the facts, circumstances, and assumptions; and state the source of the information.

   c. Describe the accounting principle(s) to be applied, including their country of origin, or the type of opinion to be expressed.

      1) If appropriate, the report should describe the reasons for the conclusions.

   d. State that the responsibility for proper accounting is with the preparers of the financial statements, who should consult with their continuing accountant.

   e. State that any difference in the facts, circumstances, or assumptions may change the report.

   f. Contain a separate paragraph at the end of the report restricting its use to specified (and identified) parties.

5. Stop and review! You have completed the outline for this subunit. Study multiple-choice questions 25 and 26 on page 619.

19.10 COMPLIANCE ATTESTATION (AT 601)

1. **Overview**. A practitioner may be asked to provide assurance about the entity's **compliance with requirements** of specified laws, regulations, rules, contracts, or grants. The engagement also may be directed toward the responsible party's written assertion about compliance. For example, management might make the assertion: "Z Company complied with the restrictive covenants in paragraph 20 of its Loan Agreement with Y Bank dated January 1, year 1, as of and for the 3 months ended March 31, year"

   a. The practitioner also may be asked to provide this type of assurance concerning the **effectiveness of internal control over compliance** with laws, regulations, etc.

   b. This standard describes the conditions under which a practitioner may accept a compliance engagement, the types of engagements, the responsibilities of the parties, and the reports that should be issued. AT 101, *Attestation Standards*, provides the framework for application of this standard.

2. **Applicability**. The standard provides guidance for engagements related to reporting on compliance with requirements that are either financial or nonfinancial.

   a. The general, field work, and reporting attestation standards (AT 101) are applicable to this type of engagement.

   b. The standard does not

      1) Affect the auditor's responsibility in an audit of financial statements

      2) Apply to governmental audit engagements unless the terms of the engagement specify an attestation report under this standard

      3) Apply to compliance reporting based solely on an audit of financial statements

      4) Apply to letters for underwriters and certain other requesting parties (AU 634)

   c. A compliance attestation does not provide a legal determination of an entity's compliance.

3. **Scope of Services**. A practitioner may perform **agreed-upon procedures** or an **examination**. However, there is no compliance attestation **review** service.

    a. In an **agreed-upon procedures engagement**, the users of the report decide the procedures to be performed by the practitioner and take responsibility for those procedures.

       1) The practitioner has no obligation to perform procedures beyond the agreed-upon procedures. However, if noncompliance comes to the practitioner's attention by other means, such information should be included in the report.

       2) The practitioner's report should be in the form of procedures and findings but should **not provide negative assurance** about whether an entity is in compliance or whether the responsible party's assertion is fairly stated.

       3) The report

          a) Has a title that includes the word "independent"

          b) Describes the nature and scope of the service

          c) Limits use to specified parties

          d) Is dated as of the completion of the agreed-upon procedures

    b. In an **examination** of an entity's compliance with specified requirements (or of a written assertion thereon), the practitioner gathers evidence to support an opinion on whether an entity is in compliance, in all material respects, based on established or agreed-upon criteria.

       1) The practitioner also may examine the effectiveness (or the responsible party's assertion about the effectiveness) of internal control over compliance, provided reasonable criteria have been established by a recognized body or are stated in, or attached to, the practitioner's report.

4. **Conditions for Engagement Performance**

    a. General. A practitioner cannot accept an engagement unless (s)he believes the subject matter to be capable of reasonably consistent evaluation against suitable, available criteria. In addition, a practitioner may perform a compliance attestation engagement if the responsible party

       1) Accepts responsibility for the entity's compliance with specified requirements and the effectiveness of the entity's internal control over compliance

       2) Evaluates compliance or effectiveness

       3) Provides the practitioner with a written assertion about compliance.

    b. An examination may be performed if, in addition to the general conditions, sufficient evidence exists or can be developed to support the responsible party's evaluation.

5. **Examination Engagement**. The purpose is to express an opinion on whether an entity is in compliance (or on whether the responsible party's assertion about such compliance is fairly stated), in all material respects, based on established or agreed-upon criteria. To express an opinion, the practitioner must gather sufficient evidence to reduce attestation risk to an acceptably low level. Attestation risk is similar to the audit risk concept used in Statements on Auditing Standards.

    a. The practitioner seeks to obtain reasonable, not absolute, assurance of compliance.

    b. Based on the extent to which (s)he wishes to restrict attestation risk and the assessments of inherent risk and control risk, the practitioner determines the acceptable level of detection risk. This level will determine the nature, timing, and extent of the necessary compliance tests.

c. The consideration of materiality differs from that in an audit of financial statements in accordance with GAAS. The following should be considered:

1) The nature of the compliance requirements, which may not be quantifiable in monetary terms

2) The nature and frequency of noncompliance identified, with appropriate consideration of sampling risk

3) Qualitative considerations, including the needs and expectations of users

d. **Performing an examination engagement**. The practitioner should use due care and exercise professional skepticism to achieve reasonable assurance that material noncompliance will be detected. The following summarizes the practitioner's procedures and considerations in an examination engagement:

1) Obtain an understanding of the specified compliance requirements.

2) Plan the engagement, including the potential use of specialists and internal auditors.

3) Obtain an understanding of the relevant portions of internal control over compliance to plan the engagement and to assess control risk. If control risk is to be assessed below the maximum, tests of controls must be performed.

4) Perform procedures to provide reasonable assurance of detecting material noncompliance, including obtaining a written representation letter from the responsible party.

5) Consider subsequent events (the requirement is similar to that established by AU 560, *Subsequent Events*, for a financial statement audit).

6) Form an opinion.

e. The practitioner's report on an examination should contain introductory, scope, and opinion paragraphs and

1) Have a title that includes the word "independent"

2) Identify the specified requirements, period covered, and responsible party

3) Describe management's and the practitioner's responsibilities

4) State that the examination was conducted in accordance with AICPA attestation standards

5) Express an opinion on an entity's compliance (or on the fairness of the responsible party's assertion)

6) Be dated as of the completion of the procedures

f. The standard report should limit use when criteria are suitable only for limited specific users or are available only to the specified parties.

g.   Example of a standard report on compliance with specified requirements based on an examination:

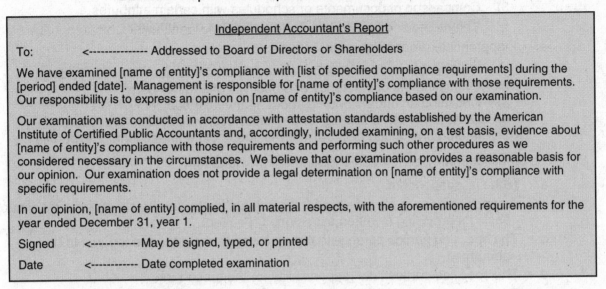

Standard Report on Compliance Based on an Examination

> ### Independent Accountant's Report
>
> To: <--------------- Addressed to Board of Directors or Shareholders
>
> We have examined [name of entity]'s compliance with [list of specified compliance requirements] during the [period] ended [date]. Management is responsible for [name of entity]'s compliance with those requirements. Our responsibility is to express an opinion on [name of entity]'s compliance based on our examination.
>
> Our examination was conducted in accordance with attestation standards established by the American Institute of Certified Public Accountants and, accordingly, included examining, on a test basis, evidence about [name of entity]'s compliance with those requirements and performing such other procedures as we considered necessary in the circumstances. We believe that our examination provides a reasonable basis for our opinion. Our examination does not provide a legal determination on [name of entity]'s compliance with specific requirements.
>
> In our opinion, [name of entity] complied, in all material respects, with the aforementioned requirements for the year ended December 31, year 1.
>
> Signed   <------------ May be signed, typed, or printed
>
> Date   <------------ Date completed examination

h.   Report modifications

   1)   Material noncompliance. When an examination discloses noncompliance with specified requirements that the practitioner believes have a material effect on the entity's compliance, the report should be modified. Depending on materiality, the practitioner should express either a qualified (except for) or an adverse opinion on compliance. An explanatory paragraph (before the opinion paragraph) should be added to the report.

   2)   Scope limitations. The practitioner should qualify or disclaim an opinion depending on materiality (e.g., if management refuses to provide a written representation letter).

   3)   Report based, in part, on the report of another practitioner. The practitioner should either refer to the other practitioner or issue the standard report (see the general guidance provided by AU 543, *Part of Audit Performed by Other Independent Auditors*).

6.   Stop and review! You have completed the outline for this subunit. Study multiple-choice questions 27 through 30 beginning on page 620.

19.11 ENGAGEMENTS TO APPLY AGREED-UPON PROCEDURES (AT 201)

1.   An agreed-upon procedures engagement is one in which a practitioner is engaged by a client to issue a report of findings based on specific procedures performed on subject matter.

   a.   Specified parties assume responsibility for the sufficiency of the procedures.

   b.   The report is in the form of procedures and findings, and neither an opinion nor negative assurance should be provided.

   c.   The general, field work, and reporting standards for attestation engagements apply (Study Unit 1). However, a written assertion is generally not required in an agreed-upon procedures engagement unless specifically required by another attest standard.

      d.   Appropriate procedures might include

         1)   Inspection of specified documents for attributes
         2)   Confirmation of specific information with third parties
         3)   Comparison of documents or schedules with certain attributes
         4)   Performance of mathematical computations or sampling

      e.   Inappropriate procedures might include

         1)   Mere reading of the work performed by others to describe their findings
         2)   Evaluating the competency or objectivity of another party
         3)   Obtaining an understanding about a particular subject
         4)   General review, checking, or any other overly subjective procedure
         5)   Interpreting documents outside the scope of the practitioner's expertise

2.   The practitioner may perform an engagement provided that

      a.   (S)he is independent.
      b.   A specified party is responsible for the subject matter (or the client has a reasonable basis for providing a written assertion, if required).
      c.   The specified parties agree with the practitioner about the procedures to be performed.
      d.   The specified parties take responsibility for the procedures.
      e.   Procedures are expected to result in reasonably consistent findings.
      f.   Criteria to be used in the determination of findings are agreed upon.
      g.   Reasonably consistent subject matter measurement can be expected.
      h.   Evidence providing a reasonable basis for findings can be collected.
      i.   There is agreement on materiality limits for reporting when applicable.
      j.   Use of the report is restricted to specified parties.

3.   To assure that specified parties take responsibility for the sufficiency of the procedures, the practitioner should do one of the following:

      a.   Communicate directly with, and obtain affirmative acknowledgment from, the parties.
      b.   Distribute the engagement letter to the specified parties.
      c.   Distribute a draft of the anticipated report to the specified parties.
      d.   Consider written requirements of the specified parties.
      e.   Discuss procedures with appropriate representatives of the specified parties.
      f.   Review contracts with or correspondence from the specified parties.

4.   Attestation documentation should be prepared.

5. The following is an example report:

Independent Accountant's Report on Applying Agreed-Upon Procedures

To the Audit Committee and Managements of ABC Inc. and XYZ Fund:

We have performed the procedures enumerated below, which were agreed to by the audit committees and managements of ABC Inc. and XYZ Fund, solely to assist you in evaluating the accompanying Statement of Investment Performance Statistics of XYZ Fund (prepared in accordance with the criteria specified therein) for the year ended December 31, 20X1. XYZ Fund's management is responsible for the statement of investment performance statistics. This agreed-upon procedures engagement was conducted in accordance with attestation standards established by the American Institute of Certified Public Accountants. The sufficiency of these procedures is solely the responsibility of those parties specified in this report. Consequently, we make no representation regarding the sufficiency of the procedures described below either for the purpose for which this report has been requested or for any other purpose.

[Include paragraphs to enumerate procedures and findings.]

We were not engaged to and did not conduct an examination, the objective of which would be the expression of an opinion on the accompanying Statement of Investment Performance Statistics of XYZ Fund. Accordingly, we do not express such an opinion. Had we performed additional procedures, other matters might have come to our attention that would have been reported to you.

This report is intended solely for the information and use of the audit committees and managements of ABC Inc. and XYZ Fund, and is not intended to be and should not be used by anyone other than these specified parties.

[Signature]
[Date]

---

6. Stop and review! You have completed the outline for this subunit. Study multiple-choice questions 31 and 32 on page 621.

QUESTIONS

19.1 Interim Financial Information (AU 722)

1. The objective of a review of interim financial information of a public entity is to provide an accountant with a basis for reporting whether

A. A reasonable basis exists for expressing an updated opinion regarding the financial statements that were previously audited.

B. Material modifications should be made to conform with generally accepted accounting principles.

C. The financial statements are presented fairly in accordance with standards of interim reporting.

D. The financial statements are presented fairly in accordance with generally accepted accounting principles.

Answer (B) is correct. *(CPA, adapted)*
REQUIRED: The objective of a review of interim financial information.
DISCUSSION: The review provides the accountant with a basis for reporting whether (s)he is aware of material modifications that should be made for such information to conform with GAAP. This objective differs significantly from that of an audit, which is to provide a basis for expressing an opinion (AU 722).
Answer (A) is incorrect because the review of interim financial information does not provide a basis for expressing an opinion. Answer (C) is incorrect because reporting on whether the statements are fairly presented is the expression of an opinion. Answer (D) is incorrect because reporting on whether the statements are fairly presented is the expression of an opinion.

2. Which of the following procedures ordinarily should be applied when an independent accountant conducts a review of interim financial information of a publicly held entity?

A. Verify changes in key account balances.

B. Read the minutes of the board of directors' meetings.

C. Inspect the open purchase order file.

D. Perform cutoff tests for cash receipts and disbursements.

Answer (B) is correct. *(CPA, adapted)*
REQUIRED: The procedure applied in a review of interim financial information.
DISCUSSION: A review involves (1) establishing an understanding with the client; (2) obtaining knowledge of the entity's business and controls; (3) performing analytical procedures, making inquiries, and applying other limited procedures; (4) obtaining written representations from management; and (5) evaluating the results of procedures. The specific procedures performed include reading the minutes of meetings of shareholders, the board of directors, and committees of the board of directors, and inquiring about the results of meetings for which minutes are unavailable.

3. Which of the following circumstances requires modification of the accountant's report on a review of interim financial information of a publicly held entity?

	Substantial Doubt About the Entity's Ability to Continue as a Going Concern	Inadequate Disclosure
A.	Yes	Yes
B.	No	No
C.	Yes	No
D.	No	Yes

Answer (D) is correct. *(CPA, adapted)*
REQUIRED: The reasons, if any, for modifying a review report on interim statements.
DISCUSSION: Modification of the report on a review of interim financial statements is necessary because of departures from GAAP, including inadequate disclosure. Uncertainties, however, do not cause a modification of a review report.

19.2 Letters for Underwriters and Certain Other Requesting Parties (AU 634)

4. Comfort letters ordinarily are signed by the client's

A. Independent accountants.

B. Underwriters of securities.

C. Audit committee.

D. Senior management.

Answer (A) is correct. *(CPA, adapted)*
REQUIRED: The persons who sign a comfort letter.
DISCUSSION: A common condition of an underwriting agreement in connection with the offering for sale of securities registered with the SEC under the Securities Act of 1933 is that the accountants furnish a comfort letter to the underwriters. Hence, the independent accountants sign the comfort letter.

5. Comfort letters ordinarily are addressed to

A. The Securities and Exchange Commission.

B. The intermediary who negotiated the agreement with the client.

C. Creditor financial institutions.

D. The client's audit committee.

Answer (B) is correct. *(CPA, adapted)*
    REQUIRED: The addressee of a comfort letter.
    DISCUSSION: The letter should not be addressed or given to anyone other than the client and the named underwriters, broker-dealer, intermediary, or buyer or seller. "The appropriate addressee is the intermediary who has negotiated the agreement with the client, and with whom the accountants will deal in discussions regarding the letter" (AU 634).

6. Which of the following matters is covered in a typical comfort letter?

A. Negative assurance concerning whether the entity's internal control activities operated as designed during the period being audited.

B. An opinion regarding whether the entity complied with laws and regulations under Government Auditing Standards and the Single Audit Act.

C. Positive assurance concerning whether unaudited condensed financial information complied with generally accepted accounting principles.

D. An opinion as to whether the audited financial statements comply in form with the accounting requirements of the SEC.

Answer (D) is correct. *(CPA, adapted)*
    REQUIRED: The item in a typical letter for underwriters.
    DISCUSSION: A typical comfort letter expresses an opinion on whether audited financial statements and schedules "included in the registration statement comply as to form in all material respects with the applicable accounting requirements of the Act and the related published rules and regulations" (AU 634). However, the comfort letter does not state or repeat an opinion about the fairness of presentation of the statements.
    Answer (A) is incorrect because comfort letters concern financial information contained in registration statements filed with the SEC under the Securities Act of 1933. Answer (B) is incorrect because comfort letters concern financial information contained in registration statements filed with the SEC under the Securities Act of 1933. Answer (C) is incorrect because comfort letters concern financial information contained in registration statements filed with the SEC under the Securities Act of 1933.

7. When an accountant issues to an underwriter a comfort letter containing comments on data that have not been audited, the underwriter most likely will receive

A. Positive assurance on supplementary disclosures.

B. Negative assurance on capsule information.

C. A disclaimer on prospective financial statements.

D. A limited opinion of pro forma financial statements.

Answer (B) is correct. *(CPA, adapted)*
    REQUIRED: The most likely assurance or lack thereof provided in a comfort letter commenting on unaudited data.
    DISCUSSION: According to AU 634, capsule information is unaudited summarized interim information for subsequent periods used to supplement the audited financial statements or unaudited condensed interim financial information in a registration statement. The accountant may give negative assurance regarding conformity with GAAP if the capsule information is in accordance with the disclosure requirements of APB 28, *Interim Financial Reporting*, and if the accountants have performed a review of the underlying financial statements in accordance with AU 722, *Interim Financial Information*.
    Answer (A) is incorrect because a comfort letter expresses, at most, negative assurance. Answer (C) is incorrect because prospective statements do not appear in a registration statement. Answer (D) is incorrect because a limited opinion is not a permissible form of reporting.

8. Which of the following statements is true concerning letters for underwriters, commonly referred to as comfort letters?

A. Letters for underwriters are required by the Securities Act of 1933 for the initial public sale of registered securities.

B. Letters for underwriters typically give negative assurance on unaudited interim financial information.

C. Letters for underwriters usually are included in the registration statement accompanying a prospectus.

D. Letters for underwriters ordinarily update auditors' opinions on the prior year's financial statements.

Answer (B) is correct. *(CPA, adapted)*
    REQUIRED: The true statement concerning letters for underwriters.
    DISCUSSION: Comments in the comfort letter about unaudited interim financial statements appearing in the registration statement should always be in the form of negative assurance.
    Answer (A) is incorrect because letters for underwriters are in response to a request from the underwriter and are not required by the Securities Act of 1933. Answer (C) is incorrect because letters for underwriters are not required as part of a registration statement. Answer (D) is incorrect because a comfort letter should not alter the previously expressed opinion on the financial statements.

19.3 Filings Under Federal Securities Statutes (AU 711)

9. An independent accountant's report is based on a review of interim financial information. If this report is presented in a registration statement, a prospectus should include a statement clarifying that the

A. Accountant's review report is not a part of the registration statement within the meaning of the Securities Act of 1933.

B. Accountant assumes no responsibility to update the report for events and circumstances occurring after the date of the report.

C. Accountant's review was performed in accordance with standards established by the Securities and Exchange Commission.

D. Accountant obtained corroborating evidence to determine whether material modifications are needed for such information to conform with GAAP.

Answer (A) is correct. *(CPA, adapted)*
REQUIRED: The statement in a review report on interim financial information included in a registration statement.
DISCUSSION: According to AU 711, when an independent accountant has reviewed interim information and his/her report is presented or incorporated by reference in a registration statement, the SEC requires that a prospectus containing a statement about the accountant's involvement clarify that the report "is not a 'report' or 'part' of the registration statement within the meaning of sections 7 and 11 of the Securities Act of 1933." The prospectus should state that reliance on the report should be restricted given the limited procedures applied and that the accountant is not subject to the liability provisions of section 11.
Answer (B) is incorrect because the registration statement contains audited financial statements. Thus, procedures should be extended from the date of the audit report to the effective date of the filing. Answer (C) is incorrect because the wording suggested by AU 711 is that "the independent public accountants have reported that they have applied limited procedures in accordance with professional standards for a review of such information." Answer (D) is incorrect because accountants make inquiries and apply analytical procedures to determine whether modifications are needed for financial information to conform with GAAP. They do not collect corroborating evidence in a review.

10. A registration statement filed with the SEC contains the reports of two independent auditors on their audits of financial statements for different periods. The predecessor auditor who audited the prior-period financial statements generally should obtain a letter of representation from the

A. Successor independent auditor.

B. Client's audit committee.

C. Principal underwriter.

D. Securities and Exchange Commission.

Answer (A) is correct. *(CPA, adapted)*
REQUIRED: The party from whom the predecessor auditor should obtain a letter of representation.
DISCUSSION: An auditor who has audited the financial statements for prior periods but not for the most recent period included in a registration statement has a responsibility for material subsequent events affecting the prior-period statements. Thus, the predecessor auditor who audited the prior-period financial statements generally should obtain a letter of representation from the successor auditor.
Answer (B) is incorrect because the predecessor auditor would not normally obtain representations from the client's audit committee. Answer (C) is incorrect because the predecessor auditor would not normally obtain representations from the principal underwriter. Answer (D) is incorrect because the predecessor auditor would not normally obtain representations from the SEC.

11. The Securities and Exchange Commission has authority to

A. Prescribe specific auditing procedures to detect fraud concerning inventories and accounts receivable of companies engaged in interstate commerce.

B. Deny lack of privity as a defense in third-party actions for gross negligence against the auditors of public companies.

C. Determine accounting principles for the purpose of financial reporting by companies offering securities to the public.

D. Require a change of auditors of governmental entities after a given period of years as a means of ensuring auditor independence.

Answer (C) is correct. *(CPA, adapted)*
REQUIRED: The authority of the SEC.
DISCUSSION: The SEC has the authority to regulate the form and content of all financial statements, notes, and schedules filed with the SEC, and also the financial reports to shareholders if the company is subject to the Securities Exchange Act of 1934. Accounting principles applied must have substantial authoritative support. The SEC recognizes GAAP and has stated that financial statements conforming to FASB standards will be presumed to have substantial authoritative support. However, the SEC reserves the right to substitute its principles for those of the accounting profession.
Answer (A) is incorrect because the SEC may not prescribe specific auditing procedures. Answer (B) is incorrect because the SEC may not deny lack of privity as a defense. Answer (D) is incorrect because the SEC may not require a change of auditors of governmental entities.

19.4   Other Information in Documents Containing Audited Financial Statements (AU 550)

12. When audited financial statements are presented in a client's document containing other information, the auditor must

A.   Perform inquiry and analytical procedures to ascertain whether the other information is reasonable.

B.   Add an explanatory paragraph to the auditor's report without changing the opinion on the financial statements.

C.   Perform the appropriate substantive auditing procedures to corroborate the other information.

D.   Read the other information to determine that it is consistent with the audited financial statements.

Answer (D) is correct.   *(CPA, adapted)*
   REQUIRED: The auditor's responsibility for other information appearing in a document with audited financial statements.
   DISCUSSION: AU 550 states that the auditor is obligated only to read the other information and consider whether it and its manner of presentation are consistent with the financial statements on which (s)he is expressing an opinion or whether it contains a material misstatement.
   Answer (A) is incorrect because the auditor has no obligation to perform any procedures to corroborate the other information. However, the auditor is permitted to express an opinion of the other information in relation to the basic financial statements taken as a whole if it has been subjected to procedures applied in the audit of those statements. Answer (B) is incorrect because the auditor need not add a paragraph unless the other information in the client's document is materially inconsistent with the financial statements and the client has not revised it. Answer (C) is incorrect because the auditor has no obligation to perform any procedures to corroborate the other information. However, the auditor is permitted to express an opinion of the other information in relation to the basic financial statements taken as a whole if it has been subjected to procedures applied in the audit of those statements.

13. An auditor concludes that there is a material inconsistency in the other information in an annual report to shareholders containing audited financial statements. However, the auditor has not performed procedures to corroborate the other information. If the auditor concludes that the financial statements do not require revision, but the client refuses to revise or eliminate the material inconsistency, the auditor may

A.   Revise the auditor's report to include a separate explanatory paragraph describing the material inconsistency.

B.   Express a qualified opinion after discussing the matter with the client's directors.

C.   Consider the matter closed because the other information is not in the audited statements.

D.   Disclaim an opinion on the financial statements after explaining the material inconsistency in a separate paragraph.

Answer (A) is correct.   *(CPA, adapted)*
   REQUIRED: The auditor action when the client presents other information with a material inconsistency.
   DISCUSSION: If the other information contains a material inconsistency, the auditor should determine whether the statements or the report need revision. If they do not, (s)he should request the client to revise the other information. If revision is not made, (s)he should consider revising the report to include an explanatory paragraph, withholding use of the report, or withdrawing from the engagement. The action taken will depend on the circumstances and the significance of the inconsistency.
   Answer (B) is incorrect because, if the opinion is expressed on the financial statements only, the inconsistency in the other information does not affect that opinion. Answer (C) is incorrect because the auditor may not ignore a material inconsistency in other information. Answer (D) is incorrect because the auditor's decision to disclaim an opinion is not affected by the other information.

19.5   Required Supplementary Information (RSI) (AU 558)

14. If management declines to present supplementary information required by the Governmental Accounting Standards Board (GASB), the auditor should express

A.   An adverse opinion.

B.   A qualified opinion with an explanatory paragraph.

C.   An unqualified opinion.

D.   An unqualified opinion with an additional explanatory paragraph.

Answer (D) is correct.   *(CPA, adapted)*
   REQUIRED: The effect on the auditor's opinion of failure to disclose required supplementary information.
   DISCUSSION: Failure to present supplementary information required by GAAP does not affect the auditor's opinion on the fairness of presentation of the statements because such information does not change the standards of financial accounting and reporting that were followed in preparing the financial statements (AU 558). Instead, the auditor should express an unqualified opinion with an additional explanatory paragraph stating that required supplementary information was omitted. The supplementary information itself need not be presented by the auditor.

15. What is an auditor's responsibility for supplementary information that is outside the basic financial statements but required by the FASB?

   A. The auditor has no responsibility for required supplementary information as long as it is outside the basic financial statements.

   B. The auditor's only responsibility for required supplementary information is to determine that such information has not been omitted.

   C. The auditor should apply certain limited procedures to the required supplementary information and report deficiencies in, or omissions of, such information.

   D. The auditor should apply tests of details of transactions and balances to the required supplementary information and report any material misstatements in such information.

Answer (C) is correct. *(CPA, adapted)*
   REQUIRED: The auditor's responsibility for supplementary information outside the basic financial statements but required by the FASB.
   DISCUSSION: The FASB regards required supplementary information outside the basic statements as essential to reporting and has established guidelines for its measurement and presentation. Although the auditor has no responsibility to audit this information, (s)he should apply limited procedures and report deficiencies in, or the omission of, such information (AU 558).
   Answer (A) is incorrect because the auditor has a responsibility to apply limited procedures to supplementary information. Answer (B) is incorrect because the application of limited procedures extends beyond determining whether the information has been omitted. Answer (D) is incorrect because the auditor is not obligated to apply more than limited procedures.

19.6 Reporting on Information Accompanying the Basic Financial Statements in Auditor-Submitted Documents (AU 551)

16. Information accompanying the basic financial statements in an auditor-submitted document should not include

   A. An analysis of inventory by location.

   B. A statement that the allowance for doubtful accounts is adequate.

   C. A statement that the depreciable life of a new asset is 20 years.

   D. An analysis of revenue by product line.

Answer (B) is correct. *(CPA, adapted)*
   REQUIRED: The item not included in information accompanying the basic financial statements in an auditor-submitted document.
   DISCUSSION: An auditor may express an opinion on a specified account unless such reporting is equivalent to expressing a piecemeal opinion (AU 623). However, this opinion is contained in a separate report, not in the report on the financial statements or in the accompanying information.
   Answer (A) is incorrect because the accompanying information includes additional details or explanations of items in or related to the basic financial statements. Answer (C) is incorrect because the accompanying information includes additional details or explanations of items in or related to the basic financial statements. Answer (D) is incorrect because the accompanying information includes additional details or explanations of items in or related to the basic financial statements.

17. What is an auditor's reporting responsibility concerning information accompanying the basic financial statements in an auditor-submitted document?

   A. The auditor should report on all the accompanying information included in the document.

   B. The auditor should report on the accompanying information only if the auditor participated in its preparation.

   C. The auditor should report on the accompanying information only if the auditor did not participate in its preparation.

   D. The auditor should report on the accompanying information only if it contains obvious material misstatements.

Answer (A) is correct. *(CPA, adapted)*
   REQUIRED: The reporting responsibility regarding information accompanying the basic financial statements in auditor-submitted documents.
   DISCUSSION: The auditor is responsible for expressing an opinion on the financial statements and all the other information reported with the financial statements (i.e., footnotes). When an auditor submits a document containing audited financial statements, (s)he must report on all the information included.
   Answer (B) is incorrect because, regardless of whether the auditor has participated in the preparation of the information, management is responsible for its content, and the auditor is responsible for reporting on its fairness. Answer (C) is incorrect because, regardless of whether the auditor has participated in the preparation of the information, management is responsible for its content, and the auditor is responsible for reporting on its fairness. Answer (D) is incorrect because the auditor must report fully on accompanying information.

18. If information accompanying the basic financial statements in an auditor-submitted document has been subjected to auditing procedures, the auditor may express an opinion that the accompanying information is fairly stated in

A. Conformity with generally accepted accounting principles.

B. All material respects in relation to the basic financial statements taken as a whole.

C. Conformity with standards established by the AICPA.

D. Accordance with generally accepted auditing standards.

Answer (B) is correct. *(CPA, adapted)*
REQUIRED: The auditor's reporting responsibility when (s)he submits a document containing "accompanying information."
DISCUSSION: The auditor is responsible for reporting on all the information included. The objective of the auditor is the same as when (s)he is reporting on the statements: to describe clearly the character of the service provided and the responsibility taken. The report on the accompanying information should include an opinion on its fairness in relation to the basic financial statements taken as a whole if it has been subjected to the auditing procedures applied in the audit. If not, the auditors must disclaim an opinion (AU 551).
Answer (A) is incorrect because the opinion on the accompanying information concerns the fairness of its relationship to the basic statements, not GAAP. Answer (C) is incorrect because the opinion on the accompanying information concerns the fairness of its relationship to the basic statements, not AICPA standards. Answer (D) is incorrect because the opinion on the accompanying information concerns the fairness of its relationship to the basic statements, not GAAS.

19. Investment and property schedules are presented for purposes of additional analysis in an auditor-submitted document. The schedules are not required parts of the basic financial statements, but they accompany the basic financial statements. When reporting on such additional information, the measurement of materiality is the

A. Same as that used in forming an opinion on the basic financial statements taken as a whole.

B. Lesser of the individual schedule of investments or schedule of property taken by itself.

C. Greater of the individual schedule of investments or schedule of property taken by itself.

D. Combined total of both the individual schedules of investments and property taken as a whole.

Answer (A) is correct. *(CPA, adapted)*
REQUIRED: The measure of materiality required for the purpose of reporting on information presented for additional analysis in an auditor-submitted document.
DISCUSSION: "When reporting in this manner, the measurement of materiality is the same as that used in forming an opinion on the basic financial statements taken as a whole. Accordingly, the auditor need not apply procedures as extensive as would be necessary to express an opinion on the information taken by itself" (AU 551).

19.7 Reporting on Condensed Financial Statements and Selected Financial Data (AU 552)

20. An auditor may report on condensed financial statements that are derived from complete audited financial statements if the

A. Auditor indicates whether the information in the condensed financial statements is fairly stated in all material respects.

B. Condensed financial statements are presented in comparative form with the prior year's condensed financial statements.

C. Auditor describes the additional review procedures performed on the condensed financial statements.

D. Condensed financial statements are distributed only to management and the board of directors.

Answer (A) is correct. *(CPA, adapted)*
REQUIRED: The requirement that permits an auditor to report on condensed financial statements.
DISCUSSION: The report on condensed financial statements should indicate (1) that the auditor has audited and expressed an opinion on the complete financial statements, (2) the date of that report, (3) the type of opinion expressed, and (4) whether, in the auditor's opinion, the information in the condensed statements is fairly stated in all material respects in relation to the complete financial statements.
Answer (B) is incorrect because the condensed statements need not be presented in comparative form; rather they should be read in conjunction with the most recent complete financial statements. Answer (C) is incorrect because the auditor need not perform additional review procedures. Answer (D) is incorrect because distribution of the report is not restricted.

21. In the standard report on condensed financial statements that are derived from a public entity's audited financial statements, a CPA should indicate that the

A. Condensed financial statements are prepared in conformity with another comprehensive basis of accounting.

B. CPA has audited and expressed an opinion on the complete financial statements.

C. Condensed financial statements are not fairly presented in all material respects.

D. CPA expresses limited assurance that the financial statements conform with GAAP.

Answer (B) is correct. *(CPA, adapted)*
REQUIRED: The indication in a standard report on condensed financial statements.
DISCUSSION: The report should state that the auditor has audited and expressed an opinion on the complete statements, the date of that report, the type of opinion expressed, and an opinion as to whether the condensed statements are fairly stated in all material respects in relation to the complete statements (AU 552).
Answer (A) is incorrect because condensed financial statements are prepared from GAAP-based financial statements. Answer (C) is incorrect because condensed financial statements may be fairly presented. Answer (D) is incorrect because the CPA expresses an opinion.

22. An auditor is engaged to report on selected financial data that are included in a client-prepared document containing audited financial statements. Under these circumstances, the report on the selected data should

A. Be limited to data derived from the audited financial statements.

B. Be distributed only to senior management and the board of directors.

C. State that the presentation is a comprehensive basis of accounting other than GAAP.

D. Indicate that the data are not fairly stated in all material respects.

Answer (A) is correct. *(CPA, adapted)*
REQUIRED: The basis of a report on selected data.
DISCUSSION: An auditor may report on selected data included in a client-prepared document containing audited statements. Selected financial data are not a required part of the basic financial statements, and management is responsible for determining the specific data to be presented. The report should be limited to data derived from the audited statements (AU 552).
Answer (B) is incorrect because the report need not be limited in distribution. Answer (C) is incorrect because the selected data are based upon the audited financial statements in accordance with GAAP. Answer (D) is incorrect because the report should state whether the information in the selected financial data is fairly stated in all material respects in relation to the complete statements.

19.8 Reporting on Financial Statements Prepared for Use in Other Countries (AU 534)

23. The financial statements of KCP America, a U.S. entity, are prepared for inclusion in the consolidated financial statements of its non-U.S. parent. These financial statements are prepared in conformity with the accounting principles generally accepted in the parent's country and are for use only in that country. Which is an appropriate report on the financial statements for KCP America's auditor to issue?

I. A U.S.-style report (unmodified)

II. A U.S.-style report modified to report on the accounting principles of the parent's country

III. The report form of the parent's country

A. I only.

B. II only.

C. II and III only.

D. I, II, and III.

Answer (C) is correct. *(CPA, adapted)*
REQUIRED: The proper reporting on the financial statements of a U.S. entity prepared for inclusion in the consolidated financial statements of its non-U.S. parent.
DISCUSSION: According to AU 534, if financial statements prepared in conformity with accounting principles generally accepted in another country are prepared for use only outside the U.S., the auditor may use either a U.S.-style report modified to report on the accounting principles of the other country or, if appropriate, the report form of the other country. An unmodified U.S.-style report is inappropriate because of the departures from GAAP contained in statements prepared in conformity with principles generally accepted in the other country.

24. Before reporting on the financial statements of a U.S. entity that have been prepared in conformity with another country's accounting principles, an auditor practicing in the U.S. should

A. Understand the accounting principles generally accepted in the other country.

B. Be certified by the appropriate auditing or accountancy board of the other country.

C. Notify management that the auditor is required to disclaim an opinion on the financial statements.

D. Receive a waiver from the auditor's state board of accountancy to perform the engagement.

Answer (A) is correct. *(CPA, adapted)*
REQUIRED: The requirement for reporting on financial statements of a U.S. entity prepared in conformity with another country's accounting principles.
DISCUSSION: AU 534 states that an independent auditor practicing in the U.S. may report on the financial statements of a U.S. entity prepared in conformity with accounting principles generally accepted in another country. However, the auditor must clearly understand, and obtain written representations from management about, the purpose and uses of the statements. (S)he must also comply with the general and field work standards of U.S. GAAS.
Answer (B) is incorrect because the accountant needs to be a CPA in the U.S. Answer (C) is incorrect because the accountant can express an opinion on the fairness of the financial statements. Answer (D) is incorrect because no waiver is required to perform this service.

19.9 Reports on the Application of Accounting Principles (AU 625)

25. Blue, CPA, has been asked to report on the application of accounting principles to a specific transaction by an entity that is audited by another CPA. Blue may accept this engagement, but should

A. Consult with the continuing CPA to obtain information relevant to the transaction.

B. Report the engagement's findings to the entity's audit committee, the continuing CPA, and management.

C. Disclaim any opinion that the hypothetical application of accounting principles conforms with generally accepted accounting principles.

D. Notify the entity that the report is for general use.

Answer (A) is correct. *(CPA, adapted)*
REQUIRED: The proper action of a CPA who accepts an engagement to report on the application of accounting principles.
DISCUSSION: The reporting accountant should consult with the continuing accountant to determine the available facts relevant to a professional judgment. The continuing accountant may provide information not otherwise available to the reporting accountant, who should explain to the entity's management the need to consult with the continuing accountant, request permission, and request authorization for the continuing accountant to respond fully (AU 625).
Answer (B) is incorrect because the accountant's written report should be addressed to the requesting entity (e.g., management or the board). Answer (C) is incorrect because the report should contain a statement describing the appropriate accounting principles to be applied, and, if appropriate, the reasons for the conclusions, not an opinion or a disclaimer. Also, the engagement may not involve reporting on the application of accounting principles to a hypothetical transaction. Answer (D) is incorrect because the use of the report is restricted to specified parties.

26. In connection with a proposal to obtain a new audit client, an accountant in public practice is asked to prepare a report on the application of accounting principles to a specific transaction. The report should include a statement that

A. The engagement was performed in accordance with Statements on Standards for Accounting and Review Services.

B. Responsibility for the proper accounting treatment rests with the preparers of the financial statements.

C. The evaluation of the application of accounting principles is hypothetical and may not be used for opinion-shopping.

D. The guidance is provided for general use.

Answer (B) is correct. *(CPA, adapted)*
REQUIRED: The statement included in a report on the application of accounting principles to a specific transaction.
DISCUSSION: The addressee of the accountant's report is the requesting entity. It should contain (1) a description of the engagement and whether it was in accordance with AICPA standards; (2) a description of the transaction; (3) a description of the accounting principles applied (including their country of origin); (4) a statement that the responsibility for proper accounting is with the preparers of the financial statements; and (5) a statement that any difference in facts, circumstances, or assumptions may change the report (AU 625).
Answer (A) is incorrect because the engagement is conducted in accordance with applicable AICPA standards. Answer (C) is incorrect because no such language appears in the report. Moreover, such a report may not be provided on a hypothetical transaction. Answer (D) is incorrect because the use of the report is restricted to specified parties.

19.10 Compliance Attestation (AT 601)

27. According to Statement on Standards for Attestation Engagements, *Compliance Attestation*,

    A. The field work and reporting but not the general attestation standards apply to this type of engagement.

    B. The practitioner may accept an engagement to perform an examination about the effectiveness of internal control over compliance only if the assertion is provided to the practitioner by the client.

    C. A compliance attestation engagement is intended to result in a legal determination of an entity's compliance with specified requirements.

    D. The practitioner must accept responsibility for the entity's compliance with the specified requirements.

Answer (B) is correct. *(Publisher)*
REQUIRED: The true statement about compliance attestation engagements.
DISCUSSION: The written assertion may be provided to the practitioner in a representation letter or may be presented in a separate report that will accompany the practitioner's report.
    Answer (A) is incorrect because the general attestation standards also apply. Answer (C) is incorrect because the report does not provide a legal determination on compliance with specified requirements, but it may be useful to legal counsel or others in making such determinations. Answer (D) is incorrect because the responsible party, typically management, must accept responsibility over compliance.

28. What service(s) may a practitioner perform in a compliance attestation engagement?

	Application of Agreed-Upon Procedures	Examination	Review
A.	Yes	Yes	Yes
B.	No	Yes	Yes
C.	Yes	Yes	No
D.	No	No	Yes

Answer (C) is correct. *(Publisher)*
REQUIRED: The service(s) that may be performed in a compliance attestation engagement.
DISCUSSION: The practitioner may perform agreed-upon procedures as long as the specified users participate in establishing the procedures to be applied and take responsibility for the adequacy of such procedures for their purposes. The practitioner may also conduct an examination in which (s)he gathers evidence to support an opinion. Both types of engagements may be performed with respect to compliance with specified requirements or about the effectiveness of internal control over compliance. However, the standard does not provide for a review engagement.

29. A practitioner's report on agreed-upon procedures related to an entity's compliance with specified requirements should contain

    A. A statement of restrictions on the use of the report.

    B. An opinion about whether management complied with the specified requirements.

    C. Negative assurance that control risk has not been assessed.

    D. An acknowledgment of responsibility for the sufficiency of the procedures.

Answer (A) is correct. *(CPA, adapted)*
REQUIRED: The statement in a report on a compliance attestation engagement to apply agreed-upon procedures.
DISCUSSION: The fourth attestation standard of reporting indicates that a report should be restricted to specified parties "when the report is on an attest engagement to apply agreed-upon procedures to the subject matter."
    Answer (B) is incorrect because the report on agreed-upon procedures should be in the form of a summary of procedures and findings, not an opinion. Answer (C) is incorrect because negative assurance about whether an entity is in compliance or whether management's assertion is fairly stated is not permitted in reports on applying agreed-upon procedures. Answer (D) is incorrect because the parties who agreed to the procedures are responsible for their sufficiency.

30. Mill, CPA, was engaged by a group of royalty recipients to apply agreed-upon procedures to financial data supplied by Modern Co. regarding Modern's written assertion about its compliance with contractual requirements to pay royalties. Mill's report on these agreed-upon procedures should contain a(n)

A. Disclaimer of opinion about the fair presentation of Modern's financial statements.

B. List of the procedures performed (or reference thereto) and Mill's findings.

C. Opinion about the effectiveness of Modern's internal control activities concerning royalty payments.

D. Acknowledgment that the sufficiency of the procedures is solely Mill's responsibility.

Answer (B) is correct. *(CPA, adapted)*
REQUIRED: The statement in a report on a compliance attestation engagement to apply agreed-upon procedures.
DISCUSSION: The practitioner's report should be in the form of procedures and findings but should not provide negative assurance about whether the entity is in compliance or whether the responsible party's assertion is fairly stated (AT 201).
Answer (A) is incorrect because the report should not contain a disclaimer of opinion on the fair presentation of Modern's financial statements. However, it should contain a paragraph stating that the independent accountant was not engaged to and did not perform an examination of the financial data regarding the written assertion about compliance with contractual requirements to pay royalties. It should also state that the objective of an examination would have been an expression of opinion on compliance with the specified requirements and that no such opinion is expressed. Answer (C) is incorrect because an agreed-upon procedures engagement typically results in a summary of findings, not an opinion. Answer (D) is incorrect because the specified parties who agreed to the procedures are responsible for their sufficiency.

19.11 Engagements to Apply Agreed-Upon Procedures (AT 201)

31. Negative assurance may be expressed when a practitioner is requested to report agreed-upon procedures to specified

	Elements of a Financial Statement	Accounts of a Financial Statement
A.	Yes	Yes
B.	Yes	No
C.	No	No
D.	No	Yes

Answer (C) is correct. *(Publisher)*
REQUIRED: The report in which negative assurance may be expressed.
DISCUSSION: The practitioner does not provide an opinion or negative assurance. Instead, the practitioner's report on agreed-upon procedures should be in the form of procedures and findings.

32. A practitioner may accept an agreed-upon procedures engagement to calculate the rate of return on a specified investment and verify that the percentage agrees with the percentage in an identified schedule provided that

A. The practitioner's report does not enumerate the procedures performed.

B. The practitioner accepts responsibility for the sufficiency of the procedures.

C. Use of the practitioner's report is restricted.

D. The practitioner is also the entity's continuing auditor.

Answer (C) is correct. *(CPA, adapted)*
REQUIRED: The condition of an engagement to apply agreed-upon procedures.
DISCUSSION: An independent practitioner may accept such an engagement if the specified parties agree to the procedures and take responsibility for their sufficiency, the subject matter is subject to reasonably consistent measurement, evidence is expected to exist providing a reasonable basis for the findings, the use of the report is restricted, and other conditions are met. The report should state that it is intended solely for the information and use of the specified parties and is not intended to be used and should not be used by anyone other than these specified parties.
Answer (A) is incorrect because the procedures performed must be enumerated. Answer (B) is incorrect because the client or specified parties take responsibility for the sufficiency of the procedures. Answer (D) is incorrect because the practitioner need not be a continuing auditor.

Use Gleim's *CPA Test Prep* for interactive testing with over 2,000 additional multiple-choice questions!

19.12 PRACTICE SIMULATION

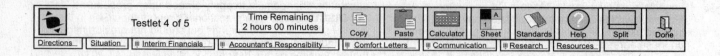

---

1. Directions

In the following simulation, you will be asked to complete various tasks related to miscellaneous reporting topics. The simulation will provide you with all of the information necessary to do your work. For full credit, be sure to view and complete all work tabs.

Resources may be available to you under the tab marked RESOURCES. You may want to review what is included in the resources before beginning the simulation.

---

2. Situation

You are the auditor for a large client and face several additional reporting requirements, such as reporting on financial statements prepared for use in other countries and reporting on interim financial information.

---

3. Interim Financial Statements

Determine whether each of the following statements relating to an engagement to perform and report on an interim review of a public company's financial information is true. Check the shaded box to the right of the statement if the item is true.

Statement	True
1. The objective of a review of interim financial information is to provide an opinion of whether the financial statements are in accordance with GAAP.	
2. A review primarily involves performing analytical procedures and inquiries.	
3. To perform a public company's review, the accountant must be the auditor of the annual statements.	
4. To perform a review of interim financial statements, the accountant must gain knowledge of the entity's business sufficient to identify types of typical misstatements that might prevail.	
5. To perform a review of interim financial statements, the accountant must obtain an attorney's letter concerning litigation, claims, and assessments.	
6. To perform a review of interim financial information, the accountant must obtain a client representation letter.	
7. A significant scope limitation results in a qualified review report.	
8. Each page of the reviewed financial statements should state "Reviewed by Auditor."	
9. A departure from GAAP in the financial statements may result in a modified review report.	
10. As a result of the review, the accountant should communicate any significant fraud or illegal acts to the audit committee.	

4. Accountant's Responsibility for Various Types of Information

This question has a matching format that requires you to select the correct responses from a drop-down list. Write the answers in the shaded columns. Each choice may be used once, more than once, or not at all.

The accountant will encounter various types of information presented by clients. Listed below are four types of information defined in the standards. In the first column (a), match each type of information with a corresponding example of the type in List 1, and in the second column (b), match the appropriate procedure to apply from List 2.

Type of Information	Example of Information (a)	Accountant's Procedures (b)
1. Other information		
2. Required supplementary		
3. Accompanying in an auditor submitted document		
4. Condensed or selected		

List 1
A) Oil and gas reserve information
B) Schedule of fixed assets
C) Summary of financial results
D) President's letter

List 2
E) Audit
F) Applied limited procedures
G) Read for consistency with financial statements
H) Determine if stated fairly relative to complete financial statements

5. Comfort Letters

This question has a matching format that requires you to select the correct responses from a drop-down list. Write the answer in the shaded column. Each choice may be used once, more than once, or not at all.

For each of the following, select the appropriate term from the choices listed that matches the description relating to comments on information other than audited financial statements typically contained in a comfort letter.

Description	Answer
1. Comments on this information must always be in the form of negative assurance.	
2. The accountants must have this information if they comment on unaudited condensed information, capsule information, financial forecasts, or changes in capital stock, increases in long-term debt, and decreases in selected items.	
3. This information consists of unaudited summarized interim information for subsequent periods used to supplement the audited financial statements or unaudited condensed interim financial information in a registration statement.	
4. The accountants should not comment on this information unless they have acquired the appropriate level of knowledge, such as that obtained from auditing or reviewing the historical statements.	
5. To apply agreed-upon procedures, the accountants must perform compilation procedures on this information and should attach the report to the comfort letter.	
6. Comments that attestations are in accordance with the applicable attestation pronouncement may be made, but no comments on nonfinancial data or the compliance with the forms required by SEC rules should be made.	
7. Comments on these matters ordinarily concern whether a change has occurred in capital stock, long-term debt has increased, or other specified financial statement items have increased or decreased during the change period.	

Choices
A) Forecasts
B) Capsule financial information
C) Pro forma financial information
D) Subsequent changes
E) Unaudited condensed interim financial statements
F) Management's discussion and analysis
G) Knowledge of the internal control system

6. Communication

A large company has hired your firm to prepare a report on the application of accounting principles to a specific transaction. Prepare a memorandum to an audit associate discussing the performance and reporting standards for an engagement regarding the application of accounting principles. Type your communication in your word processor program and print out the copy in a memorandum style format.

REMINDER: Your response will be graded for both technical content and writing skills. You should demonstrate your ability to develop, organize, and express your ideas. Do not convey information in the form of a table, bullet point list, or other abbreviated presentation.

> To: Audit associate
> From: CPA
> Subject: Report on application of accounting principles to a specific transaction

7. Research

Find the answer to the following question in the Professional Standards using the materials available in the Resources tab. Print the appropriate citation in its entirety from the source you choose. This is a copy-and-paste item.

Copy the appropriate auditing standard paragraph that outlines the reporting standards for a U.S.-style report modified to report on financial statements prepared in conformity with accounting principles generally accepted in another country that are intended for use only outside the United States.

Unofficial Answers

3. Interim Financial Statements (10 Gradable Items)

1. <u>Not correct</u>.
2. <u>Correct</u>.
3. <u>Correct</u>.
4. <u>Correct</u>.
5. <u>Not correct</u>.
6. <u>Correct</u>.
7. <u>Not correct</u>.
8. <u>Not correct</u>.
9. <u>Correct</u>.
10. <u>Correct</u>.

4. Accountant's Responsibilities for Various Types of Information (8 Gradable Items)

1. (a) <u>D) - President's letter</u>
    (b) <u>G) - Read for consistency with financial statements</u>

2. (a) <u>A) - Oil and gas reserve information</u>
    (b) <u>F) - Apply limited procedures</u>

3. (a) <u>B) - Schedule of fixed assets</u>
    (b) <u>E) - Audit</u>

4. (a) <u>C) - Summary of financial results</u>
    (b) <u>H) - Determine if stated fairly relative to complete financial statements</u>

5. Comfort Letters (7 Gradable Items)

1. <u>E) - Unaudited condensed interim financial statements</u>
2. <u>G) - Knowledge of the internal control system</u>
3. <u>B) - Capsule financial information</u>
4. <u>C) - Pro forma financial information</u>
5. <u>A) - Forecasts</u>
6. <u>F) - Management's discussion and analysis</u>
7. <u>D) - Subsequent changes</u>

6. Communication (5 Gradable Items; For grading instructions, please refer to page 11.)

To: Audit associate
From: CPA
Subject: Performing and reporting on an engagement concerning the application of accounting principles to a specific transaction

In performing the engagement, the reporting accountant should consider the circumstances in which the report or advice is requested, the purpose, and the intended use. Also, the reporting accountant should exercise due professional care, have adequate technical training and proficiency, plan the engagement adequately, and supervise assistants. The information gathered should be sufficient to provide a reasonable basis for the professional judgment rendered. Accordingly, the reporting accountant must obtain an understanding of the form and substance of the transaction(s), review applicable GAAP, and consult with other professionals or experts if appropriate. Moreover, (s)he should consider the existence of creditable precedents or analogies. To obtain evidence that may not be otherwise available, the reporting accountant should consult with the continuing accountant of the entity to determine all the relevant facts, including disputes with management. Thus, the reporting accountant should explain to the management of the entity the need for consultation with the continuing accountant, request permission, and request authorization for the continuing accountant to respond fully.

The addressee of the accountant's written report is the requesting entity. The report should accomplish several objectives. It should briefly describe the engagement and state that it was in accordance with applicable AICPA standards. This should be followed by a listing of the basic facts: identification of the specific entity; description of the transaction(s); description of the facts, circumstances, and assumptions; and the source of the information. The report should next describe the accounting principle(s) to be applied, including their country of origin, or the type of opinion to be expressed. The report also should state that the responsibility for proper accounting is with the preparers of the financial statements, who should consult with their continuing accountant. Moreover, the report should caution that any difference in the facts, circumstances, or assumptions may change the report. Finally, it should contain a separate concluding paragraph restricting its use to specified (and identified) parties.

7. Research (6 Gradable Items)

AU Section 534 -- *Reporting on Financial Statements Prepared for Use in Other Countries*

Reporting Standards -- Use Only Outside the United States

.09 A U.S.-style report modified to report on financial statements prepared in conformity with accounting principles generally accepted in another country that are intended for use only outside the United States should include-

a. A title that includes the word "independent."

b. A statement that the financial statements identified in the report were audited.

c. A statement that refers to the note to the financial statements that describes the basis of presentation of the financial statements on which the auditor is reporting, including identification of the nationality of the accounting principles.

d. A statement that the financial statements are the responsibility of the Company's management and that the auditor's responsibility is to express an opinion on the financial statements based on his/her audit.

e. A statement that the audit was conducted in accordance with auditing standards generally accepted in the United States of America (and, if appropriate, with the auditing standards of the other country).

f. A statement that U.S. standards require that the auditor plan and perform the audit to obtain reasonable assurance about whether the financial statements are free of material misstatement.

g. A statement that an audit includes:

1) Examining, on a test basis, evidence supporting the amounts and disclosures in the financial statements,
2) Assessing the accounting principles used and significant estimates made by management, and
3) Evaluating the overall financial statement presentation.

h. A statement that the auditor believes that his audit provides a reasonable basis for his opinion.

i. A paragraph that expresses the auditor's opinion on whether the financial statements are presented fairly, in all material respects, in conformity with the basis of accounting described. If the auditor concludes that the financial statements are not fairly presented on the basis of accounting described, all substantive reasons for that conclusion should be disclosed in an additional explanatory paragraph (preceding the opinion paragraph) of the report, and the opinion paragraph should include appropriate modifying language as well as a reference to the explanatory paragraph.

j. If the auditor is auditing comparative financial statements and the described basis of accounting has not been applied in a manner consistent with that of the preceding period and the change has had a material effect on the comparability of the financial statements, the auditor should add an explanatory paragraph to his report (following the opinion paragraph) that describes the change in accounting principle and refers to the note to the financial statements that discusses the change and its effect on the financial statements.

k. The manual or printed signature of the auditor's firm.

l. Date.

Scoring Schedule:

	Correct Responses		Gradable Items		Weights		
Tab 3	_____	÷	10	×	20%	=	_____
Tab 4	_____	÷	8	×	20%	=	_____
Tab 5	_____	÷	7	×	20%	=	_____
Tab 6	_____	÷	5	×	30%	=	_____
Tab 7	_____	÷	6	×	10%	=	_____

(Your Score)

Use Gleim's **CPA Review Online** to practice more simulations in a realistic environment.

STUDY UNIT TWENTY
GOVERNMENTAL AUDITS

(12 pages of outline)

20.1   Overview 629
20.2   Audits in Accordance with AU 801, Compliance Auditing Considerations in Audits of
       Governmental Entities and Recipients of Governmental Financial Assistance 630
20.3   Additional Government Auditing Standards 632
20.4   Federal Audit Requirements and the Single Audit Act 639
20.5   Practice Simulation 650

Subunit 20.1 presents an overview of the basic characteristics of governmental auditing sufficient to answer most of the related questions on recent CPA exams. However, the trend has been to increase the coverage of governmental auditing. Thus, the other subunits provide a more detailed outline of material that is likely to be covered on future exams.

20.1 OVERVIEW

1.   The **Government Accountability Office (GAO)** establishes **generally accepted government auditing standards (GAGAS)** and issues *Government Auditing Standards* (referred to as the Yellow Book). GAGAS pertain to auditors' professional qualifications and the quality of their work, the performance of field work, and the characteristics of meaningful reporting. The types of government audits and attestation engagements include

a.   **Financial audits.**

1)   **Financial statement audits**. These audits are primarily concerned with whether financial statements are presented fairly in all material respects with GAAP or with a comprehensive basis of accounting other than GAAP.

a)   GAGAS require related reporting on internal control; compliance with laws, regulations, and contract provisions; and fraud and illegal acts.

b)   The auditor conducting a governmental audit accepts a greater scope and assumes more responsibility than in an audit of a business entity.

2)   **Other objectives**. These engagements provide for different levels of assurance and entail various scopes of work such as

a)   Special reports for specified elements, accounts or items of a financial statement.

b)   Reviewing interim financial information.

c)   Issuing letters for underwriters and certain other requesting parties.

d)   Reporting on the processing of transactions by service organizations.

e)   Auditing compliance with regulations relating to federal award expenditures and other governmental financial assistance in conjunction with or as a by-product of a financial statement audit.

b. **Attestation engagements**. These engagements concern examining, reviewing, or performing agreed-upon procedures on a subject matter or an assertion about a subject matter and reporting on the results. They include reporting on

1) An entity's internal control over financial reporting or other reporting.
2) An entity's compliance with requirements of specified laws, regulations, rules, contracts, or grants.
3) Management discussion and analysis (MD&A).
4) Prospective financial statements or pro forma financial information.
5) The reliability of performance measures.
6) Allowable, reasonable, or final contract cost.

c. **Performance audits**. These audits encompass many objectives, including assessing program effectiveness and results; economy and efficiency; internal control; and compliance with legal requirements. They also may provide prospective analyses, guidance, or summary information.

2. **Single Audit Act**. Prior to 1984, agencies of the federal government that provided awards to state and local governments audited specific grants, contracts, subsidies, etc. This process often resulted in numerous audits of a recipient by various agencies and a wasteful duplication of effort. In other cases, large amounts of federal awards went unaudited. In 1984, Congress passed the Single Audit Act (amended in 1996), which requires one (a single) audit or a program-specific audit of a nonfederal entity that expends a total amount of federal awards equal to or in excess of $500,000. A single audit is required if the entity expends federal awards under more than one federal program.

a. Each federal agency shall, with regard to awards provided by that agency, monitor the use of such awards. Moreover, each nonfederal agency shall be assigned a single federal agency to assess the quality of audits and provide technical assistance.

b. Reporting packages are delivered to a federal clearinghouse. These packages include financial statements, audit reports, a schedule of expenditures of federal awards, and a corrective action plan.

c. The Office of Management and Budget (OMB) prescribes policies and procedures for the single audit. Those policies and procedures are issued in **OMB Circulars** (e.g., OMB Circular A-133, *Audits of States, Local Governments, and Non-Profit Organizations*) and **compliance supplements**.

d. The audit focus is greater for major programs, which are selected on the basis of risk-based criteria subject to certain limitations based on dollar expenditures.

3. Stop and review! You have completed the outline for this subunit. Study multiple-choice questions 1 through 5 beginning on page 641.

20.2 AUDITS IN ACCORDANCE WITH AU 801, *COMPLIANCE AUDITING CONSIDERATIONS IN AUDITS OF GOVERNMENTAL ENTITIES AND RECIPIENTS OF GOVERNMENTAL FINANCIAL ASSISTANCE*

1. **Introduction and Applicability**

a. AU 801 is applicable when the auditor is engaged to audit a governmental entity under GAAS and to test and report on compliance with laws and regulations under *Government Auditing Standards* or when certain other circumstances exist involving governmental awards (e.g., a single or other organization-wide audit such as that required under the Single Audit Act).

b. AU 801 provides general guidance to the auditor to

1) Apply pronouncements defining an auditor's responsibilities regarding illegal acts that have a direct and material effect on amounts in financial statement audits of governmental entities and other recipients of governmental awards

2) Perform a financial audit in accordance with *Government Auditing Standards*

3) Perform a single or organization-wide audit or a program-specific audit in accordance with federal audit requirements

4) Communicate with management if the auditor becomes aware that the entity is subject to an audit requirement that may not be encompassed by the terms of the engagement

2. **Effects of Laws on Financial Statements**

a. Governmental entities are subject to laws and regulations that affect their financial statements. For example, these laws and regulations may address the fund structure required by law, regulation, or bond covenant; procurement; debt limitations; and legal authority for transactions.

b. Federal, state, and local governmental entities provide awards to other entities, including not-for-profit organizations and business enterprises that are either primary recipients, subrecipients, or beneficiaries. Among the forms of governmental awards are grants of cash and other assets, loans, loan guarantees, interest-rate subsidies, and cost-reimbursement contracts. By accepting such awards, both governmental and nongovernmental entities may be subject to laws and regulations that have a direct and material effect on the determination of amounts in their financial statements.

c. Management is responsible for ensuring compliance with laws and regulations, including identifying applicable laws and regulations and establishing internal controls to provide reasonable assurance that the entity complies with those laws and regulations.

d. The auditor's responsibility for considering laws and regulations is to plan and perform the audit to obtain reasonable assurance about whether the financial statements are free of material misstatement, whether caused by errors, fraud, or illegal acts having direct and material effects.

e. The auditor should obtain an understanding of the possible effects on financial statements of laws and regulations that are generally recognized by auditors to have a direct and material effect on the determination of amounts in the financial statements. The auditor may consider performing the following procedures:

1) Consider knowledge about laws and regulations obtained from prior years' audits.

2) Discuss applicable laws and regulations with the entity's chief financial officer, legal counsel, or grant administrators.

3) Obtain written representations from management regarding the completeness of management's identification.

4) Review directly related agreements, such as those related to grants and loans.

5) Review the minutes of meetings (e.g., legislative body or governing board).

6) Inquire of the office of the federal, state, or local auditor or other appropriate audit oversight organization about the laws and regulations, including statutes and uniform reporting requirements.

7) Review information about compliance requirements (e.g., compliance supplements issued by the OMB).

3. **GAAP Hierarchies for Governmental Entities**

    a.   State and Local

        1)   GASB Statements and Interpretations, plus AICPA and FASB pronouncements if made applicable to state and local governments by GASB Statements or Interpretations

        2)   GASB Technical Bulletins and, if specifically made applicable to state and local governments by the AICPA, AICPA Audit and Accounting Guides and AICPA SOPs

        3)   Consensus positions of the GASB Emerging Issues Task Force and AICPA Practice Bulletins if specifically made applicable to state and local governments by the AICPA

        4)   "Qs and As" published by the GASB staff, as well as practices that are widely recognized and prevalent in state and local government

        5)   Other accounting literature, depending on its relevance in the circumstances

    b.   Federal

        1)   Federal Accounting Standards Advisory Board (FASAB) Statements and Interpretations, as well as AICPA and FASB pronouncements specifically made applicable to federal governmental entities by FASAB Statements or Interpretations

        2)   FASAB Technical Bulletins and, if specifically made applicable to federal governmental entities by the AICPA and cleared by the FASAB, AICPA Audit and Accounting Guides and AICPA Statements of Position

        3)   AICPA Accounting Standards Executive Committee (AcSEC) Practice Bulletins if specifically made applicable to federal governmental entities and cleared by the FASAB, as well as Technical Releases of the Accounting and Auditing Policy Committee of the FASAB

        4)   Implementation guides published by the FASAB staff, as well as practices that are widely recognized and prevalent in the federal government

        5)   Other accounting literature, depending on its relevance in the circumstances

4.   Stop and review! You have completed the outline for this subunit. Study multiple-choice questions 6 through 8 beginning on page 642.

20.3 ADDITIONAL *GOVERNMENT AUDITING STANDARDS*

1.   *Government Auditing Standards* contains standards for "audits and attestation engagements of government entities, programs, activities, and functions and of government assistance administered by contractors, nonprofit entities, and other nongovernment entities."

2. In the standards for financial audits, *Government Auditing Standards* incorporates AICPA standards of field work and reporting. The document stipulates different general standards and prescribes additional field work and reporting standards.

    a. **Independence**. The following is a general standard:

        "In all matters relating to the audit work, the audit organization and the individual auditor, whether government or public, should be free both in fact and appearance from **personal, external, and organizational** impairments to independence."

        1) The rules on **personal impairments** are similar to the AICPA rules. An auditor may not have a direct financial interest or material indirect financial interest in a client, audit work of a close family member, seek employment with the audited entity, or be biased. Furthermore, auditors must consider whether performing **nonaudit services** creates a personal impairment. When assessing whether nonaudit services impair independence, the audit organization applies **two overarching principles**:

            a) The audit organization should not provide nonaudit services that involve performing management functions or making management decisions.

            b) The audit organization should not audit its work or provide nonaudit services that are significant/material to the subject matter of audits.

        2) **External impairments** occur when auditors are deterred from acting objectively and exercising professional skepticism by pressures, actual or perceived, from management or employees of the audited entity or oversight organizations. For example, an external impairment may result from a threat of replacement of the auditor over a disagreement with the contents of the audit report.

        3) **Organizational impairments** may be created by the audit organization's place within government or the structure of the audited entity. Government auditors can be presumed to be free from organizational impairments to independence when **reporting externally to third parties** if their audit organization is organizationally independent from the audited entity. A government internal audit organization can be presumed to be free from organizational impairments to independence when **reporting internally to management** if the head of the audit organization is accountable to the head or deputy head of the government entity, required to report the results of the audit organization's work to the head or deputy head of the government entity, and located organizationally outside the staff or line management function of the unit under audit.

    b. **Professional judgment**. The following is a general standard:

        "Professional judgment should be used in planning and performing audits and attestation engagements and in reporting the results."

    c. **Competence**. The following is a general standard:

        "The staff assigned to perform the audit or attestation engagement should collectively possess adequate professional competence for the tasks required."

        1) Each auditor must earn every two years at least 24 hours of CPE directly related to government auditing.

d. **Quality control and assurance**. The following is a general standard:

"Each audit organization performing audits and/or attestation engagements in accordance with GAGAS should have an appropriate internal quality control system in place and should undergo an external peer review."

1) The peer review should be done at least every three years.

e. **Auditor communication**. The following is an additional field work standard:

"Auditors should communicate information regarding the nature, timing, and extent of planned testing and reporting and the level of assurance provided to officials of the audited entity and to the individuals contracting for or requesting the audit."

f. **Considering results of previous engagements**. The following is an additional field work standard:

"Auditors should consider the results of previous audits and attestation engagements and follow up on known significant findings and recommendations that directly relate to the objectives of the audit being undertaken."

g. **Detecting material misstatements resulting from contract or grant violations or from abuse**. The following is an additional field work standard:

"Auditors should design the audit to provide reasonable assurance of detecting material misstatements resulting from violations of contracts or grant agreements that have a direct and material effect on the determination of financial statement amounts or other financial data significant to the audit objectives." Moreover, "Auditors should be alert to situations or transactions that could be indicative of abuse."

1) Specific information may come to the auditors' attention about violations having material indirect effects. They also may become aware of indications of significant abuse. In these cases, the auditors should apply procedures specifically directed to determine whether violations or abuses have occurred.

h. **Audit documentation**. The following is an additional field work standard:

"Audit documentation related to planning, conducting, and reporting on the audit should contain sufficient information to enable an experienced auditor who has had no previous connection with the audit to ascertain from the audit documentation the evidence that supports the auditors' significant judgments and conclusions. Audit documentation should contain support for findings, conclusions, and recommendations before auditors issue their report."

i. **Compliance with GAGAS**. The following is an additional reporting standard:

"Audit reports should state that the audit was performed in accordance with GAGAS."

j. **Internal control and compliance with laws, regulations, and contract or grant provisions**. The following summarizes an additional reporting standard:

The report on financial statements (or separate reports) should describe the scope of the auditors' testing of internal control over financial reporting and compliance with laws and regulations and grant or contract provisions. The results of those tests (or an opinion if sufficient work was performed) should be included in the report.

k. **Deficiencies in internal control, fraud, illegal acts, violations of contracts or grant agreements, and abuse**. The following summarizes an additional reporting standard:

All deficiencies in internal control (reportable conditions), all fraud and illegal acts unless clearly inconsequential, and significant violations of contracts or grant agreements and abuse should be included in the auditors' report. In some cases, auditors may need to report this information to external parties.

l. **Views of responsible officials**. The following summarizes an additional reporting standard:

"If the auditors' report discloses deficiencies in internal control, fraud, illegal acts, violations of contracts or grant agreements, or abuse, auditors should obtain and report the views of responsible officials concerning the findings, conclusions, and recommendations, as well as planned corrective actions."

m. **Privileged and confidential information**. The following is an additional reporting standard:

"If certain pertinent information is prohibited from general disclosure, the audit report should state the nature of the information omitted and the requirement that makes the omission necessary."

n. **Report issuance and distribution**. The following summarizes an additional reporting standard:

Audit reports are to be submitted to the appropriate officials, oversight bodies, and funding organizations. Unless restricted by law or regulation, copies should be made available for public inspection.

3.   The following is an example of an unqualified audit report referring to *Government Auditing Standards* and the separately presented internal control and compliance reports:

Auditor's Unqualified Report on General-Purpose Financial Statements

---

Independent Auditor's Report

To: <---------- Oversight Body

We have audited the accompanying general-purpose financial statements of City of Example, Any State, as of and for the year ended June 30, year 1. These general-purpose financial statements are the responsibility of City of Example's management. Our responsibility is to express an opinion on these general-purpose financial statements based on our audit.

We conducted our audit in accordance with auditing standards generally accepted in the United States of America and the standards applicable to financial audits contained in *Government Auditing Standards*, issued by the Comptroller General of the United States. Those standards require that we plan and perform the audit to obtain reasonable assurance about whether the financial statements are free of material misstatement. An audit includes examining, on a test basis, evidence supporting the amounts and disclosures in the financial statements. An audit also includes assessing the accounting principles used and the significant estimates made by management, as well as evaluating the overall financial statement presentation. We believe that our audit provides a reasonable basis for our opinion.

In our opinion, the general-purpose financial statements referred to above present fairly, in all material respects, the financial position of City of Example, Any State, as of June 30, year 1, and the results of its operations and cash flows of its proprietary fund types and nonexpendable trust funds* for the year then ended in conformity with accounting principles generally accepted in the United States of America.

In accordance with *Government Auditing Standards*, we have also issued a report dated [*date of report*] on our consideration of the City of Example's internal control over financial reporting and on our tests of its compliance with certain provisions of laws, regulations, contracts, and grants. That report is an integral part of an audit performed in accordance with *Government Auditing Standards* and should be read in conjunction with this report in considering the results of our audit.

Signature   <---------- May be signed, typed, or printed

Date   <---------- Date of completion of field work

NOTE: *The GASB has substantially revised its financial accounting and reporting model. That revision is contained in SGAS 34, *Basic Financial Statements - and Management's Discussion and Analysis - for State and Local Governments*. Among many other changes, SGAS 34 eliminates expendable and nonexpendable trust funds.

4. The following is an example of a separate report on compliance given no material instances of noncompliance:

Auditor's Standard Report on Compliance with Laws and Regulations

---

<u>Independent Auditor's Report</u>

To: <---------- Oversight Body

We have audited the general-purpose financial statements of City of Example, Any State, as of and for the year ended June 30, year 1, and have issued our report thereon dated August 15, year 1.

We conducted our audit in accordance with auditing standards generally accepted in the United States of America and *Government Auditing Standards* issued by the Comptroller General of the United States. Those standards require that we plan and perform the audit to obtain reasonable assurance about whether the financial statements are free of material misstatement.

Compliance with laws, regulations, contracts, and grant applicable to City of Example, Any State, is the responsibility of City of Example, Any State's management. As part of obtaining reasonable assurance about whether the financial statements are free of material misstatement, we performed tests of City of Example, Any State's compliance with certain provisions of laws, regulations, contracts, and grants. However, the objective of our audit of the general-purpose financial statements was not to provide an opinion on overall compliance with such provisions. Accordingly, we do not express such an opinion.

The results of our tests disclosed no instances of noncompliance that are required to be reported herein under *Government Auditing Standards*.

This report is intended for the information of the audit committee, management, and [*specify legislative or regulatory body*]. However, this report is a matter of public record and its distribution is not limited.

Signature <---------- May be signed, typed, or printed

Date <---------- Date of completion of field work

5.   The following is an example of a separate report on internal control:

Auditor's Standard Report on Internal Control

<u>Independent Auditor's Report</u>

To: <---------- Oversight Body

We have audited the general-purpose financial statements of City of Example, Any State, as of and for the year ended June 30, year 1, and have issued our report thereon dated August 15, year 1.

We conducted our audit in accordance with auditing standards generally accepted in the United States of America and *Government Auditing Standards* issued by the Comptroller General of the United States. Those standards require that we plan and perform the audit to obtain reasonable assurance about whether the general-purpose financial statements are free of material misstatement.

The management of City of Example, Any State, is responsible for establishing and maintaining internal control. In fulfilling this responsibility, estimates and judgments by management are required to assess the expected benefits and related costs of internal controls. The objectives of internal controls are to provide management with reasonable, but not absolute, assurance that assets are safeguarded against loss from unauthorized use or disposition, and that transactions are executed in accordance with management's authorization and recorded properly to permit the preparation of general-purpose financial statements in accordance with accounting principles generally accepted in the United States of America. Because of inherent limitations in internal controls, errors or fraud may nevertheless occur and not be detected. Also, projection of evaluation of controls to future periods is subject to the risk that procedures may become inadequate because of changes in conditions or that the effectiveness of the design and operation of controls may deteriorate.

In planning and performing our audit of the general-purpose financial statements of City of Example, Any State, for the year ended June 30, year 1, we obtained an understanding of internal control components. With respect to internal control, we obtained an understanding of the design of relevant policies and procedures and whether they have been placed in operation, and we assessed control risk in order to determine our auditing procedures for the purpose of expressing our opinion on the general-purpose financial statements and not to provide an opinion on internal control. Accordingly, we do not express such an opinion.

We noted certain matters involving internal control and its operation that we consider to be reportable conditions under standards established by the American Institute of Certified Public Accountants. Reportable conditions involve matters coming to our attention relating to significant deficiencies in the design or operation of internal control that, in our judgment, could adversely affect the entity's ability to record, process, summarize, and report financial data consistent with the assertions of management in the general-purpose financial statements.

[Include paragraphs to describe the reportable conditions noted.]

A material weakness is a reportable condition in which the design or operation of one or more of the specific internal control components does not reduce to a relatively low level the risk that errors or fraud in amounts that would be material in relation to the general-purpose financial statements being audited may occur and not be detected within a timely period by employees in the normal course of performing their assigned functions.

Our consideration of internal control would not necessarily disclose all matters in internal control that might be reportable conditions and, accordingly, would not necessarily disclose all reportable conditions that are also considered to be material weaknesses as defined above. However, we believe none of the reportable conditions described above is a material weakness.

We also noted other matters involving internal control and its operation that we have reported to the management of City of Example, Any State, in a separate letter dated August 15, year 1.

This report is intended for the information of the audit committee, management, and *[specify legislative or regulatory body]*. However, this report is a matter of public record and its distribution is not limited.

Signature   <---------- May be signed, typed, or printed

Date   <---------- Date of completion of field work

---

6.   Stop and review! You have completed the outline for this subunit. Study multiple-choice questions 9 through 21 beginning on page 643.

20.4 FEDERAL AUDIT REQUIREMENTS AND THE SINGLE AUDIT ACT

1. **Overview of Federal Audit Requirements**

   a. According to the Single Audit Act, the auditor must conduct the audit in accordance with GAGAS. The scope of the audit extends to

      1) Expressing or disclaiming an opinion on whether the financial statements are presented fairly in all material respects in conformity with GAAP. (This requirement includes reporting on compliance with laws and regulations and internal control for expenditures not covered explicitly below.)

      2) Expressing or disclaiming an opinion on whether the schedule of expenditures of federal awards is presented fairly in all material respects in relation to the financial statements taken as a whole.

      3) Performing procedures to obtain an understanding of internal control sufficient to plan the audit to support a low assessed level of control risk for major programs, planning tests of controls to support that assessment for the assertions relevant to compliance requirements for each major program, and performing tests of controls. (Planning and performing tests are not required if the controls are likely to be ineffective.)

         a) The report on internal control related to the financial statements and major programs should describe the scope of testing and the results of tests, and, if applicable, it should refer to the schedule of findings and questioned costs.

         b) Reportable conditions that are individually or cumulatively material should be identified.

      4) Expressing or disclaiming an opinion on whether the auditee has complied with laws, regulations, and the provisions of contracts or grants that may have a direct and material effect on each major program.

      5) Following up.

      6) Reporting a schedule of findings and questioned costs.

   b. Compliance requirements applicable to awards made by many federal programs are covered in the **Compliance Supplement** to OMB Circular A-133, *Audits of States, Local Governments, and Non-Profit Organizations.* Its focus is on compliance requirements that could have a direct and material effect on a major program.

      1) This Supplement lists and describes the types of compliance requirements and related audit objectives and procedures that should be considered in every audit to which it relates. It also discusses objectives, procedures, and compliance requirements that are specific to each federal program included.

2. **Other Requirements of the Single Audit Act**

   a. The Single Audit Act requires nonfederal entities that expend $500,000 or more of federal awards in a fiscal year to have a single audit in accordance with the Single Audit Act unless they properly elect to have a program-specific audit.

      1) The single audit is in lieu of any financial audit required under individual federal awards. It encompasses the entity's financial statements and schedule of expenditures of federal awards.

      2) The single audit covers the operations of the entire entity, or, at the option of the entity, it may include a series of audits of the organizational subunits that expended or administered federal awards.

b.   Auditee management is responsible for identifying federal awards and the related programs and preparing a schedule of the expenditures of federal awards. The auditee is also responsible for maintaining control over federal programs; complying with laws, regulations, and the provisions of contracts and grants; preparing financial statements; ensuring that required audits are performed and submitted when due; and following up and taking corrective action.

1)   The auditee must submit to the designated clearinghouse a data collection form providing information about the auditee, its federal programs, and the results of the audit. The auditee must also submit a reporting package that includes financial statements, a summary schedule of audit findings, the auditor's reports, and the corrective action plan.

c.   The auditor uses a **risk-based approach** in determining which federal programs are major programs. Current and prior audit experience, oversight by federal agencies and pass-through entities, inherent risk, and amounts of federal awards expended are the criteria considered.

1)   A federal agency or pass-through entity may request that the auditee have a program audited as a major program.

d.   The **schedule of audit findings and questioned costs** includes any instances of known questioned costs greater than $10,000 or of known questioned costs when likely questioned costs exceed $10,000 for compliance requirements for a major program. Likely questioned costs (a projection) also must be considered when evaluating the effects of questioned costs on the audit opinion. Furthermore, known questioned costs greater than $10,000 for a nonmajor program also should be included.

1)   Audit findings should be sufficiently detailed to permit the auditee to prepare a corrective action plan and to take such action.

e.   For the purpose of **reporting an audit finding**, the auditor's determination of whether a deficiency in internal control is a reportable condition or whether an instance of noncompliance is material is in relation to a type of compliance requirement for a major program or an audit objective identified in the OMB Circular A-133 Compliance Supplement. In contrast, materiality is considered in relation to the financial statements in an audit under GAAS.

f.   Under the Single Audit Act, a federal agency or the U.S. Comptroller General may, upon request, obtain access to the auditor's working papers to provide information for a quality review, to resolve audit findings, or to carry out oversight responsibilities. Access includes the right to obtain copies.

3.   Stop and review! You have completed the outline for this subunit. Study multiple-choice questions 22 through 25 beginning on page 648.

QUESTIONS

20.1 Overview

1. Which of the following bodies promulgates standards for audits of recipients of federal awards?

   A. Governmental Accounting Standards Board.

   B. Financial Accounting Standards Board.

   C. Government Accountability Office.

   D. Governmental Auditing Standards Board.

Answer (C) is correct. *(CPA, adapted)*
   REQUIRED: The body that sets standards for audits of federal awards recipients.
   DISCUSSION: The federal agency concerned with accounting and auditing standards for U.S. government programs and services is the Government Accountability Office. The GAO promulgates generally accepted government auditing standards.
   Answer (A) is incorrect because the GASB promulgates standards for financial accounting and reporting by state and local governments. Answer (B) is incorrect because the FASB promulgates standards for financial accounting and reporting by nongovernmental entities. Answer (D) is incorrect because there is no Governmental Auditing Standards Board. The committee of the GAO that promulgates government auditing standards is the Advisory Council on *Government Auditing Standards*.

2. *Government Auditing Standards* relates to which of the services provided to government entities, programs, activities, and functions?

	Financial Audits	Nonaudit Services	Performance Audits
A.	Yes	Yes	No
B.	Yes	No	Yes
C.	Yes	Yes	Yes
D.	No	No	Yes

Answer (B) is correct. *(Publisher)*
   REQUIRED: The scope of *Government Auditing Standards*.
   DISCUSSION: *Government Auditing Standards* relates to financial audits, attestation engagements, and performance audits of government entities, programs, activities, and functions, and of government assistance administered by contractors, nonprofit entities and other nongovernmental activities. Although GAGAS are not applicable to nonaudit services, they may affect an audit organization's independence to conduct audits.

3. An objective of a performance audit is to determine whether an entity's

   A. Pro forma information is presented fairly.

   B. Operational information is in accordance with generally accepted government auditing standards.

   C. Financial statements present fairly the results of operations.

   D. Specific operating units are functioning economically and efficiently.

Answer (D) is correct. *(CPA, adapted)*
   REQUIRED: The objective of a performance audit.
   DISCUSSION: Performance audits include economy and efficiency audits. The objectives of these audits are to determine (1) whether the entity is acquiring, protecting, and using its resources economically and efficiently; (2) the causes of any inefficiencies; and (3) whether the entity has complied with laws and regulations concerning matters of economy and efficiency.
   Answer (A) is incorrect because pro forma information is the subject of attestation engagements. Answer (B) is incorrect because the conduct of the audit and the audit report, not operational information, should be in accordance with *Government Auditing Standards*. Answer (C) is incorrect because determining whether financial statements present fairly the results of operations is an objective of a financial statement audit.

4. An auditor was engaged to conduct a performance audit of a governmental entity in accordance with *Government Auditing Standards*. These standards do not require the auditor to report

   A. The audit objectives and the audit scope and methodology.

   B. All significant instances of noncompliance and instances of abuse.

   C. The views of the audited program's responsible officials concerning the auditor's findings.

   D. A concurrent opinion on the financial statements taken as a whole.

Answer (D) is correct. *(CPA, adapted)*
   REQUIRED: The action not required of an auditor engaged in a performance audit of a governmental entity in accordance with *Government Auditing Standards*.
   DISCUSSION: Performance audits relate to assessing program effectiveness and results; economy and efficiency; internal control; compliance with legal requirements; or providing prospective analyses, guidance, or summary information. There is no requirement that a financial audit be conducted simultaneously or concurrently with a performance audit.

5. Which of the following statements is a standard applicable to financial statement audits in accordance with *Government Auditing Standards* (the Yellow Book)?

    A. An auditor should report on the scope of the auditor's testing of compliance with laws and regulations.

    B. An auditor should assess whether the entity has reportable measures of economy and efficiency that are valid and reliable.

    C. An auditor should report recommendations for actions to correct problems and improve operations.

    D. An auditor should determine the extent to which the entity's programs achieve the desired results.

Answer (A) is correct. *(CPA, adapted)*
    REQUIRED: The scope of an audit under *Government Auditing Standards*.
    DISCUSSION: According to additional reporting standards for financial statement audits, the report on the financial statements should either (1) describe the scope of the auditors' testing of compliance with laws and regulations and internal controls over financial reporting and present the results of those tests or (2) refer to separate report(s) containing that information. If the scope of the work performed is sufficient, an opinion on internal control and compliance can be expressed. In presenting the results of those tests, auditors should report fraud, illegal acts, other material noncompliance, and reportable conditions in internal controls over financial reporting. In some circumstances, auditors should report fraud and illegal acts directly to parties external to the audited entity.
    Answer (B) is incorrect because economy and efficiency are subjects of performance audits rather than financial audits. Answer (C) is incorrect because advice may be provided on the correction of problems and the improvement of operations, but the auditor is not required to provide a report. Answer (D) is incorrect because achievement of desired results is a subject of performance audits rather than financial audits.

20.2 Audits in Accordance with AU 801, *Compliance Auditing Considerations in Audits of Governmental Entities and Recipients of Governmental Financial Assistance*

6. Because of the pervasive effects of laws and regulations on the financial statements of governmental units, an auditor should consider obtaining written representations from management regarding

    A. Completeness of management's identification of laws and regulations that have a direct and material effect on its financial statements.

    B. Implementation of internal controls designed to detect all illegal acts.

    C. Expression of both positive and negative assurance to the auditor that the entity complied with all laws and regulations.

    D. Employment of internal auditors who can report their findings, opinions, and conclusions objectively.

Answer (A) is correct. *(CPA, adapted)*
    REQUIRED: The audit procedure that should be considered in a governmental audit.
    DISCUSSION: The auditor should obtain an understanding of the possible financial statement effects of laws and regulations widely recognized by auditors as having direct and material effects. The auditor should also assess whether management has identified such laws and regulations. Thus, the auditor may consider obtaining written representations from management about the completeness of management's identification (AU 801).
    Answer (B) is incorrect because internal control typically safeguards assets and promotes the reliability of financial statements but, given its inherent limitations, cannot be expected to prevent or detect all illegal acts. Answer (C) is incorrect because management does not express assurance, either positive or negative, that it has complied with all laws and regulations in an audit. Answer (D) is incorrect because the entity will decide whether to employ internal auditors.

7. When auditing an entity's financial statements in accordance with *Government Auditing Standards* (the Yellow Book), an auditor is required to report on

I. Recommendations for actions to improve operations

II. The scope of the auditor's tests of compliance with laws and regulations

    A. I only.

    B. II only.

    C. Both I and II.

    D. Neither I nor II.

Answer (B) is correct. *(CPA, adapted)*
    REQUIRED: The true statement(s), if any, about reporting under *Government Auditing Standards*.
    DISCUSSION: *Government Auditing Standards* imposes more stringent reporting requirements than GAAS. Under GAGAS, the report on the financial statements should either describe the scope of the auditor's testing of compliance with laws and regulations and internal control over financial reporting and present the results of those tests or refer to separate reports containing that information. Auditors should report recommendations for actions to correct problems and to improve operations in a performance audit, not in a financial audit.
    Answer (A) is incorrect because an auditor is required to report on the scope of the auditor's tests of compliance with laws and regulations. Answer (C) is incorrect because auditors should report recommendations for actions to correct problems and to improve operations in a performance audit, not in a financial audit. Answer (D) is incorrect because an auditor is required to report on the scope of the auditor's tests of compliance with laws and regulations.

14. In auditing a not-for-profit entity that receives governmental awards, the auditor has a responsibility to

    A. Issue a separate report that describes the expected benefits and related costs of the auditor's suggested changes to the entity's internal control.

    B. Assess whether management has identified laws and regulations that have a direct and material effect on the entity's financial statements.

    C. Notify the governmental agency providing the awards that the audit is not designed to provide any assurance of detecting errors and fraud.

    D. Express an opinion concerning the entity's continued eligibility for the governmental awards.

Answer (B) is correct. *(CPA, adapted)*
    REQUIRED: The responsibility of an auditor of a not-for-profit entity that receives governmental awards.
    DISCUSSION: Management is responsible for ensuring compliance with laws and regulations. The auditor's responsibility is to understand the possible effects of laws and regulations having direct and material effects on the financial statements and to assess whether management has identified such laws and regulations (AU 801).
    Answer (A) is incorrect because the auditor need not identify the relative costs and benefits related to the client's internal control. However, the auditor must communicate reportable conditions. Answer (C) is incorrect because the audit should be designed to provide reasonable assurance of detecting material fraud. Answer (D) is incorrect because the report should express an opinion on the financial statements and present the results of tests of compliance and of internal control over financial reporting, but it does not express an opinion on continued eligibility.

15. In reporting on compliance with laws and regulations during a financial statement audit in accordance with *Government Auditing Standards*, an auditor should include in the auditor's report

    A. A statement of assurance that all controls over fraud and illegal acts were tested.

    B. Material instances of fraud and illegal acts that were discovered.

    C. The materiality criteria used by the auditor in considering whether instances of noncompliance were significant.

    D. An opinion on whether compliance with laws and regulations affected the entity's goals and objectives.

Answer (B) is correct. *(CPA, adapted)*
    REQUIRED: The issues included in an auditor's report in accordance with *Government Auditing Standards*.
    DISCUSSION: An auditor's report, in accordance with *Government Auditing Standards*, should present the results of tests of internal control over financial reporting and compliance with laws and regulations. In presenting these results, the auditor should report fraud, illegal acts, other material noncompliance, and reportable conditions in internal control over financial reporting.
    Answer (A) is incorrect because no assurance need be provided that all controls over fraud and illegal acts were tested. Answer (C) is incorrect because the materiality criteria need not be reported. Answer (D) is incorrect because no opinion need be expressed.

16. Reporting on internal control under *Government Auditing Standards* differs from reporting under generally accepted auditing standards in that *Government Auditing Standards* requires a

    A. Written report describing the entity's internal control activities specifically designed to prevent fraud and illegal acts.

    B. Written report describing each reportable condition observed, including identification of those considered material weaknesses.

    C. Statement of negative assurance that the internal control activities not tested have an immaterial effect on the entity's financial statements.

    D. Statement of positive assurance that internal control activities designed to detect material errors and fraud were tested.

Answer (B) is correct. *(CPA, adapted)*
    REQUIRED: The difference between *Government Auditing Standards* and GAAS regarding reports on internal control.
    DISCUSSION: According to the second additional standards of reporting for financial audits of governmental entities, the report on the financial statements or a separate report should present the results of tests of compliance with laws and regulations and internal control over financial reporting. This report should present the reportable conditions in internal control over financial reporting, including identification of those that are individually or cumulatively material weaknesses. Moreover, deficiencies that are not reportable conditions should be communicated to the auditee. If such deficiencies have been communicated in a management letter, the auditor should refer to that letter when reporting on internal control. However, the report need not provide any assurance on internal control design or effectiveness.
    Answer (A) is incorrect because *Government Auditing Standards* does not require the auditor to list internal control activities specifically designed to prevent fraud or illegal acts. Answer (C) is incorrect because the auditor is not required to provide a statement of positive or negative assurance regarding internal control. However, positive assurance in the form of an opinion may be provided if the scope of the work is sufficient. Answer (D) is incorrect because the auditor is not required to provide a statement of positive or negative assurance regarding internal control. However, positive assurance in the form of an opinion may be provided if the scope of the work is sufficient.

17. Which of the following statements is a standard applicable to financial statement audits in accordance with *Government Auditing Standards*?

   A. An auditor should assess whether the entity has reportable measures of economy and efficiency that are valid and reliable.

   B. An auditor should report on the scope of the auditor's testing of internal control over financial reporting.

   C. An auditor should briefly describe in the auditor's report the method of statistical sampling used in performing tests of controls and substantive tests.

   D. An auditor should determine the extent to which the entity's programs achieve the desired level of results.

Answer (B) is correct. *(CPA, adapted)*
   REQUIRED: The standard applicable to financial statement audits in accordance with *Government Auditing Standards*.
   DISCUSSION: The auditor is required, as part of a governmental audit, to report on compliance with laws and regulations and internal control over financial reporting. This report should include a description of the scope of the auditor's testing and present the results of those tests.
   Answer (A) is incorrect because a performance audit, not a financial audit, includes an evaluation of economy and efficiency. Answer (C) is incorrect because governmental audit reports ordinarily do not include identification of the methods of statistical sampling used. However, in presenting material fraud, illegal acts, or other noncompliance, an auditor should follow the reporting standards for performance audits that pertain to, among other things, methodology. Thus, when sampling significantly supports the audit findings, the auditor should describe the sample design and state why it was chosen. Answer (D) is incorrect because performance audits, not financial audits, include the entity's achievement of desired results.

18. An auditor most likely will be responsible for assuring that management communicates significant deficiencies in the design of internal controls

   A. To a court-appointed creditors' committee when the client is operating under Chapter 11 of the Federal Bankruptcy Code.

   B. To shareholders with significant influence (more than 20% equity ownership) when the reportable conditions are deemed to be material weaknesses.

   C. To the Securities and Exchange Commission when the client is a publicly held entity.

   D. To specific legislative and regulatory bodies when reporting under *Government Auditing Standards*.

Answer (D) is correct. *(CPA, adapted)*
   REQUIRED: The circumstance in which an auditor is likely responsible for assuring communication of significant deficiencies in internal control.
   DISCUSSION: An auditor is required to include reportable conditions in internal control over financial reporting in a report prepared under *Government Auditing Standards*. The report is required to be distributed to the appropriate officials of the organization being audited, officials of the organizations requiring or arranging for the audit, other officials who have legal oversight authority or who may be responsible for taking action, and others who may be authorized to receive the report.
   Answer (A) is incorrect because management would be responsible for providing audited financial statements to a creditors' committee. Answer (B) is incorrect because the auditor's report is included with the audited financial statements in the annual report, a document that is available to all shareholders. Answer (C) is incorrect because management is responsible for providing audited financial information to the SEC. However, the auditor has certain responsibilities for reporting illegal acts to the SEC under the Private Securities Litigation Reform Act of 1995.

19. When auditing an entity's financial statements in accordance with *Government Auditing Standards* (the Yellow Book), an auditor is required to report on

I. Positive aspects of the program applicable to audit objectives

II. The scope of the auditor's testing of internal controls

   A. I only.

   B. II only.

   C. Both I and II.

   D. Neither I nor II.

Answer (B) is correct. *(CPA, adapted)*
   REQUIRED: The true statement(s), if any, about reporting under *Government Auditing Standards*.
   DISCUSSION: *Government Auditing Standards* imposes more stringent reporting requirements than GAAS. Under GAGAS, the report on the financial statements should describe the scope of the auditor's testing of compliance with laws and regulations and internal control over financial reporting and present the results of those tests or refer to separate reports containing that information. The report on internal control must separately identify reportable conditions and material weaknesses but need not provide any assurance on internal control design or effectiveness. Accomplishments of the program, especially those management improvements in one area that may be applicable elsewhere, should be reported in a performance audit, not a financial audit, if they relate to audit objectives.
   Answer (A) is incorrect because an auditor is required to report on the scope of the auditor's testing of internal controls. Answer (C) is incorrect because an auditor need not report on noteworthy accomplishments of the program in a financial audit. Answer (D) is incorrect because an auditor is required to report on the scope of the auditor's testing of internal controls.

20. In reporting under *Government Auditing Standards*, an auditor most likely would be required to report a falsification of accounting records directly to a federal inspector general when the falsification is

    A. Discovered after the auditor's report has been made available to the federal inspector general and to the public.

    B. Reported by the auditor to the audit committee as a significant deficiency in internal control.

    C. Voluntarily disclosed to the auditor by low-level personnel as a result of the auditor's inquiries.

    D. Communicated by the auditor to the auditee and the auditee fails to make a required report of the matter.

Answer (D) is correct. *(CPA, adapted)*

    REQUIRED: The time when an auditor is required to report externally under *Government Auditing Standards*.

    DISCUSSION: Under *Government Auditing Standards*, auditors must report fraud and illegal acts directly to parties outside the auditee (for example, to a federal inspector general or a state attorney general) in two circumstances. These requirements are in addition to any legal requirements for direct reporting. First, if auditors have communicated such fraud or illegal acts to the auditee, and it fails to report them, the auditors should communicate their awareness of that failure to the auditee's governing body. If the auditee does not make the required report as soon as practicable after the auditors' communication with its governing body, the auditors should report the fraud or illegal acts directly to the external party specified in the law or regulation. Second, management is responsible for taking timely and appropriate steps to remedy fraud or illegal acts that auditors report to it. When fraud or an illegal act involves assistance received directly or indirectly from a government agency, auditors may have a duty to report it directly if management fails to take remedial steps. If auditors conclude that such failure is likely to cause them to depart from the standard report or resign from the audit, they should communicate that conclusion to the auditee's governing body. Then, if the auditee does not report the fraud or illegal act as soon as practicable to the entity that provided the government assistance, the auditors should report directly to that entity.

21. Which of the following statements represents a quality control requirement under government auditing standards?

    A. A CPA who conducts government audits is required to undergo an annual external peer review when an appropriate internal quality control system is not in place.

    B. A CPA seeking to enter into a contract to perform an audit should provide the CPA's most recent external peer review report to the party contracting for the audit.

    C. An external peer review of a CPA's practice should include a review of the working papers of each government audit performed since the prior external quality control review.

    D. A CPA who conducts government audits may not make the CPA's external quality control review report available to the public.

Answer (B) is correct. *(CPA, adapted)*

    REQUIRED: The quality control requirement under government auditing standards.

    DISCUSSION: According to the fourth general standard stated in *Government Auditing Standards*, an audit organization conducting an audit in accordance with these standards must have an appropriate internal quality control system in place and undergo an external peer review. For example, a CPA seeking to enter into a contract to perform an audit should provide the CPA's most recent external peer review report to the party contracting for the audit.

    Answer (A) is incorrect because organizations conducting audits in accordance with the *Government Audit Standards* should have an external peer review at least once every 3 years. Answer (C) is incorrect because an external peer review consists of evaluating a sample of audits performed and working papers prepared since the last external peer review. Answer (D) is incorrect because audit organizations should ordinarily make their external peer review reports available to auditors during their work and to appropriate oversight bodies. It is recommended that the report be made available to the public as well.

20.4 Federal Audit Requirements and the Single Audit Act

22. Although the scope of audits of recipients of federal awards in accordance with federal audit regulations varies, audits under the Single Audit Act generally have which of the following elements in common?

A. The auditor is to determine whether the federal financial assistance has been administered in accordance with applicable laws and regulations.

B. The materiality levels are lower and are determined by the government entities that provided the federal awards to the recipient.

C. The auditor should obtain written management representations that the recipient's internal auditors will report their findings objectively without fear of political repercussion.

D. The auditor is required to express both positive and negative assurance that illegal acts that could have a material effect on the recipient's financial statements are disclosed to the inspector general.

Answer (A) is correct. *(CPA, adapted)*
REQUIRED: The common element in federal audit regulations.
DISCUSSION: According to the Single Audit Act, the scope of federal audits may vary, but the auditor must

1. Determine whether the financial statements are presented fairly in all material respects in conformity with GAAP.

2. Determine whether the schedule of expenditures of federal awards is presented fairly in all material respects in relation to the financial statements taken as a whole.

3. With respect to controls over compliance, obtain an understanding of those controls, assess control risk, and perform tests of controls unless the controls are ineffective.

4. Determine whether the nonfederal entity has complied with the provisions of laws, regulations, and contracts or grants that have a direct and material effect on each major program.

5. Report audit findings in a schedule of findings and questioned costs.

Answer (B) is incorrect because materiality is determined by the auditor in relation to a type of compliance requirement for a major program or an audit objective identified in the OMB Circular A-133 Compliance Supplement. Answer (C) is incorrect because, although the auditor should obtain written management representations, no specific requirements concerning the entity's internal auditors are stipulated. Answer (D) is incorrect because the auditor is required to report illegal acts but not to provide positive or negative assurance about them.

23. Wolf is auditing an entity's compliance with requirements governing a major federal program in accordance with the Single Audit Act. Wolf detected noncompliance with requirements that have a material effect on the program. Wolf's report on compliance should express

A. No assurance on the compliance tests.

B. Reasonable assurance on the compliance tests.

C. A qualified or adverse opinion.

D. An adverse opinion or a disclaimer of opinion.

Answer (C) is correct. *(CPA, adapted)*
REQUIRED: The assurance about compliance given noncompliance with material requirements.
DISCUSSION: Under the Single Audit Act, the auditor should express an opinion on compliance with requirements applicable to a major federal program or state that an opinion cannot be expressed. When the compliance audit detects noncompliance with those requirements that the auditor believes have a material effect on the program, the auditor should express a qualified or adverse opinion. The auditor should state the basis for such an opinion in the report.
Answer (A) is incorrect because the auditor should express an opinion on compliance. Answer (B) is incorrect because the auditor's report should state that the audit was planned and performed to provide reasonable assurance about whether material noncompliance occurred. Answer (D) is incorrect because a disclaimer is not appropriate when the auditor has detected material noncompliance.

24. In an audit of compliance with requirements governing awards under major federal programs performed in accordance with the Single Audit Act, the auditor's consideration of materiality differs from materiality under generally accepted auditing standards. Under the Single Audit Act, materiality for the purpose of reporting an audit finding is

A. Calculated in relation to the financial statements taken as a whole.

B. Determined in relation to a type of compliance requirement for a major program.

C. Decided in conjunction with the auditor's risk assessment.

D. Ignored, because all account balances, regardless of size, are fully tested.

Answer (B) is correct. *(CPA, adapted)*
REQUIRED: The materiality determination under the Single Audit Act.
DISCUSSION: Under the Single Audit Act, the emphasis of the audit effort is on major programs related to federal awards administered by nonfederal entities. According to OMB Circular A-133 issued pursuant to the Single Audit Act, the schedule of findings and questioned costs includes instances of material noncompliance with laws, regulations, contracts, or grant agreements related to a major program. The auditor's determination of whether a noncompliance is material for the purpose of reporting an audit finding is in relation to a type of compliance requirement for a major program or an audit objective identified in the OMB Circular A-133 Compliance Supplement. Examples of types of compliance requirements include activities allowed or unallowed; allowable costs/cost principles; cash management; eligibility; matching, level of effort, and earmarking; and reporting.
Answer (A) is incorrect because, in a for-profit financial statement audit, materiality is related to the financial statements taken as a whole. Answer (C) is incorrect because risk assessment is performed in planning the audit, but once the auditor makes a finding, the decision to report it is contingent on the materiality to the major program. Answer (D) is incorrect because materiality must be considered in determining the appropriate tests to be applied.

25. A CPA has performed an examination of the general purpose financial statements of Big City. The examination scope included the additional requirements of the Single Audit Act. When reporting on Big City's internal control over the administration of federal awards, the CPA should

A. Communicate reportable conditions that are material in relation to the general purpose financial statements.

B. Express an opinion on the systems used to administer awards under major federal programs and express negative assurance on the systems used to administer awards under nonmajor federal programs.

C. Communicate reportable conditions that are material in relation to a type of compliance requirement for the federal program.

D. Express negative assurance on the systems used to administer awards under major federal programs and express no opinion on the systems used to administer awards under nonmajor federal programs.

Answer (C) is correct. *(CPA, adapted)*
REQUIRED: The requirement of a report on internal controls used in administering awards under a federal program.
DISCUSSION: Under the Single Audit Act, the auditor's determination of whether a deficiency in internal control is a reportable condition is in relation to a type of compliance requirement for a major program or an audit objective identified in the OMB Circular A-133 Compliance Supplement. The auditor also must identify reportable conditions that are individually or cumulatively material weaknesses.
Answer (A) is incorrect because materiality in an audit under GAAS is measured relative to the financial statements. Answer (B) is incorrect because, although an auditor conducting a single audit is required to report on controls that relate to the systems used to administer awards under federal programs, the auditor is not required to provide assurance. Answer (D) is incorrect because auditors are required to express an opinion (or disclaim an opinion) as to whether the auditee complied with laws, regulations, and the provisions of contracts or grant agreements that could have a direct and material effect on each major program.

20.5 PRACTICE SIMULATION

[icon]	Testlet 4 of 5	Time Remaining 2 hours 00 minutes	Copy	Paste	Calculator	Sheet	Standards	Help	Split	Done

| Directions | Situation | ⊞ Government Auditing | ⊞ Independence | ⊞ GAS- Laws and Regulations | ⊞ Communication | ⊞ Research | Resources |

1. Directions

In the following simulation, you will be asked to complete various tasks related to governmental reporting. The simulation will provide you with all of the information necessary to do your work. For full credit, be sure to view and complete all work tabs.

Resources are available to you under the tab marked RESOURCES. You may want to review the resources before beginning the simulation.

2. Situation

Toxic Waste Disposal Co., Inc. (TWD) is a not-for-profit organization that receives grants and fees from various state and municipal governments. TWD engaged Hall & Hall, CPAs, to audit its financial statements for the year ended July 31, in accordance with *Government Auditing Standards*. Accordingly, the auditor's reports are to be submitted by TWD to the granting government agencies, which make the reports available for public inspection.

3. Government Auditing Standards

The auditor's separate report on compliance with laws and regulations that was drafted by a staff accountant of Hall & Hall at the completion of the engagement contained the following seven statements. It was submitted to the engagement partner who reviewed matters thoroughly and properly concluded that no material instances of noncompliance were identified.

This question is presented in a multiple-choice format that requires you to select the correct response from a drop-down list. Write the answer in the shaded column. Determine whether each of the following seven statements is an appropriate element of a report on compliance with laws and regulations and, if it is inappropriate, the reason.

Statements	Answers
1. A statement that the audit was conducted in accordance with GAAS and with *Government Auditing Standards* issued by the Government Accountability Office.	

Choices
A) Appropriate.
B) Inappropriate because a governmental audit should not refer to GAAS.
C) Inappropriate because *Government Auditing Standards* is not issued by the U.S. Comptroller General.

Statements	Answers
2. A statement that the auditor's procedures included tests of compliance.	

Choices
A) Appropriate.
B) Inappropriate because the auditor's procedures should not include tests of compliance.
C) Inappropriate because a statement on the auditor's procedures should not be included within the report on compliance.

Continued on next page.

3. Government Auditing Standards -- Continued

Statements	Answers
3. A statement that management is responsible for compliance with laws, regulations, contracts, and grants.	

Choices

A) Appropriate.

B) Inappropriate because the auditor is responsible for compliance with laws, regulations, contracts, and grants.

C) Inappropriate because this statement is not required to be included within the report on compliance.

Statements	Answers
4. A statement that the standards require the auditor to plan and to perform the audit to detect all instances of noncompliance with applicable laws and regulations.	

A) Appropriate.

B) Inappropriate because the auditor is required to plan and perform the audit to provide reasonable assurance of detecting all instances of noncompliance having a direct effect on the financial statements, not all instances of noncompliance.

C) Inappropriate because the auditor is required to plan and perform the audit to detect instances of noncompliance having a direct and material effect on the financial statements, not all instances of noncompliance.

Statements	Answers
5. A statement that the auditor's objective was to provide an opinion on compliance with the provisions of laws and regulations equivalent of that to be expressed on the financial statements.	

A) Appropriate.

B) Inappropriate because expressing an opinion is a lower level of reporting than the positive and negative assurance required by *Government Auditing Standards*.

C) Inappropriate because the report does not express an opinion.

Statements	Answers
6. A statement of negative assurance that, with respect to items tested, nothing came to the auditor's attention that caused the auditor to believe that the entity had not complied, in all material respects, with the provisions of laws, regulations, contracts, and grants.	

A) Appropriate.

B) Inappropriate because no assurance should be provided.

C) Inappropriate because *Government Auditing Standards* requires positive assurance.

Statements	Answers
7. A statement that the report is intended only for the information of the specific legislative or regulatory bodies, and that this restriction is intended to limit the distribution of the report.	

A) Appropriate.

B) Inappropriate because *Government Auditing Standards* requires that the report be intended only for the use of management.

C) Inappropriate because *Government Auditing Standards* requires that, unless restricted by law or regulation, copies of the reports should be made available for public inspection.

4. Independence

This question has a matching format that requires you to select the correct response from a drop-down list. Write the answer in the shaded column. Each choice may be used once, more than once, or not at all. Independence is an important consideration for governmental auditors. *Government Auditing Standards* identifies three types of impairments of auditor independence. For each of the statements below, match the type of impairment with the statement.

Statement	Answer
1. Auditors are deterred from acting objectively by employees of the audited entity.	
2. Auditors should not provide nonaudit services that involve performing management functions of the audited entity.	
3. Auditors are pressured to reduce professional skepticism by an oversight agency of the audited entity.	
4. The impairment that parallels requirements by the AICPA.	
5. Auditors should not have a direct financial interest in the client.	
6. The auditor should be mentally unbiased.	
7. The head of internal auditing does not report results to the head or deputy head of the government entity.	
8. The audit organization should not audit its own work.	

Impairment
A) Personal impairment
B) External impairment
C) Organizational impairment

5. Effects of Laws and Regulations Related to Government Auditing Standards

This question is presented in a check-the-box format that requires you to select the correct responses from a given list. Each of the statements below represents potential responsibilities of the auditor or management of Toxic Waste Disposal Co., Inc.

Description	Auditor	Management	Neither Management nor the Auditor
1. Ensure compliance with laws and regulations			
2. Consider laws and regulations to plan and perform the audit			
3. Determine whether applicable laws and regulations are fair			
4. Gain an understanding of the possible effects of laws and regulations that may have a direct and material effect on the financial statements			
5. Obtain written representations about laws and regulations			
6. Review minutes of meeting for evidence concerning compliance with laws and regulations			
7. Identify laws and regulations requiring compliance			
8. Suggest new regulations to authorities			
9. Establish internal controls pertaining to compliance with laws and regulations			
10. Provide positive assurance that no laws or regulations have been violated by employees			

6. Communication

A manager of Toxic Waste Disposal Co., Inc. has called you and indicated that he had learned that the entity may be subject to a single audit under the Single Audit Act. He requests you to explain the differences between a single audit and a program-specific audit. In a brief memorandum to TWD, explain the differences. Type your communication in your word processor program and print out the copy in a memorandum style format.

REMINDER: Your response will be graded for both technical content and writing skills. You should demonstrate your ability to develop, organize, and express your ideas. Do not convey information in the form of a table, bullet point list, or other abbreviated presentation.

To: Client
From: CPA
Subject: Differences between a single audit and a program-specific audit

7. Research

Use the research materials available to you to find the answers to the following question in the AICPA Professional Standards. Write the appropriate professional standard AU in the box provided.

Locate the specific summary paragraph/table from the generally accepted auditing standards that relates to the generally accepted accounting principles (GAAP) hierarchies applicable to various entities (non-governmental, state and local governments and federal governmental entities). Write this standard number and paragraph in the box below.

AU [   ]

Unofficial Answers

3. Government Auditing Standards (7 Gradable Items)

1.   A) - The second paragraph of the report should indicate that the audit was conducted in accordance with both GAAS and *Government Auditing Standards*.

2.   A) - The report should state that the auditor has "performed tests of (name of entity)'s compliance with certain laws, regulations, contracts, and grants."

3.   A) - The report states that management is responsible for compliance with laws, regulations, contracts, and grants.

4.   B) - The report should state, "Those standards require that we plan and perform the audit to obtain reasonable assurance about whether the financial statements are free of material misstatement."

5.   C) - The report should describe the scope of testing of compliance with laws and regulations and present the results of those tests, including fraud, illegal acts, and other material noncompliance. It need not express an opinion. However, reporting the scope of testing includes reporting whether the tests provided sufficient evidence to support an opinion and whether the auditor is providing such an opinion.

6.   B) - No assurance on compliance, either positive or negative, need be expressed under *Government Auditing Standards*.

7.   C) - The last paragraph states that "this report is a matter of public record and its distribution is not limited."

4. Independence (8 Gradable Items)

1.   B) External impairment; Auditors are deterred from acting objectively by employees of the audited entity.

2.   A) Personal impairment; Auditors should not provide nonaudit services that involve performing management functions of the audited entity.

3.   B) External impairment; Auditors are pressured to reduce professional skepticism by an oversight agency of the audited entity.

4.   A) Personal impairment; The impairment that parallels requirements by the AICPA.

5.   A) Personal impairment; Auditors should not have a direct financial interest in the client.

6.   A) Personal impairment; The auditor should be mentally unbiased.

7.   C) Organizational impairment; The head of the internal audit organization should be accountable and report results to the head or deputy head of the government entity.

8.   A) Personal impairment; The audit organization should not audit its own work.

5. Effects of Laws and Regulations Related to Government Auditing Standards (10 Gradable Items)

1.   Management

2.   Auditor

3.   Neither Management nor the Auditor

4.   Auditor

5.   Auditor

6.   Auditor

7.   Management

8.   Neither Management nor the Auditor

9.   Management

10.   Neither Management nor the Auditor

6. Communication (5 Gradable Items; For grading instructions, please refer to page 11.)

To:	Client
From:	CPA
Subject:	Differences between a single audit and a program-specific audit

This memorandum addresses our discussion about the distinctions between a single audit and a program-specific audit.

The Single Audit Act requires one (a single) audit or a program-specific audit of a nonfederal entity that expends a total amount of federal awards equal to or in excess of $500,000. A single audit is required if the entity expends federal awards under more than one federal program. A program-specific audit is an audit of one governmental financial assistance program in accordance with federal or state laws, regulations, or audit guides.

A recipient of federal awards may be subject to a single or organization-wide audit or to a program-specific audit. A number of federal audit regulations permit the recipient to "elect" to have a program-specific audit, whereas other federal audit regulations require a program-specific audit in certain circumstances. In planning the audit, the auditor should determine and consider the specific federal audit requirements applicable to the engagement, including the issuance of additional reports. Federal audit regulations for both single or organization-wide audits and program-specific audits generally require consideration of internal control beyond what is normally required by GAAS and *Government Auditing Standards* and a determination of whether applicable compliance requirements have been met.

If you have any questions or comments, please contact us at your convenience.

7. Research (6 Gradable Items)

AU 411.18

Scoring Schedule:

	Correct Responses		Gradable Items		Weights		
Tab 3	_____	÷	7	×	20%	=	_____
Tab 4	_____	÷	8	×	20%	=	_____
Tab 5	_____	÷	10	×	20%	=	_____
Tab 6	_____	÷	5	×	30%	=	_____
Tab 7	_____	÷	6	×	10%	=	_____

(Your Score)

Use Gleim's *CPA Review Online* to practice more simulations in a realistic environment.

APPENDIX A
AUDITING PRONOUNCEMENT SUMMARY

This appendix provides a brief summary of each authoritative pronouncement tested on the Auditing section, but memorization of citations for specific pronouncements is not required. Thus, a question such as, "What does SAS 99 cover?" will not be on the exam.

Throughout this book, sources of official pronouncements document the information provided and facilitate further study. Thus, a candidate should understand the content of most, if not all, auditing pronouncements and their application to general or specific situations (the focus of the study outlines and answer explanations in this book).

AUDITING AUTHORITATIVE PRONOUNCEMENT SUMMARIES

The Auditing Standards Board of the AICPA issues Statements on Auditing Standards (SASs). Along with the 10 standards, SASs are deemed to have the status of auditing standards. Thus, an AICPA member who conducts an audit is required by the Code of Professional Conduct to comply with the SASs. They are issued as separate pronouncements in sequence but are also codified within the framework of the 10 standards and organized into the following sections:

100 Statements on Auditing Standards -- Introduction
200 The General Standards
300 The Standards of Field Work
400 The First, Second, and Third Standards of Reporting
500 The Fourth Standard of Reporting
600 Other Types of Reports
700 Special Topics
800 Compliance Auditing
900 Special Reports of the Committee on Auditing Procedure

The codifications of SASs are cited using the AU prefix followed by a three-digit number.

The following summaries extend through SAS 101. The SASs are listed by their codified numbers (AU xxx) rather than in chronological order to make it easier to relate the material to the applicable sections. Basic concepts set forth in the pronouncements should be understood.

Also see the Auditing Pronouncement Cross-Reference on pages 12 and 13, which contains a listing of these authoritative pronouncements and the study units in which they are covered.

AU SECTIONS

AU 110 - Responsibilities and Functions of the Independent Auditor

The object of independent audits is to express an opinion on whether the financial statements, in all material respects, are presented fairly in conformity with GAAP. Thus, the auditor must plan and perform the audit to obtain reasonable assurance about whether the financial statements are free of material misstatement, whether caused by error or fraud. Both the financial statements and internal controls are the responsibility of management. Auditors must comply with professional standards and have adequate education and experience.

AU 150 - Generally Accepted Auditing Standards (GAAS)

GAAS are measures of audit quality and set the objectives of audit procedures. They include the 10 standards and the SASs. The 10 standards consist of three general standards, three standards of field work, and four standards of reporting. The three general standards concern

1. Adequate technical training and proficiency as an auditor
2. Independence
3. Due professional care

The three standards of field work concern

1. Adequate planning and supervision

2. Understanding internal control sufficiently to plan the audit and to determine the nature, timing, and extent of tests to be performed

3. Obtaining sufficient competent evidence to afford a reasonable basis for an opinion regarding the financial statements

The four standards of reporting concern

1. Conformity of the statements with GAAP

2. The requirement that the report identify those circumstances in which such principles have not been consistently observed in the current period in relation to the preceding period(s)

3. Full and adequate disclosure in the statements

4. The expression of an opinion on the financial statements, taken as a whole, or an assertion that an opinion cannot be expressed, with an explanation of why no opinion can be expressed; and clear-cut indication of the character of the audit work and the degree of responsibility taken

Auditing standards must be applied by auditors. Interpretive publications, including appendixes to SASs, should be considered by auditors but need not be applied if the auditor is prepared to explain how (s)he complied with the SAS sections interpreted. Other auditing publications have no authority.

AU 161 - The Relationship of Generally Accepted Auditing Standards to Quality Control Standards

Conduct Rule 202 requires auditors to comply with GAAS. Firms should also establish quality control policies and procedures. They are dependent upon the firm's size, structure, practice, cost-benefit issues, and the separation between personnel and practice departments. GAAS relate to audits, and quality control relates to the firm's overall practice.

AU 201 - Nature of the General Standards

The general standards refer to the qualifications of the auditor and the quality of his/her work.

AU 210 - Training and Proficiency of the Independent Auditor

Education, experience, and supervision are necessary. An independent and objective auditor must have seasoned judgment to accept final responsibility for an opinion.

AU 220 - Independence

An auditor must always have an independent state of mind. (S)he must also be independent in appearance. The SEC also stresses auditor independence. Many companies encourage independence by having the auditors appointed by the board or elected by shareholders.

AU 230 - Due Professional Care in the Performance of Work

Due professional care relates to the auditor's activities and performance. (S)he must have the degree of skill commonly possessed by other auditors and must exercise it with reasonable care and diligence and professional skepticism, i.e., with a questioning mind and a critical assessment of evidence that assumes neither that management is dishonest nor unquestionably honest. The auditor must obtain only reasonable assurance that the statements are free of material misstatements caused by error or fraud. Fraud is characterized by (1) concealment through collusion; (2) withholding, misrepresenting, or falsifying documents; and (3) management's ability to override even apparently effective controls. Thus, collusion may defeat a properly performed audit because apparently persuasive evidence may be false. Moreover, an audit rarely requires authentication of documents, a process for which auditors are not trained. Documents may be modified through undisclosed side agreements with third parties, and management may override controls unpredictably.

AU 310 - Appointment of the Independent Auditor

The auditor should be appointed as early as possible. Appointment near or after the close of the period raises the issue of whether an adequate audit can be made or whether a qualified opinion or a disclaimer is necessary. Early appointment allows a significant portion of the audit to be carried out before year-end. The auditor should establish an understanding with the client regarding the services to be performed. This understanding ordinarily includes the objective of the audit and management's responsibility for (1) the financial statements and internal control, (2) ensuring that the entity complies with laws and regulations, (3) providing all financial records and information to the auditor, (4) correcting material misstatements, and (5) providing a representation letter. These and other matters may be communicated in an engagement letter.

AU 311 - Planning and Supervision

Planning and supervision relate to the first standard of field work. Planning requires developing an overall strategy. The nature, extent, and timing of planning vary with the size of the entity and other factors. A written audit program is required. It instructs assistants in work to be done and details necessary procedures. The audit program should be based on the knowledge of the client's business, including the methods used for computer processing of significant accounting information. The auditor may need to consider whether specialized skills are needed, e.g., with regard to computer processing. Supervision relates to all aspects of an audit. Assistants should know what is expected of them and what procedures to follow concerning disagreements on accounting and auditing issues.

AU 312 - Audit Risk and Materiality in Conducting an Audit

Audit risk and materiality relate to the nature, timing, and extent of audit procedures and their evaluation. Audit risk is the risk that the auditor may unknowingly fail to modify the opinion on materially misstated financial statements. It includes inherent risk, the susceptibility of an assertion to material misstatement assuming no related controls; control risk, the risk that a material misstatement could occur that will not be prevented or detected by internal control; and detection risk, the risk that the auditor will not detect a material misstatement that exists in an assertion. Financial statements are materially misstated if they contain misstatements that, singly or in the aggregate, are important enough to cause them not to be fairly presented, in all material respects, in conformity with GAAP. Misstatements can result from errors or fraud. The auditor's conclusion about aggregated misstatements should be documented. Their nature and effect also should be documented. Materiality is based on the auditor's professional judgment as to the needs of a reasonable person who will rely on the financial statements.

AU 313 - Substantive Tests prior to the Balance-Sheet Date

Application of substantive tests at interim dates, i.e., prior to year-end, increases the risk that undetected misstatements may exist at year-end. Accordingly, auditors should apply some substantive tests to the remaining period (from the date substantive tests were performed to yearend). But, if control risk is assessed at the maximum, the auditor must consider whether the effectiveness of the tests covering the remaining period will be impaired. Also, all auditing procedures must be coordinated, e.g., those applied to related party transactions. In other words, the tests applied during the remaining period and at year-end need to be based on the interim work.

AU 315 - Communications between Predecessor and Successor Auditors

A successor auditor is required to communicate with the predecessor auditor before accepting an auditing engagement. The successor should request permission from the client to make an inquiry of the predecessor before final acceptance of the engagement. Thus, the successor should ask the client to authorize the predecessor to respond fully to inquiries. The successor auditor should inquire about reasons for the change in auditors; disagreements with management about accounting principles and auditing procedures; facts bearing on management's integrity; and communications to audit committees or others regarding fraud, illegal acts by clients, and internal-control-related matters. The predecessor should respond promptly and fully, but, if circumstances require a limited response, the limited nature of that response must be clearly indicated. The successor should also request the client to permit review of the predecessor's working papers. The predecessor auditor ordinarily permits the successor to review working papers. The successor auditor's communications with the predecessor auditor may have a bearing on the audit of opening balances and the evaluation of the consistency of application of accounting principles. An auditor who is considering accepting an engagement for a reaudit is a successor auditor, and the previous auditor is a predecessor auditor.

AU 316 - Consideration of Fraud in a Financial Statement Audit

Fraud differs from error because it is an intentional act. The relevant misstatements are those arising from (1) fraudulent financial reporting and (2) misappropriation of assets. The conditions for fraud are (1) incentives or pressures; (2) opportunity; and (3) attitude, character, or set of values. Auditors must exercise professional skepticism when considering fraud risk (risk of material misstatement due to fraud). Audit planning must include discussions, such as "brainstorming," among audit team members about potential fraud. The field work involves identifying fraud risks by obtaining information through making inquiries of management and others and consideration of (1) the results of analytical procedures, (2) fraud risk factors, and (3) certain other information.

AU 317 - Illegal Acts by Clients

The auditor's responsibility for illegal acts having a direct and material effect on the financial statements is the same as that for errors or fraud. The responsibility for illegal acts having material but indirect effects is that (s)he must be aware that they may occur but need not apply specific procedures to detect them unless information comes to his/her attention indicating their existence.

AU 319 - Consideration of Internal Control in a Financial Statement Audit

The second standard of field work requires that a sufficient understanding of internal control be obtained to plan the audit and to determine the nature, timing, and extent of tests to be performed. Internal control has five components: the control environment, risk assessment, control activities, information and communication, and monitoring. The standard requires that the understanding extend in every audit to components that affect financial reporting, that it be documented, and that it include procedures to understand the design of relevant controls and determine whether they are in operation. The understanding permits the auditor to identify potential types of misstatements, consider factors affecting risk, and design tests of controls (if applicable) and substantive tests. Moreover, the auditor considers how IT affects relevant control components and the ways in which transactions are initiated, recorded, processed, and reported.

Another important feature of the standard is its integration of concepts of audit evidence and audit risk with internal control principles. The process of evidence gathering and evaluation is structured with respect to particular financial statement assertions, and audit risk and its components (inherent, control, and detection risk) are assessed in terms of those assertions. Thus, the auditor obtains an understanding of the five components of internal control and assesses control risk. If that assessment is to be below the maximum, the auditor must identify specific internal controls relevant to specific financial statement assertions, perform procedures to evaluate the design effectiveness of the controls, and perform tests of the controls to evaluate their operating effectiveness. See Study Unit 4 for a full outline.

AU 322 - The Auditor's Consideration of the Internal Audit Function in an Audit of Financial Statements

External auditors may consider an internal audit function in determining the nature, timing, and extent of audit work. The auditor should obtain an understanding of this function as part of the understanding of internal control. The purpose is to identify internal audit activities relevant to a financial statement audit. If the auditor concludes that it is efficient to consider how the internal audit function may affect the audit work, the auditor must evaluate and test the internal auditors' work and assess their competence and objectivity. Even if the internal auditors' work is expected to affect the audit procedures, the reporting responsibility continues to rest solely with the external auditor. Moreover, the external auditor must make judgments about whether, and to what extent, (s)he must directly test financial statement assertions after considering the work of the internal auditors. Issues of materiality, inherent and control risk, and the subjectivity involved in the evaluation of audit evidence must be weighed. Even if the internal audit function is deemed not to be relevant to the audit, the external auditor must assess the competence and objectivity of the internal auditors and evaluate and supervise their work if their direct assistance is sought.

AU 324 - Service Organizations

This section concerns audits of service organizations and of clients of service organizations. It applies to a financial statement audit of an entity that uses another organization's services as part of its own information system. Such services affect the initiation of transactions; accounting records, supporting information, and accounts; accounting processing; and the financial reporting process.

AU 325 - Communication of Internal Control Related Matters Noted in an Audit

An auditor must communicate all reportable conditions related to any of the internal control components. Reportable conditions constitute a broader category than material weaknesses. The standard states the obligations of an auditor regarding reportable conditions, discusses agreements with the client to report matters beyond those contemplated by the pronouncement, defines reportable conditions (and material weaknesses if the auditor wishes or has been requested to separately identify and communicate them), and describes the form and content of a report on reportable conditions, including a statement restricting its use to internal users. No report is issued if no reportable conditions were identified except in audits in accordance with Government Auditing Standards.

AU 326 - Evidential Matter

Most audit work entails obtaining and evaluating evidence about financial statement assertions. These assertions are management representations embodied in financial statement components. They are classified into five categories: existence or occurrence, completeness, rights and obligations, valuation or allocation, and presentation and disclosure. Auditors develop audit objectives and design substantive tests based on these assertions. Objectives do not vary depending on whether processing is manual or electronic, but audit procedures are influenced by the type of processing. In many cases, auditors must use information technology to access certain information, and the nature of electronic processing may require tests of controls. The basic evidential matter supporting the financial statements is the underlying accounting data and corroborating information. This evidential matter is increasingly found in the form of electronic messages, for example, as a result of the use of EDI. Evidence, whether written or electronic, must be competent and sufficient. However, the auditor most often relies on persuasive rather than convincing evidence.

AU 328 - Auditing Fair Value Measurements and Disclosures

An auditor must consider the measurement and disclosure of assets, liabilities, and equity components at fair value in financial statements. Thus, an auditor must obtain sufficient competent evidence that FVMD conform with GAAP. For this purpose, the auditor obtains an understanding of (1) the entity's process for arriving at FVMD, and (2) the relevant controls. The auditor then tests the entity's FVMD after assessing the risk of material misstatement. Testing addresses management's significant assumptions, the valuation model, and the underlying data. These procedures may include (1) development of independent estimates of fair value to corroborate management's and (2) review of subsequent events. Written representations about the reasonableness of significant assumptions also must be obtained in most cases. Moreover, the auditor must communicate with the audit committee about management's process for developing especially sensitive fair value estimates and should consider other communications. This standard has not yet been approved by the Public Company Accounting Oversight Board.

AU 329 - Analytical Procedures

This standard is intended to improve the effectiveness of audits by requiring that analytical procedures be applied in the planning and overall review phases of an audit. Use of analytical procedures as substantive tests of particular financial statement assertions is discretionary. However, documentation requirements must be met when an analytical procedure is the principal substantive test of a significant assertion. AU 329 also clarifies the definition of analytical procedures by stressing that the study and comparison based on expected relationships among data require the auditor to develop specific expectations regarding recorded amounts.

AU 330 - The Confirmation Process

Confirmation is "the process of obtaining and evaluating a direct communication from a third party in response to a request for information about a particular item affecting financial statement assertions." This pronouncement defines confirmation, relates confirmation procedures to the assessment of audit risk, discusses the design of the confirmation request and the performance of procedures, describes alternative procedures, states the factors used in evaluating the evidence obtained, and provides specific guidance with respect to confirmation of accounts receivable.

AU 331 - Inventories

Observation of physical inventories is a generally accepted auditing procedure. Auditors must make test counts when observing physical inventories. Inventories in public warehouses may be verified by direct confirmation. In addition, if the inventories are material, the auditors must evaluate the warehouse's internal controls (or obtain a report thereon from an independent accountant).

AU 332 - Auditing Derivative Instruments, Hedging Activities, and Investments in Securities

The guidance provided concerns planning and performing audit procedures to test assertions about derivatives and hedging activities accounted for under SFAS 133. The guidance also applies to all debt and equity securities, as defined by SFAS 115, but it extends to assertions about securities not accounted for under SFAS 115, e.g., equity-based investments. For an outline, see Study Unit 13.

AU 333 - Management Representations

Auditors are required to obtain written representations about such items as (1) availability and completeness of all financial data, (2) management's acceptance of responsibility for compliance with GAAP and controls for preventing and detecting fraud, (3) management's belief that the effects of uncorrected misstatements aggregated by the auditor are immaterial, (4) related party transactions, (5) absence of unrecorded transactions, (6) knowledge of fraud or suspected fraud affecting the entity, and (7) other representations related to management's assertions. If management refuses to provide written representations, an unqualified audit opinion cannot be expressed.

AU 334 - Related Parties

Material related party transactions must be disclosed and accounted for to reflect their substance. Auditors must perform procedures, e.g., inquiries of management, to determine the existence of related parties and to examine related party transactions.

AU 336 - Using the Work of a Specialist

Auditors may rely on specialists, e.g., engineers or actuaries, to value assets, make actuarial determinations, etc. The auditor must consider whether the findings support the related assertion. A documented understanding of the work to be done by the specialist should exist among the auditor, client, and specialist.

AU 337 - Inquiry of a Client's Lawyer Concerning Litigation, Claims, and Assessments

Auditors should question management about contingent liabilities. The client should send a letter to its attorneys describing all contingent liabilities including unasserted claims. The letter should request that the attorney confirm the correctness of the client's understanding regarding these claims. The letter should also ask for confirmation that the attorney will advise the client when unasserted claims require disclosure.

AU 339 - Audit Documentation

Audit documentation is the principal record of the audit procedures applied, the evidence obtained, and the conclusions reached. It serves to provide the principal support for the auditor's report and to aid in the conduct and supervision of the audit. Audit documentation should be sufficient to enable members of the audit team to understand the nature, timing, extent, and results of the work performed. It should also indicate who performed and reviewed the work and show that the accounting records agree or reconcile with the financial statements. Audit documentation may be in electronic or other media.

AU 341 - The Auditor's Consideration of an Entity's Ability to Continue as a Going Concern

The auditor must evaluate whether "there is a substantial doubt about the entity's ability to continue as a going concern for a reasonable period of time." (S)he need not apply specific procedures for this purpose. (S)he may have to obtain additional evidence as well as information about management's plans to mitigate the effects of the conditions or events indicative of the substantial doubt. Furthermore, the auditor must document the conditions or events leading to the belief that a substantial doubt exists, the work done to evaluate management's plans, the conclusion about whether the substantial doubt remains, and the consideration and effect of the conclusion on the statements and reports. A substantial doubt requires an explanatory paragraph following the opinion paragraph that includes the terms "substantial doubt" and "going concern."

AU 342 - Auditing Accounting Estimates

Accounting estimates are specifically addressed in the scope paragraph of the standard audit report (see AU 508). This standard defines accounting estimates, gives examples, describes management's responsibilities, and provides guidance for the auditor's evaluation.

AU 350 - Audit Sampling

Internal control should prevent or detect most monetary misstatements or deviations from controls. Substantive tests should detect most remaining material misstatements. Sampling risk is the possibility that samples do not represent populations; nonsampling risk refers to auditor errors in using sampling techniques, e.g., failure to evaluate sample items correctly. Regarding sampling risk for a substantive test of details, auditors should be concerned with both incorrect acceptance (the critical risk) and incorrect rejection. They must also be concerned with two aspects of sampling risk for a test of controls: the risk of assessing control risk too low (the critical risk) or too high. As the assessed levels of control risk, inherent risk, and detection risk for other substantive tests decrease (increase), the allowable risk of incorrect acceptance for a given substantive test of details increases (decreases). Both judgmental and statistical sampling are appropriate. Statistical sampling permits efficient sampling plans and quantification of sample precision and reliability (materiality and risk).

AU 380 - Communication with Audit Committees

Certain audit matters must be communicated to those who oversee the financial reporting process. It applies if the entity has an audit committee or its equivalent or if the audit constitutes an SEC engagement. The matters to be communicated are described in the outline in Study Unit 9, subunit 9.2.

AU 390 - Consideration of Omitted Procedures after the Report Date

This statement provides guidance for an auditor who, subsequent to the date of the report on audited financial statements, concludes that one or more necessary auditing procedures were omitted from the audit, but there is no indication that those statements are not fairly presented in conformity with GAAP or with another comprehensive basis of accounting. Once (s)he has reported, an auditor has no responsibility to carry out any retrospective review. However, reports and working papers relating to particular engagements may be subjected to post-issuance review for various reasons, and the omission of a necessary procedure may be disclosed. When the auditor concludes that a necessary procedure was omitted, (s)he should assess its importance. If the auditor concludes that the omission of a necessary procedure impairs his/her current ability to support the previously expressed opinion, and (s)he believes there are persons currently relying, or likely to rely, on the report, (s)he should promptly undertake to apply the omitted procedure(s) that would provide a satisfactory basis for the opinion. If (s)he cannot apply the omitted procedure, (s)he should seek advice about his/her legal responsibilities.

AU 410 - Adherence to GAAP

Generally accepted accounting principles include methods of application as well as accounting principles and practices. External auditors must express an opinion as to whether the client's financial statements adhere to GAAP.

AU 411 - The Meaning of Present Fairly in Conformity with GAAP in the Independent Auditor's Report

GAAP are the "conventions, rules, and procedures necessary to define accepted accounting practice at a particular time." The nongovernmental GAAP hierarchy is given in Study Unit 16, subunit 16.1. The GAAP hierarchy for state and local governments has five tiers. The first tier [category (a)] consists of sources of officially established accounting principles (GASB Statements and Interpretations, and, if specifically made applicable to state and local governments by GASB Statements or Interpretations, AICPA and FASB pronouncements). The next three tiers contain other sources of established accounting principles. The fifth tier includes other accounting literature. The federal hierarchy has a similar structure, but the Federal Accounting Standards Advisory Board (FASAB) is the source of category (a) guidance.

AU 420 - Consistency of Application of GAAP

If comparability among periods has been materially affected by changes in accounting principles, the auditor should appropriately modify the report. Consistency is not mentioned in the report, however, if no change with a material effect has occurred. Accounting changes that affect consistency and require recognition in audit reports include changes in principle, changes in the reporting entity not resulting from a transaction or event, correction of an error in principle, and changes in principle that are inseparable from a change in estimate. Modification of the report for an inconsistency is not necessary when a pooling of interests is not accounted for by restating prior period financial statements presented comparatively, but a qualified or adverse opinion would be expressed for the departure from GAAP. A change in the policy for determining the items treated as cash equivalents in a statement of cash flows is a change in principle requiring retroactive restatement. The audit report should recognize this change in an explanatory paragraph. Changes that do not affect consistency and do not require modification of the audit report include changes in estimate, error corrections not involving accounting principles, changes in classification, substantially different transactions or events, changes having a material future but not current effect, and changes in the reporting entity resulting from a transaction or event.

AU 431 - Adequacy of Disclosure in Financial Statements

Fairness contemplates adequate disclosure relating to form, content, arrangement of statements, terminology, classifications, and detail. If disclosure is not adequate, the auditor must express a qualified or adverse opinion.

AU 504 - Association with Financial Statements

An accountant is associated with financial statements when his/her name is used in a report or document containing the financial statements. This section is based on the fourth standard of reporting, which is intended to prevent misinterpretation of the accountant's responsibility when his/her name is associated with those statements. Accountants should not allow their names to be associated with unaudited financial statements unless the statements are clearly marked "unaudited" and an indication is provided that the accountants do not express an opinion. Negative assurance should never be given if a disclaimer of opinion is issued.

AU 508 - Reports on Audited Financial Statements

This standard describes the auditor's report and the conditions for modification. The introductory paragraph refers to an audit and explicitly states management's and the auditor's responsibilities regarding the identified statements. The scope paragraph includes a description of an audit. This paragraph states that the conduct of the audit is intended to provide reasonable assurance about the existence of material misstatements. It also clarifies that the auditor examines evidence on a test basis, assesses accounting principles and estimates, and evaluates statement presentation. The opinion paragraph states whether the financial statements are presented fairly, in all material respects, in conformity with GAAP. The country of origin of GAAS and GAAP also is identified. The auditor may express an unqualified, qualified, or adverse opinion; disclaim an opinion; or add explanatory language to the report while expressing an unqualified opinion. For example, a lack of consistency having material effects and a substantial doubt about an entity's ability to continue as a going concern require explanatory language, but an uncertainty, by itself, does not.

AU 530 - Dating of the Independent Auditor's Report

Audit reports should be dated as of the completion of field work. If a subsequent event occurs after completion of the field work but before the issuance of the statements, and it is reflected in the financial statements, the report may be dual dated, i.e., dated as of the completion of field work except for the additional disclosure, which is dated as of its discovery. The alternative is to date the report as of the date of the subsequent event. If audit reports are reissued, they should use the last day of field work.

AU 532 - Restricting the Use of an Auditor's Report

An auditor's "general-use report" is one that is not restricted as to specified parties. An example is an audit report on financial statements prepared in accordance with GAAP or another comprehensive basis of accounting. An auditor's "restricted-use report" is intended for specified parties. Examples are reports on subject matter or presentations based on measurement or disclosure criteria in contracts or regulatory provisions, reports based on procedures performed to meet the needs of specified parties who accept responsibility for their sufficiency, and reports that are by-products of a financial statement audit. A restricted-use report should indicate that the report is intended solely for the information and use of specified parties, identify those parties, and state that the report is not intended to be used and should not be used by anyone other than the specified parties.

AU 534 - Reporting on Financial Statements Prepared for Use in Other Countries

A U.S. auditor may be engaged to report on the financial statements of a U.S. entity that have been prepared in conformity with accounting principles accepted in another country for use outside the U.S. The auditor should understand, and obtain written representations about, the purpose and uses of such financial statements. If the auditor uses the standard report of another country, and the financial statements will have general distribution in that country, (s)he should consider whether any additional legal responsibilities are involved. The auditor should perform the procedures that are necessary to comply with the general and field work standards of U.S. GAAS, although they may need to be modified because the assertions in the statements differ from those prepared according to GAAP. The auditor should understand the accounting principles generally accepted in the other country. The auditor may also be requested to apply the auditing standards of the other country and should thus comply with that nation's general and field work standards. A modified U.S.-style report or the report form of the other country may be used. The auditor may report on two sets of statements for the entity: one based on GAAP and the other on principles generally accepted in the other country. The other country's reporting standards must be complied with.

AU 543 - Part of Audit Performed by Other Independent Auditors

When an audit is conducted by two or more auditors, the principal auditor must determine whether his/her participation in the audit is sufficient for recognition as the principal auditor. For this purpose, (s)he must have knowledge of the overall statements and an understanding of the individual components. The principal auditor makes a basic decision whether to accept responsibility for the other auditor. If responsibility is accepted, there is no mention of the other auditor in the audit report. If the auditor wishes to divide responsibility, the audit report indicates the magnitude of the portion of the financial statements audited by the other auditor as a percentage of total assets, income, or other criterion. If no reference is made to the other auditor, the principal auditor must gain assurance of the independence, professional reputation, and quality of the other auditor's work. Whether or not (s)he refers to the other auditor, the principal auditor should make inquiries of the professional reputation of the other auditor, and obtain assurances about his/her independence. Furthermore, the other auditor must understand his/her relationship with the principal auditor.

AU 544 - Lack of Conformity with GAAP

If financial statements of regulated companies depart from GAAP, a qualified or adverse opinion will ordinarily be issued. But an additional paragraph of the report should express an opinion as to conformity with the basis of accounting prescribed by a regulatory body.

AU 550 - Other Information in Documents Containing Audited Financial Statements

The auditor should read the other financial information in the annual reports to determine that there is no inconsistency between the other material and the financial statements. Any material misstatements, inconsistencies, etc., require modification by the client, modification of the audit report (an additional paragraph), or withdrawal. An auditor may express an opinion on the other information in relation to the basic statements if it has been subjected to audit procedures in connection with an audit of the basic financial statements.

AU 551 - Reporting on Information Accompanying the Basic Financial Statements in Auditor-Submitted Documents

Auditors should report on all information included in the documents submitted to clients that include audited financial statements. This accompanying information typically includes schedules that support the financial statement accounts. The auditor's report should identify this information and state that it is not part of the basic financial statements. The audit opinion should be modified to cover the accompanying information. If the auditor disclaims an opinion on the accompanying information, it should be clearly marked "unaudited." If required supplementary information (RSI) is presented outside the basic statements in an auditor-submitted document, the auditor should (1) express an opinion if engaged to examine the RSI, (2) report in accordance with AU 551 if the RSI has been audited in connection with the audit of the basic statements, or (3) disclaim an opinion.

AU 552 - Reporting on Condensed Financial Statements and Selected Financial Data

This pronouncement concerns reporting in a client-prepared document on condensed statements derived from audited statements of a public entity required to file complete audited statements with a regulatory agency. It also concerns reporting on selected financial data derived from audited statements of any entity presented either in a client-prepared document that includes audited statements or, with respect to a public entity, in a client-prepared document that incorporates audited statements by reference to regulatory agency filings. The auditor's report on condensed statements or selected data should indicate that the auditor has audited and expressed an opinion on the complete statements, state the type of opinion expressed, and provide an opinion as to whether the information set forth is fairly stated in all material respects in relation to the complete statements from which it was derived. In the case of condensed statements, the report should also indicate the date of the report on the complete statements. If the selected data include other information not derived from the complete statements, the auditor should specifically identify the data on which (s)he is reporting.

AU 558 - Required Supplementary Information

This standard concerns supplementary information required by GAAP. Auditors must report (i.e., add an additional paragraph to the standard report) on RSI only when (1) it is omitted, (2) it contains material misstatements, (3) the auditor is unable to complete the prescribed procedures, (4) the auditor is unable to remove substantial doubts about whether the information conforms to prescribed guidelines, or (5) the RSI is not clearly marked "unaudited" when it is in fact not audited and is not placed outside the basic statements. If the RSI is audited in connection with the audit of the basic statements, the auditor may be able to expand the audit report accordingly if the procedures applied to the RSI are sufficient to express an opinion. Auditors should determine whether supplementary information is required and whether it meets the prescribed guidelines.

AU 560 - Subsequent Events

There are two types of subsequent events: (1) those that require reflection in the financial statements and (2) those that require disclosure only. Events that merely confirm situations existing at the balance sheet date should be reflected in the financial statements; e.g., the receivables of a bankrupt debtor should be written off on the statements even though the debtor went bankrupt after the yearend. Other events should be merely disclosed, e.g., the bankruptcy of a debtor arising from a fire that occurred after year-end.

AU 561 - Subsequent Discovery of Facts Existing at the Date of the Auditor's Report

Subsequent to the issuance of the financial statements, an auditor may become aware of information affecting the report that existed at the report date. If the effects of these facts can be promptly determined, the report ordinarily should be reissued. If the client refuses to cooperate, the auditor should notify the board, the client, regulatory agencies, and others relying on the statements. If the discovery occurs after the report date but before issuance of the statements, AU 560 applies.

AU 623 - Special Reports

This pronouncement establishes the auditor's responsibility for reports on financial statements that are prepared in conformity with a comprehensive basis of accounting other than GAAP. It also provides guidance for an engagement to express an opinion on specified elements, accounts, or items of a financial statement. Other topics covered are compliance reports required by contractual agreements and regulatory agencies (however, AU 801 applies when the auditor tests compliance with laws and regulations in accordance with *Government Auditing Standards*), special-purpose financial presentations required by contractual agreements or regulatory agencies, and financial information presented in prescribed forms or schedules.

AU 625 - Reports on the Application of Accounting Principles

An accountant in public practice (reporting accountant), may prepare a written report on the application of accounting principles to specific transactions, either completed or proposed. An accountant also may provide a written report on the type of opinion that may be expressed on a specific entity's financial statements. This standard also governs oral advice on the application of accounting principles to a specific transaction and the type of opinion that may be expressed on financial statements when the reporting accountant concludes the advice is intended to be used by a principal to the transaction as an important decision factor. An accountant must not provide a written report on a hypothetical transaction. The reporting accountant should (1) exercise due care, (2) have adequate training and proficiency, (3) plan the engagement adequately, (4) supervise the work of any assistants, and (5) accumulate sufficient information to provide a reasonable basis for the professional judgment described in the report. Moreover, (s)he considers the circumstances under which the report or advice is requested, the purpose of the request, and the intended use of the report. Also, the continuing accountant should be consulted. Use of the report is restricted to specified parties.

AU 634 - Letters for Underwriters and Certain Other Requesting Parties

This pronouncement concerns "comfort letters." It states whether independent accountants acting in their professional capacity may comment on specified matters, and, if so, what the form of comment should be. Practical suggestions are offered on such matters as forms of comfort letters suitable to various circumstances, the way in which a particular form of letter may be agreed upon, the dating of letters, and the steps that may be taken when information requiring special mention in a letter comes to the accountants' attention. Also, ways are suggested to reduce or avoid the uncertainties regarding the nature and extent of accountants' responsibilities.

AU 711 - Filings under Federal Securities Statutes

An accountant has a defense against lawsuits regarding false or misleading statements if (s)he had reasonable grounds, after reasonable investigation, to believe and did believe that statements were true and not misleading at the effective date of the registration statement. The accountant should extend procedures from the date of the report to the effective date of the registration statement. The investigation consists of reading statements, making inquiries, and obtaining a written representation letter from the client about subsequent events. Although the accountant has not expressed an opinion on the unaudited interim information, (s)he still must comment on any noncompliance with GAAP in the report. A predecessor accountant also has subsequent-event responsibility and must read the applicable portions of any prospectus and registration statement.

AU 722 - Interim Financial Information

Interim financial information (IFI) is financial information for less than a full year or for 12 months ending on a date other than the fiscal year end. The objective of a review of IFI is to provide a basis for the independent accountant to communicate awareness of any material modifications necessary for the IFI to conform with GAAP (negative assurance). A review primarily involves performance of analytical and inquiry procedures. The accountant is required (1) to communicate with the predecessor prior to accepting the engagement and (2) to reach an understanding with the client in writing about the parties' responsibilities and the objectives and limitations of the review. The accountant also must obtain sufficient knowledge of the client's business and internal control to (1) identify types of misstatements, (2) consider their likelihood, and (3) select procedures. Certain procedures are mandatory, e.g., inquiring of management about financial and accounting matters and obtaining written representations. The accountant must then evaluate the results of the procedures and make appropriate communications with management, the audit committee, and others. The accountant need not report in writing on a review of IFI, but the SEC requires a registrant's IFI included in quarterly reports to the SEC to be reviewed. In addition, an accountant's engagement to review IFI must be appropriately documented.

AU 801 - Compliance Auditing Considerations in Audits of Governmental Entities and Recipients of Governmental Financial Assistance

AU 801 provides general guidance on the auditor's responsibilities under GAAS, *Government Auditing Standards*, and federal requirements for audits of governmental entities or recipients of federal awards. It states the standards for reporting on compliance with laws and regulations and on internal control.

AU 901 - Public Warehouses -- Controls and Auditing Procedures for Goods Held

This pronouncement describes public warehouse operations and related controls. It also describes audit procedures for goods in the warehouse's custody and the audit procedures by the auditor of the owner of the goods.

STATEMENTS ON STANDARDS FOR ATTESTATION ENGAGEMENTS (SSAEs)

AICPA bodies issue standards for a variety of attest services other than the traditional financial statement audit. The codification of the 12 SSAEs is presented in Section AT of the AICPA Professional Standards (Vol. 1). It covers pronouncements on attest engagements (AT 101), agreed-upon procedures engagements (AT 201), financial forecasts and projections (AT 301), reporting on pro forma financial information (AT 401), reporting on an entity's internal control over financial reporting (AT 501), compliance attestation (AT 601), and management's discussion and analysis (AT 701).

The summaries of the standards beginning below are presented in their codified numerical sequence.

SSAE SECTIONS

AT 101 - Attest Engagements

An attest engagement is one in which a practitioner is engaged to issue or does issue an examination, a review, or an agreed-upon procedures report on subject matter, or an assertion about the subject matter, that is the responsibility of another party. Standards for all attest engagements, which are a natural extension of (but do not supersede) the 10 standards, are summarized in Study Unit 1.

AT 101 permits two levels of attest assurance in general use reports. Positive assurance should be given in reports that express conclusions on the basis of an **examination**. Negative assurance should be given in reports that express conclusions on the basis of a **review**. Some engagements may result in a restricted use report. For example, an agreed-upon procedures attest engagement is based on the application of specific procedures for which no assurance is provided, but the results of the procedures are provided in a report that is designed for restricted use.

The practitioner should establish an understanding with the client regarding the services to be performed. The understanding should include the objectives of the engagement, management's responsibilities, the practitioner's responsibilities, and the limitations of the engagement. Practitioners performing attest engagements should prepare and maintain attest documentation (working papers) appropriate for the circumstances of the engagement. The attest documentation is the principal record of the attest procedures applied, information gathered, and conclusions or findings reached. It is the principal support for the report and aids the practitioner in conducting and supervising the attest engagement. The attest documentation is the property of the practitioner.

AT 201 - Agreed-Upon Procedures Engagements

This attestation standard describes agreed-upon procedure engagements in which a practitioner is engaged by the client to help specified parties to evaluate subject matter or an assertion. The practitioner reports findings based on specific procedures performed on subject matter. An assertion, which is not required to be written unless required by another attest standard, is any declaration or set of declarations about whether the subject matter is based on or in conformity with the criteria selected. Unlike an audit or review, the practitioner provides neither an opinion nor negative assurance. The report should be in the form of procedures performed and the findings based on those procedures, and its use should be restricted. Furthermore, the specified parties and the practitioner should agree upon the procedures to be performed, and the specified parties should accept responsibility for their sufficiency. The practitioner must be independent, the assertion need not be in writing, unless required by another attest standard, and the agreed-upon procedures should not be overly subjective or open to varying interpretations (e.g., general review, check, or test).

AT 301 - Financial Forecasts and Projections

A practitioner who either (1) submits prospective financial statements (PFSs) that (s)he has assembled or assisted in assembling to clients or others or (2) reports on PFSs should either compile, examine, or apply agreed-upon procedures to them if those statements are, or reasonably might be, expected to be used by another (third) party.

A **financial forecast** presents an entity's expected financial position, results of operations, and cash flows. It is based on the responsible party's assumptions reflecting conditions it expects to exist and the course of action it expects to take. It may be expressed in specific monetary amounts as a single point estimate of forecasted results or as a range if the responsible party selects key assumptions to form a range within which it reasonably expects, to the best of its knowledge and belief, the item or items subject to the assumptions to actually fall. Certain minimum presentation guidelines apply.

A **financial projection** differs from a forecast in that it is based on the responsible party's assumptions reflecting conditions it expects would exist and the course of action it expects would be taken, given one or more hypothetical assumptions. A projection is sometimes prepared to present one or more hypothetical courses of action for evaluation, as in response to a question such as "What would happen if . . . ?"

AT 401 - Reporting on Pro Forma Financial Information

This pronouncement is applicable to a practitioner who examines or reviews and reports on pro forma financial information (PFFI). It does not apply to post-balance-sheet-date transactions reflected in the historical financial statements or to PFFI required by GAAP.

PFFI indicates what the effects on historical information might have been if a consummated or proposed transaction or event, such as a business combination, had occurred earlier.

A practitioner may report on an examination (positive assurance) or review (negative assurance) of PFFI if three conditions are met.

1.   The appropriate complete historical financial statements are included in the document.

2.   The pertinent historical financial statements have been examined or reviewed, and the assurance given by the practitioner is commensurate with that given on those statements.

3.   The reporting practitioner should have appropriate knowledge of the accounting and reporting practices of each significant constituent part of the combined entity.

AT 501 - Reporting on an Entity's Internal Control over Financial Reporting

This statement is primarily concerned with an engagement to examine the effectiveness of an entity's internal control over financial reporting at a moment in time (or on an assertion thereon) and to issue a report on such an examination. It states the conditions for performance of the engagement, defines the components of internal control, and describes the limitations of a system. This pronouncement also provides guidance for planning an engagement to express an opinion on whether the entity's internal control is effective based on the control criteria or on whether management's assertion about the effectiveness of internal control is fairly stated. AT 501 also provides guidance about obtaining an understanding of internal control, evaluating the effectiveness of the design and operation of controls, and forming an opinion. Moreover, it establishes reporting standards and describes the practitioner's responsibility to communicate deficiencies of which (s)he becomes aware. The PCAOB has issued Auditing Standard No. 2, *Audits of Internal Control over Financial Reporting in Conjunction with an Audit of Financial Statements*. AS No. 2 is conceptually similar to AT 501, but it expands responsibilities for both the client and auditor.

AT 601 - Compliance Attestation

Compliance attestation engagements and the accompanying reporting obligations should be conducted in accordance with the attestation standards. The practitioner may perform an examination leading to an opinion on whether an entity is in compliance or whether management's assertions about such compliance is fairly stated. Agreed-upon procedures (but not a review) may also be performed. These engagements concern (a) the entity's compliance with specified requirements (e.g., covenants of a contract, either financial or otherwise) or (b) the effectiveness of the entity's internal control over compliance.

The standard does not relate to engagements subject to *Government Auditing Standards*, which requires reporting on an entity's compliance with laws and regulations as well as on internal control, unless the terms of the engagement specify an attestation report under AT 601.

If management's written assertion is in a representation letter and not in a separate report that will accompany the practitioner's report, the practitioner should state that assertion in the introductory paragraph. The report will ordinarily be for general use, but the practitioner may restrict its use.

AT 701 - Management's Discussion and Analysis

This standard provides guidance to a practitioner performing an attestation engagement on management's discussion and analysis (MD&A) of financial position and results of operations. The MD&A may be presented in an annual report and other documents. The MD&A section of an entity's financial statements discloses information regarding liquidity, capital resources, results of operations, and the effects of inflation and changing prices. It also presents forward-looking information. The MD&A presentation, in accordance with SEC rules, constitutes a written assertion that may be examined or reviewed. However, a report on a review engagement cannot be filed with the SEC.

ASSURANCE SERVICES

Assurance services are independent professional services that improve the quality of information, or its context, for decision makers. They encompass audit and other attestation services but also other, nonstandard, services. Thus, unless they fall under the AICPA's attestation standards, assurance services do not require written assertions. Also, they do not encompass consulting services. Assurance and consulting services are delivered using a similar body of knowledge and skills, but assurance services differ in two ways: They focus on improving information rather than providing advice, and they usually involve situations in which one party wants to monitor another (often within the same company) rather than the two-party arrangements common in consulting engagements. The AICPA has identified a number of assurance services including: risk assessment; evaluation of performance measurement systems; assessment of information systems reliability (for example, SysTrust); evaluation of care for the elderly; assurance about health care effectiveness; and assessment of the security, privacy, and reliability of electronic commerce (for example, WebTrust).

COMPILATION ENGAGEMENTS AND REVIEW ENGAGEMENTS

Accountants may not be associated with unaudited financial statements of nonpublic companies unless they are reviewed or compiled. Unaudited statements of public companies are covered by AU 504. The unaudited statements of nonpublic entities are covered by the eleven Statements on Standards for Accounting and Review Services (SSARSs) promulgated by the AICPA. These pronouncements have been codified in section AR of AICPA Professional Standards (Vol. 2).

AR 50 - Standards for Accounting and Review Services

An AICPA member who performs compilations and reviews must comply with SSARSs. The accountant must be able to justify departures from them. Interpretive publications (Interpretations of, and appendices to, SSARSs and guidance in Audit and Accounting Guides and SOPs) are not standards. However, the accountant should be aware of and consider them. Moreover, (s)he must be able to explain how SSARSs provisions were complied with if such guidance is not followed. Other compilation and review publications are not authoritative but may be aids to understanding SSARSs.

AR 100 - Compilation and Review of Financial Statements

Accountants may compile financial statements from client information without performing any procedures to verify, corroborate, or review that information. **Compilation** involves presenting the representations of management (owners) without expressing any assurance on the statements. The accountant should have knowledge of the accounting principles and practices of the industry. (S)he also should have a general understanding of the entity's business, its accounting records, the qualifications of its accountants, the accounting basis of the statements, and the form and content of the statements. Before submission of the financial statements, the accountant must read them and determine whether their form is appropriate and whether they contain obvious material errors. When an accountant reports on a compilation or submits statements **reasonably expected to be used by a third party**, a report should be included stating that the statements were compiled in accordance with SSARSs issued by the AICPA, what a compilation is, that no audit or review was undertaken, and that no opinion or other assurance is expressed. When an accountant submits financial statements that are **not reasonably expected to be used by a third party**, the required communication may consist either of a compilation report or of the **documentation of an understanding** with the client. A **submission** is a presentation to a client or a third party of statements the accountant has prepared either manually or through use of computer software. A **third party** is anyone other than managers who are knowledgeable about the procedures applied and the basis of accounting and assumptions used.

When accountants undertake **review** engagements, they express limited assurance. They must be independent to perform this service. A review does not include evaluation of internal control, tests of transactions and account balances, and other auditing procedures. An accountant's **review report** consists of three paragraphs. The introductory paragraph states that a review was performed in accordance with SSARSs and that the information is the representation of management. The scope paragraph states that a review consists principally of inquiries of company personnel and analytical procedures applied to the financial data. The accountant is also required to obtain written representations from management. Moreover, this paragraph states that a review does not constitute an audit in accordance with GAAS, and no opinion is expressed. In the third paragraph, the accountant states that (s)he is not aware of any material modifications that should be made to the financial statements to conform with GAAP.

If accountants undertaking compilation and review engagements believe that the financial statements are not in conformity with GAAP, they must have the client make necessary corrections or make the necessary disclosures in their compilation or review report.

AR 200 - Reporting on Comparative Financial Statements

AR 200 establishes standards for reporting on comparative financial statements of nonpublic entities when financial statements of one or more periods presented have been compiled or reviewed.

AR 300 - Compilation Reports on Financial Statements Included in Certain Prescribed Forms

This pronouncement provides an alternative compilation report for financial statements included in a prescribed form (e.g., of a regulatory body) that calls for a departure from GAAP. It also provides further guidance applicable to reports on financial statements included therein.

AR 400 - Communications between Predecessor and Successor Accountants

This pronouncement concerns communications by a successor accountant with his/her predecessor regarding acceptance of an engagement to compile or review financial statements of a nonpublic entity.

AR 600 - Reporting on Personal Financial Statements Included in Written Personal Financial Plans

AR 600 provides an exemption from AR 100 for personal financial statements included in written personal financial plans prepared by an accountant if the statement will be used solely by the client and his/her advisers and will not be used for any other purpose than to develop the client's personal financial goals and objectives.

GOVERNMENT AUDITING STANDARDS

Audits of certain governmental entities are required to be performed in accordance with the 2003 revision of *Government Auditing Standards* (the Yellow Book). It was promulgated by the Government Accountability Office (GAO) and applies to financial audits, attestation engagements, and performance audits. *Government Auditing Standards* incorporate GAAS for reporting and field work for financial audits and any relevant new AICPA standards unless formally excluded by the GAO. *Government Auditing Standards* also state supplementary standards. They require either separate reports on internal control over financial reporting and on compliance with laws and regulations or one report integrated into the overall report on the audit. *Government Auditing Standards* are covered in Study Unit 20, "Governmental Audits."

REVIEW CHECKLIST

Your objective is to prepare to pass this section of the CPA exam. It is **not** to do a certain amount of work or spend a certain amount of time with this book or other CPA review material/courses. Rather, you **must**

1. Understand the CPA exam thoroughly -- study *CPA Review: A System for Success* and the Introduction in this book.

2. Understand the subject matter in the 20 study units in this book. The list of subunits in each of the 20 study units (presented below and on the following page) should bring to mind core concepts, basic rules, principles, etc.

3. If you have not already done so, prepare a 1- to 2-page summary of each study unit for your final review just before you go to the exam (do not bring notes into the examination room).

Study Unit 1: Engagement Responsibilities

1.1 Attest Engagements
1.2 Audit Engagements
1.3 Audit Programs
1.4 Compilations and Reviews
1.5 Financial Forecasts and Projections
1.6 Reporting on Pro Forma Financial Information
1.7 Assurance Services
1.8 Quality Control

Study Unit 2: Risk Engagement

2.1 Pre-Engagement Acceptance Activities
2.2 Planning and Supervision
2.3 Understanding the Entity's Business
2.4 Analytical Procedures
2.5 Audit Risk and Materiality
2.6 Consideration of Fraud in a Financial Statement Audit
2.7 Illegal Acts by Clients

Study Unit 3: Strategic Planning Issues

3.1 The Auditor's Consideration of the Internal Audit Function
3.2 Using the Work of a Specialist
3.3 Related Parties
3.4 Accounting Estimates and Fair Value Measures
3.5 Consideration of Omitted Procedures after the Report Date

Study Unit 4: Internal Control Concepts and Information Technology

4.1 Definition of Internal Control
4.2 Internal Control Components and Considerations
4.3 Internal Control for Computer Systems
4.4 Understanding Internal Control
4.5 Flowcharting

Study Unit 5: Internal Control – Sales-Receivables-Cash Receipts Cycle

5.1 Responsibilities/Organizational Structure
5.2 Sales-Receivables Flowchart
5.3 Cash Receipts Flowchart
5.4 Controls in a Cash Sale Environment
5.5 Other Sales-Receivables Related Transactions
5.6 Technology Considerations for the Sales-Receivable-Cash Receipts Cycle

Study Unit 6: Internal Control – Purchases-Payables Cash Disbursements Cycle

6.1 Responsibilities/Organizational Structure
6.2 Purchases-Payables-Cash Disbursements Manual System Flowchart
6.3 Technology Considerations for the Purchases-Payables-Cash Disbursements Cycle
6.4 Electronic Data Interchange (EDI)

Study Unit 7: Internal Control – Payroll and Other Cycles

7.1 Responsibilities/Organizational Structure
7.2 Payroll Manual System Flowchart
7.3 Technology Considerations for the Payroll Cycle
7.4 Other Cycles

Study Unit 8: Tests of Controls

8.1 Assessing Control Risk
8.2 Evidence to Support the Assessed Level of Control Risk
8.3 Correlation of Control Risk and Detection Risk
8.4 Assessing Control Risk in a Computer Environment

Study Unit 9: Internal Control Communications

9.1 Communication of Internal Control Related Matters Noted in an Audit
9.2 Communication with Audit Committees
9.3 Reporting on an Entity's Internal Control over Financial Reporting
9.4 Service Organizations

Study Unit 10: Evidence – Objectives and Nature

10.1 Nature, Competence, and Sufficiency
10.2 The Confirmation Process
10.3 Audit Documentation
10.4 The Computer as an Audit Tool

Study Unit 11: Evidence – The Sales-Receivables-Cash Cycle

11.1 Substantive Testing of Sales and Receivables
11.2 Substantive Testing of Cash

Study Unit 12: Evidence – The Purchases-Payables-Inventory Cycle

12.1 Substantive Testing of Accounts Payable and Purchases
12.2 Substantive Testing of Inventory

Study Unit 13: Evidence – Other Assets, Liabilities, And Equities

13.1 Substantive Testing of Property, Plant, and Equipment
13.2 Substantive Testing of Investments
13.3 Substantive Testing of Long-Term Debt
13.4 Substantive Testing of Equity
13.4 Substantive Testing of Payroll

Study Unit 14: Evidence – Key Considerations

14.1 Substantive Tests Prior to the Balance Sheet Date
14.2 Inquiry of a Client's Lawyer Concerning Litigation, Claims, and Assessments
14.3 Subsequent Events
14.4 Subsequent Discovery of Facts Existing at the Date of the Auditor's Report
14.5 Management Representations
14.6 The Auditor's Consideration of an Entity's Ability to Continue as a Going Concern

Study Unit 15: Evidence – Sampling

15.1 Sampling Fundamentals
15.2 Statistical Sampling in Test of Controls (Attribute Sampling)
15.3 Classical Variables Sampling (Mean-per-Unit)
15.4 Probability-Proportional-to-Size (PPS) or Dollar-Unit Sampling (DUS)

Study Unit 16: Reports – Standard, Qualified, Adverse, and Disclaimer

16.1 GAAS – The Reporting Standards
16.2 The Auditor's Standard Report
16.3 Addressing and Dating the Report
16.4 Qualified Opinions
16.5 Adverse Opinions
16.6 Disclaimers of Opinion

Study Unit 17: Reports – Other Modifications

17.1 Part of Audit Performed by Other Independent Auditors
17.2 Consistency of Application of GAAP
17.3 Uncertainties and Going Concern
17.4 Comparative Financial Statements
17.5 Emphasis of a Matter

Study Unit 18: Review, Compilation, and Special Reports

18.1 Compilation
18.2 Review
18.3 Other Considerations
18.4 Uses of Special Reports
18.5 Reporting on Financial Statements Prepared in Conformity with an Other Comprehensive Basis of Accouting (OCBOA)
18.6 Specified Elements, Accounts, or Items of a Financial Statement
18.7 Other Presentations
18.8 Financial Information Presented in Prescribed Forms of Schedules That Require a Prescribed Form of Auditor's Report

Study Unit 19: Related Reporting Topics

19.1 Interim Financial Information
19.2 Letters for Underwriters and Certain Other Requesting Parties
19.3 Filings under Federal Securities Statutes
19.4 Other Information in Documents Containing Audited Financial Statements
19.5 Required Supplementary Information
19.6 Reporting on Information Accompanying the Basic Financial Statements in Auditor-Submitted Documents
19.7 Reporting on Condensed Financial Statements and Selected Financial Data
19.8 Reporting on Financial Statements Prepared for Use in Other Countries
19.9 Reports on the Application of Accounting Principles
19.10 Compliance Attestation
19.11 Engagements to Apply Agreed-Upon Procedures

Study Unit 20: Governmental Audits

20.1 Overview
20.2 Audits in Accordance with AU 801, Compliance Auditing Considerations in Audits of Governmental Entities and Recipients of Governmental Financial Assistance
20.3 Additional Government Auditing Standards
20.4 Federal Audit Requirements and the Single Audit Act

INDEX

10 standards, auditing 21

Absolute assurance. 68
Acceptable level, detection risk 254
Accounting
   And Review Services Committee 23
   Considerations 421
   Estimates. 109, 283
   Principles. 490, 595, 605
Accounts receivable 324, 351
Achieved upper deviation limit 457
ACL 328
Act
   Foreign Corrupt Practices, of 1977 290
   Sarbanes-Oxley, of
    2002 . . . . 17, 33, 133, 284, 290, 326
   SEC, of 1934 133
   Securities, of 1933 596
   Single Audit, of 1984 . . . . 630, 639
Adequacy of disclosure 106, 566
Adverse opinion 493, 499
Aggregated misstatements. 67
Agreed upon
   Criteria 281
   Procedures 607, 609
     Attest engagement 20
     PFSs. 26
AI 328
AICPA Peer Review Program (PRP) 31
Analytical procedures 64, 69, 560, 594
Antifraud programs and controls 69
APB
   20. 531
   28. 597
Applicability 285, 605, 606
Application controls. 141
AR
   100. . . . . 23, 557
   200. 563
   300. 563
   400. 564
   500. 563
   600. 564
Artificial intelligence. 328
Assertions 21, 249, 285, 317
Assessed level of control risk 250
Assessing control risk 249
Assessments 421, 594
Assets, safeguarding. 134
Assurance 634
   Absolute 68
   Attest 20
   Reasonable 68, 136
   Services 28
AT
   201 609
   401 597
   701 597

Attestation
   Compliance 606
   Engagement 17
   Engagements. 630
   Services 29, 285
   Standards 18
Attribute sampling 454
AU
   150 60
   161 31
   230 22
   310 60
   311 62
   312 . . . . 63, 66, 109
   313 419
   315 60
   316 68
   317 70
   319 . . . . 133, 150
   322 101
   324 290
   325 279
   326 . . . . 249, 317
   329 64
   330 320
   332 397
   333 426
   334 106
   336 104
   337 421
   339 324
   341 . . . . 428, 533
   342 109
   350 . . . . 254, 451
   380 282
   390 113
   508 . . . . 21, 492, 494, 499, 500, 533, 538, 563
   530 493
   534 603
   543 . . . . 527, 609
   550 599
   551 601
   552 602
   558 600
   560 . . . . 423, 608
   561 . . . . 288, 425
   623 . . . . 564, 565, 566, 567, 568
   625 605
   634 596
   711 598
   722 . . . . 593, 597
   801 630

Audit

Adjustments 283
Around/through computers 257
Command language 328
Considerations 421
Difficulties in performing 284
Documentation 324, 634
Engagements 21
Federal requirements 639
Financial statements 629
Findings 325
Governmental 629
Hooks 259
Objectives 317
Partly performed by other independent auditor . . 527
Performance 630
Planning 291
Procedures 21, 106, 429
    In the subsequent period 424
Programs 23
Review 32
Risk and materiality 66
Sampling 451
Standards 21
Auditor's standard report 492
Departure from by other auditor 530

Backup and recovery 142
Balance sheet 565
Basic precision 468
Block sampling 453

CAAT 327
Cash sales environment, internal controls 186
Center for Public Company Audit Firms Peer Review
    Program (PRP) 31
Claims 421, 594
Classical variables sampling 459
Code of Professional Conduct 22
Comfort letters 596
Committee of Sponsoring Organizations of the
Treadway Commission 133
Communication
    Audit committee 282
    Auditor 634
Competence 633
    Evidential matter 320
    Internal auditors 102
Compilation
    Financial statements 24
    PFSs 26
    Procedures 558
    Services 557
Compilation and Review of Financial Statements . . 23
Completeness assertion 21, 249, 317
Compliance
    Attestation 606
    Contractual agreements or regulatory
        requirements 567
    GAGAS 634
    Standards, other countries 603

Computer

-Assisted audit technique 327
Environment, assessing control risk 255
Systems
    Access controls 145
    Development controls 149
    Input controls 147
    Internal controls 138
    Output controls 149
    Processing controls 148
    Risk assessment 142
    Trojan horse 143
    Worms 143
Conduct rule 301 60
Confidence level 452
Confirmation process 320
Consideration of
    Conditions and events 429
    Effects on the auditor's report 431
    Entity's ability to continue as a going concern . . 428
    Financial statements effects 431
    Fraud in a financial statement audit 68
    Internet audit function 101
    Management's plans 430
    Omitted procedures after the report date 113
Consulting services 29
Control
    Activities 135, 144, 280
    Deficiency 290
    Design 251
    Environment 134, 141, 280
    Risk 67, 249, 398, 452
        Correlation to detection risk 254
    Tests 249
Controls placed in operation 291
Coordination, internal and external auditors 103
Corroborating evidential matter 319
COSO report 133
COVES 317
CPA
    Performance review 30
    Risk advisory 29
Cumulative balance 466
Current
    Files 325
    Items 397

Decision
    Not to make reference 528
    To make reference 528
Derivatives 397
Detection risk 67, 249
    Correlation to control risk 254
Difference estimation 454
Digital signatures, encryption 145
Direct and material effect 70
Disclaimer of opinion 493, 500
Disclaimers 489
Disclosure 108
Division of responsibility 528
Documentation
    Attest 21
    Audit 324
    Controls, computer systems 149
    Going concern 431
Document flowchart 153

Dollar-unit sampling 454, 462
Domain database 328
Dual-purpose tests 255
Due diligence 596
DUS 454, 462

E-Commerce 188
EDI 210
ElderCare Services 29
Electronic data interchange 210
Embedded audit module 259
Emphasis of a matter 538
Engagement
    Acceptance conditions 285
    Agreed upon procedures 607, 609
    Attestation 17, 630
    Completion documentation 326
    Examination 286, 607
    Letter 24, 60
    Objectives and limitations 594
    Performance 285, 607
    Responsibilities 17
    Review 32
Evaluation, evidential matter 320
Evidence
    Assessed level of control risk 252
    Key considerations 419
    Liabilities, equities, other assets 395
    Objectives and nature 317
    Purchases-payables-inventory cycle 377
    Sales-receivables-cash cycle 351
    Sampling 451
Evidential matter 319
Examination 18, 26, 607
    Engagement 286, 607
Existence or occurrence assertion 21, 249, 317
Expert systems 328
Explanatory language added to the auditor's
    standard report 493
Extending audit conclusions 420
External
    Impairments 633
    Matters 429

Fair value 112
    Measurements and disclosures 112
FCPA 290
Field work, standards 22, 325, 603
Filings, federal securities statutes 598
Financial
    Difficulties 429
    Forecast 24
    Reporting, fraudulent 68
    Statements
        Accounting of 566
        Assertions 21, 317
        Audits 629
        Comparative 534
        Condensed 602
        Conformity with OCBOA 564
        Dissemination 557
        Laws 631
        Other information contained in 284, 599
        Specified elements or items of 566
        Use in other countries 603

Financing cycle 234
Flowchart
    Cash receipts 184
    Internal controls 153
    Payroll computer system 233
    Payroll manual system 230
    Purchases-payables-cash disbursement manual
        system 204
    Sales-receivables 181
FOB
    Destination 378
    Shipping point 352, 378
Foreign Corrupt Practices Act of 1977 290
Fraud 635
    Financial statements 68
    Risk 68
FVMD 112

GAAP 112, 595
    Consistency of application 530
    Departures from 496
    Hierarchies 632
    Hierarchy, nongovernmental entities 490
GAAS 21, 152, 283, 490
GAGAS 629
GAO 629
General
    Controls 140
    Standards, auditing 21
    Use, PFSs 25
Generalized audit software 327
Generally accepted
    Accounting principles 21
    Auditing standards 21
    Government auditing standards 629
Going concern
    Issues 428, 594
    Uncertainties 533
Government accountability office 629
Governmental audits 629
Government Auditing Standards 630, 632

Hardware, internal controls 138, 144
Heading 326
Healthcare effectiveness 30
Hedges 397
Hedging activities 398
Heuristics 329
Hypothetical transaction 605

IA 468
IDEA 328
IFI 593
Illegal acts, clients 70
Impairments to independence 633
Incremental allowance for misstatements 468
Independence 633
Index numbers 326
Inference engine 328
Information
    Privileged 635
    Systems, financial reporting 151
    Technology, internal controls 133

Inherent risk. 67, 249, 398
Input controls, computer systems 147
Inquiries. 560, 594
Integrated test facility 259
Interactive Data Extraction and Analysis 328
Interim financial information 593
Internal
   Audit function 101
   Controls
      Accounting estimates 110
      Classification 140
      Communications. 279
      Components 134, 280, 285
      Concepts. 133
      Cycles, other 229
      Deficiencies 286, 635
      Design. 288
      Documenting the understanding 152
      Human resources 135
      Information
         And communication. 136, 280
         Technology 133
      Monitoring 136, 280
      Payroll and other cycles. 229
      Purchases-payables-cash disbursement
        cycle 203
      Regulatory agency criteria 289
      Sales-receivables-cash receipts cycle 179
      Segments 288
      Understanding 150
   Matters 429
Internet security 143
Interpretive publications 22
Inventory and warehousing cycle 235
Investing cycle 234
Investments 530
IT
   Internal controls 133, 137
   Risks. 137, 151

Judgment (nonstatistical) sampling 451

Knowledge databases 328

Lead
   Auditor 33
   Schedules 324
Letter
   Audit inquiry. 422, 423
   Comfort 596
   Engagement 24, 60
   Management representation. 427
   Representation. 62, 594
Liabilities 395
Limited
   Procedures 600
   Use, PFSs 26
Litigation 421, 594

Management
   Disagreements with. 284
   Judgment. 283
   Override, controls 69
   Representation. 398, 426
   Responsibilities 594
   Written representations 595
Material
   Misstatement 68, 112, 634
   Weakness 282, 287, 290
Materiality, audit risk 21, 66
Mean-per-unit. 454, 459
Minimum presentation guidelines 25
Misappropriation of assets 68
Misstatement 67, 595, 634

Negative
   Assurance 20, 593, 607
   Confirmation. 322
   Trends. 429
Neural networks 329
Noncurrent items 397
Nonsampling risk 452

Objectivity, internal auditors 102
Observable market price 112
OCBOA 557, 565
Office of Management and Budget 630
OMB 630
Oral advice 605
Organizational
   Chart. 153, 179
   Impairments 633
Output controls, computer systems 149

Parallel simulation. 258
Partial presentation 25
Payroll cycles 229
PCAOB 17, 31
Peer review 32
Performance
   Engagement 285, 607
   Standards 605
Permanent files 325
Personal impairments 633
PFSs. 24
Piecemeal opinion. 500
Planning and supervision 62
Plant, property, and equipment cycle 234
Positive
   Assurance 20
   Confirmation. 322
PPS 454
PR 100 32
Practitioner 18
Pre-engagement acceptance activities. 60
Prescribed forms. 568
Presentation and disclosure assertion 249
Presentations
   Financial 568
   Other. 567
Principal auditor, course of action 527
Probability-proportional-to-size sampling 454, 462

Procedures
    Auditing 21
    Confirmation 321
    Coordinating timing 420
    Decision not make reference 529
    Decision to make reference 529
Processing controls, computer systems 148
Professional
    Judgment 633
    Skepticism 68
Pro forma financial information, reporting 27
Program
    Controls, computer systems 149
    Flowchart 153
Prospective financial statements 24
Public Company Accounting Oversight Board . . 17, 31
Purchases-payables-cash disbursement cycle 203

Qualified opinion 493, 494
Quality control 634
    Engagements 31

Random sampling 453
Ratio estimation 454
Reasonable assurance 68, 136
Reasonableness, accounting estimates 111
Related parties 106
Relevant controls 112, 134
Report
    Adverse 489
    Controls placed in operation 291
    Issuance and distribution 635
    Modifications 287, 527
    Modified 559, 562
    Qualified 489
    Review 32
    Service auditor 292
    Special 557
        Uses 564
    Standard 489
        Compilation 558
        Review 561
    Types 493
Reportable conditions 280
Reporting 281, 593
    Financial statements 601
    Internal control 285
    Pro Forma Financial Information 27
    Responsibility 601
    Standards 22, 287, 490, 604
Representation letter 62, 594
Representations, written 293, 595
Request design 321
Required supplementary information 600
Responsible party 286
Revenue
    Accounts 68
    Recognition, improper 69
Revenues 397
Review 24, 27, 559
    Audit 18, 32
    Services 557, 607
Reviewing partner 33
Rights and obligations assertion 21, 249, 317

Risk
    Assessment 59, 135, 142, 280, 291, 321
    Audit 66, 249, 254
    Fraud 68
    Incorrect acceptance 452
    Incorrect rejection 452
    IT 137, 151
    Materiality 21
    Nonsampling 452
    Sampling 452
    Substantive test of details 254
Roles, auditors 101
RSI 600

SAB 101 351
Sales-receivables-cash
    Cycle 351
    Receipts cycle 179
Sample
    Deviation rate 457
    Population, definition 464
    Size 465
Sampling
    Fundamentals 451
    Interval 465
    Objectives 464
    Unit 464
Sarbanes-Oxley Act of
2002 . . . . 17, 33, 133, 284, 290, 326
SAS
    82 22
    94 133
    99 codified as AU 316 68
SASs 17, 22
Scope
    Limitations 288, 428, 494
        Lawyer's response 422
    Restriction 595
SEC
    Act of 1934 133
    Requirements 596
Second partner review 33
Securities Act of 1933 596
Security, Internet 143
Segment disclosures 497
Selected financial data 603
Service
    Auditor 291, 292
    Organizations 290
SFAS 57 . . . . 106, 108
Significant
    Accounting principles 283
    Deficiency 290
Single Audit Act of 1984 . . . . 630, 639
Software, internal controls 139
Specialist 112
Specialists, use of work of 104
Specialized audit software 329
Special reports 557
SQCSs 31
SSAE 10
    Chapter 1 17
    Chapter 3 24
    Chapter 4 27
    Chapter 5 285
SSARSs 17, 23, 557

SSCSs 17
Standard financial institution confirmation form 355
Standards
  Attestation 18
  Auditing 21
  Field work 22, 325, 603
  General 21, 603
  Performance 605
    And reporting on peer review 32
  Reporting 22, 287, 490, 604
Statement
  Of
    Cash flow 565
    Comprehensive income 558, 561
    Financial position 565
    Income 565
    Operations 565
    Retained earnings 558, 561
Statement of
  Presentation and disclosure assertion 21, 317
Statements on
  Auditing standards 17
  Presentation and disclosure assertion 397
  Quality Control Standards 31
  Standards for
    Accounting and Review Services 23, 557
    Attestation Engagements 17
    Consulting Services 17
Statistical
  (Probability or random) sampling 451
  Plan 453
  Sampling, tests of controls 454
Strategic planning issues 101
Stratification 453
Submission, financial statements 24
Subsequent
  Discovery of facts 425
  Events 288, 292, 423
    Procedures 598
  Period 424
Substantive testing
  Accounts payable and purchases 377
  Cash 354
  Design 317
  Equity 401
  Inventory 379
  Investments 397
  Long-term debt 400
  Payroll 402
  Prior to the balance sheet date 419
  Property, plant, and equipment 395
  Sales and receivables 351
  Variables sampling 451
Sufficiency, evidential matter 320
System
  Flowchart 153
  Review 32
Systematic sampling 453
SysTrust 30

Technology
  Payroll cycle 232
  Purchases-payables-cash 208
  Sales-receivables-cash 187
Test data approach 257

Tests
  Controls 249, 451
    Steps 455
  Dual-purpose 255
  FVMD 112
  Substantive 317
Third party 559
Tick marks 326
Transactions, sales-receivables 186
Trojan horse, computer systems 143

Unasserted claims 422
Uncertainties, going concern 533
Underlying accounting data 319
Understanding
  Client and the industry 558, 559
  Entity's business 63
Unqualified opinion 493
User
  Auditor 291
  Organization 291

Valuation
  Method, FVMD 112
  Model, FVMD 112
  Or allocation assertion 21, 249, 317
Variable sampling 451
  Primary methods 454
Virus protection 143

WebTrust 30
Working
  Papers 21, 324
  Trial balance 324
Worms, computer systems 143
Written
  Assertions 285
  Audit program 23
  Representations 426, 560

Yellow Book 629, 630

COMPLETE GLEIM CPA SYSTEM with REVIEW ONLINE

All 4 parts, including 5[1] books, 4 audios, CPA Test Prep software, Review Online, plus bonus book bag.   ☐ $924.95

Also, available by exam part @ $256.95 each (Does not inlude book bag.)

GLEIM CPA SET

All 4 parts, including 5[1] books, 4 audios, CPA Test Prep software, plus bonus book bag.   ☐ $539.95

Also, available by exam part @ $143.95 each (Does not inlude book bag.)

[1]Fifth book *System for Success* $_____

COMPLETE GLEIM CMA/CFM SYSTEM with ONLINE COURSE for the UNCHANGED EXAM

Includes: books, software, audios, and Online Courses, plus bonus book bag.

☐ CMA $739.95   ☐ CFM $728.95   ☐ CMA/CFM $913.95

Also, available by exam part @ $213.95 each (Does not inlude book bag.)

GLEIM 4 PART SET for the UNCHANGED EXAM

Includes 4-part set (books, software, and audios) plus bonus book bag.   ☐ CMA $453.95   ☐ CFM $453.95

Also, available by exam part @ $120.95 each (Does not inlude book bag.)

GLEIM 4 PART SET for the REORGANIZED EXAM

Includes 4-part set (books, software, and audios) plus bonus book bag.   ☐ CMA $453.95

Also, available by exam part @ $135.95 each (Does not inlude book bag.) $_____

COMPLETE GLEIM CIA SYSTEM with ONLINE COURSE

Includes: books, software, audios, and Online Courses, plus bonus book bag.   ☐ $824.95

Also, available by exam part @ $224.95 each (Does not inlude book bag.)

GLEIM CIA SET

All 4 parts, including books, audios, CIA Test Prep software, plus bonus book bag.   ☐ $483.80

Also, available by exam part @ $120.95 each (Does not inlude book bag.) $_____

GLEIM EA REVIEW SYSTEM

Includes: books and EA Test Prep software   ☐ $279.80

Also, available by exam part @ $69.95 each (Does not inlude book bag.) $_____

"THE GLEIM SERIES" EXAM QUESTIONS AND EXPLANATIONS

Includes: 5 books and EQE Test Prep software   ☐ $112.25

Also, available by part @ $29.95 each (Does not inlude book bag.)

GLEIM CPE[2]

Includes book and service

[2]For our online CPE courses and course catalogue, please visit www.gleim.com/CPE $_____

Contact
GLEIM PUBLICATIONS
for further assistance:

www.gleim.com
(800) 874-5346
sales@gleim.com

SUBTOTAL $_____

Complete your
order on the
next page

GLEIM PUBLICATIONS, INC.

P. O. Box 12848   Gainesville, FL 32604

TOLL FREE: (888) 87-GLEIM
LOCAL: (352) 375-0772
FAX: (888) 375 -6940 (toll free)
INTERNET   www.gleim.com
E-MAIL: sales@gleim.com

Customer service is available (Eastern Time):
8:00 a.m. - 7:00 p.m., Mon. - Fri.
9:00 a.m. - 2:00 p.m., Saturday
Please have your credit card ready,
or save time by ordering online!

Select   ☐ CD   ☐ Cassette
for CPA and CMA UNCHANGED audios

SUBTOTAL (from previous page) $_____
Add applicable sales tax for shipments within Florida.   _____
Shipping (nonrefundable)   15.00

TOTAL $_____

Fax or write for prices/instructions on shipments outside the 48 contiguous states, or simply order online.

NAME (please print) _____

ADDRESS _____ Apt. _____
         (street address required for UPS)

CITY _____ STATE _____ ZIP _____

____ MC/VISA/DISC ____ Check/M.O.   Daytime Telephone (____)____

Credit Card No. _____ - _____ - _____ - _____

Exp. ____/____   Signature _____
     Month / Year

E-mail address _____

1. We process and ship orders daily, within one business day over 98.8% of the time. Call by 3:00 pm for same day service.
2. Please PHOTOCOPY this order form for others.
3. No CODs. Orders from individuals must be prepaid.
4. Gleim Publications, Inc. guarantees the immediate refund of all resalable texts and unopened software and audios if returned within 30 days. Applies only to items purchased direct from Gleim Publications, Inc. Our shipping charge is nonrefundable.
5. Components of specially priced package deals are nonrefundable.

Printed 11/04. Prices subject to change without notice.

For updates and other important information, visit our website.

GLEIM
KNOWLEDGE
TRANSFER
SYSTEMS®

www.gleim.com

CPA Review: Auditing, Thirteenth Edition, First Printing -- Please complete and mail to us pages 681 and 682 the week following the CPA exam. The information requested on these pages is in full compliance with the AICPA's policy on candidate disclosure of exam information.

681

Please forward your suggestions, corrections, and comments concerning typographical errors, etc., to **Irvin N. Gleim • c/o Gleim Publications, Inc. • P.O. Box 12848 • University Station • Gainesville, Florida • 32604.** Please include your name and address so we can properly thank you for your interest.

1. _____

2. _____

3. _____

4. _____

5. _____

6. _____

7. _____

8. _____

9. _____

10. _____

11. _____

12. _____

13. _____

14. _____

15. _____

16. _____

17. _____

18. _____

Remember, for superior service: <u>Mail</u>, <u>e-mail</u>, or <u>fax</u> questions about our books or software.
<u>Telephone</u> questions about orders, prices, shipments, or payments.

Name: _____

Address: _____

City/State/Zip: _____

Telephone: Home: _____   Work: _____   Fax: _____

E-mail: _____